Abnormal Psychology

Abnormal Psychology

Eighth Edition

Susan Nolen-Hoeksema

Mc Graw Hill Education

ABNORMAL PSYCHOLOGY, EIGHTH EDITION

Published by McGraw-Hill Education, 2 Penn Plaza, New York, NY 10121.

This book is printed on acid-free paper.

4 5 6 7 8 9 LWI 21 20 19

ISBN 978-1-260-50018-9 (bound edition)
MHID 1-260-50018-7 (bound edition)

ISBN 978-1-260-08046-9 (loose-leaf edition)
MHID 1-260-08046-3 (loose-leaf edition)

Portfolio Manager: *Ryan Treat*
Product Development Manager: *Dawn Groundwater*
Marketing Managers: *Augustine Laferrera; Olivia Kaiser*
Lead Content Project Managers: *Sandy Wille; Jodi Banowetz*
Senior Buyer: *Laura Fuller*
Senior Design: *Matt Backhaus*
Senior Content Licensing Specialist: *Melisa Seegmiller*
Cover Image: *©DrAfter123/DigitalVision Vectors/Getty Images*
Compositor: *Lumina Datamatics, Inc.*

Library of Congress Cataloging-in-Publication Data

Names: Nolen-Hoeksema, Susan, 1959-2013, author.
Title: Abnormal psychology / Susan Nolen-Hoeksema, Yale University.
Description: Eighth edition. | New York, NY : MHE, [2020] | Includes bibliographical references and indexes.
Identifiers: LCCN 2018044989| ISBN 9781260500189 (alk. paper) | ISBN 9781260080469 (loose-leaf edition)
Subjects: LCSH: Psychology, Pathological–Textbooks. | Mental illness–Textbooks.
Classification: LCC RC454.N64 2020 | DDC 616.89–dc23
LC record available at https://lccn.loc.gov/2018044989

mheducation.com/highered

ABOUT THE AUTHOR

Courtesy of Susan Nolen-Hoeksema

Susan Nolen-Hoeksema (1959–2013) In January 2013 we lost our esteemed author and friend, Susan Nolen-Hoeksema. Susan was a renowned scholar, teacher, mentor, and academic leader. She was recognized internationally for her work on how people regulate their feelings and emotions and how particular patterns of thinking can make people vulnerable to and recover slowly from emotional problems, especially depression. Her research shaped the field's perspective on depression in women and girls, and countless empirical studies and theoretical contributions followed as she developed her groundbreaking theory of rumination and depression.

In her words: "My career has focused on two parallel goals. The first is to use empirical methods to address important social and mental health problems (depression, rumination, women's mental health). The second goal is to disseminate psychological science. I also believe in taking science to the public, through my textbook on Abnormal Psychology and books for the general public on women's mental health."

Susan taught at Stanford University, the University of Michigan, and Yale University. Susan's work focused on depression, mood regulation, and gender, for which she was recognized and received the David Shakow Early Career Award from Division 12, the Distinguished Leadership Award from the Committee on Women of American Psychological Association, the James McKeen Cattell Fellow Award from the Association for Psychological Science, a Research Career Award, and multiple grants from the National Institute of Mental Health. In addition, she was the founding editor of the *Annual Review of Clinical Psychology,* now the most highly cited journal in the field of clinical psychology.

In addition to being an accomplished professor, scholar, teacher, and writer, Susan was a loving and devoted mother, wife, daughter, sister, friend, and mentor. Susan touched and inspired the lives of many people both professionally and personally, and she will be dearly missed.

ABOUT THE CONTRIBUTOR

Courtesy of Brett Marroquín

Brett Marroquín is an assistant professor of psychology at Loyola Marymount University in Los Angeles, California. He received his Ph.D. in clinical psychology from Yale University under the mentorship of Susan Nolen-Hoeksema, and completed a National Institute of Mental Health (NIMH) postdoctoral fellowship in biobehavioral issues in physical and mental health at the University of California, Los Angeles. His research examines interpersonal influences on emotion, emotion regulation, and cognitive processing in healthy functioning and mood disorders. His current work focuses on the roles of social contexts and romantic relationships in emotional adjustment to negative events, including cancer diagnosis and treatment, and how effective or ineffective support from partners affects couples' physical and mental health.

BRIEF CONTENTS

CONTENTS

PREFACE

Abnormal Psychology connects proven scholarship with student performance. Through an integrated, personalized learning program, the eighth edition gives students the insight they need to study smarter and improve performance.

McGraw-Hill Education Connect® is a digital assignment and assessment platform that strengthens the link between faculty, students, and course work. Connect for *Abnormal Psychology* includes assignable and assessable videos, quizzes, exercises, and interactivities, all associated with learning objectives for *Abnormal Psychology,* Eighth Edition.

Mc Graw Hill Education connect®

A PERSONALIZED EXPERIENCE THAT LEADS TO IMPROVED LEARNING AND RESULTS

How many students think they know everything about abnormal psychology but struggle on the first exam? Students study more effectively with Connect and SmartBook.

- SmartBook helps students study more efficiently by highlighting what to focus on in the chapter, asking review questions, and directing them to resources until they understand.
- Connect's assignments help students contextualize what they've learned through application, so they can better understand the material and think critically.
- SmartBook creates a personalized study path customized to individual student needs.
- Connect reports deliver information regarding performance, study behavior, and effort so instructors can quickly identify students who are having issues or focus on material that the class hasn't mastered.

Mc Graw Hill Education SMARTBOOK®

Experience the Power of Data

Abnormal Psychology harnesses the power of data to improve the instructor and student experiences.

BETTER DATA, SMARTER REVISION, IMPROVED RESULTS

For this new edition, data were analyzed to identify the concepts students found to be the most difficult, allowing for expansion upon the discussion, practice, and assessment of challenging topics. The revision process for a new edition used to begin with gathering information from instructors about what they would change and what they would keep. Experts in the field were asked to provide comments that pointed out new material to add and dated material to review. Using all these reviews, authors would revise the material. But now, a new tool has revolutionized that model.

McGraw-Hill Education authors have access to student performance data to analyze and to inform their revisions. These data are anonymously collected from the many students who use SmartBook, the adaptive learning system that provides students with individualized assessment of their own progress. Because virtually every text paragraph is tied to several questions that students answer while using SmartBook, the specific concepts with which students are having the most difficulty are easily pinpointed through empirical data in the form of a "heat map" report.

POWERFUL REPORTING

Whether a class is face-to-face, hybrid, or entirely online, McGraw-Hill Connect provides the tools needed to reduce the amount of time and energy instructors spend administering their courses. Easy-to-use course management tools allow instructors to spend less time administering and more time teaching, while reports allow students to monitor their progress and optimize their study time.

- The **At-Risk Student Report** provides instructors with one-click access to a dashboard that identifies students who are at risk of dropping out of the course due to low engagement levels.
- The **Category Analysis Report** details student performance relative to specific learning objectives and goals, including APA learning goals and outcomes and levels of Bloom's taxonomy.
- **Connect Insight** is a one-of-a-kind visual analytics dashboard—now available for both instructors and students—that provides at-a-glance information regarding student performance.

New to this edition, SmartBook is now optimized for mobile and tablet and is accessible for students with disabilities. Content-wise, it has been enhanced with improved learning objectives that are measurable and observable to improve student outcomes. SmartBook personalizes learning to individual student needs, continually adapting to pinpoint knowledge gaps and focus learning on topics that need the most attention. Study time is more productive and, as a result, students are better prepared for class and coursework. For instructors, SmartBook tracks student progress and provides insights that can help guide teaching strategies.

INFORMING AND ENGAGING

McGraw-Hill Connect offers several ways to actively engage students.

Power of Process guides students through the process of critical reading and analysis. Faculty can select or upload content, such as journal articles, and assign guiding questions to move students toward higher-level thinking and analysis.

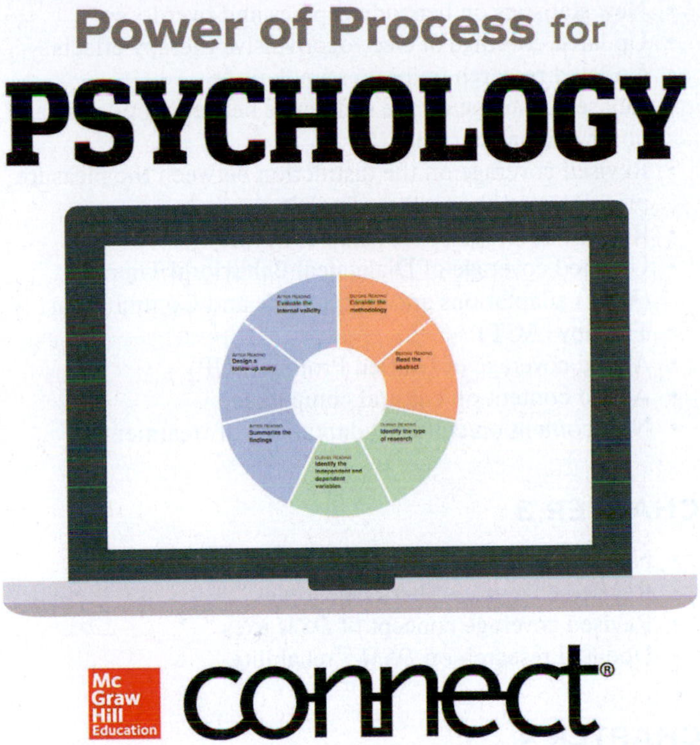

Through the connection of psychology to students' own lives, concepts become more relevant and understandable. **NewsFlash** exercises tie current news stories to key psychological principles and learning objectives. After interacting with a contemporary news story, students are assessed on their ability to make the link between real life and research findings. Topics include brain chemistry and depression, eating disorders in boys, and criticisms of the *DSM*-5.

Thinking Critically About Abnormal Psychology

Updated with *DSM-5* content, **Faces of Abnormal Psychology** connects students to real people living with psychological disorders. Through its unique video program, Faces of Abnormal Psychology helps students gain a deeper understanding of psychological disorders and provides an opportunity for critical thinking.

Interactive Case Studies help students understand the complexities of psychological disorders. Co-developed with psychologists and students, these immersive cases bring the intricacies of clinical psychology to life in an accessible, gamelike format. Each case is presented from the point of view of a licensed psychologist, a social worker, or a psychiatrist. Students observe sessions with clients and are asked to identify major differentiating characteristics associated with each of the psychological disorders presented. Interactive Case Studies are assignable and assessable through McGraw-Hill Education's Connect.

SUPPORTING INSTRUCTORS WITH TECHNOLOGY

With McGraw-Hill Education, you can develop and tailor the course you want to teach.

McGraw-Hill Campus (www.mhcampus.com) provides faculty with true single-sign-on access to all of McGraw-Hill's course content, digital tools, and other high-quality learning resources from any learning management system. McGraw-Hill Campus includes access to McGraw-Hill's entire content library, including eBooks, assessment tools, presentation slides, and multimedia content, among other resources, providing faculty open, unlimited access to prepare for class, create tests/quizzes, develop lecture material, integrate interactive content, and more.

With **Tegrity,** you can capture lessons and lectures in a searchable format and use them in traditional, hybrid, "flipped classes," and online courses. With Tegrity's personalized learning features, you can make study time efficient. Its ability to affordably scale brings this benefit to every student on campus. Patented search technology and real-time learning management system (LMS) integrations make Tegrity the market-leading solution and service.

With McGraw-Hill Education's **Create**, faculty can easily rearrange chapters, combine material from other content sources, and quickly upload content you have written, such as your course syllabus or teaching notes, using McGraw-Hill Education's Create. Find the content you need by searching through thousands of leading McGraw-Hill Education textbooks. Arrange your book to fit your teaching style. Create even allows you to personalize your book's appearance by selecting the cover and adding your name, school, and course information. Order a Create book, and you will receive a complimentary print review copy in three to five business days or a complimentary electronic review copy via email in about an hour. Experience how McGraw-Hill Education empowers you to teach your students your way. **http://create.mheducation.com**

TRUSTED SERVICE AND SUPPORT

McGraw-Hill Education's Connect offers comprehensive service, support, and training throughout every phase of your implementation. If you're looking for some guidance on how to use Connect, or want to learn tips and tricks from super-users, you can find tutorials as you work. Our Digital Faculty Consultants and Student Ambassadors offer insight into how to achieve the results you want with Connect.

INTEGRATION WITH YOUR LEARNING MANAGEMENT SYSTEM

McGraw-Hill integrates your digital products from McGraw-Hill Education with your school's learning management system (LMS) for quick and easy access to best-in-class content and learning tools. Build an effective digital course, enroll students with ease, and discover how powerful digital teaching can be.

Available with Connect, integration is a pairing between an institution's LMS and Connect at the assignment level. It shares assignment information, grades, and calendar items from Connect into the LMS automatically, creating an easy-to-manage course for instructors and simple navigation for students. Our assignment-level integration is available with **Blackboard Learn, Canvas by Instructure,** and **Brightspace by D2L,** giving you access to registration, attendance, assignments, grades, and course resources in real time, in one location.

Instructor Supplements

Instructor's Manual The instructor's manual provides a wide variety of tools and resources for presenting the course, including learning objectives and ideas for lectures and discussions.

Test Bank By increasing the rigor of the test-bank development process, McGraw-Hill Education has raised the bar for student assessment. A coordinated team of subject-matter experts methodically vetted each question and each set of possible answers for accuracy, clarity, effectiveness, and accessibility; each question has been annotated for level of difficulty, Bloom's taxonomy, APA learning outcomes, and corresponding coverage in the text. Organized by chapter, the questions are designed to test factual, conceptual, and applied understanding. All test questions are available within TestGen™ software and as Word documents.

PowerPoint Presentations The PowerPoint presentations, available in both dynamic lecture-ready and accessible WCAG-compliant versions, highlight the key points of the chapter and include supporting visuals. All of the slides can be modified to meet individual needs.

Image Gallery The Image Gallery features the complete set of downloadable figures and tables from the text. These can be easily embedded by instructors into their own PowerPoint slides.

CHAPTER-BY-CHAPTER CHANGES

Revisions based on the student heat map are reflected primarily in Chapters 2, 5, 7, 9, and 15. Other content changes include the following:

CHAPTER 1

- Updated coverage on the dimensions of abnormality on a continuum
- Revised coverage of the cognitive revolution
- Increased attention to disadvantages of deinstitutionalization
- Revised coverage on the role of correctional facilities
- Updated coverage of the Affordable Care Act and mental health

CHAPTER 2

- New statistics on benzodiazepines and overdoses
- Updated coverage of electroconvulsive therapy effects
- Updated research on brain stimulation
- Revised coverage on the difference between modeling and observational learning
- Revised coverage on the distinction between the pleasure principle and the reality principle
- Revised coverage of Freudian concepts
- Updated coverage of Dialectical Behavioral Therapy (DBT) adaptations and Acceptance and Commitment Therapy (ACT)
- Added coverage of Unified Protocol (UP)
- Added content on cultural competence
- New content on cultural adaptations of treatment

CHAPTER 3

- New coverage on computerized assessment
- Revised coverage of key *DSM* topics
- Revised coverage concept of *DSM* axes
- Updated research on *DSM*-5 reliability

CHAPTER 4

- Revised presentation of correlation
- Strengthened coverage (with new examples) of the difference between correlation and causation
- Revised presentation of demand characteristics
- New example for placebo control group for therapy
- Strengthened coverage on the limitations of laboratory studies
- Revised coverage of the types of genetic studies
- Revised presentation of adoption studies
- Strengthened coverage of meta-analysis
- Added coverage of Research Domain Criteria (RDoC)

CHAPTER 5

- Revised coverage with new example of dissociation in trauma
- Clarified distinction between *nervios* and *ataque de nervios*
- Revised presentation of neuroimaging findings related to trauma

- Strengthened presentation (with examples) of exposure therapy in cognitive-behavioral therapy (CBT)
- Revised coverage of prolonged exposure and cognitive processing therapy
- Strengthened coverage of exposure treatment for phobia
- Revised coverage of social anxiety disorder
- Revised coverage of panic disorder diagnosis
- New coverage of the cognitive aspect of panic
- Integrated coverage of cognitive factors of posttraumatic stress disorder (PTSD)
- Revised coverage of benzodiazepines in treating PTSD
- Improved coverage of general anxiety disorder definition (GAD)
- Added coverage of emotion regulation therapy (ERT) for GAD
- Revised presentation of obsessive compulsive disorder (OCD) diagnosis
- New example of compulsions
- Revised coverage of body dysmorphic disorder

CHAPTER 6

- Revised coverage of the reliability and controversies of *DSM-5*
- Updated treatment coverage
- Revised presentation of research on stress and maltreatment
- Updated coverage of prognosis relating to conversion disorders
- Updated coverage of the science on theories of dissociative identity disorder (DID)
- New coverage of treatment outcome research
- Revised coverage of dissociative fugue

CHAPTER 7

- Clarified definition and organization of subtypes of depression
- Revised coverage relating to the different bipolar disorders
- Strengthened coverage of bipolar episodes and diagnoses
- Revised presentation of cyclothymia
- New material on the distinction between episodes and general reactivity in bipolar disorder
- Improved coverage, with examples, of creativity in mood disorders
- Strengthened coverage of hopelessness in depression
- New material on the different bipolar disorders
- Revised coverage of cohort effects
- Revised coverage of gender differences in depression
- New material on puberty and gender differences in depression
- New material on racial and ethnic differences
- Updated material on genetic and brain findings relating to depression
- Added coverage of psychosocial contributors to bipolar disorders
- Added example of reward sensitivity
- Updated findings on selective serotonin reuptake inhibitors (SSRIs) and suicide
- Revised coverage of selective serotonin-norepinephrine reuptake inhibitors (SNRI)
- Revised coverage of the pros and cons of lithium
- Added lamotrigine to medical treatments for bipolar disorders
- Updated coverage of suicide epidemiology and demographics
- Added coverage of African American suicide rates and updated all coverage of ethnicity rates
- Added coverage of anxiety and suicide
- Added content on new media and suicide
- Updated research on impulsivity
- Added content on the interpersonal theory of suicide
- Added definitions of treatment vs. prevention
- Updated coverage of nonsuicidal self-injury

CHAPTER 8

- Added historical factors in discussion of delusions
- Updated research on hallucinations in general population
- Added research on anticipatory emotion
- Updated research on prognoses for psychotic disorders, including for suicide
- Integration of cognitive and biosocial theories of schizophrenia
- Added material on schizophrenia and bipolar family comorbidity
- Updated status of social drift research
- Updated status of stressful events research
- Updated evidence on treatment efficacy

CHAPTER 9

- New material on cognitive treatment for schizotypal personality disorder
- Added example of splitting
- Updated status of pharmacological treatment for borderline personality disorder
- Clarified coverage of therapy for histrionic personality disorder
- Revised coverage of narcissism subtypes
- Clarified difference between avoidant and schizoid personality disorders
- Clarified distinction between obsessive-compulsive personality disorder and obsessive-compulsive disorder
- Clarified and updated coverage of alternative dimensional models for personality disorders

CHAPTER 10

- Updated coverage of attention-deficit/hyperactivity disorder (ADHD)
- Updated status of psychosocial factors
- Update on cognitive-behavioral therapy for adult ADHD
- New material on genetic research
- Added research on name processing
- Updated status of autism spectrum disorder (ASD) medications
- Updated statistics on sports traumatic brain injury
- Added research on early identification
- Updated coverage of delirium research and treatment

CHAPTER 11

- Updated contradictory findings on physiological reactivity in conduct disorders
- Updated findings on Fast Track and conduct disorders
- Updated coverage on drugs are not first-line treatments for conduct disorder and oppositional defiant disorder
- New coverage of genetic and epigenetic findings in antisocial personality disorder
- Updated findings on amygdala and striatum

CHAPTER 12

- Updated with *DSM*-5 prevalence of anorexia nervosa
- Updated with *DSM*-5 prevalence of bulimia nervosa
- New research on leveling-out of prevalence of bulimia nervosa since 2000s
- Updated *DSM*-5 and international prevalence of binge-eating disorder
- Revised coverage of *DSM*-5 categories eating disorders not otherwise specified (EDNOS) and other specified feeding or eating disorder
- Updated coverage of obesity drugs
- Added coverage of male eating disorders and muscularity ideal
- Updated research on thinness ideal
- Revised coverage of the treatment of eating disorders
- New coverage of treatment access, Internet-based intervention, and prevention of eating disorders

CHAPTER 13

- New title: Sexual Disorders and Gender Diversity
- Updated coverage of sexual desire prevalence
- Added material on cognitions to include men
- New material on culture and gender roles
- Updated research on testosterone
- Updated research on biological treatments for women
- Revised heterosexual-specific language for early ejaculation treatment
- Revised heading of LGB section to separate sexual orientation from disorders
- Added unique considerations for LGB sexual dysfunction
- Revised coverage of nonpathological consensus and position on conversion therapy
- Emphasized continuum aspect of sadism/masochism
- Added evidence regarding sadism disorder in offenders
- Revised heading for treatment of paraphilic disorders to emphasize the disorders rather than the interests and behaviors
- Updated coverage of cognitive-behavioral therapy for paraphilias
- Significant revision of the gender dysphoria (GD) section to emphasize distress and impairment criteria
- Updated research on GD prevalence, associated psychopathology, and risk factors for HIV
- Added new coverage of gender diversity and transgender along the continuum
- Updated findings on brain in GD
- New coverage of GD in childhood and persistence into adulthood
- Added coverage of biological treatment of GD in children

CHAPTER 14

- Updated U.S. and world statistics throughout (prevalence of use, abuse, ER visits, and deaths)
- Increased emphasis on recent increases in use/abuse of methamphetamine and opioids
- Updated coverage of e-cigarettes
- Added coverage of opioid epidemic
- Updates on laws regarding medical and recreational uses of marijuana
- Updated coverage of gambling diagnosis and treatment
- Added coverage of Internet gaming disorder and other behavioral addictions

CHAPTER 15

- Updated epidemiology and statistics throughout
- Revised coverage of link between psychological diagnosis and physical health
- Updated cancer intervention research
- Updated status of research on psychosocial treatment and coronary heart disease (CHD)
- Streamlined coverage of depression and CHD
- Added discussion of culturally sensitive interventions
- New coverage of mobile health interventions (along with updates to Internet intervention)
- Clarified sleep brain-wave language
- Added examples for sleep study
- Updated research on narcolepsy as autoimmune problem
- Revised definition of hypoventilation

- Updated prevalence of sleep apnea
- Revised coverage of circadian rhythm disorders
- Revised coverage of arousal
- Increased coverage of confusional arousals
- Added examples for REM sleep disorder
- Added coverage of medications for nightmare disorder

CHAPTER 16

- Updated research on violence
- Added prevalence of incompetence to stand trial
- Revised coverage of states' use of insanity rules
- New introduction to section on justice system
- Updated rates of mental illness in prisons

ACKNOWLEDGMENTS

We are grateful to Brett Marroquín, Loyola Marymount University, for his invaluable contributions to this edition.

Chapter 1

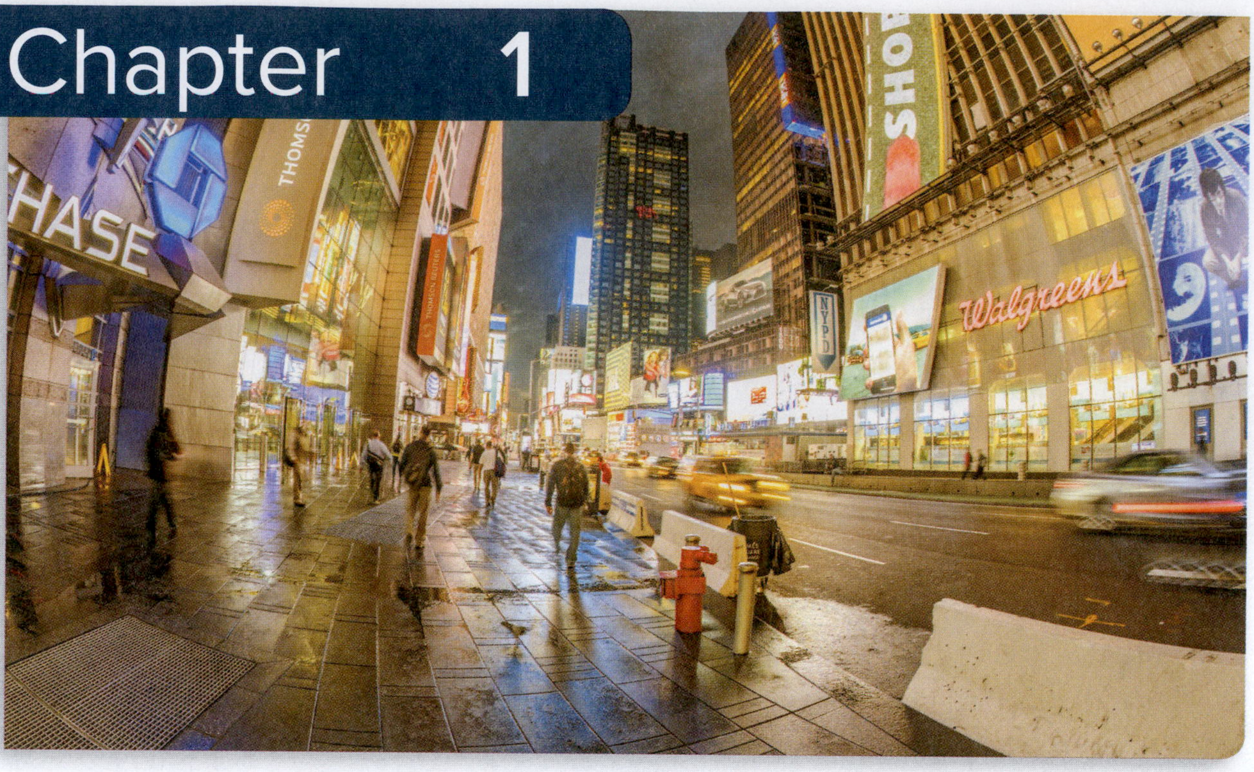

©travelview/Shutterstock

Looking at Abnormality

CHAPTER OUTLINE

Abnormality Along the Continuum

Behaviors, thoughts, and feelings are the following:

- Typical for the social context
- Not distressing to the individual
- Not interfering with social life or work/school
- Not dangerous

(Example: College students who are self-confident and happy, perform to their capacity in school, and have good friends)

Socially established division between normal and abnormal

Behaviors, thoughts, and feelings are one or more of the following:

- Highly unusual for the social context
- The source of significant individual distress
- Significantly interfering with social or occupational functioning
- Highly dangerous to the individual or others

(Example: College students who are hopeless about the future, are self-loathing, chronically abuse drugs, fail courses, and have alienated all their friends)

Normal — **Abnormal**

Behaviors, thoughts, and feelings are one or more of the following:

- Somewhat unusual for the social context
- Distressing to the individual
- Interfering with social or occupational functioning
- Dangerous

(Example: College students who are often unsure and self-critical, occasionally abuse prescription drugs, fail some courses, and avoid friends who disapprove of their drug use)

As humans, we think, we feel, we behave. Most of the time, our thoughts, feelings, and behaviors help us function in everyday life and are in the service of important goals or values we hold. Sometimes, however, we all have thoughts that upset us, experience feelings we'd rather not have, and act in ways that are self-defeating or detrimental to others. We may find ourselves in situations in which we can't think, feel, or behave as others would—as when, for example, we can't let go of a failed relationship. We may become upset over a situation that others don't find distressing, such as getting an average grade on an exam. Our thoughts, feelings, or behaviors may be interfering with our functioning in everyday life—for example, if we become afraid to walk alone after being mugged. Or we may be acting in ways that are dangerous to ourselves or others, such as driving a car when intoxicated.

Problems in thoughts, feelings, and behavior vary from normal to abnormal, as illustrated in the diagram above. We'd like to think there is a clear dividing line between normal variations in thoughts, emotions, and behaviors and what we would label "abnormal." Once an individual's behaviors or feelings crossed that line, we would be justified in saying that there is something wrong with that person or that he or she has a disorder. As we discuss in this chapter and throughout this book, however, there is increasing evidence that no such dividing line exists, perhaps for any of the mental health problems that are currently recognized. As you can see above, it can be hard to determine when behaviors, thoughts, and feelings become unusual, distressing, functionally impairing, or dangerous—key determinants of abnormality. We make decisions about where to draw the line that indicates a sufficient amount of abnormality to warrant a diagnosis or treatment. You will see that this **continuum model of abnormality** applies to all the disorders we discuss in this book. In this chapter, we discuss some of the factors that influence how thoughts, emotions, and behaviors are labeled abnormal.

Extraordinary People

My illness began slowly, gradually, when I was between the ages of 15 and 17. During that time reality became distant and I began to wander around in a sort of haze, foreshadowing the delusional world that was to come later. I also began to have visual hallucinations in which people changed into different characters, the change indicating to me their moral value. For example, the mother of a good friend always changed into a witch, and I believed this to be indicative of her evil nature. Another type of visual hallucination I had at this time is exemplified by an occurrence during a family trip through Utah: The cliffs along the side of the road took on a human appearance, and I perceived them as women, bedraggled and weeping. At the time I didn't know what to make of these changes in my perceptions. On the one hand, I thought they came as a gift from God, but on the other hand, I feared that something was dreadfully wrong. However, I didn't tell anyone what was happening; I was afraid of being called insane. I also feared, perhaps incredibly, that someone would take it lightly and tell me nothing was wrong, that I was just having a rough adolescence, which was what I was telling myself.

Source: Anonymous, 1992.

The study of abnormal psychology is the study of people, like the young woman in the Extraordinary People feature, who suffer mental, emotional, and often physical pain, often referred to as **psychopathology.** Sometimes the experiences of people with psychopathology are as unusual as those this young woman describes. Sometimes, however, people with psychopathology have experiences that are familiar to many of us but more extreme, as when everyday sadness transforms into life-altering depression.

In this book we explore the lives of people with troubling psychological symptoms to understand how they think, what they feel, and how they behave. We investigate what is known about the causes of these symptoms and the appropriate treatments for them. The purpose of this book is not only to provide you with information, facts and figures, theories, and research but also to help you understand the experience of people with psychological symptoms. The good news is that, thanks to an explosion of research in the past few decades, effective biological and psychological treatments are available for many of the mental health problems we discuss.

DEFINING ABNORMALITY

In popular culture, there are a lot of words for people and behaviors that seem abnormal: around the bend, bananas, barmy, batty, berserk, bonkers, cracked, crazy, cuckoo, daft, delirious, demented, deranged, dingy, erratic, flaky, flipped out, freaked out, fruity, insane, kooky, lunatic, mad, mad as a March hare, mad as a hatter, maniacal, mental, moonstruck, nuts, nutty, nutty as a fruitcake, of unsound mind, out of one's mind, out of one's tree, out to lunch, potty, psycho, screw loose, screwball, screwy, silly, touched, unbalanced, unglued, unhinged, unzipped, wacky. People talk as if they have an intuitive sense of what abnormal behavior is. Let's explore some of the ways abnormality has been defined.

Mental Illness

A common belief is that behaviors, thoughts, or feelings can be viewed as pathological or abnormal if they are symptoms of a *mental illness.* This implies that a disease process, much like hypertension or diabetes, is present. For example, when many people say that an individual "has schizophrenia" (which is characterized by unreal perceptions and severely irrational thinking), they imply that he or she has a disease that should show up on some sort of biological test, just as hypertension shows up when a person's blood pressure is taken.

To date, however, no biological test is available to diagnose any of the types of abnormality we discuss in this book (Hyman, 2010). This is not just because we do not yet have the right biological tests. In modern conceptualizations, mental disorders are not viewed as singular diseases with a common pathology that can be identified in all people with the disorder. Instead, mental health experts view mental disorders as collections of problems in thinking or cognition, in emotional responding or regulation, and in social behavior (Cuthbert & Insel, 2013; Hyman, 2010). Thus, for example, a person diagnosed with schizophrenia has a collection of problems in rational thinking and in responding emotionally and behaviorally in everyday life, and it is this collection of problems that we label schizophrenia. It is still possible, and in the case of schizophrenia likely, that biological factors are associated with these problems in thinking, feeling, and behaving. But it is unlikely that a singular disease process underlies the symptoms we call schizophrenia.

Cultural Norms

Consider these behaviors:

1. A man driving a nail through his hand
2. A woman refusing to eat for several days
3. A man barking like a dog and crawling on the floor on his hands and knees
4. A woman building a shrine to her dead husband in her living room and leaving food and gifts for him at the altar

Do you think these behaviors are abnormal? You might reply, "It depends." Several of these behaviors are accepted in certain circumstances. In many religious traditions, for example, refusing to eat for a period of time, or fasting, is a common ritual of cleansing and penitence. You might expect that some of the other behaviors listed, such as driving a nail through one's hand or barking like a dog, are abnormal in all circumstances, yet even these behaviors are accepted in certain situations. In Mexico, some Christians have themselves nailed to crosses on Good Friday to commemorate the crucifixion of Jesus. Among the Yoruba of Africa, traditional healers act like dogs during healing rituals (Murphy, 1976). Thus, the context, or circumstances surrounding a behavior, influences whether the behavior is viewed as abnormal.

Cultural norms play a large role in defining abnormality. A good example is the behaviors people are expected to display when someone they love dies (Rosenblatt, 2008). In cultures dominated by Shinto and Buddhist religions, it is customary to build altars to honor dead loved ones, to offer them food and gifts, and to speak with them as if they were in the room. In cultures dominated by Christian and Jewish religions, such practices would potentially be considered quite abnormal.

Cultures have strong norms for what is considered acceptable behavior for men versus women, and these gender-role expectations also influence the labeling of behaviors as normal or abnormal (Addis, 2008). In many cultures, men who display sadness or anxiety or who choose to stay home to raise their children while their wives work are at risk of being labeled abnormal, while women who are aggressive or who don't want to have children are at risk of being labeled abnormal.

Cultural relativism is the view that there are no universal standards or rules for labeling a behavior abnormal; instead, behaviors can be labeled abnormal only relative to cultural norms (Snowden & Yamada, 2005). The advantage of this perspective is that it honors the norms and traditions of different cultures, rather than imposing the standards of one culture on judgments of abnormality. Yet opponents of cultural relativism argue that dangers arise when cultural norms are allowed to dictate what is normal or abnormal. In particular, psychiatrist Thomas Szasz (1961, 2011) noted that throughout history, societies have labeled individuals and groups abnormal in order to justify controlling or silencing them. Hitler branded Jews abnormal and used this label as one justification for the Holocaust. The former Soviet Union sometimes branded political dissidents mentally ill and confined them in mental hospitals. When the slave trade was active in the United States, slaves who tried to escape their masters could be diagnosed with a mental disease that was said to cause them to desire freedom; the prescribed treatment for this disease was whipping and hard labor.

Most mental health professionals these days do not hold an extreme relativist view on abnormality, recognizing the dangers of basing definitions of abnormality solely on cultural norms. Yet even those who reject an extreme cultural-relativist position recognize that culture and gender have a number of influences on the expression of abnormal behaviors and on the way those behaviors are treated. First, culture and gender can influence the ways people express symptoms. People who lose touch with reality often believe that they have divine powers, but whether they believe they are Jesus or Mohammed depends on their religious background.

Second, culture and gender can influence people's willingness to admit to certain types of behaviors or feelings (Snowden & Yamada, 2005). People in Eskimo and Tahitian cultures may be reluctant to admit to feeling anger because of strong cultural norms against the expression of anger. The Kaluli of

In Mexico, some Christians have themselves nailed to a cross to commemorate the crucifixion of Jesus. ©AARON FAVILA/AP Images

When the slave trade was active, slaves who tried to escape were sometimes labeled as having mental illness and were beaten to "cure" them. *©Jean Baptiste Debret/Getty Images*

New Guinea and the Yanomamo of Brazil, however, value the expression of anger and have elaborate and complex rituals for expressing it (Jenkins, Kleinman, & Good, 1991).

Third, culture and gender can influence the types of treatments deemed acceptable or helpful for people exhibiting abnormal behaviors. Some cultures may view drug therapies for psychopathology as most appropriate, while others may be more willing to accept psychotherapy (Snowden & Yamada, 2005). Throughout this book, we will explore these influences of culture and gender on behaviors labeled abnormal.

The Four Ds of Abnormality

If we do not want to define abnormality only on the basis of cultural norms, and if we cannot define abnormality as the presence of a mental illness because no singular, identifiable disease process underlies most psychological problems, how do we define abnormality? Modern judgments of abnormality are influenced by the interplay of four dimensions, often called "the four Ds": dysfunction, distress, deviance, and dangerousness. Behaviors, thoughts, and feelings are *dysfunctional* when they interfere with the person's ability to function in daily life, to hold a job, or to form close relationships. The more dysfunctional behaviors and feelings are, the more likely they are to be considered abnormal by mental health professionals. For example, thinking that is out of touch with reality (such as believing you are Satan and should be punished) makes it difficult to function in everyday life and so is considered dysfunctional.

Behaviors and feelings that cause *distress* to the individual or to others around him or her are also likely to be considered abnormal. Many of the problems we discuss in this book cause individuals tremendous emotional and even physical pain; in other cases, the person diagnosed with a disorder is not in distress but causes others distress—for example, through chronic lying, stealing, or violence.

Highly *deviant* behaviors, such as hearing voices when no one else is around, lead to judgments of abnormality. What is deviant is influenced by cultural norms, of course. Finally, some behaviors and feelings, such as suicidal gestures, are of potential harm to the individual, whereas other behaviors and feelings, such as excessive aggression, could potentially

SHADES OF GRAY

Consider the following descriptions of two students.

In the year between her eighteenth and nineteenth birthdays, Jennifer, who is 5′6″, dropped from a weight of 125 pounds to 105 pounds. The weight loss began when Jennifer had an extended case of the flu and lost 10 pounds. Friends complimented her on being thinner, and Jennifer decided to lose more weight. She cut her intake of food to about 1,200 calories, avoiding carbs as much as possible, and began running a few miles every day. Sometimes she is so hungry she has trouble concentrating on her schoolwork. Jennifer values her new lean look so much, however, that she is terrified of gaining the weight back. Indeed, she'd like to lose a few more pounds so she could fit into a size 2.

Mark is what you might call a "heavy drinker." Although he is only 18, he has ready access to alcohol, and most nights he typically drinks at least five or six beers. He rarely feels drunk after that much alcohol, though, so he might also throw back a few shots, especially when he is out partying on Saturday nights. He's been caught a few times and received tickets for underage drinking, but he proudly displays them on his dorm wall as badges of honor. Mark's grades are not what they could be, but he finds his classes boring and has a hard time doing the work.

Do you find Jennifer's or Mark's behaviors abnormal? How would you rate their level of dysfunction, distress, deviance, and danger? (Discussion appears at the end of this chapter.)

harm others. Such *dangerous* behaviors and feelings are often seen as abnormal.

The four Ds together make up mental health professionals' definition of behaviors or feelings as abnormal or *maladaptive*. The experiences of the woman described in Extraordinary People presented at the beginning of this chapter would be labeled abnormal based on these criteria because the symptoms interfere with her daily functioning, cause her suffering, are highly unusual, and are potentially dangerous to her.

We are still left making subjective judgments, however. How much emotional pain or harm must a person be suffering? How much should the behaviors be interfering with daily functioning? We return to the continuum model to acknowledge that each of the four Ds lies along its own continuum. A person's behaviors and feelings can be more or less dysfunctional, distressing, deviant, or dangerous. Thus, there is no sharp line between what is normal and what is abnormal.

HISTORICAL PERSPECTIVES ON ABNORMALITY

Across history, three types of theories have been used to explain abnormal behavior. The **biological theories** have viewed abnormal behavior as similar to physical diseases, caused by the breakdown of systems in the body. The appropriate cure is the restoration of bodily health. The **supernatural theories** have viewed abnormal behavior as a result of divine intervention, curses, demonic possession, and personal sin. To rid the person of the perceived affliction, religious rituals, exorcisms, confessions, and atonement have been prescribed. The **psychological theories** have viewed abnormal behavior as a result of traumas, such as bereavement, or of chronic stress. According to these theories, rest, relaxation, a change of environment, and certain herbal medicines are sometimes helpful. These three types of theories have influenced how people acting abnormally have been regarded in the society. A person thought to be abnormal because he or she was a sinner, for example, would be regarded differently from a person thought to be abnormal because of a disease.

Ancient Theories

Our understanding of prehistoric people's conceptions of abnormality is based on inferences from archaeological artifacts—fragments of bones, tools, artwork, and so on—as well as from ancient writings about abnormal behavior. It seems that humans have always viewed abnormality as something needing special explanation.

Driving Away Evil Spirits

Historians speculate that even prehistoric people had a concept of insanity, probably one rooted in supernatural beliefs (Selling, 1940). A person who acted oddly was suspected of being possessed by evil spirits. The typical treatment for abnormality, according to supernatural theories, was exorcism—driving the evil spirits from the body of the suffering person. Shamans, or healers, would recite prayers or incantations, try to talk the spirits out of the body, or make the body an uncomfortable place for the spirits to reside—often through extreme measures such as starving or beating the person. At other times, the person thought to be possessed by evil spirits would simply be killed.

One treatment for abnormality during the Stone Age and well into the Middle Ages may have been to drill holes in the skull of a person displaying abnormal behavior to allow the spirits to depart (Tatagiba, Ugarte, & Acioly, 2015). Archaeologists have found skulls dating back to a half-million years ago in which sections of the skull have been drilled or cut away. The tool used for this drilling is called a trephine, and the operation is called **trephination.** Some historians believe that people who were seeing or hearing things that were not real and people who were chronically sad were subjected to this form of brain surgery (Feldman & Goodrich, 2001). Presumably, if the person survived this surgery, the evil spirits would have been released and the person's abnormal behavior would decline. However, we cannot know with certainty that trephination was used to drive away evil spirits. Other historians suggest that it was used primarily for the removal of blood clots caused by stone weapons during warfare and for other medical purposes (Maher & Maher, 1985).

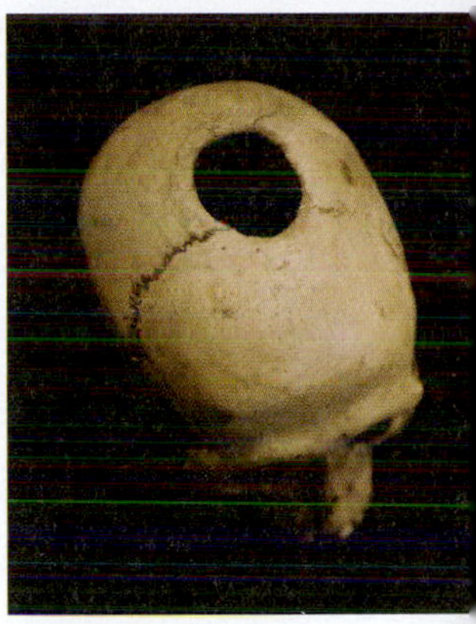

Some scholars believe that holes found in ancient skulls are from trephination, a crude form of surgery possibly performed on people acting abnormally. *©PHAS/Getty Images*

Ancient China: Balancing Yin and Yang

Some of the earliest written sources on abnormality are ancient Chinese medical texts (Tseng, 1973). The *Nei Ching* (Classic of Internal Medicine) was probably written around 2674 BCE by Huang Ti, the legendary third emperor of China.

Ancient Chinese medicine was based on the concept of yin and yang. The human body was said to contain a positive force (yang) and a negative force (yin), which confronted and complemented each other. If the two forces were in balance, the individual was healthy. If not, illness, including insanity, could result. For example, excited insanity was considered the result of an excessive positive force:

> The person suffering from excited insanity initially feels sad, eating and sleeping less; he then becomes grandiose, feeling that he is very smart and noble, talking and scolding day and night, singing, behaving strangely, seeing strange things,

> hearing strange voices, believing that he can see the devil or gods, etc. As treatment for such an excited condition, withholding food was suggested, because food was considered to be the source of positive force and the patient was thought to be in need of a decrease in such force. (Tseng, 1973, p. 570)

Chinese medical philosophy also held that human emotions were controlled by internal organs. When the "vital air" was flowing on one of these organs, an individual experienced a particular emotion. For example, when air flowed on the heart, a person felt joy; when on the lungs, sorrow; when on the liver, anger; when on the spleen, worry; and when on the kidney, fear. This theory encouraged people to live in an orderly and harmonious way so as to maintain the proper movement of vital air.

Although the perspective on psychological symptoms represented by ancient texts was largely a biological one, the rise of Taoism and Buddhism during the Chin and T'ang dynasties (420–618 CE) led to some religious interpretations of abnormal behavior. Evil winds and ghosts were blamed for bewitching people and for inciting people's erratic emotional displays and uncontrolled behavior. Religious theories of abnormality declined in China after this period (Tseng, 1973).

Some of the earliest writings on mental disorders are from ancient Chinese texts. This illustration shows a healer at work. ©*Mary Evans Picture Library/The Image Works*

Ancient Egypt, Greece, and Rome: Biological Theories Dominate

Other ancient writings on abnormal behavior are found in the papyri of Egypt and Mesopotamia (Veith, 1965). The oldest of these, a document known as the Kahun Papyrus after the ancient Egyptian city in which it was found, dates from about 1900 BCE. This document lists a number of disorders, each followed by a physician's judgment of the cause of the disorder and the appropriate treatment.

Several of the disorders apparently left people with unexplainable aches and pains, sadness or distress, and apathy about life, such as "a woman who loves bed; she does not rise and she does not shake it" (Veith, 1965, p. 3). These disorders were said to occur only in women and were attributed to a "wandering uterus." The Egyptians believed that the uterus could become dislodged and wander throughout a woman's body, interfering with her other organs. Later, the Greeks, holding to the same theory of anatomy, named this disorder *hysteria* (from the Greek word *hystera,* which means "uterus"). These days, the term "hysteria" is used to refer to physiological symptoms that probably are the result of psychological processes. In the Egyptian papyri, the prescribed treatment for this disorder involved the use of strong-smelling substances to drive the uterus back to its proper place.

Beginning with Homer, the Greeks wrote frequently of people acting abnormally (Wallace & Gach, 2008). The physician Hippocrates (460–377 BCE) described a case of a common phobia: A man could not walk alongside a cliff, pass over a bridge, or jump over even a shallow ditch without feeling unable to control his limbs or his vision becoming impaired.

Most average Greeks and Romans saw abnormal behavior as an affliction from the gods. Those afflicted retreated to temples honoring the god Aesculapius, where priests held healing ceremonies. Plato (423–347 BCE) and Socrates (469–399 BCE) argued that some forms of abnormal behavior were divine and could be the source of great literary and prophetic gifts.

For the most part, however, Greek physicians rejected supernatural explanations of abnormal behavior (Wallace & Gach, 2008). Hippocrates, often regarded as the father of medicine, argued that abnormal behavior was like other diseases of the body. According to Hippocrates, the body was composed of four basic humors: blood, phlegm, yellow bile, and black bile. All diseases, including abnormal behavior, were caused by imbalances in the body's essential humors. Based on careful observation of his many patients, which included listening to their dreams, Hippocrates classified abnormal behavior into four categories: epilepsy, mania, melancholia, and brain fever.

The treatments prescribed by the Greek physicians were intended to restore the balance of the four humors.

Sometimes these treatments were physiological and intrusive, such as bleeding a patient to treat disorders that were thought to result from an excess of blood. Other treatments consisted of rest, relaxation, a change of climate or scenery, a change of diet, or living a temperate life. Some nonmedical treatments prescribed by these physicians sound remarkably like those prescribed by modern psychotherapists. Hippocrates, for example, believed that removing a patient from a difficult family could help restore mental health. Plato argued that insanity arose when the rational mind was overcome by impulse, passion, or appetite. Sanity could be regained through a discussion with the individual that was designed to restore rational control over emotions (Maher & Maher, 1985).

Among the Greeks of Hippocrates' and Plato's time, the relatives of people considered insane were encouraged to confine their afflicted family members to the home. The state claimed no responsibility for insane people; it provided no asylums or institutions, other than the religious temples, to house and care for them. The state could, however, take rights away from people declared insane. Relatives could bring suit against those they considered insane, and the state could award the property of insane people to their relatives. People declared insane could not marry or acquire or dispose of their own property. Poor people who were considered insane were simply left to roam the streets if they were not violent. If they were violent, they were locked away. The general public greatly feared insanity of any form, and many people thought to be insane were shunned or even stoned (Maher & Maher, 1985).

Medieval Views

The Middle Ages (around 400–1400 CE) are often described as a time of backward thinking dominated by an obsession with supernatural forces, yet even within Europe supernatural theories of abnormal behavior did not dominate until the late Middle Ages, between the eleventh and fifteenth centuries (Neugebauer, 1979). Prior to the eleventh century, witches and witchcraft were accepted as real but were considered mere nuisances, overrated by superstitious people. Severe emotional shock and physical illness or injury most often were seen as the causes of bizarre behaviors. For example, English court records attributed mental health problems to factors such as a "blow received on the head," explained that symptoms were "induced by fear of his father," and noted that "he has lost his reason owing to a long and incurable infirmity" (Neugebauer, 1979, p. 481). While laypeople probably did believe in demons and curses as causes of abnormal behavior, there is strong evidence that physicians and government officials in the early Middle Ages attributed abnormal behavior to physical causes or traumas.

Witchcraft

Beginning in the eleventh century, the power of the Catholic Church in Europe was threatened by the breakdown of feudalism and by rebellions. The Church interpreted these threats in terms of heresy and Satanism. The Inquisition was established originally to rid the Earth of religious heretics, but eventually those practicing witchcraft or Satanism also became the focus of hunts. The witch hunts continued long after the Reformation, perhaps reaching their height during the fifteenth to seventeenth centuries—the period known as the Renaissance (Mora, 2008).

Some psychiatric historians have argued that persons accused of witchcraft must have been mentally ill (Veith, 1965; Zilboorg & Henry, 1941). Accused witches sometimes confessed to speaking with the devil, flying on the backs of animals, or engaging in other unusual behaviors. Such people may have been experiencing delusions (false beliefs) or hallucinations (unreal perceptual experiences), which are signs of some psychological disorders. However, confessions of such experiences may have been extracted through torture or in exchange for a stay of execution (Spanos, 1978).

In 1563, Johann Weyer published *The Deception of Dreams,* in which he argued that those accused of being witches were suffering from melancholy (depression) and senility. The Church banned Weyer's writings. Twenty years later, Reginald Scot, in his *Discovery of Witchcraft* (1584), supported Weyer's beliefs: "These women are but diseased wretches suffering from melancholy, and their words, actions, reasoning, and gestures show that sickness has affected their brains and impaired their powers of judgment" (Castiglioni, 1946, p. 253). Again, the Church—joined

Some people burned at the stake as witches may have had mental disorders that caused them to act abnormally. ©*Bettmann/Getty Images*

this time by the state—refuted the arguments and banned Scot's writings.

As is often the case, change came from within. In the sixteenth century, Teresa of Avila, a Spanish nun who was later canonized, explained that the mass hysteria that had broken out among a group of nuns was not the work of the devil but was the result of infirmities or sickness. She argued that these nuns were *comas enfermas,* or "as if sick." She sought out natural causes for the nuns' strange behaviors and concluded that they were due to melancholy, a weak imagination, or drowsiness and sleepiness (Sarbin & Juhasz, 1967).

The culture so completely accepted the existence of witches and witchcraft that some perfectly sane people may have self-identified as witches. In addition, most writings of medieval and Renaissance times, as well as writings from the witch hunt period in Salem, Massachusetts, clearly distinguish between people who were mad and people who were witches. The distinction between madness and witchcraft continues to this day in cultures that believe in witchcraft.

Psychic Epidemics

Psychic epidemics are defined as a phenomenon in which large numbers of people engage in unusual behaviors that appear to have a psychological origin. During the Middle Ages, reports of dance frenzies or manias were frequent. A monk, Peter of Herental, described a rash of dance frenzies that broke out over a 4-month period in 1374 in Germany:

> Both men and women were abused by the devil to such a degree that they danced in their homes, in the churches and in the streets, holding each other's hands and leaping in the air. While they danced they called out the names of demons, such as Friskes and others, but they were unaware of this nor did they pay attention to modesty even though people watched them. At the end of the dance, they felt such pains in the chest, that if their friends did not tie linen clothes tightly around their waists, they cried out like madmen that they were dying. (Cited in Rosen, 1968, pp. 196–197)

Bedlam—the Hospital of Saint Mary of Bethlehem in London—was famous for the chaotic and deplorable conditions in which people with mental disorders were kept. ©SCIENCE SOURCE/Science Source

Other instances of dance frenzy were reported in 1428 during the feast of Saint Vitus, at Schaffhausen, at which a monk danced himself to death. In 1518 a large epidemic of uncontrolled dance frenzy occurred at the chapel of Saint Vitus at Hohlenstein, near Zabern. According to one account, more than 400 people danced during the 4 weeks the frenzy lasted. Some writers of the time began to call the frenzied dancing Saint Vitus' dance.

A similar phenomenon, *tarantism,* was noted in Italy as early as the fourteenth century and became prominent in the seventeenth century. People suddenly developed an acute pain, which they attributed to the bite of a tarantula. They jumped around and danced wildly in the streets, tearing at their clothes and beating each other with whips. Some people dug holes in the earth and rolled on the ground; others howled and made obscene gestures. At the time, many people interpreted dance frenzies and tarantism as the results of possession by the devil. The behaviors may have been the remnants of ancient rituals performed by people worshipping the Greek god Dionysus.

We see episodes of psychic epidemics in modern times. On February 8, 1991, a number of students and teachers in a high school in Rhode Island thought they smelled noxious fumes coming from the ventilation system. The first person to detect these fumes, a 14-year-old girl, fell to the floor, crying and saying that her stomach hurt and her eyes stung. Other students and the teacher in that room then began to experience symptoms. They were moved into the hallway with a great deal of commotion. Soon students and teachers from adjacent rooms, who could see clearly into the hallway, began to experience symptoms. Eventually, 21 people (17 students and 4 teachers) were admitted to the local hospital emergency room. All were hyperventilating, and most complained of dizziness, headache, and nausea. Although some initially showed symptoms of mild carbon monoxide intoxication in blood tests, no evidence of toxic gas in the school could be found. The physicians treating the children and teachers concluded that the outbreak was a case of mass hysteria prompted by the fear of chemical warfare during the Persian Gulf War (Rockney & Lemke, 1992).

Psychic epidemics are no longer viewed as the result of spirit possession or the bite of a tarantula. Rather, psychologists attempt to understand them through research from social psychology on the influence of others on individuals' self-perceptions. The social context can affect even our perceptions of our own bodies, as we will see when we discuss people's differing reactions to psychoactive substances such as marijuana (see the chapter "Substance Use and Gambling Disorders") and people's interpretations of their physical sensations (see the chapter "Somatic Symptom and Dissociative Disorders").

The Spread of Asylums

As early as the twelfth century, many towns in Europe took some responsibility for housing and caring for people considered mentally ill (Kroll, 1973). Remarkable among these towns was Gheel, Belgium, where townspeople regularly took into their homes the mentally ill who were visiting the shrine of Saint Dymphna for cures.

In about the eleventh or twelfth century, general hospitals began to include special rooms or facilities for people exhibiting abnormal behavior. The mentally ill were little more than inmates in these early hospitals, housed against their will, often in extremely harsh conditions. One of the most famous of these hospitals was the Hospital of Saint Mary of Bethlehem, in London, which officially became a mental hospital in 1547. This hospital, nicknamed Bedlam, was famous for its deplorable conditions. At Bedlam and other mental hospitals established in Europe in the sixteenth, seventeenth, and eighteenth centuries, patients were exhibited to the public for a fee. They lived in filth and confinement, often chained to the wall or locked inside small boxes. The following description of the treatment of patients in La Bicêtre Hospital, an asylum for male patients in Paris, provides an example of typical care:

> The patients were ordinarily shackled to the walls of their dark, unlighted cells by iron collars which held them flat against the wall and permitted little movement. Often there were also iron hoops around the waists of the patients and both their hands and feet were chained. Although these chains usually permitted enough movement that the patients could feed themselves out of bowls, they often kept them from being able to lie down at night. Since little was known about dietetics, and the patients were presumed to be animals anyway, little attention was paid to whether they were adequately fed or whether the food was good or bad. The cells were furnished only with straw and were never swept or cleaned; the patient remained in the midst of all the accumulated ordure. No one visited the cells except at feeding time, no provision was made for warmth, and even the most elementary gestures of humanity were lacking. (Adapted from Selling, 1940, pp. 54–55)

The laws regarding the confinement of the mentally ill in Europe and the United States were concerned with the protection of the public and the ill person's relatives (Busfield, 1986; Scull, 1993). For example, Dalton's 1618 edition of *Common Law* states that "it is lawful for the parents, kinsmen or other friends of a man that is mad, or frantic ... to take him and put him into a house, to bind or chain him, and to beat him with rods, and to do any other forcible act to reclaim him, or to keep him so he shall do no hurt" (Allderidge, 1979).

The first Act for Regulating Madhouses in England was passed in 1774, with the intention of cleaning up the deplorable conditions in hospitals and madhouses and protecting people from being unjustly jailed for insanity. This act provided for the licensing and inspection of madhouses and required that a physician, a surgeon, or an apothecary sign a certificate before a patient could be admitted. The act's provisions applied only to paying patients in private madhouses, however, and not to the poor people confined to workhouses.

These asylums typically were established and run by people who thought that abnormal behaviors were medical illnesses. For example, Benjamin Rush (1745–1813), one of the founders of American psychiatry, believed that abnormal behavior was caused by

In the medieval and early modern periods, doctors used bleeding to treat people with mental disorders and many other ailments. ©Jean-Loup Charmet/Science Source

excessive blood in the brain and prescribed bleeding the patient, or drawing huge amounts of blood from the body. Thus, although the supernatural theories of the Middle Ages have often been decried as leading to brutal treatment of people with mental illnesses, the medical theories of those times and of the next couple of centuries did not always lead to better treatment.

Moral Treatment in the Eighteenth and Nineteenth Centuries

The eighteenth and nineteenth centuries saw the growth of a more humane treatment of people with mental health problems, a period known as the **mental hygiene movement.** This new treatment was based on the psychological view that people developed problems because they had become separated from nature and had succumbed to the stresses imposed by the rapid social changes of the period (Rosen, 1968). The prescribed treatment, including prayers and incantations, was rest and relaxation in a serene and physically appealing place.

A leader of the movement for **moral treatment** of people with abnormality was Philippe Pinel (1745–1826), a French physician who took charge of La Bicêtre in Paris in 1793. Pinel argued, "To detain maniacs in constant seclusion and to load them with chains; to leave them defenceless, to the brutality of underlings ... in a word, to rule them with a rod of iron ... is a system of superintendence, more distinguished for its convenience than for its humanity or success" (Grob, 1994, p. 27). Pinel believed that many forms of abnormality could be cured by restoring patients' dignity and tranquility.

Pinel ordered that patients be allowed to walk freely around the asylum. They were provided with clean and sunny rooms, comfortable sleeping quarters, and good food. Nurses and professional therapists were trained to work with the patients to help them regain their sense of tranquility and engage in planned social activities. Although many physicians thought Pinel himself was mad for releasing the patients from confinement, his approach was remarkably successful. Many people who had been locked away in darkness for decades became able to control their behavior and reengage in life. Some improved so much that they could be released from the asylum. Pinel later successfully reformed La Salpêtrière Hospital, a mental hospital for female patients in Paris (Grob, 1994).

In 1796 the Quaker William Tuke (1732–1822) opened an asylum in England, called The Retreat, in direct response to the brutal treatment he saw being delivered at other facilities to people with abnormal behavior. Tuke's treatment was designed to restore patients' self-restraint by treating them with respect and dignity and encouraging them to exercise self-control (Grob, 1994).

One of the most militant crusaders for moral treatment of the insane was Dorothea Dix (1802–1887). A retired schoolteacher living in Boston, Dix visited a jail on a cold Sunday morning in 1841 to teach a Sunday school class to women inmates. There she discovered the negligence and brutality that characterized the treatment of poor people exhibiting abnormal behavior, many of whom were simply warehoused in jails.

That encounter began Dix's tireless quest to improve the treatment of people with mental health problems. Dix's lobbying efforts led to the passage of laws and appropriations to fund the cleanup of mental hospitals and the training of mental health professionals dedicated to the moral treatment of patients.

Philippe Pinel, a leader in the moral movement in France, helped free mental patients from the horrible conditions of the hospitals. *©RAPHO AGENCE/Science Source*

Between 1841 and 1881, Dix personally helped establish more than 30 mental institutions in the United States, Canada, Newfoundland, and Scotland. Hundreds more public hospitals for the insane established during this period by others were run according to humanitarian perspectives.

Unfortunately, the moral treatment movement grew too fast. As more asylums were built and more people went into them, the capacity of the asylums to recruit mental health professionals and to maintain a humane, individual approach to each patient declined (Grob, 1994; Scull, 1993). The physicians, nurses, and other caretakers simply did not have enough time to give each patient the calm and dedicated attention needed. The fantastic successes of the early moral treatment movement gave way to more modest successes, and to many outright failures, as patients remained impaired or their condition worsened. Even some patients who received the best moral treatment could not benefit from it because their problems were not due to a loss of dignity or tranquility. With so many patients receiving moral treatment, the number of patients who failed to benefit from it increased, and questions about its effectiveness grew louder (Grob, 1994).

At the same time, the rapid pace of immigration into the United States in the late nineteenth century meant that an increasing percentage of its asylum patients were from different cultures and often from the lower socioeconomic classes. Prejudice against these "foreigners," combined with increasing attention to the failures of moral treatment, led to declines in public support for funding such institutions. Reduced funding led to even greater declines in the quality of care. At the turn of the twentieth century, many public hospitals were no better than warehouses (Grob, 1994; McGovern, 1985; Scull, 1993).

Effective treatments for most major mental health problems were not developed until well into the twentieth century. Until then, patients who could not afford private care were warehoused in large, overcrowded, physically isolated state institutions that did not offer treatment (Deutsch, 1937).

THE EMERGENCE OF MODERN PERSPECTIVES

Although the treatment of people who exhibited abnormal behavior deteriorated somewhat at the turn of the twentieth century, the early twentieth century saw tremendous advances in the scientific study of disorders. These advances laid the groundwork for the biological, psychological, and social theories of abnormality that now dominate psychology and psychiatry.

The Beginnings of Modern Biological Perspectives

Basic knowledge of the anatomy, physiology, neurology, and chemistry of the body increased rapidly in the late nineteenth century. With the advancement of this basic knowledge came an increasing focus on biological causes of abnormality. In 1845, German psychiatrist Wilhelm Griesinger (1817–1868) published *The Pathology and Therapy of Psychic Disorders,* presenting a systematic argument that all psychological disorders can be explained in terms of brain pathology. In 1883 one of Griesinger's followers, Emil Kraepelin (1856–1926), also published a text emphasizing the importance of brain pathology in psychological disorders. More important, Kraepelin developed a scheme for classifying symptoms into discrete disorders that is the basis for our modern classification systems (Kendler & Engstrom, 2016), as we will discuss in the chapter "Assessing and Diagnosing Abnormality." Having a good classification system gives investigators a common set of labels for disorders as well as a set of criteria for distinguishing between them, contributing immensely to the advancement of the scientific study of the disorders.

Dorothea Dix fought for the moral treatment of mental patients in the United States. *Source: Library of Congress, Prints & Photographs Division, Reproduction number LC-USZ62-9797 (b&w film copy neg.)*

One of the most important discoveries underpinning modern biological theories of abnormality was the discovery of the cause of **general paresis,** a disease that leads to paralysis, insanity, and eventually death (Duffy, 1995). In the mid-1800s, reports that patients with paresis also had a history of syphilis led to the suspicion that syphilis might be a cause of paresis. In 1897, Viennese psychiatrist Richard Krafft-Ebing injected paretic patients with matter from syphilitic sores. None of the patients developed syphilis, and Krafft-Ebing concluded that they must already have been infected with it. The discovery that syphilis is the cause of one form of insanity lent great weight to the idea that biological factors can cause abnormal behaviors (Duffy, 1995).

Emil Kraepelin (1856–1926) developed a classification system for mental disorders that remains influential today. *©Hulton Archive/Getty Images*

As we will discuss in more detail in the chapter "Theories and Treatment of Abnormality," modern biological theories of the psychological disorders have focused on the role of genetics, structural and functional abnormalities in the brain, and biochemical imbalances. The advances in our understanding of the biological aspects of psychological disorders have contributed to the development of therapeutic medications.

The Psychoanalytic Perspective

The development of psychoanalytic theory begins with the odd story of Franz Anton Mesmer (1734–1815), an Austrian physician who believed that people have a magnetic fluid in the body that must be distributed in a particular pattern in order to maintain health. The distribution of magnetic fluid in one person could be influenced by the magnetic forces of other people, as well as by the alignments of the planets. In 1778 Mesmer opened a clinic in Paris to treat all sorts of diseases by applying animal magnetism.

The psychological disorders that were the focus of much of Mesmer's treatment were the hysterical disorders, in which people lose functioning or feeling in some part of the body for no apparent physiological reason. His patients sat in darkness around a tub containing various chemicals, and the affected areas of their bodies were prodded by iron rods emerging from the tub. With music playing, Mesmer emerged wearing an elaborate robe, touching each patient as he passed by, supposedly realigning people's magnetic fluids through his own powerful magnetic force. This process, Mesmer said, cured illness, including psychological disorders.

Mesmer eventually was labeled a charlatan by a scientific review committee that included Benjamin Franklin. Yet his methods, known as **mesmerism,** continued to fuel debate long after he had faded into obscurity. The "cures" Mesmer effected in his psychiatric patients were attributed to the trancelike state that Mesmer seemed to induce in his patients. Later this state was labeled hypnosis. Under hypnosis, Mesmer's patients appeared very suggestible, and the mere suggestion that their ailments would disappear seemed enough to make them actually disappear.

The connection between hypnosis and hysteria fascinated several leading scientists of the time, although not all scientists accepted this connection. In particular, Jean Charcot (1825–1893), head of La Salpêtrière Hospital in Paris and the leading neurologist of his time, argued that hysteria was caused by degeneration in the brain. The work of two physicians practicing in the French town of Nancy, Hippolyte-Marie Bernheim (1840–1919) and Ambroise-Auguste Liebault (1823–1904), eventually won over Charcot, however. Bernheim and Liebault showed that they could induce the symptoms of hysteria, such as paralysis in an arm or the loss of feeling in a leg, by suggesting these symptoms to patients who were hypnotized. Fortunately, they could also remove these symptoms under hypnosis. Charcot was so impressed by the evidence that hysteria has psychological roots that he became a leading researcher of the psychological causes of abnormal behavior. The experiments of Bernheim and Liebault, along with the leadership of Charcot, did a great deal to advance psychological perspectives on abnormality.

One of Charcot's students was Sigmund Freud (1856–1939), a Viennese neurologist who went to study with Charcot in 1885. In the course of this work, Freud became convinced that much of the mental life of an individual remains hidden from consciousness. This view was further supported by Freud's interactions with Pierre Janet (1859–1947) in Paris. Janet was investigating multiple personality disorder, in which people appear to have multiple, distinct personalities, each of which operates independently of the others, often not knowing the others exist (Matarazzo, 1985).

When he returned to Vienna, Freud worked with Josef Breuer (1842–1925), another physician interested in hypnosis and in the unconscious processes behind psychological problems. Breuer had discovered that encouraging patients to talk about their problems while under hypnosis led to a great upwelling and release of emotion, which eventually was called catharsis. The patient's discussion of his or her problems under hypnosis was less censored than conscious discussion, allowing the therapist to elicit important psychological material more easily.

Breuer and Freud collaborated on a paper published in 1893 as *On the Psychical Mechanisms of Hysterical Phenomena,* which laid out their discoveries about hypnosis, the unconscious, and the therapeutic value of catharsis. This paper proved to be a foundation stone in the development of **psychoanalysis,** the study of the unconscious. Freud introduced his ideas to America in 1909 in a series of lectures at Clark University in Worcester, Massachusetts, at the invitation of G. Stanley Hall, one of the founders of American psychology.

Freud wrote dozens of papers and books on his theory of psychoanalysis (discussed in detail in the chapter "Theories and Treatment of Abnormality"), and he became the best-known figure in psychiatry and psychology. The impact of Freud's theories on the development of psychology over the next century cannot be overstated. Freudian ideas not only influenced the professional literature on psychopathology but also are used heavily in literary theory, anthropology, and other humanities. They pervade popular notions of psychological processes to this day.

The Roots of Behaviorism

In what now seems like a parallel universe, while psychoanalytic theory was being born, the roots of behaviorism were being planted first in Europe and then in the United States. Ivan Pavlov (1849–1936), a Russian physiologist, developed methods and theories for understanding behavior in terms of stimuli and responses rather than in terms of the internal workings of the unconscious mind. He discovered that dogs could be conditioned to salivate when presented with stimuli other than food if the food was paired with these other stimuli—a process later called **classical conditioning.** Pavlov's discoveries inspired American John Watson (1878–1958) to study important human behaviors, such as phobias, in terms of classical conditioning (see the chapter "Trauma, Anxiety, Obsessive-Compulsive, and Related Disorders"). Watson rejected psychoanalytic and biological theories of abnormal behaviors such as phobias and explained them entirely on the basis of the individual's history of conditioning. Watson (1930) went so far as to boast that he could train any healthy child to become any kind of adult he wished:

> Give me a dozen healthy infants, well-formed, and my own specified world to bring them up in, and I'll guarantee to take any one at random and train him to be any type of specialist I might select—doctor, lawyer, artist, merchant-chief, and yes, even beggar-man and thief, regardless of his talents, penchants, tendencies, abilities, vocations, and the race of his ancestors. (p. 104)

At the same time, two other psychologists, E. L. Thorndike (1874–1949) and B. F. Skinner (1904–1990), were studying how the consequences of behaviors shape their likelihood of recurrence. They argued that behaviors followed by positive consequences are more likely to be repeated than are behaviors followed by negative consequences. This process came to be known as operant, or instrumental, conditioning. This idea may seem simple to us now (one sign of how much it has influenced thinking over the past century), but at the time it was considered radical to argue that even complex behaviors, such as violence against others, can be explained by the reinforcement or punishment these behaviors have received in the past.

Behaviorism—the study of the impact of reinforcements and punishments on behavior—has had as profound an impact on psychology and on our common knowledge of psychology, as has psychoanalytic theory. Behavioral theories have led to many of the effective psychological treatments for disorders that we will discuss in this book.

The Cognitive Revolution

In the 1950s, some psychologists argued that behaviorism was limited in its explanatory power by its refusal to look at internal thought processes that mediate the relationship between stimulus and response. It wasn't until the 1970s that psychology shifted its focus substantially to the study of **cognitions**. Cognitions are thought processes—like attention, interpretation of events, and beliefs—that influence behavior and emotion. The cognitive revolution shifted perspectives toward such internal processes. An important player in this cognitive revolution was Albert Bandura, a clinical psychologist trained in behaviorism who had contributed a great deal to the application of behaviorism to psychopathology (see the chapters "Theories and Treatment of Abnormality" and "Trauma, Anxiety, Obsessive-Compulsive, and Related Disorders"). Bandura argued that people's beliefs about their ability to execute the behaviors necessary to control important events—which he called **self-efficacy beliefs**—are crucial in determining people's well-being. Again, this idea seems obvious to us now, but only because it took hold in both professional psychology and lay notions of psychology.

Another key figure in cognitive perspectives was Albert Ellis, who argued that people prone to psychological disorders are plagued by irrational negative assumptions about themselves and the world. Ellis developed a therapy for emotional problems based on his theory called rational-emotive therapy. This therapy was controversial because it required therapists to challenge, sometimes harshly, their patients' irrational belief systems. It became very popular, however, and moved psychology into the study of the thought processes behind serious emotional problems. Another therapy, developed by Aaron Beck, focused on the irrational thoughts of people with psychological problems. Beck's cognitive therapy has become one of the most widely used therapies for many disorders (see the chapter "Theories and Treatment of Abnormality"). Since the 1970s, theorists have continued to emphasize cognitive factors in psychopathology, although behavioral theories have remained strong as interpersonal theories, which we examine in the chapter "Theories and Treatment of Abnormality," have become more prominent.

MODERN MENTAL HEALTH CARE

Halfway through the twentieth century, major breakthroughs were made in drug treatments for some of the major forms of abnormality. In particular, the discovery of a class of drugs that can reduce hallucinations and delusions, known as the phenothiazines (see the chapter "Theories and Treatment of Abnormality"), made it possible for many people who had been institutionalized for years to be released from asylums and hospitals. Since then, there has been an explosion of new drug therapies for psychopathology. The biomedical approach has revolutionized the way we understand and treat mental disorders as biological phenomena. In addition, as we will discuss in the chapter "Theories and Treatment of Abnormality," several types of psychotherapy have been developed that have proven effective in treating a wide range of psychological problems. However, there are still significant problems in the delivery of mental health care, some of which began with the deinstitutionalization movement of the mid-twentieth century.

Deinstitutionalization

By 1960 a large and vocal movement known as the **patients' rights movement** had emerged. Patients' rights advocates argued that mental patients can recover more fully or live more satisfying lives if they are integrated into the community, with the support of community-based treatment facilities–a process known as **deinstitutionalization.** While many of these patients would continue to need around-the-clock care, it could be given in treatment centers based in neighborhoods rather than in large, impersonal institutions. In the United States, the **community mental health movement** was officially launched in 1963 by President John Kennedy as a "bold new approach" to mental health care. This movement attempted to provide coordinated mental health services to people in **community mental health centers,** a move that has had both positive and negative consequences.

The deinstitutionalization movement had a massive effect on the lives of people with serious psychological problems. Between 1955 and 2016, the number of patients in state psychiatric hospitals in the United States declined from a high of 559,000 to about 38,000 despite overall population growth, resulting in a rate lower than that before the moral treatment movement (Fuller, Sinclair, Geller, Quanbeck, & Snook, 2016; Lamb & Weinberger, 2016). Parallel trends were seen in Europe. Many former mental patients who had lived for years in cold, sterile facilities, receiving little useful care, experienced dramatic increases in their quality of life on their release. Moreover, they suddenly had the freedom to live where they wanted to, as they saw fit.

Several types of community-based treatment facilities were created as part of deinstitutionalization and continue to serve people with mental health problems today. *Community mental health centers* often include teams of social workers, therapists, and physicians who coordinate care. **Halfway houses** offer people with long-term mental health problems the opportunity to live in a structured, supportive environment as they try to reestablish working relationships and ties to family and friends. **Day treatment centers** allow people to obtain treatment during the day, along with occupational and rehabilitative therapies, but live at home at night.

People with acute problems that require hospitalization may go to inpatient wards of general hospitals or specialized psychiatric hospitals. Sometimes, their first contact with a mental health professional is in the emergency room of a hospital. Once their acute problems have subsided, however, they often are released back to their community treatment center rather than remaining for the long term in a psychiatric hospital.

Unfortunately, the resources to care for all the mental patients released from institutions have never been adequate. There were not enough halfway houses built or community mental health centers funded to serve the thousands of men and women who formerly were institutionalized or would have been institutionalized if the movement had not taken place (Figure 1). Meanwhile, the state psychiatric hospitals to which former patients would have retreated were closed down by the hundreds. The community mental health movement spread to Europe, with similar consequences. Twenty-eight percent of European countries have few or no community-based services for people with serious mental health problems (Semrau, Barley, Law, & Thornicroft, 2011; WHO World Mental Health Survey Consortium, 2004).

Men and women released from mental institutions began living in nursing homes and other types of group homes, where they received little mental health

FIGURE 1 **As Deinstitutionalization Led to Fewer People in Mental Hospitals, Incarceration Rates in Prisons Increased Dramatically.** Many observers believe that prisons serve as de facto institutionalization of individuals with mental illness who would previously have been served by mental health facilities.

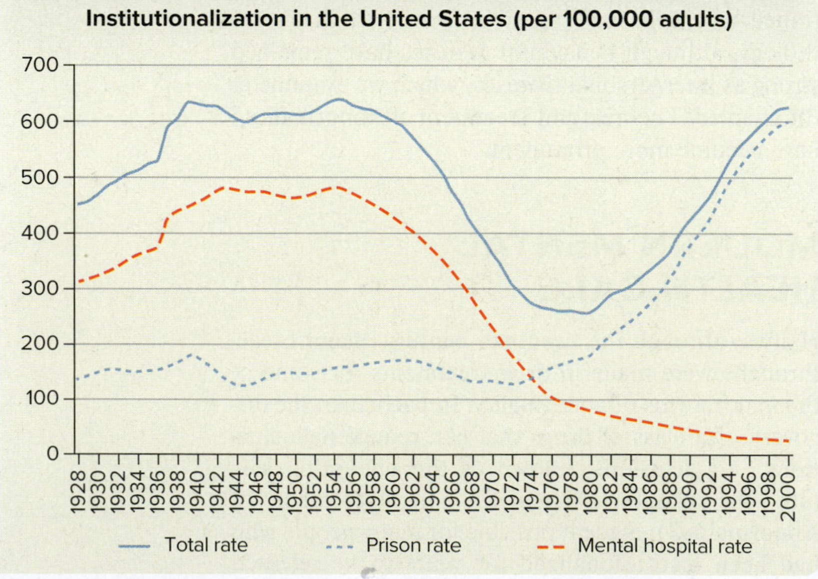

Deinstitutionalization led to a rise in homelessness among people with mental illnesses, which often go untreated. *©Sonda Dawes/The Image Works*

treatment, or with their families, many of whom were ill-equipped to handle serious mental illness (Lamb & Weinberger, 2016). Some began living on the streets. Certainly not all homeless people are mentally ill, but some researchers estimate that up to four-fifths of all long-term homeless adults in the United States and Europe have a major mental disorder, a severe substance use disorder (such as alcohol use disorder), or both (WHO World Mental Health Survey Consortium, 2004). In emergencies, these people end up in general or private hospitals that are not equipped to treat them appropriately. Many end up in jail. One study of prison inmates found that two-thirds had experienced some form of diagnosable mental disorder in their lifetime (Trestman, Ford, Zhang, & Wiesbrock, 2007). In some areas, correctional facilities are the largest providers of mental health services; some argue that following deinstitutionalization, jails have become de facto institutions (Lamb & Weinberger, 2017).

Thus, although deinstitutionalization began with laudatory goals, many of these goals were never fully reached, leaving many people who formerly would have been institutionalized in mental hospitals no better off. In recent years, the financial strains on local, state, and federal governments have led to the closing of many community mental health centers.

Managed Care

The entire system of private insurance for health care in the United States underwent a revolution in the second half of the twentieth century, when managed care emerged as the dominant means for organizing health care. **Managed care** is a collection of methods for coordinating care that ranges from simple monitoring to total control over what care can be provided and paid for. The goals are to coordinate services for an existing medical problem and to prevent future medical problems. Often, health care providers are given a set amount of money per member (patient) per month and then must determine how best to serve each patient.

Managed care can solve some of the problems created by deinstitutionalization. For example, instead of leaving it up to people with a serious psychological problem, or their families, to find appropriate care, the primary provider might find this care and ensure that patients have access to it. Suppose an individual patient reported to his physician that he was hearing voices when no one was around. The physician might refer the patient to a psychiatrist for an evaluation to determine if the patient might be suffering from schizophrenia. In some cases, the primary care physician might coordinate care offered by other providers, such as drug treatments, psychotherapy, and rehabilitation services. The primary provider also might ensure continuity of care so that patients do not "fall through the cracks." Thus, theoretically, managed care can have tremendous benefits for people with long-term, serious mental health problems. For people with less severe psychological problems, the availability of mental health care through managed care systems and other private insurance systems has led to a large increase in the number of people seeking psychotherapy and other types of mental health care.

Unfortunately, however, mental health care often is not covered fully by health insurance. Also, many people do not have any health insurance. Laws have been passed in recent years that are intended to increase the availability of coverage for mental health services, but these laws are being hotly contested. The Affordable Care Act (ACA), passed in 2010, requires insurance plans to cover mental health and substance abuse treatment, and acknowledges the increasing role of primary care providers in psychiatric treatment. The ACA expands mental health care access in the United States for those already insured, and it is estimated that millions of severely mentally ill people will newly acquire coverage (Mechanic & Olfson, 2016). However, the current mental health system has yet to fully adjust to sweeping changes, and health care policy remains a complex, controversial, and shifting political territory with clear implications for people with mental disorders. Mental health services are expensive. Because mental health problems are sometimes chronic, mental health treatment can take a long time.

CASE STUDY

Because of severe schizoaffective disorder, Rebecca J., age 56, had spent 25 years in a New York State psychiatric hospital. She lived in a group home in the community but required rehospitalization for several weeks approximately once a year when she relapsed despite taking medications. As a result of the reduction in state hospital beds (for people with mental disorders) and attempts by the state to shift readmissions for fiscal reasons, these rehospitalizations increasingly took place on the psychiatric wards of general hospitals that varied widely in quality. In 1994 she was admitted to a new hospital because the general hospital where she usually went was full. The new hospital was inadequately staffed to provide care for patients as sick as Rebecca J. In addition, the psychiatrist was poorly trained and had access to only a small fraction of Rebecca J.'s complex and voluminous past history. During her 6-week hospitalization, Rebecca J. lost 10 pounds because the nursing staff did not help her eat, had virtually all her clothing and personal effects lost or stolen, became toxic from her lithium medication, which was not noticed until she was semicomatose, and was prematurely discharged while she was still so psychotic that she had to be rehospitalized in another hospital less than 24 hours later. Meanwhile, less than a mile away in the state psychiatric hospital where she had spent many years, a bed sat empty on a ward with nursing staff and a psychiatrist who knew her case well and with her case records readily available in a file cabinet.

Source: Torrey, 2006, pp. 105–106.

The Medicaid program, which covers one-quarter of all mental health care spending in the United States, has been a target for reductions in recent years, even as the number of people seeking mental health care has risen. Many states have reduced or restricted eligibility and benefits for mental health care, increased co-payments, controlled drug costs, and reduced or frozen payments to providers (Shirk, 2008). At the same time, reductions in state and city welfare programs and other community services targeted at the poor have made daily life more difficult for poor people in general, and in particular for people with serious mental disorders, who often have exhausted their financial resources.

Only 50 to 60 percent of people in the United States with serious psychological problems receive stable mental health treatment, with much lower percentages receiving care in less-developed and poorer countries (Kessler et al., 2001; Wang et al., 2007). For example, in Europe wealthier countries such as Finland and Belgium have more than 20 mental health experts per 100,000 people, whereas poorer countries such as Turkey and Tajikistan have fewer than 2 mental health experts per 100,000 people (Semrau et al., 2011). Sometimes, people refuse care that might help them. Other times, they fall through holes in the medical safety net because of bureaucratic rules designed to shift the burden of mental health care costs from one agency to another, as in the case of Rebecca J.

As we discuss the research showing the effectiveness of various treatments for specific disorders throughout the remainder of the book, it is important to keep in mind that those treatments can work only if people have access to them.

Professions Within Abnormal Psychology

In our times, a number of professions are concerned with abnormal or maladaptive behavior. *Psychiatrists* have an MD degree and have received specialized training in the treatment of psychological problems. Psychiatrists can prescribe medications for the treatment of these problems and have been trained to conduct psychotherapies as well.

Clinical psychologists typically have a PhD in psychology, with a specialization in treating and researching psychological problems. Some have a PsyD degree from a graduate program that emphasizes clinical training more than research training. Clinical psychologists can conduct psychotherapy, but in most states they do not currently prescribe medications. (They do have limited prescription privileges in some states, and psychologists are lobbying for prescription privileges in many others.)

Marriage and family therapists specialize in helping families, couples, and children overcome problems that are interfering with their well-being. *Clinical social workers* have a master's degree in social work and often focus on helping people with psychological problems overcome social conditions that are contributing to their problems, such as joblessness or homelessness. Some states have *licensed mental health counselors,* individuals who have graduate training in counseling beyond the bachelor's degree in counseling but have not obtained a PhD. *Psychiatric nurses* have a degree in nursing, with a specialization in the treatment of people with severe psychological problems. They often work on inpatient psychiatric wards in hospitals, delivering medical care and certain forms of psychotherapy, such as group therapy to increase patients' contacts with one another. In some states, they have privileges to write prescriptions for psychotherapeutic drugs.

Each of these professions has its rewards and limitations. Students who are interested in one or more of these professions often find it helpful to volunteer as a research assistant in studies of psychological problems or for work in a psychiatric clinic or hospital. Some students find tremendous gratification working with people with psychological problems, whereas others find it more gratifying to conduct research that might answer important questions about these problems. Many mental health professionals of all types combine clinical practice and research in their careers.

CHAPTER INTEGRATION

Although the biological, psychological, and social theories of abnormality have traditionally been viewed as competing with one another to explain psychological disorders, many clinicians and researchers now believe that theories that integrate biological, psychological, and social perspectives on abnormality will prove most useful (Figure 2). For example, in the chapter "Trauma, Anxiety, Obsessive-Compulsive, and Related Disorders," we discuss theories of anxiety disorders that take into account individuals' genetic and biochemical vulnerabilities, the impact of stressful events, and the role of cognition in explaining why some people suffer debilitating anxiety. Throughout this book, we will emphasize how biological, psychological, and social factors interact with and influence one another to produce and maintain mental health problems. In other words, we will present an integrationist approach to psychological problems.

FIGURE 2 **The Integrationist Approach to Understanding Mental Health.** Many mental health theories today strive to integrate biological, psychological, and social factors in understanding mental health issues. This integrationist approach will be emphasized in this book.

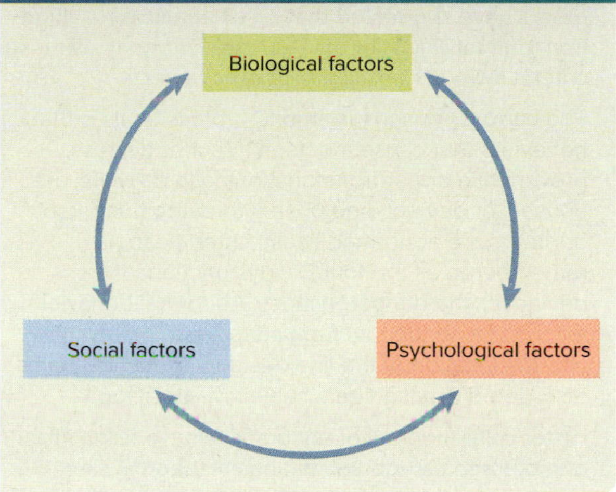

SHADES OF GRAY **DISCUSSION**

Our society highly values extreme thinness in women, and Jennifer has received substantial reinforcement for her weight loss. Thus, we see her behaviors as not very deviant. Her dieting causes her some dysfunction and distress: She is having trouble concentrating in school and is terrified of gaining weight. But her weight loss is also bringing her social benefits. Are her behaviors dangerous? Extremely thin women risk medical complications such as reduced bone density and heart arrhythmias (see the chapter "Eating Disorders"). So Jennifer's behaviors are somewhat dysfunctional, distressing, and dangerous, but they are so typical of women her age that people will differ in whether they believe her behaviors qualify as abnormal.

Mark's behaviors also seem familiar, because drinking is considered a "rite of passage" by some students. Mark drinks considerably more than most young men (see the chapter "Substance Use and Gambling Disorders"), so his level of drinking is deviant. He also has experienced some dysfunction as a result of his drinking: He has gotten in legal trouble and his grades are low. Mark certainly doesn't seem distressed about his drinking. Mark's behaviors are dangerous: He is more likely to be involved in accidents while drunk and risks alcohol poisoning from the volume he consumes. So Mark's behaviors might be considered more abnormal than Jennifer's behaviors, but people will differ on the degree of abnormality.

Would your judgments of the abnormality of these behaviors change if it were Jennifer who was drinking heavily and Mark who was dieting excessively to lose weight? Cultural norms for thinness and for drinking alcohol differ significantly for women and men. Gender strongly influences our views of normality and abnormality.

CHAPTER SUMMARY

- Cultural relativists argue that the norms of a society must be used to determine the normality of a behavior. Others have suggested that unusual behaviors, or behaviors that cause subjective distress in a person, should be labeled abnormal. Still others have suggested that only behaviors resulting from mental illness or disease are abnormal. All these criteria have serious limitations, however.
- The current consensus among professionals is that behaviors that cause a person to suffer distress, prevent him or her from functioning in daily life, are unusual or deviant, and pose a threat to the person or others are abnormal. These criteria can be remembered as the four Ds: dysfunction, distress, deviance, and dangerousness. Abnormal behaviors fall along a continuum from adaptive to maladaptive, and the location of the line designating behaviors as disordered is based on a subjective decision.
- Historically, theories of abnormality have fallen into one of three categories. Biological theories saw psychological disorders as similar to physical diseases, caused by the breakdown of a system of the body. Supernatural theories saw abnormal behavior as a result of divine intervention, curses, demonic possession, and personal sin. Psychological theories saw abnormal behavior as being a result of stress.
- In prehistoric times, people probably had largely supernatural theories of abnormal behavior, attributing it to demons or ghosts. In the Stone Age, drilling holes in the skull to allow demons to depart, a procedure known as trephination, might have been a treatment for abnormality.
- Ancient Chinese, Egyptian, and Greek texts suggest that these cultures took a biological view of abnormal behavior, although references to supernatural and psychological theories also can be found.
- During the Middle Ages, abnormal behavior may have been interpreted as being due to witchcraft.
- In psychic epidemics and mass hysterias, groups of people show similar psychological and behavioral symptoms. Usually, these have been attributed to common stresses or beliefs.
- Even well into the nineteenth and twentieth centuries, many people who acted abnormally were shut away in prisonlike conditions, tortured, starved, or ignored.
- As part of the mental hygiene movement, the moral management of mental hospitals became more widespread. Patients in these hospitals were treated with kindness and given the best biological treatments available. However, effective biological treatments for most psychological problems were not available until the mid-twentieth century.
- Modern biological perspectives on psychological disorders were advanced by Kraepelin's development of a classification system and the discovery that general paresis is caused by a syphilis infection.
- The psychoanalytic perspective began with the work of Anton Mesmer. It grew as Jean Charcot, and eventually Sigmund Freud, became interested in the role of the unconscious in producing abnormality.
- Behaviorist views on abnormal behavior began with John Watson and B. F. Skinner, who used principles of classical and operant conditioning to explain normal and abnormal behavior.
- Cognitive theorists such as Albert Ellis, Albert Bandura, and Aaron Beck focused on the role of thinking processes in abnormality.
- The deinstitutionalization movement attempted to move mental patients from mental health facilities to community-based mental health centers. Unfortunately, community-based mental health centers have never been fully funded or supported, leaving many former mental patients with few resources in the community.
- Managed care systems are meant to provide coordinated, comprehensive medical care to patients. They can be a great asset to people with long-term, serious psychological disorders.
- The professions within abnormal psychology include psychiatrists, psychologists, marriage and family therapists, clinical social workers, licensed mental health counselors, and psychiatric nurses.

KEY TERMS

continuum model of abnormality
psychopathology
cultural relativism
biological theories
supernatural theories
psychological theories
trephination
psychic epidemics
mental hygiene movement
moral treatment
general paresis
mesmerism
psychoanalysis
classical conditioning
behaviorism
cognitions
self-efficacy beliefs
patients' rights movement
deinstitutionalization
community mental health movement
community mental health centers
halfway houses
day treatment centers
managed care

Chapter 2

©ESB Professional/Shutterstock

Theories and Treatment of Abnormality

CHAPTER OUTLINE

Approaches Along the Continuum

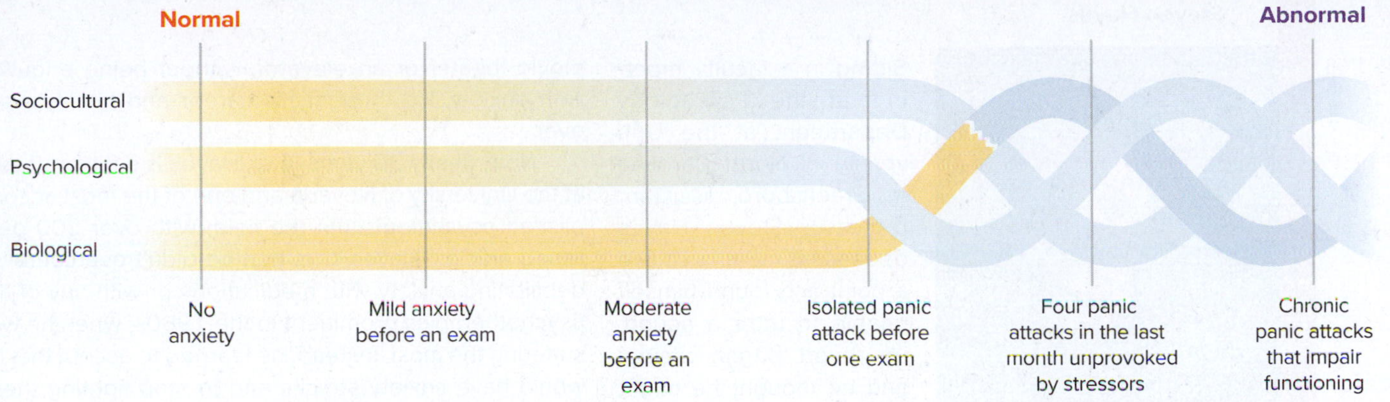

In this chapter, we discuss three general approaches to understanding psychological disorders. The **sociocultural approach** views these disorders as the result of environmental conditions and cultural norms. The **biological approach** views disorders as the result of abnormal genes or neurobiological dysfunction. The **psychological approach** views disorders as the result of thinking processes, personality styles, and conditioning.

People who favor a sociocultural approach generally view psychological disorders as falling along a continuum because they do not view these disorders as vastly different from normal functioning. Instead, they think of psychological disorders as labels that society puts on people whose behaviors and feelings differ from social and cultural norms (Chu & Leino, 2017). While they agree that these behaviors may be dysfunctional, distressing, deviant, and dangerous, they see them as understandable consequences of social stress in the individuals' lives.

A decade ago, proponents of the biological approach generally did not accept a continuum model of abnormality. Instead, they viewed psychological disorders as either present or absent—much the way they viewed medical or physical disorders (such as cancer). In recent years, however, proponents of biological approaches have embraced a continuum perspective on abnormality, seeing disorders as collections of deficits in fundamental neurobiological processes (Beauchaine & Constantino, 2017; Cuthbert & Insel, 2013; Hyman, 2010). For example, the symptoms of schizophrenia are increasingly viewed as problems in cognition and emotional processing that are due to deficits in specific areas of the brain. These problems in cognition and emotional processing can range from very mild to very severe, causing symptoms that also vary along a continuum from mild to severe. In other words, a person can have "a little bit of schizophrenia" or can exhibit significantly more symptoms, to the point of qualifying for a diagnosis of schizophrenia.

Psychological approaches to disorders have also been moving toward a continuum model of psychopathology in recent years (Clark, Cuthbert, Lewis-Fernández, Narrow, & Reed, 2017). According to these approaches, psychological processes such as cognition, learning, and emotional control also fall along a continuum that ranges from very typical to highly dysfunctional. Minor learning difficulties, for example, would be placed on the more "typical" end of the continuum, and severe mental retardation on the "dysfunctional" end. Likewise, problems in emotional control might range from feeling blue (typical) to feeling severely depressed with suicidal intentions (dysfunctional). A continuum perspective would suggest that people on the less severe end of the spectrum (who do not meet the criteria for the disorder) give us insight into the behavior of those on the more severe end (those who do meet the criteria).

As we discuss in this chapter, the sociocultural, biological, and psychological approaches are increasingly being integrated into a biopsychosocial approach to mental disorders. This integrative approach suggests that factors along the continua of biological dysfunction, psychological dysfunction, and sociocultural risks interweave to create the problems we call mental disorders.

Extraordinary People

Steven Hayes

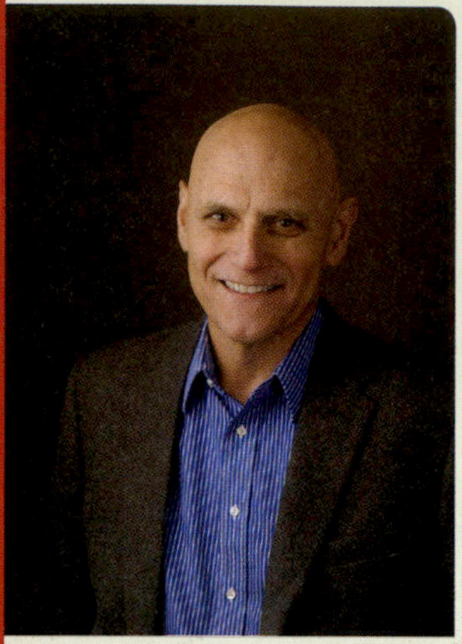

Photo by Drew Altizer, Courtesy, Steven C. Hayes

Sitting in a faculty meeting in the Psychology Department at the University of North Carolina at Greensboro, assistant professor Steven Hayes opened his mouth to make a point and found himself unable to utter a sound. His heart began racing, and he thought he might be having a heart attack. He was only 29. The episode passed, but a week later he had a similar experience in another meeting. Over the next 2 years, his attacks of absolute panic became more frequent and began dominating his life. He had great difficulty lecturing and couldn't be in an enclosed place, such as a movie theater or an elevator, without being engulfed with anxiety. He thought his career and his life were over.

Now, nearly 30 years later, Hayes is a full professor at the University of Nevada and one of the most accomplished psychologists in the field, with over 300 published articles. Hayes says that he didn't overcome his debilitating anxiety with medications or with any of the psychotherapies prominent in the 1980s, when he was suffering the most. Instead, he learned to accept that he would have anxiety attacks and to stop fighting them. Out of his experiences, he developed a new form of psychological therapy, called *acceptance and commitment therapy* or *ACT*. This therapy teaches individuals with psychological problems to be more accepting and compassionate toward themselves, to commit to their values, and to use meditation practices that help them live more in the present moment. ACT is one of the hottest of the *third-wave approaches* to psychotherapy, which we discuss later in this chapter.

Steven Hayes was able to integrate his personal experiences with his training in psychology to develop a new theory and therapy of his own. A **theory** is a set of ideas that provides a framework for asking questions about a phenomenon and for gathering and interpreting information about that phenomenon. A *therapy* is a treatment, usually based on a theory of a phenomenon, that addresses those factors the theory says cause the phenomenon.

Hayes believed that his anxiety attacks were due to the inability to accept his symptoms, but other theories suggest alternative causes. If you took a biological approach to abnormality, you would suspect that Hayes' symptoms were caused by a biological factor, such as a genetic vulnerability to anxiety, inherited from his parents. The psychological approach, like Hayes' approach, looks for the causes of abnormality in people's beliefs, life experiences, and relationships. Finally, if you took a sociocultural approach, you would consider the ways Hayes' cultural values or social environment might affect his anxiety.

Traditionally, these different approaches have been seen as incompatible. People frequently ask, "Is the cause of these symptoms biological *or* psychological *or* environmental?" This question is often called the nature-nurture question: Is the cause of psychological problems something in the nature or biology of the person, or is it in the person's nurturing or history of events to which the person was exposed? This question implies that such problems must have a single cause, rather than multiple causes. Indeed, most theories of psychological problems over history have searched for the one factor—the one gene, the one traumatic experience, the one personality trait—that causes people to develop a particular set of symptoms.

Many contemporary theorists, however, take a **biopsychosocial approach,** recognizing that the development of psychological symptoms often results from a combination of biological, psychological, and sociocultural factors. These factors are often referred to as *risk factors,* because they increase the risk of psychological problems. Risk factors can be biological, such as a genetic predisposition. They may also be psychological, such as difficulty remaining calm in stressful situations. Or they may be sociocultural, such as growing up with the stress of discrimination based on ethnicity or race.

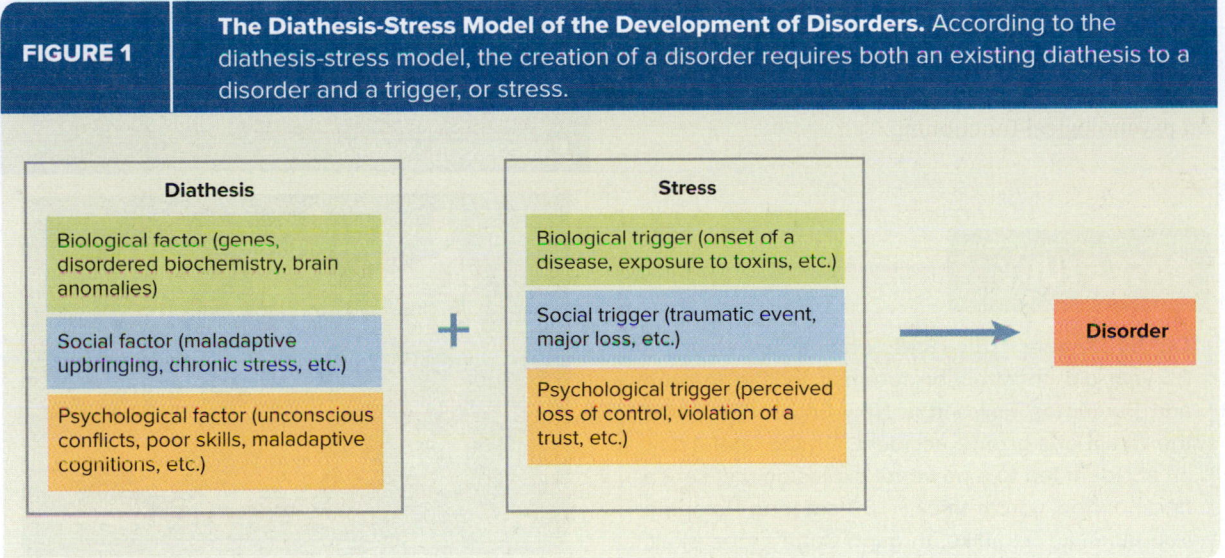

FIGURE 1 **The Diathesis-Stress Model of the Development of Disorders.** According to the diathesis-stress model, the creation of a disorder requires both an existing diathesis to a disorder and a trigger, or stress.

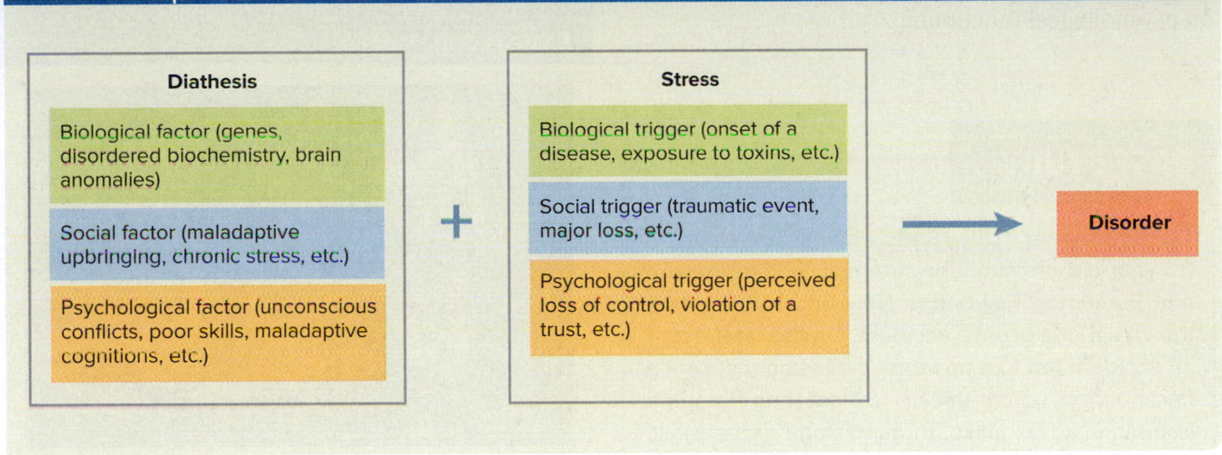

Some risk factors may lead specifically to certain types of symptoms; for example, a specific gene, known as DISC1, appears to substantially increase the risk of developing schizophrenia (Cannon et al., 2005). More commonly, however, risk factors create increased risk for a number of different problems. For instance, severe stress, such as being the victim of childhood abuse, is associated with increased risk of developing a wide range of psychopathologies (Keyes et al., 2012). Factors that increase risk for multiple types of psychological problems are referred to as *transdiagnostic risk factors* (Nolen-Hoeksema & Watkins, 2011). We will discuss several biological, psychological, and sociocultural transdiagnostic risk factors in this book.

In many cases, a risk factor may not be enough to lead a person to develop severe psychological symptoms. It may take some other experience or trigger for psychopathology to develop. Again, this trigger can be biological, such as an illness that changes a person's hormone levels. Or the trigger can be psychological or social, such as a traumatic event. Only when the risk factor and the trigger or stress come together in the same individual does the full-blown disorder emerge. This situation is often referred to as a **diathesis-stress model** (*diathesis* is another term for risk factor) (Figure 1). Although Hayes may indeed have had a genetic or personality vulnerability to anxiety (his diathesis), it may have been only when he experienced particular stressors that he developed significant anxiety.

Each of the different approaches to abnormality has led to treatments meant to relieve the symptoms people suffer. Proponents of biological theories of mental disorders most often prescribe medication, although several other types of biological treatments are discussed in this book. Proponents of psychological and some sociocultural approaches to abnormality most often prescribe psychotherapy. There are many forms of psychotherapy, but most involve a therapist (psychiatrist, psychologist, clinical social worker) talking with the person suffering from psychological problems (typically called a patient or client) about his or her symptoms and what is contributing to these symptoms. The specific topic of these conversations depends on the therapist's theoretical approach. Both medications and psychotherapy have proven effective in the treatment of many types of psychological symptoms. Medications and psychotherapy are often used together in an integrated approach, although use of medications alone has increased in recent years (Weissman & Cuijpers, 2017). Proponents of sociocultural approaches also may work to change social policies or the social conditions of vulnerable individuals so as to improve their mental health.

In this chapter, we introduce the major theories of abnormality that have dominated the field in its modern history, along with the treatments that derive from these theories. We present the theories and treatments one at a time to make them easier to understand. Keep in mind, however, that most mental health professionals now take an integrated biopsychosocial approach to understanding mental health problems, viewing them as the result of a combination of biological, psychological, and social risk factors and stresses that come together and feed off one another. We will discuss these integrated biopsychosocial approaches throughout this book.

BIOLOGICAL APPROACHES

Consider the story of Phineas Gage, one of the most dramatic examples of the effect of biological factors on psychological functioning.

CASE STUDY

On September 13, 1848, Phineas P. Gage, a 25-year-old construction foreman for the Rutland and Burlington Railroad in New England, became the victim of a bizarre accident. On the fateful day, an accident led to a powerful explosion that sent a fine-pointed, 3-cm-thick, 109-cm-long tamping iron hurling, rocketlike, through Gage's face, skull, and brain and then into the sky. Gage was momentarily stunned but regained full consciousness immediately after. He was able to talk and even walk with the help of his men. The iron landed several yards away.

Phineas Gage not only survived the momentous injury, in itself enough to earn him a place in the annals of medicine, but he survived as a different man. Gage had been a responsible, intelligent, and socially well-adapted individual, a favorite with peers and elders. He had made progress and showed promise. The signs of a profound change in personality were already evident during his convalescence under the care of his physician, John Harlow. But as the months passed, it became apparent that the transformation was not only radical but difficult to comprehend. In some respects Gage was fully recovered. He remained as able-bodied and appeared to be as intelligent as before the accident, he had no impairment of movement or speech, new learning was intact, and neither memory nor intelligence in the conventional sense had been affected. However, he had become irreverent and capricious. His respect for the social conventions by which he once abided had vanished. His abundant use of profanity offended those around him. Perhaps most troubling, he had taken leave of his sense of responsibility. He could not be trusted to honor his commitments. His employers had deemed him "the most efficient and capable" man in their employ but now they had to dismiss him. In the words of his physician, "the equilibrium or balance, so to speak, between his intellectual faculty and animal propensities" had been destroyed. In the words of his friends and acquaintances, "Gage was no longer Gage." (Adapted from Damasio et al., 1994, p. 1102)

FIGURE 2 **Phineas Gage's Brain Injury.** Modern neuroimaging techniques have helped identify the precise location of damage to Phineas Gage's brain.

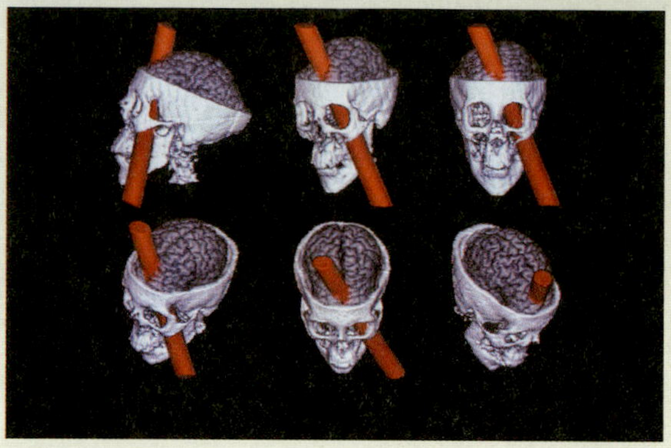

©SPL/Science Source

As a result of damage to his brain from the accident, Gage's basic personality seemed to have changed. He was transformed from a responsible, socially appropriate man into an impulsive, emotional, and socially inappropriate man. Almost 150 years later, researchers using modern neuroimaging techniques on Gage's preserved skull and a computer simulation of the tamping-iron accident determined the precise location of the damage to Gage's brain (Figure 2).

Studies of people today who suffer damage to this area of the brain reveal that they have trouble with making rational decisions in personal and social matters and with processing information about emotions. They do not have trouble, however, with following the logic of an abstract problem, with arithmetic calculations, or with memory. Like Gage, their basic intellectual functioning remains intact, but their emotional control and social judgment are impaired (Damasio, Grabowski, Frank, Galaburda, & Damasio, 1994).

The damage Gage suffered caused areas of his brain to not function properly. *Brain dysfunction* is one of three causes of abnormality on which biological approaches often focus. The other two are biochemical imbalances and genetic abnormalities. Brain dysfunction, biochemical imbalances, and genetic abnormalities can all influence one another. For example, brain dysfunction may be the result of genetic factors and may cause biochemical imbalances. We explore these three biological causes of abnormality in this section.

Brain Dysfunction

Like Phineas Gage, people whose brains do not function properly often show problems in psychological functioning. The brain can be divided into three main regions: the hindbrain, which includes all the structures located in the hind (posterior) part of the brain, closest to the spinal cord; the midbrain, located in the middle of the brain; and the forebrain, which includes the structures located in the front (anterior) part of the brain (Figures 3 and 4). The hindbrain sits on top of the spinal cord and is crucial for basic life functions. It contains the medulla, which helps control breathing and reflexes; the pons, which is important for attentiveness and the timing of sleep; the reticular formation, a network of neurons that control arousal and attention to stimuli; and the cerebellum, which is concerned primarily with the coordination of movement. The midbrain contains the superior colliculus and inferior colliculus, which relay sensory information and control movement, and the substantia nigra, a crucial part of the pathway that regulates responses to reward.

The human forebrain is relatively large and developed compared to that of other organisms. The outer layer of the cerebrum is called the **cerebral cortex** (or simply cortex; Figure 5a and b); it is this area of the brain that was damaged in Phineas Gage's accident. The cerebral cortex is involved in many of our most advanced thinking processes. It is composed of two hemispheres, on the left and right sides of the brain, that are connected by the corpus collosum. Each hemisphere is divided into four lobes (see Figure 5a and b): the frontal, parietal, occipital, and temporal lobes, large regions that perform diverse functions.

FIGURE 3 Organization of the Brain.

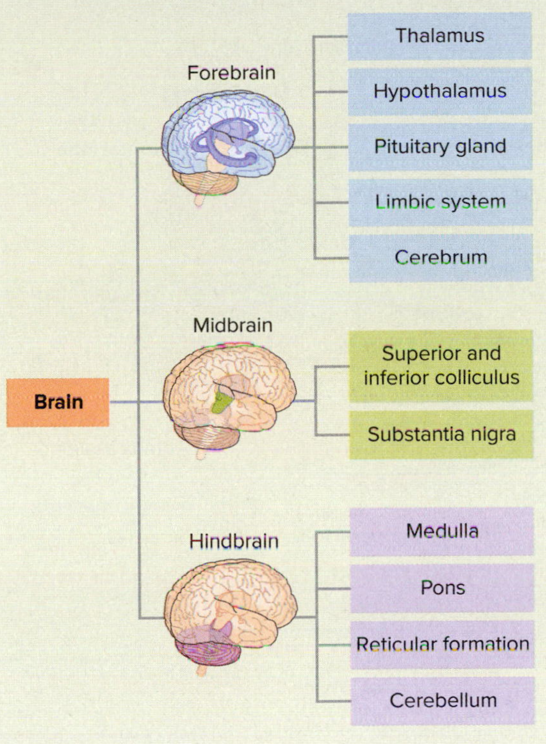

FIGURE 4 Some of the Major Structures of the Brain.

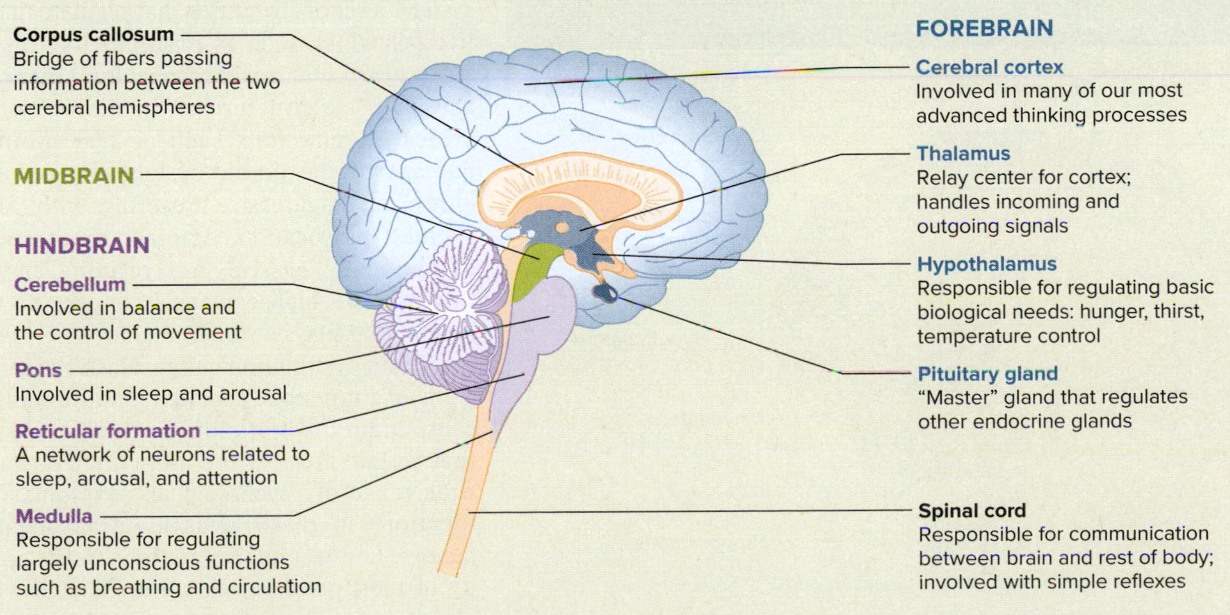

FIGURE 5 **Major Sections of the Cerebral Cortex.**

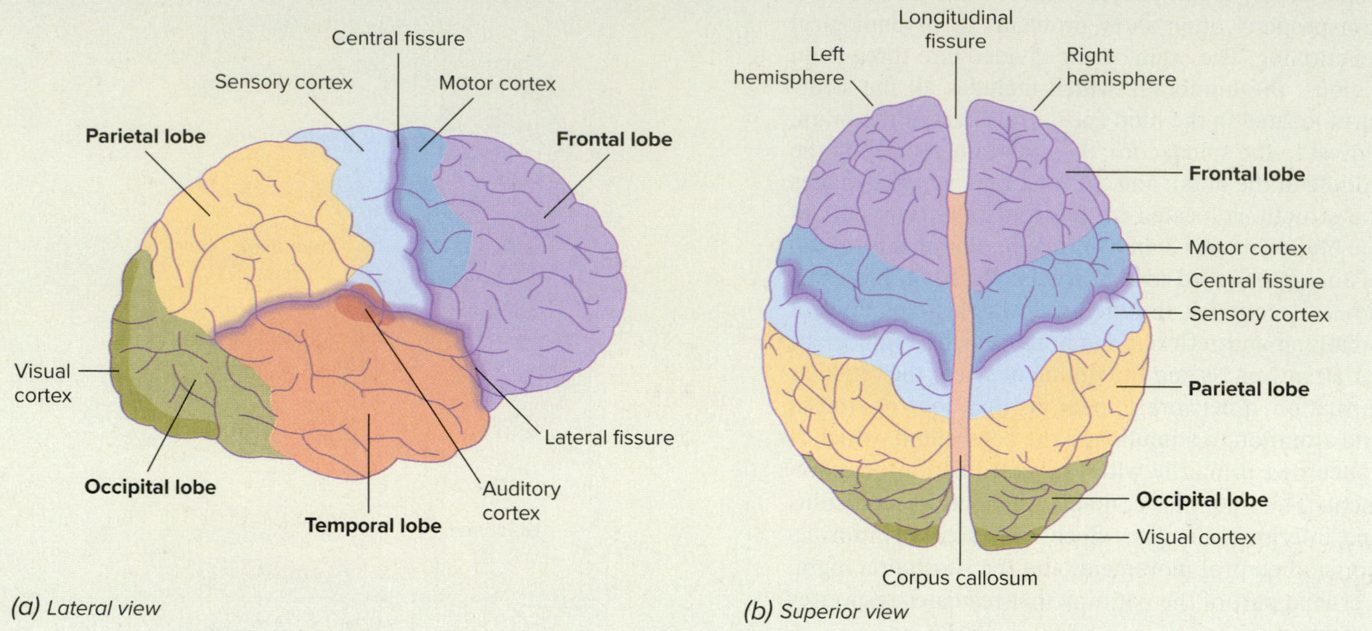

The other structures of the forebrain are found just under the cerebrum and are called *subcortical structures*. The **thalamus** directs incoming information from sense receptors (such as vision and hearing) to the cerebrum. The **hypothalamus,** a small structure just below the thalamus, regulates eating, drinking, and sexual behavior, and is involved in processing basic emotions. The pituitary gland, the most important part of the endocrine system, is discussed in the next section.

FIGURE 6 **Structures of the Limbic System.** The limbic system is a collection of structures that are closely interconnected with the hypothalamus. They appear to exert additional control over some of the instinctive behaviors regulated by the hypothalamus, such as eating, sexual behavior, and reaction to stressful situations.

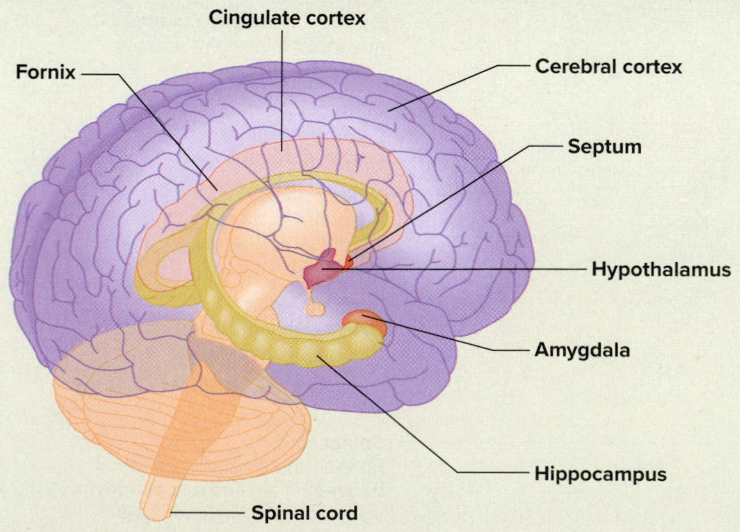

Around the central core of the brain and closely interconnected with the hypothalamus is the **limbic system,** a set of structures that regulate many instinctive behaviors, such as reactions to stressful events and eating and sexual behavior (Figure 6). The **amygdala** is a structure of the limbic system that is critical in emotions such as fear. Monkeys with damage to the limbic system sometimes become chronically aggressive, reacting with rage to the slightest provocation. At other times, they become exceptionally passive, not reacting at all to real threats. The **hippocampus** is a part of the limbic system that plays a role in memory.

Brain dysfunction can result from injury, such as from an automobile accident, and from diseases that cause brain deterioration. In this book you will see that certain areas of the brain are associated with a wide range of psychological symptoms. Thus, dysfunctions in these areas are transdiagnostic risk factors. For example, alterations in the size or activity of the frontal cortex are associated with schizophrenia, a severe disorder in which people have hallucinations (unreal perceptual experiences) and delusions (unreal beliefs); with depression; and with attention-deficit/hyperactivity disorder (ADHD), among other disorders. We will also consider examples of how environmental and psychological factors can change brain functioning. For example, a number of studies have shown that psychotherapy alone, without drug therapy, can change brain activity (Barsaglini, Sartori, Benetti, Pettersson-Yeo, & Mechelli, 2014).

Biochemical Imbalances

The brain requires a number of chemicals in order to work efficiently and effectively. These chemicals include neurotransmitters and hormones, the latter produced by the endocrine system.

Neurotransmitters

Neurotransmitters are biochemicals that act as messengers carrying impulses from one neuron, or nerve cell, to another in the brain and in other parts of the nervous system (Figure 7). Each neuron has a cell body and a number of short branches, called dendrites. The dendrites and cell body receive impulses from adjacent neurons. The impulse then travels down the length of a slender, tubelike extension, called an axon, to small swellings at the end of the axon, called synaptic terminals. Here the impulse stimulates the release of neurotransmitters.

The synaptic terminals do not actually touch the adjacent neurons. There is a slight gap between the synaptic terminals and the adjacent neurons, called the *synaptic gap* or **synapse.** The neurotransmitter is released into the synapse. It then binds to special **receptors**—molecules on the membrane of adjacent neurons. This binding works somewhat the way a key fits into a lock. The binding stimulates the adjacent neuron to initiate the impulse, which then runs through its dendrites and cell body and down its axon to cause the release of more neurotransmitters between it and other neurons.

Many biochemical theories of psychopathology suggest that the amount of certain neurotransmitters in the synapses is associated with specific types of psychopathology. The amount of a neurotransmitter available in the synapse can be affected by two processes. The process of **reuptake** occurs when the initial neuron releasing the neurotransmitter into the synapse reabsorbs the neurotransmitter, decreasing the amount left in the synapse. Another process, **degradation,** occurs when the receiving neuron releases an enzyme into the synapse that breaks down the neurotransmitter into other biochemicals. Degradation also occurs when the releasing neuron provides an enzyme. The reuptake and degradation of neurotransmitters happen naturally. When one or both of these processes malfunction, abnormally high or low levels of neurotransmitter in the synapse result.

FIGURE 7 **Neurotransmitters and the Synapse.** The neurotransmitter is released into the synaptic gap. There it may bind with the receptors on the postsynaptic membrane.

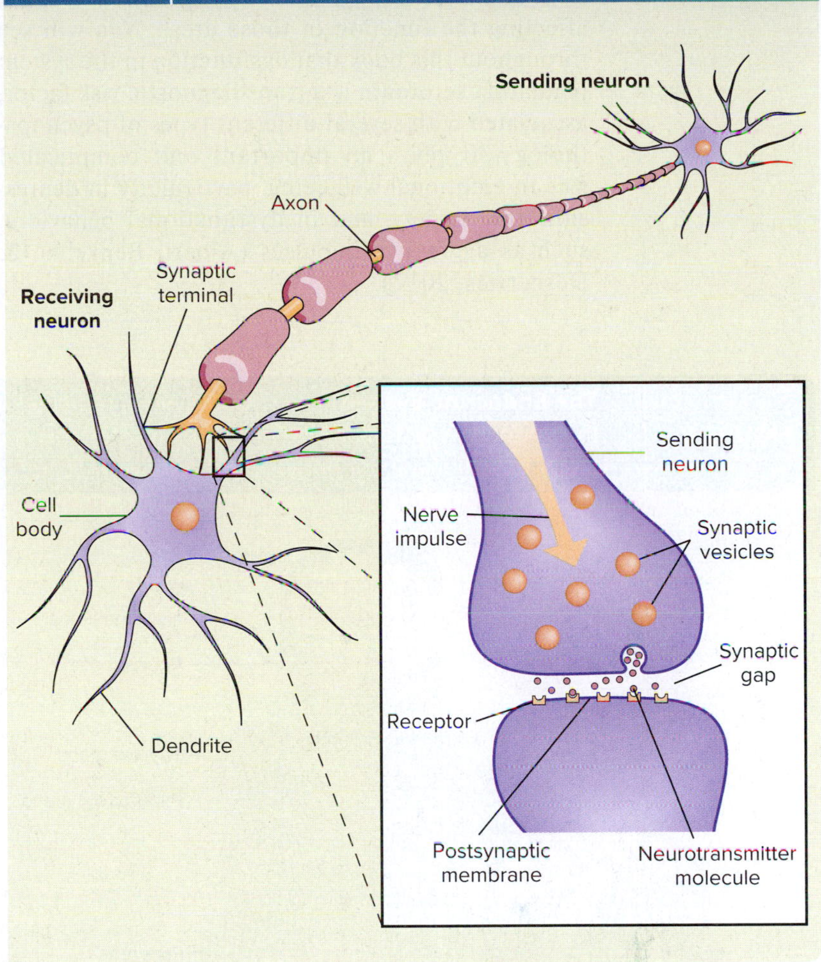

Psychological symptoms may also be associated with the number and functioning of the receptors for neurotransmitters on the dendrites. If there are too few receptors or if the receptors are not sensitive enough, the neuron will not be able to make adequate use of the neurotransmitter available in the synapse. If there are too many receptors or if they are too sensitive, the neuron may be overexposed to the neurotransmitter that is in the synapse. Within the neuron, a complex system of biochemical changes takes place as the result of the presence or absence of neurotransmitters. Psychological symptoms may be the consequence of malfunctioning in neurotransmitter systems; also, psychological experiences may cause changes in neurotransmitter system functioning.

Scientists have identified more than 100 different neurotransmitters. *Serotonin* is a neurotransmitter that travels through many key areas of the brain, affecting the function of those areas. You will see throughout this book that dysfunction in the system regulating serotonin is a transdiagnostic risk factor, associated with several different types of psychopathology. It plays an important and complicated role in emotional well-being, particularly in depression and anxiety, and in dysfunctional behaviors, such as aggressive impulses (Albert, Benkelfat, & Descarries, 2012).

FIGURE 8 **The Endocrine System.** The hypothalamus regulates the endocrine system, which produces most of the major hormones of the body.

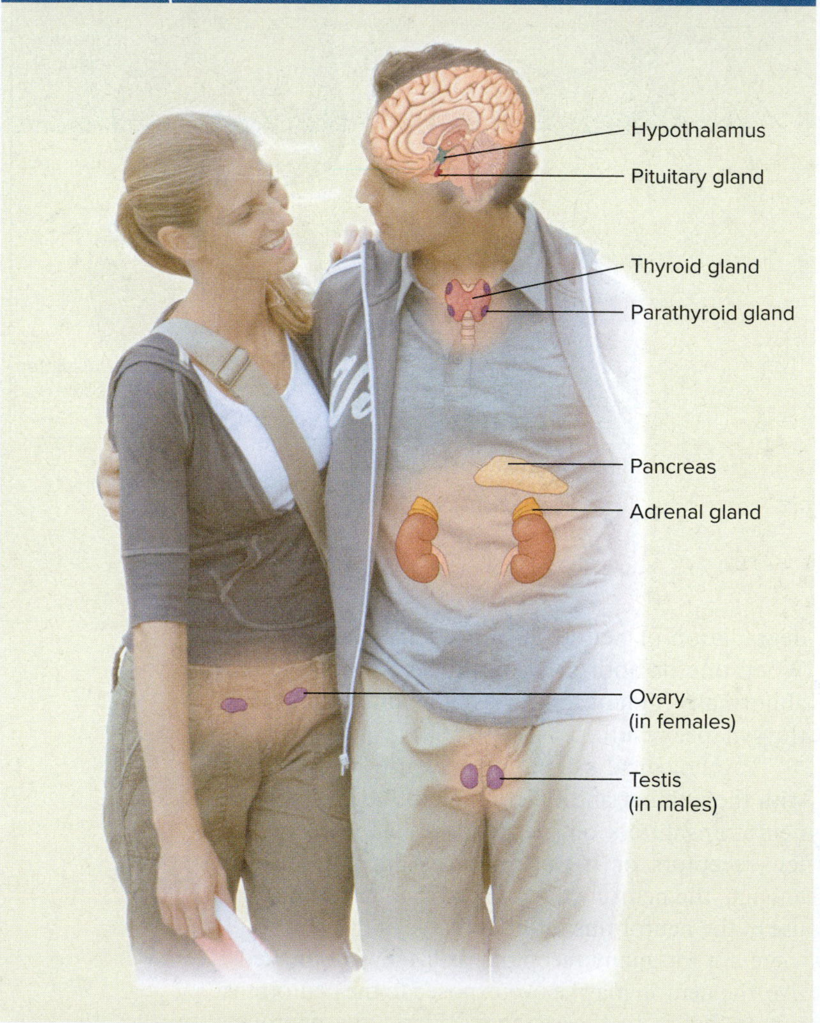

Source: King, *Experience psychology,* 2e. Copyright ©2013 McGraw-Hill Higher Education. Reprinted by permission. ©*Laurence Mouton/Getty Images*

Dopamine is a prominent neurotransmitter in those areas of the brain associated with our experience of reinforcements or rewards, and it is affected by substances, such as alcohol, that we find rewarding (Volkow, Wise, & Baler, 2017). Dopamine also is important to the functioning of muscle systems and plays a role in disorders involving control over muscles, such as Parkinson's disease. Thus, dopamine dysfunction is also a transdiagnostic risk factor.

Norepinephrine (also known as noradrenaline) is a neurotransmitter produced mainly by neurons in the brain stem. Two well-known drugs, cocaine and amphetamine, prolong the action of norepinephrine by slowing its reuptake process. Because of the delay in reuptake, the receiving neurons are activated for a longer period of time, which causes the stimulating psychological effects of these drugs, Conversely, when there is too little norepinephrine in the brain, the person's mood is depressed. Another prominent neurotransmitter is gamma-aminobutyric acid, or GABA, which inhibits the action of other neurotransmitters. Certain drugs have a tranquilizing effect because they increase the inhibitory activity of GABA. GABA is thought to play an important role in anxiety symptoms, so one contributor to Steven Hayes' anxiety could be a dysfunction in his GABA system.

The Endocrine System

Other biochemical theories of psychopathology focus on the body's **endocrine system** (Figure 8). This system of glands produces chemicals called hormones, which are released directly into the blood. A **hormone** carries messages throughout the body, potentially affecting a person's mood, level of energy, and reaction to stress. One of the major endocrine glands, the **pituitary,** has been called the *master gland* because it produces the largest number of different hormones and controls the secretion of other endocrine glands. It lies just below the hypothalamus.

The relationship between the pituitary gland and the hypothalamus illustrates the complex interactions between the endocrine and central nervous systems. For example, in response to stress (fear, anxiety, pain, and so forth), neurons in the hypothalamus secrete a substance called corticotropin-release factor (CRF). CRF is carried from the hypothalamus to the pituitary through a channel-like structure. The CRF stimulates the pituitary to release the body's major stress hormone, adrenocorticotrophic hormone (ACTH). ACTH, in turn, is carried by the bloodstream to the adrenal glands and to various other organs of the body, causing the release of about 30 hormones, each of which plays a role in the body's adjustment to emergency situations.

As we will discuss in the chapters "Trauma, Anxiety, Obsessive-Compulsive, and Related Disorders" and "Mood Disorders and Suicide," some theories of anxiety and depression suggest that these disorders result from dysregulation, or malfunctioning, of a system called the *hypothalamic-pituitary-adrenal axis* (or HPA axis). People who have a dysregulated HPA axis may have abnormal physiological reactions to stress that make it more difficult for them to cope with the stress, resulting in symptoms of anxiety and depression.

The proper working of the neurotransmitter and endocrine systems requires a delicate balance, and many forces can upset this balance. For example, chronic stress can cause dysregulation in neurotransmitter and endocrine systems that persists even after the stress has subsided.

Genetic Abnormalities

Behavioral genetics, the study of the genetics of personality and abnormality, is concerned with two questions: (1) To what extent are behaviors or behavioral tendencies inherited? and (2) What are the processes by which genes affect behavior (Loehlin, 2009)?

Let us begin by reviewing the basics of genetics. At conception, the normal fertilized embryo has 46 chromosomes, 23 from the female egg and 23 from the male sperm, making up 23 pairs of chromosomes. One of these pairs is referred to as the sex chromosomes because it determines the sex of the embryo: The XX combination results in a female embryo, and the XY combination results in a male embryo. The mother of an embryo always contributes an X chromosome, and the father can contribute either an X or a Y.

Alterations in the structure or number of chromosomes can cause major defects. Down syndrome, which is characterized by mental retardation, heart malformations, and facial features such as a flat face, a small nose, protruding lips and tongue, and slanted eyes, results when chromosome 21 is present in triplicate instead of as the usual pair.

Chromosomes contain individual genes, which are segments of long molecules of deoxyribonucleic acid (DNA; Figure 9). Genes give coded instructions to cells to perform certain functions, usually to manufacture certain proteins. Genes, like chromosomes, come in pairs. One half of the pair comes from the mother, and the other half from the father. Abnormalities in genes are much more common than major abnormalities in the structure or number of chromosomes.

For example, as noted earlier, the neurotransmitter serotonin appears to play a role in depression. One gene that influences the functioning of serotonin systems in the brain is the serotonin transporter gene. Every gene has two alleles, or coding sequences. Alleles for the serotonin transporter gene can be either short (s) or long (l). Thus, any given individual could have two short alleles (s/s genotype), two long alleles (l/l genotype), or one short and one long allele (s/l genotype). Some studies have suggested that the presence of at least one s allele on the serotonin transporter gene may increase an individual's chance of developing depression (Levinson, 2006).

Although you may often hear of scientists having discovered "the gene" for a major disorder, most disorders are associated not with a single abnormal gene but with multiple abnormal genes. Each of these

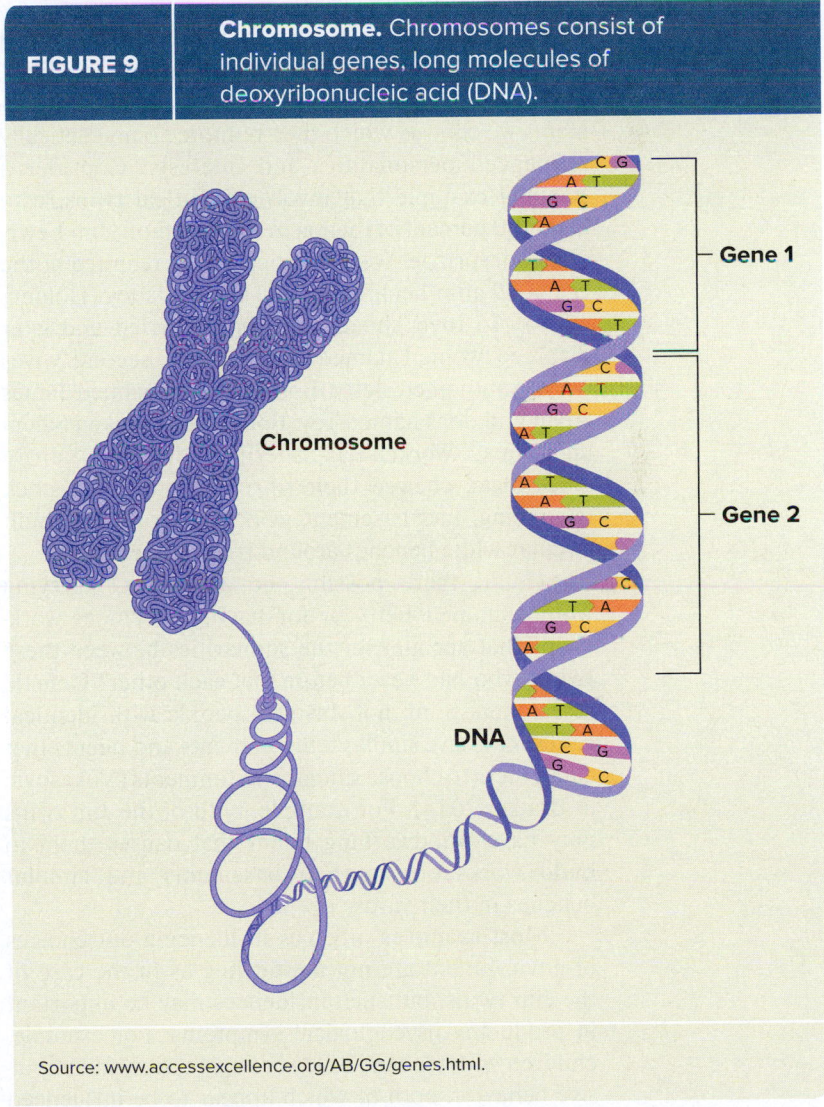

FIGURE 9 **Chromosome.** Chromosomes consist of individual genes, long molecules of deoxyribonucleic acid (DNA).

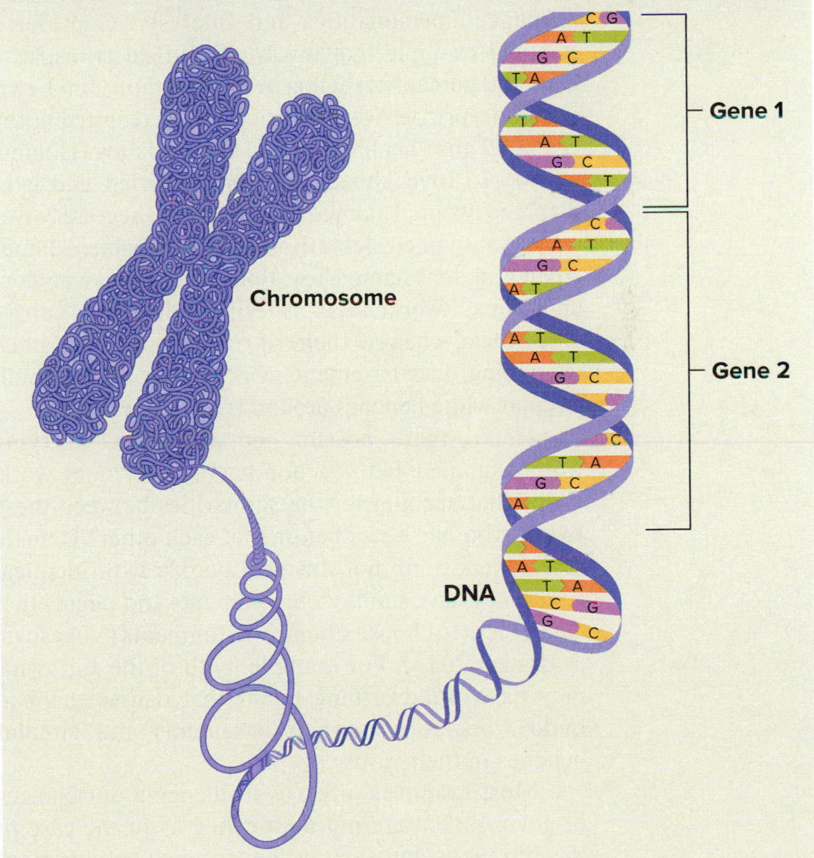

Source: www.accessexcellence.org/AB/GG/genes.html.

altered genes might make only a partial contribution to vulnerability for the disorder, some greater than others. But when a critical number of these altered genes come together, the individual may develop the disorder. This is known as a **polygenic** ("many genes") process—that is, it takes multiple genetic abnormalities coming together in one individual to create a specific disorder. A number of physiological disorders, such as diabetes, coronary heart disease, epilepsy, and cleft lip and palate, result from such polygenic processes. Most genetic models of the major types of mental disorder are also polygenic. In the case of depression, the presence of at least one s allele increases the likelihood that an individual will have depression but probably is not sufficient to cause it. Rather, a combination of genetic abnormalities is thought to contribute to depression and other disorders (Geschwind & Flint, 2015).

Studies of identical twins reared apart offer researchers many opportunities to study the relationship of genes and environment. Lily McLeod and Gillian Shaw were born in China but raised by different adoptive families in Canada where researchers are exploring these factors. In their case, the girls continue to be raised by different parents—who have agreed to let them grow up together as sisters, thereby creating a new form of blended family arrangement.
©Carlos Osorio/Getty Images

Interactions Between Genes and Environment

Genetic factors and the environment interact in a number of ways to influence our behaviors. First, genetic factors can influence the kinds of environments we choose, which then reinforce our genetically influenced personalities and interests. Consider a startling example that involves identical twins, who have 100 percent of their genes in common. Jim Lewis and Jim Springer were identical twins reunited at the age of 39 after being separated since infancy (Holden, 1980). To their shock, both had married and later divorced women named Linda. Their second wives were both named Betty. Both had sons named James Allan and dogs named Toy. Both chain-smoked Salem cigarettes, worked as sheriffs' deputies, drove Chevrolets, chewed their fingernails, enjoyed stock car racing, had basement workshops, and had built circular white benches around trees in their yards.

Could there possibly be genes for marrying women named Betty or for having basement workshops that account for the similarities between these twins, who had never before met each other? Genetic researchers think not. Instead, people with identical genes may have similar temperaments and talents that cause them to choose similar environments (Vukasović & Bratko, 2015). For example, both of the Jim twins may have woodworking talent that causes them to build workshops in their basements and circular benches in their yards.

Most examples of genes influencing our choices of environment are not as startling as in the case of the Jim twins, but such influences may be important in producing psychological symptoms. For example, children with tendencies toward aggression and impulsive behavior, both of which appear to be influenced by genetic factors, tend to choose friends who encourage their aggressive and impulsive behaviors and provide opportunities to engage in antisocial acts (Dishion & Patterson, 1997).

Second, the environment may act as a catalyst for a genetic tendency. For example, as noted earlier, the presence of at least one s allele on the serotonin transporter gene may increase an individual's chance of developing depression, but it does not determine whether the individual will develop depression. Researchers Avshalom Caspi, Terri Moffitt, and colleagues (Caspi, Sugden, et al., 2003) found that individuals who carried at least one s allele for the serotonin transporter gene were at increased risk for depression as adults only if they had a history of being maltreated as young children (Figure 10). Among individuals with no history of maltreatment, their genotype for the serotonin transporter gene had no relationship to depression. Those with the s/l genotype showed a greater probability of depression if they had been maltreated, and those with the s/s genotype showed an even greater probability of depression if they had been maltreated. Some subsequent studies have failed to replicate the findings of Caspi and colleagues (see Halldorsdottir & Binder, 2017), but this intriguing study inspired many other researchers to search for gene-environment interactions.

Third, the fascinating line of research called **epigenetics** indicates that environmental conditions

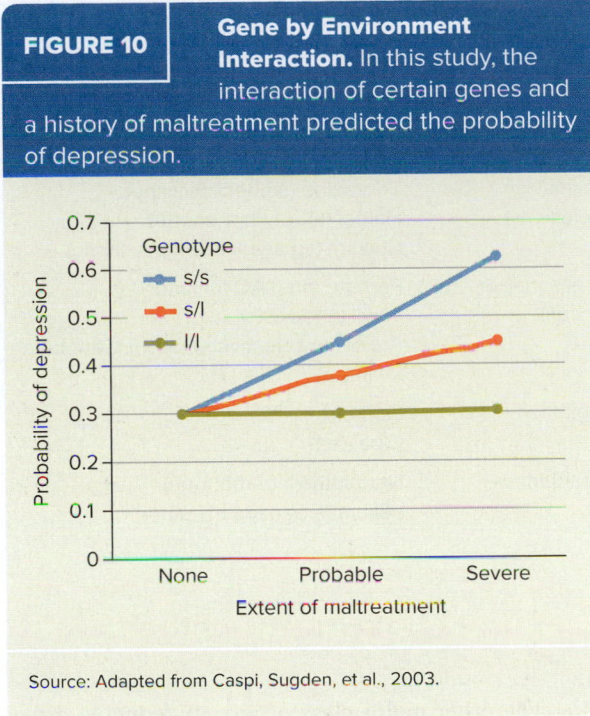

FIGURE 10 **Gene by Environment Interaction.** In this study, the interaction of certain genes and a history of maltreatment predicted the probability of depression.

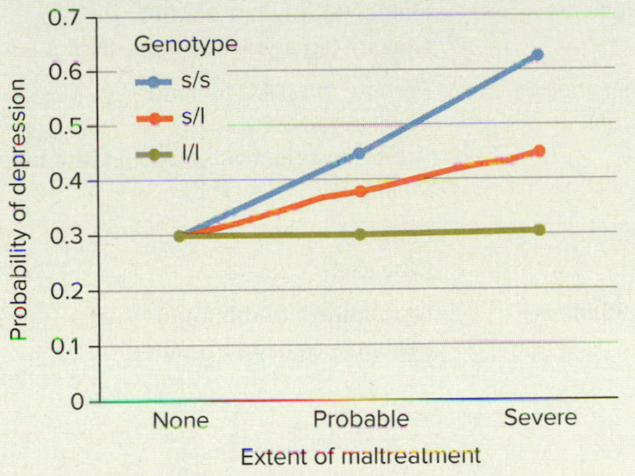

Source: Adapted from Caspi, Sugden, et al., 2003.

can affect the expression of genes. DNA can be chemically modified by different environmental conditions, resulting in genes being turned on or off. As a result, cells, tissues, and organs are altered in their development. Epigenetics is the study of heritable changes in the expression of genes without change in the gene sequence.

Researcher Michael Meany studied the effects of epigenetic processes on stress responses in rats (Hellstrom & Meaney, 2010; Meaney, 2010). Mother rats typically lick and groom their infants (called pups), but the amount of licking and grooming varies from one mother to another. Pups who are licked and groomed more tend to grow into adult rats that are less fearful and show more modest physiological responses to stress, compared to pups who are licked and groomed less. In addition, when biological offspring of mothers who lick and groom less are raised by mothers who lick and groom more, they are less fearful and physiologically reactive to stress than sibling pups that are raised by their own mothers; and when the biological offspring of mothers who lick and groom more are raised by mothers who lick and groom less, they are more fearful and physiologically reactive to stress than sibling pups raised by their own mothers. This pattern of results suggests that the mother's behavior influences the development of the pups' reactions to stress (Meaney, 2010). The amount that mother rats lick and groom pups in the first week of life affects the release of certain hormones in the pup. These hormones in turn affect the expression of a gene that influences the development of the hippocampus (refer to Figure 6), an area of the brain that influences the stress response. So the mother's behavior toward the pup during the first week of life affects the expression of key genes, changing the development of an area of the brain and, in turn, influencing the pups' behavioral and physiological responses to stress.

The role of epigenetics in psychopathology in humans is in its early stages, but it likely is very important (Barker, Walton, & Cecil, 2018). For example, epigenetic processes could help explain how identical twins who share the same DNA sequence could differ in their expression of a disorder. Both twins may carry genes that increase their risk for a disorder, but if the environments of the twins differ during fetal development or in critical stages of development after birth, the expression of these genes may differ, leading one twin but not the other to develop the disorder (see the chapter "Schizophrenia Spectrum and Other Psychotic Disorders").

Drug Therapies

Most of the biological treatments for abnormality are drug treatments (Table 1). These drugs are thought to relieve psychological symptoms by improving the functioning of neurotransmitter systems.

Antipsychotic drugs help reduce the symptoms of psychosis, which include hallucinations (unreal perceptual experiences) and delusions (fantastic, unrealistic beliefs). The first group of antipsychotic drugs was the *phenothiazines*. These drugs have been extremely helpful in reducing psychotic symptoms, but they carry a number of dangerous side effects. These side effects include severe sedation, visual disturbances, and *tardive dyskinesia,* a neurological disorder characterized by involuntary movements of the tongue, face, mouth, or jaw (see the chapter "Schizophrenia Spectrum and Other Psychotic Disorders"). Fortunately, newer medications, referred to as the atypical antipsychotics, seem to be effective in treating psychosis without inducing some of the same side effects (see the chapter "Schizophrenia Spectrum and Other Psychotic Disorders").

Antidepressant drugs reduce symptoms of depression (sadness, low motivation, and sleep and appetite disturbance). The most frequently used antidepressants, the *selective serotonin reuptake inhibitors* (SSRIs; see the chapter "Mood Disorders and Suicide"), affect the serotonin neurotransmitter system. Some of the newest antidepressant drugs, *selective serotonin-norepinephrine reuptake inhibitors* (SNRIs; see the chapter "Mood Disorders and Suicide"), are designed to target both serotonin and norepinephrine. Common side effects

TABLE 1 Drug Therapies for Mental Disorders

These are the major types of drugs used to treat several kinds of mental disorders.

Type of Drug	Purpose	Examples
Antipsychotic drugs	Reduce symptoms of psychosis (loss of reality testing, hallucinations, delusions)	Thorazine (a phenothiazine) Haldol (a butyrophenone) Clozaril (an atypical antipsychotic)
Antidepressant drugs	Reduce symptoms of depression (sadness, loss of appetite, sleep disturbances)	Parnate (an MAO inhibitor) Elavil (a tricyclic) Prozac (a selective serotonin reuptake inhibitor)
Lithium	Reduces symptoms of mania (agitation, excitement, grandiosity)	Lithobid Cibalith-S
Antianxiety drugs	Reduce symptoms of anxiety (fearfulness, worry, tension)	Nembutal (a barbiturate) Valium (a benzodiazepine)

of SSRIs and SNRIs include nausea, diarrhea, headache, tremor, daytime sedation, sexual dysfunction, and agitation. Older classes of antidepressants include the *tricyclic antidepressants* and the monoamine oxidase inhibitors (see the chapter "Mood Disorders and Suicide").

Lithium is a metallic element present in the sea, in natural springs, and in animal and plant tissue. It is widely used as a mood stabilizer, particularly in the treatment of bipolar disorder, which involves swings back and forth from depression to mania (highly elevated mood, irritability, grandiosity, and involvement in dangerous activities). Lithium's significant side effects include extreme nausea, blurred vision, diarrhea, tremors, and twitches (see the chapter "Mood Disorders and Suicide"). Other drugs, known as the **anticonvulsants,** are also used in the treatment of mania (see details in the chapter "Mood Disorders and Suicide") and have fewer side effects than lithium.

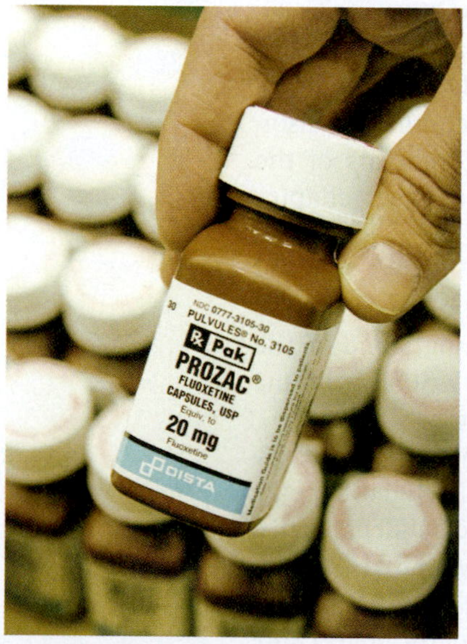

Media stories about so-called wonder drugs, including Prozac, often tout their ability to alleviate a wide range of problems beyond the treatment of serious psychological disorders. *©Darron Cummings/AP Images*

The first group of **antianxiety drugs** was the *barbiturates,* introduced at the beginning of the twentieth century. Although these drugs are effective in inducing relaxation and sleep, they are highly addictive, and withdrawal from them can cause life-threatening symptoms such as increased heart rate, delirium, and convulsions.

The other major class of anxiety-reducing drugs, the *benzodiazepines*, appears to reduce the symptoms of anxiety without interfering substantially with an individual's ability to function in daily life. A common use of these drugs is as sleeping pills. About 14 million adults receive prescriptions for benzodiazepines each year in the United States, a dramatic increase from past years (Bachhuber, Hennessy, Cunningham, & Starrels, 2016). Unfortunately, these drugs are also highly addictive. Up to 80 percent of people who take them for 6 weeks or longer show withdrawal symptoms, including heart rate acceleration, irritability, and profuse sweating. Benzodiazepines also carry risks of fatal overdose, and have increasingly figured into the United States' crisis of drug overdoses (Bachhuber et al., 2016).

Electroconvulsive Therapy and Newer Brain Stimulation Techniques

An alternative to drug therapies in the treatment of some disorders is **electroconvulsive therapy,** or **ECT.** ECT was introduced in the early twentieth century and is now most commonly used for treating severe mood disorders.

ECT consists of a series of treatments in which a brain seizure is induced by passing electrical current through the patient's brain. Patients are first anesthetized and given muscle relaxants so that they are not conscious when they have the seizure and their muscles do not jerk violently during it. Metal electrodes are taped to the head, and a current of 70 to 150 volts is passed through one side of the brain for about

½ second. Patients typically have a convulsion that lasts about 1 minute. The full series of treatments typically consists of 6 to 12 sessions. Although the mechanisms of ECT's effects are not totally clear, they may involve structural changes to the parts of the brain implicated in mood disorders (Dukart et al., 2014). ECT has shown effectiveness for severe depression, but also comes with side effects, including confusion and memory loss.

More recently, researchers have been developing alternative techniques for stimulating the brain that can be more targeted and that have fewer side effects (Slotema, Blom, Hoek, & Sommer, 2010). One procedure, known as *repetitive transcranial magnetic stimulation (rTMS),* noninvasively exposes patients to repeated, high-intensity magnetic pulses focused on particular brain structures. In the procedure known as *deep brain stimulation,* electrodes are surgically implanted in specific areas of the brain. These electrodes are then connected to a pulse generator placed under the skin that delivers stimulation to the specific brain areas. Similarly, in *vagus nerve stimulation,* electrodes are attached to the vagus nerve, a part of the nervous system that carries information to several areas of the brain, including the hypothalamus and amygdala. These electrodes are connected to a pulse generator that delivers stimulation to the vagus nerve, which in turn travels to targeted areas of the brain.

Some studies have suggested that these newer brain stimulation techniques can help relieve the symptoms of depression and auditory hallucinations (hearing voices that aren't there) in patients (Slotema et al., 2010). Electrical stimulation of neurons can result in long-term changes in neurotransmission across synapses. Patients who receive these newer brain stimulation treatments report few side effects–usually only minor headaches treatable by aspirin. Thus, there is a great deal of hope that these techniques will be effective and safe alternative therapies, particularly for people who do not respond to drug therapies and may not be able to tolerate ECT. Researchers continue to explore how these treatments affect symptoms across a wide range of disorders, and when they are better or worse treatment options (e.g., Coles, Kozak, & George, 2018).

Psychosurgery

In the chapter "Looking at Abnormality" we describe theories suggesting that prehistoric peoples performed crude brain surgery, called trephination, on people with mental disorders in order to release the evil spirits causing the disorders. In modern times, brain surgery did not become a mode of treatment for mental disorders until the early twentieth century. A Portuguese neurologist, Antonio de Egas Moniz, introduced a procedure in 1935 in which the frontal lobes of the brain are severed from the lower centers of the brain in people with psychosis. This procedure eventually developed into the procedure known as prefrontal lobotomy. Although Moniz won the Nobel Prize for his work, prefrontal lobotomies eventually were criticized as a cruel and ineffective means of treating psychosis. Patients often would experience severe and permanent side effects, including either an inability to control impulses or an inability to initiate activity, extreme listlessness and loss of emotions, seizures, and sometimes even death.

By the 1950s, the use of **psychosurgery** had declined dramatically, especially in countries outside the United States. Today psychosurgery is used rarely, and only with people who have severe disorders that do not respond to other forms of treatment. Modern neurological assessment and surgical techniques make psychosurgery more precise and safer than it was formerly, although it remains highly controversial, even among professionals (Tatagiba, Ugarte, & Acioly, 2015). Neurosurgeons attempt to lesion, or destroy, minute areas of the brain thought to be involved in a patient's symptoms. One of the greatest remaining problems in psychosurgery, however, is that we do not yet know what areas of the brain are involved in producing most psychiatric symptoms, and it is likely that many areas of the brain are involved in any given disorder.

Assessing Biological Approaches

The biological therapies have revolutionized the treatment of people with psychological disorders. We entered the twentieth century able only to house and comfort people with severe psychological disturbances. In the twenty-first century, we are able to treat many of these people so successfully that they can lead normal lives, thanks in part to the biological therapies that have been developed in recent decades. Overall, biological approaches have been remarkably effective.

Many people find biological theories appealing because they seem to erase any blame or responsibility that might be placed on the sufferer of a disorder. Indeed, many organizations that advocate for people with mental disorders argue that mental disorders should be seen as medical diseases, just like diabetes or high blood pressure. They argue that people who suffer from these disorders simply must accept that they have a disease and obtain the appropriate medical treatment.

Despite their current popularity, however, the biological therapies are not a panacea. They do not work for everyone. Indeed, some people with psychological disorders do not respond to any of the drugs or other biological treatments currently available. In addition, for some disorders, such as phobias (see the chapter "Trauma, Anxiety, Obsessive-Compulsive, and Related Disorders"), psychotherapy works better than drug therapies in alleviating symptoms.

Most of the biological therapies have significant side effects, as other chapters of this book will describe. Often these side effects are tolerable, and people endure them because the drugs offer relief from their psychological disorder. For some people, however, the side effects are worse than the disorder itself. For yet others, the side effects can be dangerous or even deadly.

Some critics of biological theories and drug therapies worry that people will turn to the drugs rather than deal with the issues in their lives that are causing or contributing to their psychological problems. Critics also argue that biological theories often ignore the role of environmental and psychological processes in biological functioning. Finally, recent research suggests that individuals who attribute their mental health problems to biological causes are more pessimistic about their prognosis for recovery than are individuals who attribute their mental health problems to nonbiological causes (Lebowitz & Ahn, 2012).

PSYCHOLOGICAL APPROACHES

We turn now to a discussion of different psychological approaches to understanding and treating abnormality. We begin with behavioral and cognitive approaches, which are the focus of much research in psychopathology. We then discuss psychodynamic and humanistic approaches, family systems approaches, and third-wave approaches.

Behavioral Approaches

Behavioral approaches focus on the influence of reinforcements and punishments in producing behavior. The two core principles or processes of learning according to behaviorism are classical conditioning and operant conditioning. Learning can also occur through modeling and observational learning.

Classical Conditioning

Around the turn of the twentieth century, Ivan Pavlov, a Russian physiologist, was conducting experiments on the salivary glands of dogs when he made discoveries that would revolutionize psychological theory. Not surprisingly, his dogs would salivate when Pavlov or an assistant put food in their mouths. Pavlov noticed that, after a while, the dogs would salivate when he or his assistant simply walked into the room.

Pavlov had paired a previously neutral stimulus (himself) with a stimulus that naturally leads to a certain response (the dish of food, which leads to salivating); eventually the neutral stimulus (Pavlov) was able to elicit that response (salivation). This process gained the name **classical conditioning.** The stimulus that naturally produces a response is the **unconditioned stimulus (US),** and the response created by the unconditioned stimulus is the **unconditioned response (UR).** Thus, in Pavlov's experiments, the dish of food was the US, and salivation in response to this food was the UR. The previously neutral stimulus is the **conditioned stimulus (CS),** and the response that it elicits is the **conditioned response (CR).** Thus, Pavlov was the CS, and when the dogs salivated in response to seeing him, this salivation became the CR (Figure 11).

Classical conditioning has been used to explain people's seemingly irrational responses to a host of neutral stimuli. For example, a college student who previously failed a test in a particular classroom may break out in a cold sweat when she enters that room again. This response is the result of classical conditioning. The room has become a conditioned stimulus, eliciting a response of anxiety, because it was paired with an unconditioned stimulus (failing an exam) that elicited anxiety.

Operant Conditioning

E. L. Thorndike observed that behaviors that are followed by a reward are strengthened, whereas behaviors that are followed by a punishment are weakened. This simple but important observation, which Thorndike labeled the law of effect, led to the development of the principles of **operant conditioning**—the shaping of behaviors by providing rewards for desired behaviors and providing punishments for undesired behaviors.

In the 1930s, B. F. Skinner showed that a pigeon will learn to press on a bar if pressing it is associated with the delivery of food and will learn to avoid pressing another bar if pressing it is associated with an electric shock. Similarly, a child will learn to make his bed if he receives a hug and a kiss from his mother each time he makes the bed, and he will learn to stop hitting his brother if he doesn't get to watch his favorite television show every time he hits his brother.

In operant conditioning, behaviors will be learned most quickly if they are paired with the reward or punishment every time the behavior is emitted. This consistent response is called a *continuous reinforcement*

FIGURE 11 **Stimulus and Response in Classical Conditioning.** Classical conditioning is a major way abnormal behaviors are learned, according to behavioral theories.

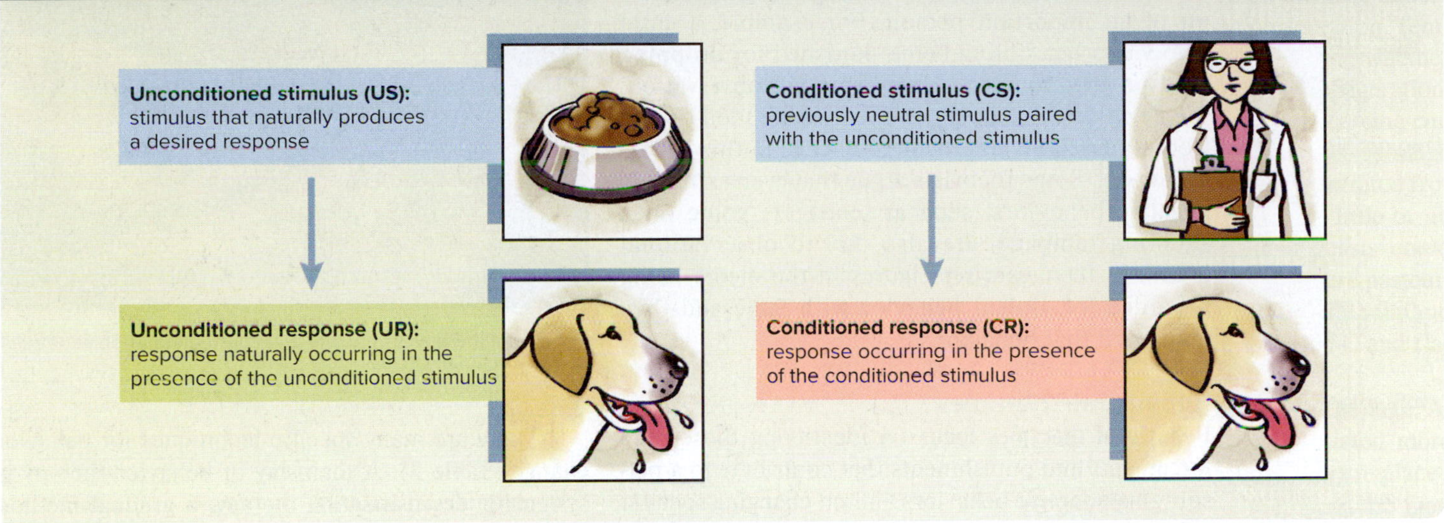

schedule. Behaviors can be learned and maintained, however, on a *partial reinforcement schedule,* in which the reward or punishment occurs only sometimes in response to the behavior. *Extinction*—eliminating a learned behavior—is more difficult when the behavior was learned through a partial reinforcement schedule than when the behavior was learned through a continuous reinforcement schedule. This is because the behavior was learned under conditions of occasional reward, so a constant reward is not needed to maintain the behavior. A good example is gambling behavior. People who frequently gamble are seldom rewarded, but they continue to gamble in anticipation of that occasional, unpredictable win.

Hobart Mowrer's (1939) two-factor model suggests that combinations of classical and operant conditioning can explain the persistence of fears. Initially, people develop fear responses to previously neutral stimuli through classical conditioning. Then, through operant conditioning, they develop behaviors designed to avoid triggers for that fear. For example, a woman may have a fear of bridges developed through classical conditioning: She fell off a bridge into icy waters as a child, and now any time she nears a bridge she feels very anxious. This woman then develops elaborate means of getting around her hometown without having to cross any bridges. Avoiding the bridges reduces her anxiety, and thus her avoidant behavior is reinforced. This woman has developed a *conditioned avoidance response* through operant conditioning. As a result, however, she never exposes herself to a bridge and never has the opportunity to extinguish her initial fear of bridges. As we shall see, many of the therapeutic techniques developed by behavioral theorists are designed to extinguish conditioned avoidance responses, which can interfere greatly with a person's ability to function in everyday life.

Gambling is reinforced by wins only occasionally, but this makes it more difficult to extinguish the behavior. ©*Syracuse Newspapers/ Dennis Nett/The Image Works*

Modeling and Observational Learning

Skinner and other "pure" behaviorists argued that humans and animals learn behaviors only by directly experiencing rewards or punishments for the behaviors. In the 1950s, however, psychologist Albert Bandura argued that people also learn behaviors by watching other people, a view that came to be known as *social learning theory*. First, in **modeling,** people learn new behaviors from imitating the behaviors modeled by important people in their lives, such as their parents. Learning through modeling is more likely to occur when the person modeling the behavior is seen as an authority figure or is perceived to be like oneself. For example, Bandura (1969) argued that children are most likely to imitate the behaviors modeled by their same-sex parent, because this parent is an authority figure and because their same-sex parent seems more similar to them than does their opposite-sex parent.

Second, **observational learning** takes place when a person observes the rewards and punishments that another person receives for his or her behavior and then behaves in accordance with those rewards and punishments. Like modeling, observational learning involves observing others, but it emphasizes observing the consequences of another's behavior, as opposed to simply the behavior of an important person. For example, a child who views her sibling being punished for dropping food on the floor will learn, through observation, the negative consequences of dropping food on the floor and will be less likely to engage in this behavior herself. Some theorists argue that even extremely negative behaviors, such as teenagers going on a shooting rampage, are also due to observational learning. Teenagers see figures in the media being rewarded for violent behavior with fame and thus may learn that behavior.

Behavioral therapy is very effective for treating phobias. ©*Vicki Beaver/Alamy Stock Photo*

Behavioral Therapies

Behavioral therapies focus on identifying those reinforcements and punishments that contribute to a person's maladaptive behaviors and on changing specific behaviors. The foundation for behavioral therapy is the *behavioral assessment* of the client's problem. The therapist works with the client to identify the specific circumstances that seem to elicit the client's unwanted behavior or emotional responses: What situations seem to trigger anxiety symptoms? When is the client most likely to begin heavy drinking? What types of interactions with other people make the client feel most distressed?

There are many specific techniques for behavior change (Table 2). A mainstay of behavior therapy is **systematic desensitization therapy,** a gradual method for extinguishing anxiety responses to stimuli and the maladaptive behavior that often accompanies this anxiety. In systematic desensitization, the client first learns relaxation exercises and then develops a hierarchy of feared stimuli, ranging from stimuli that would cause him or her only mild anxiety to stimuli that would cause severe anxiety or panic. A person with a snake phobia might put at the bottom of his hierarchy "imagining a snake in a closed container across the

TABLE 2 Behavior Change Techniques

These are some of the methods used in behavior therapy.

Label	Description
Removal of reinforcements	Removes the individual from the reinforcing situation or environment
Aversion therapy	Makes the situation or stimulus that was once reinforcing no longer reinforcing
Relaxation exercises	Help the individual voluntarily control physiological manifestations of anxiety
Distraction techniques	Help the individual temporarily distract from anxiety-producing situations; divert attention from physiological manifestations of anxiety
Flooding, or implosive, therapy	Exposes the individual to the dreaded or feared stimulus while preventing avoidant behavior
Systematic desensitization	Pairs the implementation of relaxation techniques with hierarchical exposure to the aversive stimulus
Response shaping through operant conditioning	Pairs rewards with desired behaviors
Behavioral contracting	Provides rewards for reaching proximal goals
Modeling and observational learning	Models desired behaviors, so that the client can learn through observation

room." A little further up on the hierarchy might be "watching someone else handle a snake." At the top of his hierarchy might be "touching a snake myself." Then the therapist would help him proceed through this hierarchy, starting with the least-feared stimulus. He would be instructed to vividly imagine the feared stimulus, or even be exposed to the feared stimulus for a short period, while implementing relaxation exercises to control the anxiety. When he gets to the point where he can imagine or experience the least-feared stimulus without feeling anxious, he moves on to the next-most-feared stimulus, imagining or experiencing it while implementing relaxation exercises. This process continues until he reaches the most-feared stimulus on the list and is able to experience this stimulus without anxiety. Thus, by the end of systematic desensitization therapy, a person with a snake phobia should be able to pick up and handle a large snake without becoming anxious.

Often, systematic desensitization therapy is combined with modeling—the client might watch as the therapist picks up a snake, pets it, and plays with it, observing that the therapist is not afraid, is not bitten or choked, and seems to enjoy playing with the snake. Eventually the client is encouraged to imitate the therapist's behaviors with and reactions to the snake. In some cases, people undergoing systematic desensitization are asked only to imagine experiencing the feared stimuli. In other cases, they are asked to experience these stimuli directly—actually touching and holding the snake, for example. This latter method, known as in vivo exposure, generally has stronger results than exposure only in the client's imagination (Foa & McLean, 2016).

Assessing Behavioral Approaches

Behavioral theorists set the standard for scientifically testing hypotheses about how normal and abnormal behaviors develop. The hypotheses developed from these theories are precise, and the studies that have been done to test these hypotheses are rigorously controlled and exact. As we will see in other chapters, these studies have provided strong support for behavioral explanations of many types of abnormal behavior, particularly anxiety disorders such as phobias and panic disorder. Similarly, the effectiveness of behavior therapies has been extensively and systematically supported in controlled studies (Foa & MacLean, 2016).

The behavioral theories do have limitations. How behavioral principles could account for some disorders, such as schizophrenia, is unclear. Also, most evidence for behavioral theories is from laboratory studies, but, as we discuss in the chapter "The Research Endeavor," lab results do not always apply to the complexity of the real world. Further, the behavioral theories have been criticized for not recognizing free will in people's behaviors—the active choices people make to defy the external forces acting on them.

Aaron Beck is one of the founders of cognitive theories of psychopathology. ©*Aaron Beck*

Cognitive Approaches

Cognitive theories argue that it is not simply rewards and punishments that motivate human behavior. Instead, our **cognitions**—thoughts or beliefs—shape our behavior and the emotions we experience (Beck & Bredemeier, 2016).

When something happens to us, we ask ourselves why that event happened (Abramson, Metalsky, & Alloy, 1989; Abramson, Seligman, & Teasdale, 1978). The answer to this "why" question is our **causal attribution** for the event. The attributions we make for events can influence our behavior because they impact the meaning we give to events and our expectations for similar events in the future.

The attributions we make for our own behavior can affect our emotions and self-concept. For example, if we act rudely toward another person and attribute this behavior to situational factors (we were having a stressful day), we may not feel very guilty. However, if we attribute our rude behavior to personality factors (I am a rude person), then we may feel quite guilty.

In addition to making attributions for specific events, we have broad beliefs about ourselves, our relationships, and the world. These can be either positive and helpful to us or negative and destructive. These broad beliefs are called **global assumptions.** Two prominent proponents of this view are Albert Ellis and Aaron Beck. They argued that most negative emotions or maladaptive behaviors are the result of one or more of the dysfunctional global assumptions that guide a person's life. Some of the most common dysfunctional assumptions are these:

1. I should be loved by everyone for everything I do.
2. It is better to avoid problems than to face them.
3. I should be completely competent, intelligent, and achieving in all I do.
4. I must have perfect self-control.

People who hold such beliefs often will react to situations with irrational thoughts and behaviors and negative emotions. For example, someone who believes that she must be completely competent, intelligent, and achieving in all areas of her life will be extremely upset by even minor failures or unpleasant events. If she were to score poorly on an exam, she may have thoughts such as "I am a total failure. I will

A socially anxious client may be given the behavioral assignment to talk with a stranger at a party. ©*Ingram Publishing*

never amount to anything. I should have gotten a perfect score on that exam."

Cognitive Therapies

Cognitive therapies help clients identify and challenge their negative thoughts and dysfunctional belief systems. Cognitive therapists also help clients learn more effective problem-solving techniques for dealing with the concrete problems in their lives. Cognitive therapy is designed to be short-term, on the order of 12 to 20 weeks in duration, with one or two sessions per week (Beck, Rush, Shaw, & Emery, 1979). There are three main goals in cognitive therapy (Beck, 1976):

1. Assist clients in identifying their irrational and maladaptive thoughts. A client might be asked to keep a diary of thoughts she has whenever she feels anxious.
2. Teach clients to challenge their irrational or maladaptive thoughts and to consider alternative ways of thinking. A client might be asked to evaluate the evidence for a belief or to consider how other people might think about a difficult situation.
3. Encourage clients to face their worst fears about a situation and recognize ways they could cope.

Cognitive techniques are often combined with behavioral techniques in what is known as **cognitive-behavioral therapy,** or **CBT.** The therapist may use behavioral assignments to help the client gather evidence concerning his or her beliefs, to test alternative viewpoints about a situation, and to try new methods of coping with different situations. These assignments are presented to the client as ways of testing hypotheses and gathering information that will be useful in therapy regardless of the outcome. The assignments can also involve trying out new skills, such as skill in communicating more effectively, between therapy sessions.

The following case study illustrates how a therapist might use behavioral assignments to provide a depressed student with opportunities to practice new skills and to gather information about thoughts that contribute to negative emotions.

CASE STUDY

A student was unable to complete her degree because she feared meeting with a professor to discuss an incomplete grade she had received in a course. She was quite convinced that the professor would "scream at her," and she had been unable to complete a homework assignment to call the professor's secretary to arrange a meeting. An in vivo task was agreed on in which she called the professor from her therapist's office. Her thoughts and feelings before, during, and after the call were carefully examined. As might be expected, the professor was quite glad to hear from his former student and was pleased to accept her final paper. She was able to see that her beliefs were both maladaptive and erroneous. (Adapted from Freeman & Reinecke, 1995, pp. 203–204)

Assessing Cognitive Approaches

Particularly in studies of mood disorders and anxiety disorders, and increasingly in studies of sexual disorders, eating disorders, and substance use disorders, evidence demonstrates the effect of maladaptive cognitions (Joormann & Vanderlind, 2014). Further, as we will see in other chapters, cognitive therapies have proven useful in the treatment of these disorders (Craske, 2017).

The greatest limitation of the cognitive theories has been the difficulty of proving that maladaptive cognitions precede and cause disorders, rather than being the symptoms or consequences of the disorders. For example, it is clear that depressed people think negative thoughts. But do negative thoughts cause depression, or does depression cause negative thoughts? It turns out to be harder than you might think to answer this question definitively, and to clearly delineate which aspects of cognitive therapy lead to effects (e.g., Lemmens et al., 2017).

Psychodynamic Approaches

The **psychodynamic theories** of abnormality suggest that all behaviors, thoughts, and emotions, whether normal or abnormal, are influenced to a large extent by unconscious processes (McWilliams, 2011). The psychodynamic theories began with Sigmund Freud in the late nineteenth century and have expanded to include several newer theories. These theories accept many of Freud's basic assumptions about the workings of the human mind but emphasize processes different from those that Freud emphasized.

Freud developed **psychoanalysis,** which refers to (1) a theory of personality and psychopathology, (2) a method of investigating the mind, and (3) a form of treatment for psychopathology (McWilliams, 2011). As we note in the chapter "Looking at Abnormality," Freud was a Viennese neurologist who became interested in unconscious processes while working with Jean Charcot in Paris in the late nineteenth century. He then returned to Vienna and worked with physician Josef Breuer, most notably on the case of "Anna O."

Anna O. had extensive symptoms of hysteria—physical ailments with no apparent physical cause—including paralysis of the legs and right arm, deafness, and disorganized speech. Breuer attempted to hypnotize Anna O., hoping he could cure her symptoms by suggestion. Anna O. began to talk about painful memories from her past, which apparently were tied to the development of her hysterical symptoms. She expressed a great deal of distress about these memories, but following the recounting of the memories under hypnosis, many of her symptoms went away. Breuer labeled the release of emotions connected to these memories **catharsis,** and Anna O. labeled the entire process her "talking cure."

Breuer and Freud suggested that hysteria is the result of traumatic memories that have been repressed from consciousness because they are too painful. They defined **repression** as the motivated forgetting of a difficult experience, such as being abused as a child, or of an unacceptable wish, such as the desire to hurt someone. Repression does not dissolve the emotion associated with the memory or wish. Instead, argued Breuer and Freud, this emotion is "dammed up" and emerges as symptoms.

Sigmund Freud believed that normal and abnormal behaviors are motivated by needs and drives, most of which are unconscious.
Source: Library of Congress, Prints & Photographs Division, Reproduction number LC-USZ62-139124 (b&w film copy neg.)

The Id, Ego, and Superego

Freud believed that the two basic drives that motivate human behavior are the sexual drive, which he referred to as **libido,** and the aggressive drive (McWilliams, 2011). The energy from these drives continually seeks to be released but can be channeled or harnessed by different psychological systems. Most of Freud's writings focused primarily on libido (or libidinal drive), so our discussion will do so as well.

According to Freud, three systems of the human psyche that help regulate the libido are the id, the ego, and the superego. The **id** is the system from which the libido emerges, and its drives and impulses seek immediate release. The id operates by the *pleasure principle*—the drive to maximize pleasure and minimize pain as quickly as possible to avoid psychic tension.

Freud argued that as children grow older and become aware of the world outside themselves, they also become aware that they cannot always quickly satisfy their impulses. In encountering the outside world, a part of the id splits off and becomes the **ego,** the force that seeks to gratify our wishes and needs in ways that remain within the constraints of outside reality (this is known as the *reality principle*). A preschooler who may wish to suckle at the mother's breast but is aware that this is no longer allowed may satisfy himself with cuddling in his mother's lap.

Freud further argued that the **superego** develops from the ego a little later in childhood. It is the storehouse of rules and regulations for the conduct of behavior that are learned from one's parents and from society. These rules and regulations are in the form of

TABLE 3 Defense Mechanisms

These defense mechanisms were described by Sigmund and Anna Freud.

Defense Mechanism	Definition	Example
Regression	Retreating to a behavior of an earlier developmental period to prevent anxiety and satisfy current needs	A woman abandoned by her lover curls up in a chair, rocking and sucking her fingers.
Denial	Refusing to perceive or accept reality	A husband whose wife recently died denies she is gone and actively searches for her.
Displacement	Discharging unacceptable feelings against someone or something other than the true target of these feelings	A woman who is angry at her children kicks a dog.
Rationalization	Inventing an acceptable motive to explain unacceptably motivated behavior	A soldier who killed innocent civilians rationalizes that he was only following orders.
Intellectualization	Adopting a cold, distanced perspective on a matter that actually creates strong, unpleasant feelings	An emergency room physician who is troubled by seeing young people with severe gunshot wounds every night has discussions with colleagues that focus only on the technical aspects of treatment.
Projection	Attributing one's own unacceptable motives or desires to someone else	A husband who is sexually attracted to a colleague accuses his wife of cheating on him.
Reaction formation	Adopting a set of attitudes and behaviors that are the opposite of one's true dispositions	A man who cannot accept his own homosexuality becomes homophobic.
Identification	Adopting the ideas, values, and tendencies of someone in a superior position in order to elevate self-worth	Prisoners adopt the attitudes of their captors toward other prisoners.
Sublimation	Translating wishes and needs into socially acceptable behavior	An adolescent with strong aggressive impulses train to be a boxer.

moral standards. We internalize these moral standards because living according to them reduces anxiety (McWilliams, 2011).

Freud believed that personality and psychopathology are determined by interactions among the id, ego, and superego. He believed that these mostly occur in the **unconscious,** out of our awareness. The **preconscious** is intermediate between the unconscious and the **conscious.** Some material (wishes, needs, or memories) from the unconscious can make its way into the preconscious but rarely reaches the conscious level on its own. Because these unconscious desires are often unacceptable to the individual or society, they cause anxiety if they do seep into the conscious, often prompting the ego to push them back into the unconscious. This pushing of material back into the unconscious is repression (McWilliams, 2011).

Freud—and later his daughter, Anna Freud—described certain strategies, or **defense mechanisms,** that the ego uses to disguise or transform unconscious wishes. The particular defense mechanisms that a person regularly uses shape his or her behavior and personality. Table 3 provides a list and examples of the basic defense mechanisms. Everyone uses defense mechanisms to a degree, because everyone must protect against awareness of unacceptable wishes and conform to societal norms. When a person's behavior becomes ruled by defense mechanisms or when the mechanisms themselves are maladaptive, however, these mechanisms can result in abnormal, pathological behavior.

Psychosexual Stages

Psychoanalytic theory argues that the nurturance a child receives from his or her early caregivers strongly influences personality development. A critical part of Freud's theory was his proposal that as children develop they pass through a series of universal **psychosexual stages.** In each stage, sexual drives are focused on the physical stimulation of certain body areas, and particular psychological issues can cause anxiety in the child. The responses of caregivers, usually parents, to the child's attempts to satisfy basic needs and wishes can greatly influence whether a given stage is negotiated successfully. If the parents are not appropriately responsive, helping the child learn acceptable ways of satisfying and controlling his or her drives and impulses, the child can become "fixated" at an earlier stage—that is, stuck in the specific concerns and issues of that stage and never successfully moving beyond that stage and through the subsequent stages. In essence, at each stage, unique issues emerge and must be resolved in order to proceed normally to the next stage.

According to Freud, the earliest stage of life, the *oral stage,* lasts for the first 18 months following birth. In the oral stage, libidinal impulses are best satisfied through stimulation of the mouth area, usually through feeding or sucking. At this stage, the child is entirely dependent on caregivers for gratification, and the central issues of this stage are issues of one's dependence and the reliability of others. If the child's caregiver, typically the mother, is not adequately available to the child, he or she can develop deep mistrust and fear of abandonment. Children fixated at the oral stage develop an "oral personality," characterized by excessive dependence on others but mistrust of others' love. In adults, a number of habits focused on the mouth area—for example, smoking or excessive drinking and eating—are said to reflect an oral personality.

The *anal stage* lasts from about 18 months to 3 years of age. During this phase, the focus of gratification is the anus. The child becomes very interested in toilet activities, particularly the passing and retaining of feces. Parents can cause a child to become fixated at this stage by being too harsh or critical during toilet training. Adults who fixate at this stage are said to have an "anal personality" that involves being stubborn, overly controlling, stingy, and too focused on orderliness and tidiness.

During the *phallic stage,* lasting from about age 3 to age 6, the focus of pleasure is the genitals. During this stage, one of the most important conflicts of sexual development occurs, and it occurs differently for boys and girls. Freud believed that boys become sexually attracted to their mother and hate their father as a rival. Freud labeled this the *Oedipus complex,* after the character in Greek mythology who unknowingly kills his father and marries his mother. Boys fear that their father will retaliate against them by castrating them. This fear leads them to put aside their desire for their mother and aspire to become like their father. The successful resolution of the Oedipus complex helps instill a strong superego in boys, because it results in boys identifying with their father and their father's value system.

Freud believed that, during the phallic stage, girls recognize that they do not have a penis and are horrified at this discovery. They also recognize that their mother does not have a penis and disdain their mother and all females for this deficit. Girls develop an attraction for their father, in hopes that he will provide the penis they lack. Freud labeled this the *Electra complex,* after the character in Greek mythology who conspires to murder her mother to avenge her father's death. Girls cannot have castration anxiety, because, according to Freud, they feel they have already been castrated. As a result, girls do not have as strong a motivation as boys to develop a superego. Freud argued that females never develop superegos as strong as those of males and that this leads to a greater reliance on emotion than on reason in the lives of women. Freud also thought that much of women's behavior is driven by penis envy—the wish to have the male sex organ.

The unsuccessful resolution of the phallic stage can lead to a number of psychological problems in children. If children do not fully identify with their same-sex parent, they may not develop "appropriate" gender roles or a heterosexual orientation. They also may not develop a healthy superego and may become either too self-aggrandizing or too self-deprecating. If children's sexual attraction to their parents is not met with gentle but firm discouragement, they may become overly seductive or sexualized and have a number of problems in future romantic relationships.

After the turmoil of the phallic stage, children enter the *latency stage* (ages 6–12), during which libidinal drives are quelled somewhat. Their attention turns to developing skills and interests and becoming fully socialized into the world in which they live. They play with friends of the same sex and avoid children of the opposite sex.

At about age 12, children's sexual desires emerge again as they enter puberty, and they enter the genital stage. If they have successfully resolved the phallic stage, their sexual interests turn to heterosexual relationships. They begin to pursue romantic alliances and learn to negotiate the world of dating and early sexual encounters with members of the opposite sex.

Later Psychodynamic Theories

Many of Freud's followers modified his original psychoanalytic theory, leading to a group of theories collectively referred to as *psychodynamic theories*. Anna Freud extended her work on defense mechanisms to help develop the field of **ego psychology,** emphasizing the importance of the individual's ability to regulate defenses in ways that allow healthy functioning within the realities of society. Other theorists also focused on the role of the ego as an independent force striving for mastery and competence (e.g., Jacobson, 1964; Mahler, 1968).

The **object relations** perspective integrated significant aspects of Sigmund Freud's drive theory with the role of early relationships in the development of self-concept and personality. According to proponents of this perspective—such as Melanie Klein, Margaret Mahler, and Otto Kernberg—our early relationships create unconscious mental images, or representations, of ourselves and others. We carry these mental representations throughout adulthood, and they affect all our subsequent relationships. For example, our early experiences with caregivers set up our expectations for future romantic partners. More contemporary types of psychoanalysis include **self psychology** and **relational psychoanalysis,** which emphasize the unconscious dimensions of our relationships with one another from pregnancy and infancy throughout all of life.

Carl Jung, who was a student of Freud, rejected many of Freud's ideas about the importance of sexuality in development. He argued that spiritual and religious drives were as important as sexual drives, and he suggested that the wisdom accumulated by a society over hundreds of years of human existence is stored in the memories of individuals. He referred to this wisdom as the **collective unconscious.**

Psychodynamic Therapies

Therapies based on Freud's classical psychoanalytic theory and on later psychodynamic theories focus on uncovering and resolving the unconscious processes that are thought to drive psychological symptoms. The goal of **psychodynamic therapies** is to help clients recognize their maladaptive coping strategies and the sources of their unconscious conflicts. The resulting insights are thought to free clients from the grip of the past and give them a sense of agency in making changes in the present (Safran, 2012).

Freud and others developed the method of **free association,** in which a client is taught to talk about whatever comes to mind, trying not to censor any thoughts. The therapist notices what themes seem to recur in a client's free associations, exactly how one thought seems to lead to another, and the specific memories that a client recalls.

The material the client is reluctant to talk about during psychotherapy—that is, the client's **resistance** to certain material—is an important clue to the client's central unconscious conflicts, because the most threatening conflicts are those the ego tries hardest to repress. The therapist eventually puts together these pieces of the puzzle to form a suggestion or an interpretation of a conflict the client might be facing and then voices this interpretation to the client. Sometimes the client accepts the interpretation as a revelation. At other times the client is resistant to the interpretation. The therapist might interpret resistance as a good indication that the interpretation has identified an important issue in the client's unconscious.

The client's **transference** to the therapist is also a clue to unconscious conflicts and needs. Transference occurs when the client reacts to the therapist as if the therapist were an important person in the client's early development, such as his or her father or mother. For example, a client may find himself reacting with rage or extreme fear when a therapist is just a few minutes late for an appointment, a reaction that might stem from his feelings of having been emotionally abandoned by a parent during childhood. The therapist might point out the ways the client behaves that represent transference and might then help the client explore the roots of this behavior in the client's relationships with significant others.

By **working through,** or going over and over, painful memories and difficult issues, clients are able to understand them and weave them into their self-definition in acceptable ways. This allows them to move forward in their lives. Psychodynamic therapists believe that *catharsis,* or the expression of emotions connected to memories and conflicts, is also central to the healing processes in therapy. Catharsis unleashes the energy bound in unconscious memories and conflicts, allowing this material to be incorporated into a more adaptive self-view.

What is the difference between classical psychoanalysis and modern psychodynamic therapy? Classical (Freudian) psychoanalysis typically involves three or four sessions per week over a period of many years. The focus of psychoanalysis is primarily on the interpretation of transferences and resistances, as well as on experiences in the client's past (Luborsky & Barrett, 2006). More modern psychodynamic therapy also may go on for years, but it can be as short as 12 weeks (Leichsenring & Steinert, 2018). Transferences, resistances, and the client's relationships with early caregivers are also the focus of psychodynamic therapy, but psychodynamic therapists, compared with psychoanalysts, may focus more on current situations in the client's life and tends to focus more on symptom relief than deeper self-insight.

Interpersonal therapy, or **IPT,** emerged out of modern psychodynamic theories of psychopathology, which shifted the focus from the unconscious conflicts of the individual to the client's pattern of relationships with important people in his or her life (Klerman, Weissman, Rounsaville, & Chevron, 1984; Weissman, Markowitz, & Klerman, 2017). IPT differs from psychodynamic therapies in that the therapist is much more structuring and directive in the therapy, offering interpretations much earlier and focusing on how to change current relationships. IPT is designed to be a short-term therapy, often lasting only about 12 weeks.

Assessing Psychodynamic Approaches

Psychodynamic theories are among the most comprehensive theories of human behavior established to date. For some people, they are also the most satisfying theories. They explain both normal and abnormal behavior with similar processes. Also, they have an "Aha!" quality about them that leads us to believe they offer important insights. Psychodynamic theories have played a major role in shaping psychology and psychiatry over the past century.

Psychodynamic theories also have many limitations and weaknesses. Chief among these is that it is difficult or impossible to test their fundamental assumptions scientifically (Erdelyi, 1992; but see Shedler, 2010; Westen, 1998). The processes described by these theories are abstract and difficult to measure (e.g., the Oedipus complex). Because the key factors thought to be influencing behavior are unconscious and unobservable, it is easy to provide explanations for why a particular prediction might not be borne out in a particular circumstance.

As for psychodynamic therapy, its long-term, intensive nature makes it unaffordable for many people, especially given insurance company restrictions on number of sessions. This is a challenge for many types of therapy, but partly for this reason, modern psychodynamic therapists have developed some shorter-term, more structured versions of psychodynamic therapy (Leichsenring & Steinert, 2018). Studies conducted on the effectiveness of these short-term therapies suggest that they can result in significant improvement in symptoms for people with psychological problems (Driessen et al., 2017; Leichsenring & Steinert, 2018).

This book focuses on those theories of specific disorders, and the therapies for these disorders, that have received substantial scientific support. Because psychodynamic theories and therapies have had much less empirical support than many newer psychological theories and therapies, we will not discuss them in detail in reviewing the research on most disorders.

Humanistic Approaches

Humanistic theories are based on the assumption that humans have an innate capacity for goodness and for living a full life (Rogers, 1951). Pressure from society to conform to certain norms rather than to seek one's most-developed self interferes with the fulfillment of this capacity. The humanistic theorists recognized that we often are not aware of the forces shaping our behavior and that the environment can play a large role in our happiness or unhappiness. But they were optimistic that once people recognized these forces and became freer to direct their own lives, they would naturally make good choices and be happier.

Carl Rogers (January 8, 1902–February 4, 1987) was one of the founders of the humanistic approach (or client-centered approach) to psychology. *©Bettmann/Getty Images*

Carl Rogers (1951) developed the most widely known version of humanistic theory. Rogers believed that, without undue pressure from others, individuals naturally move toward personal growth, self-acceptance, and **self-actualization**—the fulfillment of their potential for love, creativity, and meaning. Under pressure from society and family, however, people can develop rigid and distorted perspectives of the self. People often experience conflict due to differences between their true self, the ideal self they wish to be, and the self they feel they ought to be to please others. This conflict can lead to emotional distress, unhealthy behaviors, and even the loss of touch with reality.

Humanistic Therapy

The stated goal of **humanistic therapy** is to help clients discover their greatest potential through self-exploration (Krug, 2016). The job of the therapist in humanistic therapy is not to act as an authority who provides healing to the client but rather to provide the optimal conditions for the client to heal him- or herself. Humanistic therapists do not push clients to uncover repressed painful memories or unconscious conflicts. Instead, they believe that when clients are supported and empowered to grow, the clients eventually will face the past when doing so becomes necessary for their further development (Krug, 2016).

The best known of these therapies is Carl Rogers' **client-centered therapy** (**CCT;** Rogers, 1951). In CCT, the therapist communicates a genuineness in his or her role as helper to the client, which he termed *congruence,* acting as an authentic person rather than an authority figure. The therapist also shows unconditional positive regard for the client (giving the client a sense that he or she is inherently valued) and communicates an empathic understanding of the client's underlying feelings and search for self.

The main strategy for accomplishing these goals is the use of reflection. **Reflection** is a method of response in which the therapist expresses an attempt to understand what the client is experiencing and trying to communicate (Krug, 2016). The therapist does not attempt to interpret the unconscious aspects of the client's experience for the patient, but rather tries to communicate an understanding of the client and explicitly checks with the client about the accuracy of this understanding.

SHADES OF GRAY

A student comes into a therapist's office to discuss her feelings about her schoolwork and career. She says, "I'm feeling so lost in my career. Every time I seem to be getting close to doing something really good, like acing a class, I somehow manage to screw it up. I never feel like I am really using my potential. There is a block there" (Bohart, 1995, p. 101).

How might a humanistic therapist versus a psychodynamic therapist respond to this student's concerns? (Discussion appears at the end of this chapter.)

Assessing Humanistic Approaches

The humanistic theories struck a positive chord in the 1960s and still have many proponents, especially among self-help groups and peer-counseling programs. The optimism and attribution of free will of these theories are a refreshing change from the emphasis on pathology and external forces of other theories. Humanistic theories shift the focus from what is wrong with people to questions about how people can be helped to achieve their greatest potential. These theories have been criticized, however, for being vague and not subject to scientific testing.

Client-centered therapy has been used to treat people with a wide range of problems, including depression, alcoholism, schizophrenia, anxiety disorders, and personality disorders. Although some studies have shown that CCT results in better outcomes than comparison therapies, other studies have not (Elliott, Greenberg, & Lietaer, 2004). Some therapists believe that CCT may be appropriate for people who are moderately distressed but insufficient for people who are seriously distressed.

Family Systems Approaches

Family systems theories see the family as a complex interpersonal system, with its own hierarchy and rules that govern family members' behavior. The family system can function well and promote the well-being of its members, supporting their growth and accepting their change. Or the family system can be dysfunctional, creating and maintaining psychopathology in one or more members (Prochaska & Norcross, 2014).

When a member of the family has a psychological disorder, family systems theorists see it not as a problem within the individual but as an indication of a dysfunctional family system. The particular form that any individual's psychopathology takes depends on the complex interactions among the family's cohesiveness, adaptability to change, and communication style (Prochaska & Norcross, 2014).

For example, an inflexible family is resistant to and isolated from all forces outside the family and does not adapt well to changes within the family, such as a child moving into adolescence. In an enmeshed family, each member is overly involved in the lives of the others, to the point that individuals do not have personal autonomy and can feel controlled. A disengaged family, in contrast, is one in which the members pay no attention to each other and operate as independent units isolated from other family members. And in pathological triangular relationships, parents avoid dealing with conflicts with each other by always keeping their children involved in their conversations and activities (Prochaska & Norcross, 2014). So a family theorist trying to understand Steven Hayes' anxiety would examine how his family functioned as he was growing up and how that continues to influence him as an adult.

Some of the research on family systems theories of psychopathology has focused on disorders presented by the children in the family, particularly eating disorders (Treasure & Cardi, 2017). This research suggests that many young girls who develop eating disorders are members of enmeshed families. The parents of these girls are overly controlling and overinvested in their children's success, and in turn the children feel smothered and dependent on their parents. Anorexia nervosa, a disorder in which an individual refuses to eat and becomes emaciated, may be a girl's way of claiming some control over her life. The family system of these girls supports the anorexia rather than helping them overcome it. The anorexia becomes a focal point and excuse for the family's enmeshment. (See also the chapter "Eating Disorders.")

Family systems therapy is based on the belief that an individual's problems are always rooted in interpersonal systems, particularly family systems. According to this viewpoint, you cannot help an individual without treating the entire family system that created and is maintaining the individual's problems. In fact, these theorists argue that the individual may not even have a problem but rather has become the "identified patient" in the family, carrying the responsibility or blame for the dysfunction of the family system (Prochaska & Norcross, 2014).

Behavioral family systems therapy (BFST) targets family communication and problem solving, those beliefs of parents and adolescents that impede communication, and systemic barriers to problem solving. Behavioral and cognitive methods are used to teach problem-solving and communication skills and to challenge the unhelpful beliefs of parents and teens. Therapists also address dysfunctional family system characteristics, such as weak coalitions between parents. Therapists actively provide instructions, feedback, and opportunities for the rehearsal of skills and role playing.

Family therapists work with the entire family rather than with only the "identified patient."
©Nancy Sheehan/PhotoEdit

Assessing Family Systems Approaches

Family systems theories have led to therapeutic approaches that have proven useful for treating some types of disorders. Family systems therapies may be particularly appropriate in the treatment of children, because children are so much more entwined in their families than are adults. Although the details of many family systems theories have not been thoroughly tested in research, it is clear that families can contribute to or help diminish the psychological symptoms of their members (e.g., Carr, 2014). However, much more research on family systems theories and therapies is needed. Such research is difficult to carry out, because it usually involves observing people in the context of their relationships, which are difficult to capture in a laboratory setting.

Third-Wave Approaches

In recent years, a group of psychotherapeutic approaches known as **third-wave approaches** (the first wave was behavioral approaches, and the second wave was cognitive approaches) has become prominent in the theory and treatment of psychological disorders. Several of these approaches view poor regulation of emotions as a transdiagnostic risk factor at the core of many forms of psychopathology, including depression, anxiety, substance abuse, and most personality disorders (Barlow et al., 2018; Kring & Sloan, 2009). They combine techniques from behavioral and cognitive therapy with mindfulness meditation practices derived from Zen Buddhism to help individuals accept, understand, and better regulate their emotions.

The most-established third-wave approach is *dialectical behavior therapy* (DBT; Linehan, 1999). The term *dialectical* in dialectical behavior therapy refers to the constant tension between conflicting images or emotions in people prone to certain forms of psychopathology. Dialectical behavior therapy focuses on difficulties in managing negative emotions and in controlling impulsive behaviors. The therapy involves a number of behavioral and cognitive techniques and mindfulness exercises aimed at increasing problem-solving skills, interpersonal skills, and skill at managing negative emotions. DBT originally was developed by Marsha Linehan to treat people with borderline personality disorder who were suicidal, and studies comparing this therapy to control conditions suggest that it can reduce suicidal behavior and nonsuicidal self-injury (e.g., Panos, Jackson, Hasan, & Panos, 2014). Reflecting its transdiagnostic relevance, DBT has been adapted for the treatment of eating disorders (Safer, Telch, & Chen, 2009), mood disorders (Van Dijk, Jeffrey, & Katz, 2013), and other problems of emotional regulation and impulse control (Neacsiu, Eberle, Kramer, Wiesmann, & Linehan, 2014), including in children (Perepletchikova et al., 2017), and research in these areas is ongoing.

Steven Hayes, whom we met in the Extraordinary People feature at the beginning of this chapter, is the founder of *acceptance and commitment therapy* (ACT), which assumes that *experiential avoidance*—that is, avoidance of painful thoughts, memories, and feelings—is at the heart of many mental health problems. Accepting one's feelings, thoughts, and past history and learning to be present in the moment are key to achieving positive change. ACT uses a variety of techniques to help individuals accept their emotions, be present in the moment, relate to their thoughts differently (e.g., watching them as external objects), and commit to changing their behaviors in accord with their goals and values (Hayes et al., 2006). Randomized

Marsha Linehan originally developed Dialectical Behavior Therapy (DBT), one of the third wave therapies, to treat women experiencing emotion regulation problems and who had attempted suicide. *©Peter Yates/The New York Times/Redux*

controlled trials of ACT have supported its efficacy in treating a wide variety of problems, especially in anxiety, substance abuse, and physical health (A-Tjak et al., 2015).

Assessing Third-Wave Approaches

The third-wave approaches have their roots in well-established behavioral and cognitive theories and techniques, but they draw innovative ideas and techniques from spiritual and philosophical traditions, such as Buddhism, and theories of adaptive emotion regulation. Existing studies of the effectiveness of therapies based on emotion-focused approaches suggest that these therapies may be helpful in the treatment of a wide range of mental health problems. Much more research is needed, however, particularly into claims of how and why these therapies may help individuals change their behaviors and emotional reactions, and how they compare to other efficacious treatments (Dimidjian et al., 2016; Öst, 2014). An additional therapy, developed by David Barlow and colleagues, is called the Unified Protocol (UP) for emotional disorders (Barlow et al., 2018). The UP directly targets transdiagnostic processes of psychopathology, integrating techniques that have shown efficacy across other treatments for mood and anxiety disorders. The UP simplifies and organizes treatment by targeting processes common across multiple disorders (e.g., tolerating emotional distress). This approach aligns well with current continuum and transdiagnostic models of psychopathology, and a recent randomized controlled trial showed equivalent symptom reduction compared to disorder-specific treatments (Barlow et al., 2017).

Using New Technology to Deliver Treatment

The burden of mental health problems in the world is much greater than the availability of mental health professionals trained to deliver the interventions described (Kazdin & Blase, 2011). For example, recent estimates by the World Health Organization derived from studies done in 17 nations suggest that 12 to 47 percent of individuals will have symptoms that meet the criteria for diagnosis of a mental disorder in their lifetime (Kessler et al., 2009). In the United States, lifetime rates of mental disorders are estimated at 50 percent, with 25 percent of the population meeting the criteria for a diagnosis in any given year (Kessler & Wang, 2008). That amounts to about 75 million people—when there are only about 700,000 mental health professionals in the United States (Kazdin & Blase, 2011). The rate of mental health problems is especially high within disadvantaged ethnic minority groups (Alegria et al., 2008), but individuals in these groups tend to have less access to mental health services than individuals in majority groups (Cook et al., 2014). In addition, because mental health care providers tend to be concentrated in urban areas of developed countries, people living in rural areas of the United States and in developing areas of the world often have very little access to mental health care.

Increasingly, new technology, including the Internet and smart phone applications, is being used to deliver mental health care, with promising effectiveness (Andersson, 2016), including among children and adolescents (Vigerland et al., 2016). For example, a smart phone application known as Mobile Therapy prompts users to report their levels of happiness, sadness, anxiety, and anger on a touchscreen "mood map." Based on users' reports, exercises based on cognitive-behavioral therapy techniques–such as exercises to challenge negative thoughts–are provided to help individuals repair their mood. A 1-month study of the application showed that users became more self-aware of their moods and of the triggers of negativity and that their skill in coping with their negative moods increased (Morris et al., 2010).

The delivery of interventions through new technologies is a vibrant area of research in mental health, and has also thrived in the field of health psychology, as we discuss in the chapter "Health Psychology." Several studies have shown that interventions delivered through the Internet, smart phones, regular phones, and even fictional television and radio shows have improved people's diets, leading to lower levels of obesity and diabetes; decreased levels of smoking; and increased the use of condoms to prevent sexually transmitted diseases (see the chapter "Health Psychology"; Kazdin & Blase, 2011). These interventions can be made available to people living in rural areas and developing countries and to people with modest incomes, and they have been shown to be effective in these populations (e.g., Muñoz et al., 2016).

SOCIOCULTURAL APPROACHES

Sociocultural approaches suggest that we need to look beyond the individual or even the family to the larger society in order to understand people's problems. First, socioeconomic disadvantage is a transdiagnostic risk factor for a wide range of mental health problems (Snowden, 2014). Individuals who are poor tend to live in neighborhoods in which they are exposed to violence and inadequate schools and where there are few resources for everyday living (such as grocery stores) and little cohesion among neighbors. In turn, people living in poverty-stricken urban neighborhoods experience more substance abuse, juvenile delinquency, depression, and anxiety (Belle & Doucet, 2003).

Second, the upheaval and disintegration of societies due to war, famine, and natural disaster are potent transdiagnostic risk factors for mental health problems. As we discuss in the chapter "Trauma, Anxiety, Obsessive-Compulsive, and Related Disorders," individuals who live in countries ravaged by war or who must flee their homelands and live as refugees show high rates of posttraumatic stress disorder and other mental health problems.

Third, social norms and policies that stigmatize and marginalize certain groups put individuals in these groups at increased risk for mental health problems even if they do not suffer socioeconomic stress. For example, gay, lesbian, bisexual, and transgender individuals suffer higher rates of depression, anxiety, and substance use compared to heterosexuals (Hatzenbuehler, 2009; Meyer, 2003). These higher rates have been linked to the experience of discrimination based on sexual orientation and to social policies that disadvantage sexual minorities (Hatzenbuehler, 2016; Meyer, 2003). For example, data from a nationally representative study of over 34,000 participants found higher rates of mental health problems among lesbian, gay, and bisexual (LGB) respondents living in states with social policies that do not confer protection for LGB individuals (e.g., states that do not treat anti-LGB violence as a hate crime) compared to LGB respondents who reside in states with protective policies (Hatzenbuehler, Keyes, & Hasin, 2009). Another long-term study found increases in mental health problems among LGB individuals living in states that instituted bans on gay marriage in the 2004–2005 elections (Hatzenbuehler, McLaughlin, Keyes, & Hasin, 2010). Thus, sociocultural discrimination at the level of state policies can affect citizens' mental health.

Fourth, societies may influence the types of psychopathology their members show by having implicit or explicit rules about what types of abnormal behavior are acceptable (Chu & Leino, 2017). Throughout this book, we will see that the rates of disorders vary from one culture or ethnic group to another and between males and females. For example, people from "traditional" cultures, such as the Old Order Amish in the United States, appear to suffer less depression than people in modern cultures (Egeland & Hostetter, 1983). In addition, the particular manifestations of disorders seem to vary from one culture to another. For example, the symptoms of anorexia nervosa, the disorder in which people refuse to eat, appear to be different in Asian cultures than in American culture.

Indeed, some disorders appear to be specific to certain cultures (Alarcon et al., 2009). In Japan, there is a disorder called *taijin kyofusho,* in which individuals have intense fears that their body displeases, embarrasses, or is offensive to other people. Throughout Latin American and Mediterranean cultures, *ataque de nervios* is a common reaction to stress. People may feel out of control, displaying uncontrollable shouting, crying, and trembling and verbal or physical aggression. We will discuss the influence of culture on the manifestation of distress further in the chapter "Assessing and Diagnosing Abnormality."

Cross-Cultural Issues in Treatment

For the most part, people from diverse cultures who seek psychotherapy are treated with the types of psychotherapy described in this chapter, with little adaptation of these approaches to specific cultures (Chu & Leino, 2017). A number of the assumptions inherent in mainstream psychological therapies, however, can clash with the values and norms of people in certain cultures. Therefore, therapists must take a culturally sensitive approach to their clients (Chu, Leino, Pflum, & Sue, 2016; Snowden & Yamada, 2005).

First, most psychotherapies are focused on the individual—the individual's unconscious conflicts, dysfunctional ways of thinking, maladaptive behavior patterns, and so on. In contrast, many cultures focus on the group, or collective, rather than on the individual (Sue & Sue, 2003). In these cultures, the identity of the individual is not seen apart from the groups to which that individual belongs—his or her family, community, ethnic group, and religion. If therapists fail to recognize this when working with clients from collectivist cultures, they may make useless or perhaps even harmful recommendations, leading to conflicts between their clients and important groups in the clients' lives that the clients cannot handle.

Second, most psychotherapies value the expression of emotions and the disclosure of personal concerns, whereas many cultures, for example, Japanese culture, value restraint with regard to emotions and personal concerns (Sue & Sue, 2003). Some counselors may view this restraint as a problem and try to encourage their clients to become more expressive. Again, this effort can clash with the self-concepts of clients and with the norms of their culture.

Third, in many psychotherapies, clients are expected to take the initiative in communicating their concerns and desires to the therapist and in generating ideas about what is causing their symptoms and what changes they might want to make. These expectations can clash with cultural norms that require deference to people in authority (Sue & Sue, 2003). A client from a culture in which one speaks only when spoken to and never challenges an elder or an authority figure may be extremely uncomfortable with a therapist who does not directly tell the client what is wrong and how to fix it.

Fourth, many clients who are in ethnic minority groups may also be in lower socioeconomic groups, while their therapists are likely to be in middle- or upper-class socioeconomic groups. This situation can create tensions due to class differences as well as cultural differences (Miranda et al., 2005).

Some studies suggest that people from Latino, Asian, and Native American cultures are more comfortable with structured and action-oriented therapies, such as behavioral and cognitive-behavioral therapies, than with the less structured therapies (Miranda et al., 2005). The specific form of therapy may not matter as much as the cultural sensitivity the therapist shows toward the client, whatever therapy is being used. Stanley Sue and Nolan Zane (1987, pp. 42–43) give the following example of the importance of cultural sensitivity in the interaction between client and therapist. First, they describe the problems the client faced; then they describe how the therapist (one of the authors of the study) responded to these problems.

CASE STUDY

Mae C. decided to seek services at a mental health center. . . . An immigrant from Hong Kong several years ago, Mae met and married her husband (also a recent immigrant from Hong Kong). Their marriage was apparently going fairly well until six months ago when her husband succeeded in bringing over his parents from Hong Kong. . . .

After the parents arrived, Mae found that she was expected to serve them. For example, the mother-in-law would expect Mae to cook and serve dinner, to wash all the clothes, and to do other chores. . . . The parents-in-law also displaced Mae and her husband from the master bedroom. The guest room was located in the basement, and the parents refused to sleep in the basement because it reminded them of a tomb.

Mae would occasionally complain to her husband about his parents. The husband would excuse his parents' demands by indicating "They are my parents and they're getting old." In general, he avoided any potential conflict; if he took sides, he supported his parents. Although Mae realized that she had an obligation to his parents, the situation was becoming intolerable to her.

I (the therapist) indicated (to Mae) that conflicts with in-laws were very common, especially for Chinese, who are obligated to take care of their parents. I attempted to normalize the problems because she was suffering from a great deal of guilt over her perceived failure to be the perfect daughter-in-law. . . .

I discussed Mae during a case conference with other mental health personnel. . . . The staff agreed that working solely with Mae would not change the situation. . . . Confronting her in-laws was discrepant with her role of daughter-in-law, and she felt very uncomfortable in asserting herself in the situation. Trying to involve her husband or in-laws in treatment was ill advised. Her husband did not want to confront his parents. . . . Mae was extremely fearful that her family might find out that she had sought psychotherapy. Her husband as well as her in-laws would be appalled at her disclosure of family problems to a therapist who was an outsider. . . . During the case conference, we discussed the ways that Chinese handle interpersonal family conflicts which are not unusual to see. Chinese often use third-party intermediaries to resolve conflicts. . . . At the next session with Mae, I asked her to list the persons who might act as intermediaries, so that we could discuss the suitability of having someone else intervene. Almost immediately, Mae mentioned her uncle . . . whom she described as being quite understanding and sensitive. . . . After calling her uncle . . . she reported that he wanted to visit them. . . . He came for dinner, and Mae told me that she overheard a discussion between the uncle and Mae's mother-in-law. Essentially, he told her that Mae looked unhappy, that possibly she was working too hard, and that she needed a little more praise for the work that she was doing in taking care of everyone. The mother-in-law expressed surprise over Mae's unhappiness and agreed that Mae was doing a fine job. Without directly confronting each other, the uncle and his younger sister understood the subtle messages each conveyed. After this interaction, Mae reported that her mother-in-law's criticisms did noticeably diminish and that she had even begun to help Mae with the chores.

Source: Sue & Zane, 1987, pp. 42–43.

If Mae's therapist had not been sensitive to Mae's cultural beliefs about her role as a daughter-in-law and had suggested some of the solutions put forward by his colleagues in the case conference, Mae might even have dropped out of therapy. People from ethnic minority groups in the United States are much more likely than European Americans to drop out of psychosocial therapy (Snowden & Yamada, 2005). Because Mae's therapist was willing to work within the constraints of her cultural beliefs, he and Mae found a solution to her situation that was acceptable to her.

In treating children, cultural norms about childrearing practices and the proper role of doctors can make it difficult to include the family in a child's treatment. For example, in a study of behavior therapy for children, Hong Kong Chinese parents were very reluctant to be trained to engage in behavioral techniques, such as responding with praise or ignoring certain behaviors. Such techniques violated the parents' views of appropriate childrearing practices and their expectations that the therapist should be the person "curing" the child. However, several clinicians argue that family-based therapies are more appropriate than individual therapy in cultures that are highly family-oriented, including Native American, Hispanic, African American, and Asian American cultures (Miranda et al., 2005).

Jeannette Rosselló and Guillermo Bernal (2005) adapted both cognitive-behavioral therapy and interpersonal therapy to be more culturally sensitive in the treatment of depressed Puerto Rican adolescents. The Puerto Rican value of *familism,* a strong attachment to family, was incorporated into the therapy. Issues of the balance between dependence and independence were explicitly discussed in family groups. The adapted therapies proved effective in treating the adolescents' depression. In general, such culturally adapted treatments retain the key characteristics of established treatments, but seek to improve effectiveness by adding specific skills, incorporating culturally specific themes, or addressing client engagement (Chu & Leino, 2017).

Must a therapist come from the same culture as the client to fully understand the client? Research suggests that ethnic matching is not an important predictor of therapy outcome, but may affect clients' preferences and treatment attendance (Chu et al., 2016). A therapist's being from the same ethnic or racial group as the client does not mean that therapist and client share the same value system. For example, a fourth-generation Japanese American who has fully adopted the competitive and individualistic values of Americans may clash with a recent immigrant from Japan who subscribes to the self-sacrificing, community-oriented values of Japanese culture. Value differences among people of the same ethnic/racial group may explain why studies show that matching the ethnicity, race, or gender of the therapist and the client does not necessarily lead to a better outcome for the client. What matters more is therapists' "cultural competence," meaning understanding of and respect for cultural factors in treatment. Cultural competence and sensitivity can be acquired through training and experience (Chu & Leino, 2017), and they are now required elements of therapist training, partially addressing many of the issues discussed here.

Historically, studies testing treatments essentially have ignored the question of whether the effectiveness of treatments varies by cultural group or ethnicity (Miranda et al., 2005). In recent years this pattern is changing, with increased emphasis on identifying how treatments may work differently depending on culture and ethnicity, and how they can be improved (Chu & Leino, 2017).

As for gender, there is little evidence that women or men do better in therapy with a therapist of the same

Therapy adapted for Puerto Rican families may incorporate the values of familism. ©*Ariel Skelley/Getty Images*

gender, despite a good deal of research (Bhati, 2014). Women and men do tend to report that they prefer a therapist of the same gender, however (Wintersteen, Mensinger, & Diamond, 2005). Because the client's comfort with a therapist is an important contributor to a client's seeking therapy and continuing it for an entire course, gender matching may be important in therapy (Wintersteen, Mensinger, & Diamond, 2005).

Culturally Specific Therapies

Our review of the relationships between culture or gender and therapy has focused on those forms of therapy most often practiced in modern, industrialized cultures, such as behavioral, cognitive, and psychodynamic therapies. Even within modern, industrialized countries, however, cultural groups often have their own forms of therapy for distressed people (Hall, 2001; Koss-Chioino, 2000). Let us examine two of these culturally specific therapies.

Native American healing processes focus simultaneously on the physiology, psychology, and religious practices of the individual (Gone, 2010). "Clients" are encouraged to transcend the self, to experience the self as embedded in the community and as an expression of the community. Family and friends are brought together with the individual in traditional ceremonies involving prayers, songs, and dances that emphasize Native American cultural heritage and the reintegration of the individual into the cultural network. These ceremonies may be supplemented by a variety of herbal medicines that have been used for hundreds of years to treat people exhibiting physical and psychological symptoms.

Hispanics in the southwestern United States and Mexico suffering from psychological problems may consult folk healers, known as *curanderos* or *curanderas* (Valdez, 2014). Curanderos use religion-based rituals, including prayers and incantations, to overcome the folk illnesses believed to cause psychological and physical problems. Curanderos also may apply healing ointments or oils and prescribe herbal medicines.

Native Americans and Hispanics often seek help from both folk healers and mental health professionals who practice the therapies described in this chapter. Mental health professionals need to be aware of the practices and beliefs of folk healing when they treat clients from these cultural groups, keeping in mind the possibility that clients will combine the different forms of therapy and follow some recommendations of both types of healers (Chu & Leino, 2017; Valdez, 2014).

Assessing Sociocultural Approaches

The sociocultural approaches to abnormality argue that we should analyze the larger social and cultural forces that may influence people's behavior. It is not enough to look only at what is going on within individuals or their immediate surroundings. A strength of sociocultural approaches is that they avoid "blaming the victim," as other theories seem to do by placing the responsibility for psychopathology within the individual. The sociocultural approaches also raise our consciousness about our responsibility as a society to change the social conditions that put some individuals at risk for psychopathology. Community psychology and social work are two professions focused on empowering individuals to change their social conditions in order to help them improve their psychological well-being and quality of life.

The sociocultural theories can be criticized, however, for being vague about exactly how social and cultural forces lead to psychological disturbance in individuals. In what ways does social change or stress lead to depression, schizophrenia, and so on? Why do most people who are exposed to social stress and change develop no psychological disturbance at all?

PREVENTION PROGRAMS

Preventing people from developing psychopathology in the first place is better than waiting to treat it once it develops. Stopping the development of disorders before they start is called **primary prevention** (Muñoz, Cuijpers, Smit, Barrera, & Leykin, 2010). Some primary prevention strategies for reducing drug abuse and delinquency might include changing neighborhood characteristics that seem to contribute to drug use or delinquency.

Secondary prevention is focused on detecting a disorder at its earliest stages and thereby preventing the development of the full-blown disorder (Muñoz et al., 2010). Secondary prevention often involves screening for early signs of a disorder, for example, administering a questionnaire to detect mild symptoms of depression. An intervention might be administered to individuals with mild symptoms to prevent them from developing depressive disorders. Several studies have shown that administering a cognitive-behavioral intervention to an individual with mild depressive symptoms can significantly reduce the individual's chances of developing a depressive disorder (Cuijpers, van Straten, van Oppen, & Andersson, 2008).

Tertiary prevention focuses on people who already have a disorder. It seeks to prevent relapse and reduce the impact of the disorder on the person's quality of life. As we discuss in the chapter "Schizophrenia Spectrum and Other Psychotic Disorders," programs that provide job-skills training and social support to people with schizophrenia can help prevent the recurrence of psychotic episodes (Liberman, Glynn, Blair, Ross, & Marder, 2002).

COMMON ELEMENTS IN EFFECTIVE TREATMENTS

On the surface, the different types of therapy described in this chapter may seem radically different. There is evidence, however, that successful therapies share some common components, even when the specific techniques of the therapies differ greatly. These common elements seem to play a key role in treatment process and outcome (Wampold, 2015).

A positive relationship between client and therapist is important to successful treatment. ©*FilippoBacci/Getty Images*

The first common component is a *positive relationship* with the therapist (Norcross, 2002). This involves clients trusting their therapist and believing that the therapist understands them. Clients who experience positive relationships are more willing to reveal important information, engage in homework assignments, and try new skills or coping techniques suggested by the therapist. In addition, simply having a positive relationship with a caring and understanding human being helps people overcome distress and change their behaviors (Teyber & McClure, 2000).

Second, all therapies provide clients with an *explanation or interpretation* of why they are suffering (Ingram, Hayes, & Scott, 2000). For example, cognitive therapists convey to clients that the relationships among thoughts, behaviors, and emotions underlie their difficulties, whereas psychodynamic therapists might describe the role of unconscious conflicts. Simply having a label for painful symptoms and an explanation for those symptoms seems to help many people feel better. In addition, the explanations that therapies provide for symptoms usually are accompanied by a set of recommendations for how to overcome those symptoms, and following the recommendations may provide the main relief from the symptoms.

In any case, it seems clear that a client must believe the explanation given for the symptoms for the therapy to help (Frank, 1978). For example, studies of cognitive-behavioral therapy for depression have found that the extent to which clients believe and accept the rationale behind this therapy is a significant predictor of the effectiveness of the therapy (Fennell & Teasdale, 1987). Clients to whom the rationale behind cognitive therapy makes sense engage more actively in therapy and are less depressed after a course of therapy than clients who don't accept the rationale for the therapy from the outset. A major problem in drug therapies is the high dropout rate. Often, people drop out either because they do not experience quick enough relief from the drugs and therefore believe the drugs will not work or because they feel they need to talk about their problems in order to overcome them.

Third, most therapies encourage clients to *confront painful emotions* and use techniques designed to help them become less sensitive to these emotions (Barlow et al., 2018; Frank, 1978; Prochaska, 1995). In behavior therapy, systematic desensitization or flooding might be used. In psychodynamic therapy, clients are encouraged to express painful emotions and thoughts. Whatever technique is used, the goal is to help the client stop denying, avoiding, or repressing the painful emotions and become able to accept, experience, and express the emotions without being debilitated by them.

CHAPTER INTEGRATION

As we noted at the beginning of this chapter, many scientists believe that only models that integrate biological, psychological, and social risk factors can provide comprehensive explanations of psychological disorders. Only integrated models can explain why many people with disordered genes or deficiencies in neurotransmitters do not develop painful emotional symptoms or bizarre thoughts. Similarly, only integrated models can suggest how traumatic experiences and toxic interpersonal relationships can cause changes in the basic biochemistry of the brain, which then cause changes in a person's emotions, thoughts, and behaviors.

Figure 12 illustrates how some of the biological, psychological, and social risk factors discussed in this chapter might combine to contribute to symptoms of depression, for example. Initially, some people's genetic characteristics lead to poor functioning of the hypothalamic-pituitary-adrenal axis. Chronic arousal

FIGURE 12 How Some Biological, Psychological, and Social Factors Might Interact to Cause Depression.

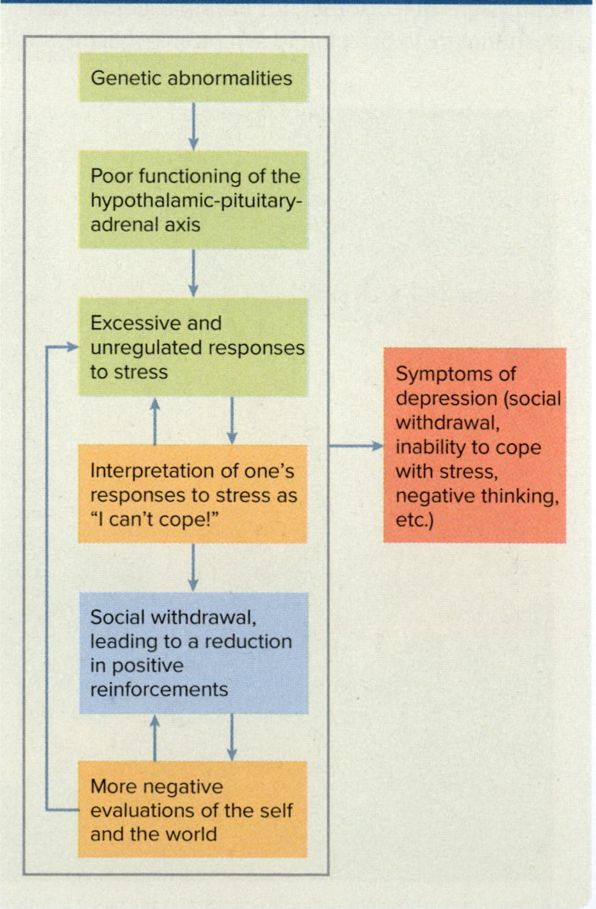

SHADES OF GRAY DISCUSSION

A humanistic therapist would provide a reflection that attempts to accurately restate what the student said and the emotions she expressed, without suggesting any interpretation of her feelings:

> **Reflection:** "It's really frustrating to screw up and kill your chances; and it feels like it's something in you that's making that happen again and again."

A psychodynamic therapist might infer that the student's expressed concerns reflect unconscious conflicts about success. When he or she feels there is enough evidence, an interpretation such as the following might be offered:

> **A psychodynamic interpretation:** "It sounds like every time you get close to success you unconsciously sabotage yourself. Perhaps success means something to you that is troubling or uncomfortable, and you are not aware of what that is."

The psychodynamic interpretation may be true, but the client-centered therapist would view it as inappropriate because it brings to the client's attention something not currently in the client's awareness (adapted from Bohart, 1995, p. 101).

of this axis may lead individuals to be overly responsive to stress. If they tend to interpret their reactions to stress in terms of "I can't cope!" they may develop a negative thinking style. This negative thinking style can then cause them to withdraw socially, leading to fewer positive reinforcements. This in turn could feed negative evaluations of themselves and of the world, further contributing to depression. Then, when they are confronted with new stressors, they might not have good strategies for coping with them and might overreact psychologically as well as physiologically. All these processes come together to produce the key symptoms of depression—social withdrawal, an inability to cope with stress, negative thinking, and so on.

CHAPTER SUMMARY

- Biological theories of psychopathology typically attribute symptoms to structural abnormalities in the brain, disordered biochemistry, or faulty genes.
- Structural abnormalities in the brain can be caused by faulty genes, by disease, or by injury. Which particular area of the brain is damaged influences the symptoms individuals show.
- Many biological theories attribute psychopathology to imbalances in neurotransmitters or to the functioning of receptors for neurotransmitters.
- Genetic theories of abnormality usually suggest that it takes an accumulation of faulty genes to cause a psychopathology.
- Genes can influence the environments people choose, which then influence the expression of genetic tendencies. Epigenetics is the study of how environmental conditions can influence the expression of genes.
- Biological therapies most often involve the use of drugs intended to regulate the functioning of the brain neurotransmitters associated with a psychological disorder or to compensate for structural brain abnormalities or the effects of genetics.
- Antipsychotic medications help reduce unreal perceptual experiences, unreal beliefs, and other symptoms of psychosis. Antidepressant drugs help reduce symptoms of depression. Lithium and anticonvulsants help reduce mania. Barbiturates and benzodiazepines help reduce anxiety.
- Electroconvulsive therapy is used to treat severe depression. Various new methods are being developed to stimulate the brain without using electricity. Psychosurgery is used in rare circumstances.
- The behavioral theories of abnormality reject notions of unconscious conflicts and focus only on the rewards and punishments in the environment that shape and maintain behavior.
- Classical conditioning takes place when a previously neutral stimulus is paired with a stimulus that naturally creates a certain response; eventually the neutral stimulus also elicits the response.
- Operant conditioning involves rewarding desired behaviors and punishing undesired behaviors.
- People also learn by imitating the behaviors modeled by others and by observing the rewards and punishments others receive for their behaviors.

- Behavior therapies focus on changing specific maladaptive behaviors and emotions by changing the reinforcements for them.
- Cognitive theories suggest that people's cognitions (e.g., attributions for events, global assumptions) influence the behaviors and emotions with which they react to situations.
- Cognitive therapies focus on changing the way a client thinks about important situations.
- Psychodynamic theories of psychopathology focus on unconscious conflicts that cause anxiety in the individual and result in maladaptive behavior. Freud argued that these conflicts arise when the impulses of the id clash with the constraints on behavior imposed by the ego and superego.
- People use various types of defense mechanisms to handle their internal conflicts. How caregivers handle a child's transitions through the psychosexual stages determines the concerns or issues the child may become fixated on.
- More recent psychodynamic theorists focus less on the role of unconscious impulses and more on the development of the individual's self-concept in the context of interpersonal relationships. They see a greater role for the environment in shaping personality and have more hope for change during adulthood than Freud had.
- Psychodynamic therapy focuses on unconscious conflicts that lead to maladaptive behaviors and emotions. Interpersonal therapies are based on psychodynamic theories but focus more on current relationships and concerns.
- Humanistic theories suggest that all humans strive to fulfill their potential for good and to self-actualize. The inability to fulfill one's potential arises from the pressures of society to conform to others' expectations and values.
- Humanistic therapies seek to help a client realize his or her potential for self-actualization.
- Family systems theories and therapies see the family as a complex interpersonal system, with its own hierarchy and rules that govern family members' behavior. When a member of the family has a psychological disorder, family systems theorists see it not as a problem within the individual but as an indication of a dysfunctional family system.
- Third-wave approaches generally combine methods and theories from the cognitive and behavioral approaches with practices derived from Buddhist mindfulness meditation to help people accept painful thoughts and emotions and regulate them more healthfully.
- Sociocultural theories suggest that socioeconomic stress, discrimination, and social upheaval can lead to mental health problems in individuals. Cultures also have implicit and explicit rules regarding the types of abnormal behavior they permit.
- Some clients may wish to work with therapists of the same culture or gender, but it is unclear whether matching therapist and client in terms of culture and gender is necessary for therapy to be effective. It is important that therapists be sensitive to the influences of culture and gender on a client's attitudes toward therapy and toward various solutions to problems.
- Prevention programs focus on preventing disorders before they develop, retarding the development of disorders in their early stages, and reducing the impact of disorders on people's functioning.
- Common components of effective therapy seem to be a good therapist-client relationship, an explanation for symptoms, and the confrontation and expression of negative emotions.

KEY TERMS

sociocultural approach
biological approach
psychological approach
theory
biopsychosocial approach
diathesis-stress model
cerebral cortex
thalamus
hypothalamus
limbic system
amygdala
hippocampus
neurotransmitters
synapse
receptors
reuptake
degradation
endocrine system
hormone
pituitary
behavioral genetics
polygenic
epigenetics
antipsychotic drugs
antidepressant drugs
lithium

anticonvulsants
antianxiety drugs
electroconvulsive therapy (ECT)
psychosurgery
behavioral approaches
classical conditioning
unconditioned stimulus (US)
unconditioned response (UR)
conditioned stimulus (CS)
conditioned response (CR)
operant conditioning
modeling
observational learning
behavioral therapies
systematic desensitization therapy
cognitive theories
cognitions
causal attribution
global assumptions
cognitive therapies
cognitive-behavioral therapy (CBT)
psychodynamic theories
psychoanalysis
catharsis
repression
libido
id
ego
superego
unconscious
preconscious
conscious
defense mechanisms
psychosexual stages
ego psychology
object relations
self psychology
relational psychoanalysis
collective unconscious
psychodynamic therapies
free association
resistance
transference
working through
interpersonal therapy (IPT)
humanistic theories
self-actualization
humanistic therapy
client-centered therapy (CCT)
reflection
family systems theories
family systems therapy
third-wave approaches
primary prevention
secondary prevention
tertiary prevention

Chapter 3

©asiseeit/Getty Images

Assessing and Diagnosing Abnormality

CHAPTER OUTLINE

Assessment and Diagnosis Along the Continuum

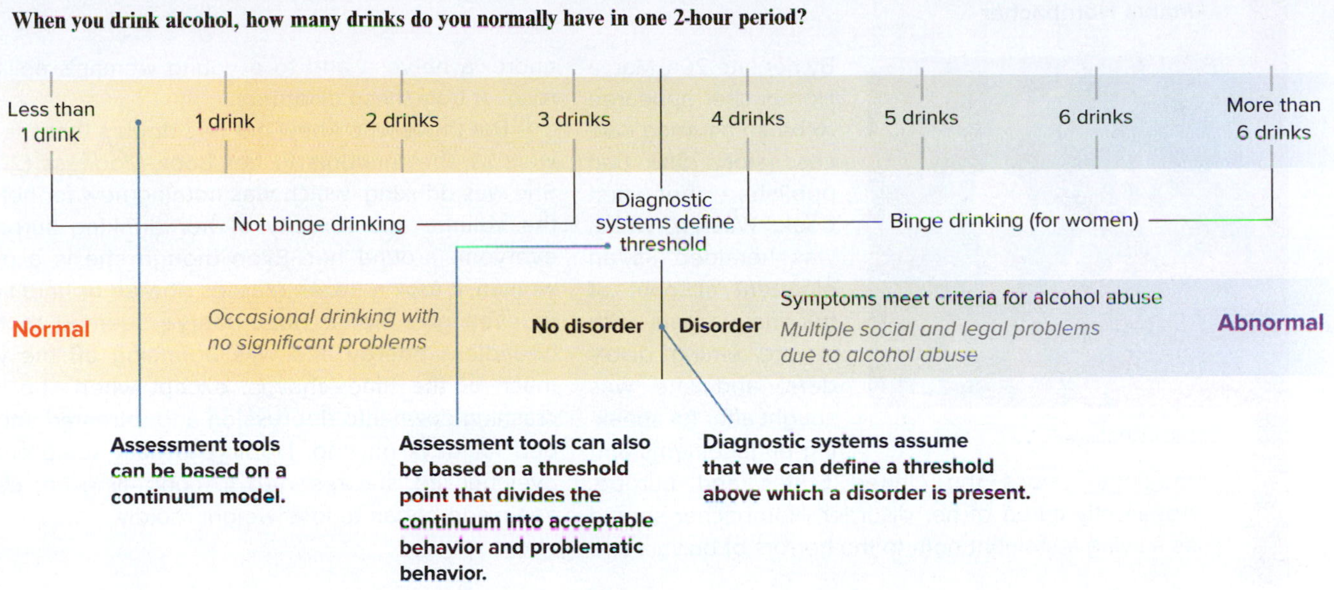

When you drink alcohol, how many drinks do you normally have in one 2-hour period?
Less than 1 drink
1 drink
2 drinks
3 drinks
4 drinks
5 drinks
6 drinks
More than 6 drinks
Not binge drinking
Diagnostic systems define threshold
Binge drinking (for women)
Normal
Occasional drinking with no significant problems
No disorder
Disorder
Symptoms meet criteria for alcohol abuse
Multiple social and legal problems due to alcohol abuse
Abnormal
Assessment tools can be based on a continuum model.
Assessment tools can also be based on a threshold point that divides the continuum into acceptable behavior and problematic behavior.
Diagnostic systems assume that we can define a threshold above which a disorder is present.

As a student, you have taken a variety of tests intended to assess your learning in different subjects. Similarly, mental health professionals use various tests or tools to assess mental health. Some assessment tools described in this chapter are based on the assumption that behaviors or feelings lie along a continuum—the task is to determine where an individual's experiences fall along that continuum. For example, a questionnaire that asked you about your drinking behavior might have several options indicating different levels of drinking. The researcher doing a study on predictors of drinking behavior might be interested in what factors predict where people fall along the continuum from little or no drinking to a great deal of drinking. A clinician may be interested in charting how a person's drinking behavior changes over the course of therapy. Other tools, however, are more like true/false tests: They are based on the assumption that there is a threshold for the behaviors they are assessing, and that either people have these behaviors or they do not. For example, some researchers set the threshold for an alcohol "binge" for women at four drinks (see the chapter "Substance Use and Gambling Disorders"). Thus, a woman who regularly drinks this amount or more in one sitting would be considered a binge drinker, whereas a woman having three drinks would not be considered a binge drinker.

Currently, the guidelines used to determine whether a person has a mental disorder use a threshold—a specific cutoff point—to make this determination and therefore seem to oppose a continuum model. Increasingly, however, researchers and clinicians are building a continuum perspective into the diagnostic process. For example, the most recent version of the manual used to diagnose disorders in the United States, the *DSM-5*, defines personality disorders at least somewhat in line with a continuum model. For most disorders, however, the *DSM-5* and other diagnostic systems set criteria for when a person's behaviors and feelings cross the line into a disorder, even in the absence of a purely scientific way to draw that line.

There are advantages and disadvantages both to a continuum approach to assessment and diagnosis and to a categorical approach that focuses on thresholds and cutoffs for identifying disorders. The continuum approach captures the nuances in people's behaviors better than does a categorical approach. The continuum approach also does not assume that we know where the cutoff is for problematic behavior. But the continuum approach can make it more difficult to communicate information about people, in part because we often think more in categorical terms. For example, saying that a person is a binge drinker may convey more information to a therapist or researcher than saying that the person drinks moderately to heavily.

Extraordinary People

Marya Hornbacher

©STR/AP Images

By her late 20s, Marya Hornbacher appeared to be an amazing success story. She had published her first book, *Wasted,* which was heralded as an eloquent account of her many years with severe eating disorders, and she was sought after for speaking engagements and readings across the United States and Europe. Apparently cured of her disorder, Hornbacher served as a living testament both to the horrors of bulimia and anorexia nervosa and to a young woman's ability to recover from these disorders.

But those who knew her had doubts that she was well, as she recounts in her book *Madness* (2008). She was drinking, which was nothing new for her. But the volume and ferocity of her drinking surprised everyone around her. Even though she is a petite woman, it took a dozen glasses of wine or hard liquor to even give her a buzz. Marya seemed to have boundless energy and was bouncing off the walls much of the time—that is, except when she went crashing down into depression and retreated into her bed for days on end. Hoping to gain some control over her life, she resorted to controlling her eating again and began to lose weight rapidly.

Marya Hornbacher presents a puzzling picture. She shows signs of alcohol abuse, mood swings, and a lingering eating disorder. Why did these symptoms emerge after she apparently had recovered from her eating disorder and had achieved success as a writer? Which of these problems is a cause of the other symptoms, and which is a consequence? How would we go about diagnosing her problems? The assessment and diagnosis of symptoms is the focus of this chapter.

Assessment is the process of gathering information about people's symptoms and the possible causes of these symptoms. Many types of information are gathered during an assessment, including information about current symptoms and ways of coping with stress, recent events and physical condition, drug and alcohol use, personal and family history of psychological disorders, cognitive functioning, and sociocultural background. The information gathered in an assessment is used to determine the appropriate diagnosis for a person's problems. A **diagnosis** is a label for a set of symptoms that often occur together. Marya Hornbacher's symptoms qualify for several diagnoses we will discuss in other chapters, including eating disorders, substance use disorders, and bipolar disorder.

In this chapter, we discuss the modern tools of assessment and how they are used both to diagnose psychological symptoms and to help us understand and treat psychological problems. Some of these tools are new, whereas others have been around for many years. These tools provide information about the individual's personality characteristics, cognitive deficits (such as learning disabilities or problems in maintaining attention), emotional well-being, and biological functioning.

We also consider modern systems of diagnosing psychological problems. A standardized system of diagnosis is crucial to communication among mental health professionals as well as to research into psychological problems. We must agree on what we mean when we use a diagnostic label. A standardized diagnostic system provides agreed-on definitions of disorders.

ASSESSMENT TOOLS

A number of assessment tools have been developed to help clinicians gather information. All assessment tools must be valid, reliable, and standardized. We first discuss these important concepts and then look at specific types of assessment tools.

Validity

If you administer a test to determine a person's behaviors and feelings, you want to be sure that the test is an accurate measure. The accuracy of a test in assessing what it is supposed to measure is called its **validity.** The best way to determine the validity of a test is to see if the results of the test yield the same information as an objective and accurate indicator of what the test is supposed to measure. For example, if there were a blood test that definitively proved whether a person had a particular psychological disorder, you would want any other test for that disorder (such as a questionnaire) to yield the same results when administered to the person.

As we discuss in the chapter "Looking at Abnormality," there are currently no definitive blood tests, brain scans, or other objective tests for any of the psychological disorders we discuss in this book. Fortunately, the validity of a test can be estimated in a number of other ways (Figure 1). A test is said to have *face validity* when, on face value, the items seem to measure what the test is intended to measure. For example, a questionnaire for anxiety that asks "Do you feel jittery much of the time?" and "Do you worry about many things?" has face validity because it seems to assess symptoms of anxiety. If it also meets other standards of validity, researchers are more likely to trust its results.

Content validity is the extent to which a test assesses all the important aspects of a phenomenon that it purports to measure. For example, if a measure of anxiety asked only about physical symptoms (nervousness, restlessness, stomach distress, rapid heartbeat) and not cognitive symptoms (apprehensions about the future, anticipation of negative events), then we might question whether it is a good measure of anxiety.

Concurrent (or *convergent*) *validity* is the extent to which a test yields the same results as other, established measures of the same behavior, thoughts, or feelings. A person's score on a new anxiety questionnaire should bear some relation to information gathered from the person's answers to an established anxiety questionnaire.

A test has *predictive validity* if it is good at predicting how a person will think, act, or feel in the future. An anxiety measure has good predictive validity if it correctly predicts which people will behave in anxious ways when confronted with stressors in the future and which people will not.

Construct validity is the extent to which a test measures what it is supposed to measure and not something else altogether (Cronbach & Meehl, 1955). Consider the construct validity of multiple-choice exams in school. They are supposed to measure a student's knowledge and understanding of content. However, they may also measure the student's ability to take multiple-choice tests—that is, their ability to determine the instructor's intent in asking each question and to recognize any tricks and obviously incorrect answer choices.

FIGURE 1 **Types of Validity for a Questionnaire or Test.** There are a number of types of validity.

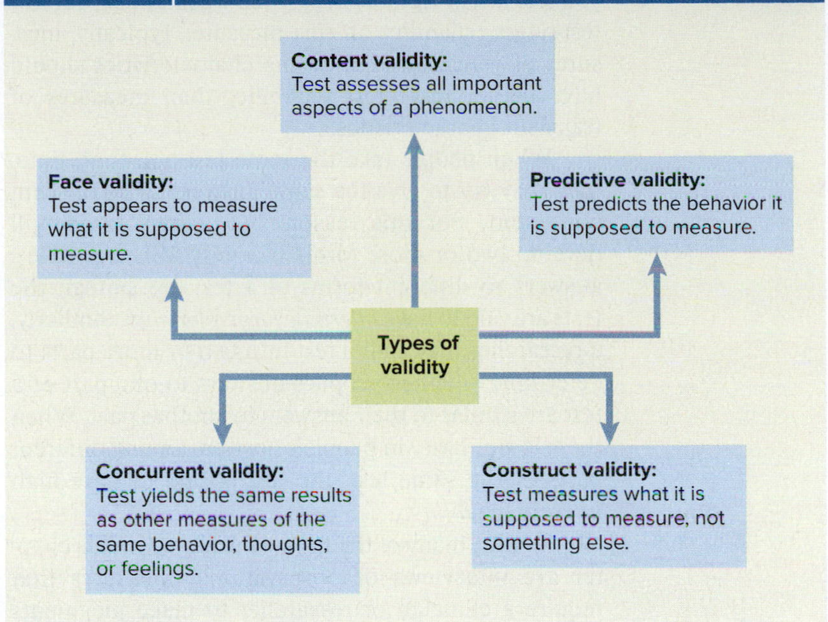

Content validity: Test assesses all important aspects of a phenomenon.
Face validity: Test appears to measure what it is supposed to measure.
Predictive validity: Test predicts the behavior it is supposed to measure.
Types of validity
Concurrent validity: Test yields the same results as other measures of the same behavior, thoughts, or feelings.
Construct validity: Test measures what it is supposed to measure, not something else.

Reliability

It is important that a test provides consistent information about a person. The **reliability** of a test indicates its consistency in measuring what it is supposed to measure. As with validity, there are several types of reliability (Figure 2). *Test-retest reliability* describes how consistent the results of a test are over time. If a test supposedly measures an enduring characteristic of a person, then the person's scores on that test should be similar when he or she takes the test at two different points in time. For example, if an anxiety questionnaire is supposed to measure people's general tendencies to be anxious, then their scores should be similar if they complete the questionnaire this week and then again next week. On the other hand, if an

FIGURE 2 **Types of Reliability for a Questionnaire or Test.** Reliability can be determined in several ways.

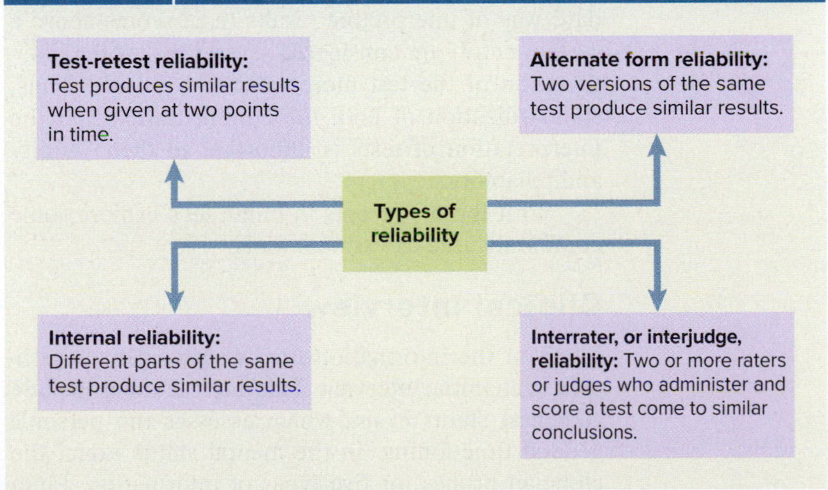

Test-retest reliability: Test produces similar results when given at two points in time.
Alternate form reliability: Two versions of the same test produce similar results.
Types of reliability
Internal reliability: Different parts of the same test produce similar results.
Interrater, or interjudge, reliability: Two or more raters or judges who administer and score a test come to similar conclusions.

anxiety questionnaire is a measure of people's current symptoms of anxiety (asking questions such as "Do you feel jittery right now?"), then we might expect low test-retest reliability on this measure. Typically, measures of general and enduring characteristics should have higher test-retest reliability than measures of transient characteristics.

When people take the same test a second time, they may try to give the same answers so as to seem consistent. For this reason, researchers often will develop two or more forms of a test. When people's answers to different forms of a test are similar, the tests are said to have *alternate form reliability*. Similarly, a researcher may split a test into two or more parts to determine whether people's answers to one part of a test are similar to their answers to another part. When there is similarity in people's answers among different parts of the same test, the test is said to have high *internal reliability*.

Finally, many of the tests we examine in this chapter are interviews or observational measures that require a clinician or researcher to make judgments about the people being assessed. These tests should have high *interrater,* or *interjudge, reliability*. That is, different raters or judges who administer and score the interview or test should come to similar conclusions when they are evaluating the same people.

Standardization

One important way to improve both validity and reliability is to standardize the administration and interpretation of tests. A standard method of administering a test prevents extraneous factors from affecting a person's response. For example, if the test administrator were to deviate from the written questions, suggesting the "right" answer to the respondents, this would reduce the validity and reliability of the test. In contrast, if the administrator of the test only read aloud the specific questions on the test, this would increase the validity and reliability of the test. Similarly, a standard way of interpreting results (e.g., scores above a certain cutoff are considered severe) makes the interpretation of the test more valid and reliable. Thus, standardization of both the administration and the interpretation of tests is important to their validity and reliability.

With these concepts in mind, let's explore some commonly used assessment tools.

Clinical Interview

Much of the information for an assessment is gathered in an initial interview. This interview may include a mental status exam, which assesses the person's general functioning. In the mental status exam, the clinician probes for five types of information. First, the clinician assesses the individual's appearance and behavior. Is he or she dressed neatly and well groomed, or does he or she appear disheveled? The ability to care for one's basic grooming indicates how well one is functioning generally. Also, the clinician will note if the individual seems to be moving particularly slowly, which may indicate depression, or seems agitated.

Second, in a mental status exam a clinician will take note of the individual's thought processes, including how coherently and quickly he or she speaks. Third, the clinician will be concerned with the individual's mood and affect. Does he or she appear down and depressed, or perhaps elated? Is the affect appropriate to the situation or inappropriate? For example, the individual may seem to laugh excessively at his own jokes, which may indicate nervousness or an inability to relate well to others. Fourth, the clinician will observe the individual's intellectual functioning—that is, how well the person speaks and any indications of memory or attention difficulties. Fifth, the clinician will note whether the individual seems appropriately oriented to place, time, and person: Does the individual understand where he or she is, what day and time it is, and who he or she is, as well as who the clinician is?

Increasingly, clinicians and researchers use a **structured interview** to gather information about individuals. In a structured interview, the clinician asks the respondent a series of questions about symptoms he or she is experiencing or has experienced in the past. The format of the questions and the entire interview is standardized, and the clinician uses concrete criteria to score the person's answers (Table 1). At the end of the interview, the clinician should be able to determine whether the respondent's symptoms qualify for a diagnosis of any major psychological problems. Structured interviews are the most reliable form of clinical interview. Recently, researchers have sought to develop computerized methods of testing that might retain validity while saving time and resources compared to face-to-face interviews; these methods are not yet widely used (Gibbons, Weiss, Frank, & Kupfer, 2016).

Symptom Questionnaires

Often, when clinicians or researchers want a quick way to determine a person's symptoms, they will ask the person to complete a **symptom questionnaire.** These questionnaires can cover a wide variety of symptoms representing several different disorders. Other questionnaires focus on the symptoms of specific disorders.

One of the most common questionnaires used to assess symptoms of depression is the Beck Depression

TABLE 1 Sample Structured Interview

ANXIETY DISORDERS

Panic Disorder Questions

Have you ever had a panic attack, when you suddenly felt frightened, anxious, or extremely uncomfortable?

If Yes: Tell me about it. When does that happen? (Have you ever had one that just seemed to come out of the blue?)

If panic attacks took place in expected situations: Did you ever have one of these attacks when you weren't in (EXPECTED SITUATION)?

Have you ever had four attacks like that in a 4-week period?

If No: Did you worry a lot about having another one? (How long did you worry?)

When was the last bad one (EXPECTED OR UNEXPECTED)?

Now I am going to ask you about that attack. What was the first thing you noticed? Then what?

During the attack . . .

. . . were you short of breath? (have trouble catching your breath?)

. . . did you feel dizzy, unsteady, or as if you might faint?

. . . did your heart race, pound, or skip?

. . . did you tremble or shake?

. . . did you sweat?

. . . did you feel as if you were choking?

. . . did you have nausea, upset stomach, or the feeling that you were going to have diarrhea?

. . . did things around you seem unreal or did you feel detached from things around you or detached from part of your body?

Source: Data from First, Spitzer, Gibbon, & Williams, 1997.

Inventory, or BDI (Beck & Beck, 1972). The most recent form of the BDI has 21 items, each of which describes four levels of a given symptom of depression ranging from feeling "I do not feel unhappy" to "I am so unhappy that I can't stand it." The respondent is asked to indicate which description best fits how he or she has been feeling in the past week. The items are scored to indicate the level of depressive symptoms the person is experiencing. Cutoff scores have been established to indicate moderate and severe levels of depressive symptoms.

Critics of the BDI have argued that it does not clearly differentiate between the clinical syndrome of depression and the general distress that may be related to an anxiety disorder or to several other disorders (see Kendall, Hollon, Beck, Hammen, & Ingram, 1987). The BDI also cannot indicate whether the respondent would qualify for a diagnosis of depression. But because the BDI is extremely quick and easy to administer and has good test-retest reliability, it is widely used, especially in research on depression.

Clinicians treating depressed people also use the BDI to monitor those individuals' symptom levels from week to week. An individual may be asked to complete the BDI at the beginning of each therapy session, and both the individual and the clinician then have a concrete indicator of any changes in symptoms.

Personality Inventories

Personality inventories usually are questionnaires meant to assess people's typical ways of thinking, feeling, and behaving. These inventories are used as part of an assessment procedure to obtain information on people's well-being, self-concept, attitudes and beliefs, ways of coping, perceptions of their environment, and social resources, and vulnerabilities.

The most widely used personality inventory in professional clinical assessments is the *Minnesota Multiphasic Personality Inventory (MMPI),* which has been translated into more than 150 languages and is used in more than 50 countries (Groth-Marnat & Wright, 2016). The original MMPI was developed in the 1930s by Starke Hathaway and Charnley McKinley. In 1989 an updated version was published under the name MMPI-2. Both versions of the MMPI present respondents with sentences describing moral and social attitudes, behaviors, psychological states, and physical conditions and ask them to respond "true," "false," or "can't say" to each sentence. Here are some examples of items from the MMPI:

I would rather win than lose in a game.

I am never happier than when alone.

My hardest battles are with myself.

I wish I were not bothered by thoughts about sex.

I am afraid of losing my mind.

When I get bored, I like to stir up some excitement.

People often disappoint me.

The MMPI was developed empirically, meaning that a large group of possible inventory items was given to psychologically "healthy" people and to people with various psychological problems. The items that reliably differentiated among groups of people were included in the inventory.

The items on the original MMPI are clustered into 10 scales that measure different types of psychological characteristics or problems, such as paranoia, anxiety, and social introversion. Another 4 scales have been added to the MMPI-2 to assess vulnerability to

TABLE 2 Clinical and Validity Scales of the Original MMPI

The MMPI is one of the most widely used questionnaires for assessing people's symptoms and personalities. It also includes scales to assess whether respondents are lying or trying to obfuscate their answers.

CLINICAL SCALES

Scale Number	Scale Name	What It Measures
Scale 1	Hypochondriasis	Excessive somatic concern and physical complaints
Scale 2	Depression	Symptomatic depression
Scale 3	Hysteria	Hysterical personality features and tendency to develop physical symptoms under stress
Scale 4	Psychopathic deviate	Antisocial tendencies
Scale 5	Masculinity-femininity	Sex-role conflict
Scale 6	Paranoia	Suspicious, paranoid thinking
Scale 7	Psychasthenia	Anxiety and obsessive behavior
Scale 8	Schizophrenia	Bizarre thoughts and disordered affect
Scale 9	Hypomania	Behavior found in mania
Scale 0	Social introversion	Social anxiety, withdrawal, overcontrol

VALIDITY SCALES

Scale Name	What It Measures
Cannot say scale	Total number of unanswered items
Lie scale	Tendency to present favorable image
Infrequency scale	Tendency to falsely claim psychological problems
Defensiveness scale	Tendency to see oneself in unrealistically positive manner

Source: Adapted from Minnesota Multiphasic Personality Inventory (MMPI).

eating disorders, substance abuse, and poor functioning at work. A respondent's scores on each scale are compared with scores from the normal population, and a profile of the respondent's personality and psychological problems is derived. Also, 4 validity scales determine whether the person responds honestly to the items on the scale or distorts his or her answers in a way that might invalidate the test (Table 2). For example, the Lie Scale measures the respondent's tendency to respond to items in a socially desirable way in order to appear unusually positive or good.

Because the items on the MMPI were chosen for their ability to differentiate people with specific types of psychological problems from people without psychological problems, the concurrent validity of the MMPI scales was "built in" during their development. The MMPI may be especially useful as a general screening device for detecting people who are functioning very poorly psychologically.

However, many criticisms have been raised about the use of the MMPI in culturally diverse samples (Groth-Marnat & Wright, 2016). The norms for the original MMPI—the scores considered "healthy"—were based on samples of people in the United States not drawn from a wide range of ethnic and racial backgrounds, age groups, and social classes. In response to this problem, the publishers of the MMPI established new norms based on more representative samples of eight communities across the United States. Still, concerns persist that the MMPI norms do not reflect variations across cultures in what is considered normal or abnormal. In addition, some question the linguistic accuracy of the translated versions of the MMPI and the comparability of these versions to the English version (Dana, 2005).

Behavioral Observation and Self-Monitoring

Clinicians often will use **behavioral observation** of individuals to assess deficits in their skills or their ways of handling situations. The clinician looks for specific behaviors and what precedes and follows these behaviors. For example, a clinician might watch a child interact with other children to determine what situations provoke aggression in the child. The clinician can then use information from the behavioral observation to help the individual learn new skills, stop negative habits, and understand and change how he or she reacts to certain situations. A couple seeking marital therapy might be asked to discuss with each other a topic on which they disagree. The clinician would observe this interaction, noting the specific ways the couple handles conflict. For example, one member of the couple may lapse into statements that blame the other member for problems in their marriage, escalating conflict to the boiling point.

Direct behavioral observation has the advantage of not relying on individuals' reporting and interpretation of their own behaviors. Instead, the clinician sees firsthand how the individuals handle important situations. One disadvantage is that individuals may alter their behavior when they are being watched. Another disadvantage is that different observers may draw different conclusions about individuals' skills; that is, direct behavioral observations may have low interrater reliability, especially in the absence of a standard means of making the observations. In addition, any individual rater may miss the details of an interpersonal interaction. For example, two raters watching a child play with others on a playground might focus on different aspects of the child's behaviors or be distracted by the chaos of the playground. For these reasons, when behavioral observation is used in research settings, the situations are highly standardized and observers watch for a set list of behaviors. Finally, direct observation may not be possible in some situations. In that case, a clinician may have a client role-play a situation, such as the client's interactions with an employer.

If direct observation or role playing is not possible, clinicians may require **self-monitoring** by individuals—that is, keeping track of the number of times per day they engage in a specific behavior (e.g., smoking a cigarette) and the conditions under which this behavior occurs. Following is an example (adapted from Thorpe & Olson, 1997, p. 149):

> Steve, a binge drinker, was asked to self-monitor his drinking behavior for 2 weeks, noting the situational context of urges to drink and his associated thoughts and feelings. These data revealed that Steve's drinking was completely confined to bar situations, where he drank in the company of friends. Gaining relief from stress was a recurring theme.

Self-monitoring is open to biases in what individuals notice about their behavior and are willing to report. However, individuals can discover the triggers of unwanted behaviors through self-monitoring, which in turn can lead them to change these behaviors.

Intelligence Tests

In clinical practice, **intelligence tests** are used to get a sense of an individual's intellectual strengths and weaknesses, particularly when mental retardation or brain damage is suspected (Ryan & Lopez, 2001). Intelligence tests are also used in schools to identify "gifted" children and children with intellectual difficulties. They are used in occupational settings and the military to evaluate adults' capabilities for certain jobs or types of service. Some examples of these tests are the *Wechsler Adult Intelligence Scale,* the *Stanford-Binet Intelligence Test,* and the *Wechsler Intelligence Scale for Children.*

These tests were designed to measure basic intellectual abilities, such as the ability for abstract reasoning, verbal fluency, and spatial memory. The term IQ is used to describe a method of comparing an individual's score on an intelligence test with the performance of individuals in the same age group. An IQ score of 100 means that the person performed similarly to the average performance of other people the same age.

Intelligence tests are controversial in part because there is little consensus as to what is meant by intelligence (Sternberg, 2015). The most widely used intelligence tests assess verbal and analytical abilities but do not assess other talents or skills, such as artistic and musical ability. Some psychologists argue that success in life is as strongly influenced by social skills and other talents not measured by intelligence tests as it is by verbal and analytical skills (Gardner, 2008; Sternberg, 2015).

Another important criticism of intelligence tests is that they are biased in favor of middle- and upper-class, educated individuals because such people are more familiar with the kinds of reasoning assessed on the tests (Sternberg, 2015). In addition, educated European Americans may be more comfortable taking intelligence tests, because testers often are also European Americans and the testing situation resembles testing situations in their educational experience. In contrast, different cultures within the United States and in other countries may emphasize forms of reasoning other than those assessed on intelligence tests, and members of these cultures may not be comfortable with the testing situation.

A "culture-fair" test would have to include items that are equally applicable to all groups or that are different for each culture but psychologically equivalent for the groups being tested. Attempts have been made to develop culture-fair tests, but the results have been disappointing. Even if a universal test were created, making statements about intelligence in different cultures would be difficult because different nations and cultures vary in the emphasis they place on "intellectual achievement."

Neuropsychological Tests

If the clinician suspects neurological impairment in a person, paper-and-pencil **neuropsychological tests** may be useful in detecting specific cognitive deficits such as a memory problem, as occurs in dementia. One frequently used neuropsychological test is the Bender-Gestalt Test (Bender, 1938). This test assesses individuals' sensorimotor skills by having them reproduce a set of nine drawings (Figure 3). People with brain damage may rotate or change parts of the drawings or be unable to reproduce the drawings. When asked to remember the drawings after a delay, they may show significant memory deficits. The Bender-Gestalt Test appears to be good at differentiating people with brain damage from those without brain damage, but it does not reliably identify the specific type of brain damage a person has (Groth-Marnat & Wright, 2016).

More extensive batteries of tests have been developed to pinpoint types of brain damage. Two of the most popular batteries are the Halstead-Reitan Test (Reitan & Davidson, 1974) and the Luria-Nebraska Test (Luria, 1973). These batteries contain several tests that provide specific information about an individual's functioning in several skill areas, such as concentration, dexterity, and speed of comprehension.

FIGURE 3 **The Bender-Gestalt Test.** On the left are the figures as presented to the clients. On the right are the figures as copied by a child with a brain tumor that is creating perceptual-motor difficulties.

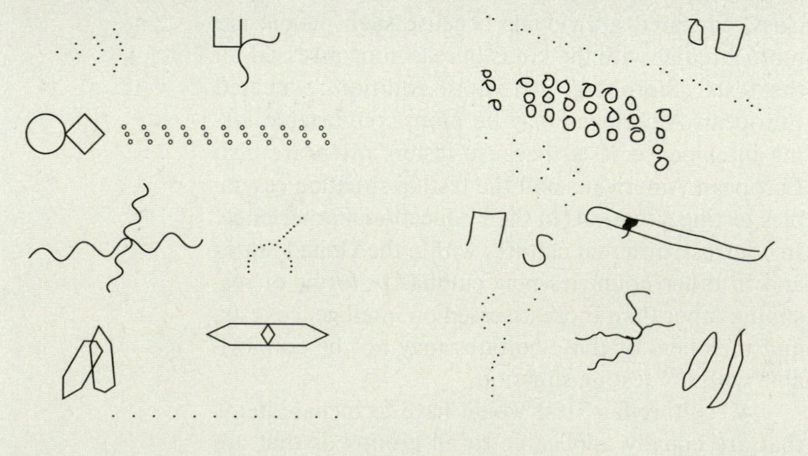

Sattler, Jerome M., *Foundations of Behavioral, Social and Clinical Assessment of Children*, 6th Edition, Figure 12-1, 399.

Brain-Imaging Techniques

Increasingly, neuropsychological tests are being used with brain-imaging techniques to identify specific deficits and possible brain abnormalities. Clinicians use brain imaging to determine if a patient has a brain injury or tumor. Researchers use brain imaging to search for differences in brain activity or structure between people with a psychological disorder and people with no disorder. Let us review existing brain-imaging technologies and what they can tell us now.

Computerized tomography (CT) is an enhancement of X-ray procedures. In CT, narrow X-ray beams are passed through the person's head in a single plane from a variety of angles. The amount of radiation absorbed by each beam is measured, and from these measurements a computer program constructs an image of a slice of the brain. By taking many such images, the computer can construct a three-dimensional image showing the brain's major structures. A CT scan can reveal brain injury, tumors, and structural abnormalities. The two major limitations of CT technology are that it exposes patients to X-rays, which can be harmful, and that it provides an image of brain structure rather than brain activity.

Positron-emission tomography (PET) can provide a picture of activity in the brain. PET requires injecting the patient with a harmless radioactive isotope, such as fluorodeoxyglucose (FDG). This substance travels through the blood to the brain. The parts of the brain that are active need the glucose in FDG for nutrition, so FDG accumulates in active parts of the brain. Subatomic particles in FDG called positrons are emitted as the isotope decays. These positrons collide with electrons, and both are annihilated and converted to two photons traveling away from each other in opposite directions. The PET scanner detects these photons and the point at which they are annihilated and constructs an image of the brain, showing those areas that are most active. PET scans can be used to show differences in the activity level of specific areas of the brain between people with a psychological disorder and people without a disorder.

Another procedure to assess brain activity is **single photon emission computed tomography,** or **SPECT.** The procedures of SPECT are much like those of PET except that a different tracer substance is injected. It is less accurate than PET but also less expensive.

Magnetic resonance imaging (MRI) has several advantages over CT, PET, and SPECT technology. It does not require exposing the patient to any radiation or injecting radioisotopes, so it can be used repeatedly for the same individual. It provides much more finely

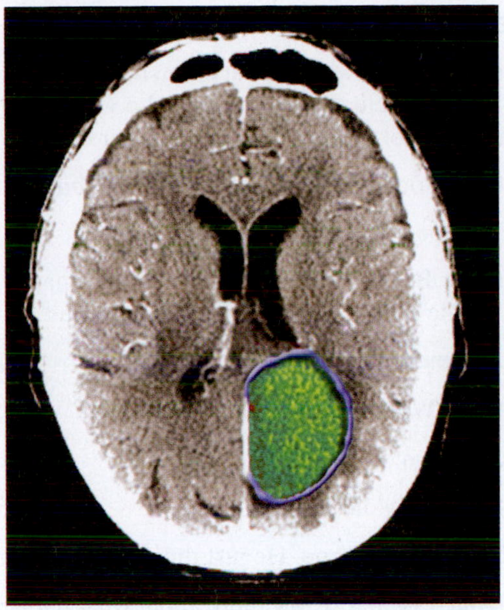

CT scans can detect structural abnormalities such as brain tumors. ©NEIL M. BORDEN/Science Source

detailed pictures of the anatomy of the brain than do other technologies, and it can image the brain at any angle. Structural MRI provides static images of brain structure. Functional MRI (fMRI) provides images of brain activity.

MRI involves creating a magnetic field around the brain that causes a realignment of hydrogen atoms in the brain. When the magnetic field is turned off and on, the hydrogen atoms change position, causing them to emit magnetic signals. These signals are read by a computer, which reconstructs a three-dimensional image of the brain. To assess activity in the brain, many images are taken only milliseconds apart, showing how the brain changes from one moment to the next or in response to some stimulus. Researchers are using MRI to study structural and functional brain abnormalities in almost every psychological disorder.

Psychophysiological Tests

Psychophysiological tests are alternative methods to CT, PET, SPECT, and MRI used to detect changes in the brain and nervous system that reflect emotional and psychological changes. An **electroencephalogram (EEG)** measures electrical activity along the scalp produced by the firing of specific neurons in the brain. EEG is used most often to detect seizure activity in the brain and can also be used to detect tumors and stroke. EEG patterns recorded over brief periods (such as ½ second) in response to specific stimuli, such as the individual's viewing of an emotional picture, are referred to as *evoked potentials* or *event-related potentials*. Clinicians can compare an individual's response to the standard response of healthy individuals.

Heart rate and respiration are highly responsive to stress and can be easily monitored. Sweat gland activity, known as *electrodermal response* (formerly called *galvanic skin response*), can be assessed with a device that detects electrical conductivity between two points on the skin. Such activity can reflect emotional arousal. Psychophysiological measures are used to assess people's emotional response to specific types of stimuli, such as the responses a veteran with posttraumatic stress disorder might have to scenes of war.

Projective Tests

A **projective test** is based on the assumption that when people are presented with an ambiguous stimulus, such as an oddly shaped inkblot or a captionless picture, they will interpret the stimulus in line with their current concerns and feelings, relationships with others, and conflicts or desires. People are thought to project these issues onto their description of the "content" of the stimulus—hence the name "projective tests." Proponents of these tests argue that they are useful in uncovering the unconscious issues or motives of a person or in cases when the person is resistant or is heavily biasing the information he or she presents to the assessor. Two of the most frequently used projective tests are the *Rorschach Inkblot Test* and the *Thematic Apperception Test (TAT).*

The Rorschach Inkblot Test, commonly referred to simply as the Rorschach, was developed in 1921 by Swiss psychiatrist Hermann Rorschach. The test consists of 10 cards, each containing a symmetrical inkblot in black, gray, and white or in color. The examiner tells the respondent something like "People may see many different things in these inkblot pictures; now tell me what you see, what it makes you think of, what it means to you" (Exner et al., 2008). Clinicians are interested in both the content and the style of the individual's responses to the inkblot. In the content of responses, they look for particular themes or concerns, such as frequent mention of aggression or fear of abandonment. Important stylistic features may include the person's tendency to focus on small details of the inkblot rather than the inkblot as a whole or hesitation in responding to certain inkblots (Exner et al., 2008).

The Thematic Apperception Test (TAT) consists of a series of pictures. The individual is asked to make up a story about what is happening in the pictures (Murray, 1943). Proponents of the TAT argue that people's stories reflect their concerns and wishes as well as their personality traits and motives. As with the Rorschach, clinicians are interested in both the content and the style of people's responses to the TAT cards. Some cards may stimulate more emotional responses than others or no response at all. These cards are considered to tap the individuals' most important concerns.

Clinicians operating from psychodynamic perspectives value projective tests as tools for assessing the underlying conflicts and concerns that individuals cannot or will not report directly. Clinicians operating from other perspectives question the usefulness of these tests. The validity and reliability of all the projective tests have not proven strong in research (Groth-Marnat & Wright, 2016; Mihura, Meyer, Dumitrascu, & Bombel, 2013). In addition, because these tests rely so greatly on subjective interpretations by clinicians, they are open to a number of biases. Finally, the criteria for interpreting the tests do not take into account an individual's cultural background (Dana, 2005).

CHALLENGES IN ASSESSMENT

Some challenges that arise in assessing people's problems include people's inability or unwillingness to provide information. In addition, special challenges arise when evaluating children and people from cultures different from that of the assessor.

Resistance to Providing Information

One of the greatest challenges to obtaining valid information from an individual can be his or her resistance to providing information. Sometimes the person does not want to be assessed or treated. For example, when a teenager is forced to see a psychologist because of parental concern about his behavior, he may be resistant to providing any information. Because much of the information a clinician needs must come directly from the person being assessed, resistance can present a formidable problem.

Even when a person is not completely resistant to being assessed, he or she may have a strong interest in the outcome of the assessment and therefore may be highly selective in the information he or she provides, may bias his or her presentation of the information, or may even lie to the assessor. Such problems often arise when assessments are part of a legal case, as when parents are fighting for custody of their children in a divorce. When speaking to psychologists who have been appointed to assess fitness for custody of the children, each parent will want to present him- or herself in the best light and also may negatively bias his or her reports on the other parent.

Evaluating Children

Consider the following conversation between a mother and her 5-year-old son, Jonathon, who was sent home from preschool for fighting with another child.

Mom: Jonathon, why did you hit that boy?

Jonathon: I dunno. I just did.

Mom: But I want to understand what happened. Did he do something that made you mad?

Jonathon: Yeah, I guess.

Mom: What did he do? Did he hit you?

Jonathon: Yeah.

Mom: Why did he hit you?

Jonathon: I dunno. He just did. Can I go now?

Mom: I need to know more about what happened. (Silence)

Mom: Can you tell me more about what happened?

Jonathon: No. He just hit me and I just hit him. Can I go now?

Anyone who has tried to have a conversation with a distressed child about why he or she misbehaved has some sense of how difficult it can be to engage a child in a discussion about emotions or behaviors. Even when a child talks readily, his or her understanding of the causes of his or her behaviors or emotions may not be very well developed. Children, particularly preschool-age children, cannot describe their feelings or associated events as easily as adults can. Young children may not differentiate among different types of emotions—often just saying that they feel "bad," for example (Harter, 1983). When distressed, children may talk about physical aches and pains rather than the emotional pain they are feeling. Or a child might show distress only in nonverbal behavior, such as making a sad face, withdrawing, or behaving aggressively.

These problems with children's self-reporting of emotional and behavioral concerns have led clinicians and researchers to rely on other people, usually adults in the children's lives, to provide information about children's functioning. Parents are often the first source of information about a child's functioning. A clinician may interview a child's parents when the child is taken for treatment, asking the parents about changes in the child's behavior and corresponding events in the child's life. A researcher studying children's functioning may ask parents to complete questionnaires assessing the children's behavior in a variety of settings.

Because parents typically spend more time with their child than any other person does, they potentially have the most complete information about the child's functioning and the best sense of how the child's behavior has or has not changed over time. Unfortunately, however, parents are not always accurate in their assessments of their children's functioning. One study found that in 63 percent of cases, parents and children disagreed on what problems had brought the child to a psychiatric clinic (Yeh & Weisz, 2001). Parents' perceptions of their children's well-being can be influenced by their own symptoms of psychopathology and by their expectations for their children's behavior (Nock & Kazdin, 2001). Indeed, parents sometimes take children for assessment and treatment of psychological problems as a way of seeking treatment for themselves.

Parents also may be the source of a child's psychological problems, and, as a result, they may be unwilling to acknowledge or seek help for the child's difficulties. The most extreme example is parents who are physically or sexually abusive. Such parents are unlikely to acknowledge the psychological or physical harm they are causing the child or to seek treatment for the child.

Cultural norms for children's behaviors differ, and parents' expectations for their children and their tolerance of deviant behavior in children are affected by these norms. For example, Jamaican parents appear to be more tolerant than American parents of unusual behaviors in children, including both aggressive behavior and behavior indicating shyness and inhibition. In turn, Jamaican parents have a higher threshold than American parents in terms of the appropriate time to take a child to a clinician (Lambert et al., 1992).

Teachers also provide information about children's functioning. Teachers and other school personnel (such as guidance counselors and coaches) are often the first to recognize that a child has a problem and to initiate an intervention to address the problem. Teachers' assessments of children, however, are often different from the assessments made by other adults, including parents and trained clinicians (De Los Reyes et al., 2015). Such discrepancies may arise because these other adults are providing invalid assessments of the children whereas the teachers are providing valid assessments. The discrepancies may also arise because children function differently in different settings. At home, a child may be well behaved, quiet, and withdrawn, while at school the same child may be impulsive, easily angered, and distractible.

Evaluating Individuals Across Cultures

A number of challenges to assessment arise when there are significant cultural differences between the assessor and the person being assessed (Dana, 2005; Paniagua & Yamada, 2013). Imagine having to obtain all the information needed to evaluate a person who comes from a culture very different from your own. The first problem you may run into is that the person may not speak your language or may speak it only partially (and you may not speak his or hers at all). Symptoms can be both underdiagnosed and overdiagnosed when the individual and the assessor do not share a language. Overdiagnosis may occur when an individual tries to describe symptoms in the assessor's language but the assessor interprets the individual's slow and confused description of symptoms as indicating more pathology than is really present. Underdiagnosis may occur when the individual cannot articulate complex emotions or strange perceptual experiences in the assessor's language and thus does not even try to do so.

One solution is to find an interpreter to translate between the clinician and the person. While interpreters can be invaluable to good communication, those who are not trained assessors themselves can misunderstand and mistranslate a clinician's questions and the person's answers, as in the following example (Marcos, 1979, p. 173):

> **Clinician to Spanish-speaking patient:** . . . Do you feel that life is not worthwhile sometimes?
>
> **Interpreter to patient:** The doctor wants to know if you feel sad. . . .
>
> **Patient's response:** No, yes, I know that my children need me . . . I prefer not to think about it.
>
> **Interpreter to clinician:** . . . [S]he says that she loves her children and that her children need her.

In this case, the interpreter did not accurately reflect the clinician's question or the patient's answer, giving the clinician a sense that the person was doing better than the person reported she was. In addition, different people from the same country can speak different dialects of a language or may have different means of expressing feelings and attitudes.

Cultural differences between clients and clinicians can lead to misinterpretations of clients' problems. ©*Zigy Kaluzny/Getty Images*

Mistranslation can occur when the interpreter does not speak the particular dialect spoken by the individual or comes from a different subculture.

Cultural biases can arise when everyone supposedly is speaking the same language but has a unique cultural background. There is evidence that African Americans in the United States are overdiagnosed as having symptoms of schizophrenia (Neighbors, Trierweiler, Ford, & Muroff, 2003). Some investigators believe that cultural differences in the presentation of symptoms play a role (Kirmayer, 2001). African Americans may present more intense symptoms than European Americans, and these symptoms then are misunderstood by European American assessors as representing more severe psychopathology. Some European American assessors may be too quick to diagnose psychopathology in African Americans because of negative stereotypes.

Even when clinicians avoid all these biases, they are still left with the fact that people from other cultures often think and talk about their psychological symptoms differently than do members of the clinician's culture. We discuss examples of cultural differences in the presentation of symptoms throughout this book. One of the most pervasive differences is in whether cultures experience and report psychological distress in emotional or somatic (physical) symptoms. European Americans tend to view the body and mind separately, whereas many other cultures do not make sharp distinctions between the experiences of the body and those of the mind (Paniagua & Yamada, 2013). Following a psychologically distressing event, European Americans tend to report that they feel anxious or sad, but members of many other cultures tend to report having physical aches and maladies. To conduct an accurate assessment, clinicians must be aware of cultural differences in the manifestation of disorders and in the presentation of symptoms, and they must use this information correctly in interpreting the symptoms individuals report. Cultural differences are further complicated by the fact that not every member of a culture conforms to what is known about that culture's norms. Within every culture, people differ in their acceptance of cultural norms for behavior.

FIGURE 4 **Syndromes as Clusters of Symptoms.** Syndromes are clusters of symptoms that frequently co-occur. The symptoms of one syndrome, such as symptoms of depression, can overlap the symptoms of another syndrome, such as symptoms of anxiety.

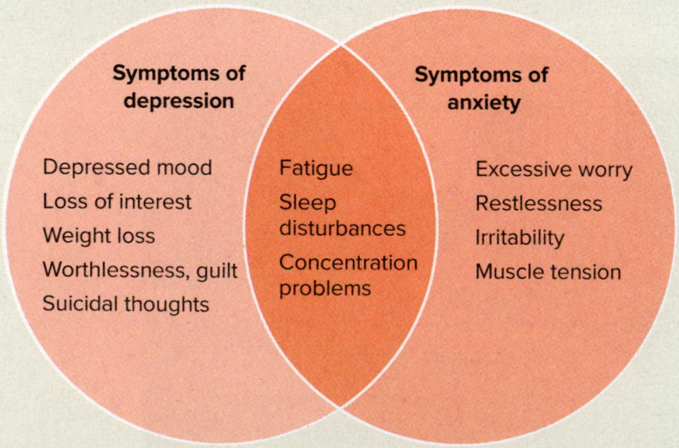

DIAGNOSIS

Recall that a *diagnosis* is a label we attach to a set of symptoms that tend to occur together. This set of symptoms is called a **syndrome.** Typically, several symptoms make up a syndrome, but people differ in which of these symptoms they experience most strongly. Some of the symptoms that make up the syndrome we call *depression* include sad mood, loss of interest in one's usual activities, sleeplessness, difficulty concentrating, and thoughts of death. But not everyone who becomes depressed experiences all these symptoms—for example, some people lose interest in their usual activities but never really feel sad or blue, and only a subset of depressed people have prominent thoughts of death.

Syndromes are not lists of symptoms that all people have all the time if they have any of the symptoms at all. Rather, they are lists of symptoms that tend to co-occur within individuals. The symptoms of one syndrome may overlap those of another. Figure 4 shows the overlap in the symptoms that make up depression (see the chapter "Mood Disorders and Suicide") and anxiety (see the chapter "Trauma, Anxiety, Obsessive-Compulsive, and Related Disorders"). Both syndromes include the symptoms fatigue, sleep disturbances, and concentration problems. However, each syndrome has symptoms more specific to it.

For centuries, people have tried to organize the confusing array of psychological symptoms into a limited set of syndromes. A set of syndromes and the rules for determining whether an individual's symptoms are part of one of these syndromes constitute a **classification system.**

One of the first classification systems for psychological symptoms was proposed by Hippocrates in the fourth century BCE. Hippocrates divided all mental disorders into mania (states of abnormal excitement), melancholia (states of abnormal depression), paranoia, and epilepsy. In 1883, Emil Kraepelin published the first modern classification system, which is the basis of our current systems. Current systems divide the world of psychological symptoms into a much larger number of syndromes than did Hippocrates. We will focus on the classification system most widely used in the United States, the ***Diagnostic and Statistical Manual of Mental Disorders,*** or ***DSM.*** The classification system used in Europe and much of the rest of the world, the *International Classification of Disease (ICD),* has many similarities to the most recent editions of the *DSM* (Clark, Cuthbert, Lewis-Fernández, Narrow, & Reed, 2017).

Diagnostic and Statistical Manual of Mental Disorders (DSM)

For more than 60 years, the official manual for diagnosing psychological disorders in the United States has been the *Diagnostic and Statistical Manual of Mental Disorders* of the American Psychiatric Association. The current, fifth edition (since 2013) is known as *DSM-5.* The first edition of the *DSM,* published in 1952, outlined the diagnostic criteria for all the mental disorders recognized by the psychiatric community at the time. These criteria were somewhat vague descriptions heavily influenced by psychoanalytic theory. For example, the diagnosis of anxiety neurosis could be manifested in a great variety of behaviors and emotions. The key to the diagnosis was whether the clinician believed that unconscious conflicts were causing the individual to experience anxiety. The second edition of the *DSM* (*DSM-II*), published in 1968, included some disorders that had been newly recognized since the publication of the first edition but otherwise was not much different.

Because the descriptions of disorders in the first and second editions of the *DSM* were so abstract and theoretically based, the reliability of the diagnoses was low. For example, one study found that four experienced clinicians using the first edition of the *DSM* to diagnose 153 patients agreed on their diagnoses only 54 percent of the time (Beck, Ward, Mendelson, Moch, & Erbaugh, 1962). This low reliability eventually led psychiatrists and psychologists to call for a radically new system of diagnosing mental disorders.

DSM-III, DSM-IIIR, DSM-IV, DSM-IV-TR, and DSM-5

In response to the reliability problems of the first and second editions of the *DSM,* in 1980 the American Psychiatric Association published the third edition of the *DSM,* known as *DSM-III.* This third edition was followed in 1987 by a revised third edition, known as *DSM-IIIR,* and in 1994 by a fourth edition, known as *DSM-IV,* revised as *DSM-IV-TR* in 2000. These newer editions improved diagnosis by replacing the vague descriptions of disorders with specific and concrete criteria for each disorder. These criteria are in the form of behaviors people must show or experience, or feelings they must report, in order to be given a diagnosis. The developers tried to be as descriptive as possible in listing the criteria for each disorder. A good example is the diagnostic criteria for panic disorder, which are given in Table 3. A person must have 4 of 13 possible symptoms as well as meet other criteria in order to be diagnosed with panic disorder. These criteria reflect the fact that not all the symptoms of panic disorder are present in every individual.

Two other elements distinguish the later editions of the *DSM* from their predecessors. First, the later editions specify how long a person must show symptoms of the disorder in order to be given the diagnosis (see Table 3, item B). Second, the criteria for most disorders require that symptoms interfere with occupational or social functioning. This emphasis on symptoms that are long-lasting and severe reflects the consensus among psychiatrists and psychologists that abnormality should be defined in terms of the impact of behaviors on the individual's ability to function and on his or her sense of well-being (see the chapter "Looking at Abnormality"). While the *DSM* attempts to precisely define the threshold between normality and abnormality, remember that the setting of the threshold along the continuum is a subjective judgment.

In 2013 the newest edition of the *DSM, DSM-5* (American Psychiatric Association, 2013), was released. (The roman numeral was replaced because it is limiting in our electronic age.) This new edition removed some diagnoses that were in the *DSM-IV-TR,* added some new diagnoses, and modified the criteria for others. In addition, the authors of the *DSM-5* (a committee of the American Psychiatric Association) attempted to incorporate a continuum or dimensional perspective, much like that described in the chapter "Looking at Abnormality," into the diagnosis of several disorders, particularly autism and the personality disorders (Clark et al., 2017). Substantial controversy has surrounded the development of the *DSM-5* (Frances & Widiger, 2012), focused on the empirical justification for the inclusion and exclusion of disorders, claims that the process of developing the *DSM-5* was clouded by secrecy and a disregard for alternative points of view, and concerns about the social impact of some of the new diagnoses (e.g., lowering the threshold for some diagnoses pathologizes normal variation in behaviors).

Throughout this book, the criteria for disorders specified by the *DSM-5* will be given. Because the *DSM-5* is relatively new, however, much of the existing research is based on disorders as defined by the *DSM-IV-TR* or earlier editions. Thus, when appropriate the differences between *DSM-5* criteria and *DSM-IV-TR* criteria will be noted, and implications for our understanding of the relevant disorders will be discussed.

TABLE 3 *DSM-5* Criteria for Panic Disorder

A. Recurrent unexpected panic attacks, defined as an abrupt surge of intense fear or intense discomfort that reaches a peak within minutes, and during which time four or more of the following symptoms occur. (*Note:* The abrupt surge can occur from a calm state or an anxious state.)
   1. Palpitations, pounding heart, or accelerated heart rate
   2. Sweating
   3. Trembling or shaking
   4. Sensations of shortness of breath or smothering
   5. Feelings of choking
   6. Chest pain or discomfort
   7. Nausea or abdominal distress
   8. Feeling dizzy, unsteady, lightheaded, or faint
   9. Chills or heat sensations
   10. Paresthesias (numbness or tingling sensations)
   11. Derealization (feelings of unreality) or depersonalization (being detached from oneself)
   12. Fear of losing control or going crazy
   13. Fear of dying

B. At least one of the attacks has been followed by 1 month (or more) of one or both of the following:
   1. Persistent concern or worry about additional Panic Attacks or their consequences (e.g., losing control, having a heart attack, "going crazy")
   2. Significant maladaptive change in behavior related to the attacks (e.g., behaviors designed to avoid having Panic Attacks, such as avoidance of exercise or unfamiliar situations)

C. The disturbance is not attributable to the direct physiological effects of a substance (e.g., a drug of abuse, a medication) or another medical condition (e.g., hyperthyroidism, cardiopulmonary disorders).

D. The disturbance is not better accounted for by another mental disorder (e.g., the Panic Attacks do not occur only in response to feared social situations in Social Anxiety Disorder, circumscribed phobic objects or situations in Specific Phobia, obsessions in Obsessive-Compulsive Disorder, reminders of traumatic events in Posttraumatic Stress Disorder, or separation from attachment figures in Separation Anxiety Disorder).

Reliability of the *DSM*

Despite the use of explicit criteria for disorders, the reliability of many of the diagnoses listed in the *DSM-III* and *DSM-IIIR* was disappointing. On average, experienced clinicians agreed on their diagnoses using these manuals only about 70 percent of the time (Kirk & Kutchins, 1992). The reliability of some of the diagnoses, particularly the personality disorder diagnoses, was much lower.

Low reliability of diagnoses can be due to many factors. Although the developers of the *DSM-III* and *DSM-IIIR* attempted to make the criteria for each disorder explicit, many criteria still were vague and required the clinician to make inferences about the individual's symptoms or to rely on the individual's willingness to report symptoms. For example, most of the symptoms of the mood disorders and the anxiety disorders are subjective experiences (e.g., sadness, apprehensiveness, hopelessness), and only the individual can report whether he or she has these symptoms and how severe they are. To diagnose any of the personality disorders, the clinician must establish that the person has a lifelong history of specific dysfunctional behaviors or ways of relating to the world. Unless the clinician has known the person his or her entire life, the clinician must rely on the person and his or her family to provide information about the person's history. Different sources of information can provide very different pictures of the person's functioning.

To increase the reliability of diagnoses in the *DSM-IV,* the task force that developed it conducted numerous field trials (see Frances & Widiger, 2012). The criteria for most of the diagnoses to be included

SHADES OF GRAY

As you read the following case study, compare Mark's symptoms to the criteria in Table 3.

When Mark went to an appointment with his physician, he looked pale and visibly nervous. He told his doctor that twice in the last month he had had an episode in which his heart suddenly started racing, he felt short of breath and cold all over, and he trembled uncontrollably. He was sure, when these feelings were happening, that he was dying of a heart attack. The symptoms lasted about 10 minutes and then subsided. His doctor asked Mark where he was when these symptoms began. Mark said the first time he felt this way was when he was about to give a presentation in an important class. The second time was when he was on his way to meet his parents for dinner.

Do Mark's symptoms meet the criteria for panic disorder? (Discussion appears at the end of this chapter.)

in the *DSM-IV* were tested in clinical and research settings. In a field trial, testing determines whether diagnostic criteria can be applied reliably and whether they fit individuals' experiences. As a result, the *DSM-IV* and *DSM-IV-TR* diagnoses had a higher reliability than their predecessors, although clearly they were not completely reliable (Widiger, 2002). Field trials were conducted during the development of the *DSM-5,* although questions have been raised about their adequacy (First, 2010). The reliability of the *DSM-5* diagnoses remains under examination (Chmielewski, Clark, Bagby, & Watson, 2015).

Nonaxial Approach in the *DSM-5*

Since the *DSM-III*, clinicians have been asked to evaluate patients on multiple "axes" in order to capture important information about them. These axes basically just refer to multiple categories of disorders and functional areas that clinicians should evaluate. The first axis included clinical disorders, and the second addressed personality disorders and intellectual disabilities. The remaining axes covered medical, psychosocial, environmental, and childhood factors that added to the clinical picture. These axes were often used by insurance companies and governmental agencies in making their professional assessments. Clinicians were never obligated to use the axes in making a mental disorder diagnosis; the axes were intended to provide as varied a clinical assessment as possible.

The *DSM-5* has moved away from the axial system to bring it more in line with the manual used internationally, the *International Classification of Diseases (ICD)*, published by the World Health

For over 60 years the *Diagnostic and Statistical Manual of the Mental Disorders*, or *DSM*, has been the official reference for diagnosing psychological disorders in the United States. The fifth edition was published in 2013. ©*murat sarica/Getty Images*

Organization (WHO). The changes reflect the globalization of research on mental health problems and the desire of researchers around the world for similar diagnostic systems.

With the publication of the *DSM-5* the former Axes I, II, and III are integrated into the overall diagnostic scheme (in other words, the clinician records just one list of diagnoses). Separate notations for important psychosocial and contextual factors (former Axis IV) and disability (former Axis V) are made by the clinician. The goal is to consider the individual's functional status separately from his or her diagnosis or symptom status.

DSM-IV Axis IV addressed psychosocial and environmental problems that might affect the diagnosis, treatment, and prognosis of mental disorders. The editors of *DSM-5* felt that this resource should no longer provide diagnostic criteria separate from those used in the *ICD*.

DSM-IV Axis V consisted of the Global Assessment of Functioning (GAF) scale, which allowed clinicians to register their judgment of an individual's overall level of functioning. The scale ran from 0 to 100, with 100 representing maximum functioning. One person might be diagnosed with depression and receive a GAF score of 40, whereas another person with the same diagnosis might receive a score of 70. Although each person has the same diagnosis, the clinical portrait of each would be seen differently. Perhaps one person is too depressed to go to work, whereas another is capable of handling most of life's responsibilities. This scale was dropped in the *DSM-5* because contributors noted its lack of conceptual clarity: for example, different clinicians might assess the same person with different scores. To provide some global measure of disability, the *DSM-5* recommends the WHO Disability Assessment Schedule (WHODAS).

Continuing Debates About the DSM

Although *DSM-5* was meant to reflect developments in our understanding of mental disorders, debates continue over fundamental questions about the classification and diagnosis of disorders. We next consider some of these debates.

Reifying Diagnoses Once a diagnosis is defined in any classification system, people tend to reify it. That means seeing the diagnosis as real and true rather than as the product of a set of judgments about how symptoms tend to occur together (Hyman, 2010). These judgments may be made by experts and be based on the best empirical science of the time, but they are highly fallible and, to some extent, always social constructions based on our society's current views of mental disorders. Moreover, as noted in the chapter "Looking at Abnormality," it's increasingly clear that certain problems in biological, psychological, and social functioning cut across many disorders (Cuthbert & Insel, 2013; Sanislow et al., 2011). The reification of diagnoses can impede progress in research and treatment as researchers focus on understanding the causes of and treatments for the diagnosis rather than on the biological, psychological, and social problems that underlie the disorder and related disorders (Hyman, 2010). Indeed, it can be difficult for researchers to obtain funding to study problems that are not official diagnoses in the *DSM* and for clinicians to be reimbursed by insurance companies to treat them.

Category or Continuum The *DSM-IV-TR* and its predecessors were *categorical* diagnostic systems, meaning that their diagnostic criteria defined where normality ends and psychopathology begins. The *DSM-5* retains the categorical system for most diagnoses, but it introduces a continuum or dimensional perspective on a number of disorders, such as the autism spectrum disorders, personality disorders, and substance use disorders. Further, a number of dimensional assessment scales for rating a person's symptoms and functioning have been added to the *DSM-5*. These moves toward a more dimensional model of diagnosis reflect the growing consensus that all behaviors fall along a continuum and that most disorders represent extremes along this continuum (Clark et al., 2017).

Yet questions have been raised about whether a continuum perspective is practical for real-world use (First, 2010). Busy clinicians have to make hundreds of decisions per day, and it may be easier to think in terms of categories than continuums. Prior versions of the *DSM* had some dimensions along which clinicians could rate patients' functioning, but there is evidence that most clinicians did not use them (First, 2010). So although in reality mental health and mental disorder may exist along continuums or dimensions, the human mind may be constructed to think more in terms of categories and the presence or absence of disorders.

Differentiating Mental Disorders from One Another A frequent complaint with the *DSM-IV* and *DSM-IV-TR* was the difficulty in differentiating the mental disorders from one another (Watson, 2009). Most people who were diagnosed with one disorder also met the criteria for at least one other disorder, a situation referred to as **comorbidity.** This overlap occurs, in part, because certain symptoms show up in the criteria for several different disorders. For example, irritability or agitation can be part of depression, mania, anxiety, schizophrenia, some of the personality disorders, and some of the childhood disorders. Some changes in the *DSM-5* were made to try to correct the problem of comorbidity. For example, many of the diagnoses of the personality disorders (see the chapter "Personality Disorders") were revised to reduce the amount of overlap in the criteria for different disorders.

Although we might want to make the diagnostic criteria for disorders more distinct, recent research suggests that much of the comorbidity among disorders exists because it reflects problems in fundamental cognitive, emotional, and behavioral processes that cut across many disorders, such as sleep problems, depressed or anxious mood, and substance use (Sanislow et al., 2011). Some experts believe that diagnostic systems of the future will specify how these dimensions come together to create different types of psychopathology, as well as how and why these psychopathologies are related (Cuthbert & Insel, 2013). The authors of the *DSM-5* developed a set of instruments to assess variations in cognitive, emotional, and behavioral processes. These instruments are not part of the *DSM-5* but are available for use by researchers and clinicians to obtain ratings for important dimensions regardless of the specific disorder with which an individual might be diagnosed (see Helzer et al., 2008).

In the meantime, however, most people who are given one diagnosis of a mental disorder will also meet the criteria for at least one other diagnosis (Kessler et al., 2005). This leads to many questions, such as which diagnosis should be considered the primary diagnosis and which the secondary diagnosis, which diagnosis should be treated first, whether people with diagnoses A and B are fundamentally different from or similar to people with diagnoses A and C, and so on.

Addressing Cultural Issues Different cultures have distinct ways of conceptualizing mental disorders. Some disorders that are defined in one culture do not seem to occur in others. Table 4 describes some of these culture-bound syndromes. In addition, there is cultural variation in the presentation of symptoms. For example, there are differences among cultures in the content of delusions (beliefs out of touch with reality) in schizophrenia. The *DSM-5* and its predecessors provide guidelines for considering cultural issues such

TABLE 4 Culture-Bound Syndromes

Certain syndromes appear to occur only in some cultures.

Syndrome	Cultures Where Found	Symptoms
Amok	Malaysia, Laos, Philippines, Polynesia, Papua New Guinea, Puerto Rico	Brooding followed by an outburst of violent, aggressive, or homicidal behavior
Ataque de nervios	Latin America and Latin Mediterranean cultures	Uncontrollable shouting, attacks of crying, trembling, heat in the chest rising into the head, verbal or physical aggression, a sense of being out of control
Dhat	India, Sri Lanka, China	Severe anxiety about the discharge of semen, whitish discoloration of the urine, feelings of weakness and exhaustion
Ghost sickness	Native American cultures	Preoccupation with death and the deceased, manifested in dreams and in severe anxiety
Koro	Malaysia, China, Thailand	Episode of sudden and intense anxiety that the penis (or, in women, the vulva and nipples) will recede into the body and possibly cause death
Mal de ojo	Mediterranean cultures	Fitful sleep, crying without apparent cause, diarrhea, vomiting, fever
Shinjingshuairuo	China	Physical and mental fatigue, dizziness, headaches, other pains, concentration difficulties, sleep disturbance, memory loss
Susto	U.S. Latinos, Mexico, Central America, South America	Appetite disturbances, sleep problems, sadness, lack of motivation, low self-worth, aches and pains; follows a frightening experience
Taijinkyofusho	Japan	Intense fear that one's body displeases, embarrasses, or is offensive to other people

as the kinds of symptoms acceptable in the individual's culture. Some critics do not believe these guidelines have gone far enough in recognizing cultural variation in what behaviors, thoughts, and feelings are considered healthy or unhealthy (Kirmayer, 2001). Throughout the remainder of this book, we will comment on cultural variations in the experience and prevalence of each disorder recognized by the *DSM*.

The Social-Psychological Dangers of Diagnosis

We noted earlier that once a diagnosis is given, people tend to see it as real rather than as a judgment. This can make people oblivious to the biases that may influence diagnoses. One influential critic of psychiatry, Thomas Szasz (1920–2012), argued that so many biases are inherent in determining who is labeled as having a mental disorder that the entire system of diagnosis is corrupt and should be abandoned. Szasz (1961) believed that people in power use psychiatric diagnoses to label and isolate people who do not "fit in." He suggested that mental disorders do not really exist and that people who seem to be suffering from mental disorders are oppressed by a society that does not accept their alternative ways of behaving and looking at the world.

Even psychiatrists and psychologists who do not fully agree with Szasz' perspective recognize that giving a person a diagnosis leads to certain judgments and expectations of them that can have unintended consequences. This point was made in a classic study of the effects of diagnoses by psychologist David Rosenhan (1973). He and seven colleagues had themselves admitted to 12 different mental hospitals by reporting to hospital staff that they had been hearing voices saying the words "empty," "hollow," and "thud." When they were questioned by hospital personnel, they told the truth about every other aspect of their lives, including the fact that they had never experienced mental health problems before. All eight were admitted to the hospitals, all but one with a diagnosis of schizophrenia (see the chapter "Schizophrenia Spectrum and Other Psychotic Disorders").

Children who are labeled as different can be ostracized by other children.
©*Wavebreakmedia/Getty Images*

Once they were admitted to the hospitals, the pseudopatients stopped reporting that they were hearing voices and behaved as normally as they usually did. When asked how they were doing by hospital staff, the pseudopatients said they felt fine and no longer heard voices. They cooperated in activities. The only thing they did differently from other patients was to write down their observations on notepads occasionally during the day.

Nevertheless, not one of the pseudopatients was ever detected as normal by hospital staff, although they remained in the hospitals for an average of 19 days. Several of the other patients in the mental hospitals detected the pseudopatients' normality, however, making comments such as "You're not crazy, you're a journalist, or a professor [referring to the continual note taking]. You're checking up on the hospital" (Rosenhan, 1973). When the pseudopatients were discharged, they were given the diagnosis of schizophrenia in remission, meaning that the physicians still believed the pseudopatients had schizophrenia but the symptoms had subsided for the time being.

Rosenhan (1973) concluded, "It is clear that we cannot distinguish the sane from the insane in psychiatric hospitals. The hospital itself imposes a special environment in which the meanings of behavior can be easily misunderstood." He also noted that, if even mental health professionals cannot distinguish sanity from insanity, the dangers of diagnostic labels are even greater in the hands of nonprofessionals: "Such labels, conferred by mental health professionals, are as influential on the patient as they are on his relatives and friends, and it should not surprise anyone that the diagnosis acts on all of them as a self-fulfilling prophecy. Eventually, the patient himself accepts the diagnosis, with all of its surplus meanings and expectations, and behaves accordingly."

Not surprisingly, Rosenhan's study created a furor in the mental health community. How could seasoned professionals have made such mistakes—admitting mentally healthy people to psychiatric hospitals on the basis of one symptom (hearing voices), not recognizing the pseudopatients' behavior as normal, allowing them to be discharged carrying a diagnosis that suggested they still had schizophrenia? Even today, Rosenhan's study is held up as an example of the abuses of the power to label people as sane or insane, normal or abnormal, good or bad. Not only do clinicians and the public begin to view the person as his or her disorder (e.g., he is a schizophrenic, she is a depressive), but people with disorders also take on the role of a disordered person, a role they may carry for the rest of their lives.

Another study of boys in grades 3 to 6 illustrates how labeling children can influence how others treat them (Harris, Milich, Corbitt, & Hoover, 1992). Researchers paired boys who were the same age. In half the pairs, one of the boys was told that his partner had a behavior disorder that made him disruptive. In reality, only some of the boys labeled as having a behavior disorder actually had a behavior disorder. In the other half of the pairs, the boys were not told anything about each other, although some of the boys actually did have a behavior disorder. All the pairs worked together on a task while researchers videotaped their interaction. After the interaction, the boys were asked several questions about each other and about their enjoyment of the interaction.

The boys who had been told that their partners had a behavior disorder were less friendly toward their partners during the task, talked with them less often, and were less involved in the interaction with their partners than were the boys who had been told nothing about their partners. In turn, the boys who had been labeled as having a behavior disorder enjoyed the interaction less, took less credit for their performance on the task, and said that their partners were less friendly toward them than did the boys who had not been so labeled. Most important, labeling a boy as having a behavior disorder influenced his partner's behaviors toward him and his enjoyment of the task regardless of whether he actually had a behavior disorder. These results show that labeling a child as having a disorder strongly affects other children's behaviors toward him or her, even when there is no reason for the child to be so labeled.

So, should we avoid psychiatric diagnoses altogether? Probably not. Despite the potential dangers of diagnostic systems, they serve vital functions. The primary role of diagnostic systems is to organize the confusing array of psychological symptoms in an agreed-upon manner. This organization facilitates communication from one clinician to another and across time.

For example, if Dr. Jones reads in a patient's history that he was diagnosed with schizophrenia according to the *DSM-5,* she knows what criteria were used to make that diagnosis and can compare the patient's diagnosis then with his symptoms now. Such information can assist Dr. Jones in making an accurate assessment of the patient's current symptoms and in determining the proper treatment for his symptoms. For example, if the patient's current symptoms also suggest schizophrenia and the patient responded to Drug X when he had schizophrenia a few years ago, this history indicates that he might respond well to Drug X now.

Having a standard diagnostic system also greatly facilitates research on psychological disorders. For example, if a researcher at University A is using the *DSM-5* criteria to identify people with obsessive-compulsive disorder and a researcher at University B is using the same criteria for the same purpose, the two researchers will be better able to compare the results of their research than if they were using different criteria to diagnose obsessive-compulsive disorder. Standardization can lead to faster advances in our understanding of the causes of and effective treatments for disorders.

CHAPTER INTEGRATION

Assessment is inherently a process of biopsychosocial integration of pieces of information about an individual. After clinicians administer a battery of assessment tests to a person, they must then integrate the information gathered from these tests to form a coherent picture of the person's characteristics, symptoms, strengths, and weaknesses. This picture weaves together information on biological functioning (major illnesses, possible genetic vulnerability to psychopathology), psychological functioning (personality, coping skills, intellectual strengths), and social functioning (support networks, work relationships, social skills) (Figure 5).

FIGURE 5 **Integration of Biological, Psychological, and Social Factors in Assessment and Diagnosis.**

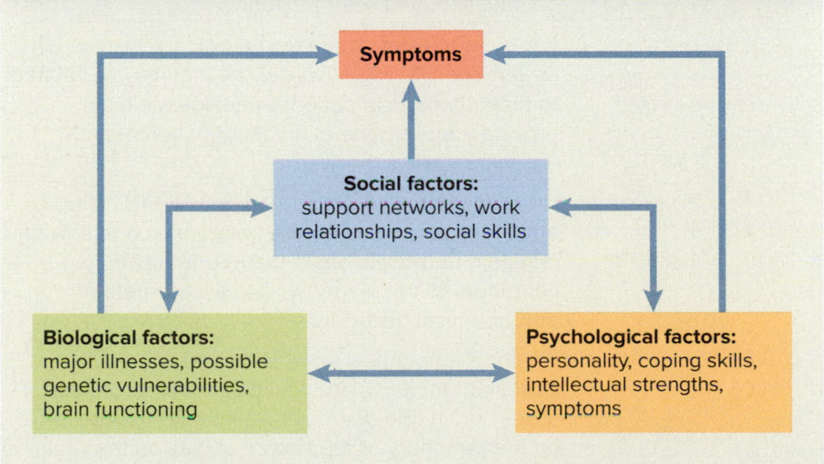

SHADES OF GRAY DISCUSSION

If you determined that Mark has experienced panic attacks, you are correct. The *DSM-5* requires four symptoms for diagnosis of a panic attack (see criterion A), and Mark reports five: rapid heartbeat, shortness of breath, chills, trembling, and feeling as though he was going to die. Further, these symptoms seem to have developed suddenly and to have increased in intensity within minutes, meeting criterion A in Table 3.

It is less clear whether Mark's symptoms meet the criterion that they are "unexpected," because his panic attacks occurred before giving an important presentation and before meeting his parents and may often (or expectedly) occur in these situations. In addition, criterion B requires him to have been persistently fearful of another panic attack or to have made significant maladaptive changes in his behavior related to panic attacks for at least a month. We cannot tell whether either of these conditions has been met. We also cannot rule out the possibility of an organic factor, such as too much coffee, or another mental disorder having caused his panic attacks, so we do not know if he meets criteria C and D. Thus, although it appears that Mark has experienced some panic attacks, we cannot currently diagnose him with panic disorder.

CHAPTER SUMMARY

- Assessment is the process of gathering information about people's symptoms and the causes of these symptoms. Diagnosis is a label we attach to symptoms that tend to co-occur.
- The validity and reliability of assessment tools indicate their quality. Validity is the accuracy of a test in assessing what it is supposed to assess. Five types of validity are face validity, content validity, concurrent validity, predictive validity, and construct validity. Reliability is the consistency of a test. Types of reliability include test-retest reliability, alternate form reliability, internal reliability, and interrater reliability. Standardization of the implementation and interpretation of an assessment tool can increase both validity and reliability.
- In a mental status exam, the clinician assesses the individual's (a) appearance and behavior, (b) thought processes, (c) mood and affect, (d) intellectual functioning, and (e) orientation.
- To assess emotional and behavioral functioning, clinicians use structured clinical interviews, symptom questionnaires, personality inventories, behavioral observation, and self-monitoring.
- Paper-and-pencil neuropsychological tests can assess specific cognitive deficits that may be related to brain damage in patients. Intelligence tests provide a more general measure of verbal and analytical skills.
- Brain-imaging techniques such as CT, PET, SPECT, and MRI scans currently are being used primarily for research purposes, but in the future they may contribute to the diagnosis and assessment of psychological disorders.
- Psychophysiological tests, including the electroencephalogram (EEG) and electrodermal responses, assess brain and nervous system activity detectable on the periphery of the body (such as on the scalp and skin).
- Projective tests present individuals with ambiguous stimuli. Clinicians interpret individuals' reactions to the stimuli. Both the validity and the reliability of these tests are low.
- During the assessment procedure, many problems and biases can be introduced. Individuals may be resistant to being assessed and thus distort the information they provide. They may be too impaired by cognitive deficits, distress, or lack of development of verbal skills to provide information. Further, many biases can arise when the clinician and the individual are from different cultures.
- A classification system is a set of definitions of syndromes and rules for determining when a person's symptoms are part of each syndrome. In the United States, the predominant classification system for psychological problems is the *Diagnostic and Statistical Manual of Mental Disorders (DSM)* of the American Psychiatric Association. Its most recent editions provide specific criteria for diagnosing each of the recognized psychological disorders, as well as information on the course and prevalence of disorders.
- The explicit criteria in the *DSM* have increased the reliability of diagnoses, but there is still room for improvement.
- The *DSM-5* provides three axes on which clinicians can assess individuals. On Axis I, major clinical syndromes and any medical conditions individuals have are noted. On Axis II, psychosocial and environmental stressors are noted. On Axis III, individuals' general levels of functioning are assessed.
- Critics point to many dangers in labeling people as having psychiatric disorders, including the danger of stigmatization. Diagnosis is important, however, to communication among clinicians and researchers. Only when a system of definitions of disorders is agreed on can communication about disorders be improved.

KEY TERMS

assessment
diagnosis
validity
reliability
structured interview
symptom questionnaire
personality inventories
behavioral observation
self-monitoring
intelligence tests
neuropsychological tests
computerized tomography (CT)
positron-emission tomography (PET)
single photon emission computed tomography (SPECT)
magnetic resonance imaging (MRI)
psychophysiological tests
electroencephalogram (EEG)
projective test
syndrome
classification system
Diagnostic and Statistical Manual of Mental Disorders (DSM)
comorbidity

Chapter 4

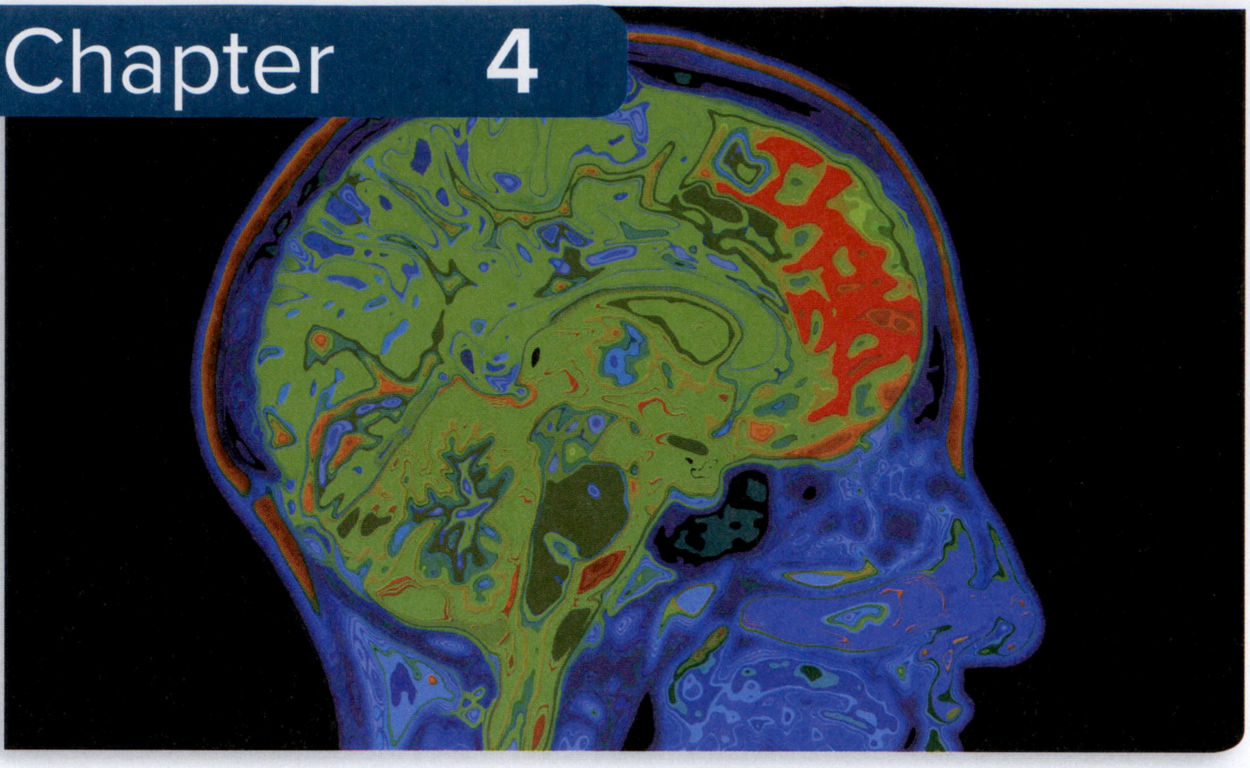

©SpeedKingz/Shutterstock

The Research Endeavor

CHAPTER OUTLINE

Research Along the Continuum

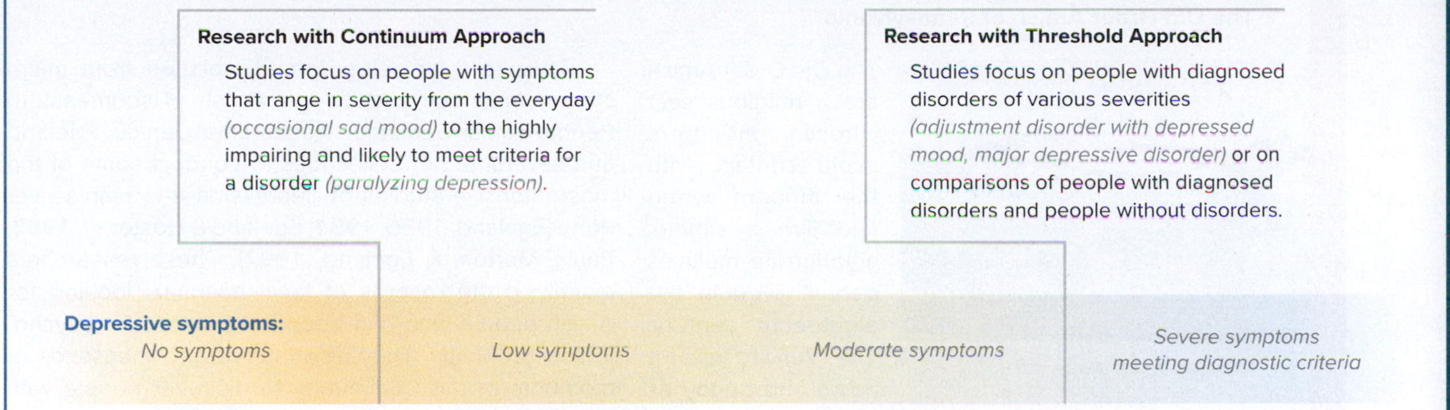

Research with Continuum Approach
Studies focus on people with symptoms that range in severity from the everyday (occasional sad mood) to the highly impairing and likely to meet criteria for a disorder (paralyzing depression).
Research with Threshold Approach
Studies focus on people with diagnosed disorders of various severities (adjustment disorder with depressed mood, major depressive disorder) or on comparisons of people with diagnosed disorders and people without disorders.
Depressive symptoms:
No symptoms
Low symptoms
Moderate symptoms
Severe symptoms meeting diagnostic criteria

This text helps you understand psychopathology using a continuum model. This model actually is a hot topic for debate in the field of abnormal psychology. Researchers disagree on whether studies should reflect a continuum model of psychopathology or instead focus only on disorders as diagnosed in the *DSM-5* and related diagnostic schemes (Lilienfeld & Treadway, 2016). The difference lies mainly in how researchers view people who have some symptoms of a disorder but do not meet the criteria for diagnosis. Researchers who favor continuum models believe that such individuals provide valuable insights into people who have diagnosable disorders. For example, they argue that the results of studies of people with moderate depression can be generalized to individuals with diagnosed depressive disorders (Angst et al., 2007). Researchers who do not support continuum models argue that people who fall short of a diagnosable disorder are inherently different from those who have a disorder and that therefore studies of these people cannot be applied to those who have a disorder. To continue our example, these researchers believe that the results of studies of people with moderate depression cannot be generalized to people with diagnosed depressive disorders (Gotlib, Lewinsohn, & Seeley, 1995).

The debate continues, with evidence supporting both points of view. Some research methods use a continuum model, such as a study of the relationship between how many stressors individuals have experienced and how many depressive symptoms they report. In contrast, investigators who are interested only in differences between people with diagnosed disorders and people who do not meet diagnostic criteria would be more likely to compare these two groups on the number of stressors they have experienced. We explore several research methods in this chapter.

It is important to remember that research is a cumulative process. No one study can definitively answer complex questions about the causes of and best treatments for mental disorders. Too often, individual studies generate a great deal of media attention, with headlines such as "Scientists Find the Gene for Schizophrenia" or "Study Shows Antidepressant Medications Do Not Work." The public can be given false hopes for breakthroughs that are dashed by future studies, leading to cynicism and reduced funding of mental health science. People with mental health problems can also come to believe that they should discontinue some treatment because one study raised doubts about its effectiveness. Only with the accumulation of evidence from multiple studies using multiple methods can we begin to have faith in the answer to a question about the causes of or appropriate treatments for a disorder.

Extraordinary People

The Old Order Amish of Pennsylvania

©Andrea Izzotti/Shutterstock

The Old Order Amish are a religious sect whose members avoid contact with the modern world and live a simple, agrarian life, much as people lived in the eighteenth century. The Amish use a horse and buggy as transportation, most of their homes do not have electricity or telephone service, and there is little movement of people into or out of their culture. The rules of social behavior among the Amish are very strict, and roles within the community are clearly set. Members who do not comply with community norms are isolated or shunned.

Despite their self-enforced isolation from mainstream American society, the Amish of southeastern Pennsylvania welcomed researcher Janice Egeland and several of her colleagues to conduct some of the most intensive studies of depression and mania ever done (Egeland, 1986, 1994; Egeland & Hostetter, 1983; Pauls, Morton, & Egeland, 1992). These researchers examined the records of local hospitals looking for Amish people who had been hospitalized for psychological problems. They also interviewed thousands of members of this community to discover people with mood disorders who had not been hospitalized. The closed society of the Amish and their meticulous recordkeeping of family histories proved a perfect setting in which to study the transmission of psychological disorders within families. The result was groundbreaking research on genetic factors that contribute to mood disorders.

Although research in abnormal psychology in many ways resembles research in other fields, the study of psychopathology presents some special challenges. One challenge is accurately measuring abnormal behaviors and feelings. We cannot see, hear, or feel other people's emotions and thoughts. Researchers often must rely on people's own accounts, or self-reports, of their internal states and experiences. Self-reports can be distorted in a number of ways, intentionally or unintentionally. Similarly, relying on an observer's assessments of a person has its own pitfalls. The observer's assessments can be biased by stereotypes involving gender and culture, idiosyncratic biases, and lack of information. A second challenge is the difficulty of obtaining the participation of populations of interest, such as people who are paranoid and hearing voices.

A third challenge, mentioned in the Research Along the Continuum feature, is that most forms of abnormality probably have multiple causes. Unless a single study can capture all the biological, psychological, and social causes of the psychopathology of interest, it cannot fully explain the causes of that abnormality. Rarely can a single study accomplish so much. Instead, we usually are left with partial answers to the question of what causes a certain disorder or symptom, and we must piece together the partial answers from several studies to get a complete picture.

Despite these challenges, researchers have made tremendous strides in understanding many forms of abnormality in the past 50 years or so. They have overcome many of the challenges of researching psychopathology by using a multimethod approach—that is, using different methods to study the same issue. Each different research method may have some limitations, but taken together the methods can provide convincing evidence concerning an abnormality.

In this chapter, we discuss the most common methods of mental health research. In our discussion, we will use various research methods to test the idea that stress contributes to depression. Of course, these research methods also can be used to test many other ideas.

THE SCIENTIFIC METHOD

Any research project involves a basic series of steps designed to obtain and evaluate, in a systematic way, information relevant to a problem. This process is often called the **scientific method.**

First, researchers must select and define a problem. In our case, the problem is to determine the relationship between stress and depression. Then a **hypothesis,** or testable statement of what we predict will happen in our study, must be formulated. Next, the method for testing the hypothesis must be chosen and implemented. Once the data have been collected and analyzed, the researcher draws the appropriate conclusions and documents the results in a research report.

Defining the Problem and Stating a Hypothesis

Throughout this chapter, we will examine the idea that stress causes depression. This simple idea is too broad and abstract to test directly. Thus, we must state a hypothesis, or a testable prediction of what relationship between stress and depression we expect to find in our study.

To generate a hypothesis, we might ask, "What kind of evidence would support the idea that stress causes depression?" If we find that people who have recently experienced stress are more likely to be depressed than people who have not recently experienced stress, this evidence would support our idea. One hypothesis, then, is that people who have recently been under stress are more likely to be depressed than people who have not. We can test this hypothesis by a number of research methods.

The alternative to our hypothesis is that people who experience stress are not more likely to develop depression than people who do not experience stress. This prediction that there is no relationship between the phenomena we are studying–in this case, stress and depression–is called the **null hypothesis.** Results often support the null hypothesis instead of the researcher's primary hypothesis.

Does support for the null hypothesis mean that the underlying idea has been disproved? No. The null hypothesis can be supported for many reasons, including flaws in the study design. Researchers often will continue to test their primary hypothesis, using a variety of methodologies. If the null hypothesis continues to get much more support than the primary hypothesis, the researchers eventually either modify or drop the primary hypothesis.

Choosing and Implementing a Method

Once we have stated a hypothesis, the next step in testing our idea that stress leads to depression is to choose how we are going to define the phenomena we are studying.

A **variable** is a factor or characteristic that can vary within an individual or between individuals. Weight, mood, and attitudes toward one's mother are all factors that can vary over time, so they are considered variables. Characteristics such as sex and ethnicity do not vary for an individual over time, but because they vary from one individual to another, they too can be considered variables. A **dependent variable** is the factor we are trying to predict in our study. In our studies of stress and depression, we will be trying to predict depression, so depression is our dependent variable. An **independent variable** is the factor we believe will affect the dependent variable. In our studies, the independent variable is the amount of stress an individual has experienced.

In order to research depression and stress, we must first define what we mean by these terms. As we discuss in the chapter "Mood Disorders and Suicide," depression is a syndrome or a collection of the following symptoms: sadness, loss of interest in one's usual activities, weight loss or gain, changes in sleep, physical agitation or slowing down, fatigue and loss of energy, feelings of worthlessness or excessive guilt, problems in concentration or indecisiveness, and suicidal thoughts (American Psychiatric Association, 2013). Researchers who adopt a continuum model of depression focus on the full range of depressive symptoms, from no symptoms to moderate symptoms to the most severe symptoms. Researchers who do not accept a continuum model would consider anyone who has some of these symptoms of depression but does not meet the criteria for one of the depressive disorders to be not depressed.

Stress is more difficult to define, because the term has been used in so many ways in research and in the popular press. Many researchers consider stressful events to be events that are uncontrollable, unpredictable, and challenging to the limits of people's abilities to cope (see the chapter "Health Psychology").

Operationalization refers to the way we measure or manipulate the variables in a study. Our definitions of depression and stress will influence how we measure these variables. For example, if we define depression as a diagnosable depressive disorder, then we will measure depression in terms of whether people's symptoms meet the criteria for a depressive disorder. If we define depression as symptoms along the entire range of severity, then we might measure depression as scores on a depression questionnaire.

In measuring stress, we might assess how often a person has encountered events that most people would consider stressful. Or we might devise a way of manipulating or creating stress so that we can then examine people's depression in response to this stress. In the remaining sections of this chapter, we will discuss different methods for testing hypotheses, as well as the conclusions that can and cannot be drawn from these methods.

SHADES OF GRAY

Imagine that you are the student member of the human participants committee that is considering the ethics of research at your school. A researcher proposes a study in which participants would believe they were taking a test that indicated their intellectual ability. In truth, half the participants would be randomly assigned to receive feedback that they had done poorly on the test, and half would be randomly assigned to receive feedback that they had done well on the test. The researcher would measure participants' moods before and after taking the test and receiving the feedback.

At a minimum, what would you require of the researcher in order to consider this study ethical? (Discussion appears at the end of this chapter.)

Ethical Issues in Research

Any research, whether experimental or some other type, must be evaluated for whether it is ethical. All colleges and universities have *human participants committees* (often referred to as human subjects committees, institutional review boards, or ethics committees). These committees review the procedures of studies done with humans to ensure that the benefits of the study substantially outweigh any risks to the participants and that the risks to the participants have been minimized. The committees ensure that each research study includes certain basic rights for all participants:

1. *Understanding the study.* Participants have the right to understand the nature of the research they are participating in, particularly any factors that might influence their willingness to participate. For example, if they are likely to experience discomfort (psychological or physical) as a result of participating in the study or if the study entails any risk to their well-being, the researcher should explain this in plain language to the participants. Individuals not capable of understanding the risks of a study, such as young children or adults with mental impairments, must have a parent, guardian, or other responsible adult make the judgment about their participation in the study.
2. *Confidentiality.* Participants should expect their identity and any information gathered from them in the course of the study to be held in strict confidence. Researchers usually report data aggregated across participants rather than data gathered from individual participants. Researchers who intend to report data gathered from individuals should obtain their explicit permission.
3. *Right to refuse or withdraw participation.* Participants should be allowed to refuse to participate in the study or to withdraw from participation once the study has begun without suffering adverse consequences. If students are participating in a study as a course requirement or as an opportunity for extra credit for a class, they should be given the choice of equitable alternative activities if they wish not to participate. Payment or other inducements for being in a study should not be so great that individuals essentially cannot afford to refuse to participate.
4. *Informed consent.* Usually, participants' consent to participate in the study should be documented in writing. In some cases, a written informed consent document is not used, as when participants are filling out an anonymous survey (in this case, their willingness to complete the survey is taken as their consent to participate). Also, if obtaining written documentation of participants' consent could put them at risk, the researcher sometimes is allowed to obtain only verbal consent. Examples of when this would be permitted include research being done in countries where a civil war is ongoing or an oppressive regime is in power, in which case participants might be at risk if it is discovered they have talked with researchers.
5. *Deception.* Researchers should use deception in studies only when doing so is absolutely essential and justified by the study's potential contributions. Participants should not be deceived about those aspects of the research that might affect their willingness to participate, such as physical risks, discomfort, or unpleasant emotional experiences. If deception is necessary, researchers should explain the deception to the participants after the research is completed.
6. *Debriefing.* At the end of the study, researchers should explain the purpose of the research and answer participants' questions.

Although these rights may seem straightforward, human participants committees must make judgment calls as to whether a given study adequately protects participants' rights and whether the potential benefits of the study outweigh any risks to the participants.

CASE STUDIES

Throughout this book, you will see **case studies**—detailed histories of individuals who have some form of psychological disorder. Case studies have been used for centuries as a way to understand the experiences of individuals and to make more general inferences about the sources of psychopathology.

If we wanted to use a case study to test our idea that stress causes depression, we would focus on an individual, interviewing him or her at length to discover the links between periods of depression and stressful events in his or her life. We might also interview close friends and family to obtain additional information. Based on the information we gathered, we would create a detailed description of the causes of his or her depressive episodes, with emphasis on the role of stressful events in these episodes.

Evaluating Case Studies

Case studies are a time-honored method of research, for several reasons. No other method captures the uniqueness of the individual as much as a case study. The nuances of an individual's life and experiences can be detailed, and the individual's own words can be used to describe these experiences. Exploring the unique experiences of individuals and honoring their perspectives on these experiences are important goals for many researchers, and in-depth case studies of individual lives have become even more popular in recent years.

Case studies can be the only way to study rare problems, because there simply are not enough people with such problems to study through another method. For example, much of the research on people with multiple personalities has come from case studies, because this form of psychopathology historically has been quite rare.

Case studies can be invaluable in helping generate new ideas and providing tentative support for those ideas. Today one of the most common uses of case studies is in drug treatment research to report unusual reactions patients have had to certain drugs. These reports can alert other clinicians to watch for similar reactions in their patients. If enough case reports of these unusual reactions emerge in the literature, larger-scale research to study the sources of the reactions may be warranted.

Actor and comedian Robin Williams struggled with mental illness for years, leading up to his death by suicide in 2014. ©*s_bukley/Shutterstock*

Case studies have drawbacks, however. The first involves **generalizability**—the ability to apply what we have learned to other individuals or groups. The conclusions drawn from the study of an individual may not apply to many other individuals. This limitation is especially obvious when case studies focus on people whose experiences may have been dramatic but unusual. For example, the circumstances leading to the deaths of such celebrities as Amy Winehouse, Kurt Cobain, or Phillip Seymour Hoffman may be interesting and relevant, but they may not tell us much about why other people commit suicide or engage in self-harming behaviors that might result in death.

The other drawback of case studies is that they can lack objectivity. This lack of objectivity can be on the part of both the individuals telling their stories and the therapists or researchers listening to the stories. People might have biased recollections of their pasts and may selectively report events that happen in the present. Moreover, the therapists or researchers might selectively remember parts of the stories that support their beliefs and assumptions about the causes of human behavior and forget parts that do not align with their theories. Thus, two case studies of the same person conducted by two different researchers may lead to different conclusions about the motivations and key events in that person's life.

CORRELATIONAL STUDIES

Correlational studies examine the relationship between an independent variable and a dependent variable without manipulating either variable. Correlational studies are the most common type of study in psychology and medicine. For example, you will often read about studies of the link between television watching and violence, smoking and heart disease, and Internet use and depression in which researchers have examined the naturally occurring relationships between variables.

There are many kinds of correlational studies. The most common type of correlational study in abnormal psychology is a study of two or more continuous variables. A **continuous variable** is measured along a continuum. For example, on a scale measuring severity of depression, scores might fall along a continuum from 0 (no depression) to 100 (extreme depression). On a scale measuring number of recent stressors, scores might fall along a continuum from 0 (no stressors) to 20 (20 or more recent stressors). If we measured severity of depression and number of recent stressors in the same group of people and then looked at the relationship between these two continuous variables, we would be doing a continuous variable correlational study. For example, we might find that people who experience more stressors also report more depressive symptoms.

Another type of correlational study is a **group comparison study.** In this type of study, researchers are interested in the relationship between people's membership in a particular group and their scores on some other variable. For example, we might be interested in the relationship between depression and whether people have experienced a specific type of stress, such as failing a test. In this case, the groups of interest are students who failed a test and students who did not. We would find people who represented these two groups, then measure depression in both groups. This is still a correlational study because we are only observing the relationship between two variables—test failure and depression—and are not manipulating any variable. In this type of study, however, at least one of the variables—group membership—is not a continuous variable.

Both continuous variable studies and group comparison studies can be either **cross-sectional**—observing people at only one point in time—or **longitudinal**—observing people on two or more occasions over time. Longitudinal studies have a major advantage over cross-sectional studies, because they can show that the independent variable precedes and predicts changes in the dependent variable over time. For example, a longitudinal study of stress and depression can show that people who are not depressed at the beginning of the study are much more likely to be depressed later in the study if they have experienced a stressful event in the interim than if they have not.

Measuring the Relationship Between Variables

In most correlational studies, the relationship between the variables is indicated by a correlation coefficient. Let us review what this statistic is and how to interpret it.

Correlation Coefficient

A **correlation coefficient** is a statistic used to represent the relationship between variables, usually denoted by the symbol *r*. A correlation coefficient can fall between −1.00 and +1.00. A positive correlation coefficient indicates that as values of the independent variable increase, values of the dependent variable also increase (Figure 1a). For example, a positive correlation between stress and depression would mean that people who report more stressors have higher levels of depression.

A negative correlation coefficient indicates that as values of the independent variable increase, values of the dependent variable decrease (Figure 1b). If we were measuring stressors and depression, a negative correlation would mean that people who report more stressors actually have lower levels of depression. This is an unlikely scenario, but there are many instances of negative correlations between variables. For example, people who receive more positive social support from others typically have lower levels of depression.

The magnitude (size) of a correlation is the degree to which the variables move in tandem with each other. It is indicated by how close the correlation coefficient is to either +1.00 or −1.00. A correlation (*r*) of 0 indicates no relationship between the variables (Figure 1c). A value of *r* of +1.00 or −1.00 indicates a perfect relationship between the two variables (as illustrated in Figure 1a and b)—the value of one variable is perfectly predicted by the value of the other variable; for example, every time people experience stress they become depressed.

Seldom do we see perfect correlations in psychological research. Instead, correlations often are in the low to moderate range (for example, .2 to .5),

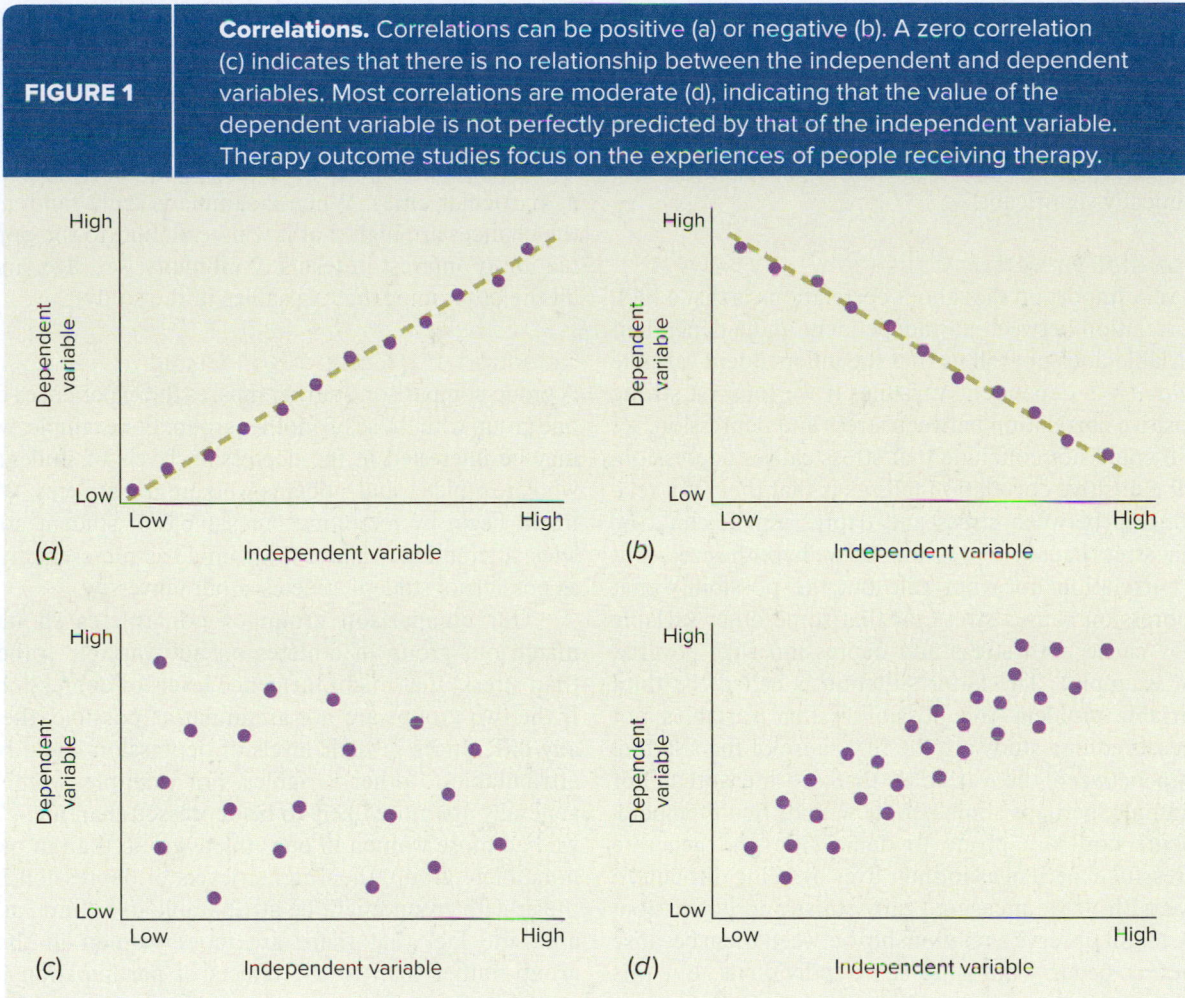

FIGURE 1 **Correlations.** Correlations can be positive (a) or negative (b). A zero correlation (c) indicates that there is no relationship between the independent and dependent variables. Most correlations are moderate (d), indicating that the value of the dependent variable is not perfectly predicted by that of the independent variable. Therapy outcome studies focus on the experiences of people receiving therapy.

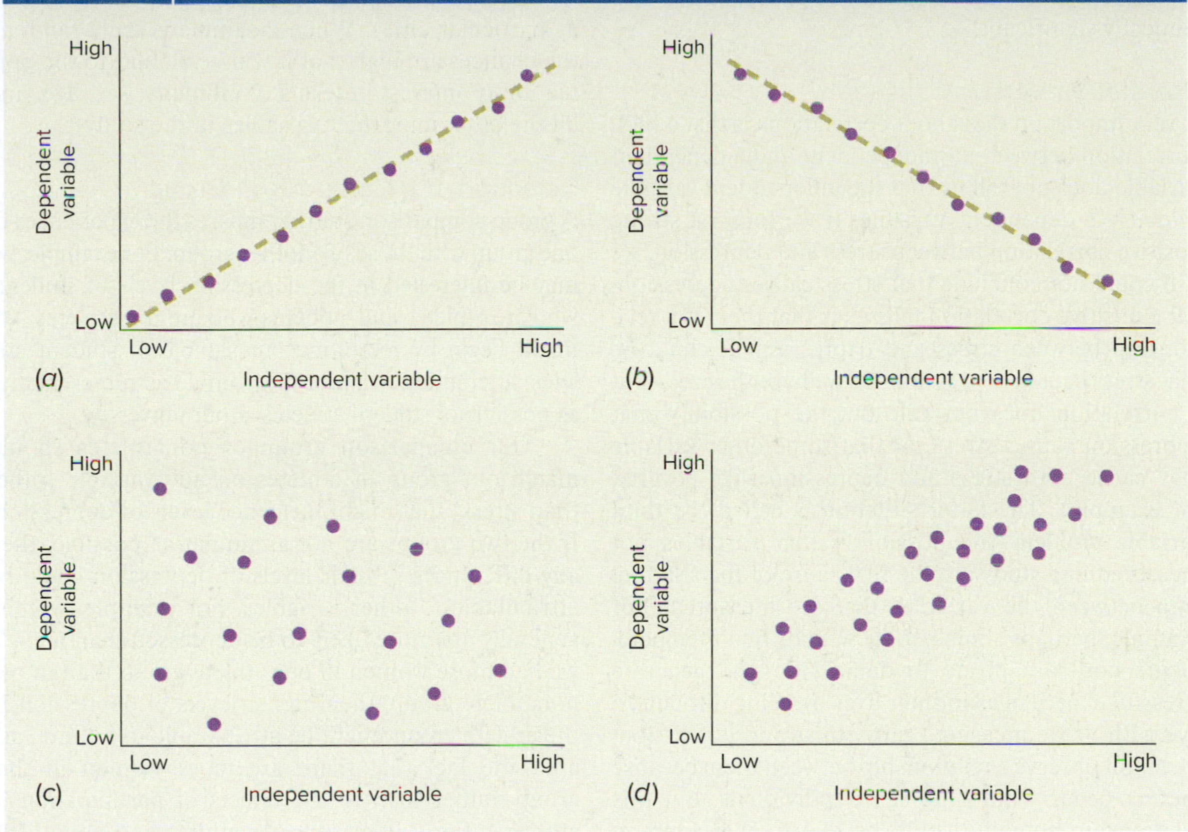

indicating some relationship between the two variables but a far from perfect relationship (Figure 1d). Many relationships between variables happen by chance and are not meaningful. Scientists evaluate the importance of a correlation coefficient by examining its statistical significance.

Statistical Significance

The **statistical significance** of a result, such as a correlation coefficient, is an index of how likely it is that the result occurred simply by chance. You will often see statements in research studies such as "The result was statistically significant at $p < .05$." This means that the probability (p) is less than 5 in 100 that the result occurred only by chance. Researchers typically accept results at this level of significance ($p < .05$) as support of their hypotheses, although the choice of an acceptable significance level is somewhat arbitrary.

Whether a correlation coefficient will be statistically significant at the $p < .05$ level is determined by its magnitude and the size of the sample on which it is based. Both larger correlations and larger sample sizes increase the likelihood of achieving statistical significance. A correlation of .30 will be significant if it is based on a large sample, say 200 or more, but will not be significant if it is based on a small sample, say 10 or fewer participants. On the other hand, a correlation of .90 will be statistically significant even if the sample is as small as 30 people.

A result can be statistically significant but not clinically significant. For example, a study of 10,000 people might find a correlation of .15 between the number of stressors people experienced and their scores on a depression questionnaire. This correlation would likely be statistically significant because of the very large sample, but it is so small as to suggest that stress is not a very good predictor of depression. Similarly, two groups may differ in their mean levels of depression to a statistically significant degree because the sample sizes of both groups are very large.

But if the two groups actually differ only by 1 or 2 points on a depression questionnaire in which scores can range from 0 to 60, the clinical significance of the difference in the two groups would be questionable. Increasingly, research is being examined for whether an effect is not only statistically significant but also clinically significant.

Correlation Versus Causation

A very important fact about correlations is that a high correlation between an independent and a dependent variable does not tell us that the independent variable *caused* the dependent variable. If we found a strong positive correlation between stress and depression, we still could not conclude that stress causes depression. All a positive correlation tells us is that there is a relationship between stress and depression. It could be that stress causes depression—as we hypothesized—but a correlation does not rule out the possibility that depression causes stress, or that some other variable may cause both stress and depression (like poverty, for example). The latter situation is called the **third variable problem**—the possibility that variables not measured in a study are the real cause of the relationship between the variables that are measured. For example, perhaps some people with difficult temperaments both are prone to depression and generate stressful experiences in their lives by being difficult to live with. If we measured only stress and depression, we might observe a relationship between them because they co-occur within the same individuals. But this relationship actually would be due to the common relationship of stress and depression to temperament.

Selecting a Sample

A critical choice in a correlational study is the choice of the sample. A **sample** is a group of people taken from the population we want to study.

Representativeness

A *representative sample* is a sample that is highly similar to the population of interest in terms of sex, ethnicity, age, and other important variables. If a sample is not representative—for example, if there are fewer women or people of color in our sample than in the general population of interest—then the sample is said to have *bias*. If our sample represents only a small or unusual group of people, then we cannot generalize the results of our study to the larger population. For example, if all the people in our study are white, middle-class females, we cannot know whether our results generalize to males, people of color, or people in other socioeconomic classes.

An effective way to obtain a representative sample of a population is to generate a random sample of that population. For example, some studies have obtained random samples of the entire U.S. population by randomly dialing phone numbers throughout the country and then recruiting into the study the people who answer the phone. Often, researchers can settle for random samples of smaller populations, such as particular cities. When a sample is truly random, the chances are high that it will be similar to the population of interest in terms of ethnicity, sex, age, and all the other important variables in the study.

Selection of a Comparison Group

A group comparison study compares the experiences of one group with those of another group. For example, we may be interested in the depression levels of students who are athletes and students who are not athletes. We might begin by recruiting our sample of student athletes, attempting to make this sample as representative as possible of student athletes at our university.

Our comparison group of nonathletes should match our group of athletes on any variable (other than stress) that might influence levels of depression. If the two groups are not as similar as possible, then any differences in their levels of depression could be attributable to other variables. For example, women generally are more likely to be depressed than men. If we had more women in our athlete group than in our nonathlete group, then higher levels of depression in the athlete group might be attributable to a third variable—the fact that there are more women in that group—rather than to the effects of participation in athletics. For this reason, our athlete and nonathlete groups should be alike on all third variables that might influence our dependent variable, depression.

Evaluating Correlational Studies

Correlational studies have provided much important information for abnormal psychology. One major advantage of correlational studies is that many of them focus on situations occurring in the real world, rather than those manipulated in a laboratory. This gives them relatively good **external validity,** the extent to which a study's results can be generalized to real-life phenomena. The results of these studies may be generalizable to wider populations and to people's actual life experiences.

Longitudinal correlational studies have several advantages over cross-sectional correlational studies. In longitudinal correlational studies, researchers can determine whether there are differences between the groups before the event of interest occurs. If there are no differences before the event but significant differences after the event, then researchers can have more confidence that it was the event that actually led to the differences between the groups. Longitudinal designs also allow researchers to follow groups long enough to assess both short-term and long-term reactions to the event.

Longitudinal studies can be time-consuming and expensive to run. The chapter "Schizophrenia Spectrum and Other Psychotic Disorders" reports studies in which children at high risk for schizophrenia were studied from their preschool years to their early adult years to determine what characteristics could predict who would develop schizophrenia and who would not (Erlenmyer-Kimling, Rock, Squires-Wheeler, & Roberts, 1991). Some of these studies have been going on for more than 25 years and have cost millions of dollars. They are producing extremely valuable data, but at a high cost in both researchers' time and research dollars.

The greatest disadvantage of all correlational studies is that they cannot indicate what is a cause and what is a consequence. For example, many stressful events that depressed people report may be the consequences of their depression rather than the causes (Hammen, 2018). The symptoms of depression can cause stress by impairing interpersonal skills, interfering with concentration on the job, and causing insomnia. The same problem exists for studies of many types of psychopathology. For example, the symptoms of schizophrenia can disrupt social relationships, alcohol abuse can lead to unemployment, and so on. A correlational study linking the two variables would not be sufficient evidence to conclude that disrupted social relationships *cause* schizophrenia, or that unemployment leads to substance abuse, because either direction is possible.

Finally, all correlational studies suffer from the third variable problem. Researchers seldom can measure all possible influences on participants' levels of depression or other psychopathologies. Third variable problems are one of the major reasons why researchers turn to experimental studies.

A study of depression in student athletes might need to include a comparison group of students who are not athletes. ©Greg Nelson/Sports Illustrated/Getty Images

EPIDEMIOLOGICAL STUDIES

Epidemiology is the study of the frequency and distribution of a disorder, or a group of disorders, in a population. An epidemiological study asks how many people in a population have the disorder and how this number varies across important groups within the population, such as men and women or people with high and low incomes.

Epidemiological research focuses on three types of data. First, research may focus on the **prevalence** of a disorder, or the proportion of the population that has the disorder at a given point or period in time. For example, a study might report the lifetime prevalence of a disorder, or the number of people who will have the disorder at some time in their life. The 12-month prevalence of a disorder would be the proportion of the population who will be diagnosed with the disorder in any 12-month period.

Table 1 shows the lifetime and 12-month prevalence of one of the more severe forms of depression—major depressive disorder—from a nationwide epidemiological study conducted in the United States (Kessler et al., 2003). Not surprisingly, the proportion of the population who will be diagnosed with major depressive disorder at some time in their life is larger than the proportion who will be diagnosed with the disorder in any 12-month period.

Table 1 illustrates the fact, mentioned earlier, that the prevalence of major depression is greater for women than for men. As we discuss in the chapter "Mood Disorders and Suicide," this fact, revealed by many epidemiological studies, has been an important focus of research into depression.

TABLE 1 Lifetime and 12-Month Prevalence of Major Depressive Disorder

	Lifetime Prevalence (%)	12-Month Prevalence (%)
Males	13.2	4.9
Females	20.2	8.6
Total	16.9	6.8

Source: Adapted from Kessler et al., 2003.

Second, epidemiological research seeks to determine the **incidence** of a disorder, or the number of new cases of the disorder that develop during a specified period of time. The 1-year incidence of a disorder is the number of people who develop the disorder during a 1-year period.

Third, epidemiological research is concerned with the **risk factors** for a disorder—those conditions or variables that are associated with a higher risk of having the disorder. If women are more likely than men to have a disorder, then being a woman is a risk factor for the disorder. In terms of our interest in the relationship between stress and depression, an epidemiological study might show that people who live in high-stress areas of a city are more likely to have depression than people who live in low-stress areas of the city.

How do researchers determine the prevalence, incidence, and risk factors for a disorder? Epidemiological researchers first identify the population of interest and next identify a random sample of that population, for example, by randomly phoning residential telephone numbers. They then use structured clinical interviews that ask specific questions of participants to assess whether they have the symptoms that make up the disorder and the risk factors, such as gender or socioeconomic status, being studied. (Recall our discussion of structured clinical interviews in the chapter "Assessing and Diagnosing Abnormality.") From these data, epidemiologists estimate how many people in different categories of risk factors have the disorder.

Evaluating Epidemiological Studies

Epidemiological studies have provided valuable information on the prevalence, incidence, and risk factors for disorders, and we discuss evidence gathered from some major nationwide and international epidemiological studies throughout this book. This research can give us important clues as to who is at highest risk for a disorder. In turn, we can use this information to test hypotheses about why those people are at higher risk.

Epidemiological studies are affected by many of the same limitations as correlational studies. First and foremost, they cannot establish that any risk factor causes a disorder. While a study may show that people living in higher-stress neighborhoods are more likely to have a disorder, this does not mean that the high-stress environment caused the disorder. Also, as in correlational studies, third variables may explain the relationship between any risk factor and the rates of a disorder.

EXPERIMENTAL STUDIES

The hallmark of **experimental studies** is control. Researchers attempt to control the independent variable and any potentially problematic third variables rather than simply observing them as they occur naturally. There are various types of experimental studies we could do to investigate whether stress leads to depression. We will examine four types in particular.

Human Laboratory Studies

To test our hypothesis that stress leads to depression, we could expose participants to a stressor in the laboratory and then determine whether it causes an increase in depressed mood. This method is known as a **human laboratory study.**

Several studies of this type have been done (see Peterson & Seligman, 1984). The stressor that is often used in this type of study is an unsolvable task or puzzle, such as an unsolvable anagram. In this case, our index of stress is participants' exposure to unsolvable anagrams. Because we are manipulating stress, not simply measuring it, we have the advantage of knowing precisely what type of stress participants are exposed to and when. We cannot create in the laboratory many of the types of stress that may cause depression in the real world, such as the destruction of a person's home in a hurricane or continual physical abuse. Instead, we create analogues—situations that capture some key characteristics of these real-world events, such as their uncontrollability and unpredictability.

Internal Validity

We want to ensure that our experiment has **internal validity,** meaning that changes in the dependent variable can confidently be attributed to our manipulation of the independent variable and not to other factors. For example, people who participate in our experiment using anagrams might become more depressed over the course of the experiment simply because participating in an experiment is a difficult experience, not because the anagrams are unsolvable. This threat to internal validity is basically the same type of third variable problem encountered in correlational and epidemiological studies.

To control third variables, researchers create a **control group** or control condition, in which participants have all the same experiences as the group of main interest in the study except that they do not receive the key manipulation—in our example, the stressor of the unsolvable puzzles. The control group for our study could be given similar but solvable anagrams. Thus, the control group's experience would be identical to that of the other group—the **experimental**

group or experimental condition—except for receiving the unsolvable puzzles.

Another threat to internal validity can arise if the participants in the experimental group (the group given the unsolvable anagrams) and in the control group (the group given the solvable anagrams) differ in important ways before beginning the experiment. If such differences exist, we cannot be sure that our manipulation is the cause of any changes in the dependent variable. Internal validity requires **random assignment,** which means that each participant must have an equal chance of being in the experimental group or the control group. Often, a researcher will use a table of random numbers to assign participants to groups.

Yet another threat to internal validity is the presence of **demand characteristics**—situations that cause participants to guess the purpose of the study and thus change their behavior. For example, if our measure of depression is too obvious, participants might guess what hypothesis we are testing and respond differently, consciously or unconsciously. To avoid the presence of demand characteristics, we could use subtler measures of depression embedded in other tests—often called *filler measures*—to obscure the real purpose of our study. Researchers also often use *cover stories,* telling participants a false story to prevent them from guessing the true purpose of the experiment. After the study, participants should be debriefed about the deception they were exposed to in the study, as well as its true purpose.

Researchers may give participants an unsolvable puzzle in order to observe the effects of stress on mental health.
©Gary He/McGraw-Hill Education

Participants' behavior in the study can be affected if they know what group they are in ahead of time. Similarly, if experimenters know what condition a participant is in, they might inadvertently behave in ways that affect how the participant responds to the manipulations. In order to reduce these demand characteristics, both the participants and the experimenters who interact with them should be unaware of whether participants are in the experimental condition or the control condition. This situation is referred to as a **double-blind experiment.**

We have instituted a number of safeguards to ensure internal validity in our study: Participants have been randomly selected and assigned, and our participants and experimenters are unaware of which condition participants are in. Now we can conduct the study. When our data are collected and analyzed, we find that, as we predicted, participants given the unsolvable anagrams showed greater increases in depressed mood than did participants given the solvable anagrams.

What can we conclude about our idea of depression, based on this study? Our experimental controls have helped us rule out third variable explanations, so we can be relatively confident that it was the experience of the uncontrollable stressor that led to the increases in depression in the experimental group. Thus, we can say that our study supports our hypothesis that people exposed to uncontrollable stress will show more depressed mood than will people not exposed to such stress.

Evaluating Human Laboratory Studies

The primary advantage of human laboratory studies is control. Researchers have more control over third variables, the independent variable, and the dependent variable in these studies than they do in any other type of study they can do with humans.

Yet human laboratory studies also have their limitations. Because we cannot know if our results generalize to what happens outside the laboratory, their external validity can be low. Is being exposed to unsolvable anagrams anything like being exposed to major, real-world uncontrollable stressors, such as the death of a loved one? Clearly, the severity of the two types of experiences differs, but is this the only important difference? Similarly, do the increases in depressed mood in the participants in our study, which probably were small, tell us anything about why some people develop extremely severe, debilitating episodes of depression? Experimental studies such as this have been criticized for their lack of generalizability to major psychopathologies that occurs in real life, as opposed to what we can capture in the laboratory.

Apart from posing problems of generalizability, human laboratory studies sometimes pose serious ethical concerns. Is it ethical to deliberately induce distress, even mild distress, in people? Different people will give different answers to this question.

Therapy Outcome Studies

Therapy outcome studies are experimental studies designed to test whether a specific therapy—a psychological therapy or a biological therapy—reduces psychopathology in individuals who receive it. Because therapies target supposed causes of psychopathology, therapy outcome studies can produce evidence that reducing these causes reduces psychopathology, which in turn supports the hypothesis that these factors played a role in creating the psychopathology in the first place.

Control Groups

Sometimes, people simply get better with time. Thus, to see whether our participants' improvement actually has anything to do with our therapy, we need to compare the experiences of people who receive our experimental therapy with those of a control group made up of people who do not receive the therapy. Sometimes, researchers use a **simple control group** consisting of participants who do not receive the experimental therapy but are tracked for the same period of time as the participants who do receive the therapy.

A variation on this simple control group is the **wait list control group.** The participants in this type of group do not receive the therapy when the experimental group does but instead are put on a wait list to receive the intervention at a later date, when the study is completed. Both groups of participants are assessed at the beginning and end of the study, but only the experimental group receives the therapy as part of the study.

Another type of control group, the **placebo control group,** is used most often in studies of the effectiveness of drugs. The participants in this group have the same interactions with experimenters as the participants in the experimental group, but they take pills that are placebos (inactive substances) rather than the drug being studied. In psychotherapy studies, the placebo control group might receive an "inactive" treatment, such as a weekly check-in that does not include the therapy. Usually, to prevent demand effects, both the participants and the experimenters in these studies are unaware of which group the participants are in; thus, this type of experiment is double-blind.

Evaluating Therapy Outcome Research

Although therapy outcome studies might seem the most ethical way of conducting research on people in distress, they have their own methodological challenges and ethical issues. Most psychological therapies involve a package of techniques for responding to people's problems. For example, depressed people in an experimental therapy group might be taught assertiveness skills, social problem-solving skills, and skills in changing self-defeating thinking. Which of these skills was most responsible for alleviating their depression? Even when a therapy works, researchers often cannot know exactly what it is about the therapy that works.

Photo of group therapy with diverse participants. ©*Wavebreak Media Ltd/123RF*

Ethical problems arise in using all three types of control groups—simple control groups, wait list control groups, and placebo control groups—in therapy outcome research. Some researchers believe it is unethical to withhold treatment or to provide a treatment believed to be ineffective for people in distress. For example, many depressed participants assigned to a control group may be in severe distress or in danger of harming themselves and therefore may need immediate treatment.

In response to this concern, many therapy outcome studies now compare the effectiveness of two or more therapies expected to have positive effects. These studies basically are a competition between rival therapies and the theories behind them. The idea is that all the participants in such studies benefit, while at the same time researchers gain useful information about the most effective type of therapy for the pathology. Regardless of which type of control or comparison group experimenters use in a therapy outcome study, participants must be informed of the types of groups the study involves and of the fact that they will be randomly assigned to one group or another (and thus run the risk of not receiving useful treatment as part of the study).

Another ethical issue concerns the obligation of the therapist to respond to the needs of the patient. How much can a therapy be modified to respond to a specific participant's needs without compromising the scientific integrity of the study? Therapists may feel the need to vary the dosage of a drug or to deviate from a study's procedure for psychological intervention. Departing too much from the standard therapy, however, will lead to significant variation in the therapy received by participants in the intervention, which could compromise the results of the study.

A related methodological issue has to do with generalizing results from therapy outcome studies to the real world. In these studies, the therapeutic intervention usually is delivered to patients in a controlled, high-quality atmosphere by the most competent therapists. Patients usually are screened so that they fit a narrow set of criteria for being included in the study, and often only patients who stick with the therapy to its end are included in the final analyses.

In the real world, mental health services are not always delivered in controlled, high-quality atmospheres by the most competent therapists. Patients are who they are, and their complicated symptom presentations and lives may not fit neatly into the criteria for an "optimal patient." Also, patients often leave and return to therapy and may not receive a full trial of the therapy before dropping out for financial or personal reasons.

Therapy outcome research that tests how well a therapy works in highly controlled settings with a narrowly defined group of people is said to test the **efficacy** of a therapy. In contrast, therapy outcome research that tests how well a therapy works in real-world settings, with all the complications mentioned, is said to test the **effectiveness** of a therapy.

Single-Case Experimental Designs

Another type of experimental study is the **single-case experimental design,** in which a single individual or a small number of individuals are studied intensively. Unlike the case studies discussed earlier, a single-case experimental design exposes the individual to some manipulation or intervention, and his or her behavior is examined before and after the intervention to determine the effects. In addition, in a single-case experimental design, the participant's behaviors are measured repeatedly over time through some standard method, whereas a case study often is based on the researcher's impressions of the participant and the factors affecting his or her behaviors, thoughts, and emotions.

ABAB Design

A specific type of single-case experimental design is the **ABAB design,** or **reversal design,** in which an intervention is introduced, withdrawn, and then reinstated and the behavior of the participant is examined both on and off the treatment. For example, in the study of the effects of a drug for depression, an individual depressed participant might be assessed for her level of depression each day for 4 weeks. This is the baseline assessment (A; Figure 2). Then the participant would be given the drug for 4 weeks (B), and her level

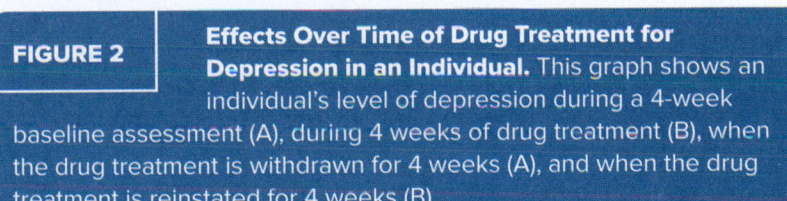

FIGURE 2 **Effects Over Time of Drug Treatment for Depression in an Individual.** This graph shows an individual's level of depression during a 4-week baseline assessment (A), during 4 weeks of drug treatment (B), when the drug treatment is withdrawn for 4 weeks (A), and when the drug treatment is reinstated for 4 weeks (B).

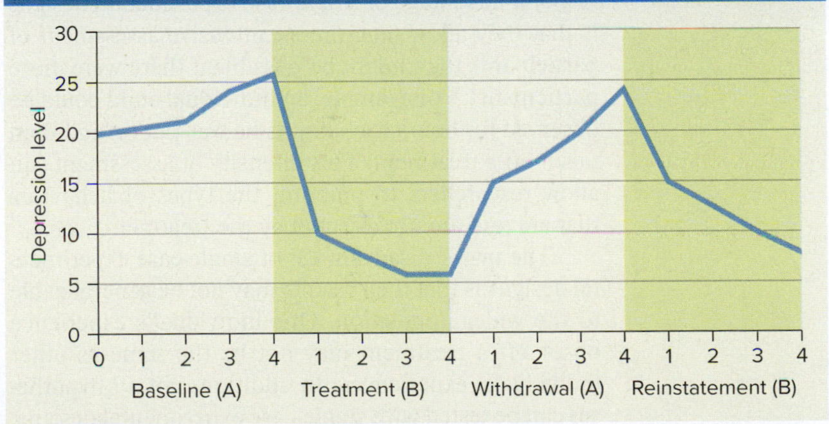

of depression would be assessed each day during that period. The drug then would be withdrawn for 4 weeks (A), and, again, her level of depression would be assessed each day. Finally, the drug would be reinstated for 4 weeks (B) and her level of depression assessed each day during that period. If the participant's levels of depression followed the pattern seen in Figure 2, this result would suggest that her depression level was much lower when she was taking the drug (B) than when she was not taking the drug (A).

Multiple Baseline Designs

In a **multiple baseline design,** an intervention might be given to the same individual but in different settings, or to different individuals at different points in time. To test whether a meditation exercise reduces depression, a researcher might teach a depressed person how to use the exercise while at work when she feels depressed. If the participant's depression decreased at work but not at home, where she did not use the meditation exercise, the researcher has some evidence that the exercise was responsible for the reduction in depression. If the participant were then told to use the meditation exercise at home and her depression decreased in this setting also, this would be further evidence of the exercise's utility.

Similarly, the researcher might teach the meditation exercise to multiple individuals, but at different points in time when their experiences are likely to be different. For example, the researcher might teach the meditation exercise to one depressed college student during the first week of classes, to another student during spring break, and to still another during exam week. If all the students experienced relief of their depression symptoms after learning the meditation exercise, despite their different levels of stress, this would be evidence that the effects of the meditation exercise were generalizable across individuals and settings.

Evaluating Single-Case Experimental Designs

A major advantage of single-case experimental designs is that they allow much more intensive assessment of participants than might be possible if there were more participants. For example, an individual child could be observed for hours each day as he was put on and then taken off a treatment. This intensity of assessment can allow researchers to pinpoint the types of behaviors that are and are not affected by the treatment.

The major disadvantage of single-case experimental designs is that their results may not be generalizable to the wider population. One individual's experience on or off a treatment may not be the same as other individuals' experiences. In addition, not all hypotheses can be tested with single-case experimental designs. Some treatments have lingering effects after they end. For example, if a person is taught new skills for coping with stress during the treatment, these skills will continue to be present even after the treatment is withdrawn.

Animal Studies

Researchers sometimes try to avoid the ethical issues involved in experimental studies with humans by conducting the studies with animals. Animal research has its own set of ethical issues, but many researchers feel it is acceptable to expose animals to situations in the laboratory that it would not be ethical to impose on humans. **Animal studies** thus provide researchers with even more control over laboratory conditions and third variables than is possible in human laboratory studies.

In a well-known series of animal studies designed to investigate depression (discussed in the chapter "Mood Disorders and Suicide"), Martin Seligman, Bruce Overmier, Steven Maier, and their colleagues subjected dogs to an uncontrollable stressor in the laboratory (Overmier & Seligman, 1967; Seligman & Maier, 1967). The experimental group of dogs received a series of uncontrollable electric shocks. Let us call this Group E, for experimental.

In addition, there were two control groups. One control group of dogs received shocks but could control them by jumping over a barrier (Figure 3). Let us call this Group J, for jump. The dogs in Groups E and J received the same number and duration of shocks. The only difference between the groups was that the dogs in Group E could not control the shocks, whereas the dogs in Group J could. The second control group of dogs received no shock. Let us call this Group N, for none.

Dogs in Group E initially responded to the shocks by jumping around their cages. Soon, however, the majority became passive. Later, when the researchers provided the dogs with an opportunity to escape the shock by jumping over a barrier, these dogs did not learn to do so. It seemed that they had learned they could not control the shock, so they did not recognize opportunities for control when offered. The researchers labeled this set of behaviors *learned helplessness deficits.*

The dogs in the controllable shock group, Group J, learned to control the shock and did not develop learned helplessness deficits. The fact that the two groups of dogs experienced the same number and duration of shocks suggests that lack of control, not the shocks alone, led to the learned helplessness deficits in the experimental group. The dogs in Group N, which received no shocks, also did not develop learned helplessness deficits.

Seligman and colleagues likened the learned helplessness deficits shown by their dogs to the symptoms

FIGURE 3 **Shuttle Box for Learned Helplessness Experiments.** Researchers used an apparatus like this to deliver controllable or uncontrollable shocks to dogs in order to investigate the phenomenon of learned helplessness.

of depression in humans: apathy, low initiation of behavior, and the inability to see opportunities to improve one's environment (see Seligman, 1975). They argued that many human depressions result from people learning that they have no control over important outcomes in their lives. This learned helplessness theory of depression seems helpful in explaining the depression and passivity seen in chronically oppressed groups, such as battered spouses and some people who grow up in poverty.

Another type of animal study is similar to therapy outcome studies. In studies of the effectiveness of drugs, animals often are given the drugs to determine their effects on different bodily systems and behaviors. Sometimes the animals are killed after receiving the drugs, to enable detailed physiological analyses of their effects. Obviously, such studies could not be done with humans. Animal studies of drugs are particularly useful in the early stages of research, when the possible side effects of the drugs are unknown.

Evaluating Animal Studies

There clearly are problems with animal studies. First, some people believe it is no more ethical to conduct painful, dangerous, or fatal experiments with animals than it is to do so with humans. Second, from a scientific vantage point, we must ask whether we can generalize the results of experiments with animals to humans. Are learned helplessness deficits in dogs really analogous to human depression? The debate over the ethical and scientific issues of animal research continues. Particularly with regard to research on drug effectiveness, however, animal research may be crucial to the advancement of our knowledge of how to help people overcome psychopathology.

GENETIC STUDIES

Identifying genetic factors associated with psychopathology involves a variety of research methods. Researchers investigate the degree to which genes play a role in a particular disorder, or its heritability, through three types of genetic studies: family history studies, twin studies, and adoption studies. To investigate specific genes that may be involved in a disorder, they may use molecular genetic studies (also called association studies) or linkage analyses.

Family History Studies

Disorders that are genetically transmitted should, on average, show up more often in families of people who have the disorder than they do in families of people who do not have the disorder. This is true whether the disorder is associated with one or with many genes. To conduct a **family history study,** scientists first identify people who clearly have the disorder in question. This group is called the *probands.* The researchers also identify a control group of people who clearly do not have the disorder. They then trace the family pedigrees, or family trees, of individuals in these two groups and determine how many of their relatives have the disorder. Researchers are most interested in first-degree relatives, such as full siblings, parents, or children, because these relatives are most genetically similar to the subjects (unless they have an identical twin, who will be genetically identical to them).

Figure 4 illustrates the degree of genetic relationship between an individual and various categories of relatives. This figure gives you an idea of why the risk of inheriting the genes for a disorder quickly decreases as the relationship between an individual and the relative with the disorder becomes more distant: The percentage of genes the individual and the relative with the disorder have in common decreases greatly with distance.

Although family history studies provide very useful information about the possible genetic transmission of a disorder, they have their problems. The most obvious is that families share not only genes but also environment. Several members of a family might have a disorder because they share the same environmental

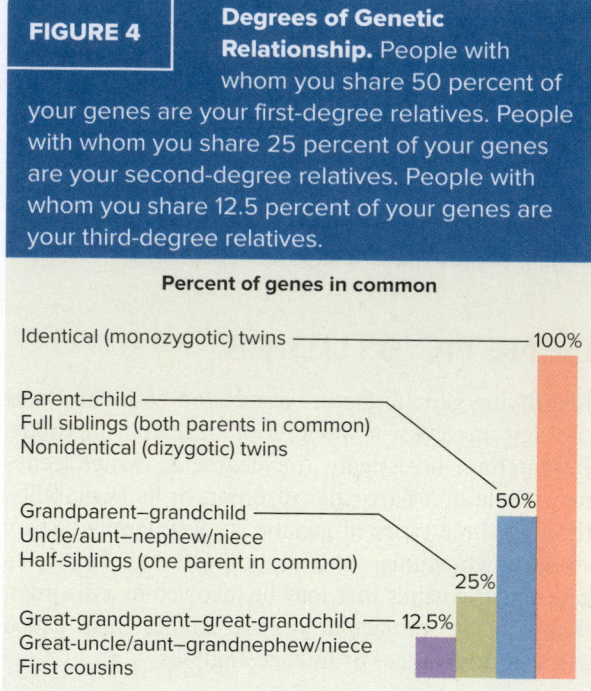

FIGURE 4 **Degrees of Genetic Relationship.** People with whom you share 50 percent of your genes are your first-degree relatives. People with whom you share 25 percent of your genes are your second-degree relatives. People with whom you share 12.5 percent of your genes are your third-degree relatives.

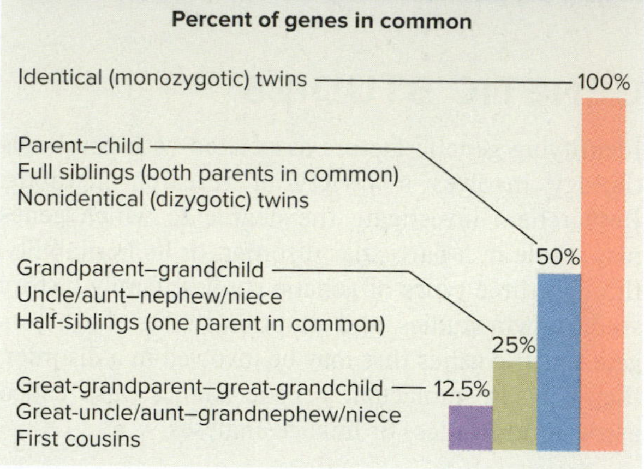

stresses. Family history studies cannot tease apart the genetic and environmental contributions to a disorder. Researchers often turn to twin studies to do this.

Twin Studies

Notice in Figure 4 that identical twins, or **monozygotic (MZ) twins**, share 100 percent of their genes. This is because they come from a single fertilized egg, which splits into two identical parts. In contrast, nonidentical twins, or **dizygotic (DZ) twins**, share, on average, 50 percent of their genes because they come from two separate eggs fertilized by separate sperm, just as non-twin siblings do.

Researchers have capitalized on this difference between MZ and DZ twins to conduct **twin studies** on the contribution of genetics to many disorders. If a disorder is determined entirely by genetics, then when one member of a monozygotic (MZ) twin pair has a disorder, the other member of the pair should always have the disorder. This probability that both twins will have the disorder if one twin has it is called the **concordance rate** for the disorder. Thus, if a disorder is entirely determined by genes, the concordance rate among MZ twins should be close to 100 percent. The concordance rate for the disorder among dizygotic (DZ) twins will be much lower than 100 percent. Even when a disorder is transmitted only partially by genes, the concordance rate for MZ twins should be considerably higher than the concordance rate for DZ twins, because MZ twins are genetically identical while DZ twins share only about half their genes.

For example, suppose the concordance rate for Disorder X for MZ twins is 48 percent, whereas the concordance rate for DZ twins is 17 percent. These concordance rates tell us two things. First, because the concordance rate for MZ twins is considerably higher than that for DZ twins, we have evidence that Disorder X is genetically transmitted. Second, because the concordance rate for MZ twins is well under 100 percent, we have evidence that a combination of a genetic predisposition and other factors (biological or environmental) causes an individual to develop Disorder X.

Twin studies do not fully separate genetic and environmental factors, because MZ twins may have more similar environments and experiences than do DZ twins. For example, MZ twins typically look alike, whereas DZ twins often do not, and physical appearance can affect other people's reactions to an individual. MZ twins also may be more likely than DZ twins to share talents that influence their opportunities. For instance, MZ twins may both be athletic or talented academically or musically, which can affect their treatment by others and their opportunities in life. Finally, parents may simply treat MZ twins more similarly than they do DZ twins. To address these problems, researchers have turned to a third method for studying heritability, the adoption study.

Adoption Studies

An **adoption study** can be carried out in a number of ways, but they all take advantage of the fact that adopted individuals share genes with biological parents who did not raise them, and do not share genes with the adoptive parents who did raise them. This allows researchers to separate the role of genetics and environment. Most commonly, researchers first identify people who have the disorder of interest who were adopted shortly after birth. They then determine the rates of the disorder in the biological relatives of these adoptees and in the adoptive relatives of the adoptees. If a disorder is strongly influenced by genetics, researchers should see higher rates of the disorder among the biological relatives of the adoptee than among the adoptive relatives. If the disorder is strongly influenced by environment, they should see higher rates of the disorder among the adoptive relatives than among the biological relatives.

Molecular Genetic Studies and Linkage Analyses

The technology for examining human genes has advanced rapidly in recent decades, allowing researchers to search for associations between specific genetic abnormalities (also referred to as genetic markers) and psychopathology in what are called **molecular genetic studies** or **association studies.** A typical study might compare a group of people who have been diagnosed with a particular disorder, such as depression, with people who have no form of psychopathology. DNA from individuals in both groups is obtained either through blood samples or by swabbing the inside of the individuals' cheeks to obtain a small amount of tissue. This DNA is then analyzed (genotyped) to determine whether each individual has a genetic characteristic or marker of interest.

Because the human genome is so vast, researchers may try to narrow down the location of the gene marker associated with a psychological disorder by looking for other characteristics that co-occur with the disorder and have known genetic markers, a process called **linkage analysis.** For example, in the study of mood disorders among the Amish described in the Extraordinary People segment at the beginning of this chapter, researchers found that two markers on chromosome 11, one for insulin and one for a known cancer gene, were linked to the presence of mood disorder in one large family (Biron et al., 1987). This suggests that a gene that plays a role in vulnerability to mood disorders may be on chromosome 11. Unfortunately, this linkage has not been replicated in other studies. In the chapter "Schizophrenia Spectrum and Other Psychotic Disorders," we discuss genetic linkage studies that have identified possible genetic markers for schizophrenia.

CROSS-CULTURAL RESEARCH

Not long ago, most psychological research was conducted with college students, most of whom were white and middle- or upper-class. Researchers believed that any results they obtained from these samples could be generalized to any other relevant sample. Only anthropologists and a handful of psychologists and psychiatrists argued that what is true of one ethnic group, culture, or gender is not necessarily true of others.

In the past few decades, however, there has been an explosion of cross-cultural research in abnormal psychology. Researchers are investigating the similarities and differences across culture in the nature, causes, and treatment of psychopathology. These cross-cultural researchers face several special challenges.

First, researchers must be careful in applying theories or concepts that were developed in studies of one culture to another culture (Rogler, 1989). Because the manifestations of disorders can differ across cultures, researchers who insist on narrow definitions of disorders may fail to identify people manifesting disorders in culturally defined ways. Similarly, theoretical variables can have different meanings or manifestations in different cultures.

A good example is the variable known as *expressed emotion.* Families high in expressed emotion are highly critical of and hostile toward other family members and emotionally overinvolved with one another. Several studies of the majority cultures in America and Europe have shown that people with schizophrenia whose families are high in expressed emotion have higher rates of relapse than those whose families are low in expressed emotion (Hooley, 2007). The meaning and manifestation of expressed emotion can differ greatly across cultures, however:

> Criticism within Anglo-American family settings, for example, may focus on allegations of faulty personality traits (e.g., laziness) or psychotic symptom behaviors (e.g., strange ideas). However, in other societies, such as those of Latin America, the same behaviors may not be met with criticism. Among Mexican-descent families, for example, criticism tends to focus on disrespectful or disruptive behaviors that affect the family but not on psychotic symptom behavior and individual personality characteristics. Thus, culture plays a role in creating the content or targets of criticism. Perhaps most importantly, culture is influential in determining whether criticism is a prominent part of the familial emotional atmosphere. (Jenkins & Karno, 1992, p. 10)

Today's researchers are more careful to search for culturally specific manifestations of the characteristics of interest in their studies and for the possibility that the characteristics or variables that predict psychopathology in one culture may be irrelevant in other cultures.

Second, even if researchers believe they can apply their theories across cultures, they may have difficulty translating their questionnaires or other assessment tools into different languages. A key concept in English, for example, may not be precisely translated into another language. Many languages contain variations of pronouns and verbs whose usage is determined by the social relationship between the speaker and the person being addressed. For example, in Spanish, the second-person pronoun *usted* ("you") connotes respect, establishes an appropriate distance in a social relationship, and is the correct way for a young interviewer to address an older respondent (Rogler, 1989). In contrast, when a young interviewer addresses a young respondent, the relationship is more informal, and the appropriate form of address is *tú* (also "you"). An interviewer who violates the social norms implicit in a language can alienate a respondent and impair the research.

Third, there may be cultural or gender differences in people's responses to the social demands of interacting with researchers. For example, people of Mexican origin, older people, and people in a lower socioeconomic class are more likely to answer yes to researchers' questions, regardless of the content, and also to attempt to answer questions in socially desirable ways than are Anglo-Americans, younger people, and people in a higher socioeconomic class. These differences appear to result from differences among groups in their deference to authority figures and concern over presenting a proper appearance (Ross & Mirowsky, 1984). Similarly, it is often believed that men are less likely than women to admit to "weaknesses," such as symptoms of distress or problems coping. If researchers do not take biases into account when they design assessment tools and analyze data, erroneous conclusions can result.

META-ANALYSIS

Often the research literature contains many studies that have investigated a particular idea (e.g., that stress leads to depression). An investigator may want to know what the overall trend across all studies is–in other words, what the evidence suggests is true when you put it all together. He or she may also want to know what factors might account for some studies supporting their hypothesis and others not. To do this, a researcher could just read over all the studies and draw conclusions about whether most of them support or do not support the hypothesis. However, these conclusions can be biased by the reader's interpretations of the studies.

A more objective way to draw conclusions about a body of research is to conduct a **meta-analysis,** a statistical technique for summarizing results across several studies. The first step in a meta-analysis is to do a thorough literature search, usually by searching scholarly databases using key words (like "depression" and "stress"). Because studies use different methods and measures for testing a hypothesis, the second step of a meta-analysis is to transform the results of each study into a statistic that then allows results to be compared across studies. You can think of this as translating the results of each separate study into a single language, so that they all make sense with respect to one another. This statistic, called the *effect size,* indicates how big the differences are between two groups (such as a group that received a specific form of therapy and one that did not) or how strong the relationship is between two continuous variables (such as the correlation between levels of stress and levels of depression). Researchers can then examine the average effect size across studies to make a conclusion about what the research literature has to say across multiple studies. They can also relate the effect size to characteristics of the study, such as the year it was published, the type of measure used, or the age or gender of the participants, to see whether those factors might play a role in differing results. For example, a meta-analysis of studies of children's depression levels found that studies done in more recent years tend to find lower levels of depression than studies done previously (Twenge & Nolen-Hoeksema, 2002). This finding raises the possibility that levels of depression among children may be decreasing.

Evaluating Meta-Analysis

Meta-analysis can overcome some of the problems resulting from small numbers of participants in an individual study because they pool the data from thousands of study participants, thereby providing more power to find significant effects. For example, the studies examined by Twenge and Nolen-Hoeksema (2002) generally had small numbers of ethnic minority children, making it difficult for each individual study to compare their depression scores with those of nonminority children. By pooling studies, however, the overall sample sizes of Hispanic and African American children were large enough to allow comparisons by race/ethnicity. The meta-analysis found that Hispanic children generally had higher depression scores than African American or white children. This is an example of a finding that meta-analyses can provide what single studies often cannot.

Meta-analyses have their problems, however. First, some published studies have methodological flaws. These flawed studies may be included in a meta-analysis along with methodologically stronger studies, influencing the overall results. Second, there is a *file drawer effect*–studies that do not support the hypothesis they are designed to test are less likely to get published than studies that do (and instead are "filed away," thus the name). For example, a study that finds that a psychotherapy is not any more effective than a wait list control is less likely to get published than a study that finds that the same psychotherapy is more effective than the wait list control. The bias toward publishing studies with positive results means that many perfectly good studies that fail to find the expected effects do not get published and therefore do not end up in meta-analyses. This file drawer effect biases the results of meta-analyses toward finding an overall positive effect of a treatment or of some other difference between groups.

CHAPTER INTEGRATION

We noted in the chapter "Theories and Treatment of Abnormality" that theories or models of psychopathology are increasingly based on the integration of concepts from biological, psychological, and social approaches. These concepts often are viewed from a vulnerability-stress perspective. The characteristics that make a person more vulnerable to abnormality might include biological characteristics, such as a genetic predisposition, or psychological characteristics, such as a maladaptive style of thinking about the world. These personal characteristics must interact with characteristics of the situation or environment to create the abnormality. For example, a woman with a genetic predisposition to depression may never develop the disorder in its full form if she has a supportive family and never faces major stressors.

Conducting research that reflects this integrationist perspective on abnormality is not easy. Researchers must gather information about people's biological, psychological, and social vulnerabilities and strengths. This work may require specialized equipment or expertise. It also may require following participants longitudinally to observe what happens when people with vulnerabilities face stressors that may trigger episodes of their disorder.

Increasingly, researchers work together in teams to share both their expertise in specialized research methods and their available resources, making multidisciplinary longitudinal research possible. Researchers also train in multiple disciplines and methods. For example, some psychologists use magnetic resonance imaging (MRI), positron-emission tomography (PET) scans, and other advanced biological methods in their investigations of abnormality.

A new and prominent movement in the area of abnormal psychology research, called the Research Domain Criteria (RDoC), encourages researches to integrate across such methods (Cuthbert & Insel, 2013). In addition to advocating the biopsychosocial approach, this initiative from the National Institute of Mental Health also directly reflects issues highlighted in the previous chapters, including increased emphasis on the continuum model of abnormality, the role of common mechanisms underlying multiple disorders, and the limitations of diagnostic categories (Clark, Cuthbert, Lewis-Fernández, Narrow, & Reed, 2017; Lilienfeld & Treadway, 2016).

If you pursue a career in researching abnormality, you might integrate methods from psychology (which have been the focus of this chapter), sociology, and biology to create the most comprehensive picture of the disorder you are investigating. This task may seem daunting, but an interactionist approach holds out the possibility of producing breakthroughs that can greatly improve the lives of people vulnerable to psychopathology.

SHADES OF GRAY DISCUSSION

Your greatest challenge in deciding the ethics of this particular study is that the study involves deception. Some ethics committees would never accept a study in which students were deceived about their results on an intelligence test. Other committees might approve this study if it ensured all or most of the basic rights discussed in the section "Ethical Issues in Research." Participants must be made aware that they may experience psychological distress as a result of participating. They must know that they may decline participation or withdraw at any point. Usually, these statements must appear in an informed consent document that individuals should read before deciding to participate. This document should also tell participants how confidential their responses in the study will be. In this case, there is no reason why participants' responses should not be confidential.

If the researcher told participants before the study began that the feedback they will receive is bogus, this clearly would affect participants' responses to the feedback. The researcher would argue that participants cannot be told in the informed consent document that the study involves deception. Your ethics committee then must decide whether the potential benefits of the information obtained in this study warrant the deception.

Following the study, the researcher should reveal the nature of the deception and the justification for using it. Many participants, especially college students, continue to believe negative feedback they receive in an experiment even after being told that they were deceived. The researchers who discovered this phenomenon recommended conducting a *process debriefing* (Ross, Lepper, & Hubbard, 1975). In such a debriefing, experimenters discuss at length the purposes and procedures of the experiment, explaining that the feedback was not a reflection of participants' abilities.

CHAPTER SUMMARY

- A hypothesis is a testable statement of what we predict will happen in a study.
- The dependent variable is the factor the study aims to predict. The independent variable is the factor used or manipulated to predict the dependent variable.
- A sample is a group taken from the population of interest to participate in the study. The sample for the study must be representative of the population of interest, and the research must be generalizable to the population of interest.

- A control group consists of people who are similar in most ways to the primary group of interest but who do not experience the variable the theory hypothesizes causes changes in the dependent variable. Matching the control group to the group of primary interest can help control third variables, which are variables unrelated to the theory that still may have some effect on the dependent variable.
- The basic rights of participants in studies include being told the risks of participation, having their information kept confidential, having the right to refuse participation or withdraw from the study, giving informed consent, not being exposed to deception unless it is well justified, and being debriefed following the study.
- Case studies of individuals provide detailed information about their subjects. They are helpful in generating new ideas and in studying rare problems. They suffer from problems in generalizability and in the subjectivity of both the person being studied and the person conducting the study.
- Correlational studies examine the relationship between two variables without manipulating the variables. A correlation coefficient is an index of the relationship between two variables. It can range from −1.00 to +1.00. The magnitude of the correlation indicates how strong the relationship between the variables is.
- A positive correlation indicates that as values of one variable increase, values of the other variable increase. A negative correlation indicates that as values of one variable increase, values of the other variable decrease.
- A result is said to be statistically significant if it is unlikely to have happened by chance. The convention in psychological research is to accept results for which there is a probability of less than 5 in 100 that they happened by chance.
- A correlational study can show that two variables are related, but it cannot show that one variable causes the other. All correlational studies have the third variable problem—the possibility that variables not measured in the study actually account for the relationship between the variables measured in the study.
- Continuous variable studies evaluate the relationship between two variables that vary along a continuum.
- A representative sample resembles the population of interest on all important variables. One way to generate a representative sample is to obtain a random sample.
- Whereas cross-sectional studies assess a sample at one point in time, longitudinal studies assess a sample at multiple points in time. A longitudinal study often assesses a sample that is expected to experience some key event in the future both before and after the event, then examines changes that occurred in the sample. Group comparison studies evaluate differences between key groups, such as a group that experienced a certain stressor and a matched comparison group that did not.
- Epidemiological studies look at the frequency and distribution of a disorder in a population. The prevalence of a disorder is the proportion of the population that has the disorder at a given point or period in time. The incidence of a disorder is the number of new cases of the disorder that develop during a specific period of time. Risk factors for a disorder are conditions or variables associated with a higher risk of having the disorder.
- Experimental studies can provide evidence that a given variable causes psychopathology. A human laboratory study has the goal of inducing the conditions that we hypothesize will lead to our outcome of interest (e.g., increasing stress to cause depression) in people in a controlled setting. Participants are randomly assigned to either the experimental group, which receives a manipulation, or a control group, which does not.
- Generalizing experimental studies to real-world phenomena sometimes is not possible. In addition, manipulating people who are in distress in an experimental study can create ethical problems.
- A therapy outcome study allows researchers to test a hypothesis about the causes of a psychopathology while providing a service to participants.
- In therapy outcome studies, researchers sometimes use wait list control groups, in which control participants wait to receive the interventions until after the studies are completed. Alternatively, researchers may try to construct placebo control groups, in which participants receive the general support of therapists but none of the elements of the therapy thought to be active. Both types of control groups have practical and ethical limitations.
- Difficult issues associated with therapy outcome studies include problems in knowing what elements of therapy were effective, questions about the appropriate control groups to use, questions about whether to allow modifications of the therapy to fit individual participants' needs, and the lack of generalizability of the results of these studies to the real world.
- Single-case experimental designs involve the intensive investigation of single individuals or small groups of individuals before and after a manipulation or intervention. In an ABAB, or reversal, design, an intervention is introduced, withdrawn, and then reinstated, and the behavior of a participant on and off the treatment is examined.
- In multiple baseline designs, an individual is given a treatment in different settings or multiple individuals are given a treatment at different times across different settings, and the effects of the treatment are systematically observed.

- Animal studies allow researchers to manipulate their subjects in ways that are not ethically permissible with human participants, although many people feel that such animal studies are equally unethical. Animal studies raise questions about their generalizability to humans.
- Genetic studies include a variety of research methods. Family history studies determine whether biological relatives of someone with a disorder are more likely to have it than are people not related to someone with the disorder. Adoption studies determine whether the biological family members of adoptees with a disorder are more likely to have the disorder than are the adoptive family members. Twin studies determine whether monozygotic twins are more alike in the presence or absence of a disorder than are dizygotic twins. Molecular genetic (or association) studies look for specific genes associated with a disorder. Linkage analyses investigate the relationship between a biological characteristic for which the genes are known and a psychological disorder for which they are not.
- Cross-cultural research poses challenges. Theories and concepts that make sense in one culture may not be applicable to other cultures. Questionnaires and other assessment tools must be translated accurately. Also, culture can affect how people respond to the social demands of research. Finally, researchers must be careful not to build into their research any assumptions that one culture is normal and another is deviant.
- Meta-analysis is a statistical technique for summarizing results across several studies. In a meta-analysis, the results of individual studies are standardized by use of a statistic called the effect size. Then the magnitude of the effect size and its relationship to characteristics of the study are examined.
- Meta-analyses reduce bias that can occur when investigators draw conclusions across studies in a more subjective manner, but they can include studies that have poor methods or exclude good studies that did not get published because they did not find significant effects.

KEY TERMS

scientific method
hypothesis
null hypothesis
variable
dependent variable
independent variable
operationalization
case studies
generalizability
correlational studies
continuous variable
group comparison study
cross-sectional
longitudinal
correlation coefficient
statistical significance
third variable problem
sample
external validity
epidemiology
prevalence
incidence
risk factors
experimental studies
human laboratory study
internal validity
control group
experimental group
random assignment
demand characteristics
double-blind experiment
therapy outcome studies
simple control group
wait list control group
placebo control group
efficacy
effectiveness
single-case experimental design
ABAB (reversal) design
multiple baseline design
animal studies
family history study
monozygotic (MZ) twins
dizygotic (DZ) twins
twin studies
concordance rate
adoption study
molecular genetic studies
association studies
linkage analysis
meta-analysis

Chapter 5

©Photographee.eu/Shutterstock

Trauma, Anxiety, Obsessive-Compulsive, and Related Disorders

CHAPTER OUTLINE

Fear and Anxiety Along the Continuum

Functional

- Fear is in response to **objectively threatening** events *(fearing you will fail a class after failing the midterm)*
- Fear is of **appropriate severity** given the threat *(being concerned because you need this class to graduate)*
- Fear **subsides when threat has passed** *(relaxing when you learn there was a grading error and you actually did well)*
- Fear leads to **adaptive behaviors** to confront or avoid threat *(asking your instructor if you can improve your grade with extra work)*

- Fear may be **somewhat unrealistic** *(fear of appearing foolish when giving a presentation in class)*
- Fear may be **somewhat more than is warranted** given the severity of the threat *(being unable to sleep the night before a presentation)*
- Fear **persists after the threat has passed** *(after you give the presentation, analyzing it and worrying about what people thought)*
- Fear **leads to behaviors that may be somewhat inappropriate** *(taking a tranquilizer before the presentation to relax)*

Potentially meets diagnostic criteria for an anxiety disorder:

- Fear is **moderately unrealistic** *(fearing a car accident if you drive on Friday the 13th)*
- Fear is **definitely more than is warranted** given the severity of the threat *(being very nervous when forced to drive on Friday the 13th)*
- Fear **persists for quite a while after the threat has passed** *(worrying about the next Friday the 13th)*
- Fear leads to **behaviors that are potentially dangerous or impairing** *(skipping class to avoid driving on Friday the 13th)*

Likely meets diagnostic criteria for an anxiety disorder:

- Fears are **completely unrealistic** *(fearing that every ache or pain is a sign of terminal illness)*
- Fears are **excessive** given the objective threat *(thinking one is dying when one feels pain)*
- Fears **persist long after the threat has passed,** and chronic anticipatory anxiety exists *(believing one has a terminal illness despite physician reassurance)*
- Fear **leads to dangerous behavior or impairment** *(seeking out surgery to cure the terminal illness your physician says you do not have)*

Dysfunctional

Think of a time when you felt fearful or anxious, perhaps on the first day of college. Chances are you felt a bit tense or jittery, you worried about what you might encounter, and there were times you wished you could just retreat back to familiar surroundings and people. This is a typical response to a new and potentially threatening situation—here the threat is that you might not like the people at your college, you might not feel you fit in, or you might not do well in your classes. Fear is adaptive when it is realistic (i.e., when there is a real threat in the environment), when it is in proportion to the threat, if it subsides when the threat has passed, and if it leads to appropriate behaviors to overcome the threat (e.g., making an effort to meet new people and become familiar with your new surroundings).

People vary greatly, however, in the situations they find threatening, in how fearful they become when they encounter a threat, and in how they behave in response to their fears. Fear can become maladaptive when it arises in situations that most people would not find threatening. For example, some people become incapacitated with fear if they have to leave their home. Fear is maladaptive if it is greatly out of proportion to the threat, for example, when people become panicked at the possibility of encountering a snake on a nature walk. Fear becomes **anxiety** when it persists long after the threat has subsided. For example, some people who have experienced traumatic events continue to be extremely fearful long after the trauma has ended. And fear can become an anxiety disorder when a person engages in maladaptive behaviors in response to a threat; for example, a person with agoraphobia may become housebound due to fear of venturing out.

Extraordinary People

David Beckham, *Perfection On and Off the Field*

©Photo Works/Shutterstock

Soccer star David Beckham's extraordinary ability to curve shots on corner kicks was immortalized in the movie *Bend It Like Beckham*. Beckham's perfectionism on the field is paralleled by his perfectionism about order and symmetry: "I've got this obsessive compulsive disorder where I have to have everything in a straight line or everything has to be in pairs" (quoted in Dolan, 2006). Beckham spends hours ordering the furniture in his house in a particular way or lining up the clothes in his closet by color. His wife, Victoria (the former Posh Spice), says, "If you open our fridge, it's all coordinated down either side. We've got three fridges—food in one, salad in another and drinks in the third. In the drinks one, everything is symmetrical. If there's three cans he'll throw away one because it has to be an even number" (quoted in Frith, 2006). Beckham has traveled around the world, playing for top teams including Real Madrid, Manchester United, Los Angeles Galaxy, and AC Milan. Each time he enters a new hotel room, he has to arrange everything in order: "I'll go into a hotel room. Before I can relax I have to move all the leaflets and all the books and put them in a drawer. Everything has to be perfect" (quoted in Frith, 2006). His teammates on Manchester United knew of his obsessions and compulsions and would deliberately rearrange his clothes or move the furniture around in his hotel room to infuriate him.

When we face any type of threat or stressor, our body mobilizes to handle it. Over evolutionary history, humans have developed a characteristic **fight-or-flight response,** a set of physical and psychological responses that help us fight a threat or flee from it. The physiological changes of the fight-or-flight response result from the activation of two systems controlled by the hypothalamus, as seen in Figure 1: the **autonomic nervous system** (in particular, the sympathetic division of this system) and the **adrenal-cortical system** (a hormone-releasing system; see the chapter "Theories and Treatment of Abnormality").

When we face a threat or stressor, the hypothalamus first activates the sympathetic division of the autonomic nervous system. This system acts directly on the smooth muscles and internal organs to produce key bodily changes: The liver releases extra sugar (glucose) to fuel the muscles, and the body's metabolism increases in preparation for expending energy on physical action. Heart rate, blood pressure, and breathing rate increase, and the muscles tense. Less essential activities, such as digestion, are curtailed. Saliva and mucus dry up, increasing the size of the air passages to the lungs. The body secretes endorphins, which are natural painkillers, and the surface blood vessels constrict to reduce bleeding in case of injury. The spleen releases more red blood cells to help carry oxygen.

In addition to the autonomic nervous system, the hypothalamus activates the adrenal-cortical system. It does this by releasing corticotropin-release factor (CRF), which signals the pituitary gland to secrete adrenocorticotropic hormone (ACTH), the body's major stress hormone. ACTH stimulates the outer layer of the adrenal glands (the adrenal cortex), releasing a group of hormones, the major one being **cortisol.** The amount of cortisol in blood or urine samples is often used as a measure of stress. ACTH also signals the adrenal glands to release about 30 other hormones, each of which plays a role in the body's adjustment to emergency situations. Eventually, when the threatening stimulus has passed, the hippocampus, a part of the brain that helps regulate emotions, turns off this physiological cascade. The fight-or-flight system thus has its own feedback loop that normally regulates the level of physiological arousal we experience in response to a stressor. In many of the disorders we discuss in this chapter, the normal response becomes abnormal, and the fight-or-flight system becomes dysregulated.

In addition to these physiological responses to a threat, characteristic emotional, cognitive, and behavioral responses occur (Table 1). Emotionally, we experience terror and dread, and we often are irritable or restless. Cognitively, we are on the lookout for danger. Behaviorally, we seek to confront the threat or escape

FIGURE 1 **The Fight-or-Flight Response.** The body's fight-or-flight response is initiated by the part of the brain known as the hypothalamus. The hypothalamus stimulates the sympathetic division of the autonomic nervous system, which acts on smooth muscles and internal organs to produce the bodily changes shown in the figure. The hypothalamus also releases corticotrophin-release factor (CRF), which triggers the pituitary gland to release adrenocorticotropic hormone (ACTH). In turn, ACTH stimulates the adrenal glands to release about 30 other hormones. The hormones act on organs and muscles to prepare the body to fight or flee.

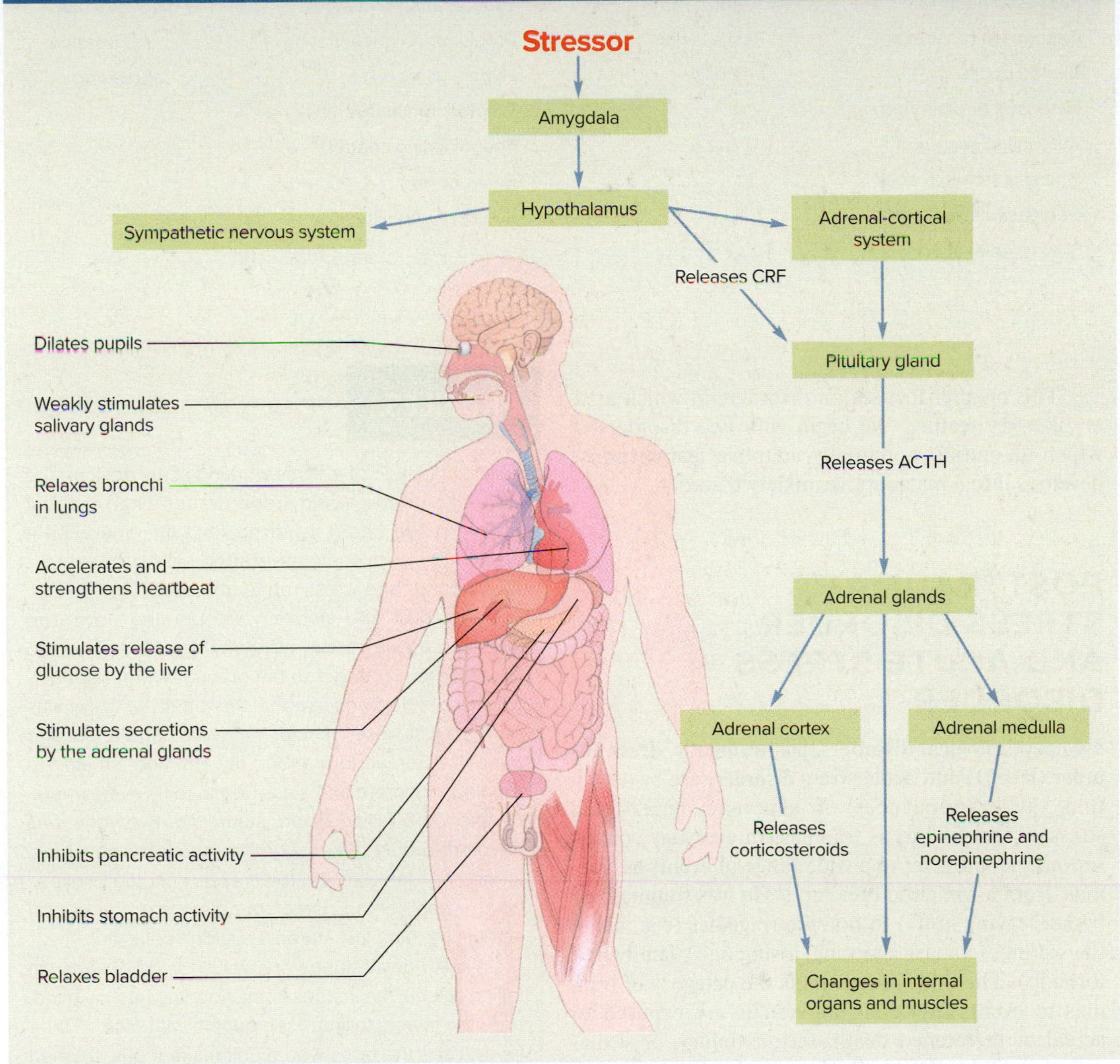

from it. In a realistic fear response, these emotional, cognitive, and behavioral responses subside when the threat subsides. In anxiety and related disorders, these responses may persist in the absence of any objective threat.

Anxiety is a part of many psychological disorders. Most people with serious depression report bouts of anxiety (Watson, 2009). People with schizophrenia often feel anxious when they believe they are slipping into a new episode of psychosis. Many people who abuse alcohol and other drugs do so to dampen anxious symptoms. In addition, people with one anxiety disorder are likely to have another (Craske & Waters, 2005).

TABLE 1 Responses to Threat

These characteristic responses to threat can also be symptoms of an anxiety disorder.

Somatic	Emotional	Cognitive	Behavioral
Tense muscles	Sense of dread	Anticipation of harm	Escape
Increased heart rate	Terror	Exaggeration of danger	Avoidance
Changes in respiration	Restlessness	Problems in concentrating	Aggression
Dilated pupils	Irritability	Hypervigilance	Freezing
Increased perspiration		Worried, ruminative thinking	
Adrenaline secretion		Fear of losing control	
Inhibited stomach acid		Fear of dying	
Decreased salivation		Sense of unreality	
Bladder relaxation			

This chapter focuses on disorders in which anxiety is a key feature. We begin with two disorders in which an initial, potentially adaptive fear response develops into a maladaptive anxiety disorder.

POSTTRAUMATIC STRESS DISORDER AND ACUTE STRESS DISORDER

Two psychological disorders, **posttraumatic stress disorder (PTSD)** and **acute stress disorder,** are by definition the consequences of experiencing extreme stressors, referred to as traumas. In everyday conversations, people refer to a wide range of events as traumas, from a romantic breakup ("He was traumatized by her leaving him") to horrific tragedies (e.g., being the victim of a mass shooting, losing one's family in a tornado). The *DSM-5* constrains the category of traumas to events in which individuals are exposed to actual or threatened death, serious injury, or sexual violation (Table 2). In addition, in the diagnostic criteria for PTSD and acute stress disorder, the *DSM-5* requires that individuals either directly experience or witness the traumatic event, learn that the event happened to someone they are close to, or experience repeated or extreme exposure to the details of a traumatic event (as do first responders at a tragedy). Blair, a survivor of the terrorist attack on the World Trade Center on September 11, 2001, describes many core symptoms of both disorders.

PROFILES

I just can't let go of it. I was working at my desk on the 10th floor of the World Trade Center when the first plane hit. We heard it but couldn't imagine what it was. Pretty soon someone started yelling, "Get out—it's a bomb!" and we all ran for the stairs.

The dust and smoke were pouring down the staircase as we made our way down. It seemed to take an eternity to get to the ground. When I got outside, I looked up and saw that the top of the tower was on fire. I just froze; I couldn't move. Then the second plane hit. Someone grabbed my arm and we started running. Concrete and glass began to fly everywhere. People were falling down, stumbling. Everyone was covered in dust. When I got far enough away, I just stood and stared as the towers fell. I couldn't believe what I was seeing. Other people were crying and screaming, but I just stared. I couldn't believe it.

Now, I don't sleep very well. I try, but just as I'm falling asleep, the images come flooding into my mind. I see the towers falling. I see people with cuts on their faces. I see the ones who didn't make it out, crushed and dead. I smell the dust and smoke. Sometimes, I cry to the point that my pillow is soaked. Sometimes, I just stare at the ceiling, as I stared at the towers as they fell. During the day, I go to work, but often it's as if my head is in another place. Someone will say something to me, and I won't hear them. I often feel as if I'm floating around, not touching or really seeing anything around me. But if I do hear a siren, which you do a lot in the city, I jump out of my skin.

TABLE 2 *DSM-5* Criteria for Posttraumatic Stress Disorder

A. Exposure to actual or threatened death, serious injury, or sexual violence in one (or more) of the following ways:

1. Directly experiencing the traumatic event(s).
2. Witnessing, in person, the event(s) as it occurred to others.
3. Learning that the traumatic event(s) occurred to a close family member or close friend. In cases of actual or threatened death of a family member or friend, the event(s) must have been violent or accidental.
4. Experiencing repeated or extreme exposure to aversive details of the traumatic event(s) (e.g., first responders collecting human remains; police officers repeatedly exposed to details of child abuse).

Note: Criterion A4 does not apply to exposure through electronic media, television, movies, or pictures, unless this exposure is work related.

B. Presence of one (or more) of the following intrusion symptoms associated with the traumatic event(s), beginning after the traumatic event(s) occurred:

1. Recurrent, involuntary, and intrusive distressing memories of the traumatic event(s).
2. Recurrent distressing dreams in which the content and/or affect of the dream are related to the traumatic event(s).
3. Dissociative reactions (e.g., flashbacks) in which the individual feels or acts as if the traumatic event(s) were recurring. (Such reactions may occur on a continuum, with the most extreme expression being a complete loss of awareness of present surroundings.)
4. Intense or prolonged psychological distress at exposure to internal or external cues that symbolize or resemble an aspect of the traumatic event(s).
5. Marked physiological reactions to internal or external cues that symbolize or resemble an aspect of the traumatic event(s).

C. Persistent avoidance of stimuli associated with the traumatic event(s), beginning after the traumatic event(s) occurred, as evidenced by one or both of the following:

1. Avoidance of or efforts to avoid distressing memories, thoughts, or feelings about or closely associated with the traumatic event(s).
2. Avoidance of or efforts to avoid external reminders (people, places, conversations, activities, objects, situations) that arouse distressing memories, thoughts, or feelings about or closely associated with the traumatic event(s).

D. Negative alterations in cognitions and mood associated with the traumatic event(s), beginning or worsening after the traumatic event(s) occurred, as evidenced by two (or more) of the following:

1. Inability to remember an important aspect of the traumatic event(s) (typically due to dissociative amnesia and not to other factors such as head injury, alcohol, or drugs).
2. Persistent and exaggerated negative beliefs or expectations about oneself, others, or the world (e.g., "I am bad," "No one can be trusted," "The world is completely dangerous," "My whole nervous system is permanently ruined").
3. Persistent, distorted cognitions about the cause or consequences of the traumatic event(s) that lead the individual to blame himself/herself or others.
4. Persistent negative emotional state (e.g., fear, horror, anger, guilt, or shame).
5. Markedly diminished interest or participation in significant activities.
6. Feelings of detachment or estrangement from others.
7. Persistent inability to experience positive emotions (e.g., inability to experience happiness, satisfaction, or loving feelings).

E. Marked alterations in arousal and reactivity associated with the traumatic event(s), beginning or worsening after the traumatic event(s) occurred, as evidenced by two (or more) of the following:

1. Irritable behavior and angry outbursts (with little or no provocation) typically expressed as verbal or physical aggression toward people or objects.
2. Reckless or self-destructive behavior.
3. Hypervigilance.
4. Exaggerated startle response.
5. Problems with concentration.
6. Sleep disturbance (e.g., difficulty falling or staying asleep or restless sleep).

(continued)

TABLE 2 ***DSM-5* Criteria for Posttraumatic Stress Disorder (*continued*)**

F. Duration of the disturbance (Criteria B, C, D, and E) is more than 1 month.

G. The disturbance causes clinically significant distress or impairment in social, occupational, or other important areas of functioning.

H. The disturbance is not attributable to the physiological effects of a substance (e.g., medication, alcohol) or another medical condition.

Specify whether:

With dissociative symptoms: The individual's symptoms meet the criteria for posttraumatic stress disorder, and in addition, in response to the stressor, the individual experiences persistent or recurrent symptoms of either of the following:

1. **Depersonalization:** Persistent or recurrent experiences of feeling detached from, and as if one were an outside observer of, one's mental processes or body (e.g., feeling as though one were in a dream; feeling a sense of unreality of self or body or of time moving slowly).
2. **Derealization:** Persistent or recurrent experiences of unreality of surroundings (e.g., the world around the individual is experienced as unreal, dreamlike, distant, or distorted).

Note: To use this subtype, the dissociative symptoms must not be attributable to the physiological effects of a substance (e.g., blackouts, behavior during alcohol intoxication) or another medical condition (e.g., complex partial seizures).

Specify if:

With delayed expression: If the full diagnostic criteria are not met until at least 6 months after the event (although the onset and expression of some symptoms may be immediate).

Immediately after the World Trade Center attacks, about 20 percent of people living nearby had symptoms meeting the diagnosis of PTSD, including reexperiencing the event (e.g., flashbacks or nightmares), feeling numb and detached, or being hypervigilant and chronically aroused (Galea et al., 2002). Even people not physically present were traumatized by the event. Nationwide studies showed that just after September 11, 2001, 44 percent of adults reported symptoms of PTSD (Schuster et al., 2001). Two months later, 21 percent of adults nationwide reported still being "quite a bit" or "extremely" bothered by distress symptoms (Stein et al., 2004). Those in this study experiencing persistent distress reported accomplishing less at work (65 percent), avoiding public gathering places (24 percent), and using alcohol or other drugs to quell worries about terrorism (38 percent).

Traumatic events such as the 2017 Harvest Country Music Festival shooting at which 59 people died and over 500 were injured, can lead to posttraumatic stress. ©*Denise Truscello/Getty Images News/Getty Images*

A wide range of specific events can induce posttraumatic stress disorder or acute stress disorder, ranging from extraordinary events such as a terrorist attack to common events such as a traffic accident. The experiences qualify as traumas under the *DSM-5* as long as they expose the individual to actual or threatened death, serious injury, or sexual violation. About 7 percent of adults will be exposed to a traumatic event and develop posttraumatic stress disorder at some time in their lives, with women at greater risk than men (Kessler et al., 2005). For some, the symptoms can be mild to moderate, permitting normal functioning. For others, however, the symptoms can be immobilizing, causing deterioration in their work, family, and social lives.

A diagnosis of PTSD requires the presence of four types of symptoms: reexperiencing of the traumatic event, avoidance, negative changes in thought or mood, and hypervigilance or chronic arousal (Table 2). The first involves repeated *reexperiencing* of the traumatic event. PTSD sufferers may experience intrusive images or thoughts, recurring nightmares, or flashbacks in which they relive the event. Memories of the World Trade Center attack intrude into Blair's consciousness against her will, particularly when she encounters something that reminds her of the event. She also relives her emotional reaction to the event, and she chronically experiences negative emotions that have not diminished with time.

The second type of symptoms in PTSD involves *persistent avoidance* of situations, thoughts, or memories associated with the trauma. People will shun activities, places, or other people that remind them of the event. The third group of symptoms involves *negative changes in thought and mood* associated with the event. People may not be able to remember aspects of the trauma. They may unrealistically blame themselves or others for the event and feel permanently damaged. They may report "survivor guilt" about having lived through the traumatic event or about things they had to do to survive. They may be chronically distressed or, like Blair, become emotionally numb and withdrawn, feeling detached from themselves and their ongoing experiences.

The fourth type of symptoms includes *hypervigilance and chronic arousal.* People with PTSD are always on guard for the traumatic event to recur. Sounds or images that remind them of their trauma can instantly create panic and flight. A war veteran, hearing a car backfire, may jump into a ditch and begin to have flashbacks of the war, reexperiencing the terror he or she felt on the front lines. Irritability and agitation are common, as is insomnia.

In addition to these symptoms, many people with PTSD experience some symptoms of *dissociation.* Dissociation is a process in which different facets of their sense of self, memories, or consciousness become disconnected from one another. For example, a person could feel like she is not in her own body, or that the world around her feels unreal (see the chapter "Somatic Symptom and Dissociative Disorders"). For some people with PTSD, dissociative symptoms are especially prominent and persistent (see Friedman et al., 2011). These people can be diagnosed with the subtype **PTSD with prominent dissociative (depersonalization/derealization) symptoms.**

Another disorder associated with traumas, acute stress disorder, occurs in response to traumas similar to those involved in PTSD but is diagnosed when symptoms arise within 1 month of exposure to the stressor and last no longer than 4 weeks. As in PTSD, the individual with acute stress disorder persistently reexperiences the trauma through flashbacks, nightmares, and intrusive thoughts; avoids reminders of the trauma; and is constantly aroused. In acute stress disorder, dissociative *symptoms* are common, including numbing or detachment, reduced awareness of surroundings, derealization (experiencing the world as unreal or dreamlike), depersonalization (feeling detached from one's body or mental processes), and an inability to recall important aspects of the trauma. Although acute stress disorder is defined as a short-term response to trauma, people who experience acute stress disorder are at high risk of continuing to experience posttraumatic stress symptoms for many months (Bryant, Friedman, Spiegel, Ursano, & Strain, 2011).

Another trauma- and stress-related diagnosis is **adjustment disorder,** which consists of emotional and behavioral symptoms (depressive symptoms, anxiety symptoms, and/or antisocial behaviors) that arise within 3 months of the experience of a stressor. The stressors that lead to adjustment disorder can be of any severity, while those that lead to PTSD and acute stress disorder are, by definition, extreme. Adjustment disorder is a diagnosis for people experiencing emotional and behavioral symptoms following a stressor who do not meet the criteria for a diagnosis of PTSD, acute stress disorder, or an anxiety or mood disorder resulting from stressful experience.

Traumas Leading to PTSD

The traumas that can lead to PTSD unfortunately are common. Among them are natural disasters such as floods, tsunamis, earthquakes, fires, hurricanes, and tornadoes. One of the largest natural disasters in recent history was the tsunami that struck south and southeast Asia on December 26, 2004. Over 280,000 people

Survivors of natural disasters, such as Super Storm Sandy in 2012, often experience posttraumatic stress disorder. ©meunierd/Shutterstock

were killed, and 1.2 million were displaced. In the state of Tamil Nadu, India, 7,983 people were killed, and 44,207 had to be relocated to camps due to damage to their homes. Two months after the tsunami, researchers found that 13 percent of adults in this area were experiencing PTSD (Kumar et al., 2007). Five months after Hurricane Katrina devastated the northern coast of the Gulf of Mexico in 2005, 30 percent of people from the New Orleans metropolitan area and 12 percent from the rest of the hurricane area were diagnosed with PTSD (Galea et al., 2007).

Search and rescue personnel who respond in the hours and days just after a disaster are at significant risk for PTSD. A meta-analysis of 28 studies of ambulance personnel, firefighters, police, and other first responders across the world found that 10 percent currently experienced PTSD, regardless of whether they had recently responded to a large-scale traumatic event (Berger et al., 2012). Ambulance workers had the highest rates of PTSD, presumably because their job involves daily exposure to people who are seriously injured and dying, in a chronically pressured work environment.

Human-made disasters such as wars, terrorist attacks, and torture may be even more likely to lead to PTSD than are natural disasters. PTSD symptoms went by different names in the two world wars and the Korean War: "combat fatigue syndrome," "war zone stress," and "shell shock." In follow-up studies of soldiers experiencing these syndromes, the soldiers showed chronic posttraumatic stress symptoms for decades after the war (Elder & Clipp, 1989; Sutker, Allain, & Winstead, 1993). PTSD became widely recognized after the Vietnam War. Almost 19 percent of Vietnam veterans had the disorder at some point, and 9 percent still had it 10 to 12 years after their service ended (Dohrenwend et al., 2006).

Recent and ongoing wars and conflicts have left thousands of PTSD sufferers in their wake. Studies of U.S. Army soldiers and Marines have found that approximately 15 to 19 percent of those deployed in Iraq and about 11 percent of those deployed in Afghanistan can be diagnosed with PTSD (Erbes, Westermeyer, Engdahl, & Johnsen, 2007; Hoge et al., 2004; Hoge, Auchterlonie, & Milliken, 2006; Sundin, Fear, Iversen, Rona, & Wessely, 2010). Follow-up studies of soldiers returning from Iraq have found that as many as 42 percent report some mental health problems, most often PTSD symptoms (Milliken, Auchterlonie, & Hoge, 2007). Army sergeant Kristofer Goldsmith, who served 4 years in active duty in Iraq, is one of those soldiers.

The citizens of countries besieged by war are also at high risk for PTSD. The Afghan people have endured decades of war and occupation, the repressive regime of the Taliban, the U.S. bombing of their country after the September 11 attacks, and, since 2001, protracted violence. Thousands of Afghanis have been killed, injured, or displaced from their homes. Many of the displaced now live in makeshift tents without adequate food or water. Posttraumatic stress disorder was found in 42 percent of Afghan citizens, and other anxiety symptoms were found in 72 percent (Cardozo et al., 2004). Afghan women may be especially likely to experience PTSD, because the Taliban deprived them of their basic human rights, killed their husbands and male relatives, and then made it impossible for them to survive without those men. Over 90 percent of these women reported some anxiety symptoms, and 42 percent were diagnosed with PTSD (see also Scholte et al., 2004). More recently, refugees fleeing internal conflict in Syria have endured similar traumas in their home country, during their flight to other countries, and, in some cases, following a negative reception in those countries. They will likely experience psychological consequences for years to come.

Sexual assault is the trauma most commonly associated with PTSD, and nearly half (46 percent) of

CASE STUDY

Kristofer Goldsmith was a 19-year-old, fresh out of high school, when he joined the Army. He was soon deployed to Sadr City, one of the most violent places in Iraq. Goldsmith's duty was to photograph and document the incidents his platoon encountered, including mutilated men, women, and children.

When his unit was back home for a while, family and friends noticed that Goldsmith was a different man. His drinking escalated to binges every day. He also seemed to get into fights or be violent in some way every day. He was constantly hypervigilant for any threats. Simply walking through a crowded shopping mall was enough to spark paranoia as he scanned every person and scene for enemies who might spring out and hurt him. Innocent remarks by clerks or being touched by someone as he was walking by could spark violent outbursts. There were times when he seemed not to know what he was doing and was totally out of control. At one party, he suddenly grabbed another guy and choked him until he stopped breathing.

Soon Goldsmith's unit was ordered to redeploy to Iraq. Believing he couldn't face the scenes of devastation and death that now haunted him, he attempted suicide, swallowing massive numbers of painkillers and gulping a liter and a half of vodka. Goldsmith survived and was eventually diagnosed with PTSD. (Gajilan, 2008) sexual assault survivors develop PTSD at some time in their lives (Zinzow et al., 2012). Most women report some PTSD symptoms shortly after a sexual assault (see Figure 2), and almost 50 percent still qualify for the diagnosis 3 months after the rape, while as many as 25 percent still experience PTSD 4 to 5 years later (Faravelli, Giugni, Salvatori, & Ricca, 2004; Foa & Riggs, 1995; Resnick, Kilpatrick, Dansky, & Saunders, 1993; Rothbaum, Foa, Riggs, & Murdock, 1992).

FIGURE 2 **Posttraumatic Symptoms in Rape Survivors.** Almost all women show symptoms of posttraumatic stress disorder severe enough to be diagnosed with it in the first or second week following a rape. Over the 3 months following a rape, the percentage of women continuing to show symptoms of PTSD declines. However, almost 50 percent of women continue to be diagnosed with PTSD 3 months after a rape.

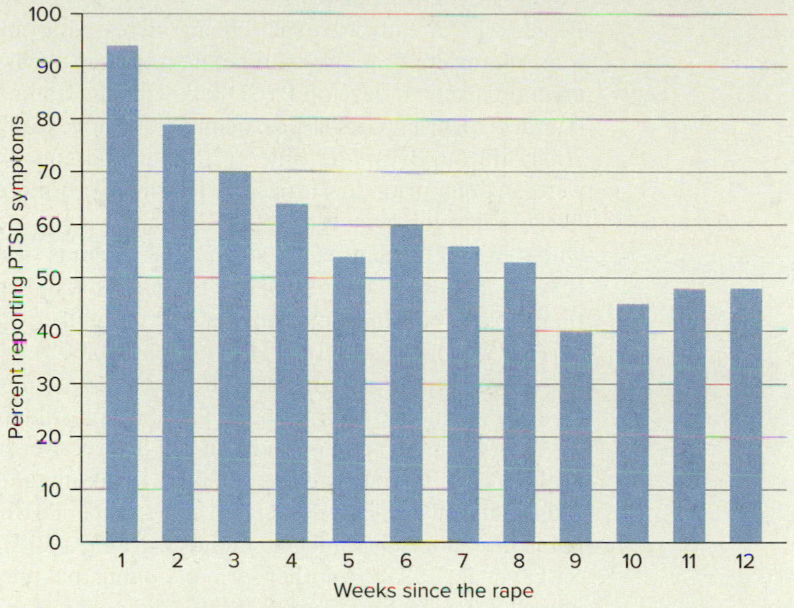

Source: Adapted from Foa & Riggs, 1995.

Theories of PTSD

If, as we have seen, traumatic experiences are relatively common, what determines abnormality? What kind of trauma is most likely to cause long-term, severe psychological impairment? And why do some people develop PTSD in the wake of trauma, whereas others do not? Researchers have identified a number of factors that seem to increase the likelihood of developing PTSD.

Environmental and Social Factors

An important set of risk factors involves the contexts in which people experience trauma. Strong predictors of people's reactions to trauma include its *severity* and *duration* and the individual's *proximity* to it (Cardozo, Vergara, Agani, & Gotway, 2000; Ehlers et al., 1998; Hoge et al., 2004; Kessler, Sonnega, Bromet, Hughes, & Nelson, 1995). People who experience more severe and longer-lasting traumas and are directly affected by a traumatic event are more prone to developing PTSD. For example, veterans are more likely to experience PTSD if they were on the front lines for an extended period (Iversen et al., 2008). People at Ground Zero during the World Trade Center attacks were more likely to develop PTSD than were those who were not at the site (Galea et al., 2002). Rape survivors who were violently and repeatedly raped over an extended period are particularly likely to experience PTSD (Epstein, Saunders, & Kilpatrick, 1997; Zinzow et al., 2012). Victims of natural disasters who are injured or who lose their homes or loved ones are more likely to experience PTSD than are those whose lives are less severely affected (Galea, Tracy, Norris, & Coffey, 2008). These examples illustrate how contextual factors affect how one person's reaction to traumatic events can differ from another person's.

Another predictor of vulnerability to PTSD is the availability of social support. People who have the emotional support of others after a trauma recover more quickly than do people who do not (Kendall-Tackett, Williams, & Finkelhor, 1993; LaGreca, Silverman, Vernberg, & Prinstein, 1996; Sutker, Davis, Uddo, & Ditta, 1995). Survivors of Hurricane Katrina who could talk with others about their experiences and who received emotional and practical

People supported by others during and after traumatic events, such as the 2001 attack on the World Trade Towers, often recover more quickly than those who do not.
Source: Library of Congress Prints and Photographs Division

support were less likely to develop PTSD than were those who did not receive such support (Galea et al., 2008). Search and rescue personnel responding to the 2010 earthquake in Haiti were unlikely to develop PTSD if they had strong social support among their colleagues and in their community (van der Velden, van Loon, Benight, & Eckardt, 2012).

Psychological Factors

People who already are experiencing increased symptoms of anxiety or depression before a trauma occurs are more likely to develop PTSD following the trauma (Cardozo, Kaiser, Gotway, & Agani, 2003; Hoge et al., 2004; Mayou, Bryant, & Ehlers, 2001). Children who were anxious prior to Hurricane Katrina were more likely to develop symptoms of PTSD than were those who were not (Weems et al., 2007). War veterans who have psychological distress or poor interpersonal relationships before they enter combat are more likely to develop symptoms of PTSD (Koenen et al., 2002).

Once trauma occurs, people's styles of coping may also influence their vulnerability. Several studies have shown that people who use self-destructive or avoidant coping strategies, such as drinking and self-isolation, are more likely to experience PTSD (Merrill, Thomsen, Sinclair, Gold, & Milner, 2001; Sutker et al., 1995). Another form of coping that may increase the likelihood of PTSD is dissociation, or psychological detachment from the trauma and ongoing traumatic events. People who dissociate may feel that they are in another place, or in someone else's body watching the trauma and its aftermath unfold. Those who dissociate shortly after a trauma are at increased risk of developing PTSD (Cardeña & Carlson, 2011; Friedman et al., 2011).

Gender and Cross-Cultural Differences

Women are more likely than men to be diagnosed with PTSD, as well as most other anxiety disorders including panic disorder, social anxiety disorders, and generalized anxiety disorder (Hanson et al., 2008; Roberts, Gilman, Brelau, & Koenen, 2011). Women may experience some of the triggers for anxiety disorders more often than men, particularly sexual abuse (Burnam, Stein, Golding, & Siegel, 1988). Women also may be more likely to develop PTSD because the types of traumas they frequently experience, such as sexual abuse, are stigmatized, decreasing the amount of social support they receive. Men are more likely to suffer traumas that carry less stigma, such as exposure to war.

Nationwide studies in the United States find that African Americans have higher rates of PTSD compared to whites, Hispanics, and Asian Americans (Roberts et al., 2011). Whites reported being exposed to the greatest number of potentially traumatizing events, but African Americans reported more traumas of certain types than did other groups, namely, witnessing domestic violence and being the victim of a violent assault. Asians had the most reports of being a refugee or a civilian in a war zone. All the racial/ethnic minority groups were less likely than whites to seek treatment for trauma-related symptoms, perhaps due to lower socioeconomic status and less access to health care or to greater stigmatization against seeking mental health treatment (Roberts et al., 2011).

Culture also appears to strongly influence the *manifestation* of anxiety. People in Latino cultures report a syndrome known as *ataque de nervios* (attack of the nerves) (see Lewis-Fernandez et al., 2010). A typical ataque de nervios might include trembling, heart palpitations, a sense of heat in the chest rising into the head, difficulty moving limbs, loss of consciousness or the mind going blank, memory loss, a sensation of needles in parts of the body (paresthesia), chest tightness, difficulty breathing (dyspnea), dizziness, faintness, and spells. Behaviorally, the person begins to shout, swear, and strike out at others. The person then falls to the ground and either experiences convulsive body movements or lies as if dead. Ataque de nervios is more common among recent trauma victims (Guarnaccia, Rivera, Franco, Neighbors, & Allende-Ramos, 1996).

More chronic anxiety-like symptoms, known as *nervios,* are common in Latino communities, particularly among the poor and uneducated (Guarnaccia et al., 1996). The term *nervios* (which is more general than ataque de nervios) encompasses a broad array of symptoms, including physical ailments (headaches, stomach problems, dizziness) and emotional symptoms (sadness, irritability, anger, absentmindedness), as well as the presence of intrusive worries or negative thoughts. One study of 942 adults in rural Mexico found that 21 percent of the women and 10 percent of the men had chronic nervios (de Snyder, Diaz-Perez, & Ojeda, 2000). The authors suggest that among the underprivileged, particularly women, nervios expresses the anger and frustration of "being at the bottom" and provides temporary release from the grinding everyday burdens of life (see also Lopez & Guarnaccia, 2000).

Biological Factors

The biological responses to threat appear to be different in people with PTSD than in people without the disorder. Genetic factors may predispose victims of threat to these different biological responses. Research on biological factors has focused on three areas: neuroimaging, biochemistry, and genetics.

Neuroimaging Findings Neuroimaging studies using positron-emission tomography (PET) and magnetic resonance imaging (MRI; see the chapter "Assessing and Diagnosing Abnormality") have shown differences in brain activity between people with PTSD and those without it in response to threatening or emotional stimuli. These differences occur in brain areas that regulate emotion, the fight-or-flight response, and memory, including the amygdala, hippocampus, and prefrontal cortex (Britton & Rauch, 2009). The amygdala, which activates when processing emotional material and threat, appears to respond more actively to emotional stimuli in those with PTSD. Further, the medial prefrontal cortex, which modulates the reactivity of the amygdala to emotional stimuli, is less active in people with more severe symptoms of PTSD than in people with less severe symptoms. Thus, the brains of people with severe PTSD may be both more reactive to emotional stimuli and less able to dampen that reactivity when it occurs (Shin et al., 2011).

Some studies also show shrinkage in the hippocampus among PTSD patients, possibly due to overexposure to neurotransmitters and hormones released in the stress response (Britton & Rauch, 2009). The hippocampus functions in memory, and damage to it may result in some of the memory problems reported by PTSD patients. It also helps regulate the body's fear response, as discussed earlier. Thus, damage to the hippocampus may interfere with returning the fear response to a normal level after the threat has passed. Together, these findings about the brain align with the types of symptoms and behaviors seen in PTSD.

Biochemical Findings Recall that one of the major hormones released as part of the fight-or-flight response is cortisol and that high levels usually indicate an elevated stress response. Interestingly, resting levels of cortisol among people with PTSD (when not exposed to trauma reminders) tend to be lower than among people without PTSD (Yehuda, Pratchett, & Pelcovitz, 2012). For example, studies that have assessed cortisol levels in people injured in a traffic accident one to two days previously have found that those with lower cortisol levels are at significantly increased risk for PTSD over the next weeks and months (Ehring, Ehlers, Cleare, & Glucksman, 2008; McFarlane, Barton, Yehuda, & Wittert, 2011). Cortisol acts to reduce sympathetic nervous system activity after stress, so lower levels may result in prolonged activity of the sympathetic nervous system following stress. As a result, some people may more easily develop a conditioned fear of stimuli associated with the trauma and subsequently develop PTSD (Ballenger et al., 2004).

Some other physiological responses to stress are exaggerated in PTSD sufferers, including elevated heart rate and increased secretion of the neurotransmitters epinephrine and norepinephrine (Ballenger et al., 2004; Pole et al., 2007). In people vulnerable to PTSD, different components of the stress response may not be working in sync with one another. The hypothalamic-pituitary-adrenal (HPA) axis may be unable to shut down the response of the sympathetic nervous system by secreting necessary levels of cortisol, resulting in overexposure of the brain to epinephrine, norepinephrine, and other neurochemicals. This overexposure may cause memories of the traumatic event to be "overconsolidated," or planted more firmly in memory (Ballenger et al., 2004; Walderhaug, Krystal, & Neumeister, 2011).

Increasing evidence suggests that exposure to extreme or chronic stress during childhood may permanently alter children's biological stress response, making them more vulnerable to PTSD—as well as to other anxiety disorders and depression—throughout their lives (Cicchetti & Toth, 2005; Nemeroff, 2004). Studies of maltreated (severely neglected or physically, emotionally, or sexually abused) children show abnormal cortisol responses to stressors (Cicchetti & Rogosch, 2001) and a diminished startle response (Klorman, Cicchetti, Thatcher, & Ison, 2003). Adults abused as children continue to have abnormal cortisol responses and elevated startle and anxiety responses to laboratory stressors, even when they no longer show symptoms of PTSD or depression (Heim, Meinlschmidt, & Nemeroff, 2003; Pole et al., 2007). Depressed women who were abused as children show lower volume of the hippocampus than depressed women who were not abused as children (Vythilingam et al., 2002). Thus, early childhood trauma may leave permanent physical and emotional scars that predispose individuals to later psychological problems, including PTSD.

Genetics Vulnerability to PTSD may be inherited (Smoller, 2016). One study of about 4,000 twins who served in the Vietnam War found that if one developed PTSD, the other was much more likely to develop it if the twins were identical rather than fraternal (True et al., 1993; Stein, Jang, Taylor, Vernon, and Livesley, 2002). The adult children of Holocaust survivors with PTSD are over three times more likely to develop it than are matched comparison groups. They also have abnormally low levels of cortisol, whether or not they have ever been exposed to traumatic events or developed PTSD (Yehuda, Blair, Labinsky, & Bierer, 2007). These findings suggest that abnormally low cortisol levels may be one heritable risk factor for PTSD. Other studies have found that the abnormalities in brain responses to emotional stimuli also appear to have a genetic basis (Stevens et al., 2014).

Treatments for PTSD

Psychotherapies for PTSD generally have three goals: exposing clients to what they fear in order to extinguish that fear, challenging distorted cognitions that contribute to symptoms, and helping clients reduce stress in their lives. These goals are addressed in cognitive-behavioral therapy for PTSD and in stress-management therapies. Some clients also benefit from antianxiety and antidepressant medications.

Cognitive-Behavioral Therapy and Stress Management

Cognitive-behavioral therapy has proven effective in the treatment of PTSD (Chard, Shuster, & Resick, 2012; Cusack et al., 2016). A major element is systematic desensitization (see the chapter "Theories and Treatment of Abnormality"). The client identifies thoughts and situations that create anxiety, ranking them from most anxiety-provoking to least. The therapist takes the client through this hierarchy, exposing the client to the trauma cues that elicit fear, avoidance, and other symptoms of PTSD, sometimes using relaxation techniques to quell the anxiety. It usually is impossible to return to the actual traumatic event, so imagining it vividly must replace actual exposure. A combat veteran being treated for PTSD imagines the bloody battles and scenes of killing and death that haunt him; a rape survivor imagines the minute details of the assault. The therapist also watches for unhelpful thinking patterns, such as survivor guilt, and helps the client challenge these thoughts.

Repeatedly and vividly imagining and describing the feared events in the safety of the therapist's office allows the client to habituate to his or her anxiety so that reactions to stimuli become less powerful, and to distinguish memory from present reality. It may also allow the client to integrate the events into his or her concepts of self and of the world (Chard et al., 2012). For example, sexual assault survivors' experience often shatters their prior belief that the world is generally safe, or confirms their previous belief that it is unsafe; cognitive-behavioral therapy can help them process the event in a more balanced and adaptive way. Two specific types of cognitive-behavioral therapy for PTSD include prolonged exposure therapy, which focuses on repeated exposure to trauma reminders, and cognitive processing therapy, which focuses on reinterpretation of the trauma (Foa & MacLean, 2016; Resick et al., 2017). Studies of rape survivors, combat veterans, survivors of traffic collisions, and refugees have found that repeated exposure therapy significantly decreases PTSD symptoms and helps prevent relapse (Ehlers et al., 2010; Institute of Medicine, 2008; Resick, Williams, Suvak, Monson, & Gradas, 2012). Studies indicate that the effects of exposure therapies on negative thoughts and beliefs may also decrease symptoms of depression, which commonly co-occurs with PTSD (Schumm, Dickstein, Walter, Owens, & Chard, 2015; Zalta et al., 2014).

Technology can provide a controlled repetitive exposure to "virtual" trauma to help people, such as this soldier, process their actual trauma. *©Ted S. Warren/AP Images*

Some clients with PTSD cannot tolerate exposure to their traumatic memories. For these clients, **stress-inoculation therapy** may be warranted. Therapists teach clients skills for overcoming problems in their lives that increase their stress and problems that may result from PTSD, such as marital problems or social isolation. Stress-inoculation therapy is an efficacious form of treatment for PTSD, but exposure-based therapies show somewhat more consistent outcomes (Cusack et al., 2016; Foa & MacLean, 2016).

As with many other disorders, the most effective treatments for PTSD may not be available to many individuals. To overcome barriers to PTSD treatment, Internet-based treatments have been developed that show early evidence of effectiveness for some people (Kuester, Niemeyer, & Knaevelsrud, 2016), including some veterans (Hobfoll, Blais, Stevens, Walt, & Gengler, 2016). Researchers are also exploring newer treatment techniques incorporating mindfulness techniques (Hopwood & Schutte, 2017), complementary approaches like yoga and meditation (Gallegos, Crean, Pigeon, & Heffner, 2017), and virtual reality technology for exposure (Rizzo et al., 2017).

Biological Therapies

The selective serotonin reuptake inhibitors (SSRIs) and, to a lesser extent, the benzodiazepines are used to treat symptoms of PTSD, particularly sleep problems, nightmares, and irritability (Ballenger et al., 2004). Although some people with PTSD benefit from these medications, the evidence for their effectiveness in treating PTSD is mixed (Institute of Medicine, 2008), and some (in particular, the benzodiazepines) can have significant side effects and addictive potential.

SPECIFIC PHOBIAS AND AGORAPHOBIA

People can develop irrational fears of many objects and situations. The *DSM-5* divides phobias into *specific phobias,* which focus on particular objects or animals (e.g., snakes) or places (e.g., heights), and *agoraphobia,* which is a generalized fear of situations in which the person might not be able to escape or get help if needed.

Specific Phobias

Specific phobias are unreasonable or irrational fears of specific objects or situations (LeBeau et al., 2010). The *DSM-5* groups specific phobias into five categories: *animal type, natural environment type, situational type, blood-injection-injury type,* and *other* (Table 3). The key symptoms of specific phobia include a marked fear or anxiety about a specific object or situation that is disproportionate to the actual danger. The diagnostic criteria also include the individual actively avoiding the object or situation, or enduring it with intense fear or anxiety. These symptoms have to last for at least six months, cause clinical distress or impairment, and cannot be better attributed to another mental or physical disorder (APA, 2013). When people with these phobias encounter their feared object or situation, their anxiety is immediate and intense, sometimes producing a panic attack. They also become anxious over the possibility of encountering the object or situation and will go to great lengths to avoid it.

Most phobias develop during childhood. Adults with phobias recognize that their anxieties are unreasonable, although children may not. As many as 13 percent of people will have a specific phobia at some time in their lives, making phobias one of the most common mental disorders (Kessler et al., 2005). Almost 90 percent of those with a specific phobia never seek treatment (Regier et al., 1993).

Animal-type phobias focus on specific animals or insects, such as dogs, cats, snakes, or spiders. Snakes and spiders are the most common objects of animal phobias, probably because it has been adaptive over evolutionary history to fear these objects (Jacobi et al., 2004). While most people who come across a feared animal or insect will startle and move away quickly, they would not be diagnosed with a phobia because

TABLE 3 *DSM-5* Criteria for Specific Phobia

A. Marked fear or anxiety about a specific object or situation (e.g., flying, heights, animals, receiving an injection, seeing blood).

B. The phobic object or situation almost always provokes immediate fear or anxiety.

C. The phobic object or situation is actively avoided or endured with intense fear or anxiety.

D. The fear or anxiety is out of proportion to the actual danger posed by the specific object or situation and to the sociocultural context.

E. The fear, anxiety, or avoidance is persistent, typically lasting 6 months or more.

F. The fear, anxiety, or avoidance causes clinically significant distress or impairment in social, occupational, or other important areas of functioning.

G. The disturbance is not better explained by the symptoms of another mental disorder, including fear, anxiety, and avoidance of situations associated with panic-like symptoms or other incapacitating symptoms (as in agoraphobia); objects or situations related to obsessions (as in obsessive-compulsive disorder); reminders of traumatic events (as in posttraumatic stress disorder); separation from home or attachment figures (as in separation anxiety disorder); or social situations (as in social anxiety disorder).

Specify if:

Code based on the phobic stimulus:

300.29 (F40.218) Animal (e.g., spiders, insects, dogs).
300.29 (F40.228) Natural environment (e.g., heights, storms, water).
300.29 (F40.23x) Blood-injection-injury (e.g., needles, invasive medical procedures).

Coding note: Select specific ICD-10-CM code as follows: **F40.230** fear of blood; **F40.231** fear of injections and transfusions; **F40.232** fear of other medical care; or **F40.233** fear of injury.

300.29 (F40.248) Situational (e.g., airplanes, elevators, enclosed places).
300.29 (F40.298) Other (e.g., situations that may lead to choking or vomiting; in children, e.g., loud sounds or costumed characters).

Coding note: When more than one phobic stimulus is present, code all ICD-10-CM codes that apply (e.g., for fear of snakes and flying, F40.218 specific phobia, animal, and F40.248 specific phobia, situational).

SHADES OF GRAY

Read the following case study.

Last week, Ramón was turning left at a light when another driver sped through the intersection and ran into his car, smashing the entire passenger side. Fortunately, Ramón was physically uninjured, thanks in part to his air bag. He got out of his car screaming at the driver who hit him but then saw that he was unconscious and bleeding. Ramón immediately called 911, and the ambulance came within a few minutes.

Since the accident, Ramón has been having nightmares in which he is in the accident again, only this time his 3-year-old daughter is in the backseat and is seriously injured. He wakes up sweating and sometimes screaming. He has to go into his daughter's bedroom and touch her to convince himself she is okay. His concentration at work is diminished because he is tired from loss of sleep and because he keeps going over the accident, thinking about how he could have prevented it. Today he was at his desk, replaying the accident again in his mind, when his boss came by to ask him a question. Ramón jumped so badly at the sound of his name that he spilled his coffee all over his desk.

Does Ramón meet the criteria for posttraumatic stress disorder or acute stress disorder? (Discussion appears at the end of this chapter.)

they do not live in terror of encountering a snake or spider or organize their lives around avoiding them.

Natural environment type phobias, which are also extremely common (LeBeau et al., 2010), focus on events or situations in the natural environment, such as storms, heights, or water. Mild to moderate fears of these natural events or situations are extremely common and are adaptive in that they help us avoid danger. A diagnosis of phobia is warranted only when people reorganize their lives to avoid the feared situations or have severe anxiety attacks when confronted with them.

Situational type phobias usually involve fear of public transportation, tunnels, bridges, elevators, flying, or driving. Claustrophobia, or fear of enclosed spaces, is a common situational phobia. One prominent person with a situational phobia is John Madden, the former coach and sports announcer. Madden is so afraid of flying that he travels over 60,000 miles a year on his personal bus to get to sports events around the United States.

Former Super Bowl–winning coach and sports television commentator John Madden. His fear of flying leads him to travel to sports events by luxury RV coach. ©*G. Paul Burnett/AP Images*

Blood-injection-injury type phobias are diagnosed in people who fear seeing blood or an injury. Whereas people with another type of specific phobia typically experience increases in heart rate, blood pressure, and other fight-or-flight responses when confronted with their feared object or situation, people with blood-injection-injury type phobia experience significant drops in heart rate and blood pressure and are likely to faint. This type of phobia runs more strongly in families than do the other types (LeBeau et al., 2010).

Agoraphobia

The term *agoraphobia* comes from the Greek for "fear of the marketplace." People with **agoraphobia** fear places where they might have trouble escaping or getting help if they become anxious. This often includes public transportation (being on a bus, train, plane, or boat), open spaces (such as a parking lot), being in shops or theaters, being in crowded places, or being alone anywhere outside their home. People with agoraphobia also often fear that they will embarrass themselves if others notice their symptoms or their efforts to escape during an attack. Actually, other people can rarely tell when a person is anxious (Craske & Barlow, 2014).

About 50 percent of people with agoraphobia have a history of panic attacks (described below) that preceded the development of the agoraphobia (Wittchen, Gloster, Beesdo-Baum, Fava, & Craske, 2010). The remaining people with agoraphobia typically have a history of another anxiety disorder, a somatic symptoms disorder (see the chapter "Somatic Symptom and Dissociative Disorders"), or depression (Wittchen et al., 2010). Agoraphobia most often begins when people are in their early 20s and is more common in women than in men.

People with agoraphobia often reach the point where they will not leave their homes alone. Sometimes, they are able to venture out with a close family member who makes them feel safe. However, family and friends may not be willing to chaperone them everywhere they go. When people with agoraphobia force themselves to enter situations that frighten them, they experience persistent and intense anxiety, causing many to retreat to their homes. Some turn to alcohol or another substance to dampen their anxiety symptoms (Wittchen et al., 2010).

Theories of Phobias

The phobias have been a battleground among various psychological approaches to abnormality. Freud (1909) argued that phobias result when unconscious anxiety is displaced onto a neutral or symbolic object. That is, people become phobic of objects or situations not because they have any real fear of them but because they have displaced their anxiety over other issues onto them.

This theory is detailed in a 150-page case history of a little boy named Hans, who had a phobia of horses after seeing a horse fall on the ground and writhe violently. How did Hans' phobia develop? According to Freud, young boys have a sexual desire for their mothers and jealously hate their fathers, but they fear that their fathers will castrate them in retaliation for this desire. As noted in the chapter "Theories and Treatment of Abnormality," this phenomenon is known as the Oedipus complex. In Freud's interpretation, little Hans unconsciously displaced this anxiety onto horses, which symbolized his father for him. Freud's evidence came from Hans' answers to a series of leading questions. After long conversations about what Hans was "really" afraid of, Hans reportedly became less fearful of horses because, according to Freud, he had gained insight into the true source of his anxiety.

There is little reason to accept Freud's theory of phobias. Hans never provided any spontaneous or direct evidence that his real problem was Oedipal concerns rather than fear of horses. In addition, Hans' phobia of horses decreased slowly over time, rather than suddenly in response to an insight. Many children have specific fears that simply fade over time. In general, psychodynamic therapy is not highly effective for treating phobias, suggesting that insight into unconscious anxieties is not what is needed in their treatment.

Behavioral Theories

In contrast to the psychodynamic theories, the behavioral theories have been very successful in explaining phobias. According to Mowrer's (1939) two-factor theory, classical conditioning leads to the fear of the phobic object, and operant conditioning helps maintain it. As discussed in the chapter "Theories and Treatment of Abnormality," in classical conditioning a previously neutral object (the conditioned stimulus) is paired with an object that naturally elicits a reaction (an unconditioned stimulus that elicits an unconditioned response) until the previously neutral object elicits the same reaction (now called the conditioned response). When a tone is paired with an electric shock, the conditioned stimulus is the tone, the unconditioned stimulus is the electric shock, the unconditioned response is anxiety in response to the shock, and the conditioned response is anxiety in response to the tone.

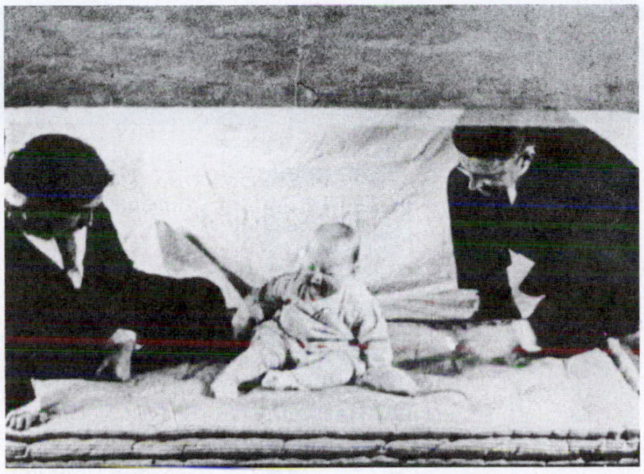

Little Albert, shown in this photo, developed a fear of white rats through classical conditioning. ©*Prof. Ben Harris*

The first application of these theories to phobias came in a series of studies done almost 100 years ago by John Watson and Rosalie Raynor (1920). Watson and Raynor placed a white rat in front of an 11-month-old boy named Little Albert. As Little Albert reached for the white rat, they banged a metal bar loudly just above his head. Naturally, Little Albert was startled and began to cry. After several more pairings of the white rat with the loud noise from the metal bar, Little Albert would have nothing to do with the rat. When presented with it, he retreated and showed distress. Little Albert's fear also generalized to other white furry animals—he would not approach white rabbits either.

Although by today's standards this experiment would raise serious ethical questions, it showed the creation of a phobia through classical conditioning. The unconditioned stimulus (US) was the loud noise from the banged bar, and the unconditioned response (UR) was Little Albert's startle response to the noise. The conditioned stimulus (CS) was the white rat, and the conditioned response (CR) was the startle-and-fear response to the white rat (Figure 3). If Little Albert had later been presented with the white rat several times without the noise, his fear of white rats should have been extinguished.

Most people who develop a phobia, however, try to avoid being exposed to their feared object, thus avoiding what could extinguish the phobia. If they are suddenly confronted with their feared object, they

FIGURE 3 **The Behavioral Account of Little Albert's Phobia.** The pairing of the banged bar (the US), which naturally leads to a startle response (the UR), and the white rat (the CS) eventually leads to the white rat producing the same startle response (now referred to as the CR).

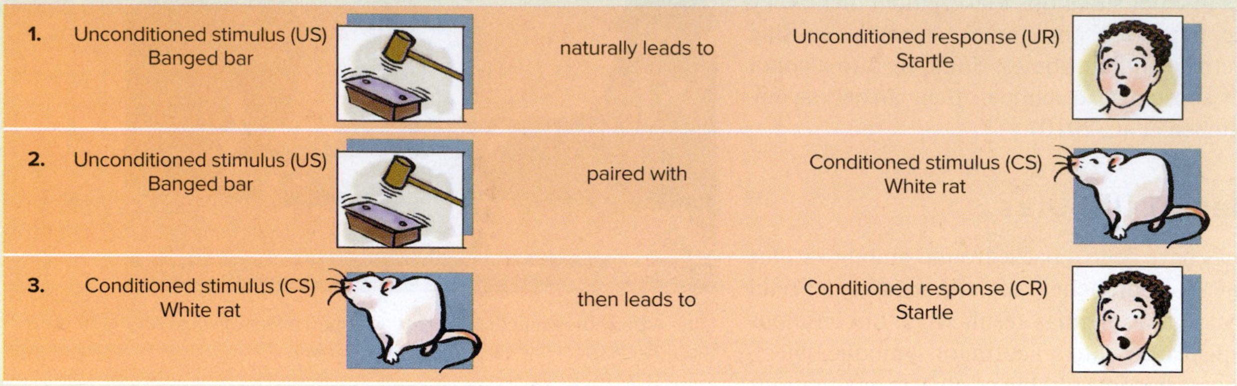

experience extreme anxiety and run away as quickly as possible. Running away reduces their anxiety; thus, their avoidance of the feared object is reinforced by the reduction of their anxiety—an operant conditioning process known as **negative reinforcement** (Mowrer, 1939). Thereafter, they avoid the feared object.

Some theorists argue that phobias can develop through observational learning as well as through direct classical conditioning (see Mineka & Zinbarg, 2006). For example, small children may learn to fear snakes if their parents show severe fright when they see a snake (Bandura, 1969; Mineka, Davidson, Cook, & Keir, 1984).

An extension of the behavioral theory of phobias may answer the question of why humans develop phobias of some objects or situations and not others (deSilva, Rachman, & Seligman, 1977; Mineka, 1985; Seligman, 1970). Phobias of spiders, snakes, and heights are common, but phobias of flowers are not. Many phobic objects appear to be things whose avoidance, over evolutionary history, has been advantageous for humans. Our distant ancestors had many nasty encounters with insects, snakes, heights, loud noises, and strangers. Those who quickly learned to fear and avoid these objects or events were more likely to survive and bear offspring. Thus, evolution may have selected for the rapid conditioning of fear to certain objects or situations. Although these are less likely to cause us harm today, we carry the vestiges of our evolutionary history and are biologically prepared to learn certain associations quickly. This theory is known as **prepared classical conditioning** (Seligman, 1970). Many objects more likely to cause us harm in today's world (such as guns and knives) have not been around long enough, evolutionarily speaking, to be selected for rapid conditioning, so phobias of them should be relatively difficult to create.

To test this idea, researchers presented subjects with pictures of objects that theoretically should be evolutionarily selected for conditioning (snakes and spiders) and objects that should not be so selected (houses, faces, and flowers). They paired the presentation of these pictures with short but painful electric shocks. The subjects developed anxiety reactions to the pictures of snakes and spiders within one or two pairings with shock, but it took four or five pairings of the pictures of houses, faces, or flowers with shock to create a fear reaction. Extinguishing the subjects' anxiety reactions to houses or faces was relatively easy once the pictures were no longer paired with shock, but the anxiety reactions to spiders and snakes were difficult to extinguish (Hugdahl & Ohman, 1977; Ohman, Fredrikson, Hugdahl, & Rimmo, 1976; Ohman & Mineka, 2001).

The behavioral theory seems to provide a compelling explanation for phobias, particularly when we add the principles of observational learning and prepared classical conditioning. It has also led to effective therapies. Its most significant problem is that many people with phobias can identify no traumatic event in their own lives or the lives of people they are close to that triggered their phobias. Without conditioned stimuli, it is hard to argue that they developed their phobias through classical conditioning or observational learning. Some individuals who develop phobias may have a chronic low-level anxiety or reactivity, which makes them more susceptible to the development of phobias given even mildly aversive experiences (Craske & Waters, 2005).

Biological Theories

The first-degree relatives (that is, parents, children, and siblings) of people with phobias are three to four times more likely to have a phobia than the first-degree relatives of people without phobias. Twin studies suggest that this is due, at least in part, to genetics (Hettema, Neale, & Kendler, 2001; Merikangas, Lieb, Wittchen, & Avenevoli, 2003). Some studies suggest that situational and animal phobias are associated with similar genes, while other studies suggest a general tendency toward phobias that is not isolated to one type of phobia (LeBeau et al., 2010).

Treatments for Phobias

A number of behavioral techniques can treat phobias. Some therapists include cognitive techniques and medications.

Behavioral Treatments

Behavioral therapies for phobias use exposure to extinguish the person's fear of the object or situation. These therapies cure the majority of phobias (Hopko, Robertson, Widman, & Lejuez, 2008). Some studies suggest that just one, intensive session of behavior therapy can lead to major reductions in phobic behaviors and anxiety (Ollendick & Davis, 2013). Three basic components of behavior therapy for phobias are systematic desensitization, modeling, and flooding.

As we have already discussed, in systematic desensitization clients formulate lists of situations or objects they fear, ranked from most to least feared. They learn relaxation techniques and begin to expose themselves to the items on their "hierarchy of fears," beginning with the least feared. A person with a severe dog phobia who has "seeing a picture of a dog in a magazine" first on her list might look at a picture of a dog. The therapist will coach her to use relaxation techniques to replace her anxiety with a calm reaction. When she can look at a picture of a dog without experiencing anxiety, she might move on to looking at a dog in a pet store window, again using relaxation techniques to lower her anxiety reaction and replace it with calm. Gradually, the client and therapist will move through the entire list, "relearning" that dogs can lead to neutral or positive consequences, until the client is able to pet a big dog without feeling overwhelming anxiety (Craske, Treanor, Conway, Zbozinek, & Vervliet, 2014).

Blood-injection-injury phobia requires a different approach, because people with this phobia experience severe decreases in heart rate and blood pressure (Öst & Sterner, 1987). Thus, therapists teach them to tense the muscles in their arms, legs, and chest until they feel the warmth of their blood rising in their faces. This **applied tension technique** increases blood pressure and heart rate and can keep people with this type of phobia from fainting when confronted with the feared object. Then systematic desensitization can help extinguish fear of blood, injury, or injections.

Modeling techniques are often adopted in conjunction with systematic desensitization. A therapist treating a person with a snake phobia may perform (model) each behavior on the client's hierarchy of fears before asking the client to perform it. The therapist will stand in the room with the snake before asking the client to do so, touch the snake before asking the client to do so, and hold the snake before the client does. Through observational learning, the client associates these behaviors with a calm response in the therapist, which reduces anxiety about engaging in the

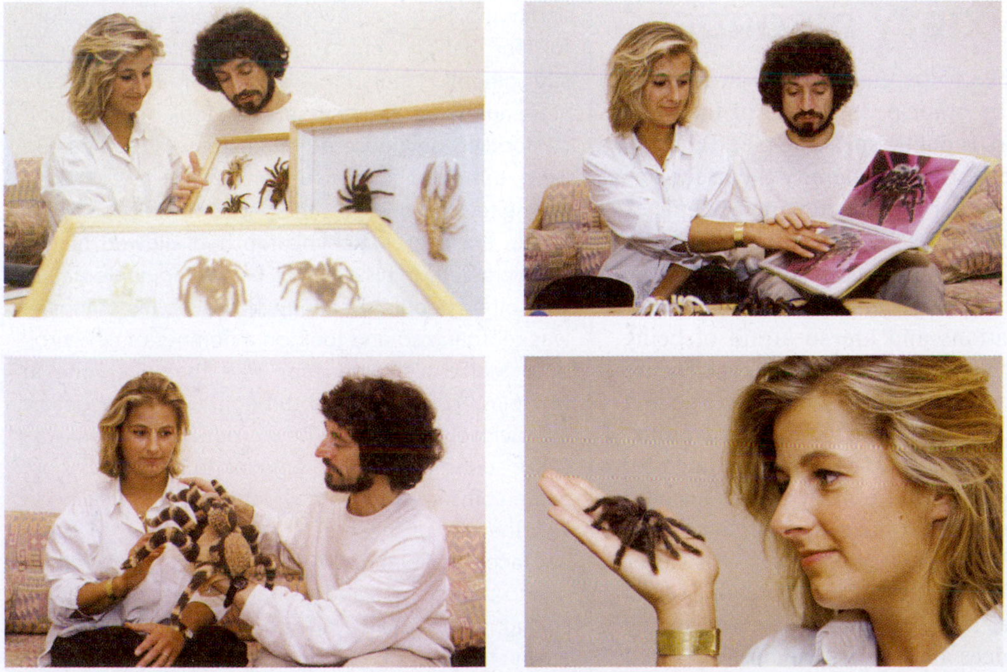

The therapist shows dead spiders behind glass to this woman as a first step in desensitizing her fear. The next step is having her touch pictures of spiders, so that she confronts a higher level of fear. Next, the woman is invited to go a step further by holding a stuffed toy spider. The process of desensitization is complete when the woman is able to hold a live spider on her hand without a problematic level of fear. *©ullstein bild/Getty Images*

behaviors. Modeling is as effective as systematic desensitization in reducing phobias (Bandura, 1969).

Flooding intensively exposes a client to his or her feared object until anxiety is extinguished. In a flooding treatment, a person with claustrophobia might lock himself in a closet for several hours, and a person with a dog phobia might spend the night in a dog kennel. The therapist typically will prepare clients with relaxation techniques they can use to reduce their fear. Flooding is as effective as systematic desensitization or modeling and often works more quickly. However, it is more difficult to get clients to agree to this type of therapy, because it is frightening to contemplate.

Biological Treatments

Some people use the benzodiazepines to reduce their anxiety when forced to confront their phobic objects; for example, they use Valium before flying or giving a presentation. These drugs produce temporary relief, but the phobia remains (Jefferson, 2001). In fact, this temporary relief provided by benzodiazepines–along with the risk of withdrawal symptoms when they wear off–can lead to benzodiazepine addiction, creating more problems than it solves. In contrast, behavioral techniques can cure most phobias in a few hours (Davis, Ollendick, & Öst, 2009). It is also important to note that although behavioral treatments are quite effective, relapse is not uncommon. Researchers are working to better understand how the extinction of irrational fears can be maintained over the long term (Vervliet, Craske, & Hermans, 2013). For now, it appears that the age-old advice to "confront your fears" through behavior therapy is the best strategy.

SOCIAL ANXIETY DISORDER

Most of us don't like to be embarrassed in front of others or rejected by other people. One of the most common social fears is public speaking (see Table 4). Nearly half of college students identify themselves as "shy" and say they get nervous meeting new people or encountering unfamiliar social situations (Heiser, Turner, & Beidel, 2003). Such concerns are normal, but people with **social anxiety disorder** become so anxious in social situations and are so afraid of being rejected, judged, or humiliated in public that they are preoccupied with worries about such events to the point that their lives may become focused on avoiding social encounters (see the *DSM-5* criteria in Table 5). Social anxiety disorder is more likely than a specific phobia to create severe disruption in a person's daily life (Bögels et al., 2010). In most cultures, it is easier to avoid snakes or spiders than it is to avoid social situations. Consider the inner pain Malcolm, in the case study, experiences and the way he has organized his life to avoid social situations.

TABLE 4 Lifetime Prevalence of Social Fears in a National Survey

Social Fear	Percentage of People Saying They Experienced the Fear in Their Lifetime
Public speaking	30.2%
Talking in front of a small group	15.2
Talking with others	13.7
Using a toilet away from home	6.6
Writing while someone watches	6.4
Eating or drinking in public	2.7
Any social fear	38.6

Source: Kessler, Stein, & Berglund, 1998, p. 614.

CASE STUDY

Malcolm was a computer expert who worked for a large software firm. One of the things he hated most was to ride the elevator at his office when there were other people riding it. He felt that everyone was watching him, commenting silently on his rumpled clothes, and noticing every time he moved. He held his breath for almost the entire elevator ride, afraid that he might say something or make an embarrassing sound. Often, he walked up the eight flights of stairs to his office rather than risk that someone might get on the elevator with him.

Malcolm rarely went anywhere except to work and home. He hated even to go to the grocery store for fear that he would run his cart into someone or say something stupid to a clerk. He found a grocery store and several restaurants that took orders online for food to be delivered to customers' homes. He liked this service because he could avoid even talking to someone over the phone to place an order.

In the past, Malcolm's job had allowed him to remain quietly in his office all day, without interacting with other people. Recently, however, his company was reorganized and took on a number of new projects. Malcolm's supervisor said that everyone in Malcolm's group needed to begin working together more closely to develop new products. Malcolm was supposed to make a presentation to his group about some software he was developing, but he called in sick the day of the presentation because he could not face the situation. Malcolm was thinking that he had to change jobs and perhaps go into private consulting, so he could work from his home and avoid having to work with anyone else.

TABLE 5 *DSM-5* Criteria for Social Anxiety Disorder

A. Marked fear or anxiety about one or more social situations in which the individual is exposed to possible scrutiny by others. Examples include social interactions (e.g., having a conversation, meeting unfamiliar people), being observed (e.g., eating or drinking), and performing in front of others (e.g., giving a speech).

B. The individual fears that he or she will act in a way or show anxiety symptoms that will be negatively evaluated (i.e., will be humiliating or embarrassing; will lead to rejection or offend others).

C. The social situations almost always provoke fear or anxiety.

D. The social situations are avoided or endured with intense fear or anxiety.

E. The fear or anxiety is out of proportion to the actual threat posed by the social situation and to the sociocultural context.

F. The fear, anxiety, or avoidance is persistent, typically lasting for 6 months or more.

G. The fear, anxiety, or avoidance causes clinically significant distress or impairment in social, occupational, or other important areas of functioning.

H. The fear, anxiety, or avoidance is not attributable to the physiological effects of a substance (e.g., a drug of abuse, a medication) or another medical condition.

I. The fear, anxiety, or avoidance is not better explained by the symptoms of another mental disorder, such as panic disorder, body dysmorphic disorder, or autism spectrum disorder.

J. If another medical condition (e.g., Parkinson's disease, obesity, disfigurement from burns or injury) is present, the fear, anxiety, or avoidance is clearly unrelated or is excessive.

Specify if:

Performance only: If the fear is restricted to speaking or performing in public.

In social situations, people with social anxiety disorder may tremble and perspire, feel confused and dizzy, have heart palpitations, and eventually have a full panic attack. Like Malcolm in the case study, they think others see their nervousness and judge them as inarticulate, weak, stupid, or crazy. Malcolm avoided speaking in public and having conversations with others for fear of being judged. People with social anxiety disorder may avoid eating or drinking in public, for fear that they will make noises when they eat, drop food, or otherwise embarrass themselves. They may avoid writing in public, afraid that others will see their hands tremble. Men with social anxiety disorder often avoid urinating in public bathrooms. The key characteristic of social anxiety disorder is that the feared situations are social in nature.

Social anxiety disorder is relatively common, with a lifetime prevalence of about 12 percent in the United States (Kessler et al., 2005) and 1 to 7 percent internationally (Stein et al., 2017). Multiple studies show that women are somewhat more likely than men to develop this disorder (Asher, Asnaani, & Aderka, 2017; Xu et al., 2012). Women with social anxiety disorder tend to have more severe social fears than men, particularly with regard to performance situations (such as giving a presentation), but men seek treatment more often, possibly because their fears often include dating situations (Asher et al., 2017).

Social anxiety disorder tends to develop in either the early preschool years or adolescence. This is when many people become self-conscious and concerned about others' opinions of them (Blöte, Miers, Heyne, & Westenberg, 2015; Bögels et al., 2010). Over 90 percent of adults with social anxiety disorder report humiliating experiences earlier in their lives that contributed to their symptoms, such as extreme teasing as a child (McCabe, Antony, Summerfeldt, Liss, & Swinson, 2003). Others report feeling uncomfortable in social situations as far back as they can remember. Social anxiety disorder often co-occurs with mood disorders and other anxiety disorders. Once it develops, social anxiety disorder tends to be chronic if left untreated, and most people do not seek treatment (Kessler, 2003).

In Japan, the term *taijinkyofu-sho* describes an intense fear of interpersonal relations. Taijinkyofu-sho is characterized by shame about and persistent fear of causing others offense, embarrassment, or even harm through one's personal inadequacies. It is most frequently encountered, at least in treatment settings, among young men. People with this disorder may fear blushing, emitting body odor, displaying unsightly body parts, speaking their thoughts aloud, or irritating others (see Lewis-Fernandez et al., 2010). This concern is in line with the emphasis in Japan on deference to others (Kirmayer, 2001).

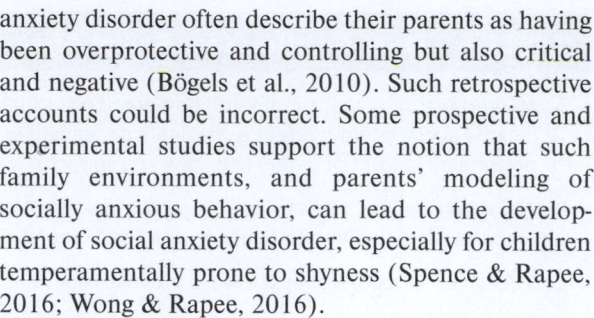

Theories of Social Anxiety Disorder

Social anxiety, or more generally shyness, runs in families, and twin studies suggest it has a genetic basis (Scaini, Belotti, & Ogliari, 2014). Genetic factors appear to lead, not specifically to anxiety about social situations, however, but instead to a more general tendency toward the anxiety disorders (Shimada-Sugimoto, Otowa, & Hettema, 2015), possibly via their role in the brain areas of the amygdala, hippocampus, and prefrontal cortex (Bas-Hoogendam et al., 2016).

Cognitive perspectives on social anxiety disorder have dominated psychological theories (Heimberg, Brozovich, & Rapee, 2010; Morrison & Heimberg, 2013). According to these perspectives, people with social anxiety disorder have excessively high standards for their social performance—for example, they believe they should be liked by everyone. They also focus on negative aspects of social interactions and evaluate their own behavior harshly. They tend to notice potentially threatening social cues (such as a grimace on the face of the person they are speaking to), misinterpret them in self-defeating ways, and overvalue social evaluation (Wong & Rapee, 2016). They are exquisitely attuned to their self-presentation and their internal feelings and tend to assume that, if they feel anxious, it is because the social interaction is not going well (Clark & Wells, 1995). They engage in a number of "safety behaviors" to reduce their anxiety. For example, they may avoid eye contact, or social interactions altogether; excessively rehearse what they will say in an interaction; and fail to self-disclose, thereby reducing the quality of the social interaction and the impression they actually leave with others (Morrison & Heimberg, 2013). After a social interaction, they ruminate excessively about their performance and the other person's reactions.

The popular singer-songwriter Sia, who often hides her face in public performances, has described paralyzing social anxiety that led to depression, substance abuse, and thoughts of suicide before she developed coping strategies.
©Frederick M. Brown/Getty Images

What creates these behavioral habits and cognitive biases? Adults with social anxiety disorder often describe their parents as having been overprotective and controlling but also critical and negative (Bögels et al., 2010). Such retrospective accounts could be incorrect. Some prospective and experimental studies support the notion that such family environments, and parents' modeling of socially anxious behavior, can lead to the development of social anxiety disorder, especially for children temperamentally prone to shyness (Spence & Rapee, 2016; Wong & Rapee, 2016).

Treatments for Social Anxiety Disorder

The selective serotonin reuptake inhibitors (SSRIs) and serotonin-norepinephrine reuptake inhibitors (SNRIs) have been shown to be efficacious in reducing symptoms of social anxiety (see meta-analysis by Mayo-Wilson et al., 2014). Symptoms tend to return when individuals stop taking these medications, however.

Cognitive-behavioral therapy (CBT) seems particularly useful for treating social anxiety (Mayo-Wilson et al., 2014; Morrison & Heimberg, 2013). The behavioral component of this therapy involves exposing clients to social situations that make them anxious, starting with the least anxiety-producing situations and working up to the more anxiety-producing situations. Therapists may role-play situations with clients (e.g., having a conversation with a store clerk), accompany clients in social situations to coach them as they engage in social encounters, and assign clients homework to carry out "experiments" in which they attempt a social interaction they believe they can't tolerate. They may teach them relaxation techniques to quell their anxiety in these situations or skills that can help them interact more effectively with others, for example, in starting conversations. They also help them recognize and eliminate their safety behaviors (e.g., avoiding eye contact). The cognitive component of therapy involves identifying negative cognitions clients have about themselves and about social situations and teaching them how to dispute these cognitions. CBT for social anxiety can be administered in a group setting in which group members form an audience for one another, providing exposure to the very situation each member fears. Individuals can practice their feared behaviors in front of the others while the therapist coaches them in the use of relaxation techniques to calm their anxiety. The group can also help the individual challenge any negative, catastrophizing thoughts about his or her behavior, as in the following excerpt from a group cognitive therapy session with Gina.

PROFILES

Therapist: So your automatic thought is, "I don't know how to have a conversation," is that right?

Gina: Yeah, I always screw it up.

Therapist: All right, let's ask the rest of the group what they think about that. Who has had a conversation with Gina or noticed her talking with someone else?

Ed: We walked out to our cars together last week and talked in the parking lot for a while. [Several other group members mention similar conversations.]

Therapist: So it sounds like you have had a number of conversations with the rest of the group.

Gina: I guess so.

Therapist: Group, how did she do? How did the conversations go?

Sally: It was fine. She was asking me about my car, because she has been looking for a new one, so we talked mostly about that. [Other group members provide similar answers.]

Therapist: Well, Gina, the rest of the group doesn't seem to agree that you don't know how to have conversations.

Gina: I guess I've always been so nervous that I never stopped to think that sometimes the conversations go OK.

(Source: Adapted from Turk, Heimberg, & Hope, 2001, pp. 124–125)

A number of meta-analyses have found that CBT is an effective treatment for social anxiety disorder, is just as effective as antidepressants in reducing symptoms over the course of therapy, and is much more effective in preventing relapse following therapy (see Morrison & Heimberg, 2013; Mayo-Wilson et al., 2014).

Mindfulness-based interventions also can prove helpful for people with social anxiety disorder (Goldin & Gross, 2010). These interventions teach individuals to be less judgmental about their own thoughts and reactions and more focused on, and relaxed in, the present moment. Therapies such as acceptance and commitment therapy (ACT)—which builds on CBT techniques to emphasize mindfulness, acceptance, and values—are similar to CBT in effectiveness for social anxiety disorder (Craske, Niles, et al., 2014).

In addition to individual therapy for social anxiety disorder, cognitive-behavioral therapies delivered in a group format have also been shown to be about equally effective (Mayo-Wilson et al., 2014; Wersebe, Sijbrandij, & Cuijpers, 2013). As you might imagine, group settings allow a natural way to engage patients in social situations, increasing exposure while also building social skills (Herbert et al., 2005), though for some clients, individual therapy is preferred. New treatments that use virtual reality technology to present a "social" scenario in individual treatment appear to have some effectiveness as well (Anderson et al., 2013), but research in this area is in its earlier stages.

PANIC DISORDER

CASE STUDY

The first time Celia had a panic attack, two days before her twentieth birthday, she was working at McDonald's. As she was handing a customer a Big Mac, the earth seemed to open up beneath her. Her heart began to pound, she felt she was suffocating, she broke into a sweat, and she was sure she was going to have a heart attack and die. After about 20 minutes of terror, the panic subsided. Trembling, she got in her car, raced home, and barely left the house for the next 3 months.

Since that time, Celia has had about three attacks a month. She does not know when they are coming. During them she feels dread, searing chest pain, suffocating and choking, dizziness, and shakiness. She sometimes thinks this is all not real and she is going crazy. She also thinks she is going to die.

(Source: Adapted from Seligman, 1993, p. 61)

Celia is suffering from **panic attacks,** short but intense periods during which she experiences many symptoms of anxiety: heart palpitations, trembling, a feeling of choking, dizziness, intense dread, and so on (Table 6). Celia's panic attacks appear to come "out of the blue," in the absence of any environmental trigger. Simply handing a customer a hamburger should not cause such terror. This is one of the baffling characteristics of some panic attacks.

Other people have panic attacks triggered by specific situations or events. Someone with a social anxiety disorder, for instance, may have a panic attack when forced into a social situation (Craske et al., 2010). Most commonly, panic attacks arise in certain situations but not every time. In all cases, however, they are terrifying experiences, causing a person intense fear or discomfort, the physiological symptoms of anxiety, and the feeling of losing control, going crazy, or dying.

TABLE 6 *DSM-5* Diagnostic Criteria for Panic Disorder

A. Recurrent unexpected panic attacks. A panic attack is an abrupt surge of intense fear or intense discomfort that reaches a peak within minutes, and during which time four (or more) of the following symptoms occur:

Note: The abrupt surge can occur from a calm state or an anxious state.

1. Palpitations, pounding heart, or accelerated heart rate.
2. Sweating.
3. Trembling or shaking.
4. Sensations of shortness of breath or smothering.
5. Feelings of choking.
6. Chest pain or discomfort.
7. Nausea or abdominal distress.
8. Feeling dizzy, unsteady, light-headed, or faint.
9. Chills or heat sensations.
10. Paresthesias (numbness or tingling sensations).
11. Derealization (feelings of unreality) or depersonalization (being detached from oneself).
12. Fear of losing control or "going crazy."
13. Fear of dying.

Note: Culture-specific symptoms (e.g., tinnitus, neck soreness, headache, uncontrollable screaming or crying) may be seen. Such symptoms should not count as one of the four required symptoms.

B. At least one of the attacks has been followed by 1 month (or more) of one or both of the following:

1. Persistent concern or worry about additional panic attacks or their consequences (e.g., losing control, having a heart attack, "going crazy").
2. A significant maladaptive change in behavior related to the attacks (e.g., behaviors designed to avoid having panic attacks, such as avoidance of exercise or unfamiliar situations).

C. The disturbance is not attributable to the physiological effects of a substance (e.g., a drug of abuse, a medication) or another medical condition (e.g., hyperthyroidism, cardiopulmonary disorders).

D. The disturbance is not better explained by another mental disorder (e.g., the panic attacks do not occur only in response to feared social situations, as in social anxiety disorder; in response to circumscribed phobic objects or situations, as in specific phobia; in response to obsessions, as in obsessive-compulsive disorder; in response to reminders of traumatic events, as in posttraumatic stress disorder; or in response to separation from attachment figures, as in separation anxiety disorder).

As many as 28 percent of adults have occasional panic attacks, especially during times of stress (Kessler, Chiu, et al., 2006). For most, the attacks are annoying but isolated events that do not change how they live their lives. A diagnosis of **panic disorder** is only made when the panic attacks are more problematic. This includes when they become a common occurrence, when they are not usually provoked by any particular situation but are unexpected, and when a person begins to worry about having them and changes behaviors as a result of this worry.

Some people with panic disorder have many episodes in a short period of time, such as every day for a week, and then go weeks or months without any episodes, followed by another period of frequent attacks. Other people have attacks less frequently but more regularly, such as once every week for months. Between full-blown attacks, they might experience minor bouts of panic.

People with panic disorder often fear that they have a life-threatening illness, and they are more likely to have a personal or family history of serious chronic illness. Even after such an illness is ruled out, they may continue to believe they are about to die of a heart attack, seizure, or other physical crisis. Another common but erroneous belief is that they are "going crazy" or "losing control." Many people with panic disorder feel ashamed and try to hide it from others. If left untreated, people with panic disorder may become demoralized and depressed (Craske & Waters, 2005).

About 3 to 5 percent of people will develop panic disorder at some time (Craske & Waters, 2005; Kessler et al., 2005), usually between late adolescence and the mid-thirties. It is more common in women and tends to be chronic (Craske & Waters, 2005). There is some evidence that panic disorder—as well as social anxiety disorder—may have a more chronic course among African Americans compared to Caucasians (Sibrava et al., 2013).

Panic disorder can be debilitating. Many sufferers also show chronic generalized anxiety, depression, and alcohol abuse (Wilson & Hayward, 2005). Those with panic disorder who are depressed or who abuse alcohol may be at an increased risk for suicide attempts (Craske et al., 2010).

Theories of Panic Disorder

Biological and cognitive theories interact to create vulnerability to panic disorder.

Biological Factors

Panic disorder clearly runs in families (Hettema et al., 2001), and family history and twin studies suggest that the heritability of panic disorder is about 43 to 48 percent (Wittchen et al., 2010). No specific genes have been consistently identified as causing panic disorder.

The fight-or-flight response appears to be poorly regulated in people who develop panic disorder, perhaps due to poor regulation of several neurotransmitters, including norepinephrine, serotonin, gamma-aminobutyric acid (GABA), and cholecystokinin (CCK; Charney et al., 2000). Panic attacks can easily be triggered in sufferers of panic disorder if they hyperventilate, inhale a small amount of carbon dioxide, ingest caffeine, breathe into a paper bag, or take infusions of sodium lactate, a substance that resembles the lactate produced during exercise (Craske & Barlow, 2014; Wittchen et al., 2010). These activities initiate the physiological changes of the fight-or-flight response. People without a history of panic attacks may experience some physical discomfort during these activities, but rarely a full-blown attack.

Neuroimaging studies show differences between people with panic disorder and those without panic disorder in several areas of the limbic system involved in the stress response, including the amygdala, hypothalamus, and hippocampus (Duval, Javanbakht, & Liberzon, 2015). People with the disorder also show dysregulation of norepinephrine systems in an area of the brain stem called the **locus ceruleus** (see Figure 4). The locus ceruleus has well-defined pathways to the limbic system. Poor regulation in the locus ceruleus may cause panic attacks, which then stimulate the limbic system, lowering the threshold for the activation of diffuse and chronic anxiety (Gorman, Papp, & Coplan, 1995). This anticipatory anxiety may, in turn, increase the likelihood of dysregulation of the locus ceruleus and thus of another panic attack.

Some women with panic disorder report increased anxiety symptoms during premenstrual periods and postpartum (Maeng & Milad, 2015). The hormone progesterone can affect the activity of both the serotonin and GABA neurotransmitter systems. Fluctuations in progesterone levels with the menstrual cycle or postpartum might lead to an imbalance or dysfunction of the serotonin or GABA systems, thereby influencing susceptibility. Increases in progesterone also can induce mild chronic hyperventilation. In women prone to panic attacks, this may be enough to induce a full-blown attack.

FIGURE 4 **Areas of the Brain Involved in Panic Disorder.** Several areas of the limbic system shown here, along with the locus ceruleus, may be involved in panic attacks.

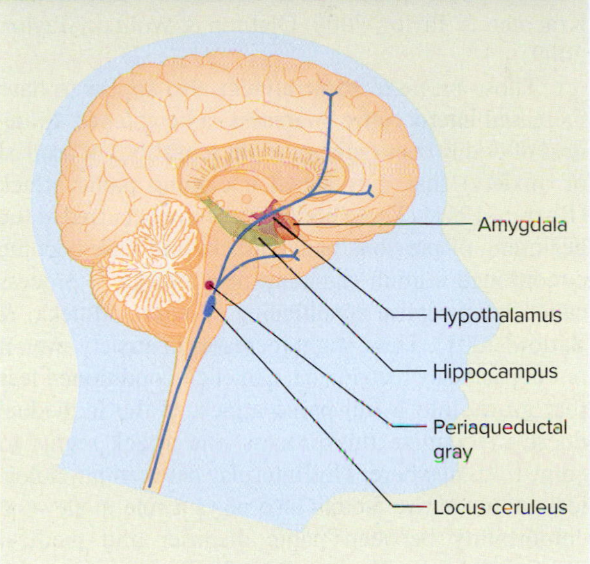

Cognitive Factors

Although many people with panic disorder may have a biological vulnerability to it, psychological factors also appear to help determine who develops the disorder. Cognitive theorists argue that people prone to panic attacks tend to (1) pay very close attention to their bodily sensations, (2) misinterpret these sensations in a negative way, and (3) engage in snowballing catastrophic thinking, exaggerating symptoms and their consequences (Barlow, 2011; Craske & Barlow, 2014). For example, a person not prone to panic disorder might feel a bit dizzy after standing up quickly and think "I'm feeling dizzy; I guess I stood up too quickly," and leave it at that. But a person prone to panic disorder might think, "I'm really dizzy. I think I'm going to faint. Maybe I'm having a seizure. Oh God, what's happening?" This kind of thinking increases the subjective sense of anxiety as well as physiological changes such as increased heart rate. The person interprets these feelings catastrophically and is on the way to a full panic attack. Between attacks, the person is hypervigilant for any bodily sensations, worrying about his or her health generally and about having more panic attacks specifically. This constant arousal makes further attacks more likely (Craske & Barlow, 2014).

The unfounded belief that bodily symptoms have harmful consequences is labeled **anxiety sensitivity** (McNally, 2002). People high in anxiety sensitivity are more likely than people low in it to have panic disorder, to have more frequent panic attacks, or to develop panic attacks over time (Hayward, Killen, Kraemer, & Taylor, 2000; Olatunji & Wolitzky-Taylor, 2009).

Those prone to panic attacks also appear to have increased **interoceptive awareness**—a heightened awareness of bodily cues (such as slight sensations of arousal or anxiety) that may signal a coming panic attack (Razran, 1961). These bodily cues have occurred at the beginning of previous panic attacks and have become conditioned stimuli signaling new attacks, a process called **interoceptive conditioning** (Bouton, Mineka, & Barlow, 2001). Thus, slight increases in anxiety, even if not consciously recognized, can elicit conditioned fear that grows into a full panic attack. If the individual doesn't recognize this process, the attack seems to come from nowhere. This interplay between physiological and cognitive factors also plays a role in elevated comorbidity between panic disorder and medical illnesses (Meuret, Kroll, & Ritz, 2017).

Beliefs about the controllability of symptoms appear to be important to the development of panic attacks. In one study, two groups of people with panic disorder were asked to wear breathing masks, which delivered air slightly enriched with carbon dioxide. Participants were warned that inhaling carbon dioxide could induce an attack. One group was told they could not control the amount of carbon dioxide that came through their masks. The other group was told they could control it by turning a knob. Actually, neither group had any control over the amount of carbon dioxide, and both groups inhaled the same amount. However, 80 percent of the people who believed they had no control experienced a panic attack, compared to 20 percent of those who believed they had control (Sanderson, Rapee, & Barlow, 1989). In summary, a number of cognitive factors contribute to panic disorder, including biased thoughts, anxiety sensitivity, high interoceptive awareness, interoceptive conditioning (learning), and beliefs about controllability.

FIGURE 5 **An Integrated Model of Panic Disorder.** Biological and psychological factors come together to create panic disorder and agoraphobia.

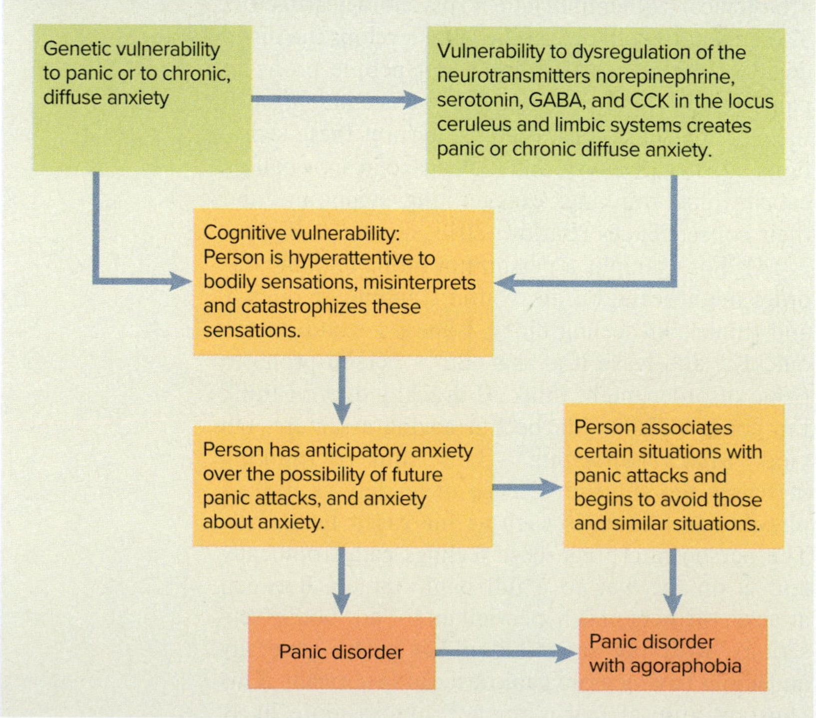
Genetic vulnerability to panic or to chronic, diffuse anxiety
Vulnerability to dysregulation of the neurotransmitters norepinephrine, serotonin, GABA, and CCK in the locus ceruleus and limbic systems creates panic or chronic diffuse anxiety.
Cognitive vulnerability: Person is hyperattentive to bodily sensations, misinterprets and catastrophizes these sensations.
Person has anticipatory anxiety over the possibility of future panic attacks, and anxiety about anxiety.
Person associates certain situations with panic attacks and begins to avoid those and similar situations.
Panic disorder
Panic disorder with agoraphobia

An Integrated Model

The biological and psychological factors of panic disorder have been integrated into the model illustrated in Figure 5 (Bouton et al., 2001; Craske & Waters, 2005). Many people who develop panic disorder seem to have a biological vulnerability to a hypersensitive fight-or-flight response. Presented with only a mild stimulus, their heart begins to race, their breathing becomes rapid, and their palms begin to sweat.

These people typically will not develop frequent panic attacks or a panic disorder, however, unless they engage in catastrophizing thinking about their physiological symptoms. Such cognitions increase the intensity of initially mild physiological symptoms to the point of a panic attack. They also make the individuals hypervigilant for signs of another panic attack, putting them at a constant mild to moderate level of anxiety. This anxiety increases the probability that they will become panicked again, and the cycle continues.

Some people then begin to associate certain situations with symptoms of panic and may begin to feel them again if they return to the situations. By avoiding these places, they reduce their symptoms, thereby reinforcing their avoidance behavior. This process is known as a **conditioned avoidance response** (Mowrer, 1939). Thus, a man who has a panic attack while sitting in a theater may later associate the theater with his symptoms and begin to feel anxious whenever he is near it. By avoiding it, he can reduce his anxiety. He may associate other places, such as his home or a specific room, with lowered anxiety levels, so being in these places is reinforcing. Eventually, he confines himself to his safe places and avoids a wide range of places he feels are unsafe. Thus he develops agoraphobia, which frequently co-occurs with panic disorder.

Treatments for Panic Disorder

Both biological and psychological treatments for panic disorder have been developed. Certain antidepressant drugs effectively treat panic attacks and agoraphobia, and the benzodiazepines can help some people. Cognitive-behavioral therapies appear to be as successful as medications in reducing symptoms and better than medications at preventing relapse.

Biological Treatments

The most common biological treatment for panic disorder is medication affecting serotonin and norepinephrine systems, including selective serotonin reuptake inhibitors (SSRIs, such as Paxil, Prozac, Zoloft), serotonin-norepinephrine reuptake inhibitors (SNRIs, such as Effexor), and tricyclic antidepressants (Batelaan, Van Balkom, & Stein, 2012; see the chapter "Theories and Treatment of Abnormality" for common side effects of these drugs). The benzodiazepines, which work quickly to reduce panic attacks and general symptoms of anxiety in most patients, are also often prescribed (Susman & Klee, 2005). Benzodiazepines suppress the central nervous system and influence functioning in the GABA, norepinephrine, and serotonin neurotransmitter systems. Unfortunately, they are physically (and psychologically) addictive and have significant withdrawal symptoms (see the chapter "Theories and Treatment of Abnormality"). Most people with panic disorder will experience a relapse of symptoms when drug therapies are discontinued if they have not also received cognitive-behavioral therapy (Batelaan et al., 2012).

FIGURE 6 **A Panic Thoughts Diary.** This man recorded the thoughts he had had during panic attacks and then worked on these thoughts in cognitive therapy.

SITUATION	SYMPTOMS AND SEVERITY	THOUGHTS
Office at work	Choking (mild) Dizziness (mild) Heart racing (mild)	Oh, I can't have an attack here. People will see me and I might get fired. I'm suffocating! I'm going to faint.
Riding subway home	Sweating (severe) Choking (severe) Shaking (severe) Heart racing (severe) Dizziness (severe)	I can't stand this! I've got to get out of here. I'm going to choke to death. I'm trapped. I'm going to faint!
At home	Sweating (mild) Heart still racing (moderate) A little faintness	I can't believe I made it home.

Cognitive-Behavioral Therapy

As in treatment for PTSD and phobias, cognitive-behavioral therapy for panic disorder has clients confront the situations or thoughts that arouse anxiety. Confrontation seems to help in two ways: It allows clients to challenge and change irrational thoughts about these situations, and it helps them extinguish anxious behaviors.

Cognitive-behavioral interventions have multiple components (Craske & Barlow, 2014). First, clients are taught relaxation and breathing exercises, which impart some control over symptoms and permit clients to engage in the other components of the therapy. Second, the clinician guides clients in identifying the catastrophizing cognitions they have about changes in bodily sensations. Clients may keep diaries of their thoughts about their bodies on days between sessions, particularly at times when they begin to feel they are going to panic. Figure 6 shows one man's panic thoughts diary. He noted mild symptoms of panic at work but more severe symptoms while riding the subway home. In both situations, he had thoughts about feeling trapped, suffocating, and fainting.

Many clients, too overwhelmed while having symptoms to pay attention to their thoughts, need to experience panic symptoms in the presence of their therapist in order to identify their catastrophizing cognitions (Craske & Barlow, 2014). The therapist may try to induce symptoms during sessions by having clients exercise to elevate their heart rate, spin to get dizzy, or put their head between their knees and then stand up quickly to get light-headed (due to sudden changes in blood pressure). None of these activities is dangerous, but all are likely to produce the kind of symptoms clients catastrophize. As clients experience these symptoms and their catastrophizing cognitions, the therapist helps them collect their thoughts.

Third, clients practice relaxation and breathing exercises while experiencing panic symptoms during the session. If attacks occur during sessions, the therapist talks clients through them, coaching them in the use of relaxation and breathing techniques, suggesting ways to improve their skills, and noting clients' success in using the skills to stop the attacks.

Fourth, the therapist challenges clients' catastrophizing thoughts about their bodily sensations and teaches them to challenge these thoughts themselves, using the cognitive techniques described in the chapter "Theories and Treatment of Abnormality." The therapist might help clients reinterpret the sensations accurately. For example, the client whose thoughts are listed in Figure 6 frequently felt as if he were choking. His therapist might explore whether his choking sensation might be due to the stuffiness of a small office or a subway on a warm summer day. If he interprets the increase in his heart rate as a heart attack, the therapist might have him collect evidence from his physician that he is in perfect cardiac health. The therapist might also explore the client's expectations that he will die of a heart attack because a relative did. If relaxation techniques allow a client to reduce panic symptoms during a therapy session, the therapist will challenge the client's belief that the symptoms are uncontrollable (Craske & Barlow, 2014).

Fifth, the therapist uses systematic desensitization therapy to expose clients gradually to the situations they fear most while helping them maintain control over their symptoms (Craske & Barlow, 2014). The client and therapist begin by listing panic-inducing situations, from most to least threatening. Then, after learning relaxation and breathing skills and perhaps gaining some control over panic symptoms induced during therapy sessions, clients begin to expose themselves to their panic-inducing situations, starting with the least threatening. The therapist might accompany clients in this exercise, coaching them in their relaxation and breathing skills and in how to challenge catastrophic cognitions that arise.

A large-scale, multisite study compared tricyclic antidepressants to cognitive-behavioral therapy (CBT) in the treatment of 312 people with panic disorder and found them equally effective in eliminating symptoms (Barlow, Gorman, Shear, & Woods, 2000). Several other studies have found that 85 to 90 percent of panic disorder patients treated with CBT experienced complete relief from their panic attacks within 12 weeks (Craske & Barlow, 2014; Schmidt & Keough, 2010). In follow-up studies of patients receiving CBT, nearly 90 percent were panic-free 2 years after treatment. Cognitive-behavioral therapy appears to be considerably better than antidepressants at preventing relapse after treatment ends, probably because this therapy teaches people strategies to prevent the recurrence of panic symptoms.

GENERALIZED ANXIETY DISORDER

PTSD, the phobias, social anxiety disorder, and panic disorder involve periods of anxiety that are acute and more or less specific to certain objects, thoughts, or situations. But some people are anxious all the time, in almost all situations. These people may be diagnosed with **generalized anxiety disorder (GAD;** Table 7). The key characteristic of GAD is uncontrollable worry. People with GAD worry about many things in their lives, as Claire describes in the following profile.

TABLE 7 *DSM-5* Criteria for Generalized Anxiety Disorder

A. Excessive anxiety and worry (apprehensive expectation), occurring more days than not for at least 6 months, about a number of events or activities (such as work or school performance).

B. The individual finds it difficult to control the worry.

C. The anxiety and worry are associated with three (or more) of the following six symptoms (with at least some symptoms having been present for more days than not for the past 6 months):

1. Restlessness or feeling keyed up or on edge.
2. Being easily fatigued.
3. Difficulty concentrating or mind going blank.
4. Irritability.
5. Muscle tension.
6. Sleep disturbance (difficulty falling or staying asleep, or restless, unsatisfying sleep).

D. The anxiety, worry, or physical symptoms cause clinically significant distress or impairment in social, occupational, or other important areas of functioning.

E. The disturbance is not attributable to the direct physiological effects of a substance (e.g., a drug of abuse, a medication) or another medical condition (e.g., hyperthyroidism).

F. The disturbance is not better explained by another mental disorder (e.g., anxiety or worry about having panic attacks in panic disorder, negative evaluation in social anxiety disorder [social phobia], contamination or other obsessions in obsessive-compulsive disorder, separation from attachment figures in separation anxiety disorder, reminders of traumatic events in posttraumatic stress disorder, gaining weight in anorexia nervosa, physical complaints in somatic symptom disorder, perceived appearance flaws in body dysmorphic disorder, having a serious illness in illness anxiety disorder, or the content of delusional beliefs in schizophrenia or delusional disorder).

PROFILES

I just feel anxious and tense all the time. It started in high school. I was a straight-A student, and I worried constantly about my grades, whether the other kids and the teachers liked me, being prompt for classes—things like that. . . . Now I vacuum four times a week and clean the bathrooms every day. There have even been times when I've backed out of going out to dinner with my husband because the house needed to be cleaned.

I get so upset and irritated over minor things. . . . I still worry about being on time to church and to appointments. Now I find I worry a lot about my husband. He's been doing a tremendous amount of traveling for his job, some of it by car, but most of it by plane. Because he works on the northeastern seaboard, and because he frequently has to travel in the winter, I worry that he'll be stuck in bad weather and get into an accident or, God forbid, a plane crash.

Oh, and I worry about my son. He just started playing on the varsity football team, so he's bound to get an injury some time. It's so nerve-wracking to watch him play that I've stopped going to his games. I'm sure my son must be disappointed . . . , but it's simply too much for me to take. (Brown, T. A., O'Leary, T. A., & Barlow, D. H., *Generalized Anxiety Disorder, Clinical Handbook of Psychological Disorders: A Step-By-Step Treatment Manual,* 3rd ed., 2001, 193–194. Copyright ©2001 Guilford Press. Reprinted with permission)

People with GAD may worry about their performance on the job, their relationships, and their health. Like Claire, they also may worry about minor issues such as being late. The focus of their worries may shift frequently, and they tend to worry about many things instead of focusing on only one issue of concern (Andrews et al., 2010). Because of anxiety and worry about situations, these individuals frequently spend inordinate amounts of time and energy preparing for feared situations or avoiding those situations, are immobilized by procrastination and indecision, and seek reassurance from others. Their worry is accompanied by physiological symptoms, including muscle tension, sleep disturbances, and chronic restlessness. People with GAD feel tired much of the time, probably due to chronic muscle tension and sleep loss (Craske & Waters, 2005).

GAD is relatively common, with longitudinal studies showing as many as 14 percent of individuals meeting the criteria for the disorder at some time in their lives (Moffitt et al., 2010) and more women than men developing the disorder (Vesga-Lopez et al., 2008). It tends to be chronic (Kessler et al., 2002). Many people with this disorder report that they have been anxious all their lives; the disorder most commonly begins in childhood or adolescence. Almost 90 percent of people with GAD have another mental disorder, most often another anxiety disorder, but there are also high rates of comorbid mood disorders and substance abuse (Grant, Stinson, Dawson, Chou, & Ruan, 2005; Newman, Llera, Erickson, Przeworski, & Castonguay, 2013). GAD—more specifically, worry—increases the risk for physical ailments as well, particularly cardiovascular disease (see Newman et al., 2013).

Theories of Generalized Anxiety Disorder

Researchers have explored the emotional, cognitive, and biological dimensions of GAD.

Emotional and Cognitive Factors

People with GAD report experiencing more intense negative emotions, even compared to people with major depression (Aldao, Mennin, Linardatos, & Fresco, 2010), and are highly reactive to negative events (Tan et al., 2012). They report feeling that their emotions are not controllable or manageable (Newman et al., 2013). In neuroimaging studies, people with GAD showed heightened reactivity to emotional stimuli in the amygdala, an area of the brain involved in processing emotion (Schienle, Hettema, Caceda, & Nemeroff, 2011). Physiologically, they show chronically elevated activity of their sympathetic nervous systems and hyperreactivity to threatening stimuli (Brosschot, Van Dijk, & Thayer, 2007; Pieper, Brosschot, van der Leeden, & Thayer, 2010).

These emotional disturbances occur alongside cognitive disturbances. Cognitively, people with GAD make a number of maladaptive assumptions, such as "It's always best to expect the worst" and "I must anticipate and prepare myself at all times for any possible danger" (Beck & Emery, 1985; Ellis, 1997). Many of these assumptions reflect concerns about losing control or being unable to tolerate uncertainty. Their maladaptive assumptions lead people with GAD to respond to situations with automatic thoughts that stir up anxiety, cause them to be hypervigilant, and lead them to overreact (Beck & Emery, 1985). For example, when facing an exam, a person with GAD might reactively think, "I don't think I can do this," "I'll fall apart if I fail this test," and "I can't predict what will be on the test, so I have to stay up all night re-reading everything in the book in case it's on there."

Even the unconscious cognitions of people with GAD appear to focus on detecting possible threats in the environment (Mathews & MacLeod, 2005). In the Stroop color-naming task, participants are presented with words printed in color on a computer

FIGURE 7 **The Stroop Color-Naming Task.** In this task, words are flashed on a computer screen for a brief period of time, and the person is asked to name the color the word is printed in. People with generalized anxiety disorder are slower to name the color of words with threatening content than that of neutral words, presumably because they are attending to the content of the threatening words.

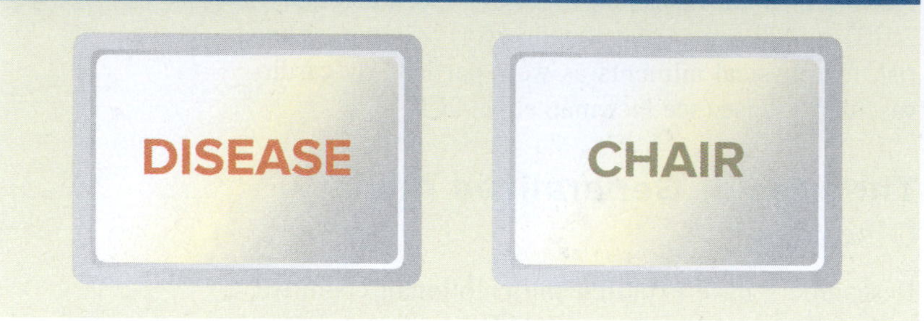

People with GAD maintain a constant level of anxiety. This level of distress may explain why such people sometimes display maladaptive behavior, including hostility, which in turn may exacerbate the GAD symptoms. *©Dmytro Zinkevych/Shutterstock*

screen (Figure 7). Their role is to say what color the word is printed in. In general, people are slower in naming the color of words that have special significance to them (such as disease or failure for people with chronic anxiety) than in naming the color of nonsignificant words. Presumably, they are paying more attention to the content of those words than to the colors (Mathews & MacLeod, 2005).

Why do some people become hypervigilant for signs of threat? One theory is that they have experienced stressors or traumas that were uncontrollable and came without warning, particularly an interpersonal trauma such as a rejection or a loss (see Newman et al., 2013). Animals given unpredictable and uncontrollable shocks often exhibit symptoms of chronic fear or anxiety. Studies have shown that the level of control and predictability in an infant monkey's life is related to the symptoms of anxiety it exhibits as an adolescent or adult (Mineka, Gunnar, & Champoux, 1986; Suomi, 1999). People who have had unpredictable and uncontrollable life experiences—such as an abusive parent—also may develop chronic anxiety (Newman et al., 2013). Other influences during childhood and adolescence may include negative parental behaviors, such as being overly controlling, demanding, protective, or rejecting.

What function does the characteristic worry of GAD serve? People with GAD say that worrying helps them avoid bad events by motivating them to engage in problem solving (Borkovec & Roemer, 1995). Yet they seldom get to the problem solving. Thomas Borkovec (Borkovec, Alcaine, & Behar, 2004), in his cognitive avoidance model of GAD, argued that worrying actually helps people with GAD avoid awareness of internal and external threats and thus helps reduce their reactivity to unavoidable negative events. Michelle Newman and Sandra Llera (2011) extended the cognitive avoidance model to suggest that by worrying about possible threats, people with GAD maintain a constant level of anxiety that is more tolerable than leaving themselves open to sudden sharp increases in negative emotion. That is, they prefer a chronic but familiar state of distress to sudden shifts in emotion in response to specific negative events, so using worry in this way is reinforced. This constant state of distress and hypervigilance may also explain why people with GAD sometimes display maladaptive interpersonal behavior—such as appearing cold, intrusive, or even hostile—which can exacerbate interpersonal problems and GAD symptoms (Przeworski et al., 2011).

Biological Factors

We've already noted that people with GAD show heightened activity of their sympathetic nervous system and greater reactivity to emotional stimuli in the amygdala, a part of the brain's limbic system. This greater activity may be associated with abnormalities in the GABA neurotransmitter system, which plays an important role in many areas of the brain, including the limbic system (Charney, 2004; Le Doux, 1996). When GABA binds to a neuronal receptor, it prevents the neuron from firing. One theory is that people with generalized anxiety disorder have a deficiency of GABA or of GABA receptors, which results in excessive firing of neurons through many areas of the brain, particularly the limbic system. As a result of excessive and chronic neuronal activity, the person experiences chronic, diffuse symptoms of anxiety.

Genetic studies suggest that GAD, as a specific disorder, has a modest heritability (Andrews et al., 2010). The more general trait of anxiety is much more clearly heritable and puts individuals at risk for GAD (Craske & Waters, 2005).

Treatments for Generalized Anxiety Disorder

The effective treatments for GAD are cognitive-behavioral or biological.

Cognitive-Behavioral Treatments

Cognitive-behavioral treatments focus on helping people with GAD confront the issues they worry about most; challenge their negative, catastrophizing thoughts; and develop coping strategies. In the following profile, a cognitive-behavioral therapist helps Claire challenge her tendency to overestimate the probability that her son will be injured while playing football.

PROFILES

Therapist: Claire, you wrote that you were afraid about your son playing in his football game. What specifically were you worried about?

Claire: That he'd get seriously hurt. His team was playing last year's state champions, so you know that those boys are big and strong.

Therapist: How specifically do you imagine your son getting hurt?

Claire: Getting a broken back or neck. Something that will result in paralysis or death. It happened to two NFL players this past year, remember?

Therapist: What happened to your son when he played in the game?

Claire: Nothing, really. He came home that afternoon with a sore thumb, but that went away after a while. He said he scored a touchdown and had an interception. I guess he played really well.

Therapist: So you had predicted that he would be injured during the game, but that didn't happen. When we're anxious, we tend to commit a common cognitive error, called "probability overestimation." In other words, we overestimate the likelihood of an unlikely event. While you were feeling anxious and worried, what was the probability in your mind that your son would be hurt, from 0 to 100 percent?

Claire: About 75 percent.

Therapist: And now what would you rate the probability of your son getting hurt in a future game?

Claire: Well, if you put it that way, I suppose around a 50 percent chance of him getting injured.

Therapist: So that means for every two times that your son plays football, he gets hurt once. Is that correct?

Claire: Umm, no. I don't think it's that high. Maybe about 30 percent.

Therapist: That would be one out of every three times that your son gets hurt. What evidence can you provide from your son's playing history to account for your belief that he'll get hurt one out of every three games?

Claire: Well, none. He had a sprained ankle during summer training, but that's it.

Therapist: So what you're saying is that you don't have very much evidence at all to prove that your son has a 30 percent chance of getting hurt in a game.

Claire: Gee, I never thought of it that way.

(Brown, T. A., O'Leary, T. A., & Barlow, D. H., *Generalized Anxiety Disorder, Clinical Handbook of Psychological Disorders: A Step-By-Step Treatment Manual,* 3rd ed., 2001, 193–194. Copyright ©2001 Guilford Press. Reprinted with permission)

Overall, cognitive-behavioral therapy for GAD appears equally effective as benzodiazepine therapy in the short term, and superior to placebos or nondirective supportive therapy (Borkovec, Newman, & Castonguay, 2003; Borkovec & Ruscio, 2001; Siev & Chambless, 2007). In one follow-up study, its positive effects remained after 2 years (Borkovec, Newman, Pincus, & Lytle, 2002). CBT for GAD also has effects on depression, which is important because GAD and depression often co-occur, and because anxiety can often precede the onset of depressive episodes (Cuijpers et al., 2014). This is a good example of how targeting common processes, like emotion dysregulation and negative thinking, can ameliorate symptoms of multiple disorders. A newer therapy, emotion regulation therapy (ERT), focuses on emotional awareness and regulation, and trials suggest it is efficacious in treating GAD with and without comorbid depression (Mennin, Fresco, O'Toole, & Heimberg, 2018).

Biological Treatments

The benzodiazepine drugs (such as Xanax, Librium, Valium, and Serax) provide short-term relief from anxiety symptoms (Gorman, 2003). However, their side effects and addictiveness preclude long-term use. Once people discontinue the drugs, their anxiety symptoms return (Davidson, 2001).

Both the tricyclic antidepressant imipramine (trade name Tofranil) and the selective serotonin reuptake inhibitor paroxetine (trade name Paxil) have been shown to be better than a placebo in reducing anxiety symptoms in GAD, and paroxetine improves anxiety more than a benzodiazepine. Venlafaxine (trade name Effexor), a serotonin-norepinephrine reuptake inhibitor, also reduces symptoms of anxiety in GAD better than a placebo (Davidson et al., 2008).

SEPARATION ANXIETY DISORDER

Children, like adults, can suffer from posttraumatic stress disorder, panic attacks, phobias, social anxiety disorder, and generalized anxiety disorder. One anxiety disorder is especially associated with childhood onset: **separation anxiety disorder** (see the *DSM-5* criteria in Table 8). Many infants become anxious and upset if they are separated from their primary caregivers. With development, however, most come to understand that their caregivers will return, and they find ways to comfort themselves while their caregivers are away.

However, some children continue to be extremely anxious when they are separated from their caregivers, even into childhood and adolescence. They may be very shy, sensitive, and demanding of adults. They may refuse to go to school because they fear separation, and they may experience stomachaches, headaches, nausea, and vomiting if forced to leave their caregivers. They may follow their caregivers around the house, have nightmares with themes of separation, and be unable to sleep at night unless they are with their caregivers. When separated from their caregivers, they worry that something bad will happen to the caregivers and harbor exaggerated fears of natural disasters, kidnappings, and accidents. Younger children may cry inconsolably. Older children may avoid activities, such as being on a baseball team, that might take them away from their caregivers.

Many children go through a few days of these symptoms after a traumatic event, such as getting lost in a shopping mall or seeing a parent hospitalized for a sudden illness. Separation anxiety disorder is not diagnosed unless symptoms persist for at least 4 weeks and significantly impair the child's functioning.

About 3 percent of children under age 11 years, more commonly girls, experience separation anxiety disorder (Rapee, Schniering, & Hudson, 2009). Left untreated, the disorder can recur throughout childhood and adolescence, significantly interfering with academic progress and peer relationships. One study examined the adult outcomes of children with separation anxiety who had refused to go to school. They had more psychiatric problems as adults than did the comparison group, were more likely to continue to live with their parents, and were less likely to have married and had children (Flakierska-Praquin, Lindstrom, & Gilberg, 1997).

In past versions of the *DSM,* separation anxiety disorder was classified among disorders diagnosed primarily in children or adolescents. In *DSM-5,* this disorder is listed under the anxiety disorders instead. In fact, up to 6 percent of U.S. adults report

TABLE 8 *DSM-5* Criteria for Separation Anxiety Disorder

A. Developmentally inappropriate and excessive fear or anxiety concerning separation from those to whom the individual is attached, as evidenced by at least three of the following:

1. Recurrent excessive distress when anticipating or experiencing separation from home or major attachment figures.
2. Persistent and excessive worry about losing major attachment figures or possible harm to them, such as illness, injury, disasters, or death.
3. Persistent and excessive worry about experiencing an untoward event (e.g., getting lost, being kidnapped, having an accident, becoming ill) that causes separation from a major attachment figure.
4. Persistent reluctance or refusal to go out, away from home, to school, to work, or elsewhere because of fear of separation.
5. Persistent and excessive fear or reluctance about being alone or without major attachment figures at home or in other settings.
6. Persistent reluctance or refusal to sleep away from home or to go to sleep without being near a major attachment figure.
7. Repeated nightmares involving the theme of separation.
8. Repeated complaints of physical symptoms (e.g., headaches, stomachaches, nausea, vomiting) when separation from major attachment figures occurs or is anticipated.

B. The fear, anxiety, or avoidance is persistent, lasting at least 4 weeks in children and adolescents and typically 6 months or more in adults.

C. The disturbance causes clinically significant distress or impairment in social, academic, occupational, or other important areas of functioning.

D. The disturbance is not better explained by another mental disorder, such as refusing to leave home because of excessive resistance to change in autism spectrum disorder; delusions or hallucinations concerning separation in psychotic disorders; refusal to go outside without a trusted companion in agoraphobia; worries about ill health or other harm befalling significant others in generalized anxiety disorder; or concerns about having an illness in illness anxiety disorder.

separation anxiety in adulthood, with over half reporting onset of symptoms in adulthood (as opposed to symptoms continuing from childhood onset). Adult separation anxiety disorder is linked with other anxiety and mood disorders as well (Bögels, Knappe, & Clark, 2013; Pini et al., 2010).

Theories of Separation Anxiety Disorder

Researchers have tended to focus on biological, psychological, and sociological theories to explain separation anxiety disorder.

Biological Factors

Children with separation anxiety disorder tend to have family histories of anxiety and depressive disorders (Biederman et al., 2001; Manicavasagar, Silove, Rapee, Waters, & Momartin, 2001). Twin studies suggest that the tendency toward anxiety is heritable, more so in girls than in boys. However, it is not clear that a specific tendency toward separation anxiety is heritable (Rapee et al., 2009). What may be inherited is a tendency toward a trait known as **behavioral inhibition.** Children high on behavioral inhibition are shy, fearful, and irritable as toddlers and cautious, quiet, and introverted as school-age children (Kagan, Reznick, & Snidman, 1987). These children tend to avoid or withdraw from novel situations, are clingy with their parents, and become excessively aroused in unfamiliar situations. Behavioral inhibition appears to be a risk factor for developing anxiety disorders in childhood (Caspi, Harrington, et al., 2003; Smoller, Cerrato, & Weatherall, 2015).

Psychological and Sociocultural Factors

Observational studies of interactions between anxious children and their parents show that the parents tend to be more controlling and intrusive both behaviorally and emotionally, and also more critical and negative in their communications with their children (Drake & Ginsburg, 2012). Some of this behavior may be in response to the children's anxious behaviors, but many parents of anxious children are themselves anxious or depressed.

Some of the best evidence that environmental and parenting factors can influence the development of anxiety disorders in youngsters comes from studies of primates (Mineka et al., 1986; Suomi, 1999). Susan Mineka and colleagues found that rhesus monkeys who, from ages 2 to 6 months, were given adequate food and water but could not control their access to them became fearful and inhibited. Other monkeys given the same amount of food and water but under conditions that allowed them to exert some control did not become fearful. This result suggests that some

Children with separation anxiety disorder often cling desperately to their parents. *©Geri Engberg/The Image Works*

human children raised in conditions over which they have little control may develop anxiety symptoms.

Moreover, Stephen Suomi (1999) found that although some rhesus monkeys seem to be born behaviorally inhibited, the extent to which they develop serious signs of fearfulness and anxiety later in life depends on the parenting they receive. Those raised by anxious mothers, who are inhibited and inappropriately responsive to the infants, are prone to develop monkey versions of anxiety disorders. Those raised by calm, responsive mothers who model appropriate reactions to stressful situations typically are no more likely to develop anxiety problems as adolescents or adults than those not born behaviorally inhibited.

Children may learn to be anxious from their parents or as an understandable response to their environment (Rapee et al., 2009). In some cases, such as in the following case study, separation anxiety disorder develops after a traumatic event.

CASE STUDY

In the early morning hours, 7-year-old Maria was abruptly awakened by a loud rumbling and violent shaking. She sat upright in bed and called out to her 10-year-old sister, Rosemary, who was leaping out of her own bed 3 feet away. The two girls ran for their mother's bedroom as their toys and books plummeted from shelves and dresser tops. The china hutch in the hallway teetered in front of them and then fell forward with a crash, blocking their path to their mother's room. Mrs. Marshall called out to them to go back and stay in their doorway. They huddled there together until the shaking finally stopped. Mrs.

(continued)

Marshall climbed over the hutch and broken china to her daughters. Although they were all very scared, they were unhurt.

Two weeks later, Maria began to complain every morning of stomachaches, headaches, and dizziness, asking to stay home with her mother. After 4 days, when a medical examination revealed no physical problems, Maria was told she must return to school. She protested tearfully, but her mother insisted, and Rosemary promised to hold her hand all the way to school. In the classroom, Maria could not concentrate on her schoolwork and was often out of her seat, looking out the window in the direction of home. She told her teacher she needed to go home to see whether her mother was okay. When told she couldn't go home, she began to cry and tremble so violently that the school nurse called Mrs. Marshall, who picked Maria up and took her home.

The next morning, Maria's protests grew stronger and she refused to go to school until her mother promised to go with her and sit in her classroom for the first hour. When Mrs. Marshall began to leave, Maria clung to her, crying, pleading for her not to leave, and following her into the hallway. The next day, Maria refused to leave the house for her Brownie meeting and her dancing lessons or even to play in the front yard. She followed her mother around the house and insisted on sleeping with her at night. "I need to be with you, Mommy, in case something happens," she declared.

Treatments for Separation Anxiety Disorder

Separation anxiety disorder is most often treated with cognitive-behavioral therapies (CBT) (Kendall, Crawford, Kagan, Furr, & Podell, 2017). Children are taught new skills for coping and for challenging cognitions that feed their anxiety. They might learn relaxation exercises to practice when they are separated from their parents. Their fears about separation are challenged, and they are taught to use self-talk to calm themselves when they become anxious.

As therapy progresses, the number and duration of periods of separation from their parents are increased. Parents must be willing to participate in therapy and to cope with their children's (and their own) reactions to increased periods of separation. Parents may need to be taught to model nonanxious reactions to separations from their children and to reinforce nonanxious behavior in their children.

Controlled clinical trials of this type of therapy show that it can be effective in the short term and maintain its effects over the long term (Rapee et al., 2009; Shortt, Barrett, & Fox, 2001; Velting, Setzer, & Albano, 2004). Philip Kendall and his colleagues (Kendall, Hudson, Gosch, Flannery-Schroeder, & Suveg, 2008) tested three treatments: individualized CBT to anxious children, family-based CBT to anxious children and their parents, and simple education and support. At the end of therapy, the children in both the individualized and the family-based CBT showed substantial declines in anxiety symptoms, while the children who received only education and support showed less improvement. With all three treatments, the declines in anxiety symptoms were sustained over a 1-year follow-up period.

Consider how Maria was treated for her separation anxiety.

CASE STUDY

Mrs. Marshall was instructed to take Maria to school and leave four times during the period she was there. Initially, Mrs. Marshall left for 30 seconds each time. Over time, she gradually increased the amount of time and distance she was away while Maria remained in the classroom. Maria was given a sticker at the end of the school day for each time she remained in her seat while her mother was out of the room. In addition, she was praised by her teacher and her mother, and positive self-statements ("My mommy will be okay; I'm a big girl and I can stay at school") were encouraged. No response was made when Maria failed to stay in her chair. Maria could exchange her stickers for prizes at the end of each week.

At home, Mrs. Marshall was instructed to give minimal attention to Maria's inquiries about her well-being and to ignore excessive, inappropriate crying. Eventually, Maria was given a sticker and praise each morning for sleeping in her own bed.

The first few times Mrs. Marshall left the classroom, Maria followed her out. Soon, however, she began to stay in her chair and receive stickers. At home, she remained in her own bed the first night, even though she was told she had to stay only 2 hours to earn her sticker. At her own request, she returned to Brownie meetings and attended summer camp.

Drugs used to treat childhood anxiety disorders include antidepressants; antianxiety drugs, such as the benzodiazepines; stimulants; and antihistamines. The selective serotonin reuptake inhibitors, such as fluoxetine and sertraline, are used most frequently and have been shown to be most consistent in effectively reducing anxiety symptoms in children (Strawn, Welge, Wehry, Keeshin, & Rynn, 2015; Walkup et al., 2008).

OBSESSIVE-COMPULSIVE DISORDER

Obsessions are thoughts, images, ideas, or urges (e.g., to harm oneself) that are persistent, that uncontrollably intrude on consciousness, and that usually cause significant anxiety or distress. **Compulsions** are repetitive behaviors or mental acts that an individual feels he or she must perform.

Obsessive-compulsive disorder (OCD; see Table 9) is diagnosed when either obsessions, compulsions, or both are present to a significant degree. Prior to the *DSM-5,* OCD was classified as an anxiety disorder because people with OCD experience anxiety as a result of their obsessional thoughts, as well as when they are unable to carry out their compulsive behaviors. OCD differs enough from the anxiety disorders, however, that the *DSM-5* authors moved OCD into its own category, along with several related disorders: *hoarding, hair-pulling disorder (also known as trichotillomania), skin-picking disorder*, and *body dysmorphic disorder* (Hirschtritt, Bloch, & Mathews, 2017). These disorders are linked by repetitive behaviors and impaired behavioral inhibition, but the removal of OCD from the anxiety disorder category is not without controversy (Abramowitz & Jacoby, 2015).

The obsessions and compulsions of some people with OCD, like David Beckham's obsession with orderliness described in the Extraordinary People feature at the beginning of this chapter, can seem simply quirky. Other patterns of obsessions and compulsions can appear much stranger, or even bizarre, as illustrated by the profile of a young boy named Zach who has OCD.

PROFILES

When I was 6 I started doing all these strange things when I swallowed saliva. . . . I had to . . . touch the ground. I didn't want to lose any saliva . . . and later I had to blink my eyes if I swallowed. I was frustrated because I couldn't stop the compulsions. Each time I swallowed I had to do something. For a while I had to touch my shoulders to my chin. . . . I had no reason. I was afraid. It was just so unpleasant if I didn't. If I tried not to do these things, all I got was failure. I had to do it, and no matter how hard I tried, I just *still* had to.

It wrecked my life. . . . I couldn't do anything. If you put it all together I did it maybe an hour and a half or sometimes three hours a day.

(Source: Rapoport, 1990, pp. 43–44)

TABLE 9 *DSM-5* Criteria for Obsessive-Compulsive Disorder

A. Presence of obsessions, compulsions, or both:

Obsessions are defined by (1) and (2):

1. Recurrent and persistent thoughts, urges, or images that are experienced, at some time during the disturbance, as intrusive and unwanted, and that in most individuals cause marked anxiety or distress.
2. The individual attempts to ignore or suppress such thoughts, urges, or images, or to neutralize them with some other thought or action (i.e., by performing a compulsion).

Compulsions are defined by (1) and (2):

1. Repetitive behaviors (e.g., hand washing, ordering, checking) or mental acts (e.g., praying, counting, repeating words silently) that the individual feels driven to perform in response to an obsession or according to rules that must be applied rigidly.
2. The behaviors or mental acts are aimed at preventing or reducing anxiety or distress, or preventing some dreaded event or situation; however, these behaviors or mental acts are not connected in a realistic way with what they are designed to neutralize or prevent, or are clearly excessive.

B. The obsessions or compulsions are time-consuming (e.g., take more than 1 hour per day) or cause clinically significant distress or impairment in social, occupational, or other important areas of functioning.

C. The obsessive-compulsive symptoms are not attributable to the physiological effects of a substance (e.g., a drug of abuse, a medication) or another medical condition.

D. The disturbance is not better explained by the symptoms of another mental disorder (e.g., excessive worries, as in generalized anxiety disorder; preoccupation with appearance, as in body dysmorphic disorder; difficulty discarding or parting with possessions, as in hoarding disorder; hair pulling, as in trichotillomania [hair-pulling disorder]; skin picking, as in excoriation [skin-picking] disorder; stereotypies, as in stereotypic movement disorder; ritualized eating behavior, as in eating disorders; preoccupation with substances or gambling, as in substance-related and addictive disorders; preoccupation with having an illness, as in illness anxiety disorder; sexual urges or fantasies, as in paraphilic disorders; impulses, as in disruptive, impulse-control, and conduct disorders; guilty ruminations, as in major depressive disorder; thought insertion or delusional preoccupations, as in schizophrenia spectrum and other psychotic disorders; or repetitive patterns of behavior, as in autism spectrum disorder).

Zach's thoughts and behaviors might seem out of touch with reality. However, an important part of OCD is that people with OCD usually know that their thoughts and behaviors are irrational. They simply cannot control them.

OCD often begins at a young age. The peak age of onset for males is between 6 and 15, and for females between 20 and 29 (Angst et al., 2004). Children often hide their symptoms, even from their parents; as a result, the symptoms can go undetected for years (Rapoport et al., 2000).

OCD tends to be chronic if left untreated (Leckman et al., 2010). Obsessional thoughts are usually distressing to people with OCD, and engaging in compulsive behaviors can be time-consuming or harmful (e.g., hand-washing to the point of bleeding). As many as 66 percent of people with OCD are also significantly depressed. Panic attacks, phobias, and substance abuse are common among OCD sufferers.

Between 1 and 3 percent of people will develop OCD at some time in their lives, and many more people will have symptoms that don't quite meet the diagnostic criteria (Kessler et al., 2005; Leckman et al., 2010). In the United States, European Americans show higher rates of OCD than African Americans or Hispanic Americans. The prevalence of OCD does not seem to differ greatly across countries that have been studied, including the United States, Canada, Mexico, England, Norway, Hong Kong, India, Egypt, Japan, and Korea (Escobar, 1993; Insel, 1984; Kim, 1993). Although some studies have found slightly higher rates in women (Angst et al., 2004), other studies have not (Edelmann, 1992; Karno & Golding, 1991).

Across cultures, the most common type of obsession in OCD is thoughts and images associated with aggression (such as thoughts of hurting one's child), sexuality (such as recurrent pornographic images), and/or religion (such as a compulsion to shout obscenities in a house of worship) (Bloch, Landeros-Weisenberger, Rosario, Pittenger, & Leckman, 2008). Although thoughts of this kind occur to most people occasionally, most of us can dismiss or ignore them. People with OCD cannot. The second most common type involves symmetry and ordering, such as David Beckham's arrangement of soda cans in the refrigerator. The third most common type of obsession concerns contamination and is often accompanied by a cleaning compulsion (Leckman et al., 2010). Howie Mandel, comedian and judge on *America's Got Talent,* has obsessions about germs and contamination that keep him from shaking hands with anyone (Mandel, 2009). He will do a fist bump with contestants but will not shake their hand. He keeps his head shaved because it helps him feel cleaner.

Often an individual's compulsion is tied logically to his or her obsession (Abramowitz & Jacoby, 2015). If Howie Mandel does touch someone's hand or an object he feels is dirty, he will wash his hands over and over until he feels clean (Mandel, 2009). The compulsive behavior becomes so extreme and repetitive that it is irrational. "Checking" compulsions, which are extremely common, are tied to obsessional doubts, as illustrated in the following profile.

PROFILES

I'm driving . . . doing 55 MPH. Out of nowhere an obsessive-compulsive disorder (OCD) attack strikes. While in reality no one is on the road, I'm intruded by the . . . thought that I *might* have hit someone . . . !

I . . . say to myself, "That's ridiculous. I didn't hit anybody." Nonetheless, a gnawing anxiety is born.

I reason, "Well, if I hit someone while driving, I would have *felt* it." This brief trip into reality helps the pain dissipate . . . for a second. Why? Because the . . . anxiety that I really did commit the illusionary accident is growing larger—so is the pain.

The pain is a terrible guilt that I have committed an unthinkable . . . act . . . I know this is ridiculous, but there's a . . . pain . . . telling me something . . . different.

I start ruminating, "Maybe I did hit someone and didn't realize it. . . . Oh, my God! I might have killed somebody! I have to go back and check." Checking is the only way to calm the anxiety. It brings me closer to truth somehow. I can't live with the thought that I actually may have killed someone—I have to check it out.

(Source: Rapoport, 1990, pp. 21–22)

The man's compulsive checking makes some sense, given what he is thinking. However, what he is thinking—that he hit someone on the road without knowing it—is highly improbable. The compulsive checking briefly quells his obsessional thoughts, but they recur with even more force.

Often, the link between the obsession and the compulsion is the result of "magical thinking" (Rapoport, 1991). Many people with OCD believe that repeating a behavior a certain number of times will ward off danger to themselves or others. Their rituals often become stereotyped and rigid, and they develop obsessions and compulsions about not performing them correctly. An individual might feel compelled to read a passage in a book 25 times perfectly, fearing that something bad will happen to his family if he does not. People with OCD vary in the degree to which they are aware of the irrationality of their obsessions and compulsions; many find themselves unable to manage their behaviors despite having insight into their irrationality.

Hoarding is a compulsive behavior that is closely related to OCD but is classified as a separate diagnosis in the *DSM-5* (see Table 10), due to evidence that hoarding has distinct features and may have different biological correlates (Frost, Steketee, & Tolin, 2012; Mataix-Cols et al., 2010). As featured in the reality TV show *Hoarding: Buried Alive*, people who hoard cannot throw away their possessions—even things that most of us consider trash, such as newspapers or take-out food containers. They stockpile these items in their homes and cars to the point of creating a hazard, making these spaces unusable. Compulsive hoarders often show emotional attachments to their possessions, equating them with their identity or imbuing them with human characteristics (Frost et al., 2012). For example, one woman bought a half dozen puppets from a TV shopping station because no one else was bidding on them and she didn't want the puppets' feelings to be hurt (Frost & Steketee, 2010). The woman fully realized her behavior wasn't rational, but she still felt bad for the puppets.

Epidemiological studies suggest that 2 to 5 percent of the population engage in hoarding (Iervolino et al., 2009). Only a small subset of people who hoard also meet the criteria for OCD, but these people also tend to have high rates of major depression, social anxiety, and generalized anxiety disorder (Frost et al., 2012; Samuels et al., 2008). People's hoarding behavior often increases as they age (Ayers, Saxena, Golshan, & Wetherell, 2009).

Hoarding differs from OCD in that people with the disorder experience thoughts about their possessions, not as intrusive, unwanted, or distressing, but instead as part of their natural stream of thought (Mataix-Cols et al., 2010). People who hoard do not experience anxiety about their hoarding behavior, but they may become extremely anxious, angry, or sad when pressured to get rid of their hoarded possessions.

People diagnosed with **hair-pulling disorder (trichotillomania)** have a history of the recurrent pulling out of their hair, resulting in noticeable hair loss. People with **skin-picking disorder** recurrently pick at scabs or places on their skin, creating significant lesions that often become infected and cause scars. People with both these disorders sometimes report

TABLE 10 *DSM-5* Criteria for Hoarding Disorder

A. Persistent difficulty discarding or parting with possessions, regardless of their actual value.

B. This difficulty is due to a perceived need to save the items and to distress associated with discarding them.

C. The difficulty discarding possessions results in the accumulation of possessions that congest and clutter active living areas and substantially compromises their intended use. If living areas are uncluttered, it is only because of the interventions of third parties (e.g., family members, cleaners, authorities).

D. The hoarding causes clinically significant distress or impairment in social, occupational, or other important areas of functioning (including maintaining a safe environment for self and others).

E. The hoarding is not attributable to another medical condition (e.g., brain injury, cerebrovascular disease, Prader-Willi syndrome).

F. The hoarding is not better explained by the symptoms of another mental disorder (e.g., obsessions in obsessive-compulsive disorder, decreased energy in major depressive disorder, delusions in schizophrenia or another psychotic disorder, cognitive deficits in major neurocognitive disorder, restricted interests in autism spectrum disorder).

Specify if:

With excessive acquisition: If difficulty discarding possessions is accompanied by excessive acquisition of items that are not needed or for which there is no available space.

Specify if:

With good or fair insight: The individual recognizes that hoarding-related beliefs and behaviors (pertaining to difficulty discarding items, clutter, or excessive acquisition) are problematic.

With poor insight: The individual is mostly convinced that hoarding-related beliefs and behaviors (pertaining to difficulty discarding items, clutter, or excessive acquisition) are not problematic despite evidence to the contrary.

With absent insight/delusional beliefs: The individual is completely convinced that hoarding-related beliefs and behaviors (pertaining to difficulty discarding items, clutter, or excessive acquisition) are not problematic despite evidence to the contrary.

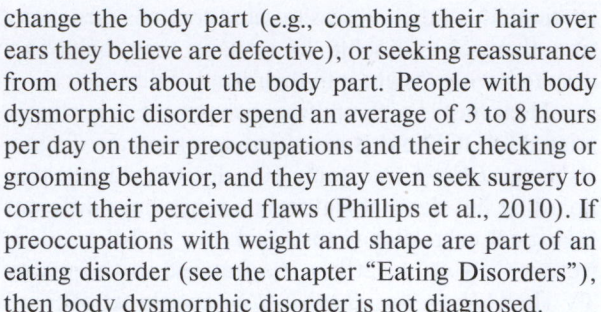

Only a small subset of people who hoard also meet the criteria for OCD, but hoarders tend to have high rates of major depression, social anxiety, and generalized anxiety disorder. *©Boston Globe/Getty Images*

tension immediately before or while attempting to resist the impulse, and pleasure or relief when giving in to it. Much of the time, however, the hair pulling or skin picking is automatic, occurring without much awareness (Stein, Grant et al., 2010).

Hair-pulling disorder and skin-picking disorder were included in the *DSM-5* category together with OCD and hoarding because they share features of repetitiveness, problems with behavioral inhibition, and show comorbidity (Lochner, Roos, & Stein, 2017; Woods & Houghton, 2014).The estimated prevalence of hair-pulling disorder is 1 to 3 percent (Christenson, Pyle, & Mitchell, 1991). It is seen most often in females, and the average age of onset is 13 (Christenson & Mansueto, 1999). The estimated prevalence of skin-picking disorder is 2 to 5 percent, and it most often begins in adolescence, often with a focus on acne lesions (Lochner et al., 2017).

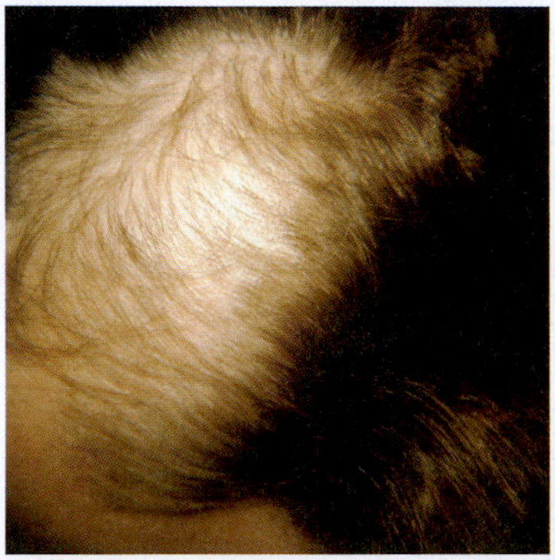

Trichotillomania is the compulsion to pull out one's own hair. *©JOHN F. WILSON, MD./Science Source*

People with **body dysmorphic disorder** are excessively preoccupied with a part of their body that they believe is defective but that others see as normal or only slightly unusual. These preoccupations most often focus on the face or head (e.g., nose, ears, skin), but they can focus on any body part (Phillips et al., 2010). As a result of their preoccupations, these people may spend a great deal of time checking themselves in the mirror, attempting to hide or change the body part (e.g., combing their hair over ears they believe are defective), or seeking reassurance from others about the body part. People with body dysmorphic disorder spend an average of 3 to 8 hours per day on their preoccupations and their checking or grooming behavior, and they may even seek surgery to correct their perceived flaws (Phillips et al., 2010). If preoccupations with weight and shape are part of an eating disorder (see the chapter "Eating Disorders"), then body dysmorphic disorder is not diagnosed.

Although it is not clear whether there are gender differences in the prevalence of this disorder, men and women with body dysmorphic disorder tend to obsess about different parts of their bodies (Phillips et al., 2010). Women seem to be more concerned with their breasts, legs, hips, and weight, whereas men tend to be preoccupied with their body build, their genitals, excessive body hair, and thinning hair. These gender differences likely represent extreme versions of societal norms concerning attractiveness in women and men.

Case studies of people with body dysmorphic disorder indicate that their perceptions of deformation can be so severe and bizarre as to be considered out of touch with reality (Phillips, Didie, Feusner, & Wilhelm, 2008). Even if they do not lose touch with reality, some people with the disorder have severe impairment in their functioning. Most people with this disorder avoid social activities because of their "deformity," many become housebound, and many obtain cosmetic surgery. About 30 percent attempt suicide (Phillips et al., 2008).

Body dysmorphic disorder tends to begin in the teenage years and to become chronic if left untreated. The average age of onset of this disorder is 16, and the average number of bodily preoccupations is about four. Body dysmorphic disorder is highly comorbid with several disorders, including anxiety and depressive disorders, personality disorders, and substance use disorders, and especially with OCD (Frías, Palma, Farriols, & González, 2015).

Theories of OCD and Related Disorders

The biological theories of OCD have dominated research in recent years. Cognitive-behavioral theories have also been proposed.

Biological Theories

Biological theories of obsessive-compulsive disorder have focused on a circuit in the brain involved in motor behavior, cognition, and emotion (Milad & Rauch, 2012). This circuit projects from specific areas of the frontal cortex to areas of the basal ganglia called the *striatum,* then through the basal ganglia to the thalamus, and then loops back to the frontal cortex

(Figure 8). People with OCD, hair-pulling disorder, and skin-picking disorder show alterations in the structure and activity level of these areas and in the connections between these areas (Milad & Rauch, 2012). People with hoarding disorder show alterations in other areas of the frontal cortex and the limbic system (Saxena, 2008). The brain activity of people with body dysmorphic disorder seems to differ from that of healthy controls when they are processing visual stimuli, including faces (Fang & Wilhelm, 2015).

For people with OCD and related disorders, dysfunction in this circuit may result in the system's inability to turn off the primitive urges (e.g., aggressive urges) or the execution of the stereotyped behaviors. When most of us think our hands are dirty, we engage in a fairly stereotyped form of cleansing: We wash them. People with OCD, however, continue to have the urge to wash their hands because their brains do not shut off their thoughts about dirt or their hand-washing behavior when the behavior is no longer necessary. Proponents of this biological theory point out that many of the obsessions and compulsions of people with OCD have to do with contamination, sex, aggression, and repeated patterns of behavior—all issues with which this brain circuit deals (Milad & Rauch, 2012; Rauch et al., 2003).

People with OCD and related disorders often get some relief from their symptoms when they take drugs that regulate the neurotransmitter serotonin, which plays an important role in the circuit's proper functioning (Micallef & Blin, 2001; Saxena et al., 2003). Those patients who respond to serotonin-enhancing drugs tend to show a greater reduction in the rate of activity in these brain areas than patients who do not respond well to the drugs (Baxter, Schwartz, Bergman, & Szuba, 1992; Saxena et al., 1999, 2003). Interestingly, people with OCD who respond to behavior therapy also tend to show decreases in the rate of activity in the caudate nucleus and the thalamus (Schwartz, Stoessel, Baxter, Martin, & Phelps, 1996).

In rare cases, a sudden onset of OCD in children is associated with a strep infection (Swedo et al., 1998). It is thought that autoimmune processes triggered by the infection affect the areas of the basal ganglia implicated in OCD in some vulnerable children, creating the symptoms of OCD (Leckman et al., 2010).

Finally, genes may help determine who is vulnerable to OCD (Mundo, Zanoni, & Altamura, 2006). Family history studies clearly show that OCD, hair pulling, and skin picking run in families, and twin studies support a substantial genetic component in obsessive and compulsive behaviors (Eley et al., 2003; Hudziak et al., 2004). Different genes may be involved in vulnerability to OCD and to hoarding or body dysmorphic disorder (Mataix-Cols et al., 2010; Phillips et al., 2010).

FIGURE 8 **OCD in the Brain.** A three-dimensional view of the human brain (with parts shown as they would look if the overlying cerebral cortex were transparent) clarifies the locations of the orbital frontal cortex and the basal ganglia—areas implicated in obsessive-compulsive disorder. Among the basal ganglia's structures are the caudate nucleus, which filters powerful impulses that arise in the orbital frontal cortex so that only the most powerful ones reach the thalamus. Perhaps the orbital frontal cortex, the caudate nucleus, or both are so active in people with obsessive-compulsive disorder that numerous impulses reach the thalamus, generating obsessive thoughts or compulsive actions.

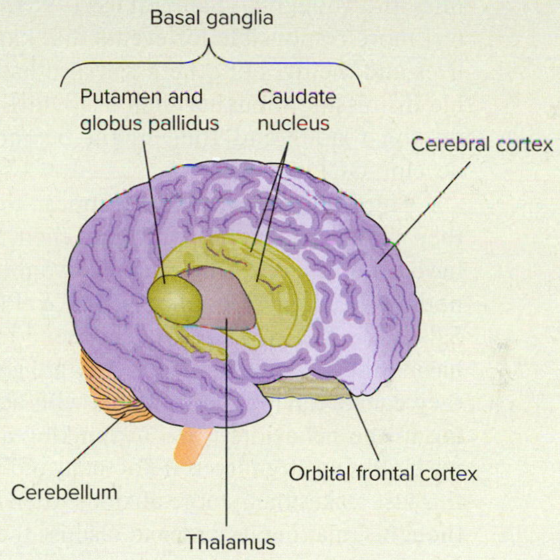

Source: Adapted from Rapoport, 1989, p. 85.

Cognitive-Behavioral Theories

Most people, including those without OCD, occasionally have negative, intrusive thoughts, including thoughts about harming others or doing something against their moral code (Angst et al., 2004; Leckman et al., 2010; Rachman & deSilva, 1978). People are more prone to having such thoughts and to engaging in rigid, ritualistic behaviors when they are distressed (Clark & Purdon, 1993; Rachman, 1997). Many new mothers, exhausted from sleep deprivation and the stress of caring for a newborn, think of harming their baby even though they are horrified by such thoughts and would never carry them out.

Most people can ignore or dismiss such thoughts, attributing them to their distress. With the passage of time, the thoughts subside. According to cognitive-behavioral theories of OCD, what differentiates people with OCD from people without the disorder is their inability to turn off these negative, intrusive thoughts (Clark, 1988; Salkovskis, 1998; Salkovskis & Millar, 2016).

Why do people who develop OCD have trouble turning off their thoughts, according to cognitive-behavioral theories? First, they may be depressed or generally anxious much of the time so that even minor negative events are likely to invoke intrusive, negative thoughts (Clark & Purdon, 1993). Second, people with OCD may have a tendency toward rigid, moralistic thinking (Rachman, 1993; Salkovskis, 1998). That is, they judge their negative, intrusive thoughts as more unacceptable than most people would and become more anxious and guilty about having them. Their anxiety then makes it harder for them to dismiss the thoughts (Salkovskis, 1998). People who feel more responsible for events that happen in their lives and the lives of others will also have more trouble dismissing thoughts such as "Did I hit someone on the road?" and thus might be more likely to develop OCD.

Third, people with OCD appear to believe that they should be able to control all their thoughts and have trouble accepting that everyone has horrific notions from time to time (Clark & Purdon, 1993; Salkovskis & Millar, 2016). They tend to believe that having these thoughts means they are going crazy, or they equate having the thoughts with actually engaging in the behaviors ("If I'm thinking about hurting my child, I'm as guilty as if I actually did"). Of course, this just makes them more anxious when they have the thoughts, making it harder to dismiss the thoughts.

According to these theories, compulsions develop largely through operant conditioning. People with anxiety-provoking obsessions discover that if they engage in certain behaviors, their anxiety is reduced. For example, the new mother might develop rituals (like praying for 5 minutes before touching the baby) to reduce anxiety caused by her intrusive thoughts. Each time the obsessions return and the person uses the behaviors to reduce them, the behaviors are negatively reinforced. Thus, compulsions are born.

Research has supported the argument put forth by this theory that people with OCD have these rigid and unrealistic beliefs (Salkovskis & Millar, 2016). Also, as we will see, cognitive-behavioral therapies based on this model have proven quite useful in treating OCD (Foa & McLean, 2016).

People with hoarding disorder also often have an exaggerated sense of responsibility, feeling guilty about wasting things, having an excessive need to "be ready just in case," and feeling responsible for not "hurting" the item (Frost et al., 2012). People who hoard also tend to believe they have a poor memory and therefore need to keep items in sight in order to remember them or to keep control over them. People with body dysmorphic disorder show biases toward appearance-specific stimuli, and overvaluation and negative interpretations of their perceived flaw (Fang & Wilhelm, 2015).

Treatment of OCD and Related Disorders

Both biological and cognitive-behavioral treatments are helpful for people with OCD.

Biological Treatments

In the 1980s, it was fortuitously discovered that antidepressant drugs affecting levels of serotonin helped relieve symptoms of OCD in many patients (Marazziti, Catena, & Pallanti, 2006). Clomipramine (trade name Anafranil) was the first such drug (Rapoport, 1989). Then the SSRIs, including fluoxetine (trade name Prozac), paroxetine (trade name Paxil), sertraline (trade name Zoloft), and fluvoxamine (trade name Luvox), proved effective. Controlled studies suggest that 50 to 80 percent of OCD patients experience decreases in their obsessions and compulsions while on these drugs, compared to only 5 percent of patients on placebos (Marazziti et al., 2006; Hurley, Saxena, Rauch, Hoehn-Saric, & Taber, 2008). These drugs can also be effective with people with hoarding disorder (Mataix-Cols et al., 2010) and body dysmorphic disorder (Phillips et al., 2010).

These drugs are not the complete answer for people with OCD and related disorders, however. A substantial number of OCD sufferers do not respond to the SSRIs. Among those who do, obsessions and compulsions are reduced only 30 to 40 percent, and patients tend to relapse if they discontinue the drugs. Significant side effects, which include drowsiness, constipation, and loss of sexual interest, prevent many people from taking them. Studies suggest that adding an atypical antipsychotic (see the chapter "Schizophrenia Spectrum and Other Psychotic Disorders") can help people who do not respond fully to the SSRIs (Bystritsky et al., 2004).

Cognitive-Behavioral Treatments

Many clinicians believe that drugs must be combined with cognitive-behavioral therapies that use **exposure and response prevention** to help people recover completely from OCD and related disorders. Exposure and response prevention therapy repeatedly exposes the client to the focus of the obsession and prevents compulsive responses to the resulting anxiety (Foa & McLean, 2016). Repeated exposure to the content of the obsession while preventing the person from engaging in the compulsive behavior extinguishes the client's anxiety about the obsession. The client learns that not engaging in the compulsive behavior does not lead to the terrible result they fear, and that their anxiety can decrease without their engaging in the behavior (Foa & McLean, 2016; Jacoby & Abramowitz, 2016).

Clients may be given homework that helps them confront their obsessions and compulsions. Early in therapy, a client might be assigned simply to refrain from cleaning the house every day and instead to clean it only every 3 days. Later he might be asked to drop a cookie on a dirty kitchen floor and then pick it up and eat it, or to drop the kitchen knives on the floor and then use them to prepare food. Because the client progressively learns to decrease anxiety without acting on compulsions, these behavioral techniques in turn decrease the distress caused by the obsessions.

The cognitive component of cognitive-behavioral therapy for OCD involves challenging the individual's moralistic thoughts and excessive sense of responsibility. For example, a woman with a germ obsession who believes she would be a bad mother if she touched her baby when she wasn't completely sure her hands were clean would be guided through exposure exercises (such as touching her baby with slightly dirty hands) with response prevention (not washing her hands), while being helped to challenge her thoughts that her baby was being harmed (by noticing that the baby was fine after being touched by slightly dirty hands).

These cognitive-behavior therapies lead to significant improvement in obsessions and compulsive behavior in 60 to 90 percent of OCD clients (Foa & McLean, 2016; Öst, Havnen, Hansen, & Kvale, 2015).

Exposure and response prevention is a treatment for OCD in which therapists help patients to face their fears step by step—in this case, walking across a bridge of planks—without engaging in the problematic compulsions patients have come to rely on for relieving distress, like counting to a certain number, or avoiding stepping on the cracks. ©*BSIP/Getty Images*

CBT for OCD is at least as effective as pharmacotherapy (e.g., SSRIs), and the combination of CBT with medication is the most effective (Romanelli, Wu, Gamba, Mojtabai, & Segal, 2014). In most clients, the improvement remains for up to 6 years. CBT can also be effective in the treatment of hoarding (Frost et al., 2012), although less research has been conducted on this disorder. Cognitive-behavioral treatment for skin-picking disorder and hair-pulling disorder often focuses on *habit reversal training* (Azrin, Nunn, & Frantz, 1980). This therapy, in which patients are led to become more aware of their behaviors and cues and to replace behaviors with healthier responses, has shown effectiveness for these conditions (Lochner et al., 2017).

Cognitive-behavioral therapies for body dysmorphic disorder focus on challenging clients' maladaptive cognitions about their body, exposing them to feared situations concerning their body, extinguishing anxiety about their body parts, and preventing compulsive responses to that anxiety (Fang & Wilhelm, 2015). For example, a client might identify her ears as her deformed body part. The client could develop her hierarchy of things she would fear doing related to her ears, ranging from looking at herself in the mirror with her hair fully covering her ears to going out in public with her hair pulled back and her ears fully exposed. After learning relaxation techniques, the client would begin to work through the hierarchy and engage in the feared behaviors, beginning with the least feared and using the relaxation techniques to quell her anxiety. Eventually, the client would work up to the most feared situation, exposing her ears in public. At first, the therapist might contract with the client that she could not engage in behaviors intended to hide the body part (such as putting her hair over her ears) for at least 5 minutes after going out in public. The eventual goal in therapy would be for the client's concerns about her ears to diminish totally and no longer affect her behavior or functioning. Empirical studies have supported the efficacy of cognitive-behavioral therapies in treating body dysmorphic disorder (Fang & Wilhelm, 2015).

ANXIETY DISORDERS IN OLDER ADULTS

Anxiety is one of the most common problems among older adults, with up to 15 percent of people over age 65 experiencing an anxiety disorder (Bryant, Jackson, & Ames, 2008; Reynolds, Pietrzak, El-Gabalawy, MacKenzie, & Sareen, 2015). Some older people have had anxiety disorders all their lives. For other people, anxiety first arises in old age. It often takes the form of worry about loved ones or about the older person's own health or safety, and it frequently exists together with medical illness and with depression, as with Mrs. Johnson in the following case study.

CASE STUDY

Mrs. Johnson is a 71-year-old female who was referred by a family practice physician working in a nearby town. Mrs. Johnson had become extremely anxious and moderately depressed following a major orthopedic surgery, a total hip replacement. She was a retired office worker.

I was immediately struck by her general level of anxiety. For example, she expressed fears about her ability to get her husband to take her to an appointment and was concerned that she might not be the right type of person for psychological treatment. Her anxiety seemed to interfere with her ability to adequately attend to and process information. For example, she seemed to have difficulty getting down the directions to my office. She stated that she was concerned about being able to find the building and that she would leave her house early in case she got lost.

Mrs. Johnson indicated that she loved all her children but that she worried about two of them. Both had been divorced and she was concerned about their well-being and that of her three grandchildren. She reported not having the desire to eat because her stomach was "fluttery." I asked, "Do you find yourself worrying about things?" to which she responded, "Yes, a lot. I worry that I've begun to be a burden for my husband. I worry about my hip and I worry about not being able to get around. I guess I'm crazy because I worry about being worried so much." I assured her that she was not crazy, just anxious, which can oftentimes make you feel like you are crazy.

(Source: Adapted from Scogin, Floyd, & Forde, 2000, pp. 117–118)

Mrs. Johnson was diagnosed with generalized anxiety disorder. Although rates of mental disorders tend to decrease in older age (Reynolds et al., 2015), older adults may worry more about health and about family issues than do younger adults (Scogin et al., 2000). Too often, their worries about health are dismissed as understandable when in fact these worries indicate that they are suffering from GAD.

Panic disorder is relatively rare in later life (Bryant et al., 2008). One epidemiological study estimated that only 0.5 percent of people over age 65 can be diagnosed with this disorder (Reynolds et al., 2015). Obsessive-compulsive disorder also is quite rare, diagnosed in only 0.8 percent of the older people in this study. The symptoms of posttraumatic stress disorder (PTSD) and acute stress disorder, however, are more common among older people, often occurring in response to the loss of a loved one (Bryant et al., 2008).

Very few older adults seek treatment for anxiety disorders, and those who do tend to consult their family physician rather than a mental health professional (Scogin et al., 2000). For those older people who do seek help, cognitive-behavioral therapy has been shown to be effective in treating their anxiety symptoms (Wetherell, Lenze, & Stanley, 2005).

Physicians frequently prescribe an antianxiety drug, such as a benzodiazepine, when an older patient complains of anxiety. With age come changes in drug absorption and distribution, metabolism, and sensitivity to side effects. Side effects such as unsteadiness can lead to falls and bone fractures (Scogin et al., 2000). Also, tolerance can develop with prolonged use of the benzodiazepines, leading to severe withdrawal effects and the rebound of anxiety symptoms when the person discontinues their use. Antidepressant drugs, including buspirone and the selective serotonin reuptake inhibitors, are increasingly used to treat anxiety symptoms and have fewer side effects and withdrawal effects than the benzodiazepines. Older adults often are taking several prescription and over-the-counter medications that can interact with psychotropic drugs. All these factors make the management of drug therapy in older adults more complex than in younger adults (Scogin et al., 2000).

CHAPTER INTEGRATION

Biology clearly influences the experience of anxiety. Evolution has prepared our bodies to respond to threatening situations with physiological changes that make it easier for us to flee from or confront a threat. For some people, this natural physiological response may be impaired, leading to overreactivity, chronic arousal, or poorly regulated arousal. These people may be more prone to severe anxiety reactions to threatening stimuli and to anxiety disorders.

Psychological and social factors also clearly play a role in anxiety and the anxiety disorders. Traumatic experiences lead to the development of some anxiety disorders, particularly PTSD. People differ in what they perceive as threatening, leading to differences in the level of anxiety they feel in potentially threatening situations. These differences may be due to specific traumas that some people have experienced or to people's upbringing. A child may develop a phobia of dogs because her mother modeled a fearful response to dogs. Another child may be chronically anxious and may believe he must be perfect because his parents punish him severely if he makes any type of mistake.

Vulnerability (diathesis)-stress models (Figure 9) stipulate that people who develop an anxiety disorder have pre-existing biological or psychological vulnerabilities due in part to trauma or severe stress and that these vulnerabilities interact with new stressors to create anxiety disorders. Such models help explain why some people, but not others, experience anxiety so severe and chronic that it develops into a disorder.

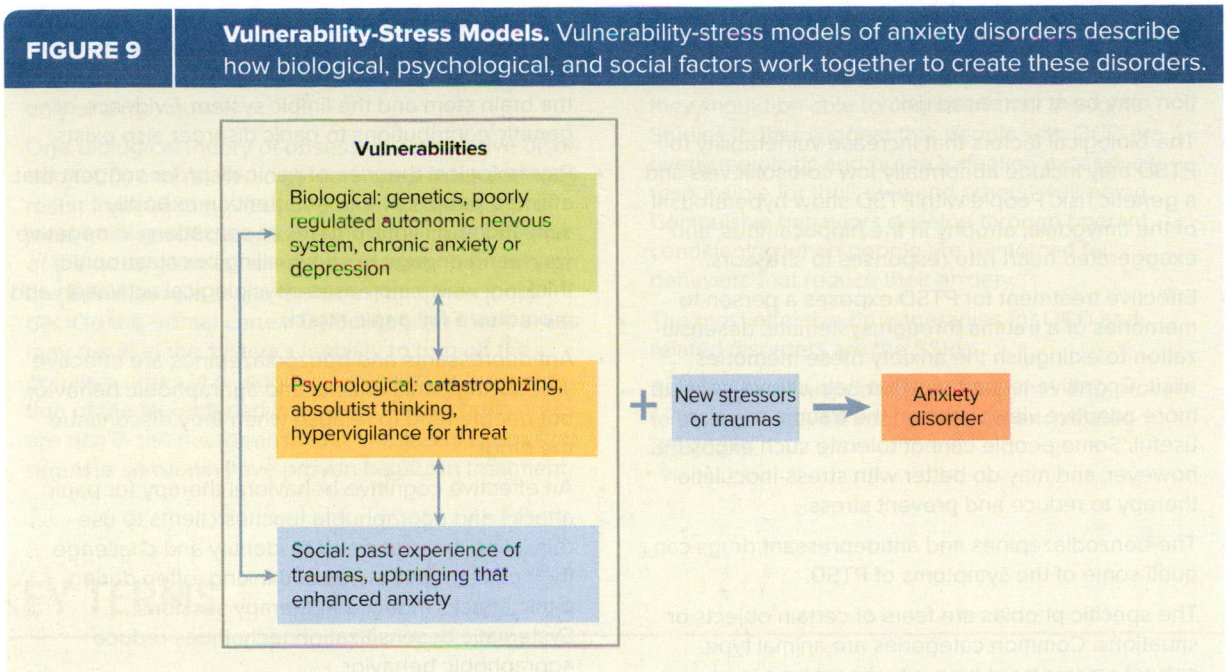

FIGURE 9 **Vulnerability-Stress Models.** Vulnerability-stress models of anxiety disorders describe how biological, psychological, and social factors work together to create these disorders.

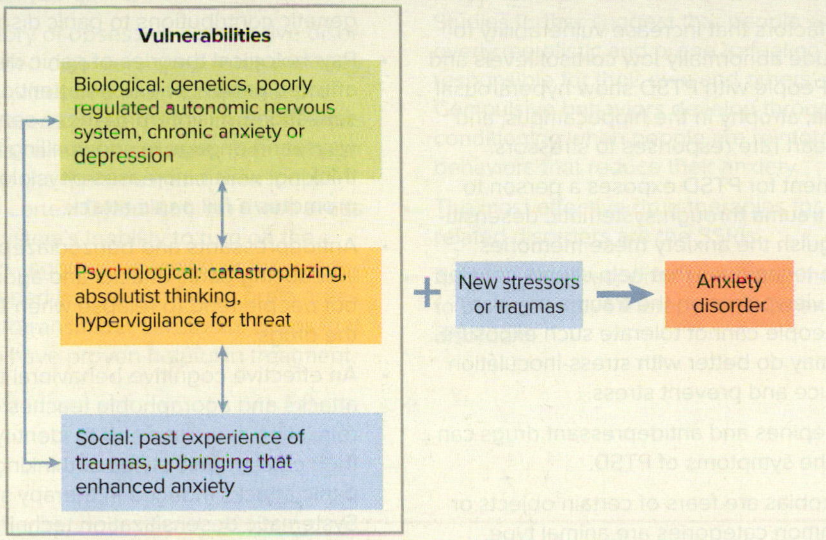

SHADES OF GRAY DISCUSSION

Neither posttraumatic stress disorder nor acute stress disorder applies to Ramón. Although his recurrent nightmares meet the reexperiencing criterion for PTSD and acute stress disorder, he actively thinks about the accident rather than avoiding thoughts of it. We have no evidence that he displays a lack of interest in activities, feels detached or estranged from others, has restricted affect, or has a sense of a foreshortened future or other negative beliefs or thoughts. We also lack evidence that Ramón has significant arousal symptoms; the exaggerated startle response he had in the interchange with his boss seems to be an isolated incident, and his sleep difficulties are caused primarily by his nightmares.

For now, Ramón appears to be having an understandable, but not diagnosable, reaction to a very frightening event. If you were his psychologist, you would want to check up in a week or two. If his nightmares and thoughts about the accident persist, and if they begin to more significantly impair his functioning, you might then diagnose him with an adjustment disorder.

CHAPTER SUMMARY

- Posttraumatic stress disorder (PTSD) occurs after exposure to actual or threatened death, serious injury, or sexual violation. It manifests four types of symptoms: (1) repeatedly reexperiencing the traumatic event through intrusive images or thoughts, recurring nightmares, flashbacks, and psychological and physiological reactivity to stimuli that remind the person of the traumatic event; (2) avoidance of anything that might arouse memories of the event; (3) negative cognitive and emotional symptoms; and (4) hypervigilance and chronic arousal.
- A subtype of PTSD is characterized by prominent dissociative (depersonalization/derealization) symptoms.
- Acute stress disorder has symptoms similar to those of PTSD but occurs within 1 month of a stressor and usually lasts less than 1 month.
- Social factors appear to influence the risk for PTSD. The more severe and longer-lasting a trauma and the more deeply involved a person is in it, the more likely he or she is to develop PTSD. People with less social support are at increased risk.

Chapter 6

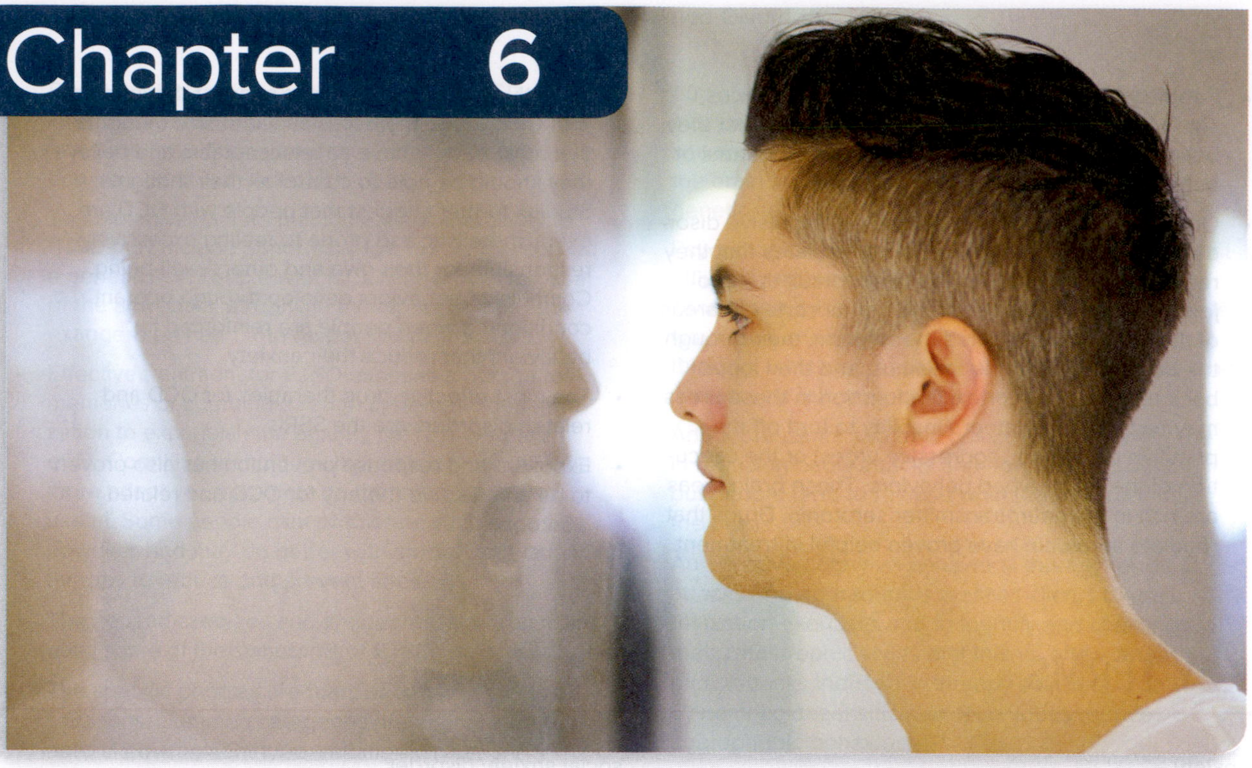

©PeopleImages/Getty Images

Somatic Symptom and Dissociative Disorders

CHAPTER OUTLINE

Somatic Symptom and Dissociative Disorders Along the Continuum

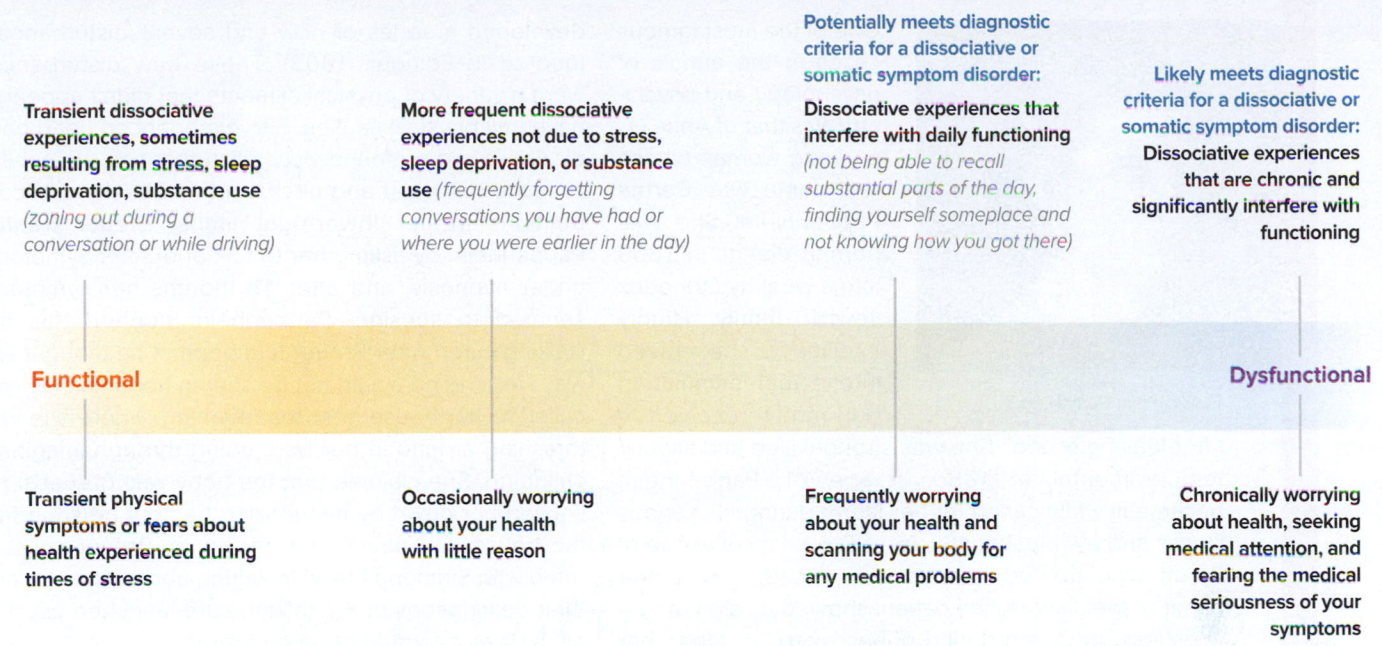

Functional

Transient dissociative experiences, sometimes resulting from stress, sleep deprivation, substance use *(zoning out during a conversation or while driving)*

More frequent dissociative experiences not due to stress, sleep deprivation, or substance use *(frequently forgetting conversations you have had or where you were earlier in the day)*

Potentially meets diagnostic criteria for a dissociative or somatic symptom disorder:
Dissociative experiences that interfere with daily functioning *(not being able to recall substantial parts of the day, finding yourself someplace and not knowing how you got there)*

Likely meets diagnostic criteria for a dissociative or somatic symptom disorder:
Dissociative experiences that are chronic and significantly interfere with functioning

Dysfunctional

Transient physical symptoms or fears about health experienced during times of stress

Occasionally worrying about your health with little reason

Frequently worrying about your health and scanning your body for any medical problems

Chronically worrying about health, seeking medical attention, and fearing the medical seriousness of your symptoms

The disorders we discuss in this chapter are considered by some theorists to be associated with a psychological process known as *dissociation,* in which different parts of an individual's identity, memory, or consciousness split off from one another. You may not realize it, but you likely have had dissociative experiences (Aderibigbe, Bloch, & Walker, 2001; Seedat, Stein, & Forde, 2003): You are driving down a familiar road, thinking about a recent conversation with a friend, and suddenly you realize that you've driven several miles and don't remember traveling that section of the road. That's a dissociative experience, as is daydreaming. When we daydream, we can lose consciousness of where we are and of what is going on around us. Becoming absorbed in a movie or a book is also a dissociative experience.

Researcher Colin Ross (1997) asked more than a thousand adults from the general community about a number of different dissociative experiences. Missing part of a conversation appears to be the most common dissociative experience (reported by 83 percent of people), followed by being unsure of whether you have actually carried through with something (such as brushing your teeth) or have only thought about doing it (reported by 73 percent). These experiences are not harmful. Farther down the list are somewhat more bizarre experiences, such as hearing voices in your head (reported by 26 percent), feeling as though your body is not your own (reported by 23 percent), and not recognizing objects or other people as real (reported by 26 percent). But even these more bizarre experiences happen, at least occasionally, to a substantial percentage of the general population. Fatigue and stress are probably the most common causes of dissociation. A study of mentally healthy soldiers undergoing survival training in the U.S. Army found that over 90 percent reported dissociative symptoms in response to the stress of the training; the symptoms included feeling separated from what was happening, as if they were watching themselves in a movie (Morgan et al., 2001). A small subset of people, however, have frequent dissociative experiences and as a result have difficulty functioning in daily life.

Just as we all experience mild dissociative symptoms, many of us "carry our stress in our body," experiencing tension and distressing or preoccupying aches, pains, and health concerns when we feel stress. This may be the result of dissociation in which our consciousness of our psychological pain is diminished and instead we are aware only of physical pain. Usually these aches and pains subside when our stress subsides. For a small number of people, however, their attention to their perceived aches and pains is chronic and they have very high levels of worry about illness, resulting in significant functional impairment. Their lives focus excessively on fears about their physical health, and they may be diagnosed with a somatic symptom disorder. Whether or not a person's symptoms are medically explained, their suffering is real.

Extraordinary People

Anna O., *The Talking Cure*

©ullstein bild/Getty Images

One of the most famous cases in the annals of psychology and psychiatry was that of Anna O., a young woman whose real name was Bertha Pappenheim. She was born in Vienna in 1859 into a wealthy Orthodox Jewish family. Highly intelligent, she craved intellectual stimulation but rarely received it after leaving school. She was strong-willed and slightly temperamental. In 1880, at age 21, Pappenheim became ill while caring for her father during his serious illness and eventual death. Josef Breuer, a colleague of Freud who treated Pappenheim, noted, "Up to the onset of the disease, the patient showed no sign of nervousness, not even during pubescence. . . . Upon her father's illness, in rapid succession there seemingly developed a series of new and severe disturbances" (quoted in Edinger, 1963). These new disturbances were a variety of physical ailments that didn't appear to have any physical causes. She experienced head pain, dizziness and profound visual disturbances, an inability to move her head and neck, and numbness and contractions in her lower-right limbs. Breuer treated Pappenheim by asking her to talk about her symptoms under hypnosis, and after 18 months her symptoms seemed to subside. Pappenheim dubbed this the "talking cure." After Breuer told her that he thought she was well and he would not be seeing her again, he was called to her house later that evening, where she was thrashing around in her bed, going through imaginary childbirth. She claimed that the baby was Breuer's. He calmed her down by hypnotizing her, but he soon fled the house and never saw her again. Breuer collaborated with Sigmund Freud in writing about Anna O., and their descriptions of the talking cure launched psychoanalysis as a form of psychotherapy.

Bertha Pappenheim, or Anna O., appeared to suffer from what the *DSM-5* calls a *somatic symptom disorder*—she experienced physiological symptoms that Breuer argued were the result of painful emotions or memories. In this chapter, we discuss the somatic symptom disorders as well as the *dissociative disorders,* in which people develop multiple separate personalities or completely lose their memory of significant portions of their lives. The somatic symptom disorders and dissociative disorders have historically been thought to result from similar processes—patients cannot confront difficult emotions and stressful experiences, so they unconsciously convert their emotions into physical and psychological symptoms. As seen in the story of Bertha Pappenheim, these phenomena provided the material for much of the early theorizing by Breuer, Freud, and other psychoanalysts. In recent years, these disorders and the idea that people can completely lose conscious access to painful memories and emotions have become controversial. We discuss this controversy at the end of the chapter.

SOMATIC SYMPTOM DISORDERS

As noted throughout this book, drawing sharp distinctions between the body and the mind is becoming increasingly unfounded as we come to understand how intertwined biological and psychological factors are. The **somatic symptom disorders** are a prime example of the fluid boundary between mind and body. People with these disorders may experience significant physical symptoms for which there is no apparent organic cause, but this seems to be the result of psychological factors. They are often excessively concerned about their symptoms and spend a great deal of time worrying and seeking medical treatment.

One difficulty in diagnosing somatic symptom disorders is the possibility that an individual has a real physical disorder that is difficult to detect or diagnose. Many of us have friends or relatives who have complained for years about symptoms that physicians attributed to "nervousness" or "attention seeking" but that later were determined to be early symptoms of serious disease. The diagnosis of somatic symptom disorder is easier when psychological factors leading to the development of the symptoms can be identified clearly or when physical examination proves that the symptoms are not physiologically possible. For example, when a child is perfectly healthy on weekends but has stomachaches in the morning just before going to school, it is possible that the stomachaches are due to distress over going to school. A more extreme example of a clear somatic symptom disorder is *pseudocyesis,* or false pregnancy, in which a woman believes she is pregnant but physical examination and laboratory tests confirm that she is not. Bertha Pappenheim apparently displayed pseudocyesis.

The category of somatic symptom disorders includes five specific disorders. The first is simply called *somatic symptom disorder*. This disorder is new to the *DSM-5* and combines a number of diagnoses from the *DSM-IV-TR* that were difficult to distinguish. Other disorders in the somatic symptom disorders category are *illness anxiety disorder* (formerly hypochondriasis), *conversion disorder,* and *factitious disorder.* One final diagnosis in this category of disorders is *psychological factors affecting other medical conditions* (sometimes referred to as psychosomatic disorders), in which people have an actual, documented physical illness or defect, such as high blood pressure, that is worsened by psychological factors. For example, depression can exacerbate a number of medical diseases, including cancer, heart disease, diabetes, arthritis, and asthma (Everson-Rose & Lewis, 2005; Katon, 2003). We will discuss the effects of psychological factors on medical conditions in detail in the chapter "Health Psychology."

In this chapter, we focus on disorders in which there are distressing somatic symptoms along with abnormal thoughts, feelings, and behaviors in response to these bodily symptoms. Medically unexplained symptoms are present to varying degrees, particularly in conversion disorder where psychological factors are assumed to underlie the symptoms.

Somatic Symptom Disorder and Illness Anxiety Disorder

A person with **somatic symptom disorder** has one or more distressing physical symptoms and spends a great deal of time and energy thinking about these symptoms and seeking medical care for them. They can be gastrointestinal symptoms (e.g., nausea, diarrhea), pain symptoms, neurological symptoms (e.g., dizziness, tremors), or symptoms affecting any part of the body. Although anyone with painful or life-threatening symptoms might be preoccupied with them and seek alternative opinions about their causes and treatments, people with somatic symptom disorder have health concerns that are excessive given their actual physical health, that persist even when they have evidence that they are well, and that interfere with their daily functioning (see Table 1). When they experience a symptom, they may assume the worst—that it is cancer, a heart attack, a stroke, and so on. They may insist on medical procedures—even surgeries—that clearly are unnecessary. They may avoid a wide range of activities, fearing exacerbation of their symptoms, to the point that they become isolated and inactive. For others, their health concerns become a core feature of

TABLE 1 *DSM-5* Diagnostic Criteria for Somatic Symptom Disorder

A. One or more somatic symptoms that are distressing or result in significant disruption of daily life.

B. Excessive thoughts, feelings, or behaviors related to the somatic symptoms or associated health concerns as manifested by at least one of the following:

1. Disproportionate and persistent thoughts about the seriousness of one's symptoms.
2. Persistently high level of anxiety about health or symptoms.
3. Excessive time and energy devoted to these symptoms or health concerns.

C. Although any one symptom may not be continuously present, the state of being symptomatic is persistent (typically more than 6 months).

Specify if:

With predominant pain, for individuals whose somatic symptoms predominantly involve pain.

Persistent: characterized by severe symptoms, marked impairment, and long duration (> 6 months).

Mild (only one Criterion B symptom); **Moderate** (two or more Criterion B symptoms); **Severe** (two or more Criterion B symptoms, and multiple or one very severe somatic complaint).

their identity and dominate their interpersonal relationships. Often, the fears and complaints focus on a particular organ system. Carlos, in the following case study, was convinced something was wrong with his bowels.

CASE STUDY

Carlos, a married man of 39, came to the clinic complaining, "I have trouble in my bowels and then it gets me in my head. My bowels just spasm on me, I get constipated." The patient's complaints dated back 12 years to an attack of "acute indigestion" in which he seemed to bloat up and pains developed in his abdomen and spread in several directions. He traced some of these pathways with his finger as he spoke. Carlos spent a month in bed at this time and then, based on an interpretation of something the doctor said, rested for another 2 months before working again. Words of reassurance from his doctor failed to take effect. He felt "sick, worried, and scared," feeling that he would never really get well again.

Carlos became very dependent on the woman he married when he was 22 years old. He left most of the decisions to her and showed little interest in sexual relations. His wife was several years older than he and did not seem to mind his totally passive approach to life. His attack of "acute indigestion" followed her death, 5 years after marriage, by 3 months during which he felt lost and hopeless. In time, he moved to a rural area and remarried. His second wife proved less willing to assume major responsibility for him than the first, and she made sexual demands on him that he felt unable to meet. He became more and more preoccupied with his gastrointestinal welfare. (Source: Adapted from Cameron & Rychlak, 1985)

TABLE 2 *DSM-5* Diagnostic Criteria for Illness Anxiety Disorder

A. Preoccupation with having or acquiring a serious illness.

B. Somatic symptoms are not present or, if present, are only mild in intensity. If another medical condition is present or there is a high risk of developing a medical condition (e.g., strong family history is present), the preoccupation is clearly excessive or disproportionate.

C. There is a high level of anxiety about health, and the individual is easily alarmed about personal health status.

D. The individual performs excessive health-related behaviors (e.g., repeatedly checking his or her body for signs of illness) or exhibits maladaptive avoidance (e.g., avoiding doctor appointments and hospitals).

E. Illness preoccupation has been present for at least 6 months, but the specific illness that is feared may change over that period of time.

F. The illness-related preoccupation is not better explained by another mental disorder, such as somatic symptom disorder, panic disorder, generalized anxiety disorder, body dysmorphic disorder, obsessive-compulsive disorder or delusional disorder, somatic type.

Specify whether:

Care-seeking type: Medical care is frequently used.

Care-avoidant type: Medical care is rarely used.

Illness anxiety disorder is very similar to somatic symptom disorder. The primary distinction in the *DSM-5* between the two disorders is that people with somatic symptom disorder actually experience physical symptoms and seek help for them, whereas people with illness anxiety disorder worry that they will develop or have a serious illness but do not always experience severe physical symptoms (Table 2). However, when they do have physical complaints, people with illness anxiety disorder become very alarmed and are more likely to seek immediate medical care. People with illness anxiety disorder may go through many medical procedures and float from physician to physician, sure that they have a dreadful disease. They may insist that toxins or other environmental conditions are affecting their health, despite evidence to the contrary. One extensive community study in Germany found that the majority of individuals had multiple concerns about the health effects of environmental toxins, most often pesticides, hormones or antibiotics in food, or genetically modified food (Rief et al., 2012).

People with somatic symptom disorder or illness anxiety disorder may be prone to periods of anxiety and depression. They may express their distress as physical symptoms or mask the distress with alcohol abuse or antisocial behavior (Feder et al., 2001; Katon, Sullivan, & Walker, 2001; Löwe et al., 2008). Their symptoms and health concerns become a large part of their identity. Moreover, changes in their symptoms mirror their emotional well-being: When they are anxious or depressed, they report more physical complaints and worries than when they are not anxious or depressed (Bekhuis, Schoevers, van Borkulo, Rosmalen, & Boschloo, 2016).

SHADES OF GRAY

Consider this description of a young boy with health worries.

Ben is a 9-year-old whose teachers refer to him as "the worrier." At least once a week, he ends up in the school nurse's office with complaints of a headache or a stomachache, insisting he needs to rest or go home. The school nurse always dutifully takes Ben's temperature, which is always normal. Still, Ben will not go back to class. His frequent absences are causing his grades to decline. Ben's mother has taken him to his pediatrician a number of times, and multiple tests have revealed no medical problems that could be causing his frequent headaches and stomachaches.

Ben's health worries seem to have started about 8 months ago, after he had a serious case of the flu that kept him home in bed for over a week. Shortly after that, his parents separated because of marital conflict that had been escalating for years. When his mother has tried to talk with Ben about the possibility that his aches and pains are connected to his parents' separation, he has acknowledged that this could be true. But within a few days, he has experienced another headache or stomachache, saying "This time it's real, and it really hurts!"

Does Ben appear to have a somatic symptom disorder? If so, which one? (Discussion appears at the end of this chapter.)

Studies find that a large percentage of the population complain of multiple somatic symptoms and health concerns that are not well-explained by a medical condition (Rief & Martin, 2014). For example, one large study of patients seeking care in cardiology, neurology, respiratory, and gastrointestinal clinics found that nearly 20 percent had excessive illness anxiety (Tyrer et al., 2011), and 1 to 7 percent of the general population experiences severe levels of illness anxiety annually (Hedman & Axelsson, 2017). Multiple symptom complaints and concerns about health are more common in older adults than in middle-aged adults, even after taking into account the increased incidence of medical illness with age (Feder et al., 2001; Ladwig, Martin-Mittag, Lacruz, Henningsen, & Creed, 2010). The cultural norms with which older adults were raised often prohibited admitting to depression or anxiety. For this reason, older adults who are depressed or anxious may be more likely to express their negative emotions in somatic complaints, which are acceptable and expected in old age. Young children also often express their distress in somatic complaints (Garber, Walker, & Zeman, 1991). While they may not have the language to express difficult emotions, they can say that they feel "bad" or that they have a stomachache or a headache.

The experience of multiple somatic symptoms and health concerns tends to be long-term and disabling. One longitudinal study found that people with many health complaints but no diagnosed medical illness were more likely to suffer disability, low income, impaired sleep, and psychological distress (Ladwig et al., 2010). They also were more likely to develop high blood pressure, obesity, and high cholesterol, were hospitalized more often, and were more likely to die in the 12-year follow-up than people with few health complaints.

It is important to note that diagnoses of somatic symptom disorder and illness anxiety disorder are new to the *DSM-5*, and their reliability and validity are not well established. Some studies indicate that these diagnoses are improvements on the *DSM-IV*, but it is not yet clear that the two disorders are fundamentally different, beyond the presence of physical symptoms and more functional impairment and psychiatric comorbidity in somatic symptom disorder (Newby, Hobbs, Mahoney, Wong, & Andrews, 2017). Some researchers are concerned that the criteria are too broad, lump too many different syndromes together, and risk mislabeling physical illness as mental illness (Frances, 2013; Rief & Martin, 2014).

Theories of Somatic Symptom Disorder and Illness Anxiety Disorder

Cognitive factors are thought to play a strong role in somatic symptom disorder and illness anxiety disorder (Hedman & Axelsson, 2017; Rief & Martin, 2014). People with these disorders often have dysfunctional beliefs about illness, assuming that serious illnesses are common, and tend to misinterpret any physical change in themselves as a sign for concern. They believe they are vulnerable to a wide range of physical illnesses and unable to tolerate pain. People with somatic symptom disorder tend to experience bodily sensations more intensely than other people, to pay more attention than others to physical symptoms and health-related information, and to catastrophize these symptoms (Rief & Martin, 2014; Witthöft et al., 2016). For example, a person with somatic symptom disorder might have a slight case of indigestion but experience it as severe chest pain and interpret the pain as a sure sign of a heart attack. The person's interpretation of his experience may have a direct influence on his physiological processes by increasing his heart rate or blood pressure, thereby maintaining and exacerbating the pain. Further, his cognitions will influence the way he presents his symptoms to his physician and his family. As a result, the physician may prescribe more potent medication or order more diagnostic tests, and family members may express more sympathy, excuse the person from responsibilities, and otherwise encourage passive behavior (Turk & Ruby, 1992). In this way, the person's misinterpretation and catastrophizing of his symptoms are reinforced, increasing the likelihood that he will interpret future symptoms similarly.

Multiple health complaints and excessive health concerns run in families, primarily among female relatives (Phillips, 2001). Anxiety and depression are also common in the female relatives of people with these symptoms (Garber et al., 1991). The male relatives of people with multiple, excessive health complaints also have higher than usual rates of alcoholism and antisocial personality disorder. It is not clear that the transmission of multiple somatic symptoms and health concerns in families is related to genetics (Gillespie, Zhu, Heath, Hickie, & Martin, 2000). The children of parents who catastrophize their somatic symptoms may model their parents' thinking styles and health behaviors (Marshall, Jones, Ramchandrani, Stein, & Bass, 2007). Parents who somatize also are more likely to neglect their children, and the children may learn that the only way to receive care and attention is to be ill. This finding is in accord with a behavioral account of somatic complaints and health concerns, which views them as the result of reinforcements for "sickness behavior" that individuals have received over much of their lives (Ullman & Krasner, 1975).

Somatic symptom disorder and illness anxiety disorder may be part of posttraumatic stress disorder experienced by a person who has survived a severe stressor (Katon et al., 2001). For example, refugees and recent immigrants who have posttraumatic stress disorder also have been shown to have an increased risk of somatic symptoms and health concerns (Cervantes, Salgado de Snyder, & Padilla, 1989). One study of Hmong immigrants to the United States, who had fled Cambodia during the Khmer Rouge regime, found that 17 percent had posttraumatic stress disorder characterized by moderate to severe somatic symptoms (Westermeyer, Bouafuely, Neider, & Callies, 1989). Trauma earlier in life, such as childhood physical and sexual abuse, has also been linked with somatic symptoms in adulthood (Nelson, Baldwin, & Taylor, 2012). Future research is needed to understand how traumatic stress might cause emotional distress to be expressed somatically.

Treatment of Somatic Symptom Disorder and Illness Anxiety Disorder

Convincing people with these disorders that they need psychological treatment is not easy. They may continue to insist that they are physically ill despite dozens of physicians telling them they are not and hundreds of medical tests establishing no physical illness. Psychodynamic therapies focus on providing insight into the connections between emotions and physical symptoms by helping people recall events and memories that may have triggered their symptoms. Behavioral therapies attempt to determine the reinforcements individuals receive for their symptoms and health complaints and to eliminate these reinforcements while increasing positive rewards for healthy behavior. Cognitive therapies for these disorders help people learn to interpret their physical symptoms appropriately and to avoid catastrophizing them, similar to the cognitive treatment of panic symptoms (see the chapter "Trauma, Anxiety, Obsessive-Compulsive, and Related Disorders"; Hedman & Axelsson, 2017). Cognitive-behavioral treatments that focus on identifying and challenging illness beliefs and misinterpretations of physical sensations, as well as exposing clients to their anxiety triggers, have shown positive effects (Olatunji et al., 2014). More recent treatments incorporating mindfulness and acceptance skills, including acceptance and commitment therapy, have shown promise as well (Eilenberg, Fink, Jensen, Rief, & Frostholm, 2016), as have trials of Internet-delivered CBT (Newby et al., 2018). Antidepressants can also reduce somatic symptoms.

Some clinicians use the belief systems and cultural traditions of individuals they are treating to motivate them to engage in therapy and help them overcome their physical complaints. Following is a case study that shows the use of cultural beliefs in treating a Hispanic woman with somatic symptom disorder.

CASE STUDY

Ellen was a 45-year-old woman who consulted many doctors for "high fever, vomiting, diarrhea, inability to eat, and rapid weight loss." After numerous negative lab tests, her doctor told her, "I can't go on with you; go to one of the *espiritistas* or a *curandera* [traditional healers]." A cousin then took her to a Spiritist center "for medicine." She was given herbal remedies—some baths and a tea of *molinillo* to take in the morning before eating. But the treatment focused mainly on the appearance of the spirit of a close friend who had died a month earlier from cancer. The spirit was looking for help from Ellen, who had not gone to help during her friend's illness because of her own family problems. The main thrust of the healer's treatment plan was to help Ellen understand how she had to deal with the feelings of distress related to the stress of a paralyzed husband and caring for two small daughters alone. The spirit's influence on Ellen's body was an object lesson that was aimed at increasing her awareness of how her lifestyle was causing her to neglect the care of her own body and feelings much as she had neglected her dying friend. (Source: Adapted from Koss, 1990, p. 22)

The spiritual healer in Ellen's case recognized the cause of her somatic complaints as stress, anger, and guilt; helped her link her physical symptoms to these emotions; and helped her find ways to cope more adaptively with the emotions. The context for this intervention was not cognitive therapy or another type of psychotherapy used by the dominant, non-Hispanic culture but rather the cultural belief system concerning the role of spirits in producing physical symptoms.

Conversion Disorder (Functional Neurological Symptom Disorder)

A dramatic type of somatic symptom disorder is **conversion disorder.** People with this disorder lose neurological functioning in a part of their bodies, apparently not due to medical causes. Some of the most common conversion symptoms are paralysis, blindness, mutism, seizures, loss of hearing, severe loss of coordination, and anesthesia in a limb. The diagnostic criteria require at least one symptom of altered motor or sensory function that is not due to recognized neurobiological or medical conditions, and not attributable to another disorder (American Psychiatric Association, 2013). One particularly dramatic conversion symptom is glove anesthesia, in which people lose all feeling in one hand, as if they were wearing a glove that wiped out physical sensation. As Figure 1 shows, however, the nerves in the hand are distributed in a way that makes this pattern of anesthesia highly unlikely. Conversion disorder typically involves one specific symptom, such as blindness or paralysis, but a person can have repeated episodes of conversion involving different parts of the body. The name "conversion disorder" presumes that psychological distress, often over a traumatic event, is "converted" into a physical symptom. Patients and physicians alike often object to this presumption (Stone et al., 2011), so the *DSM-5* parenthetically labels this disorder **functional neurological symptom disorder,** a more neutral name that doesn't presume a psychological cause. Unexplained neurological symptoms are relatively common. It has been estimated that 20 percent of patients in neurological clinics have symptoms with no apparent medical cause (Feinstein, 2011). The number of individuals meeting full criteria for persistent conversion disorder is very low, perhaps around 20 in 100,000 (Feinstein, 2011).

Theories of Conversion Disorder

Freud and his contemporaries viewed conversion symptoms as the result of the transfer of the psychic energy attached to repressed emotions or memories to physical symptoms. The symptoms often symbolized the specific concerns or memories being repressed. The reduction in anxiety was referred to as the *primary gain*. In addition, patients receive attention and concern from others and may be relieved of obligations and expectations, reinforcing the conversion symptoms. Freud called this the *secondary gain*.

FIGURE 1 **Glove Anesthesia.** In the conversion symptom called glove anesthesia, the entire hand from fingertips to wrist becomes numb. Actual physical damage to the ulnar nerve, in contrast, causes anesthesia in the ring finger and little finger and beyond the wrist partway up the arm; damage to the radial nerve causes anesthesia only in parts of the ring, middle, and index fingers and the thumb and partway up the arm.

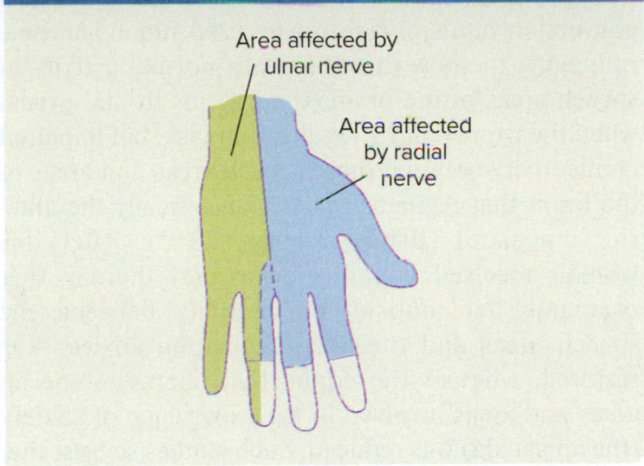

Behavioral theories don't infer that conversion symptoms represent transferred unconscious anxiety, but they do emphasize the role conversion symptoms play in alleviating distress by removing the individual from difficult environments and allowing him or her to avoid unwanted responsibilities or situations (Deary, Chalder, & Sharpe, 2007).

Conversion symptoms apparently were quite common during the two world wars, when soldiers inexplicably would become paralyzed or blind and therefore unable to return to the front (Ironside & Batchelor, 1945). Many of the soldiers seemed unconcerned about their paralysis or blindness, a phenomenon called *la belle indifference*. Sometimes, the physical symptoms represented traumas the soldiers had witnessed. For example, a soldier who had shot a civilian in the chest might have chest pains.

Children can also have conversion symptoms. Most often, their symptoms mimic those of someone close to them who has a physical illness or impairment (de Gusmão et al., 2014; Spierings, Poels, Sijben, Gabreels, & Renier, 1990). For example, a child whose cherished grandfather has had a stroke and has lost functioning on his right side may become unable to use his right arm.

Research suggests that people with conversion symptoms are highly hypnotizable (Roelofs et al., 2002; Stone et al., 2011). This supports the idea that conversion symptoms result from spontaneous self-hypnosis, in which sensory or motor functions are dissociated, or split off, from consciousness in reaction to extreme stress. Some evidence indicates that stressful life events and emotional or physical maltreatment are associated with conversion symptoms (Ludwig et al., 2018).

Neurological models suggest that conversion symptoms arise when sensory or motor areas of the brain are impaired by anxiety (Aybek & Vuilleumier, 2016). For example, in a case study of a woman with conversion mutism, researchers used functional neuroimaging to show that there was normal activity in speech areas of the brain (the inferior frontal gyrus) when the woman did a vocalization task, but impaired connectivity between these speech areas and areas of the brain that regulate anxiety (specifically the anterior cingulate) (Bryant & Das, 2012). After this woman received cognitive-behavioral therapy that overcame her mutism, connectivity between the speech areas and the areas regulating anxiety was restored, whereas the connectivity between speech areas and areas involved in the experience of anxiety (the amygdala) was reduced. Such studies suggest that conversion disorder does not involve impaired activity in areas of the brain associated specifically with the loss of functioning (such as speech areas in mutism) but instead changes in connectivity between these areas and areas associated with the generation and regulation of anxiety.

Treatment of Conversion Disorder

People with conversion disorder can be difficult to treat because they do not believe there is anything wrong with them psychologically, and prognosis is generally poor (Gelauff & Stone, 2016). Psychoanalytic treatment for conversion disorder focuses on the expression of painful emotions and memories and on insight into the relationship between these and the conversion symptoms (Feinstein, 2011). Cognitive-behavioral treatments focus on relieving the person's anxiety centered on the initial trauma that caused the conversion symptoms and on reducing any benefits the person is receiving from the conversion symptoms (Lehn et al., 2016). For example, the treatment of a rape victim (we will call her Jane) who developed conversion symptoms for the secondary gain they afforded her might involve both systematic desensitization therapy and exposure therapy (see the chapters "Theories and Treatment of Abnormality" and "Trauma, Anxiety, Obsessive-Compulsive, and Related Disorders"). A hierarchy of situations that Jane avoided—mostly situations that reminded her of her rape—was constructed. For the exposure therapy, Jane was aided in approaching those situations that made her feel anxious and in progressing through her hierarchy to increasingly more feared situations while practicing relaxation techniques. During the imagery sessions, Jane recounted the details of the assault first in general terms and later in great detail, including both the details of the situation and the details of her physiological and cognitive reactions to the assault. At first, Jane was able to describe the assault only in a whisper, but she cried at full volume. After crying, Jane's speech became increasingly louder, with occasional words uttered at full volume. Eventually, she regained a full-volume voice. Following treatment, Jane's PTSD symptoms also decreased, and they diminished further over the next year (Rothbaum & Foa, 1991).

Factitious Disorder

The final diagnosis in the *DSM-5* somatic symptom disorder category we will consider is **factitious disorder,** in which a person deliberately fakes an illness specifically to gain medical attention and play the sick role. Factitious disorder is also referred to as *Munchhausen's syndrome*. Factitious disorder differs from somatic symptom disorder in that factitious disorder involves evidence that the individual is providing false information or behaving deceptively. Factitious disorder differs from **malingering,** in which people fake a symptom or a disorder in order to avoid an unwanted situation, such as military service, or in order to gain something, such as an insurance payment. The major difference between malingering and factitious disorder is the motivation for faking symptoms. In malingering the symptoms help an individual avoid an unwanted situation, while in factitious disorder the symptoms are intentionally created to gain medical attention.

Factitious disorder imposed on another (formerly referred to as *factitious disorder by proxy*) is diagnosed when an individual falsifies illness in another (e.g., child, pet, older adult). For example, parents fake or even create illnesses in their children in order to gain attention for themselves. They act as devoted and long-suffering protectors of their children, drawing praise for their dedicated nursing. Their children are subjected to unnecessary and often dangerous medical procedures and may actually die from their parents' attempts to make them ill.

Seven-year-old Jennifer Bush appeared to be one victim of factitious disorder imposed on another. Jennifer underwent almost 200 hospitalizations and 40 operations in efforts to cure the puzzling array of ailments she seemed to have. Her mother, Kathleen Bush, was with her through it all, dealing with medical professionals and standing by as the family's finances were ruined by Jennifer's medical bills. All the while, however, it seems Kathleen Bush was actually causing her daughter's illnesses by giving her unprescribed drugs, altering her medications, and even putting fecal bacteria in her feeding tube. Bush eventually was arrested and convicted of child abuse and fraud and served 3 years in prison (Toufexis, Blackman, & Drummond, 1996).

DISSOCIATIVE DISORDERS

Scientific interest in dissociative disorders has waxed and waned over the past century (Kihlstrom, 2005). There was a great deal of interest in dissociation in nineteenth-century France and in the United States among neurologists and psychologists such as Charcot, Freud, Carl Jung, and William James. French neurologist Pierre Janet viewed **dissociation** as a process in which components of mental experience are split off from consciousness but remain accessible through dreams and hypnosis. One case he investigated was that of a woman named Irene, who had no memory of the fact that her mother had died. However, during her sleep, Irene physically dramatized the events surrounding her mother's death.

After about 1910, interest in dissociative phenomena waned, partly because of the rise within psychology of behaviorism and biological approaches, which rejected the concept of repression and the use of techniques such as hypnosis in therapy. Ernest Hilgard (1977/1986) revitalized interest in dissociation in his experiments on the *hidden observer* phenomenon. He argued that there is an active mode to consciousness, which includes our conscious plans and desires and our voluntary actions. In its passive receptive mode, the conscious registers and stores information in memory without being aware that the information has been processed, as if a person has internal hidden observers that watch and record events in that person's life without that person being aware of it.

Hilgard and his associates conducted experimental studies in which participants were hypnotized and given a suggestion that they would feel no pain during a painful procedure but would remember the pain when the hypnotist gave them a specific cue. These subjects indeed showed no awareness of pain during the procedure. When cued, they reported memories of the pain in a matter-of-fact fashion, as if a lucid, rational observer of the event had registered the event for the subject. Other research showed that some anesthetized surgical patients could later recall, under hypnosis, specific pieces of music played during the surgery. Again, it was as if a hidden observer was registering the events of the operation even while the patient was completely unconscious under anesthesia (see Kihlstrom, 2001; Kihlstrom & Couture, 1992).

For most people, the active and receptive modes of consciousness weave our experiences together so seamlessly that we do not notice any division between them. People who develop dissociative disorders, however, may have chronic problems integrating their active consciousness with their receptive consciousness (Hilgard, 1992; Lynn, Lilienfeld, Merckelbach, Giesbrecht, & van der Kloet, 2012). That is, the different aspects of consciousness in these people do not integrate with each other in normal ways but instead remain split and operate independently of each other.

We begin our discussion of specific dissociative disorders with dissociative identity disorder (DID), formerly known as multiple personality disorder. We then move to dissociative amnesia and depersonalization/derealization disorder. All these disorders involve frequent experiences in which various aspects of a person's "self" are split off from each other and felt as separate.

CASE STUDY

Eve White was a quiet, proper, and unassuming woman, a full-time homemaker and devoted mother to a young daughter. She sought help from a psychiatrist for painful headaches that were occurring with increasing frequency. The psychiatrist decided that her headaches were related to arguments she was having with her husband over whether to raise their young daughter in the husband's church (which was Catholic) or in her church (which was Baptist). After undergoing some marital therapy, Mrs. White's marriage improved and her headaches subsided for a year or so.

Then, her husband recontacted her therapist, alarmed over changes in his wife's behavior. She had gone to visit a favorite cousin in a town 50 miles away and during the visit had behaved in a much more carefree and reckless manner than she usually did. Mrs. White told her husband over the phone that she was not going to return home, and the two had a terrible fight that ended in an agreement to divorce. When Mrs. White did return home a few days later, however, she said she had no memory of the fight with her husband or, for that matter, of the visit with her cousin.

Shortly thereafter, Mrs. White apparently went shopping and bought hundreds of dollars worth of elaborate clothing, which the couple could not afford. When confronted by her husband about her expenditures, Mrs. White claimed to have no memory of buying the clothing.

At the urging of her husband, Mrs. White made an appointment with the therapist whom she had originally consulted about her headaches. In the session, she admitted that her headaches had returned and were much more severe now than before. Eventually, she also tearfully admitted that she had

(continued)

begun to hear a voice other than her own speaking inside her head and that she feared she was going insane. The therapist asked her more questions about the clothes-buying spree, and Mrs. White became more tense and had difficulty getting words out to discuss the incident. Then, as her therapist reported,

> The brooding look in her eyes became almost a stare. Eve seemed momentarily dazed. Suddenly her posture began to change. Her body slowly stiffened until she sat rigidly erect. An alien, inexplicable expression then came over her face. This was suddenly erased into utter blankness. The lines of her countenance seemed to shift in a barely visible, slow, rippling transformation. For a moment there was the impression of something arcane. Closing her eyes, she winced as she put her hands to her temples, pressed hard, and twisted them as if to combat sudden pain. A slight shudder passed over her entire body.
>
> Then the hands lightly dropped. She relaxed easily into an attitude of comfort the physician had never before seen in this patient. A pair of blue eyes popped open. There was a quick reckless smile. In a bright, unfamiliar voice that sparked, the woman said, "Hi, there, Doc!"
>
> Still busy with his own unassimilated surprise, the doctor heard himself say, "How do you feel now?"
>
> "Why just fine—never better! How you doing yourself, Doc? . . . She's been having a real rough time. There's no doubt about that," the girl said carelessly. "I feel right sorry for her sometimes. She's such a damn dope though. . . . What she puts up with from that sorry Ralph White—and all her mooning over that little brat . . . ! To hell with it, I say!" . . .
>
> The doctor asked, "Who is 'she'?"
>
> "Why, Eve White, of course. Your long-suffering, saintly, little patient."
>
> "But aren't you Eve White?" he asked.
>
> "That's for laughs," she exclaimed, a ripple of mirth in her tone. . . . "Why, I'm Eve Black," she said. . . . "I'm me and she's herself," the girl added. "I like to live and she don't. . . . Those dresses—well, I can tell you about them. I got out the other day, and I needed some dresses. I like good clothes. So I just went into town and bought what I wanted. I charged 'em to her husband, too!" She began to laugh softly. "You ought've seen the look on her silly face when he showed her what was in the cupboard!" (Thigpen, C. H., and Cleckley, H. M., *The Three Faces of Eve.* Copyright ©1957 by McGraw-Hill Education. All rights reserved. Used with permission.)

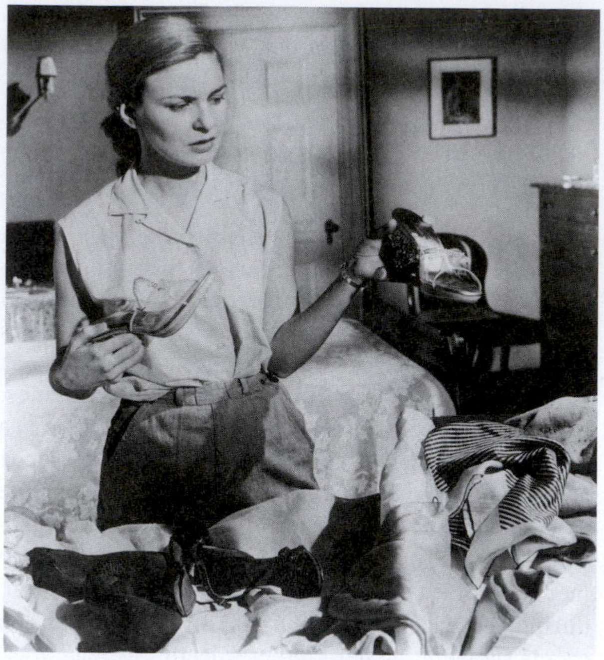

The movie *The Three Faces of Eve* depicts the story of a woman with dissociative identity disorder. Here, she has discovered extravagant articles of clothing in her closet that she doesn't remember buying. *©20th Century-Fox Film Corp. All Rights Reserved. Courtesy of Everett Collection*

Dissociative Identity Disorder

The story of Eve White, depicted in the movie *The Three Faces of Eve,* is one of the most detailed and gripping accounts of a person diagnosed with **dissociative identity disorder (DID).** In later sessions, Eve Black told the psychiatrist of escapades in which she had stayed out all night drinking and then had gone "back in" in the morning to let Eve White deal with the hangover. At the beginning of therapy, Eve White had no consciousness of Eve Black or of more than 20 personalities eventually identified during therapy. Eve White eventually recovered from her disorder, integrating the aspects of her personality represented by Eve Black and her other personalities into one entity and living a healthy, normal life.

Dissociative identity disorder is one of the most controversial and fascinating disorders recognized in clinical psychology and psychiatry. People with this disorder appear to have more than one distinct identity or personality state, and many have more than a dozen (Table 3). Each personality has different ways of perceiving and relating to the world, and each takes control over the individual's behavior on a regular basis. As was true of Eve White/Black, the alternate personalities can be extremely different from one another, with distinct facial expressions, speech characteristics, physiological responses, gestures, interpersonal styles, and attitudes (International Society for

TABLE 3 *DSM-5* Diagnostic Criteria for Dissociative Identity Disorder

A. Disruption of identity characterized by two or more distinct personality states, which may be described in some cultures as an experience of possession. The disruption in identity involves marked discontinuity in sense of self and sense of agency, accompanied by related alterations in affect, behavior, consciousness, memory, perception, cognition, and/or sensory-motor functioning. These signs and symptoms may be observed by others or reported by the individual.

B. Recurrent gaps in the recall of everyday events, important personal information, and/or traumatic events that are inconsistent with ordinary forgetting.

C. The symptoms cause clinically significant distress or impairment in social, occupational, or other important areas of functioning.

D. The disturbance is not a normal part of a broadly accepted cultural or religious practice. Note: In children, the symptoms are not better explained by imaginary playmates or other fantasy play.

E. The symptoms are not attributable to the direct physiological effects of a substance (e.g., blackouts or chaotic behavior during intoxication) or another medical condition (e.g., complex partial seizures).

the Study of Trauma and Dissociation [ISSTD], 2011). Often they are different ages and different genders and perform specific functions.

The cardinal symptom in dissociative identity disorder is the apparent presence of multiple personalities with distinct qualities, referred to as *alters* or alternate identities. These alters can take many forms and perform many functions. Child alters—alters that are young children, who do not age as the individual ages—appear to be the most common type of alter (Ross, 1997). Childhood trauma is often associated with the development of dissociative identity disorder. A child alter may be created during a traumatic experience to take on the role of victim in the trauma, while the *host* personality escapes into the protection of psychological oblivion. Or an alter may be created as a type of big brother or sister to protect the host personality from trauma. When a child alter is "out," or in control of the individual's behavior, the adult may speak and act in a childlike way.

Another type of alter is the persecutor personality. These alters inflict pain or punishment on the other personalities by engaging in self-mutilative behaviors, such as self-cutting or -burning and suicide attempts (Coons & Milstein, 1990; Ross, 1997). A persecutor alter may engage in a dangerous behavior, such as taking an overdose of pills or jumping in front of a truck, and then "go back inside," leaving the host personality to experience the pain. Persecutors may believe that they can harm other personalities without harming themselves.

Yet another type of alter is the protector, or helper, personality. The function of this personality is to offer advice to other personalities or perform functions the host personality is unable to perform, such as engaging in sexual relations or hiding from abusive parents. Helpers sometimes control the switching from one personality to another or act as passive observers who can report on the thoughts and intentions of all the other personalities (Ross, 1997).

People with dissociative identity disorder typically report significant periods of amnesia, or blank spells. They describe being completely amnesic for the periods when other personalities are in control or having one-way amnesia between certain personalities. In these instances, one personality is aware of what the other is doing, but the second personality is completely amnesic for periods when the first personality is in control. As with Eve White, people with dissociative identity disorder may suddenly discover unknown objects in their home or may lose objects. People they do not recognize might approach them on the street, claiming to know them. They may consistently receive mail or phone calls addressed to someone with a different first or last name. Verifying reports of amnesia is difficult, but some studies suggest that information and memories tend to transfer between identities, even in individuals who believe that certain personalities experience amnesia (Kong, Allen, & Glisky, 2008; Lynn et al., 2012).

Posttraumatic stress disorder is frequently comorbid with DID (Spiegel et al., 2013). Self-injurious behavior is common among people with dissociative identity disorder and often is the reason they seek or are taken for treatment. Their behavior includes self-inflicted burns or other injuries, wrist slashing, and drug overdoses. About three-quarters of patients with dissociative identity disorder have a history of suicide attempts, and over 90 percent report recurrent suicidal thoughts (Ross, 1997).

Like adults, children diagnosed with dissociative identity disorder exhibit a host of behavioral and emotional problems (Silberg, 2014). Their performance in school may be erratic, sometimes very good and sometimes very poor. They are prone to antisocial behavior, such as stealing, fire setting, and aggression. They may engage in sexual relations and abuse alcohol or illicit drugs at an early age. They tend to show many symptoms of posttraumatic stress disorder

(PTSD; see the chapter "Trauma, Anxiety, Obsessive-Compulsive, and Related Disorders"), including hypervigilance, flashbacks to traumas they have endured, traumatic nightmares, and an exaggerated startle response. Their emotions are unstable, alternating among explosive outbursts of anger, deep depression, and severe anxiety.

Most children and many adults with dissociative identity disorder report hearing voices inside their head. Some report awareness that their actions or words are being controlled by other personalities. For example, Joe, an 8-year-old boy with dissociative identity disorder, described how "a guy inside of me," called B. J. (for Bad Joey), would make him do "bad things."

PROFILES

Well, say B. J. hears someone call me names, then he would strike me to do something, like I'd be running at the other kid, but it wouldn't be my legs, I'd be saying to my legs, "no . . . , stop . . . , " but they'd keep going on their own because that's B. J. doing that. Then my arm would be going at the other kid, hitting him, and I could see my arm doing that, but I couldn't stop it, and it wouldn't hurt when my hand hit him, not until later when B. J. goes back in and then my arm is my own arm. Then it starts hurting. (Source: Hornstein & Putnam, 1992, p. 1081)

Reliable estimates of the prevalence of dissociative identity disorder in the general population are hard to come by. Studies of patients in psychiatric care find that between 1 and 6 percent of patients can be diagnosed with DID (Dorahy et al., 2014; Foote, Smolin, Kaplan, Legatt, & Lipschitz, 2006). The vast majority of people diagnosed with this disorder are adult women.

Issues in Diagnosis

Dissociative identity disorder was rarely diagnosed before about 1980, after which there was a great increase in the number of reported cases. This is due in part to the fact that dissociative identity disorder was first included as a diagnostic category in the *DSM* in its third edition, published in 1980. The availability of specific diagnostic criteria for this disorder made it more likely to be diagnosed. At the same time, the diagnostic criteria for schizophrenia were made more specific in the 1980 version of the *DSM,* possibly leading to some cases that earlier would have been diagnosed as schizophrenia being diagnosed as dissociative identity disorder. One final, and important, influence on diagnostic trends was the publication of a series of influential papers by psychiatrists describing persons with dissociative identity disorder whom they had treated (Coons, 1980; Greaves, 1980; Rosenbaum, 1980). These cases aroused interest in the disorder within the psychiatric community.

Still, most mental health professionals are reluctant to give this diagnosis. Most people diagnosed with dissociative identity disorder have previously been diagnosed with other disorders. Some of the other disorders diagnosed may be secondary to or the result of the dissociative identity disorder. For example, one study of patients with dissociative identity disorder found that 97 percent could also be diagnosed with major depression; 90 percent had an anxiety disorder, most often posttraumatic stress disorder; 65 percent were abusing substances; and 38 percent had an eating disorder (Ellason, Ross, & Fuchs, 1996). In addition, most people with dissociative identity disorder also are diagnosed with a personality disorder (Dorahy et al., 2014). Some of the earlier diagnoses may be misdiagnoses of the dissociative symptoms. For example, when people with dissociative identity disorder report hearing voices talking inside their heads, they may be misdiagnosed as having schizophrenia (ISSTD, 2011).

While the diagnostic criteria for DID had not changed very much since *DSM-III, DSM-5* includes some important changes. *DSM-5* added the words "or an experience of possession" to Criterion A (see Table 4) to make the criteria more applicable to diverse cultural groups by identifying a common presentation of DID in non-Western cultures as well as subgroups in Western cultures (e.g., immigrant and some conservative or fundamentalist religious groups; Spiegel et al., 2013). Many features of DID can be influenced by an individual's cultural background and the fragmented identities may take the form of possessing spirits, deities, demons, animals, or mythical figures considered to be real. In contrast to culturally normative possession states that may be part of a spiritual practice, abnormal possession DID is experienced as involuntary, distressing, and uncontrollable, and often involves conflict between the individual and social, cultural, or religious norms (Criterion D). Research has shown that cases of pathological possession with dissociative symptoms occur in many countries (Cardeña, van Duijl, Weiner, & Terhune, 2009), and one study showed that nearly 60 percent of patients with DID in Western settings felt as if they were possessed (Ross, 2011). Other *DSM-5* changes include that transitions in identity do not have to be directly observed by others but instead could be self-reported (Criterion A), and problems with recall (amnesia) include everyday events and not just traumatic experiences (Criterion B).

TABLE 4 *DSM-5* Diagnostic Criteria for Dissociative Amnesia

A. An inability to recall important autobiographical information, usually of a traumatic or stressful nature, that is inconsistent with ordinary forgetting. Note: Dissociative amnesia most often consists of localized or selective amnesia for a specific event or events; or generalized amnesia for identity and life history.

B. The symptoms cause clinically significant distress or impairment in social, occupational, or other important areas of functioning.

C. The disturbance is not attributable to the direct physiological effects of a substance (e.g., alcohol or other drug of abuse, a medication) or a neurological or other medical condition (e.g., partial complex seizures, sequelae of a traumatic brain injury, other neurological condition).

D. The disturbance is not better explained by dissociative identity disorder, posttraumatic-stress disorder, acute stress disorder, somatic symptom disorder, or major or mild neurocognitive disorder.

Specify if:

With Dissociative Fugue: Apparently purposeful travel or bewildered wandering that is associated with amnesia for identity or for other important autobiographical information.

Dissociative identity disorder is diagnosed more frequently in the United States than in Great Britain, Europe, India, or Japan (Dorahy et al., 2014; Saxena & Prasad, 1989; Takahashi, 1990). Some studies suggest that Latinos, both within and outside the United States, may be more likely than other ethnic groups to experience dissociative symptoms in response to traumas. For example, a study of Vietnam veterans found that Latino veterans were more likely than non-Latino veterans to show dissociative symptoms (Koopman et al., 2001). Another study conducted with Latino survivors of community violence in the United States found that those who were less acculturated to mainstream U.S. culture were more likely to show dissociative symptoms than were those who were more acculturated (Marshall & Orlando, 2002). Dissociative symptoms may be part of the syndrome *ataque de nervios,* a culturally accepted reaction to stress among Latinos that involves transient periods of loss of consciousness, convulsive movements, hyperactivity, assaultive behaviors, and impulsive acts (see the chapter "Trauma, Anxiety, Obsessive-Compulsive, and Related Disorders"). Some researchers have argued that psychiatrists in the United States are too quick to diagnose dissociative identity disorder; others argue that psychiatrists in other countries misdiagnose it as another disorder (Coons, Cole, Pellow, & Milstein, 1990; Fahy, 1988).

Substantial controversy has revolved around claims by some people with dissociative disorders that during adulthood they have recovered memories of severe abuse after years of not remembering the abuse. We discuss this controversy in detail at the end of this chapter.

Theories of Dissociative Identity Disorder

Many theorists who study dissociative identity disorder view it as the result of coping strategies used by persons faced with intolerable trauma—most often childhood sexual and/or physical abuse—that they are powerless to escape (ISSTD, 2011; Putnam, Zahn, & Post, 1990; Schimmenti & Caretti, 2016). As Ross (1997, p. 64) describes:

> The little girl being sexually abused by her father at night imagines that the abuse is happening to someone else, as a way to distance herself from the overwhelming emotions she is experiencing. She may float up to the ceiling and watch the abuse in a detached fashion. Now not only is the abuse not happening to her, but she blocks it out of her mind—that other little girl remembers it, not the original self. In this model, DID is an internal divide-and-conquer strategy in which intolerable knowledge and feeling is split up into manageable compartments. These compartments are personified and take on a life of their own.

Indeed, most studies find that the majority of people diagnosed with dissociative identity disorder self-report having been a victim of sexual or physical abuse during childhood (e.g., Ross & Ness, 2010; see Dorahy et al., 2014). In turn, dissociative experiences are commonly reported by survivors of child sexual abuse (Kisiel & Lyons, 2001; Vonderlin et al., 2018). For example, in a study of 135 persons with dissociative identity disorder, 92 percent reported having been sexually abused, and 90 percent reported having been repeatedly physically abused (Ellason et al., 1996; see also Putnam, Guroff, Silberman, & Barban, 1986). Researchers have found similar results in studies in which patients' reports of abuse were corroborated by at least one family member or by emergency room reports (Coons, 1994; Coons & Milstein, 1986). The abuse most often was carried out by parents or other family members and was chronic over an extended period of childhood. Other types of trauma that have been associated with the development of dissociative identity disorder include kidnapping, natural disasters, war, famine, and religious persecution (Ross, 1999). Some people with DID report having been the victim of torture and abuse by cults, human trafficking, multigenerational abusive family systems, pedophile networks, or even aliens or government "mind experiments" (ISSTD, 2011).

Some evidence indicates that people who develop dissociative identity disorder tend to be highly suggestible and hypnotizable and may use self-hypnosis to dissociate and escape their traumas (Dell, 2018; Kihlstrom, Glisky, & Angiulo, 1994). They may create the alternate personalities to help them cope with their traumas, much as a child might create imaginary playmates to ease pangs of loneliness. These alternate personalities can provide the safety, security, and nurturing that they are not receiving from their caregivers. Retreating into their alternate personalities or using these personalities to perform frightening functions becomes a chronic way of coping with life.

However, not all researchers believe trauma plays the determining role in dissociative identity disorder (see Lynn et al., 2012). A contrasting view is the sociocognitive model (Spanos, 1994; see Lynn et al., 2012), which argues that the alternate identities are created by patients who adopt the idea or narrative of dissociative identity disorder as an explanation that fits their lives. The identities are not true personalities with clear-cut demarcations but rather metaphors used by the patients to understand their subjective experiences. Patients are not faking their multiple personalities but rather are playing out a role that helps them deal with stresses in their lives and is reinforced by attention and concern from others, and by cultural narratives, psychotherapy, and media. Both trauma and sociocognitive factors likely play a role (Sar, Krüger, Martínez-Taboas, Middleton, & Dorahy, 2013).

A few family history studies suggest that dissociative identity disorder may run in some families (Coons, 1984; Dell & Eisenhower, 1990). In addition, studies of twins and of adopted children have found evidence that the tendency to dissociate is substantially affected by genetics (Becker-Blease et al., 2004; Pieper, Out, Bakermans-Kranenburg, & van IJzendoorn, 2011). The ability and tendency to dissociate as a coping response may to some extent be biologically determined.

Treatment of Dissociative Identity Disorder

Treating dissociative identity disorder can be extremely challenging. The goal of treatment is integrating all the alter personalities into one coherent personality and helping the patient rebuild the capacity for coping with distress and trusting healthy relationships (Brand, Loewenstein, & Spiegel, 2014; ISSTD, 2011). This integration is sometimes achieved by "giving voice" to each identity and helping the identities become aware of one another, determining the function or role of each personality, helping each personality confront and work through the traumas that led to the disorder and the concerns each one has or represents, and negotiating with the personalities for unification into one personality who has learned adaptive styles of coping with stress. Building trust and therapeutic alliance is critical, as patients with DID often have experienced traumas that have completely shattered their trust in others. The therapist may interact with each of the alters to engage them in the process of reviewing and understanding the trauma history and integrating their memories and strengths into one coherent personality. Hypnosis is sometimes used in the treatment of dissociative identity disorder (Putnam & Lowenstein, 1993). Possession-form DID likely requires culturally adapted treatments, perhaps involving indigenous healers (Martinez-Taboas, 2005; Spiegel et al., 2013).

One of the few studies to empirically evaluate the treatment of DID found that patients who were able to integrate their personalities through treatment remained relatively free of symptoms over the subsequent 2 years (Ellason & Ross, 1997). These patients also reported few symptoms of substance abuse or depression and were able to reduce their use of antidepressants and antipsychotic medications. In contrast, patients who had not achieved integration during treatment continued to show symptoms of DID and a number of other disorders. A more recent study (using clinician reports) suggests that DID treatment can improve functioning for as long as 6 years (Myrick et al., 2017). These studies did not compare the outcome of the patients who received therapy with that of patients who did not, nor did they compare different types of therapy.

Dissociative Amnesia

In dissociative identity disorder, individuals claim to have amnesia for those periods of time when their alternate personalities are in control. Yet some people have significant periods of amnesia without assuming new personalities or identities. They cannot remember important facts about their lives and their personal identities and typically are aware of large gaps in their memory or knowledge of themselves. These people are said to have **dissociative amnesia** (Table 4).

Amnesia is considered to be either organic or psychogenic (Table 5). **Organic amnesia** is caused by brain injury resulting from disease, drugs, accidents (such as blows to the head), or surgery. Organic amnesia that involves the inability to remember new information is known as **anterograde amnesia. Psychogenic amnesia** arises in the absence of any brain injury or

TABLE 5 Differences Between Psychogenic and Organic Amnesia

There are several important differences between psychogenic amnesia and organic amnesia.

Psychogenic Amnesia	Organic Amnesia
Caused by psychological factors	Caused by biological factors (such as disease, drugs, and blows to the head)
Seldom involves anterograde amnesia (inability to learn new information acquired since onset of amnesia)	Often involves anterograde amnesia
Can involve retrograde amnesia (inability to remember events from the past)	Can involve retrograde amnesia
Retrograde amnesia often only for personal information, not for general information	Retrograde amnesia usually for both personal and general information

disease and is thought to have psychological causes. Psychogenic amnesia rarely involves anterograde amnesia.

Retrograde amnesia, the inability to remember information from the past, can have both organic and psychogenic causes. For example, people who have been in a serious car accident can have retrograde amnesia for the few minutes just before the accident. This retrograde amnesia can be due to brain injury resulting from blows to the head during the accident, or it can be a motivated forgetting of the events leading up to the trauma. Retrograde amnesia can also occur for longer periods of time.

When retrograde amnesias are due to organic causes, people usually forget everything about the past, including both personal information, such as where they lived and people they knew, and general information, such as the identity of the president and major historical events of the period. They typically retain memory of their personal identity, however; while they may not remember their children, they know their own name. When long-term retrograde amnesias are due to psychological causes, people typically lose their identity and forget personal information but retain their memory for general information. The following case study describes a man with a psychogenic retrograde amnesia.

Loss of memory due to alcohol intoxication is common, but usually the person forgets only the events occurring during the period of intoxication. People who have severely abused alcohol much of their lives can develop a more global retrograde amnesia, known as Korsakoff's syndrome, in which they cannot remember much personal or general information for a period of several years or decades. However, the type of retrograde amnesia in the case study, which apparently involved only one episode of heavy drinking and the loss of only personal information, typically has psychological causes.

CASE STUDY

Some years ago a man was found wandering the streets of Eugene, Oregon, not knowing his name or where he had come from. The police, who were baffled by his inability to identify himself, called in Lester Beck . . . , a psychologist they knew to be familiar with hypnosis, to see if he could be of assistance. He found the man eager to cooperate and by means of hypnosis and other methods was able to reconstruct the man's history. . . .

Following domestic difficulties, the man had gone on a drunken spree completely out of keeping with his earlier social behavior, and he had subsequently suffered deep remorse. His amnesia was motivated in the first place by the desire to exclude from memory the mortifying experiences that had gone on during the guilt-producing episode. He succeeded in forgetting all the events before and after this behavior that reminded him of it. Hence the amnesia spread from the critical incident to events before and after it, and he completely lost his sense of personal identity. (Source: Hilgard 1977/1986, p. 68)

A subtype of dissociative amnesia is a **dissociative fugue,** in which the individual travels to a new place and may assume a new identity with no memory of his or her previous identity. People in a dissociative fugue may behave quite normally in their new environment and not find it odd that they cannot remember anything from their past. Just as suddenly, they may return to their previous identity and home, resuming their life as if nothing had happened, with no memory of what they did during the fugue. The autobiographical memory loss in a dissociative fugue may be especially long-lasting and resistant to "relearning." A fugue may last for days or years, and a person may experience repeated fugue states or a single episode. Dissociative fugue diagnoses are extremely rare.

As in DID, some theorists argue that psychogenic amnesias may be the result of using dissociation as a defense against intolerable memories or stressors (Freyd, 1996; Gleaves, Smith, Butler, & Spiegel, 2004). Psychogenic amnesias most frequently occur following traumatic events, such as wars or sexual and/or physical abuse of increased severity, frequency, and violence. Alternatively, amnesia for a specific event may occur because individuals are in such a high state of arousal during the event that they do not encode and store information during it and thus are unable to retrieve information about it later.

Amnesias for specific periods of time around traumas appear to be fairly common, but generalized retrograde amnesias for an individual's entire past and identity appear to be very rare. Studies of people in countries that have been the site of attempted genocides, ethnic cleansings, and wars have suggested that the rate of dissociative amnesias in these countries may be elevated. For example, a study of 810 Bhutanese refugees in Nepal found that almost 20 percent of those who had been tortured during conflicts in their countries could be diagnosed with dissociative amnesia (van Ommeren et al., 2001).

One complication that arises in diagnosing amnesias is the possibility that the amnesias are being faked by people trying to escape punishment for crimes they committed during the periods for which they claim to be amnesic. True amnesias also can occur in conjunction with the commission of crimes. Many crimes are committed by persons under the influence of alcohol or other drugs, and the drugs can cause blackouts for the periods of intoxication (Go, 2017). Similarly, people who incur a head injury while committing a crime—for example, by falling while trying to escape the scene of a crime—can have amnesia for the commission of the crime.

Amnesia is seen most often in homicide cases, with 10 to 70 percent of persons accused of murder claiming to have amnesia for the killings (Go, 2017). In most of these cases, the victims are closely related to the killers (lovers, spouses, close friends, or family members), the killings appear to be unpremeditated, and the killers are in a state of extreme emotional arousal at the time of the killings. More rarely, the killers appear to have been in a psychotic state at the time of the killings.

There is no clear-cut way to differentiate true amnesias from feigned ones. Moderate or severe head injuries leading to amnesia may be detectable through neuroimaging of the brain. Feigned amnesia is more common in individuals with financial, sexual, or legal problems, or a wish to escape stressful circumstances. Some clinicians advocate the use of hypnosis to help people remember events around crimes if it is suspected that the amnesia is due to psychological causes. However, the possibility that hypnosis will "create" memories through the power of suggestion has led many courts to deny the use of hypnosis in such cases. In most cases, it is impossible to determine whether the amnesia is real.

Lorena Bobbit cut off her husband's penis after years of experiencing his abuse. She claimed to have amnesia for the act of cutting it off.
©Consolidated News Pictures/Getty Images

People suffering from dissociative amnesia or dissociative fugue may recover on their own. Psychotherapy involves helping patients recall and understand the trauma that contributed to their dissociation, but there are few empirical studies of psychotherapy's effectiveness for these disorders (Staniloiu & Markowitsch, 2014).

Depersonalization/ Derealization Disorder

People with **depersonalization/derealization disorder** have frequent episodes during which they feel detached from their own mental processes or body, as if they are outside observers of themselves (Table 6). Occasional experiences of depersonalization or derealization are common, particularly when people are sleep-deprived or under the influence of drugs (Baker et al., 2003). Approximately half of all adults report having had at least one brief episode of depersonalization or derealization, usually following a significant stressor (American Psychiatric Association, 2013). The worldwide lifetime prevalence of depersonalization/derealization disorder is between 0.8 percent and 2.8 percent, and is equally common among men and women.

TABLE 6 *DSM-5* Diagnostic Criteria for Depersonalization/Derealization Disorder
A. The presence of persistent or recurrent experiences of depersonalization, derealization, or both: 1. Depersonalization: Experiences of unreality, detachment, or being an outside observer with respect to one's thoughts, feelings, sensations, body, or actions (e.g., perceptual alterations, distorted sense of time, unreal or absent self, emotional and/or physical numbing). 2. Derealization: Experiences of unreality or detachment with respect to surroundings (e.g., individuals or objects are experienced as unreal, dreamlike, foggy, lifeless, or visually distorted).
B. During the depersonalization or derealization experiences, reality testing remains intact.
C. The symptoms cause clinically significant distress or impairment in social, occupational, or other important areas of functioning.
D. The disturbance is not attributable to the direct physiological effects of a substance (e.g., a drug of abuse, medication) or another medical condition (e.g., seizures).
E. The disturbance is not better explained by another mental disorder, such as schizophrenia, panic disorder, major depressive disorder, acute stress disorder, posttraumatic stress disorder, or another dissociative disorder.

Depersonalization/derealization disorder is diagnosed when episodes are so frequent and distressing that they interfere with the individual's ability to function. One study of people diagnosed with the disorder found that the average age of onset was about 23 years and that two-thirds reported having had chronic experiences of depersonalization/derealization since the onset (Baker et al., 2003). Seventy-nine percent reported impaired social or work functioning, and the majority also had another psychiatric diagnosis, most often depression. People diagnosed with this disorder often report a history of childhood emotional, physical, or sexual abuse (Simeon, Guralnik, Schmeidler, Sirof, & Knutelska, 2001).

Controversies Around the Dissociative Disorders

Surveys of psychiatrists in the United States and Canada find that less than one-quarter of them believe there is strong empirical evidence that the dissociative disorders are valid diagnoses (Lalonde, Hudson, Gigante, & Pope, 2001; Pope, Oliva, Hudson, Bodkin, & Grueber, 1999). Skeptics argue that the disorders are artificially created in suggestible clients by clinicians who reinforce clients for creating symptoms of a dissociative disorder and who may even induce symptoms of the disorder through hypnotic suggestion (see Kihlstrom, 2005; Lynn et al., 2012; Loftus, 2011; Spanos, 1994).

Controversy over the diagnosis of dissociative amnesia increased in response to claims that some survivors of childhood sexual abuse repressed their memories of the abuse for years and then eventually recalled these memories, often in the context of psychotherapy. These repressed memories represent a form of dissociative amnesia. Those who believe in repressed memories argue that the clinical evidence for dissociative or psychogenic amnesia is ample and that the empirical evidence is growing (DePrince & Freyd, 2014). Nonbelievers argue that the empirical evidence against the validity of dissociative amnesia is ample and that the supportive evidence is biased (Kihlstrom, 2005; Loftus, 2011).

Most of the evidence for the phenomenon of repressed memories comes from studies of people who either are known to have been abused or self-report abuse and who claim to have forgotten or repressed their abuse at some time in the past. For example, Linda Williams (1995) surveyed 129 women who had documented histories of having been sexually abused sometime between 1973 and 1975. These women, who were between 10 months and 12 years old at the time of their abuse, were interviewed about 17 years after their abuse. Williams found that 49 of these 129 women either had no memory of the specific abuse events that were documented or had forgotten about the abuse completely.

John Briere and Jon Conte (1993) located 450 therapy patients who self-identified as abuse victims. Briere and Conte asked these people if there had ever been a time before their eighteenth birthday when they "could not remember" their abuse. Fifty-nine percent answered yes to this question. As another example, Judith Herman and Mary Harvey (1997) examined interviews of 77 women who had reported memories of childhood trauma. They found that 17 percent spontaneously reported having had some delayed recall of the trauma and that 16 percent reported a period of complete amnesia following the trauma.

Nonbelievers in repressed memories have raised questions about the methods and conclusions of these studies (Kihlstrom, 2005; Loftus, 2003; McNally, 2003, 2017). For example, regarding the Williams study, it turns out that 33 of the 49 women who said they could not remember the specific abuse incidents they were asked about could remember other childhood abuse incidents. Thus, they had not completely forgotten or repressed all memories of abuse. Instead, they simply could not remember the specific incident about which they were being asked. Williams did not give any additional information about the 16 women who could remember no incidents of childhood molestation. They may simply have been too young to remember the incidents, because memory for anything that happens before about age 3 tends to be sketchy.

Nonbelievers in repressed memories also cite numerous studies from the literature on eyewitness identification and testimony indicating that people can be made to believe certain events occurred that in fact never happened (Ceci & Bruck, 1995; Frenda, Nichols, & Loftus, 2011; Laney & Loftus, 2013) and that these beliefs can persist for months or years (Zhu et al., 2012). For example, Elizabeth Loftus and her colleagues developed a method for instilling a childhood memory of being lost on a specific occasion at age 5 (Loftus, 2003). This method involved a trusted family member engaging the subject in a conversation about the time he or she was lost (Loftus, 1993, p. 532):

> Chris (14 years old) was convinced by his older brother Jim that he had been lost in a shopping mall when he was 5 years old. Jim told Chris this story as if it were the truth: "It was 1981 or 1982. I remember that Chris was 5. We had gone shopping in the University City shopping mall in Spokane. After some panic, we found Chris being led down the mall by a tall, oldish man (I think he was wearing a flannel shirt). Chris was crying and holding the man's hand. The man explained that he had found Chris walking around crying his eyes out just a few moments before and was trying to help him find his parents." Just two days later, Chris recalled his feelings about being lost: "That day I was so scared that I would never see my family again. I knew that I was in trouble." On the third day, he recalled a conversation with his mother: "I remember Mom telling me never to do that again." On the fourth day: "I also remember that old man's flannel shirt." On the fifth day, he started remembering the mall itself: "I sort of remember the stores." In his last recollection, he could even remember a conversation with the man who found him: "I remember the man asking me if I was lost." . . . A couple of weeks later, Chris described his false memory and he greatly expanded on it. "I was with you guys for a second and I think I went over to look at the toy store, the Kay-Bee Toy and uh, we got lost and I was looking around and I thought, 'Uh-oh, I'm in trouble now.' You know. And then I . . . I thought I was never going to see my family again. I was really scared you know. And then this old man, I think he was wearing a blue flannel, came up to me. . . . He was kind of old. He was kind of bald on top. . . . He had like a ring of gray hair . . . and he had glasses."

Other studies have found that repeatedly asking adults about childhood events that never actually happened leads perhaps 20 to 40 percent eventually to "remember" these events and even explain them in detail (Frenda et al., 2011; Laney & Loftus, 2013). For example, in one study, 40 percent of a British sample said they had seen footage of a bus exploding in the 2005 London terrorist attacks, when such footage did not exist (Ost, Granhag, Udell, Roos, & Hjelmsater, 2008). Thirty-five percent of these described memories of details that they could not have seen.

The percentage of participants developing false memories of events that never happened can be increased by procedures that mimic some of the psychotherapeutic methods used with people who "recover" repressed memories (Scoboria et al., 2017). For example, family photo albums are sometimes reviewed in psychotherapy to help people remember traumatic events. In false memory experiments, showing participants photographs of themselves or other family members in the context of telling a story of a false memory makes participants more likely to believe the false memory with strong confidence (Lindsay, Hagen, Read, Wade, & Garry, 2004). Simply having a psychologist suggest that an individual's dreams reflect repressed memories of childhood events leads a majority of subjects subsequently to report that the events depicted in their dreams actually happened (Mazzoni & Loftus, 1998).

Critics of this line of work question the application of these studies to claims of repressed memories of sexual abuse (Brewin & Andrews, 2017; Gleaves, Hernandez, & Warner, 2003). They argue that although people might be willing to go along with experimenters who try to convince them that they were lost in a shopping mall as a child, they are unlikely to be willing to go along with a therapist who tries to convince them that they were sexually abused if such abuse did not in fact happen. Abuse is such a terrible thing to remember, and the social consequences of admitting the abuse and confronting the abuser are so negative, that people simply would not claim the memory was true if it was not.

Researchers have used paradigms from cognitive psychology to test hypotheses about the reality of repressed memories. In a series of studies, Richard McNally and colleagues (McNally, 2003; McNally, Clancy, & Schacter, 2001; McNally, Clancy, Schacter, & Pitman, 2000a, 2000b) have found that individuals reporting recovered memories of either childhood sexual abuse or abduction by space aliens have a greater tendency to form false memories during certain laboratory tasks. For example, one task required participants to say whether they recognized words similar to, but not exactly the same as, other words they previously had learned. People who claimed to have recovered memories of alien abductions were more prone than comparison groups to falsely recognize words they had not seen previously (Clancy, Schacter, McNally, & Pitman, 2000; Clancy, McNally, Schacter, Lenzenweger, & Pitman, 2002). The researchers argue that these people are characterized by an information-processing style that may render them more likely to believe they have experienced specific events, such as childhood sexual abuse, when in fact they have experienced other, broadly similar events, such as physical abuse or emotional neglect.

Jennifer Freyd and colleagues have argued that the kinds of cognitive tasks McNally and colleagues used do not tap into the specific cognitive phenomena associated with repressed memories. Specifically, they suggest that individuals who dissociate from, and forget, their abusive experiences are most likely to differ from other individuals in the performance of cognitive tasks that require divided attention—that is, paying attention to more than one thing at a time—because a division of attention is critical to dissociation (DePrince & Freyd, 2014; Freyd, Martorella, Alvarado, Hayes, & Christman, 1998). One divided-attention task requires participants to press a key on a keyboard in response to a secondary task while attending to words on a computer screen and committing them to memory. Under these divided-attention conditions, people who score high on measures of dissociation recall fewer trauma-related words but more neutral words they previously had been instructed to remember, while low-dissociation participants show the opposite pattern. This suggests that people high in dissociation are better able to keep threatening information from their explicit awareness, particularly if they can instead turn their attention to other tasks or other events in their environment.

The repressed memory debate is likely to continue for some time (see Brewin & Andrews, 2017; McNally, 2017). Researchers are striving to apply scientific techniques to support their views, with significant real-world implications. Psychologists are being called on to testify in court cases involving claims of recovered or false memories. Through all the controversy, people trying to understand their distressing symptoms find themselves at the center of this scientific maelstrom.

CHAPTER INTEGRATION

Philosophers and scientists have long debated the mind-body problem: Does the mind influence bodily processes? Do changes in the body affect a person's sense of "self"? Exactly how do the body and the mind influence each other?

As noted earlier, the dissociative and somatic symptom disorders provide compelling evidence that the mind and the body are complexly interwoven (Figure 2). In conversion disorder, psychological stress causes the person to lose eyesight, hearing, or functioning in another important physiological system. In somatic symptom disorder, a person under psychological stress experiences physiological symptoms, such as severe headaches. An underlying theme of these disorders is that some people find it easier or more acceptable to experience psychological distress through changes in their body than to express it more directly as sadness, fear, or anger, perhaps because of cultural or social norms.

We all somatize our distress to some degree—we feel more aches and pains when we are upset about something than when we are happy. People who develop somatic symptom disorders, and perhaps dissociative disorders, may somatize their distress to an extreme degree. Their tendency to differentiate between what is going on in their mind and what is going on in their body may be minimal, and they may favor an extreme bodily expression of what is going on in their mind.

FIGURE 2 **Mind and Body in the Somatic Symptom and Dissociative Disorders.**

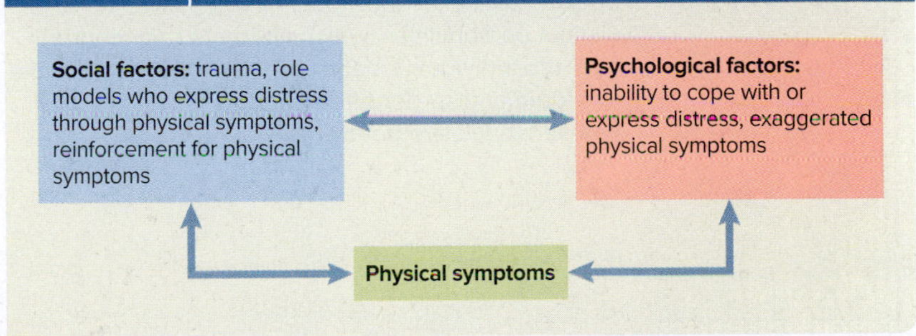

SHADES OF GRAY **DISCUSSION**

Ben's health concerns do seem to be linked to his parents' separation and not to a medical condition. His insistence of real pain and his refusal to return to class signal that he experiences significant physical and emotional distress over his perceived headaches and stomachaches. Therefore, his symptoms are more in line with a somatic symptom disorder than with illness anxiety disorder.

CHAPTER SUMMARY

- The somatic symptom disorders are a group of disorders in which the individual experiences distressing physical symptoms and abnormal thoughts, feelings, and behaviors in response to these symptoms.
- Somatic symptom disorder involves a long history of physical complaints for which an individual has sought treatment. Medically unexplained symptoms are present to various degrees and are a key feature in conversion disorder. People with these disorders show high rates of anxiety and depression.
- People with illness anxiety disorder fear becoming ill, although they may not experience actual symptoms of illness.
- The cognitive theory of the somatic symptom disorders is that affected people believe they are vulnerable to illness, focus excessively on physical symptoms, and catastrophize these symptoms. They are reinforced by the attention and concern they receive from others. Treatment involves helping people have more realistic perspectives on their health, removing reinforcements for illness behavior, and teaching people to cope better with stress.
- In conversion disorder, individuals lose all sensory and/or motor functioning in a part of their body, such as the eyes or the legs. Conversion symptoms often occur after trauma or stress. People with conversion disorder tend to have high rates of depression, anxiety, alcohol abuse, and antisocial personality disorder. Treatment for the disorder focuses on the expression of associated emotions or memories.
- In the dissociative disorders, the individual's identity, memories, and consciousness become separated, or dissociated, from one another. In dissociative identity disorder (DID), the individual develops two or more distinct personalities, which alternate their control over the individual's behavior. Persons with dissociative identity disorder often engage in self-injurious and self-mutilative behaviors.
- The vast majority of diagnosed cases of dissociative identity disorder are women, and they tend to have a history of severe childhood sexual and/or physical abuse. The alternate personalities may have been formed during the traumatic experiences as a way of psychologically managing these experiences, particularly among people who are highly hypnotizable. The treatment of dissociative identity disorder typically involves helping the various personalities become integrated into one functional personality.
- Dissociative, or psychogenic, amnesia involves the loss of memory due to psychological causes. It differs from organic amnesia, which is caused by brain injury and in which a person may have difficulty remembering new information (anterograde amnesia), a rare condition in psychogenic amnesia. In addition, with organic amnesia loss of memory for the past (retrograde amnesia) usually is generalized, whereas with psychogenic amnesia memory loss is limited to personal information.
- Psychogenic amnesia typically occurs following traumatic events. It may be due to motivated forgetting of events, to poor storage of information during events due to hyperarousal, or to avoidance of the emotions experienced during traumatic events and of the memories associated with these events.
- Dissociative fugue is a subtype of dissociative amnesia in which the person suddenly moves away from home and assumes an entirely new identity, with complete amnesia for the previous identity.
- Depersonalization/derealization disorder involves frequent episodes in which individuals feel detached from their mental processes or their body. Transient depersonalization/derealization experiences are common, especially in people who are sleep-deprived or under the influence of drugs.

KEY TERMS

somatic symptom disorders
illness anxiety disorder
conversion disorder (functional neurological symptom disorder)
factitious disorder
malingering
factitious disorder imposed on another
dissociation
dissociative identity disorder (DID)
dissociative amnesia
organic amnesia
anterograde amnesia
psychogenic amnesia
retrograde amnesia
dissociative fugue
depersonalization/derealization disorder

Chapter 7

©ximagination/123RF

Mood Disorders and Suicide

CHAPTER OUTLINE

Mood Disorders Along the Continuum

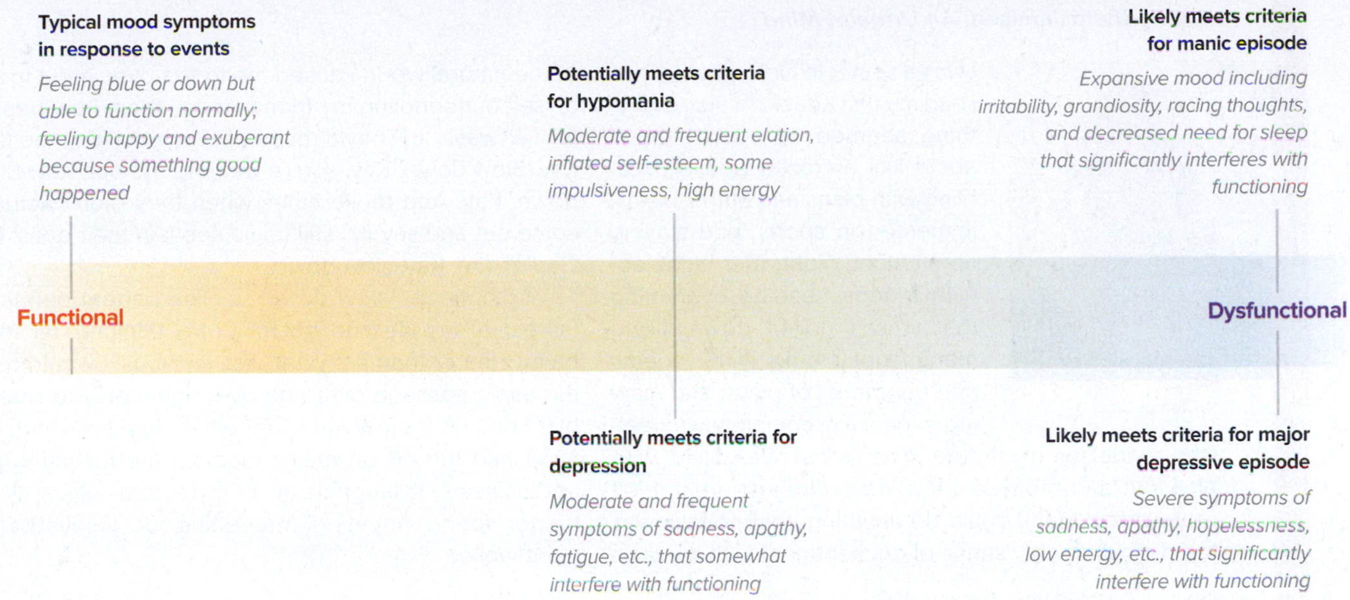

"I'm depressed" is a phrase you may have uttered, perhaps after you didn't do as well as you expected on an exam or when a friend became angry and wouldn't speak to you. Such events often sap our energy and motivation, shake our self-esteem, and make us feel down and blue—all symptoms of depression.

More significant events, such as the death of a loved one, the breakup of a marriage, or the loss of a job, can lead to more serious symptoms of depression. In some people, the symptoms may be mild or moderate and not interfere with daily functioning. Sometimes, however, symptoms of depression following negative events become debilitating and can last for a long period of time. In some cases, severe symptoms of depression emerge without any obvious cause. A diagnosis of depression depends on both the severity and the duration of symptoms.

Like symptoms of depression, symptoms of mania also vary in severity and duration. Perhaps you've experienced a "fizzing over" feeling of exuberance when something in your life is going particularly well—such as getting an acceptance to college or beginning a relationship with somebody special. As in depression, moderate symptoms of mania usually are tied to specific situations and lessen as those situations pass. Symptoms of a manic episode, however, go beyond feeling happy when something good has happened. People diagnosed with mania are often irritable and impatient with others. Their extreme self-confidence may lead them to carry out grandiose schemes to earn money or influence others, or to engage in extremely risky or impulsive behaviors.

Drawing the line between normal mood responses to common or uncommon events and the mood disorders has been very challenging for researchers and clinicians. When you are saddened by a loss, how long is too long for these feelings to last before they should be diagnosed as a disorder? One of the biggest controversies in the development of the *DSM-5* was the question of how to define bereavement-related depressive disorders (Frances & Widiger, 2012). Some argue that in the vast majority of cases, depressive symptoms following a loss should not be diagnosed as a disorder, whereas others argue that excluding bereavement-related depressions from diagnoses fails to recognize the negative impact of these depressions on people's lives and the need for treatment.

On the other hand, being extremely self-confident, possessing grand and risky ideas, and having boundless energy are a recipe for success in our go-go, high-tech world. Historically, these are traits that many leaders and innovators in business, politics, government, and the arts have possessed (Jamison, 1993). Where do we draw the line between mania and creative genius or entrepreneurialism?

Extraordinary People

Kay Redfield Jamison, *An Unquiet Mind*

©Thomas Traill

I was a senior in high school when I had my first attack. At first, everything seemed so easy. I raced about like a crazed weasel, bubbling with plans and enthusiasms, immersed in sports, and staying up all night, night after night, out with friends, reading everything that wasn't nailed down, filling manuscript books with poems and fragments of plays, and making expansive, completely unrealistic plans for my future. The world was filled with pleasure and promise; I felt great. Not just great, I felt really great. I felt I could do anything, that no task was too difficult. . . . My sense of enchantment with the laws of the natural world caused me to fizz over, and I found myself buttonholing my friends to tell them how beautiful it all was. . . . [They'd respond:] You're talking too fast, Kay. Slow down, Kay. You're wearing me out, Kay. Slow down, Kay. And those times when they didn't actually come out and say it, I still could see it in their eyes: For God's sake, Kay, slow down.

I did, finally, slow down. . . . The bottom began to fall out of my life and my mind. My thinking, far from being clearer than a crystal, was tortuous. I would read the same passage over and over again only to realize that I had no memory at all for what I had just read. My mind had turned on me: It mocked me for my vapid enthusiasms; it laughed at all my foolish plans; it no longer found anything interesting or enjoyable or worthwhile.

(Source: Adapted from Jamison, 1995, pp. 35–38)

The emotional roller-coaster ride Kay Jamison describes is known as **bipolar disorder,** or *manic-depression.* First, Jamison had **mania,** with great energy and enthusiasm for everything, talking and thinking so fast that her friends could not keep up with her. Eventually, though, she crashed into a **depression.** Her energy and enthusiasm were gone, and she was slow to think, to talk, and to move. The joy had been drained from her life. Bipolar disorder is one of the two major types of mood disorders. The other type is **depressive disorders.** People with depressive disorders experience only depression, and not mania.

CHARACTERISTICS OF DEPRESSIVE DISORDERS

We will consider depressive disorders first. In depressive disorders, the symptoms of depression take over the whole person—emotions, bodily functions, behaviors, and thoughts.

Symptoms of Depression

A cardinal symptom of depression is depressed mood out of proportion to any cause. Many people diagnosed with depression report that they have lost interest in everything in life, a symptom referred to as *anhedonia.* Even when they try to do something enjoyable, they may feel no emotion. As Kay Jamison (1995, p. 110) writes, she was "unbearably miserable and seemingly incapable of any kind of joy or enthusiasm."

In depression, changes in appetite, sleep, and activity levels can take many forms. Some people with depression lose their appetite, while others find themselves eating more, perhaps even binge eating. Some people with depression want to sleep all day; others find it difficult to sleep and might awaken before dawn and not be able to go back to sleep.

Behaviorally, many people with depression are slowed down, a condition known as *psychomotor retardation.* They walk more slowly, gesture more slowly, and talk more slowly and quietly. They have more accidents because they cannot react quickly enough to avoid them. Many people with depression lack energy and report feeling chronically fatigued. A subset of people with depression exhibit *psychomotor agitation* instead of psychomotor retardation—these people feel physically agitated, cannot sit still, and may move around or fidget aimlessly.

The thoughts of people with depression may be filled with themes of worthlessness, guilt, hopelessness, and even suicide. They often have trouble concentrating and making decisions. Some people with severe depression lose touch with reality, experiencing delusions (beliefs with no basis in reality) and hallucinations (seeing, hearing, or feeling things that are not real). These delusions and hallucinations usually are negative. People with depression may have delusions that they have committed a terrible sin, that they are being punished, or that they have killed or hurt someone. They may hear voices accusing them of having committed an atrocity or instructing them to kill themselves.

Diagnosing Depressive Disorders

Depression takes several forms. A severe bout of depressive symptoms lasting 2 weeks or more can be diagnosed as a **major depressive disorder.** The diagnosis of major depressive disorder requires that a person experience either depressed mood or loss of interest in usual activities, plus at least four other symptoms of depression, chronically for at least 2 weeks (Table 1). In addition, these symptoms must be severe enough to interfere with the person's ability to function in everyday life. People who experience only one depressive episode receive a diagnosis of *major depressive disorder, single episode*. Two or more episodes separated by at least 2 consecutive months without symptoms merit the diagnosis of *major depressive disorder, recurrent episode*.

The *DSM-5* criteria in Table 1 include a note to clinicians that a "normal and expected" depressive response to a negative event such as a loss should not be diagnosed as a major depressive disorder unless other, more atypical symptoms are present, including worthlessness, suicidal ideas, psychomotor retardation, and severe impairment. In addition, research has shown that a syndrome labeled *complicated grief* is

TABLE 1 *DSM-5* Criteria for Major Depressive Disorder

A. Five (or more) of the following symptoms have been present during the same 2-week period and represent a change from previous functioning; at least one of the symptoms is either (1) depressed mood or (2) loss of interest or pleasure. (Note: Do not include symptoms that are clearly attributable to another medical condition.)

1. Depressed mood most of the day, nearly every day, as indicated by either subjective report (e.g., feels sad, empty, hopeless) or observation made by others (e.g., appears tearful). (Note: In children and adolescents, can be irritable mood.)
2. Markedly diminished interest or pleasure in all, or almost all, activities most of the day, nearly every day (as indicated by either subjective account or observation).
3. Significant weight loss when not dieting or weight gain (e.g., a change of more than 5% of body weight in a month), or decrease or increase in appetite nearly every day. (Note: In children, consider failure to make expected weight gain.)
4. Insomnia or hypersomnia nearly every day.
5. Psychomotor agitation or retardation nearly every day (observable by others, not merely subjective feelings of restlessness or being slowed down).
6. Fatigue or loss of energy nearly every day.
7. Feelings of worthlessness or excessive or inappropriate guilt (which may be delusional) nearly every day (not merely self-reproach or guilt about being sick).
8. Diminished ability to think or concentrate, or indecisiveness, nearly every day (either by subjective account or as observed by others).
9. Recurrent thoughts of death (not just fear of dying), recurrent suicidal ideation without a specific plan, or a suicide attempt or a specific plan for committing suicide.

B. The symptoms cause clinically significant distress or impairment in social, occupational, or other important areas of functioning.

C. The episode is not attributable to the physiological effects of a substance or to another medical condition. Note: Criteria A–C represent a major depressive episode.

Note: Responses to a significant loss (e.g., bereavement, financial ruin, losses from a natural disaster, a serious medical illness or disability) may include the feelings of intense sadness, rumination about the loss, insomnia, poor appetite, and weight loss noted in Criterion A, which may resemble a depressive episode. Although such symptoms may be understandable and considered appropriate to the loss, the presence of a major depressive episode in addition to the normal response to a significant loss should be carefully considered. This decision inevitably requires the exercise of clinical judgment based on the individual's history and the cultural norms for the expression of distress in the context of loss.

D. The occurrence of the major depressive episode is not better explained by schizoaffective disorder, schizophrenia, schizophreniform disorder, delusional disorder, or other specified and unspecified schizophrenia spectrum and other psychotic disorders.

E. There has never been a manic episode or a hypomanic episode. Note: This exclusion does not apply if all the manic-like or hypomanic-like episodes are substance-induced or are attributable to the physiological effects of another medical condition.

shown by 10 to 15 percent of bereaved people, characterized by strong yearning for the deceased person and preoccupation with the loss, persistent regrets about one's own or others' behavior toward the deceased, difficulty accepting the finality of the loss, and a sense that life is empty and meaningless (Horowitz et al., 1997). People who show complicated grief after a loss are more likely to be functioning poorly 2 to 3 years after the loss than are those who show milder grief reactions or those who show only symptoms of major depressive disorder (Bonanno et al., 2007; Bonanno, Westphal, & Mancini, 2011).

More chronic forms of depression have been reformulated in *DSM-5*. **Persistent depressive disorder** (formerly *dysthymic disorder* and *chronic major depressive disorder* in *DSM-IV*) has as its essential feature depressed mood for most of the day, for more days than not, for at least 2 years. In children and adolescents, persistent depressive disorder requires depressed or irritable mood for a duration of at least 1 year. In addition, its diagnosis requires the presence of two or more of the following symptoms: (a) poor appetite, (b) insomnia or hypersomnia, (c) low energy or fatigue, (d) low self-esteem, (e) poor concentration, and/or (f) hopelessness. During these 2 years (1 year in youth), the person must never have been without symptoms of depression for longer than a 2-month period. When an individual meets diagnostic criteria for major depressive disorder for 2 years, he or she is also given the diagnosis of persistent depressive disorder. *DSM-5* combined the *DSM-IV* categories of dysthymic and chronic major depressive disorder because research failed to find a meaningful difference between these two conditions, despite the *DSM-IV* notion that dysthymic disorder was a less severe form of depression. In fact, individuals with persistent depressive disorder show a higher risk for comorbid disorders than those with major depressive disorder alone, particularly anxiety and substance use disorders, and tend to experience worse functional consequences.

More than 70 percent of people diagnosed with major depressive or persistent depressive disorder also have another psychological disorder at some time in their lives. The most common disorders that are comorbid with (occur with) depression are substance abuse, such as alcohol abuse; anxiety disorders, such as panic disorder; and eating disorders (Kessler et al., 2003). Sometimes the depression precedes and may cause the other disorder. In other cases the depression follows and may be the consequence of the other disorder.

Although the *DSM-5* criteria determine when to diagnose a major depressive episode, depression can take many different forms. These are called subtypes, and the *DSM-5* recognizes several specific subtypes (see Table 2 for their names and key symptoms). The first subtype is depression with *anxious distress*. Anxiety is extremely common in depression (Watson, 2009), and people with this subtype have prominent anxiety symptoms as well as depressive symptoms. The second subtype of depression is with *mixed features*. People with this subtype meet the criteria for a major depressive disorder and have at least three symptoms of mania, but they do not meet the full criteria for a manic episode (discussed below in the section on bipolar disorder). The third subtype is depression with *melancholic features*, in which the physiological symptoms of depression are particularly prominent. The fourth subtype is depression with *psychotic features*, in which people experience delusions and hallucinations. The content of delusions and hallucinations may be consistent with typical depressive themes of personal

TABLE 2 Subtypes of Major Depressive Episodes

Subtype	Characteristic Symptoms
Anxious distress	Prominent anxiety symptoms
Mixed features	Presence of at least three manic/hypomanic symptoms, but does not meet criteria for a manic episode
Melancholic features	Inability to experience pleasure, distinct depressed mood, depression regularly worse in morning, early morning awakening, marked psychomotor retardation or agitation, significant anorexia or weight loss, excessive guilt
Psychotic features	Presence of mood-congruent or mood-incongruent delusions or hallucinations
Catatonic features	Catatonic behaviors: not actively relating to environment, mutism, posturing, agitation, mimicking another's speech or movements
Atypical features	Positive mood reactions to some events, significant weight gain or increase in appetite, hypersomnia, heavy or leaden feelings in arms or legs, long-standing pattern of sensitivity to interpersonal rejection
Seasonal pattern	History of at least 2 years in which major depressive episodes occur during one season of the year (usually the winter) and remit when the season is over
Peripartum onset	Onset of major depressive episode during pregnancy or in the 4 weeks following delivery

inadequacy, guilt, death, or punishment (mood-congruent), or their content is unrelated to depressive themes or mixed (mood-incongruent). In the fifth subtype, depression with *catatonic features*, people show the strange behaviors collectively known as catatonia, which can range from a complete lack of movement to excited agitation. The sixth subtype is depression with *atypical features*–the criteria for this subtype are an odd assortment of symptoms, and are not particularly unusual, as the label would suggest (see Table 2).

The seventh subtype of major depressive disorder is depression with *seasonal pattern,* also referred to as **seasonal affective disorder,** or **SAD.** People with SAD have a history of at least 2 years of experiencing and fully recovering from major depressive episodes. They become depressed when the daylight hours are short and recover when the daylight hours are long. In the Northern Hemisphere, this means that people are depressed from November through February and not depressed from June through August. Some people with this disorder actually develop mild forms of mania or have full manic episodes during the summer months and are diagnosed with bipolar disorder with seasonal pattern. In order to be diagnosed with seasonal affective disorder, a person's mood changes cannot be the result of psychosocial events, such as regularly being unemployed during the winter. Rather, the mood changes must seem to come on without reason or cause.

Although many of us may experience mood changes with the seasons, only about 5 percent of the U.S. population have a diagnosable seasonal affective disorder, and only 1 to 5 percent internationally (Rohan, Roecklein, & Haaga, 2009; Westrin & Lam, 2007). SAD is more common among people in latitudes with fewer hours of daylight in the winter months. For example, a study in Greenland found a relatively high rate of SAD (9 percent) and found that individuals living in northern latitudes were more likely to meet the criteria for SAD than individuals living in southern latitudes (Kegel, Dam, Ali, & Bjerregaard, 2009). Similarly, in the United States the rate is only 1.4 percent in Florida but 9.9 percent in Alaska (Rohan, Roecklein, & Haaga, 2009).

The eighth subtype is depression with **peripartum onset.** This diagnosis is given to women when the onset of a major depressive episode occurs during pregnancy or in the 4 weeks following childbirth. Because 50 percent of "postpartum" major depressive episodes actually begin prior to delivery, *DSM-5* refers to these episodes collectively as peripartum episodes. More rarely, some women develop mania postpartum and are given the diagnosis of bipolar disorder with peripartum onset. In the first few weeks after giving birth, as many as 30 percent of women experience the postpartum blues–emotional lability (unstable and quickly shifting moods), frequent crying, irritability, and fatigue. For most women, these symptoms cease completely within 2 weeks of the birth. About 1 in 10 women experiences postpartum depression serious enough to warrant a diagnosis of a major depressive disorder with peripartum onset (O'Hara & McCabe, 2013). Many of the risk factors for postpartum depression are similar to those for depressive episodes in general, but specific biological factors (like hormonal changes) and psychosocial factors (such as support from partners and parents) relevant to childbirth may play specific roles as well (Yim, Tanner Stapleton, Guardino, Hahn-Holbrook, & Dunkel Schetter, 2015).

The last depressive disorder to be discussed is **premenstrual dysphoric disorder.** This is not a subtype of major depressive disorder, but instead is a separate disorder in *DSM-5*. Some women regularly experience significant increases in distress during the premenstrual phase of their menstrual cycle. Their symptoms are often a mixture of depression, anxiety and tension, and irritability and anger, which may occur in mood swings during the week before the onset of menses, improve once menses has begun, and become minimal or absent in the week postmenses. These women also often report physical symptoms such as breast tenderness or swelling, bloating and weight gain, and joint and muscle pain. These women can be diagnosed with premenstrual dysphoric disorder. Although many women experience mild premenstrual symptoms, only about 2 percent of women meet the diagnostic criteria for premenstrual dysphoric disorder (Epperson et al., 2012).

Prevalence and Course of Depressive Disorders

Sixteen percent of Americans experience an episode of major depression at some time in their life (Kessler, Merikangas, & Wang, 2007). International studies in North America, Latin America, Europe, and Japan show that the lifetime prevalence of major depression ranges from 3 percent in Japan to the 16 percent rate in the United States (Andrade et al., 2003).

In the United States, 18- to 29-year-olds are most likely to have had a major depressive episode in the past year (Kessler et al., 2003). Rates of depression in the past year go down steadily and are lowest in people over age 65 (Kessler et al., 2010). However, the rates of depression rise among people over age 85. When it does occur, depression in older people tends to be severe, chronic, and debilitating (Fiske, Wetherell, & Gatz, 2009).

It may be surprising that the rate of depression is so low among adults over age 65. Diagnosing depression in older adults is complicated (Fiske et al., 2009). First, older adults may be less willing than younger adults to report the symptoms of depression because they grew up in a society less accepting of depression.

Second, depressive symptoms in older adults often occur in the context of a serious medical illness, which can interfere with making an appropriate diagnosis (Kessler et al., 2010). Third, older people are more likely than younger people to have mild to severe cognitive impairment, and it is often difficult to distinguish between a depressive disorder and the early stages of a cognitive disorder (see the chapter "Neurodevelopmental and Neurocognitive Disorders").

Although these factors are important, other researchers suggest that the low rate is valid, and they have offered several explanations for it (Lyness, 2004). The first is quite grim: Depression appears to interfere with physical health, and as a result people with a history of depression may be more likely to die before they reach old age. The second explanation is more hopeful: As people age, they may develop more adaptive coping skills and a psychologically healthier outlook on life (Fiske et al., 2009). We consider a third explanation, that there have been historical changes in people's vulnerability to depression, later in this chapter.

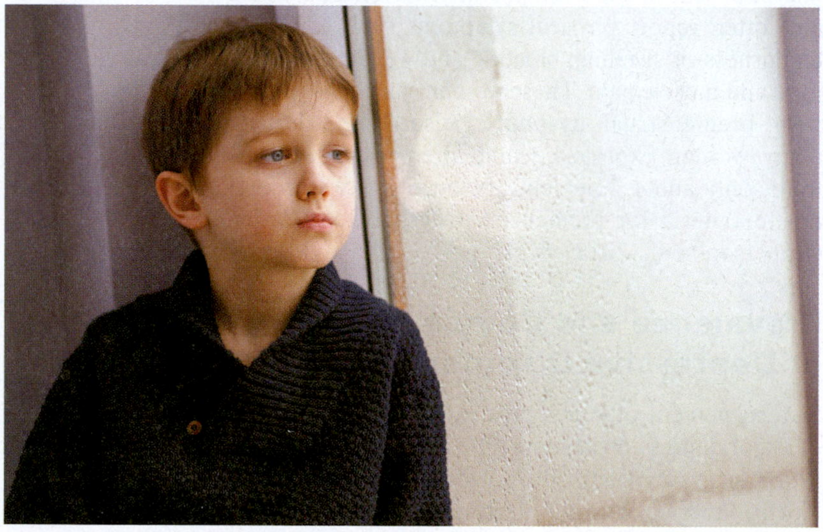

Depression is less common among children than among adults. Still, at any point in time, as many as 2.5 percent of children and 8.3 percent of adolescents can be diagnosed with major depression. *©Daniel Jędzura/123RF*

Depression is less common among children than among adults. Still, at any point in time, as many as 2.5 percent of children and 8.3 percent of adolescents can be diagnosed with major depression, and as many as 1.7 percent of children and 8.0 percent of adolescents can be diagnosed with persistent depressive disorder (see Garber & Horowitz, 2002; Kessler et al., 2012; Merikangas & Knight, 2009). As many as 24 percent of youth will experience an episode of major depression at some time before age 20. Children will often show irritability instead of sadness; also, rather than lose weight, they may simply fail to gain the weight expected for their developmental period.

Women are about twice as likely as men to experience both mild depressive symptoms and severe depressive disorders (Nolen-Hoeksema & Hilt, 2013). This gender difference in depression has been found in many countries, in most ethnic groups, and in all adult age groups. We discuss possible reasons for these differences later in the chapter.

Depression appears to be a long-lasting, recurrent problem for some people. One nationwide study found that people with major depression had spent an average of 16 weeks during the previous year with significant symptoms of depression (Kessler et al., 2003). The picture that emerges is of depressed people spending much of their time at least moderately depressed. After recovery from one episode of depression, people with depression remain at high risk for a relapse. As many as 75 percent of people who experience a first episode of depression will experience subsequent episodes (Kessing, Hansen, & Andersen, 2004; Solomon et al., 2000). People with a history of multiple episodes of depression are more likely to remain depressed for long periods of time.

Depression is a costly disorder, both to the individual and to society. People who have a diagnosis of major depression lose an average of 27 days of work per year because of their symptoms. Depression in workers costs employers an estimated $37 billion per year in lost productivity alone (not including the cost of treatment) (Kessler et al., 2007).

SHADES OF GRAY

Consider the following case study of a college student, who may resemble someone you know.

Carmen's friends were shocked to find her passed out in her dorm room with an empty bottle of sleeping pills on the floor next to her. Carmen had experienced years of unhappiness, a sense of low self-worth, pessimism, and chronic fatigue. She often told her friends she couldn't remember a time when she was happy for more than a few days at a time. Since the beginning of the winter term, however, Carmen's depressed mood had deepened, and she had spent days on end locked in her bedroom, apparently sleeping. She had said it was no use going to class because she couldn't concentrate. She had been skipping meals and had lost 12 pounds.

Based on the time frame and symptoms described, what diagnosis would Carmen most likely receive? (Discussion appears at the end of the chapter.)

The good news is that when people undergo treatment for their depression, they tend to recover much more quickly than they would without treatment and to reduce their risk of relapse. The bad news is that many people with depression either never seek care or wait years after the onset of symptoms before they seek care (Kessler et al., 2003). We might ask why people experiencing the terrible symptoms of depression don't seek treatment. One reason is that they may lack insurance or the money to pay for care. Often, however, they expect to get over their symptoms on their own. They believe that their symptoms are simply a phase that will pass with time and that won't affect their lives over the long term.

CHARACTERISTICS OF BIPOLAR DISORDER

PROFILES

There is a particular kind of pain, elation, loneliness, and terror involved in this kind of madness. When you're high it's tremendous. The ideas and feelings are fast and frequent like shooting stars and you follow them until you find better and brighter ones. Shyness goes, the right words and gestures are suddenly there, the power to seduce and captivate others a felt certainty. There are interests found in uninteresting people. Sensuality is pervasive and the desire to seduce and be seduced irresistible. Feelings of ease, intensity, power, well-being, financial omnipotence, and euphoria now pervade one's marrow.

But, somewhere, this changes. The fast ideas are far too fast and there are far too many; overwhelming confusion replaces clarity. Memory goes. Humor and absorption on friends' faces are replaced by fear and concern. Everything previously moving with the grain is now against—you are irritable, angry, frightened, uncontrollable, and enmeshed totally in the blackest caves of the mind. You never knew those caves were there. It will never end. (Source: Goodwin & Jamison, 1990, pp. 17–18)

The person in the profile is describing an episode of bipolar disorder. When she is manic, she has tremendous energy and vibrancy, her self-esteem is soaring, and she is filled with ideas and confidence. Then, when she becomes depressed, she is despairing and fearful, she doubts herself and everyone around her, and she wishes to die. This alternation between periods of mania and periods of depression is the classic manifestation of bipolar disorder.

Symptoms of Mania

We have already discussed the symptoms of depression in detail, so here we focus on the symptoms of mania (Table 3). The mood of people who are manic can be elated, but that elation is often mixed with irritation and agitation. Variations in manic symptoms

TABLE 3 *DSM-5* Criteria for a Manic Episode

A. A distinct period of abnormally and persistently elevated, expansive, or irritable mood and abnormally and persistently increased goal-directed activity or energy, lasting at least 1 week and present most of the day, nearly every day (or any duration if hospitalization is necessary).

B. During the period of mood disturbance and increased energy or activity, three (or more) of the following symptoms (four if the mood is only irritable) are present to a significant degree, and represent a noticeable change from usual behavior:

1. Inflated self-esteem or grandiosity
2. Decreased need for sleep (e.g., feels rested after only 3 hours of sleep)
3. More talkative than usual or pressure to keep talking
4. Flight of ideas or subjective experience that thoughts are racing
5. Distractibility (i.e., attention too easily drawn to unimportant or irrelevant external stimuli), as reported or observed
6. Increase in goal-directed activity (either socially, at work or school, or sexually) or psychomotor agitation (i.e., purposeless non-goal-directed activity)
7. Excessive involvement in activities that have a high potential for painful consequences (e.g., engaging in unrestrained buying sprees, sexual indiscretions, or foolish business investments)

C. The mood disturbance is sufficiently severe to cause marked impairment in social or occupational functioning or to necessitate hospitalization to prevent harm to self or others, or there are psychotic features.

D. The episode is not attributable to the direct physiological effects of a substance (e.g., a drug of abuse, a medication, or other treatment), or to another medical condition.

Note: At least one lifetime manic episode is required for the diagnosis of bipolar I disorder.

can lead to one of four bipolar disorder diagnoses: *bipolar I disorder, bipolar II disorder, cyclothymic disorder,* and *rapid cycling bipolar disorder*. We will first discuss the symptoms of mania, and then how the specific disorders are defined.

People with mania have unrealistically positive and grandiose (inflated) self-esteem. They experience racing thoughts and impulses. At times, these grandiose thoughts are delusional and may be accompanied by grandiose hallucinations. People experiencing a manic episode may speak rapidly and forcefully, trying to convey a rapid stream of fantastic thoughts. Some people may become agitated and irritable, particularly with people they perceive as "getting in the way." They may engage in a variety of impulsive behaviors, such as sexual indiscretions or spending sprees. Often, they will frenetically pursue grand plans and goals.

In order to be diagnosed with a manic episode, an individual must show an elevated, expansive, or irritable mood for at least 1 week, as well as at least three of the other symptoms listed in Table 3. These symptoms must impair the individual's functioning.

People who experience manic episodes meeting these criteria are said to have **bipolar I disorder.** Almost all these people eventually will fall into a depressive episode; mania without any depression is rare (Goodwin & Jamison, 2007). For some people with bipolar I disorder, the depressions are as severe as major depressive episodes, whereas for others the episodes of depression are relatively mild and infrequent. Some people diagnosed with bipolar I disorder have mixed episodes in which they experience the full criteria for manic episodes and at least three key symptoms of major depressive episodes in the same day, every day for at least 1 week.

Whereas people with bipolar I disorder experience mania, people with **bipolar II disorder** experience **hypomania.** Hypomania involves the same symptoms as mania, but the episodes are milder (Table 4). The major difference is that in hypomania these symptoms are not severe enough to interfere with daily functioning, do not involve hallucinations or delusions, and last at least 4 consecutive days (rather than a week). Whereas depression is common in bipolar I disorder but not required for the diagnosis, for bipolar II disorder, in addition to hypomania the person also has to experience major depressive episodes.

The third form of bipolar disorder is **cyclothymic disorder**, which is less severe but more chronic. A person with cyclothymic disorder alternates between periods of some hypomanic symptoms and periods of some depressive symptoms, chronically over at least a 2-year period. The defining feature is that the hypomanic and depressive symptoms are of insufficient number, severity, or duration to meet full criteria for hypomania or major depressive episode, respectively. During the periods of hypomanic symptoms, the person may be able to function reasonably well. Often, however, the periods of depressive symptoms significantly interfere with daily functioning, although the episodes are less severe than major depressive episodes. People with cyclothymic disorder are at increased risk of developing bipolar disorder (Goodwin & Jamison, 2007).

About 90 percent of people with bipolar disorder have multiple episodes or cycles during their lifetimes (Merikangas et al., 2007). The length of an individual episode of bipolar disorder varies greatly from one person to the next. Some people are in a manic state for several weeks or months before moving into a depressed state. More rarely, people switch from mania to depression and back within a matter of days or, as noted above, even in the same day. The number of lifetime episodes also varies tremendously from one person to the next, but a relatively common pattern is for episodes to become more frequent

TABLE 4 Criteria for Bipolar I and Bipolar II Disorders

Bipolar I and II disorders differ in the presence of major depressive episodes, episodes meeting the full criteria for mania, and hypomanic episodes.

Criteria	Bipolar I	Bipolar II
Major depressive episodes	Can occur but are not necessary for diagnosis	Are necessary for diagnosis
Episodes meeting full criteria for mania	Are necessary for diagnosis	Cannot be present for diagnosis
Hypomanic episodes	Can occur between episodes of severe mania or major depression but are not necessary for diagnosis	Are necessary for diagnosis

and closer together over time. Four or more mood episodes that meet criteria for manic, hypomanic, or major depressive episode within 1 year lead to a diagnosis of **rapid cycling bipolar disorder.** Interestingly, there appears to be a seasonal aspect to bipolar disorder for some people, as in unipolar depression. Some studies show that up to 25 percent of people with bipolar disorder experience their depressive or manic episodes in a seasonal pattern (Geoffroy et al., 2013; Goikolea et al., 2007).

Importantly, the episodes in bipolar disorder are periods with multiple symptoms of mania or depression. You have probably heard the phrase "he's so bipolar" to refer to someone who experiences day-to-day moodiness, unpredictability, or emotional reactivity. Although it is true that people with bipolar disorder show some symptoms (like irritability) even between episodes, this loose terminology for subthreshold fluctuations does not truly capture the episodic nature that defines the disorder, and can lead to stigma.

One area of great interest and controversy is bipolar disorder in youth. Until the past decade or so, it was assumed that bipolar disorder could not be diagnosed reliably until individuals were in their late teens or early adulthood. Increasingly, researchers and clinicians have become interested in identifying early signs of bipolar disorder in children and young teenagers so interventions can be initiated and researchers can investigate the causes and course of the disorder in youth (Brotman, Sharif-Askary, Dickstein, & Leibenluft, 2016).

Although some children show the alternating episodes of mania and depression interspersed with periods of normal mood characteristic of bipolar disorder (Birmaher et al., 2006), others show chronic symptoms and rapid mood switches. Individuals in the latter group tend toward severe irritability characterized by frequent temper tantrums or rages. These children are at increased risk of developing anxiety and depressive disorders later in life but do not tend to develop classic bipolar disorder (Stringaris, Cohen, Pine, & Leibenluft, 2009). In addition, it is difficult to distinguish the agitation and risky behavior that accompany mania in youth from the symptoms of attention-deficit/hyperactivity disorder (ADHD; see the chapter "Neurodevelopmental and Neurocognitive Disorders"), which include hyperactivity, poor judgment, and impulsivity, or from the symptoms of oppositional defiant disorder (see the chapter "Disruptive, Impulse-Control, and Conduct Disorders"), which include chronic irritability and refusal to follow rules. There has been considerable debate as to whether these agitated, irritable children have bipolar disorder, ADHD, or oppositional defiant disorder, none of which seems to fit their symptoms perfectly.

Some children who regularly throw temper tantrums may have bipolar disorder or another condition, such as the new *DSM-5* category called disruptive mood dysregulation disorder.
©Steve Wisbauer/Getty Images

The authors of the *DSM-5* decided to distinguish children with these temper tantrums from children with more classic bipolar disorder by adding a new diagnosis for youth age 6 and older called **disruptive mood dysregulation disorder.** To qualify for this diagnosis, a young person must show severe temper outbursts that are grossly out of proportion in intensity and duration to a situation and inconsistent with developmental level. During an outburst, these children may rage at others verbally and become physically violent toward others. Between outbursts, their mood is persistently and obviously irritable and angry. To receive the diagnosis, a child must have at least three temper outbursts per week for at least 12 months and in at least two settings (e.g., home and school).

Prevalence and Course of Bipolar Disorder

Bipolar disorder is less common than depressive disorders. Internationally, only 0.6 percent of people will experience bipolar I disorder and only 0.4 percent of people bipolar II disorder in their lifetimes (Merikangas et al., 2011). Men and women seem equally likely to develop the disorder, and there are no consistent differences in the prevalence of the disorder among ethnic groups or across cultures. These facts suggest that biological factors may be more responsible for bipolar disorder than for depressive disorders, which show more variability across cultures. Most people who develop bipolar disorder do so in late adolescence or early adulthood (Merikangas et al., 2011).

Like people with depressive disorders, people with bipolar disorder often face chronic problems on the job and in their relationships (Marangell, 2004). The majority of people with bipolar disorders also meet the criteria for other psychiatric disorders, most often an anxiety disorder (Merikangas et al., 2011). In addition, people with bipolar disorder often abuse substances such as alcohol and hard drugs, which impairs their control over their disorder, their willingness to take medications, and their functioning. Despite the impairment resulting from their symptoms, most people with bipolar disorder, especially those in developing countries, do not receive any treatment (Merikangas et al., 2011).

Creativity and the Mood Disorders

As noted in Mood Disorders Along the Continuum, some theorists have argued that the symptoms of mania—increased self-esteem, a rush of ideas and the courage to pursue those ideas, high energy, little need for sleep, excessive optimism, and decisiveness—can actually have benefits in certain settings. In turn, the melancholy of depression is often seen as inspirational for artists. Indeed, some of the most influential people in history—including political leaders, religious figures, and artists—have suffered, and perhaps benefited, from bipolar disorder or depression (Jamison, 1993).

Rap artist and actor DMX (aka Earl Simmons) has publicly acknowledged struggling with depression. *©hurricanehank/123RF*

Winston Churchill had periods of manic symptoms that may have been both an asset and a liability. *Source: Library of Congress Prints and Photographs Division [LC-DIG-npcc-17934]*

Political leaders including Abraham Lincoln, Alexander Hamilton, Winston Churchill, Napoleon Bonaparte, and Benito Mussolini and religious leaders including Martin Luther and George Fox (founder of the Society of Friends, or Quakers) have been posthumously diagnosed by psychiatric biographers as having had periods of mania, hypomania, or depression (Jamison, 1993). Although during periods of depression these leaders often were incapacitated, during periods of mania and hypomania they accomplished extraordinary feats. While manic, they devised brilliant and daring strategies for winning wars and solving national problems and had the energy, self-esteem, and persistence to carry out these strategies.

Writers, artists, and composers have a higher-than-normal prevalence of mania and depression. For example, a study of 1,005 famous twentieth-century artists, writers, and other professionals found that the artists and writers experienced two to three times the rate of mood disorders, psychosis, and suicide attempts than comparably successful people in business, science, and public life. The poets in this group were most likely to have been manic (Ludwig, 1992). More recently, actors Jim Carrey, Kirsten Dunst, and Zach Braff, game-show host Drew Carey, rapper DMX, and singers Demi Lovato and Mariah Carey are among the celebrities who have publicized their mood disorder.

Although many creative people with bipolar disorder may have been able to learn from their periods of depression and to exploit their periods of mania, many also have found the highs and lows of the disorder unbearable and have attempted or completed suicide. In general, the mood disorders substantially impair thinking and productivity. As Elizabeth Wurtzel (1995, p. 295) notes:

> While it may be true that a great deal of art finds its inspirational wellspring in sorrow, let's not kid ourselves in how much time each of those people wasted and lost by being mired in misery. So many productive hours slipped by as paralyzing despair took over. This is not to say that we should deny sadness its rightful place among the muses of poetry and of all art forms, but let's stop calling it madness, let's stop pretending that the feeling itself is interesting. Let's call it depression and admit that it is very bleak.

THEORIES OF DEPRESSION

Depression is one of the most researched of all the psychological disorders. We will discuss biological, behavioral, cognitive, interpersonal, and sociocultural theories.

Biological Theories of Depression

A number of different biological processes appear to be involved in depression, including genetics, neurotransmitter systems, structural and functional abnormalities of the brain, and neuroendocrine systems.

Genetic Factors

Family history studies find that the first-degree relatives of people with major depressive disorder are two to three times more likely to also have depression than are the first-degree relatives of people without the disorder (Flint & Kendler, 2014). Twin studies of major depression find higher concordance rates for monozygotic twins than for dizygotic twins, implicating genetic processes in the disorder (Kendler, Myers, Prescott, & Neale, 2001). Depression that begins early in life appears to have a stronger genetic base than depression that begins in adulthood.

It is probable that multiple genetic abnormalities contribute to depression. Several studies suggest that the serotonin transporter gene may play a role (Flint & Kendler, 2014; Saveanu & Nemeroff, 2012). As we will discuss below, serotonin is one of the neurotransmitters implicated in depression. Abnormalities on the serotonin transporter gene could lead to dysfunction in the regulation of serotonin, which in turn could affect the stability of individuals' moods. In a landmark longitudinal study, Av-shalom Caspi and colleagues (Caspi, Sugden, et al., 2003) found that people with abnormalities on the serotonin transporter gene were at increased risk for depression when they faced negative life events (see also Kaufman et al., 2004, 2006). Not all studies have replicated these findings (see Risch et al., 2009), but a recent meta-analysis supported the interaction between the serotonin transporter gene and early stress in the prediction of later depression (Karg, Burmeiester, Shedden, & Sen, 2011). Other genes have been linked with depression and also show evidence of gene-environment interactions (Dunn et al., 2015).

Neurotransmitter Theories

The neurotransmitters that have been implicated most often in depression are the **monoamines,** specifically, **norepinephrine, serotonin,** and, to a lesser extent, **dopamine.** These neurotransmitters are found in large concentrations in the limbic system, a part of the brain associated with the regulation of sleep, appetite, and emotional processes. The early theory of the role of these neurotransmitters in mood disorders was that depression is caused by a reduction in the amount of norepinephrine or serotonin in the synapses between neurons (Glassman, 1969; Schildkraut, 1965).

As our understanding of the functioning of neurotransmitters in the brain has increased, theories of their role in depression have become much more complex (Saveanu & Nemeroff, 2012). A number of processes within brain cells that affect the functioning of neurotransmitters may go awry in depression (Figure 1). For example, serotonin and norepinephrine are synthesized in neurons from tryptophan and tyrosine, respectively, and some studies suggest that abnormalities in this synthesis process may contribute to depression (Zhang, Beaulieu, Sotnikova, Gainetdinov, & Caron, 2004). Both serotonin and norepinephrine are released by one neuron (referred to as the presynaptic neuron) into the synapse and then bind to receptors on other neurons (referred to as the postsynaptic neurons; see Figure 1). The release process, which is regulated by the serotonin transporter gene, may be abnormal in depression. In addition, the receptors for serotonin and norepinephrine on the postsynaptic neurons may be less sensitive than normal in people with depression, or they may sometimes malfunction (Saveanu & Nemeroff, 2012).

Structural and Functional Brain Abnormalities

Neuroimaging studies have found consistent abnormalities in at least four areas of the brain in people with depression: the prefrontal cortex, anterior cingulate, hippocampus, and amygdala (Figure 2).

Critical functions of the prefrontal cortex include attention, working memory, planning, and

FIGURE 1 **Neurotransmitter Abnormalities Implicated in Depression.** Several problems in the production and regulation of serotonin and norepinephrine may contribute to depression.

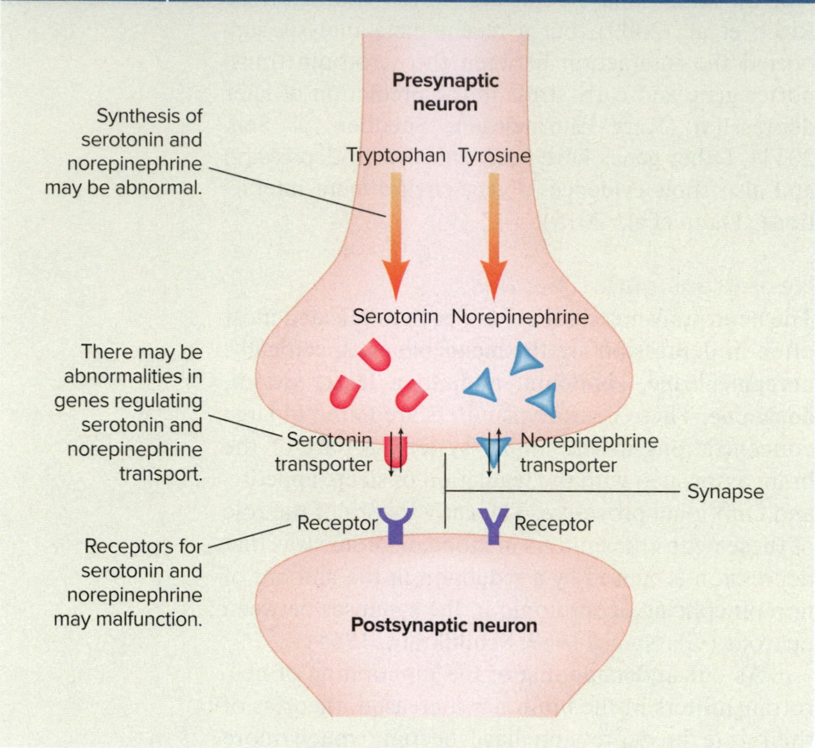

FIGURE 2 **Areas of the Brain Implicated in Major Depression.** Neuroimaging studies have found abnormalities in the prefrontal cortex, anterior cingulate, amygdala, and hippocampus.

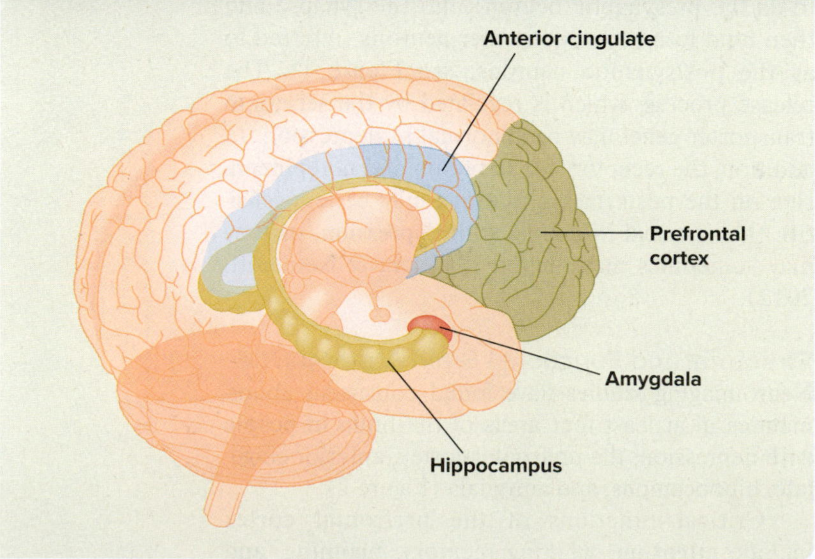

novel problem solving. Many studies have shown reduced metabolic activity and a reduction in the volume of gray matter in the prefrontal cortex, particularly on the left side, in people with serious depression (Saveanu & Nemeroff, 2012; Thase, Hahn, & Berton, 2015). In addition, electroencephalographic (EEG) studies show lower brain-wave activity on the left side of the prefrontal cortex in depressed people compared to nondepressed people (Davidson, Pizzagalli, Nitschke, & Putnam, 2002). The left prefrontal cortex is particularly involved in motivation and goal orientation, and inactivity in this region may be associated with motivational difficulties like those seen in depression. The successful treatment of depression with antidepressant medications is associated with increases in metabolic and brain-wave activity in the left prefrontal cortex (Kennedy et al., 2001).

The anterior cingulate, a subregion of the prefrontal cortex, plays an important role in the body's response to stress, in emotional expression, and in social behavior. People with depression show different levels of activity in the anterior cingulate relative to controls (Singh & Gotlib, 2014; Thase et al., 2015). This altered activity may be associated with problems in attention, in the planning of appropriate responses, and in coping, as well as with anhedonia found in depression. Again, activity normalizes in this region of the brain when people are successfully treated for their depression (Dougherty & Rauch, 2007).

The hippocampus is critical in memory and in fear-related learning. Neuroimaging studies show smaller volume and lower metabolic activity in the hippocampus of people with major depression (Cole, Costafreda, McGuffin, & Fu, 2011). Damage to the hippocampus could be the result of chronic arousal of the body's stress response. As we will discuss, people with depression show chronically high levels of the hormone cortisol, particularly in response to stress, indicating that their bodies overreact to stress and their levels of cortisol do not return to normal as quickly as those of nondepressed people. The hippocampus contains many receptors for cortisol, and chronically elevated levels of this hormone may kill or inhibit the development of new neurons in the hippocampus (Pittenger & Duman, 2008). Treatment with antidepressants or electroconvulsive therapy results in the growth of new cells in the hippocampus in rats (Pittenger & Duman, 2008).

Abnormalities in the structure and functioning of the amygdala also are found in depression (Singh & Gotlib, 2014; Thase et al., 2015). The amygdala helps direct attention to stimuli that are emotionally salient and have major significance for the individual. Studies of people with mood disorders show an enlargement and increased activity in this part of the brain, and activity in the amygdala has been observed to decrease to normal levels in people successfully treated for depression (Singh & Gotlib, 2014; Thase et al., 2015). The effects of overactivity in the amygdala are not yet entirely clear, but the overactivity may bias people toward aversive or emotionally arousing information and lead to rumination over negative memories and negative aspects of the environment (Davidson, Pizzagalli, & Nitschke, 2009).

Interestingly, differences in brain function may begin emerging in childhood, even before a depressive episode. Girls who are at high risk for depression (because their mothers have had depression) exhibit decreased neural reactivity to rewarding stimuli, as early as age 9 (Kujawa, Proudfit, & Klein, 2014; Sharp et al., 2014). Such patterns could be due to a number of factors, but they suggest that vulnerability to depression can have neural aspects early in life.

Neuroendocrine Factors

Hormones have long been thought to play a role in mood disorders, especially depression. The neuroendocrine system regulates a number of important hormones, which in turn affect basic functions such as sleep, appetite, sexual drive, and the ability to experience pleasure (to review the neuroendocrine system, see the chapter "Theories and Treatment of Abnormality"). These hormones also help the body respond to environmental stressors.

Three key components of the neuroendocrine system—the hypothalamus, pituitary, and adrenal cortex—work together in a biological feedback system richly interconnected with the amygdala, hippocampus, and cerebral cortex. This system, often referred to as the **hypothalamic-pituitary-adrenal axis,** or **HPA axis,** is involved in the fight-or-flight response (see the chapter "Trauma, Anxiety, Obsessive-Compulsive, and Related Disorders").

Normally, when we are confronted with a stressor, the hypothalamus releases corticotropin-releasing hormone (CRH) onto receptors on the anterior pituitary (Figure 3). This results in secretion of corticotropin into the plasma in the bloodstream, stimulating the adrenal cortex to release cortisol into the blood. This process helps the body fight the stressor or flee from it. The hypothalamus has cortisol receptors that detect when cortisol levels have increased and normally responds by decreasing CRH to regulate the stress response. Thus, this biological feedback loop both helps activate the HPA system during stress and calms the system when the stress is over.

People with depression tend to show elevated levels of cortisol and CRH, indicating chronic hyperactivity in the HPA axis and difficulty in the HPA axis's returning to normal functioning following a stressor (Saveanu & Nemeroff, 2012). In turn, the excess hormones produced by heightened HPA activity seem to have an inhibiting effect on receptors for the monoamine neurotransmitters. One model for the development of depression proposes that people exposed to chronic stress may develop poorly regulated neuroendocrine systems. Then, when they are exposed to even minor stressors later in life, the HPA axis overreacts and does not easily return to baseline. This overreaction changes the functioning of the monoamine neurotransmitters in the brain, and an episode of depression is likely to follow (Southwick, Vythilingam, & Charney, 2005). In addition, chronic excessive exposure to cortisol may account for the volume reductions in several brain areas seen in depressed people, including the hippocampus, the prefrontal cortex, and the amygdala.

Early traumatic stress, such as being the victim of sexual and/or physical abuse, suffering severe neglect,

FIGURE 3 **The Hypothalamic-Pituitary-Adrenal Axis.** The hypothalamus synthesizes corticotropin-releasing hormone (CRH). CRH is transported to the pituitary gland, where it stimulates the synthesis and release of adrenocorticotropic hormone (ACTH), which then circulates to the adrenal glands, producing cortisol. Cortisol then inhibits the production of further ACTH and CRH. Normally, this process prevents too much or too prolonged physiological arousal following a stressor. In major depression, however, people often show abnormal cortisol functioning, suggesting that there is dysregulation in the hypothalamic-pituitary-adrenal (HPA) axis.

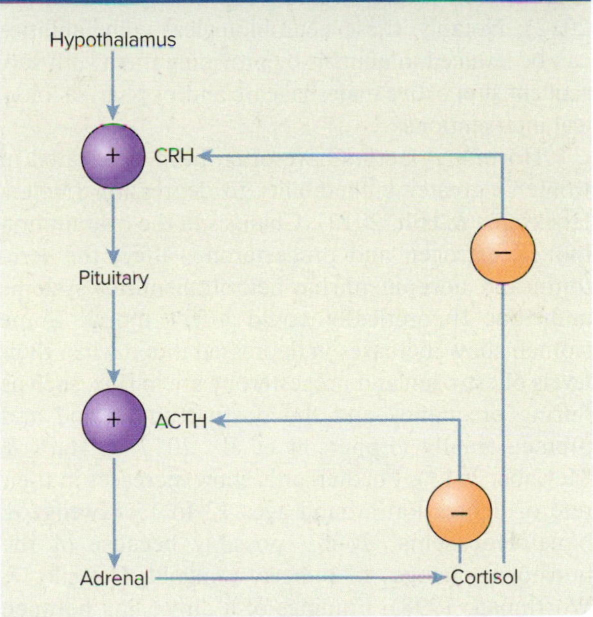

or being exposed to other serious chronic stress, may lead to some of the neuroendocrine abnormalities that predispose people to depression (Southwick et al., 2005). Studies of children who have been abused or neglected show that their biological responses to stress—particularly the response of their HPA axis—often are either exaggerated or blunted (Cicchetti & Toth, 2016). Christine Heim and colleagues (Heim & Nemeroff, 2001; Heim, Plotsky, & Nemeroff, 2004) have found that women who were sexually abused as children show altered HPA responses to stress as adults, even when they are not depressed. Similarly, animal studies show that early stress (such as separation from the mother) promotes exaggerated neurobiological stress reactivity and a vulnerability to depression-like responses to future stressors (Saveanu & Nemeroff, 2012). Notably, these neurobiological vulnerabilities can be reduced in animals by providing them with subsequent supportive maternal care and/or pharmacological interventions.

Hormonal factors have often been implicated in women's greater vulnerability to depression (Nolen-Hoeksema & Hilt, 2013). Changes in the ovarian hormones, estrogen and progesterone, affect the serotonin and norepinephrine neurotransmitter systems and thus theoretically could affect mood. Some women show increases in depressed mood when their levels of estrogen and progesterone are in flux, such as during pregnancy and the postpartum period and premenstrually (Epperson et al., 2012; O'Hara & McCabe, 2013). Further, girls show increases in their rate of depression around ages 13 to 15 (Twenge & Nolen-Hoeksema, 2002), possibly because of the hormonal changes of puberty (Angold, Castello, & Worthman, 1998). Findings of a direct link between changes in estrogen and progesterone levels and vulnerability to depression have not been consistent, however. The hormonal changes of puberty, the menstrual cycle, the peripartum period, and menopause may trigger depression only in women with a genetic or other biological vulnerability to the disorder (Steiner, Dunn, & Born, 2003; Young & Korzun, 1999).

Psychological Theories of Depression

Behavioral theorists have focused on the role of uncontrollable stressors in producing depression. Cognitive theorists have argued that the ways people think can contribute to, and maintain, depression. Interpersonal theorists have considered the role of relationships in causing and maintaining depression. Sociocultural theorists have focused on explanations for the differences in rates of depression among sociodemographic groups.

Behavioral Theories

Depression often arises as a reaction to stressful negative events, such as the breakup of a relationship, the death of a loved one, a job loss, or a serious medical illness (Hammen, 2018; Monroe, 2010). Up to 80 percent of people with depression report a negative life event prior to the onset of their depression (Mazure, 1998). People with depression are more likely than people without depression to have chronic life stressors, such as financial strain or a bad marriage. They also tend to have a history of traumatic life events, particularly events involving loss (Hammen, 2018).

Behavioral theories of depression suggest that life stress leads to depression because it reduces the positive reinforcers in a person's life (Hollon & Dimidjian, 2015; Lewinsohn & Gotlib, 1995). The person begins to withdraw, which results in a further reduction in reinforcers, which leads to more withdrawal, creating a self-perpetuating chain.

For example, a man having difficulty in his marriage may initiate interactions with his wife less often because these interactions are no longer as positively reinforcing as they once were. This only worsens the communication between him and his wife, so the relationship deteriorates. He then withdraws further and becomes depressed about this area of his life. Behavioral theorists suggest that such a pattern is especially likely in people with poor social skills, because they are more likely to experience rejection by others and also more likely to withdraw in response to rejection than to find ways to overcome it (Lewinsohn, 1974). In addition, once a person begins engaging in depressive behaviors, these behaviors are reinforced by the sympathy and attention they engender in others. Integrating this psychosocial perspective with a biological account, Pizzagalli (2014) has argued that life stress also contributes to the anhedonia and behavioral withdrawal of depression by affecting interrelated biological pathways of stress (such as neuroendocrine pathways) and reward processing (such as dopamine systems).

Another behavioral theory—the **learned helplessness theory**—suggests that the type of stressful event most likely to lead to depression is an uncontrollable negative event (Seligman, 1975). Such events, especially if they are frequent or chronic, can lead people to believe they are helpless to control important outcomes in their environment. In turn, this belief in helplessness leads people to lose their motivation and to reduce actions on their part that might control the environment as well as leaving them unable to learn how to control situations that are controllable. These learned helplessness deficits are similar to the symptoms of depression: low motivation, passivity, and indecisiveness (Seligman, 1975). For example, battered women may develop the belief that they cannot control their beatings or other parts of their lives. This belief may explain their high rates of depression and their tendency to remain in abusive relationships (Koss & Kilpatrick, 2001).

Cognitive Theories

Aaron Beck (1967) argued that people with depression look at the world through a **negative cognitive triad:** They have negative views of themselves, the world, and the future. They then commit errors in thinking that support their negative cognitive triad, such as ignoring good events and exaggerating negative events. Their negative thinking both causes and perpetuates their depression. Many studies have demonstrated that people with depression show these negative ways of thinking, and some longitudinal studies have shown that these thinking styles predict depression over time (Abramson et al., 2002; Joormann & Vanderlind, 2014). Beck's theory led to one of the most widely used and successful therapies for depression—cognitive-behavioral therapy.

The loss of a loved one can increase the risk of depression. ©*Anjo Kan/Shutterstock*

Another cognitive theory of depression, the **reformulated learned helplessness theory,** explains how cognitive factors might influence whether a person becomes helpless and depressed following a negative event (Abramson, Seligman, & Teasdale, 1978; Peterson & Seligman, 1984). This theory focuses on people's causal attributions for events. A causal attribution is an explanation of why an event happened. According to this theory, people who habitually explain negative events by causes that are internal, stable, and global tend to blame themselves for these negative events, expect negative events to recur in the future, and expect to experience negative events in many areas of their lives. In turn, these expectations lead them to experience long-term learned helplessness deficits as well as loss of self-esteem in many areas of their lives.

People who attribute negative events, such as taking an exam, to internal ("*I*" failed), stable ("I *always* fail), and global causes (I always fail at *everything*") may be at greater risk for depression. ©*Digital Vision/Getty Images*

For example, consider a student who becomes depressed after failing a psychology exam. The reformulated learned helplessness theory would suggest that she has blamed her failure on internal causes (she didn't study hard enough) rather than external causes (the exam was too hard). Further, she has assumed that the failure was due to stable causes, such as a lack of aptitude in psychology, rather than to unstable causes, such as the instructor not allowing enough time. Therefore, she expects to fail again. Finally, she has attributed her failure to a global cause, such as her difficulty learning the material. This global attribution then leads her to expect failure in other academic areas.

A related cognitive theory involves *hopelessness depression.* Hopelessness depression develops when people make pessimistic attributions for the most important events in their lives and perceive that they have no way to cope with the consequences of these events (Abramson, Metalsky, & Alloy, 1989). For example, the student above might not only conclude that she didn't study hard enough, but also that there is no way she can ever graduate. Both the reformulated learned helplessness theory and the hopelessness theory have led to much additional research (Abramson et al., 2002). One of the most definitive studies of the hopelessness theory of depression was a long-term study of college students (Alloy, Abramson, & Francis, 1999). The researchers interviewed first-year students at two universities and identified those with hopeless attributional styles and those with optimistic attributional styles. They then tracked these students for the next 2 years, interviewing them every 6 weeks. Among the students with no history of depression, those with a hopeless attributional style were much more likely to develop a first onset of major depression than were those with an optimistic attributional style (17 percent versus 1 percent). In addition, among students with a history of depression, those with a hopeless style were more likely to have a relapse of depression than were those with an optimistic style (27 percent versus 6 percent). Thus, a pessimistic attributional style predicted both first onset and relapse of depression.

Another cognitive theory, the ruminative response styles theory, focuses more on the process of thinking than on the content of thinking as a contributor to depression (Nolen-Hoeksema, Wisco, & Lyubomirsky, 2008). Some people, when they are sad, blue, and upset, focus intently on how they feel–their symptoms of fatigue and poor concentration and their sadness and hopelessness–and can identify many possible causes. They do not attempt to do anything about these causes, however, and instead continue to engage in **rumination** about their depression. Several studies have shown that people with this more ruminative coping style are more likely to develop major depression (Nolen-Hoeksema et al., 2008). Ruminative thinking is one way in which, for some people, stressful experiences can give rise to depression (Ruscio et al., 2015). The cognitive phenomenon of rumination has also been linked with genetic, neural, and physiological processes, consistent with the biopsychosocial approach (Mandell, Siegle, Shutt, Feldmiller, & Thase, 2014; Woody, McGeary, & Gibb, 2014).

People who are depressed show a bias toward negative thinking in basic attention and memory processes (Harvey, Watkins, Mansell, & Shafran, 2004; Joormann & Vanderlind, 2014). Depressed people are more likely than nondepressed people to dwell on negative stimuli, such as sad faces (Gotlib, Krasnoperova, Yue, & Joormann, 2004) and to have trouble disengaging their attention from negative stimuli (Joormann, 2004). After learning a list of words and then being surprised with the task of recalling those words, depressed people tend to recall more negative words than positive words, while nondepressed people show the opposite memory bias (Blaney, 1986; Matt, Vasquez, & Campbell, 1992). These biases in attention to and memory for negative information could form the basis of depressed people's tendency to see the world in a negative light and may help maintain this tendency.

In addition, depressed people tend to show overgeneral memory (Williams et al., 2007). When given a simple word cue such as "angry" and asked to describe a memory prompted by that cue, depressed people are more likely than nondepressed people to offer memories that are highly general (e.g., "People who are mean") instead of concrete (e.g., "Jane being rude to me last Friday"). Mark Williams and colleagues (2007) suggest that depressed people develop the tendency to store and recall memories in a general fashion as a way of coping with a traumatic past (see also Ono, Devilly, & Shum, 2016). Vague, general memories are less emotionally charged and painful than memories that are rich in concrete detail, and thus they help reduce the emotional pain depressed people feel over their past. Interestingly, the one other disorder characterized by overgeneral memory is posttraumatic stress disorder (see the chapter "Trauma, Anxiety, Obsessive-Compulsive, and Related Disorders"), which develops specifically in response to traumatic events (Williams et al., 2007).

Interpersonal Theories

The interpersonal relationships of people with depression often are fraught with difficulty. The **interpersonal theories of depression** focus on these relationships (Coyne, 1976; Hames, Hagan, & Joiner, 2013). Interpersonal difficulties and losses frequently precede depression and are the stressors most commonly reported as triggering depression (Hammen, 2018; Rudolph, 2008). Depressed people are more likely than nondepressed people to have chronic conflict in their relationships with family, friends, and co-workers (Hammen, 2018).

Depressed people may act in ways that engender interpersonal conflict, in part due to deficits in social and communication skills (Hammen, 2018; Hames et al., 2013). Some depressed people have a heightened need for approval and expressions of support from others (Leadbeater, Kuperminc, Blatt, & Herzog, 1999; Rudolph & Conley, 2005) but at the same time easily perceive rejection by others, a characteristic called **rejection sensitivity** (Downey & Feldman, 1996). They engage in excessive reassurance seeking, constantly looking for assurances from others that they are accepted and loved (Joiner & Timmons, 2009). They never quite believe the affirmations other people give, however, and anxiously keep going back for more. After a while, their family and friends can become weary of this behavior and may become frustrated or hostile. The insecure person picks up on these cues of annoyance and panics over them. The person then feels even more insecure and engages in excessive reassurance seeking. Eventually the person's social support may be withdrawn altogether, leading to increased and longer depression. The self-defeating interpersonal behaviors of depressed individuals may be a result of such various influences as negative thinking patterns, history of maltreatment, and even genetic vulnerabilities (Liu, 2013).

Just as depression is characterized by certain social behaviors, social and interpersonal factors also affect the internal factors of depression. How parents interact with their children affects the child's development of cognitive and behavioral factors implicated in depression later on, as do interactions with peers in adolescence (e.g., Eisenberg, Spinrad, & Eggum, 2010). In fact, exemplifying the biopsychosocial approach to depression, a longitudinal study of adolescents found that genetic and neural predictors of depression at age 18 depend on parenting behaviors when the child is age 12 (Little et al., 2015). In adulthood, too, an individual's social relationships can influence how he or she copes with negative events. Having more close relationships (and, especially, high-quality relationships) can provide protection against maladaptive coping patterns and depressive symptoms (Marroquín & Nolen-Hoeksema, 2015).

Sociocultural Theories

Sociocultural theorists have focused on how differences in the social conditions of demographic groups lead to differences in vulnerability to depression. Three demographic factors are especially relevant to sociocultural theories of depression: cohort effects (meaning generational differences), gender, and ethnicity/race.

Cohort Effects A **cohort effect** exists when people's difference on some psychological variable depends not on their age per se, but instead on the era in which they were born and lived. Historical and cultural changes may have put more recent generations at higher risk for depression than previous generations (Kessler et al., 2003; Klerman & Weissman, 1989). For example, fewer than 20 percent of people born before 1915 appear to have experienced major depression, whereas over 40 percent of people born after 1955 appear to be at risk for major depression at some time in their lives. Some theorists suggest that more-recent generations are at higher risk for depression because of the rapid changes in social values beginning in the 1960s and the disintegration of the family unit (Klerman & Weissman, 1989). Another possible explanation is that younger generations have unrealistically high expectations for themselves that older generations did not have, and thus more vulnerability to depression.

Gender Differences We noted earlier that women are about twice as likely as men to suffer from depression. Several explanations have been offered for this gender difference (Nolen-Hoeksema & Hilt, 2013).

One is that men and women differ in how they respond to, or cope with, negative feelings. When faced with distress, men are more likely than women to turn to alcohol to cope and to deny that they are distressed, while women are more likely than men to ruminate about their feelings and problems (Nolen-Hoeksema & Hilt, 2013). Men therefore may be more likely to develop disorders such as alcohol abuse, while women's tendency to ruminate appears to make them more likely to develop depression. These different responses to stress may be due to social norms—it is more acceptable for men to turn to alcohol and for women to ruminate (Addis, 2008; Nolen-Hoeksema & Hilt, 2013).

Perhaps also due to gender socialization, women tend to be more interpersonally oriented than men (Feingold, 1994). On one hand, women's strong interpersonal networks may give them support in times of need. On the other hand, when bad things happen to others or when there is conflict in their relationships, women are more likely than men to experience depressive symptoms (Hammen, 2003; Rudolph, 2008). Women also appear more likely than men to base their self-worth on the health of their relationships (Jack, 1991). In addition, women in most societies have less status and power than do men, and as a result they experience more prejudice, discrimination, and violence (Nolen-Hoeksema & Hilt, 2013). Sexual abuse, particularly in childhood, occurs more often to girls and women, and contributes to depression throughout their lifetime (Widom, DuMont, & Czaja, 2007).

Earlier in this chapter, we noted biological explanations for women's greater vulnerability to depression compared to men. Biological and sociocultural factors likely interact to lead to the large gender difference in the incidence of depression (Nolen-Hoeksema & Hilt, 2013). For example, the increase in gender differences coincides with puberty, and social aspects of puberty—such as its timing relative to one's peers—play a role in depression (e.g., Alloy, Hamilton, Hamlat, & Abramson, 2016).

Ethnicity/Race Differences As society becomes increasingly diverse, ethnic and racial differences in the prevalence and patterns of depression support sociocultural theories. In the United States, compared to Caucasian Americans, Latinos show similar rates of depression overall (Kessler et al., 2003). However, rates vary widely depending on specific culture of origin, first versus second generation status, and acculturation (González, Tarraf, Whitfield, & Vega, 2010; Wassertheil-Smoller et al., 2014). Interestingly, Latinos born in the United States have higher rates of depression than those who immigrated from other countries. Relative to Caucasian Americans, Latinos show more chronic courses of depression and receive less adequate treatment (González et al., 2010; Wassertheil-Smoller et al., 2014).

Adult studies indicate that African Americans have lower rates of depression than Caucasian Americans (Anderson & Mayes, 2010; Kessler et al., 2003). This may seem puzzling given the disadvantaged status of African Americans in U.S. society. However, African Americans have high rates of anxiety disorders, suggesting that the stress of their social status may make them especially prone to anxiety disorders rather than to depression. Other studies have found extremely high rates of depression among Native Americans, especially the young (Saluja et al., 2004). Depression among Native American youth is tied to poverty, hopelessness, and alcoholism.

Asian Americans show lower rates of depression than other ethnic groups. Some findings indicate that, because of cultural differences, people of Asian descent may experience depression in a more somatic form—for example, reporting a headache rather than negative thinking (e.g., Ryder et al., 2008), although evidence for this claim is mixed (Kim & Lopez, 2014). Ethnic/racial differences not only shed light on sociocultural factors in depression across demographics, but also help guide treatment and prevention efforts.

THEORIES OF BIPOLAR DISORDER

Most existing theories of bipolar disorder focus on biological causes. In recent years, however, there has been increasing interest in psychological and social contributors to new episodes in people with bipolar disorder.

Biological Theories of Bipolar Disorder

Genetic Factors

Bipolar disorder is strongly and consistently linked to genetic factors, although the specific genetic abnormalities that contribute to bipolar disorder are not yet known. First-degree relatives (parents, children, and siblings) of people with bipolar disorder have 5 to 10 times higher rates of both bipolar disorder and depressive disorders than relatives of people without bipolar disorder (Craddock & Sklar, 2013). Also, the identical twins of individuals with bipolar disorder are 45 to 75 times more likely to develop the disorder than are people in the general population (McGuffin et al., 2003). Ongoing research seeks to identify the specific genes implicated in bipolar disorder, some of which likely contribute to other disorders like schizophrenia (Craddock & Sklar, 2013).

Structural and Functional Brain Abnormalities

Like the depressive disorders, bipolar disorder is associated with abnormalities in the structure and functioning of the amygdala, which is involved in the processing of emotions (Figure 4), and the prefrontal cortex, which is involved in cognitive control of emotion, planning, and judgment (Garrett et al., 2012; Phillips & Swartz, 2014). Some evidence also indicates alterations in the size or functioning of the hippocampus.

An area of the brain called the striatum, part of a structure called the basal ganglia, is involved in the

FIGURE 4 **Amygdala Activation in Youth with Bipolar Disorder.** Youth with bipolar disorder showed significantly greater amygdala activation (yellow area) than did healthy youth when rating their fear of neutral faces.

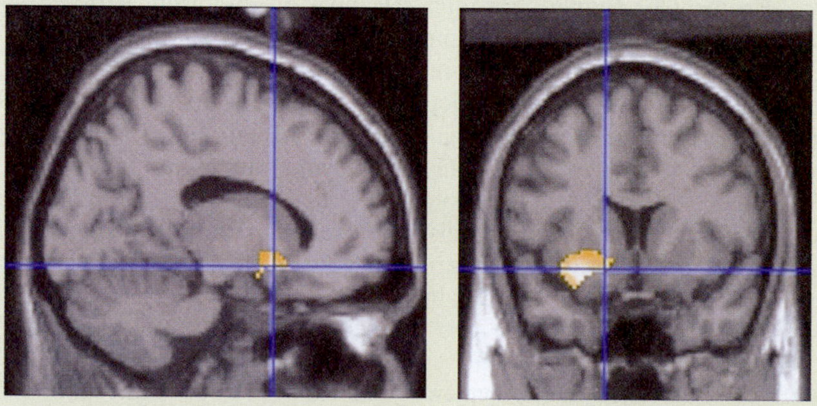

processing of environmental cues of reward. For example, this brain structure becomes active when rewarding stimuli, such as tasty food or opportunities to earn money, are perceived by the individual. This area of the brain is activated abnormally in people with bipolar disorder but not consistently so in people with major depression, suggesting that people with bipolar disorder may be neurobiologically hypersensitive to rewarding cues in the environment (Nusslock et al., 2012). A circuit from the prefrontal cortex through the striatum to the amygdala is involved in adaptation to changing contingencies of reward (i.e., knowing when you should drop one strategy in favor of another in order to get a reward). Some researchers suggest that individuals with bipolar disorder have abnormalities in the functioning of this circuit that lead them to have inflexible responses to reward (Brotman et al., 2016; Philips & Swartz, 2014). When they are in a manic phase, they inflexibly and excessively seek reward; when they are in a depressive phase, they are highly insensitive to reward. Even between manic or depressive episodes, though, people with bipolar disorder respond to incentives and social rewards with more positive emotion, and this reactivity is linked with activity in the striatum (Dutra, Cunningham, Kober, & Gruber, 2015).

Some studies suggest that youth with bipolar disorder have abnormalities in the white matter of the brain, particularly in the prefrontal cortex (Frazier et al., 2007; Kafantaris et al., 2009). White matter is tissue that connects various structures in the brain and transmits messages between them. White-matter abnormalities are found in children at their first episodes of bipolar disorder, before they have been medicated (Adler et al., 2006), and in children at risk for bipolar disorder because of family history (Frazier et al., 2007). White-matter abnormalities could result in the brain's prefrontal area having difficulty communicating with and exerting control over other areas, such as the amygdala, leading to the disorganized emotions and extreme behavior characteristic of bipolar disorder (Brady et al., 2017; Garrett et al., 2012).

Neurotransmitter Factors

The monoamine neurotransmitters have been implicated in bipolar disorder as well as in major depressive disorder. In particular, several studies have suggested that dysregulation in the dopamine system contributes to bipolar disorder (Brotman et al., 2016). High levels of dopamine are thought to be associated with high reward seeking, while low levels are associated with insensitivity to reward. Thus, dysregulation in the dopamine system may lead to excessive reward seeking during the manic phase and a lack of reward seeking in the depressed phase (Ashok et al., 2017).

Psychosocial Contributors to Bipolar Disorder

Although biological theories of bipolar disorder have received the most attention, psychosocial approaches have identified other important factors, including reward sensitivity, stress, and changes to bodily and social routines.

In line with biological evidence that dysregulation of reward systems plays a role in bipolar disorder, psychologists have been examining relationships between bipolar disorder and behavioral indicators of sensitivity to reward. Reward sensitivity refers to the degree to which people experience emotional, behavioral, and biological responses to positive events they experience or anticipate. In some of these studies, individuals play games on the computer, such as gambling games, that assess their willingness to take risks in order to pursue possible rewards and their ability to detect what kinds of behaviors will be rewarded. These studies confirm that people with bipolar disorder, even when they are asymptomatic, show greater sensitivity to reward than do people without the disorder (Alloy et al., 2008; Johnson, Fulford, & Carver, 2012). In addition, a study that followed people with bipolar disorder for nearly 3 years found that those with greater sensitivity to reward relapsed into manic or hypomanic symptoms sooner than did those with lower sensitivity to reward (Alloy et al., 2008). Whereas a person without bipolar disorder might enjoy a fun evening out with friends and then go home to relax, a person with bipolar disorder might find the evening so rewarding that she stays up through the night. In contrast, individuals with high sensitivity to punishment relapse into depressive episodes sooner than those with lower sensitivity to punishment.

Another psychological factor that has been studied in people with bipolar disorder is stress. Experiencing stressful events and living in an unsupportive family may trigger new episodes of bipolar disorder (Altman et al., 2006; Frank, Swartz, & Kupfer, 2000; Hlastala, Frank, Kowalski, Sherrill, & Tu, 2000). Even positive events can trigger new episodes of mania or hypomania, particularly if they involve striving for goals seen as highly rewarding. A study of college students found that among those with bipolar disorder, preparing for and completing exams tended to trigger hypomanic symptoms, particularly among students who were highly sensitive to rewards (Nusslock, Abramson, Harmon-Jones, Alloy, & Hogan, 2007). Thus, goal-striving situations may trigger high reward sensitivity, which in turn triggers manic or hypomanic symptoms in people with bipolar disorder.

Changes in bodily rhythms or usual routines also can trigger episodes in people with bipolar disorder (Frank et al., 2000). For example, changes in sleep and eating patterns can lead to relapse. Irregular or inadequate sleep, in particular, appears to be a characteristic of many individuals with bipolar disorder that can lead to increased symptoms (Harvey, 2008b; Ng et al., 2015). Significant changes in daily routine can do the same, particularly if they are due to changes in the social climate, such as starting a new job. Some researchers believe that there is a close relationship between social and bodily rhythms and disruption in the neural and psychological systems underlying reward (Alloy, Nusslock, & Boland, 2015). A psychosocial therapy we discuss later in this chapter, interpersonal and social rhythm therapy, helps people with bipolar disorder keep their bodily and social rhythms regular.

TREATMENT OF MOOD DISORDERS

Many forms of treatment are now available for sufferers of mood disorders. In any given year, however, only about half the people who have bipolar disorder and about 60 percent of the people having an episode of major depression seek treatment in the United States, and many fewer seek treatment in developing nations (Kessler et al., 2003; Merikangas et al., 2011). Most often, those who eventually do seek treatment do so a number of years after the onset of their symptoms.

Biological Treatments for Mood Disorders

Most of the biological treatments for depression and bipolar disorder are drug treatments. In addition to being treated with drugs, some people with mood disorders are treated with electroconvulsive therapy (ECT). Three new treatments for mood disorders—repetitive transcranial magnetic stimulation (rTMS), vagus nerve stimulation, and deep brain stimulation—hold out hope for many people. People with seasonal affective disorder (SAD) can benefit from a simple therapy: exposure to bright lights.

The Federal Drug Administration (FDA) requires warnings for SSRIs saying that they may increase the risk of suicide. ©*Robin Nelson/PhotoEdit*

Drug Treatments for Depression

The late twentieth century saw rapid growth in the number of drugs available for depression and in the number of people using them. Several classes of drugs are commonly used in treating depressive disorders and the depressive symptoms of bipolar disorder; these drugs include selective serotonin and/or norepinephrine reuptake inhibitors, tricyclic antidepressants, and monoamine oxidase inhibitors. Initially, they were thought to work by altering levels of the neurotransmitters serotonin, norepinephrine, or dopamine in synapses or by affecting the receptors for these neurotransmitters. However, these changes occur within hours or days of taking the drugs, whereas reductions in depressive symptoms typically don't appear for weeks. More recent theories suggest that these drugs have slow-emerging effects on intracellular processes in the neurotransmitter systems discussed in the section on genetic factors in depression (see Figure 1) and on the action of genes that regulate neurotransmission, the limbic system, and the stress response (Gitlin, 2015).

All of the different antidepressant drugs currently available reduce depression in about 50 to 60 percent of people who take them (Gitlin, 2015). These medications appear to work better for treating severe and persistent depression than for treating mild-to-moderate depression. A meta-analysis of 718 patients from six studies found that antidepressants were substantially better than a placebo in reducing symptoms only in very severely depressed patients; in patients with mild-to-moderate depression, the effects of the antidepressants were small to nonexistent (Fournier et al., 2010; see also Khan, Leventhal, Khan, & Brown, 2002; Kirsch et al., 2008).

The choice of which drug to begin treatment with tends to be based on the experience of the physician and concerns about the patient's ability to tolerate side effects. It typically takes a few weeks to know whether a person will respond to a drug. Most people try more than one medication before they find the one that works for them. These days, antidepressant drugs are used to relieve the acute symptoms of depression. Then individuals usually are maintained on antidepressant drugs for at least 6 months after their symptoms have subsided, to prevent relapse. Discontinuing antidepressant use during the first 6 to 9 months after symptoms subside seems to double the risk of relapse in severe depression (Geddes, Burgess, Hawton, Jamison, & Goodwin, 2004). People with bipolar disorder often take antidepressants continually to prevent a relapse of depression.

Selective Serotonin Reuptake Inhibitors The **selective serotonin reuptake inhibitors**, or **SSRIs**, are widely used to treat depressive symptoms. SSRIs are not more effective in the treatment of depression than the other available antidepressants, but they have fewer difficult-to-tolerate side effects (Gitlin, 2015). In addition, they are much safer if taken in overdose than many of the older antidepressants, such as the tricyclic antidepressants and the monoamine oxidase inhibitors, described below. Finally, they have positive effects on a wide range of symptoms that co-occur with depression, including anxiety, eating disorders, and impulsiveness.

The SSRIs do have side effects, however, and 5 to 10 percent of people have to discontinue their use because of these side effects (Gitlin, 2015). The most common side effects are gastrointestinal symptoms (e.g., nausea and diarrhea), tremor, nervousness, insomnia, daytime sleepiness, diminished sex drive, and difficulty achieving orgasm. When people first begin taking an SSRI, they sometimes report feeling "jittery" or having a feeling of "crawling out of one's skin." Some people who have bipolar disorder may develop manic symptoms when they take an SSRI. The agitation some people experience while taking an SSRI may contribute to an increase in suicidal thought and behavior, but this can also be due to increased motivation and energy as depression begins to lift. Some studies have suggested that SSRIs can increase suicidal behavior among children and adolescents, but overall, it seems SSRIs decrease such behavior in children and adults (Garland, Kutcher, Virani, & Elbe, 2016).

Selective Serotonin-Norepinephrine Reuptake Inhibitors The **selective serotonin-norepinephrine reuptake inhibitors (SNRIs)** were designed to affect levels of norepinephrine as well as serotonin. They act in the same way as SSRIs (that is, by influencing neurotransmission), but perhaps because these drugs influence both neurotransmitters, they show a slight advantage over the selective serotonin reuptake inhibitors in preventing a relapse of depression (Nemeroff et al., 2007). The dual action of these drugs also may account for their slightly broader array of side effects compared to the SSRIs.

Bupropion: A Norepinephrine-Dopamine Reuptake Inhibitor Bupropion affects the norepinephrine and dopamine systems and thus is known as a **norepinephrine-dopamine reuptake inhibitor.** It may be especially useful in treating people suffering from psychomotor retardation, anhedonia, hypersomnia, cognitive slowing, inattention, and craving–for example, bupropion can help people stop craving cigarettes. In addition, bupropion appears to overcome the sexual dysfunction side effects of the SSRIs and thus sometimes is used in conjunction with them. The effects of bupropion address the role of dopamine in pleasure, reward, and movement (see the chapter "Theories and Treatment of Abnormality" for reminders of how these various neurotransmitters work).

Tricyclic Antidepressants The **tricyclic antidepressants** were some of the first drugs shown to consistently relieve depression. However, they are used much less frequently these days than the other drugs reviewed in this section. The primary reason for this is that they have numerous side effects. Many of these are anticholinergic effects, so called because they are related to levels of the neurotransmitter acetylcholine. The tricyclic antidepressants also can cause a drop in blood pressure and cardiac arrhythmia in people with heart problems. Further, the tricyclics can be fatal in overdose, and an overdose is only three to four times the average daily prescription for the drug. For this reason, physicians are wary of prescribing these drugs, particularly for people with depression who might be suicidal.

Monoamine Oxidase Inhibitors Another older class of drugs that is no longer used frequently to treat depression is the **monoamine oxidase inhibitors (MAOIs).** MAO is an enzyme that causes the breakdown of the monoamine neurotransmitters in the synapse. MAOIs decrease the action of MAO and thereby increase the levels of these neurotransmitters in the synapses.

The MAOIs are as effective as the tricyclic antidepressants, but their side effects are potentially quite dangerous. When people taking MAOIs ingest aged cheese, red wine, or beer, they can experience a potentially fatal rise in blood pressure. The MAOIs also can interact with several drugs, including antihypertension medications and over-the-counter drugs such as antihistamines. The MAOIs also can cause liver damage, weight gain, severe lowering of blood pressure, and several of the same side effects caused by the tricyclic antidepressants.

Mood Stabilizers

People with bipolar disorder may take antidepressants to relieve their depressive symptoms, but they also usually take a mood stabilizer (lithium or an anticonvulsant medication) to relieve or prevent symptoms of mania. Lithium can also have positive effects on depressive symptoms in people with depression. In addition, many people are prescribed atypical antipsychotic medications to control mood swings.

Lithium Lithium may work by improving the functioning of the intracellular processes that appear to be abnormal in the mood disorders (Malhi, Tanious, Das, Coulston, & Berk, 2013). Most people with bipolar disorder take lithium even when they have no symptoms of mania or depression in order to prevent relapses. People maintained on adequate doses of lithium have significantly fewer relapses of mania and depression than people with bipolar disorder not maintained on lithium (Geddes et al., 2004; Ketter, Miller, Dell'Osso, & Wang, 2016). Lithium is also quite effective in reducing suicide risk, as we discuss later in this chapter.

Although lithium has literally been a lifesaver for many people with mood disorders, it poses some problems. The main problem is that the difference between an effective dose of lithium and a toxic dose is small, leaving a narrow window of therapeutic effectiveness. People who take lithium must be monitored carefully by a physician, who can determine whether the dosage of lithium is adequate to relieve their symptoms but not so large as to induce toxic side effects. The side effects of lithium range from annoying to life threatening. Many patients experience abdominal pain, nausea, vomiting, diarrhea, tremors, and twitches. Some people on lithium complain of blurred vision and problems in concentration and attention that interfere with their ability to work. Lithium can cause diabetes, hypothyroidism, and kidney dysfunction and can contribute to birth defects if taken during the first trimester of pregnancy. Up to 55 percent of patients develop resistance to lithium within 3 years, and only about 33 percent of patients remain symptom-free on lithium (Nemeroff, 2000). Physicians and patients need to work together to ensure that the major benefits of lithium are balanced with these significant drawbacks.

Anticonvulsant and Atypical Antipsychotic Medications In the mid-1990s it was discovered that a medication that helps reduce seizures, valproate (trade name Depakote), also helped stabilize mood in people with bipolar disorder. Other anti-epileptic medications, carbamazepine (trade names Tegretol, Equetro) and lamotrigine (trade name Lamictal), have been approved for use in treating bipolar disorder. The side effects of these drugs include blurred vision, fatigue, vertigo, dizziness, rash, nausea, drowsiness, and liver disease. Valproate seems to induce fewer side effects and is used more often than carbamazepine. Lamotrigine is used especially for maintenance treatment and preventing episode recurrence. But the anti-epileptics can cause birth defects if women take them while pregnant, and they do not prevent suicide as effectively as lithium does. The anti-epileptics may work by restoring the balance between the neurotransmitter systems in the amygdala.

The atypical antipsychotic medications, which are described in more detail in the chapter "Schizophrenia Spectrum and Other Psychotic Disorders," are also used to quell the symptoms of severe mania. These drugs, which include olanzapine (Zyprexa), ariprizole (Abilify), quetiapine (Seroquel), and risperidone (Risperdal), reduce functional levels of dopamine and seem to be especially useful in the treatment of psychotic manic symptoms (Ketter et al., 2016). The side effects of these drugs can include weight gain and problematic metabolic changes (e.g., increased risk of diabetes and increased insulin, glucose, and low-density lipoprotein cholesterol levels).

With the increased recognition of bipolar disorder and related syndromes in children, such as disruptive mood regulation disorder, there has been an increase in the use of medications to treat children. These medications include mood stabilizers, atypical antipsychotics, and antidepressants. Existing studies show that these drugs can help stabilize children's moods, but the number of well-controlled, large group studies is small, and there are significant concerns about both the short-term and the long-term toxic effects of these drugs on children's developing brains and bodies (Liu et al., 2011).

Electroconvulsive Therapy

Perhaps the most controversial of the biological treatments for mood disorders is electroconvulsive therapy (ECT). ECT was introduced in the early twentieth century, originally as a treatment for schizophrenia (see the chapter "Theories and Treatment of Abnormality"). It consists of a series of treatments in which a brain seizure is induced by passing electrical current through the patient's head. Patients are first anesthetized and given muscle relaxants so they are not conscious when they have the seizure and so their muscles do not jerk violently during the seizure. Metal electrodes are taped to the head, and a current of 70 to 130 volts is passed through one side of the brain for about 1 second. Patients typically have a convulsion that lasts about 1 minute. The full ECT treatment consists of 6 to 12 sessions. Neuroimaging studies show that ECT results in decreases in metabolic activity in several regions of the brain, including the frontal cortex and the anterior cingulate, although the mechanisms by which ECT relieves depressive symptoms are not completely clear (Dukart et al, 2014; Henry, Schmidt, Matochik, Stoddard, & Potter, 2001; Oquendo et al., 2001).

ECT can lead to memory loss and difficulty learning new information, particularly in the days following

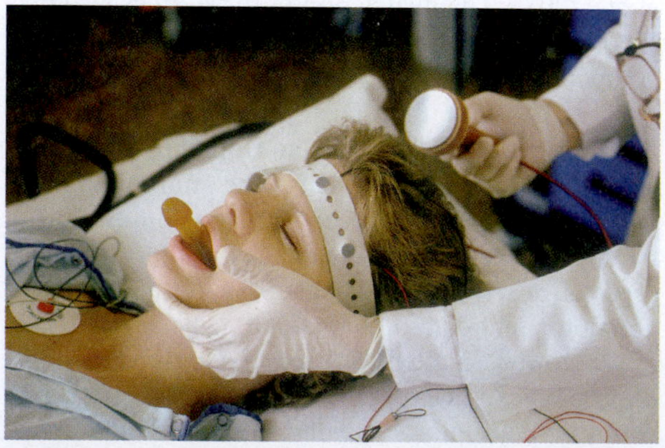

Electroconvulsive therapy is an effective treatment for severe depression, but it is controversial, in part because of outdated depictions of it in the media. *©W & D McINTYRE/Science Source*

treatment (Sackeim et al., 2007). When ECT was first developed, it was administered to both sides of the brain, and the effects on memory and learning sometimes were severe and permanent. These days, ECT usually is delivered to only one side of the brain—usually the right side, because this side is less involved in learning and memory. As a result, patients undergoing modern ECT are less likely to experience significant or long-term memory loss or learning difficulties, but people who have undergone ECT still experience a significant increase in memory problems (Sackeim et al., 2007). In addition, because this unilateral administration sometimes is not as effective as bilateral administration, some people are still given bilateral ECT. Although ECT can be extremely effective in eliminating the symptoms of depression, the relapse rate among people who have undergone ECT can be as high as 85 percent, with over 30 percent of patients relapsing in the first 6 months after ECT (Fink, 2001; Jelovac, Kolshus, & McLoughlin, 2013).

Newer Methods of Brain Stimulation

In recent years, researchers have been investigating new methods of stimulating the brain without applying electric current. Each of these methods has been shown in randomized clinical trials to result in more improvement in depressive symptoms than a placebo in patients with depressive disorders or bipolar disorder whose depressive symptoms have not responded to other forms of treatment (Slotema, Blom, Hoek, & Sommer, 2010).

In the procedure known as **repetitive transcranial magnetic stimulation (rTMS),** scientists expose patients to repeated, high-intensity magnetic pulses focused on particular brain structures (Figure 5a). This procedure involves placing a machine around specific locations of the brain, but is noninvasive and can be done on an outpatient basis. In treating people with depression, researchers have targeted the left prefrontal cortex, which tends to show abnormally low metabolic activity in some people with depression.

FIGURE 5 **Newer Methods of Brain Stimulation.** (a) Repetitive transcranial magnetic stimulation exposes patients to repeated, high-intensity magnetic pulses focused on particular brain structures. (b) In vagus nerve stimulation, electrodes are attached to the vagus nerve, a part of the autonomic nervous system that carries information to several areas of the brain. (c) In deep brain stimulation, electrodes are implanted deep in the brain and connected to a pulse generator placed under the skin. The generator then delivers stimulation to targeted brain areas.

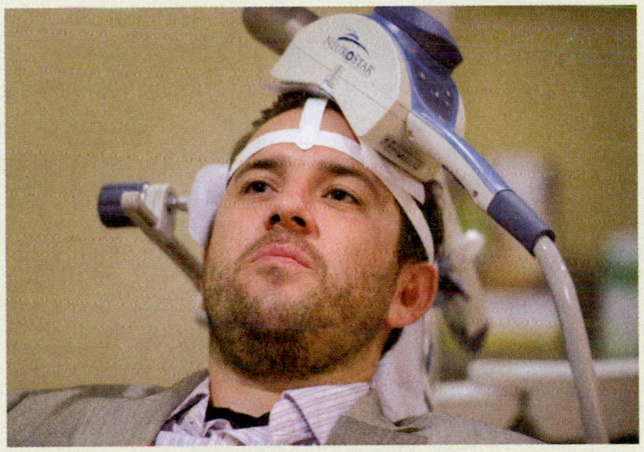

©Sacramento Bee/Getty Images

(a)

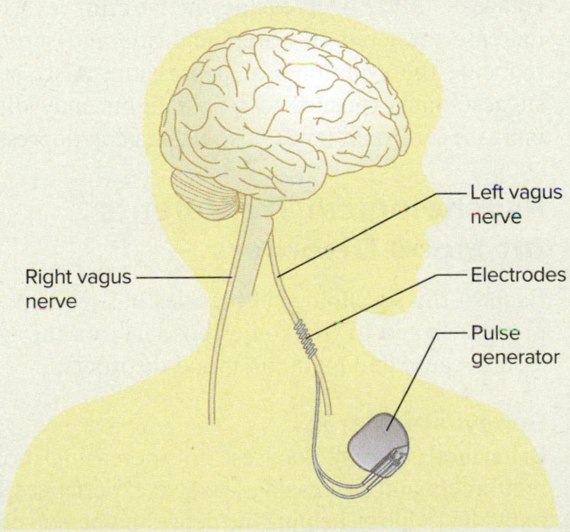

(b)

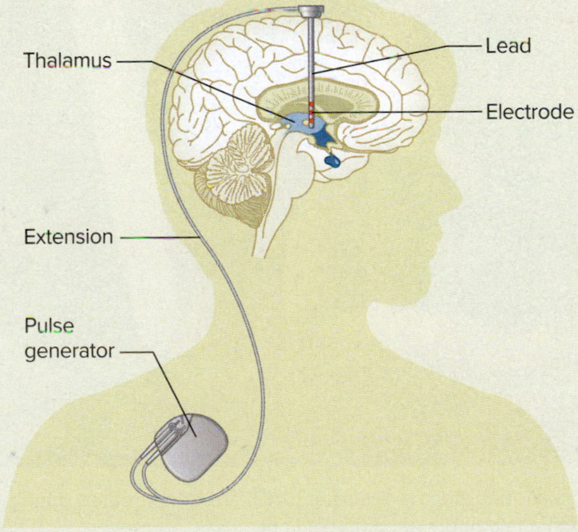

(c)

Patients who receive rTMS report few side effects—usually only minor headaches treatable by over-the-counter pain relievers. Patients can remain awake, rather than having to be anesthetized as in electroconvulsive therapy (ECT), thereby avoiding possible complications of anesthesia.

Another newer method that holds considerable promise in the treatment of serious depression is **vagus nerve stimulation** (VNS; Figure 5b). The vagus nerve, part of the autonomic nervous system, carries information from the head, neck, thorax, and abdomen to several areas of the brain, including the hypothalamus and amygdala, which are involved in depression. In vagus nerve stimulation, the vagus nerve is stimulated by a small electronic device, much like a cardiac pacemaker, that is surgically implanted under the patient's skin in the left chest wall. How VNS relieves depression is not entirely clear, but positron-emission studies show that VNS results in increased activity in the hypothalamus and amygdala, which may have antidepressant effects (Slotema et al., 2010).

The newest and least studied procedure to date is **deep brain stimulation.** In this procedure, electrodes are surgically implanted in specific areas of the brain (Figure 5c). The electrodes are connected to a pulse generator that is placed under the skin and stimulates these brain areas. Very small trials of deep brain stimulation have shown promise in relieving intractable depression (Mayberg et al., 2005). Understanding how these newer treatments for depression actually work is an important goal of researchers seeking to maximize effectiveness and minimize risks (e.g., Coles, Kozak, & George, 2018; De Raedt, Vanderhasselt, & Baeken, 2015).

People diagnosed with seasonal affective disorder (SAD) are often treated during darker winter months with a few hours each day of light.
©Rocky89/Getty Images

Light Therapy

Recall that seasonal affective disorder (SAD) is a form of mood disorder in which people become depressed during the winter months, when there are the fewest hours of daylight. Their moods improve in the summer months, when there are more hours of daylight each day. People with SAD may have deficient retinal sensitivity to light, meaning that their bodies react more strongly than most people's to changes in the amount of light each day (Rohan, Roecklein, Lacy, & Vacek, 2009). It turns out that exposing people with SAD to bright light for a few hours each day during the winter months, known as **light therapy,** can significantly reduce some people's symptoms. One study found that 57 percent of people with SAD who completed a trial of light therapy showed remission of their symptoms and 79 percent of those who had both light therapy and cognitive therapy (described below) showed remission, compared to 23 percent of a control group who did not receive intervention (Rohan et al., 2007; see also Rohan et al., 2015).

One theory is that light therapy helps reduce seasonal affective disorder by resetting circadian rhythms, natural cycles of biological activity that occur every 24 hours. The production of several hormones and neurotransmitters varies over the course of the day according to these rhythms, which are regulated by internal clocks but can be affected by environmental stimuli, including light. People with depression sometimes show dysregulation of their circadian rhythms. Light therapy may work by resetting circadian rhythms, thereby normalizing the production of hormones and neurotransmitters (Rohan, Roecklein, & Haaga, 2009).

Another theory is that light therapy works by decreasing levels of the hormone melatonin, which is secreted by the pineal gland (Rohan, Roecklein, & Haaga, 2009). Decreasing melatonin levels can increase the levels of norepinephrine and serotonin, reducing the symptoms of depression. Also, studies suggest that exposure to bright lights may directly increase serotonin levels, also decreasing depression.

Psychological Treatments for Mood Disorders

Each of the psychological theories has led to a treatment designed to overcome those factors the theory asserts cause and maintain mood disorders.

Behavioral Therapy

Behavioral therapy focuses on increasing positive reinforcers and decreasing aversive experiences in an individual's life by helping the depressed person change his or her patterns of interaction with the environment

CASE STUDY

Mark worked constantly. When he was not actually at work, he was working at home. He had a position of considerable responsibility and was convinced that if he didn't stay focused on his job, he'd miss something that would result in his being fired or kicked off the career ladder. Mark had not taken a vacation in several years. Although he wanted to continue to get pay raises and promotions, as he has each year, he was also painfully aware that life was passing him by. He felt stressed, depressed, and hopeless about ever having a "normal" life.

Mark clearly felt rewarded for his one-dimensional life with praise, pay raises, promotions, and the absence of mistakes for which he might be punished. Mark's behavior was governed by his work focus. He engaged in no social activities, lived alone, and did not organize his time to include anything but his work. The behavior therapist suggested that if he wanted to improve his quality of life, and his outlook on life, he must learn some very specific new behaviors. Mark was encouraged to schedule time for social and recreational opportunities. He learned that he needed to actively and deliberately do things that are fun and pleasurable. He and the therapist practiced new ways to meet people and form social relationships (friendships, dating). The therapist also taught him relaxation skills to reduce his stress. Eventually, Mark felt a new sense of control over his life, and his depression lifted. (Source: Adapted from Yapko, 1997)

and with other people (Dimidjian, Barrera, Martell, Muñoz, & Lewinsohn, 2011; Hollon & Dimidjian, 2015). Behavioral therapy is designed to be short-term, lasting about 12 weeks.

The first phase of behavioral therapy involves a functional analysis of the connections between specific circumstances and the depressed person's symptoms. When does the depressed person feel worst? Are there any situations in which he or she feels better? This analysis helps the therapist pinpoint the behaviors and interaction patterns that need to be the focus of therapy. It also helps the client understand the intimate connections between his or her symptoms and his or her daily activities or interactions.

Once the circumstances that precipitate the client's depressive symptoms are identified, therapists help the client change aspects of the environment that are contributing to the depression, such as isolation. They teach depressed clients skills for changing their negative circumstances, particularly negative social interactions. They also help clients learn new skills, such as relaxation techniques, for managing their moods in unpleasant situations. Several of these techniques are illustrated in the previous case study.

Cognitive-Behavioral Therapy

Cognitive-behavioral therapy (CBT) represents a blending of cognitive and behavioral theories of depression (Beck, Weissman, Lester, & Trexler, 1974; Ellis & Harper, 1961; Lewinsohn, Muñoz, Youngren, & Zeiss, 1986; Rehm, 1977; see Hollon & Dimidjian, 2015). This therapy has two general goals. First, it aims to change the negative, hopeless patterns of thinking described by the cognitive models of depression. Second, it aims to help people with depression solve concrete problems in their lives and develop skills for being more effective in their world so they no longer have the deficits in reinforcers described by behavioral theories of depression.

CASE STUDY

Susan was a young, single, 24-year-old woman. Her goals for therapy were to learn how to overcome chronic feelings of depression and temptations to overeat. Susan was unemployed and living with her aunt and uncle in a rural area. She had no means of personal transportation. Hypersensitivity to the reactions of significant others and the belief that they could control her feelings seemed to be central to her negative self-concept and feelings of helplessness. Susan described her mother as knowing which "buttons to push." This metaphor was examined and challenged. She was questioned as to how her mother controlled her emotions: Where were these buttons? Once again, the principle was asserted that it is not the actions of others that cause emotions, but one's cognitions about them.

. . . During the last stage of therapy, Susan's mother visited. This provided a real test of the gains Susan had made, as it was her mother's criticism that she feared the most. At first, she reported feeling easily wounded by her mother's criticism. These examples were used as opportunities to identify and challenge self-defeating thoughts. Soon, Susan was able to see her mother's critical statements as her mother's problem, not her own. She also discovered that, as she became better at ignoring her mother's critical remarks and not taking them to heart, her mother began to be more relaxed and open around her and criticized her less. (Source: Adapted from Thorpe & Olson, 1997, pp. 225–227)

Like behavioral therapy, cognitive-behavioral therapy is designed to be brief and time-limited. The therapist and client usually will agree on a set of goals they wish to accomplish in 6 to 12 weeks. These goals focus on specific problems that clients believe are connected to their depression, such as problems in their marriage or dissatisfaction with their job. From the beginning of therapy, the therapist urges clients to set their own goals and make their own decisions.

The first step in cognitive-behavioral therapy is to help clients discover the negative automatic thoughts they habitually have and understand the link between those thoughts and their depression. Often, the therapist will assign clients the homework of keeping track of times when they feel sad or depressed and writing down on record sheets, such as the one in Figure 6, what is going through their mind at such times.

The second step in cognitive-behavioral therapy is to help clients challenge their negative thoughts. People with depression often believe that there is only one way to interpret a situation—their negative way. Therapists use a series of questions to help clients consider alternative ways of thinking about a situation and the pros and cons of these alternatives, such as "What is the evidence that you are right in the way you are interpreting this situation?" "Are there other ways of looking at this situation?" and "What can you do if the worst-case scenario comes true?"

The third step in cognitive-behavioral therapy is to help clients recognize the deeper, basic beliefs or assumptions they might hold that are fueling their depression. These might be beliefs such as "If I'm not loved by everyone, I'm a failure" or "If I'm not a complete success at everything, my life is worthless." The therapist will help clients question such beliefs and decide if they truly want to base their lives on them. The case of Susan illustrates some of the cognitive components of cognitive-behavioral therapy.

Cognitive-behavioral therapists also use behavioral techniques to train clients in new skills they might need to cope better. Often people with depression are unassertive in making requests of other people or in standing up for their rights and needs. This lack of assertiveness can be the result of their negative

FIGURE 6 **An Automatic Thoughts Record Used in Cognitive-Behavioral Therapy.** In cognitive-behavioral therapy, patients keep a record of the negative thoughts that arise when they feel negative emotions. This record is then used in therapy to challenge the patients' depressive thinking.

Date	Event	Emotion	Automatic thoughts
April 4	Boss seemed annoyed.	Sad, anxious, worried	Oh, what have I done now? If I keep making him mad, I'm going to get fired.
April 5	Husband didn't want to make love.	Sad	I'm so fat and ugly.
April 7	Boss yelled at another employee.	Anxious	I'm next.
April 9	Husband said he's taking a long business trip next month.	Sad, defeated	He's probably got a mistress somewhere. My marriage is falling apart.
April 10	Neighbor brought over some cookies.	A little happy, mostly sad	She probably thinks I can't cook. I look like such a mess all the time. And my house was a disaster when she came in!

automatic thoughts. For example, a person who often thinks "I can't ask for what I need because the other person might get mad and that would be horrible" is not likely to make even reasonable requests of other people. The therapist first will help clients recognize the thoughts behind their actions (or lack of action). The therapist then may work with the clients to devise exercises or homework assignments in which they practice new skills, such as assertiveness, between therapy sessions.

Interpersonal Therapy

In interpersonal therapy (IPT), therapists look for four types of problems in depressed individuals (Table 5; Weissman & Verdeli, 2013). First, many depressed people are grieving the loss of a loved one, perhaps not from death but instead from the breakup of an important relationship. Interpersonal therapists help clients face such losses and explore their feelings about them. Therapists also help clients begin to invest in new relationships.

A second type of problem on which interpersonal therapy focuses is interpersonal role disputes, which arise when people do not agree on their roles in a relationship. For example, a college student and a parent may disagree on the extent to which the student should follow the parent's wishes in choosing a career. Interpersonal therapists first help the client recognize the dispute and then guide him or her in making choices about what concessions might be made to the other person in the relationship. Therapists also may need to help clients modify and improve their patterns of communicating with others in relationships. For example, a student who resents his parents' intrusions into his private life may tend to withdraw and sulk rather than directly confront his parents about their intrusions. He would be helped to develop more effective ways of communicating his distress over his parents' intrusions.

The third type of problem addressed in interpersonal therapy is role transitions, such as the transition from college to work or from work to full-time motherhood. People sometimes become depressed over the role they must leave behind. Therapists help clients develop more realistic perspectives toward roles that are lost and learn to regard new roles in a more positive manner. If a client feels unsure about his or her ability to perform a new role, the therapist helps the client develop a sense of mastery in the new role. Sometimes, clients need help developing new networks of social support to replace the support systems they have left behind in their old roles.

Fourth, people with depression also turn to interpersonal therapy for help with problems caused by deficits in interpersonal skills. Such skill deficits can be the reason people with depression have inadequate social support networks. The therapist reviews with clients their past relationships, especially important childhood relationships, and helps them understand these relationships and how they might be affecting their current relationships. The therapist also might directly teach clients social skills, such as assertiveness.

Interpersonal and Social Rhythm Therapy and Family-Focused Therapy

Interpersonal and social rhythm therapy (ISRT) is an enhancement of interpersonal therapy designed specifically for people with bipolar disorder (Frank et al., 2005). When people with bipolar disorder experience disruptions in either their daily routines or their social environment, they sometimes experience an upsurge in symptoms. ISRT combines interpersonal therapy

TABLE 5 Interpersonal Therapy

Interpersonal therapists focus on four types of interpersonal problems as sources of depression.

Type of Problem	Therapeutic Approach
Grief, loss	Help the client accept feelings and evaluate a relationship with a lost person; help the client invest in new relationships
Interpersonal role disputes	Help the client make decisions about concessions willing to be made and learn better ways of communicating
Role transitions	Help the client develop more realistic perspectives toward roles that are lost and regard new roles in a more positive manner
Interpersonal skills deficits	Review the client's past relationships, helping the client understand these relationships and how they might be affecting current relationships; directly teach the client social skills, such as assertiveness

Source: Hollon et al., 2005.

techniques with behavioral techniques to help patients maintain regular routines of eating, sleeping, and activity, as well as stability in their personal relationships. By having patients self-monitor their patterns over time, therapists help patients understand how changes in sleep patterns, circadian rhythms, and eating habits can provoke symptoms. Then therapists and patients work together to develop a plan to stabilize the patients' routines and activities. Similarly, patients learn how stressors in their family and work relationships affect their moods, and they develop better strategies for coping with these stressors. Studies show that patients who receive ISRT in conjunction with medication show fewer symptoms and relapses over time than patients who do not receive ISRT (Frank et al., 2005; Haynes, Gengler, & Kelly, 2016). Targeting the important role of sleep in bipolar disorder, related treatments increasingly address insomnia and other sleep problems directly. Preliminary evidence indicates that this emphasis may reduce relapses and improve functioning (Harvey et al., 2015).

Family-focused therapy (FFT) is also designed to reduce interpersonal stress in people with bipolar disorder, particularly within the context of families. Patients and their families are educated about bipolar disorder and trained in communication and problem-solving skills. Studies comparing family-focused therapy with standard therapy (medication with periodic individual checkups with a psychiatrist) have found that adults receiving family-focused therapy show lower relapse rates over time (Miklowitz & Chung, 2016). In addition, applications of FFT to adolescents with or at risk of developing bipolar disorder show promise in helping these youths and their families manage symptoms and reduce the impact of the disorder on the adolescents' functioning and development (Miklowitz et al., 2013). More generally, patients with bipolar disorder are strongly affected by their social environments (and vice versa). Including the family appears to be an overall positive addition to psychosocial treatment (Reinares et al., 2016).

Comparison of Treatments

Which of the many treatments for mood disorders is best? In the past few decades, several studies have compared behavioral, cognitive-behavioral, interpersonal, and drug therapies in the treatment of depressive disorders. Perhaps surprisingly, these therapies, despite their vast differences, appear to be about equally effective in treating most people with depression (Cuijpers, van Straten, van Oppen, & Andersson, 2008; DeRubeis, Gelfand, Tang, & Simons, 1999; Dimidjian et al., 2006; Hollon & Dimidjian, 2015; Weissman & Verdeli, 2013). For example, in one study, 240 people with major depression were randomly assigned to receive either the SSRI paroxetine (Paxil) or cognitive-behavioral therapy for 16 weeks (DeRubeis et al., 2005). At the end of treatment, about 60 percent in each group no longer experienced major depression. Another study compared the results of behavioral therapy, cognitive therapy (without behavioral interventions), and drug therapy (paroxetine) in 240 patients with major depressive disorder (Dimidjian et al., 2006). In this study, behavioral therapy led to improvement in the greatest number of patients, followed by cognitive therapy and then drug therapy.

We might expect the combination of psychotherapy and drug therapy to be more effective in treating people with persistent depressive disorder than either type of therapy alone, and some studies support this expectation (Cuijpers, Dekker, Hollon, & Andersson, 2009; Cuijpers, van Straten, Warmerdam, & Andersson, 2009; see Weissman & Cuijpers, 2017). For example, in one study, 681 patients with persistent depressive disorder were randomly assigned to receive a serotonin modulator (nefazadone, a drug no longer sold because of adverse side effects), cognitive-behavioral therapy, or both for 12 weeks (Keller et al., 2000). About 50 percent of the people receiving medication or cognitive-behavioral therapy alone experienced relief from their depression, while 85 percent of the patients receiving both medication and cognitive-behavioral therapy experienced relief.

Relapse rates in depression are quite high, even among people whose depressions completely disappear with treatment. For this reason, many psychiatrists and psychologists argue that people with a history of recurrent depression should be kept on a maintenance level of therapy even after their depression is relieved (Gitlin, 2015). Usually, the maintenance therapy is a drug therapy, and many people remain on antidepressant drugs for years after their initial episodes of depression have passed. Studies of behavioral therapy, interpersonal therapy, and cognitive-behavioral therapy show that maintenance levels of these therapies—usually consisting of once-a-month meetings with therapists—also can substantially reduce relapse rates (Hollon & Dimidjian, 2015; Cuijpers, Donker, Weissman, Ravitz, & Cristea, 2016).

Even when maintenance doses of psychotherapy are not available, people who have had any of the empirically supported psychotherapies appear to be less likely to relapse than those who have had only drug therapy (Weissman & Cuijpers, 2017). For example, researchers followed the 240 patients in one of the studies described earlier for a year after they had recovered from acute depression. They found that those who had had cognitive-behavioral therapy showed a lower rate of relapse than those who continued with the drug therapy (paroxetine) only and that both groups had much lower rates of relapse than those who were taking

FIGURE 7 **Relapse Rates After Drug Versus Cognitive-Behavioral Therapy for Major Depression.** Patients with major depression who had received CBT showed lower relapse rates in the next year than those who continued to take only an SSRI. Both groups showed lower rates of relapse than patients who received a placebo pill.

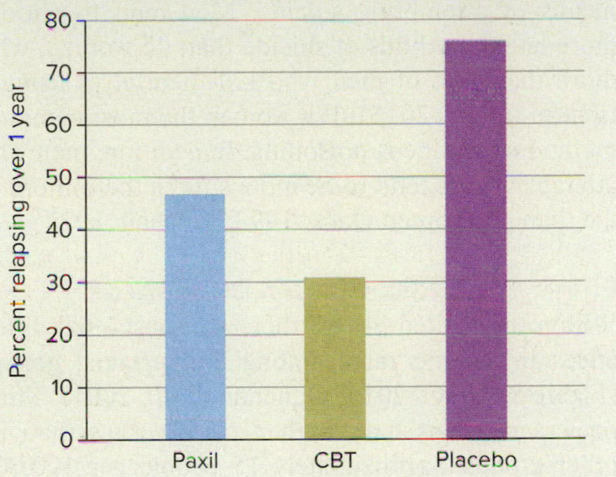

a placebo pill over those 12 months (Figure 7; Hollon et al., 2005). Interventions that specifically emphasize relapse prevention may be especially helpful for people at higher risk for depression relapse (Bockting, Hollon, Jarrett, Kuyken, & Dobson, 2015).

In the case of bipolar disorder, combining drug treatment with the psychological therapies may reduce the rate at which patients stop taking their medication and may lead more patients to achieve full remission of their symptoms, compared to lithium treatment alone (Miklowitz, 2010; Swartz & Frank, 2001). Psychotherapy can help people with bipolar disorder understand and accept their need for lithium treatment as well as help them cope with the impact of the disorder on their lives.

In addition to treating mood disorders after their onset, another priority is preventing episodes before they emerge. Prevention programs can be effective in eliminating or delaying the onset of symptoms, especially if they are targeted at high-risk groups based on risk factors for depression (Muñoz, Beardslee, & Leykin, 2012). For example, programs aimed at women prior to childbirth appear somewhat effective in preventing postpartum depression (Sockol, Epperson, & Barber, 2013).

SUICIDE

Suicide is among the three leading causes of death worldwide among people ages 15 to 44 (World Health Organization [WHO], 2017). Around the world, more people die from suicide than from homicide. Suicide is associated with mood disorders, and thus we address it in the final section of this chapter. Note, however, that the risk of suicide is increased in people with any mental disorder.

Defining and Measuring Suicide

The Centers for Disease Control and Prevention (CDC), one of the federal agencies in the United States that tracks suicide rates, defines **suicide** as "death from injury, poisoning, or suffocation where there is evidence (either explicit or implicit) that the injury was self-inflicted and that the decedent intended to kill himself/herself." As clear as this definition seems, there is great variability in the form that suicide takes, and whether to call particular types of death suicide is open to debate. We may easily agree that a young man who is despondent and shoots himself in the head has committed suicide. It is harder to agree on whether an unhappy young man who goes on a drinking binge and crashes his car into a tree has committed suicide. Is an elderly person who refuses life support when dying from a painful disease committing suicide? Is a middle-aged person with severe heart disease who continues to smoke cigarettes, eat fatty foods, and drink excessive amounts of alcohol committing suicide? Clearly, suicide-like behaviors fall along the type of continuum we discuss throughout this book.

We can distinguish among *completed suicides,* which end in death; **suicide attempts,** which may or may not end in death; and **suicidal ideation** or thought. Many people with mental disorders think about committing suicide but never attempt to kill themselves. Also, actual suicide attempts are much more common than completed suicides, with some studies estimating that suicide attempts are 20 times as common as completed suicides (WHO, 2017).

Given the difficulty of defining suicide, it is not surprising that accurate suicide rates are difficult to obtain. Many deaths are ambiguous, particularly when no notes are left behind and no clues exist as to the victim's mental state before death. Recorded rates probably are low, because the stigma against suicide is a great incentive for labeling a death anything but a suicide. Accurate data on nonlethal suicide attempts are even harder to obtain.

Even so, the statistics indicate that suicide is more common than we would like to believe. More than 40,000 people kill themselves each year in the United States, an average of 113 people per day, or 1 every 13 minutes (CDC, 2015). In addition, as many as 3 percent of the population make a suicide attempt (with intent to die) sometime in their lives (Nock & Kessler, 2006), and more than 13 percent report having had suicidal thoughts at some time (Borges, Angst,

Nock, Ruscio, & Kessler, 2008). Suicide is not just an American phenomenon, however. Internationally, an estimated 800,000 people die by suicide each year, or 1 person about every 40 seconds (WHO, 2017).

In the context of the tragic statistics just reviewed, *DSM-5* approaches suicide risk and behavior more deliberately than did *DSM-IV*. Throughout *DSM-5*, particular characteristics that make people more vulnerable to suicide are highlighted, and those mental disorders that are associated with an elevated risk for suicide are identified specifically (e.g., not just mood or personality disorders, but schizophrenia, anorexia, and posttraumatic stress disorder). By describing the suicidal patterns associated with a range of diagnoses, *DSM-5* encourages clinicians to attend to suicide risk early and often in treatment. In addition, *DSM-5* includes two new conditions for further research study in a special section toward the end of the manual. These include proposed criteria sets for suicidal behavior disorder and nonsuicidal self-injury, for which future research is encouraged, both of which represent major problems on college campuses. While the proposed criteria sets are *not* intended for clinical use (and are not yet officially recognized as disorders), their inclusion provides increased emphasis on suicide and self-harm as an important focus of future clinical research.

Gender Differences

While two to three times more women than men attempt suicide (Nock & Kessler, 2006), men are four times more likely than women to complete suicide (CDC, 2015). This gender difference is true across all age groups, as seen in Figure 8. Many people assume that suicide rates are highest among adolescents. Although rates are increasing in that age group (see below), in fact the most "typical" suicide in the United States involves a middle-aged, Caucasian man (CDC, 2015).

The gender difference in rates of completed suicide may be due in part to gender differences in the means of attempting suicide. Men tend to choose more lethal methods of suicide than do women, with more than half of men who kill themselves using a firearm (CDC, 2015). For women the most common method of suicide is poisoning. In addition, men who attempt suicide tend to be more sure in their intent to die than are women (Jack, 1992; Linehan, 1973).

Ethnic and Cross-Cultural Differences

Within the United States, there are substantial differences in suicide rates among ethnic/racial groups (Figure 9; CDC, 2015; Oquendo et al., 2001). European Americans have higher suicide rates than all other groups—approximately 15 people per 100,000 population—and Native Americans are close behind, at approximately 13 per 100,000 (CDC, 2015). Suicide among Native Americans is tied to poverty, lack of education and hope, discrimination, substance abuse, limited access to care, and the easy availability of firearms (Wexler et al., 2015). Suicide rates among African American males have increased greatly in

FIGURE 8 **Gender, Age, and Suicide.** In many nations of the world, males are more likely to commit suicide than females across almost all age groups.

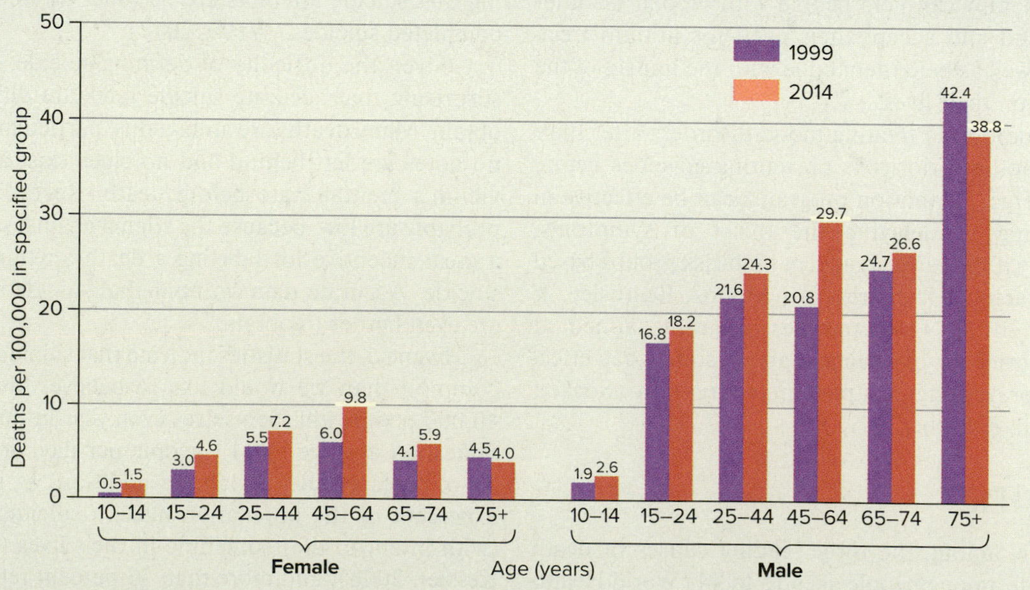

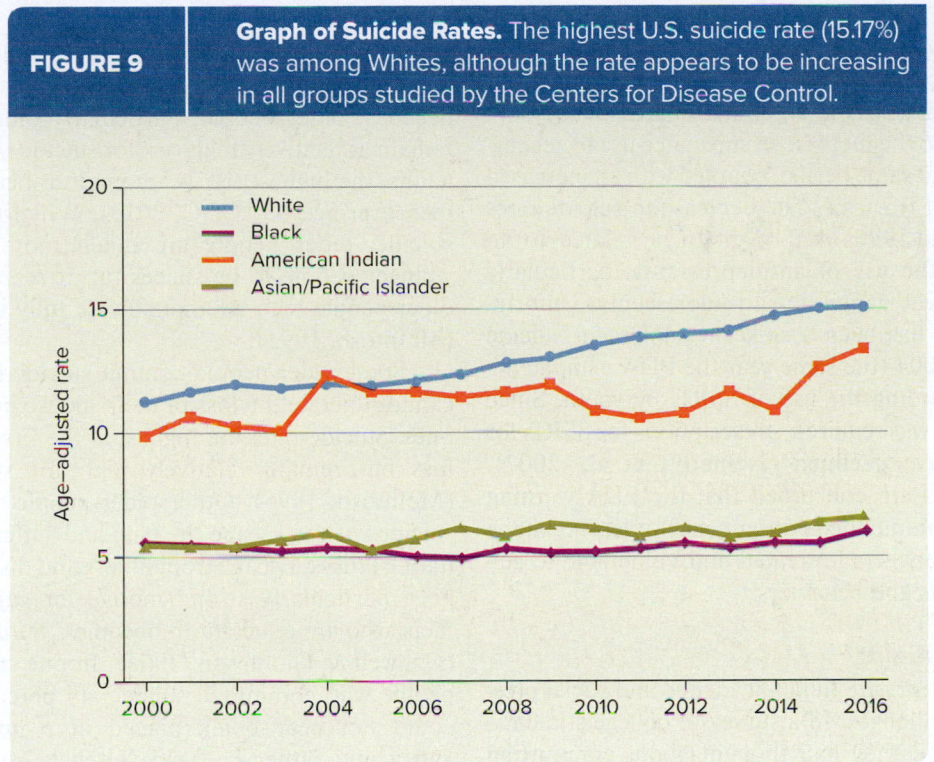

FIGURE 9 **Graph of Suicide Rates.** The highest U.S. suicide rate (15.17%) was among Whites, although the rate appears to be increasing in all groups studied by the Centers for Disease Control.

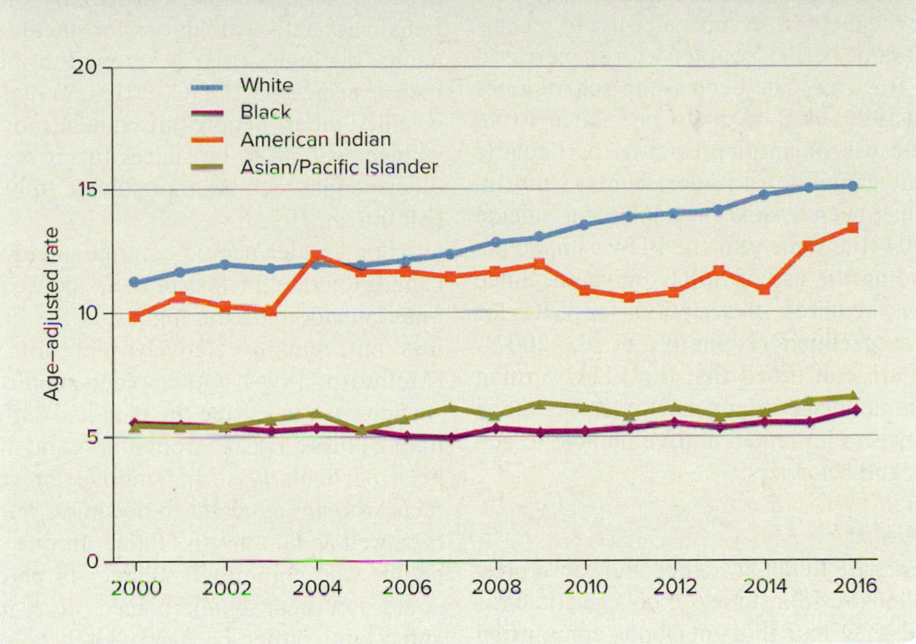

recent decades, but African Americans generally commit suicide at lower rates than other groups (about 6 per 100,000; CDC, 2015). One possible explanation is relatively strong family support structures and higher levels of religious involvement among African Americans (Taylor, Chatters, & Joe, 2011). Latino suicide rates are similar, but have increased markedly in recent years among young Latina females (CDC, 2015; Silva & Van Orden, 2018).

There are also cross-national differences in suicide rates. Higher rates are found in much of Europe, the former Soviet Union and China, and lower rates in Latin America and South America (WHO, 2017). The suicide rates in Australia, the United States, Canada, and England fall between these two extremes. The differences may be due in part to cultural and religious norms. Followers of religions that expressly forbid suicide are less likely to attempt it (Gearing & Alonzo, 2018; O'Donnell, O'Donnell, Wardlaw, & Stueve, 2004).

Suicide in Children and Adolescents

Although suicide is relatively rare in young children, it is not unheard of. The rate of suicide increases substantially in early adolescence. Each year, 17 percent of teenagers in the United States seriously consider suicide, 15 percent devise a specific plan to attempt suicide, more than 8 percent attempt suicide, and about 2 percent make a serious suicide attempt that requires medical attention (Jacobson & Gould, 2009). Suicide may become more common in adolescence than in childhood because the rates of several types of psychopathology tied to suicide, including depression, anxiety disorders, and substance abuse, increase in adolescence. Suicide rates also may rise during the teen years because adolescents are more sophisticated than children in their thinking and can contemplate suicide more clearly. Finally, adolescents simply may have readier access to the means to commit suicide (e.g., drugs and guns) than do children.

As is the case for adults, girls are much more likely to attempt suicide than boys, but boys are more likely to succeed (Jacobson & Gould, 2009). Males are up to six times more likely than females in this age range to commit suicide (CDC, 2015; Hawton, Saunders, & O'Connor, 2012). Gay, lesbian, and bisexual adolescents have rates of suicide attempts 2 to 6 times higher than those of heterosexual adolescents (Jacobson & Gould, 2009).

Hispanic females have especially high rates of suicidal thoughts and plans and attempted suicides compared to Hispanic males and adolescents from other racial/ethnic groups (Jacobson & Gould, 2009; Silva & Van Orden, 2018). Luis Zayas and colleagues (Zayas, Lester, Cabassa, & Fortuna, 2005) suggest that these high rates are linked to clashes between Hispanic girls, who are highly acculturated to American values, and their parents, who may hold traditional cultural values of *familism* (centrality of family to one's life) and may reject their daughters' bids for independence.

Rates of suicide among children and teenagers more than doubled between the 1950s and the early 1990s, but they have steadily declined since 1994 (Hawton et al., 2012). The initial increase may have been linked to the increase in substance use by teenagers during that same period, coupled with an increased availability of firearms. The decrease in suicide rates since the mid-1990s is thought to be related to an increase in the use of antidepressants, particularly SSRIs, to treat depression in adolescents. Unfortunately, there has been a spike in adolescent suicide rates since 2004—the same year the FDA mandated a warning regarding the use of SSRIs by youth. Since that warning was required, prescriptions for SSRIs for teenagers have declined (Nemeroff et al., 2007). Some experts are concerned that the FDA warning has had the unintended consequence of leaving many depressed teenagers untreated and vulnerable to suicidal thoughts and behaviors.

College Students

The college years are full of academic and social pressures and challenges. In a survey of college students, 9 percent said they had thought about committing suicide since entering college, and 1 percent said they had attempted suicide while at college (Furr, Westefeld, McConnell, & Jenkins, 2001). Students who had contemplated or attempted suicide were more likely than those who had not to have experienced depression and hopelessness, loneliness, and problems with their parents. Regrettably, only 20 percent of the students who had contemplated suicide had sought any type of counseling. However, rates of suicidal thinking among college students are about the same as their same-age peers; rates of suicide attempts are somewhat lower (CDC, 2015).

Illness is often a precursor to suicide among older adults. ©*Jack Spratt/The Image Works*

Suicide in Older Adults

Although there has been a 50 percent decline in suicide rates among adults over age 65 in the past few decades, older people, particularly older men, still remain at relatively high risk for suicide. Among older adults, the highest risk is among European American men over age 85 (CDC, 2015). When they attempt suicide, older people are much more likely than younger people to be successful. It seems that most older people who attempt suicide fully intend to die (McIntosh, 1995).

Some older people commit suicide because they cannot tolerate the loss of their spouse or other loved ones. Suicide rates are highest in the first year after a loss but remain relatively high for several years (McIntosh, 1995). Other older people who commit suicide wish to escape the pain and suffering of debilitating illness. Escape from illness and disabilities may be a particularly strong motive for suicide among men, who are reluctant to become a burden to others (Conwell & Thompson, 2008). In one study of older people who committed suicide, 44 percent said they could not bear being placed in a nursing home and would rather be dead (Loebel, Loebel, Dager, Centerwall, & Reay, 1991).

Most older people who lose a spouse or become ill do not commit suicide. Those with a history of depression or other psychological problems are at greatest risk for responding to the challenges of old age with suicide (Harwood, Hawton, Hope, & Jacoby, 2000). Higher suicide rates among older adults may also reflect the impairments in cognitive abilities (such as problem solving and resisting impulses) that older adults sometimes experience during depressive episodes (Wang & Blazer, 2015).

Nonsuicidal Self-Injury

Some people—often adolescents—repeatedly cut, burn, puncture, or otherwise significantly injure their skin with no intent to die, a behavior known as **nonsuicidal self-injury,** or **NSSI** (Nock, 2010). NSSI seems to be relatively common, with lifetime prevalence of up to 18 percent internationally (Muehlenkamp, Claes, Havertape, & Plener, 2012). NSSI is especially prevalent among adolescents (17 percent) compared to young adults (13 percent) and adults (5.5 percent; Swannell, Martin, Page, Hasking, & St. John, 2014). Clinicians, teachers, and other health professionals report a dramatic increase in NSSI in recent years, but longitudinal data do not support this (Muehlenkamp et al., 2012; Swannell et al., 2014).

Individuals who engage in NSSI are at increased risk for suicide attempts (Klonsky, May, & Saffer, 2016; Nock, 2010). NSSI occurs at an elevated rate across most mood and anxiety disorders (Bentley, Cassiello-Robbins, Vittorio, Sauer-Zavala, & Barlow,

2015), as well as being a prominent feature of borderline personality disorder (see the chapter "Personality Disorders"). Theories of NSSI suggest that it functions as a way of regulating emotion and/or influencing the social environment (Fox, Toole, Franklin, & Hooley, 2017). People who engage in NSSI often report that the experience of feeling the pain and seeing the blood actually calms them and releases tension. There is some evidence that individuals who engage in NSSI do have more difficulty regulating their emotions, and use their behavior to regulate distress (Davis et al., 2014; Fox et al., 2017; Weinberg & Klonsky, 2012). Self-injury also draws support and sympathy from others or may punish others (Nock, 2008). Some risk factors for NSSI are similar to those for suicide, such as hopelessness (Fox et al., 2015), but much more research on what triggers self-injury is needed.

Understanding Suicide

Our ability to understand the causes of suicide is hampered by many factors. First, although suicide is more common than we would hope, it is still rare enough to make studying it difficult. Second, in the wake of a suicide, family members and friends may selectively remember certain information about the victim (e.g., evidence that he or she was depressed) and forget other information. Third, most people who kill themselves do not leave a note. The notes that are left often do not provide much understanding of what led the people to take their lives (Jamison, 1993). In this section, we briefly discuss historical perspectives on suicide and then discuss research findings on the factors contributing to suicide.

Historical Perspectives on Suicide

Freud argued that depressed people express anger at themselves instead of at the people they feel have betrayed or abandoned them. When that anger becomes so great in depressed people that they wish to annihilate the image of the lost person, they destroy themselves. For example, teenagers who cannot express anger at their parents may attempt suicide to punish them. Like many of Freud's theories, this idea is difficult to test because it involves emotions that people are unable or unwilling to express or acknowledge.

In his classic work on suicide, sociologist Émile Durkheim (1897) focused on the mind-sets certain societal conditions can create that increase the risk for suicide. He proposed that there are three types of suicide. **Egoistic suicide** is committed by people who feel alienated from others, empty of social contacts, and alone in an unsupportive world. The patient with schizophrenia who kills herself because she is completely isolated from society may be committing egoistic suicide. **Anomic suicide** is committed by people who experience severe disorientation because of a major change in their relationship to society. A man who loses his job after 20 years of service may feel *anomie,* a complete confusion of his role and his worth in society, and may commit anomic suicide. Finally, **altruistic suicide** is committed by people who believe that taking their life will benefit society. For instance, during the Vietnam War, Buddhist monks publicly immolated themselves to protest the war.

Durkheim's theory suggests that social ties and integration into a society will help prevent suicide if the society discourages suicide and supports individuals in overcoming negative situations in ways other than suicide. However, if a society supports suicide as a beneficial act in some situations, then ties with such a society may promote suicide. For example, some terrorist groups promote suicide as an honorable, even glorious, act in the service of striking at enemies.

Modern empirical research has identified a number of psychological, biological, and environmental factors that increase the risk for suicide. We turn now to this research.

Psychological Disorders and Suicide

More than 90 percent of people who commit suicide probably have been suffering from a diagnosable mental disorder (Borges et al., 2010; Jacobson & Gould, 2009; Joiner, Brown, & Wingate, 2005). Depression increases the odds of a suicide attempt by approximately 6 times, and bipolar disorder increases the odds of a suicide attempt by 7 times (Nock et al., 2008). Internationally, one in every four people with bipolar I disorder, and one in every five people with bipolar II disorder, has a history of suicide attempts (Merikangas et al., 2011). The mood disorders are most closely associated with suicide, but borderline personality disorder, substance abuse, and, to a lesser extent, anxiety disorders are also predictors of suicidal behavior (Bentley et al., 2016; Klonsky et al., 2016).

By far the best predictor of future suicidal thoughts and behavior is past suicidal thoughts and behavior (Borges et al., 2008, 2010; O'Connor & Nock, 2014). Among adolescents, a history of a previous suicide attempt increases the odds of suicide by 30 times among boys and by 3 times among girls (Shaffer et al., 1996). Thus, it is critically important that suicidal thoughts and behaviors be assessed and that intervention be made, regardless of what other psychological problems they may be related to.

Stressful Life Events and Suicide

Studies across cultures have shown that the risk of suicide is increased by a variety of stressful life events, especially events related to abuse, interpersonal loss, perceived failure, economic hardship, and physical illness (Borges et al., 2010; O'Connor & Nock, 2014). A large cross-national study found that interpersonal violence, especially sexual abuse, is the traumatic event most strongly linked to suicidal thoughts and attempts (Stein et al., 2010). Such experiences not only are immediate triggers of suicidal thoughts and behavior but also are associated with increased risk over the victim's life span. For example, a nationwide study in the United States found that a history of child sexual abuse increased the odds of a suicide attempt by 2 to 4 times for women and by 4 to 11 times for men (Molnar, Berkman, & Buka, 2001), and risk increases with more instances of abuse (Bruffaerts et al., 2010).

Loss of a loved one through death, divorce, or separation is also consistently related to suicide attempts or completions (O'Connor & Nock, 2014). People feel they cannot go on without the lost relationship and wish to end their pain. Physical abuse by a partner is also a potent predictor of suicide attempts (McLaughlin, O'Carroll, & O'Connor, 2012).

Another stressful event consistently linked to increased vulnerability to suicide is economic hardship (Borges et al., 2010; Fanous, Prescott, & Kendler, 2004). Loss of a job, for example, can precipitate suicidal thoughts and attempts (Platt & Hawton, 2000). Increases in the suicide rate among African American males may be tied to perceptions that their economic futures are uncertain as well as to comparisons of their economic status to that of the majority culture. Rates of suicide among African American males in the United States are highest in communities where the occupational and income inequalities are greatest (Joe & Kaplan, 2001).

Finally, a large international study found that physical illness, especially if it occurred early in life, was a risk factor for suicidal ideation, plans, and attempts even in people who did not have a mental disorder (Scott et al., 2010). The illness most strongly related to suicidal thoughts and behavior was epilepsy.

Could media coverage of school shootings, such as the one at Santa Fe High School in Texas on May 18, 2018, and suicide inspire other students to commit similar acts?
©Bob Levey/Getty Images

Suicide Contagion

Can suicide be contagious? When a well-known member of society commits suicide, people who closely identify with that person may see suicide as more acceptable. When two or more suicides or attempted suicides are nonrandomly bunched together in space or time, such as a series of suicide attempts in the same high school or a series of completed suicides in response to the suicide of a celebrity, scientists refer to them as a **suicide cluster** (Haw, Hawton, Niedzwiedz, & Platt, 2013). Suicide clusters seem to occur primarily among adolescents (Haw et al., 2013).

Suicide clusters appear likeliest among people who knew the person who committed suicide. One well-documented example is that of a high school with about 1,500 students in which 2 students committed suicide within 4 days. At that school, over the next 18 days, 7 other students attempted suicide, and an additional 23 students reported having suicidal thoughts (Brent et al., 1989). Many of those who attempted suicide or had active suicidal thoughts were friends of one another and of the students who had completed suicide.

Other suicide clusters occur not among close friends but among people who are linked by media exposure to the suicide of a stranger, often a celebrity. Some studies have suggested that suicide rates, at least among adolescents, increase after a publicized suicide (Haw et al., 2013). For example, researchers in Taiwan interviewed 438 individuals suffering from depression shortly after massive media coverage of the suicide of popular television star M. J. Nee. They found that 38.8 percent of the depressed individuals reported that the media coverage had increased their own thoughts about suicide, and 5.5 percent said it had led them to make a suicide attempt (Cheng, Hawton, Lee, & Chen, 2007). Individuals who had themselves attempted suicide in the month prior to the media coverage of the celebrity suicide were nearly 12 times more likely to report having made another suicide attempt in response to the media coverage than were individuals who had not recently attempted suicide.

What is the reason for suicide clustering? Some theorists have examined the role of the media in **suicide contagion** (see Pirkis, Mok, Robinson, & Nordentoft, 2016). "Contagion" may occur when survivors who become suicidal are modeling the behavior of the friend or admired celebrity who committed suicide. That suicide also may make the idea of suicide more acceptable and thus lower inhibitions for suicidal behavior in survivors. For example, among the depressed individuals in the Taiwanese study described above, several said "His case showed that suicide is not shameful" and "He was a courageous martyr for me to follow elegantly" (Cheng et al., 2007, pp. 72–73). In addition, the local and media attention given to a suicide can be attractive to some people who are feeling alienated and abandoned. After the murder-suicide rampage of two teenagers at Columbine High School in Littleton, Colorado, some teenagers said that receiving media attention like the attention that was given to the shooters would be an attractive way to "go out." Such phenomena may become more prevalent with newer technologies that allow exposure to suicide or other negative peer influences via social media, although research in this area is only emerging (Twenge, Joiner, Rogers, & Martin, 2018).

Personality and Cognitive Factors in Suicide

One personality characteristic that seems to predict suicide is **impulsivity,** the general tendency to act on one's impulses rather than to inhibit them when it is appropriate to do so (Joiner et al., 2005). This trait has long been viewed as a risk factor for suicide, but the connection may not be as strong as once believed (Anestis, Soberay, Gutierrez, Hernández, & Joiner, 2014; Klonsky et al., 2016). Nevertheless, when impulsivity is overlaid on another psychological problem—such as depression, substance abuse, or living in a chronically stressful environment—it can be a contributor to suicidal thinking and behavior. One family history study showed that the children of parents with a mood disorder who also scored high on measures of impulsivity were at much greater risk of attempting suicide (Brent et al., 2002).

The cognitive variable that has most consistently predicted suicide is **hopelessness**—the feeling that the future is bleak and there is no way to make it more positive (Beck, Steer, Kovacs, & Garrison, 1985). Thomas Joiner (2005) suggested that hopeless feelings about being a burden on others and about never belonging with others are especially linked to suicide. This theory, known as the interpersonal theory of suicide, merges cognitive and social factors and has been supported by research (Chu et al., 2017). Hopelessness also may be one reason many people who are suicidal do not seek treatment. Other cognitive factors in suicide include cognitive rigidity, rumination, perfectionism, and poor problem solving (O'Connor & Nock, 2014).

Biological Factors in Suicide

As in the mood disorders, biological contributors to suicide include genetic predisposition and neurotransmitter dysfunction. Suicide runs in families. For example, one study found that the children of parents who had attempted suicide were 6 times more likely to also attempt suicide than were the children of parents who had a mood disorder but had not attempted suicide (Brent et al., 2002, 2003).

Although some of this clustering of suicide within families may be due to environmental factors, such as family members modeling each other or sharing common stressors, twin and adoption studies suggest that genetics is involved as well (Joiner et al., 2005). Twin studies estimate that the risk of suicide attempts increases by 5.6 times if a person's monozygotic twin has attempted suicide, and by 4.0 times if a person's dizygotic twin has attempted suicide (Glowinski et al., 2001; Joiner et al., 2005). Strong evidence of a genetic component to suicide remained when researchers controlled for histories of psychiatric problems in the twins and their families, for recent and past negative life events, for how close the twins were to each other socially, and for personality factors.

Many studies have found a link between suicide and low levels of the neurotransmitter serotonin (see Mann, 2013). For example, postmortem studies of the brains of people who committed suicide find low levels of serotonin (Costanza et al., 2014; Gross-Isseroff, Biegon, Voet, & Weizman, 1998). Also, people with a family history of suicide or who have attempted suicide are more likely to have abnormalities on genes that regulate serotonin (Antypa, Serretti, & Rujescu, 2013; Courtet et al., 2004; Joiner et al., 2005). People with low serotonin levels who attempt suicide are more likely to make another suicide attempt than are people with higher serotonin levels, and as in depression, the effects of genes and serotonin are stronger under conditions of negative life events (e.g., Ghasemi, Seifi, Baybordi, Danaei, & Rad, 2018) Differences in serotonin transmission are linked to suicidal tendencies even in people who are not depressed, suggesting that the connection between serotonin and suicide is not due entirely to a common connection to depression.

Treatment and Prevention

Some intervention and prevention programs appear to reduce the risk of suicide. Intervention programs target people immediately at risk of suicide. They include crisis intervention services (e.g., suicide hotlines) and dialectical behavior therapy. Prevention programs target the public in general, or people who have risk factors but are not immediately in crisis. Prevention programs have focused on educating people broadly about suicide risk and the steps to take if they are suicidal or know of someone who is suicidal. Because access to guns is associated with higher suicide rates, some prevention efforts focus on removing access to guns, which might reduce the chances of a person taking his or her own life impulsively.

Treatment of Suicidal Persons

A person who is gravely suicidal needs immediate care. Sometimes people require hospitalization to prevent an imminent suicide attempt. They may voluntarily agree to be hospitalized. If they do not agree, they can be hospitalized involuntarily for a short period of time (usually about 3 days). We will discuss the pros and cons of involuntary hospitalization in the chapter "Mental Health and the Law."

Community-based *crisis intervention programs* are available to help suicidal people deal in the short term with their feelings and then refer them to mental health specialists for longer-term care. Some crisis intervention is done over the phone, on suicide hotlines. Some communities have walk-in clinics or suicide prevention centers, which may be part of a more comprehensive mental health system.

Crisis intervention aims to reduce the risk of an imminent suicide attempt by providing suicidal persons someone to talk with who understands their feelings and problems. The counselor can help them mobilize support from family members and friends and can make a plan to deal with specific problem situations in the short term. The crisis intervention counselor may contract with the suicidal person that he or she will not attempt suicide, or at least will contact the counselor as soon as suicidal feelings return. The counselor will help the person identify other people he or she can turn to when feeling panicked or overwhelmed and make follow-up appointments with the suicidal person or refer him or her to another counselor for long-term treatment.

The medication most consistently shown to reduce the risk of suicide is lithium. A review of 33 published treatment studies of people with major depression or bipolar disorder found that those not treated with lithium were 13 times more likely to commit or attempt suicide than those treated with lithium (Baldessarini, Tondo, & Hennen, 2001).

The selective serotonin reuptake inhibitors also may reduce the risk of suicide, because they reduce depressive symptoms and because they regulate levels of serotonin, which may have an independent effect on suicidal intentions (Gitlin, 2015; Mann, 2013). As we discussed earlier, however, there is some evidence that the serotonin reuptake inhibitors can increase the risk of suicide in some children and adolescents. Clinicians must weigh the potential benefits and risks and carefully monitor individuals for signs of increased suicidal thoughts when they begin taking an SSRI (Garland et al., 2016).

Psychological therapies designed to treat depression can be effective in treating suicidal individuals. *Dialectical behavior therapy (DBT)* was developed to treat people with borderline personality disorder, who frequently attempt suicide (see the chapter "Personality Disorders"; Linehan, 1999). This therapy focuses on managing negative emotions and controlling impulsive behaviors. It aims to increase problem-solving skills, interpersonal skills, and skill at managing negative emotions. Studies show that dialectical behavior therapy and cognitive-behavioral therapy can reduce suicidal thoughts and behaviors (Asarnow, Hughes, Babeva, & Sugar, 2017; Linehan et al., 2006; Ougrin, Tranah, Stahl, Moran, & Asarnow, 2015). Similar to other clinical issues, clinicians and researchers are developing mobile technologies for addressing NSSI and suicide (Franklin et al., 2016).

What is clearest from the literature on the treatment of suicidal people is that they are woefully undertreated. Most people who are suicidal never seek treatment (Bruffaerts et al., 2011). Even when their families know they are suicidal, they might not be taken for treatment because of denial and a fear of being stigmatized. Recall that a suicide attempt is the strongest predictor of future suicide attempts and completed suicide. Suicide attempts tend to increase in intent and lethality after the first attempt (Goldston et al., 2015), so receiving professional attention early on is critical for suicidal individuals.

Suicide Prevention

Suicide hotlines and crisis intervention centers provide help to suicidal people in times of their greatest need, hoping to prevent a suicidal act until the suicidal feelings have passed. In addition, many prevention programs aim to educate entire communities about suicide. These programs often are based in schools or colleges. Students are given information about the rate of suicide in their age group, the risk factors for suicide, and actions to take if they or a friend is suicidal.

Some such programs have been shown to affect suicidal thinking and behavior (e.g., Schilling, Lawless, Buchanan, & Aseltine, 2014). Unfortunately, the evidence supporting broad-based prevention or education programs is mixed, and some may even do harm (Calear et al., 2016; Gould, Greenberg, Velting, & Shaffer, 2003). One major problem with these programs is that they often simultaneously target both the general population of students and those students at high risk for suicide. The programs may attempt to destigmatize suicide by making it appear quite common and by not mentioning that most suicidal people are suffering from a psychological disorder, in hopes that suicidal students will feel freer to seek help. But such messages can backfire with students who are not suicidal, making suicide seem like an understandable response to stress. In addition, studies of school-based suicide prevention programs have found that adolescents who had made prior suicide attempts generally reacted negatively to the programs, saying that they were less inclined to seek help after attending the program than before (Gould, Greenberg, et al., 2003).

Researchers have tailored suicide prevention messages to specific populations—particularly high-risk populations—in hopes of getting the right kind of help to the neediest people. David Shaffer and his colleagues have designed a program that involves screening adolescents for risk of suicide, doing a diagnostic interview with high-risk adolescents, and then interviewing them to determine the most appropriate referral to a mental health specialist (Shaffer & Gould, 2000). This program has had some success in identifying high-risk youth and getting them into effective treatment. Similar programs have been developed for college students. In addition, clinicians and school administrators are increasingly aware of the prevalence of NSSI in adolescence and young adulthood, and of research showing that it presents a risk for suicidal behavior. Although interventions for NSSI are early in development, several appear promising and may affect suicide prevention as well (Glenn, Franklin, & Nock, 2015).

Parents and school officials often worry that asking teenagers about thoughts of suicide might "put the idea in their head." One study addressed this concern directly (Gould et al., 2005). The researchers randomly assigned more than 2,000 teenagers to complete questionnaires that either included or did not include questions about suicidal thoughts and behaviors. Two days later the researchers had all the teenagers fill out a measure of suicidal thought. Teenagers who had completed the suicide questionnaire did not report any more (or less) suicidal thought or distress than the teenagers who had not been asked about suicide. Thus, there was no evidence that answering questions about suicide induced teenagers to consider suicide or made them highly distressed.

Guns and Suicide

In the United States, 50 percent of suicides involve guns (CDC, 2015). Purchase of a gun can indicate suicidal intent: A longitudinal study of people who had purchased handguns in California found that their risk of suicide increased 57 times in the first week after the purchase (Wintemute, Parham, Beaumont, Wright, & Drake, 1999). The majority of people who commit suicide by gun, however, use a gun that has been in their household for some time; the presence of a gun in the home increases the risk of suicide by 4 to 5 times (Houtsma, Butterworth, & Anestis, 2018; Miller & Hemenway, 2008). As mentioned, one explanation for higher rates of suicide deaths in men, despite higher rates of attempts in women, is that men use guns—a highly lethal method—more often than women do.

Indeed, the most frequent use of a gun in the home is for suicide. Researchers examined 398 consecutive deaths by gun in the homes of families who owned guns (usually handguns). Of these deaths, only 0.5 percent involved intruders shot by families protecting themselves. In contrast, 83 percent were suicides of adolescent or adult family members. Another 12 percent were homicides of one adult in the home by another family member, usually in the midst of a quarrel. The final 3 percent of deaths were due to accidental shootings of a family member (Kellermann, Rivara, Somes, & Reay, 1992).

Restricting access to guns appears to lower suicide rates. ©*Cbenjasuwan/Shutterstock*

The mere presence of a firearm in the home appears to be a risk factor for suicide when other risk factors are taken into account, especially when handguns are improperly secured or are kept loaded (Houtsma et al., 2018; Miller & Hemenway, 2008). These suicides do not occur only among people with mental disorders. One study found that while the presence of a gun in the home increased the risk of suicide by 3 times for people with a mental disorder, it increased the risk of suicide by 33 times for people without a mental disorder (Kellerman et al., 1992). This apparently counterintuitive finding is the result of the dramatic increase in impulsive suicides seen among residents of homes containing a loaded gun, even among people without a known risk factor such as psychopathology (Brent & Bridge, 2003; Westefeld, Gann, Lustgarden, & Yeates, 2016).

Can the number of such suicides be reduced by laws that restrict access to guns? Several studies have found that suicide rates are lower in cities, states, or countries with strict antigun legislation that limits people's access to guns (e.g., Anestis & Anestis, 2015). For example, one international study showed that the percentage of suicides by gun decreased proportionately with the number of households owning guns; in addition, after countries enacted stricter gun control laws, the percentage of suicides involving guns decreased (Ajdacic-Gross et al., 2006). Similarly, in the United States, in states with unrestrictive firearm laws (e.g., Alaska, Kentucky, Montana) rates of suicide by firearm are much higher than in states with restrictive firearm laws (e.g., New York, Connecticut, Rhode Island) (Anestis & Anestis, 2015; Houtsma et al., 2018). Such patterns related to gun laws and suicide are found even after controlling for differences in socioeconomic status, race/ethnicity, and urbanization (Anestis & Anestis, 2015).

Although people who are intent on committing suicide can find other means to do so when guns are not available, restricting ready access to them appears to reduce impulsive suicides with guns. Suicides by means other than guns (e.g., by jumping off a building or inhaling carbon monoxide) show no increase when access to guns is restricted, suggesting that people do not consistently substitute different means of committing suicide when guns are not available (Miller & Hemenway, 2008; Westefeld et al., 2016). Instead, the unavailability of guns seems to give people a cooling off period during which their suicidal impulses can wane.

What to Do if a Friend Is Suicidal

What should you do if you suspect that a friend or family member is suicidal? The Depression and Bipolar Support Alliance (2008), a patient-run advocacy group, makes the following suggestions in *Suicide and Depressive Illness:*

1. Take the person seriously. Although most people who express suicidal thoughts do not go on to attempt suicide, most people who do commit suicide have communicated their suicidal intentions to friends or family members beforehand.
2. Get help. Call the person's therapist, a suicide hotline, 911, or any other source of professional mental health care.
3. Express concern. Tell the person concretely why you think he or she is suicidal.
4. Pay attention. Listen closely, maintain eye contact, and use body language to indicate that you are attending to everything the person says.
5. Ask direct questions about whether the person has a plan for suicide and, if so, what that plan is.
6. Acknowledge the person's feelings in a nonjudgmental way. For example, you might say something like "I know you are feeling really horrible right now, but I want to help you get through this" or "I can't begin to completely understand how you feel, but I want to help you."
7. Reassure the person that things can be better. Emphasize that suicide is a permanent solution to a temporary problem.
8. Don't promise confidentiality. You need the freedom to contact mental health professionals and tell them precisely what is going on.
9. Make sure guns, old medications, and other means of self-harm are not available.
10. If possible, don't leave the person alone until he or she is in the hands of professionals. Go with him or her to the emergency room if need be. Then, once he or she has been hospitalized or has received other treatment, follow up to show you care.
11. Take care of yourself. Interacting with a person who is suicidal can be extremely stressful and disturbing. Talk with someone you trust about it—perhaps a friend, family member, or counselor—particularly if you worry about how you handled the situation or that you will find yourself in that situation again.

CHAPTER INTEGRATION

The mood disorders affect the whole person. Depression and mania involve changes in every aspect of functioning, including biology, cognitions, personality, social skills, and relationships. Some of these changes may be causes of the depression or mania, while others may be consequences.

The fact that the mood disorders are phenomena affecting the whole person illustrates the intricate connections among biology, cognitions, personality, and social interactions. These areas of functioning are so intertwined that major changes in any one area almost necessarily will provoke changes in other areas. Many recent models of the mood disorders suggest that most people who become depressed carry a vulnerability to depression for much of their lives. This may be a biological vulnerability, such as dysfunction in the neurotransmitter systems, or a psychological vulnerability, such as overdependence on others. Not until these vulnerabilities interact with certain stressors is a full-blown depression triggered, however (Figure 10).

FIGURE 10 **An Integrative Model of Depression.**

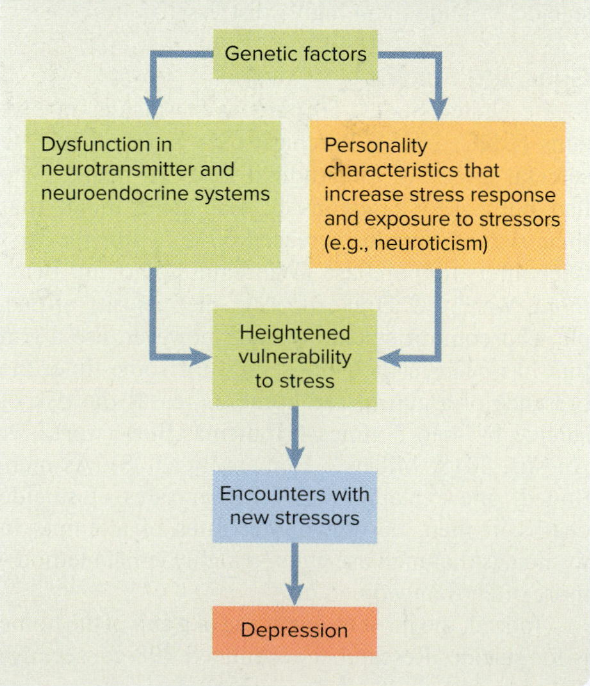

Fortunately, the interconnections among these areas of functioning may mean that improving functioning in one area can improve functioning in other areas: Improving people's biological functioning can improve their cognitive and social functioning and their personalities, improving people's cognitive and social functioning can improve their biological functioning, and so on. Thus, although there may be many pathways into mood disorders (biological, psychological, and social), there also may be many pathways out.

SHADES OF GRAY DISCUSSION

Carmen's symptoms—currently severe depressed mood in the context of long-standing unhappiness, excessive sleep every day (hypersomnia), difficulty concentrating to a degree that interfered with her ability to engage in her college classes, feelings of worthlessness, and significant weight loss (likely greater than 5 percent of her body weight) because she's skipping meals—are characteristic of a major depressive episode. We know she "spent days on end in her bedroom," but we are not entirely clear if her current symptoms meet the criterion of 2 consecutive weeks to receive a diagnosis of major depressive disorder. What we know more certainly is that she has experienced many years (> 2) struggling with moderately low mood, low self-esteem, pessimism, and chronic fatigue. Thus, she would clearly meet criteria for persistent depressive disorder, likely early onset (before age 21), severe, but we would need to get more information to add the specifier of "with intermittent major depressive episodes, with current episode." The addition of the specifier would indicate that full criteria for a major depressive episode are currently met, but she has experienced periods of at least 2 months in the past 2 years with symptoms that fall below the threshold for a full major depressive episode.

Because Carmen's more severe symptoms began in the winter term, you may wonder if she is experiencing a major depressive disorder with seasonal pattern, or what used to be known as seasonal affective disorder (SAD). "With seasonal pattern" is a specifier that applies to recurrent major depressive disorder and highlights a temporal relationship between the onset of major depressive episodes and a particular time of year (e.g., in the fall or winter). The addition of this specifier is not currently warranted because (a) it requires evidence that Carmen has experienced seasonal changes in mood in the last 2 years, and we only have evidence that Carmen's depression has worsened in this year, and (b) the specifier requires that Carmen's depressive symptoms lift during the spring or summertime. Instead, Carmen's depressive symptoms seem to persist throughout the year.

CHAPTER SUMMARY

- People with depressive disorders experience only the symptoms of depression (sad mood, loss of interest, disruption in sleep and appetite, motor retardation or agitation, loss of energy, feelings of worthlessness and guilt, suicidal thoughts and behavior).
- People with bipolar disorder experience symptoms of both depression and hypomania or mania (elated or agitated mood, grandiosity, little need for sleep, racing thoughts and speech, increase in goals, and dangerous behavior). The presence of one or more hypomanic or manic episodes is the core feature of the bipolar disorders (see Table 4).
- Major depressive disorder is the classic condition among the depressive disorders. It is characterized by discrete episodes of depressed mood and/or loss of interest or pleasure and other symptoms that lasts at least 2 weeks. In addition, there are several subtypes of major depressive disorder: with mixed features, with anxiety features, with melancholic features, with psychotic features, with catatonic features, with atypical features, with seasonal pattern, and with peripartum onset.
- Persistent depressive disorder (dysthymia) is a chronic form of depression that continues for at least 2 years in adults or 1 year in youth. It can be less severe than major depressive disorder (full criteria are not met in last 2 years) or it may represent intermittent or persistent major depressive episodes, and includes many of the same subtypes as major depressive disorder.
- Premenstrual dysphoric disorder is diagnosed in women who show increases in symptoms of distress in the week before the onset of menses, with relief of symptoms after menses begins.
- Cyclothymic disorder is a less severe but more chronic form of bipolar II disorder that does not include major depressive episodes.
- Depression is one of the most common disorders, but there are substantial age, gender, and cross-cultural differences in depression. Bipolar disorder is much less common than the depressive disorders and tends to be a lifelong problem. The length of individual episodes of bipolar disorder, as in depression, varies dramatically from one person to the next and over the life course.

- The neurotransmitters norepinephrine, serotonin, and dopamine have been implicated in the mood disorders. Disordered genes may lead to dysfunction in these neurotransmitter systems. In addition, neuroimaging studies show abnormal structure or activity in several areas of the brain, including the prefrontal cortex, hippocampus, anterior cingulate, and amygdala. There is evidence that people with depression have chronic hyperactivity in the hypothalamic-pituitary-adrenal axis, which may make them more susceptible to stress.
- Behavioral theories of depression suggest that people with much stress in their lives may have too low a rate of reinforcement and too high a rate of punishment, leading to depression. Stressful events also can lead to learned helplessness—the belief that nothing you do can control your environment—which also is linked to depression.
- The cognitive theories argue that depressed people have negative views of themselves, the world, and the future and engage in biased thinking that promotes this negativity. People who ruminate in response to distress are more prone to depression.
- Interpersonal theories suggest that people prone to depression are highly sensitive to rejection and engage in excessive reassurance seeking. Levels of interpersonal stress and conflict are high in the lives of depressed people.
- Sociocultural theorists have tried to explain the differences in rates of depression among different demographic groups. The decreased risk of depression in older adults may be due to historical cohort effects. Women's greater risk for depression may be due to differences in the ways women and men respond to distress and to women's greater interpersonal orientation, lesser power and status, and higher rates of victimization. High rates of depression in Hispanic Americans may be due to low socioeconomic status.
- Bipolar disorder has an even greater connection to genetic factors than does depression. The areas of the brain most implicated in bipolar disorder are the amygdala, prefrontal cortex, and striatum. Adolescents with bipolar disorder show abnormalities in white-matter tissue. Dopamine is the neurotransmitter most implicated in bipolar disorder.
- People with bipolar disorder may have dysfunctional reward systems: They are hypersensitive to reward when in a manic state and insensitive to reward when in a depressed state.
- Most of the biological therapies for mood disorders are drug therapies, including antidepressants and mood stabilizers. Electroconvulsive therapy is used to treat severe depression that does not respond to drugs. Newer methods of stimulating the brain, including repetitive transcranial magnetic stimulation, vagus nerve stimulation, and deep brain stimulation, hold promise for the treatment of mood disorders. Light therapy is helpful in treating major depressive disorder with seasonal pattern.
- Behavior therapies focus on increasing positive reinforcers and decreasing negative events by building social skills and teaching clients how to engage in pleasant activities and cope with their moods. Cognitive-behavioral therapies help people with depression develop more adaptive ways of thinking. Interpersonal therapy helps people with depression identify and change the patterns in their relationships.
- Interpersonal social rhythm therapy helps people with bipolar disorder manage their social relationships and daily rhythms to try to prevent relapse. Family-focused therapy may help people with bipolar disorder manage their disorder.
- Direct comparisons of various psychotherapies and drug therapies show that they tend to be equally effective in treating depression. Psychotherapies may be more effective than drug therapies in reducing relapse.
- Suicide is defined as death from injury, poisoning, or suffocation when there is evidence (either explicit or implicit) that the injury was self-inflicted and that the decedent intended to kill him- or herself.
- Women are more likely than men to attempt suicide, but men are more likely than women to complete suicide. Cross-cultural differences in suicide rates may have to do with religious proscriptions, stressors, or cultural norms about suicide. Young people are less likely than adults to commit suicide, but suicide rates among youth have been fluctuating dramatically in recent decades. The elderly, particularly elderly men, are at high risk for suicide.
- Several mental disorders, including depression, bipolar disorder, substance abuse, schizophrenia, and anxiety disorders, increase the risk for suicide.
- Several negative life events or circumstances, including economic hardship, serious illness, loss, and abuse, increase the risk for suicide.
- Suicide clusters (also called suicide contagion) occur when two or more suicides or attempted suicides are nonrandomly bunched together in a place or time.
- Impulsivity and hopelessness predict suicidal behavior.
- Family history, twin, and adoption studies all suggest a genetic vulnerability to suicide. Many studies have found a link between low serotonin levels and suicide.
- Drug treatments for suicidal patients most often involve lithium or antidepressant medications. Psychotherapies for suicide are similar to those for depression. Dialectical behavior therapy addresses skill deficits and thinking patterns in people who are recurrently suicidal.
- Suicide hotlines and crisis intervention programs provide immediate help to people who are highly suicidal. Community prevention programs aim to educate the public about suicide and to encourage suicidal people to enter treatment.
- Guns are involved in the majority of suicides, and some research suggests that restricting access to guns can reduce the number of suicide attempts.

KEY TERMS

bipolar disorder
mania
depression
depressive disorders
major depressive disorder
persistent depressive disorder
seasonal affective disorder (SAD)
peripartum onset
premenstrual dysphoric disorder
bipolar I disorder
bipolar II disorder
hypomania
cyclothymic disorder
rapid cycling bipolar disorder
disruptive mood dysregulation disorder
monoamines
norepinephrine
serotonin
dopamine
hypothalamic-pituitary-adrenal axis (HPA axis)
behavioral theories of depression
learned helplessness theory
negative cognitive triad
reformulated learned helplessness theory
rumination
interpersonal theories of depression
rejection sensitivity
cohort effect
selective serotonin reuptake inhibitors (SSRIs)
selective serotonin-norepinephrine reuptake inhibitors (SNRIs)
norepinephrine-dopamine reuptake inhibitor
tricyclic antidepressants
monoamine oxidase inhibitors (MAOIs)
repetitive transcranial magnetic stimulation (rTMS)
vagus nerve stimulation (VNS)
deep brain stimulation
light therapy
behavioral therapy
interpersonal and social rhythm therapy (ISRT)
family-focused therapy (FFT)
suicide
suicide attempts
suicidal ideation
nonsuicidal self-injury (NSSI)
egoistic suicide
anomic suicide
altruistic suicide
suicide cluster
suicide contagion
impulsivity
hopelessness

Chapter 8

©Phovoi R/AGE Fotostock

Schizophrenia Spectrum and Other Psychotic Disorders

CHAPTER OUTLINE

Schizophrenia Spectrum and Other Psychotic Disorders Along the Continuum

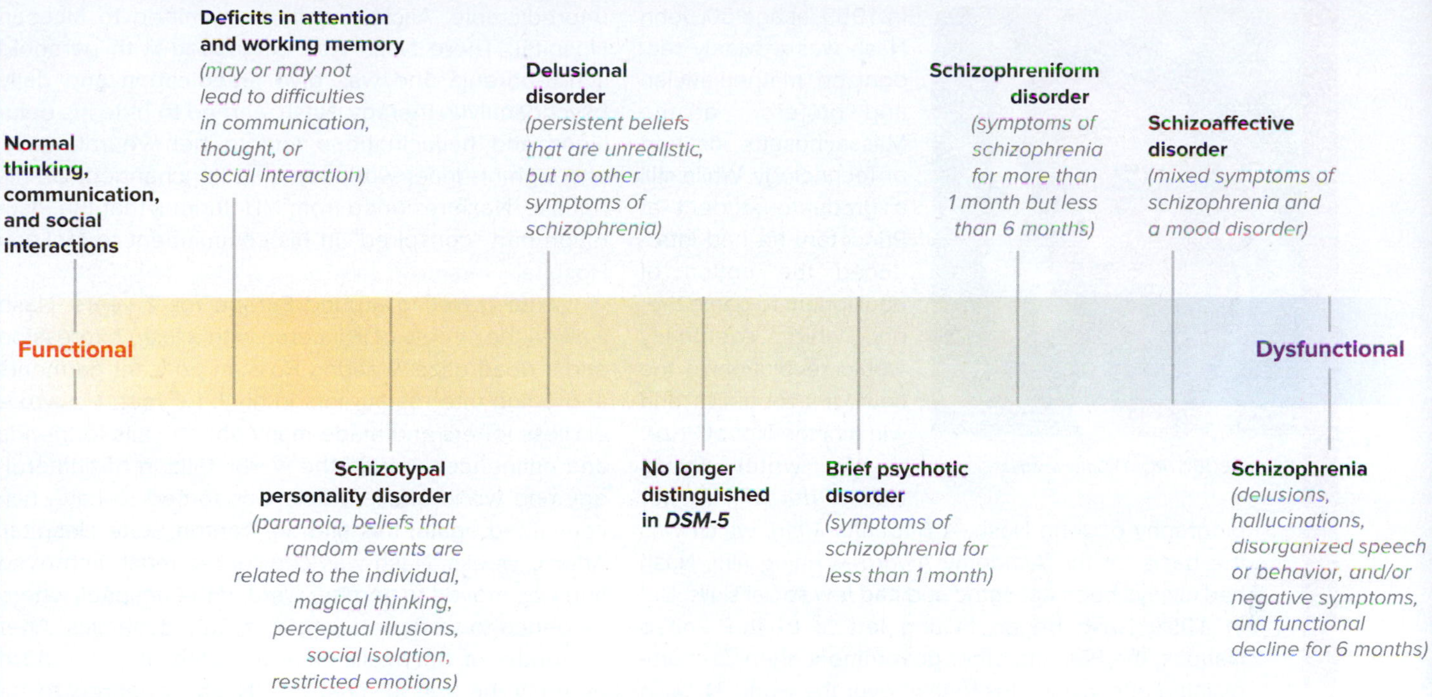

Schizophrenia is one of those disorders you've probably seen depicted in the media. People with this disorder see, hear, and feel things that aren't real (hallucinations) and may have fixed beliefs—for example, that they are going to be harmed by some organization or that their thoughts have been "removed" by some outside force (delusions). Such experiences and beliefs that are out of touch with reality are called *psychotic*. People with psychosis may speak incoherently and act in an unpredictable manner. Although you might think schizophrenia is so different from normal experience that it couldn't possibly be on a continuum, the symptoms that make up schizophrenia can appear in mild to moderate form in many people who do not meet the full criteria for any disorder (Ahmed, Buckley, & Mabe, 2012; Linscott & van Os, 2010). For example, in a study of 8,580 people from an unselected community sample, 28 percent reported having had at least one symptom characteristic of schizophrenia, such as hearing voices that no one else heard or believing that their thoughts were being controlled by someone else (Johns et al., 2004). In addition, biological family members of people with schizophrenia often show problems in attention and memory, as well as neurological abnormalities similar to those seen in schizophrenia, but less severe.

The *DSM-5* recognizes the continuum of psychotic experiences by listing schizophrenia and other psychotic disorders in order of severity. The first disorder along the continuum is *schizotypal personality disorder*, which involves moderate symptoms resembling those of schizophrenia but with a retained grasp on reality. People with this personality disorder often speak in odd and eccentric ways, have unusual beliefs or perceptions, and have difficulty relating to other people. Farther along the continuum are disorders in which people lose touch with reality. In *delusional disorder,* individuals have persistent beliefs that are contrary to reality, but they lack other symptoms of schizophrenia and often are not impaired in their functioning. Their delusions tend to be about things that are possible but untrue. In *brief psychotic disorder,* individuals have symptoms of schizophrenia for 1 month or less. In *schizophreniform* disorder, individuals have symptoms of schizophrenia for 1 to 6 months but usually resume their normal lives. *Schizoaffective disorder* presents a mixed picture of schizophrenia and major depression or mania. Other psychotic disorders, including *substance-induced psychotic disorder* and *psychotic* (or *catatonic*) *disorder associated with another medical condition,* are psychoses specifically brought on by a substance or an illness, respectively. They may be short-term or longer lasting.

The continuum of disorders illustrated here represents what the *DSM-5* calls the schizophrenia spectrum—a set of psychotic disorders that share similarities with schizophrenia but are not as severe or persistent.

Extraordinary People

John Nash, *A Beautiful Mind*

©BOB STRONG/Getty Images

In 1959, at age 30, John Nash was a widely recognized mathematician and professor at the Massachusetts Institute of Technology. While still a graduate student at Princeton, he had introduced the notion of equilibrium to game theory, which eventually would revolutionize the field of economics and win him the Nobel Prize.

As writer Sylvia Nasar details in her biography of John Nash, *A Beautiful Mind,* which was the basis for the Academy Award–winning film, Nash had always been eccentric and had few social skills. But in 1959 Nash began writing letters to the United Nations, the FBI, and other government agencies complaining of conspiracies to take over the world. He also began talking openly about his belief that powers from outer space, or perhaps from foreign governments, were communicating with him through the front page of the *New York Times*. Nash later described one of his delusions:

> I got the impression that other people at MIT were wearing red neckties so I would notice them. As I became more and more delusional, not only persons at MIT but people in Boston wearing red neckties [would seem significant to me] . . . [there was some relation to] a cryptocommunist plot. (Nasar, 1998, p. 242)

Nash's wife, Alicia, saw him become increasingly distant and cold toward her. His behavior grew more and more bizarre:

> Several times, Nash had cornered her with odd questions when they were alone, either at home or driving in the car. "Why don't you tell me about it?" he asked in an angry, agitated tone, apropos of nothing. "Tell me what you know," he demanded. (Nasar, 1998, p. 248)

In April 1959, after his threats to harm her became more severe and his behavior became increasingly unpredictable, Alicia had him committed to McLean Hospital. There Nash was diagnosed with paranoid schizophrenia and was given medication and daily psychoanalytic therapy. Nash learned to hide his delusions and hallucinations and to behave rationally, although his inner world remained unchanged. On his release, Nash resigned from MIT, furious that the institution had "conspired" in his commitment to McLean Hospital.

After traveling around Europe for 2 years, Nash walked the streets of Princeton with a fixed expression and a dead gaze, wearing Russian peasant garments and going into restaurants in his bare feet. He wrote endless letters and made many phone calls to friends and eminences around the world, talking of numerology and world affairs. Alicia was forced to have him committed again, this time in Trenton State Hospital. After 6 weeks, Nash was considered much improved and was moved to another ward of the hospital, where he began to work on a paper on fluid dynamics. After 6 months of hospitalization, a month after his 33rd birthday, he was discharged. Nash appeared to be well for some time, but then his thinking, speech, and behavior began to slip again. Eventually he ended up living with his mother in Roanoke, Virginia.

His daily rounds extended no farther than the library or the shops at the end of Grandin Road, but in his mind he traveled to the remotest reaches of the globe and lived in refugee camps, foreign embassies, prisons, and bomb shelters. At other times he felt that he was inhabiting an inferno, a purgatory, or a polluted heaven. His many identities included a Palestinian refugee, a Japanese shogun, and even, at times, a mouse (Nasar, 1998).

After his mother died, Nash returned to Princeton and lived with Alicia. During the 1970s and 1980s, his illness gradually subsided without treatment. Nash was awarded the Nobel Prize in economics for his contributions to game theory. He and Alicia lived in Princeton, where Nash worked on his mathematical theories and helped care for their son, Johnny, who obtained his PhD in mathematics and who also developed paranoid schizophrenia. Although Johnny has received the newest treatments for schizophrenia, they help only a little, and he is hospitalized frequently. His father and mother died in a traffic accident in 2015.

What must it be like to walk around with perceptions that do not map onto reality, as John Nash did during the acute phases of his illness? You might see things that do not really exist. You might hear voices that are not coming from other people but are only in your head. You might believe that the ideas you are having are being broadcast over television, so that others already know what you are thinking. If you are unable to tell the difference between what is real and what is unreal, you are experiencing **psychosis.**

Psychosis can take many forms. One of the most severe and puzzling psychotic disorders is **schizophrenia.** At times, people with schizophrenia think and communicate clearly, have an accurate view of reality, and function well in daily life. At other times, during the active phase of their illness, their thinking and speech are disorganized, they lose touch with reality, and they have difficulty caring for themselves.

Schizophrenia and other psychotic disorders exact a heavy toll, including high medical costs. In any given year, more than 90 percent of people with psychotic disorders seek treatment in a mental health facility or general medicine facility (Narrow et al., 1993). International studies show that nations spend up to 3 percent of their health care budgets treating people with psychotic disorders, and tens of billions of dollars more are lost in declines in productivity (Gustavsson et al., 2011; Jin & Mosweu, 2017). Most people who develop psychotic disorders do so in their late teenage or early adult years, when they are ready to begin contributing to society. Then the disorder strikes. Instead of pursuing their education, a career, or a family, they may need continual services, including residential care, rehabilitative therapy, subsidized income, and the help of social workers to obtain needed resources—and they may need these services for the rest of their lives, because schizophrenia tends to be chronic.

Within the United States, 1 to 2 percent of the population will develop schizophrenia at some time in their lives (Lieberman, Stroup, & Perkins, 2012; Walker, Kestler, Bollini, & Hochman, 2004). Similarly, studies around the globe find that between 0.5 and 2 percent of the general population will develop schizophrenia (Gottesman, 1991; Linscott & van Os, 2010).

E. Fuller Torrey (2013) compiled data from several sources to estimate where people with schizophrenia are living. Torrey determined that the majority of people with schizophrenia live independently or with their family. He also reported that there are almost as many people with schizophrenia in jails, prisons, and homeless shelters and on the street as there are in hospitals and nursing homes. The criminal justice system and shelters often are repositories for people with schizophrenia who do not have a family to support them or the resources to receive psychiatric help.

SYMPTOMS, DIAGNOSIS, AND COURSE

Schizophrenia is a complex disorder with psychosis as its core diagnostic symptom. *DSM-5* refers to the **schizophrenia spectrum** to reflect the fact that there are five domains of symptoms that define psychotic disorders, and their number, severity, and duration distinguish psychotic disorders from each other. People with schizophrenia may show all or just some psychotic symptoms, and the disorder can look different across individuals. The five domains of psychotic symptoms include four kinds of *positive symptoms*—namely, delusions, hallucinations, disorganized thought (speech), and disorganized or abnormal motor behavior (including catatonia)—and *negative symptoms* (e.g., restricted emotional expression or affect). People with schizophrenia also often show numerous *cognitive deficits* that research has shown are linked to declines in functioning, although cognitive symptoms are not part of the diagnostic criteria.

Positive Symptoms

The **positive symptoms** of schizophrenia include delusions, hallucinations, disorganized thought and speech, and disorganized speech. These are described as positive because they are overt expressions of unusual perceptions, thoughts, and behaviors.

Delusions

Delusions are ideas that an individual believes are true but that are highly unlikely and often simply impossible. Of course, most people occasionally hold beliefs that are likely to be wrong, such as the belief that they will win the lottery. These kinds of self-deceptions differ from delusions in at least three ways (Strauss, 1969). First, self-deceptions are at least possible, whereas delusions often are not. It is possible, if highly unlikely, that you are going to win the lottery, but it is not possible that your body is dissolving and floating into space. Second, people harboring self-deceptions may think about these beliefs occasionally, but people harboring delusions tend to be preoccupied with them. Delusional people look for evidence in support of their beliefs, attempt to convince others of these beliefs, and take actions based on them, such as filing lawsuits against the people they believe are trying to control their mind. Third, people holding self-deceptions typically acknowledge that their beliefs may be wrong, but people holding delusions often are highly resistant to arguments or compelling facts that contradict their delusions. They may view the arguments others make against their beliefs as a conspiracy to silence them and as evidence of the truth of their beliefs.

TABLE 1 Types of Delusions

These are some types of delusions that are often woven together in a complex and frightening system of beliefs.

Type of Delusion	Definition	Example
Persecutory delusion	False belief that oneself or one's loved ones are being persecuted, watched, or conspired against by others	Belief that the CIA, FBI, and local police are conspiring to catch you in a sting operation
Delusion of reference	Belief that everyday events, objects, or other people have an unusual personal significance	Belief that a newscaster is reporting on your movements, or that a random manhole cover was put there so you could see it
Grandiose delusion	False belief that one has great power, knowledge, or talent or that one is a famous and powerful person	Belief that you are Martin Luther King, Jr., reincarnated
Delusion of being controlled	Belief that one's thoughts, feelings, or behaviors are being imposed or controlled by an external force	Belief that an alien has taken over your body and is controlling your behavior
Thought broadcasting	Belief that one's thoughts are being broadcast from one's mind for others to hear	Belief that your thoughts are being transmitted via the Internet against your will
Thought insertion	Belief that another person or object is inserting thoughts into one's mind	Belief that your spouse is inserting blasphemous thoughts into your mind
Thought withdrawal	Belief that thoughts are being removed from one's mind by another person or by an object	Belief that your roommate is stealing all your thoughts while you sleep
Delusion of guilt or sin	False belief that one has committed a terrible act or is responsible for a terrible event	Belief that you have killed someone or that you are responsible for a disaster (e.g., flood)
Somatic delusion	False belief that one's appearance or part of one's body is diseased or altered	Belief that your intestines have been replaced by snakes

Table 1 lists some of the more common types of delusions. Most common are **persecutory delusions** (Bentall et al., 2008; Cannon & Kramer, 2012). People with persecutory delusions may believe they are being watched or tormented by people they know, such as their professors, or by agencies or persons in authority with whom they have never had direct contact, such as the FBI or a particular member of Congress. Pamela Spiro Wagner, a person with schizophrenia, writes about delusions she had after having a tooth filled at the dentist's office.

PROFILES

A few days later, I came to understand that amalgam is not all the dentist filled the tooth with. I realize from various signs and evidence around me that he implanted a computer microchip for reasons I can't yet determine. The computers at the drugstore across the street, programmed by the Five People, have tapped into my TV set and monitor my activities with radar. If I go out, special agents keep every one of my movements under surveillance. (Wagner & Spiro, 2005, p. 205)

Another common type of delusion is the **delusion of reference,** in which people believe that random events or comments by others are directed at them. People with delusions of reference may believe that the comments of a local politician at a rally are directed at them. John Nash believed that people in Boston were wearing red neckties so he would notice them as part of a cryptocommunist plot.

Grandiose delusions are beliefs that one is a special being or possesses special powers (Knowles, McCarthy-Jones, & Rowse, 2011). A person may believe herself a deity incarnated, or she may believe that she is the most intelligent person on earth or has discovered the cure for a disease. Another common type of delusion is **delusions of thought insertion,** or beliefs that one's thoughts are being controlled by outside forces.

Delusional beliefs can be simple and transient, such as when a person with schizophrenia believes the pain he has just experienced in his stomach is the result of someone across the room shooting a laser beam at him. However, delusional beliefs often are complex and elaborate, with the person clinging to these beliefs for long periods. The following profile illustrates how several types of delusions—grandiose delusions, persecutory delusions, delusions of reference, and delusions of thought insertion—may work together in one person's belief system. Although the passage is written by a person with schizophrenia about his own experience, he speaks of himself in the third person.

PROFILES

A drama that profoundly transformed David Zelt began at a conference on human psychology. David respected the speakers as scholars and wanted their approval of a paper he had written about telepathy. A week before the conference, David had sent his paper "On the Origins of Telepathy" to one speaker, and the other speakers had all read it. He proposed the novel scientific idea that telepathy could only be optimally studied during the process of birth. . . .

David's paper was viewed as a monumental contribution to the conference and potentially to psychology in general. If scientifically verified, his concept of telepathy, universally present at birth and measurable, might have as much influence as the basic ideas of Darwin and Freud. Each speaker focused on David. By using allusions and nonverbal communications that included pointing and glancing, each illuminated different aspects of David's contribution. Although his name was never mentioned, the speakers enticed David into feeling that he had accomplished something supernatural in writing the paper. . . . David was described as having a halo around his head, and the Second Coming was announced as forthcoming. Messianic feelings took hold of him. His mission would be to aid the poor and needy, especially in underdeveloped countries. . . .

David's sensitivity to nonverbal communication was extreme; he was adept at reading people's minds. His perceptual powers were so developed that he could not discriminate between telepathic reception and spoken language by others. He was distracted by others in a way that he had never been before. It was as if the nonverbal behavior of people interacting with him was a kind of code. Facial expressions, gestures, and postures of others often determined what he felt and thought.

Several hundred people at the conference were talking about David. He was the subject of enormous mystery, profound in his silence. Criticism, though, was often expressed by skeptics of the anticipated Second Coming. David felt the intense communication about him as torturous. He wished the talking, nonverbal behavior, and pervasive train of thoughts about him would stop. (Source: Zelt, 1981, pp. 527–531)

David's grandiose delusions were that he had discovered the source of telepathy, that all the scientists thought highly of him, and that he might be the Messiah. These grandiose delusions were accompanied by persecutory delusions—that the scientists were criticizing him because they were jealous. David's delusions of reference were that all the scientists were talking about him, both directly and indirectly. David believed that he could read others' minds. Finally, he had delusions of thought control—that the scientists were determining his feelings with their facial expressions, gestures, and postures.

Delusions also occur in other disorders. In particular, individuals with severe forms of depression or bipolar disorder (see the chapter "Mood Disorders and Suicide") often have delusions that are consistent with their moods: When they are depressed, they might believe they have committed some unforgivable sin, and when they are manic, they might believe they are a deity (Bentall et al., 2008).

Although the types of delusions we have discussed likely occur in all cultures, the specific content of delusions can differ across cultures (Suhail & Cochrane, 2002; Tateyama, Asai, Hashimoto, Bartels, & Kasper, 1998). For example, one study found that many of the delusions of British people with schizophrenia focused on being controlled by televisions, radios, and computers, but this focus was rare among Pakistani people with schizophrenia, whose delusions were more likely to involve being controlled by black magic (Suhail & Cochrane, 2002). These differences in the content of delusions probably reflect differences in the cultures' belief systems as well as differences in the people's environments. Studies comparing Japanese people and Western Europeans with schizophrenia have found that, among the Japanese, delusions of being slandered by others and delusions that others know something terrible about them are relatively common, perhaps due to the emphasis in Japanese culture on being thought well of by others. In contrast, among Germans and Austrians with schizophrenia, religious delusions of having committed a sin (e.g., "Satan orders me to pray to him; I will be punished") are relatively common, perhaps due to the influence of Christianity in Western Europe (Tateyama et al., 1993). Even within a culture, delusional content differs across time based on sociocultural factors. For example, delusional content in the United States disproportionately focused on Germans during World War II, Communists during the Cold War, and technology in recent years (Cannon & Kramer, 2012).

Some theorists argue that odd or impossible beliefs that are part of a culture's shared belief system cannot be considered delusions (Fabrega, 1993). If the people of a particular culture believe that the spirits of dead relatives watch over the living, then individuals in that culture who hold that belief are not considered delusional. However, people who hold extreme manifestations of their culture's shared belief systems are considered delusional. For example, a person in the culture described who believed that her dead relatives were causing her heart to rot would be considered delusional. *DSM-5* also changed the definition of delusions to "fixed beliefs that are not amenable to change in light of conflicting evidence" from "erroneous beliefs" (as in *DSM-IV*) because it is often highly difficult to establish the fully false nature of a belief (Coltheart, Langdon, & McKay, 2011).

Hallucinations

Have you ever had a strange perceptual experience, such as thinking you saw someone when no one was near, thinking you heard a voice talking to you, or feeling as though your body was floating through the air? In one study, 15 percent of mentally healthy college students reported sometimes hearing voices, such as their "conscience" giving them advice or two voices (usually both their own) debating a topic (Chapman, Edell, & Chapman, 1980). Subsequent studies differ widely in the estimated prevalence of such experience, but it is clear that they are not particularly uncommon (Johns et al., 2014). Most of these students probably would not be diagnosed with schizophrenia, because their auditory "hallucinations" are occasional and brief—often occurring when they are tired, stressed, or under the influence of alcohol or other drugs—and do not impair their daily functioning in any way. In addition, the hallucinations that occur due to alcohol or drug use usually are arbitrary perceptual experiences, such as flashes of light or blasts of noise.

The **hallucinations**—unreal perceptual experiences—of people with schizophrenia tend to be more frequent, persistent, complex, sometimes more bizarre, and often entwined with delusions than these college students' hallucinations. They also are not precipitated simply by sleep deprivation, stress, or drugs, as the person in the profile above describes.

The specific content of hallucinations and delusions may be influenced by culture. ©KEVIN FRAYER/AP Images

PROFILES

At one point, I would look at my co-workers and their faces would become distorted. Their teeth looked like fangs ready to devour me. Most of the time I couldn't trust myself to look at anyone for fear of being swallowed. I had no respite from the illness. Even when I tried to sleep, the demons would keep me awake, and at times I would roam the house searching for them. I was being consumed on all sides whether I was awake or asleep. I felt I was being consumed by demons. (Long, 1996)

Hallucinations can involve any of the senses. *Auditory hallucinations* (hearing voices, music, and so on) are the most common hallucinations. They may consist of a voice speaking the individual's thoughts aloud or carrying on a running commentary on the person's behavior, a collection of voices speaking about the individual in the third person, or voices issuing commands and instructions. The voices may seem to come either from inside the person's head or from somewhere outside. They often have a negative quality, criticizing or threatening the individuals or telling them to hurt themselves or others. People with schizophrenia may talk back to the voices even as they are trying to talk to people who are actually in the room with them. The second most common type of hallucination is *visual hallucinations,* often accompanied by auditory hallucinations. For example, a woman may see a figure of a man standing at her bedside, telling her she is damned and must die. An individual's hallucinations may be consistent with her delusions—the person who sees Satan telling her she must die may think that she is related to Satan.

Tactile hallucinations involve the perception that something is happening to the outside of the person's body—for example, that bugs are crawling up her back. *Somatic hallucinations* involve the perception that something is happening inside the person's body—for example, that worms are eating his intestines. These hallucinations often are very frightening (Torrey, 2013).

Hallucinations do not occur only in schizophrenia and other psychotic disorders. One study of individuals with visual hallucinations (Gauntlett-Gilbert & Kuipers, 2003) found that 60 percent were diagnosed with schizophrenia or schizoaffective disorders (described below) but that 25 percent were diagnosed with depression and 15 percent with bipolar disorder (see the chapter "Mood Disorders and Suicide").

As with delusions, the types of hallucinations people experience in different cultures appear similar, but the content of the hallucinations can be culturally specific. For example, Asians with hallucinations might see the ghosts of ancestors haunting them, but this hallucination is not common among Europeans (Browne, 2001). As with delusions, clinicians must understand hallucinations in their cultural context (Larøi et al., 2014). For example, a Puerto Rican woman might be diagnosed with schizophrenia by a European American interviewer because she believes she has special powers to anticipate events and because she describes what sound like hallucinations, such as "I see images of saints and virgins in the house. I also see the image of Jesus Christ, with the crown of thorns and bleeding." Interviewers who know Puerto Rican culture, however, might recognize this woman's beliefs and experiences as consistent with a spiritual group common in Latin America that believes in clairvoyance and religious visions (Guarnaccia, Guevara-Ramos, Gonzales, Canino, & Bird, 1992).

Disorganized Thought and Speech

The disorganized thinking of people with schizophrenia is often referred to as a **formal thought disorder.** One of the most common forms of disorganization in schizophrenia is a tendency to slip from one topic to a seemingly unrelated topic with little coherent transition, often referred to as *loose associations* or *derailment*. For example, one person with schizophrenia posted this "announcement":

> Things that relate, the town of Antelope, Oregon, Jonestown, Charlie Manson, the Hillside Strangler, the Zodiac Killer, Watergate, King's trial in L.A., and many more. In the last 7 years alone, over 23 Starwars scientists committed suicide for no apparent reason. The AIDS coverup, the conference in South America in 87 had over 1,000 doctors claim that insects can transmit it. To be able to read one's thoughts and place thoughts in one's mind without the person knowing it's being done. Realization is a reality of bioelectromagnetic control, which is thought transfer and emotional control, recording individual brain-wave frequencies of thought, sensation, and emotions.

The person who wrote this announcement saw clear connections among the events he listed in the first half of the paragraph and between these events and his concerns about mind reading and bioelectromagnetic control. However, it is difficult for us to see these connections.

A person with schizophrenia may answer questions with unrelated or barely related comments. For example, when asked why he is in the hospital, a man with schizophrenia might answer, "Spaghetti looks like worms. I really think it's worms. Gophers dig tunnels but rats build nests." At times the person's speech is so disorganized as to be totally *incoherent* to the listener, a form of speech known as "word salad." For example, "Much of abstraction has been left unsaid and undone in these products milk syrup, and others, due to economics, differentials, subsidies, bankruptcy, tools, buildings, bonds, national stocks, foundation craps, weather, trades, government in levels of breakages and fuses in electronics too all formerly states not necessarily factuated" (Maher, 1966, p. 395). The person may make up words that mean something only to him or her, known as *neologisms.* Or the person may make associations between words based on the sounds of the words rather than on the content, known as *clangs,* or may repeat the same word or statement over and over again.

Men with schizophrenia tend to show more severe deficits in language than do women with schizophrenia, possibly because language is controlled more bilaterally—that is, by both sides of the brain—in women than in men (see Mendrek & Mancini-Marie, 2016). Thus, the brain abnormalities associated with schizophrenia may not affect women's language and thought as much as they do men's because women can use both sides of their brain to compensate for deficits. In contrast, language is more localized in men, so when these areas of the brain are affected by schizophrenia, men may not be as able to compensate for the deficits.

Disorganized or Catatonic Behavior

The disorganized behavior of people with schizophrenia often frightens others. People with schizophrenia may display unpredictable and apparently untriggered agitation—suddenly shouting, swearing, or pacing rapidly. These behaviors may occur in response to hallucinations or delusions. For example, a man who believes he is being persecuted may hallucinate a frightening figure chasing him; in response, he screams and runs. Another man who believes a computer chip has been implanted under his skin to control him may pace agitatedly because no one will believe him and offer him the help he thinks he needs.

People with schizophrenia often have trouble organizing their daily routines of bathing, dressing properly, and eating regularly. Because their attention and memory are impaired, it takes all their concentration to accomplish even one simple task, such as brushing their teeth. They may engage in socially unacceptable behavior, such as public masturbation. Many are disheveled and dirty, sometimes wearing few clothes on a cold day or heavy clothes on a very hot day.

Catatonia is disorganized behavior that reflects unresponsiveness to the environment. This ranges from a lack of response to instructions (*negativism*),

A significant percentage of people with schizophrenia end up homeless and on the streets.
©McGraw-Hill Education/Christopher Kerrigan

to showing a rigid, inappropriate, or bizarre posture, to a complete lack of verbal or motor responses (e.g., *mutism*). In *catatonic excitement*, the person shows purposeless and excessive motor activity for no apparent reason. The individual may articulate a number of delusions or hallucinations or may be incoherent (Mueser & Jeste, 2008).

Negative Symptoms

You might say to yourself that all the symptoms of schizophrenia seem negative. However, specific psychotic symptoms are explicitly labeled **negative symptoms** because they involve the loss of certain qualities of the person, rather than behaviors or thoughts that the person expresses overtly (Marder & Galderisi, 2017). The core negative symptoms in schizophrenia are restricted affect and avolition/asociality. Although the positive symptoms of schizophrenia may strike you as more severe and debilitating than the negative symptoms, the presence of strong negative symptoms is more associated with poor outcome than is the presence of strong positive symptoms, in part because the negative symptoms tend to be persistent and more difficult to treat (Galderisi et al., 2012; Strauss, Harrow, Grossman, & Rosen, 2010). Negative symptoms are less prominent in other psychotic disorders.

Restricted Affect

Restricted affect refers to a severe reduction in or absence of emotional expression in people with schizophrenia. People with schizophrenia show fewer facial expressions of emotion, may avoid eye contact, and are less likely to use gestures to communicate emotional information than people without the disorder. Their tone of voice may be flat, with little change in emphasis, intonation (speech melody), rhythm, tempo, or loudness to indicate emotion or social engagement.

Do people with schizophrenia actually experience less affect than people without the disorder? Self-report questionnaires often find that people with schizophrenia report significant *anhedonia*, or a loss of the ability to experience pleasure (see Kring & Elis, 2013). Yet in laboratory studies in which individuals' responses to standardized positive stimuli (e.g., pleasant outdoor scenes or photos of food) are assessed, people with schizophrenia often report as much positive affect as people without the disorder (Minor & Cohen, 2010; Kring & Moran, 2008). Similarly, some studies have shown emotionally charged films to people with and without schizophrenia while recording their facial expressions and physiological arousal (Kring & Neale, 1996). The people with schizophrenia showed less facial responsiveness to the films than did the normal group, but they reported experiencing just as much emotion and showed even more physiological arousal. Thus, people with schizophrenia who show no emotion may be experiencing intense emotion that they cannot express. The self-reports of anhedonia by people with schizophrenia may reflect limitations in self-report questionnaires or secondary problems with depression, which is common in schizophrenia (Marder & Galderisi, 2017). Moreover, multiple studies show that even when emotion experience is intact, people with schizophrenia have trouble predicting future emotional experience, which can lead to problems in motivation and decision making (e.g., Moran & Kring, 2018).

Avolition/Asociality

Avolition is an inability to initiate or persist at common, goal-directed activities, including those at work, at school, and at home. The person is physically slowed down in his or her movements and seems unmotivated. He or she may sit around all day doing almost nothing. Personal hygiene and grooming are lacking. Avolition may be expressed as asociality, the lack of desire to interact with other people. Individuals with schizophrenia are often withdrawn and socially isolated. Some of this social isolation may be the result of the stigma of schizophrenia—many people with schizophrenia are shunned by their families and other people. Asociality should be diagnosed only when the individual has access to welcoming family and friends but shows no interest in socializing with them (Marder & Galderisi, 2017).

Cognitive Deficits

People with schizophrenia show deficits in basic cognitive processes, including attention, memory, and processing speed (Savla, Moore, & Palmer, 2008).

Compared to people without schizophrenia, they have greater difficulty focusing and maintaining their attention at will—for example, in tracking a moving object with their eyes. In addition, people with schizophrenia show deficits in working memory, the ability to hold information in memory and manipulate it (Barch & Sheffield, 2017). These deficits in attention and working memory make it difficult for people with schizophrenia to pay attention to relevant information and to suppress unwanted or irrelevant information. As a result, they find it difficult to distinguish the thoughts in their mind that are relevant to the situation at hand and to ignore stimuli in their environment that are not relevant to what they are doing. These deficits taken together may contribute to the hallucinations, delusions, disorganized thought and behavior, and avolition of people with schizophrenia (Barch & Sheffield, 2017). Information and stimulation constantly flood their consciousness, and they are unable to filter out what is irrelevant or to determine the source of the information. This makes it difficult for them to concentrate, maintain a coherent stream of thought or conversation, perform a basic task, or distinguish real from unreal. Social relationships and work performance are severely affected, and daily functioning is impaired (Bowie et al., 2008). Delusions and hallucinations may develop as individuals try to make sense of the thoughts and perceptions bombarding their consciousness (Beck & Rector, 2005; Garety & Freeman, 2013).

The immediate relatives of people with schizophrenia also show many of these cognitive deficits to a less severe degree, even if they do not show the symptoms of schizophrenia (Snitz, MacDonald, & Carter, 2006). In addition, longitudinal studies of people who develop schizophrenia suggest that many show these cognitive deficits before they develop acute symptoms of the disorder (Cannon et al., 2003), and cognitive deficits often do not improve over the course of the disorder or with treatment. Cognitive deficits may be an early marker of risk for schizophrenia and may contribute to the development of other symptoms (Gur et al., 2007) and strongly contribute to the disability of the illness (Green, Kern, Braff, & Mintz, 2000).

Diagnosis

Schizophrenia has been recognized as a psychological disorder since the early 1800s (Gottesman, 1991). In 1883, German psychiatrist Emil Kraepelin labeled the disorder *dementia praecox* (precocious dementia) because he believed that the disorder results from premature deterioration of the brain. He viewed the disorder as progressive, irreversible, and chronic (Lavretsky, 2008).

Eugen Bleuler disagreed with Kraepelin's view that this disorder develops at an early age and always leads to severe deterioration of the brain (Lavretsky, 2008). Bleuler introduced the label *schizophrenia* for this disorder, from the Greek words *schizein*, meaning "to split," and *phren*, meaning "mind." Bleuler believed that this disorder involves the splitting of usually integrated psychic functions of mental associations, thoughts, and emotions. (Bleuler did not view schizophrenia as the splitting of distinct personalities, as in dissociative identity disorder, nor do modern psychiatrists and psychologists.)

Bleuler argued that the primary problem underlying the symptoms of schizophrenia is the "breaking of associative threads"—that is, a breaking of associations among thought, language, memory, and problem solving. He argued that the attentional problems seen in schizophrenia are due to a lack of the necessary links between aspects of the mind, and that the disorganized behavior is similarly due to an inability to maintain a train of thought (Lavretsky, 2008).

The *DSM-5* states that, in order to be diagnosed with schizophrenia, an individual must show two or more symptoms of psychosis, at least one of which should be delusions, hallucinations, or disorganized speech (see Table 2). These symptoms must be consistently and acutely present for at least 1 month, referred to as the *acute phase* of the disorder. In addition, the individual must have some symptoms of the disorder for at least 6 months to a degree that impairs social or occupational functioning. These symptoms cannot be due to a medical disease, a mood disorder, or ingestion of a substance (see the chapter "Mood Disorders and Suicide"). When symptoms of catatonia are present, these symptoms are specified in the diagnosis.

During the 6 months before and after the active phase (meeting Criterion A in Table 2), the individual may show predominantly negative symptoms, with milder forms of the positive symptoms. These are often referred to as **prodromal symptoms** (before the acute phase) and **residual symptoms** (after the acute phase). When experiencing prodromal and residual symptoms, people with schizophrenia may be withdrawn and uninterested in others. They may express beliefs that are unusual but not delusional (Nelson & Yung, 2008). They may have strange perceptual experiences, such as sensing another person in the room, without reporting full-blown hallucinations. They may speak in a somewhat disorganized and tangential way but remain coherent. Their behavior may be peculiar—for example, collecting scraps of paper—but not grossly disorganized. During the prodromal phase, family members and friends may perceive the person with schizophrenia as "gradually slipping away" (Torrey, 2013). Left untreated, schizophrenia is both

TABLE 2 *DSM-5* Diagnostic Criteria for Schizophrenia

A. Two (or more) of the following, each present for a significant portion of time during a 1-month period (or less if successfully treated). At least one of these must be 1, 2, or 3:
   1. Delusions
   2. Hallucinations
   3. Disorganized speech (i.e., frequent derailment or incoherence)
   4. Grossly disorganized or catatonic behavior
   5. Negative symptoms (i.e., diminished emotional expression or avolition)

B. For a significant portion of the time since the onset of the disturbance, level of functioning in one or more major areas, such as work, interpersonal relations, or self-care, is markedly below the level achieved prior to the onset (or when the onset is in childhood or adolescence, there is failure to achieve expected level of interpersonal, academic, or occupational functioning).

C. Continuous signs of the disturbance persist for at least 6 months. This 6-month period must include at least 1 month of symptoms (or less if successfully treated) that meet Criterion A (i.e., active-phase symptoms) and may include periods of prodromal or residual symptoms. During these prodromal or residual periods, the signs of the disturbance may be manifested by only negative symptoms or by two or more symptoms listed in Criterion A present in an attenuated form (e.g., odd beliefs, unusual perceptual experiences).

D. Schizoaffective disorder and depressive or bipolar disorder with psychotic features have been ruled out because either (1) no major depressive or manic episodes have occurred concurrently with the active-phase symptoms, or (2) if mood episodes have occurred during active-phase symptoms, they have been present for a minority of the active and residual periods of the illness.

E. The disturbance is not attributable to the physiological effects of a substance (e.g., a drug of abuse, a medication) or another medical condition.

F. If there is a history of autism spectrum disorder or communication disorder of childhood onset, the additional diagnosis of schizophrenia is made only if prominent delusions or hallucinations in addition to the other required symptoms of schizophrenia are also present for at least 1 month (or less if successfully treated).

Specify if:

With catatonia

chronic and episodic; after the first onset of an acute episode, individuals may have chronic residual symptoms punctuated by relapses into acute episodes.

The odd behaviors and asociality seen in schizophrenia can resemble the symptoms of autism spectrum disorders (see the chapter "Neurodevelopmental and Neurocognitive Disorders"). To distinguish the two disorders, the diagnostic criteria for schizophrenia specify that schizophrenia can be diagnosed only if delusions and/or hallucinations are clearly present. In addition, the severe deficits in social interaction control to autism spectrum disorder begin very early in the developmental period.

The impact of schizophrenia symptoms on people's lives is enormous. One review of 37 longitudinal studies that had followed individuals for an average of 3 years after their first episode of acute schizophrenia symptoms found that only about 40 percent were employed or in school and only about 37 percent had recovered a good level of functioning (Menezes, Arenovich, & Zipursky, 2006). Difficulties in functioning are tied to the negative symptoms of schizophrenia–the lack of motivation and appropriate emotional responding–as well as to the positive symptoms. People with schizophrenia who show many negative symptoms have lower levels of educational attainment and less success holding jobs, poorer performance on cognitive tasks, and a poorer prognosis than do those with predominantly positive symptoms (Andreasen, Flaum, Swayze, Tyrell, & Arndt, 1990; Marder & Galderisi, 2017). In addition, the negative symptoms are less responsive to medication than are the positive symptoms: With medication, a person with schizophrenia may be able to overcome the hallucinations, delusions, and thought disturbances but may not be able to overcome the restricted affect and avolition. Thus, the person may remain chronically unresponsive, unmotivated, and socially isolated even when not acutely psychotic (Marder & Galderisi, 2017).

You may have heard the media refer to people with schizophrenia as "paranoid schizophrenics." Prior versions of the *DSM* listed subtypes of schizophrenia, the best known of which was paranoid schizophrenia. People with this type of schizophrenia, such as John Nash, have delusions and hallucinations that involve themes of persecution and grandiosity. Their delusions often focus on being hunted, spied on, persecuted and conspired against by others, including government agencies, the media, family and friends, and complete strangers, perhaps because they have special knowledge or powers. They may believe that anyone who disagrees with their delusions is part of the conspiracy. They can become angry, suspicious, and even violent, as John Nash did. They often do not show grossly disorganized speech or behavior. They may be lucid and articulate, relating elaborate stories of plots against them.

Although paranoia is still recognized as a common symptom in schizophrenia, the *DSM-5* dropped the *DSM-IV* subtypes of schizophrenia because evidence supporting their diagnostic stability, validity, and usefulness is not strong (Linscott, Allardyce, & van Os, 2009).

Prognosis

Schizophrenia is one of the most severe and debilitating mental disorders, and many people with the disorder suffer symptoms and impairment for many years, even with treatment (Harrow, Grossman, Jobe, & Herbener, 2005; Jobe & Harrow, 2010). Between 50 and 80 percent of people hospitalized for one episode of active-phase schizophrenia will be rehospitalized sometime in their lives (Eaton, Moortensenk, Herrman, & Freeman, 1992; Harrow et al., 2005). The life expectancy of people with schizophrenia is between 10 and 20 years shorter than that of people without schizophrenia (Laursen, Nordentoft, & Mortensen, 2014). People with schizophrenia suffer from infectious and circulatory diseases at a higher rate than do people without the disorder, due in part to underdiagnosis of physical illness, less access to care, higher rates of smoking, and being overweight due to diet, exercise, and side effects of medications (Laursen et al., 2014). Between 5 and 10 percent of people with schizophrenia commit suicide, with the highest rates among those recently diagnosed or experiencing a first psychotic episode (Laursen et al., 2014; Ventriglio et al., 2016). The following account of a woman's suicidal thoughts gives a sense of the psychological pain that many people with schizophrenia live with and wish to end through suicide.

PROFILES

I had major fantasies of suicide by decapitation and was reading up on the construction of guillotines. I had written several essays on the problem of the complete destruction of myself; I thought my inner being to be a deeply poisonous substance. The problem, as I saw it, was to kill myself, but then to get rid of my essence in such a way that it did not harm creation. (Anonymous, 1992, p. 334)

Despite the dire statistics, many people with schizophrenia do not show a progressive deterioration in functioning across the life span but instead stabilize within 5 to 10 years of their first episode, showing few or no relapses and regaining a moderately good level of functioning (Eaton et al., 1992; Eaton, Thara, Federman, & Tien, 1998; Menezes et al., 2006). For example, one 15-year study found that 41 percent of people with schizophrenia had at least one or more periods of complete recovery lasting at least 1 year (Harrow et al., 2005), and a substantial subset of patients was able to maintain functioning even without antipsychotic medication (Harrow & Jobe, 2013).

Gender and Age Factors

Women with schizophrenia tend to have a better prognosis than men with the disorder (Seeman, 2008). For example, in a 20-year study of people with schizophrenia, 61 percent of the women had periods of recovery, compared to 41 percent of the men (Grossman, Harrow, Rosen, Faull, & Strauss, 2008). Women are hospitalized less often than men and for briefer periods of time, show milder negative symptoms between periods of active-phase symptoms, and have better social adjustment when they are not psychotic (Grossman et al., 2008). The reasons for these gender differences are not entirely clear. Women diagnosed with schizophrenia tend to have better prior histories than men: They are more likely to have graduated from high school or college, to have married and had children, and to have developed good social skills (Seeman, 2008). This may be, in part, because the onset of schizophrenia in women tends to be in the late twenties or early thirties, whereas men more often develop schizophrenia in their late teens or early twenties. Women with schizophrenia also show fewer cognitive deficits than men with the disorder (Mendrek & Mancini-Marie, 2016). All these factors lead to expectations of a better prognosis for women but do not entirely explain it (Grossman et al., 2008).

Estrogen may affect the regulation of dopamine, a neurotransmitter implicated in schizophrenia, in ways that are protective for women (Mendrek & Mancini-Marie, 2016; Seeman, 2008). Some of the sex differences, particularly in cognitive deficits, may also be due to normal sex differences in the brain. The pace of prenatal brain development, which is hormonally regulated, is slower in males than in females and may place males at higher risk than females for abnormal brain development. Exposure to toxins and illnesses in utero increases the risk for abnormal brain development and the development of schizophrenia. Several studies suggest that males with schizophrenia show greater abnormalities in brain structure and functioning than do females with schizophrenia (Mendrek & Mancini-Marie, 2016).

In both men and women with schizophrenia, functioning seems to improve with age (Jablensky, 2000; Harrow et al., 2005). Why? Perhaps they find treatments that help them stabilize, or maybe they and their families learn to recognize the early symptoms of a relapse and seek earlier treatment before the symptoms become acute (Torrey, 2013). Alternatively, the aging of the brain might somehow reduce the likelihood of new episodes of schizophrenia. Some think this might be related to a reduction in dopamine levels in the brain with age; as we will discuss, high dopamine levels have been implicated in schizophrenia.

Sociocultural Factors

Culture appears to play a strong role in the course of schizophrenia. Schizophrenia tends to have a more benign course in developing countries than in developed countries (Hopper, 2008; Jablensky, 2000). Cross-national studies find that persons who develop schizophrenia in countries such as India, Nigeria, and Colombia are less disabled by the disorder in the long term than are persons who develop schizophrenia in countries such as Great Britain, Denmark, and the United States (Figure 1; Hopper, 2008; Jablensky, 2000).

The social environment of people with schizophrenia in developing countries may facilitate adaptation and recovery better than the social environment of people with schizophrenia in developed countries (Hopper, 2008; Larøi et al., 2014). In developing countries, broader and closer family networks surround people with schizophrenia (Karno & Jenkins, 1993; Myers, 2010). This ensures that no one person is solely responsible for the care of a person with schizophrenia, a situation that is risky for both the person with schizophrenia and the caregiver. Families in some developing countries also score lower on measures of hostility, criticism, and overinvolvement than do families in some developed countries (Hooley, 2007). This may help lower relapse rates for their family members with schizophrenia.

Whatever the reasons for variations in the course of schizophrenia across cultures and between men and women, the conventional wisdom that schizophrenia is inevitably a progressive disorder, marked by more deterioration with time, has been replaced by new evidence that many people with schizophrenia achieve a good level of functioning over time.

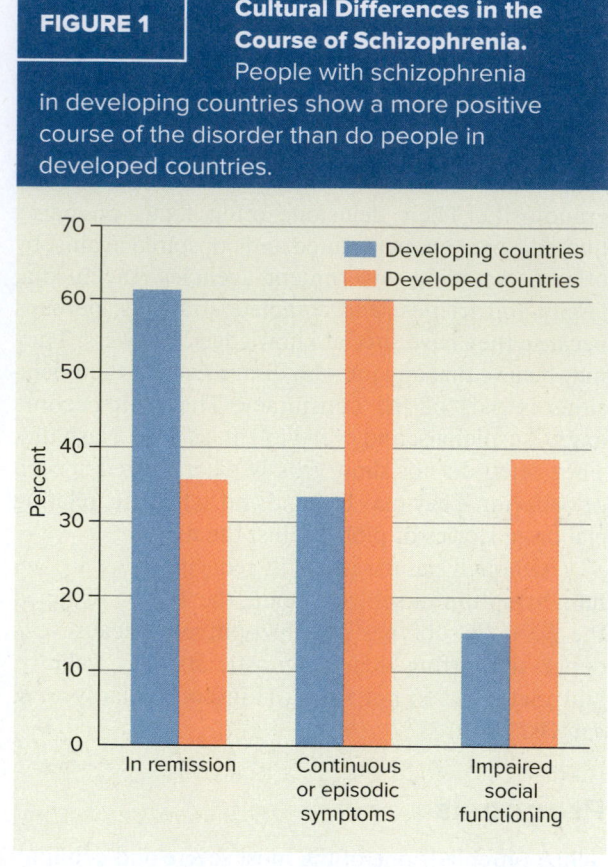

FIGURE 1 **Cultural Differences in the Course of Schizophrenia.** People with schizophrenia in developing countries show a more positive course of the disorder than do people in developed countries.

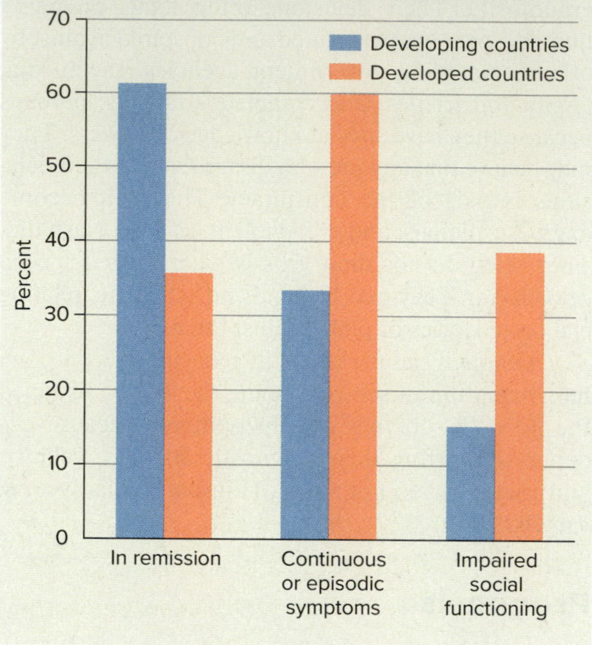

Other Psychotic Disorders

The *DSM-5* recognizes other psychotic disorders that share features with schizophrenia. These disorders fall along a continuum of severity. Schizophrenia has the worst long-term outcome of these disorders, followed by schizoaffective disorder, schizophreniform disorder, and the other psychotic disorders shown in the chapter-opening feature, "Schizophrenia Spectrum and Other Psychotic Disorders Along the Continuum." **Schizoaffective disorder** is a mix of schizophrenia and a mood disorder (Table 3). People with schizoaffective disorder simultaneously experience psychotic symptoms (delusions, hallucinations, disorganized speech and behavior, and/or negative symptoms) and prominent mood symptoms meeting the criteria for a major depressive or manic episode (see the chapter "Mood Disorders and Suicide"). Mood symptoms must be present for the majority of the period of illness. Unlike mood disorders with psychotic features, schizoaffective disorder requires at least 2 weeks of hallucinations or delusions without mood symptoms.

TABLE 3 *DSM-5* Diagnostic Criteria for Schizoaffective Disorder

A. An uninterrupted period of illness during which there is a major mood episode (major depressive or manic) current with Criterion A of schizophrenia. Note: The major depressive episode must include Criterion A1: Depressed mood.

B. Delusions or hallucinations for 2 or more weeks in the absence of a major mood episode (depressive or manic) during the lifetime duration of the illness.

C. Symptoms that meet criteria for a major mood episode are present for the majority of the total duration of the active and residual portions of the illness.

D. The disturbance is not attributable to the effects of a substance (e.g., a drug of abuse, a medication) or another medical condition.

Specify type:

Bipolar type: A manic episode is part of the presentation. Major depressive episodes may also occur.

Depressive type: If only major depressive episodes are part of the presentation.

Specify if:

With catatonia

TABLE 4 *DSM-5* Diagnostic Criteria for Schizophreniform Disorder

A. Criteria A, D, and E of Schizophrenia are met (see Table 2).

B. An episode of the disorder lasts at least 1 month but less than 6 months. When the diagnosis must be made without waiting for recovery, it should be qualified as "provisional."

Specify if:

With good prognostic features: as evidenced by two or more of the following:

1. Onset of prominent psychotic symptoms within 4 weeks of the first noticeable change in usual behavior or functioning
2. Confusion or perplexity
3. Good premorbid social and occupational functioning
4. Absence of blunted or flat affect

Without good prognostic features

With catatonia

The diagnosis of **schizophreniform disorder** requires that individuals meet Criteria A, D, and E for schizophrenia but show symptoms that last only 1 to 6 months (Table 4). The 1- to 6-month duration requirement is intermediate between that for brief psychotic disorder (discussed next) and schizophrenia. Although functional impairments may be present, they are not necessary for a diagnosis of schizophreniform disorder. Individuals with this disorder who have a good prognosis have a quick onset of symptoms, functioned well previously, and experience confusion but not blunted or flat affect. Individuals who do not show two or more of these features are said to be without good prognostic features. The majority (about two-thirds) of individuals with schizophreniform disorder will eventually receive a diagnosis of schizophrenia or schizoaffective disorder (American Psychiatric Association, 2013).

Individuals with **brief psychotic disorder** show a sudden onset of delusions, hallucinations, disorganized speech, and/or disorganized behavior. However, the episode lasts only for 1 day to 1 month, after which

TABLE 5 *DSM-5* Diagnostic Criteria for Brief Psychotic Disorder

A. Presence of one (or more) of the following symptoms. At least one of these must be (1), (2), or (3):
 1. Delusions
 2. Hallucinations
 3. Disorganized speech (e.g., frequent derailment or incoherence)
 4. Grossly disorganized or catatonic behavior

 Note: Do not include a symptom if it is a culturally sanctioned response.

B. Duration of an episode of the disturbance is at least 1 day but less than 1 month, with eventual full return to premorbid level of functioning.

C. The disturbance is not better explained by major depressive or bipolar disorder with psychotic features or another psychotic disorder such as schizophrenia or catatonia, and is not attributable to the physiological effects of a substance (e.g., substance of abuse, a medication) or another medical condition.

Specify if:

With marked stressor(s) (brief reactive psychosis): if symptoms occur in response to events that, singly or together, would be markedly stressful to almost anyone in similar circumstances in the individual's culture.

Without marked stressor(s): if symptoms do not occur in response to events that, singly or together, would be markedly stressful to almost anyone in similar circumstances in the individual's culture.

With postpartum onset: if onset is during pregnancy or within 4 weeks postpartum

With catatonia

the symptoms completely remit (Table 5). Symptoms sometimes emerge after a major stressor, such as being in an accident. At other times, no stressor is apparent. Approximately 1 in 10,000 women experience brief psychotic episodes shortly after giving birth (Steiner, Dunn, & Born, 2003; VanderKruik et al., 2017). Although risk of relapse is high, most people show an excellent outcome.

Individuals with **delusional disorder** (Table 6) have delusions lasting at least 1 month regarding situations that occur in real life, such as being followed, being poisoned, being deceived by a spouse, or having a disease. Unlike schizophrenia, they do not show any other psychotic symptoms. Other than the behaviors that may follow from their delusions, they do not act oddly or have difficulty functioning. In the general population, delusional disorder may be rare, with an estimated lifetime prevalence of 0.2 percent. It appears to affect females more than males. Onset tends to be later in life than most disorders, with an average age of first admission to a psychiatric facility of 40 to 49 (Munro, 1999).

Finally, people with **schizotypal personality disorder** (Table 7) have a lifelong pattern of significant oddities in their self-concept, their ways of relating to others, and their thinking and behavior. They do not have a strong and independent sense of self and may have trouble setting realistic or clear goals. Their emotional expression may be restricted, as in schizophrenia, or odd for the circumstances. They may have few close relationships and trouble understanding the behaviors of others. They tend to perceive other people as deceitful and hostile and may be socially anxious and isolated because of their suspiciousness. People with schizotypal personality disorder think and behave in ways that are very odd, although they maintain their grasp on reality. They may believe that random events or circumstances are related to them. For example, they may think it highly significant that a fire occurred in a store in which they had shopped only yesterday. Their perceptions are also odd—for example, thinking they see people in the patterns of wallpaper. They may be easily distracted or fixate on an object for long periods of time, lost in thought or fantasy. On neuropsychological tests (see the chapter "Assessing and Diagnosing Abnormality"), people with schizotypal personality disorder show deficits in working memory, learning, and recall similar to, but less severe than, those shown by people with schizophrenia (Barch & Sheffield, 2017). They also share some of the same genetic traits and neurological abnormalities of people with schizophrenia (Cannon, van Erp, & Glahn, 2002). Some people diagnosed with schizotypal personality disorder have episodes symptomatic of brief psychotic disorder, and some eventually develop the full syndrome of schizophrenia. Although

TABLE 6 *DSM-5* Diagnostic Criteria for Delusional Disorder

A. The presence of one (or more) delusions with a duration of 1 month or longer.

B. Criterion A of schizophrenia has never been met. Note: Hallucinations, if present, are not prominent and are related to the delusional theme (e.g., the sensation of being infested with insects associated with delusions of infestation).

C. Apart from the impact of the delusion(s) or its ramifications, functioning is not markedly impaired, and behavior is not obviously bizarre or odd.

D. If manic or major depressive episodes have occurred, these have been brief relative to the duration of the delusional periods.

E. The disturbance is not attributable to the physiological effects of a substance or another medical condition and is not better explained by another mental disorder, such as body dysmorphic disorder or obsessive-compulsive disorder.

Specify whether:

Erotomanic type: The central theme of the delusion is that another person is in love with the individual.

Grandiose type: The central theme of the delusion is the conviction of having some great (but unrecognized) talent or insight or having made some important discovery.

Jealous type: The central theme of the delusion is that one's spouse or lover is unfaithful.

Persecutory type: The central theme of the delusion is the belief that one is being conspired against, cheated, spied on, followed, poisoned or drugged, maliciously maligned, harassed, or obstructed in the pursuit of long-term goals.

Somatic type: The central theme of the delusion involves bodily functions or sensations.

Mixed type: No one delusional theme predominates.

Unspecified type: The dominant delusional belief cannot be clearly determined or is not described in the specific types (e.g., referential delusions without a prominent persecutory or grandiose theme).

Specify if:

With bizarre content: If delusions are clearly implausible, not understandable, and not derived from ordinary life experiences (e.g., delusional belief that one's internal organs have been removed by a stranger and replaced with someone else's organs without leaving any wounds or scars).

TABLE 7 Diagnostic Criteria for Schizotypal Personality Disorder

A. A pervasive pattern of social and interpersonal deficits marked by acute discomfort with, and reduced capacity for, close relationships as well as by cognitive or perceptual distortions and eccentricities of behavior, beginning by early adulthood and present in a variety of contexts, as indicated by five or more of the following:

1. Ideas of reference (excluding delusions of reference).
2. Odd beliefs or magical thinking that influences behavior and is inconsistent with subcultural norms (e.g., superstitiousness, belief in clairvoyance, telepathy, or "sixth sense"; in children and adolescents, bizarre fantasies or preoccupations).
3. Unusual perceptual experiences, including bodily illusions.
4. Odd thinking and speech (e.g., vague, circumstantial, metaphorical, overelaborate, or stereotyped).
5. Suspiciousness or paranoid ideation.
6. Inappropriate or constricted affect.
7. Behavior or appearance that is odd, eccentric, or peculiar.
8. Lack of close friends or confidants other than first-degree relatives.
9. Excessive social anxiety that does not diminish with familiarity and tends to be associated with paranoid fears rather than negative judgments about self.

B. Does not occur exclusively during the course of schizophrenia, a bipolar disorder or depressive disorder with psychotic features, another psychotic disorder, or autism spectrum disorder. Note: If criteria are met prior to the onset of schizophrenia, add "premorbid," e.g., "schizotypal personality disorder (premorbid)."

SHADES OF GRAY

Read the following case study (adapted from Andreasen, 1998).

Jeff, age 19, had been a normal but somewhat shy kid until about 2 years ago. On a high school trip to France, he had become acutely anxious and returned home early. After that, Jeff began to withdraw. He no longer wanted to be with friends, and he dropped off the football team. His grades plummeted from his usual A's and B's, but he was able to graduate. His parents commented that a gradual but dramatic personality change had taken place over the past 2 years, and he just seemed "empty." All their efforts to encourage him, to help him find new directions, or to reassess his goals seemed to have led nowhere.

Jeff had begun coursework in college but was unable to study and dropped out. He got a job delivering pizzas but couldn't even find his way around town—the town he had grown up in—to deliver the pizzas to the right addresses. His parents reported that he seemed suspicious much of the time and that he had no desire to be around friends or peers. Jeff didn't seem to care about anything. His grooming and hygiene had deteriorated. The apartment he rented was filthy and full of decaying food and dirty laundry. He had no history of drug abuse of any type.

When interviewed by a psychiatrist, Jeff said he did not feel sad or blue, just "empty." Jeff reported no experiences of hearing voices when no one was around, seeing things that other people can't see, or feeling like he'd lost control of his mind or body.

Does Jeff have schizophrenia or one of the disorders along the schizophrenia spectrum? (Discussion appears at the end of this chapter.)

schizotypal personality disorder falls below the threshold required for a diagnosis of a psychotic disorder, *DSM-5* recognizes it as part of the schizophrenia spectrum of disorders (Heckers et al., 2013). The *DSM-5* also considers it to be a personality disorder. More information about schizotypal personality disorder is presented in the chapter "Personality Disorders."

BIOLOGICAL THEORIES

Given the similarity in the symptoms and prevalence of schizophrenia across cultures and time, biological factors have long been thought key to its development. There are several biological theories of schizophrenia. First, evidence indicates genetic transmission, although genetics does not fully explain who develops this disorder. Second, some people with schizophrenia show structural and functional abnormalities in specific areas of the brain, which may contribute to the disorder. Third, many people with schizophrenia have a history of birth complications or prenatal exposure to viruses, which may affect brain development. Fourth, neurotransmitter theories hold that excess levels of dopamine contribute to schizophrenia; newer research also focuses on the neurotransmitters serotonin, GABA, and glutamate.

Genetic Contributors to Schizophrenia

Family, twin, and adoption studies all indicate the presence of a genetic component to the transmission of schizophrenia (Allen et al., 2008). Many scientists believe that no single genetic abnormality accounts for this complex disorder. Indeed, it may be that different genes are responsible for different symptoms of the disorder; for example, one set of genes may contribute to the positive symptoms, and a different set of genes may contribute to the negative symptoms (Gur et al., 2007).

Family Studies

Psychologist Irving Gottesman compiled more than 40 studies to determine the lifetime risk of developing schizophrenia for people with various familial relationships to a person with schizophrenia (Gottesman & Shields, 1976). His conclusions are summarized in Figure 2. The children of two parents with schizophrenia and monozygotic (identical) twins of people with schizophrenia share the greatest number of genes with people with schizophrenia. As the top bars of the graph in Figure 2 show, these individuals also have the greatest risk of developing schizophrenia at some time in their lives.

As the genetic similarity to a person with schizophrenia decreases, an individual's risk of developing schizophrenia also decreases. Thus, a first-degree relative of a person with schizophrenia (e.g., a nontwin sibling), who shares about 50 percent of genes with the person with schizophrenia, has about a 10 percent chance of developing the disorder. In contrast, a niece or nephew of a person with schizophrenia, who shares about 25 percent of genes with the person with schizophrenia, has only a 3 percent chance of developing the disorder. The general population has a risk of developing the disorder of about 1 to 2 percent. The relationship between an individual's degree of genetic similarity to a schizophrenic relative and the individual's own risk of developing schizophrenia strongly suggests that genes play a role in its development.

Having a biological relative with schizophrenia increases an individual's risk for the disorder but does not mean that the individual will develop it. For example, of all children who have one parent with schizophrenia, 87 percent will not develop the disorder. Also, 63 percent of people with schizophrenia have no first- or second-degree relative with the disorder (Gottesman & Erlenmeyer-Kimling, 2001). Interestingly, family members of people with schizophrenia are at elevated risk of having bipolar disorder—and vice versa—suggesting shared genetic factors (Lichtenstein et al., 2009).

Adoption Studies

Even when the child of a person with schizophrenia develops the disorder, it may not be due to genetics. A home with a parent with schizophrenia is likely to be a stressful environment. When a parent is psychotic, the child may be exposed to illogical thought, mood swings, and chaotic behavior. Even when the parent is not actively psychotic, the residual negative symptoms of schizophrenia—restriction of affect, lack of motivation, and disorganization—may impair the parent's child-care skills.

Several adoption studies addressing the question of genes versus environment indicate that genetics plays an important role in schizophrenia. For example, Seymour Kety and colleagues (1994) found that the biological relatives of adoptees with schizophrenia were 10 times more likely to have a diagnosis of schizophrenia than were the biological relatives of adoptees who did not have schizophrenia. In contrast, the adoptive relatives of adoptees with schizophrenia showed no increased risk for the disorder.

In one of the largest adoption studies, Pekka Tienari (Tienari et al., 2003; Tienari, Wahlberg, & Wynne, 2006) tracked 155 offspring of mothers with schizophrenia and 185 children of mothers without schizophrenia; all the children had been given up for adoption early in life. Approximately 10 percent of the children whose biological mother had schizophrenia developed schizophrenia or another psychotic disorder, compared to about 1 percent of the children whose biological mother did not have schizophrenia.

Twin Studies

Figure 2 also shows the compiled results of several twin studies of schizophrenia. The results show a concordance rate for monozygotic (identical) twins of 46 percent, and a concordance rate for dizygotic (fraternal) twins of 14 percent. A study that assessed all twins born in Finland between 1940 and 1957 using statistical modeling estimated that 83 percent of the variation in schizophrenia is due to genetic factors (Cannon, Kapiro, Lonnqvist, Huttunen, & Koskenvuo, 1998).

Even when a person carries a genetic risk for schizophrenia, however, many other biological and

FIGURE 2 **Risk for Schizophrenia and Genetic Relatedness.** One's risk of developing schizophrenia decreases substantially as one's genetic relationship to a person with schizophrenia becomes more distant.

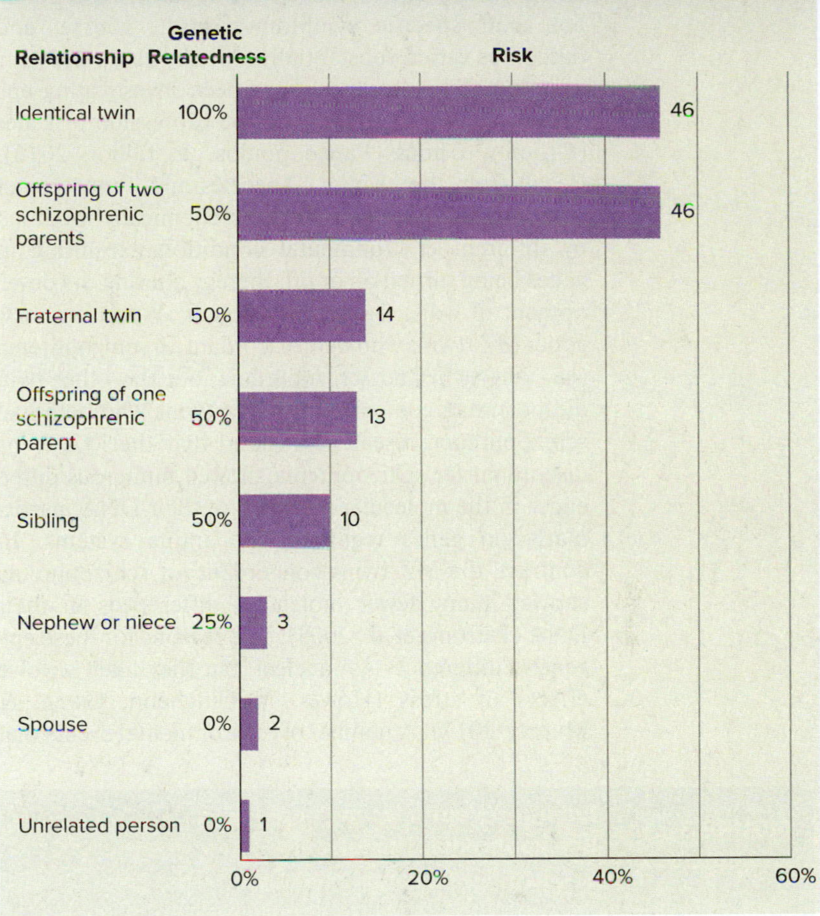

The Genain quadruplets all later developed schizophrenia, but the specific forms of the disorder differed among the sisters.
©AP Images

environmental factors may influence whether and how he or she manifests the disorder. The classic illustration of this point is the story of the Genain quadruplets, who shared the same genes and family environment. All of them developed schizophrenia, but their specific symptoms, onset, course, and outcomes varied substantially (Mirsky et al., 2000).

Recently researchers have been investigating epigenetic factors that influence the expression of genes (Cromby, Chung, Papadopoulos, & Talbot, 2016). Recall from the chapter "Theories and Treatment of Abnormality" that DNA can be chemically modified by different environmental conditions, resulting in genes being turned on or off, thereby altering the development of cells, tissues, and organs. When monozygotic (MZ) twins who were discordant for schizophrenia (i.e., one twin had schizophrenia, but the other twin did not) were compared with MZ twins who both had schizophrenia, researchers found that the MZ twins discordant for schizophrenia showed numerous differences in the molecular structure of their DNA, particularly on genes regulating dopamine systems. In contrast, the MZ twins concordant for schizophrenia showed many fewer molecular differences in their DNA (Petronis et al., 2003). The reasons for these epigenetic differences are unclear, but they likely involve effects of stress (Howes, McCutcheon, Owen, & Murray, 2017). A number of environmental events that could affect development in utero appear to increase the risk for schizophrenia. Some of these events might alter genes that guide brain development (Diwadkar, Bustamante, Rai, & Uddin, 2014).

FIGURE 3 **Enlarged Ventricles in People with Schizophrenia.** The left panel shows the brain of a healthy male. The right panel shows the brain of his identical twin, who has schizophrenia. Notice the larger ventricles (blue spaces midbrain) in the brain of the twin with schizophrenia.

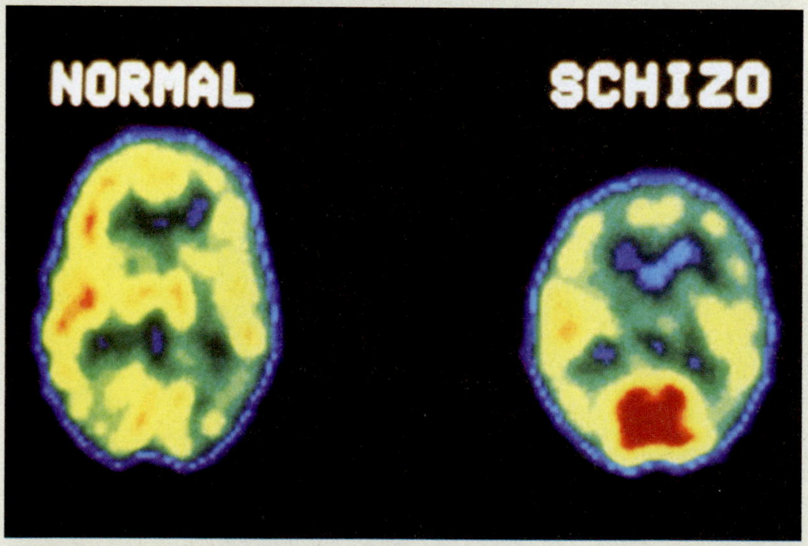

©SCIENCE SOURCE/Science Source

Structural and Functional Brain Abnormalities

Clinicians and researchers have long believed that the brains of people with schizophrenia differ fundamentally from those of people without schizophrenia. With the development of technologies such as positron-emission tomography (PET scans), computerized axial tomography (CAT scans), and magnetic resonance imaging (MRI), scientists have been able to examine in detail the structure and functioning of the brain. These new technologies have shown major structural and functional deficits in the brains of some people with schizophrenia (Barch & Sheffield, 2017; Karlsgodt, Sun, & Cannon, 2010). Most theorists think of schizophrenia as a neurodevelopmental disorder, in which a variety of factors lead to abnormal development of the brain in the uterus and early in life.

The most consistent finding is a gross reduction in gray matter in the cortex of people with schizophrenia, particularly in the medial, temporal, superior temporal, and prefrontal areas (Figure 3; Karlsgodt et al., 2010). In addition, people who are at risk for schizophrenia because of a family history but have not yet developed the disorder show abnormal activity in the prefrontal cortex (Lawrie, McIntosh, Hall, Owens, & Johnstone, 2008). The prefrontal cortex is important in language, emotional expression, planning, and carrying out plans. The prefrontal cortex connects to all other cortical regions, as well as to the limbic system, which is involved in emotion and cognition, and to the basal ganglia, which is involved in motor movement. Thus, it seems logical that a person with an unusually small or inactive prefrontal cortex would show the deficits in cognition, emotion, and social interactions seen with schizophrenia, such as difficulty holding a conversation, responding appropriately to social situations, and carrying out tasks.

The prefrontal cortex undergoes major development in the years from adolescence to young adulthood (Galván & Tottenham, 2016). Aberrations in the normal development of the prefrontal cortex during mid- to late adolescence may help explain the emergence of the disorder during this period (Cannon et al., 2003). Neuroimaging studies of individuals who developed schizophrenia in adolescence show significant structural changes across the cortex, particularly in the prefrontal cortex, from before to after development of symptoms (Figure 3; Sun et al., 2009).

The hippocampus is another brain area that consistently differs from the norm in people with schizophrenia (Karlsgodt et al., 2010). The hippocampus plays a critical role in the formation of long-term memories. In some studies, people with schizophrenia show abnormal hippocampal activation when doing tasks that require them to encode information for storage in their memory or to retrieve information from memory (Barch, Csernansky, Conturo, & Snyder, 2002; Schacter, Chiao, & Mitchell, 2003). Other studies show that people with schizophrenia have abnormalities in the volume and shape of their hippocampus and at the cellular level (Knable, Barci, Webster, Meador-Woodruff, & Torrey, 2004; Lieberman et al., 2018). Similar abnormalities in the hippocampus are found in the first-degree relatives of people with schizophrenia (Seidman et al., 2002).

In addition to reductions in gray matter, the brains of people with schizophrenia show reductions and abnormalities in white matter (material that forms the connections between areas of the brain), particularly in areas associated with working memory (Karlsgodt et al., 2008). These white-matter abnormalities are present in individuals before they develop overt symptoms of schizophrenia, suggesting that they are early signs of the disorder rather than consequences of the disease process (Karlsgodt, Niendam, Bearden, & Cannon, 2009). White-matter abnormalities can impair the ability of various areas of the brain to work together, which could lead to the severe deficits seen in schizophrenia.

Along with these changes in the structure and activity of cortical and other brain areas, people with schizophrenia show enlargement of ventricles, fluid-filled spaces in the brain (Lawrie et al., 2008). Enlarged ventricles suggest atrophy, or deterioration, in other brain tissue. People with schizophrenia with enlarged ventricles tend to show social, emotional, and behavioral deficits long before they develop the core symptoms of schizophrenia. They also tend to have more severe symptoms than other people with schizophrenia and are less responsive to medication. These characteristics suggest gross alterations in the functioning of the brain, which are difficult to alleviate with treatment.

Damage to the Developing Brain

What causes the neuroanatomical abnormalities in schizophrenia? Genetic factors and epigenetic factors seem to play a major role (Howes et al., 2017). In addition, these abnormalities may be tied to birth complications, traumatic brain injury, viral infections, nutritional deficiencies, and deficiencies in cognitive stimulation (Barch & Sheffield, 2017; Howes & Murray, 2014).

Birth Complications Serious prenatal and birth difficulties are more frequent in the histories of people with schizophrenia than in those of people without schizophrenia and may play a role in the development of neurological difficulties (Cannon et al., 2003; Kotlicka-Antczak et al., 2017). Moreover, a longitudinal study of individuals at high risk for schizophrenia found that those with a history of obstetric difficulties were more likely to develop the full syndrome of schizophrenia than were those without such a history (Mittal et al., 2009).

One type of birth complication that may be especially important in neurological development is perinatal hypoxia (oxygen deprivation at birth or in the few weeks before or after birth) (Goldstein et al., 2000). As many as 30 percent of people with schizophrenia have a history of perinatal hypoxia. A prospective study of 9,236 people born in Philadelphia between 1959 and 1966 found that the odds of an adult diagnosis of schizophrenia increased in direct proportion to the degree of perinatal hypoxia (Cannon, Rosso, Bearden, Sanchez, & Hadley, 1999). The authors of this study suggest that the effects of oxygen deprivation interact with a genetic vulnerability to schizophrenia, resulting in a person's developing the disorder. Most people experiencing oxygen deprivation prenatally or at birth do not develop schizophrenia, however.

Prenatal Viral Exposure Epidemiological studies have shown high rates of schizophrenia among persons whose mothers were exposed to viral infections while pregnant (Cannon et al., 2003). For example, people whose mothers were exposed to the influenza epidemic that swept Helsinki, Finland, in 1957 were significantly more likely to develop schizophrenia than were people whose mothers were not exposed. The link was particularly strong among people whose mothers were exposed during the second trimester of pregnancy (Mednick, Machon, Huttunen, & Bonett, 1988; Mednick et al., 1998). The second trimester is a crucial period for the development of the central nervous system of the fetus. Disruption in this phase of brain development could cause the major structural deficits found in the brains of some people with schizophrenia. Interestingly, people with schizophrenia are somewhat more likely to be born in the spring months than at other times of the year (Ellman & Cannon, 2008). Pregnant women may be more likely to contract influenza and other viruses at critical phases of fetal development if they are pregnant during the fall and winter.

Other types of prenatal insults also seem to increase risk for schizophrenia. For example, individuals whose mothers were pregnant during the famine in China from 1959 to 1961 had a twofold risk of developing schizophrenia compared to individuals whose mothers were not pregnant during times of famine (Xu et al., 2009). Another study found that individuals whose mothers had been exposed to the herpes simplex virus while pregnant were more likely to have a psychotic disorder, most often schizophrenia (Buka et al., 2008). The authors of this study suggest that viral infections prompt a mother's immune system to be more active, which can negatively impact the development of brain cells and dopamine systems in the fetus (see also Kneeland & Fatemi, 2013).

Neurotransmitters

The neurotransmitter dopamine has long been thought to play a role in schizophrenia (Howes, McCutcheon, & Stone, 2015). The original dopamine theory was that the symptoms of schizophrenia are caused by excess levels of dopamine in the brain, particularly in the prefrontal cortex and the limbic system.

This theory was supported by several lines of evidence. First, drugs that tend to reduce the symptoms of schizophrenia, the **phenothiazines** or **neuroleptics,** block the reuptake of dopamine, reducing the functional level in the brain. Second, drugs that increase the functional level of dopamine in the brain, such as amphetamines, tend to increase the incidence of the positive symptoms of schizophrenia (Davis, Kahn, Ko, & Davidson, 1991). Third, neuroimaging studies suggest the presence of more receptors for dopamine and higher levels of dopamine in some areas of the brain in people with schizophrenia than in people without the disorder.

The original dopamine theory of schizophrenia proved too simple (Davis et al., 1991; Howes et al., 2015). Many people with schizophrenia do not respond to the phenothiazines. In addition, even people with schizophrenia who do respond to the phenothiazines tend to experience more relief from positive symptoms (hallucinations and delusions) than from negative symptoms. This suggests that simple dopamine depletion does not fully explain the negative symptoms. Furthermore, levels of dopamine change relatively soon after drug therapy begins, while changes in symptoms often take longer. This suggests that the level of dopamine in the brain is not the only determinant of symptoms (Hengartner & Moncrieff, 2018).

Kenneth Davis and colleagues (1991) proposed a revised theory suggesting that different types of dopamine receptors and different levels of dopamine in various areas of the brain can account for the symptoms of schizophrenia. First, there may be excess dopamine activity in the **mesolimbic pathway,** a subcortical part of the brain involved in the processing of salience and reward (Figure 4). Abnormal functioning in this area of the brain may lead individuals to attribute salience to otherwise innocuous stimuli, contributing to hallucinations and delusions and to deficits in motivation (Howes et al., 2015). Newer drugs in the treatment of schizophrenia, the *atypical antipsychotics,* may work to reduce the symptoms of schizophrenia by binding to a specific type of dopamine receptor common in the mesolimbic system, blocking the action of dopamine.

Second, there may be unusually low dopamine activity in the prefrontal area of the brain, which is involved in attention, motivation, and the organization of behavior (Barch & Sheffield, 2017; Howes et al., 2015). Low dopamine activity here may lead to the negative symptoms of schizophrenia: lack of motivation, inability to care for oneself in daily functions, and the restriction of affect. This idea is consistent with the evidence associating structural and functional abnormalities in this part of the brain with the negative symptoms of schizophrenia. It also helps explain why the phenothiazines, which reduce dopamine activity, do not effectively alleviate the negative symptoms.

Although the revised version of the dopamine hypothesis was proposed over two decades ago, many of its components continue to be supported (see Howes et al., 2015). Dysregulation of dopamine systems seem to be involved in multiple forms of psychosis (and mood disorders), not just in schizophrenia.

Other neurotransmitters also play an important role in schizophrenia. Serotonin neurons regulate dopamine neurons in the mesolimbic system, and some of the newest drugs for treating schizophrenia bind to serotonin receptors (Howes et al., 2015). The interaction between serotonin and dopamine may be critical in schizophrenia. Still other research has found abnormal levels of the neurotransmitters glutamate and gamma-aminobutyric acid (GABA) in people with schizophrenia (Howes et al., 2015). Glutamate and GABA are widespread in the brain, and deficiencies could contribute to cognitive and emotional symptoms. Glutamate neurons are the

FIGURE 4 **Areas of Abnormal Dopamine Activity in the Brain in Schizophrenia.**
There may be excess dopamine activity in the mesolimbic pathway, which begins in the ventral tegmental area and projects to the hypothalamus, amygdala, and hippocampus. But there may be unusually low dopamine activity in the prefrontal cortex.

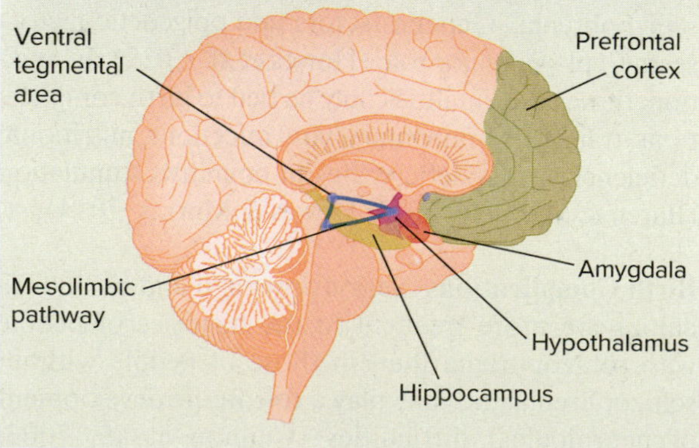

major excitatory pathways linking the cortex, limbic system, and thalamus, regions of the brain shown to behave abnormally in people with schizophrenia. Drugs, such as PCP and ketamine, that block glutamate receptors cause hallucinations and delusions in otherwise healthy individuals.

PSYCHOSOCIAL PERSPECTIVES

Although schizophrenia is strongly linked to biological factors, social factors can influence its onset, course, and outcome.

Social Drift and Urban Birth

People with schizophrenia are more likely than people without schizophrenia to experience chronically stressful circumstances, such as living in impoverished inner-city neighborhoods and having low-status occupations or being unemployed (Dohrenwend, 2000). Some research supports a **social drift** explanation for this link: Because schizophrenia symptoms interfere with a person's ability to complete an education and hold a job, people with schizophrenia tend to drift downward in social class compared to the class of their family of origin.

A classic study showing social drift tracked the socioeconomic status of men with schizophrenia and compared it to the status of their brothers and fathers (Goldberg & Morrison, 1963). The men with schizophrenia tended to end up in socioeconomic classes well below those of their fathers. In contrast, the healthy brothers of the men with schizophrenia tended to end up in socioeconomic classes equal to or higher than those of their fathers. Some other recent data support the social drift theory, but other evidence supports the opposite causal direction—that social status and environments affect schizophrenia (Heinz, Deserno, & Reininghaus, 2013). Of course, both directions are possible or even likely (e.g., Lund & Cois, 2018), and the link may reflect other associated risk factors, such as genetics (Sariaslan et al., 2016).

Several studies also have shown that people with schizophrenia and other forms of psychosis are more likely to have been born in a large city than in a small town (e.g., Lewis, David, Andreasson, & Allebeck, 1992; Takei et al., 1995; van Os, Hanssen, Bijl, & Vollebergh, 2001; see Heinz et al., 2013; March et al., 2008). For example, studies in the United States find that people with psychotic disorders are as much as five times more likely to have been born and raised in a large metropolitan area than in a rural area. Does the stress of the city lead to psychosis? E. Fuller Torrey and Robert Yolken (1998) argue that the link between urban living and psychosis is due not to stress but to overcrowding, which increases the risk that a pregnant woman or a newborn will be exposed to infectious agents. Many studies have shown that the rates of many infectious diseases—including influenza, tuberculosis, respiratory infections, herpes, and measles—are higher in crowded urban areas than in less crowded areas (Heinz et al., 2013). As noted earlier, there is a link between prenatal or perinatal exposure to infectious disease and schizophrenia. However, it is clear that social factors related to stress, including poverty, discrimination, and marginalization, also play a role (Heinz et al., 2013; Howes et. al., 2017; March et al., 2008).

Stress and Relapse

Although stressful circumstances alone might not cause someone to develop schizophrenia, they might trigger new episodes in people with the disorder. Researchers have found higher levels of stress occurring shortly before the onset of a new episode compared to other times in the lives of people with schizophrenia (Norman & Malla, 1993). For example, in one study, researchers followed a group of people with schizophrenia for 1 year, interviewing them every 2 weeks to determine whether they had experienced any stressful events and/or any increase in their symptoms. Those who experienced relapses of psychosis were more likely than those who did not to have experienced negative life events in the month before their relapse (Ventura, Neuchterlein, Lukoff, & Hardesty, 1989). Stressful events in adulthood may be especially important among people who experienced adverse events in childhood (Beards et al., 2013; Lataster, Myin-Germeys, Lieb, Wittchen, & van Os, 2011).

One major stressor linked to an increased risk for episodes in schizophrenia is immigration (Alegría, Álvarez, & DiMarzio, 2017). Recent immigrants often have left behind extended networks of family and friends to move to a new country where they may know few people. They may face financial stress, particularly if the education they received in their native country isn't recognized in their new country. They may not know the language of their new country and may not be comfortable in the new culture. Studies in the United States and Britain have found that first- and second-generation immigrants have a higher incidence of acute schizophrenia symptoms than individuals from their ethnic group who have been in the country longer or individuals native to the country (Cantor-Graae & Selten, 2005; Coid et al., 2008; Kirkbride et al., 2006).

It is important not to overstate the link between stressful life events and new episodes of schizophrenia. In the study that followed people with schizophrenia for a year, more than half the participants who had a relapse of active psychotic symptoms in the year they were followed had not experienced a negative life

The role of family interaction in schizophrenia is an example of how biological, psychological, and social factors combine in mental illness. ©*Eric Risberg/AP Images*

event just before their relapse (Ventura et al., 1989). In addition, other studies suggest that many of the life events that people with schizophrenia experience prior to relapse actually may be caused by prodromal symptoms that occur just before their relapse into psychosis (Dohrenwend et al., 1987). For example, one prodromal symptom of psychosis relapse is social withdrawal. Those negative life events that most often precede a relapse, such as the breakup of a relationship or the loss of a job, might be caused partially by the person's social withdrawal.

Schizophrenia and the Family

Historically, theorists blamed schizophrenia on mothers. Early psychodynamic theorists suggested that schizophrenia results when mothers are at the same time overprotective and rejecting of their children (Fromm-Reichmann, 1948). These schizophrenogenic (schizophrenia-causing) mothers dominated their children, not letting them develop an autonomous sense of self and simultaneously making the children feel worthless and unlovable. Similarly, Gregory Bateson and his colleagues (1956) argued that parents (particularly mothers) of children who develop schizophrenia put their children in a double bind by constantly communicating conflicting messages to their children. Such a mother might physically comfort her child when he falls down and is hurt but, at the same time, be verbally hostile to and critical of the child. Children chronically exposed to such mixed messages supposedly cannot trust their feelings or their perceptions of the world and thus develop distorted views of themselves, of others, and of their environment that contribute to schizophrenia. These theories did not hold up to scientific scrutiny, but they heaped guilt on the family members of people with schizophrenia.

One factor in family interaction that research shows is associated with multiple episodes of schizophrenia is **expressed emotion.** Families high in expressed emotion are overinvolved with one another, are overprotective of the family member with schizophrenia, and voice self-sacrificing attitudes toward the family member while at the same time being critical, hostile, and resentful toward him or her (Hooley, 2007). Although these family members do not doubt their loved one's illness, they talk as if the ill family member can control his or her symptoms (Hooley & Campbell, 2002). They often have ideas about how the family member can improve his or her symptoms or functioning.

Expressed emotion has been assessed through lengthy interviews with people with schizophrenia and their families, through projective tests, and through direct observation of family interactions. A number of studies have shown that people with schizophrenia whose families are high in expressed emotion are more likely to suffer relapses of psychosis than are those whose families are low in expressed emotion (e.g., Hooley, 2007). More recently, a longitudinal study of individuals at high risk for schizophrenia found that those living in a family characterized by low warmth and high criticism (components of high expressed emotion) were more likely to develop the full syndrome of schizophrenia than were those living in a family with greater warmth and less criticism (Schlosser et al., 2010). Being in a family with high expressed emotion may create stresses for persons with schizophrenia that overwhelm their ability to cope and thus trigger first or new episodes of psychosis.

The link between high levels of family expressed emotion and higher relapse rates has been replicated in studies of several cultures, including those of Europe, the United States, Mexico, and India. In Mexico and India, however, families of people with schizophrenia tend to score lower on measures of expressed emotion than do their counterparts in Europe or the United States (Figure 5; Karno & Jenkins, 1993; Karno et al., 1987). The lower levels of expressed emotion in families in developing countries may help explain the lower relapse rates of people with schizophrenia in these countries.

Critics of the literature on expressed emotion argue that the hostility and intrusiveness observed in some families of people with schizophrenia might be the result of the symptoms exhibited by the person with schizophrenia rather than contributors to relapse (Parker, Johnston, & Hayward, 1988). Although families often are forgiving of the positive symptoms of schizophrenia (e.g., hallucinations, delusions) because they view them as uncontrollable, they can be unforgiving of the negative symptoms (e.g., lack of

FIGURE 5 Cultural Differences in the Prevalence of Expressed Emotion in Families of People with Schizophrenia. Families of people with schizophrenia from developing countries tend to show lower levels of expressed emotion than do families of people with schizophrenia from developed countries. This may be one reason why people with schizophrenia from developing countries have fewer relapses than do those from developed countries.

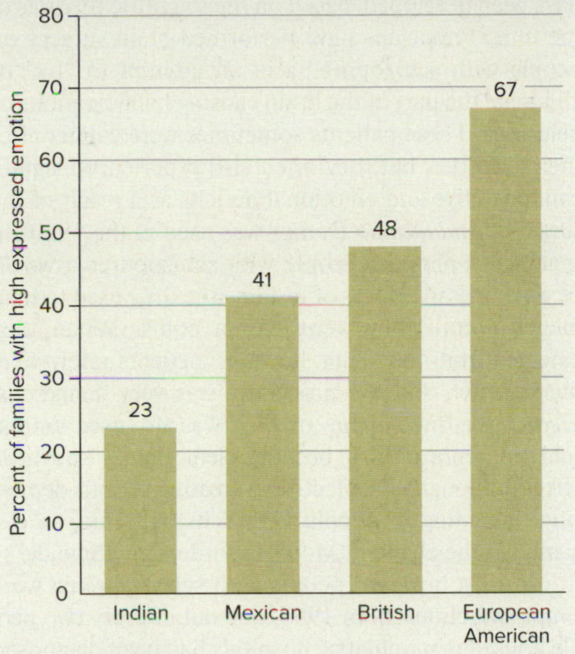

motivation, blunted affect), viewing them as controllable by the person with schizophrenia (Hooley & Campbell, 2002). People with more of the negative symptoms may elicit more expressed emotion from their families. They also may be especially prone to relapse, but for reasons other than exposure to expressed emotion.

Family members who rate particularly high on expressed emotion are themselves more likely to have some form of psychopathology (Goldstein, Talovic, Nuechterlein, & Fogelson, 1992). Thus, people with schizophrenia in these families may have high rates of relapse because they have a greater genetic loading for psychopathology, rather than because their family members show high levels of expressed emotion. Perhaps the best evidence that family expressed emotion does in fact influence relapse in people with schizophrenia is that interventions to reduce family expressed emotion tend to reduce the relapse rate in family members with schizophrenia (Hooley, 2007).

Cognitive Perspectives

Aaron Beck and Neil Rector (Beck & Rector, 2005) suggest that fundamental difficulties in attention, inhibition, and adherence to the rules of communication lead people with schizophrenia to try to conserve their limited cognitive resources. One way they do this is by using certain biases or thinking styles for understanding the overwhelming information streaming through their brain. Delusions arise as the person with schizophrenia tries to explain strange perceptual experiences, and "jumps to conclusions" based on limited evidence. Hallucinations result from a hypersensitivity to perceptual input, coupled with a tendency to attribute experiences to external sources. Rather than thinking "I'm hearing things," the person with schizophrenia will think "Someone is trying to talk to me." The negative symptoms of schizophrenia arise from expectations that social interactions will be aversive and from the need to withdraw and conserve scarce cognitive resources.

This cognitive conceptualization has received empirical support and has led to cognitive treatments for people with schizophrenia (Garety & Freeman, 2013). Researchers and clinicians increasingly recognize the role of cognition in combination with emotional, biological, and social factors in schizophrenia (Garety & Freeman, 2013; Howes & Murray, 2014). Cognitive therapies help patients identify and cope with stressful circumstances associated with the development and worsening of symptoms. They also teach patients to dispute their delusional beliefs or hallucinatory experiences. Negative symptoms are treated by helping patients develop the expectation that being more active and interacting more with other people will have positive benefits. This cognitive intervention has shown greater success in reducing symptoms than does simply providing patients with support (Beck & Rector, 2005; Garety & Freeman, 2013).

Cross-Cultural Perspectives

Different cultures vary greatly in how they explain schizophrenia (Hopper, 2008; Karno & Jenkins, 1993; Larøi et al., 2014). Most have a biological explanation for the disorder, including the general idea that it runs in families. Intermingled with biological explanations are theories that attribute the disorder to stress, lack of spiritual piety, and family dynamics. Kevin Browne (2001) offers a case study of a woman from Java, whose understanding of her schizophrenia symptoms included all these factors.

Anik's experience illustrates the interweaving in people with schizophrenia symptoms of traditional beliefs and practices and modern biological treatments.

CASE STUDY

Anik is a 29-year-old Javanese woman who was born in a rural area but has lived in the city of Yogyakarta for the past 4 years. She has been married 1½ years but is very unhappy in her marriage, feeling her husband is lacking in openness and compassion. Anik has been unable to care for her 8-month-old daughter for the past several months, so the daughter was living with Anik's aunt in Jakarta. When her illness began, Anik first became withdrawn and didn't sleep or eat. She developed hallucinations of accusatory voices criticizing her husband, his family, and their landlady. Anik also suffered from jealous delusions that her husband was having an affair. She was taken to the hospital by her brother, where her symptoms included *mondar-mandir* ("wandering without purpose"), *ngamuk* ("being irritable"), being easily offended and suspicious, talking to herself, crying, insomnia, *malmun* ("daydreaming"), and quickly changing emotions. Her sister-in-law reported that she had been chronically fearful and irritable for some time and would frequently slam doors and yell. In Javanese culture, the control of emotions in social situations is of great importance, so Anik's outbursts were seen as clear signs of some sort of pathology.

Anik had several explanations for her behavior. First and foremost, she believed that she was in a bad marriage, and this stress was a contributing factor. Shortly before her symptoms began, her landlady said something harsh to her, and Anik believed that her startle reaction to this (*goncangan*) led to *sajithati,* literally "liver sickness." In addition, Anik's mother had a brief period during Anik's childhood when she "went crazy," becoming loud and violent, and Anik believes she may have inherited this tendency from her mother. Anik initially sought to overcome her symptoms by increasing the frequency with which she repeated Muslim prayers and asking to be taken to a Muslim boarding house. Once she was taken to the hospital, she agreed to take antipsychotic medications, which helped her symptoms somewhat. She was discharged from the hospital after a short time but was rehospitalized multiple times over the next year. (Brown, T. A., O'Leary, T. A., & Barlow, D. H., 2001, in Barlow, D. H. (Ed.) "Generalized Anxiety Disorder," *Clinical Handbook of Psychological Disorders: A Step-by-Step Treatment Manual,* Third Edition, p. 502.

Although she agreed to take antipsychotic medications, the understanding she and her family had of her symptoms was not primarily a biological one but rather one rooted in concerns about stress and, to some extent, religion.

TREATMENT

Comprehensive treatment for people with schizophrenia includes medications to help reduce psychotic symptoms, therapy to help people cope with the consequences of the disorder, and social services to support community integration and to ensure their access to the resources they need to participate in daily life.

Biological Treatments

Over the centuries, many treatments for schizophrenia have been developed, based on the scientific theories of the time. Physicians have performed brain surgery on people with schizophrenia in an attempt to "fix" or eliminate the part of the brain causing hallucinations or delusions. These patients sometimes were calmer after their surgeries, but they often also experienced significant cognitive and emotional deficits as a result of the surgery. *Insulin coma therapy* was used in the 1930s to treat schizophrenia. People with schizophrenia would be given massive doses of insulin—the drug used to treat diabetes—until they went into a coma. When they emerged from the coma, however, patients rarely were much better, and the procedure was very dangerous. *Electroconvulsive therapy*, or *ECT*, was also used to treat schizophrenia until it became clear that it had little effect (although it is effective in treating serious depression, including in people with schizophrenia, as discussed in the chapter "Mood Disorders and Suicide").

Mostly, however, people with schizophrenia were simply warehoused. In 1955, one out of every two people housed in psychiatric hospitals had been diagnosed with schizophrenia, although by today's standards of diagnosis some may actually have had different disorders (Rosenstein, Milazzo-Sayre, & Manderscheid, 1989). These patients received custodial care—they were bathed, fed, and prevented from hurting themselves, often with the use of physical restraints—but few received any treatment that actually reduced their symptoms and improved their functioning. Not until the 1950s was an effective drug treatment for schizophrenia—chlorpromazine—introduced. Since then, several other antipsychotic drugs (also called *neuroleptics*) have been added to the arsenal of treatments for schizophrenia. More recently, the atypical antipsychotics hold out the promise of relieving positive symptoms while inducing fewer intolerable side effects than the traditional or typical antipsychotics.

Typical Antipsychotic Drugs

In the early 1950s, French researchers Jean Delay and Pierre Deniker found that **chlorpromazine** (Thorazine), one of a class of drugs called the phenothiazines, calms agitation and reduces hallucinations and delusions in patients with schizophrenia. Other phenothiazines that became widely used include trifluoperazine

(Stelazine), thioridazine (Mellaril), fluphenazine (Prolixin), and perphenazine (Trilafon). These drugs appear to block receptors for dopamine, thereby reducing its action in the brain. For the first time, many people with schizophrenia could control the positive symptoms of the disorder (hallucinations, delusions, thought disturbances) by taking these drugs even when they were asymptomatic.

Thanks to these drugs, by 1971 the number of people with schizophrenia who required hospitalization had decreased to half of what would have been expected without the use of the drugs (Lavretsky, 2008). Other classes of antipsychotic drugs introduced after the phenothiazines include the *butyrophenones* (such as Haldol) and the *thioxanthenes* (such as Navane).

Although the typical antipsychotic drugs revolutionized the treatment of schizophrenia, about 25 percent of people with schizophrenia do not respond to them (Adams, Awad, Rathbone, & Thornley, 2007). Among people who do respond, the typical antipsychotics are more effective in treating the positive symptoms of schizophrenia than in treating the negative symptoms (lack of motivation and interpersonal deficits). Many people with schizophrenia who take these drugs are not actively psychotic but still are unable to hold a job or build positive social relationships. People with schizophrenia typically must take an antipsychotic drug all the time in order to prevent new episodes of active symptoms. If the drug is discontinued, about 78 percent of people with schizophrenia relapse within 1 year and 98 percent relapse within 2 years, compared to about 30 percent of people who continue on their medications (Gitlin et al., 2001).

Unfortunately, however, these drugs have significant side effects that cause many people to want to discontinue their use (Adams et al., 2007). The side effects include grogginess, dry mouth, blurred vision, drooling, sexual dysfunction, visual disturbances, weight gain or loss, constipation, menstrual irregularities in women, and depression. Another common side effect is *akinesia,* which includes slowed motor activity, monotonous speech, and an expressionless face. Patients taking the phenothiazines often show symptoms similar to those seen in Parkinson's disease, including muscle stiffness, freezing of the facial muscles, tremors and spasms in the extremities, and *akathesis,* an agitation that causes people to pace and be unable to sit still (Adams et al., 2007). The fact that Parkinson's disease is caused by a lack of dopamine in the brain suggests that these side effects occur because the drugs reduce the functional levels of dopamine.

One serious side effect is **tardive dyskinesia,** a neurological disorder that involves involuntary movements of the tongue, face, mouth, or jaw. People with this disorder may involuntarily smack their lips, make sucking sounds, stick out their tongue, puff their cheeks, or make other bizarre movements over and over again. Tardive dyskinesia often is irreversible and may occur in over 20 percent of persons with long-term use of the phenothiazines.

The side effects of the neuroleptics can be reduced by lowering dosages. For this reason, many clinicians prescribe for people with schizophrenia the lowest dosage possible that still keeps active symptoms at bay, known as a maintenance dose. Unfortunately, maintenance doses often do not restore an individual to full functioning. The negative symptoms of schizophrenia may still be strongly present, along with mild versions of the positive symptoms, making it hard for the individual to function in daily life. Some people with schizophrenia have frequent hospitalizations and ongoing difficulties outside the hospital.

Atypical Antipsychotics

Fortunately, newer drugs, the **atypical antipsychotics,** seem to be more effective in treating schizophrenia than the neuroleptics, without the neurological side effects of the latter (Sharif, Raza, & Ratakonda, 2000; Walker et al., 2009). One of the most common of these drugs, *clozapine* (sold in the United States as Clozaril), binds to the D4 dopamine receptor, but it also influences several other neurotransmitters, including serotonin (Sajatovic, Madhusoodanan, & Fuller, 2008). Clozapine has helped many people with schizophrenia who never responded to the phenothiazines, and it appears to reduce the negative symptoms as well as the positive symptoms in many patients (Sharif et al., 2000).

Although clozapine does not induce tardive dyskinesia, it does have some side effects, including dizziness, nausea, sedation, seizures, hypersalivation, weight gain, and tachycardia. In addition, in 1 to 2 percent of the people who take clozapine, a condition called *agranulocytosis* develops (Sharif et al., 2000). This is a deficiency of granulocytes, substances produced by bone marrow that fight infection. The condition can be fatal, so patients taking clozapine must be carefully monitored. Due to these side effects, clozapine often is used only after other atypical antipsychotics have been tried.

A number of other atypical antipsychotics have been introduced over the past two decades, including risperidone (trade name Risperdal), olanzapine (Zyprexa), quetiapine (Seroquel), and ziprasidone (Geodone, Zeldox). These drugs do not tend to induce agranulocytosis, but they can cause a number of side effects, including significant weight gain and increased risk for diabetes, as well as sexual dysfunction, sedation, low blood pressure, seizures, gastrointestinal problems, vision problems, and problems with concentration.

A randomized clinical trial conducted by the National Institute of Mental Health in several sites across the United States compared the effectiveness of five of these drugs (quetiapine, perphenazine, risperidone, olanzapine, and ziprasidone) in over

1,000 patients with schizophrenia (Levine, Rabinowitz, Ascher-Svanum, Faries, & Lawson, 2011). The focus of the trial was how many patients would show remission of symptoms over an 18-month follow-up period. Unfortunately, only 44.5 percent of the patients experienced remission of any duration during this period, 21.0 percent showed remission for at least 3 months, and only 11.7 percent showed remission for at least 6 months. For the five medications, 6-month remission rates were highest (12.4 percent) for the olanzapine treatment group, followed by quetiapine (8.2 percent), perphenazine (6.8 percent), ziprasidone (6.5 percent), and risperidone (6.3 percent). Although the atypical antipsychotics are superior to older medications, more work is needed to determine which of them are safest and most effective, and for which patients (Samara et al., 2016).

Psychological and Social Treatments

Even when antipsychotic medications do help reduce the psychotic symptoms of schizophrenia, they often do not completely restore the life of a person with schizophrenia, as the following profile illustrates.

PROFILES

Medicine did not cause sanity; it only made it possible. Sanity came through a minute-by-minute choice of outer reality, which was often without meaning, over inside reality, which was full of meaning. Sanity meant choosing reality that was not real and having faith that someday the choice would be worth the fear involved and that it would someday hold meaning. (Anonymous, 1992, p. 335)

Many individuals who are able to control the positive symptoms of schizophrenia with drugs still experience many of the negative symptoms, particularly problems in motivation and in social interactions. Psychological interventions can help these individuals increase their social skills and reduce their isolation and apathy. Such interventions also can help people with schizophrenia and their families reduce the stress and conflict in their lives, thereby reducing the risk of relapse into psychosis (Pharoah, Mari, Rathbone, & Wong, 2010; Turner, van der Gaag, Karyotaki, & Cuijpers, 2014). In addition, the lack of effectiveness of the antipsychotic drugs suggested by the studies reviewed in the preceding section is due in part to people discontinuing the drugs either because they do not think they need them or because they find the side effects intolerable (Barkhof, Meijer, de Sonneville, Linszen, & de Haan, 2012). Psychological interventions can help people with schizophrenia understand their disorder, appreciate the need to remain on their medications, and cope more effectively with the side effects of the medications. Because of the severity of their disorder, many people with schizophrenia have trouble finding or holding a job, feeding and sheltering themselves, and obtaining necessary medical or psychiatric care. Psychologists, social workers, and other mental health professionals can assist people with schizophrenia in meeting these basic needs.

Behavioral, Cognitive, and Social Treatments

Most experts in the treatment of schizophrenia argue for a comprehensive approach that addresses the wide array of behavioral, cognitive, and social deficits in schizophrenia and is tailored to the specific deficits of each individual with the disorder (Liberman, 2008; Mueser, Deavers, Penn, & Cassisi, 2013). These treatments are given in addition to medication and can increase patients' level of everyday functioning and significantly reduce the risk of relapse (see review by Barkhof et al., 2012).

Cognitive treatments include helping people with schizophrenia recognize and change demoralizing attitudes they may have toward their illness so that they will seek help when needed and participate in society to the extent that they can (Beck & Rector, 2005; Garety & Freeman, 2013). Behavioral treatments, based on social learning theory (see the chapter "Theories and Treatment of Abnormality"), include the use of operant conditioning and modeling to teach persons with schizophrenia skills such as initiating and maintaining conversations with others, asking for help or information from physicians, and persisting in an activity, such as cooking or cleaning (Liberman, 2008). These interventions may be administered by the family. In that case, a therapist would teach a client's family members to ignore schizophrenia symptoms, such as bizarre comments, and instead reinforce socially appropriate behavior by giving it attention and positive emotional responses. In psychiatric hospitals and residential treatment centers, token economies sometimes are established, based on the principles of operant conditioning. Patients earn tokens that they can exchange for special privileges (such as additional outings beyond what is ordinarily provided) by completing daily self-care tasks (such as showering or changing clothing) or even by simply engaging in appropriate conversations with others.

Social interventions include increasing contact between people with schizophrenia and supportive others, often through self-help support groups (Liberman, 2008). These groups discuss the impact of the disorder on their lives, the frustration of trying to make people understand their disorder, their fear of relapse, their experiences with various medications, and other day-to-day concerns. Group members also can help one another learn social and problem-solving skills by giving feedback and providing a forum in which individual members can role-play new skills. People with schizophrenia also are often directly taught problem-solving skills applicable to common social situations. For example, they may practice generating and role-playing solutions for when a receptionist tells them no one is available at a company to interview them for a potential job.

Although behavioral, cognitive, and social treatments can improve functioning, studies show that the effects can be rather small, especially in the long term (Jauhar et al., 2014; Turner et al., 2014). Current research aims to understand how these treatments can be improved and tailored to individuals and their particular symptoms.

Family Therapy

Recall that high levels of expressed emotion within the family of a person with schizophrenia can substantially increase the risk and frequency of relapse. Many researchers have examined the effectiveness of family-oriented therapies for people with schizophrenia. Successful therapies combine basic education on schizophrenia with the training of family members in coping with their loved one's inappropriate behaviors and the disorder's impact on their lives (Hogarty et al., 1991; Pharaoh et al., 2010; see review by Barkhof et al., 2012).

In the educational portion of these therapies, families are taught about the disorder's biological causes, its symptoms, and the medications and their side effects. The hope is that this information will reduce self-blame in family members, increase their tolerance for the uncontrollable symptoms of the disorder, and allow them to monitor their family member's use of medication and possible side effects. Family members also learn communication skills to reduce harsh, conflictual interactions, as well as problem-solving skills to help manage issues in the family such as lack of money, in order to reduce the overall level of stress in the family. They also learn specific behavioral techniques for encouraging appropriate behavior and discouraging inappropriate behavior on the part of their family member with schizophrenia.

These family-oriented interventions, when combined with drug therapy, appear to be more effective at reducing relapse rates than drug therapy alone. On average, approximately 24 percent of people who receive family-oriented therapy in addition to drug therapy relapse into schizophrenia, compared to 64 percent of people who receive routine drug therapy alone (Pitschel-Walz, Leucht, Baumi, Kissling, & Engel, 2001). Family-based therapies also can increase patients' adherence to taking antipsychotic medications. For example, Guo et al. (2010) randomly assigned 1,268 patients with early-stage schizophrenia to receive antipsychotic medication alone or medication plus family therapy, which included skills training and cognitive-behavioral interventions. Over the year the patients were followed, 33 percent of the patients receiving family-based intervention discontinued their medications, compared to 47 percent of the patients receiving medication alone. The patients receiving family-based intervention also experienced less relapse of symptoms and greater improvement in social functioning and quality of life than those who received medication alone.

For people with schizophrenia to be cared for by their family and to be deeply embedded in it is more likely in some cultures than in others. Family-oriented interventions may be even more critical for people in these cultures (Barrio & Yamada, 2010; Lopez, Kopelowicz, & Canive, 2002). The interventions must be culturally sensitive. One study found that behavior therapies to increase communication actually backfired in some Hispanic families, perhaps because these families already had low levels of expressed emotion and found the techniques suggested by the therapists to violate their cultural norms for how family members should interact (Telles et al., 1995). For example, some of the most traditional family members in this study expressed great discomfort during exercises that encouraged them to establish eye contact or express negative feelings to authority figures, because these actions were considered disrespectful. As with other disorders, therapists must take into account the culture of their clients in designing interventions.

Assertive Community Treatment Programs

Some people with schizophrenia lack families to care for them. Even those with families have such a wide array of needs—for the monitoring and adjustment of their medications, occupational training, assistance in receiving financial resources (such as Social Security and Medicaid), social skills training, emotional support, and sometimes basic housing—that comprehensive community-based treatment programs are necessary. **Assertive community treatment programs** provide comprehensive services for people with schizophrenia, relying on the expertise of medical professionals, social workers, and psychologists to meet the variety of patients' needs 24 hours a day (Bustillo, Lauriello, Horan, & Keith, 2001).

In the chapter "Looking at Abnormality" we discussed the community mental health movement, which was initiated by President Kennedy in the 1960s to transfer the care of people with serious mental disorders from primarily psychiatric hospitals to comprehensive community-based programs. The idea was that people with schizophrenia and other serious disorders would spend time in the hospital when severe symptoms required it but when discharged from the hospital would go to community-based programs, which would help them reintegrate into society, maintain their medications, gain needed skills, and function at their highest possible level. Hundreds of halfway houses, group homes, and therapeutic communities were established for people with serious mental disorders who needed a supportive place to live.

One classic example of such programs was The Lodge, a residential treatment center for people with schizophrenia established by George Fairweather and his colleagues (Fairweather, Sanders, Maynard, & Cressler, 1969). At The Lodge, mental health professionals were available for support and assistance, but residents ran the household and worked with other residents to establish healthy behaviors and discourage inappropriate behaviors. The residents also established their own employment agency to assist with finding jobs. Follow-up studies showed that Lodge residents fared much better than people with schizophrenia who were simply discharged from the hospital into the care of their families or into less intensive treatment programs (Fairweather et al., 1969). For example, Lodge residents were less likely to be rehospitalized and much more likely to hold a job than were those in a comparison group, even after The Lodge closed.

FIGURE 6 **Effects of Home-Based Treatment on Need for Institutional Care.** In one study, patients with schizophrenia who received intensive home-based skills training and care were much less likely to be hospitalized for psychotic symptoms or to need other types of institutional care.

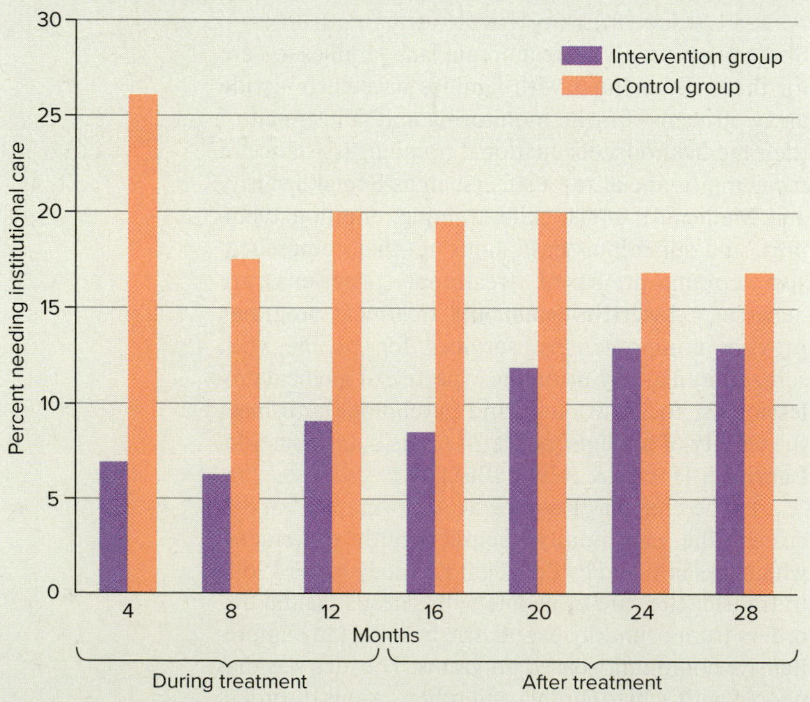

Other comprehensive treatment programs provide skills training, vocational rehabilitation, and social support to people with schizophrenia who live at home. Studies of these programs find that they reduce the amount of time spent in the hospital and, as a result, can be cost-effective.

A program known as *assertive community therapy* has become the gold standard for community-based interventions (Test & Stein, 1980; see Bond & Drake, 2015). The model program of this type of therapy was first established in a study done in Madison, Wisconsin. Mental health professionals worked with chronically disabled people with schizophrenia. Interventions were provided in the homes or communities of the patients for 14 months, and then the patients were followed for another 28 months. Their progress was compared with that of another group of patients, who received standard hospital treatment for their positive symptoms. Both groups were treated with antipsychotic medications. The patients who received the home-based intensive skills interventions were less likely than the control-group patients to be hospitalized and more likely to be employed both during the treatment and in the 28 months of follow-up (Figure 6). The home-based intervention group also showed lower levels of emotional distress and of positive symptoms during the intervention than did the control group. The difference in levels of symptoms between the two groups diminished after the intervention period ended. In general, the gains that people in skills-based interventions make tend to decline once the interventions end, suggesting that these interventions need to be ongoing. However, their benefits can be great. Since the original tests of assertive community treatment, dozens of additional randomized clinical trials have supported the effectiveness of this type of treatment over most types of controls (Catty et al., 2002; Williams, Firn, Wharne, & Macpherson, 2011).

Although 38 states in the United States have adopted assertive community treatment as the gold standard for care for people with schizophrenia and other serious mental disorders, only 2 percent of individuals with these disorders are currently being served by such programs (Padgett & Henwood, 2011). Unfortunately, the *community mental health movement* was never funded at a level that could support its lofty goals. With the changes in medical insurance in recent years, funding for mental health care for the seriously mentally ill has been even tighter. Although billions of dollars are spent on mental health care each year in the United States, much of that money goes not to direct services to people with schizophrenia but instead to subsistence programs such as Social Security disability payments and to community services for people with less serious mental disorders (Torrey, 2013). Much of the financial burden of caring for people with schizophrenia falls to state and local governments, which lack the necessary resources, or to families, who too often are bankrupted by the cost of care.

As a result, 40 to 60 percent of people with schizophrenia receive little or no care in a given year (Torrey, 2013). Those who do receive care often are hospitalized only when their symptoms are acute, and they remain in the hospital for an inadequate period of time to allow their symptoms to stabilize. They may be discharged with little or no follow-up. Some return to their families, but many end up in nursing homes, where they receive only custodial care, or in single-room-occupancy hotels or rooming houses, often in run-down inner-city neighborhoods. Many end up homeless or in prison (Torrey, 2013).

Some modern treatment facilities provide people with schizophrenia with comprehensive services in a positive, pleasant setting. ©*Skyland Trail, Atlanta, GA*

Cross-Cultural Treatments: Traditional Healers

In developing countries and in parts of industrialized countries, the symptoms of schizophrenia sometimes are treated by folk or religious healers, according to cultural beliefs about the meaning and causes of the symptoms. Anthropologists and cultural psychiatrists have described four models that traditional healers tend to follow in treating schizophrenic symptoms (Karno & Jenkins, 1993). According to the *structural model,* there are interrelated levels of experience–such as the body, emotion, and cognition or the person, society, and culture–and symptoms arise when the integration of these levels is lost. Healing thus involves reintegrating these levels through a change of diet or environment, the prescription of herbal medicines, or rituals.

The *social support model* holds that symptoms arise from conflictual social relationships, and healing involves mobilizing a patient's kin to support him or her through the crisis and reintegrating the patient into a positive social support network. The *persuasive model* suggests that rituals can transform the meaning of symptoms for patients, diminishing their pain. Finally, in the *clinical model,* the faith the patient has in the traditional healer to provide a cure for the symptoms is sufficient. In developing countries, care for people with schizophrenia is more likely to be carried out by the extended family than by a mental health institution (Karno & Jenkins, 1993). Thus, it may be especially important in these countries that interventions for a person with schizophrenia also include his or her family.

CHAPTER INTEGRATION

There is probably more consensus among mental health professionals about the biological roots of schizophrenia than of any other psychopathology discussed in this book. The evidence that the fundamental vulnerability to schizophrenia is biological is compelling, yet there is growing consensus that psychosocial factors also contribute to the risk for schizophrenia among people who have a biological vulnerability. Theorists are increasingly developing models that integrate the biological and psychosocial contributors to schizophrenia in order to provide comprehensive explanations of the development of this disorder (Figure 7; Cannon, 2009; Howes et al., 2017).

Genetic factors clearly play a role in vulnerability to schizophrenia. Environmental factors early in a person's life, such as exposure to toxins or to viruses in utero or hypoxia during childbirth, can interact with a genetic liability stemming from epigenetic processes to increase the person's vulnerability to developing schizophrenia. If a person with this biological vulnerability to schizophrenia is raised in a supportive, low-expressed-emotion family and escapes exposure to major stressors, he or she may never develop the full syndrome of schizophrenia. The person still may have mild symptoms, however, because the biological underpinnings of this disorder play such an important role. Alternatively, a person who has a biological vulnerability and grows up in a stressful atmosphere is more likely to develop the full syndrome of schizophrenia. Psychosocial stress also clearly contributes to new episodes of psychosis in people with this disorder.

There is widespread consensus among mental health professionals that the most effective therapies for schizophrenia are those that address both the biological and the psychosocial contributors to the disorder.

FIGURE 7 **Interaction of Biological and Psychosocial Factors in Schizophrenia.**

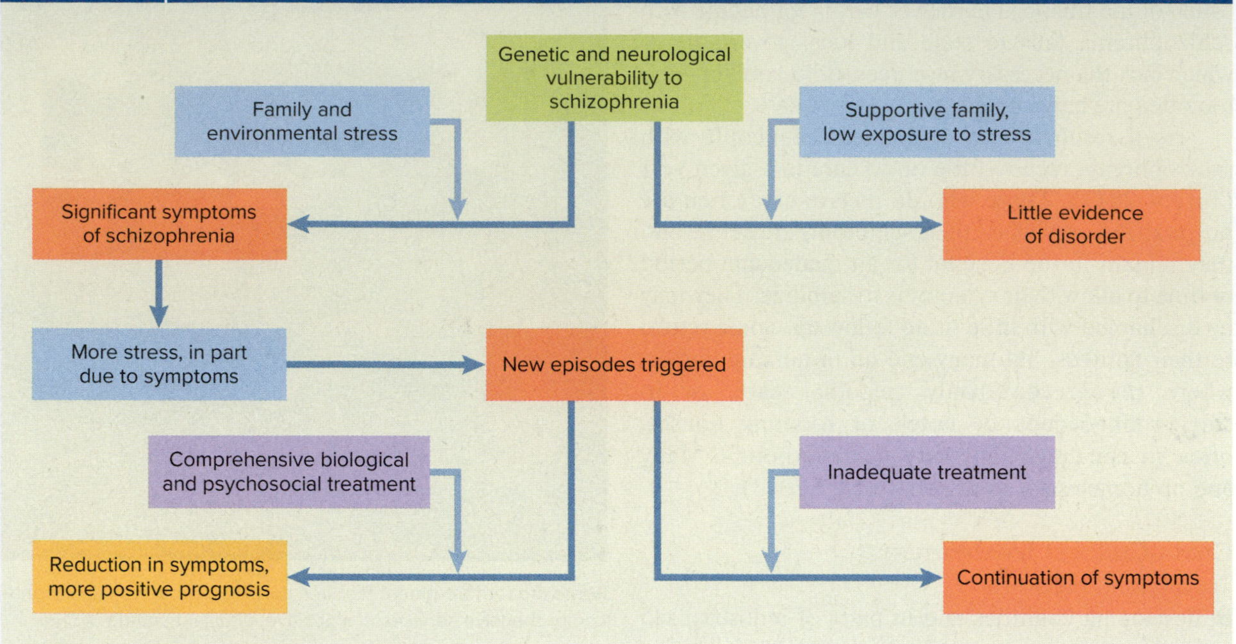

SHADES OF GRAY DISCUSSION

As you may have noticed, Jeff's symptoms do not fit neatly into any of the categories in the *DSM-5*. You might wonder if he is depressed, because he reports feelings of emptiness. But because he does not show most of the other symptoms of depression (see the chapter "Mood Disorders and Suicide"), this is not an appropriate diagnosis. His emptiness, social isolation, lack of motivation, and general deterioration in functioning all look like negative symptoms of schizophrenia. However, he does not appear to have the positive symptoms—delusions, hallucinations, or incoherence in speech or thought.

The psychiatrist treating Jeff believed that he was showing prodromal or early symptoms of schizophrenia, which often are predominantly negative. He was given antipsychotic medications and allowed to go home with his parents. Remaining isolated and apathetic, he stopped taking the medications. Two months later, he said he was experiencing severe electrical sensations in his head that he believed were being transmitted through his father's mind. He also began to have "horrible thoughts" that were put there by his father. He became agitated and one night grabbed a knife, went into his parents' bedroom, and threatened to kill his father if he would not stop tormenting him. Fortunately, his father was able to talk him into dropping the knife and going to the emergency room.

Jeff was admitted to the hospital, given a diagnosis of schizophrenia, and placed on a higher dose of antipsychotic medications. His positive symptoms diminished, but his negative symptoms remained. (Adapted from Andreasen, 1998)

CHAPTER SUMMARY

- There are five domains of symptoms that define psychotic disorders. They include positive and negative symptoms.
- The positive symptoms of schizophrenia include delusions (fixed beliefs that are held strongly despite conflicting evidence), hallucinations (unreal perceptual experiences), thought disturbances (incoherent thought and speech), and grossly disorganized or catatonic behavior.
- The negative symptoms of schizophrenia include restricted affect and avolition (the inability to initiate and persist in goal-directed activities) or asociality. Separate prodromal and residual symptoms are mild versions of the positive and negative symptoms that occur before and after episodes of acute symptoms.
- Cognitive deficits in schizophrenia include problems in attention, working memory, processing speed, learning and memory, abstraction, and problem solving.

- Estimates of the prevalence of schizophrenia in various countries range from about 0.1 to 2.0 percent, but most estimates are between 0.5 and 1.0 percent. There are some slight ethnic differences in rates of schizophrenia, but these may be due to differences in socioeconomic status.
- The content of delusions and hallucinations varies somewhat across cultures, but the form of these symptoms remains similar, and many clinicians and researchers believe that schizophrenia can be diagnosed reliably across cultures.
- A number of other psychotic disorders are recognized by the *DSM-5*. Schizoaffective disorder is diagnosed when symptoms of schizophrenia occur with periods of major depression or mania. Individuals with schizophreniform disorder meet the criteria for schizophrenia but for a period of only 1 to 6 months. Those with brief psychotic disorder meet the criteria for schizophrenia but for a period of less than 1 month and sometimes in response to a major stressor. Delusional disorder is characterized by just one kind of psychotic symptoms, delusions. Schizotypal personality disorder is characterized by a life-long pattern of severe oddities in thought, behavior, and self-concept that fall short of psychosis.
- Biological theories of schizophrenia focus on genetics, structural and functional abnormalities in the brain, and neurotransmitters. There is clear evidence of a genetic transmission of schizophrenia. People with schizophrenia show abnormal functioning in the cortical areas of the brain, particularly prefrontal areas and the hippocampus, as well as enlarged ventricles. Many people with schizophrenia have a history of prenatal difficulties, such as exposure to the influenza virus during the second trimester of gestation, or birth complications, including perinatal hypoxia. Brain abnormalities and dysfunction in dopamine systems play a role in schizophrenia.
- Stressful events probably cannot cause schizophrenia in people who lack a vulnerability to the disorder, but they may trigger new episodes of psychosis in people with the disorder.
- Expressed emotion theorists argue that some families of people with schizophrenia are simultaneously overprotective and hostile and that this increases the risk of relapse.
- Cognitive theories suggest that some psychotic symptoms are attempts by the individual to understand and manage cognitive deficits.
- Drugs known as the phenothiazines, introduced in the 1950s, brought relief to many people with schizophrenia. The phenothiazines reduce the positive symptoms of schizophrenia but often are not effective in reducing the negative symptoms. Major side effects include tardive dyskinesia, an irreversible neurological disorder characterized by involuntary movements of the tongue, face, mouth, or jaw.
- Atypical antipsychotics, most of which were introduced in the past two decades, seem to induce fewer side effects than the phenothiazines and are effective in treating both the positive symptoms and the negative symptoms of schizophrenia for many people. Still, many people with schizophrenia do not respond or respond only partially to these drugs.
- Psychological and social treatments focus on helping people with schizophrenia reduce stress, improve family interactions, learn social skills, manage their illness, and cope with the impact of the disorder on their lives. Comprehensive treatment programs combining drug therapy with an array of psychological and social treatments have been shown to reduce relapse significantly.

KEY TERMS

psychosis
schizophrenia
schizophrenia spectrum
positive symptoms
delusions
persecutory delusions
delusion of reference
grandiose delusions
delusions of thought insertion
hallucinations
formal thought disorder
catatonia
negative symptoms
restricted affect
avolition
prodromal symptoms
residual symptoms
schizoaffective disorder
schizophreniform disorder
brief psychotic disorder
delusional disorder
schizotypal personality disorder
phenothiazines
neuroleptics
mesolimbic pathway
social drift
expressed emotion
chlorpromazine
tardive dyskinesia
atypical antipsychotics
assertive community treatment programs

Chapter 9

©Dunca Daniel/123RF

Personality Disorders

CHAPTER OUTLINE

Personality Disorders Along the Continuum

Functional

Long-standing patterns of behavior, thought, and feeling that lead to positive social and occupational functioning

A student who is interested in classes, has good relationships with friends, can regulate his or her emotions, and reflects on him- or herself accurately

Long-standing patterns of behavior, thought, and feeling that are unusual but do not interfere with social or occupational functioning

A student who is awkward or sometimes inappropriate with others; struggles with his or her sense of self, self-esteem, or life goals; and/or sometimes overreacts emotionally

Potentially meets diagnostic criteria for a personality disorder:

Long-standing patterns of behavior, thought, and feeling that somewhat interfere with social and/or occupational functioning

A student who is often inappropriate with others or socially withdrawn, is having significant difficulties understanding him- or herself or others, and/or frequently overreacts emotionally or behaviorally

Likely meets diagnostic criteria for a personality disorder:

Long-standing patterns of behavior, thought, and feeling that substantially interfere with social and/or occupational functioning

A student who is chronically inappropriate with others or socially withdrawn; has severe difficulties with identity, self-esteem, or self-direction; and/or becomes out of control emotionally in distressing situations

Dysfunctional

Your personality affects your daily life constantly. It determines how you perceive the events of your day, how you feel, and how you interact with others. A core aspect of your personality is your sense of self, or *identity* (Krueger & Markon, 2014). On the functional end of the personality continuum are people who have a sense of self that is relatively stable and is distinct from others. They have a sense of meaning and purpose in their life and the ability to pursue personally important goals that are socially acceptable. Another core aspect of personality is the way we *relate to others* (Krueger & Markon, 2014). People with adaptive personalities can empathize and cooperate with others, can be intimate with others appropriately, and appreciate the uniqueness of the different people in their life.

Some people have difficulty in their sense of self and in their relationships to others. Their identity may be diffuse and their self-esteem unstable, prone to deflation by mild slights or inflation by simple compliments. They may wander through life without meaningful goals or constructive internal standards of behavior. Or their identity may be too rigid, unable to adapt to changes in their circumstances, as when they lose a job or develop an illness. People also vary greatly in their ability to form and maintain good interpersonal relationships. Some people find it difficult to care about others appropriately, being either too self-sacrificing or too self-absorbed to empathize with others. Some people have difficulty tolerating differing perspectives and differentiating their own needs and desires from those of others. Some may find interpersonal relationships too distressing or unrewarding and withdraw from other people altogether. When individuals have significant deficits in their identity and their capacity for interpersonal relationships, they may be diagnosed with a personality disorder.

We've noted throughout this book that drawing a line between normal and abnormal, between functional and dysfunctional, is problematic for all the mental disorders. Personality disorders have presented especially great challenges in defining where unhealthy functioning that constitutes a disorder begins. The *DSM-5* includes two models of personality disorders. Its current categorical model is nearly the same as *DSM-IV*. Its alternative dimensional model is based on ample evidence that personality disorders, for the most part, represent extreme versions of typical personality traits (Krueger & Markon, 2014; Morey, Benson, Busch, & Skodol, 2015; Widiger & Mullins-Sweatt, 2009).

Extraordinary People

Susanna Kaysen, *Girl, Interrupted*

©Boston Globe/Getty Images

Susanna Kaysen was 18, depressed, drifting through life and endlessly oppositional toward her parents and teachers. She tried to commit suicide and eventually was hospitalized, remaining in the hospital for nearly 2 years. Later, Kaysen discovered that her diagnosis had been borderline personality disorder. In her autobiography, *Girl, Interrupted,* she raises many questions about this diagnosis.

After locating a copy of the *DSM*, she saw that many of her behaviors were characteristic of borderline personality disorder. "It's a fairly accurate picture of me at eighteen, minus a few quirks like reckless driving and eating binges," she has written.

Kaysen recognizes that sometimes symptoms of a disorder seem like normal developmental processes when she wryly likens the *DSM*'s description of the instability of self-image, interpersonal relationships, and mood characteristic of borderline personality disorder to the typical life of an adolescent.

She sees in the *DSM* other characteristics of her own, such as self-mutilating behavior and a chronic feeling of emptiness. "My chronic feelings of emptiness and boredom," she reports, "came from the fact that I was living a life based on my incapacities, which were numerous." She lists many aspects of school life that she simply couldn't manage.

At times Kaysen felt she was "crazy," asking herself and other people if something she did or said seemed disturbed. "I start a lot of sentences with 'Maybe I'm totally nuts,' or, 'Maybe I've gone round the bend.' If I do something out of the ordinary—take two baths in one day, for example—I say to myself, 'Are you crazy?'"

Was Susanna Kaysen just a mixed-up teenager whose parents expected too much of her and locked her away when she didn't comply? Or was she a deeply troubled young woman whose stay in the hospital prevented her complete psychological deterioration? Is the diagnosis of borderline personality disorder valid, or is it a label we attach to people who don't conform? Kaysen's *Girl, Interrupted* (which was made into a film starring Winona Ryder) brings life to the enduring debate about the validity and ethics of the diagnosis of borderline personality disorder.

Source: Adapted from Kaysen, 1993.

In your daily conversations, you likely refer to people's personalities all the time. **Personality** is enduring patterns of perceiving, feeling, thinking about, and relating to oneself and the environment. You might say that a person you just met is outgoing, or that you tend to be disorganized, or that a friend of yours is highly emotional. A **personality trait** is a prominent aspect of personality that is relatively consistent across time and across situations, such as being outgoing, caring and compassionate, exploitive or hostile, impulsive or unstable.

One of the leading theories of personality is the **five-factor model,** a dimensional perspective that posits that everyone's personality is organized along five broad personality traits, or factors. These factors are often referred to as the *Big 5:* negative emotionality, extraversion, openness to experience, agreeableness, and conscientiousness (McCrae & Costa, 1999, 2013). Each factor has a number of facets, or dimensions, as shown in Table 1. The table lists the facets that make up each of the five factors (in the leftmost column), and descriptions of people who are high on that facet (in the second column) and descriptions of people low on that facet (in the third column). These descriptions give a sense of the two ends of each dimension. Basically, all people vary on each of these dimensions, and these dimensions cluster under the Big 5. Considerable research supports the five-factor model of personality. These traits seem to capture a great deal of the variation in people's personalities, and they have been replicated in cultures very different from that of the United States (Benet-Martinez & John, 1998; Yang et al., 2002; see Carlo, Knight, Roesch, Opal, & Davis, 2014). The personality traits, especially the facet dimensions, in the five-factor model appear to be strongly influenced by genetics (Briley & Tucker-Drob, 2012; Jang et al., 2006; Sanchez-Roige, Gray, MacKillop, Chen, & Palmer, 2018). You can probably find yourself among the traits and facets of the Big 5.

TABLE 1 The Big 5 Personality Factors

Each of the Big 5 personality factors is composed of different facets, or components.

Facet	Individuals high on this facet are	Individuals low on this facet are
FACTOR 1: NEGATIVE EMOTIONALITY VERSUS EMOTIONAL STABILITY		
Anxiousness	fearful, apprehensive	relaxed, unconcerned, cool
Angry hostility	angry, bitter	even-tempered
Depressiveness	pessimistic, glum	optimistic
Self-consciousness	timid, embarrassed	self-assured, glib, shameless
Impulsivity	tempted, urgent	controlled, restrained
Vulnerability	helpless, fragile	clear-thinking, fearless, unflappable
FACTOR 2: EXTRAVERSION VERSUS INTROVERSION		
Warmth	cordial, affectionate, attached	cold, aloof, indifferent
Gregariousness	sociable, outgoing	withdrawn, isolated
Assertiveness	dominant, forceful	unassuming, quiet, resigned
Activity	unassuming, quiet, resigned	passive, lethargic
Excitement seeking	reckless, daring	cautious, monotonous, dull
Positive emotions	high-spirited	placid, anhedonic
FACTOR 3: OPENNESS VERSUS CLOSEDNESS TO ONE'S OWN EXPERIENCE		
Fantasy	dreamers, unrealistic, imaginative	practical, concrete
Aesthetics	aberrant interests, aesthetic	uninvolved, no aesthetic interests
Feelings	self-aware	constricted, unaware
Actions	unconventional, eccentric	routine, predictable, habitual, stubborn
Ideas	unusual, creative	pragmatic, rigid
Values	permissive, broad-minded	traditional, inflexible, dogmatic
FACTOR 4: AGREEABLENESS VERSUS ANTAGONISM		
Trust	gullible, naïve, trusting	skeptical, cynical, suspicious, paranoid
Straightforwardness	confiding, honest	cunning, manipulative, deceptive
Altruism	sacrificial, giving	stingy, selfish, greedy, exploitative
Compliance	docile, cooperative	oppositional, combative, aggressive
Modesty	meek, self-effacing, humble	confident, boastful, arrogant
Tender-mindedness	soft, empathetic	tough, callous, ruthless
FACTOR 5: CONSCIENTIOUSNESS VERSUS UNDEPENDABILITY		
Competence	perfectionistic, efficient	lax, negligent
Order	ordered, methodical, organized	haphazard, disorganized, sloppy
Dutifulness	rigid, reliable, dependable	casual, undependable, unethical
Achievement	workaholic, ambitious	aimless, desultory
Self-discipline	dogged, devoted	hedonistic, negligent
Deliberation	cautious, ruminative, reflective	hasty, careless, rash

Source: Widiger & Mullins-Sweatt, 2009.

As mentioned earlier, the *DSM-5* includes two models of personality disorders. Similar to the *DSM-IV-TR,* the first model is categorical and defines 10 different personality disorders in terms of distinct criteria sets. The categorical model is intended for current clinical use. An alternative trait-specific, or dimensional, model was developed for *DSM-5* and is included in a different section of the manual designated for further study. It makes use of a continuum model of personality disorders such as that represented in the Big 5 model. The alternative model essentially assumes that normal and abnormal personality fall on an integrated continuum of personality, with personality disorders representing more extreme and maladaptive variants of personality traits, as described in this chapter's Along the Continuum feature. We will first describe the *DSM-5*'s current model before turning to a review of its limitations and the *DSM-5*'s alternative model of personality disorders.

GENERAL DEFINITION OF PERSONALITY DISORDER

The *DSM-5* carries forward the categorical perspective first established in *DSM-III* in 1980. It treats personality disorders as if they were entirely different from "normal" personality traits. Unlike prior manuals, however, the *DSM-5* provides a general definition of **personality disorder** that applies to each of the 10 specific personality disorders (Table 2). The general criteria for a personality disorder specify that an individual's personality pattern must *deviate markedly from the expectations of his or her culture* as shown in *styles of thinking about oneself, others, or events; emotional experience and expression; interpersonal functioning; and/or impulse control.* An individual's personality pattern must be *pervasive and inflexible* across situations, be *stable* over time, have an *onset in adolescence or early adulthood*, and lead to *significant distress or functional impairment*. An individual's long-term pattern of functioning also cannot be better explained as a manifestation or consequence of another mental, substance use, or medical disorder.

By definition, a personality disorder is an enduring pattern of thinking, feeling, and behaving that is relatively stable over time, and the particular personality features must be evident by early adulthood. For a personality disorder to be diagnosed in an individual younger than 18 years, the personality patterns must have been present for at least 1 year (with the exception of antisocial personality disorder, which cannot be diagnosed before age 18). Most clinicians will thus assess the stability of personality traits over time and across different situations, taking into account ethnic, cultural, and social background influences and taking care to distinguish the personality traits that define the personality disorders from characteristics that emerge in response to situational stressors or more transient mental states like mood, anxiety, or substance use disorders.

The *DSM-5* also moved away from a multiaxial system of diagnosis, first introduced in *DSM-III,* and collapsed Axes I and II into a common section (see the chapter "Assessing and Diagnosing Abnormality"). Until the *DSM-5,* the personality disorders were treated differently and placed on Axis II, because it was believed that personality disorders were especially pervasive and chronic, rather than occurring in more discrete or acute episodes, which characterize the clinical disorders coded on Axis I. Although most people diagnosed with a personality disorder also experience another clinical disorder at some time in their life (Grant, Stinson, et al., 2004), the *DSM-5* had as one of its goals to reduce comorbidity and no longer regarded the Axis I and Axis II distinction as clinically useful (Links & Eynan, 2013; Morey et al., 2015).

The *DSM-5* groups 10 distinct personality disorders into three clusters based on their descriptive similarities (Table 3). Importantly, *DSM-5* explicitly recognizes that this clustering system is limited, has not been consistently validated, and fails to account for the fact that individuals often show co-occurring personality disorders from different clusters. *Cluster A* includes three disorders characterized by *odd or eccentric behaviors and thinking:* paranoid personality disorder, schizoid personality disorder, and schizotypal personality disorder. Each of these has some of the features of schizophrenia, but people diagnosed with these personality disorders are not out of touch with reality. Their behaviors often appear odd,

TABLE 2 Personality Disorder

The general criteria for a personality disorder specify that an individual's personality pattern must deviate significantly from the expectations of his or her culture as shown in the styles of thinking about oneself, others, or events; emotional experience and expression; interpersonal functioning; and/or impulse control.

TABLE 3 Personality Disorder Clusters

The *DSM-5* groups personality disorders into three clusters based on descriptive similarities.

CLUSTER A: ODD-ECCENTRIC PERSONALITY DISORDERS

People with these disorders have symptoms similar to those of people with schizophrenia, including inappropriate or flat affect, odd thought and speech patterns, and paranoia. People with these disorders maintain their grasp on reality, however.

CLUSTER B: DRAMATIC-EMOTIONAL PERSONALITY DISORDERS

People with these disorders tend to be manipulative, volatile, and uncaring in social relationships. They are prone to impulsive, sometimes violent behaviors that show little regard for their own safety or the safety or needs of others.

CLUSTER C: ANXIOUS-FEARFUL PERSONALITY DISORDERS

People with these disorders are extremely concerned about being criticized or abandoned by others and thus have dysfunctional relationships with others.

eccentric, and inappropriate. For example, they may be chronically suspicious of others or speak in odd ways that are difficult to understand.

Cluster B includes four disorders characterized by *dramatic, erratic, or emotional behavior and interpersonal relationships:* antisocial personality disorder, histrionic personality disorder, borderline personality disorder, and narcissistic personality disorder. People diagnosed with these disorders tend to be manipulative, volatile, and uncaring in social relationships and prone to impulsive behaviors. They may behave in exaggerated ways or even attempt suicide to try to gain attention.

Cluster C includes three disorders characterized by *anxious and fearful emotions and chronic self-doubt:* dependent personality disorder, avoidant personality disorder, and obsessive-compulsive personality disorder. People diagnosed with these disorders have little self-confidence and difficulty in relationships.

CLUSTER A: ODD-ECCENTRIC PERSONALITY DISORDERS

The behavior of people diagnosed with the odd-eccentric personality disorders (Table 4) is similar to that of people with schizophrenia, but these people retain their grasp on reality to a greater degree than do people who are psychotic. They may be paranoid, speak in odd and eccentric ways that make them difficult to understand, have difficulty relating to

TABLE 4 Cluster A: Odd-Eccentric Personality Disorders

People with an odd-eccentric personality disorder may exhibit mild signs of schizophrenia.

Label	Key Features	Relationship to Schizophrenia
Paranoid personality disorder	A pattern of distrust and suspiciousness such that others' motives are interpreted as malevolent	Weak relationship
Schizoid personality disorder	A pattern of detachment from social relationships and a restricted range of emotional expression	Unclear relationship
Schizotypal personality disorder	A pattern of acute discomfort in close relationships, cognitive or perceptual distortions, and eccentricities of behavior	Strong relationship—considered a mild version of schizophrenia

other people, and have unusual beliefs or perceptual experiences that fall short of delusions and hallucinations. Many researchers consider this group of personality disorders to be part of the *schizophrenia spectrum,* particularly schizotypal personality disorder (Nelson, Seal, Pantelis, & Phillips, 2013), though they are below the threshold for the diagnosis of a psychotic disorder (see the chapter "Schizophrenia Spectrum and Other Psychotic Disorders"). That is, these disorders show some attenuated schizophrenia-like symptoms and, especially regarding schizotypal personality disorder, may be precursors to schizophrenia in a small proportion of people. These disorders also more often occur in people with first-degree relatives who have schizophrenia or persecutory type delusional disorder.

Paranoid Personality Disorder

The defining feature of **paranoid personality disorder** is a pattern of pervasive distrust and suspiciousness of others such that their motives are interpreted as malevolent. People diagnosed with this disorder believe that other people are chronically trying to deceive or exploit them, and they are preoccupied with concerns about being victimized or mistreated by others. They are hypervigilant for evidence confirming their suspicions. Often they are penetrating observers of situations, noting details most other people miss. For example, they notice a slight grimace on the face of their boss or an apparently trivial slip of the tongue by their spouse that would go unnoticed by everyone else. Moreover, people diagnosed with paranoid personality disorder consider these events to be highly meaningful and spend a great deal of time trying to decipher such clues to other people's true intentions. They are also very sensitive and angrily reactive to real or perceived criticism and tend to bear grudges.

People with paranoid personality disorder tend to misinterpret situations in line with their suspicions. For example, a husband might interpret his wife's cheerfulness one evening as evidence that she is having an affair with someone at work. These people are resistant to rational arguments against their suspicions and may consider the fact that another person is arguing with them as evidence that the person is part of the conspiracy against them. Some are secretive and withdraw from other people in an attempt to protect themselves, but others become hostile and argumentative, sure that their way of looking at the world is right and superior and that the best defense against the conspiring of others is a good offense. Felix, in the following case study, was diagnosed with paranoid personality disorder.

CASE STUDY

Felix is a 59-year-old construction worker who worries that his co-workers might hurt him. Last week, while he was using a table saw, Felix's hand slipped and his fingers came very close to being cut badly. Felix wonders if someone sabotaged the saw, so that somehow the piece of wood he was working with slipped and drew his hand into the saw blade. Since this incident, Felix has observed his co-workers looking at him and whispering to each other. He mentioned his suspicion that the saw had been tampered with to his boss, but the boss told him that was a crazy idea and that Felix obviously had just been careless.

Felix does not have any close friends. Even his brothers and sisters avoid him, because he frequently misinterprets things they say to be criticisms of him. Felix was married for a few years, but his wife left him when he began to demand that she not see any of her friends or go out without him, because he suspected she was having affairs with other men. Felix lives in a middle-class neighborhood in a small town that has very little crime. Still, he owns three handguns and a shotgun, which are always loaded, in expectation of someone breaking into his house.

Epidemiological studies suggest that between 0.7 and 5.1 percent of people in the general population can be diagnosed with paranoid personality disorder (Lenzenweger, 2008; Trull, Jahng, Tomko, Wood, & Sher, 2010). People diagnosed with this disorder appear to be at increased risk for a number of clinical disorders, including major depression, anxiety disorders, substance abuse, and psychotic episodes (Grant, Stinson, et al., 2004; Trull et al., 2010), as well as impaired vocational functioning (McGurk et al., 2013). Not surprisingly, they are difficult to get along with, and their interpersonal relationships, including intimate relationships, tend to be unstable. Retrospective studies suggest that their prognosis generally is poor, with their symptoms intensifying under stress, sometimes experiencing very brief psychotic episodes.

Theories of Paranoid Personality Disorder

Some family history studies have shown that paranoid personality disorder is more common in the families of people with schizophrenia than in the families of healthy control subjects. This finding suggests that paranoid personality disorder may be part of the schizophrenia spectrum of disorders. One twin study found the heritability of paranoid personality disorder to be .50 (Coolidge, Thede, & Jang, 2004).

Cognitive theorists view paranoid personality disorder as the result of an underlying belief that other people are malevolent and deceptive, combined with a lack of self-confidence about being able to defend oneself against others (Beck, Davis, & Freeman, 2015). Thus, the person must always be vigilant for signs of others' deceit or criticism and must be quick to act against others. A study of 17 patients diagnosed with paranoid personality disorder found that they endorsed beliefs as predicted by this cognitive theory more than did patients diagnosed with other personality disorders (Beck et al., 2001).

As in many disorders, there are also social contributors to paranoid personality disorder. In the United States, African Americans report higher rates of paranoid personality disorder than whites. This disparity is likely due in part to increased exposure in this group to social and environmental risk factors that may lead individuals to be more mistrustful or suspicious. Differential exposure to discrimination, prejudice, childhood trauma, and especially socioeconomic status appear to contribute to this demographic disparity (Iacovino, Jackson, & Oltmanns, 2014).

Treatment of Paranoid Personality Disorder

People diagnosed with paranoid personality disorder usually come into contact with clinicians only when they are in crisis. They may seek treatment for severe symptoms of depression or anxiety, but they often do not feel a need for treatment of their paranoia. Their guarded and suspicious style will often undercut the development of a trusting, therapeutic relationship. In addition, therapists' attempts to challenge their paranoid thinking are likely to be misinterpreted in line with their paranoid belief system. For these reasons, treating paranoid personality disorder can be quite difficult (Millon, Grossman, Millon, Meagher, & Ramnath, 2004).

In order to gain the trust of a person diagnosed with a paranoid personality disorder, the therapist must be calm, respectful, and extremely straightforward. The therapist cannot directly confront the client's paranoid thinking but instead must rely on indirect means of raising questions in the client's mind about his or her typical way of interpreting situations. Although many therapists do not expect paranoid clients to achieve full insight into their problems, they hope that, by developing at least some degree of trust in the therapist, the client can learn to trust others a bit more and thus develop somewhat improved interpersonal relationships.

Cognitive therapy for people diagnosed with this disorder focuses on increasing their sense of self-efficacy in dealing with difficult situations, thus decreasing their fear and hostility toward others. As an example, consider the following interchange between a cognitive therapist and a woman, Ann, who believed that her co-workers were intentionally trying to annoy her and to turn her supervisor against her.

PROFILES

Therapist: You're reacting as though this is a very dangerous situation. What are the risks you see?

Ann: They'll keep dropping things and making noise to annoy me.

Therapist: Are you sure nothing worse is at risk?

Ann: Yeah.

Therapist: So you don't think there's much chance of them attacking you or anything?

Ann: Nah, they wouldn't do that.

Therapist: If they do keep dropping things and making noises, how bad will that be?

Ann: Like I told you, it's real aggravating. It really bugs me.

Therapist: So it would continue pretty much as it's been going for years now.

Ann: Yeah. It bugs me, but I can take it.

Therapist: And you know that if it keeps happening, at the very least you can keep handling it the way you have been—holding the aggravation in, then taking it out on your husband when you get home. Suppose we could come up with some ways to handle the aggravation even better or to have them get to you less. Is that something you'd be interested in?

Ann: Yeah, that sounds good.

Therapist: Another risk you mentioned earlier is that they might talk to your supervisor and turn her against you. As you see it, how long have they been trying to do this?

Ann: Ever since I've been there.

Therapist: How much luck have they had so far in doing that?

Ann: Not much.

Therapist: Do you see any indications that they're going to have any more success now than they have so far?

Ann: No, I don't guess so.

(continued)

Therapist: So your gut reaction is as though the situation at work is really dangerous. But when you stop and think it through, you conclude that the worst they're going to do is to be really aggravating, and that even if we don't come up with anything new, you can handle it well enough to get by. Does that sound right?

Ann: [Smiling] Yeah, I guess so.

Therapist: And if we can come up with some ways to handle the stress better or handle them better, there will be even less they can do to you.

(Beck, A. T. & Freeman, A. M., *Cognitive Therapy of Personality Disorders,* pp. 245–247. New York: Guilford Press. Copyright ©2009 by Guilford Press. Reprinted with permission.)

In this interchange, the therapist did not directly challenge Ann's beliefs about her co-workers' intentions but did try to reduce the sense of danger Ann felt about her workplace by helping her redefine the situation as aggravating rather than threatening. The therapist also enlisted Ann in an effort to develop new coping skills that might further reduce her aggravation and develop a sense of self-efficacy.

Schizoid Personality Disorder

You may have heard the term "schizoid" used to describe people who strongly prefer to turn their attention inward and away from the outside world, often engaging in solitary activities. People diagnosed with **schizoid personality disorder** show a pervasive pattern of detachment from social relationships and a restricted range of emotional expression in their interactions with others. They seem indifferent to opportunities to develop close relationships and derive little, if any, pleasure from family or social interactions. Their experience and expression of positive emotions are very low, and their interest in having sexual experiences with another person is typically very limited. Other people describe them as emotionally aloof or cold, "loners," or "bland," uninteresting, and humorless. People diagnosed with this disorder are often indifferent to others' praise or criticism, and they take pleasure in few activities. While they tend to view relationships with others as unrewarding, messy, and intrusive, in those few situations in which they may temporarily feel comfortable talking about themselves, they may acknowledge having painful feelings, particularly related to social interactions. The man described next shows several of these symptoms.

CASE STUDY

Roy was a successful sanitation engineer involved in the planning and maintenance of water resources for a large city; his job called for considerable foresight and independent judgment but little supervisory responsibility. In general, he was appraised as an undistinguished but competent and reliable employee. There were few demands of an interpersonal nature made of him, and he was viewed by most of his colleagues as reticent and shy and by others as cold and aloof.

Difficulties centered around his relationship with his wife. At her urging they sought marital counseling, for, as she put it, "he is unwilling to join in family activities, he fails to take interest in the children, he lacks affection, and he is disinterested in sex."

The pattern of social indifference, flatness of affect, and personal isolation that characterized much of Roy's behavior was of little consequence to those with whom a deeper or more intimate relationship was not called for; with his immediate family, however, these traits took their toll. (Source: Millon, 1969, p. 224)

Roy would be diagnosed with schizoid personality disorder because of his long-standing avoidance of relationships with other people and his lack of close relationships with family members.

Schizoid personality disorder is uncommon, with about 0.8 to 1.7 percent of adults manifesting the disorder at some time in their life (Lenzenweger, 2008; Trull et al., 2010). This disorder appears to occur somewhat more often in men than women (Trull et al., 2010; Zimmerman, Rothschild, & Chelminski, 2005). People with schizoid personality disorder can function in society, particularly in occupations that do not require frequent interpersonal interactions.

Theories of Schizoid Personality Disorder

There is a slightly increased rate of schizoid personality disorder in the relatives of persons with schizophrenia, but the link between the two disorders is not clear (Kendler, Neale, Kessler, Heath, & Eaves, 1993). Twin studies of the personality traits associated with schizoid personality disorder, such as low sociability and low warmth, strongly suggest that these personality traits may be partially inherited (Widiger & Costa, 2013). The evidence for the heritability of schizoid personality disorder is only indirect, however.

Treatment of Schizoid Personality Disorder

As you might expect, people with schizoid personality disorder may not be very motivated for treatment, and the interpersonal closeness of therapy may be experienced as stressful instead of supportive. Despite these treatment challenges, psychosocial treatments for schizoid personality disorder focus on increasing the person's awareness of his or her own feelings, as well as increasing his or her social skills and social contacts (Beck et al., 2015). The therapist may model the expression of feelings for the client and help the client identify and express his or her own feelings. Social skills training, done through role-playing with the therapist and homework assignments in which the client tries out new social skills with other people, is an important component of cognitive therapies. Some therapists recommend group therapy for people with schizoid personality disorder. In the context of group sessions, the group members can model interpersonal relationships, and each person with schizoid personality disorder can practice new social skills directly with other group members.

Schizotypal Personality Disorder

People diagnosed with **schizotypal personality disorder** show symptoms similar to those of schizophrenia but in milder form. Like schizoid and paranoid personality disorders, people with schizotypal personality disorder tend to be socially isolated, to have a restricted range of emotions, and to be uncomfortable in interpersonal interactions (Table 5). As children, they are passive, socially unengaged, and hypersensitive to criticism (Olin et al., 1999), and they may attract teasing because they appear "odd" or "eccentric."

The distinguishing characteristics of schizotypal personality disorder are the cognitive and perceptual distortions and odd and eccentric behaviors. These characteristics generally fall into four categories (Beck et al., 2015).

The first category is paranoia or suspiciousness. As in paranoid personality disorder, people diagnosed with schizotypal personality disorder perceive other people as deceitful and hostile, and much of their social anxiety emerges from this paranoia. The second category is ideas of reference. People diagnosed with schizotypal personality disorder tend to believe that random events or circumstances have a particular meaning just for them. For example, they may think it highly significant that a fire occurred in a store in which they had shopped only yesterday. The third category is odd beliefs and magical thinking. For example, they may believe that others know what they are thinking. The fourth category is illusions that are just short of hallucinations. For example, they may think they see people in the patterns of wallpaper.

In addition to demonstrating cognitive and perceptual distortions, people diagnosed with schizotypal personality disorder tend to have speech that is tangential, circumstantial, vague, or overelaborate. In interactions with others, they may have inappropriate emotional responses or no emotional response to what other people say or do. Their behaviors also are odd, sometimes reflecting their odd thoughts. They may be easily distracted or may fixate on an object for a long period of time, lost in thought or fantasy.

Although these oddities of thought, speech, and behavior are similar in quality to those seen in schizophrenia, their severity is not as great as in schizophrenia, and people diagnosed with schizotypal personality disorder retain basic contact with reality. The man in the following case study shows many of the oddities of schizotypal personality disorder.

TABLE 5 Schizotypal Personality Disorder*

A pervasive pattern of social and interpersonal deficits marked by acute discomfort with, and reduced capacity for, close relationships as well as by cognitive or perceptual distortions and eccentricities of behavior, beginning by early adulthood.

—Symptoms include:

- Restricted range of emotion
- Uncomfortable interpersonal interactions
- Odd and eccentric behavior
- Paranoia

—Prevalence rate is 3.9 percent of general population

—More commonly diagnosed in males than in females

*The information presented in this table is based solely on the author's interpretation of *DSM-5*. It does not reflect the exact language that appears in *DSM-5* and is not, therefore, formally endorsed by the American Psychological Association.

CASE STUDY

A 41-year-old man was referred to a community mental health center's activities program for help in improving his social skills. He had a lifelong pattern of social isolation, with no real friends, and spent long hours worrying that his angry thoughts about his older brother would cause his brother harm. He had previously worked as a clerk in civil service but had lost his job because of poor attendance and low productivity.

On interview the patient was distant and somewhat distrustful. He described in elaborate and often irrelevant detail his rather uneventful and routine daily life. For two days he had studied the washing instructions on a new pair of jeans: Did "Wash before wearing" mean that the jeans were to be washed before wearing the first time, or did they need, for some reason, to be washed each time before they were worn? He did not regard concerns such as these as senseless, though he acknowledged that the amount of time spent thinking about them might be excessive. He could recite from memory his most recent monthly bank statement, including the amount of every check and the running balance as each check was written. He knew his balance on any particular day, but he sometimes got anxious if he considered whether a certain check or deposit had actually cleared. (Reprinted with permission from the *DSM-IV Casebook: A Learning Companion to the Diagnostic and Statistical Manual of Mental Disorders,* Fourth Edition. Copyright ©1994 by American Psychiatric Association. All Rights Reserved.)

The prevalence of schizotypal personality disorder in the general population is 3.9 percent (Pulay et al., 2009) and is more commonly diagnosed in males than in females (Trull et al., 2010; Zimmerman et al., 2005). People diagnosed with schizotypal personality disorder are at increased risk for depression and for schizophrenia or isolated psychotic episodes (Kwapil & Barrantes-Vidal, 2012).

For a person to be given a diagnosis of schizotypal personality disorder, his or her odd or eccentric thoughts cannot be part of cultural beliefs, such as a cultural belief in magic or specific superstitions. Still, some psychologists have argued that people of color are diagnosed more often with schizophrenia-like disorders, such as schizotypal personality disorder, than are whites because white clinicians often misinterpret culturally bound beliefs as evidence of schizotypal thinking (Snowden & Cheung, 1990; see Schwartz & Blankenship, 2014). One large study of people in treatment found that African American patients were more likely than white or Hispanic patients to be diagnosed with schizotypal personality disorder on both self-report and standardized diagnostic interviews (Chavira et al., 2003). This finding suggests that African Americans may be diagnosed with this disorder relatively frequently even when steps are taken to avoid clinician bias. It is possible that African Americans are more likely to be exposed to conditions that enhance a biological vulnerability to schizophrenia-like disorders. These conditions include urban living and low socioeconomic status (see the chapter "Schizophrenia Spectrum and Other Psychotic Disorders" for a discussion of these conditions in schizophrenia).

Theories of Schizotypal Personality Disorder

Schizotypal personality disorder is the most well-researched of the cluster A personality disorders. Family history, adoption, and twin studies all suggest that schizotypal personality disorder is transmitted genetically (Nelson et al., 2013). Indeed, a twin study found the heritability of schizotypal personality disorder to be .81 (Coolidge et al., 2004). In addition, schizotypal personality disorder is much more common in the first-degree relatives of people with schizophrenia than in the relatives of either psychiatric patients or healthy control groups (Kendler et al., 1993; Kwapil & Barrantes-Vidal, 2012). This supports the view that schizotypal personality disorder is a mild form of schizophrenia that is transmitted through genes in ways similar to those in schizophrenia. A gene that regulates the NMDA receptor system has been associated with both schizophrenia and schizotypal personality disorder (Ohi et al., 2012).

People with schizotypal personality disorder show many of the same cognitive deficits as people with schizophrenia, including difficulties in verbal fluency, in inhibiting information when a task calls for it, and in memory (Barch & Sheffield, 2017; Cochrane, Petch, & Pickering, 2012; Mitropoulou et al., 2003). People with schizotypal personality disorder, like people with schizophrenia, tend to show dysregulation of the neurotransmitter dopamine in the brain (Abi-Dargham et al., 2004). Thus, like people with schizophrenia, people with schizotypal personality disorder may have abnormally high levels of dopamine in some areas of the brain.

Although people with schizotypal personality disorder show abnormalities in the same areas of the brain as people with schizophrenia, these abnormalities tend to be less severe in schizotypal personality disorder than in schizophrenia, perhaps reflecting the less severe symptoms (Barch & Sheffield, 2017; Kwapil & Barrantes-Vidal, 2012). For example, one study showed that people with both disorders show gray matter reductions in areas of the temporal lobe of the brain compared to controls, but the reductions were less in people with schizotypal personality disorder than in people with schizophrenia (Takahashi et al., 2011). Some research finds that people with schizotypal personality disorder do not tend to show the abnormalities in the prefrontal areas of the brain shown by people with schizophrenia (e.g., Suzuki et al., 2005), perhaps reflecting the less severe symptoms in schizotypal personality disorder.

People with schizotypal personality disorder also tend to have more frequent histories of a wide range of childhood adversities compared to the general population, including physical, emotional, and sexual abuse and having a parent who was battered, abused substances, or spent time in jail.

Treatment of Schizotypal Personality Disorder

Schizotypal personality disorder is most often treated with the same drugs used to treat schizophrenia, including traditional neuroleptics such as haloperidol and thiothixene and atypical antipsychotics such as olanzapine, and typically at lower doses (Ripoll, Triebwasser, & Siever, 2011). As in schizophrenia, these drugs appear to relieve psychotic-like symptoms, which include distorted ideas of reference, magical thinking, and illusions. Antidepressants sometimes are used to help people with schizotypal personality disorder who are experiencing significant distress.

Although there are few psychological theories of schizotypal personality disorder, psychological therapies have been developed to help people with this disorder overcome some of their symptoms. In psychotherapy for schizotypal personality disorder, it is especially important for the therapist to first establish a good relationship with the client, because these clients typically have few close relationships and tend to struggle with paranoid thoughts and excessive social anxiety (Beck et al., 2015). The next step in therapy is to help the client increase social contacts and learn socially appropriate behaviors through social skills training. Group therapy may be especially helpful in increasing clients' social skills.

The crucial component of cognitive therapy with clients diagnosed with schizotypal personality disorder is teaching them to look for objective evidence in the environment to support their thoughts and to disregard bizarre thoughts. For example, a client who frequently thinks she is not real can be taught to identify that thought as bizarre and to discount the thought when it occurs, rather than taking it seriously and acting on it. This psychotherapy approach is similar to cognitive-behavioral approaches to psychotic disorders (see the chapter "Schizophrenia Spectrum and Other Psychotic Disorders"). Because symptoms are typically less severe than in schizophrenia, techniques like challenging perceptions and thoughts may be more readily accepted by the patient (Beck & Rector, 2005; Garety & Freeman, 2013).

CLUSTER B: DRAMATIC-EMOTIONAL PERSONALITY DISORDERS

People diagnosed with the dramatic-emotional personality disorders engage in behaviors that are dramatic and impulsive, and they often show little regard for their own safety or the safety of others (Table 6). For example, they may engage in suicidal behaviors

TABLE 6 Cluster B Personality Disorders: Dramatic-Emotional

People with dramatic-emotional personality disorders tend to have unstable emotions and to engage in dramatic and impulsive behavior.

Label	Key Features	Similar Disorders
Antisocial personality disorder	A pattern of disregard for, and violation of, the rights of others; criminal, impulsive, deceitful, or callous behavior; lack of remorse	Conduct disorder (evidenced by age 15)
Borderline personality disorder	A pattern of instability in self-image, mood, and interpersonal relationships and marked impulsivity; transient dissociative states; highly reactive to real or imagined abandonment	Mood disorders
Histrionic personality disorder	A pattern of excessive emotionality and attention seeking; dramatic, seductive, or provocative behavior; suggestible; shallow emotional expression and relationships	Somatoform disorders, mood disorders
Narcissistic personality disorder	A pattern of grandiosity, need for admiration, and lack of empathy; entitled, arrogant, and exploitative attitudes and behavior	Manic symptoms

or self-damaging acts such as self-cutting. They also may act in hostile, even violent, ways against others. One core feature of this group of disorders is a lack of concern for others. Two of the disorders in this cluster, borderline personality disorder and antisocial personality disorder, have been the focus of a great deal of research, whereas the other two, histrionic personality disorder and narcissistic personality disorder, have not. Because antisocial personality disorder shares important symptom patterns that have a developmental continuity with conduct disorder, it is discussed in the chapter "Disruptive, Impulse-Control, and Conduct Disorders."

Borderline Personality Disorder

Recall that Susanna Kaysen, whom we met in the Extraordinary People feature, suffered a variety of symptoms and received a diagnosis of **borderline personality disorder,** which she later questioned. In the following case study, a clinician describes her introduction to another woman who later was diagnosed with borderline personality disorder.

CASE STUDY

At the initial meeting, Cindy was a 30-year-old, white, married woman with no children who was living in a middle-class suburban area with her husband. She had a college education and had successfully completed almost 2 years of medical school. Cindy was referred by her psychiatrist of 11 years, who was no longer willing to provide more than pharmacotherapy following a recent hospitalization for a near-lethal suicide attempt. In the 2 years prior to referral, Cindy had been hospitalized at least 10 times (one lasting 6 months) for psychiatric treatment of suicidal ideation; had engaged in numerous instances of parasuicidal behavior, including at least 10 instances of drinking Clorox bleach, multiple deep cuts, and burns; and had had three medically severe or nearly lethal suicide attempts, including cutting an artery in her neck.

Until age 27 Cindy was able to function well in work and school settings, and her marriage was reasonably satisfactory to both partners, although the husband complained of Cindy's excessive anger. When Cindy was in the second year of medical school, a classmate she knew only slightly committed suicide. Cindy stated that when she heard about the suicide, she immediately decided to kill herself also but had very little insight into what about the situation actually elicited the inclination to kill herself. Within weeks she left medical school and became severely depressed and actively suicidal. Although Cindy presented herself as a person with few psychological problems before the classmate's suicide, further questioning revealed a history of severe anorexia nervosa, bulimia nervosa, and alcohol and prescription medication abuse, originating at age 14.

Over the course of therapy, a consistent pattern associated with self-harm became apparent. The chain of events would often begin with an interpersonal encounter (almost always with her husband), which culminated in her feeling threatened, criticized, or unloved. These feelings would often be followed by urges either to self-mutilate or to kill herself, depending somewhat on her levels of hopelessness, anger, and sadness. Decisions to self-mutilate and/or to attempt suicide were often accompanied by the thought "I'll show you." At other times, hopelessness and a desire to end the pain permanently seemed predominant. Following the conscious decision to self-mutilate or attempt suicide, Cindy would then immediately dissociate and at some later point cut or burn herself, usually while in a state of "automatic pilot." Consequently, Cindy often had difficulty remembering specifics of the actual acts. At one point, Cindy burned her leg so badly (and then injected it with dirt to convince the doctor that he should give her more attention) that reconstructive surgery was required. (Source: Linehan, M. M., Cochran, B. N., & Kehrer, K. C., "Dialectical Behavior Therapy for Borderline Personality Disorder," in D. H. Barlow (Ed.), *Clinical Handbook of Psychological Disorders: A Step-by-Step Treatment Manual,* Third Edition, pp. 502–504. Copyright ©2001 by Guilford Press. Reprinted with permission.)

Cindy's symptoms represent some of the benchmarks of borderline personality disorder: out-of-control emotions that cannot be smoothed, a hypersensitivity to abandonment, a tendency to cling too tightly to other people, and a history of hurting oneself (see the *DSM-5* criteria in Table 7). This disorder is characterized by fundamental deficits in identity and in interpersonal relationships. The self-concept of people with borderline personality disorder is unstable, with periods of extreme self-doubt alternating with periods of grandiose self-importance and accompanied by a need for others to support their self-esteem. Further, like Cindy, people with this disorder are prone to transient dissociative states, in which they feel unreal, lose track of time, and may even forget who they are.

TABLE 7 Borderline Personality Disorder*

A pervasive pattern of instability of interpersonal relationships, self-image, and affect and marked impulsivity beginning by early adulthood.
—Symptoms include: • Out-of-control emotions • Unstable interpersonal relationships • Concerns about abandonment • Self-damaging behavior • Impulsivity • Frequently accompanied by depression, anxiety, or anger —Prevalence rate is 5.9 percent of general population —More commonly diagnosed in females than in males

*The information presented in this table is based solely on the author's interpretation of *DSM-5*. It does not reflect the exact language that appears in *DSM-5* and is not, therefore, formally endorsed by the American Psychological Association.

Their interpersonal relationships are extremely unstable—they can switch from idealizing others to despising them without provocation. People with borderline personality disorder often describe an emptiness that leads them to cling to new acquaintances or therapists in an attempt to fill their internal void. They worry about abandonment and misinterpret other people's everyday actions as desertion or rejection. For example, if a therapist has to cancel an appointment because of illness, a client with borderline personality disorder might interpret this as rejection by the therapist and become very depressed or angry.

Along with instability of self-concept and interpersonal relationships, the mood of people with borderline personality disorder is unstable, with bouts of severe depression, anxiety, or anger seeming to arise frequently, often without cause. People with this disorder also show a strong tendency to engage in impulsive, self-damaging behaviors, including self-mutilating or suicidal behavior. Cindy's self-mutilating behavior was to cut and burn herself.

The variety of symptoms in borderline personality disorder and their shifting nature make it a complex disorder to diagnose and treat. This complexity is heightened by the fact that people with borderline personality disorder frequently are also diagnosed with another mental disorder, such as substance abuse, depression, generalized anxiety disorder, a simple phobia, agoraphobia, posttraumatic stress disorder, panic disorder, or somatization disorder (Eaton et al., 2011; Hasin et al., 2011). About 75 percent of people with borderline personality disorder attempt suicide, and about 10 percent die by suicide (Soloff & Chiapetta, 2012). The greatest risk for suicide appears to be in the first year or two after diagnosis with the disorder, possibly because people often are not diagnosed until a crisis brings them to the attention of the mental health system.

A large nationwide study of adults in the United States found that 5.9 percent could be diagnosed with borderline personality disorder (Zanarini, Frankenburg, Reich, & Fitzmaurice, 2012). In clinical settings, borderline personality disorder is diagnosed much more often in women than in men, but the gender difference in a large nationwide study of adults in the community was small. It is somewhat more commonly diagnosed in people of color than in whites, and in people in the lower socioeconomic classes than in people in other classes (Chavira et al., 2003; De Genna & Feske, 2013). A large study of people in treatment for personality disorders found that Hispanics were more likely than whites or African Americans to be diagnosed with borderline personality disorder (Chavira et al., 2003). This could be because factors that contribute to the disorder, such as extreme stress, are more common among Hispanics. Or clinicians may overdiagnose the disorder in Hispanic people because they do not take into account Hispanic cultural norms that permit greater expression of strong emotions such as anger, aggressiveness, and sexual attraction (Chavira et al., 2003).

Although borderline personality disorder has been viewed as a chronic, intractable disorder by clinicians, recent studies have shown that over 85 percent of people diagnosed with this disorder show remission of symptoms within 10 to 15 years and that only a minority of those in remission have a relapse of the disorder (Gunderson, Stout, et al., 2011; Zanarini,

Frankenburg, et al., 2012). The ability of these individuals to hold a job significantly improved over the time period studied, but they continued to show difficulty in having stable, positive social relationships. Stressful life events and lack of social support are triggers for relapse in individuals whose symptoms have remitted (Gunderson, Stout, et al., 2011).

Theories of Borderline Personality Disorder

Given the emotional instability characteristic of borderline personality disorder, it is not surprising that several theorists have argued that people with this disorder have fundamental deficits in regulating emotion (Baer, Peters, Eisenlohr-Moul, Geider, & Sauer, 2012; Carpenter & Trull, 2013; Selby, Anestis, Bender, & Joiner, 2009). People with borderline personality disorder score higher than healthy subjects on measures of difficulty in regulating emotion and in laboratory tasks assessing unwillingness to tolerate emotional distress in order to reach a goal (Gratz, Moore, & Tull, 2016; Gratz, Rosenthal, Tull, Lejuez, & Gunderson, 2010). In one study, participants carried beepers that randomly cued them to provide ratings of their moods. People with borderline personality disorder showed greater variability in their moods, particularly with regard to hostility, fear, and sadness, than people with no personality disorder (Trull et al., 2008). A similar set of studies tracked the emotions of patients with borderline personality disorder during their days and found that, compared to healthy individuals, patients experienced a more negative emotional baseline, more emotional variability, and somewhat slower return to their emotional baseline (Ebner-Priemer et al., 2015).

Cognitively, people with borderline personality disorder are hyperattentive to negative emotional stimuli in the environment, their memories tend to be more negative, and they tend to make negatively biased interpretations of situations (Baer et al., 2012). While they frequently try to suppress their negative thoughts, their attempts usually are unsuccessful, and they end up ruminating about the negative thoughts or acting out impulsively or aggressively in response to them (Selby et al., 2009). The combination of emotional and cognitive dysfunction in borderline personality disorder is also linked with the disruption in interpersonal behavior that can cause so much impairment. Laboratory and observational studies show that individuals with the disorder tend to hold more negative views of others and of relationships, sometimes struggle to empathize with others' perspectives, and engage in poor problem solving in social scenarios (Lazarus, Cheavens, Festa, & Rosenthal, 2014).

What do these difficulties in processing and regulating emotion stem from? Empirical studies have found that people with borderline personality disorder are more likely than people without the disorder to report a childhood marked by instability, neglect, and parental psychopathology (Gunderson, Zanarini, et al., 2011; Helgeland & Torgersen, 2004). They often have a history of physical and sexual abuse during childhood (Afifi et al., 2011; Martins, de Carvalho Tofoli, Von Werne Baes, & Juruena, 2011). This abuse, neglect, and instability could contribute to difficulties in regulating emotions and in attaining a positive, stable identity through several mechanisms.

Marsha Linehan (see Neacsiu & Linehan, 2014) suggests that a history of exposure to abuse, neglect, criticism, and emotional invalidation by significant others makes it difficult for people with borderline personality disorder to learn appropriate emotion-regulation skills and to understand and accept their emotional reactions to events. People with this disorder come to rely on others to help them cope with difficult situations but do not have enough self-confidence to ask for this help in mature or effective ways. They become "manipulative" and indirect in their attempt to gain support from others (for example, by injuring themselves or creating crises), and their extreme emotional reactions to situations lead to impulsive actions.

Psychoanalytic theorists, particularly those in the object relations school (Kernberg, 1979; Klein, 1952), suggest that people with borderline personality disorder never learned to fully differentiate their view of themselves from their view of others, making them extremely reactive to others' opinions of them and to the possibility of abandonment. When they perceive others as rejecting them, they reject themselves and may engage in self-punishment or self-mutilation. They also have never been able to integrate the positive and negative qualities of either their self-concept or their concept of others, because their early caregivers rewarded them when they remained dependent and compliant, but became hostile when they tried to separate from the caregivers. They tend to see themselves and other people as either all good or all bad and to vacillate between these two views, a process known as *splitting*. The instability in their emotions and interpersonal relationships is due to such splitting, reflecting their vacillation between the all-good and the all-bad self and the all-good and the all-bad other. For example, a person with borderline personality disorder might view her partner as the sweetest, most caring person in the world when they are getting along, but when he does something frustrating, she might suddenly view him as totally unsupportive, unintelligent, and selfish, with no sense that he could have a mix of these positive and negative characteristics.

Neuroimaging studies show that the amygdala and hippocampus of people with borderline personality disorder are smaller in volume than those of people without the disorder (Ruocco, Amirthavasagam, & Zakzanis, 2012). Recall that the amygdala is a part of the brain that is important in the processing of emotion and that the hippocampus is involved in the regulation of stress and in memory. In addition, people with borderline personality disorder have greater activation of the amygdala in response to pictures of emotional faces, which may partly explain the difficulty they have in regulating their moods (Donegan et al., 2003; Mier et al., 2012). Neuroimaging studies also have found structural and metabolic abnormalities in the prefrontal cortex of patients with borderline personality disorder (Soloff et al., 2012). This area of the brain is important in the regulation of emotional reactions and control of impulsive behavior. Impaired functioning in the amygdala and prefrontal cortex has been linked with the emotional lability and dysregulation found in people with borderline personality disorder (Silvers et al., 2016).

The neurobiological differences between people with borderline personality disorder and healthy individuals could be due to genetic factors. The disorder runs in families (Gunderson, Zanarini, et al., 2011), and twin studies provide evidence that the symptoms of borderline personality disorder are heritable (Distel et al., 2009). Early abuse and maltreatment also are associated with changes in the structure and organization of the brain, particularly the amygdala and hippocampus, which may explain in part why child abuse could contribute to the deficits seen in people with the disorder (Ruocco et al., 2012).

Treatment of Borderline Personality Disorder

One of the first psychotherapies shown to have positive effects in patients with borderline personality disorder was **dialectical behavior therapy** (Neacsiu & Linehan, 2014). This therapy focuses on helping clients gain a more realistic and positive sense of self, learn adaptive skills for solving problems and regulating emotions, and correct dichotomous thinking. Therapists teach clients to monitor self-disparaging thoughts and black-or-white evaluations of people and situations and to challenge these thoughts and evaluations. Therapists also help clients learn appropriate assertiveness skills to use in close relationships so that they can express their needs and feelings in a mature manner. Clients may learn how to control their impulsive behaviors by monitoring situations most likely to lead to such behaviors and learning alternative ways to handle those situations. Controlled clinical trials comparing dialectical behavior therapy to wait list controls have found that the therapy reduces depression, anxiety, and self-mutilating behavior while increasing interpersonal functioning (e.g., Bohus et al., 2004; Linehan et al., 2006; see Choi-Kain, Finch, Masland, Jenkins, & Unruh, 2017; Panos, Jackson, Hasan, & Panos, 2014).

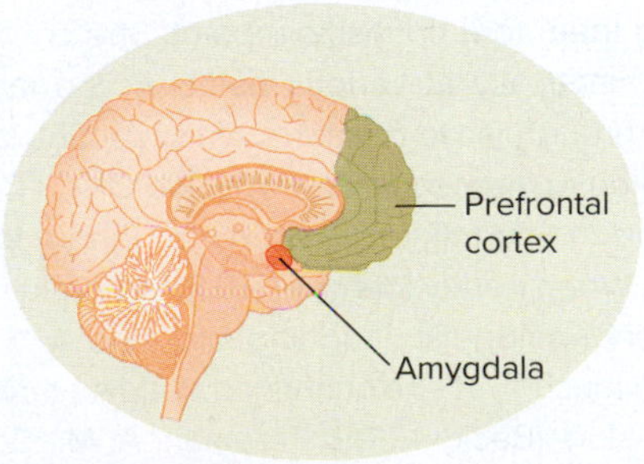

The amygdala and the prefrontal cortex have been implicated in borderline personality disorder.

Cognitive therapy treatments for borderline personality disorder have also proven helpful. *Systems training for emotional predictability and problem solving* (STEPPS) is a group intervention for people with borderline personality disorder that combines cognitive techniques challenging irrational and maladaptive cognitions and behavioral techniques addressing self-management and problem solving. A clinical trial of STEPPS compared to usual therapy (support plus medication) showed that clients receiving STEPPS showed greater improvement in negative affect, impulsivity, and functioning than clients receiving the usual therapy (Blum et al., 2008). Similarly, trials of cognitive-behavioral therapy focusing on challenging patients' maladaptive core beliefs and teaching them more adaptive ways to function in daily life resulted in significant reductions in hospitalizations and suicide attempts, as well as greater improvements in mood, compared to patients receiving general support (Davidson et al., 2006; Giesen-Bloo et al., 2006; Sempértegui, Karreman, Arntz, & Bekker, 2013).

Psychodynamically oriented therapies also show promise in the treatment of borderline personality disorder. **Transference-focused therapy** uses the relationship between patient and therapist to help patients develop a more realistic and healthier understanding of themselves and their interpersonal relationships. Patients with borderline personality disorder receiving this therapy showed reductions in suicidality, impulsivity, aggression, and anger (Clarkin, Levy, Lenzenweger, & Kernberg, 2007). **Mentalization-based treatment** is based on the theory that people with borderline personality disorder have fundamental difficulty understanding the mental states of themselves and others because of traumatic experiences in

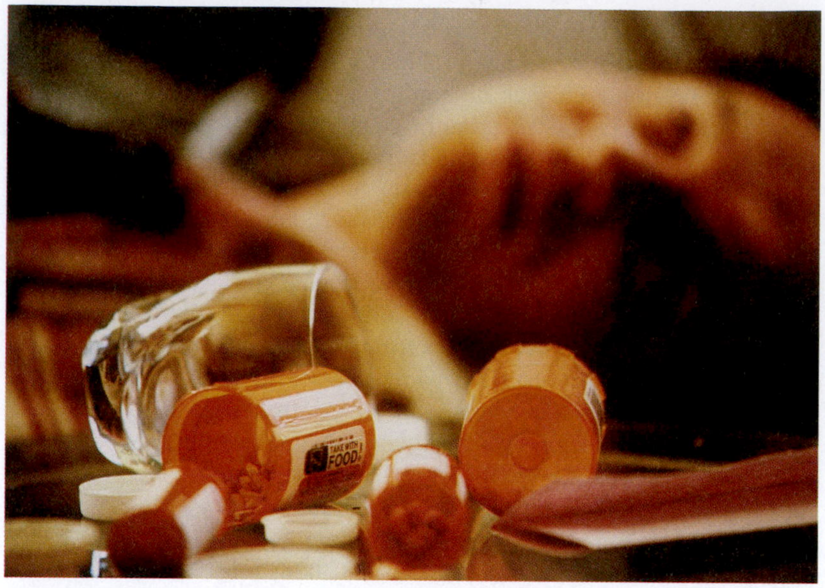

Suicidal behavior is common among people with borderline personality disorder.
©Esbin-Anderson/The Image Works

childhood and poor attachment to their caregivers (Fonagy & Bateman, 2008). This psychodynamically oriented therapy provides patients with validation and support. Further, it attempts to help patients appreciate alternatives to their own subjective sense of self and others by using the relationship between the patient and the therapist, and the patient and others, to illustrate those alternatives. One long-term study found significant improvement in mood and functioning in patients receiving mentalization-based therapy compared to patients receiving typical community care. Also, over a 5-year follow-up, patients receiving mentalization-based therapy needed less medication, had fewer suicide attempts, and continued to function better on several dimensions than patients receiving the usual care (Bateman & Fonagy, 2008).

The first-line treatment for borderline personality disorder is psychotherapy (Choi-Kain et al., 2017). Some medications may be useful in treatment, including the mood stabilizers aripiprazole and lamotrigine and the atypical antipsychotics, such as olanzapine and quetiapine (Black et al., 2014; Zanarini, Schulz, et al., 2012; see Stoffers & Lieb, 2015). You might expect serotonin reuptake inhibitors to improve mood and reduce aggressiveness and impulsivity in people with borderline personality disorder, but so far evidence of their effectiveness is lacking (Stoffers & Lieb, 2015). Overall, the results of drug treatment studies have been mixed. Adding a drug treatment to an effective psychotherapy such as dialectical behavior therapy does not appear to improve recovery rates, and is recommended primarily for comorbid disorders (Choi-Kain et al., 2017; Neacsiu & Linehan, 2014; Simpson et al., 2004).

Histrionic Personality Disorder

Histrionic personality disorder shares features with borderline personality disorder, including rapidly shifting emotions and intense, unstable relationships. However, people with borderline personality disorder also show self-destructiveness, angry disruptions in close relationships, and chronic feelings of inner emptiness, while people with histrionic personality disorder behave in ways to draw attention to themselves across situations. A person with borderline personality disorder may desperately cling to others as an expression of self-doubt and unstable identity, but a person with histrionic personality disorder simply wants flattering nurturance and preferential attention. He or she may be overly trusting of and influenced by others, particularly strong authority figures. Individuals with histrionic personality disorder pursue others' attention by being highly dramatic (e.g., gregarious, exaggerated emotional expression) and overtly seductive and by flamboyantly emphasizing the positive qualities of their physical appearance. Others see them as self-centered and shallow, unable to delay gratification, demanding, and overly dependent, and they often end up alienating friends with the demands for constant attention. Debbie, in the following case study, was diagnosed with histrionic personality disorder.

CASE STUDY

Debbie was a 26-year-old woman who worked as a salesclerk in a trendy clothing store and who sought therapy for panic disorder with agoraphobia. She dressed flamboyantly, with an elaborate and dramatic hairdo. Her appearance was especially striking, since she was quite short (under 5 feet tall) and at least 75 pounds overweight. She wore sunglasses indoors throughout the evaluation and constantly fiddled with them, taking them on and off nervously and waving them to emphasize a point. She cried loudly and dramatically at various points in the interview, going through large numbers of tissue. She continually asked for reassurance. ("Will I be OK?" "Can I get over this?") She talked nonstop throughout the evaluation. When gently interrupted by the evaluator, she was very apologetic, laughing and saying, "I know I talk too much," yet she continued to do so throughout the session. (Beck, A. T. & Freeman, A. M., *Cognitive Therapy of Personality Disorders,* pp. 211–212. Copyright ©1990 by Guilford Press. Reprinted with permission.)

National epidemiological survey data from 2001 to 2002 suggest a prevalence of histrionic personality disorder of 1.84 percent (Grant, Hasin, Stinson, et al., 2004), with women more likely to be diagnosed with the disorder than men in clinical settings. People with this disorder are more likely to be separated or divorced than married (Disney, Weinstein, & Oltmanns, 2012). Like people with the somatoform disorders, they tend to exaggerate medical problems and make more medical visits than the average person, and this group has an increased rate of suicidal threats and behavior to coerce attentive caregiving (Kraus & Reynolds, 2001). People with this disorder most often seek treatment for depression or anxiety (Fabrega, Ulrich, Pilkonis, & Mezzich, 1991).

Theories of Histrionic Personality Disorder

Although discussions of histrionic personalities date back to the ancient Greek philosophers, little is known about causes or effective treatments, and the disorder is the focus of little research (Blashfield, Reynolds, & Stennett, 2012). Family history studies indicate that histrionic personality disorder clusters in families, along with borderline and antisocial personality and somatic symptom disorders. Whether this disorder is genetically caused or results from processes within the family or the environment is unclear.

Treatment of Histrionic Personality Disorder

Psychodynamic treatments focus on uncovering repressed emotions and needs and helping people with histrionic personality disorder express these emotions and needs in more socially appropriate ways (for example, by reaching out calmly for support, and offering support to others as well). Cognitive therapy focuses on identifying clients' assumptions that they cannot function on their own and helping them formulate goals and plans for their life that do not rely on the approval of others (Beck et al., 2015). Therapists attempt to help clients tone down their dramatic evaluations of situations by challenging these evaluations and suggesting more adaptive ones. Several case-related studies of treatments that aim to promote appropriate behavior in daily life contexts have shown reductions in self-reported depression and interpersonal difficulties (Callaghan, Summers, & Weidman, 2003; Kellett, 2007). None of the therapies for this disorder have been tested empirically.

Narcissistic Personality Disorder

Most of us have encountered narcissists before—people who think they are better than everyone else and should get their way in all circumstances and who will walk all over others to accomplish their goals. The word *narcissist* comes from the Greek myth of Narcissus, who fell in love with the reflection of himself in a pool, was unable to leave it, and died as a result.

The characteristics of **narcissistic personality disorder** are similar to those of histrionic personality disorder. In both disorders, individuals act in a dramatic manner, seek admiration from others, and are shallow in their emotional expressions and relationships with others. Whereas people with histrionic personality disorder look to others for approval, people with narcissistic personality disorder rely on their inflated self-evaluations and see dependency on others as weak and threatening. As the name implies, grandiosity is a distinguishing feature, as they are preoccupied with thoughts of their self-importance and with fantasies of power and success, and they view themselves as superior to most other people. In interpersonal relationships, they make entitled demands on others to follow their wishes, ignore or devalue the needs and wants of others, exploit others to gain power, and are arrogant and condescending. In contrast to borderline personality disorder, they do not experience the same abandonment concerns, despite needing the admiration of others. David, in the following case study, has been diagnosed with narcissistic personality disorder.

The word *narcissist* comes from the Greek myth of Narcissus, who fell in love with the reflection of himself in a pool, was unable to leave it, and died as a result. *©Alinari Archives/Alinari/Getty Images*

CASE STUDY

David was an attorney in his early 40s when he sought treatment for depressed mood. He cited business and marital problems as the source of his distress and wondered if he was having a midlife crisis. David had grown up in a comfortable suburb of a large city, the oldest of three children and the only son of a successful businessman and a former secretary. David spoke of being an "ace" student and a "super" athlete but could not provide any details that would validate a superior performance in these areas. He also recollected that he had his pick of girlfriends, as most women were "thrilled" to have a date with him.

David went to college, fantasizing about being famous in a high-profile career. He majored in communications, planning to go on to law school and eventually into politics. He met his first wife during college, the year she was the university homecoming queen. They married shortly after their joint graduation. He then went on to law school, and she went to work to support the couple.

During law school, David became a workaholic, fueled by fantasies of brilliant work and international recognition. He spent minimal time with his wife and, after their son was born, even less time with either of them. At the same time, he continued a string of extramarital affairs, mostly brief sexual encounters. He spoke of his wife in an annoyed, devaluing way, complaining about how she just did not live up to his expectations. He waited until he felt reasonably secure in his first job so that he could let go of her financial support and then he sought a divorce. He continued to see his son occasionally, but he rarely paid his child support.

After his divorce, David decided that he was totally free to just please himself. He loved spending all his money on himself, and he lavishly decorated his condominium and bought an attention-getting wardrobe. He constantly sought the companionship of attractive women. He was very successful at making initial contacts and getting dates, but he rarely found anyone good enough to date more than once or twice.

At work, David believed that because he was "different" from other people, they had no right to criticize him. But he had every right to criticize others. He also believed that other people were weak and needed contact with someone like him in order to bring direction or pleasure into their lives. He saw no problem in taking advantage of other people if they were "stupid" enough to allow him to do so. (Beck, A. T. & Freeman, A. M., *Cognitive Therapy of Personality Disorders,* 211–212. Copyright ©1990 by Guilford Press. Reprinted with permission.)

People with narcissistic personality disorder can be successful in societies that reward self-confidence and assertiveness, such as the United States (Millon, Grossman, Millon, Meagher, & Ramnath, 2004). When they grossly overestimate their abilities, however, they can make poor choices in their careers and may experience many failures, and they annoy and often alienate the important people in their lives (Miller, Campbell, & Pilkonis, 2007). People with this disorder seek treatment most often for depression and for trouble adjusting to life stressors (Fabrega et al.,1991).

A nationwide study in the United States found that 7.7 percent of men and 4.8 percent of women could be diagnosed with narcissistic personality disorder (Stinson et al., 2008). These data also suggest that narcissistic personality disorder is more prevalent among younger adults, possibly supporting the impression that narcissistic personality disorder is on the rise as a result of social and economic conditions that support more extreme versions of self-focused individualism (Bender, 2012; but see Wetzel et al., 2017). People diagnosed with the disorder have high rates of substance abuse and of mood and anxiety disorders. In addition, they have increased rates of physical and sexual aggression, impulsivity, homicidal thoughts, and suicidal behaviors (Pincus et al., 2009; Ronningstam, 2011a).

Theories of Narcissistic Personality Disorder

Psychodynamically oriented theorists suggest that the symptoms of narcissistic personality disorder are maladaptive strategies for managing emotions and self-views (Ronningstam, 2011b). People with this disorder did not develop a realistically positive view of themselves or adaptive strategies for handling stress and distress as children, so they rely on the praise and domination of others for their self-esteem (Kernberg, 1993; Kohut, 1977). Cognitive theorists have argued that some people with narcissistic personality disorder develop unrealistically positive assumptions about their self-worth as the result of indulgence and overvaluation by significant others during childhood (Beck et al., 2015). Other people with this disorder develop the belief that they are unique or exceptional as a defense against rejection or unmet basic emotional needs by important people in their lives. One study found that people diagnosed with narcissistic personality disorder were significantly more likely to endorse beliefs such as "I don't have to be bound by rules that apply to other people" than were people diagnosed with other disorders (Beck et al., 2001).

Researchers and clinicians often distinguish two different subtypes of narcissism: grandiose narcissism and vulnerable narcissism (Miller, Lynam, Hyatt, & Campbell, 2017; Pincus & Lukowitzky, 2010). The grandiose narcissist copes with difficulties in self-esteem by viewing himself as superior and unique and by engaging in grandiose fantasies. Such people are arrogant, entitled, manipulative, exploitative, envious, and aggressive, particularly when distressed. They may engage in criminal or violent acts toward others. David, from the case study above, would be considered a grandiose narcissist. A vulnerable narcissist, by contrast, copes with difficulties in self-esteem by engaging in grandiose fantasies to quell intense shame. Such people are self-focused, hypersensitive to rejection and criticism, distrustful, and thus avoid others. For example, a vulnerable narcissist might feel extreme shame at being passed over for a job, and respond to this shame by claiming she was overqualified. There is evidence of these two subtypes of narcissism in the behaviors and thoughts endorsed by people who have narcissistic personality disorder or who score high on measures of narcissism (Miller et al., 2017; Pincus & Lukowitzky, 2010; Ronningstam, 2011a). What the two subtypes share in common is the personality trait of interpersonal antagonism (Miller et al., 2017).

Like borderline personality disorder, narcissistic personality disorder is associated with a history of childhood adversity, including physical abuse and neglect, and with having a parent who was abused or who had a mental health problem (Afifi et al., 2011). Some evidence indicates that overly permissive or overly controlling parenting may give rise to grandiose and vulnerable narcissism, respectively, but more research is needed (Miller et al., 2017).

Treatment of Narcissistic Personality Disorder

People with narcissistic personality disorder tend not to seek treatment except when they develop depression or are confronted with severe interpersonal problems (Ronningstam, 2011b). In general, they see any problems they encounter as due to the weakness and problems of others. Not surprisingly, narcissistic personality traits pose significant challenges to the development of a stable working alliance between a client and therapist. By emphasizing a collaborative therapeutic approach, a therapist using cognitive techniques can help these clients develop more realistic expectations of their abilities and more sensitivity to the needs of others by teaching them to challenge their initially self-aggrandizing ways of interpreting situations (Beck et al., 2015). Such self-understanding and changes in self-serving biases don't come easily for people with narcissistic personality disorder, and often they do not remain in therapy once their acute symptoms or interpersonal problems lessen. Like histrionic personality disorder, however, no systematic psychotherapy or medication treatment studies have been published (Dhawan, Kunik, Oldham, & Coverdale, 2010; Stoffers et al., 2011).

CLUSTER C: ANXIOUS-FEARFUL PERSONALITY DISORDERS

The cluster C anxious-fearful personality disorders—avoidant personality disorder, dependent personality disorder, and obsessive-compulsive personality disorder—are characterized by a chronic sense of anxiety or fearfulness and behaviors intended to ward off feared situations (Table 8). People with each of the three disorders fear something different, but they are all nervous and unhappy.

TABLE 8 Cluster C: Anxious-Fearful Personality Disorders

People with the anxious-fearful personality disorders are often anxious or fearful.

Label	Key Features	Similar Disorders
Avoidant personality disorder	A pattern of social inhibition, feelings of inadequacy, and a fear of being criticized, which lead to the avoidance of social interactions and nervousness	Social phobia
Dependent personality disorder	A pattern of submissive and clinging behavior related to an excessive need to be taken care of, and leading to high levels of dependence on others	Separation anxiety disorder, persistent depressive disorder (dysthymia)
Obsessive-compulsive personality disorder	A pattern of preoccupation with orderliness, extreme perfectionism, and control, leading to emotional constriction, rigidity in one's activities and relationships, and anxiety about even minor disruptions in one's routines	Obsessive-compulsive disorder

Avoidant Personality Disorder

People with **avoidant personality disorder** have low self-esteem, are prone to shame, and are extremely anxious about being criticized by others and thus avoid interactions in which there is any possibility of being criticized (see Table 9). They might choose occupations that are socially isolated, such as wilderness park rangers. The two pathological personality traits that characterize them are negative affectivity and detachment. When they must interact with others, people with avoidant personality disorder are restrained, nervous, and hypersensitive to signs of being evaluated or criticized. They are terrified of saying something silly or doing something to embarrass themselves. They tend to be depressed and lonely. While they may crave relationships with others, they feel unworthy of these relationships and isolate themselves, as the following case study illustrates.

CASE STUDY

Ruthann is a 32-year-old postal employee who petitioned her supervisors to assign her to a rural route where she wouldn't have to talk with anyone most of the day. Ruthann has always been terrified of interacting with others, believing that they would judge her. When she was forced to interact, she was sure other people found her stupid and ugly and caught the many "social mistakes" she felt she committed in these interactions. Ruthann lived alone and did not date because she was sure men would find her unattractive and silly and would reject her.

Nationwide studies in the United States find that up to 2.4 percent of people can be diagnosed with avoidant personality disorder, with more women than men diagnosed (Grant, Hasin, Stinson, et al., 2004). People with this disorder are prone to persistent depressive disorder, including bouts of major depression and severe anxiety (Grant, Stinson, et al., 2004; Sanislow, da Cruz, Gianoli, & Reagan, 2012).

There is overlap between the characteristics of avoidant personality disorder and those of social anxiety disorder (see the chapter "Trauma, Anxiety, Obsessive-Compulsive, and Related Disorders"), so much so that they may be alternate forms of the same disorder. In particular, people with either disorder are highly self-critical about their social interactions (Cox, Turnbull, Robinson, Grant, & Stein, 2011). People with avoidant personality disorder tend to have more severe and generalized anxiety about social situations than people with social anxiety disorder and are more chronically impaired by their anxiety (Sanislow et al., 2012). Nonetheless, they also may desire acceptance and affection and sometimes fantasize about idealized relationships with others. Note that this is different from schizoid personality disorder; although both disorders involve social isolation, in avoidant personality disorder this is due to anxious avoidance, as opposed to the social detachment of schizoid personality disorder.

Theories of Avoidant Personality Disorder

Twin studies show that genetics plays a role in avoidant personality disorder and that some of the same genes likely are involved in avoidant personality disorder and social anxiety disorder (Torvik et al., 2016). Unlike other personality disorders, avoidant personality disorder does not have a strong relationship to

TABLE 9 Avoidant Personality Disorder

People with avoidant personality disorder may choose professions that allow them to avoid other people.

—Symptoms include:

- Prone to shame
- Hypersensitive to criticism
- Restrained and detached
- Isolated from others
- Severe anxiety about social situations

—Prevalence rate is 2.4 percent of general population

—More commonly diagnosed in females than in males

—Frequently accompanied by depression and anxiety

sexual or physical abuse in childhood, although people with this disorder do report higher rates of emotional neglect (Afifi et al., 2011).

Cognitive theorists suggest that people with avoidant personality disorder develop dysfunctional beliefs about being worthless as a result of rejection by important others early in life (Beck et al., 2015). They contend that children whose parents reject them conclude, "If my parents don't like me, how could anyone?" Thus, they avoid interactions with others. Their thoughts are of this sort: "Once people get to know me, they see I'm really inferior." When they must interact with others, they are unassertive and nervous, thinking, "I must please this person in every way or she will criticize me." They also tend to discount any positive feedback they receive from others, believing that other people are simply being nice or do not see how incompetent they really are. A study of 130 patients with avoidant personality disorder found that they endorsed such beliefs more often than patients with other personality disorders (Beck et al., 2001).

Treatment of Avoidant Personality Disorder

Cognitive and behavioral therapies have proven helpful for people with avoidant personality disorder. These therapies have included graduated exposure to social settings, social skills training, and challenges to negative automatic thoughts about themselves and social situations. People receiving these therapies show increases in the frequency and range of social contacts, decreases in avoidance behaviors, and increases in comfort and satisfaction when engaging in social activities (Emmelkamp et al., 2006).

The serotonin reuptake inhibitors are sometimes used to reduce the social anxiety of people with avoidant personality disorder, but little research on their effectiveness in treating avoidant personality disorder separate from social anxiety has been done (Ripoll, Triebwasser, & Siever, 2011; Silk & Feurino, 2012).

Dependent Personality Disorder

People with **dependent personality disorder** are anxious about interpersonal interactions, but their anxiety stems from a deep need to be cared for by others, rather than from a concern that they will be criticized. Their desire to be loved and taken care of by others leads people with dependent personality disorder to deny any of their own thoughts and feelings that might displease others and result in disagreements, to submit to even the most unreasonable or unpleasant demands, and to cling frantically to others. People with this personality disorder have difficulty making everyday decisions, instead heavily relying on others for advice and reassurance, and they do not initiate new activities except in an effort to please others. In contrast to people with avoidant personality disorder, who avoid relationships unless certain of being liked, people with dependent personality disorder can function only within a relationship and will overly accommodate others to obtain care and support. They deeply fear the loss of relationship supports and the prospect of having to assume independent responsibility, and they may allow themselves to be exploited and abused to maintain relationships, as in the following case of Francesca.

People with avoidant personality disorder may choose professions that allow them to avoid other people. *©kali9/Getty Images*

CASE STUDY

Francesca was in a panic because her husband seemed to be getting increasingly annoyed with her. Last night, he became very angry when Francesca asked him to cancel an upcoming business trip because she was terrified of being left at home alone. In a rage, her husband shouted, "You can't ever be alone! You can't do anything by yourself! You can't even decide what to have for dinner by yourself! I'm sick of it. Grow up and act like an adult!"

It was true that Francesca had a very difficult time making decisions for herself. While she was in high school, she couldn't decide which courses to take and talked with her parents and friends for hours about what she should do, finally doing whatever her best friend or her mother told her to do.

(continued)

When she graduated from high school, she didn't feel smart enough to go to college, even though she had gotten good grades in high school. She drifted into a job because her best friend had a job with the same company and she wanted to remain close to that friend. The friend eventually dumped Francesca, however, because she was tired of Francesca's incessant demands for reassurance. Francesca frequently bought gifts for the friend and offered to do the friend's laundry or cooking, in obvious attempts to win the friend's favor. But Francesca also kept the friend for hours in the evening, asking her whether she thought Francesca had made the right decision about some trivial issue, such as what to buy her mother for Christmas and how she thought Francesca was performing on the job.

Soon after her friend dumped her, Francesca met her future husband, and when he showed some interest in her, she quickly tried to form a close relationship with him. She liked the fact that he seemed strong and confident, and when he asked her to marry him, Francesca thought that perhaps finally she would feel safe and secure. But especially since he has begun to get angry with her frequently, Francesca has been worrying constantly that he is going to leave her.

National epidemiologic survey data suggest a relatively low estimated lifetime prevalence of dependent personality disorder of 0.49 percent (Grant, Hasin, Stinson, et al., 2004). Higher rates of the disorder are found with self-report methods than with structured clinical interviews, suggesting that many people feel they have this disorder when clinicians would not diagnose it in them. More women than men are diagnosed with this disorder (Fabrega et al., 1991; Trull et al., 2010). Depressive and anxiety disorders commonly co-occur in people with dependent personality disorder, often triggered by interpersonal conflict or relationship disruption (Bornstein, 2012; Grant, Stinson, et al., 2004). Dependent personality disorder increases the risk for physical illness, partner and child abuse, suicidal behavior, and high levels of functional impairment and health care costs (Bornstein, 2012; Loas, Cormier, & Perez-Diaz, 2011).

Theories of Dependent Personality Disorder

Dependent personality disorder runs in families, and one twin study estimated the heritability of this disorder to be .81 (Coolidge et al., 2004). Children and adolescents with a history of separation anxiety disorder or chronic physical illness appear to be more prone to developing dependent personality disorder.

Cognitive theories argue that people with dependent personality disorder have exaggerated and inflexible beliefs related to their depending needs, such as "I am needy and weak," which in turn drive their dependent behaviors. A study of 38 patients with dependent personality disorder found that they endorsed such beliefs more often than patients with other personality disorders (Beck et al., 2001).

Treatment of Dependent Personality Disorder

Unlike people with many of the other personality disorders, persons with dependent personality disorder frequently seek treatment (Millon et al., 2004) and are likely to show greater insight and self-awareness. Their desire to strengthen ties to caring authority figures likely facilitates early development of a positive working alliance with the therapist, although it also presents challenges (Bornstein, 2012; Paris, 1998). Although many psychosocial therapies are used in the treatment of this disorder, none have been systematically tested for their effectiveness. Psychodynamic treatment focuses on helping clients gain insight into the early experiences with caregivers that led to their dependent behaviors, often by examining their relationship style with the therapist and interpreting the transference process with the goal of increased independence. Nondirective and humanistic therapies may be helpful in fostering autonomy and self-confidence in persons with dependent personality disorder (Millon et al., 2004).

Cognitive-behavioral therapy for dependent personality disorder includes behavioral techniques designed to increase assertive behaviors and decrease anxiety, as well as cognitive techniques designed to challenge clients' assumptions about the need to rely on others (Beck et al., 2015). Clients might be given graded exposure to anxiety-provoking situations, such as making everyday and then more important decisions independently. For example, they and their therapists might develop a hierarchy of increasingly difficult independent actions that the clients gradually attempt on their own, beginning with deciding what to have for lunch and ending with deciding what job to take. After making each decision, clients are encouraged to recognize their competence and to challenge any negative thoughts they had about making the decision. They also may be taught relaxation skills to enable them to overcome their anxiety enough to engage in homework assignments. Regardless of the therapeutic approach, it is important for the therapist to consider the dependent person's social network. Sometimes marital or family therapy can help elucidate relationship patterns that foster dependency, reinforce feelings of helplessness and anxiety, and interfere with independent decision making (Bornstein, 2012).

SHADES OF GRAY

Ellen Farber, a single 35-year-old insurance company executive, came to a psychiatric emergency room of a university hospital with complaints of depression and the thought of driving her car off a cliff. . . . She reported a 6-month period of increasingly persistent dysphoria and lack of energy and pleasure. Feeling as if she were "made of lead," Ms. Farber had recently been spending 15 to 20 hours a day in her bed. She also reported daily episodes of binge-eating, when she would consume "anything I can find," including entire chocolate cakes or boxes of cookies. She reported problems with intermittent binge-eating since adolescence, but these episodes had recently increased in frequency, resulting in a 20-pound weight gain over the past few months. . . .

She attributed her increasing symptoms to financial difficulties. Ms. Farber had been fired from her job 2 weeks before coming to the emergency room. She claimed it was because she "owed a small amount of money." When asked to be more specific, she reported owing $150,000 to her former employers and another $100,000 to various local banks due to spending sprees.

In addition to lifelong feelings of emptiness, Ms. Farber described chronic uncertainty about what she wanted to do in life and with whom she wanted to be friends. She had many brief, intense relationships with both men and women, but her quick temper led to frequent arguments and even physical fights. Although she had always thought of her childhood as happy and carefree, when she became depressed she began to recall episodes of abuse by her mother. Initially, she said she had dreamt that her mother had pushed her down the stairs when she was only 6, but then she began to report previously unrecognized memories of beatings or verbal assaults by her mother. (Reprinted with permission from the *DSM-IV Casebook: A Learning Companion to the Diagnostic and Statistical Manual of Mental Disorders*, Fourth Edition. Copyright ©1994 by American Psychiatric Association. All Rights Reserved.)

What diagnosis would you give Ms. Farber? (Discussion appears at the end of this chapter.)

Obsessive-Compulsive Personality Disorder

Self-control, attention to detail, perseverance, and reliability are highly valued in many societies, including U.S. society. Some people, however, develop these traits to an extreme and become rigid, perfectionistic, dogmatic, ruminative, and emotionally blocked. These people are said to have **obsessive-compulsive personality disorder.** People with this disorder base their self-esteem on their productivity and on meeting unreasonably high goals. They are compulsive; preoccupied with rules, details, and order; and perfectionistic. They tend to persist in a task even when their approach is failing, leading them to experience negative affect. Interpersonally, they have difficulty appreciating others or tolerating their quirks and may be rigidly bound to rules. They are often stubborn and may force others to follow strict standards of performance.

Many of the disorder's features overlap with "type A" personality characteristics.

This disorder shares features with obsessive-compulsive disorder (OCD; see the chapter "Trauma, Anxiety, Obsessive-Compulsive, and Related Disorders") and has a small to moderate comorbidity with OCD (Diedrich & Voderholzer, 2015; Lochner et al., 2011). But obsessive-compulsive personality disorder involves a more general way of interacting with the world than does OCD, which often involves only specific obsessional thoughts and compulsive behaviors. While people with obsessive-compulsive disorder will be focused on very specific thoughts, images, ideas, or behavior and may feel very anxious if they do not engage in these (e.g., becoming anxious if they cannot check whether they have turned off the stove), people with obsessive-compulsive personality disorder will be more generally prone to being perfectionistic, rigid, and concerned with order. Recall that people with OCD experience obsessions and compulsions as intrusive and unwanted; by contrast, people with obsessive-compulsive personality disorder typically view their concerns as part of their personalities.

People with obsessive-compulsive personality disorder often seem grim and austere, tensely in control of their emotions, and lacking in spontaneity (Millon et al., 2004). They are workaholics who see little need for leisure activities or friendships. Other people experience them as stubborn, stingy, possessive, moralistic, and officious. They tend to relate to others in terms of rank or status and are ingratiating and deferential to "superiors" but dismissive, demeaning, or authoritarian toward "inferiors." Although they are extremely concerned with efficiency, their perfectionism and obsession about following rules often interfere with completing tasks and getting along with others, as in the following case study.

CASE STUDY

Ronald Lewis is a 32-year-old accountant who is "having trouble holding on to a woman." He does not understand why, but the reasons become very clear as he tells his story. Mr. Lewis is a remarkably neat and well-organized man who tends to regard others as an interference to the otherwise mechanically perfect progression of his life. For many years he has maintained an almost inviolate schedule. On weekdays he arises at 6:47, has two eggs soft-boiled for 2 minutes, 45 seconds, and is at his desk at 8:15. Lunch is at 12:00, dinner at 6:00, bedtime at 11:00. He has separate Saturday and Sunday schedules, the latter characterized by a methodical and thorough trip through the *New York Times*. Any change in schedule causes him to feel varying degrees of anxiety, annoyance, and a sense that he is doing something wrong and wasting time.

Orderliness pervades Mr. Lewis's life. His apartment is immaculately clean and meticulously arranged. His extensive collections of books, records, and stamps are all carefully catalogued, and each item is reassuringly always in the right and familiar place. Mr. Lewis is highly valued at his work because his attention to detail has, at times, saved the company considerable embarrassment. . . . His perfectionism also presents something of a problem, however. He is the slowest worker in the office and probably the least productive. He gets the details right but may fail to put them in perspective. His relationships to co-workers are cordial but formal. He is on a "Mr. and Ms." basis with people he has known for years in an office that generally favors first names. Mr. Lewis's major problems are with women and follow the same repetitive pattern.

At first, things go well. Soon, however, he begins to resent the intrusion upon his schedule a woman inevitably causes. This is most strongly illustrated in the bedtime arrangements. Mr. Lewis is a light and nervous sleeper with a rather elaborate routine preceding his going to bed. He must spray his sinuses, take two aspirin, straighten up the apartment, do 35 sit-ups, and read two pages of the dictionary. The sheets must be of just the right crispness and temperature and the room must be noiseless. Obviously, a woman sleeping over interferes with his inner sanctum and, after sex, Mr. Lewis tries either to have the woman go home or sleep in the living room. No woman has put up with this for very long. (Spitzer, R. L., Skodol, A. E., Gibbon, M., & Williams, J. B. W., *Psychopathology: A Case Book*, pp. 63–64. Copyright ©1983 by The McGraw-Hill Companies, Inc. All rights reserved. Reprinted with Permission.)

Obsessive-compulsive personality disorder is the most prevalent personality disorder, with up to 7.9 percent of the U.S. population meeting the criteria for a diagnosis and no gender differences in its prevalence (Diedrich & Voderholzer, 2015; Grant, Hasin, Stinson, et al., 2004). People with this disorder are prone to depressive, anxiety, and eating disorders, but not to the same extent as people with the other personality disorders already discussed (Grant, Stinson, et al., 2004). Interestingly, the majority of individuals with OCD do not also have obsessive-compulsive personality disorder, but when they co-occur OCD and depression symptoms are more severe (Diedrich & Voderholzer, 2015; Gordon, Salkovskis, Oldfield, & Carter, 2013).

Theories of Obsessive-Compulsive Personality Disorder

Cognitive theories suggest that people with this disorder harbor beliefs such as "Flaws, defects, or mistakes are intolerable." One study found that people diagnosed with obsessive-compulsive personality disorder endorsed such beliefs significantly more often than people diagnosed with other personality disorders (Beck et al., 2001), but a more recent study found that they did not (Arntz, Weertman, & Salet, 2011).

Obsessive-compulsive personality disorder appears to be related to genetic factors similar to those found in obsessive-compulsive disorder (Lochner et al., 2011; Taylor, Asmundson, & Jang, 2011). People with obsessive-compulsive personality disorder have a slightly greater history of physical neglect than people with no disorder (Afifi et al., 2011).

Treatment of Obsessive-Compulsive Personality Disorder

There are no controlled psychological treatment studies focusing primarily on obsessive-compulsive personality disorder, and only one medication trial. Supportive therapies may assist people with this disorder in overcoming the crises that bring them in for treatment, and behavioral therapies can decrease their compulsive behaviors (Beck et al., 2015; Millon et al., 2004). For example, a client may be given the assignment to alter his usual rigid schedule for the day, first by simply getting up 15 minutes later than usual and then by gradually changing additional elements of his schedule. The client may be taught to use relaxation techniques to overcome the anxiety created by alterations in the schedule. He might also write down the automatic negative thoughts he has about changes in the schedule ("Getting up 15 minutes later is going to put my entire day off"). In the next therapy session, he and the therapist might discuss the evidence for and against these automatic thoughts, gradually replacing maladaptive thoughts and rigid expectations

People with obsessive-compulsive personality disorder are very concerned with orderliness, structure, and rules. ©*IPGGutenbergUKLtd/iStock/Getty Images*

with more flexible beliefs and attitudes that include valuing close relationships, leisure and recreation, and feelings. Sometimes the selective serotonin reuptake inhibitor medications (e.g., Prozac) may be used to reduce obsessionality.

ALTERNATIVE *DSM-5* MODEL FOR PERSONALITY DISORDERS

The *DSM-5*'s definition of personality disorder and the criteria used for diagnosing the personality disorders reviewed in this chapter have not changed from those in the *DSM-IV-TR*. In fact, its categorical scheme for understanding personality disorders has remained in place for over 30 years since the publication of the *DSM-III* in 1980. However, the *DSM-5* includes an alternative model for diagnosing personality disorders that incorporates a *dimensional,* or continuum, perspective. It is presented in a separate section of the *DSM-5* designated for further study (Section III) and is not meant for current clinical use. It is reviewed here to provide a perspective on the evolution of the diagnosis of personality disorders, as well as one approach to responding to the problems with a categorical diagnostic system.

Over the years, many limitations of the *DSM*'s categorical approach to the diagnosis of personality disorders have been recognized by clinicians and researchers (see Krueger & Markon, 2014; Morey et al., 2015). Some of the most significant limitations include that the 10 separate personality disorders have a good deal of overlap in their diagnostic criteria (Grant, Stinson, Dawson, Chou, & Ruan, 2005; Zimmerman et al., 2005). Indeed, it appears that although the different personality disorders are distinguished by their unique symptoms discussed above, there is also a more general personality pathology factor that is common across multiple personality disorders (Sharp et al., 2015). There was poor agreement among clinicians as to whether individuals met the criteria for these disorders (Morey et al., 2015; Zanarini et al., 2000). Although the personality disorders are conceptualized as stable characteristics of an individual, longitudinal studies found that people diagnosed with these disorders varied over time in how many symptoms they exhibited and in the severity of these symptoms, going into and out of the diagnosis (Shea et al., 2002). In particular, people often seemed as if they had a personality disorder when they were suffering from an acute disorder, such as major depressive disorder, but then their personality disorder symptoms seemed to diminish when their depressive symptoms subsided. Finally, despite having 10 different personality disorder diagnoses, the *DSM* criteria did not fit many people who seemingly had pathological personalities, nor did the criteria reflect the extensive literature on fundamental personality traits that are consistent across cultures (Verheul & Widiger, 2004).

The alternative *DSM-5* model characterizes personality disorders in terms of impairments in personality *functioning* and pathological personality *traits*. There are three steps in diagnosing a personality disorder under this alternative model (see Waugh et al., 2017). The first step in diagnosing a personality disorder is determining an individual's level of functioning in terms of their sense of self (or identity) or their relationships

A core personality trait involves the extent to which people are appropriately outgoing and trusting of others (left) or tend to be withdrawn, avoidant, and untrusting (right). *Left: ©JGI/Jamie Grill/Blend Images/Getty Images; Right: ©L. Mouton/PhotoAlto*

with others on a scale that goes from little or no impairment to extreme impairment. To diagnose a personality disorder under this system, the person must have at least moderate impairment.

The second step in diagnosing a personality disorder is determining whether the individual has any pathological personality traits. Although there is tremendous variability across people in the specific nature of their personalities, as noted at the beginning of this chapter regarding, for instance, the Big 5 model, there appears to be a relatively small set of personality traits or dimensions along which people's personalities vary (Krueger & Markon, 2014; McCrae & Terracciano, 2005). The pathological personality traits used in the alternative model have significant overlap with the Big 5 traits, but also some differences (Suzuki, Griffin, & Samuel, 2017).

There are five pathological traits assessed in the alternative model. One fundamental trait is the extent to which people tend to be even-tempered and calm, secure, and able to handle stress, versus being emotionally labile, insecure, and overreactive to stress, a dimension referred to in personality theories as *neuroticism* (McCrae & Costa, 1999) or in *DSM-5* alternative model terms as **negative affectivity.** A second core personality trait, **detachment,** involves the extent to which people are appropriately outgoing and trusting of others versus tending to be withdrawn, avoidant, and untrusting. The third dimension, **antagonism,** is anchored at the positive end by characteristics such as honesty, appropriate modesty, and concern for others and at the negative end by characteristics such as deceitfulness, grandiosity, and callousness. A fourth domain, called **disinhibition,** ranges from a tendency to be responsible, organized and cautious to a tendency to be impulsive, risk-taking, and irresponsible. The fifth dimension, **psychoticism,** captures personality characteristics that are relatively rare in the general population but are important aspects of certain types of dysfunction (Krueger & Markon, 2014; Watson, Clark, & Chmielewski, 2008). People high on this dimension have highly unusual beliefs and perceptions and tend to be quite eccentric.

Taken together, the alternative *DSM-5* model specifies that, in order to diagnose an individual with a personality disorder, he or she must show significant difficulties in identity and interpersonal functioning and significant pathological personality traits. In addition, these difficulties and traits must be unusual for the individual's developmental stage and sociocultural environment. For example, if an individual believed he could speak to dead relatives but this was a common belief in his culture, then he might not be rated high on the psychoticism trait domain. Finally, as in the official categorical model in the *DSM-5*, in the alternative model these difficulties and pathological traits cannot be due to ingesting a substance, such as hallucinatory perceptions while on a narcotic, or to a medical condition, such as a blow to the head, or better explained by another mental disorder.

Although the *DSM-5* explicitly incorporates a continuum approach into its general criteria in the alternative model for a personality disorder, it also includes six specific personality disorders—*antisocial, avoidant, borderline, narcissistic, obsessive-compulsive,* and *schizotypal*—with which individuals may be diagnosed based on their identified traits. Note that four personality disorders discussed in this chapter are not specifically recognized in the alternative model.

The third step in the diagnosis of personality disorders under this model is determining whether individuals meet the criteria for any of these six specific disorders. If an individual doesn't meet the criteria for any of these disorders but still has significant difficulties in his or her sense of self and relationships together with pathological personality traits, the diagnosis *personality disorder–trait specified* is given. For example, a person who does not meet the definition for antisocial, avoidant, borderline, narcissistic, obsessive-compulsive, or schizotypal personality disorder but is highly prone to being anxious about whether other people like him and also behaves irresponsibly in an attempt to get attention from others might be diagnosed as having personality disorder–trait specified.

When clinicians diagnose someone with personality disorder–trait specified, they then specify which pathological personality traits the person has. Thus, the *DSM-5* approach to personality disorders is a *hybrid model;* that is, it combines a dimensional or continuum approach with the categorical approach more typical of other types of disorders.

This hybrid dimensional-categorical model and its components aim to address the significant limitations of a purely categorical approach to personality disorders. The authors of the *DSM-5* included the model in a separate section of the manual to encourage research that might support the model in the diagnosis and care of people with personality disorders, as well as contribute to improved understanding of the causes and treatments of personality pathology.

Understanding how pathological personality traits factor into more than one personality disorder and relate to other mental disorders is a major motivation for the alternative model. Research on the dimensional model suggests that pathological personality traits can capture the maladaptive aspects of personality and their role in poor functioning (Clark et al., 2015; Wright et al., 2015). More research is needed to determine whether this newer approach should replace the official categorical system, but studies suggest that it is useful in both research and clinical application (Waugh et al., 2017). The more dimensional perspective on personality disorders may also help researchers and clinicians better understand the complexities of mental disorders more broadly (Wright et al., 2012). Future research relating the alternative *DSM-5* model to general personality traits (e.g., the Big 5) might also facilitate integration of normal and pathological personality (Morey et al., 2015; Suzuki et al., 2017).

The approach to personality disorders in *DSM-5* is an excellent example of how the field of abnormal psychology continually faces the issues of defining abnormality and categorizing and diagnosing mental disorders discussed in this book's early chapters. This dimensional approach may also improve researchers' ability to understand how personality pathology develops in childhood and adolescence. This aspect is key not only to understanding pathology but also to prevention and intervention. As personality traits are viewed as more variable than they were in the past, and as diagnoses are less clearly categorical, studies of the biological predispositions and psychosocial factors in the development of personality pathology play an increasingly important role (De Fruyt & De Clercq, 2014).

CHAPTER INTEGRATION

Several of the personality disorders discussed in this chapter, as well as antisocial personality disorder (see the chapter "Disruptive, Impulse-Control, and Conduct Disorders"), are associated with a history of adversity in childhood, including abuse and neglect, and parental instability and psychopathology (Afifi et al., 2011). There are several possible explanations for this relationship (see Figure 1). It may be the result of genetic factors that create both parental psychopathology (which leads to neglectful and abusive parenting and an unstable household) and vulnerability to a personality disorder in children. Abuse and neglect, along with a genetic predisposition, may produce permanent changes in the developing brain of some children that result in symptoms of certain personality disorders (Ruocco et al., 2012). Abuse, neglect, and poor parenting resulting from parental psychopathology could also lead children to develop maladaptive ways of thinking about themselves and the world and poor regulation of their emotions (Beck et al., 2015; Millon et al., 2004). Genetic factors may also contribute to

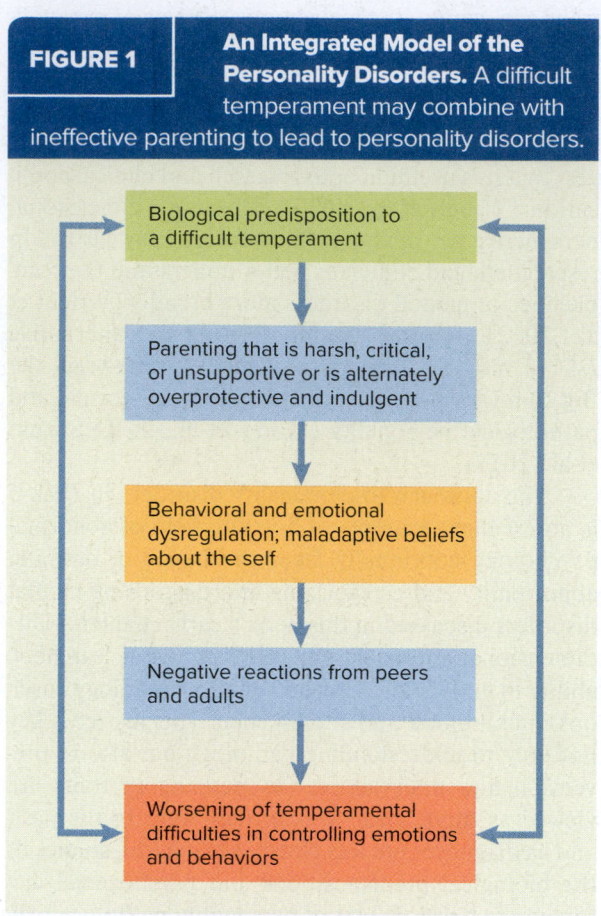

FIGURE 1 **An Integrated Model of the Personality Disorders.** A difficult temperament may combine with ineffective parenting to lead to personality disorders.

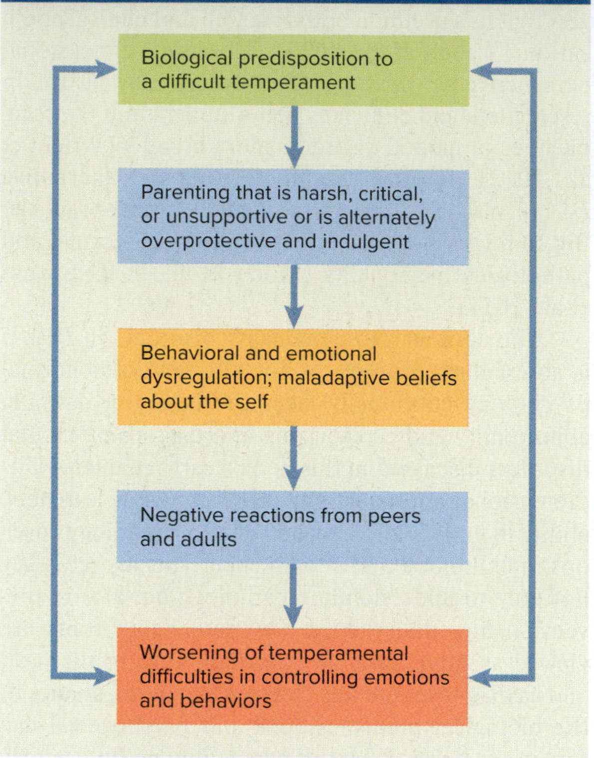

the children developing maladaptive cognitions and emotion regulation strategies. Children who show early symptoms of personality disorders likely are more difficult to parent, which may lead to more hostile or neglectful behavior on the part of their parents. On the other hand, children born with a vulnerability to personality disorder symptoms but have parents who validate their children's emotional experiences, are responsive to their needs, and help them develop an appropriate view of themselves and adaptive ways to cope with stress and relate to the world may never develop a full-blown personality disorder.

SHADES OF GRAY DISCUSSION

Ms. Farber shows signs of a mood disorder, with dysphoria, lack of energy or pleasure, and suicidal thoughts. Her sleeping and eating patterns have changed dramatically as well. This could suggest that she has a major depressive disorder, but other details of her story point to the possibility of a personality disorder. Ms. Farber's spending sprees, intense and even violent relationships with others, feelings of emptiness, and unstable sense of herself and her relationships suggest borderline personality disorder. This case illustrates a common problem clinicians face in making the diagnosis of a personality disorder: People with a personality disorder often come to the attention of mental health professionals when they are in a crisis, making it difficult to diagnose whether they have an acute disorder, such as depression, and/or a personality disorder.

CHAPTER SUMMARY

- Personality refers to a person's enduring patterns of perceiving, feeling, thinking about, and relating to oneself and the environment. A personality trait is a prominent aspect of personality that is relatively consistent across time and situations.
- The *DSM-5* defines personality disorder as an enduring pattern of inner experience and behavior (e.g., ways of perceiving and interpreting self, others, events; emotional responses; impulse control; interpersonal functioning) that deviates markedly from the expectations of an individual's culture. The personality pattern is pervasive and inflexible across time and situations, with onset in adolescence or early adulthood, and leads to clinically significant distress and/or functional impairment.

- Like *DSM-IV-TR,* the *DSM-5* takes a categorical approach toward classifying personality disorders and assumes that there is a dividing line between normal personality and pathological personality. However, the *DSM-5* no longer classifies personality disorders on a separate axis, as in *DSM-IV-TR.*
- It divides the personality disorders into three clusters based on their descriptive similarities: Cluster A includes the odd-eccentric disorders, cluster B includes the dramatic-emotional disorders, and cluster C consists of the anxious-fearful disorders.
- The cluster A odd-eccentric personality disorders include paranoid personality disorder (extreme mistrust of others), schizoid personality disorder (extreme social withdrawal and detachment), and schizotypal personality disorder (discomfort in close relationships, odd behavior, inappropriate social interactions, and cognitive-perceptual distortions). These disorders, particularly schizotypal personality disorder, may be genetically linked to schizophrenia and may represent mild versions of schizophrenia. People with these disorders tend to have poor social relationships and to be at increased risk for depression and schizophrenia.
- Psychotherapies for the odd-eccentric disorders have not been empirically tested for their efficacy. They may be treated with traditional and atypical antipsychotics.
- The cluster B dramatic-emotional personality disorders include four disorders characterized by dramatic, erratic, and emotional behavior and interpersonal relationships: antisocial personality disorder (see the chapter "Disruptive, Impulse-Control, and Conduct Disorders"), borderline personality disorder, histrionic personality disorder, and narcissistic personality disorder. People with borderline personality disorder show profound instability in self-concept, emotional regulation, and interpersonal relationships, along with impulsive behavior. People with histrionic personality disorder show rapidly shifting moods, unstable relationships, a need for attention and approval, and dramatic, seductive behavior. People with narcissistic personality disorder show grandiosity, arrogance, and exploitation of others.
- Theories of borderline personality disorder argue that it is due to difficulties in self-concept and regulating emotions. These difficulties may be related to childhood adversity (especially abuse), which is commonly (though not always) reported by people with this disorder. The disorder is also associated with smaller volume in the hippocampus and amygdala, greater reactivity of the amygdala to emotional stimuli, and less activity in the prefrontal cortex, possibly leading to impulsive behavior and emotion regulation difficulties.
- Dialectical behavior therapy has been shown to be effective in treating people with borderline personality disorder. This therapy focuses on helping clients gain a more realistic and positive sense of self; learn adaptive skills for managing distress, regulating emotions, and solving problems; and correct dichotomous thinking. Cognitive and psychodynamic therapies (i.e., transference-focused and mentalization-based treatments) are also helpful. Mood stabilizers and atypical antipsychotics may be the most helpful medications.
- Treatments for histrionic and narcissistic personality disorders are less well developed, and people with these disorders tend not to seek therapy unless they develop significant distress (e.g., depression) or problems. Cognitive therapy may be helpful to them.
- The cluster C anxious-fearful personality disorders include three disorders characterized by anxious and fearful emotions and chronic self-doubt, leading to maladaptive behaviors: dependent personality disorder (extreme need to be cared for and fear of rejection), avoidant personality disorder (social anxiety and sense of inadequacy leading to social avoidance), and obsessive-compulsive personality disorder (rigidity in activities and interpersonal relationships).
- Genetic factors and childhood experiences of rejection by significant others are implicated in the development of avoidant personality disorder. Treatment involves cognitive-behavioral interventions to expose people to the interpersonal situations that make them anxious and to help them change the way they interpret criticism from others.
- People with obsessive-compulsive personality disorder often also have obsessive-compulsive disorder, and the disorders share some of the same genetic risk factors. Treatment with behavioral interventions to reduce compulsions and cognitive techniques to challenge rigid, perfectionistic beliefs can be helpful.
- In addition to the current categorical model for diagnosing personality disorders, the *DSM-5* includes an alternative dimensional trait model in a separate section of the manual designated for further study. The alternative model requires clinicians to diagnose a personality disorder based on particular difficulties in personality functioning and on specific patterns of pathological personality traits. The alternative model may represent how the diagnosis of personality disorders will evolve in the future and may facilitate integration of normal and pathological personality theories and research.

KEY TERMS

personality
personality trait
five-factor model
personality disorder
paranoid personality disorder
schizoid personality disorder
schizotypal personality disorder
borderline personality disorder
dialectical behavior therapy
transference-focused therapy
mentalization-based treatment
histrionic personality disorder
narcissistic personality disorder
avoidant personality disorder
dependent personality disorder
obsessive-compulsive personality disorder
negative affectivity
detachment
antagonism
disinhibition
psychoticism

Chapter 10

©Olesia Bilkei/123RF

Neurodevelopmental and Neurocognitive Disorders

CHAPTER OUTLINE

Neurodevelopmental and Neurocognitive Disorders Along the Continuum

One of the most fascinating discoveries in the last few decades is how much the human brain changes across the life span. The pace of brain development is extraordinary in early life, with dramatic growth in its size and complexity in infancy and childhood, followed by further shaping and maturation into early adulthood (Casey, Tottenham, Liston, & Durston, 2005). The brain continues to change throughout adulthood in response to people's lifestyles, experiences, and health. Then, as people grow older, come gradual declines in the structural and functional integrity of the brain but adaptations in the ways the brain processes information that allow most people to retain a high level of functioning well into old age (Park & Reuter-Lorenz, 2009; Sowell et al., 2003).

Yet there is tremendous variability across people in the development and aging of the brain and in related cognitive, emotional, and behavioral functioning. Parents of young children often anxiously chart their child's progress on major milestones of development, such as talking, walking, and reading. Although some children reach these milestones later than others, most eventually gain the critical skills that allow them to function in everyday life. Some children, however, continue to have major problems with basic academic skills, such as reading, writing, and mathematics. Others have more global cognitive deficits that interfere with their ability to function in many domains of life. For others, the deficits are in their ability to regulate their emotions and behaviors and to understand social interactions. Although such difficulties may stem in part from adverse environmental experiences, such as trauma or poverty, they often have their roots in atypical brain development.

Similarly, as our brains age in middle age and older adulthood, they decrease in size and efficiency, leading most of us to experience gradual declines in how quickly we perceive and process information, in our ability to hold and manipulate information in working memory, and in long-term memory (see Figure 1). Most of us can use our accumulated knowledge and expertise to compensate for these declines in cognitive-processing ability. However, for some people, deterioration in the brain is more severe and widespread than usual, leading to moderate or severe deficits in the processing of information and thus in their ability to function in daily life.

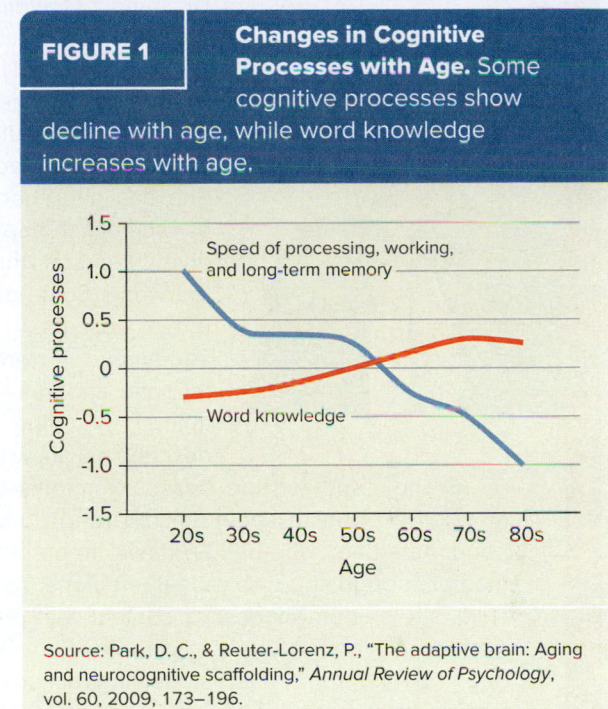

FIGURE 1 **Changes in Cognitive Processes with Age.** Some cognitive processes show decline with age, while word knowledge increases with age.

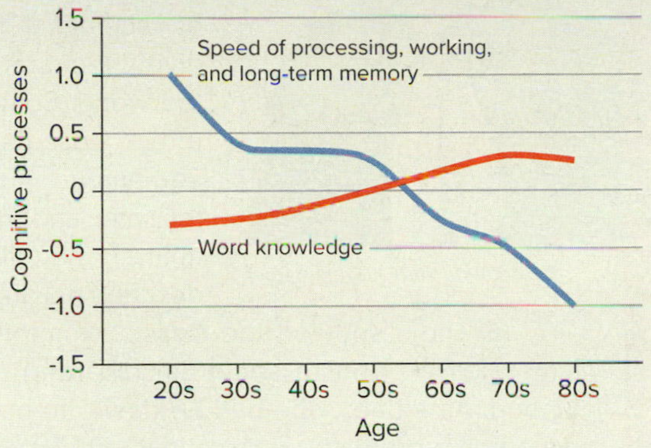

Source: Park, D. C., & Reuter-Lorenz, P., "The adaptive brain: Aging and neurocognitive scaffolding," *Annual Review of Psychology*, vol. 60, 2009, 173–196.

Brain dysfunction in either childhood or older age can be understood only in the context of what is typical or functional for individuals in those periods of life. Psychologists who focus on functional and dysfunctional development in children are referred to as *developmental psychopathologists*. Those concerned with functional and dysfunctional changes in older age are referred to as *geropsychologists*.

Extraordinary People

Temple Grandin, *Thinking in Pictures*

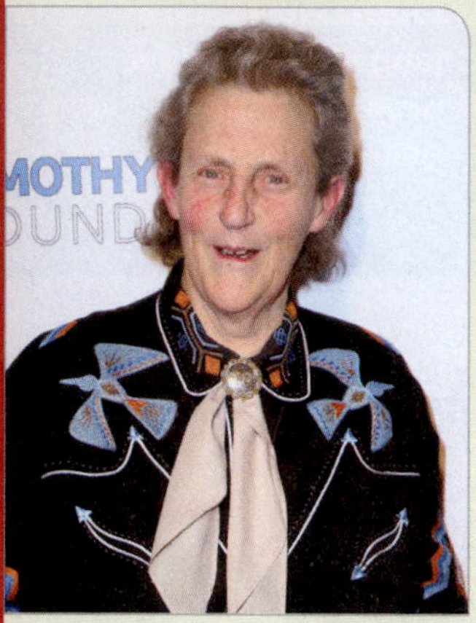

©MediaPunch/REX/Shutterstock

Dr. Temple Grandin, professor of animal sciences at Colorado State University, has designed one-third of the livestock-handling facilities in the United States. She has published dozens of scientific papers and gives lectures throughout the world. Some of her lectures describe her new equipment and procedures for safer and more humane animal handling. Others describe her life with autism.

Grandin showed the classic symptoms of autism (now called autism spectrum disorder) during childhood. As a baby, she had no desire to be held by her mother, though she was calm if left alone. As a young child, she seldom made eye contact with others and seemed to lack interest in people. She frequently threw wild tantrums. If left alone, she rocked back and forth or spun around repeatedly. She could sit for hours on the beach, watching sand dribble through her fingers, in a trancelike state. At age 2, she still had not begun talking and was labeled "brain-damaged" because doctors at that time did not know about autism spectrum disorder.

Fortunately, Grandin's mother was determined to find good teachers, learn ways to calm her daughter, and encourage her to speak and engage with others. Grandin did learn to speak by the time she entered elementary school, although most of her social interaction deficits remained. When she was 12, Grandin scored 137 on an IQ test (which falls in the very superior range) but still was thrown out of a regular school because she didn't fit in. She persisted, however, and eventually went to college, where she earned a degree in psychology, and then to graduate school, where she earned a PhD in animal sciences.

Grandin has been able to thrive in her career and personal life. Still, she finds it very difficult to understand emotions and social relationships. She does not "read" other people well and often finds herself offending others or being stared at because of her social awkwardness:

> I have always felt like someone who watches from the outside. I could not participate in the social interactions of high school life. ... My peers spent hours standing around talking about jewelry or some other topic with no real substance. What did they get out of this? I just did not fit in. I never fit in with the crowd, but I had a few friends who were interested in the same things, such as skiing and riding horses. Friendship always revolved around what I did rather than who I was. (Grandin, 1995, p. 132)

Still, Grandin does not regret that she has autism. She says,

> If I could snap my fingers and be a nonautistic person, I would not. Autism is part of what I am. (p. 60)

Source: Grandin, T., *Thinking in pictures and my other reports from my life with autism*. New York: Vintage Books, 1995, 132.

All the disorders in this book are related to dysfunction in the brain to one degree or another. The disorders we discuss in this chapter are classified in the *DSM-5* specifically as neurological disorders. We consider a group of disorders that typically arise first in childhood, known as the **neurodevelopmental disorders:** attention-deficit/hyperactivity disorder; autism spectrum disorder; intellectual disability; and learning, communication, and motor disorders. Then we consider disorders that typically arise in older age. These are known as the **neurocognitive disorders:** various major and mild neurocognitive disorders, and delirium.

ATTENTION-DEFICIT/ HYPERACTIVITY DISORDER

"Pay attention! Slow down! You're so hyper today!" Most parents say this at least occasionally. A major focus of socialization is helping children learn to pay attention, control their impulses, and organize their behaviors so that they can accomplish long-term goals. Some children have tremendous trouble learning these skills, however, and may be diagnosed with **attention-deficit/hyperactivity disorder,** or **ADHD** (see the *DSM-5* criteria in Table 1). Eddie in the following case study is a young boy with ADHD.

TABLE 1 *DSM-5* Criteria for Attention-Deficit/Hyperactivity Disorder

A. A persistent pattern of inattention and/or hyperactivity that interferes with functioning or development, as characterized by (1) and/or (2):

1. *Inattention:* Six (or more) of the following symptoms have persisted for at least 6 months to a degree that is inconsistent with developmental level and that negatively impacts directly on social and academic/occupational activities: Note: The symptoms are not solely a manifestation of oppositional behavior, defiance, hostility, or failure to understand tasks or instructions. For older adolescents and adults (age 17 and older), at least five symptoms are required.
   a. Often fails to give close attention to details or makes careless mistakes in schoolwork, at work, or during other activities (e.g., overlooks or misses details, work is inaccurate)
   b. Often has difficulty sustaining attention in tasks or play activities (e.g., has difficulty remaining focused during lectures, conversations, or lengthy reading)
   c. Often does not seem to listen when spoken to directly (e.g., mind seems elsewhere, even in the absence of any obvious distraction)
   d. Often does not follow through on instructions and fails to finish schoolwork, chores, or duties in the workplace (e.g., starts tasks but quickly loses focus and is easily sidetracked)
   e. Often has difficulty organizing tasks and activities (e.g., difficulty managing sequential tasks; difficulty keeping materials and belongings in order; messy, disorganized work; poor time management; tends to fail to meet deadlines)
   f. Often avoids, dislikes, or is reluctant to engage in tasks that require sustained mental effort (e.g., schoolwork or homework; for older adolescents and adults, preparing reports, completing forms, or reviewing lengthy papers)
   g. Often loses things necessary for tasks or activities (e.g., school materials, pencils, books, tools, wallets, keys, paperwork, eyeglasses, mobile telephones)
   h. Is often easily distracted by extraneous stimuli (for older adolescents and adults, may include unrelated thoughts)
   i. Is often forgetful in daily activities (e.g., doing chores, running errands; for older adolescents and adults, returning calls, paying bills, keeping appointments)

2. *Hyperactivity and impulsivity:* Six (or more) of the following symptoms have persisted for at least 6 months to a degree that is inconsistent with developmental level and that negatively impacts directly on social and academic/occupational activities. Note: The symptoms are not solely a manifestation of oppositional behavior, defiance, hostility, or a failure to understand tasks or instructions. For older adolescents and adults (age 17 and older), at least five symptoms are required.
   a. Often fidgets with or taps hands or feet or squirms in seat
   b. Often leaves seat in situations when remaining seated is expected (e.g., leaves his or her place in the classroom, office or other workplace, or other situations that require remaining in place)
   c. Often runs about or climbs in situations where it is inappropriate (Note: In adolescents or adults, may be limited to feeling restless)
   d. Often unable to play or engage in leisure activities quietly
   e. Is often "on the go," acting as if "driven by a motor" (e.g., is unable to be or uncomfortable being still for an extended time, as in restaurants, meetings; may be experienced by others as being restless and difficult to keep up with)
   f. Often talks excessively
   g. Often blurts out an answer before a question has been completed (e.g., completes people's sentences; cannot wait for turn in conversation)
   h. Often has difficulty waiting his or her turn (e.g., while waiting in line)
   i. Often interrupts or intrudes on others (e.g., butts into conversations, games, or activities; may start using other people's things without asking or receiving permission; for adolescents or adults, may intrude into or take over what others are doing)

B. Several inattentive or hyperactive-impulsive symptoms were present prior to age 12 years.

C. Several inattentive or hyperactive-impulsive symptoms are present in two or more settings (e.g., at home, school, or work; with friends or relatives; in other activities).

D. There is clear evidence that the symptoms interfere with, or reduce the quality of, social, academic, or occupational functioning.

E. The symptoms do not occur exclusively during the course of schizophrenia or another psychotic disorder and are not better explained by another mental disorder (e.g., mood disorder, anxiety disorder, dissociative disorder, personality disorder, substance intoxication or withdrawal).

Specify Based on Current Presentation

Combined Presentation: If both Criterion A1 (Inattention) and Criterion A2 (Hyperactivity-Impulsivity) are met for the past 6 months.

Predominantly Inattentive Presentation: If Criterion A1 (Inattention) is met but Criterion A2 (Hyperactivity-Impulsivity) is not met for the past 6 months.

Predominantly Hyperactive/Impulsive Presentation: If Criterion A2 (Hyperactivity-Impulsivity) is met and Criterion A1 (Inattention) is not met for the past 6 months.

CASE STUDY

Eddie, age 9, was referred to a child psychiatrist at the request of his school because of the difficulties he creates in class. His teacher complains that he is so restless that his classmates are unable to concentrate. He is hardly ever in his seat and mostly roams around talking to other children while they are working. In his seat, he fidgets with his hands and feet and drops things on the floor. His most recent suspension from school was for swinging from the fluorescent light fixture over the blackboard. Because he was unable to climb down again, the class was in an uproar.

His mother says that Eddie's behavior has been difficult since he was a toddler and that, as a 3-year-old, he was extremely hyperactive and demanding. He has always required little sleep and awoken before anyone else. When he was small, "he got into everything," particularly in the early morning, when he would get up at 4:30 or 5:00 and go downstairs by himself. His parents would awaken to find the living room or kitchen "demolished." When he was 4, he unlocked the door of the apartment and wandered off into a busy street; fortunately, he was rescued by a passerby.

Eddie has no interest in TV and dislikes games or toys that require any concentration or patience. He is not popular with other children and at home prefers to be outdoors, playing with his dog or riding his bike. If he plays with toys, his games are messy and often broken. His mother cannot get him to keep his things in any order. (Source: *DSM Casebook: A Learning Companion to the Diagnostic and Statistical Manual of Mental Disorders,* Fifth Edition. American Psychiatric Association, 2013.)

Most elementary-school-age children can sit still for some period of time and engage in games that require patience and concentration. They can inhibit their impulses to jump up in class or walk into traffic. Eddie cannot. His behavior is driven and disorganized, as is common in children with ADHD.

There are three subtypes or presentations of ADHD in the *DSM-5*. The *combined presentation* requires six or more symptoms of inattention and six or more symptoms of hyperactivity-impulsivity. The *predominantly inattentive presentation* is diagnosed if six or more symptoms of inattention but less than six symptoms of hyperactivity-impulsivity are present. The *predominantly hyperactive/impulsive presentation* is diagnosed if six or more symptoms of hyperactivity-impulsivity but less than six symptoms of inattention are present. Eddie appears to have this last presentation of ADHD.

By definition, ADHD begins in childhood. One of the major changes in the diagnostic criteria for ADHD in the *DSM-5* is that the age limit for the onset of symptoms was raised from 7 years to 12 years, in response to research suggesting that the cutoff of 7 years failed to capture many children who eventually show ADHD but a cutoff of 12 years captured 95 percent of individuals who develop ADHD (Barkley, 2014; Frick & Nigg, 2012; Kieling et al., 2010). Epidemiological studies based on the earlier cutoff of 7 years of age indicate that 5 to 7 percent of children develop ADHD (Polanczyk & Jensen, 2008; Polanczyk, Willcutt, Salum, Kieling, & Rohde, 2014); this likely is an underestimate of the prevalence according to the new *DSM-5* criterion of onset by 12 years of age (Voort, He, Jameson, & Merikangas, 2014). Boys are a little more than two times more likely than girls to develop ADHD in childhood and early adolescence, although this difference narrows as they age into adulthood (Hinshaw, 2018). Girls with ADHD tend to present primarily with inattentive features and have less disruptive behavior than boys with ADHD, which may lead to an underidentification of ADHD in girls (Biederman et al., 2002). ADHD is found across most cultures and ethnic groups. Although the percentage of children with ADHD is similar across countries, children in the United States are diagnosed at somewhat higher rates (Hinshaw, 2018; Polanczyk et al., 2014). Like Eddie, most children with ADHD are diagnosed in elementary school.

Children with ADHD often do poorly in school (Langberg et al., 2012). Because they cannot pay attention or calm their hyperactivity, they do not learn the material and often perform below their intellectual capabilities. In addition, 20 to 25 percent of children with ADHD may have a specific learning disorder that makes it doubly hard for them to concentrate in school and to learn (Wilens, Biederman, & Spencer, 2002).

Children with ADHD may have poor relationships with other children and, like Eddie, often are rejected outright (Hoza et al., 2005). When interacting with their peers, children with ADHD may be intrusive, irritable, and demanding. They want to play by their own rules and sometimes show mood and temper problems. When things do not go their way, they may become aggressive.

The behavior problems of some children with ADHD worsen over the course of development, and become severe enough to be diagnosed as a conduct disorder. This is particularly true for ADHD children with the combined presentation. Children with conduct disorders grossly violate the social and cultural norms for appropriate behavior toward others by acting in uncaring and even antisocial ways (see the chapter "Disruptive, Impulse-Control, and Conduct Disorders"). Between 45 and 60 percent of children

Children normally have high energy levels, but only a minority of children can be labeled hyperactive. *©Petri Artturi Asikainen/Gorilla Creative Images/Getty Images*

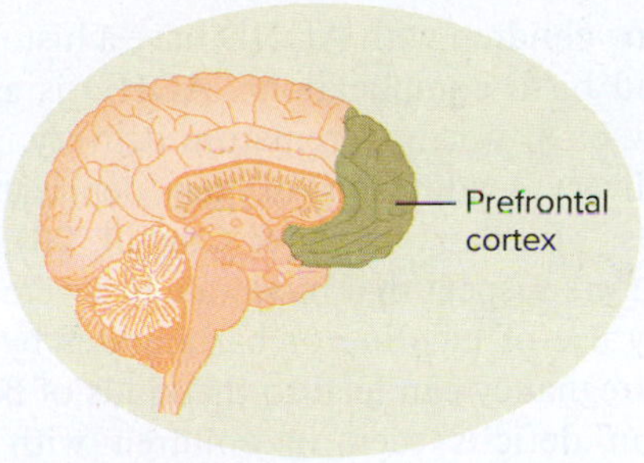

The prefrontal cortex is smaller and shows abnormal activity in children with ADHD.

with ADHD develop a conduct disorder, abuse drugs or alcohol, or violate the law (Ahmad & Hinshaw, 2016; Frick & Nigg, 2012). For some individuals, conduct problems persist into adulthood.

The long-term outcomes for children with ADHD vary considerably. Symptoms persist into young adulthood in about 50 percent of cases (Klassen, Katzman, & Chokka, 2010; Hinshaw, 2018). Adults diagnosed with ADHD as children are at increased risk for antisocial personality disorder, substance abuse, mood and anxiety disorders, marital problems, traffic accidents, legal infractions, and frequent job changes (Fischer & Barkley, 2006; Wilens et al., 2002). Some adults who have had lifelong problems achieving success in school and at work and difficulties in social relationships might have had undiagnosed and untreated ADHD as children. An epidemiological study of the United States found that 4.4 percent of adults could be diagnosed with ADHD (Kessler, Adler, et al., 2006). They were more likely to be male, and they showed a wide range of difficulties at work and in their social lives. Most had not received treatment for ADHD specifically, although many had been treated for other disorders. Adults with ADHD are at higher risk for depression, anxiety disorders, substance abuse, and antisocial personality disorder (Asherson, Buitelaar, Faraone, & Rohde, 2016; Klassen et al., 2010).

Biological Factors

The difficulties in attention, planning and carrying through with activities, and impulse control seen in ADHD appear to be tied to fundamental abnormalities in the brain (Cubillo, Halari, Smith, Taylor, & Rubia, 2012; Hoogman et al., 2017). Abnormal activity has been seen in several areas, including the prefrontal cortex, which is key to the control of cognition, motivation, and behavior; the striatum, which is involved in working memory and planning; and the cerebellum, which is involved in motor behaviors. The cerebral cortex is smaller in volume in children, and there is less connectivity between frontal areas of the cortex and areas of the brain that influence motor behavior, memory and attention, and emotional reactions. Because the cortex continues to develop well into adolescence, one hypothesis is that children with ADHD are neurologically immature—that is, their brains are slower to develop than the brains of unaffected children—leaving them unable to maintain attention and control their behavior at an age-appropriate level. This immaturity hypothesis helps explain why in some children the symptoms of ADHD, especially hyperactivity symptoms, decline with age (Cubillo et al., 2012; Hoogman et al., 2017).

The catecholamine neurotransmitters, particularly dopamine and norepinephrine, appear to function abnormally in individuals with ADHD (del Campo, Chamberlain, Sahakian, & Robbins, 2011). We have previously discussed the role of these neurotransmitters in mood, but they also play important roles in sustained attention, inhibition of impulses, and processing of errors. Drugs that affect levels of these neurotransmitters are useful in treating ADHD.

ADHD is strongly tied to genetic factors (Larsson, Chang, D'Onofrio, & Lichtenstein, 2014). Siblings of children with ADHD are three to four times more likely to develop it than siblings of children without the disorder (Todd, Lobos, Sun, & Neuman, 2003). Several other disorders also tend to run in the families of children with ADHD, including antisocial personality disorder, alcoholism, and depression (Ahmad & Hinshaw, 2016; Faraone, Biederman, Keenan, & Tsuang, 1991). Twin studies and adoption studies suggest that genetic factors play a role in vulnerability to ADHD (Pingault et al., 2015). Attentional and hyperactivity symptoms of ADHD both seem to have a genetic basis (Nikolas & Burt, 2010). Molecular genetics studies suggest that genes that influence dopamine, noradrenaline, and serotonin may be abnormal in individuals with ADHD (Li, Chang, Zhang, Gao, & Wang, 2014).

Many children with ADHD have a history of prenatal and birth complications. ADHD is associated with low birth weight, premature delivery, and difficult delivery leading to oxygen deprivation (see Sciberras, Mulraney, Silva, & Coghill, 2017). Some investigators suspect that moderate to severe drinking or heavy use of nicotine or barbiturates by mothers during pregnancy can lead to the kinds of behavioral inhibition deficits seen in children with ADHD. Others regard these associations as a result of shared genetic risk among ADHD and drinking and smoking habits. Some studies have found small to moderate risk associated with exposure to lead during childhood, including through ingesting lead-based paint (Goodlad, Marcus, & Fulton, 2013).

The links between diet and symptoms of ADHD are inconsistent. An unhealthy "Western" diet full of fat, sodium, sugar, and food additives is associated with greater symptoms of hyperactivity both in healthy children and in children with ADHD, but it is not clear that this diet causes ADHD or other forms of psychopathology (Howard et al., 2011). A small number of children with ADHD show improvement in their symptoms when synthetic food colorings are removed from their diet (Nigg, Lewis, Edinger, & Falk, 2012).

Psychological and Social Factors

Children with ADHD are more likely than children without a psychological disorder to belong to families that experience frequent disruptions and in which the parents are prone to aggressive and hostile behavior and substance abuse (Ahmad & Hinshaw, 2016; Harold et al., 2013). Some of these associations may be due to shared genetic effects on impulsivity and cognitive problems, which lead to both the parental behaviors and the children's ADHD symptoms. However, it appears that genetic factors in ADHD prompt disruptive behavior in children and, in turn, hostile parenting, even in adoptive (i.e., genetically unrelated) parents (Harold et al., 2013). Family interaction patterns, especially in early childhood, influence the course and severity of ADHD, including the development of conduct problems (e.g., Musser, Karalunas, Dieckmann, Peris, & Nigg, 2016).

Treatments for ADHD

Most children with ADHD are treated with stimulant drugs, such as Ritalin, Dexedrine, and Adderall (Barkley, 2014). It may seem odd to give a stimulant to a hyperactive child, but 70 to 85 percent of ADHD children respond to these drugs with decreases in demanding, disruptive, and noncompliant behavior (Chan, Fogler, & Hammerness, 2016; Swanson et al., 2008). The children also show increases in positive mood, in the ability to be goal-directed, and in the quality of their interactions with others. The stimulants may work by increasing levels of dopamine in the synapses of the brain, enhancing release and inhibiting reuptake of this neurotransmitter (Swanson, Baler, & Volkow, 2011).

The side effects of stimulants include reduced appetite, insomnia, edginess, and gastrointestinal upset. Stimulants also can increase the frequency of tics in children with ADHD. There has been concern that stimulants may stunt growth, and some evidence exists that children with ADHD who begin taking stimulants show a decrease in their growth rate (Swanson et al., 2017). Stimulants also carry a risk of abuse by people looking for a high, to make money by resale, or hoping to gain an edge in high school, college, or the workplace (see the chapter "Substance Use and Gambling Disorders").

Nationwide, the number of children prescribed stimulant medications in the United States increased by 200 to 300 percent in the 1980s and 1990s, and then increased more slowly after 2000 (Zuvekas & Vitiello, 2012). However, rates of prescriptions continue to increase, especially among adolescents and adults (Safer, 2016). Some researchers argue that this increase reflects greater recognition of children and adults with ADHD and of their need for treatment. Others say that it represents an inappropriate overuse of the drugs, particularly for children who are difficult to control (Angold, Erkanli, Egger, & Costello, 2000). There is scant empirical evidence on which to judge these competing claims.

In a longitudinal study of children in the southeastern United States, 72 percent of those with ADHD received stimulants at some point during the 4 years they were followed, suggesting that most children with ADHD are being treated (Angold et al., 2000). In this study, however, the majority of the children taking stimulants did not have symptoms meeting the diagnostic criteria for ADHD, suggesting that stimulants were misprescribed, especially for the boys and the younger children in the study. More research is needed to determine whether stimulants are being used appropriately in treating children.

Other drugs that treat ADHD include atomoxetine, clonidine, and guanfacine, which are not stimulants but affect norepinephrine levels. These drugs can help reduce tics, common in children with ADHD, and increase cognitive performance (del Campo et al., 2011; Kratochvil et al., 2007). Side effects of these drugs include dry mouth, fatigue, dizziness, constipation, and sedation.

Children and adolescents with ADHD are sometimes prescribed antidepressant medications, particularly if they also have depression. These drugs have some positive effects on cognitive performance but are not as effective for ADHD as the stimulants

SHADES OF GRAY

Read the following description of Jake, a college student.

Jake had just earned a 2.4 GPA in his freshman year at the University of Washington when his parents took him to see a psychologist about his academic performance. At the meeting with the psychologist, his parents described their middle son as lazy, unmotivated, stubborn, and disorganized. His brothers were successful at school, as his parents had been. Growing up, Jake had seemed smart, but he often sabotaged his grades by forgetting to do his homework, quitting in the middle of assignments, and not finishing tests. When he completed a project, he would often leave it behind or lose it. He could be engrossed in TV or a video game, but when it came to his homework, he lacked focus. His parents also noted that he was constantly late and didn't seem to care about making everyone else wait for him.

When the psychologist spoke with Jake alone, Jake seemed like a nice, polite teenager. Jake felt discouraged and confused about school. He agreed that he didn't get the good grades his brothers did and knew his parents expected more of him. When he was younger he did well in school, and in elementary school he thought of himself as smart. But his grades had slipped when he transitioned into middle school, then again when he entered high school, and now again in college. He thought he understood what was going on in class but was always forgetting or losing things, and his mind would often wander. Outside of the classroom, he had a small but supportive group of friends, and he was involved in a wide variety of sports and activities. He denied any involvement with drugs or illegal activity. (Source: Adapted from Vitkus, J., *Casebook in abnormal psychology*. New York: McGraw-Hill, 2004, pp. 193–199)

What might be causing Jake's problems? What additional information would you want before making a diagnosis? (Discussion appears at the end of this chapter.)

(Wilens et al., 2002). Bupropion, an antidepressant with particularly strong effects on dopamine levels, appears to be more effective for ADHD than some other antidepressants. Unfortunately, the gains made by ADHD children treated with medications alone are short-term. As soon as medication is stopped, symptoms often return.

Behavioral therapies for ADHD focus on reinforcing attentive, goal-directed, and prosocial behaviors and extinguishing impulsive and hyperactive behaviors (Barkley, 2014; Evans, Owens, Wymbs, & Ray, 2018). These therapies typically engage parents and teachers in changing rewards and punishments in many aspects of the child's life. A child and his parents might agree that he will earn a chip every time he obeys a request to wash his hands or put away his toys. At the end of each week, he can exchange his chips for fun activities. Each time the child refuses to comply, he loses a chip. Such techniques can help parents break the cycle of engaging in arguments with their children that escalate problem behaviors, which in turn lead to more arguments and perhaps physical violence. The children learn to anticipate the consequences of their behaviors and to make less impulsive choices. They are taught to interact more appropriately with others, including waiting their turn in games, finding nonaggressive ways to express frustration, and listening when others speak. Meta-analyses of hundreds of studies have found strong and consistent evidence that behavioral therapy is highly effective in reducing symptoms of ADHD in children (Catala-Lopez et al., 2017; Fabiano et al., 2009). For adults with ADHD, cognitive-behavioral treatments that incorporate organizational, planning, and time management skills appear to be effective as well (Knouse, Teller, & Brooks, 2017).

Some studies suggest that the combination of stimulant therapy and psychosocial therapy is more likely to produce short-term improvements than either therapy alone. In one multi-site study, 579 children with ADHD were randomly assigned to receive the combination of Ritalin and behavior therapy, one therapy alone, or routine community care

In behavioral therapies for ADHD, a child and her parents might agree that she will earn a chip every time she obeys a request to wash her hands. At the end of each week, she can exchange her chips for fun activities such as eating an ice cream cone or extra television time. ©*Adam Gault/OJO Images/Getty Images*

(Jensen et al., 2001). After 14 months, 68 percent of the combined-treatment group had reduced or discontinued their ADHD behaviors, such as aggression and lack of concentration. In the medication-alone group, 56 percent showed reduced or discontinued symptoms. Behavior therapy alone reduced symptoms in only 34 percent of group members, and only 25 percent of those given routine community care showed reductions in their symptoms. In follow-ups 3, 6, and 8 years later, all three treatment groups continued to have fewer ADHD symptoms than they had had before treatment, but there were no differences between treatment groups in outcome (Jensen et al., 2007; Molina et al., 2009). In addition, 6 and 8 months after treatment ended, all three groups still had more symptoms than classmates who had not been diagnosed with ADHD (Molina et al., 2009).

AUTISM SPECTRUM DISORDER

Autism spectrum disorder (ASD) involves impairment in two fundamental behavior domains—deficits in social interactions and communications and restricted, repetitive patterns of behaviors, interests, and activities (see Table 2). Richard, a child with autism spectrum disorder, shows a range of deficits characteristic of this disorder.

TABLE 2 *DSM-5* Diagnostic Criteria for Autism Spectrum Disorder

A. Persistent deficits in social communication and social interaction across multiple contexts, as manifested by the following, currently or by history (examples are illustrative, not exhaustive; see text [of the *DSM-5*]):

1. Deficits in social-emotional reciprocity; ranging from abnormal social approach and failure of normal back-and-forth conversation, to reduced sharing of interests, emotions, or affect or failure to initiate or respond to social interactions.
2. Deficits in nonverbal communicative behaviors used for social interaction, ranging, for example, from poorly integrated verbal and nonverbal communication, to abnormalities in eye contact and body language, to deficits in understanding and use of gestures, or to a total lack of facial expression or nonverbal communication.
3. Deficits in developing, maintaining, and understanding relationships, ranging, for example, from difficulties adjusting behavior to suit various social contexts, to difficulties in sharing imaginative play or in making friends, or to an absence of interest in peers.

B. Restricted, repetitive patterns of behavior, interests, or activities as manifested by at least two of the following, currently or by history (examples are illustrative, not exhaustive; see text [of the *DSM-5*]):

1. Stereotyped or repetitive motor movements, use of objects, or speech (e.g., simple motor stereotypies, lining up toys or flipping objects, echolalia, idiosyncratic phrases).
2. Insistence on sameness, inflexible adherence to routines, or ritualized patterns of verbal or nonverbal behavior (such as extreme distress at small changes, difficulties with transitions, rigid thinking patterns, greeting rituals, need to take same route or eat same food each day).
3. Highly restricted, fixated interests that are abnormal in intensity or focus (such as strong attachment to or preoccupation with unusual objects, excessively circumscribed or perseverative interests).
4. Hyper- or hyporeactivity to sensory input or unusual interest in sensory aspects of environment (such as apparent indifference to pain/temperature, adverse response to specific sounds or textures, excessive smelling or touching of objects, fascination with lights or movement).

C. Symptoms must be present in the early developmental period (but may not become fully manifest until social demands exceed limited capacities, or may be masked by learned strategies in later life).

D. Symptoms cause clinically significant impairment in social, occupational, or other important areas of current functioning.

E. These disturbances are not better explained by intellectual disability or global developmental delay. Intellectual disability and autism spectrum disorder frequently co-occur; to make comorbid diagnoses of autism spectrum disorder and intellectual disability, social communication (Criteria A) must be below that expected for general developmental level.

CASE STUDY

Richard, age 3½, appeared to be self-contained and aloof from others. He did not greet his mother in the mornings or his father when he returned from work, though if left with a baby-sitter, he tended to scream much of the time. He had no interest in other children and ignored his younger brother. His babbling had no conversational intonation. It was not until age 3 that he could understand simple practical instructions. His speech consisted of echoing some words and phrases he had heard in the past, with the original speaker's accent and intonation; he could use one or two such phrases to indicate his simple needs. For example, if he said, "Do you want a drink?" he meant he was thirsty. He did not communicate by facial expression or use gesture or mime, except for pulling someone along with him and placing his or her hand on an object he wanted. He was fascinated by bright lights and spinning objects and would stare at them while laughing, flapping his hands, and dancing on tiptoe. He was intensely attached to a miniature car, which he held in his hand, day and night, but he never played imaginatively with this or any other toy. From age 2 he had collected kitchen utensils and arranged them in repetitive patterns all over the floors of the house. These pursuits, together with occasional periods of aimless running around, constituted his whole repertoire of spontaneous activities.

The major management problem was Richard's intense resistance to any attempt to change or extend his interests. Removing his toy car, even retrieving, for example, an egg whisk or a spoon for its legitimate use in cooking, or trying to make him look at a picture book precipitated temper tantrums that could last an hour or more, with screaming, kicking, and the biting of himself or others. These tantrums could be cut short by restoring the status quo.

His parents had wondered if Richard might be deaf, but his love of music, his accurate echoing, and his sensitivity to some very soft sounds, such as those made by unwrapping chocolate in the next room, convinced them that this was not the cause of his abnormal behavior. Psychological testing gave Richard a mental age of 3 years in non-language-dependent skills (such as assembling objects) but only 18 months in language comprehension. (Source: *DSM Casebook: A Learning Companion to the Diagnostic and Statistical Manual of Mental Disorders,* Fifth Edition. American Psychiatric Association, 2013.)

The deficits in social interactions and communications of **autism** may first show up in infants' and toddlers' interactions with their parents, which are usually characterized by reciprocal adoration. Compared to normally developing children, infants with autism spectrum disorder may not smile and coo in response to their caregivers or initiate play with their caregivers. They may not want to cuddle with their parents, even when they are frightened. They may hardly ever make eye contact relative to cultural norms or show joint attention (i.e., failure to follow a caregiver's pointing or eye gaze). Other early symptoms often include delayed language development. When they are a bit older, children with autism spectrum disorder may not be interested in playing with other children, preferring solitary play. They also do not seem to react to other people's emotions. In the chapter opener, Temple Grandin describes how she had to work hard to overcome her lack of understanding of social interactions.

Approximately 50 percent of children with autism spectrum disorder do not develop useful speech. Those who do develop language may not use it as other children do. In the case study about Richard, he showed several of the communication problems characteristic of children with autism spectrum disorder. Rather than generating his own words, he simply echoed what he had just heard, a behavior called **echolalia.** He reversed pronouns, using *you* when he meant *I*. When he did try to generate his own words or sentences, his language was one-sided and lacked social reciprocity and he did not modulate his voice for expressiveness, instead sounding almost like a monotone voice-generating machine.

The second group of deficits concerns the activities and interests of children with autism spectrum disorder. Rather than engaging in symbolic play with toys, they are preoccupied with one feature of a toy or an object. Richard was preoccupied with his miniature car, carrying it everywhere without playing with it, and Temple Grandin was interested only in watching sand dribble through her fingers. They may engage in bizarre, repetitive behaviors with toys. Rather than using two dolls to play "house," a child with autism spectrum disorder might take the arm off one doll and simply pass it back and forth between her two hands. Routines and rituals often are extremely important to children with autism spectrum disorder. When any aspect of their daily routine is changed—for example, if their mother stops at the bank on the way to school—they may become excessively frightened and highly distressed. Some children perform stereotyped and repetitive behaviors using some part of their body, such as incessantly flapping their hands or banging their head against a wall. These behaviors sometimes are referred to as *self-stimulatory behaviors,* under the

In the movie *Rain Man*, Dustin Hoffman plays a man with autism who had some extraordinary abilities. Most people with autism do not fall into this category of "savants" portrayed in the film.
©United Artists/courtesy of Everett Collection

assumption that these children engage in such behaviors for self-stimulation. It is not clear, however, that this is their true purpose.

Children with autism spectrum disorder often do poorly on measures of intellectual ability, such as IQ tests, with approximately 50 percent of autistic children showing at least moderate intellectual disability (Mattila et al., 2011; Sigman, Spence, & Wang, 2006). The deficits of some children with autism spectrum disorder are confined to skills that require language and understanding others' points of view, and they may score in the average range on tests that do not require language skills. Temple Grandin is clearly of above-average intelligence despite her autism spectrum disorder. Much has been made in the popular press about the special talents of some children with autism spectrum disorder, such as the ability to play music without having been taught or to draw extremely well, or exceptional memory and mathematical calculation abilities as depicted in the movie *Rain Man*. These persons sometimes are referred to as *savants*. Such cases are quite rare, however (Bölte & Poustka, 2004).

For the diagnosis of autism spectrum disorder, symptoms must have their onset in early childhood. It is important to note that there is wide variation in the severity and outcome of this disorder. One study followed 68 individuals who had been diagnosed with autism as children and who had a performance (nonverbal) IQ of at least 50 (Howlin, Goode, Hutton, & Rutter, 2004). As adults, 13 of them had been able to obtain some sort of academic degree, 5 had gone on to college, and 2 had obtained a postgraduate degree. Of the 68 people in the study, 23 were employed and 18 had close friendships. The majority, however, required ongoing support from their parents or required some form of residential care. Fifty-eight percent, or 39 individuals, had overall outcomes that were rated "poor" or "very poor." They were unable to live alone or hold a job, and they had persistent problems in communication and social interactions.

By far the best predictor of the outcome of autism spectrum disorder is a child's IQ and the amount of language development before age 6 (Anderson, Liang, & Lord, 2014; Howlin et al., 2004). Children who have an IQ above 50 and communicative speech before age 6 have a much better prognosis than do others. People diagnosed with autism spectrum disorder who had an IQ of 70 or above were especially likely to achieve a "good" or "very good" outcome (Howlin et al., 2004).

In the *DSM-IV-TR* (published in 1994), autism was one of multiple diagnoses in the category **pervasive developmental disorders (PDDs),** and it required the presence of two symptoms of social impairment (from a list of four possible symptoms) and one symptom each of communication problems and repetitive/stereotyped behaviors (from lists of four possible symptoms each); in addition, the onset had to be before age 3. Asperger's disorder was another PDD and was often considered a high-functioning form of autism involving deficits in social interactions and restricted, repetitive behavior but no significant communication deficits. Two other relatively rare variants (Rett's disorder and childhood disintegrative disorder) were also in the PDD category, along with pervasive developmental disorder not otherwise specified (PDD-NOS). The lifetime prevalence of all PDDs combined was estimated to be about 1 to 2 percent (Baird et al., 2006; Fombonne, 2009; Kim et al., 2011).

In the *DSM-5*, the PDD category has been dropped, and there is only one autism spectrum disorder, as defined in Table 2. These changes were made due to evidence that the distinctions between the different PDDs, especially autism and Asperger's disorder, were difficult to make reliably and that the PDDs seemed to share common etiologies (Lord & Bishop, 2015; Swedo et al., 2012). Moreover, because the disorder presents differently depending on symptom severity, developmental level (e.g., IQ), and age, *DSM-5* uses the term "spectrum" to capture the range of related but varied presentations. The impact of the changes in the treatment of autism spectrum disorders in the *DSM-5* is a matter of some debate and concern. Several initial studies that reanalyzed data on children diagnosed under the *DSM-IV-TR* criteria found that the *DSM-5* criteria for autism spectrum disorder captured only about 50 to 60 percent of children who previously would have been diagnosed with autism, Asperger's disorder, or PDD-NOS (Mattila et al., 2011; McPartland, Reichow, & Volkmar, 2012). These studies indicated that the children most likely not to fit the *DSM-5* criteria for autism spectrum disorder are those who have higher IQs and who lack deficits in verbal communications. Only about one-quarter of individuals previously diagnosed with Asperger's syndrome or PDD-NOS meet the criteria for autism spectrum disorder based on the *DSM-5* criteria (McPartland et al., 2012). These findings raised concerns about the effects of these changes on access to services for individuals who have previously been diagnosed with autistic disorders other than classic, low-functioning autism (McPartland et al., 2012). The most recent and largest study of this kind, however, found that *DSM-5* criteria identified 91 percent of children with established *DSM-IV* PDD diagnoses (Huerta, Bishop, Duncan, Hus, & Lord, 2012), suggesting that most children would remain eligible for the diagnosis and related services. Future studies will likely further clarify the impact of these changes to the diagnostic criteria.

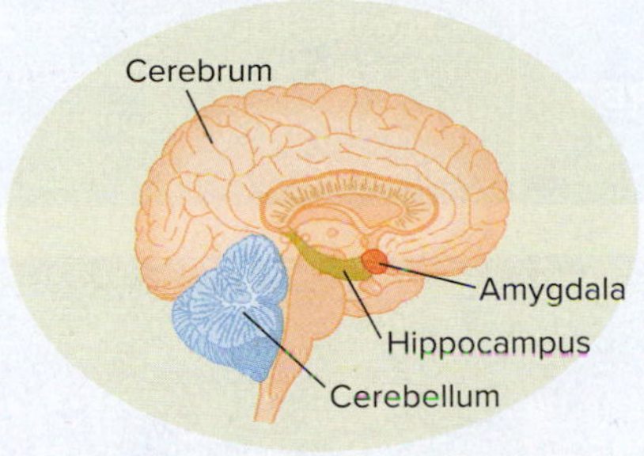

These areas of the brain have been implicated in autism.

Contributors to Autism Spectrum Disorder

Over the years, a wide variety of theories of autism have been proposed. The psychiatrist who first described autism, Leo Kanner (1943), thought that autism was caused by a combination of biological factors and poor parenting. He and later psychoanalytic theorists (Bettelheim, 1967) described the parents of children with autism as cold, distant, and uncaring. The child's symptoms were seen as a retreat inward to a secret world of fantasies in response to unavailable parents. However, research over the decades has shown clearly that unresponsive parenting plays little or no role in the development of autism.

Several biological factors have been implicated in the development of autism spectrum disorder. Family and twin studies strongly suggest that genetics plays a role in the development of the disorder. The siblings of children with autism spectrum disorder are 50 times more likely to have the disorder than are the siblings of children without autism spectrum disorder (Sigman et al., 2006). Twin studies show concordance rates for autism spectrum disorder to be about 60 percent for monozygotic (MZ) twins and 0 to 30 percent for dizygotic (DZ) twins (Chen, Peñagarikano, Belgard, Swarup, & Geschwind, 2015; Hallmayer et al., 2011). In addition, about 90 percent of the MZ twins of children with autism spectrum disorder have a significant cognitive impairment, compared to 10 percent of DZ twins. Also, children with autism spectrum disorder have a higher-than-average rate of other genetic disorders associated with cognitive impairment, including fragile X syndrome and PKU (Chen et al., 2015; Volkmar, State, & Klin, 2009). These data suggest that a general vulnerability to several types of cognitive impairment, only one of which is manifested as autism spectrum disorder, runs in families. No single gene seems to cause autism spectrum disorder; instead, abnormalities in several genes have been associated with autism spectrum disorder (Chen et al., 2015).

Neurological factors probably play a role in autism spectrum disorder. The array of deficits seen in autism spectrum disorder suggests disruption in the normal development and organization of the brain (Chen et al., 2015). In addition, approximately 30 percent of children with autism spectrum disorder develop seizure disorders by adolescence, suggesting a severe neurological dysfunction (Fombonne, 1999). A consistent finding is greater head and brain size in children with the disorder than in children without it (Lotspeich et al., 2004; Via, Radua, Cardoner, Happé, & Mataix-Cols, 2011).

Neuroimaging studies have suggested a variety of structural abnormalities in the brains of individuals with autism spectrum disorder, including in the cerebellum, the cerebrum, the amygdala, and possibly the hippocampus (Chen et al., 2015; Via et al., 2011). When children with autism spectrum disorder are doing tasks that require perception of facial expressions, joint attention with another person, empathy, or thinking about social situations, they show abnormal functioning in areas of the brain that are recruited for such tasks. For example, when shown photos of faces, children with autism spectrum disorder show less activation than do typically developing children in an area of the brain involved in facial perception called the fusiform gyrus (Figure 2; Schultz, 2005). Another study showed that adults with autism spectrum disorder show atypical patterns of brain activation when hearing their own name (Nijhof, Dhar, Goris, Brass, & Wiersema, 2018). Difficulty in perceiving and understanding facial expressions and verbal communications could contribute to these children's deficits in social interactions.

Neurological dysfunctions could be the result of genetic factors. Alternatively, children with autism have a higher-than-average rate of prenatal and birth complications, and these complications might create the neurological abnormality (Chen et al., 2015). Furthermore, studies have found differences between children with and without autism spectrum disorder in levels of the neurotransmitters serotonin and dopamine; more research is needed to understand how these neurotransmitters factor into the disorder (Muller, Anacker, & Veenstra-VanderWeele, 2016).

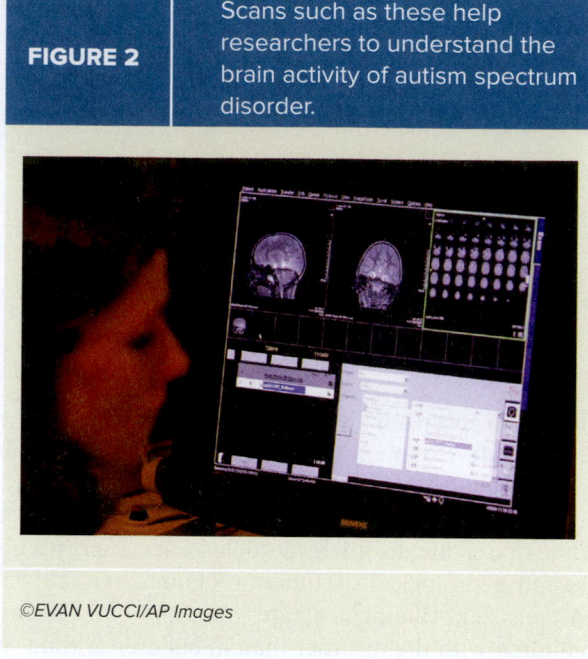

FIGURE 2 Scans such as these help researchers to understand the brain activity of autism spectrum disorder.

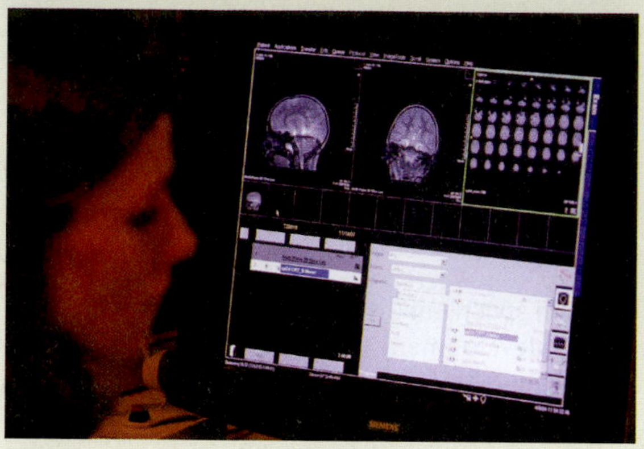

©EVAN VUCCI/AP Images

Treatments for Autism Spectrum Disorder

A number of drugs have been shown to improve some of the symptoms of autism spectrum disorder, including overactivity, stereotyped behaviors (e.g., head banging and hand flapping), sleep disturbances, and tension. However, although medications are often prescribed, the evidence for their effectiveness is quite mixed (Madden et al., 2017; Stepanova, Dowling, Phelps, & Findling, 2017). The selective serotonin reuptake inhibitors appear to reduce repetitive behaviors and aggression and improve social interactions in some, but not all, people with autism spectrum disorder. The atypical antipsychotic medications have shown more reliable effectiveness; they are used to reduce obsessive and repetitive behaviors and to improve self-control. Finally, stimulants are used to improve attention. Although these drugs do not alter the core features of autism spectrum disorder, they sometimes make it easier for people with autism spectrum disorder to participate in school and in behavioral treatments.

Psychosocial therapies for autism spectrum disorder combine behavioral techniques and structured educational services (Reichow, Barton, Boyd, & Hume, 2012; Vismara & Rogers, 2010; Wong et al., 2015). Operant conditioning strategies are used to reduce excessive behaviors, such as repetitive or ritualistic behaviors, tantrums, and aggression, and to alleviate deficits or delays, such as deficits in communication and in interactions with others. These techniques may be implemented in highly structured schools designed especially for children with autism spectrum disorder or in regular classrooms if children are mainstreamed. The specific deficits a child has in cognitive, motor, or communication skills are targeted, and materials that reduce possible distractions (such as books that do not have words printed in bright colors) are used. Parents may be taught to implement the techniques consistently when the children are at home.

One pioneering study showed that 47 percent of children with autism spectrum disorder who are given this intensive behavioral treatment for at least 40 hours a week for at least 2 years achieved normal intellectual and educational functioning by age 7, compared to only 2 percent of children with autism who received institutional care alone (Lovaas, 1987). Several other studies have shown strong improvements in cognitive skills and behavioral control in children with autism spectrum disorder who were treated with a comprehensive behavior therapy administered both by their parents and in their school setting from an early age (see meta-analysis by Eldevik et al., 2009).

INTELLECTUAL DISABILITY

Intellectual disability (ID) (or intellectual developmental disorder), formerly referred to as mental retardation, involves significant deficits in intellectual abilities and life functioning. The first *DSM-5* criterion for intellectual disability requires significant deficits in intellectual functioning, such as abstract thinking, reasoning, learning, problem solving, and planning (Table 3, American Psychiatric Association, 2013). The *DSM* requires that these deficits be confirmed by clinical assessment and formal assessments such as IQ tests.

The second criterion for the diagnosis involves deficits in functioning in three broad domains of daily living, such that the person cannot live reasonably independently without some support (American Psychiatric Association, 2013). First, in the conceptual domain, individuals show deficits in skills such as language, reading, writing, math, reasoning, knowledge, memory, and problem solving. Second, in the social domain, individuals have difficulty in being aware of and understanding others' experiences, in interpersonal communication skills, in the ability to make and keep friends, in social judgment, and in regulating their own reactions in social interactions. Third, in the practical domain, individuals show deficits in managing personal care (such as maintaining hygiene, grocery shopping, cooking), managing their own finances, recreation, transportation, and organizing themselves to hold a job or attend school. People with intellectual disability also often have problems with motor skills, such as eye-hand coordination

TABLE 3 *DSM-5* Criteria for Intellectual Disability (ID)

Intellectual disability (intellectual developmental disorder) is a disorder with an onset during the developmental period that includes both intellectual and adaptive functioning deficits in conceptual, social, and practical domains. The following three criteria must be met:

A. Deficits in intellectual functions, such as reasoning, problem solving, planning, abstract thinking, judgment, academic learning, and learning from experience, confirmed by both clinical assessment and individualized, standardized intelligence testing.

B. Deficits in adaptive functioning that result in failure to meet developmental and sociocultural standards for personal independence and social responsibility. Without ongoing support, the adaptive deficits limit functioning in one or more activities of daily life, such as communication, social participation, and independent living, across multiple environments, such as home, school, work, and community.

C. Onset of intellectual and adaptive deficits during the developmental period.

The severity of intellectual disability can be classified as mild, moderate, severe, or profound, on the basis of adaptive function (and not IQ alone) and the level of supports required.

and balance. These deficits have to be significant compared to other people who are the same age and have a similar sociodemographic background and culture.

The *DSM-5* classifies intellectual disability into four levels of severity: mild, moderate, severe, and profound. Children and adults with a *mild level of intellectual disability* generally have some limitations in their ability to acquire typical academic or job-related skills, may seem immature in social interactions and overly concrete in their communications with others, show limited social judgment and understanding of risk, and may be able to care for themselves reasonably well except in complex situations such as making legal or health decisions. Adults with mild intellectual disability often hold competitive jobs that don't emphasize conceptual skills.

Children with a *moderate level* of *intellectual disability* typically have significant delays in language development, such as using only 4 to 10 words by age 3. They may be physically clumsy and have some trouble dressing and feeding themselves. They typically do not achieve beyond the second-grade level in academic skills but, with special education, can acquire simple vocational skills. As adults, they may be able to hold a job requiring only an elementary-school level of conceptual skills, but they likely will require considerable assistance. With extensive training, they can learn to care for their personal needs (eating, personal hygiene). Their social interactions may be impaired by communication difficulties, and they may show poor social judgment.

Individuals with *severe* intellectual disability have a very limited vocabulary and may speak in two- or three-word sentences. As children they may have significant deficits in motor development and may play with toys inappropriately (e.g., banging two dolls together). As adults, they can feed themselves with a spoon and dress themselves if the clothing is not complicated (with many buttons or zippers). They cannot travel alone for any distance and cannot shop or cook for themselves. Some individuals may be able to learn some unskilled manual labor, but many are unable to do so. In the social domain, they generally lack awareness of risk, and may easily be led by others due to naiveté in social situations. They require support for all aspects of daily living.

At the *profound level* of intellectual disability, individuals often don't develop conceptual skills beyond simple matching of concrete physical features of objects. Co-occurring sensory and motor impairments may prevent functional use of objects and limit participation in everyday activities to watching. In the social domain, the individual may only be able to understand simple concrete instructions and gestures. Even in adulthood, the individual is fully dependent on others for all aspects of daily living, including physical care, health, and safety. Maladaptive behavior is present in a significant minority of individuals with profound intellectual disability.

Individually administered intelligence tests are used to assess the level of intellectual functioning of a person suspected of having intellectual disability. Intelligence tests measure verbal comprehension, working memory, perceptual reasoning, quantitative reasoning, abstract thought, and processing speed. Individuals with intellectual disability generally have scores of two standard deviations below the mean IQ score of the general population of 100; in other words, an IQ score of 70 (± 5, or 65–75) or lower. However, *DSM-5* deemphasizes intelligence test scores in the diagnostic criteria to determine level of severity, and rather focuses clinicians' attention on the individual's level of adaptive functioning across the conceptual, social, and practical domains, in part because IQ scores can be misleading or misused. It is estimated that 1 to 3 percent of the population has intellectual development disorder (Humeau, Gambino, Chelly, & Vitale, 2009).

Advocates of mainstreaming argue that individuals with intellectual disabilities should be integrated into everyday life.
©John Birdsall/Shutterstock

Biological Causes of Intellectual Disability

Many biological factors can cause intellectual disability, including chromosomal and gestational disorders, exposure to toxins prenatally or in early childhood, infections, brain injury or malformations, metabolism and nutrition problems, and some kinds of seizure disorders (e.g., infantile spasms). We examine these factors first and then turn to sociocultural factors.

Genetic Factors

Nearly 300 genes affecting brain development and functioning have been implicated in the development of intellectual disability (Ellison, Rosenfeld, & Shaffer, 2013). These genes do not lead to the disorder as such but rather to one or more of the types of deficits people with ID show. It is not surprising, then, that families of children with intellectual disability tend to have high incidences of a variety of intellectual problems, including the different levels of intellectual disability and autism spectrum disorder (Ellison et al., 2013; Humeau et al., 2009).

Two metabolic disorders that are genetically transmitted and that cause intellectual disability are phenylketonuria (PKU) and Tay-Sachs disease. PKU is carried by a recessive gene and occurs in about 1 in 20,000 births. Children with PKU are unable to metabolize phenylalanine, an amino acid. As a result, phenylalanine and its derivative, phenylpyruvic acid, build up in the body and cause brain damage. Fortunately, children who from an early age receive a special diet free of phenylalanine can attain an average level of intelligence. Most states mandate testing for PKU in newborns. If left untreated, children with PKU typically have an IQ below 50 and severe or profound ID.

Tay-Sachs disease also is carried by a recessive gene and occurs primarily in Jewish populations. When an affected child is 3 to 6 months old, a progressive degeneration of the nervous system begins, leading to mental and physical deterioration. These children usually die before age 6, and there is no effective treatment.

Several types of chromosomal disorders can lead to intellectual disability (Williams, 2010). Normally children are born with 23 pairs of chromosomes. Twenty-two of these pairs are known as autosomes, and the twenty-third pair contains the sex chromosomes. One of the best-known causes of intellectual disability is Down syndrome, which occurs when chromosome 21 is present in triplicate rather than in duplicate. (For this reason, Down syndrome is also referred to as trisomy 21.) Down syndrome occurs in about 1 in every 800 children born in the United States.

From childhood, almost all people with Down syndrome have intellectual disability, although the severity level varies from mild to profound. Their ability to care for themselves, live somewhat independently, and hold a job depends on their level of intellectual deficit and the training and support they receive. Children with Down syndrome have a round, flat face and almond-shaped eyes; a small nose; slightly protruding lip and tongue; and short, square hands. They tend to be short in stature and somewhat obese. Many have congenital heart defects and gastrointestinal difficulties. As adults, they seem to age more rapidly than normal, and their life expectancy is shorter than average. People with Down syndrome have abnormalities in the neurons in their brains that resemble those found in Alzheimer's disease. Nearly all individuals with Down syndrome past age 40 develop the thinking and memory deficits characteristic of a neurocognitive disorder due to Alzheimer's disease (see the section later in this chapter, "Neurocognitive Disorder Due to Alzheimer's Disease") and lose the ability to care for themselves (Visser et al., 1997).

Fragile X syndrome, another common cause of intellectual disability, is caused when a tip of the X chromosome breaks off (Turk, 2011). This syndrome affects primarily males because they do not have a second, normal X chromosome to balance the mutation. The syndrome is characterized by severe to profound intellectual disability, speech defects, and severe deficits in interpersonal interaction. Males with fragile X syndrome have large ears, a long face, and enlarged testes. Females with the syndrome tend to have a less severe level of intellectual disability (Koukoui & Chaudhuri, 2007). Two other chromosomal abnormalities that cause severe intellectual disability and shortened life expectancy are trisomy 13 (chromosome 13 is present in triplicate) and trisomy 18 (chromosome 18 is present in triplicate).

The risk of having a child with Down syndrome or any other chromosomal abnormality increases with the age of the parents. This may be because the older a parent is, the more likely chromosomes are to have degenerated or to have been damaged by toxins.

Brain Damage During Gestation and Early Life

Intellectual development can be profoundly affected by the fetus's prenatal environment (King, Hodapp, & Dykens, 2005). When a pregnant woman contracts the rubella (German measles) virus, the herpes virus,

CASE STUDY

Abel Dorris was adopted when he was 3 years old by Michael Dorris. Abel's mother had been a heavy drinker throughout the pregnancy and after Abel was born. She had subsequently died at age 35 of alcohol poisoning. Abel had been born almost 7 weeks premature, with low birth weight. He had been abused and malnourished before being removed to a foster home. At age 3, Abel was small for his age, was not yet toilet-trained, and could only speak about 20 words. He was diagnosed with a mild intellectual disability. His adoptive father hoped that, in a positive environment, Abel could catch up.

Yet, at age 4, Abel was still in diapers and weighed only 27 pounds. He had trouble remembering the names of other children, and his activity level was unusually high. When alone, he would rock back and forth rhythmically. At age 4, he suffered the first of several severe seizures, which caused him to lose consciousness for days. No drug treatments seemed to help.

When he entered school, Abel had trouble learning to count, to identify colors, and to tie his shoes. He had a short attention span and difficulty following simple instructions. Despite devoted teachers, when he finished elementary school, Abel still could not add, subtract, or identify his place of residence. His IQ was in the mid-60s.

Eventually, at age 20, Abel entered a vocational training program and moved into a supervised home. His main preoccupations were his collections of stuffed animals, paper dolls, newspaper cartoons, family photographs, and old birthday cards. At age 23, he was hit by a car and killed. (Source: Adapted from Dorris, M., *The unbroken cord*. New York: Harper & Row, 1989; Lyman, R., "Michael Dorris dies at 52: Wrote of his son's suffering," *New York Times*, April 15, 1997, 24.)

or syphilis, there is a risk of damage to the fetus that can cause intellectual disability. Chronic maternal disorders, such as high blood pressure and diabetes, can interfere with fetal nutrition and brain development and thereby affect the intellectual capacities of the fetus. If these maternal disorders are treated effectively throughout the pregnancy, the risk of damage to the fetus is low.

Children whose mothers abuse alcohol during pregnancy are at increased risk for **fetal alcohol syndrome** (**FAS;** see Mukherjee, Hollins, & Turk, 2006). Children with fetal alcohol syndrome have a below average IQ of 68 and have poor judgment, distractibility, and difficulty understanding social cues. As adolescents, their academic functioning is at only the second- to fourth-grade level, and they have trouble following directions. It is estimated that 2 to 15 children per 10,000 in the United States have fetal alcohol syndrome, and three times that number are born with lesser alcohol-related neurological and birth defects (CDC, 2018d). Abel Dorris, in the case study above, was born with fetal alcohol syndrome.

Children whose mothers abuse alcohol during pregnancy are at increased risk for *fetal alcohol syndrome.* ©*Realistic Reflections*

Even low to moderate levels of drinking during pregnancy can lead to negative outcomes, such as higher rates of miscarriage, delivery before full gestation, lower birth weight, congenital abnormalities, and impaired social and cognitive development (Jacobson & Jacobson, 2000; Kelly, Day, & Streissguth, 2000; Olson, Feldman, Streissguth, Sampson, & Boostein, 1998). For example, longitudinal studies of children exposed prenatally to alcohol show negative effects on growth at age 6 and on learning and memory skills at age 10, even if the children do not evidence the full syndrome of FAS (Cornelius, Goldschmidt, Day, & Larkby, 2002). One study found that a mother's consumption of even one to three drinks per week during pregnancy was associated with significant deficits in young children's social engagement and interaction skills (Brown, Olson, & Croninger, 2010).

Severe head traumas that damage children's brains also can lead to intellectual disability. Shaken baby syndrome results when a baby is shaken, leading to intracranial injury and retinal hemorrhage (see Mian et al., 2015). Babies' heads are relatively large and heavy compared to the rest of their body, and their neck muscles are too weak to control their head when they are shaken. The rapid movement of their head when shaken can lead to their brain's being banged against the inside of the skull and bruised. Bleeding in and around the brain or behind the eyes can lead to seizures, partial or total blindness, paralysis, intellectual disability, or death. Although the shaking of a baby may be part of a pattern of chronic abuse, shaken baby syndrome can occur when an otherwise nonabusive parent becomes frustrated and shakes the baby only once.

Young children face a number of other hazards that can cause brain damage. Exposure to toxic substances–such as lead, arsenic, and mercury–during early childhood can lead to intellectual disability by damaging areas of the brain. Children also can incur traumatic brain injury leading to intellectual disability through accidents, including motor vehicle accidents in which they are not properly restrained.

Sociocultural Factors

Children with intellectual disability are more likely to come from low socioeconomic backgrounds (Emerson, Shahtahmasebi, Lancaster, & Berridge, 2010). It may be that their parents also have intellectual disability and have not been able to acquire well-paying jobs. The social disadvantages of being poor also may contribute to lower-than-average intellectual development. Poor mothers are less likely to receive good prenatal care, increasing the risk of premature birth. Children living in lower socioeconomic areas are at increased risk for exposure to lead, because many older buildings have lead paint, which chips off and can be ingested. Poor children are concentrated in poorly funded schools, where those with lower IQs receive less favorable attention from teachers and fewer learning opportunities, especially if they are also members of a minority group. Poor children also are less likely to have parents who read to them and are involved in their schooling. These factors may directly affect a child's intellectual development and exacerbate the biological conditions that impede a child's cognitive development (Zigler, Gilliam, & Jones, 2006).

Treatments for Intellectual Disability

Interventions for children and adults with intellectual disability must be comprehensive, intensive, and long-term to show benefits (Singh, 2016; Zigler et al., 2006; Zigler & Styfco, 2004, 2008).

Drug Therapy

Medications are used to reduce seizures, which are common in people with intellectual disability; to control aggressive or self-injurious behavior; and to improve mood (Matson & Neal, 2009). Neuroleptic medications (see the chapter "Schizophrenia Spectrum and Other Psychotic Disorders") can reduce aggressive, destructive, and antisocial behavior; however, the potential for neurological side effects has made these medications controversial. The atypical antipsychotics, such as risperidone, have been shown to reduce aggression and self-injurious behavior in adults with intellectual disability without having serious neurological side effects (Unwin & Deb, 2011). Antidepressant medications can reduce depressive symptoms, improve sleep patterns, and help control self-injurious behavior in individuals with intellectual disability.

Behavioral Strategies

A child's parents or caregivers and teachers can work together using behavioral strategies to enhance the child's positive behaviors and reduce negative behaviors. These strategies help children and adults learn new skills, from identifying colors correctly to applying vocational skills. Social and communication skills also may be taught. Individuals may learn to initiate conversations by asking questions and to articulate what they want to say more clearly. The desired behavior may be modeled in incremental steps and rewards given to the individual as he or she comes closer to mastering the skill. Behavioral strategies also can help reduce self-injurious and other maladaptive behaviors. Typically, behavioral methods do not simply focus on isolated skills but rather are integrated into a comprehensive program designed to maximize the individual's ability to function in the community (Feldman, 2004).

Social Programs

Social programs have focused on integration of the child into the mainstream where possible, on placement in group homes that provide comprehensive care, and on institutionalization when necessary. The earlier these interventions begin, the greater the chance that the child will develop to his or her full potential.

Early Intervention Programs Many experts recommend beginning comprehensive interventions with children at risk for intellectual development disorder from the first days of life. These measures include intensive one-on-one interventions to enhance their development of basic skills; efforts to reduce the social conditions that might interfere with the children's development, such as child abuse, malnutrition, or exposure to toxins; and adequate medical care (Perry, Koudys, & Blacklock, 2016; Zigler & Styfco, 2004).

One such program was the Infant Health and Development Program (Gross, Brooks-Gunn, & Spiker, 1992), which focused on children with a birth weight of 2,500 grams (5½ pounds) or less and a gestational age of 37 completed weeks or less. This program had three components. First, specially trained counselors visited each child's home during the first 3 years of the child's life, providing support to the mother and fostering parent-child activities that would enhance the child's development. The mothers were given training in good parenting practices and in ways to facilitate their children's cognitive development. For example, they were taught ways to calm their babies (who tended to be irritable), provide appropriate levels of stimulation as well as opportunities for exploration, and reduce stress in the family's environment. Second, the children went daily to a child development center with specially trained teachers, who worked to overcome the children's intellectual and physical deficits. Third, parent support groups were started to help the parents cope with the stresses of parenting.

At 36 months of age, the children in the intervention group were significantly less likely to have IQ scores in the low range than were those in the control group, who received only medical care (Infant Health and Development Program, 1990). The children who received the program intervention also showed fewer behavioral and emotional problems at age 36 months than did the children in the control group.

What accounted for the positive effects of the intervention? Several factors were noted. The home environments of the children in the intervention group improved significantly (Berlin, Brooks-Gunn, McCartoon, & McCormick, 1998; McCormick, McCarton, Brooks-Gunn, Belt, & Gross, 1998). More learning materials were available, and their mothers more actively stimulated the children's learning. The mothers of the children in the intervention program were better able to assist their children in problem solving, remaining more responsive and persistent with their children. In turn, these children showed more enthusiasm for and involvement in learning tasks. In addition, the mothers in the intervention program reported better mental health than the mothers in the control group and also were less likely to use harsh discipline with their children. All these factors were associated with better outcomes for the children in the intervention group.

Mainstreaming Controversy exists over whether children with intellectual disability should be placed in special education classes or instead be mainstreamed—that is, put into regular classrooms. On one hand, special education classes can provide children with extra training in skills they lack. On the other hand, some critics argue that these classes stigmatize children and provide them with an education that asks less of them than they are capable of achieving.

Placing children with intellectual disability in a classroom with children of average intelligence can put them at certain disadvantages. One study found that children with intellectual disability were viewed negatively by the other children in their classrooms (Zigler & Hodapp, 1991). Also, children with intellectual disability who are mainstreamed may not receive the special training they need. Studies comparing the academic progress of children with intellectual disability in special education programs and in regular classrooms have reported mixed results (Dessemontet, Bless, & Morin, 2012; Freeman & Alkin, 2000). Many children today spend some time in special education, where they receive intensive training to overcome skills deficits, and some time in regular classrooms over the course of the week.

Group Homes Many adults with intellectual disability live in group homes, where they receive assistance in performing daily tasks (e.g., cooking, cleaning) and training in vocational and social skills. They may work in sheltered workshops during the day, performing unskilled or semiskilled labor. Increasingly, they are being mainstreamed into the general workforce, often in service-related jobs (e.g., in fast-food restaurants or as baggers in grocery stores). Some community-based programs for adults with intellectual disability have been shown to be effective in enhancing their social and vocational skills (Chilvers, Macdonald, & Hayes, 2006; Toogood, Totsika, Jones, & Lowe, 2016).

Institutionalization In the past, most children with intellectual disability were institutionalized for life. Institutionalization is much less common these days, even for children with severe intellectual disability. African American and Latino families are less likely than European American families to institutionalize their children with intellectual disability (Blacher, Hanneman, & Rousey, 1992). This may be because African American and Latino families are less likely than European American families to have the financial resources to place their children in high-quality institutions, or it may be because African American and Latino cultures place a stronger emphasis on caring for ill or disabled family members within the family.

LEARNING, COMMUNICATION, AND MOTOR DISORDERS

Rather than having deficits in a broad array of skills, as in intellectual disability, children with learning, communication, or motor disorders have deficits or abnormalities in specific skills or behaviors. These disorders are not due to intellectual disability, global developmental delay, neurological disorders, or general external factors like economic disadvantage. The severity of these disorders can range from mild to severe.

Specific Learning Disorder

Individuals with **specific learning disorder** have deficits in one or more academic skills: reading, written expression, and/or mathematics (see Table 4). The *DSM-5* diagnosis is given only when the individual's

TABLE 4 *DSM-5* Criteria for Specific Learning Disorder

A. Difficulties learning and using academic skills, as indicated by the presence of at least one of the following symptoms that have persisted for at least 6 months, despite the provision of interventions that target those difficulties:

1. Inaccurate or slow and effortful word reading (e.g., reads single words aloud incorrectly or slowly and hesitantly, frequently guesses words, has difficulty sounding out words).
2. Difficulty understanding the meaning of what is read (e.g., may read text accurately but not understand the sequence, relationships, inferences, or deeper meanings of what is read).
3. Difficulties with spelling (e.g., may add, omit, or substitute vowels or consonants).
4. Difficulties with written expression (e.g., makes multiple grammatical or punctuation errors within sentences; employs poor paragraph organization; written expression of ideas lacks clarity).
5. Difficulties mastering number sense, number facts, or calculation (e.g., has poor understanding of numbers, their magnitude, and relationships; counts on fingers to add single-digit numbers instead of recalling the math fact that peers do; gets lost in the midst of arithmetic computation and may switch procedures).
6. Difficulties with mathematical reasoning (e.g., has severe difficulty applying mathematical concepts, facts, or procedures to solve quantitative problems).

B. The affected academic skills are substantially and quantifiably below those expected for the individual's chronological age, and cause significant interference with academic and occupational performance, or with activities of daily living. Skill impairments are confirmed by individually administered standardized achievement measures and comprehensive clinical assessment. For individuals ≥17 years, a documented history of impairing learning difficulties may be substituted for the standardized assessment.

C. The learning difficulties begin during school-age years and may not become fully manifest until the demands for those affected academic skills exceed the individual's limited capacities (e.g., as in timed tests, reading, or writing lengthy complex reports for a tight deadline, excessively heavy academic loads).

D. The learning difficulties are not better accounted for by intellectual disabilities, uncorrected visual or auditory acuity, other mental or neurological disorders, psychosocial adversity, lack of proficiency in the language of academic instruction, or inadequate educational instruction.

Specify all academic domains and subskills that are impaired. When more than one domain is impaired, each one should be coded according to the following specifiers:

With impairment in reading:
- Word reading accuracy
- Reading rate or fluency
- Reading comprehension

With impairment in written expression:
- Spelling accuracy
- Grammar and punctuation accuracy
- Clarity or organization of written expression

With impairment in mathematics:
- Number sense
- Memorization of arithmetic facts
- Accurate or fluent calculation
- Accurate math reasoning

performance in one or more of these domains is significantly below that expected for his or her age, schooling, and overall level of intelligence. Although the threshold for diagnosis of a specific learning disorder is somewhat arbitrary, unexpected low performance on individually administered, culturally and linguistically appropriate, standardized academic achievement tests is a generally used criterion for school-age individuals (e.g., ≤ 1 or 1.5 standard deviations below the age-based population mean).

Difficulties in reading, often referred to as *dyslexia,* are usually apparent by the fourth grade and represent the most common specific learning disorder. Reading impairments include poor word reading accuracy, slow reading rate, and reading comprehension weaknesses. They are seen in about 7 percent of children, more commonly boys (Peterson & Pennington, 2015; Rutter et al., 2004). Difficulties in mathematics may include problems in understanding mathematical terms, recognizing numerical symbols, clustering objects into groups, counting, mastering math facts, and understanding mathematical principles. Although many people feel that they are not great at math, deficits in math skills severe enough to warrant this diagnosis occur in only about 1 percent of children (Tannock, 2005). Difficulties in written expression involve significant weaknesses in spelling, constructing a sentence or paragraph, or grammar and punctuation.

Children with learning disorders often struggle with low academic performance or have to put forth extraordinarily high levels of effort to achieve average grades. They can become demoralized or disruptive in class. If left untreated, they are at high risk for dropping out of school, with as many as 40 percent never finishing high school. As adults, they may have problems getting and keeping a good job, and often avoid leisure or work activities that require reading, arithmetic, and/or writing. The emotional side effects of their learning disorder may also affect their social relationships (Fletcher, Lyon, Fuchs, & Barnes, 2018).

Learning disorders can lead to frustration and low self-esteem.
©*Image 100 Ltd*

Communication Disorders

The **communication disorders** involve persistent difficulties in the acquisition and use of language and other means of communication (see Table 5).

TABLE 5 Diagnostic Features of Communication Disorders

Disorder	Description
Language Disorder	Persistent difficulties in the acquisition and use of language in speech, written or sign language due to deficits in the comprehension or production of vocabulary, sentence structure, or discourse.
Speech Sound Disorder	Persistent difficulty with speech sound production that interferes with speech intelligibility or prevents verbal communication of messages. Includes deficits in the phonological knowledge of speech sounds and/or difficulty coordinating movements of the jaw, tongue, or lips for clear speech with breathing and vocalizing for speech.
Childhood-Onset Fluency Disorder (Stuttering)	A disturbance in the normal fluency and time patterning of speech (e.g., sound syllable repetitions, sound prolongations of consonants and vowels, pauses within words).
Social (Pragmatic) Communication Disorder	Persistent difficulties with pragmatics or the social use of language and nonverbal communication in naturalistic contexts, which affects the development of social relationships and social participation. Symptoms are not better explained by autism spectrum disorder, intellectual disability, or low abilities in the domains of word structure and grammar or general cognitive ability.

Source: *Diagnostic and Statistical Manual of Mental Disorders,* Fifth Edition. American Psychiatric Association, 2013.

Children with **language disorder** have difficulties with spoken language, written language, and other language modalities (e.g., sign language). Their symptoms may include problems with vocabulary, grammar, narrative (i.e., knowing how to describe something or put together a story), and other pragmatic language abilities. Children with **speech sound disorder** have persistent difficulties in producing speech. They may not use speech sounds appropriate for their age or dialect, or they may substitute one sound for another (e.g., use a *t* for a *k* sound) or omit certain sounds (such as final consonants on words). Their words come out sounding like baby talk. They might say *wabbit* for *rabbit,* or *bu* for *blue* (Kartheiser, Ursano, & Barnhill, 2007).

A third *DSM-5* communication disorder is **childhood-onset fluency disorder** or stuttering. Children who stutter have significant problems with speaking evenly and fluently, often voicing frequent repetitions of sounds or syllables (such as "I-I-I-I see him"). Some children also repeat whole words or short phrases, for example, "Kids tease me about my, about my s-s-s-stutter." The severity of their speech problems varies by the situation but usually is worse when they are under pressure to speak well, as when giving an oral report. Stuttering often begins gradually and almost always starts before age 10. Estimates of the prevalence of stuttering range from 0.3 percent to 5 percent, with roughly twice as many boys as girls diagnosed (Howell, 2007; McKinnon, McLeod, & Reilly, 2008; Proctor, Yairi, Duff, & Zhang, 2008). As many as 80 percent of children who stutter recover on their own by age 16 (Drayna & Kang, 2011). Others, however, continue to stutter as adults. Stuttering can lower children's self-esteem and cause them to limit their goals and activities.

Finally, children with **social communication disorder** have deficits in using verbal and nonverbal communication for social purposes, such as greeting and sharing information, in a manner that is appropriate for the social context. Because children with social communication disorder have difficulty changing their communication to match the needs of the listener or following rules for conversation and storytelling, their social participation and social relationships are often impaired. Note that children with autism spectrum disorder have difficulties in social communication. The *DSM-5* specifies that the diagnosis of social communication disorder can be given only if the child's communication difficulties are not better explained by autism spectrum disorder, and thus the child cannot currently or by history also show evidence of restricted/repetitive patterns of behavior, interests, or activities.

Causes and Treatment of Learning and Communication Disorders

Genetic factors are implicated in all the learning and communication disorders (Carrion-Castillo, Franke, & Fisher, 2013; Davis, Haworth, & Plomin, 2009; Drayna & Kang, 2011). While there may not be specific genes responsible for specific disorders in most cases, certain genetic abnormalities may account for a number of different learning disorders (Davis, Haworth, & Plomin, 2009; Peterson & Pennington, 2015).

Abnormalities in brain structure and functioning have long been thought to cause learning disorders. Studies of people with difficulties in reading have identified three areas of the brain involved in three separate but interrelated skills (Shaywitz & Shaywitz, 2008). An area of the inferior frontal gyrus called *Broca's area* is involved in the ability to articulate and analyze words. An area in the parietotemporal region is involved in the ability to map the visual perception of the printed word onto the basic structures of language. Another area, in the occipitotemporal region, is involved in the rapid, automatic, fluent identification of words (Shaywitz & Shaywitz, 2008). In individuals with dyslexia, a condition in which the individual has difficulty with accurate and fluent word recognition, neuroimaging studies show unusually low activity in the parietotemporal and occipitotemporal regions (Shaywitz, 2003).

Environmental factors linked to the learning disorders include lead poisoning, birth defects, sensory deprivation, and low socioeconomic status (Fletcher et al., 2018). These conditions may create the risk of damage to critical brain areas. Children whose environments offer fewer opportunities to develop language skills are less likely to overcome biological contributors to learning problems (Peterson & Pennington, 2015; Shaywitz & Shaywitz, 2008).

The treatment of these disorders usually involves therapies designed to build the missing skills (Fletcher et al., 2018). Under the provisions of the Individuals with Disabilities Education Act, these interventions are bundled in a child's comprehensive Individualized Education Plan (IEP). The IEP describes the child's specific skills deficits as determined by formal tests and observations by parents and teachers. The plan also involves parents and teachers in strategies to help the child overcome these deficits. A child with dyslexia might receive systematic instruction in word recognition while in school, supplemented with practice at home, possibly using computerized exercises. Such programs appear to significantly improve skills in children with learning disorders (Scammacca et al., 2016).

Studies suggest that specialized instruction to overcome skills deficits actually can change brain functioning. In one study, children with dyslexia received daily individual tutoring. Before, immediately after, and 1 year after the intervention, the children underwent neuroimaging. Children who received this intervention not only improved their reading but also demonstrated increased activation in the parietotemporal and occipitotemporal regions (Shaywitz et al., 2004). Other researchers also have seen neural effects of specialized training to overcome learning problems (Gabrieli, 2009; Temple et al., 2003).

Motor Disorders

The *DSM-5* specifies four **motor disorders** (see Table 6). Two of these are tic disorders, **Tourette's disorder** and **persistent motor or vocal tic disorder (PMVTD).** They are relatively common, with prevalences of 1 percent and 3 to 4 percent, respectively (Roessner, Hoekstra, & Rothenberger, 2011). **Tics** are sudden, rapid, recurrent, nonrhythmic motor movements or vocalizations. Examples of motor tics include jerking of the head, arm, or leg; eye blinking; facial grimacing; and neck stretching. Vocal tics can be almost any sound or noise, but common ones include throat clearing, sniffing, and grunting (Singer, 2005). People with Tourette's disorder have multiple motor tics and at least one or more vocal tics that have persisted for more than a year since the first tic onset. About 10 percent of people with Tourette's have a complex form of vocal tic that involves uttering or shouting obscenities or other socially objectionable words or phrases (Singer, 2005). People with PMVTD have *only* motor *or* vocal tics, not both. People with these disorders often feel a premonition that a tic is imminent and an urge just before the tic occurs; the urge to tic is temporarily reduced by the tic behavior (Flessner, 2011). The frequency of tics in both disorders increases when people are under stress or do not have alternative activities to occupy them.

The distinctions between Tourette's disorder and PMVTD may seem minor, and studies show that similar genetic and other biological factors may underlie both tic disorders (e.g., Harris & Singer, 2006). Tourette's disorder, especially with the presence of complex vocal tics, is more debilitating and more often comorbid with other disorders than is PMVTD such as ADHD or OCD, so the authors of the *DSM-5* chose to keep them as separate diagnoses (Walkup, Ferraõ, Leckman, Stein, & Singer, 2010).

People with **stereotypic movement disorder** engage in repetitive, seemingly driven, and apparently purposeless motor behavior, such as hand shaking or waving, hair twirling, body rocking, head banging, and self-biting. These behaviors differ from tics in that the individual may continue to engage in them for an extended period of time (Stein, Grant, et al., 2010). They are often seen in individuals with other disorders, particularly autism spectrum disorder, intellectual disability, and attention-deficit/hyperactivity disorder (Stein, Grant, et al., 2010).

All three of these motor disorders typically begin in childhood and increase in adolescence and then decline in adulthood (Roessner et al., 2011; Walkup et al., 2010). All three are highly comorbid with

TABLE 6 Criteria for Motor Disorders

Disorder	Description
Tourette's Disorder	Both multiple motor *and* one or more vocal tics that have been present at some time during the illness, although not necessarily concurrently
Persistent Motor or Vocal Tic Disorder	Single motor *or* vocal tics, persistent for at least 1 year, and with onset before age 18
Stereotypic Movement Disorder	Repetitive, seemingly driven, and apparently purposeless motor behavior (e.g., hand shaking or waving, body rocking, head banging, self-biting) causing clinically significant distress or functional impairment
Developmental Coordination Disorder	Motor performance that is substantially below expected levels, given the person's chronologic age and previous opportunities for skill acquisition (e.g., poor balance, clumsiness, dropping or bumping into things; marked delays in acquiring basic motor skills such as walking, crawling, sitting, catching, throwing, cutting, coloring, or printing)

Note: For tic disorders that do not meet the criteria for Tourette's Disorder or Persistent Motor or Vocal Tic Disorder, the *DSM-5* provides diagnoses of Other Specified or Unspecified Tic Disorder.

obsessive-compulsive disorder and likely share common causes with OCD (Walkup et al., 2010). Specifically, these three motor disorders and OCD co-occur in families and may be due to similar genetic factors. Further, these disorders are associated with dysfunctions in dopamine systems in areas of the brain involved in control of motor behavior, such as the cerebrum, basal ganglia, and frontal cortex, as is the case in OCD (see reviews in Roessner et al., 2011; Stein, Grant, et al., 2010; Walkup et al., 2010). Tourette's syndrome and PMVTD both respond to drugs that alter dopamine systems, such as atypical antipsychotic medications (Roessner et al., 2013; Walkup et al., 2010). All three motor disorders also can be treated with a behavioral therapy called *habit reversal therapy* (Azrin & Nunn, 1973), in which the triggers for and signs of impending tics or stereotypic behaviors are identified and clients are taught to engage in competing behaviors (e.g., squeezing their hands when they feel a vocal tic coming on, crossing their arms when they feel they are about to engage in hand flapping). Habit reversal therapy and related behavioral treatments have shown positive results in randomized controlled trials (McGuire et al., 2014).

Developmental coordination disorder is another motor disorder involving fundamental deficits or significant delays in the development of basic motor skills, such as sitting, crawling, walking, running, simple athletic skills (throwing or catching a ball), and motor skills involved in writing, cutting, or coloring. These deficits cannot be due to a medical condition such as muscular dystrophy. Significant deficits such as these are fairly common, with a prevalence of 5 to 6 percent in children (affecting more boys than girls), and can cause moderate to severe distress and dysfunction in a child's life (Blank, Smits-Engelsman, Polatajko, & Wilson, 2012). These deficits are frequently comorbid with other disorders, especially ADHD (Sigurdsson, van Os, & Fombonne, 2002). The causes of developmental coordination disorder are not known, and may be highly heterogeneous (Blank et al., 2012). The disorder is most often treated with physical or occupational therapy.

TABLE 7 *DSM-5* Criteria for Major Neurocognitive Disorder (NCD)

A. Evidence of significant cognitive decline from a previous level of performance in one or more cognitive domains (complex attention, executive function, learning and memory, language, perceptual-motor, or social cognition) based on:
   1. Concern of the individual, a knowledgeable informant, or the clinician that there has been a significant decline in cognitive function; *and*
   2. A substantial impairment in cognitive performance, preferably documented by standardized neuropsychological testing or, in its absence, another quantified clinical assessment.

B. The cognitive deficits interfere with independence in everyday activities (i.e., at a minimum, requiring assistance with complex instrumental activities of daily living such as paying bills or managing medications).

C. The cognitive deficits do not occur exclusively in the context of delirium.

D. The cognitive deficits are not better explained by another mental disorder (e.g., major depressive disorder, schizophrenia).

Note: NCDs are specified by their etiological subtypes, such as whether, for example, they are due to Alzheimer's disease, frontotemporal lobar degeneration, Lewy body disease, traumatic brain injury, or substance/medication use.

MAJOR AND MILD NEUROCOGNITIVE DISORDERS

In the remainder of the chapter, we discuss disorders that most often arise later in life, namely the neurocognitive disorders (NCDs), which include major and mild NCD and delirium. These disorders result from medical conditions that cause impairment in cognition or from substance intoxication or withdrawal. Cognitive problems include memory deficits, language disturbances, perceptual disturbances, impairment in the capacity to plan and organize, and failure to recognize or identify objects. We begin our discussion with major and mild neurocognitive disorder.

Major neurocognitive disorder is more commonly known as **dementia** when referring to older adults with degenerative disorders like Alzheimer's disease (see the *DSM-5* criteria in Table 7). People with this disorder cannot remember the most fundamental facts of their lives, express themselves through language or carry out basic everyday tasks. Milder versions of this disorder that involve modest cognitive decline from a previous level of performance, but do not yet result in significant impairment in functioning, can be diagnosed as **mild neurocognitive disorder.**

Major neurocognitive disorder (NCD) typically occurs in late life. The estimated prevalence of the most common type of major NCD—that due to Alzheimer's disease—is 5 to 10 percent of people over age 65 (Alzheimer's Association, 2018; Hebert, Weuve,

Scherr, & Evans, 2013). The prevalence of most types of major NCD increases with age, and experts estimate that 30 percent of individuals age 85 and older are living with major NCD (Ferri et al., 2005).

Symptoms of Major Neurocognitive Disorder

Major neurocognitive disorder is characterized by a decline in cognitive functioning severe enough to interfere with daily living (see Table 7). Memory deficits are prominent. In the early stages of major NCD, the memory lapses may be similar to those we all experience from time to time–forgetting the name of someone we know casually, our phone number, or what we went into the next room to get. Most of us eventually remember what we temporarily forgot, either spontaneously or by using tricks that jog our memory. The difference in major NCD is that memory does not return spontaneously and may not respond to reminders or other cues.

People in the early stages of major NCD, or who have mild neurocognitive disorder, may repeat questions because they do not remember asking them moments ago or do not remember getting an answer. They frequently misplace items, such as keys or wallets. They may try to compensate for their memory loss. For example, they may carefully write down their appointments or things they need to do. Eventually, however, they forget to look at their calendars or lists. As memory problems become more significant, they may become angry when asked questions or may make up answers in an attempt to hide their memory loss. As the disorder progresses, they may become lost in familiar surroundings and be unable to find their way when not accompanied by someone.

Eventually, long-term memory also becomes impaired. People with major NCD will forget the order of major events in their life, such as graduation from college, marriage, and the birth of their children. After a time, they will be unable to recall the events at all and may not even know their own name.

Another cognitive deficit of major NCD is **aphasia,** a deterioration of language. People with major NCD will have tremendous difficulty producing the names of objects or people and often may use terms such as *thing* or vague references to the objects or people to hide their inability to produce concrete names. If asked to identify a cup, for example, they may say that it is a thing for drinking but be unable to name it as a cup. They also may be unable to understand what another person is saying or to follow simple requests such as "Turn on the lights and shut the door." In advanced stages of major NCD, people may exhibit echolalia, simply repeating what they hear, or **palilalia,** repeating sounds or words over and over.

Another common cognitive deficit is **apraxia,** impairment of the ability to execute common actions such as waving good-bye or putting on a shirt. This deficit is not caused by problems in motor functioning (e.g., moving the arm), in sensory functioning, or in comprehending what action is required. People with major NCD simply are unable to carry out actions that are requested of them or that they wish to carry out.

Agnosia is the failure to recognize objects or people. People with major NCD may not be able to identify common objects, such as chairs or tables. At first, they fail to recognize casual friends or distant family members. With time, they may not recognize their spouse or children or even their own reflection in a mirror.

Most people with major NCD eventually lose **executive functions,** those brain functions that involve the ability to plan, initiate, monitor, and stop complex behaviors. Cooking Thanksgiving dinner, for example, requires executive functioning. Each menu item (the turkey, the stuffing, the pumpkin pie) requires different ingredients and preparation. The cooking of various menu items must be coordinated so that all the items are ready at the same time. People with mild NCD may attempt to cook Thanksgiving dinner but forget important components (such as the turkey) or fail to coordinate the dinner, burning certain items and undercooking others. People with major NCD are unable even to initiate such a complex task.

Deficits in executive functioning also involve difficulty in the kind of abstract thinking required to evaluate new situations and respond appropriately to these situations. For example, if a man with major NCD is presented with the proverb "People who live in glass houses shouldn't throw stones," he might be unable to interpret the abstract meaning of the proverb and instead interpret it concretely to mean "People don't want their windows broken."

In addition to these cognitive deficits, people with major NCD often show changes in emotional functioning and personality. Shoplifting and exhibitionism are common manifestations of a decline in judgment and an inability to control impulses. People with NCDs may become depressed when they recognize their cognitive deterioration. Often, however, they do not recognize or admit to their cognitive deficits. This can lead them to engage in unrealistic or dangerous actions, such as driving a car when

Former President Ronald Reagan, who died in 2004 at age 93, was diagnosed with Alzheimer's disease. *Source: National Archives and Records Administration (NLS-WHPO-A-C584(12))*

they are too impaired to do so safely. They may become paranoid and angry with family members and friends, whom they see as thwarting their desires and freedom. They may accuse others of stealing belongings they have misplaced. They may believe that others are conspiring against them—the only conclusion left to them when they simply do not remember conversations in which they agreed to some action (e.g., starting a new medication or moving into a treatment facility for people with major NCD). Violent outbursts and combative behavior sometimes occur, particularly in moderate to severe stages of major NCDs.

Types of Major and Mild Neurocognitive Disorder

There are several types of neurocognitive disorder based on their causes. *DSM-5* recommends that the type of major or mild NCD be specified based on its medical or substance/medication-induced cause(s). The most common is Alzheimer's disease, which accounts for up to two-thirds of all cases of neurocognitive disorders (Gatz, 2007). These disorders also can be caused by vascular disease (blockage or leakage of blood to the brain, commonly referred to as a stroke); by traumatic brain injury; by progressive diseases, such as Parkinson's disease and HIV disease; and by chronic substance abuse.

FIGURE 3 **Neurofibrillary Tangles and Beta-Amyloid Plaques in Alzheimer's Disease.** Protein deposits build up and cause neurofibrillary tangles and beta-amyloid plaques in neurons in the brains of people with Alzheimer's disease.

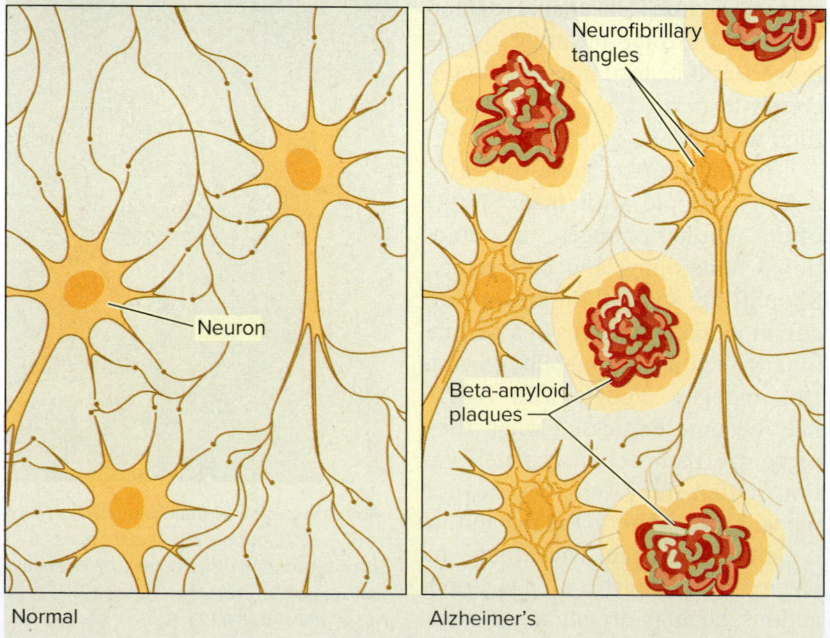

Neurocognitive Disorder Due to Alzheimer's Disease

People with neurocognitive disorder due to **Alzheimer's disease** meet the criteria for major or mild NCD, and show clear evidence of decline in learning and memory. The disease typically begins with mild memory loss, but as the disease progresses the memory loss and disorientation quickly become profound. About two-thirds of Alzheimer's patients show psychiatric symptoms, including agitation, irritability, apathy, and dysphoria. Often these emotional and behavioral symptoms are as difficult for caregivers of people with Alzheimer's disease to deal with as the cognitive symptoms. As the disease worsens, sufferers may become violent and may experience hallucinations and delusions. The disease usually begins after age 65, but there is an early-onset type of Alzheimer's disease that tends to progress more quickly than the late-onset type (Gatz, 2007; Scheltens et al., 2016). On average, people with this disease die within 8 to 10 years of its diagnosis, usually as a result of physical decline or independent diseases common in old age, such as heart disease.

Brain Abnormalities in Alzheimer's Disease What we now call Alzheimer's disease was first described in 1906 by Alois Alzheimer. He observed severe memory loss and disorientation in a 51-year-old female patient. Following her death at age 55, an autopsy revealed that filaments within nerve cells in her brain were twisted and tangled. These **neurofibrillary tangles** are common in the brains of Alzheimer's patients but rare in people without an NCD (Figure 3). The tangles, which are made up of a protein called tau, impede nutrients and other essential supplies from moving through cells to the extent that cells eventually die. Another brain abnormality seen in Alzheimer's disease *is* plaques (see Figure 3). **Plaques** are deposits of a class of protein, called **beta-amyloid,** that are neurotoxic and accumulate in the spaces between the cells of the cerebral cortex, hippocampus, amygdala, and other brain structures critical to memory and cognition (Villemagne, Doré, Burnham, Masters, & Rowe, 2018).

There is extensive cell death in the cortex of Alzheimer's patients, resulting in shrinking of the cortex and enlargement of the ventricles of the brain (Figure 4). The remaining cells lose many of their dendrites—the branches that link one cell to other cells (Figure 5). The result of all these brain abnormalities is profound memory loss and an inability to coordinate self-care and other daily activities.

Causes of Alzheimer's Disease Genetic factors appear to predispose some people to the brain changes seen in Alzheimer's disease. Family history

FIGURE 4 **Cortical Regions in Alzheimer's Disease.** Cell death causes shrinkage of cortical regions in the brains of people with advanced Alzheimer's disease (left; compare to healthy brain on right).

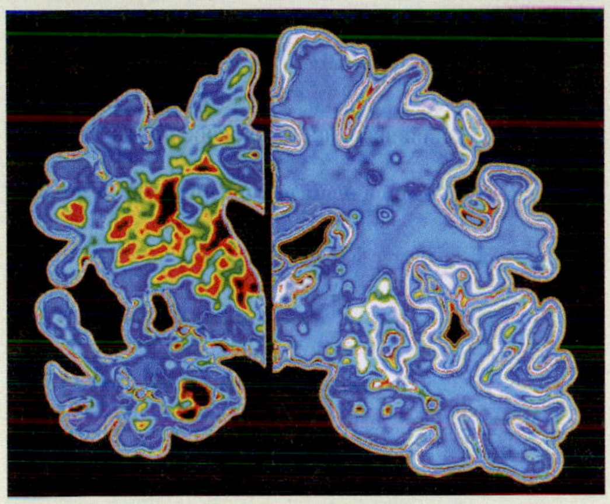

©SPL/Science Source

FIGURE 5 **Cell Damage in Alzheimer's Disease.** Cells lose their dendrites, which connect cells to one another, in the brains of people with Alzheimer's disease.

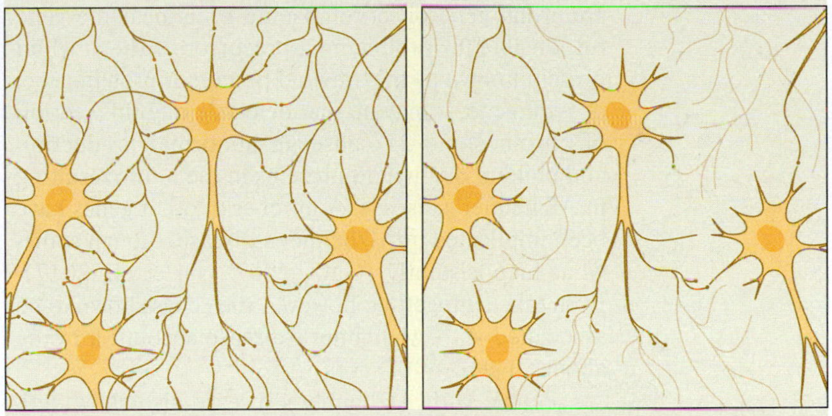

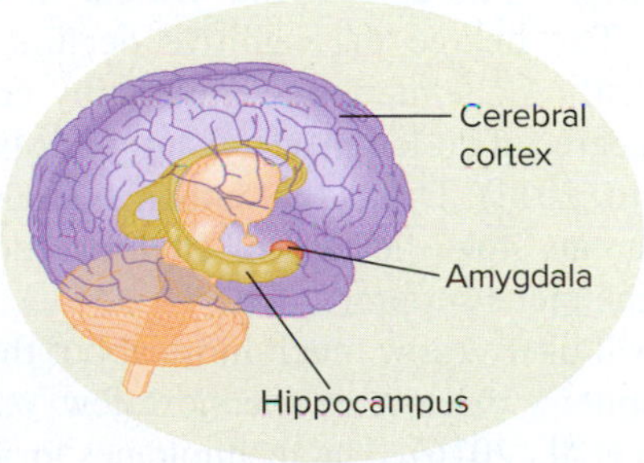

Plaques accumulate between cells in these and other areas of the brain in Alzheimer's disease.

studies suggest that 24 to 49 percent of first-degree relatives of patients with Alzheimer's disease eventually develop the disease (Gatz, 2007). The lifetime risk of developing Alzheimer's disease is 1.8 to 4.0 times higher for people with a family history of the disorder than for those without such a history. Twin studies confirm an important role of genetics in the risk for Alzheimer's disease, as well as for other types of NCD. Concordance rates for all types of NCD in monozygotic twins are 44 percent for men and 58 percent for women; concordance rates for dizygotic twins are 25 percent for men and 45 percent for women (Gatz, Reynolds, et al., 2006).

Several genes have been linked to Alzheimer's disease. The gene most consistently associated with the disease is the apolipoprotein E gene (ApoE), which is on chromosome 19. This gene regulates the ApoE protein, which is involved in the transport of cholesterol through the blood. ApoE also binds to beta-amyloid protein and may play a role in its regulation. The ApoE gene has three alleles, or versions: e2, e3, and e4. People who inherit an e4 allele from one parent have a 2 to 4 times greater risk of developing Alzheimer's disease than people who do not inherit an e4 allele, and people who inherit e4 alleles from both parents have an 8 to 12 times greater risk of developing the disorder (Coon et al., 2007; Naj et al., 2017).

Neuroimaging studies show that people with the e4 version of the ApoE gene have reduced cortex and hippocampus volume compared to people without the e4 version of the ApoE gene, even as children or adolescents (Jack et al., 2007; Shaw et al., 2007; Thompson et al., 2004). As adults, people with the e4 version of the ApoE gene show greater cognitive deficits and earlier onset of Alzheimer's disorder (Perneczky, Alexopoulos, Wagenpfeil, & Kurz, 2012).

Other genes are implicated in the development of less common forms of Alzheimer's disease, which begin in middle age and are more strongly familial. One of these genes is on chromosome 21 (Naj et al., 2017; Webb & Murphy, 2012). The first clue that a defective gene on chromosome 21 might be linked with Alzheimer's disease came from the fact that people with Down syndrome are more likely than people in the general population to develop Alzheimer's disease in late life. Researchers hypothesized that the gene responsible for some forms of Alzheimer's disease may be on chromosome 21 and that people with Down syndrome are more prone to Alzheimer's disease because they have an extra chromosome 21.

This hypothesis has been supported by studies of families with high rates of Alzheimer's disease. These studies have found links between the presence of the disease and the presence of an abnormal gene on chromosome 21 (Webb & Murphy, 2012). Also, this abnormal gene on chromosome 21 is near the gene responsible for producing a precursor of the amyloid protein known as the amyloid precursor protein gene, or APP gene. It may be that defects along this section of chromosome 21 cause an abnormal production and buildup of amyloid proteins in the brain, resulting in Alzheimer's disease. A number of other genes have been implicated in Alzheimer's disease, though somewhat inconsistently (Gatz, 2007; Naj et al., 2017). Even taken altogether, however, the genes shown to be associated with Alzheimer's disease account for only about 50 percent of cases.

People with Alzheimer's disease also show deficits in a number of neurotransmitters, including acetylcholine, norepinephrine, serotonin, somatostatin (a corticotropin-releasing factor), and peptide Y (Micheau & Marighetto, 2011). The deficits in acetylcholine are particularly noteworthy because this neurotransmitter is thought to be critical in memory function. The degree of cognitive decline seen in patients with Alzheimer's is significantly correlated with the degree of deficit in acetylcholine (Micheau & Marighetto, 2011). Drugs that enhance levels of acetylcholine can slow the rate of cognitive decline in some Alzheimer's sufferers.

We will likely know much more about the causes of Alzheimer's disease in the next few years (see Scheltens et al., 2016). The technologies for studying the genetic and neurological processes of the disease are advancing rapidly, and many researchers are investigating this disorder. Five and a half million people in the United States and 18 million people worldwide are estimated to have Alzheimer's disease, and this number is expected to increase by at least 300 percent by 2050 (Alzheimer's Association, 2018; Hebert et al., 2013). The annual cost of caring for people with neurocognitive disorder in the United States is expected to be $400 billion by 2050 (Lyketsos et al., 2012). We can hope that by then we will understand the disorder well enough to treat it effectively.

Vascular Neurocognitive Disorder

Another common type of neurocognitive disorder is **vascular neurocognitive disorder.** People with this disorder meet the criteria for major or mild NCD, depending on the severity of cognitive symptoms and functional decline. The most prominent cognitive symptoms are significant declines in processing speed, in the ability to pay attention, and in the executive functions described earlier. In addition, there must be evidence of a recent vascular event or cerebrovascular disease. **Cerebrovascular disease** occurs when the blood supply to areas of the brain is blocked, causing tissue damage in the brain. Neuroimaging techniques, such as PET and MRI, can detect areas of tissue damage and reduced blood flow in the brain, confirming cerebrovascular disease.

Sudden damage to an area of the brain due to the blockage of blood flow or to hemorrhaging (bleeding) is called a **stroke.** Vascular NCD can occur after one large stroke or after an accumulation of small strokes. Cerebrovascular disease can be caused by high blood pressure and the accumulation of fatty deposits in the arteries, which block blood flow to the brain. It also can be a complication of diseases that inflame the brain and of traumatic brain injuries.

About 25 percent of stroke patients develop cognitive deficits severe enough to qualify for a diagnosis of neurocognitive disorder (Burhan, Moradizadeh, & Marlatt, 2018; Stephens et al., 2004). A greater risk of developing vascular NCD is seen in stroke patients who are older (over age 80), who have less education, who have a history of strokes, or who have diabetes.

Even stroke patients who do not immediately develop NCD are at increased risk of cognitive decline compared to people the same age who do not suffer a stroke (Burhan et al., 2018; Hachinski, 2008). The patients most likely to eventually develop NCD tend to have additional strokes over time, some of which were obvious and others that were "silent" (or without obvious symptoms) and detected only later. In addition, patients who have medical events or conditions that cause widespread oxygen or blood deficiency—such as seizures, cardiac arrhythmias, congestive heart failure, and pneumonia—are more likely to develop vascular NCDs.

Neurocognitive Disorders Associated with Other Medical Condition

A variety of other serious medical conditions can produce neurocognitive disorders, including Lewy body disease, Parkinson's disease, the human immunodeficiency virus (HIV), and Huntington's disease. Parkinson's disease is a degenerative brain disorder that affects about 0.3 percent of people in the general population and 2 percent of people over age 65 (Poewe et al., 2017). Muhammed Ali, who died in 2016, and Michael J. Fox are two well-known people with Parkinson's disease. Its primary symptoms are tremors, muscle rigidity, and the inability to initiate movement. The symptoms result from the death of brain cells that produce the neurotransmitter dopamine. Approximately 75 percent of people with Parkinson's disease develop neurocognitive disorder (Aarsland & Kurz, 2009).

Michael J. Fox is a well-known person suffering from Parkinson's disease. Despite his symptoms, he continues his acting career and is an active advocate. ©*Mike Coppola/MJF2015/Getty Images Entertainment/Getty Images*

Neurocognitive disorder due to Lewy body disease is the second most common type of progressive neurocognitive disorder after Alzheimer's disease. It is caused by abnormal round structures that develop in the brain. Its characteristic symptoms include changes in attention and alertness, visual hallucinations, and the symptoms of Parkinson's disease. There is some evidence that it is related to both Alzheimer's disease and Parkinson's disease.

The human immunodeficiency virus (HIV), the virus that causes AIDS, can cause a mild or major NCD. People's memory and concentration become impaired. Their mental processes slow—they may have difficulty following conversations or may take much longer to organize their thoughts and to complete simple, familiar tasks. They may withdraw socially and lose their spontaneity. Weakness in the legs or hands, clumsiness, loss of balance, and lack of coordination are also common. If the neurocognitive disorder progresses, the deficits worsen. Speech becomes increasingly impaired, as does the understanding of language. People become confined to bed, often indifferent to their surroundings.

HIV-associated major NCD is diagnosed when the deficits and symptoms become severe and global, with significant disruption of daily activities and functioning. As antiretroviral therapies have become widely used in treating people with HIV, new onsets of HIV-related neurocognitive disorder have decreased, as has its severity. On the other hand, as more patients with HIV survive into older age due to these drugs, the number of people with HIV-related NCD is increasing, particularly among people who abused drugs or also had a hepatitis C infection (Nath et al., 2008).

Huntington's disease is a rare genetic disorder that afflicts people early in life, usually between ages 25 and 55. People with this disorder eventually develop a major NCD and chorea—irregular jerks, grimaces, and twitches. Huntington's disease is transmitted by a single dominant gene on chromosome 4 (Ross et al., 2014). If one parent has the gene, his or her children have a 50 percent chance of inheriting the gene and developing the disorder. Huntington's disease affects many neurotransmitters in the brain, but which of these changes causes chorea and neurocognitive disorder remains unclear.

Mild and major neurocognitive disorder can also be caused by a rare disorder called prion disease (also known as Creutzfeld-Jacob's disease); by brain tumors; by endocrine conditions, such as hypothyroidism; by nutritional conditions, such as deficiencies of thiamine, niacin, and vitamin B12; by infections, such as syphilis; and by other neurological diseases, such as multiple sclerosis. In addition, the chronic heavy use of alcohol, inhalants, and sedatives, especially in combination with nutritional deficiencies, can cause brain damage and neurocognitive disorder. As many as 10 percent of chronic alcohol abusers may develop neurocognitive disorder (Ridley, Draper, & Withall, 2013). Alcohol-related neurocognitive disorder usually has a slow, insidious onset. While it can be slowed with nutritional supplements, it often is persistent, particularly when use was prolonged and as age increases.

Traumatic brain injury, another potential cause of neurocognitive disorder, can result from penetrating injuries, such as those caused by gunshots, or closed head injuries, typically caused by impact to the head and/or concussive forces such as caused by motor vehicle accident, explosion, or sports injury. In the United States, falls account for 28 percent of traumatic brain injuries, motor vehicle accidents for 20 percent, being struck by an object for 19 percent, violence for 11 percent, and bicycle accidents for 3 percent (Langlois, Rutland-Brown, & Wald, 2006). Leland, in the case study below, developed a major NCD after a motor vehicle accident.

CASE STUDY

A 41-year-old factory worker named Leland was returning home along a rural road one night after work. A drunk driver ran a stop sign and collided at a high rate of speed with the driver's side of Leland's car. Leland was not wearing a seat belt. The collision sent Leland through the windshield and onto the pavement. He lived but sustained a substantial brain injury, as well as many broken bones and cuts. Leland

(continued)

was unconscious for more than 2 weeks and then spent another 2 months in the hospital, recovering from his injuries.

When he returned home to his family, Leland was not himself. Before the accident, he was a quiet man who doted on his family and frequently displayed a wry sense of humor. After the accident, Leland was sullen and chronically irritable. He screamed at his wife or children for the slightest annoyance. He even slapped his wife once when she confronted him about his verbal abuse of the children.

Leland did not fare much better at work. He found he now had great trouble concentrating on his job, and he could not follow his boss's instructions. When his boss approached Leland about his inability to perform his job, Leland could not express much about the trouble he was having. He became angry at his boss and accused him of wanting to fire him. Leland had always been much liked by his co-workers, and they welcomed him back after the accident with sincere joy, but soon he began to lash out at them, as he was lashing out at his wife and children. He accused a close friend of stealing from him. These symptoms continued acutely for about 3 months. Gradually, they declined. Finally, about 18 months after the accident, Leland's emotional and personality functioning appeared to be back to normal. His cognitive functioning also improved greatly, but he still found it more difficult to pay attention and to complete tasks than he did before the accident.

Leland's symptoms are characteristic of people with a severe **traumatic brain injury.** He showed changes both in his cognitive abilities and in his usual emotional and personality functioning. Fortunately, Leland's symptoms subsided after several months. Many victims of moderate to severe brain injury never fully recover.

Neurocognitive disorders that follow single closed head injuries are typically mild and more likely to dissipate with time than are NCDs that follow repeated closed head injuries, such as those experienced by boxers, some soldiers, or people in multiple motor vehicle accidents. Between 2001 and 2012, over 3 million traumatic brain injuries in the United States were the result of sports and recreation activities; boys and young men are most likely to suffer neurocognitive disorder due to brain injury because they take more risks associated with brain injuries than do other groups (Coronado et al., 2015).

Soldiers who have served in Iraq and Afghanistan have had high rates of traumatic brain injury due to blasts from roadside bombs and other explosive devices. It is estimated that 22 percent of all injuries in these wars are traumatic brain injuries (Committee on Gulf War and Health, 2008). Soldiers with traumatic brain injuries show declines in neurocognitive function similar to those seen in neurocognitive disorder, as well as depression, aggressive behavior, long-term unemployment, and problems in their social relationships.

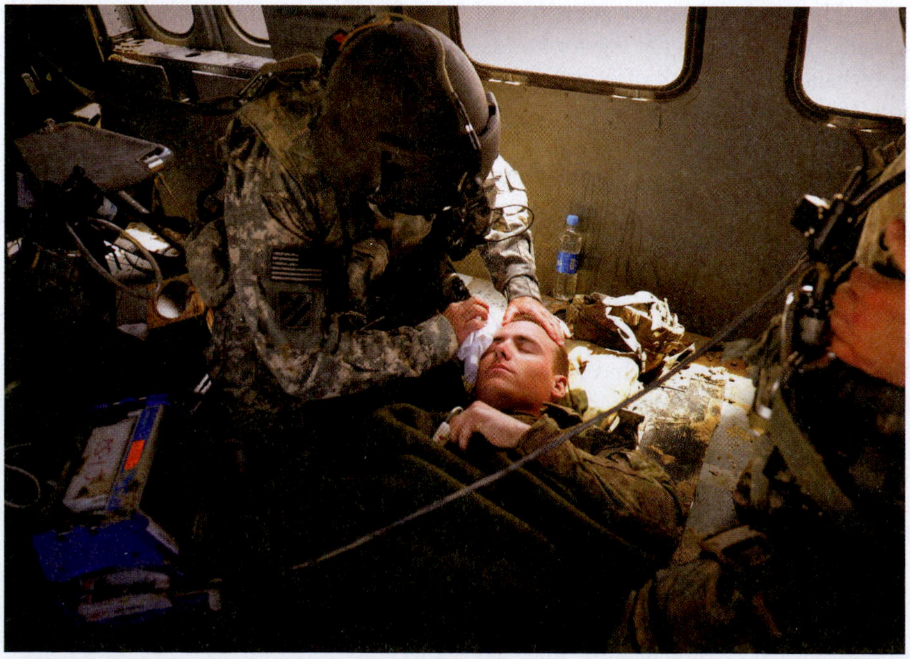

Soldiers who have served in Iraq and Afghanistan have had high rates of traumatic brain injury.
©PETER PARKS/AFP/Getty Images

The Impact of Gender, Culture, and Education on Neurocognitive Disorder

There are more elderly women than elderly men with neurocognitive disorder, particularly Alzheimer's disease (Gatz, 2007). This may be simply because women tend to live longer than men and thus live long enough to develop an age-related neurocognitive disorder. Among people with the same degree of the brain changes due to Alzheimer's, women tend to show greater cognitive impairment than men (Barnes et al., 2005; Perneczky, Drzezga, Diehl-Schmid, Li, & Kurz, 2007). The reasons for these gender differences are not known.

In general, African Americans are diagnosed with neurocognitive disorder more frequently than European Americans (Chin, Negash, & Hamilton, 2011; Chui & Gatz, 2005). African Americans have higher rates of hypertension and cardiovascular disease, both of which contribute to vascular neurocognitive disorder. However, the genetic factors leading to neurocognitive disorder may be more prevalent in European Americans than in African Americans.

Differences in people's level of education also may contribute to differences in rates of neurocognitive disorder. Studies in the United States, Europe, Israel, and China show that people with lower levels of education are more likely to be diagnosed with neurocognitive disorder than are people with higher levels of education (Chen et al., 2012; Katzman, 1993; Stern, Gurland, Tatemichi, & Tang, 1994). Neuroimaging studies of people with neurocognitive disorder find that those with less education show more of the brain deterioration associated with neurocognitive disorder than do those with more education. It may be that people with more education have a higher socioeconomic status, which in turn provides them with better nutrition and health care that protect them against the conditions contributing to Alzheimer's disease. Education and, more generally, cognitive activity throughout one's life actually may increase brain resources in ways that forestall the development of neurocognitive disorder in people prone to the disorder (Gatz, Prescott, & Pedersen, 2006; Scheltens et al., 2016).

The likelihood that a person with neurocognitive disorder will be institutionalized rather than cared for in the family is greater among European Americans than among Asians or Hispanics and Latinos (Chin et al., 2011; Mausbach et al., 2004; Torti, Gwyther, Reed, Friedman, & Schulman, 2004). One reason may be that European Americans are more likely to have the substantial financial resources it takes to treat family members with neurocognitive disorder (Chin et al., 2011). In addition, Asian and Latino cultures may have a more positive view of caring for sick and elderly family members than European American culture. Asian and Latino cultures also exert greater societal pressure to care for ill family members in the home.

Treatments for and Prevention of Neurocognitive Disorder

Two classes of drugs are approved for treatment of the cognitive symptoms of neurocognitive disorder (Martorana, Esposito, & Koch, 2010). The first class is cholinesterase inhibitors, such as donepezil (Aricept), rivastigmine (Exelon), and galantamine (Reminyl). These drugs help prevent the breakdown of the neurotransmitter acetylcholine, and randomized trials show that they have a modest positive effect on neurocognitive disorder symptoms (Martorana et al., 2010). The side effects of these drugs include nausea, diarrhea, and anorexia. The second class is drugs that regulate the activity of the neurotransmitter glutamate, which plays an essential role in learning and memory; memantine (Namenda) is one such drug. Developing new drugs is an international priority due to projected increases in the number of people with neurocognitive disorder (Cummings et al., 2016).

Many other drugs used to treat people with neurocognitive disorder affect the secondary symptoms of the disorder rather than the primary cognitive symptoms. Antidepressants and antianxiety drugs may be used to help control emotional symptoms. Antipsychotic drugs may help control hallucinations, delusions, and agitation (Scheltens et al., 2016; Sultzer et al., 2008).

Behavior therapies can be helpful in controlling patients' angry outbursts and emotional instability (Fitzsimmons & Buettner, 2002; Teri et al., 2003). Often, family members are given training in behavioral techniques to help them manage patients at home. These techniques not only reduce stress and emotional distress in family caregivers but also may result in fewer behavior problems in the family member with neurocognitive disorder (Teri et al., 2003).

Many people are interested in behavioral means of reducing their risk for neurocognitive disorder. Aerobic exercise and mental activity may have some protective value (Deeny et al., 2008; Valenzuela, 2008). Reducing the risk factors for stroke—for example, avoiding smoking, obesity, and hypertension—may reduce the risk for vascular neurocognitive disorder (Gatz, 2007; Scheltens et al., 2016). Although some memory decline is typical of aging,

The School Sisters of Notre Dame have participated in a fascinating study of the effects of early intellectual activity on mental and physical health in old age. ©*SCOTT TAKUSHI/Newscom*

research shows that some people who notice a significant decline are in fact in the early stages of dementia (Rabin, Smart, & Amariglio, 2017). Early identification of memory problems and treatment with cognitive training may help slow the progression into major neurocognitive disorder (Smart et al., 2017).

One of the most fascinating studies to show a link between intellectual activity beginning early in life and a reduced risk of Alzheimer's disease is the Nun Study, a longitudinal study of several hundred elderly nuns in the School Sisters of Notre Dame. Nuns who entered old age with greater intellectual strengths were less likely to develop severe neurocognitive disorder, even when their brain showed evidence of significant neurofibrillary tangles and senile plaques (Snowdon, 1997, 2003). For example, the level of linguistic skill the nuns showed in journal writings when they were in their twenties significantly predicted their risk of developing neurocognitive disorder in later life (Snowdon et al., 1996). The best example was Sister Mary, who had high cognitive test scores right up until her death at age 101. An evaluation of Sister Mary's brain revealed that Alzheimer's disease had spread widely through her brain, even though her cognitive test scores slipped only from the "superior" range to the "very good" range as she aged. Other results from this study showed that tiny strokes may lead a mildly deteriorating brain to develop a major neurocognitive disorder (Snowdon et al., 1997).

DELIRIUM

Delirium is characterized by disorientation, recent memory loss, and a clouding of attention (Table 8). A delirious person has difficulty focusing, sustaining, or shifting attention. These signs arise suddenly, within several hours or days. They fluctuate over the course of a day and often become worse at night, a condition known as *sundowning*. The duration of these signs is short–rarely longer than a month. Delirious patients often are agitated or frightened. They also may experience disrupted sleep-wake cycles, incoherent speech, delusions, and hallucinations.

TABLE 8 *DSM-5* Criteria for Delirium

A. A disturbance in attention (i.e., reduced ability to direct, focus, sustain, and shift attention) and orientation to the environment and awareness (reduced orientation to the environment).

B. The disturbance develops over a short period of time (usually hours to a few days), and represents a change from baseline attention and awareness, and tends to fluctuate in severity during the course of a day.

C. An additional disturbance in cognition (e.g., memory deficit, disorientation, language, visuospatial ability, or perception).

D. The disturbances in Criteria A and C are not better explained by another preexisting, established, or evolving neurocognitive disorder and do not occur in the context of a severely reduced level of arousal, such as coma.

E. There is evidence from the history, physical examination, or laboratory findings that the disturbance is a direct physiological consequence of another medical condition, substance intoxication or withdrawal, or exposure to a toxin, or due to multiple etiologies.

The symptoms of delirium usually follow a common progression (Inouye, Westendorp, & Saczynski, 2014). In the early phase, patients report mild symptoms such as fatigue, decreased concentration, irritability, restlessness, or depression. They may experience mild cognitive impairments or perceptual disturbances, or even visual hallucinations. As the delirium worsens, the person's orientation becomes disrupted. A patient may think she is in her childhood home instead of in the hospital. If undetected, the delirium progresses, and the person's orientation to familiar people becomes distorted. For example, a delirious person may misidentify his wife or fail to recognize his child. Immediate memory is the first to be affected, followed by intermediate memory (memories of events occurring in the past 10 minutes) and finally by remote, or distant, memory. When intervals of these symptoms alternate with intervals of lucid functioning and the symptoms become worse at night, a diagnosis of delirium is likely. If the person is not disoriented (to time, place, or person) or if recent memory loss is absent, then a diagnosis of delirium is unlikely.

The onset of delirium may be dramatic, as when a normally quiet person suddenly becomes loud, verbally abusive, and combative or when a compliant hospital patient tries to pull out his intravenous tube. Sometimes, though, the onset of delirium manifests as an exaggerated form of an individual's normal personality traits. For example, a generally cranky person recovering from surgery may complain loudly and harshly about the "inadequate" care she is receiving from the attending nurses. It would be easy for attending staff to regard her irritability as consistent with her personality style: "She must be feeling better; she's beginning to complain." In this type of case, the delirium may go unrecognized until more severe symptoms emerge.

Sometimes, delirious individuals simply appear confused. People who know the person well might say, "He just doesn't seem like himself." These delirious individuals may call an acquaintance by the wrong name or forget how to get to a familiar location, such as their room. In such cases, the first indication of delirium often comes from the observations of family or medical staff. They notice that the person seems calm during the day but becomes agitated at night. It is important to monitor such a person around the clock. Detecting delirium also may require the frequent testing of the person's orientation (by asking his or her name, the date and time, and the location). Close monitoring is also important because, with delirium, accidents such as falling out of bed or stepping into traffic are common.

Delirium typically signals a serious medical condition. When it is detected and the underlying medical condition is treated, delirium is temporary and reversible (Cole, Ciampi, Belzile, & Zhong, 2009). The longer delirium continues, however, the more likely the person is to suffer permanent brain damage, because the causes of delirium, if left untreated, can induce permanent changes in the functioning of the brain.

Causes of Delirium

Neurocognitive disorder is the strongest predictor of delirium, increasing the risk fivefold (Inouye et al., 2014). A wide range of medical disorders, including stroke, congestive heart failure, infectious diseases, a high fever, and HIV infection, is associated with a risk for delirium. Intoxication with illicit drugs and withdrawal from these drugs or from prescription medications also can lead to delirium. Other possible causes include fluid and electrolyte imbalances, medication side effects, and toxic substances.

Delirium may be caused when a medical condition, a drug, or a toxic substance affects the level of acetylcholine in the brain. Abnormalities in a number of other neurotransmitters, including dopamine, serotonin, and GABA, are seen in people who are delirious.

Delirium is probably the most common psychiatric syndrome found in general hospitals, particularly in older people. About 18 to 35 percent of older people are delirious on admission to the hospital for a serious illness, and another 11 to 14 percent develop delirium while in the hospital (Inouye et al., 2014).

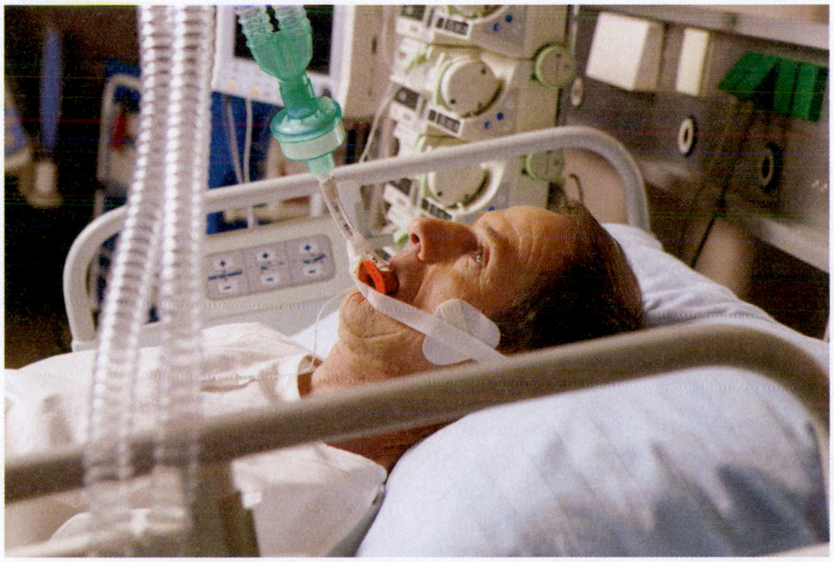

Delirium is a common problem in older adult hospital patients. ©*Fuse/Getty Images*

Older people often experience delirium following surgery. The delirium may be the result of the person's medical disorder or the effect of medications. It also may result from sensory isolation. A syndrome known as ICU/CCU psychosis—a type of delirium—occurs in intensive care and cardiac care units (Brown, 2014). Patients who are kept in unfamiliar surroundings that are monotonous may hear noises from machines as human voices, see the walls quiver, or hallucinate that someone is tapping them on the shoulder. Among the elderly, a high mortality rate is associated with delirium (Inouye et al., 2014). The typical reason is that the underlying condition or the cause of the delirium is very serious. Delirium also has negative effects on health, functioning, and survival well after the episode itself, and can increase risk for dementia as well (Inouye et al., 2014).

Some people are at increased risk for delirium. Risk factors include age (the older the person, the higher the risk), gender (males are at greater risk than females), and preexisting brain damage or neurocognitive disorder. African Americans have higher rates of delirium than European Americans, possibly because African Americans are less likely to have health insurance and thus do not receive early intervention for a serious illness. As a result, their illness may be more likely to become severe enough to cause delirium.

Treatments for Delirium

It is extremely important that delirium be recognized and treated quickly. If a delirious person is not already hospitalized, immediate referral to a physician should be made. If another medical condition is associated with the delirium (e.g., stroke or congestive heart failure), the first priority is to treat that condition. Drugs that may contribute to the delirium must be discontinued. Antipsychotic medications sometimes are used to treat the person's confusion and agitation, although they do not seem to affect prognosis of delirium (Inouye et al., 2014). It also may be necessary to prevent people with delirium from harming themselves accidentally. Often, nursing care is required to monitor people's state and prevent them from wandering off, tripping, or ripping out intravenous tubes and to manage their behavior if they should become noncompliant or agitated and combative. In some instances, restraints are necessary. Providing a reassuring atmosphere filled with familiar personal belongings, such as family photographs and the person's own clothing, can help patients prone to delirium be less agitated and feel more secure and in control. Psychosocial treatments that improve sleep, address sensory issues, and encourage mobility and therapeutic activity have shown some promise but require further research (Inouye et al., 2014).

CHAPTER INTEGRATION

As noted in the Along the Continuum feature at the beginning of this chapter, both developmental psychopathologists and geropsychologists emphasize the importance of understanding the neurodevelopmental and neurocognitive disorders in the context of normal development and aging. Development and aging are not simply biological processes but rather involve the interaction of biological, environmental, and psychosocial processes, as depicted in Figure 6.

All the disorders in this chapter are related to genetic abnormalities, but the environment can affect the expression of genes through epigenetic processes (see the chapter "Theories and Treatment of Abnormality"). For example, there is evidence that the risk of autism spectrum disorder is higher among children whose biological fathers are older (e.g., over 40) at the time of conception (see Hultman et al., 2011). This may be because sperm deteriorate due to aging, or it may be that accumulated exposure to toxins over the lifespan causes DNA damage that results in a higher risk for autism spectrum disorder in their children.

FIGURE 6 **Integrating Biological, Environmental, and Psychosocial Factors in Neurodevelopmental and Neurocognitive Disorders.**

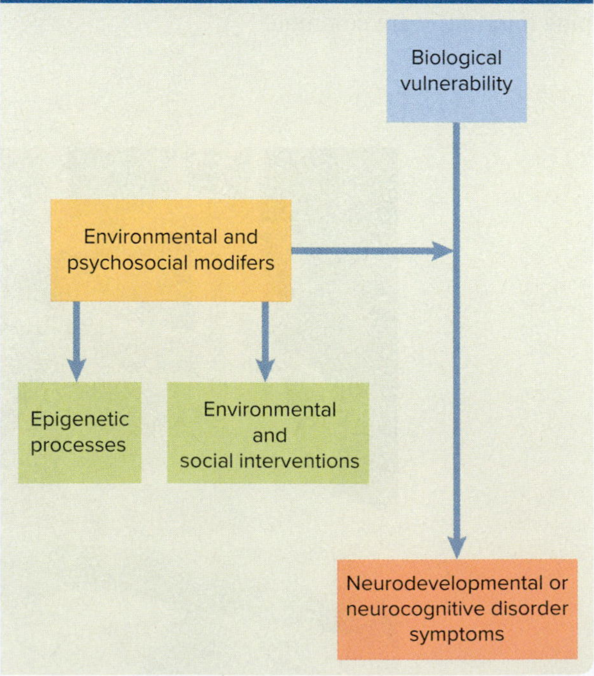

In addition, the impact of biological vulnerabilities to neurodevelopmental or neurocognitive disorders on functioning can be significantly influenced by the environment and people's behavior. Children with autism spectrum disorder who receive early, intense behavioral intervention may eventually function very similarly to a child without the disorder, whereas children with autism spectrum disorder who receive no intervention are much less likely to develop typical functioning. As another example, the likelihood of developing many diseases in old age is substantially influenced by a person's behavior as a younger adult—people who keep mentally active into middle and old age may be less likely to develop Alzheimer's disease or develop less severe versions of NCDs.

Similarly, the social and emotional environment can affect the severity of deficits among people with neurodevelopmental and neurocognitive disorders. A child with ADHD whose parents are overwhelmed by his behavior and withdraw or become aggressive in response is less likely to develop the ability to regulate his behavior than is a child whose parents respond more effectively. If an older adult who is easily confused or forgetful is further stressed by family members who frequently become annoyed with her or expect too much of her, then her cognitive deficits can become even more severe. Thus, even though the neurodevelopmental or neurocognitive disorders are rooted in brain malfunction, psychosocial factors can influence the severity and manifestation of these disorders.

SHADES OF GRAY DISCUSSION

Before giving Jake a diagnosis, there are several possibilities worth considering. First, you might consider whether Jake has a learning disability that is hurting his academic performance. You might administer testing to see if this is the case. Second, you may note that people with the inattentive type of ADHD are not hyperactive and often may seem absent-minded. Jake's tendencies to forget things, to leave projects incomplete, to have his mind wander, and to be late all fit the symptoms of a predominantly inattentive presentation of ADHD. However, they also could be caused by depression. Jake's parents often were critical of him and felt that he wasn't living up to their expectations, and difficulty with concentration, memory, and work completion are common features of depression. Also, the fact that Jake's grades tended to drop at times of transition could suggest trouble coping with change. You would need to thoroughly investigate these possibilities before making a diagnosis. More than just the presence of symptoms, an accurate diagnosis of ADHD requires that symptoms have a childhood onset, be developmentally inappropriate and persistent, be present in multiple settings, cause significant functional problems, and not be due to any other psychiatric disorder.

CHAPTER SUMMARY

- Attention-deficit/hyperactivity disorder (ADHD) is characterized by inattentiveness and hyperactivity. Children with ADHD often do poorly in school and in peer relationships and are at increased risk for developing behavior problems. ADHD is more common in boys than in girls.
- Biological factors that have been implicated in the development of ADHD include genetics, exposure to toxins prenatally and early in childhood, and abnormalities in neurological functioning.
- Treatments for ADHD usually involve stimulant drugs and behavior therapy designed to decrease children's impulsivity and hyperactivity and help them increase attention.
- Autism spectrum disorder is characterized by significant impairment in social interaction, communication with others, and everyday behaviors, interests, and activities. Many children with autism spectrum disorder score in the intellectual disability range on IQ tests. Outcomes of autism spectrum disorder vary widely, although the majority of people must receive continual care, even as adults. The best predictors of a good outcome in autism spectrum disorder are an IQ above 50 and language development before age 6.
- Possible biological causes of autism spectrum disorder include a genetic predisposition to cognitive impairment, central nervous system damage, prenatal complications, and neurotransmitter imbalances.

- Drugs reduce some symptoms in autism spectrum disorder but do not eliminate the core of the disorder. Behavior therapy is used to reduce inappropriate and self-injurious behaviors and encourage prosocial behaviors.
- Intellectual disability is defined as significant deficits in conceptual, social, and practical skills that affect everyday functioning with onset during the developmental period. It is not diagnosed by low IQ alone, and its level of severity is determined by adaptive functioning deficits.
- A number of biological factors are implicated in intellectual disability, including metabolic disorders (PKU, Tay-Sachs disease); chromosomal disorders (Down syndrome, fragile X, trisomy 13, trisomy 18); prenatal exposure to rubella, herpes, syphilis, or drugs (especially alcohol, as in fetal alcohol syndrome); premature delivery; and traumatic brain injury (such as that arising from being shaken as an infant).
- There is some evidence that intensive and comprehensive educational interventions, administered very early in a child's life, can help decrease the level of intellectual disability.
- Specific learning disorder affects skills in reading, mathematics, or written expression.
- The communication disorders involve persistent difficulties in the acquisition and use of language and other means of communication.
- Children with language disorder have difficulties with spoken language, written language, and other language modalities (e.g., sign language). Their symptoms may include problems with vocabulary, grammar, narrative (i.e., knowing how to describe something or put together a story), and other pragmatic language abilities.
- Children with speech disorder have persistent difficulties in producing speech.
- Children with social communication disorder have difficulties in the acquisition and use of spoken or written language or other, nonverbal forms of communication for social communication in naturalistic settings that interfere with their social relationships.
- Some of the learning and communication disorders may have genetic roots. Abnormalities in brain structure and functioning have been implicated in these disorders. Environmental factors, including lead poisoning, birth defects, sensory deprivation, and low socioeconomic status, may contribute to brain dysfunction.
- Treatment of the learning and communication disorders usually focuses on building skills in problem areas through specialized training, as well as computerized exercises.
- Tourette's disorder and chronic motor or vocal tic disorder are motor disorders involving the presence of persistent tics. Stereotypic movement disorder is a motor disorder characterized by repetitive, seemingly driven, and apparently purposeless motor behavior. These disorders are highly comorbid with obsessive-compulsive disorder and may be related to similar biological factors.
- Developmental coordination disorder involves deficits in fundamental motor skills.
- Neurocognitive disorders involve deterioration in cognitive functioning, often accompanied by emotional and behavioral changes. Cognitive impairments in neurocognitive disorder include memory impairment, aphasia, apraxia, agnosia, and loss of executive functioning.
- The most common type of neurocognitive disorder is that due to Alzheimer's disease. The brain of an Alzheimer's patient shows neurofibrillary tangles, plaques made up of beta-amyloid protein, and cortical atrophy. Recent theories of Alzheimer's disease focus on genes that might contribute to the buildup of beta-amyloid protein in the brain of Alzheimer's patients, particularly the ApoE gene.
- Neurocognitive disorder also can be caused by cerebrovascular disease, traumatic brain injury, and progressive disorders such as Parkinson's disease, Lewy body disease, HIV infection, Huntington's disease, and prion disease (Creutzfeldt-Jakob disease). Chronic substance abuse and the nutritional deficiencies that often accompany it also can lead to neurocognitive disorder.
- Drugs may help reduce the cognitive symptoms of neurocognitive disorder and the accompanying depression, anxiety, and psychotic symptoms in some patients.
- Delirium is characterized by disorientation, recent memory loss, and a global attention disturbance. Delirium typically is a signal of a serious medical condition, such as a stroke, congestive heart failure, an infectious disease, a high fever, or drug or medication intoxication or withdrawal. It is a common syndrome in hospitals, particularly among elderly surgical patients.
- Treating delirium involves treating the underlying condition leading to the delirium and keeping the patient safe until the symptoms subside.

KEY TERMS

neurodevelopmental disorders
neurocognitive disorders
attention-deficit/hyperactivity disorder (ADHD)
autism spectrum disorder (ASD)
autism
echolalia
pervasive developmental disorders (PDDs)
intellectual disability (ID)
fetal alcohol syndrome (FAS)
specific learning disorder
communication disorders
language disorder
speech sound disorder
childhood-onset fluency disorder
social communication disorder
motor disorders
Tourette's disorder
persistent motor or vocal tic disorder (PMVTD)
stereotypic movement disorder
developmental coordination disorder
major neurocognitive disorder
dementia
mild neurocognitive disorder
aphasia
palilalia
apraxia
agnosia
executive functions
Alzheimer's disease
neurofibrillary tangles
plaques
beta-amyloid
vascular neurocognitive disorder
cerebrovascular disease
stroke
traumatic brain injury
delirium

©Westend61/SuperStock

Chapter 11

Disruptive, Impulse-Control, and Conduct Disorders

CHAPTER OUTLINE

Disorders of Conduct and Impulse Control Along the Continuum

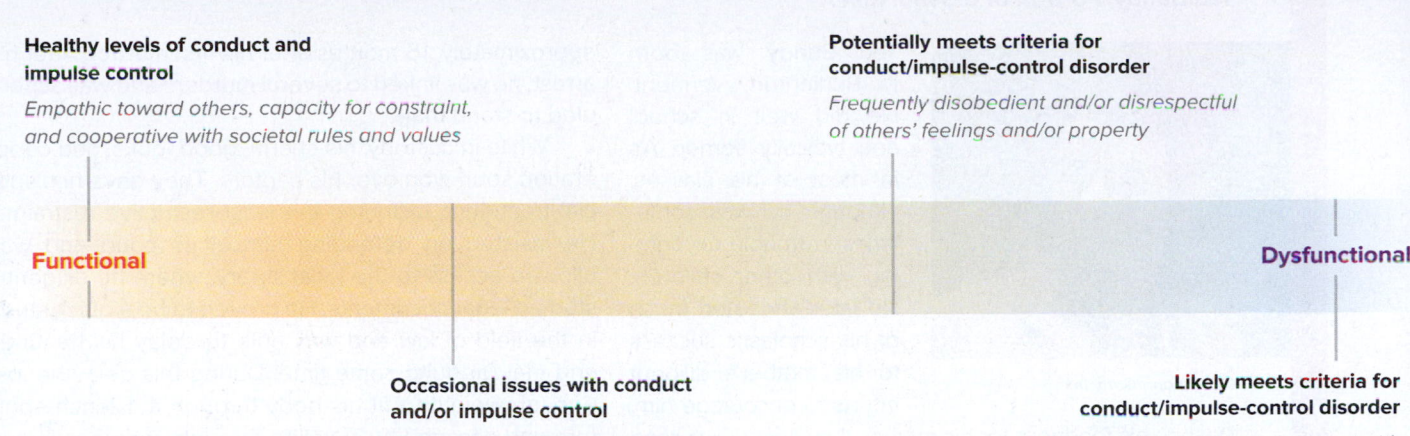

Healthy levels of conduct and impulse control
Empathic toward others, capacity for constraint, and cooperative with societal rules and values

Occasional issues with conduct and/or impulse control
Generally compassionate and law-abiding, but occasionally breaks rules or defies authority

Potentially meets criteria for conduct/impulse-control disorder
Frequently disobedient and/or disrespectful of others' feelings and/or property

Likely meets criteria for conduct/impulse-control disorder
Callous and/or unemotional contact with others, cruel and/or unlawful behavior

Functional — Dysfunctional

The disorders discussed in this chapter all involve disruptive, impulsive, and antisocial behavior that violates major social norms. You've no doubt observed that people vary in how cooperative they are with social norms and in how empathetic and caring they are toward other people. On one end of the continuum are people who exemplify a strong social and moral code and who deeply care for others, even sacrificing their own well-being on behalf of others (think Mother Teresa). Most of us are a little farther along the continuum: Although we generally are law-abiding and try to be compassionate toward others, we break a few rules now and then (e.g., driving too fast) and are sometimes unkind to others, especially when we are stressed or in a bad mood. Yet farther along the continuum are people who think some social norms don't apply to them and who can be downright cruel toward others, particularly when it helps them accomplish their goals, such as Kevin Spacey's character Francis Underwood in the television program *House of Cards* or Prince Joffrey in *Game of Thrones*.

The individuals who receive the diagnoses discussed in this chapter persistently break basic social rules regulating behavior and often treat others very badly, even being aggressive or violent toward others. Two of the disorders we discuss apply only to children. Children diagnosed with *oppositional defiant disorder* are chronically angry and irritable; are argumentative and defiant, refusing to comply with adult requests; and are vindictive toward others, often blaming others for their own mistakes and bad behavior. Children diagnosed with *conduct disorder* act in even more antisocial ways, repeatedly being aggressive and cruel toward animals and people, vandalizing and destroying others' property, stealing and lying, and violating basic family and school rules. The other two disorders are diagnosed only in individuals age 18 and older. *Intermittent explosive disorder* is characterized by repeated outbursts of verbal or physical aggression toward others that is far out of proportion to any provocation. *Antisocial personality disorder* is characterized by a chronic pattern of disregard for the basic rights of others. People with this disorder are selfish, manipulative, deceitful, cruel, and often aggressive toward others in order to get what they want.

Throughout this chapter, we discuss biological and psychosocial factors that appear to contribute to the development of these disorders. These factors may also help account for bad behavior that falls short of meeting any of the diagnoses—the everyday bad behavior we see in people with whom we interact or people in the media. Fundamentally, all behavior, good and bad, moral and immoral, is tied to biological and psychosocial factors. This raises the following question: What are the implications of identifying causes of bad behavior for how society should deal with people who violate major social norms and hurt others?

Extraordinary People

Ted Bundy, *Portrait of a Serial Killer*

©Bettmann/Getty Images

Ted Bundy was born in Burlington, Vermont. He did well in school and typically earned A's in most of his classes, although he was sometimes in trouble for fighting with other children. He later attributed much of his scholastic success to his mother's diligent efforts to encourage him. Despite his fondness for his mother, they never discussed personal matters, and he stated that their relationship was not an open one. Bundy reported that he found it difficult to socialize and often chose to be alone or engage in solitary hobbies when in high school. Although he was described as charming, intelligent, and attractive, he had limited social contacts because he did not enjoy drinking and preferred the role of a scholar. He also had relatively few experiences with girls in high school and only went on one date.

After graduation, Bundy became involved with politics and worked on several successful campaigns, where he was described as being responsible, dedicated, and hardworking. Through this experience he was able to establish a wide social network. Bundy used his charm and quick wit to establish himself as an up-and-coming politician and even was referred to as a "young JFK" for his political savvy.

At age 27, Bundy began abducting, raping, and murdering young women. He often lured these women into his car by deception, such as by impersonating a police detective. The brutal murders included bludgeoning, mutilation, and rape. The murders attracted media and police attention, yet Bundy continued to abduct women and evade detection. He planned and executed the kidnappings with great care, in order to avoid discovery. His colleagues found him charming and endearing, and they could not imagine that he was capable of such acts. Bundy was finally arrested approximately 15 months after his first murder. After his arrest, he was linked to several murders and was scheduled to stand trial.

While in custody, his charm, good looks, and cooperation soon won over his captors. They gave him special treatment, including the least restrictive restraints. He insisted on defending himself in court and was allowed access to the local library, where he diligently studied legal documents. He proved to be a quick study in the field of law and was able to delay his hearings and trial for quite some time. During this delay he lost enough weight to fit his body through a 12-inch aperture and escaped by crawling through openings above the jail cells and offices.

After escaping custody he settled near Florida State University. Not long after, he was once again raping, beating, and killing women. During this time, he lived under a false name and supported himself by using stolen credit cards. He was eventually arrested after bludgeoning to death many members of a sorority house as they slept. He was subsequently found guilty and twice sentenced to death. However, his legal acumen was so high during the trial that, after sentencing him, the judge stated that Bundy "should have been a lawyer." These legal skills continued to serve him while in prison as he delayed his execution for 10 years. Others, however, suggested that his arrogant self-confidence contributed to a failure to obtain competent legal counsel and that his effort to serve as his own lawyer ultimately was harmful to his defense.

While in prison, Bundy granted numerous interview requests and revealed that he committed the murders as a way to gain full possession of the women. He claimed that the rapes were not brutal and that he had attempted to make the murders as painless as possible for the victims. Bundy never expressed any explicit or compelling feelings of remorse for the murders. In fact he withheld the identities of many of his victims as a way to delay his execution. (Adapted from T. A. Widiger, personal communication, 2009)

Ted Bundy was one of the most extreme examples of what many people call a *psychopath* or *sociopath.* He could be charming, charismatic, cunning, and hideously sadistic, deriving great pleasure from inflicting pain on others. He never accepted responsibility for his actions, blaming his unlawful behavior on the bad influence of the violent pornography he was attracted to as a youth.

The disorders we consider in this chapter all reflect the tendency to engage in behavior that violates the basic rights of others or major social norms. In most cases these antisocial behaviors are nowhere near as extreme as Ted Bundy's, but they can still exact a heavy toll on the targets of the behavior. We start with conduct disorder and oppositional defiant disorder, which by definition begin during childhood. Then we discuss intermittent explosive disorder, which, as the name implies, is characterized by intermittent but recurrent aggressive outbursts. Finally, we cover antisocial personality disorder, which is diagnosed only in adults and could be applied to Ted Bundy.

CONDUCT DISORDER AND OPPOSITIONAL DEFIANT DISORDER

Have you ever lied, stolen something, or hit someone? Most of us would have to answer yes to at least one of these. However, relatively few would answer yes to the following questions:

- Have you ever pulled a knife or a gun on another person?
- Have you ever forced someone into sexual activity at knifepoint?
- Have you ever deliberately set a fire with the hope of damaging someone's property?
- Have you ever broken into someone else's car or house with the intention of stealing?

Many young people who have **conduct disorder** answer yes to these questions and engage in other serious transgressions of societal norms for behavior (see the *DSM-5* criteria in Table 1). These children have a chronic pattern of unconcern for the basic rights of others. Consider Phillip, in the following case study.

CASE STUDY

Phillip, age 12, was suspended from a small-town Iowa school and referred for psychiatric treatment by his principal, who sent the following note:

> This child has been a continual problem since coming to our school. He does not get along on the playground because he is mean to other children. He disobeys school rules, teases the patrol children, steals from the other children, and defies all authority. Phillip keeps getting into fights with other children on the bus.
>
> The truth is not in Phillip. When caught in actual misdeeds, he denies everything and takes upon himself an air of injured innocence. He believes we are picking on him. His attitude is sullen when he is refused anything. He pouts, and when asked why he does these things, he points to his head and says, Because I'm not right up here. This boy needs help badly. He does not seem to have any friends. His aggressive behavior prevents the children from liking him. Our school psychologist tested Phillip, and the results indicated average intelligence, but his school achievement is only at the third- and low fourth-grade level. (Source: Jenkins, R. L., *Behavior disorders of childhood and adolescence*. Springfield, IL: Charles C Thomas, 1973, 60–64.)

The behaviors of children with conduct disorder fall into four categories: (1) aggression to people and animals, (2) destruction of property, (3) deceitfulness or theft, and (4) serious violations of rules. Approximately 3 to 7 percent of children and adolescents exhibit behaviors serious enough to warrant a diagnosis of conduct disorder (Canino, Polanczyk, Bauermeister, Rohde, & Frick, 2010; Maughan, Rowe, Messer, Goodman, & Meltzer, 2004). These children are highly likely to engage in violent and criminal behavior (Frick & Nigg, 2012). In the United States, vandalism by juveniles is estimated to cost schools more than $600 million annually.

An important distinction is made between conduct disorder that begins in childhood and conduct disorder that begins in adolescence (Frick & Nigg, 2012; Moffitt, 2006), and *DSM-5* requires that conduct disorder be specified based on its age at onset. Children with **childhood-onset conduct disorder** (beginning before age 10) often show behavioral problems in preschool or early elementary school, and their problems tend to worsen as they grow older. They are more likely than individuals with **adolescent-onset conduct disorder** (beginning at age 10 or later) to continue to engage in antisocial behavior into adolescence and adulthood, a pattern called **life-course-persistent antisocial behavior** (Moffitt, Caspi, Harrington, & Milne, 2002; Odgers et al., 2008). For example, as adolescents, about 50 percent of those diagnosed with childhood-onset conduct disorder engage in criminal behavior and drug abuse. As adults, about 75 to 85 percent are chronically unemployed, have a history of unstable personal relationships, frequently engage in impulsive physical aggression, or abuse their spouse (Moffitt et al., 2008). Between 35 and 40 percent are diagnosed with antisocial personality disorder as adults.

The *DSM-5* allows another specifier for the diagnosis—*"with limited prosocial emotions"*—which can be applied to children who meet the full criteria for conduct disorder and show at least two of the following characteristics in multiple relationships and settings: (a) lack of remorse or guilt for their actions, (b) lack of empathy for others (callousness), (c) lack of concern about performance at school, at work, or in other important

TABLE 1 *DSM-5* Criteria for Conduct Disorder

A. A repetitive and persistent pattern of behavior in which the basic rights of others or major age-appropriate societal norms or rules are violated, as manifested by the presence of at least three of the following 15 criteria in the past 12 months from any of the categories below, with at least one criterion present in the past 6 months:

Aggression to People and Animals

1. Often bullies, threatens, or intimidates others
2. Often initiates physical fights
3. Has used a weapon that can cause serious physical harm to others (e.g., a bat, brick, broken bottle, knife, gun)
4. Has been physically cruel to people
5. Has been physically cruel to animals
6. Has stolen while confronting a victim (e.g., mugging, purse snatching, extortion, armed robbery)
7. Has forced someone into sexual activity

Destruction of Property

8. Has deliberately engaged in fire setting with the intention of causing serious damage
9. Has deliberately destroyed others' property (other than by fire setting)

Deceitfulness or Theft

10. Has broken into someone else's house, building, or car
11. Often lies to obtain goods or favors or to avoid obligations (e.g., "cons" others)
12. Has stolen items of nontrivial value without confronting a victim (e.g., shoplifting, but without breaking and entering; forgery)

Serious Violations of Rules

13. Often stays out at night despite parental prohibitions, beginning before age 13 years
14. Has run away from home overnight at least twice while living in the parental or parental surrogate home, or once without returning for a lengthy period
15. Is often truant from school, beginning before age 13 years

B. The disturbance in behavior causes clinically significant impairment in social, academic, or occupational functioning.

C. If the individual is age 18 years or older, criteria are not met for antisocial personality disorder.

activities, and (d) shallow or deficient emotions (e.g., insincerity in emotions, using emotions to manipulate others). Children with this callous, unemotional presentation are less reactive to signs of fear and distress in others and less sensitive to punishment (Frick, 2012, 2016). They tend to be fearless and thrill-seeking. These traits characterize **psychopathy,** a more severe, aggressive, and difficult-to-treat pattern predictive of more long-term problems into adulthood (Cleckley, 1941/1982; Hare & Neumann, 2008; Kimonis et al., 2015). Because psychopathy has been studied more in adults than in children, we will discuss it below in relation to antisocial personality disorder.

The *DSM-5* also recognizes a less severe pattern of chronic misbehavior, **oppositional defiant disorder** (see Table 2). Note that the symptoms are grouped into three types, reflecting both emotional and behavioral symptom categories. Unlike children with conduct disorder, children with oppositional defiant disorder are not aggressive toward people or animals, do not destroy property, and do not show a pattern of theft and deceit. They are, however, chronically negativistic, defiant, disobedient, and hostile (Frick & Nigg, 2012). We see several symptoms of oppositional defiant disorder in 9-year-old Jeremy in the following case study.

TABLE 2 *DSM-5* Criteria for Oppositional Defiant Disorder

A. A pattern of angry/irritable mood, argumentative/defiant behavior, or vindictiveness lasting at least 6 months as evidenced by at least four symptoms from any of the following categories, and exhibited during interaction with at least one individual who is not a sibling.

Angry/Irritable Mood

1. Often loses temper
2. Is often touchy or easily annoyed
3. Is often angry and resentful

Argumentative/Defiant Behavior

4. Often argues with authority figures, or for children and adolescents, with adults
5. Often actively defies or refuses to comply with requests from authority figures or with rules
6. Often deliberately annoys others
7. Often blames others for his or her mistakes or misbehavior

Vindictiveness

8. Has been spiteful or vindictive at least twice within the past 6 months

Note: The persistence and frequency of these behaviors should be used to distinguish a behavior that is within normal limits from a behavior that is symptomatic. For children under 5 years of age, the behavior should occur on most days for a period of at least 6 months unless otherwise noted (Criterion A8). For individuals 5 years or older, the behavior should occur at least once per week for at least 6 months, unless otherwise noted (Criterion A8). While these frequency criteria provide guidance on a minimal level of frequency to define symptoms, other factors should also be considered, such as whether the frequency and intensity of the behaviors are outside a range that is normative for the individual's developmental level, gender, and culture.

B. The disturbance in behavior is associated with distress in the individual or others in his or her immediate social context (e.g., family, peer group, work colleagues), or it impacts negatively on social, educational, occupational, or other important areas of functioning.

C. The behaviors do not occur exclusively during the course of a psychotic, substance use, depressive, or bipolar disorder. Also, the criteria are not met for disruptive mood dysregulation disorder.

CASE STUDY

Jeremy has been increasingly difficult to manage since nursery school. At school, he teases and kicks other children, trips them, and calls them names. He is described as bad tempered and irritable, though at times he seems to enjoy school. Often he appears to be deliberately trying to annoy other children, though he always claims that others have started the arguments. He does not get in serious fights but does occasionally exchange a few blows with another child.

Jeremy sometimes refuses to do what his two teachers tell him to do, and this year he has been particularly difficult during arithmetic, art, and science lessons. He gives many reasons why he should not have to do his work and argues when told to do it. At home, Jeremy's behavior varies. Some days he is defiant and rude to his mother, needing to be told to do everything several times, though he usually complies eventually. Other days he is charming and volunteers to help, but his unhelpful days predominate. His mother says, "The least little thing upsets him, and then he shouts and screams." Jeremy is described as spiteful and mean with his younger brother, Rickie. His mother also says that he tells many minor lies, though when pressed he is truthful about important things. (Source: *DSM Casebook: A Learning Companion to the Diagnostic and Statistical Manual of Mental Disorders,* Fifth Edition. American Psychiatric Association, 2013.)

Symptoms of oppositional defiant disorder often begin during the toddler and preschool years. Being defiant and obstinate are common characteristics of "the terrible twos," and concerns have been raised that the diagnosis of oppositional defiant disorder pathologizes a behavior that is typical in young children. Indeed, some children who meet the criteria for oppositional defiant disorder seem to outgrow these behaviors by late childhood or early adolescence. Children diagnosed with oppositional defiant disorder, however, are significantly more likely than children who do not meet the criteria for the diagnosis to go on to develop conduct disorder, substance use disorders, and mood and anxiety disorders (Erskine et al., 2016; Loeber, Burke, & Pardini, 2009b).

Across cultures, boys are about three times more likely than girls to be diagnosed with conduct disorder or oppositional defiant disorder; this discrepancy is less stark in adolescence than in childhood (Canino et al., 2010; Frick & Nigg, 2012). Males are 10 to 15 times more likely than females to have life-course-persistent antisocial behavior (Moffitt, 2006). The biological and psychosocial causes of these disorders may be present more often in boys than in girls. Also, boys with conduct disorder tend to be more physically aggressive than girls with conduct disorder and thus more likely to draw attention (Maughan, Pickles, Rowe, Costello, & Angold, 2000; Tiet, Wasserman, Loeber, McReynolds, & Miller, 2001).

Some researchers have suggested that antisocial behavior is not rarer in girls than in boys but just looks different (Crick, Ostrov, & Kawabata, 2007). Girls' aggression is more likely to be indirect and verbal rather than physical. Girls appear to engage in relational aggression, such as excluding their peers, gossiping about them, and colluding with others to damage the social status of their targets (Crick et al., 2007).

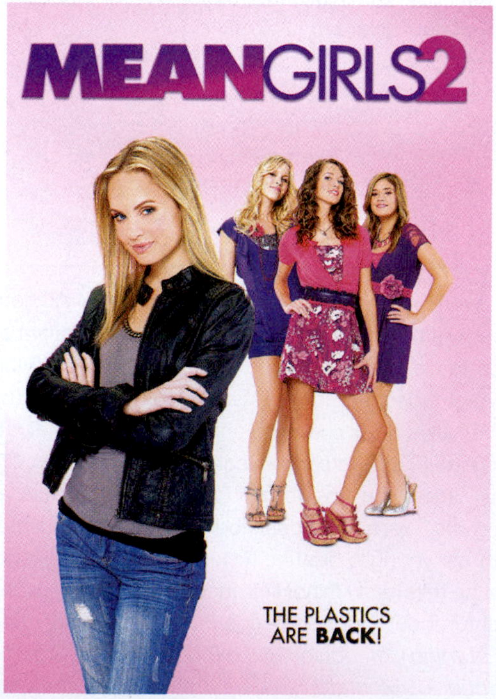

Girls may be aggressive toward others in different ways than boys. ©AF archive/Alamy Stock Photo

However, girls and boys with conduct disorder are equally likely to engage in stealing, lying, and substance abuse (Tiet et al., 2001). Long-term studies of girls diagnosed with conduct disorder find that, as adolescents and adults, they also show high rates of depression and anxiety disorders, severe marital problems, criminal activity, and early, unplanned pregnancies (Loeber & Burke, 2011; Moffitt, Caspi, Rutter, & Silva, 2001).

Contributors to Conduct Disorder and Oppositional Defiant Disorder

The risk factors for conduct disorder and oppositional defiant disorder are largely the same, so we discuss them together, referring primarily to conduct disorder because the majority of the research has focused on this disorder.

Biological Factors

Children with conduct disorder are more likely than children without the disorder to have parents with a history of antisocial behavior (Salvatore & Dick, 2016). Twin and adoption studies indicate that this aggregation of antisocial behaviors in families is due to both genetic and environmental factors (Polderman et al., 2015; Silberg, Maes, & Eaves, 2012). Genetics appears to play a particularly strong role in childhood-onset conduct disorder. Several specific genes have been associated with an increased risk of conduct disorder and oppositional defiant disorder, primarily genes involved in the regulation of the neurotransmitters dopamine, serotonin, and norepinephrine (Moffitt et al., 2008; Salvatore & Dick, 2016). One of these genes is the monoamine oxidase A (MAOA) gene, which encodes an enzyme that metabolizes serotonin, dopamine, and norepinephrine (see meta-analyses by Ficks & Waldman, 2014; Taylor & Kim-Cohen, 2007). Several studies have found that children who have both an abnormal variant of the MAOA gene and a history of childhood maltreatment (including physical and sexual abuse as well as neglect) are especially likely to develop aggressive traits in general, and conduct disorder in particular (e.g., Caspi et al., 2002). This is another example of interactions between genes and environment contributing to psychopathology. As in other disorders, however, more recent findings on such interactions in conduct disorder and oppositional defiant disorder are more mixed (Dick et al., 2015; Salvatore & Dick, 2016).

The exact mechanisms by which genetic and environmental vulnerabilities create conduct disorder are

SHADES OF GRAY

Consider the description below of Jake.

Jake has been larger than most kids from the day he was born. Now, at age 10, he towers over all the other boys and is 15 pounds heavier than most, with most of the extra weight being muscle. Over the last couple of years, Jake's parents encouraged him to channel his size and energies into sports, but he wasn't very coordinated and was teased by other kids, who called him "the gorilla." When this happened, Jake would sometimes lash out at the child who teased him, punching or kicking him. Given Jake's size advantage, this behavior usually resulted in moderate to severe injury for the other child. In the last 6 months Jake has been ambushing children who have been mean to him in the past on their way home from school and beating them up fairly severely. This has accomplished Jake's goals—the retribution against the other children feels good, and he doesn't get teased much anymore. Lately he's taken to ambushing children who have never teased him, just to send a message to others to stay clear of him and treat him with respect.

Could Jake be diagnosed with a conduct disorder based on the information in the description? (Discussion appears at the end of this chapter.)

still being mapped (Dodge, 2009; Frick, 2016). Children with conduct disorder may have neurological deficits in those brain systems responsible for planning and controlling behavior and processing reward and punishment (Matthys, Vanderschuren, & Schutter, 2013). They have high rates of comorbid attention-deficit/hyperactivity disorder (ADHD; see the chapter "Neurodevelopmental and Neurocognitive Disorders"; Beauchaine, Hinshaw, & Pang, 2010), a fundamentally neurological disorder characterized by difficulties in attention, impulsivity, and hyperactivity. Neuroimaging studies show abnormalities in the functional areas of the prefrontal cortex involved in responding to emotional stimuli, including the anterior cingulate (Stadler et al., 2007; Sterzer, Stadler, Krebs, Kleinschmidt, & Poustka, 2005). They also show less amygdala activity in response to emotional stimuli (Sterzer et al., 2005), possibly suggesting that children with conduct disorder do not process emotional cues the way healthy children do (see Matthys et al., 2013). Indeed, children with conduct disorder show deficits on tasks that measure planning and organizing ability and the processing of emotional cues (Forslund, Brocki, Bohlin, Granqvist, & Eninger, 2016; Hobson, Scott, & Rubia, 2011).

In addition to genetics, another source of the neurological deficits these children have may be exposure to neurotoxins and drugs prenatally or during the preschool years. Boys whose mothers smoke during pregnancy are 2.6 times more likely to demonstrate oppositional behavior in early childhood, followed by increasingly more aggressive and severe antisocial behavior as they grow older (Wakschlag, Pickett, Kasza, & Loeber, 2006).

The role of serotonin in violent behavior has been the focus of many studies. One study of a large community-based sample found that young men with high blood serotonin levels relative to the levels of other men their age were much more likely to have committed a violent crime (Moffitt et al., 1998). Several other studies, but not all, have found an association between measures of serotonin activity and antisocial behavior in children (Matthys et al., 2013).

Several studies have shown that children with conduct disorder have a slower heart rate than children without the disorder, both while resting and especially when confronted with a stressor (Fanti, 2018; Ortiz & Raine, 2004). They also show abnormal cortisol levels both at rest and in response to a stressor (Matthys et al., 2013). Because they become less physiologically aroused than other children when confronted by stressors, children with conduct disorder may be more willing to take risks and may have more difficulty learning from being punished for their behavior. However, children with conduct disorder who also experience anxiety symptoms and emotion dysregulation may show more, rather than less, physiological reactivity (Fanti, 2018).

People often link aggressive behavior to the hormone testosterone. A meta-analysis of studies of testosterone and aggression in humans found a small but statistically significant correlation of .14 (Book, Starzyk, & Quinsey, 2001). The association between testosterone and aggression depends on the social context of the participants. In a study of 9- to 15-year-old boys, higher testosterone levels were associated with more conduct disorder symptoms in boys whose peers engaged in socially deviant behaviors (Rowe, Maughan, Worthman, Costello, & Angold, 2004). In boys whose peers did not engage in such behaviors, testosterone was associated with leadership rather than with conduct disorder symptoms.

Social Factors

Conduct disorder and oppositional defiant disorder are found more frequently in children in lower socioeconomic classes and in urban areas than in children in higher socioeconomic classes and in rural areas (Shaw & Shelleby, 2014; Yoshikawa, Aber, & Beardslee, 2012). An "experiment of nature" provided evidence that poverty may play a causal role in antisocial behavior. For several years, researchers had been following 1,420 children in rural North Carolina, about one-quarter of whom were Native American (Costello, Compton, Keeler, & Angold, 2003). During the study, a casino operated by Native Americans opened, providing a sudden and substantial increase in income for the families of some of these children. The rates of conduct and oppositional defiant disorder decreased in those Native American children whose families benefited from the casino money.

The quality of parenting that children receive, particularly children with vulnerability to conduct disturbances, is strongly related to whether they develop the full syndrome of conduct disorder (Kim-Cohen, Caspi, Rutter, Polo Tomas, & Moffitt, 2006; Loeber, Burke, & Pardini, 2009a; Shaw & Shelleby, 2014). Children who develop conduct disorder symptoms tend to have been difficult babies, toddlers, and younger children, at least as reported by their parents (Forbes, Rapee, Camberis, & McMahon, 2017). They are described as having been irritable, demanding, disobedient, and impulsive. They seemed to lack self-control and responded to frustration with aggression. Some theorists argue that such children are born with a biologically based difficult temperament that interacts with parenting and environmental factors to produce behavioral problems (Caspi, Harrington, et al., 2003).

Children who are physically abused or severely neglected by their parents are more likely to develop disruptive and delinquent behavior (Stouthamer-Loeber, Loeber, Homish, & Wei, 2001). Children whose parents are not involved in their everyday life—for example, whose parents do not know who their children's friends are or what their children are doing in school—are more likely to develop conduct disturbances. When parents do interact with their children with conduct disturbances, the interactions often are characterized by hostility, physical violence, and ridicule. Such parents frequently ignore their children or are absent from home, but when the children transgress, the parents lash out violently (Kim-Cohen et al., 2006; Shaw & Shelleby, 2014; Smith & Farrington, 2004). These parents are likely to physically punish boys more severely than girls, which may account partially for the higher rate of conduct disturbances in boys than in girls.

Young people living in such families may turn to their peers to receive validation and escape their parents. Unfortunately, their peer group may consist of others with similar conduct disturbances who tend to encourage delinquent acts and even provide opportunities for those acts. For example, they may dare a new group member to commit a robbery to "show he is a man" and even provide him with a weapon and a getaway car. Children who become part of a deviant peer group are especially likely to begin abusing alcohol and illicit drugs, which in turn leads to further deviant acts (Loeber et al., 2009a).

Children are more likely to exhibit disruptive and delinquent behavior if they have been physically abused. *©Piotr Wawrzyniuk/Shutterstock*

Individuals with antisocial tendencies also tend to choose mates with similar tendencies (Smith & Farrington, 2004). Conversely, those who form close relationships with others who do not have a conduct disturbance are much more likely to outgrow their behaviors. Delinquent young men who marry young women with no history of conduct problems tend to cease their delinquent acts permanently (Sampson & Laub, 1992).

Cognitive Factors

Children with conduct disorder tend to process information about social interactions in ways that promote aggressive reactions (Forslund et al., 2016). They assume that others will be aggressive toward them, and they use these assumptions—rather than cues from specific situations—to interpret the actions of their peers (Helseth, Waschbusch, King, & Willoughby, 2015). For example, when accidentally bumped into by another child, a child with conduct disorder will assume that the bump was intentional and meant to provoke a fight. Children with conduct disorder tend to consider a narrow range of responses to perceived provocation by a peer, usually including aggression (see Fontaine & Dodge, 2006). When pressed to consider other responses, they generate ineffective or vague ideas and often judge anything besides aggression as a useless or unattractive response (Crick & Ladd, 1990; Helseth et al., 2015).

Children who think about social interactions this way are likely to act aggressively toward others. Others then may retaliate—other children will hit back, parents and teachers will punish them, and people will perceive them negatively. These reactions feed the children's assumption that the world is against them, causing them to misinterpret future actions by others. A cycle of interactions can be built that maintains and encourages aggressive, antisocial behaviors.

Again, the best evidence that thinking patterns are causes, rather than simply correlates, of antisocial behavior in children comes from studies showing that changing children's aggressive thinking patterns can reduce their aggressive behavior. We will look to these and other interventions as they are used with children with conduct disorder.

An Integrative Model

Biological, social, and cognitive factors contributing to conduct disorder often may coincide and interact, sending a child on a trajectory toward antisocial behaviors that is difficult to stop (Figure 1) (Dodge, 2009; Dodge & Pettit, 2003; Frick, 2016; Loeber et al., 2009a). Antisocial parents appear both to confer on their children a genetic vulnerability to conduct disturbances and to parent them in ways that engender antisocial behaviors—for example, exhibiting violence and hostility, neglect, and a lack of warmth (Frick, 2016; Loeber et al., 2009a; Silberg et al., 2012). These children also may be exposed to maternal drug use, poor prenatal nutrition, pre- and postnatal exposure to toxic agents, child abuse, poverty, and the stress of growing up in a violent neighborhood (Jennings, Perez, & Reingle Gonzalez, 2018; Loeber et al., 2009a; Silberg et al., 2003). Infants and toddlers with the neuropsychological problems seen in children with conduct disorder are more irritable, impulsive, awkward, overreactive, inattentive, and slow to learn than their peers. This makes them difficult to care for and puts them at increased risk for maltreatment and neglect. Early symptoms of aggression and oppositional behavior in a child lead to and interact with harsh discipline and a lack of warmth from parents and conflicts with aggressive peers. These children are at risk for academic and social problems in school, which can motivate them to turn to deviant peer groups that encourage antisocial behavior. Along the way, such children learn that the world is hostile and that they must defend themselves rapidly and aggressively. They are prone to impulsive behaviors or rash reactions to others. These children enter adulthood with a long history of negative interactions with others, violent and impulsive outbursts, and alienation from mainstream society. All these factors feed on one another, perpetuating the cycle of antisocial behavior into adulthood.

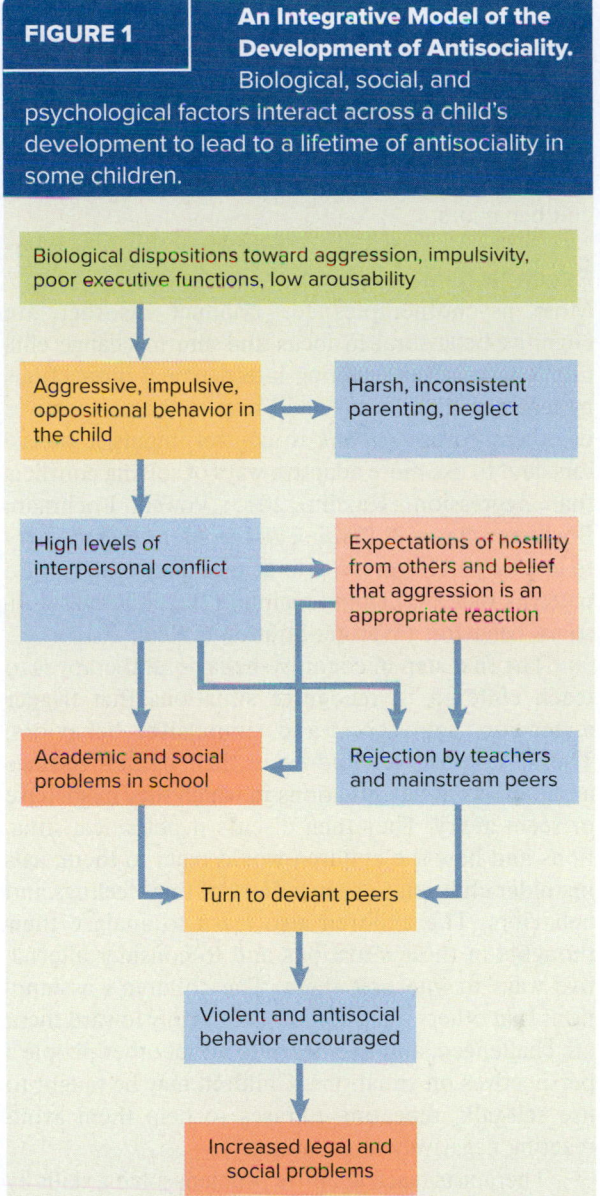

FIGURE 1 **An Integrative Model of the Development of Antisociality.** Biological, social, and psychological factors interact across a child's development to lead to a lifetime of antisociality in some children.

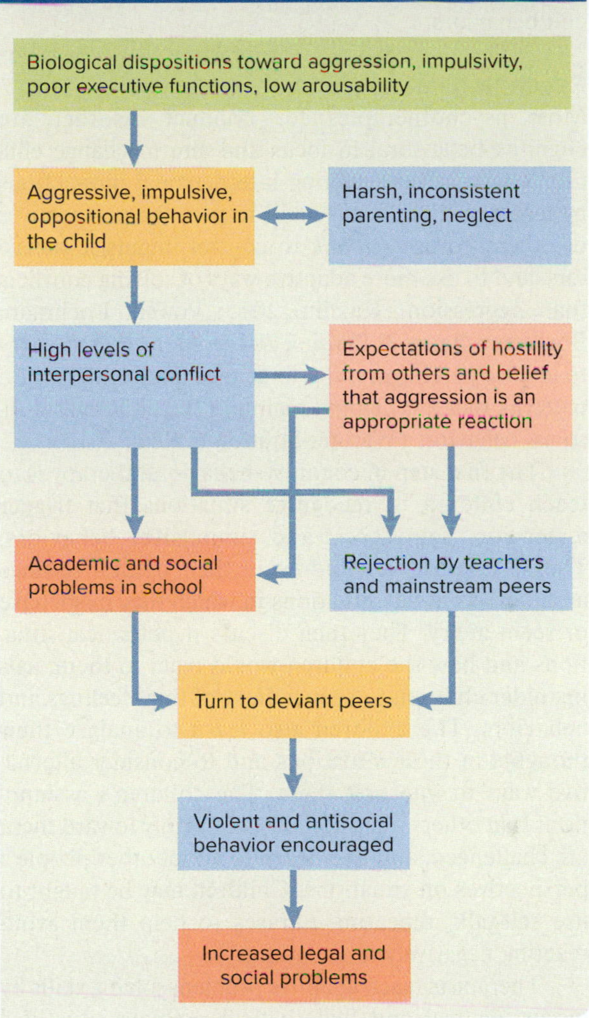

In a longitudinal study following children from age 3 into adulthood, Terri Moffitt, Avshalom Caspi, and colleagues (Moffitt & Caspi, 2001; Moffitt et al., 2001) found that the combination of a biological disposition toward cognitive deficits and a difficult temperament plus growing up in a risky environment characterized by inadequate parenting and disrupted family bonds tended to lead to conduct disorder that developed in childhood and persisted into adulthood. In contrast, youth who were antisocial only in adolescence were much less likely to have this combination of biological and environmental risk factors. Another study found impulsivity in boys to be linked to a greater risk for late-adolescent delinquency only among those who grew up in poor and violent neighborhoods (Lynam et al., 2000).

Treatments for Conduct Disorder and Oppositional Defiant Disorder

Psychological and social treatments can reduce violent and disruptive behavior in children with these disorders. Some children are also given medications to decrease their emotional dysregulation and difficult behaviors.

Psychological and Social Therapies

Most psychotherapies for conduct disorder are cognitive-behavioral in focus and aim to change children's ways of interpreting interpersonal interactions by teaching them to take and respect the perspectives of others, to use *self-talk* to control impulsive behaviors, and to use more adaptive ways of solving conflicts than aggression (Kazdin, 2015; Powell, Lochman, Boxmeyer, Barry, & Pardini, 2017). Many therapies try to involve parents in order to change family interaction patterns that are helping maintain the children's antisocial behaviors (Webster-Stratton & Reid, 2017).

The first step in cognitive-behavioral therapy is to teach children to recognize situations that trigger anger or aggressive and impulsive behaviors. Therapists observe children in their natural settings and then point out situations in which they misbehave or seem angry. They then discuss hypothetical situations and how the children would react to them, asking older children to keep a diary of their feelings and behaviors. The children also learn to analyze their thoughts in these situations and to consider alternative ways to interpret them. The children's assumptions that others intentionally act meanly toward them are challenged, and they learn to adopt other people's perspectives on situations. Children may be taught to use self-talk, repeating phrases to help them avoid reacting negatively to situations.

Therapists teach adaptive problem-solving skills by discussing real and hypothetical problem situations with children and helping them generate positive solutions. For example, if a therapist and a child are discussing how to respond to another child who has cut in line in the lunchroom, the therapist initially might model an assertive (rather than aggressive) response, such as saying "I would like you to move to the back of the line" to the child cutting in. Then the child in therapy might practice the assertive response, perhaps also pretending to be the child cutting in line in order to gain some perspective on the other child's behavior.

Some psychosocial therapies for children with conduct disorder include parents, particularly if the family dynamics support the children's behavior (Kazdin, 2017, 2018). Parents learn to reinforce positive behaviors in their children and to discourage aggressive or antisocial behaviors. They also are given nonviolent discipline techniques and strategies for controlling their own angry outbursts. These behavioral techniques are especially important in treating younger children, who may not be able to analyze and challenge their thinking and problem-solving processes.

Unfortunately, it can be difficult to get those parents who need the most improvement in parenting skills to participate in therapy (Kazdin, 2017). Therapists also need to be sensitive to cultural differences in behavioral norms for children and parents. For example, in families of color it often is useful to engage the extended family (grandparents, aunts, uncles) in family therapy as well as the parents, depending on cultural values and norms (Chu & Leino, 2017).

All these cognitive-behavioral therapies—particularly interventions made in the home, in the classroom, and in peer groups—reduce aggressive and impulsive behaviors in children (Kazdin, 2015; Webster-Stratton & Reid, 2017). Unfortunately, many children relapse, particularly if their parents have poor parenting skills, a history of alcoholism or drug abuse, or some other psychopathology. Interventions are most likely to have long-term positive effects if they begin early in a child's life, and booster sessions after a course of initial therapy can help a child avoid relapse (Kazdin, 2017; Shaw & Shelleby, 2014).

One ambitious program attempted to delay or prevent the onset of conduct disorder in children who showed a number of risk factors, such as a parental history of antisocial behavior. This program, called Fast Track, provided intensive cognitive-behavioral therapy to children and behavioral training to parents as described above, as well as academic tutoring from kindergarten through grade 10. After the first 3 years, the children in the intervention group showed better social interaction skills and peer relations and less aggressive behavior in the classroom than children in the control group, who received no intervention (Conduct Problems Prevention Research Group, 2002). After 5 years, 22 percent of the intervention group had conduct disorder compared to 29 percent of the control group (Conduct Problems Prevention Research Group, 2007). As adolescents, those in the intervention group reported less antisocial behavior and were less likely to seek outpatient care for mental health problems (Jones et al., 2010). At age 25, those in the intervention group reported fewer internalizing, externalizing, and substance abuse symptoms (59 percent) than those in the control group (69 percent), as well as fewer crime convictions, less risky sexual behavior, and higher well-being (Conduct Problems Prevention Research Group, 2015).

Drug Therapies

Non-pharmacological treatment is considered the "first-line" treatment for conduct disorder and oppositional defiant disorder, but many children who exhibit severely aggressive behavior have been prescribed a variety of drugs. Stimulants are the most widely prescribed drugs for conduct disorder in the United States, Canada, and many other countries, in part because conduct disorder often is comorbid with ADHD. A meta-analysis of clinical trials found that stimulants are highly effective in relieving ADHD symptoms in children with conduct disorder, and moderately effective in reducing aggression in these children (Balia, Carucci, Coghill, & Zuddas, 2018; Pappadopulos et al., 2006). Antidepressants, particularly the selective serotonin reuptake inhibitors and the serotonin-norepinephrine reuptake inhibitors, may help reduce episodes of irritable and agitated behavior in children (Balia et al., 2018; Savill et al., 2015). Children with conduct disorder and oppositional defiant disorder sometimes are prescribed atypical antipsychotics, which seem to suppress aggressive behavior (Balia et al., 2018). Whether they affect other symptoms of conduct disorder, such as lying and stealing, is unclear. Traditional antipsychotic medications, such as Haldol and Mellaril, also have been used to treat children with conduct disorder, with some success (Balia et al., 2018; Pappadopulos et al., 2006). However, the neurological side effects of these drugs (for additional information on these issues with conduct disorder, see the chapter "Schizophrenia Spectrum and Other Psychotic Disorders") have discouraged many physicians from prescribing them. Some controlled studies suggest that mood stabilizers, including lithium and anticonvulsants (see the chapter "Mood Disorders and Suicide"), may effectively treat children with aggressive conduct disorder (Balia et al., 2018).

ANTISOCIAL PERSONALITY DISORDER

In the Extraordinary People feature at the beginning of this chapter, you read the chilling account of Ted Bundy, the serial rapist and killer. People like Bundy who exhibit chronic antisocial behaviors are diagnosed as having **antisocial personality disorder** (**ASPD**; Table 3). ASPD diagnostic criteria are presented in the "Personality Disorders" chapter in the *DSM-5,* but ASPD is also dual-coded as a conduct disorder in *DSM-5.* ASPD is reviewed in this chapter because it is very closely connected to the spectrum of disruptive, impulse-control, and conduct disorders, including in its developmental origins, while still sharing the key features of a personality disorder (see the chapter "Personality Disorders").

The key features of antisocial personality disorder, as defined by the *DSM-5,* are an impairment in the ability to form positive relationships with others, a tendency to engage in behaviors that violate basic rights of others and major social norms and values, and a focus on doing whatever it takes to gratify one's personal desires. People with this disorder are

TABLE 3 *DSM-5* Diagnostic Criteria for Antisocial Personality Disorder

A. A pervasive pattern of disregard for and violation of the rights of others, occurring since age 15 years, as indicated by three (or more) of the following:
   1. Failure to conform to social norms with respect to lawful behaviors, as indicated by repeatedly performing acts that are grounds for arrest.
   2. Deceitfulness, as indicated by repeated lying, use of aliases, or conning others for personal profit or pleasure.
   3. Impulsivity or failure to plan ahead.
   4. Irritability and aggressiveness, as indicated by repeated physical fights or assaults.
   5. Reckless disregard for safety of self or others.
   6. Consistent irresponsibility, as indicated by repeated failure to sustain consistent work behavior or honor financial obligations.
   7. Lack of remorse, as indicated by being indifferent to or rationalizing having hurt, mistreated, or stolen from another.

B. The individual is at least age 18 years.

C. There is evidence of conduct disorder with onset before age 15 years.

D. The occurrence of antisocial behavior is not exclusively during the course of schizophrenia or bipolar disorder.

deceitful, repeatedly lying or conning others for personal profit or pleasure. Like Ted Bundy, they may commit violent criminal offenses against others—including assault, murder, and rape—in order to gain pleasure or get what they want. When caught, they tend to have little remorse and seem indifferent to the pain and suffering they have caused others.

A prominent characteristic of antisocial personality disorder is poor impulse control. People with this disorder have low frustration tolerance and often act impetuously, with no apparent concern for the consequences of their behavior. They often take chances and seek thrills, with no concern for danger. They are easily bored and restless, unable to endure the tedium of routine or to persist at the day-to-day responsibilities of marriage or a job (Millon, Grossman, Millon, Meagher, & Ramnath, 2004). As a result, they tend to drift from one relationship to another and often have lower-status jobs. They may impulsively engage in criminal activity—50 to 80 percent of men and about 20 percent of women in prison may be diagnosable with antisocial personality disorder (Cale & Lilienfeld, 2002; Fazel & Danesh, 2002; Warren et al., 2002).

We noted earlier that Ted Bundy would be called a *psychopath* by some theorists. The definition of *psychopathy* by pioneers in the field such as Hervey Cleckley (1941/1982) and Robert Hare (Hare & Neumann, 2008) extends the *DSM-5* criteria for antisocial personality disorder, emphasizing certain broad personality traits. The *DSM-5* criteria for antisocial personality disorder and definitions of psychopathy overlap, but are not entirely the same. Psychopaths are characterized by a superficial charm, a grandiose sense of self-worth, a tendency toward boredom and a need for stimulation, a history of pathological lying, cunning and manipulativeness, and a lack of remorse. People with psychopathy are cold and callous, gaining pleasure by competing with and humiliating everyone and anyone. They can be cruel and malicious. They often insist on being seen as faultless and are dogmatic in their opinions. However, when they need to, people with psychopathy can be gracious and cheerful—until they get what they want. Then they may revert to being brash and arrogant. Cleckley (1941/1982) noted that although psychopaths often end up in prison or dead, many become successful businesspeople and professionals. He suggested that the difference between successful psychopaths and those who end up in prison is that the successful ones are better able to maintain an outward appearance of normality. They may be able to do this because they have superior intelligence and can put on a "mask of sanity" and superficial social charm in order to achieve their goals.

Epidemiological studies assessing antisocial personality disorder as defined by the *DSM-IV* suggest that it is one of the most common personality disorders, with as many as 4.1 percent of the general population being diagnosed with the disorder at some time in their life (Glenn, Johnson, & Raine, 2013; Werner, Few, & Bucholz, 2015). Men are substantially more likely than women to be diagnosed with this disorder. Epidemiological studies have not found ethnic or racial differences in rates of diagnosis.

As many as 80 percent of people with antisocial personality disorder abuse substances such as alcohol and illicit drugs (Trull, Jahng, Tomko, Wood, & Sher, 2010). Substance use, such as binge drinking, may be just one form of impulsive behavior that is part of antisocial personality disorder. Substance use probably feeds impulsive and antisocial behavior in people with this personality disorder. Alcohol and other substances may reduce any inhibitions they do have, making them more likely to lash out violently at others. People with this disorder also are at somewhat increased risk for suicide attempts (particularly females) and violent death (Cale & Lilienfeld, 2002).

Adults with antisocial personality disorder typically have shown a disregard for societal norms and a tendency toward antisocial behavior since childhood, and most would have been diagnosed with conduct disorder by mid-adolescence (see Table 3, Criterion C). For some people with this disorder, however, there is a tendency for their antisocial behavior to diminish as they age. This is particularly true of people who were not antisocial as children but became antisocial as adolescents or young adults (Moffitt, 1993). This tendency may be due to psychological or biological maturation or to the possibility that many people with this disorder have been jailed or otherwise constrained by society from acting out their antisocial tendencies.

In part because antisocial personality disorder is defined in terms of behaviors that involve rule-breaking, a large proportion of prisoners meet criteria for this disorder.
©*Ingram Publishing*

Contributors to Antisocial Personality Disorder

Because most adults diagnosed with antisocial personality disorder have exhibited antisocial tendencies since childhood, the biological and psychosocial factors associated with this disorder are similar to those associated with conduct disorder. Here we summarize those factors, focusing on studies that have been done with adults with antisocial tendencies. Many of these studies have used samples of individuals (mostly men) exhibiting criminal behaviors, rather than those specifically with antisocial personality disorder.

There is substantial evidence of a genetic influence on antisocial behaviors, particularly criminal behaviors (Baker, Jacobson, Raine, Lozano, & Bezdjian, 2007; Ferguson, 2010; Rosenström et al., 2017). Twin studies find that the concordance rate for such behaviors is nearly 50 percent in monozygotic twins, compared to 20 percent or lower in dizygotic twins (Larsson et al., 2007; Rosenström et al., 2017). Adoption studies find that the criminal records of adopted sons are more similar to the criminal record of their biological father than to that of their adoptive father (Cloninger & Gottesman, 1987; Mednick, Reznick, Hocevar, & Baker, 1987).

Those genes most frequently implicated in adult antisociality are genes associated with functioning in the serotonin system, which is involved in impulsivity and aggression (Ficks & Waldman, 2014). Although not all studies support the role of these specific genes (Vassos, Collier, & Fazel, 2014), there may be complex interactions between these genes and others in the production of antisocial personality disorder (e.g., Arias et al., 2011). As in studies of children, studies of adults find that those who have a genotype that influences serotonin functioning and who grow up in socioeconomically deprived circumstances are at particularly increased risk for developing symptoms of antisocial personality disorder (Lyons-Ruth et al., 2007). Some newer epigenetic research suggests that early environmental factors might affect gene expression, including genes involved in serotonin and oxytocin, in ways that affect antisocial behavior (e.g., Checknita et al., 2015; see Raine, 2018).

People with antisocial personalities tend to show deficits in verbal skills and in the executive functions of the brain: the ability to sustain concentration, abstract reasoning, concept and goal formation, the ability to anticipate and plan, the capacity to program and initiate purposive sequences of behavior, self-monitoring and self-awareness, and the ability to shift from maladaptive patterns of behavior to more adaptive ones (Raine, 2018). In turn, studies have found differences between antisocial adults and the general population in the structure or functioning of specific areas of the prefrontal cortex of the brain. These areas are involved in a wide range of advanced cognitive processes, such as decision making, planning, impulse control, regulation of emotions, learning from punishments and rewards, and feeling empathy for others (Ogilvie, Stewart, Chan, & Shum, 2011; Siever, 2008). For example, Adrian Raine and colleagues (2000) observed an 11 percent reduction in the volume of gray matter in the prefrontal cortex of males with antisocial personality disorder compared to males without the disorder. In another study, Raine and colleagues (2011) observed reductions in the volume of the prefrontal cortex of both males and females with symptoms of antisocial personality disorder compared to individuals with no symptoms. In addition, across the sample as a whole, males had less volume in the prefrontal cortex than females, and the differences between males and females in prefrontal cortex volume accounted for the differences in the number of antisocial symptoms they had. Thus, Raine and colleagues suggest that a tendency toward less gray matter in specific areas of the prefrontal cortex in males compared to females helps explain the gender differences in rates of antisocial personality disorder. In addition to decreased volume in the prefrontal cortex, studies have found decreased volume and activity in the amygdala, which processes emotion and threat, and increased volume and activity in the striatum, which is involved in reward processing (Raine, 2018).

These deficits in structure and brain functioning could be tied to the genetic abnormalities that have been seen in people with antisocial personality disorder. They may also be caused by medical illnesses or exposure to toxins during infancy and childhood, both of which are more common among people who develop antisocial and criminal behavior than among those who do not. Whatever their causes, the deficits in executive functions, empathy for others, and learning from punishment might contribute to stimulation seeking, poor impulse control, and difficulty in anticipating the consequences of one's actions.

The risk taking, fearlessness, and difficulty in learning from punishment seen in people with antisocial personality disorder have also been tied to low levels of arousability as measured by a relatively low resting heart rate, low skin conductance activity, or excessive slow-wave electroencephalogram readings (Latvala, Kuja-Halkola, Almqvist, Larsson, & Lichtenstein, 2015; Sylvers, Brubaker, Alden, Brennan, & Lilienfeld, 2008). One interpretation of these data is that low levels of arousal indicate low levels of fear in response to threatening situations (Raine, 2018). Fearlessness can be put to good use—bomb disposal experts and British paratroopers also show low levels of arousal (McMillan & Rachman, 1987; O'Connor, Hallam, & Rachman, 1985). However, fearlessness also may predispose some people to antisocial and violent behaviors that require fearlessness to execute, such as fighting and robbery. In addition, low-arousal individuals may not fear punishment and thus may not be deterred from antisocial behavior by the threat of punishment.

Chronically low arousal also may be an uncomfortable state and may lead to stimulation seeking (Eysenck, 1994). If an individual seeks stimulation through prosocial or neutral acts, such as skydiving, this trait may not lead to antisocial behavior. Some individuals, however, may seek stimulation through antisocial acts that are dangerous or impulsive, such as fighting. The direction stimulation seeking takes—toward antisocial activities or toward more neutral activities—may depend on the reinforcement individuals receive for their behaviors. Those who are rewarded for antisocial behaviors by family and peers may develop antisocial personalities, whereas those who are consistently punished for such behaviors and are given alternative, more neutral options for behavior may not.

Like the other personality disorders, antisocial personality disorder is linked to a history of childhood adversity and maltreatment. A study of a nationally representative sample found that adults diagnosed with antisocial personality disorder had elevated rates of having been battered by a caregiver and of having a parent who had a substance use problem, who went to jail, and/or who attempted suicide (Afifi et al., 2011). They also had over twice the rates of physical, emotional, and sexual abuse as individuals without the disorder.

As in children with conduct disorder, the genetic, neurobiological, and social factors associated with antisocial personality disorder probably interact (see Figure 1 in the section "An Integrative Model") to create a cycle of violence in the lives of people with the disorder. They then perpetuate that violence in their own relationships and families.

Treatments for Antisocial Personality Disorder

People with antisocial personality disorder tend to believe they do not need treatment. They may submit to therapy when forced to because of marital discord, work conflicts, or incarceration, but they are prone to blaming others for their current situation rather than accepting responsibility for their actions. As a result, many clinicians do not hold much hope for effectively treating persons with this disorder through psychotherapy (Kraus & Reynolds, 2001; Millon et al., 2004).

When clinicians do attempt psychotherapy, they tend to focus on helping the person with antisocial personality disorder gain control over his or her anger and impulsive behaviors by recognizing triggers and developing alternative coping strategies (Kraus & Reynolds, 2001). Some clinicians also try to increase the individual's understanding of the effects of his or her behaviors on others (Hare & Hart, 1993).

Lithium and the atypical antipsychotics have been used successfully to control impulsive and aggressive behaviors in people with antisocial personality disorder (Markovitz, 2004; Ripoll, Triebwasser, & Siever, 2011). Antiseizure drugs also have been used to reduce impulsiveness and aggressiveness (Ripoll et al., 2011).

INTERMITTENT EXPLOSIVE DISORDER

Children with conduct disorder and adults with antisocial personality disorder often engage in aggressive acts, which may be impulsive outbursts or premeditated behavior that unfolds over a longer period of time. The diagnosis of **intermittent explosive disorder** is given to individuals age 6 and older who engage in relatively frequent impulsive acts of aggression (see Table 4). The aggression may be verbal or physical (though noninjurious), and must be grossly out of proportion to the situation (e.g., angrily throwing a water bottle at a salesperson who won't give you a discount). The outbursts can't be the kind that are calculated to gain some advantage, such as a baseball player yelling at an umpire who has called a strike on him. Instead, they must be "out of control" as the result of anger, and represent an inability to inhibit the impulse to be aggressive in the immediate context of frustration or a perceived stress that would not typically result in an aggressive outburst. Epidemiological studies suggest that between 3.5 and 7 percent of the population could be diagnosed with intermittent explosive disorder (Coccaro, Fanning, & Lee, 2017; Kessler, Coccaro, et al., 2006). It typically begins in late childhood or adolescence and rarely onsets after age 40. This chronic disorder can lead to legal difficulties and to failed relationships and loss of employment (McCloskey, Noblett, Deffenbacher, Gollan, & Coccaro, 2008).

One theory of intermittent explosive disorder is that the impulsive aggressive behavior is caused by an imbalance in serotonin levels, although only a small amount of research has been conducted (Coccaro, Lee, & Kavoussi, 2010). The disorder runs in families, but it is not known whether this is due to genetic factors or to environmental and parenting factors (Coccaro, 2012).

Cognitive-behavioral treatments for intermittent explosive disorder help individuals identify and avoid triggers for explosive outbursts and appraise situations

TABLE 4 *DSM-5* Criteria for Intermittent Explosive Disorder

A. Recurrent behavioral outbursts representing a failure to control aggressive impulses as manifested by either of the following:

1. Verbal aggression (e.g., temper tantrums, tirades, verbal arguments or fights) or physical aggression toward property, animals, or other individuals, occurring twice weekly, on average, for a period of 3 months. The physical aggression does not result in damage or destruction of property and does not result in physical injury to animals or other individuals.
2. Three behavioral outbursts involving damage or destruction of property and/or physical assault involving physical injury against animals or other individuals occurring within a 13-month period.

B. The magnitude of aggressiveness expressed during the recurrent outbursts is grossly out of proportion to the provocation or to any precipitating psychosocial stressors.

C. The recurrent aggressive outbursts are not premeditated (i.e., are impulsive and/or anger-based) and are not committed to achieve some tangible objective (e.g., money, power, intimidation).

D. The recurrent aggressive outbursts cause either marked distress in the individual or impairment in occupational or interpersonal functioning, or are associated with financial or legal consequences.

E. Chronological age is at least 6 years (or equivalent developmental level).

F. The recurring aggressive outbursts are not better explained by another mental disorder (e.g., major depressive disorder, bipolar disorder, disruptive mood dysregulation disorder, a psychotic disorder, antisocial personality disorder, borderline personality disorder) and are not attributable to another medical condition (e.g., head trauma, Alzheimer's disease) or to the physiological effects of a substance (e.g., a drug of abuse, a medication). For children 6–18 years, aggressive behavior that occurs as part of an adjustment disorder should not be considered for this diagnosis.

Note: This diagnosis can be made in addition to attention-deficit/hyperactivity disorder, conduct disorder, oppositional defiant disorder, or autism spectrum disorder when recurrent impulsive aggressive outbursts are in excess of those usually seen in these disorders and warrant independent clinical attention.

in ways that do not provoke aggression on their part. One study found that both individual and group cognitive-behavioral therapy were more effective than a wait-list control in reducing anger, aggression, hostile thinking, and depressive symptoms while improving anger control in individuals with intermittent explosive disorder (McCloskey et al., 2008). Serotonin and norepinephrine reuptake inhibitors and mood stabilizers (e.g., lithium) have been shown to reduce aggression in individuals with this disorder in small, uncontrolled studies (Myrseth & Pallesen, 2010).

CHAPTER INTEGRATION

We noted earlier that integrative models of the disruptive, impulse-control, and conduct disorders view them as the result of interactions between biological and psychosocial factors. The reciprocal effects of these factors on each other in these disorders are striking (see Figure 2). Parents who are antisocial pass on their genes to their children, and parent them in ways that promote uncontrolled, aggressive, rule-breaking behavior. In addition, families whose members engage in antisocial behavior may experience *downward social drift:* The adults in these families cannot keep good jobs, and the families'

FIGURE 2 Reciprocal Effects Between Biological and Psychosocial Factors in the Disruptive, Impulse-Control, and Conduct Disorders

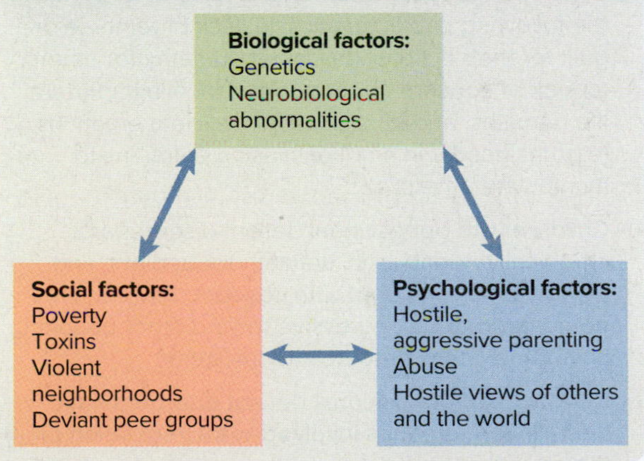

socioeconomic status tends to decline, leading to the children growing up in poor surroundings, where they are exposed to toxins that can damage their developing brains.

These children tend to be irritable and difficult and thus draw hostility from their parents, teachers, and peers. The negative reactions of others feeds these children's own hostile tendencies, convincing them that the world is against them. They join deviant peer groups, whose members reinforce their bad behavior. Their lack of achievement in school, inability to get along with others, and criminal behavior cause them to live in poverty. Then, when they have children of their own, the cycle begins again.

SHADES OF GRAY **DISCUSSION**

The criteria for conduct disorder require three symptoms over a 12-month period, one of which is present in the past 6 months. Jake's current behavior of ambushing other children would likely meet the criteria if it continues—he's initiating fights, being physically cruel, and intimidating others intentionally. Prior to his beginning to ambush other kids, the fights he got into were provoked by teasing, so it's not clear that they would count toward a diagnosis of conduct disorder.

Jake seems to have turned into a bully, repeatedly harassing and victimizing innocent and often helpless others (Olweus, 2011). A study of American students found that 11 percent have been victims of bullying, 13 percent have been bullies, and 6 percent have been both (Tanner, 2001). Adults can be bullies, too, as in Michael Douglas's portrayal of Gordon Gekko in the movie *Wall Street*. Bullying is associated with a broad array of antisocial behaviors in children and adults, including physical fights, school and work attendance problems, cruelty to animals, stealing, and harassment (Vaughn et al., 2010). Bullies are significantly more likely than nonbullies to be diagnosed with conduct disorders as children and to have a history of parental antisocial behavior. As adults, they are more likely to commit crimes and to be diagnosed with antisocial personality disorder and substance use disorders (Ttofi, Farrington, & Lösel, 2012; Vaughn et al., 2010).

CHAPTER SUMMARY

- Conduct disorder is characterized by a persistent pattern of (a) aggression toward people and animals, (b) destruction of property, (c) deceitfulness or theft, and (d) serious violations of rules and social norms.
- Conduct disorder is more common in boys than in girls and is highly stable across childhood and adolescence. Childhood-onset conduct disorder is more persistent than adolescent-onset conduct disorder.
- A diagnosis of conduct disorder with limited prosocial emotions is given to children who meet the full criteria for conduct disorder and have at least two of the following characteristics: (a) lack of remorse or guilt for their actions, (b) lack of empathy for others, (c) lack of concern about performance in important life domains, and (d) shallow or deficient emotions (e.g., insincerity in emotions, using emotions to manipulate others).
- Children with oppositional defiant disorder are chronically negativistic, defiant, disobedient, and hostile. Unlike children with conduct disorder, they do not tend to be aggressive toward other people or animals, to steal, or to destroy property.
- Conduct and oppositional defiant disorders have been linked to genes involved in the regulation of the neurotransmitters dopamine, serotonin, and norepinephrine. The combination of certain genes and a history of maltreatment is especially strongly linked to conduct disorder.
- Children with conduct disorder show a range of neurological deficits in brain systems responsible for controlling behavior and impulses. These deficits may be caused by genetic factors and/or exposure to toxins.
- Abnormal serotonin levels, low physiological arousal, and high testosterone levels may also be linked to conduct disorder.
- Poverty, maltreatment, parenting characterized by harsh discipline with a lack of warmth, and deviant peer groups are social factors associated with conduct disorder.
- Children with conduct disorder tend to process information about social interactions in hostile ways and to see aggression as the only way to respond.
- The treatment for conduct disorder is most often cognitive-behavioral therapy, focusing on changing children's ways of interpreting interpersonal situations and helping them control their angry impulses. Parents are taught methods to control their children's behavior with appropriate punishments and

reinforcements. Antipsychotic drugs, antidepressants, and stimulant drugs also are sometimes used to treat conduct disorder.

- Antisocial personality disorder is characterized by an impairment in the ability to form positive relationships with others, a tendency to engage in behaviors that violate basic rights of others and social norms and values, deceit and manipulativeness, and a focus on doing whatever it takes to gratify one's personal desires.
- Psychopathy is not recognized in *DSM-5* but overlaps with antisocial personality disorder. Psychopathy extends the criteria for antisocial personality disorder beyond persistent violations of others' rights and social norms to include traits like egocentricity, shallow emotions, manipulativeness, and lack of empathy, guilt, and remorse.
- Genetic factors, particularly those that affect serotonin and dopamine systems, may play a role in antisocial personality disorder. As in conduct disorder, the interaction between certain genes and growing up in deprived circumstances is associated with antisocial behavior.
- People with antisocial personalities tend to show deficits in areas of the brain associated with verbal skills, planning, and control of behavior.
- Low levels of arousability may contribute to the risk taking, fearlessness, and difficulty in learning from experience in people with antisocial personality disorder.
- Psychotherapy is not considered to be very effective for people with antisocial personality disorder. Lithium, antipsychotic drugs, and antiseizure drugs may help control their impulsive behaviors.
- Intermittent explosive disorder is characterized by persistent intermittent anger-based outbursts of noninjurious and nondestructive physical or verbal aggression greatly out of proportion to the circumstances (e.g., in response to a minor stress).
- Intermittent explosive disorder may be related to imbalances in serotonin systems or to genetic factors, but little research into its causes has been done.
- Cognitive-behavioral treatments for intermittent explosive disorder help individuals identify and avoid triggers for explosive outbursts and appraise situations in ways that do not provoke aggression on their part. Serotonin and norepinephrine reuptake inhibitors and mood stabilizers (e.g., lithium) have been shown to reduce aggression in individuals with this disorder.

KEY TERMS

conduct disorder
childhood-onset conduct disorder
adolescent-onset conduct disorder
life-course-persistent antisocial behavior
psychopathy
oppositional defiant disorder
antisocial personality disorder (ASPD)
intermittent explosive disorder

Chapter 12

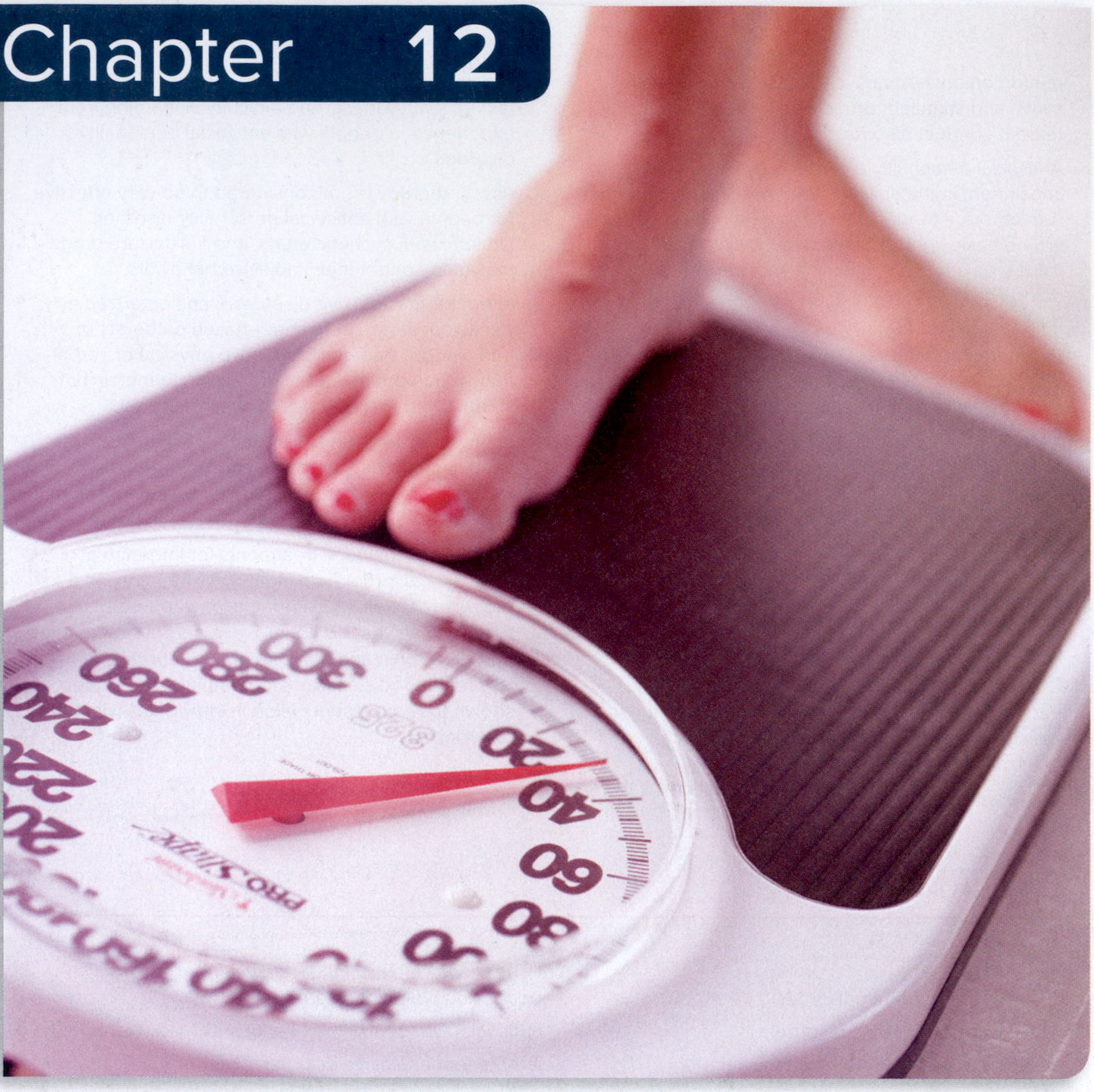

©PhotoDisc/Getty Images

Eating Disorders

CHAPTER OUTLINE

Eating Disorders Along the Continuum

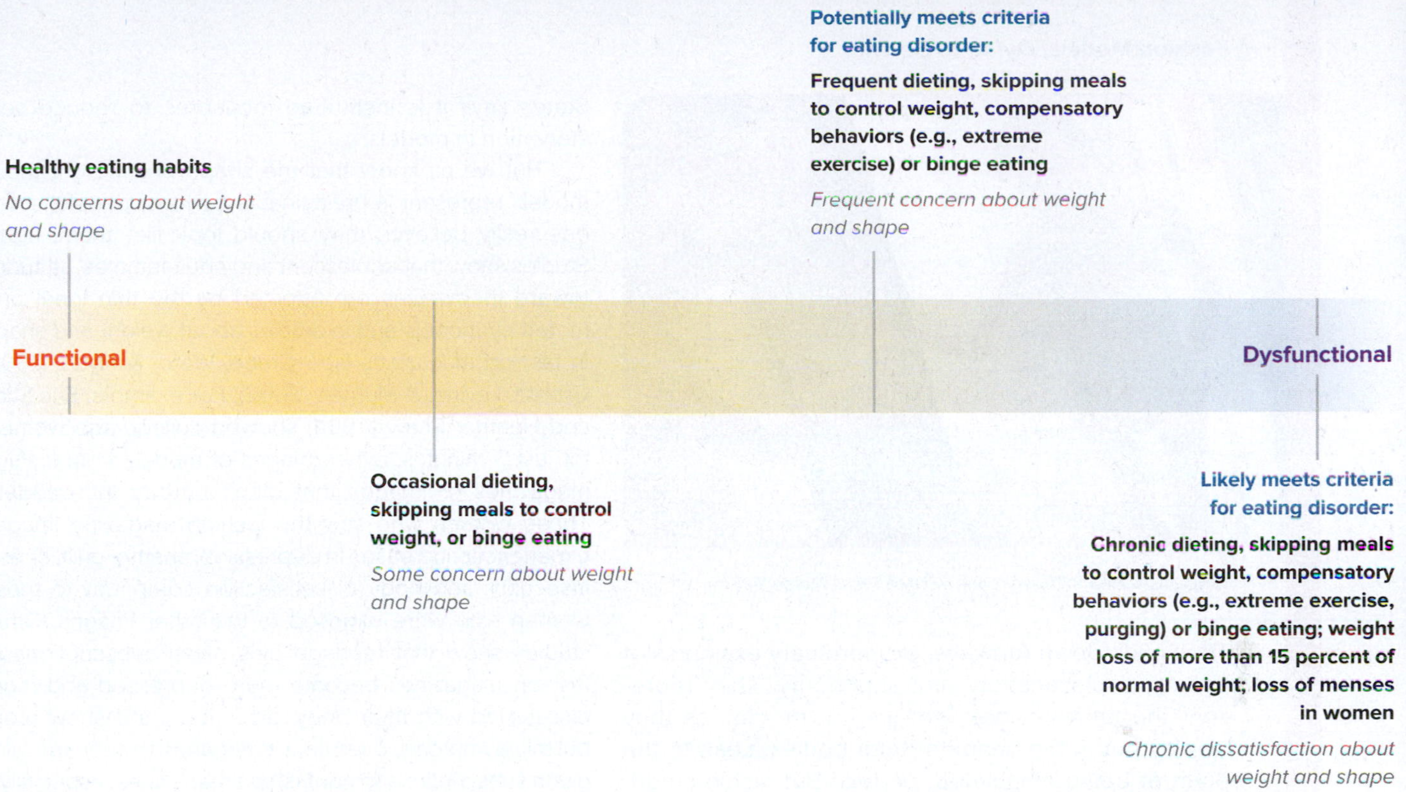

Potentially meets criteria for eating disorder:
Frequent dieting, skipping meals to control weight, compensatory behaviors (e.g., extreme exercise) or binge eating
Frequent concern about weight and shape
Healthy eating habits
No concerns about weight and shape
Functional
Dysfunctional
Occasional dieting, skipping meals to control weight, or binge eating
Some concern about weight and shape
Likely meets criteria for eating disorder:
Chronic dieting, skipping meals to control weight, compensatory behaviors (e.g., extreme exercise, purging) or binge eating; weight loss of more than 15 percent of normal weight; loss of menses in women
Chronic dissatisfaction about weight and shape

A "normative discontent"—that's how researchers 30 years ago labeled the dissatisfaction with weight and shape that is rampant among women, particularly young women, in developed countries (Rodin, Silberstein, & Striegel-Moore, 1984). Sadly, this discontent has only gotten worse in the last 30 years, and it has spread worldwide through mass media (Becker et al., 2011). In the United States, 84 percent of young women want to be thinner than they are (Neighbors & Sobal, 2007). A study in Iceland found that 64 percent of women who were of normal weight felt they needed to lose weight (Matthiasdottir, Jonsson, & Kristjansson, 2012). Although men are less likely to be concerned with their weight, in recent years men have become increasingly concerned with attaining the lean lower body and strong, toned upper body celebrated in pop culture and the media. Nearly half of men and 90 percent of adolescent boys want to be leaner and more muscular than they are (Murray et al., 2017; Neighbors & Sobal, 2007; Tiggemann, Martins, & Kirkbride, 2007).

Dieting is the most common way people try to overcome their body dissatisfaction. Most people diet at least occasionally. A study of college students found that only 33 percent of the women said they "never" diet, compared to 58 percent of college men (Rozin, Bauer, & Catanese, 2003). Other behaviors you might associate with eating disorders are also common, especially among young adults. A study of 2,200 students in six colleges around the United States found that 15 percent of the women surveyed admitted to having engaged in some purging behavior (e.g., self-induced vomiting) and that 28 percent classified themselves as obsessed with their weight (Rozin et al., 2003). Rates for men responding to these questions were 4 percent and 11 percent, respectively.

At the far end of the continuum are people whose concerns about weight become so preoccupying and whose behaviors surrounding eating get so out of control that they have an eating disorder. There are three specific types of eating disorders: anorexia nervosa, bulimia nervosa, and binge-eating disorder. *Anorexia nervosa* is a pursuit of thinness that leads people to starve themselves. *Bulimia nervosa* is a cycle of bingeing followed by extreme behaviors to prevent weight gain, such as self-induced vomiting. *Binge-eating disorder* is applied to people who regularly binge but do not purge what they eat. As you will see in this chapter, while relatively few people meet the full criteria for these eating disorders, many more people have some symptoms, what researchers call *partial-syndrome eating disorders* (Lewinsohn, Striegel-Moore, & Seeley, 2000).

In this chapter, we discuss the diagnosis and epidemiology of eating disorders; the causes of eating disorders, including the psychological and biological factors that may lead some people to develop the disorders; and effective treatments for eating disorders.

Extraordinary People

Fashion Models, *Dying to Be Thin*

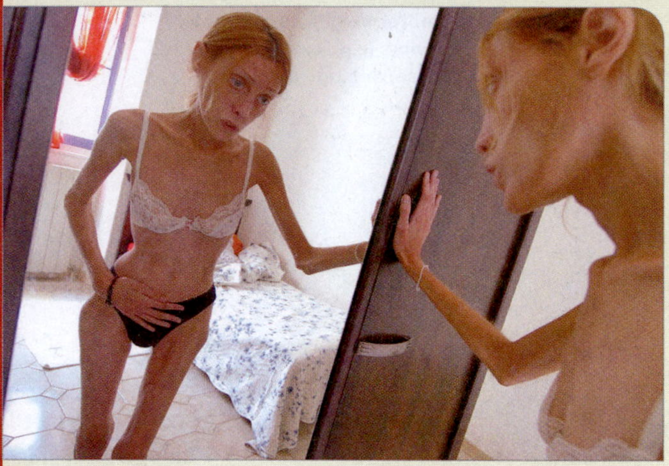

Isabele Caro *©Thierry Lopez/ZUMA Press/Marseille/France*

They glide down runways, extraordinary examples of beauty, sophistication, and superiority. They represent the ultimate look, not just in the clothes they display but in the shape of their bodies. Lean to the point of being emaciated, perfect. But fashion models are literally dying in their attempt to attain and maintain the extreme thinness demanded by the industry. When French model and actress Isabele Caro was photographed in an Italian advertising campaign about the fashion industry's insistence that models be ultrathin, she weighed 60 pounds (she was 5 feet 4 inches tall). She survived on just one chocolate square and a cup of tea per day. She had lost her hair and several teeth. More than once she had lapsed into a coma. But the notoriety that her anorexic photos gained her landed her a spot as a judge on the French version of "America's Next Top Model." A couple of years later she was dead at the age of 28. Before Caro's death, Brazilian model Ana Carolina Reston died at the age of 21, weighing only 88 pounds. Model Luisel Ramos of Uruguay died from heart failure resulting from self-starvation just after stepping off a fashion show runway. In 2010, male model Jeremy Gillitzer died from complications of anorexia nervosa at age 38. When he had spoken to reporters a couple of years earlier, he had weighed only 88 pounds.

The deaths of models from complications of self-starvation have prompted European cities such as Madrid to set minimum weight standards for fashion models. In March 2012 the Israeli government passed a law requiring a minimum weight for any models working in that country. The fashion industry in the United States says it is instituting measures to reduce self-starvation in models.

But we all know that the shape and weight these models represent is unattainable by most people, so no one really believes they should look like them, right? Studies show that adolescent and adult females' attitudes toward themselves *are* affected by the thin ideal promoted by models and in articles about weight and shape in fashion magazines (see Grabe, Ward, & Hyde, 2008; Groesz, Levine, & Murnen, 2002). For example, Eric Stice and Heather Shaw (1994) showed college-age women, for just 3 minutes, either images of models from fashion magazines or images that didn't portray thin models. Those women who saw the fashion magazine images experienced increases in depression, shame, guilt, stress, insecurity, and body dissatisfaction compared to those women who were exposed to the other images. Other studies show that teenage girls given subscriptions to fashion magazines become more depressed and more dissatisfied with their body, diet more, and show more bulimic symptoms over time compared to teenage girls given subscriptions to nonfashion magazines, especially if the girls already expressed dissatisfaction with their body and had little social support (Stice, Spangler, & Agras, 2001). Similar results have been found in studies that expose adolescent or adult males to media depictions of idealized male bodies (Blond, 2008).

Obviously, not everyone who reads fashion magazines or sees fashion models on television becomes obsessed with his or her weight and shape or develops symptoms of an eating disorder. Later in this chapter, we discuss factors that enhance vulnerability to these pressures. But there is good reason to think that the extraordinary standards set by fashion models and media stars do affect how women and men view and treat their own bodies.

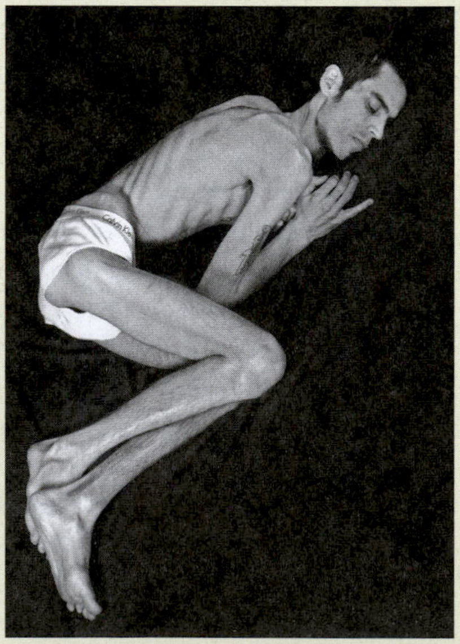

Jeremy Gillitzer *©Nick Vlcek/Barcroft Media Ltd.*

Does the following profile, excerpted from a college student's diary, sound like someone you know?

PROFILES

This morning I had a half of a grapefruit for breakfast, and some coffee—no sugar or cream. For lunch, I had an apple and a diet soda. For dinner, I had some plain white rice and a salad with just some lemon squeezed over it. So I was feeling really good about myself, really virtuous. That is, until Jackie came over, and completely messed up my day. She brought over a movie to watch, which was fine. But then she insisted on ordering a pizza. I told her I didn't want any, that I wasn't hungry (which was a lie, because I was starving). But she ordered it anyway. The pizza arrived, and I thought I could be good and not have any. But it was just sitting there on the table, and I couldn't think of anything except having some. I couldn't concentrate on the movie. I kept smelling the pizza and feeling the emptiness in my stomach. Like a weakling, I reached out and got one piece, a small piece. It was ice cold by then, and kind of greasy, but I didn't care. I ate that piece in about 5 seconds flat. Then I had another piece. And another. I stopped after four pieces. But I still couldn't pay attention to the movie. All I could think about was what a pig I was for eating that pizza, and how I'll never lose 10 pounds so I can fit into size 2 jeans. Jackie's gone now, and I still keep thinking about how ugly and fat I am, and how I have no willpower. I didn't deserve to have that pizza tonight, because I haven't lost enough weight this month. I'm going to have to skip breakfast and lunch tomorrow, and exercise for a couple of hours, to make up for being a complete pig tonight.

Being overweight can have many negative consequences, such as high blood pressure, heart disease, and diabetes, as we discuss later in this chapter. But most people care about their weight because what a person weighs is equated with a person's self-worth in our society. Eating has become more than a source of nourishment, and exercise more than a means of improving health. What people eat and how much they exercise have become linked to feelings of worth, merit, guilt, sin, rebelliousness, and defiance, in turn affecting people's self-esteem.

In this chapter we focus on people whose concern with weight and shape, and whose eating behaviors, are severe enough not only to interfere with their functioning in daily life but also to threaten their lives. As discussed in Eating Disorders Along the Continuum, however, people's attitudes and behaviors toward food and their bodies cover a wide range of problems.

CHARACTERISTICS OF EATING DISORDERS

Although we discuss anorexia nervosa, bulimia nervosa, and binge-eating disorder separately, most individuals who initially meet the criteria for one of these disorders "migrate" between them, meeting the criteria for two or more of the disorders at different times (Hilbert et al., 2014; Keel, Brown, Holland, & Bodell, 2012). Moreover, many individuals show behaviors and concerns characteristic of one or more of the eating disorders without meeting the full criteria for one of these diagnoses. Such individuals may be given the diagnosis *other specified feeding or eating disorder.*

Anorexia Nervosa

People with **anorexia nervosa** starve themselves, subsisting on little or no food for very long periods of time, yet they remain convinced that they need to lose more weight. As a result, their body weight is significantly below what is minimally normal for their age and height (see the *DSM-5* criteria in Table 1). For example, Isabele Caro, described in the Extraordinary People feature, was 5 feet 4 inches tall and weighed only 60 pounds. The extreme weight loss often causes women and girls who have begun menstruating to stop having menstrual periods, a condition known as **amenorrhea,** although some women who meet the other *DSM-5* criteria for anorexia nervosa still report some menstrual activity (Attia & Roberto, 2009). In fact, *DSM-5* eliminated the *DSM-IV* requirement for amenorrhea from its diagnostic criteria.

Despite being emaciated, people with anorexia nervosa have a distorted image of their body, often believing that they are disgustingly fat and need to lose more weight. They struggle with an intense fear of gaining weight or of becoming fat, yet despite low weight they routinely engage in behavior that interferes with any weight gain. They feel good and worthwhile only when they have complete control over their eating and when they are losing weight. Their weight loss causes people with anorexia to be chronically fatigued, yet they drive themselves to exercise excessively and to keep up a grueling schedule at work or school.

People with anorexia nervosa often develop elaborate rituals around food, as writer Marya Hornbacher describes in her autobiography, *Wasted.*

TABLE 1 *DSM-5* Criteria for Anorexia Nervosa

A. Restriction of energy intake relative to requirements, leading to a significantly low body weight in the context of age, sex, developmental trajectory, and physical health. Significantly low weight is defined as a weight that is less than minimally normal or, for children and adolescents, less than that minimally expected.

B. Intense fear of gaining weight or of becoming fat, or of persistent behavior that interferes with weight gain, even though at a significantly low weight.

C. Disturbance in the way in which one's body weight or shape is experienced, undue influence of body weight or shape on self-evaluation, or persistent lack of recognition of the seriousness of the current low body weight.

Specify current subtype:

Restricting type: During the last 3 months, the individual has not engaged in recurrent episodes of binge eating or purging behavior (i.e., self-induced vomiting or the misuse of laxatives, diuretics, or enemas). Weight loss is accomplished primarily through dieting, fasting, and/or excessive exercise.

Binge-Eating/Purging type: During the last 3 months, the individual has engaged in recurrent episodes of binge eating or purging behavior (i.e., self-induced vomiting or the misuse of laxatives, diuretics, or enemas).

PROFILES

I would spread my paper out in front of me, set the yogurt aside, check my watch. I'd read the same sentence over and over, to prove that I could sit in front of food without snarfing it up, to prove it was no big deal. When five minutes had passed, I would start to skim my yogurt. . . . You take the edge of your spoon and run it over the top of the yogurt, being careful to get only the melted part. Then let the yogurt drip off until there's only a sheen of it on the spoon. Lick it—wait, be careful, you have to only lick a teeny bit at a time, the sheen should last at least four or five licks, and you have to lick the back of the spoon first, then turn the spoon over and lick the front, with the tip of your tongue. Then set the yogurt aside again. Read a full page, but don't look at the yogurt to check the melt progression. Repeat. Repeat. Do not take a mouthful, do not eat any of the yogurt unless it's melted. Do not fantasize about toppings, crumbled Oreos, or chocolate sauce. Do not fantasize about a sandwich. A sandwich would be so complicated. (Hornbacher, 1998, pp. 254–255)

Hornbacher describes one of the two types of anorexia nervosa—the restricting type (Table 2). People with the **restricting type of anorexia nervosa** simply refuse to eat and/or engage in excessive exercise as a way of preventing weight gain. Some people attempt to go for days without eating anything; most eat very small amounts of food each day, in part simply to stay alive and in part in response to pressure from others to eat. Hornbacher survived for months on one cup of yogurt and one fat-free muffin per day. Daphne, in the following case study, also has the restricting type of anorexia nervosa, one that includes excessive exercise as part of her weight-loss behavior pattern.

CASE STUDY

Daphne is 5 feet 11 inches tall and weighs 102 pounds. She has felt "large" since her height soared above her schoolmates in the fifth grade. She has been on a diet ever since. During her junior year in high school, Daphne decided that she had to take drastic measures to lose more weight. She began by cutting her calorie intake to about 1,000 calories per day. . . . Each day, Daphne would not let herself eat until she had run at least 10 miles. Then she would have just a few vegetables and a handful of cereal. . . . Daphne dropped to 110 pounds, and she stopped menstruating. Her mother expressed some concern about how little Daphne was eating, but as her mother tended to be overweight, she did not discourage Daphne from dieting.

When it came time to go to college, Daphne was excited but also frightened, because she had always been a star student . . . and wasn't sure she could

TABLE 2 Comparison of Eating Disorders

The eating disorders vary on several characteristics.

Characteristic	Anorexia Nervosa Restricting Type	Anorexia Nervosa Binge/Purge Type	Bulimia Nervosa	Binge-Eating Disorder
Body weight	Significantly underweight	Significantly underweight	Often normal weight or overweight	Often significantly overweight
Body image	Severely disturbed	Severely disturbed	Overconcerned with weight and shape	Often very distressed with overweight
Bingeing	No	Yes	Yes	Yes
Purging or other compensatory behaviors	No	Yes	Yes	No
Sense of lack of control over eating	No	During binges	Yes	Yes

maintain her straight A's in college. In the first examination period in college, Daphne got mostly A's but one B. She felt very vulnerable, like a failure, and as if she were losing control. She also was unhappy with her social life, which, by the middle of the first semester, was going nowhere. Daphne decided that things might be better if she lost more weight, so she cut her food intake to two apples and a handful of cereal each day. She also ran at least 15 miles each day. By the end of fall semester, she was down to 102 pounds. She was also chronically tired, had trouble concentrating, and occasionally fainted. Still, when Daphne looked in the mirror, she saw a fat, homely young woman who needed to lose more weight. (Source: *DSM Casebook: A Learning Companion to the Diagnostic and Statistical Manual of Mental Disorders,* Fifth Edition. American Psychiatric Association, 2013.)

The other type of anorexia is the **binge/purge type of anorexia nervosa,** in which people periodically engage in binge eating or purging behaviors (e.g., self-induced vomiting or the misuse of laxatives or diuretics). This disorder is different from bulimia nervosa in that people with the binge/purge type of anorexia nervosa continue to be substantially below a healthy body weight, whereas people with bulimia nervosa typically are at normal weight or somewhat overweight. Often, a person with the binge/purge type of anorexia nervosa does not engage in binges in which large amounts of food are eaten. If even a small amount of food is eaten, the person feels as if she has binged and will purge this food (Stoving et al., 2012).

As in the *DSM-IV,* individuals with anorexia nervosa are required by Criterion A (see Table 1) to be at a significantly low body weight. *DSM-5,* however, provides guidance regarding how to determine whether an individual is at a significantly low weight and severity specifiers. For example, *DSM-5* suggests using a body mass index (BMI) of 18.5 kg/m^2 as the lower limit of normal body weight, a benchmark employed by the Centers for Disease Control and Prevention (CDC) and the World Health Organization (WHO). The level of severity of anorexia nervosa would be mild if BMI $\geq$ 17 kg/m^2, moderate if BMI = 16–16.99 kg/m^2, severe if BMI = 15–15.99 kg/m^2, and extreme if BMI < 15 kg/m^2. However, the level of severity is not based only on BMI, but can be adjusted based on clinical symptoms, the degree of functional disability, or the need for supervision.

Large, community-based studies in the United States and Europe using *DSM-IV* criteria found that the lifetime prevalence of anorexia nervosa was 0.9 percent in adult women (Hudson, Hiripi, Pope, & Kessler, 2007; Preti et al., 2009) and 0.3 percent in adolescent girls (Swanson, Crow, et al., 2011). The rate among males was 0.3 percent in the U.S. studies (Hudson et al., 2007; Swanson, Crow, et al., 2011), and no men with anorexia nervosa were found in the community samples in the European study (Preti et al., 2009). These rates are based on the *DSM-IV* criteria, which are stricter than the *DSM-5* criteria. In the *DSM-IV*, an individual was required to be at least 15 percent below normal weight and women were required to show amenorrhea to obtain a diagnosis of anorexia nervosa. Newer studies using the *DSM-5* criteria have found higher prevalence rates. One study followed girls for 8 years from adolescence to early adulthood and found that 0.8 percent had diagnosable anorexia nervosa by age 20 (Stice, Marti, & Rohde, 2013). Some estimate lifetime prevalence among adult women to be up to 4 percent (Smink, van Hoeken, & Hoek, 2013).

In the United States, Caucasians are more likely than African Americans and Hispanic Americans to develop the disorder (Perez, Ohrt, & Hoek, 2016; Striegel-Moore & Franko, 2008; Swanson, Crow, et al., 2011). This may be because Caucasians are more likely to accept the thin ideal promoted in the media (Smolak & Striegel-Moore, 2001). Similarly, there is some evidence that cultures that do not value thinness in females have lower rates of anorexia nervosa than those in the United States and Europe (Hoek et al., 2005).

The incidence of anorexia nervosa has increased substantially since the early part of the twentieth century (Gordon, 2017). For example, a study of over 30,000 Swedish twins found significantly higher rates of anorexia nervosa among those born after 1945 than among those born before 1945 (Bulik et al., 2006). The motivations for self-starvation also seem to vary across culture and time. In centuries past, and outside the United States and Europe, the stated motivations for excessive fasting have had less to do with weight concerns than with stomach discomfort or religious considerations (Keel & Klump, 2003). Patients with anorexia nervosa in Asian countries do not have the distorted body image characteristic of anorexia in the United States and Europe and readily admit to being very thin. Nonetheless, they stubbornly refuse to eat, as illustrated by the following case study of one Chinese woman.

CASE STUDY

Miss Y, age 31, was 5 foot 3 inches. She had formerly weighed 110 pounds but now weighed 48 pounds. Her anorexia began 4 years previously, when she was suddenly deserted by her boyfriend. . . . Miss Y started to complain of abdominal discomfort and reduced her food intake. She became socially withdrawn and unemployed. At her psychiatric examination, she wore long hair and was shockingly emaciated—virtually a skeleton. She had sunken eyes, hollow cheeks, and pale, cold skin. She recognized her striking wasting readily but claimed a complete lack of hunger and blamed the weight loss on an unidentifiable abdominal problem. . . . When asked whether she consciously tried to restrict the amount she ate, she said, "No." When questioned why she had gone for periods of 8 or more waking hours without eating anything, she said it was because she had no hunger and felt distended, pointing to the lower left side of her abdomen. . . . Miss Y . . . resisted all attempts to discuss this loss in detail and all other psychological and medical treatments. Miss Y later died of cardiac arrest. Postmortem examination revealed no specific pathology other than multiple organ atrophy due to starvation. (Adapted from Sing, 1995, pp. 27–29)

One question that can be raised is whether self-starvation in the absence of expressed weight concerns can be called anorexia nervosa, given that weight concerns are a defining feature of the disorder in the *DSM-5* (see Table 1, Criterion B). Alternatively, it is possible that the more culturally sanctioned rationale for dietary restriction involving gastrointestinal discomfort was put forth by Miss Y, substituting for the expression of weight concerns. *DSM-5* Criterion B was expanded to include not only overtly expressed fear of weight gain but also persistent behavior that interferes with weight gain; Miss Y clearly shows the latter. While the *DSM-5* itself is a culture-bound document, representing views of mental disorders in "Western" cultures, its text often addresses culture-related diagnostic issues in understanding and describing illness experiences.

Anorexia nervosa usually begins in adolescence or young adulthood (Hudson et al., 2007; Preti et al., 2009; Stice et al., 2013; Swanson, Crow, et al., 2011). The course of the disorder varies greatly from person to person. Long-term studies suggest that the median number of years from onset to remission of the disorder is 7 years for women and 3 years for men, even among patients in treatment (Stoving, Andries, Brixen, Bilenberg, & Horder, 2011). Ten to 15 years after onset of the diagnosis, about 70 percent of patients no longer qualify for a diagnosis, but many continue to have eating-related problems or other psychopathology, particularly depression (Stoving et al., 2011; Wade, Bergin, Tiggemann, Bulik, & Fairburn, 2006). Individuals with the binge/purge type of anorexia nervosa tend to have more comorbid psychopathology than people with the restricting type, particularly impulsive, suicidal, and self-harming behaviors (Peat, Mitchell, Hoek, & Wonderlich, 2009), and a more chronic course of the disorder (Stoving et al., 2012).

Anorexia nervosa is a dangerous disorder, with a death rate of 5 to 9 percent (Arcelus, Mitchell, Wales, & Nielson, 2011; Erdur et al., 2012). Some of the most serious consequences of anorexia are cardiovascular complications, including bradycardia (extreme slowing of heart rate), arrhythmia (irregular heart beat), and heart failure. Another potentially serious complication of anorexia is acute expansion of the stomach, to the point of rupturing. Bone strength is an issue for women who have amenorrhea, presumably because low estrogen levels reduce bone strength. Kidney damage has been seen in some people with anorexia, and impaired immune system functioning may make people with anorexia more vulnerable to medical illnesses. In addition, the suicide rate among people with anorexia nervosa is 31 times the rate in the general population (Preti, Rocchi, Sisti, Camboni, & Miotto, 2011).

Bulimia Nervosa

The core characteristic of **bulimia nervosa** is uncontrolled eating, or **bingeing,** followed by behaviors intended to prevent weight gain from the binges (see the *DSM-5* criteria in Table 3). Mild presentations of bulimia include an average of 1 to 3 episodes of inappropriate compensatory behavior per week, while more extreme forms involve an average of 14 or more episodes per week. The *DSM-5* defines a binge as occurring over a discrete period of time, such as 1 or 2 hours, and involving an amount of food definitely larger than most people would eat during a similar period of time and in similar circumstances. People with eating disorders show tremendous variation in the size of their binges, however. Some people consume 3,000 to 4,000 calories in one sitting, focusing on food high in fat and carbohydrates; in other cases, the binge is between 1,200 and 2,000 calories (Hilbert, Wilfley, Dohm, & Striegel-Moore, 2011; Wolfe, Baker, Smith, & Kelly-Weeder, 2009). What makes these lesser amounts binges is people's sense that they are violating some dietary rule they have set for themselves and that they have no control over their eating but feel compelled to eat even though they are not hungry (Goldschmidt et al., 2016; Wolfe et al., 2009). Recognizing this aspect of binges, the *DSM-5* criteria for a binge include a sense of lack of control over eating (Criterion A2).

The behaviors people with bulimia use to control their weight include self-induced vomiting; the abuse of laxatives, diuretics, or other purging medications; fasting; and excessive exercise. Like people with anorexia nervosa, people with bulimia nervosa have self-evaluations that are heavily influenced by their body shape and weight. When they are thin, they feel like a "good person." However, people with bulimia nervosa, unlike people with anorexia nervosa, do not tend to show gross distortions in their body images. Whereas a woman with anorexia nervosa who is absolutely emaciated looks in the mirror and sees herself as obese, a woman with bulimia nervosa has a more realistic perception of her actual body shape and weight. Still, people with bulimia nervosa are constantly dissatisfied with their shape and weight and concerned about losing weight.

Self-induced vomiting is the behavior people most often associate with bulimia. Bulimia is often discovered by family members, roommates, and friends when people with the disorder are caught vomiting or leave messes after they vomit. Dentists also recognize people with bulimia because frequent vomiting can rot teeth due to exposure to stomach acid. The cycle of bingeing and then purging or using other compensatory behaviors to control weight becomes a way of life.

Other people use excessive exercise or fasting to control their weight. The man in the following profile fasted for a day or longer after a binge to control his weight. As the pressures of his job and a failed marriage increased, his bulimic pattern of bingeing and then fasting grew more serious.

TABLE 3 *DSM-5* Criteria for Bulimia Nervosa

A. Recurrent episodes of binge eating. An episode of binge eating is characterized by both of the following:
   1. Eating, in a discrete period of time (e.g., within any 2-hour period), an amount of food that is definitely larger than most people would eat during a similar period of time under similar circumstances.
   2. A sense of lack of control over eating during the episode (e.g., a feeling that one cannot stop eating or control what or how much one is eating).

B. Recurrent inappropriate compensatory behaviors in order to prevent weight gain, such as self-induced vomiting; misuse of laxatives, diuretics, or other medications; fasting; or excessive exercise.

C. The binge eating and inappropriate compensatory behaviors both occur, on average, at least once per week for 3 months.

D. Self-evaluation is unduly influenced by body shape and weight.

E. The disturbance does not occur exclusively during episodes of anorexia nervosa.

PROFILES

I would sigh with relief when Sunday evening came, since I had no work responsibilities until the next morning, and I would have just returned my son to his mother's custody. I would then carefully shop at convenience stores for "just right" combinations of cheese, lunch meats, snack chips, and sweets such as chocolate bars. I would also make a stop at a neighborhood newsstand to buy escapist paperback novels (an essential part of the binge) and then settle down for a three-hour session of reading and slow eating until I could barely keep my eyes open. My binges took the place of Sunday dinner, averaging approximately 6,000 calories in size. Following the binge, my stomach aching with distension, I would carefully clean my teeth, wash all the dishes, and fall into a drugged slumber. I would typically schedule the following day as a heavy working day with evening meetings in order to distract myself from increasing hunger as I fasted. I began running. . . . I would typically run for one hour, four to five days per week, and walked to work as a further weight control measure. . . . As time went on, I increased the frequency of these binges, probably because of the decreasing structured demands for my time. . . . I was physically exhausted most of the time, and my hands, feet, and abdomen were frequently puffy and edematous, which I, of course, interpreted as gain in body fat and which contributed to my obsession with weight and food. I weighed myself several times per day in various locations, attending to half pound variations as though my life depended on them. (Source: Wilps, 1990)

Based on *DSM-IV* criteria, the lifetime prevalence of bulimia nervosa is estimated to be 0.5 percent in adults (Hudson et al., 2007) and 0.9 percent in adolescents (Swanson, Crow, et al., 2011). It is much more common in females than in males (Swanson, Crow, et al., 2011). As with anorexia nervosa, the criteria for the diagnosis of bulimia nervosa were loosened somewhat in the *DSM-5* (by reducing the minimum average number of times per week binge/purge behaviors must occur from two to one). Partly due to this change, studies using *DSM-5* criteria find higher lifetime prevalence of up to 2.6 percent among women (Smink et al., 2013; Stice et al., 2013). Men with bulimia nervosa are more likely than women with the disorder to exercise excessively to control their weight and to be focused on developing a lean, muscular look rather than on being excessively thin (Murray et al., 2017).

Men with bulimia nervosa are more likely than women with bulimia nervosa to use excessive exercising to control their weight. *©Pierre Charriau/AGE Fotostock*

There is clear evidence of cultural, racial/ethnic, and historical differences in the prevalence of bulimia nervosa. In the United States, it is more common in Caucasians and Hispanic Americans than in African Americans (Perez et al., 2016; Striegel-Moore & Franko, 2008; Swanson, Crow, et al., 2011), and a meta-analysis found that bulimia nervosa is considerably more common in Westernized cultures than in non-Westernized cultures (Keel & Klump, 2003). In addition, the prevalence of bulimia nervosa increased significantly in the second half of the twentieth century. Some studies indicate that rates in the United States, Europe, and Australia reached a peak in the 1990s, remaining stable or decreasing somewhat in the 2000s (Crowther, Armey, Luce, Dalton, & Leahey, 2008; Keel, Heatherton, Dorer, Joiner, & Zalta, 2006; Smink et al., 2016).

The onset of bulimia nervosa most often occurs in adolescence (Hudson et al., 2007; Swanson, Crow, et al., 2011). Although the death rate among people with bulimia is not as high as among people with anorexia, bulimia also has serious medical complications and a death rate nearly double that in the general population (Arcelus et al., 2011). One of the most serious complications is an electrolyte imbalance, which results from fluid loss following excessive and chronic vomiting, laxative abuse, and diuretic abuse. Imbalances in electrolytes can lead to heart failure. The suicide rate among people with bulimia nervosa is 7.5 times higher than in the general population (Preti et al., 2011).

Bulimia nervosa tends to be a chronic condition. A long-term study of people seeking treatment found that 15 years after the disorder about 50 percent showed remission of their symptoms but the other 50 percent still had symptoms qualifying for a diagnosis (Stoving et al., 2011). The frequent use of purging is a predictor of a poorer outcome (Stoving et al., 2012).

TABLE 4 *DSM-5* Criteria for Binge-Eating Disorder

A. Recurrent episodes of binge eating. An episode of binge eating is characterized by both of the following:
   1. Eating, in a discrete period of time (e.g., within any 2-hour period), an amount of food that is definitely larger than most people would eat in a similar period of time under similar circumstances.
   2. A sense of lack of control over eating during the episode (e.g., a feeling that one cannot stop eating or control what or how much one is eating).

B. The binge-eating episodes are associated with three (or more) of the following:
   1. Eating much more rapidly than normal.
   2. Eating until feeling uncomfortably full.
   3. Eating large amounts of food when not feeling physically hungry.
   4. Eating alone because of feeling embarrassed by how much one is eating.
   5. Feeling disgusted with oneself, depressed, or very guilty afterward.

C. Marked distress regarding binge eating is present.

D. The binge eating occurs, on average, at least once a week for 3 months.

E. The binge eating is not associated with the recurrent use of inappropriate compensatory behavior and does not occur exclusively during the course of bulimia nervosa or anorexia nervosa.

Binge-Eating Disorder

Binge-eating disorder was included in *DSM-IV* as a proposed condition in need of further study. As a result of extensive research supporting its clinical usefulness and validity over the past 20 years, it is included in *DSM-5* as a mental disorder. **Binge-eating disorder** resembles bulimia nervosa, except that a person with binge-eating disorder does not regularly engage in purging, fasting, or excessive exercise to compensate for binges (Table 4). People with binge-eating disorder may eat continuously throughout the day, with no planned mealtimes (Masheb, Grilo, & White, 2011). Others engage in discrete binges of large amounts of food, often in response to stress and to feelings of anxiety or depression (Munsch, Meyer, Quartier, & Wilhelm, 2012; Wonderlich, Gordon, Mitchell, Crosby, & Engel, 2009). They may eat very rapidly and appear almost in a daze as they eat, as the man in the following case study describes.

CASE STUDY

"The day after New Year's Day I got my check cashed. I usually eat to celebrate the occasion, so I knew it might happen. On the way to the bank I steeled myself against it. I kept reminding myself of the treatment and about my New Year's resolution about dieting. . . .

"Then I got the check cashed. And I kept out a hundred. And everything just seemed to go blank. I don't know what it was. All of my good intentions just seemed to fade away. They just didn't seem to mean anything anymore. I just said, 'What the hell,' and started eating, and what I did then was an absolute sin."

He described starting in a grocery store where he bought a cake, several pieces of pie, and boxes of cookies. Then he drove through heavy midtown traffic with one hand, pulling food out of the bag with the other hand and eating as fast as he could. After consuming all of his groceries, he set out on a furtive round of restaurants, staying only a short time in each and eating only small amounts. Although in constant dread of discovery, he had no idea what "sin" he felt he was committing. He knew only that it was not pleasurable. "I didn't enjoy it at all. It just happened. It's like a part of me just blacked out. And when that happened there was nothing there except the food and me, all alone." Finally he went into a delicatessen, bought another $20 worth of food and drove home, eating all the way, "until my gut ached." (Stunkard, A. J., 2003)

People with binge-eating disorder often are significantly overweight and say they are disgusted with their body and ashamed of their bingeing (Stunkard, 2011; Wonderlich et al., 2009). They typically have a history of frequent dieting, membership in weight-control programs, and family obesity (Fairburn et al., 1997). In fact, as many as 30 percent of people currently in weight-loss programs may have binge-eating disorder (Stunkard, 2011). In the United States the rate in the general population is 2 to 3.5 percent (Hudson et al., 2007; Smink et al., 2013); in other countries the rates are somewhat lower (Kessler et al., 2013).

Binge-eating disorder is somewhat more common in women than in men, both in the general community and among people in weight-loss programs, although the gender difference is not significant in some studies (Hudson et al., 2007; see Ágh et al., 2015). In the United States, there do not appear to be racial or ethnic differences in rates of binge-eating disorder (Perez et al., 2016; Striegel-Moore & Franko, 2008). People with this disorder also have high rates of depression and anxiety and possibly a higher incidence of alcohol abuse and personality disorders (Striegel-Moore & Franko, 2008). Binge-eating disorder tends to be chronic; one retrospective study found the mean duration of the disorder to be 8 years (Hudson et al., 2007), and another study found a mean duration of 14.4 years (Pope et al., 2006).

Other Specified Feeding or Eating Disorder

As noted in Eating Disorders Along the Continuum, subclinical symptoms of eating disorders are quite common, particularly among adolescent and young adult women. Researchers in Oregon followed a large group of adolescents for several years, examining the ebb and flow of what they called *partial-syndrome eating disorders*—syndromes that don't meet the full criteria for anorexia nervosa or bulimia nervosa (Lewinsohn et al., 2000; Striegel-Moore, Seeley, & Lewinsohn, 2003). Adolescents with partial-syndrome eating disorders may binge a couple of times a month but not every week. They may be underweight but not severely so. They tend to be highly concerned with their weight and judge themselves on the basis of their weight, but their symptoms don't add up to a full-blown eating disorder.

The researchers found that adolescents with partial-syndrome eating disorders, the vast majority of whom were girls, were just as likely as those with full-blown eating disorders to have several psychological problems, both in adolescence and in their 20s. These problems included anxiety disorders, substance abuse, depression, and attempted suicide. Almost 90 percent had a diagnosable psychiatric disorder when they were in their early 20s. Those diagnosed with partial-syndrome eating disorders also had lower self-esteem, poorer social relationships, poorer physical health, and lower levels of life satisfaction than those with no signs of an eating disorder. They were less likely to have earned a bachelor's degree and more likely to be unemployed.

The *DSM-5* created a new diagnostic category called **other specified feeding or eating disorder** to capture presentations of an eating disorder that cause clinically significant distress or impairment but do not meet the full diagnostic criteria for any of the eating disorders previously discussed. The partial-syndrome eating disorders would fit into this new category. *DSM-IV* included a similar category called eating disorders not otherwise specified (EDNOS). In fact, about 5 percent of the general population experiences EDNOS as defined in *DSM-IV* (Fairburn et al., 2007; Wade et al., 2006). Not only was *DSM-IV* EDNOS more prevalent than either anorexia nervosa or bulimia nervosa, it also tended to be as severe and persistent (Fairburn et al., 2007), raising questions about the validity of the diagnostic classifications. This issue was addressed in *DSM-5* through the addition of other specified feeding or eating disorder, the broadening of the criteria for anorexia nervosa and bulimia nervosa, and the addition of binge-eating disorder. Rates of EDNOS are now significantly lower (Smink et al., 2013).

The *DSM-5* other specified feeding or eating disorder category includes disorders like **atypical anorexia nervosa** wherein all the criteria for anorexia nervosa are met, except that despite significant weight loss, the individual's weight is within or above the normal range. Another example is *bulimia nervosa of low frequency and/or limited duration,* which involves meeting all of the criteria for bulimia nervosa, except that the binge eating and inappropriate compensatory behaviors occur, on average, less than once a week and/or for less than 3 months. One last example is **night eating disorder,** a new disorder introduced in *DSM-5*. People with this disorder regularly eat excessive amounts of food after dinner and into the night (Allison, 2017). The eating behavior is not part of cultural or social norms—this is not the typical ordering of pizza with friends after a party or the occasional bout of the late-night munchies. People with night eating disorder feel an overwhelming desire to eat at night most nights of the week and are highly distressed that they cannot control their eating behavior. They experience frequent insomnia and may believe they need to eat in order to fall asleep. They typically are not hungry in the morning and skip breakfast. Night eating disorder most often begins in early adulthood and tends to be long-lasting. People with this disorder often are overweight and suffer from depression. Night eating disorder differs from *sleep-eating*, which can occur in some sleep disorders (see the chapter "Health Psychology"), in that people with night eating disorder are awake and aware when they are eating while people who sleep-eat are not.

Obesity

Although obesity is not included in *DSM-5* as a mental disorder, it is common among people with binge-eating disorder and is one of the greatest public health concerns internationally (Brownell & Walsh, 2017; Gearhardt et al., 2012). It is included here because obesity is highly associated with numerous mental disorders, is a risk factor for the development of some mental disorders (e.g., depressive disorders), and is the result of psychotropic medication side effects (e.g., atypical antipsychotics; see the chapter "Schizophrenia Spectrum and Other Psychotic Disorders").

Obesity (excess body fat) is defined as a body mass index (BMI) of 30 or over. BMI is based on kg/m^2; using the Imperial system of measurement, it is calculated as your weight in pounds multiplied by 703, then divided by the square of your height in inches (CDC, 2018b). Between 1980 and 2002, the prevalence of obesity in the United States doubled in adults and tripled in children and adolescents (Flegal, Carroll, Ogden, & Johnson, 2002; Hedley et al., 2004; Ogden, Flegal, Carroll, & Johnson, 2002). Rates have continued to climb, and currently it is estimated that nearly 40 percent of American adults and 19 percent of American children are obese (CDC, 2018b; Ogden, Carroll, Kit, & Flegel, 2012). African Americans and Hispanic Americans have the highest obesity rate, followed by non-Hispanic whites and Asian Americans (CDC, 2018b; Figure 1). Rates of obesity also are climbing around the world, particularly in countries where the standard of living and access to American fast foods are increasing (Novak & Brownell, 2011; WHO, 2018c).

Obesity is associated with an increased risk of coronary heart disease, hypertension and stroke, type 2 diabetes, and some kinds of cancer (Novak & Brownell, 2011). In the United States, 5 to 7 percent of all health care costs are due to the effects of obesity. People with obesity suffer not only more physical illnesses but also a lower quality of life and more emotional problems, due in part to the stigmatization of obese people (Gearhardt et al., 2012; Pearl, 2018). For example, experimental studies have shown that employers are less likely to hire or promote individuals described in vignettes as overweight than they are to hire or promote individuals with identical credentials not described as overweight (Roehling, Pichler, & Bruce, 2013). Children and adolescents who are obese report frequent teasing and bullying and report that they skip school as a result (Van Geel, Vedder, & Tanilon, 2014). Although many laypeople think such stigmatization could serve as motivation for obese people to lose weight, experimental studies show that exposure to stigmatizing media portrayals leads obese people to eat more rather than less (Pearl, 2018; Pearl, Puhl, & Brownell, 2012).

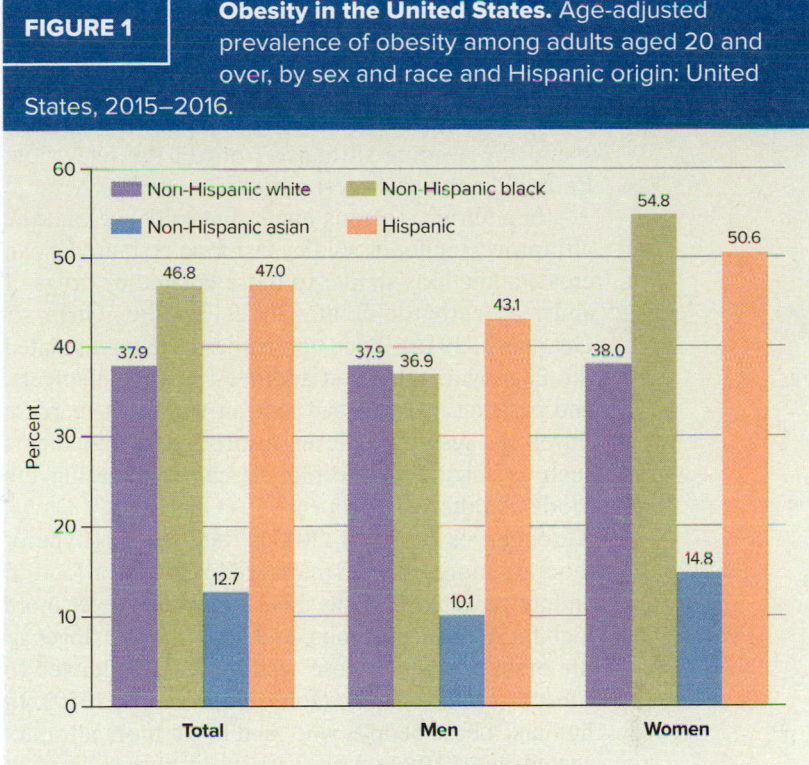

FIGURE 1 **Obesity in the United States.** Age-adjusted prevalence of obesity among adults aged 20 and over, by sex and race and Hispanic origin: United States, 2015–2016.

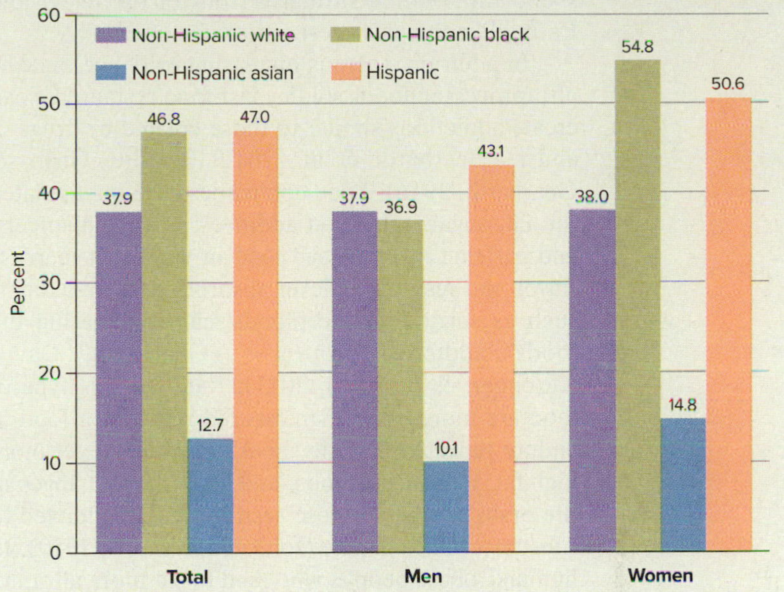

Source: https://www.cdc.gov/nchs/products/databriefs/db288.htm

The dramatic historical increases in obesity point to environmental causes. Researcher Kelly Brownell argues that we live in a toxic environment of high-fat, high-calorie, inexpensive food and advertisers who promote the consumption of large quantities of this food (Brownell & Horgen, 2004; Brownell & Walsh, 2017; Gearhardt et al., 2012). Added to this "Super-Size Me" culture is a significant reduction over the past several decades in the amount of physical activity people engage in. More than 60 percent of Americans do not get 30 minutes of physical exercise per day, and 25 percent get no exercise at all (Godfrey & Brownell, 2008). In the United States, only 2 percent of high schools, 8 percent of middle schools, and 4 percent of elementary schools require daily physical education (Story, Nanney, & Schwartz, 2009). A typical day for many Americans involves driving to work or school, passing through the drive-through at a fast-food restaurant to get a fat- and cholesterol-laden breakfast sandwich, sitting at work or school all day, getting up only to go to another fast-food restaurant for a lunch that may have thousands of calories, and then driving home to spend the evening sitting in front of the television. Eating like this is a prescription for obesity.

In addition, there is increasing evidence that the ultraprocessed foods sold by fast-food restaurants can create addictions similar to those created by drugs of abuse (Gearhardt et al., 2012; Schulte, Grilo, & Gearhardt, 2016). Food companies have manipulated the fat, sugar, salt, food additives, flavor enhancers, and caffeine in processed food in ways that increase flavor and result in quicker absorption of ingredients such as sugar into the bloodstream, increasing the foods' addictive properties (Gearhardt, Davis, Kuschner, & Brownell, 2011). Rats fed this type of food are more likely than rats fed regular rat food to endure repeated electric shocks in order to get more high-fat, high-sugar foods, and they show changes in the brain similar to those seen in people addicted to substances like cocaine (Johnson & Kenny, 2010). In humans, obese people, who tend to eat more ultraprocessed foods, show more activity in reward areas of the brain associated with drug abuse when exposed to photos of such foods than do lean people (Rothemund et al., 2007; Stoeckel et al., 2008). Obese people show less activity in certain reward areas of the brain than do lean people when they actually consume such food, however, suggesting that changes in the brain similar to those seen in drug addicts occur after chronic exposure to ultraprocessed foods (Stice, Spoor, Bohon, Veldhuizen, & Small, 2008; Stice, Spoor, Ng, & Zald, 2009). Finally, people who show behavioral signs of food addiction, such as craving, tolerance, and withdrawal from high-fat, high-sugar ultraprocessed foods, have brain activity in response to viewing food photos and consuming processed foods similar to that of obese people (and drug addicts) (Gearhardt, Yokum, et al., 2011; Schulte et al., 2016). Cravings may be especially cued by food stimuli in the environment (Joyner, Kim, & Gearhardt, 2017). Thus, the environments and ultraprocessed foods that are the staple of American and, increasingly, international diets may be causing addictions to these foods that make them hard to resist.

Other evidence that a toxic food environment contributes to obesity comes from studies of immigrants. One study compared Pima Indian women who migrated to Arizona to their female relatives who remained in Mexico. The women in Arizona had an average dietary fat intake of 41 percent of all calories, an average body weight of 198 pounds, and an average BMI of 37. In comparison, the women in Mexico had an average dietary fat intake of only 23 percent of all calories, an average body weight of 154 pounds, and an average BMI of 25 (Ravussin, Valencia, Esparza, Bennett, & Schulz, 1994).

Not everyone living in a toxic food environment becomes overweight or obese. Genes appear to account for a substantial percentage of the variability in obesity (Albuquerque, Stice, Rodríguez-López, Manco, & Nóbrega, 2015). Genes affect the number of fat cells and the likelihood of fat storage, the tendency to overeat, and the activity level in the brain in response to food. These genetic factors interact with the toxic environment to contribute to obesity. For example, Eric Stice and colleagues (Stice, Spoor, et al., 2008; Stice, Yokum, Bohon, Marti, Smolen, 2010) found that individuals who showed atypical activity in reward areas of the brain in response to tasty food were at risk for future weight gain only if they had a certain variant of a gene associated with reward processing.

Millions of people try to lose weight on their own, with the aid of self-help books; millions of others participate in commercial weight-loss programs such as Weight Watchers. Evaluations of popular weight-loss programs suggest that they can result in modest weight loss (Gearhardt et al., 2012). For example, Christopher Gardner and colleagues (2007) randomly assigned women with a BMI of 27 to 40 to follow the Atkins (carbohydrate-restricted), the Ornish (fat-restricted), the Zone (macronutrients balance), or the LEARN (exercise and changes in eating patterns) program. At the end of 1 year, the women on the Atkins program had lost an average of about 10 pounds, significantly more weight loss than that of women on the Zone program (3.5 pounds) but not significantly different from that of women on the Ornish program (4.8 pounds) or the LEARN program (5.7 pounds). Another study that included both men and women found that the Atkins, Ornish, Zone, and Weight Watchers programs all resulted in similar weight loss (Dansinger, Gleason, Griffith, Selker, & Schaefer, 2005). Weight Watchers led to an average loss of 4 to 7 pounds, but only 50 to 65 percent of people stuck to the diet for 1 year. Even for those who do stick to these programs, the modest weight loss is discouraging, especially given the advertisements suggesting that these programs can result in much greater weight loss for obese people. Yet even a modest weight loss of 5 to 10 percent of body weight can result in significant health improvements for obese people.

Weight-loss drugs, such as orlistat (Xenical), lorcaserin (Belviq), liraglutide (Saxenda), and phentermine/topirimate (Qysmia) can suppress appetite and can help people lose weight. Randomized controlled trials have shown that these drugs can lead to weight loss of 3 to 9 percent over a year (Yanovski &

TV weatherman Al Roker underwent bariatric surgery to lose weight. *Left:* ©*Nick Elgar/Hulton Archive/Getty Images; Right:* ©*Jason LaVeris/FilmMagic/Getty Images.*

Yanovski, 2014). However, all these medications have side effects, including gastrointestinal upset (orlistat), nausea and increased heart rate (liraglutide), and risk of birth defects among pregnant women (phentermine/topirimate). Lifestyle changes are currently recommended first.

For obese people with a BMI between 30 and 39, low-calorie diets (900 to 1,200 calories per day), often using prepackaged, portion-controlled servings (such as meal replacement shakes), are recommended (Wadden, Neiberg, et al., 2011). Individuals also are encouraged to increase their level of physical activity. Such a program results in significantly more weight loss than when individuals consume a self-selected diet of conventional food (Berkowitz et al., 2011). For extremely obese people with a BMI of 40 or over who have at least one severe health problem (e.g., diabetes), bariatric surgery is an option. A small pouch is created at the base of the esophagus, severely limiting food intake, and the stomach may be stapled, banded, or bypassed. Such surgery can result in a substantial weight loss, on average 60 percent of excess weight (Chang et al., 2014). One person who underwent bariatric surgery is TV weatherman Al Roker.

It is difficult for overweight and obese people to lose weight, and even more difficult to keep it off. To combat the discouragement many people feel about losing weight, researchers are encouraging obese people to adopt reasonably modest goals for weight loss and to focus on increasing their physical activity, both of which can lead to substantial improvements in cardiac functioning and diabetes risk (Wadden, Wilson, Stunkard, & Berkowitz, 2011). In general, the proven methods for preventing weight gain and reducing weight are these:

- Eat more nutrient-dense foods and fewer foods with empty calories.
- Aim for a minimum of 30 minutes of physical activity daily.
- Structure your environment so that healthy choices are easier to make; for example, keep low-fat foods readily available in your house and purge your cabinets of junk food.
- Be more active throughout the day: Use the stairs rather than the elevator, park in the farthest spot from the building rather than the closest, and seek other opportunities that encourage movement over standing or sitting (Godfrey & Brownell, 2008).

UNDERSTANDING EATING DISORDERS

A number of biological, sociocultural, and psychological factors have been implicated in the development of the eating disorders. As we have discussed, people frequently "migrate" between the eating disorder

SHADES OF GRAY

Read the following case study.

At the insistence of her parents, Rachel, a 19-year-old freshman at a competitive liberal arts college, received a psychiatric evaluation during spring break. According to her parents, Rachel had lost 16 pounds since her precollege physical the previous August. She now weighed 104 pounds at a height of 5 feet 5 inches, when a healthy weight for a small-framed woman her height is about 120 pounds. Rachel explained that she had been a successful student and field hockey player in high school. After deciding not to play field hockey in college, she began running several mornings each week during the summer and "cut out junk food" to protect herself from gaining "that freshman 15." Rachel lost a few pounds that summer and received compliments from friends and family for looking so "fit." She reported feeling more confident and ready for college than she had expected. Once she began school, Rachel increased her running to daily, often skipped breakfast in order to get to class on time, and selected from the salad bar for her lunch and dinner. She worked hard in school and made the dean's list the first semester.

When Rachel returned home for Christmas vacation, her family noticed that she looked thin and tired. Despite encouragement to catch up on rest, she awoke early each morning to run. She returned to school in January and thought she might be developing depression. Courses seemed less interesting, and she wondered whether the college she attended was right for her after all. She was sleeping less well and felt cold much of the day. The night Rachel returned home for spring break, her parents asked her to step on the bathroom scale. Rachel was surprised to learn that her weight had fallen to 104 pounds, and she agreed to a visit to her pediatrician, who found no evidence of a medical illness and recommended a psychiatric consultation. (Source: Adapted from Attia & Walsh, 2007, p. 164.)

Does Rachel have an eating disorder? What criteria does she meet? Are there any criteria that she doesn't meet? (Discussion appears at the end of this chapter.)

diagnoses and symptoms, so as you might expect, some of the risk factors are shared among the disorders (Hilbert et al., 2014). As we discuss at the end of this chapter, it is likely that it takes an accumulation of several of these factors for any individual to develop an eating disorder. In this section, however, we consider each factor separately.

Biological Factors

Like most psychological disorders, anorexia nervosa, bulimia nervosa, and binge-eating disorder tend to run in families (Trace, Baker, Peñas-Lledó, & Bulik, 2013). A study of more than 30,000 twins found a heritability of 56 percent for anorexia nervosa (Bulik et al., 2006). A twin study of binge-eating disorder found a heritability of 41 percent (Bulik, Sullivan, & Kendler, 2003). Genes appear to carry a general risk for eating disorders rather than a specific risk for one type of eating disorder (Bulik et al., 2010; Culbert, Racine, & Klump, 2015). A genetic risk for developing eating disorders appears to interact with the biological changes of puberty to contribute to the onset of eating disorders in girls, but not in boys (Klump et al., 2012). That is, in girls changes in hormones at puberty may activate a genetic risk for the eating disorders. The biological changes of puberty are accompanied by changes in girls' social worlds that likely contribute to their risk for eating disorders, as we discuss below.

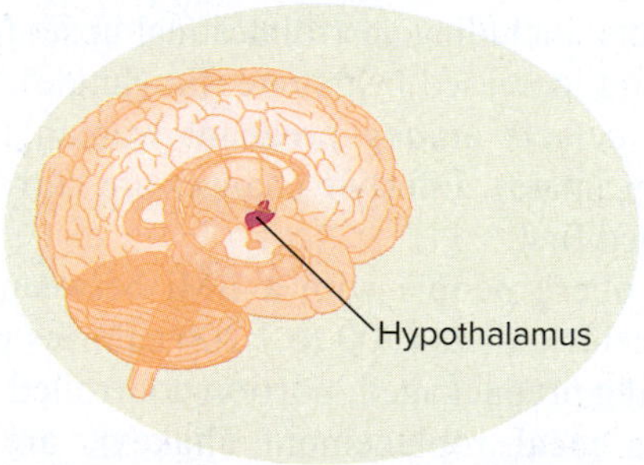

The hypothalamus plays a central role in regulating eating and is implicated in the disordered eating behaviors characteristic of bulimia nervosa and anorexia nervosa.

Much of the current research on the biological causes of the eating disorders focuses on those bodily systems that regulate appetite, hunger, satiety, initiation of eating, and cessation of eating (Stice & Shaw, 2017; Trace et al., 2013). The hypothalamus plays a central role in regulating eating (Berthoud & Morrison, 2008). It receives messages about the body's recent food consumption and nutrient level and sends messages to cease eating when the body's nutritional needs are met. These messages are carried by a variety of neurotransmitters, including norepinephrine, serotonin, and dopamine, and by a number of hormones, including cortisol and insulin. Disordered eating behavior might be caused by imbalances in or dysregulation of any of the neurochemicals involved in this system or by structural or functional problems in the hypothalamus (Culbert et al., 2015). For example, disruptions of this system could cause the individual to have trouble detecting hunger accurately or to stop eating when full, both of which are characteristics of people with eating disorders.

People with anorexia nervosa show lowered functioning of the hypothalamus and abnormalities in the levels of several hormones important to its functioning, including serotonin and dopamine (Culbert et al., 2015; Stice & Shaw, 2017). Whether these disruptions are causes or consequences of the self-starvation of anorexia is unclear. Some studies have found that people with anorexia continue to show abnormalities in hypothalamic and hormonal functioning and neurotransmitter levels after they gain some weight, whereas other studies have found that these abnormalities disappear with weight gain (Polivy & Herman, 2002).

Many people with bulimia show abnormalities in the systems regulating the neurotransmitter serotonin (Culbert et al., 2015; Keel et al., 2012). Deficiencies in serotonin might lead the body to crave carbohydrates, and people with bulimia often binge on high-carbohydrate foods. These people may then engage in self-induced vomiting or some other type of purge in order to avoid gaining weight from carbohydrates.

Thus, a number of biological abnormalities have been found to be associated with anorexia nervosa and bulimia nervosa. These abnormalities could contribute to disordered eating behavior by causing the body to crave certain foods or by making it difficult for a person to read the body's signals regarding hunger and fullness. Exactly why people with eating disorders also develop a distorted body image and the other cognitive and emotional problems seen in the eating disorders is not clear.

Sociocultural and Psychological Factors

Societal pressures to be thin and attractive probably play a role in the eating disorders, although, as noted earlier, many people who are exposed to these pressures do not develop an eating disorder. Certain psychological factors may also need to come into play for an eating disorder to develop.

Social Pressures and Cultural Norms

Psychologists have linked the historical and cross-cultural differences in the prevalence of the eating disorders to differences in the standards of beauty for women at different historical times and in different cultures (Garner & Garfinkel, 1980; Keel & Klump, 2003; McCarthy, 1990; Sobal & Stunkard, 1989). In addition, certain groups within a culture, such as athletes, may have standards for appearance that put them at greater risk for developing an eating disorder.

The Thin Ideal and Body Dissatisfaction The ideal shape for women in many developed nations has become thinner and thinner since the mid-twentieth century (Keel & Klump, 2003). Models in fashion magazines, winners of the Miss America and Miss Universe pageants, and Barbie dolls—icons of beauty for women—all have been getting thinner for years, something that is only recently beginning to change. Also, as discussed in the Extraordinary People feature, the average model in a fashion magazine these days is pencil-thin, with a figure that is physically unattainable by most adult women. Several studies show that women who internalize the thin ideal promoted in the media are at risk for eating disorders (see Hausenblas et al., 2013; Keel & Forney, 2013; Stice, 2002).

Both anorexia nervosa and bulimia nervosa are much more common in females than in males, perhaps because thinness is more valued and more strongly encouraged in females than in males. For example, studies of popular women's and men's magazines find 10 times more diet articles in women's magazines than in men's magazines (Andersen & DiDomenico, 1992; Grieve & Bonneau-Kaya, 2007). As discussed in the Extraordinary People feature, the more exposure young females have to media pressure to be thin, the more dissatisfied they become with their bodies (Grabe et al., 2008; Groesz et al., 2002; Hausenblas et al., 2013). Body dissatisfaction fed by pressures to be thin is one of the strongest predictors of risk for the development of eating disorders in young women. In one longitudinal study of high school girls, 24 percent of those with the greatest body dissatisfaction developed a diagnosable eating disorder, compared to 6 percent of those with less body dissatisfaction (Stice, Marti, & Durant, 2011). Media portrayals of male beauty emphasize muscularity over thinness, and have done so increasingly in recent years. Coinciding with this increase, boys' and men's body dissatisfaction and disordered eating has increased (Murray et al. 2017).

People can avoid some pressures to conform to the ideal of thinness by avoiding fashion magazines and other media depictions. People can't completely avoid their friends, however, and sometimes peers are the most effective carriers of appearance-related messages. Stice and colleagues had women college students talk to another college woman they thought was simply another student but actually was an accomplice in the study (Stice, Maxfield, & Wells, 2003). This accomplice was a

Boys and men are increasingly experiencing dissatisfaction with their bodies just as women have, especially when they compare themselves to celebrities such as Zac Efron. ©Frederick M. Brown/Getty Images Entertainment/Getty Images

thin, attractive 19-year-old woman. In the pressure condition, the accomplice complained about how dissatisfied she was with her weight and discussed her extreme exercise routine and restrictive diet. In the neutral condition, the accomplice talked about classes she was currently taking and her plans for the weekend. The target women in the pressure condition became significantly more dissatisfied with their bodies after talking with the thin accomplice about her weight concerns. In contrast, the women in the neutral condition did not become more dissatisfied with their bodies after talking with the same woman about matters unrelated to weight or dieting.

A study of adolescent girls in Fiji demonstrated the dual influences of peers and the media on eating behavior (Becker et al., 2011). In Fiji's indigenous population, access to popular media (television and the Internet) varies greatly from one region to another. Girls who had more direct media exposure had more eating disorder symptoms, but the strongest predictor of symptoms was the amount of media exposure the girls' friends had. Those girls whose friends watched the most television and had the most Internet access had the highest scores on a measure of eating pathology. When a girl is barraged by messages promoting the thin ideal in the media and these messages are reinforced in her peer network, her risk of developing an eating disorder increases significantly.

The thin ideal remains a strong sociocultural factor in eating disorders, but evidence suggests that its power may be decreasing. A meta-analysis of studies of body dissatisfaction found that thinness-oriented body dissatisfaction among girls and women has decreased over time (Karazsia, Murnen, & Tylka, 2017). It may be that increases in body-accepting messages in the media, visibility of fuller-sized models and celebrities, and ethnic diversity have begun to have psychological effects. Notably, the study showed no comparable decrease in muscularity-oriented body dissatisfaction among men.

Athletes and Eating Disorders One group with additional pressure to maintain a specific weight and body shape is athletes, especially those participating in sports in which weight is considered an important factor in competitiveness, such as gymnastics, ice skating, dancing, horse racing, wrestling, and bodybuilding (Joy, Kussman, & Nattiv, 2016; Smolak, Murnen, & Ruble, 2000). Researchers in Norway assessed all 522 elite female athletes between ages 12 and 35 for the presence of eating disorders. They found that those participating in sports classified as "aesthetic" or "weight-dependent," including diving, figure skating, gymnastics, dance, judo, karate, and wrestling, were most likely to have anorexia nervosa or bulimia nervosa (Table 5; Sundgot-Borgen, 1994; see also Krentz & Warschburger, 2011). Many of the women athletes with eating disorders reported feeling that the physical changes of puberty had decreased their competitive edge. They had started dieting severely to try to maintain their prepubescent figure. The case of Heidi, described by her therapist, illustrates several of these triggers.

TABLE 5 Rates of Eating Disorders in Elite Women Athletes

Sports that emphasize weight are especially likely to encourage eating disorders.

Sport	Percentage with an Eating Disorder
Aesthetic sports (e.g., figure skating, gymnastics)	35%
Weight-dependent sports (e.g., judo, wrestling)	29
Endurance sports (e.g., cycling, running, swimming)	20
Technical sports (e.g., golf, high jumping)	14
Ball game sports (e.g., volleyball, soccer)	12

Source: Data from Sundgot-Borgen, 1994.

Some people with eating disorders may control their weight through excessive exercise. ©*Thinkstock Images/Stockbyte/Getty Images*

CASE STUDY

Heidi arrived in my office after gymnastics practice. . . . We talked about gymnastics, which Heidi had been involved in since she was 6. At that time, she was selected to train with the university coaches. Now she trained 4 hours a day, 6 days a week. She didn't expect to make an Olympic team, but she anticipated a scholarship to a Big Ten Conference school.

Heidi glowed when she talked about gymnastics, but I noticed her eyes were red and she had a small scar on the index finger of her right hand. (When a finger is repeatedly stuck down the throat, it can be scarred by the acids in the mouth.) I wasn't surprised when she said she was coming in for help with bulimia.

Heidi said, "I've had this problem for two years, but lately it's affecting my gymnastics. I am too weak, particularly on the vault, which requires strength. It's hard to concentrate.

"I blame my training for my eating disorder," Heidi continued. "Our coach has weekly weigh-ins where we count each other's ribs. If they are hard to count we're in trouble."

. . . Coach took her and the other gymnasts to a steak house. Heidi ordered a double cheeseburger and onion rings. After she ate, she obsessed about the weigh-in the next day, so she decided, just this once, to get rid of her meal. She slipped into the restaurant bathroom and threw up.

. . . "It was harder than you would think. My body resisted, but I was able to do it. It was so gross that I thought, 'I'll never do that again,' but a week later I did. At first it was weekly, then twice a week. Now it's almost every day. (Source: Adapted from Pipher, 1994, pp. 165–168)

Among men, bodybuilding is an increasingly popular sport, but bodybuilders routinely have substantial weight fluctuations as they shape their bodies for competition and then binge in the off-season. Male bodybuilders tend to have a pattern of eating and exercising as obsessive as that of men with eating disorders, but with a focus on gaining muscle rather than on losing fat (Murray et al., 2017). In one study of male bodybuilders, 46 percent reported bingeing after most competitions, and 85 percent reported gaining significant weight (an average of 15 pounds) in the off-season. Then they dieted to prepare for competition, losing an average of 14 pounds. In a parallel study of female bodybuilders and weight lifters, 42 percent reported having been anorexic at some time in their life, 67 percent were terrified of being fat, and 58 percent were obsessed with food (Anderson, Bartlett, Morgan, & Brownell, 1995). A study of female weight lifters found that they often abused ephedrine, a stimulant that helps reduce body fat, particularly if they had symptoms of an eating disorder (Gruber & Pope, 1998).

There is mixed evidence as to whether amateur athletics contributes to eating-disorder behaviors. One study of women college students found that varsity athletes showed the highest rates of eating-disorder behaviors, but club athletes and independent exercisers still had higher rates of some eating-disorder behaviors than did women who did not exercise (Holm-Denoma, Scaringi, Gordon, van Orden, & Joiner, 2009). However, a meta-analysis of studies concluded that, although elite athletes do show increased rates of eating disorders, nonelite athletes—particularly those participating in sports in which thinness is not emphasized—showed lower rates of eating problems than nonathletes (Smolak et al., 2000).

Cognitive Factors

When the body dissatisfaction that comes from social pressures to achieve a certain shape or weight is combined with low self-esteem and perfectionism, the result is a toxic mix of cognitive factors that strongly predict the development of an eating disorder (Boone, Soenens, & Luyten, 2014; Culbert et al., 2015; Fairburn, Cooper, Shafra, Bohn, & Hawker, 2008; Vohs et al., 2001). Women who feel they need a perfect body, are dissatisfied with their body, and have low self-esteem will engage in maladaptive strategies to control their weight, including excessive dieting and purging.

In addition, people with eating disorders tend to be more concerned with the opinions of others and are more conforming to others' wishes, perhaps making them more susceptible to social pressures to be thin (Fairburn et al., 2008; Wade et al., 2008). People with eating disorders tend to have a dichotomous thinking style, judging things as either all good or all bad. For example, if they eat one cookie, they may think that they have blown their diet and might as well eat the whole box of cookies. They will say that they cannot break their rigid eating routines or they will completely lose control over their eating. They obsess over their eating routines and plan their days around these routines, down to the smallest detail (Abramson, Bardone-Cone, Vohs, Joiner, & Heatherton, 2006).

Women with eating disorders may be concerned with body size at an unconscious level (see Keel et al., 2012). Women with and without symptoms of bulimia were shown photos of women who varied in terms of both their body size and the emotions shown on their faces. The participants were not told that these were the critical dimensions along which the photos varied. Women with bulimic symptoms were more likely than the other women in the study to attend to information about body size rather than to information about facial emotion and to classify the photos on the basis of body size rather than facial emotion (Viken, Treat, Nosofsky, McFall, & Palmeri, 2002). Thus, women who show bulimic symptoms unconsciously organize their perceptions of the world around body size more so than do women who do not show significant bulimic symptoms.

Emotion Regulation Difficulties

Eating-disorder behaviors may sometimes serve as maladaptive strategies for dealing with painful emotions (Fairburn et al., 2009; Kober & Boswell, 2018; Oldershaw, Lavender, Sallis, Stahl, & Schmidt, 2015; Svaldi, Griepenstroh, Tuschen-Caffier, & Ehring, 2012). Individuals suffering depressive symptoms or, more generally, negative affect are at risk for the development of anorexic, bulimic, and binge-eating disorder symptoms (Leehr et al., 2015; Stice, 2016; Stice, Burton, & Shaw, 2004; Stice, Presnell, & Spangler, 2002). Stice and colleagues (2002) followed a group of adolescent girls over a period of 2 years and found that girls who engaged in emotional eating—eating when they felt distressed in an attempt to feel better—were significantly more likely to develop chronic binge eating over those 2 years.

Stice and colleagues have identified two subtypes of disordered eating patterns involving binge eating (Stice et al., 2002; Stice, Bohon, Marti, & Fischer, 2008). One subtype is connected to excessive attempts to lose weight. Women with this *dieting subtype* are greatly concerned about their body shape and size and try their best to maintain a strict low-calorie diet, but they frequently abandon their regimen and engage in binge eating. They then often use vomiting or exercise to try to purge themselves of the food or of the weight it puts on their bodies. The other subtype is the *depressive subtype*. Women with this subtype also are concerned about their weight and body size, but they are plagued by feelings of depression and low self-esteem and often eat to quell these feelings.

Women with the depressive subtype of disordered eating patterns suffer greater social and psychological consequences over time than do women with the dieting subtype (Stice et al., 2002; Stice, Bohon, et al., 2008). They face more difficulties in their relationships with family and friends; are more likely to suffer significant psychiatric disorders, such as anxiety disorders; and are less likely to respond well to treatment. Longitudinal studies find that women with the depressive subtype are more likely to be diagnosed with major depression or an anxiety disorder over time and also are more likely to continue to engage in severe binge eating, compared to women with the dieting subtype (Stice & Fairburn, 2003; Stice, Bohon, et al., 2008). Over an 8-year follow-up, 80 percent of the women with the depressive subtype developed major depression. Among those women who suffered both elevated depressive symptoms and body dissatisfaction, 43 percent developed a diagnosable eating disorder (Stice et al., 2011).

Family Dynamics

Hilde Bruch (1973, 1982), a pioneer in the study of eating disorders, argued that anorexia nervosa often occurs in girls who have been unusually "good girls"—high achievers, dutiful and compliant daughters who are always trying to please their parents and others by being "perfect." These girls tend to have parents who are overinvested in their daughters' compliance and achievements, are overcontrolling, and will not allow the expression of feelings, especially negative feelings (see also Minuchin, Rosman, & Baker, 1978). As a result, the daughters do not learn to identify and accept their own feelings and desires. Instead, they learn to monitor closely the needs and desires of others and to comply with others' demands, as can be seen in the case of Renee and her family.

CASE STUDY

Renee is a 16-year-old with anorexia nervosa. Her parents are highly educated and very successful, having spent most of their careers in the diplomatic corps. Renee, her two brothers, and her parents are "very close, as are many families in the diplomatic corps, because we move so much," although the daily care of the children has always been left to nannies. The children had to follow strict rules for appropriate conduct, both in and outside the home. These rules were driven partly by the requirements of the families of diplomats to "be on their best behavior" in their host country and partly by Renee's parents' very conservative religious beliefs. Renee, as the only daughter in the family, always had to behave as "a proper lady" to counteract the stereotype of American girls as brash and sexually promiscuous. All the children were required to act mature beyond their years, controlling any emotional outbursts, accepting defeats and disappointments without complaint, and happily picking up and moving every couple of years when their parents were reassigned to another country.

Renee's anorexic behaviors began when her parents announced they were leaving the diplomatic corps to return to the United States. Renee had grown very fond of their last post in Europe, because she had finally found a group of friends that she liked and of whom her parents approved and she liked her school. She had always done well in school but often had hated the harshly strict teachers. In her present school, she felt accepted by her teachers as well as challenged by the work. When Renee told her parents she would like to finish her last year of high school in this school rather than go to the United States with them, they flatly refused to even consider it. Renee tried to talk with her parents, suggesting she stay with the family of one of her friends, who was willing to have her, but her parents cut her off and told her they would not discuss the idea further. Renee became sullen and withdrawn and stopped eating shortly after the family arrived in the United States.

One important task of adolescence is separation and individuation from one's family. Bruch argues that girls from overcontrolling families deeply fear separation because they have not developed the ability to act and think independently of their family. They also fear involvement with peers, especially sexual involvement, because they neither understand their feelings nor trust their judgment. Yet at some level they recognize their need to separate from their family. They harbor rage against their parents for their overcontrol and become angry, defiant, and distrustful. They also discover that controlling their food intake both gives them a sense of control over their life and elicits concern from their parents. Their rigid control of their body provides a sense of power over the self and the family that they have never had before. It also provides a way of avoiding peer relationships—the girl dons the persona of an anorexic, presenting herself as sickly, distant, untouchable, and superior in her self-control.

Research has confirmed that the families of girls with eating disorders have high levels of conflict, discourage the expression of negative emotions, and emphasize control and perfectionism (Holtom-Viesel & Allan, 2014; Wade, Gillespie, & Martin, 2007; see Treasure & Cardi, 2017). Several of these negative characteristics are also prevalent in the families of children with depression, anxiety disorders, and several other forms of psychopathology. What may distinguish families in which anorexia nervosa or bulimia nervosa develops is that the mothers in these families believe their daughters should lose more weight, criticize their daughters' weight, and are themselves more likely to show disordered eating patterns (Arroyo, Segrin, & Andersen, 2017; Hill & Franklin, 1998). One longitudinal study showed that eating and weight-related concerns in 10-year-old children were predicted by the amount of conflict over eating habits and issues of control during mealtimes when the children were 5 years old (Stein et al., 2006). In addition, a lack of awareness of their bodily sensations may allow some girls in these families to ignore even the most severe hunger pangs (Leon, Fulkerson, Perry, & Early-Zald, 1995). Girls from these troubled families who cannot completely ignore their hunger may fall into the binge/purge type of anorexia nervosa or into bulimia nervosa.

Studies of adult women with binge-eating disorder suggest that the combination of low parental warmth and high parental demands or control seems to distinguish girls and women who develop binge-eating disorder from those who develop other forms of psychopathology (Striegel-Moore et al., 2005; Wilfley, Pike, & Striegel-Moore, 1997). Another family characteristic that distinguishes people with binge-eating disorder from individuals with other mental disorders is a history of binge eating among other family members (Striegel-Moore et al., 2005). Thus, individuals who develop the tendency to binge may come from families that modeled and reinforced bingeing behavior (e.g., Braden et al., 2014).

Unfortunately, the majority of studies of the families and personality characteristics associated with eating disorders have compared people who already have an eating disorder with those who do not. As a

One theory of eating disorders emphasizes the role of overcontrolling families.
©STOCK4B-RF/Getty Images

result, we do not know to what extent these family and personality characteristics actually are causes of eating disorders. The controlling nature of parents' behaviors toward their child may be a consequence as well as a cause of the disorder, with parents exerting control in order to try to save their child's life.

TREATMENTS FOR EATING DISORDERS

In this section, we discuss psychotherapies and drug treatments for people with eating disorders. There are many more studies of treatments for bulimia nervosa and binge-eating disorder than for anorexia nervosa, in part because the prevalence of anorexia nervosa is low.

Psychotherapy for Anorexia Nervosa

It can be difficult to engage people with anorexia nervosa in psychotherapy. Because they so highly value the thinness they have achieved and believe they must maintain absolute control over their behaviors, people with anorexia nervosa can be resistant to therapy in general, and to therapists' attempts to change their behaviors or attitudes in particular. Regardless of the type of psychotherapy a therapist uses with a client with anorexia, he or she must do much work to win the client's trust and encourage participation in the therapy and to maintain this trust and participation as the client begins to regain the dreaded weight (Wade & Watson, 2012).

Winning the trust of someone with anorexia can be especially difficult if the therapist is forced to hospitalize the client because she has lost so much weight that her life is in danger. However, hospitalization and forced refeeding sometimes are necessary (Olmsted et al., 2010). Because people with anorexia nervosa typically do not seek treatment themselves, often they do not come to the attention of a therapist until they are so malnourished that they have a medical crisis, such as a cardiac problem, or until their families fear for their life. During hospitalization, the therapist will try to engage the client in facing and solving the psychological issues causing her to starve herself.

Psychotherapy can help many people with anorexia, particularly adolescents, but it typically is a long process, often marked by many setbacks (Wade & Watson, 2012). Along the way, many people with anorexia who have an initial period of recovery–with restoration of normal weight and healthy eating patterns–relapse into bulimic or anorexic behaviors (Carter et al., 2012). They often continue to have self-esteem issues, family problems, and periods of depression and anxiety.

Cognitive-behavioral therapies are the most researched treatment for anorexia nervosa (Linardon, Wade, de la Piedad Garcia, & Brennan, 2017). The client's overvaluation of thinness is confronted, and rewards are made contingent on the person's gaining weight. If the client is hospitalized, certain privileges in the hospital are used as rewards, such as going outside the hospital for a shopping trip or receiving family visits (assuming all parties agree to this plan). The client also may be taught relaxation techniques to use as she becomes extremely anxious about ingesting food. Randomized clinical trials find that cognitive-behavioral therapy can lead to weight gains and reductions in symptoms, although a substantial percentage of patients drop out of therapy or return to anorexic behaviors over time (Linardon et al., 2017; Wade & Watson, 2012). So far, comparisons of cognitive-behavioral treatments with other active treatments (e.g., supportive and family treatments) have shown them to be similar in efficacy (Byrne et al., 2017; Linardon et al., 2017).

In family therapy, the person with anorexia and her family are treated as a unit. The best-studied family therapy is the Maudsley model (Lock & le Grange, 2013). The intervention involves 10 to 20 sessions over 6 to 12 months. Parents are initially coached to take control of their child's eating and weight as the child's weight increases to a stable level. As the therapy progresses, the child gains greater autonomy over her eating, in collaboration with her family and therapist. There is evidence that family therapy can be successful in treating girls with anorexia nervosa (Lock, Agras, Bryson, & Kraemer, 2005; Rienecke, 2017).

Psychotherapy for Bulimia Nervosa and Binge-Eating Disorder

Cognitive-behavioral therapy (CBT) has received the most empirical support for treating bulimia nervosa (Fairburn, 2005; Linardon et al., 2017). CBT for bulimia nervosa is based on the view that the extreme concerns about shape and weight are the central features of the disorder (Fairburn et al., 2008). The therapist teaches the client to monitor the cognitions that accompany her eating, particularly the binge episodes and purging episodes. Then the therapist helps the client confront these cognitions and develop more adaptive attitudes toward weight and body shape. An interchange between a therapist and a client might go like this:

Therapist: What were you thinking just before you began to binge?

Client: I was thinking that I felt really upset and sad about having no social life. I wanted to eat just to feel better.

Therapist: And as you were eating, what were you thinking?

Client: I was thinking that the ice cream tasted really good, that it was making me feel good. But I was also thinking that I shouldn't be eating this, that I'm bingeing again. But then I thought that my life is such a wreck that I deserve to eat what I want to make me feel better.

Therapist: And what were you thinking after you finished the binge?

Client: That I was a failure, a blimp, that I have no control, that this therapy isn't working.

Therapist: Okay, let's go back to the beginning. You said you wanted to eat because you thought it would make you feel better. Did it?

Client: Well, as I said, the ice cream tasted good and it felt good to indulge myself.

Therapist: But in the long run, did bingeing make you feel better?

Client: Of course not. I felt terrible afterward.

Therapist: Can you think of anything you might say to yourself the next time you get into such a state, when you want to eat in order to make yourself feel better?

Client: I could remind myself that I'll feel better only for a little while, but then I'll feel terrible.

Therapist: How likely do you think it is that you'll remember to say this to yourself?

Client: Not very likely.

Therapist: Is there any way to increase the likelihood?

Client: Well, I guess I could write it on a card or something and put the card near my refrigerator.

Therapist: That's a pretty good idea. What else could you do to prevent yourself from eating when you feel upset? What other things could you do to relieve your upset, other than eat?

Client: I could call my friend Keisha and talk about how I feel. Or I could go for a walk—someplace away from food—like up in the hills, where it's so pretty. Walking up there always makes me feel better.

Therapist: Those are really good ideas. It's important to have a variety of things you can do, other than eat, to relieve bad moods.

The behavioral components of this therapy involve introducing forbidden foods (such as bread) back into the client's diet and helping the client confront her irrational thoughts about these foods, such as "If I have just one doughnut, I'm inevitably going to binge." Similarly, the client is taught to eat three healthy meals a day and to challenge the thoughts she has about these meals and about the possibility of gaining weight. Cognitive-behavioral therapy for bulimia usually lasts about 3 to 6 months and involves 10 to 20 sessions.

Controlled studies of the efficacy of cognitive-behavioral therapy for bulimia find that about half the clients completely stop the binge/purge cycle (Fairburn, 2005; Shapiro et al., 2007). Clients undergoing this therapy also show a decrease in depression and anxiety, an increase in social functioning, and a lessening of concern about dieting and weight. Cognitive-behavioral therapy is more effective than drug therapies in producing complete cessation of binge eating and purging and in preventing relapse over the long term (Fairburn, 2005; Linardon et al., 2017). Expanded cognitive-behavioral therapies that also address emotion-regulation difficulties are especially effective in people with a combination of eating disorders and depression (Fairburn et al., 2009).

Other studies of the treatment of bulimia have compared cognitive-behavioral therapy (CBT) with three other types of psychotherapy: interpersonal therapy (IPT), supportive-expressive psychodynamic therapy, and behavioral therapy without a focus on cognitions (Agras, Walsh, Fairburn, Wilson, & Kraemer, 2000; Fairburn, Jones, Peveler, & Carr, 1991; Fairburn et al., 1995; Garner, Rockert, Davis, & Garner, 1993; Wilson et al., 1999; Wilson, Fairburn, Agras, Walsh, & Kraemer, 2002; see Linardon et al.,

2017). In interpersonal therapy, the client and the therapist discuss interpersonal problems related to the client's eating disorder, and the therapist works actively with the client to develop strategies to solve these problems. In supportive-expressive psychodynamic therapy, the therapist also encourages the client to talk about problems related to the eating disorder—especially interpersonal problems—but in a highly nondirective manner. In behavioral therapy, the client is taught how to monitor her food intake, is reinforced for introducing avoided foods into her diet, and is taught coping techniques for avoiding bingeing. In the studies, all the therapies resulted in significant improvement in the clients' eating behaviors and emotional well-being, but the cognitive-behavioral and interpersonal therapy clients showed the greatest and most enduring improvements (Linardon et al., 2017). Comparisons of CBT and IPT suggest that CBT is significantly more effective than IPT in treating bulimia and works more quickly, with substantial improvement being shown by 3 to 6 weeks into treatment with CBT (Agras et al., 2000; Fairburn et al., 2015; Wilson et al., 1999, 2002). CBT and IPT appear to be comparably effective in preventing relapse in 1- and 6-year follow-ups (Agras et al., 2000; Linardon et al., 2017).

For binge-eating disorder, cognitive-behavioral therapy has been shown to be more effective than other psychotherapies or antidepressant medications (Brownley et al., 2016; Linardon et al, 2017). CBT reduces binges as well as overconcern with weight, shape, and eating in people with binge-eating disorder.

Despite the efficacy of psychotherapy for eating disorders, and CBT in particular, good treatment can be hard to access (Kazdin, Fitzsimmons-Craft, & Wilfley, 2017). Efforts to improve treatment access include modifying treatment for delivery online and through mobile apps (Agras, Fitzsimmons-Craft, & Wilfley, 2017). In addition, especially because eating disorders tend to develop in adolescence and early adulthood, researchers have developed promising prevention programs that target risk factors such as media exposure and internalization of the thinness ideal (Becker & Stice, 2017; Le, Barendregt, Hay, & Mihalopoulos, 2017).

Biological Therapies

The selective serotonin reuptake inhibitors (SSRIs), such as fluoxetine (trade name Prozac), have been the focus of much research on biological treatments for bulimia nervosa. These drugs appear to reduce binge-eating and purging behaviors, but often they fail to restore the individual to normal eating habits (see meta-analyses by Flament, Bissada, & Spettigue, 2012; Linardon et al., 2017; Reas & Grilo, 2008). Adding cognitive-behavioral therapy to antidepressant treatment increases rates of recovery (Fairburn, 2005). Antidepressants are often used to treat anorexia nervosa, and they result in reduction of symptoms in half the studies conducted (see Flament et al., 2012). Olanzapine, an atypical antipsychotic (see the chapter "Schizophrenia Spectrum and Other Psychotic Disorders"), leads to increases in weight in people with anorexia nervosa (see Flament et al., 2012). Meta-analyses of medications for binge eating found that a number of drugs, including the SSRIs, antiepileptic medications (such as topiramate), and obesity medications (such as orlistat), all are better than a placebo in reducing binge eating but do not tend to reduce concerns about body shape or weight (Brownley et al., 2016; Flament et al., 2012; Reas & Grilo, 2008).

CHAPTER INTEGRATION

Experts generally have suggested that biological, psychological, and social factors interact to cause the eating disorders (see Brownell & Walsh, 2017; Culbert et al., 2015). Any one factor alone may not be enough to lead someone to develop anorexia nervosa or bulimia nervosa, but combined they may do so (Figure 2).

First, societal pressures for thinness clearly provide a potent influence on the development of unhealthy attitudes toward eating, especially for women. If these pressures were simply toward achieving a healthy weight and maintaining fitness, they would not be so dangerous. However, the ideal weight for women promoted by beauty symbols in developed countries is much lower than that considered healthy and normal for the average woman, and thus women may develop a negative body image. This leads them to engage in excessive dieting. Unfortunately, excessive dieting sets up conditions for impulsive binge eating, which leads to negative emotions and even lower self-esteem.

Second, biological factors may interact with these societal pressures to make some people more likely than others to develop an eating disorder. People who develop eating disorders may have a genetic predisposition to these disorders or to dysregulation of the hormone or neurotransmitter system. Exactly how the genetic vulnerabilities lead to the symptoms of eating disorders is unclear, but they may contribute to an

FIGURE 2 Multiple Pathways into the Eating Disorders.

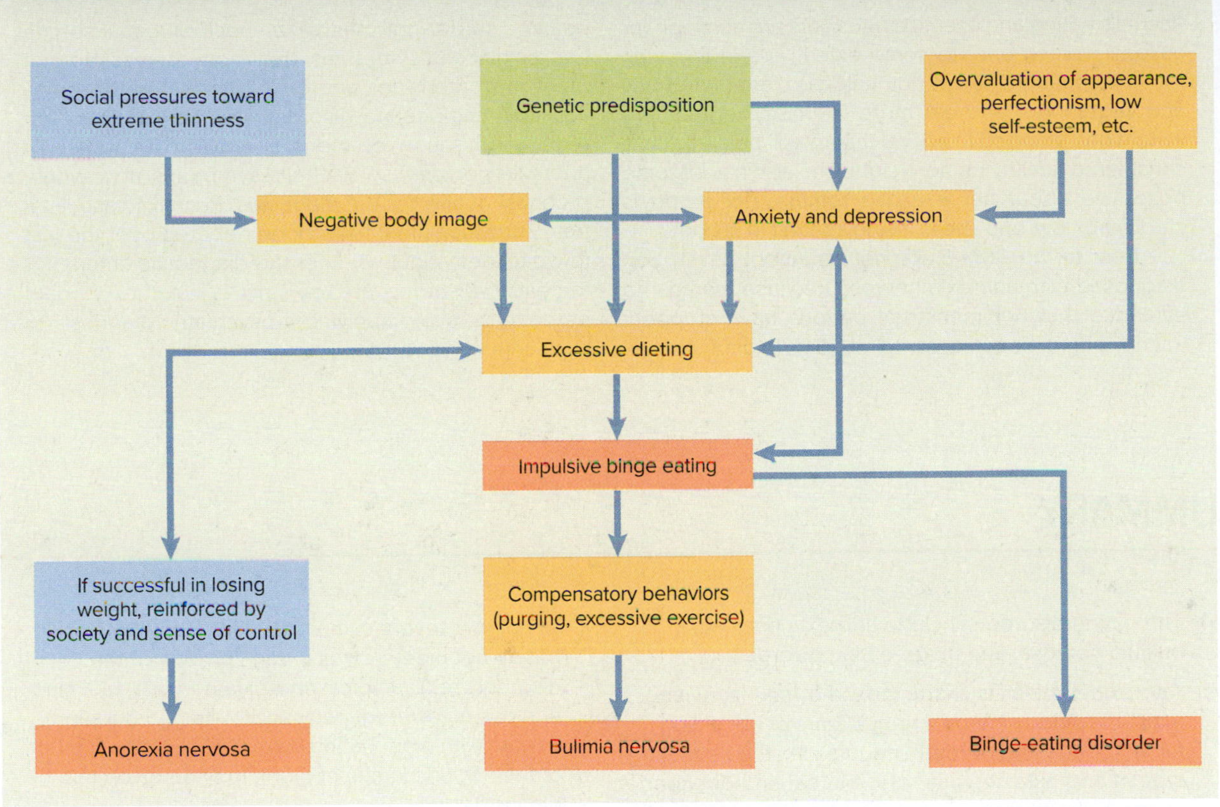

ability to diet excessively. Another biological factor that may predispose some people to acquiesce to the pressures to diet and to be thin is a tendency toward anxiety or mild depression. Many people with eating disorders, especially people with bulimia nervosa, are often depressed and eat impulsively in response to their moods. Although problems in mood in people with an eating disorder may be the result of environmental circumstances or of the stresses of the disorder, they also may have a biological origin in some people.

Third, personality factors may interact with societal pressures to be thin and/or with the biological predispositions described to lead some people to develop an eating disorder. Perfectionism, all-or-nothing thinking, and low self-esteem may make people more likely to engage in extreme measures to control their weight in pursuit of an ideal of attractiveness. These personality characteristics are more likely to develop in children whose parents are lacking in affection and nurturance and who at the same time are controlling and demanding of perfection.

Whatever pathway an individual takes into the eating disorders, these behaviors tend to be maintained once they begin. The excessive concern over weight among people with anorexia or bulimia nervosa is constantly reinforced by societal images, and any weight loss they do achieve is reinforced by peers and family. People with anorexia also may be reinforced by the sense of control they gain over their lives by highly restrictive dieting. People with bulimia nervosa and binge-eating disorder may greatly desire control but are unable to maintain it, so they fall into binge eating to escape negative emotions. The compensatory behaviors of bulimia nervosa help the individual regain some sense of control, however fragile, and thereby are reinforced.

Thus, it may take a mixture of these factors, rather than any single factor, to lead someone to develop a diagnosable eating disorder. Once the disorder sets in, however, it tends to be reinforced and perpetuated. Note also that many of the same factors contribute to each different eating disorder.

SHADES OF GRAY DISCUSSION

Rachel's eating and exercise behaviors are common for college women and, to some extent, are in line with recommendations to cut out junk food, eat more fruits and vegetables, and get more exercise. Yet Rachel's weight has dropped to a level that is well below what is considered healthy for her height. She also has become obsessive about her exercise routine, her mood is chronically low, and she is losing interest in school.

Prior to the *DSM-5,* Rachel would not have been diagnosed with anorexia nervosa because there is no evidence that her menstrual periods have stopped. Rachel might have received a *DSM-IV* diagnosis of eating disorder not otherwise specified because she has significant symptoms that nonetheless do not meet the criteria for anorexia nervosa, bulimia nervosa, or binge-eating disorder. The *DSM-5* does not require cessation of menses for the diagnosis of anorexia nervosa, so Rachel's symptoms now would probably qualify for the diagnosis. Rachel's case illustrates questions that have been debated over the last few decades about whether the diagnostic criteria for the eating disorders are too strict or whether it would be better to avoid applying a psychiatric diagnosis to such common behavior.

CHAPTER SUMMARY

- The eating disorders include anorexia nervosa, bulimia nervosa, and binge-eating disorder.
- Anorexia nervosa is characterized by self-starvation, a distorted body image, intense fears of becoming fat, and often amenorrhea. People with the restricting type of anorexia nervosa refuse to eat and/or engage in excessive exercise in order to prevent weight gain. People with the binge/purge type periodically engage in bingeing and then purge to prevent weight gain.
- The lifetime prevalence of anorexia is under 1 percent, with 90 to 95 percent of cases seen in females. Anorexia nervosa usually begins in adolescence, and the course is variable from one person to another. It is a very dangerous disorder with a relatively high death rate from complications of self-starvation and suicide.
- Bulimia nervosa is characterized by uncontrolled bingeing followed by inappropriate compensatory behaviors designed to prevent weight gain from the binges (e.g., self-induced vomiting, misuse of laxatives or diuretics, excessive exercise).
- Bulimia nervosa is more common in females than in males. The onset of bulimia nervosa most often is in adolescence. Although people with bulimia do not tend to be underweight, bulimia nervosa has several dangerous medical complications.
- People with binge-eating disorder engage in bingeing, but not in purging or in behaviors designed to compensate for the binges. People with the disorder tend to be significantly overweight.
- The *DSM-5* diagnosis other specified feeding or eating disorder replaced the *DSM-IV* eating disorder not otherwise specified. It may be given to individuals who show severe symptoms of an eating disorder but do not meet the full criteria for one of the eating disorders (e.g., atypical anorexia nervosa, bulimia nervosa of low frequency and/or limited duration). People with night eating disorder, who ingest much of their caloric intake at night, may be given this diagnosis.
- Obesity is defined as a body mass index of 30 or more. Obesity rates have skyrocketed in recent years, largely due to increases in the intake of high-fat, low-nutrient food and decreases in physical activity. Treatments for obesity include commercial weight-loss programs, medications, low-calorie diets, and bariatric surgery.
- The biological factors implicated in the development of the eating disorders include genetics, the dysregulation of hormone and neurotransmitter systems, and generally lower functioning in the hypothalamus.
- Sociocultural theorists have attributed the eating disorders to pressures to be thin, especially in developed nations.
- Eating disorders may develop in some people as maladaptive strategies for coping with negative emotions. Also, certain cognitive factors, including overvaluation of appearance, perfectionism, low self-esteem, excessive concern about others' opinions, and a rigid, dichotomous thinking style, may contribute to the development of the eating disorders.
- The families of girls with eating disorders may be overcontrolling, overprotective, and hostile and may not allow the expression of feelings, especially negative feelings. In adolescence, these girls may develop eating disorders as a way of exerting control.

- Cognitive-behavioral therapy and family therapy have been shown to be effective in the treatment of anorexia nervosa.
- Cognitive-behavioral therapy has proven to be the most effective therapy for reducing the symptoms of bulimia and binge-eating disorder and preventing relapse. Interpersonal therapy, supportive-expressive psychodynamic therapy, and behavioral therapy also appear to be effective in treating bulimia nervosa.
- Antidepressants can reduce symptoms in anorexia nervosa, bulimia nervosa, and binge-eating disorder. The atypical antipsychotic olanzapine can help restore weight in people with anorexia nervosa.

KEY TERMS

anorexia nervosa
amenorrhea
restricting type of anorexia nervosa
binge/purge type of anorexia nervosa
bulimia nervosa
bingeing
binge-eating disorder
other specified feeding or eating disorder
atypical anorexia nervosa
night eating disorder
obesity

Chapter 13

©praetorianphoto/E+/Getty Images

Sexual Disorders and Gender Diversity

CHAPTER OUTLINE

Sexuality and Gender Along the Continuum

Functional — **Dysfunctional**

Sexual functioning, sexual practices, and gender identity that bring the individual positive well-being and relationships

- **Occasional difficulties in sexual functioning that do not cause distress or relationships difficulties** *(occasional difficulty reaching orgasm)*
- **Atypical sexual practices that do not cause distress or difficulties in social functioning** *(use of objects as part of sex play with a consenting partner)*
- **Questions about gender identity that eventually are resolved**

Potentially meets diagnostic criteria for a sexual disorder:

- **Difficulties in sexual functioning that cause moderate distress or difficulties in relationships** *(frequent difficulty reaching orgasm)*
- **Atypical sexual practices that cause distress or difficulties in social functioning** *(one's partner disapproves of the objects used in sexual practice)*
- **Uncertainty about gender identity**

Likely meets diagnostic criteria for a sexual disorder:

- **Chronic difficulties in sexual functioning that cause significant distress or difficulties in relationships** *(complete lack of sexual desire)*
- **Atypical sexual practices that cause significant distress or difficulties in social functioning** *(inappropriate objects become the sole focus of sexual activities, arrests for illegal sexual behavior)*
- **Significant distress regarding gender identity, desire to change genders**

Before the work of researchers William Masters and Virginia Johnson in the 1950s and 1960s, we knew little about typical or atypical **sexual functioning**—that is, what happens in the body during sexual activity. They argued that the sexual response cycle can be divided into five phases: desire, arousal or excitement, plateau, orgasm, and resolution, as reviewed later in this chapter. Occasional problems with sexual functioning, such as difficulty reaching orgasm or lack of sexual desire, are extremely common. When people have difficulties in sexual functioning that are persistent and that cause significant distress or interpersonal difficulty, they may be diagnosed with *a sexual dysfunction* (Balon, Segraves, & Clayton, 2007; Wincze & Weinberg, 2015). Studies around the world suggest that 40 to 45 percent of women and 20 to 30 percent of men frequently experience sexual dysfunctions (Lewis et al., 2010).

The activities and objects that people find arousing vary tremendously. When people focus their sexual activity on something considered inappropriate by society—for example, nonliving objects, prepubescent children, nonconsenting adults, or suffering or humiliation—they may be diagnosed with a *paraphilic disorder.* Many people have occasional paraphilic fantasies. One study found that 62 percent of men fantasized about having sex with a young girl, 33 percent fantasized about raping a woman, and 12 percent fantasized about being humiliated during sex (Crepault & Couture, 1980). People diagnosed with a paraphilic disorder often feel compelled to engage in their paraphilias, even though their behaviors cause them distress or create social, occupational, or legal problems.

Finally, individuals also vary in their **gender identity**—their perception of themselves as male, female, another gender, or without gender. Gender identity differs from *gender roles,* which are society's expectations for how males and females should act. Many females engage in behaviors considered part of the traditional masculine gender role, such as playing aggressive sports or pursuing competitive careers, but still have a fundamental sense of themselves as female. Similarly, many males engage in behaviors considered part of the traditional feminine gender role, such as caring for children, cooking, or sewing, but still have a fundamental sense of themselves as male. When an individual believes he or she was born with the body of the wrong gender and experiences significant distress, the *DSM-5* defines this as *gender dysphoria* (formerly called gender identity disorder). People with gender dysphoria feel trapped in the wrong body, wish to be rid of their genitals, and want to live as a member of the other gender.

The *DSM-5* definitions of sexual disorders are controversial because they single out some sexual behaviors as abnormal and disordered but not others. For example, adults whose sexual fantasies, urges, and behaviors focus on women's breasts can be diagnosed with a sexual disorder, but adults who prefer sexual activity with prostitutes may not be diagnosed under the *DSM-5* criteria.

Extraordinary People

David Reimer, *The Boy Who Was Raised as a Girl*

In April 1966, 8-month-old Bruce Reimer underwent a routine circumcision to alleviate a painful medical condition on his penis. The operation went terribly wrong, however, and Bruce's penis was accidentally severed. None of the doctors whom Bruce's anguished parents consulted could offer any hope of restoring the penis and suggested that he would never be able to function as a normal male. But Dr. John Money offered them a solution: Raise Bruce as a girl and have him undergo sex reassignment therapy. Dr. Money firmly believed that male or female identity depends on the environment in which a child is raised, not on genes or the genitals with which he or she is born. Bruce's condition presented Dr. Money with the perfect opportunity to prove his theory. Not only had Bruce been born male, but he had an identical twin brother as well. If surgically reassigning Bruce's sex and raising him as a girl resulted in Bruce fully accepting himself as a girl, when his twin brother identified himself as a boy, Money's theories of gender identity would be soundly supported.

Bruce's parents renamed him Brenda Lee and began dressing him in feminine clothes. The child underwent a bilateral orchidectomy—removal of both testicles—at the age of 22 months. Brenda's parents then furnished her with dolls and tried to reinforce her identity as a girl. Brenda, however, resisted. As brother Brian recalled, "When I say there was nothing feminine about Brenda . . . I mean there was nothing feminine. She walked like a guy. Sat with her legs apart. We both wanted to play with guys, build forts and have snowball fights and play army. She'd get a skipping rope for a gift, and the only thing we'd use that for was to tie people up, whip people with it" (Colapinto, 2000, p. 57).

As Brenda grew up, she refused surgery to create a vagina for her and insisted on urinating standing up. Beginning at age 12, Brenda was given estrogen, and as a result she began to develop breasts. However, her voice began to crack, just like her brother's. Finally, when Brenda was 14, her father told her the truth about the botched circumcision and her parents' decision to raise her as a girl. Brenda said, "I was relieved. . . . Suddenly it all made sense why I felt the way I did. I wasn't some sort of weirdo. I wasn't crazy" (Colapinto, 2000, p. 180).

Brenda immediately decided to revert to her biological sex. She renamed herself David, after the biblical king and giant-slayer. David began to take injections of testosterone and in 1980 underwent a double mastectomy to remove the breasts he had grown. Then, a month before his sixteenth birthday, he had surgery to create a rudimentary penis. Still, David's reentry into life as a boy was difficult. He still looked and talked differently from other boys and, as a result, was teased and shunned. The artificial genitals that had been fashioned for him frequently became blocked, and he went through several additional surgeries and treatments. Over the next few years, David attempted suicide and secluded himself in a mountain cabin for months at a time.

Finally, after his twenty-second birthday, David had a new kind of surgery to create a more acceptable and functional penis. In 1990, David married a young woman named Jane, and things went well for a while. But after losing his job, experiencing financial difficulties, and separating from his wife, David committed suicide in 2004. According to his mother, he had also been grieving the death of his brother, which had occurred 2 years before the suicide. In a news story after David's death, John Colapinto, his biographer, noted, "David's blighted childhood was never far from his mind. Just before he died, he talked to his wife about his sexual 'inadequacy,' his inability to be a true husband. Jane tried to reassure him. But David was already heading for the door" (*Colapinto,* 2004).

David Reimer's story raises many questions about the biological and social contributors to our self-concept as male or female, our sexual preferences, and the role of sexuality and gender in our psychological well-being. In this chapter, we consider how biology interacts with social norms and psychological factors to produce both sexual health and sexual disorders.

As noted in Sexuality and Gender Along the Continuum, much of what we know about what happens in the human body during sexual activity is rooted in Masters and Johnson's (1970) groundbreaking work. They observed people engaging in a variety of sexual practices in a laboratory setting and recorded the physiological changes that occurred, concluding that the human sexual response cycle consists of five phases of physical and emotional change: desire, arousal or excitement, plateau, orgasm, and resolution (Figure 1). **Sexual desire** is

FIGURE 1 **The Sexual Response Cycle.** Masters and Johnson divided the sexual response cycle into five phases (see discussion in Sexuality Along the Continuum).

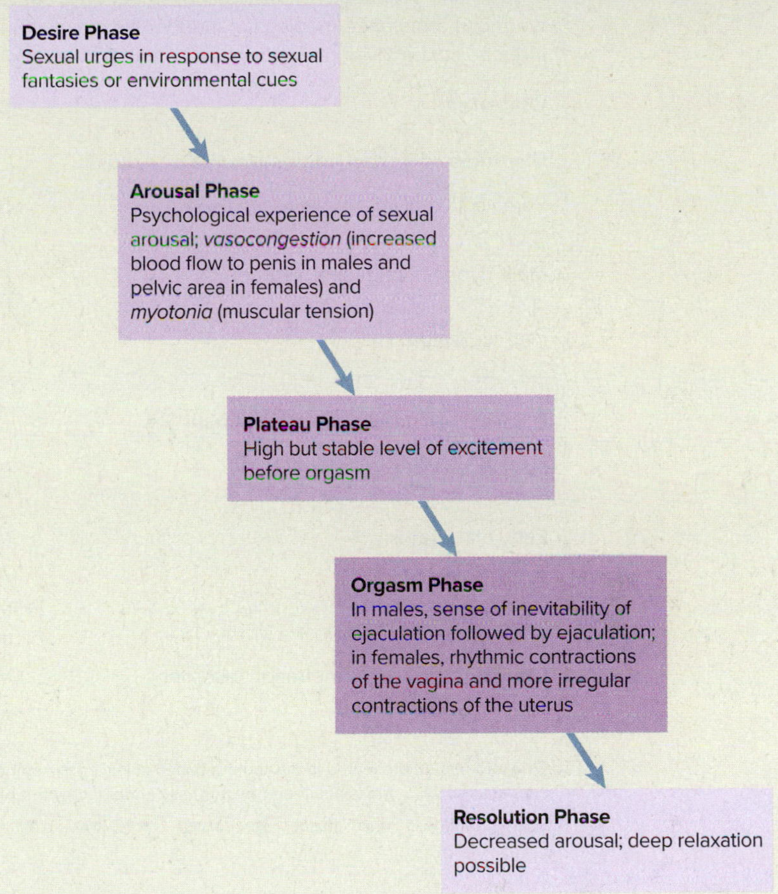

Desire Phase
Sexual urges in response to sexual fantasies or environmental cues
Arousal Phase
Psychological experience of sexual arousal; vasocongestion (increased blood flow to penis in males and pelvic area in females) and myotonia (muscular tension)
Plateau Phase
High but stable level of excitement before orgasm
Orgasm Phase
In males, sense of inevitability of ejaculation followed by ejaculation; in females, rhythmic contractions of the vagina and more irregular contractions of the uterus
Resolution Phase
Decreased arousal; deep relaxation possible

Source: Masters & Johnson, 1970.

the urge to engage in any type of sexual activity, even imaginal, such as fantasy. The **arousal phase,** or excitement phase, combines a psychological experience of pleasure and the physiological changes known as *vasocongestion* and *myotonia*. Vasocongestion, or *engorgement,* occurs when blood vessels and tissues fill with blood. In males, erection of the penis is caused by an increase in the flow of blood into the arteries of the penis, accompanied by a decrease in the outflow of blood from the penis through the veins. In females, vasocongestion causes the clitoris to enlarge, the labia to swell, and the vagina to become moist. Myotonia is muscular tension. During the arousal phase, many muscles in the body become tenser, culminating in the muscular contractions known as orgasm.

After arousal is the **plateau phase,** when excitement remains at a high but stable level. This period is pleasurable in itself, and some people try to extend the plateau phase as long as possible before reaching **orgasm,** the discharge of the neuromuscular tension built up during the excitement and plateau phases. In males, orgasm involves rhythmic contractions of the prostate and the entire length of the penis and urethra, accompanied by the ejaculation of semen. After ejaculation, a *refractory* period, lasting from a few minutes to a few hours, occurs in which the male cannot achieve full erection and another orgasm, regardless of the type or intensity of sexual stimulation. In females, orgasm generally involves rhythmic contractions of the vagina and more irregular contractions of the uterus, which are not always felt. Because females do not have a refractory period, they are capable of experiencing additional orgasms immediately following one. However, not all women find multiple orgasms easy to achieve or desirable. Following orgasm, the entire musculature of the body relaxes, and men and women tend to experience a state of deep relaxation, the stage known as **resolution.**

If you are sexually active, you may or may not have recognized all these phases in your sexual response cycle. People vary greatly in the length and distinctiveness of each phase. Although the work of Masters and Johnson was critical to our understanding of sexual functioning, it soon became clear that people vary tremendously in the extent to which they consciously experience each of these phases anytime they engage in sexual activity. For example, Masters and Johnson's depiction of the sexual response cycle may be more characteristic of men than of women, as women's responses tend to be more variable than men's (Basson et al., 2001; Giraldi, Kristensen, & Sand, 2015). Sometimes, the excitement phase is short for a female, and she reaches a discernible orgasm quickly. At other times, the excitement phase is longer, and she may or may not experience a full orgasm.

Occasional difficulties at one or more of the phases of the sexual response cycle are common (Michael, Gagnon, Laumann, & Kolata, 1994). As we discuss later, these difficulties may be tied to stresses in individuals' lives, medications they are taking, illness, or problems in their relationships. Individuals who have persistent difficulties that cause them distress or interfere with their social or occupational functioning may be diagnosed with a sexual dysfunction.

SEXUAL DYSFUNCTIONS

The **sexual dysfunctions** are a set of disorders in which people have difficulty responding sexually or experiencing sexual pleasure (Table 1). To qualify for a diagnosis of a sexual dysfunction, the difficulty must be more than occasional or transient, and must

TABLE 1 *DSM-5* Sexual Dysfunctions*

The sexual dysfunction disorders can be roughly divided into disorders of sexual desire and arousal and disorders of orgasm and sexual pain. If a sexual dysfunction is caused by a substance (e.g., alcohol) or medication, it is given the diagnosis substance/medication-induced sexual dysfunction. All sexual dysfunctions (except substance/medication-induced sexual dysfunction) require a minimum duration of approximately 6 months.

Disorder	Description
Disorders of Sexual Interest/Desire or Arousal	
Female sexual interest/arousal disorder	Persistent lack of, or significantly reduced, interest in sexual activity and/or lack of arousal in response to sexual activity
Male hypoactive desire disorder	Persistently absent or deficient sexual/erotic thoughts or fantasies, or desire for sexual activity
Erectile disorder	Recurrent inability to attain or maintain an erection or a marked decrease in erectile rigidity
Disorders of Orgasm or Sexual Pain	
Female orgasmic disorder	Reduced intensity, or recurrent delay or absence of orgasm during sexual activity
Early ejaculation	Recurrent ejaculation within 1 minute of initiation of partnered sexual activity when not desired
Delayed ejaculation	Marked delay, infrequency, or absence of ejaculation during sexual encounters
Genito-pelvic pain/penetration disorder	Marked difficulties having vaginal penetration; pain or tightening of pelvic floor muscles during penetration

*The information presented in this table is based solely on the author's interpretation of *DSM-5*. It does not reflect the exact language that appears in *DSM-5* and is not, therefore, formally endorsed by the APA.

Source: *Diagnostic and Statistical Manual of Mental Disorders,* Fifth Edition. American Psychiatric Association, 2013.

cause significant distress or interpersonal difficulty. The distress and impairment criteria are especially important when considering a diagnosis of sexual dysfunction, because there is a great deal of variability in what is considered a normal human sexual experience. The *DSM-5* recognizes seven distinct sexual dysfunction disorders, which can roughly be divided into disorders of desire and arousal and disorders of orgasm and sexual pain (see Table 1). To be diagnosed with any of these disorders, the dysfunction must occur most of the time for at least 6 months, must cause significant distress or impairment, and must not be due to another, nonsexual psychiatric problem (e.g., depression); a substance or medication; a general medical condition; or stressors. If individuals do have a sexual dysfunction caused by a substance (such as chronic alcohol abuse) or a medication (such as an antidepressant), they may be diagnosed with *substance/medication-induced sexual dysfunction.* In reality, these dysfunctions overlap significantly, and many people who seek treatment for a sexual problem have more than one nonsexual dysfunction.

When considering whether or not someone suffers from a sexual dysfunction, clinicians should assess for several factors that may contribute to the symptoms, in order to fully understand the patient and as a tool in formulating interventions. These factors include partner factors such as health issues and sexual problems; relationship factors, including conflict and communication issues; individual vulnerability factors such as a history of abuse; cultural or religious beliefs; and relevant medical conditions (*DSM-5*, p. 423).

Disorders of Sexual Interest/ Desire and Arousal

Sexual desire can be manifested in a person's sexual thoughts and fantasies, a person's interest in initiating or participating in sexual activities, and a person's awareness of sexual cues from others (Krakowsky & Grober, 2016; Sand & Fisher, 2007). People vary tremendously in their levels of sexual desire or interest, and an individual's level of sexual desire or interest can vary greatly across time (Michael et al., 1994). Low sexual desire or arousal is among the most common problems for which people seek treatment (Leiblum, 2010; Wincze, Bach, & Barlow, 2008).

Male Hypoactive Sexual Desire Disorder

Men with **male hypoactive sexual desire disorder** have little desire for sex and have deficient or absent sexual thoughts or fantasies—they do not fantasize about sex or initiate sexual activity and may be unresponsive when a partner initiates sex (American Psychiatric Association, 2013). This lack of sexual desire causes them marked distress or interpersonal difficulty. In some rare cases, men report never having had much interest in sex, either with other people or privately (e.g., viewing of erotic films, masturbation, or fantasy). These men are diagnosed with *lifelong male hypoactive sexual desire disorder,* as the disturbance has always been present. In most cases, the man used to enjoy sex but has lost interest in it, a condition diagnosed as *acquired male hypoactive sexual desire disorder.* Inhibited desire can be either generalized to all partners and situations or specific to certain partners or types of stimulation. Obviously, the judgment about when a man's sexual desire has been too low for too long is subjective. The *DSM-5* specifies that the clinician should make this determination with consideration of other aspects of the person's life, including age. Between 15 and 20 percent of men report frequent problems involving hypoactive sexual desire, with higher rates among older men than among younger men (Krakowsky & Grober, 2016; McCabe et al., 2016).

Female Sexual Interest/Arousal Disorder

The nature of sexual desire or interest may be different for men and women. For men, the *DSM-5* defines desire as the presence of sexual fantasies and yearning to have sex, but many women say they seldom engage in sexual fantasies or yearning for sex yet do desire and enjoy sex (Sand & Fisher, 2007). In addition, sexual interest or desire and sexual arousal seem to be more intimately connected with each other in women than in men. In some women, sexual interest precedes arousal, while in others it follows it. As a result of these differences between women and men, and because for women problems with arousal and desire frequently coexist, the *DSM-5* combines difficulties in sexual interest or arousal into one diagnosis for women, **female sexual interest/arousal disorder.** In order to receive this diagnosis, a woman must, for at least 6 months, report at least three of the following symptoms: absent or significantly reduced interest in sexual activity, in sexual or erotic thoughts or fantasies, in initiation of sex or receptiveness to sex, in excitement or pleasure in most sexual encounters, in sexual responsiveness to erotic cues, or in genital or nongenital responses to sexual activity. As in male hypoactive sexual disorder, female sexual interest/arousal disorder can be either lifelong or acquired. It is important to note that female sexual interest/arousal disorder should not be diagnosed simply when there is a difference of interest between sexual partners, and that "most" in the criteria refers to having absent or significantly reduced excitement or pleasure in approximately 75 to 100 percent of sexual encounters.

The data we have on these problems in women come mostly from the *DSM-IV* diagnostic scheme, which separated sexual desire problems and sexual arousal problems in women. More than 30 percent of women report an occasional lack of desire for sex (McCabe et al., 2016). In a study of over 31,000 women, unusually low sexual desire was diagnosed in 9.5 percent of them (Clayton, 2007). Rates of low sexual desire increase to 26 percent in postmenopausal women (Leiblum, Koochaki, Rodenberg, Barton, & Rosen, 2006). For diagnosable levels of low desire, researchers estimate prevalence of 8.9 percent of women between 18 and 44, 12.3 percent between 45 and 64, and 7.4 percent age 65 or older (Parish & Hahn, 2016). Women with low sexual desire are more likely than men to report anxiety, depression, and life stress. About 20 percent of women report difficulties with lubrication or arousal during sexual activity (Laumann, Paik, & Rosen, 1999; Lewis et al., 2010; McCabe et al., 2016). The study of over 31,000 women found that 5.4 percent could be diagnosed with a *DSM-IV* sexual arousal disorder (Clayton, 2007). Some discrepancy in prevalence rates has been reported depending on whether or not "distress" accompanies reported symptoms. Some women who experience problems with arousal and desire are not distressed by this (APA, 2013, p. 435).

Erectile Disorder

Erectile disorder in men (sometimes referred to as *impotence*) involves the recurrent inability to attain or maintain an erection until the completion of sexual activity or a marked decrease in erectile rigidity. Men with the lifelong form of erectile disorder have never been able to sustain an erection for a desired period of time. Men with the acquired form of the disorder were able to sustain an erection in the past but no longer can. Occasional problems in achieving or sustaining an erection are common, with as many as 30 million men in the United States having erectile problems at some time in their life. Such problems do not constitute a disorder until they become persistent and significantly interfere with a man's interpersonal

Thanks in part to endorsements by celebrities such as baseball player Rafael Palmeiro, former Senator Bob Dole, and former Chicago Bears coach Mike Ditka (pictured), sales of medications to treat erectile disorder have skyrocketed. ©*Shutterstock*

relationships or cause him distress. The criteria for erectile disorder specify that a man must fail to achieve or maintain an erection until completion of sexual activity on all or almost all (75 to 100 percent) occasions over a period of approximately 6 months.

One nationwide study (Saigal et al., 2006) found that one in five men over age 20 could be diagnosed with erectile dysfunction; similar or slightly lower rates have been found internationally (McCabe et al., 2016). The prevalence of erectile dysfunction increases dramatically with age, with over 77 percent of men over age 75 affected by it (Lewis et al., 2010; McCabe et al., 2016; Saigal et al., 2006). The *DSM-5* reports that many clinicians have noted that lifelong dysfunction is associated with psychological contributors that are often amenable to treatment, whereas acquired cases are more often associated with biological causes. Problems with erectile functioning can be both the result and the cause of other difficulties in a couple's relationship.

Disorders of Orgasm or Sexual Pain

Individuals can desire to have sex, become aroused during sexual activity, but not experience an orgasm. In addition, women can experience significant pain or tightening of the pelvic muscles upon penetration.

Female Orgasmic Disorder

Women with **female orgasmic disorder,** or *anorgasmia*, experience markedly reduced intensity of orgasms, or delay or absence of orgasm, after having reached the excitement phase of the sexual response cycle in at least 75 percent of sexual encounters. Female orgasmic disorder can be either lifelong or acquired.

About one in four women reports occasional difficulty reaching orgasm (Laumann et al., 1999; McCabe et al., 2016), and 4.7 percent can be diagnosed with orgasmic disorder (Clayton, 2007). The problem is greater among postmenopausal women, with about one in three reporting some problem reaching orgasm during sexual stimulation (Clayton, 2007). As has been found with female sexual interest/arousal disorder, some women who have symptoms of female orgasmic disorder are not distressed by this and therefore would not warrant a diagnosis.

Early Ejaculation and Delayed Ejaculation

The most common form of orgasmic disorder in males is **early or premature ejaculation.** Men with this disorder persistently ejaculate with minimal sexual stimulation before they wish to ejaculate. Again, it is a judgment call as to when early ejaculation becomes a sexual dysfunction. The *DSM-5* specifies that, in order to receive this diagnosis, a man must ejaculate within 1 minute of penetration in partnered sexual activity and before the man wishes it on 75 percent of occasions over a period of at least 6 months. It can be either lifelong or acquired. The *DSM-5* also notes that early ejaculation may be applied to nonpenetrative sexual activities, but specific duration criteria are not known.

Edward Laumann and colleagues (1999) found that 21 percent of men reported problems with early ejaculation; others report rates as high as 40 percent (Williams & Johnson, 2016). Some men seeking treatment for this problem simply cannot prevent ejaculation before their partner reaches orgasm. Others ejaculate after very little stimulation, long before their partner is fully aroused. A community-based study found that 13 percent of men could be diagnosed with premature ejaculation by the *DSM-IV-TR* criteria, which were less specific than the *DSM-5* criteria in defining early ejaculation or requiring that it occur at least 75 percent of the time (Patrick et al., 2005). When the one-minute criterion is applied, the prevalence of men who meet the criteria for the disorder falls to 1 to 3 percent (APA, 2013, p. 444).

Men try to manage problems with early ejaculation by applying desensitizing cream to the penis before sex, wearing multiple condoms, distracting themselves with other thoughts while having sex, not allowing their partner to touch them, and masturbating multiple times shortly before having sex (Althof, 1995). These tactics generally are unsuccessful and can make the man's partner feel shut out of the sexual encounter, as in the following case study.

Men with **delayed ejaculation** experience a marked delay in or the absence of orgasm following the excitement phase of the sexual response cycle in at least 75 percent of sexual encounters. Unlike early ejaculation, the definition of "delay" is not precisely defined and research does not yet suggest a clear definition. In most cases of this disorder, a man cannot ejaculate during intercourse but can ejaculate with manual or oral stimulation. Eight percent of men report problems reaching orgasm (Laumann et al., 1999; see also McCabe et al., 2016); it is estimated that less than 3

CASE STUDY

Bill and Margaret were a couple in their late 20s who had been married for 2 years. They had had a tumultuous dating relationship before marriage. A therapist helped Bill and Margaret deal with issues in their relationship. However, the therapist made an incorrect assumption that with increased intimacy and the commitment of marriage, Bill's ejaculatory control problem would disappear. . . .

Margaret saw the early ejaculation as a symbol of lack of love and caring on Bill's part. As the problem continued over the next 2 years, Margaret became increasingly frustrated and withdrawn. She demonstrated her displeasure by resisting his sexual advances, and their intercourse frequency decreased from three or four times per week to once every 10 days. A sexual and marital crisis was precipitated by Margaret's belief that Bill was acting more isolated and distant when they did have intercourse. When they talked about their sexual relationship, it was usually in bed after intercourse, and the communication quickly broke down into tears, anger, and accusations. Bill was on the defensive and handled the sexual issue by avoiding talking to Margaret, which frustrated her even more.

Unbeknownst to Margaret, Bill had attempted a do-it-yourself technique to gain better control. He had bought a desensitizing cream he'd read about in a men's magazine and applied it to the glans of his penis (the caplike structure at the end of the penis) 20 minutes before initiating sex. During intercourse he tried to keep his leg muscles tense and think about sports as a way of keeping his arousal in check. Bill was unaware that Margaret felt emotionally shut out during sex. Bill was becoming more sensitized to his arousal cycle and was worrying about erection. He was not achieving better ejaculatory control, and he was enjoying sex less. The sexual relationship was heading downhill, and miscommunication and frustration were growing. (McCarthy, B. W., Cognitive-behavioral strategies and techniques in the treatment of early ejaculation. In Leiblum, S. R. & Rosen, R. C. (Eds.), *Principles and practice of sex therapy: Update for the 1990s.* New York: Guilford Press, 1989, 151–152. Used with permission.)

percent of men could be diagnosed with delayed ejaculation (Perelman & Rowland, 2008).

Genito-Pelvic Pain/Penetration Disorder

In community surveys, 12 to 39 percent of women report frequent pain during intercourse (Farmer, Kukkonen, & Binik, 2008; McCabe et al., 2016). The pain may be shallow during intromission (insertion of the penis into the vagina) or deep during penile thrusting. Some women also experience pain when inserting tampons, having a gynecological exam, riding a bike, or even walking (Farmer, Kao, & Binik, 2009). The pain can be the result of dryness of the vagina caused by antihistamines or other drugs, infection of the clitoris or vulval area, injury or irritation to the vagina, or tumors of the internal reproductive organs. Pain during intercourse is rare in men, but when it does occur, it involves painful erections or pain during thrusting (Farmer et al., 2009).

In addition, some women experience involuntary contraction of the muscles surrounding the outer third of the vagina when penetration with a penis, finger, tampon, or speculum is attempted. These contractions are often called vaginismus. These women may experience sexual arousal and have an orgasm when their clitoris is stimulated. In other women, even the anticipation of vaginal insertion may result in this muscle spasm. It is estimated that 1 to 9 percent of women experience such muscle tightening (Perez, Brown, & Binik, 2016).

Women who for approximately 6 months recurrently experience either pain or muscle tightening during sex, or who have marked fear or anxiety about experiencing such pain, can be diagnosed with **genito-pelvic pain/penetration disorder.**

Causes of Sexual Dysfunctions

Most sexual dysfunctions probably have multiple causes, including both biological and psychosocial causes.

Biological Causes

The *DSM-5* specifies that to receive a diagnosis of any sexual dysfunction, the dysfunction cannot be caused exclusively by a medical condition. Still, many medical illnesses can cause problems in sexual functioning in both men and women. One of the most common contributors to sexual dysfunction is diabetes, which can lower sexual drive, arousal, enjoyment, and satisfaction, especially in men (Maiorino, Bellastella, & Esposito, 2014). Diabetes often goes undiagnosed, leading people to believe that psychological factors are causing their sexual dysfunction when the cause actually is undiagnosed diabetes. Other diseases that are common causes of sexual dysfunction, particularly in men, are cardiovascular disease, multiple sclerosis, kidney failure, vascular disease, spinal cord injury, and injury to the autonomic nervous system due to surgery or radiation (Lewis et al., 2010).

As many as 40 percent of cases of erectile disorder are caused by one of these medical conditions (Lewis, Yuan, & Wangt, 2008). In men with cardiovascular disease, sexual dysfunction can be caused directly by the disease, which can reduce blood flow to the penis, or it may be a psychological response to the presence of the disease. For example, a man who recently has had a heart attack may fear he will have another one if he engages in sex.

In men, abnormally low levels of the androgen hormones, especially testosterone, or high levels of the hormones estrogen and prolactin can cause sexual dysfunction (Isidori et al., 2014). In women, levels of both androgens and estrogens may play a role in sexual dysfunction, although less consistently so than in men (Meston & Bradford, 2007). Estrogen problems in women may result in low arousal due to reduced vaginal lubrication. Levels of estrogen drop greatly at menopause; thus, postmenopausal women often complain of lowered sexual desire and arousal. Similarly, women who have had a radical hysterectomy—which removes the main source of estrogen, the ovaries—can experience reductions in both sexual desire and arousal. Androgens seem to play a role in the maintenance of sexual desire and mood and also may enhance the function of vaginal tissue.

Vaginal dryness or irritation, which causes pain during sex and therefore lowers sexual desire and arousal, can be caused by antihistamines, douches, tampons, vaginal contraceptives, radiation therapy, endometriosis, and infections such as vaginitis or pelvic inflammatory disease (Meston & Bradford, 2007). Injuries during childbirth that have healed poorly, such as a poorly repaired episiotomy, can cause sexual pain in women (Salvatore, Redaelli, Baini, & Candiani, 2016). Women who have had gynecological cancers sometimes report pain, changes in the vaginal anatomy, and problems with their body image or sexual self-concept (Sears, Robinson, & Walker, 2018).

Although many people drink alcohol to decrease their sexual inhibitions, alcohol also can impair sexual performance. *©Blend Images—DreamPictures/Brand X Pictures/Getty Images*

Several prescription drugs can diminish sexual drive and arousal and interfere with orgasm (Clayton, 2007; Montejo, Montejo, & Navarro-Cremades, 2015). These include antihypertensive drugs taken by people with high blood pressure, antipsychotic drugs, antidepressants, lithium, and tranquilizers. Indeed, sexual dysfunction is one of the most common side effects of the widely used selective serotonin reuptake inhibitors (Meston & Bradford, 2007; Montejo et al., 2015).

Many recreational drugs, including marijuana, cocaine, amphetamines, and nicotine, can impair sexual functioning (Lewis et al., 2010). Although people often drink alcohol to make them feel sexier and less inhibited, even small amounts of alcohol can significantly impair sexual functioning. Chronic alcohol abusers and alcohol dependents often have diagnosable sexual dysfunctions (Lewis et al., 2008). As noted previously, when a sexual dysfunction is caused by substance use, it is given the diagnosis **substance-induced sexual dysfunction.**

To determine whether a man is capable of attaining an erection, clinicians can do a psychophysiological assessment with devices that directly measure men's erections. In a laboratory, strain gauges can be attached to the base and glans of a man's penis to record the magnitude, duration, and pattern of arousal while he watches erotic films or listens to erotic audio recordings (Lewis et al., 2008). For women, the physical ability to become aroused can be measured with a vaginal photoplethysmograph, a tampon-shaped device inserted into a woman's vagina that records the changes accompanying vasocongestion, the rush of blood to the vagina during arousal.

Psychological Causes

People's emotional well-being and beliefs and attitudes about sex greatly influence their sexuality.

Mental Disorders Again, the *DSM-5* criteria for the diagnosis of sexual dysfunction exclude that caused by other (nonsexual) mental disorders, but a number of mental disorders can cause sexual dysfunction (Waldinger, 2015). A person with depression may have no desire for sex or may experience any of the problems in sexual arousal and functioning discussed in this chapter. Unfortunately, the medications used to treat depression often lead to problems in sexual functioning. Similarly, people with an anxiety disorder, such as generalized anxiety disorder, panic disorder, or obsessive-compulsive disorder, may find their sexual desire and functioning waning. Loss of sexual desire and functioning also is common in people with schizophrenia (Waldinger, 2015).

Attitudes and Cognitions People who have been taught that sex is dirty, disgusting, or sinful or is a "necessary evil" understandably may lack the desire to have sex. They also may know so little about their own body and sexual responses that they do not know how to make sex pleasurable.

Although such negative attitudes toward sex may be less common among younger people these days, many younger and older women still report a fear of "letting go," which interferes with orgasm (Nobre & Pinto-Gouveia, 2006; Peixoto & Nobre, 2014). They say they fear losing control or acting in some way that will embarrass them. This fear of loss of control may result from a distrust of one's partner, a sense of shame about sex, a poor body image, or a host of other factors. Cognitions among men that can contribute to dysfunction include all-or-nothing beliefs about erection quality, satisfying one's partner, and viewing foreplay as a waste of time (Peixoto & Nobre, 2014).

Another set of attitudes that interfere with sexual functioning is often referred to as performance concerns or **performance anxiety** (Masters & Johnson, 1970). People worry so much about whether they are going to be aroused and have an orgasm that this worry interferes with their sexual functioning: "What if I can't get an erection? I'll die of embarrassment!" "I've got to have an orgasm, or he'll think I don't love him!" These worry thoughts are so distracting that people experiencing them cannot focus on the pleasure that sexual stimulation is giving them and thus do not become as aroused as they want to or need to in order to reach orgasm (Figure 2; Barlow, Sakheim, & Beck, 1983; Perelman & Watter, 2016).

In addition, many people engage in *spectatoring:* They anxiously attend to reactions and performance during sex as if they were spectators rather than participants (Masters & Johnson, 1970). Spectatoring distracts from sexual pleasure and interferes with sexual functioning. Unfortunately, people who have had some problems in sexual functioning only develop more performance concerns, which then further interfere with their functioning. By the time they seek treatment for sexual dysfunction, they may be so anxious about "performing" sexually that they avoid all sexual activity.

FIGURE 2 A Model Showing How Anxiety and Cognitive Interference Can Produce Erectile Dysfunction and Other Sexual Disorders.

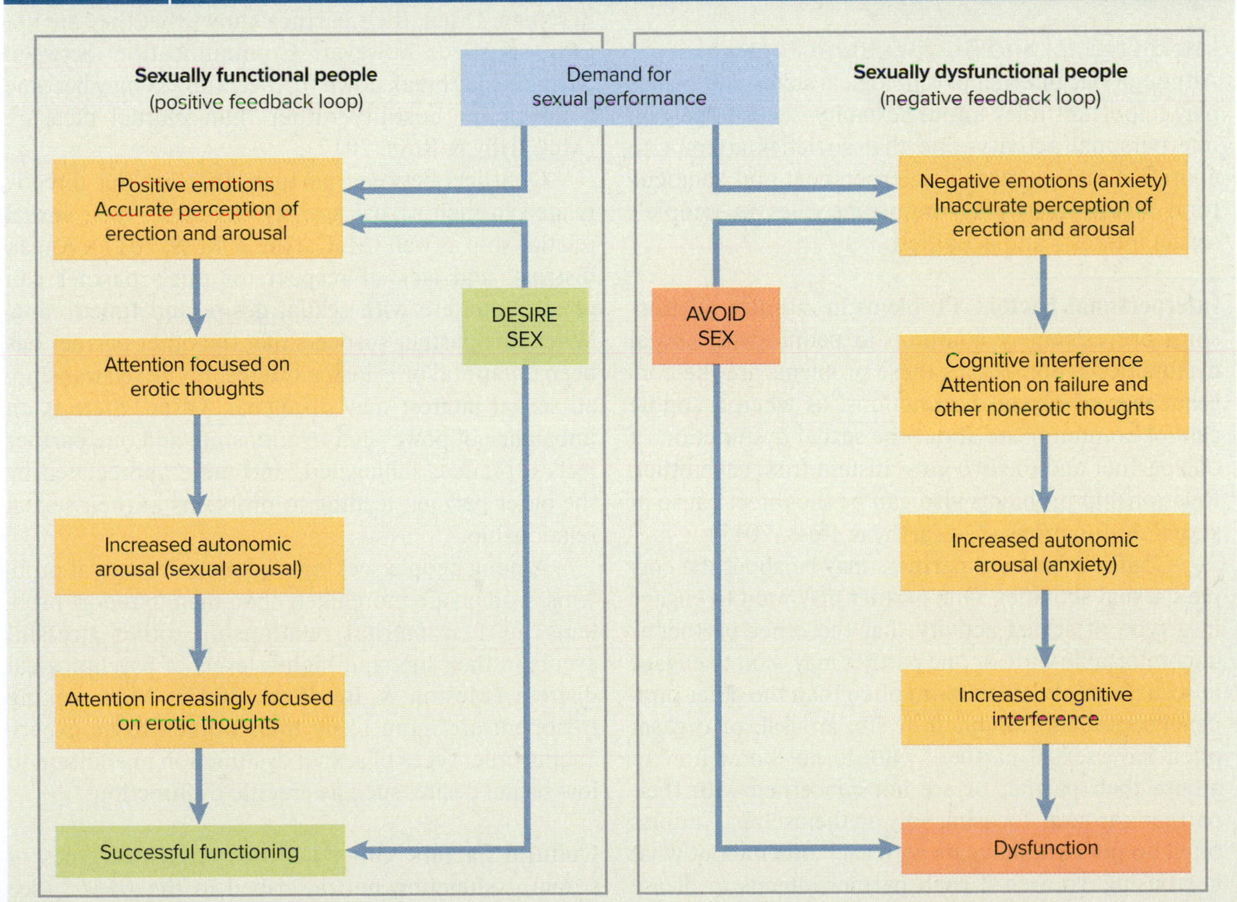

Source: Barlow, 1986.

Trauma Reductions in sexual desire and functioning often follow personal trauma, such as the loss of a loved one, the loss of a job, or the diagnosis of severe illness in one's child. Unemployment may contribute to declines in sexual desire and functioning in men. Traumas such as unemployment can challenge a person's self-esteem, interfering with his or her sexual self-concept. Trauma can also cause a person to experience a depression that includes a loss of interest in most pleasurable activities, including sex. In such cases, clinicians typically focus on treating the depression, with the expectation that sexual desire will resume once the depression has lifted.

One type of personal trauma often associated with sexual desire disorders in women is sexual assault or sexual abuse (Waldinger, 2015). A woman who has been sexually assaulted or abused may lose all interest in sex and become disgusted or extremely anxious when anyone, particularly a man, touches her. Her sexual aversion may become tied to a sense of vulnerability and loss of control or to a conditioned aversion to all forms of sexual contact. In addition, male partners of women who have been sexually assaulted sometimes cannot cope with the trauma and withdraw from sexual encounters with the sexual assault survivor. Survivors then may feel victimized yet again, and their interest in sex may decline even further.

Interpersonal and Sociocultural Factors

Although our internal psychological states and beliefs play important roles in our sexuality, sex is largely an interpersonal activity–one that societies attempt to control. For this reason, interpersonal and sociocultural factors also play important roles in people's sexual interests and activities.

Interpersonal Factors Problems in intimate relationships are extremely common in people with sexual dysfunctions. Sometimes these problems are the consequences of sexual dysfunctions, as when a couple cannot communicate about the sexual dysfunction of one partner and the two grow distant from each other. Relationship problems also can be the direct cause of sexual dysfunctions (McCarthy & Ross, 2017).

Conflicts between partners may be about the couple's sexual activities. One partner may want to engage in a type of sexual activity that the other partner is uncomfortable with, or one partner may want to engage in sexual activity much more often than the other partner. People with inhibited desire, arousal, or orgasm often have sexual partners who do not know how to arouse their partner or are not concerned with their partner's arousal, focusing only on themselves. Couples often do not communicate with each other about what is arousing, so even if each partner intends to please the other, neither knows what the other desires.

Anorgasmia (lack of orgasm) characteristic of female orgasmic disorder may be tied to lack of communication between a woman and her partner about what the woman needs to reach orgasm (McCarthy & Ross, 2017). In sexual encounters between men and women, men still are more likely to decide when to initiate sex, how long to engage in foreplay, when to penetrate, and what position to use during intercourse. A man's pattern of arousal often is not the same as a woman's pattern of arousal, and he may be making these decisions on the basis of his level of arousal and needs for stimulation, not understanding that hers may be different.

Most women have difficulty reaching orgasm by coitus alone and need oral or manual stimulation of the clitoris to become aroused enough to reach orgasm (Carpenter, Williams, & Worly, 2017). Because many men and women believe that men should be able to bring women to orgasm by penile insertion and thrusting alone, women may never receive the stimulation they need to be sufficiently aroused to orgasm. They may feel inhibited from telling their partner that they would like him to stimulate their clitoris more, because they are afraid of hurting their partner's feelings or angering him or because they believe they do not have the right to ask for the kind of stimulation they want. Some women fake an orgasm to protect their partner's ego. Often, their partner knows that they are not fully satisfied, however. Communication between partners may break down further, and sex may become a forum for hostility rather than mutual pleasure (McCarthy & Ross, 2017).

Conflicts between partners that are not directly related to their sexual activity can affect their sexual relationship as well (McCarthy & Ross, 2017). Anger, distrust, and lack of respect for one's partner can greatly interfere with sexual desire and functioning. When one partner suspects that the other partner has been unfaithful or is losing interest in the relationship, all sexual interest may disappear. Often, there is an imbalance of power in a relationship, and one partner feels exploited, subjugated, and underappreciated by the other partner, leading to problems in their sexual relationship.

Among people seeking treatment for sexual problems, women are more likely than men to report problems in their marital relationship, other stressful events in their life, and higher levels of psychological distress (Meston & Bradford, 2007). Men seeking treatment are more likely than women to be experiencing other types of sexual dysfunction in addition to low sexual desire, such as erectile dysfunction.

Cultural Factors Other cultures recognize types of sexual dysfunction not described in the *DSM-5* (see Hall, 2016; Hall & Graham, 2013). For example, both the traditional Chinese medical system and the Ayurvedic medical system, which is native to India, teach that loss of semen is detrimental to a man's health (Dewaraja & Sasaki, 1991). Masturbation is strongly discouraged because it results in semen loss without the possibility of conception. A study of 1,000 consecutive patients seeking treatment in a sexual clinic in India found that 77 percent of the male patients reported difficulties with premature ejaculation and 71 percent were concerned about nocturnal emissions associated with erotic dreams (Verma, Khaitan, & Singh, 1998).

A depersonalization syndrome known as *Koro,* thought to result from semen loss, has been reported among Malaysians, Southeast Asians, and southern Chinese. This syndrome involves an acute anxiety state, characterized by a feeling of panic and impending death, and a delusion that the penis is shrinking into the body and disappearing (American Psychiatric Association, 2013). To stop the penis from disappearing into the body, the patient or his relatives may grab and hold the penis until the attack of Koro is ended.

In Polynesian culture, there is no word for erection problems in men (Mannino, 1999). If a man does not have an erection, it is assumed that he does not want sex. In some African cultures, the preference is for a woman's vagina to be dry and tight for sexual intercourse (Brown, Ayowa, & Brown, 1993). Several herbal treatments are used to achieve this dryness.

In addition to cultures' recognition of unique disorders, aspects of culture such as gender roles and religion affect the expression of disorders recognized in the *DSM-5* (Hall & Graham, 2013). For example, in cultures in which women's desire for sex is not expected, female sexual interest/arousal disorder is less prevalent and is likely experienced differently. For men, premature ejaculation is a primary complaint across cultures. By contrast, Western women seek treatment for sexual desire problems most often, whereas women in non-Western and more male-centric cultures seek treatment for vaginismus and genito-pelvic pain/penetration disorder (Hall, 2016).

In surveys in the United States, less educated and poorer men and women tend to experience more sexual dysfunctions. Problems include having pain during sex, not finding sex pleasurable, being unable to reach orgasm, lacking interest in sex, climaxing too early, and, for men, having trouble maintaining an erection (Laumann, Gagnon, Michael, & Michaels, 1994; Lewis et al., 2010). People in lower educational and income groups may have more sexual dysfunctions because they are under more psychological stress, because their physical health is worse, or because they have not had the benefit of educational programs that teach people about their bodies and about healthy social relationships. In addition, people from cultural backgrounds that teach negative attitudes toward sex are more likely to develop sexual dysfunctions resulting from these attitudes (Hall & Graham, 2013).

Trends Across the Life Span

Our culture conveys the message that young adults, particularly men, can't get enough sex but that sexual activity declines steadily with age. Supposedly, older adults (i.e., over about age 65) hardly ever have sex. Although younger adults tend to engage in more sexual activity than older adults, many adults remain sexually active well into old age (Lindau et al., 2007; Hillman, 2017).

Age-related biological changes can affect sexual functioning (Hillman, 2017). Both men and women need adequate levels of testosterone to maintain sexual desire. Testosterone levels begin to decline in a person's 50s and continue to decrease steadily throughout the rest of the person's life. Lower testosterone levels and age-related decreases in blood flow are associated with increased difficulty in achieving and maintaining an erection, increased time to ejaculation, and less intense orgasms (Hillman, 2017; Hockenberry & Masson, 2016). Diminished estrogen levels in postmenopausal women can lead to vaginal dryness and lack of lubrication and thus to a reduction in sexual responsivity (Hillman, 2017). In many cases of sexual dysfunction in older adults, the cause is not age itself but instead medical conditions, which are more common in older age.

For both older men and older women, the loss of a lifelong spouse, losses of other family members and friends, health concerns, and discomfort with one's own aging can contribute to sexual problems. Conflicts and dissatisfactions in a couple's relationship can worsen as the couple spends more time together following retirement and/or their children's moving out of the house. Older couples may need to learn to be more flexible and patient with each other as their bodies change and to try new techniques for stimulating each other. A number of biological and psychosocial treatments are available for sexual dysfunctions in both older and younger people.

Treatments for Sexual Dysfunctions

Because most sexual dysfunctions have multiple causes, treatment may involve a combination of approaches, often including biological interventions, psychosocial therapy focusing on problems in a relationship or on the concerns of an individual client, and sex therapies to help clients learn new skills for increasing their sexual arousal and pleasure.

Many older adults remain sexually active and experience little decline in sexual functioning. *©Ronnie Kaufman/Blend Images LLC*

Biological Therapies

If a sexual dysfunction is the direct result of another medical condition, such as diabetes, treating the medical condition often will reduce the sexual dysfunction (Maiorino et al., 2014). Similarly, if medications are contributing to a sexual dysfunction, adjusting the dosage or switching to a different type of medication can relieve sexual difficulties. Also, getting a person to stop using recreational drugs such as marijuana can often cure sexual dysfunction.

A number of biological treatments are available for men with erectile disorder (Bennett, 2016). The drug that has received the most media attention in recent years is sildenafil (trade name Viagra). This drug has proven effective both in men whose erectile dysfunction has no known organic cause and in men whose erectile dysfunction is caused by a medical condition, such as hypertension, diabetes, or spinal cord injury. Three other drugs, Cialis, Levitra, and Stenyx, have similar positive effects. These drugs do have side effects, though, including headaches, flushing, and stomach irritation, and they do not work for about a third of men (Chen et al., 2015).

Some antidepressants, particularly the selective serotonin reuptake inhibitors (SSRIs), can cause sexual dysfunctions (Montejo et al., 2015). Other drugs can be used in conjunction with these antidepressants to reduce their sexual side effects. One drug that has proven helpful in this regard is bupropion, which goes by the trade names Wellbutrin and Zyban. Bupropion appears to reduce the sexual side effects of the SSRIs and can itself be effective as an antidepressant. Sildenafil also may help men whose erectile dysfunction is caused by taking antidepressants, allowing them to continue taking the antidepressants without losing sexual functioning.

In men with erectile disorder, certain drugs can be injected directly into the penis to induce an erection. Although this method is effective, it has the obvious drawback of requiring injections (Bednarchik, Kottwitz, & Geiger, 2016). Mechanical interventions are also available for men with erectile dysfunction (Köhler & McVary, 2016). One device includes a cylinder that fits over the penis and connects to a manual or battery-powered vacuum pump, which induces engorgement of the penis with blood. Alternatively, prosthetic devices can be surgically implanted into the penis to make it erect. One prosthesis consists of a pair of rods inserted into the penis. The rods create a permanent erection, which can be bent either up or down against the body. Another type is a hydraulic inflatable device, which allows a man to create an erection by pumping saline into rods inserted in the penis and then to relieve the erection by pumping out the saline. Erections achieved with these devices technically are full erections but frequently do not evoke bodily or mental feelings of sexual arousal.

For men suffering from premature ejaculation, some antidepressants can be helpful, including fluoxetine (Prozac), clomipramine (Anafranil), and sertraline (Zoloft). Several studies suggest that these drugs significantly reduce the frequency of premature ejaculation (Rowland & Cooper, 2017).

Several studies have examined the effects of hormone therapy, specifically the use of testosterone, to increase sexual desire in men and women with hypoactive sexual desire disorder. Hormone replacement therapy can be very effective for men whose low levels of sexual desire or arousal are linked to low levels of testosterone; they are not effective for men whose low sexual desire or arousal is not linked to low levels of testosterone (Hockenberry & Masson, 2016; Isidori et al., 2014). In multiple randomized controlled trials, testosterone also appears to be effective in women with low levels of desire or arousal, particularly postmenopausal women (Achilli et al., 2017). Side effects can include increased hair growth in a minority of cases. Bupropion has proven helpful in treating some women with hypoactive sexual desire (Parish & Hahn, 2016).

Large controlled studies investigating the effects of sildenafil for women with sexual dysfunctions report mixed results (see Brotto, 2017). The drug does increase vasocongestion and lubrication in women, but these physiological changes do not consistently lead to greater subjective arousal, and sildenafil has been largely discarded as a pharmacological treatment for women. A newer medication, filbanserin (Addyi), was approved in the United States in 2015 and dubbed by some as the "female Viagra." Flibanserin acts on multiple neurotransmitters and has shown very modest effects on sexual desire (Brotto, 2017). It is taken daily and the woman cannot use alcohol while taking it, due to risk of developing severe low blood pressure. Because the drawbacks often outweigh the benefits, this drug is not widely prescribed.

Psychotherapy and Sex Therapy

The introduction of drugs, such as sildenafil, that can overcome sexual dysfunctions, at least in men, has dramatically changed the nature of treatments for these disorders. Given the financial and time constraints imposed by managed care, many people seeking treatment for a sexual dysfunction are offered only a medication and not psychotherapy (McCarthy & Ross, 2017). Also, many people want only a medication and do not want to engage in psychotherapy to address possible psychological and interpersonal contributors to their sexual problems.

A variety of psychotherapeutic techniques have been developed, however, and have been shown to help people with sexual dysfunctions (see Frühauf, Gerger, Schmidt, Munder, & Barth, 2013; McCarthy & Ross, 2017; Peterson, 2017). One option is individual psychotherapy in which individuals explore the thoughts and previous experiences that impede them from enjoying a positive sexual life. Couples therapy often helps couples develop more satisfying sexual relationships. As part of both individual and couples therapy, behavioral techniques are used to teach people skills to enhance their sexual experiences and to improve communication and interactions with their sexual partners.

Individual and Couples Therapy A therapist begins treatment by assessing the attitudes, beliefs, and personal history of an individual client or of both members of a couple in order to discover experiences, thoughts, and feelings that might be contributing to sexual problems. Cognitive-behavioral interventions often are used to address attitudes and beliefs that interfere with sexual functioning (McCarthy & Ross, 2017; Wincze & Weinberg, 2015). For example, a man who fears that he will embarrass himself by not sustaining an erection in a sexual encounter may be challenged to examine the evidence of this having happened to him in the past. If this has been a common occurrence for the man, his therapist would explore the thought patterns surrounding the experience and then help the man challenge these cognitions and practice more positive ones. Similarly, a woman who has low sexual desire because she was taught by her parents that sex is dirty would learn to challenge this belief and to adopt a more accepting attitude toward sex.

Many busy couples do not take time for activities that can maintain their sexual interest in each other. *©sturti/iStock/Getty Images*

When one member of a couple has a sexual dysfunction, it may be the result of problems in the couple's relationship, or, conversely, it may be contributing to problems in the relationship. For this reason, many therapists prefer to treat sexual dysfunctions in the context of the couple's relationship, if possible, rather than focusing only on the individual with the sexual dysfunction. The therapist may use role playing during therapy sessions to observe how the couple discusses sex and how the partners perceive each other's role in their sexual encounters (McCarthy & Ross, 2018).

Some couples in long-term relationships have abandoned the seduction rituals—those activities that arouse sexual interest in both partners—they followed when they were first together (McCarthy & Ross, 2018). Couples in which both partners work may be particularly prone to try squeezing in sexual encounters late at night, when both partners are tired and not really interested in sex. These encounters may be rushed or not fully satisfying and can lead to a gradual decline in interest in any sexual intimacy. A therapist may encourage a couple to set aside enough time to engage in seduction rituals and satisfying sexual encounters. For example, partners may decide to hire a babysitter for their children, have a romantic dinner out, and then go to a hotel, where they can have sex without rushing or being interrupted by their children.

Partners often differ in their scripts for sexual encounters—their expectations about what will take place during a sexual encounter and about what each partner's responsibilities are. Resolving these differences in scripts may be a useful goal in therapy.

For example, if a woman lacks desire for sex because she feels her partner is too rough during sex, a therapist may encourage the partner to slow down and show the woman the kind of gentle intimacy she needs to enjoy sex. In general, therapists help partners understand what each wants and needs from sexual interactions and helps them negotiate mutually acceptable and satisfying repertoires of sexual exchange.

When the conflicts between partners involve matters other than their sexual practices, the therapist will focus primarily on these conflicts and only secondarily on the sexual dysfunction. Such conflicts may involve an imbalance of power in the relationship, distrust or hostility, or disagreement over important values or decisions. Cognitive-behavioral, psychodynamic, and family systems therapies are all applied to couple problems, including those affecting sexual dysfunction. Cognitive-behavioral therapies have been researched more than other types of couple therapy and have been shown to be effective for several types of sexual dysfunction (see Benson & Christensen, 2016; Johnson, Simakhodskaya, & Moran, 2018; Wincze & Weinberg, 2015).

Sex Therapy Whether a therapist uses a cognitive-behavioral or some other therapeutic approach to address the psychological issues involved in a sexual dysfunction, direct sex therapy using behavioral techniques may be a part of the therapy. When a sexual dysfunction seems to be due, at least in part, to inadequate sexual skill on the part of the client and his or her partner, sex therapy that focuses on practicing skills can be useful (Frühauf et al., 2013). Some people have never learned what gives them or their partner pleasure or have fallen out of the habit of engaging in some practices. Sex therapy both teaches skills and helps partners develop a regular pattern of engaging in satisfying sexual encounters.

Sex therapy often includes teaching or encouraging clients to masturbate (Heiman, 2000). The goals of masturbation are for people to explore their bodies to discover what is arousing and to become less inhibited about their sexuality. Then individuals are taught to communicate their newly discovered desires to their partners. This technique can be especially helpful for anorgasmic women, many of whom have never masturbated and have little knowledge of what they need in order to become aroused (Meston & Bradford, 2007). Studies show that more than 80 percent of anorgasmic women are able to have an orgasm when they learn to masturbate and that 20 to 60 percent are able to have an orgasm with their partner after learning to masturbate (Heiman, 2000). These women also report increased enjoyment and satisfaction from sex, a more relaxed attitude toward sex and life, and increased acceptance of their body.

The client's cognitions while engaging in new sexual skills can be evaluated and used as a focus of therapy sessions (McCarthy & Ross, 2017). For example, a woman who is learning how to masturbate for the first time may realize that while she is masturbating, she has thoughts such as "I'm going to get caught, and I'll be so embarrassed"; "I shouldn't be doing this—this is sinful"; and "Only pathetic people do this." A cognitive-behavioral therapist can then help the woman address the accuracy of these thoughts and decide whether she wants to maintain this attitude toward masturbation. If the woman is in psychodynamic therapy, the therapist might explore the origins of the woman's attitudes about masturbation in her early relationships. Thus, the behavioral techniques of sex therapy not only directly teach the client new sexual skills but also provide material for discussion in therapy sessions.

Sensate Focus Therapy One of the mainstays of sex therapy is **sensate focus therapy** (Masters & Johnson, 1970; Weiner & Avery-Clark, 2017). In the early phases of this therapy, partners are instructed not to be concerned about or even to attempt intercourse. Rather, they are told to focus intently on the pleasure created by the exercises. These instructions are meant to reduce performance anxiety and any concern about achieving orgasm.

In the first phase of sensate focus therapy, partners spend time gently touching each other, but not around the genitals. They are instructed to focus on the sensations and to communicate with each other about what does and does not feel good. The goal is to

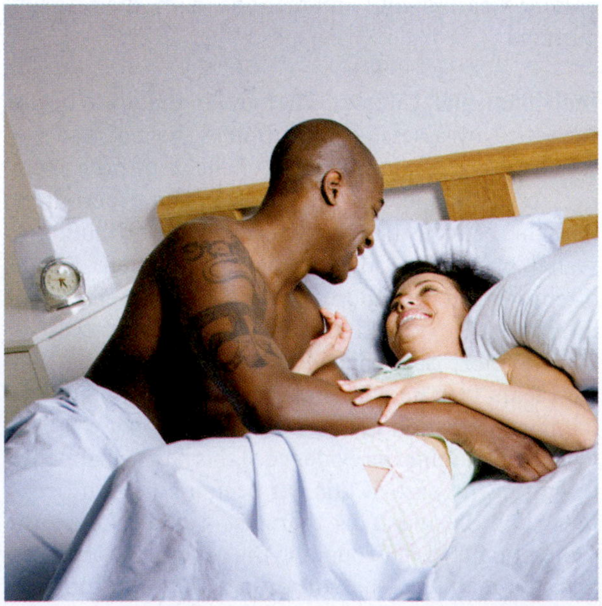

In sensate focus therapy, couples are encouraged to spend time exploring what sexually arouses each of them without feeling pressured to reach orgasm. *©Andersen Ross/Blend Images/Getty Images*

have the partners spend intimate time together communicating, without pressure for intercourse. This first phase may continue for several weeks, until the partners feel comfortable with the exercises and have learned what gives each of them pleasure.

In the second phase of sensate focus therapy, the partners spend time directly stimulating each other's breasts and genitals, but still without attempting intercourse. If the problem is a female sexual interest/arousal disorder, the woman guides her partner to stimulate her in arousing ways. It is acceptable for a woman to be aroused to orgasm during these exercises, but the partners are instructed not to attempt intercourse until she regularly becomes fully aroused by her partner during the sensate focus exercises. If the problem is a male erectile disorder, the man guides his partner in touching him in ways that feel arousing. If he has an erection, he is to let it come and go naturally. Intercourse is forbidden until he is able to have erections easily and frequently during the sensate focus exercises.

Throughout these exercises, the partner with the problem is instructed to be selfish and to focus only on the arousing sensations and on communicating with his or her partner about what feels good. The touching should proceed in a relaxed and nondemanding atmosphere. Once the partner with the problem regularly experiences arousal with genital stimulation, the partners may begin having intercourse, but the focus remains on enhancing and sustaining pleasure rather than on orgasm or performance.

Sensate focus therapy has been shown to be effective for disorders of desire, arousal, and orgasm, often in combination with other therapies (Linschoten, Weiner, & Avery-Clark, 2016). The following case study indicates how the behavioral techniques of sensate focus therapy can help couples recognize and confront the complex personal and interpersonal issues that may be interfering with their enjoyment of sex.

CASE STUDY

Murray, a 53-year-old successful insurance agent, and his wife, a 50-year-old nutritional counselor, had been married for 28 years. With the exception of time spent on vacation, Murray had a 7-year history of erectile dysfunction. The frequency of their lovemaking had gradually declined to its current level of once every 4 months. Murray reported considerable performance anxiety, enhanced by his competitive personality style. He summed up his dilemma: "When you have a life full of successes, you don't get much practice at how to deal with inadequacy."

During the first hour of therapy, sensate focus exercises were suggested and instructions given to engage in sensual nongenital touching. They returned in a week, noting how difficult it had been to find time to pleasure one another. Their mutual avoidance was discussed and understood as a means of warding off feelings of inadequacy. Working through the resistance allowed the couple to engage in the exercises three times over the course of the next week. With the pleasuring, Murray began to achieve good, long-lasting erections.

Therapy then progressed to include genital touching. After the first week, they talked about their problem of "silliness." They realized that humor had been used to cope with the dysfunction. Now, however, joking in bed seemed to inhibit sexual closeness. Murray's good erections were maintained, although he was having trouble concentrating on his sensations. Further exploration revealed that he was focusing his attention in a driven, intense manner. To counter this, the therapist redirected him to maintain a relaxed awareness akin to meditation. Murray found this analogy helpful, and the couple felt ready to proceed with vaginal containment. During the following week, they "disobeyed" and moved on to have mutually satisfying intercourse. They feared the recurrence of the old problem, but it did not return, and the remaining two sessions were spent talking about their sexual life. Despite otherwise good communication, they had never been able before to broach this topic with one another. (Althof, S. E., "Erectile dysfunction: Psychotherapy with men and couples." In Leiblum, S. R. & Rosen, R. C. (Eds.), *Principles and Practice of Sex Therapy*, 3rd ed., New York, NY: Guilford Press, 270. Copyright © 2000 by Guilford Press. Reprinted by permission.)

Techniques for Treating Early Ejaculation Two techniques are useful in helping a man with early ejaculation gain control over his ejaculations: the stop-start technique (Semans, 1956) and the squeeze technique (Masters & Johnson, 1970). The **stop-start technique** can be carried out either through masturbation or with a partner. In the first phase, the man is told to stop stimulating himself or to tell his partner to stop stimulating him just before he is about to ejaculate. He then relaxes and concentrates on the sensations in his body until his level of arousal declines. At that point, he or his partner can resume stimulation, again stopping before the point of ejaculatory inevitability. If stimulation stops too late and the man ejaculates, he is encouraged not to feel angry or disappointed but to enjoy the ejaculation and reflect on what he has learned about his body and then resume the exercise.

If a man is engaging in this exercise with a partner, they are instructed not to engage in intercourse until he has sufficient control over his ejaculations during his partner's manual stimulation of him.

In the second phase of this process, when a female partner is involved, the man lies on his back with his female partner on top of him, and she inserts his penis into her vagina but then remains quiet (a similar position can be used with a male partner). Most men with premature ejaculation have intercourse only in the on-top position, with quick and short thrusting during intercourse, which makes it very difficult for them to exert control over their ejaculations. The goal is for the man to enjoy the sensation of penetration without ejaculating. During the exercise, he is encouraged to touch or massage his partner and for them to communicate about what they are experiencing. If he feels he is reaching ejaculatory inevitability, he can request that his partner dismount and lie next to him until his arousal subsides. Partners are encouraged to engage in this exercise for at least 10 to 15 minutes, even if they must interrupt it several times to prevent the man from ejaculating.

In the third phase of the stop-start technique, the man's partner creates some thrusting motion while still on top of him but uses slow, long strokes. The partners typically reach orgasm and experience the entire encounter as highly intimate and pleasurable. Female partners of men with premature ejaculation often have trouble reaching orgasm during intercourse themselves, because the men lose their erection after ejaculating, long before the women are highly aroused, and tension is high between the partners during sex. The stop-start technique can create encounters in which men's partners receive the stimulation they need to reach orgasm as well.

The **squeeze technique** is used somewhat less often because it is harder to teach to partners (McCarthy, 2001). The man's partner stimulates him to an erection, and then, when he signals that ejaculation is imminent, his partner applies a firm but gentle squeeze to his penis, either at the head or at the base, for 3 or 4 seconds. This results in a partial loss of erection. The partner then can stimulate him again to the point of ejaculation and use the squeeze technique to stop the ejaculation. The goal of this technique, as with the stop-start technique, is for the man with a premature ejaculation disorder to learn to identify the point of ejaculatory inevitability and control his arousal level at that point.

Techniques for Treating Pelvic Muscle Tightening

Pelvic muscle tightening is often treated by deconditioning the woman's automatic tightening of her vaginal muscles (Stein, 2016). She is taught about the muscular tension at the opening of her vagina and the need to learn to relax those muscles. In a safe setting, she is instructed to insert her fingers into her vagina. She examines her vagina in a mirror and practices relaxation exercises. She may also use silicon or metal vaginal dilators made for this exercise. Gradually, she inserts larger and larger dilators as she practices relaxation exercises and becomes accustomed to the feel of the dilator in her vagina. If she has a partner, his or her fingers may be used instead of the dilator. If the woman has a male partner, eventually she guides his penis into her vagina while remaining in control.

Some physical therapists specifically treat sexual dysfunctions by focusing on weakness of the pelvic floor muscles, problems with blood flow in the penis, joint dysfunction, and pain associated with intercourse. They utilize techniques of muscle reeducation, nerve and joint mobilization, and massage.

Considerations for Gay, Lesbian, and Bisexual People

Gay, lesbian, and bisexual people experience sexual dysfunctions for the same reasons as heterosexual people, such as medical disorders, medications, aging, or conflicts with partners, and do so at similar rates (Cohen & Savin-Williams, 2017). Gay, lesbian, and bisexual people face additional stressors related to their sexuality due to continuing stigma and discrimination against them, which can affect sex and health (Gilman et al., 2001; Plöderl & Tremblay, 2015).

Therapists treating gay, lesbian, or bisexual clients must be sensitive to the psychological stresses these clients face as a result of society's rejection of their sexual orientation, as well as to the contributions of these stresses to their sexual functioning. Compared to heterosexual people, these clients may be influenced by unique developmental influences on identity and sexuality (such as coming out processes or cultural expectations) that affect the various domains of sexual function (Cohen & Savin-Williams, 2017). Most of the sex therapy treatments can readily be adapted for gay, lesbian, or bisexual couples.

Gay, lesbian, and bisexual people are discussed here to emphasize unique characteristics relevant to this population's experience of the sexual disorders. Researchers and clinicians do not consider minority sexual orientation itself as pathological. The attitude of clinical psychology as a profession toward homosexuality changed several decades ago. Early versions of the *DSM* listed homosexuality, particularly *ego-dystonic homosexuality* (which meant that the person did not want to be homosexual), as a mental disorder. Gay men, lesbians, and bisexual people argue that their sexual orientation is a natural part of themselves. Apart from society's homophobia, their orientation causes them no discomfort. Ample psychological research supports this idea; moreover, there is little evidence that psychotherapy can lead a homosexual person to become heterosexual, and substantial evidence that it can do harm. In 1973 the American Psychiatric Association removed homosexuality from its list of recognized psychological disorders (Spitzer, 1981). All of the major American mental health organizations explicitly reject the classification of minority sexual orientation as a disorder, as well as the use of so-called "conversion" therapies (e.g., American Psychological Association, 2009).

PARAPHILIC DISORDERS

People vary greatly in the sexual activities they find arousing (see Table 2). Atypical sexual preferences have been called *paraphilias* (Greek for "besides" + "love"). Paraphilias are sometimes divided into those that involve the consent of others (e.g., some sadomasochistic practices) and those that involve nonconsenting others (e.g., voyeurism). They also can be divided into those that involve contact with others (e.g., pedophilia) and those that do not necessarily involve contact with others (e.g., some fetishes). The *DSM-5* specifies that paraphilias are not in and of themselves mental disorders, and cannot be diagnosed as a **paraphilic disorder.** A paraphilic disorder is a paraphilia that is currently causing the individual significant distress or impairment, or entails personal harm or risk of harm to others. Table 3 lists the paraphilic disorders recognized by the *DSM-5.*

The definitions of the paraphilias and paraphilic disorders are highly controversial. The *DSM-5* attempted to tighten the definition of a paraphilic disorder by specifying that the presence of a paraphilia does not constitute a disorder and that a diagnosis can be given only when the behaviors cause the person distress or impairment or cause others harm. However, questions remain as to why some variations in sexual behavior are considered mental disorders while

TABLE 2 The Kinds of Sexual Practices People Find Appealing

A national survey of 18- to 44-year-olds found that many different sexual practices appeal to people, with men finding more activities appealing than do women.

	Percent Saying "Very Appealing"	
Practice	**Men**	**Women**
Vaginal intercourse	83%	78%
Watching partner undress	50	30
Receiving oral sex	50	33
Giving oral sex	37	19
Group sex	14	1
Anus stimulated by partner's fingers	6	4
Using dildos/vibrators	5	3
Watching others do sexual things	6	2
Having a same-gender sex partner	4	3
Having sex with a stranger	5	1

Source: Michael et al., 1994.

TABLE 3 Paraphilic Disorders

The paraphilic disorders involve atypical, recurrent, intense sexually arousing fantasies, sexual urges, or behaviors that cause the individual significant distress or impairment, or entail harm to others or the risk of harm.

Diagnosis	Object of Fantasies, Urges, or Behaviors
Fetishistic disorder	Nonliving objects (e.g., female undergarments) or nongenital body part(s)
Transvestic disorder	Cross-dressing
Sexual sadism disorder	Acts (real, not simulated) involving the physical or psychological suffering (including humiliation) of another person
Sexual masochism disorder	Acts (real, not simulated) of being humiliated, beaten, bound, or otherwise made to suffer
Voyeuristic disorder	Act of observing an unsuspecting person who is naked, in the process of undressing, or engaged in sexual activity
Exhibitionistic disorder	Exposure of one's genitals to an unsuspecting stranger
Frotteuristic disorder	Touching and rubbing against a nonconsenting person
Pedophilic disorder	Sexual activity with a prepubescent child or children

others are not (Beech, Miner, & Thornton, 2016). On the other hand, labeling sexual behaviors that involve victims, such as pedophilia, as mental disorders runs the risk of providing an "excuse" for behaviors that society wishes to forbid and punish.

Some researchers wanted to include a disorder called paraphilic coercive disorder in the *DSM-5*; this diagnosis would apply to individuals who derive sexual pleasure from coercing others into nonconsensual sex (i.e., rape). Not surprisingly, this proposal raised a firestorm of concern (Frances & First, 2011; Knight, 2010; Wollert & Cramer, 2011), and the authors of the *DSM-5* decided to reject the proposal, once again confirming that rape is not a mental disorder but a criminal act (Beech et al., 2016). Another diagnosis proposed but rejected for inclusion in *DSM-5* is hypersexual disorder, which is characterized by excessive preoccupation with sexual fantasies, urges, and activities (sometimes referred to as sexual addiction) and lasts at least 6 months. Again, initial proposals to include this diagnosis in the *DSM-5* (Kafka, 2010) met with sharp criticism that there was insufficient evidence for its validity as a psychiatric disorder (Halpern, 2011; Moser, 2011; see Beech et al., 2016), though a later study suggested high reliability and validity when applied in a clinical setting (Reid et al., 2012). The problem of sexual addiction awaits further study, while those individuals with such behavior (such as excessive pornography use) and associated distress or impairment will seek treatment for a problem that is not yet defined as a mental disorder.

Drag queens such as RuPaul perform in exaggerated female dress and behavior, often as a form of performance art. Most identify as gay men, and do not dress as women for sexual arousal or as an expression of transgender identity. ©*Mark Boster/Los Angeles Times/Getty Images*

These controversies are difficult to resolve because they involve moral judgments and powerful social norms. In addition, the research literature on most paraphilic disorders is limited and inconsistent, providing little information on which to base judgments about how pathological these behaviors are (Beech et al., 2016).

Fetishistic Disorder and Transvestic Disorder

Fetishistic disorder involves the use of nonliving objects or nongenital body parts for sexual arousal or gratification. Commonly eroticized body parts include feet, toes, and hair. Soft fetishes are objects that are soft, furry, or lacy, such as frilly lingerie, stockings, and garters. Hard fetishes are objects that are smooth, harsh, or black, such as spike-heeled shoes, black gloves, and garments made of leather or rubber (Darcangelo, Hollings, & Paladino, 2008). These soft and hard objects are somewhat arousing to many people and, indeed, are promoted as such by their manufacturers. For most people, however, the objects simply add to the sexiness of the people wearing them, and their desire is for sex with those people. For the person with a fetish, the desire is for the object itself (Darcangelo et al., 2008).

Fetishistic disorder is almost exclusively reported in males in clinical samples. Although many men may engage in fetishistic behavior, perhaps less than 1 percent would be diagnosed with a disorder, because their behavior does not cause significant distress or impairment (Darcangelo, 2008).

One variation on fetishism is **transvestic disorder,** or dressing in the clothes of the other sex as a means of becoming sexually aroused. The diagnosis requires that the cross-dressing behavior cause the individual significant distress or impairment. Transvestic disorder can be distinguished from transvestism, which is cross-dressing behavior that may or may not be for the purposes of sexual arousal or gratification (Wheeler, Newring, & Draper, 2008). One community-based study found that 2.8 percent of men and 0.4 percent of women reported engaging in cross-dressing for sexual arousal (Langstrom & Zucker, 2005).

For many men who engage in cross-dressing, it is not the women's clothes themselves that are sexually arousing but instead the activity of dressing in women's clothes. They may surreptitiously wear only one women's garment, such as a pair of women's underpants. Or they may dress fully in women's garments, complete with makeup and a wig. Some men engage in cross-dressing alone. Others participate in transvestite subcultures, in which groups of men gather for drinks, meals, and dancing while dressed as women (Wheeler et al., 2008). About half of men who engage in cross-dressing for sexual gratification find the behavior acceptable and thus might not meet the *DSM-5* criteria for the disorder (Langstrom & Zucker, 2005). Some men with transvestic disorder are sexually aroused by thoughts of being a woman—having a woman's physical traits or functions (for example, breasts or menstruation) or engaging in traditionally feminine tasks, such as sewing. This accompanying arousal is called autogynephilia and is distinct from both gender dysphoria and transgender identity (discussed below).

Most adults who engage in cross-dressing report that the behavior began secretly prior to or during puberty (Wheeler et al., 2008). The function of the cross-dressing at young ages may not be explicitly sexual but instead may be more generally pleasurable or exciting or may alleviate negative psychological states associated with male gender roles. With puberty, cross-dressing activities increasingly are paired with sexual behavior. Most men who engage in cross-dressing are married and have children (Langstrom & Zucker, 2005). With age, the sexual function of cross-dressing may diminish even as men continue to cross-dress as a self-soothing behavior to achieve feelings of comfort or well-being (Newring, Wheeler, & Draper, 2008).

Sexual Sadism and Sexual Masochism Disorders

Sexual sadism disorder and **sexual masochism disorder** are two separate diagnoses, although sadistic and masochistic sexual practices often are considered together as a pattern referred to as **sadomasochism.** In sexual sadism disorder, a person's sexual fantasies, urges, or behaviors involve inflicting pain and humiliation on his or her sex partner. Further, for the diagnosis to be given, the urges must cause the person significant distress or impairment in functioning or the person must have acted on these urges with a nonconsenting person. In sexual masochism disorder, a person's sexual fantasies, urges, or behaviors involve suffering pain or humiliation during sex, and they must cause the person significant distress or impairment in functioning. In both disorders, distress may manifest as guilt, shame, loneliness, or intense sexual frustration.

Some people occasionally engage in mild or moderately sadistic or masochistic behaviors during sex or simulate such behaviors without actually carrying through with the infliction of pain or suffering (Hucker, 2008). These people probably would not be given a diagnosis, especially if their behaviors occur in the context of a trusting relationship in which boundaries have been set and safety measures are in place (e.g., having a "safe word" that, when uttered by either partner,

Sexual sadism and sexual masochism exist along a continuum. More moderate forms that occur between consenting adults, such as those portrayed in the blockbuster romance *Fifty Shades of Grey,* by E. L. James, would likely not qualify for a *DSM-5* diagnosis. ©*Chuck Zlotnick/Focus/Universal/Kobal/Shutterstock*

stops the behavior). This is a good example of sexuality along the continuum, as well as the challenges in defining abnormality in the sexual disorders (Beech et al., 2016). People diagnosed with sexual sadism disorder or sexual masochism disorder typically engage in sadistic and masochistic behaviors as their preferred or exclusive form of sexual gratification.

The sexual rituals in sadism and masochism disorders are of four types: physical restriction, which involves the use of bondage, chains, or handcuffs as part of sex; the administration of pain, in which one partner inflicts pain or harm on the other with beatings, whippings, electrical shock, burning, cutting, stabbing, strangulation, torture, mutilation, or even death; hypermasculinity practices, including the aggressive use of enemas, fists, and dildos in the sexual act; and humiliation, in which one partner verbally and physically humiliates the other during sex (Sandnabba, Santtila, Alison, & Nordling, 2002). The partner who is the victim in such encounters may be either a masochist and a willing "victim" or a nonconsenting victim. A variety of props may be used in these encounters, including black leather garments, chains, shackles, whips, harnesses, and ropes. Men are much more likely than women to enjoy sadomasochistic sex, in the roles of both sadist and masochist (Sandnabba et al., 2002). Some women find such activities exciting, but many consent to them only to please their partners or because they are paid to do so, and some are nonconsenting victims of sadistic men.

Although sadomasochistic sex between consenting adults typically does not result in physical injury, the activities can get out of control or go too far. A particularly dangerous activity is hypoxyphilia, which involves sexual arousal by means of oxygen deprivation, obtained by placing a rope around the neck, putting a plastic bag or mask over the head, or exerting severe chest compression (Hucker, 2008). Accidents involving hypoxyphilia can result in permanent injury or death. Unsurprisingly given the role of lack of consent in the diagnosis, sexual sadism disorder is found at higher rates among forensic populations of sexually motivated murderers and sex offenders (Beech et al., 2016).

Voyeuristic, Exhibitionistic, and Frotteuristic Disorders

Voyeurism, as a form of sexual arousal, involves watching another person undress, do things in the nude, or have sex. Voyeurism is probably the most common illegal paraphilia (Beech et al., 2016; Langstrom, 2009). A survey of 2,450 randomly selected adults from the general population of Sweden found that 12 percent of the men and 4 percent of the women reported at least one incident of being sexually aroused by spying on others having sex (Langstrom & Seto, 2006). A study of 60 male college students in the United States suggested that 42 percent had secretly watched others in sexual situations (Templeman & Stinnet, 1991).

For a diagnosis of **voyeuristic disorder** to be made, the voyeuristic behavior must be repeated over 6 months and must be compulsive. Further, for a diagnosis to be given, the urges must cause the person significant distress or impairment in functioning or the voyeur must have acted on these urges with a nonconsenting person. Most people who engage in voyeurism are men who watch women (Lavin, 2008). They may masturbate during or immediately after the act of watching.

The person who engages in *exhibitionism* obtains sexual gratification by exposing his or her genitals to involuntary observers, who usually are strangers. The survey in Sweden cited above found that 4.1 percent of men and 2.1 percent of women reported having experienced sexual arousal from exposing their genitals to a stranger at least once in their life (Langstrom & Seto, 2006). In order to obtain the diagnosis of **exhibitionistic disorder,** individuals must have acted on their urges to engage in the behavior, or the behavior must cause significant distress or impairment. Most exhibitionists are men, and their targets tend to be women, children, or adolescents (Murphy & Page, 2008). Clinically, it is important to know that exhibitionists who target children may also have a co-occurring pedophilic disorder. The exhibitionist typically confronts his victim in a public place, such as at a park or on a bus. His arousal comes from observing the victim's surprise, fear, or disgust or from a fantasy that his victim is becoming sexually aroused. His behavior often is compulsive and impulsive—he feels a sense of excitement, fear, restlessness, and sexual arousal and then feels compelled to find relief by exhibiting himself (Murphy & Page, 2008). Some people who engage in exhibitionism masturbate while exhibiting themselves. Others draw on memories or fantasies of exposing themselves to arouse themselves while masturbating.

People who engage in exhibitionism are more likely than most sex offenders to get caught, in part because of the public nature of their behavior. In addition, some of them repeatedly return to places where they have already exhibited themselves. The danger of being caught heightens their arousal. People who engage in exhibitionism are also likely to continue their behavior after having been caught (Murphy & Page, 2008).

Frotteurism is a paraphilia that often co-occurs with voyeurism and exhibitionism. The person who engages in frotteurism gains sexual gratification from rubbing against and fondling parts of the body of a nonconsenting person. Often, this happens in crowded places, such as an elevator, and the target may not recognize the contact as sexual (Krueger & Kaplan, 2008). In order to receive the diagnosis of **frotteuristic disorder,** individuals must have acted on their urges to engage in the behavior, or the urges must be causing significant distress or impairment. Most people who engage in frotteurism are males, and the onset of the disorder most often is in adolescence or early adulthood (Beech et al., 2016; Lussier & Pichê, 2008).

Pedophilic Disorder

People with **pedophilic disorder** have sexual fantasies, urges, and behaviors focused on prepubescent children. To be diagnosed with pedophilic disorder, the individual must have acted on the urges, or the urges must have caused significant distress or impairment. Most people with pedophilic disorder are heterosexual men attracted to young girls (Seto, 2008). Homosexual men with pedophilia typically are attracted to young boys. Women can have pedophilia, but this situation is rarer.

DSM-5 recognizes that pedophilic disorder can be exclusive (i.e., attracted only to children) or nonexclusive. Additional specifiers indicate whether an individual is sexually attracted to males, females, or both, and whether the pedophilic behavior is limited to incest.

Not all individuals with pedophilic fantasies engage in sexual contact with children; instead, many use child pornography to become sexually aroused (Seto, 2009). Still, most of what we know about pedophilia is based on studies conducted with individuals who have committed sexual offenses with children. Sexual encounters between people with pedophilic disorder and their child victims often are brief, although they may recur frequently. People with pedophilic disorder may threaten children with harm, physically restrain them, or tell them that they will punish them or their loved ones if the children do not comply. Other people with pedophilic disorder are loving, caring, and gentle to the child, using emotional closeness to gain sexual access to the child. This is especially true in incestuous relationships, in which people with pedophilic disorder may see themselves as simply being good, loving parents. They believe that what they do to the child is not sexual but loving (Seto, 2009). Some predatory individuals with pedophilic disorder develop elaborate plans for gaining access to children, such as winning the trust of the mother or marrying the mother, trading children with other people with pedophilic disorder, or, in rare cases, abducting children or adopting children from foreign countries (McConaghy, 1998).

The impact on the child victims of people with pedophilic disorder can be great. The most frequent symptoms shown by sexually abused children are fearfulness, complex posttraumatic stress disorder, conduct disorder and hyperactivity, sexualized behaviors (promiscuity and sexual behavior inappropriate for their age), and poor self-esteem (Kendall-Tackett, Williams, & Finkelhor, 1993; McConaghy, 1998; Murray, Nguyen, & Cohen, 2014). More severe symptoms are experienced by children who endure frequent abuse over a long period, who are penetrated by the perpetrator, who are abused by a family member (typically, a father or stepfather), and whose mother does not provide support on learning of the abuse. About two-thirds of victimized children show significant recovery from their symptoms within 12 to 18 months following cessation of the abuse, but significant numbers of abused children continue to experience psychological problems even into adulthood (Nelson, Baldwin, & Taylor, 2012; Kendall-Tackett et al., 1993; Vonderlin et al., 2018).

CASE STUDY

Dr. Crone, a 35-year-old, single child psychiatrist, had been arrested and convicted of fondling several neighborhood girls, ages 6 to 12. Friends and colleagues were shocked and dismayed, as he had been considered by all to be particularly caring and supportive of children.

Dr. Crone's first sexual experience was at age 6, when a 15-year-old female camp counselor performed fellatio on him several times over the course of the summer—an experience that he had always kept to himself. As he grew older, he was surprised to notice that the age range of girls who attracted him sexually did not change, and he continued to have recurrent erotic urges and fantasies about girls between ages 6 and 12. Whenever he masturbated, he would fantasize about a girl in that age range, and on a couple of occasions over the years, he had felt himself to be in love with such a youngster.

Intellectually, Dr. Crone knew that others would disapprove of his many sexual involvements with young girls. He never believed, however, that he had caused any of these youngsters harm, feeling instead that they were simply sharing pleasurable feelings together. He frequently prayed for help and that his actions would go undetected. He kept promising himself that he would stop, but the temptations were such that he could not. (Source: *DSM-IV-TR Casebook: A Learning Companion to the Diagnostic and Statistical Manual of Mental Disorders,* Fourth Edition, Text Revision. American Psychiatric Association, 2000.)

Causes of Paraphilias

Behavioral theories of the paraphilias explain them as being due to an initial classical pairing of intense early sexual arousal with a particular stimulus (Figure 3). For example, a child may become aroused when spying on the babysitter's lovemaking with her boyfriend or while being held down and tickled erotically. This may be followed by intensive operant conditioning in which the stimulus is present during masturbation. For example, the individual may repeatedly fantasize about a particular scenario, such as watching the babysitter have sex, while masturbating. This reinforces the association between the stimulus and sexual arousal. The individual may try to suppress the undesired arousal or behaviors, but these attempts at inhibition increase the frequency and intensity of the fantasies. Eventually, the sexual arousal may generalize to other stimuli similar to the initial fantasy, such as actually watching other people's lovemaking, leading to paraphilic behavior (e.g., voyeurism). Some people with paraphilia appear to have a strong sex drive and masturbate often, providing many opportunities for the pairing of their fantasies with sexual gratification (Kafka & Hennen, 2003). Often, the person with a paraphilia also has few opportunities for other types of sexual reinforcement and has difficulty relating appropriately to other adults.

FIGURE 3 A Behavioral Account of the Development of Paraphilias.

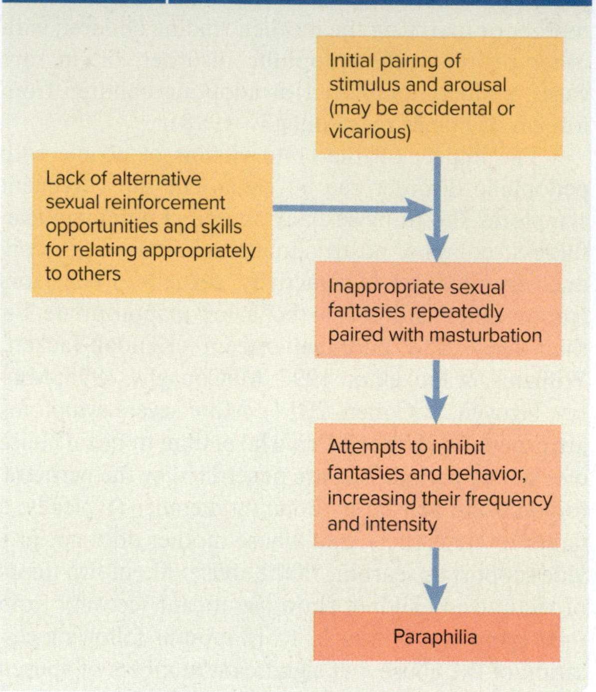
Initial pairing of stimulus and arousal (may be accidental or vicarious)
Lack of alternative sexual reinforcement opportunities and skills for relating appropriately to others
Inappropriate sexual fantasies repeatedly paired with masturbation
Attempts to inhibit fantasies and behavior, increasing their frequency and intensity
Paraphilia

These classic behavioral theories have been supplemented with principles of social learning theory (see the chapter "Theories and Treatment of Abnormality"), which suggest that the larger environment of a child's home and culture influences his or her tendency to develop deviant sexual behavior. Children whose parents frequently use corporal punishment and engage in aggressive contact with each other are more likely to engage in impulsive, aggressive, and perhaps sexualized acts toward others as they grow older. Many people with pedophilia have poor interpersonal skills and feel intimidated when interacting sexually with adults (Seto, 2008).

A study of 64 convicted sex offenders with various types of paraphilia found that they had higher rates of childhood abuse and family dysfunction than did offenders who had committed property crimes and did not have a paraphilia (Lee, Jackson, Pattison, & Ward, 2002). Childhood sexual abuse was a particularly strong predictor of pedophilia. Similarly, studies of juvenile sex offenders, most of whom assaulted a younger child, find that many likely suffered sexual abuse (Gerardin & Thibaut, 2004).

Cognitive theorists have also identified a number of distortions and assumptions that people with a paraphilia have about their behaviors and the behaviors of their victims (Gerardin & Thibaut, 2004; Maletzky, 1998). These distortions may have been learned from parents' deviant messages about sexual behavior. They are used to justify the person's victimization of others when that is part of the behavior.

Several lines of evidence suggest that alterations in the development of the brain and hormonal systems may contribute to pedophilia (Seto, 2008). Men with pedophilia are more likely to have had a head injury before age 13, to have cognitive and memory deficits, to have lower intelligence, and to have differences in brain structure volume (Cantor et al., 2008). In addition, some small studies suggest that men with pedophilia have dysfunctions in the frontal areas of the brain involved in regulating impulsive and aggressive behavior and in testosterone levels (Jordan, Fromberger, Stolpmann, & Müller, 2011). How these factors specifically contribute to pedophilia is not yet clear.

Treatments for the Paraphilic Disorders

Most people with a paraphilia or a paraphilic disorder do not seek treatment for their behaviors (Darcangelo et al., 2008). Treatment is often forced on those who are arrested after engaging in illegal acts including voyeurism, exhibitionism, frotteurism, or pedophilia. Simple incarceration does little to change these behaviors, and convicted sex offenders are likely to become repeat offenders (Seto, 2008).

Biological interventions generally are aimed at reducing the sex drive in order to reduce paraphilic behavior. Surgical castration, which removes the testes and thereby almost completely eliminates the production of androgens, lowers repeat offense rates among sex offenders (Maletzky & Field, 2003; Seto, 2009). Castration has been performed on hundreds of convicted sex offenders in the Netherlands, Germany, and the United States, although it is rarely used today (Seto, 2009).

Sex offenders can also be treated by chemical castration, in which they are given antiandrogen drugs that suppress the production of testosterone and thereby reduce the sex drive. These drugs typically are used in conjunction with psychotherapy and can be useful for hypersexual men who are motivated to change their behavior (Holoyda & Kellaher, 2016). Follow-up studies have shown that people with a paraphilia treated with antiandrogen drugs show reductions in their paraphilic behavior (Garcia, Delavenne, Assumpção, & Thibaut, 2013; Holoyda & Kellaher, 2016). These drugs have a number of side effects, however, including fatigue, sleepiness, depression, weight gain, leg cramps, breast formation, hair loss, and osteoporosis. Seven U.S. states have laws that require some sex offenders who want to be paroled to take antiandrogen drugs or undergo surgical castration.

The selective serotonin reuptake inhibitors (SSRIs) have been used to reduce sexual drive and paraphilic behavior (Holoyda & Kellaher, 2016). Some studies find that these drugs have positive effects on sexual drive and impulse control, although the effects are not totally consistent across studies.

Behavior modification therapies commonly are used to treat paraphilia and can be successful if people with a paraphilia are willing to change their behavior. **Aversion therapy** is used to extinguish sexual responses to objects or situations a person with a paraphilia finds arousing. During such therapy, a person with a paraphilia might be exposed to painful but harmless electric shocks or loud bursts of noise while viewing photographs of what arouses them, such as children, or while actually touching objects that arouse them, such as women's panties. Desensitization procedures may be used to reduce the person's anxiety about engaging in normal sexual encounters with other adults. For example, people with a paraphilia might be taught relaxation exercises, which they then use to control their anxiety as they gradually build up fantasies of interacting sexually with other adults in ways that are fulfilling to them and to their partners (Maletzky, 1998). These behavioral treatments generally are effective in the treatment of nonpredatory paraphilias such as fetishism (Darcangelo et al., 2008).

Cognitive interventions may be combined with behavioral interventions designed to help people learn more socially acceptable ways to approach and interact with people they find attractive (e.g., Kaplan & Krueger, 2012; Wong Sarver & Gros, 2014). Role playing might be used to give the person with a paraphilia practice in approaching another person and eventually negotiating a positive sexual encounter with him or her. Also, group therapy in which people with paraphilias support one another through changes in their behavior can be helpful. Multiple studies find that these combined cognitive-behavioral treatments can effectively treat nonpredatory paraphilias in individuals motivated to change (Darcangelo et al., 2008; Kaplan & Krueger, 2012).

Cognitive-behavioral therapy also has been used to help people with a predatory paraphilia (e.g., pedophilia, exhibitionism, voyeurism) identify and challenge thoughts and situations that trigger their behaviors and serve as justifications for the behaviors (Kaplan & Krueger, 2012). Some clinical trials of cognitive-behavioral therapy for sex offenders have found a significantly lower recidivism rate in men who received the therapy compared to those who did not (Marshall & Marshall, 2015). However, the evidence base is small and somewhat mixed (Kaplan & Krueger, 2012; Marques, Wiederanders, Day, Nelson, & van Ommeren, 2005).

GENDER DYSPHORIA

Gender dysphoria is a new *DSM-5* diagnostic category that replaces *DSM-IV*'s *gender identity disorder.* While gender identity disorder emphasized cross-gender identification, *DSM-5*'s gender dysphoria is diagnosed when there is a discrepancy between individuals' gender identity (i.e., sense of themselves as male or female) and their biological sex (Table 4). Stephanie, in the following case study, would be diagnosed with gender dysphoria.

DSM-5 acknowledges the wide variation of gender-incongruent conditions and provides separate criteria sets for gender dysphoria in children and in adolescents and adults, the latter of which are more

TABLE 4 *DSM-5* Criteria for Gender Dysphoria in Adolescents or Adults

A. A marked incongruence between one's experienced/expressed gender and assigned gender, of at least 6 months duration, as manifested by at least two of the following:

1. A marked incongruence between one's experienced/expressed gender and primary and/or secondary sex characteristics (or, in young adolescents, the anticipated secondary sex characteristics)
2. A strong desire to be rid of one's primary and/or secondary sex characteristics because of a marked incongruence with one's experienced/expressed gender (or, in young adolescents, a desire to prevent the development of the anticipated secondary sex characteristics)
3. A strong desire for the primary and/or secondary sex characteristics of the other gender
4. A strong desire to be of the other gender (or some alternative gender different from one's assigned gender)
5. A strong desire to be treated as the other gender (or some alternative gender different from one's assigned gender)
6. A strong conviction that one has the typical feelings and reactions of the other gender (or some alternative gender different from one's assigned gender)

B. The condition is associated with clinically significant distress or impairment in social, occupational, or other important areas of functioning.

CASE STUDY

Stephanie was 30 when she first attended our clinic. She gave a history of conviction that she was, in fact, male and wished to rid herself of identifiably female attributes and acquire male traits and features. She said she had been cross-living and employed as a male for about 1 year, following the breakdown of a 10-year marriage. She was taking testosterone prescribed by her family physician. She presented at our clinic with a request for removal of her uterus and ovaries.

She did not give a childhood history of tomboy attitudes, thoughts, or behavior. She said social interaction with other children, boys or girls, was minimal. Desperate for a friend, she fantasized "an articulate and strong" boy, exactly her age, named Ronan. They were always together and they talked over everything: thoughts and feelings and the events of her life. Cross-dressing in her father's clothing also began during childhood. There was no history of sexual arousal associated with or erotic fantasy involving cross-dressing.

Puberty at age 12 and the accompanying bodily changes apparently did not overly distress Stephanie. Sexual and romantic feelings focused on "slender, feminine-appearing men." . . .

At 19, she met a slender, good-looking man. They were compatible and married soon after. The marriage was a success. Stephanie's preferred position for intercourse was with both kneeling, she behind her husband, rubbing her pubic area against him while masturbating him. She would imagine she had a penis and was penetrating him. . . . She decided to live full-time in the male role as Jacob. While on the West Coast, she started treatment with male hormones. She moved back east and presented at our clinic for assessment. She saw herself as a male, primarily attracted to gay or gay-appearing males. (Dickey & Stephens, 1995, pp. 442–443)

detailed (see Table 4; Zucker, Lawrence, & Kreukels, 2016). Importantly, the diagnosis of gender dysphoria requires significant distress or impairment associated with the gender incongruence; the incongruence is not in itself viewed as a disorder. As with adults, children with gender dysphoria experience incongruence between their assigned gender and the way they experience themselves as male or female. *Gender dysphoria in children* is a rare condition in which a child persistently rejects his or her anatomic sex and strongly desires to be or insists he or she is a member of the other sex. Girls with this disorder seek masculine-type activities and male peer groups to a degree far beyond that of a tomboy. Sometimes these girls express the belief that they will eventually grow a penis. Boys with the disorder seek feminine-type activities and female peer groups and tend to begin cross-dressing in girls' clothes at a very early age (Zucker & Wood, 2011). They express disgust with their penis and wish it would disappear. The onset of these behaviors typically is in the preschool years. Boys are referred more often than girls for concerns regarding gender dysphoria. This may reflect a greater prevalence of gender dysphoria in males than in females, or it may reflect a greater concern on the part of parents with violations of gender roles in boys than in girls (Zucker & Cohen-Kettenis, 2008).

Adults with gender dysphoria might cross-dress or dress in gender-nonconforming ways, either occasionally or regularly. Unlike people with transvestic disorder, these people are not sexually aroused by this practice; they simply believe they are putting on the clothes of the gender to which they really belong. The sexual preferences of individuals with gender dysphoria vary. Some individuals are asexual, having little interest in either sex; some are heterosexual; and some are homosexual (Lawrence, 2008). People with gender dysphoria who can afford it may seek a sex-change operation.

Gender dysphoria is rare. Studies of prevalence vary, but a meta-analysis estimated prevalence of 6.8 in 100,000 natal (born) males and 2.6 in 100,000 natal females (Arcelus et al., 2015). Some people with gender dysphoria are so disturbed by their misassignment of gender and its social consequences that they develop mood and anxiety disorders, and to a lesser degree, alcohol and other substance abuse problems (Yarbrough, 2018; Zucker et al., 2016). Rates of suicide, suicide attempts, and nonsuicidal self-injury are also elevated in this group. Low self-esteem and psychological distress also result from their rejection by others. High rates of HIV infection among people with gender dysphoria have been reported in some studies, especially among individuals who also face poverty, racism, and employment discrimination (American Psychological Association, 2015; Wiewel, Torian, Merchant, Braunstein, & Shepard, 2016). HIV may be contracted through risky sexual behaviors or through the sharing of needles during drug use or hormone injections. Many people with gender dysphoria avoid seeking medical attention because of negative interactions with physicians. Indeed, some physicians refuse to treat people with gender dysphoria.

The diagnosis of gender dysphoria represents one piece—and a quite controversial piece—of gender diversity more broadly (Zucker & Duschinsky, 2016; Zucker et al., 2016). A number of terms are used by

In recent years the experiences of transgender individuals have become more visible in the culture, including the coming out of Caitlyn Jenner (previously Bruce Jenner), an Olympic athlete and reality TV star. *Left: ©Focus On Sport/Getty Images Sport/Getty Images; Right: ©Joe Seer/Shutterstock*

and for people whose gender identity or expression does not correspond with binary, biologically based male/female categories, and who would not necessarily be diagnosed with gender dysphoria. These terms include "transgender," "gender variant," "genderqueer," "gender nonconforming," "nonbinary," and "transsexual," among others. The term **transgender** (or "trans") is currently the most widely used, and refers to the broad spectrum of individuals who transiently or persistently identify with a gender different from their natal sex. This may include nontraditional gender identity that is recognized as neither male nor female. The term "transsexual," more widely used in the past, refers primarily to people who have chosen to undergo sexual reassignment surgery or hormonal treatment to align their biology with their gender identity (American Psychological Association, 2015). It is a more medically based term than the broader, socially based "transgender" umbrella term, and is considered offensive by some. The term "cisgender" applies to people whose gender identity aligns with their natal sex.

People who identify as transgender may or may not be diagnosed with gender dysphoria, depending on whether their gender incongruence causes distress or impairment. This was a major concern in the development of the *DSM-5* criteria (Zucker et al., 2016). Some transgender groups advocated for removing gender identity disorder altogether, just as homosexuality was removed in 1973. However, it was retained in order to maintain access to care for people distressed by their gender incongruence, and was reformulated to emphasize this incongruence rather than cross-sex identification (Zucker et al., 2016). Notably, whereas gender dysphoria is quite rare, population-based studies in the United States estimate that 0.6 percent identify as

Awareness of issues of gender dysphoria and transgender identity has increased in recent years, due in part to increased depiction in film and television. *©Lionsgate TV/Netflix/Kobal/Shutterstock*

transgender (Flores, Herman, Gates, & Brown, 2016). Like the sexual disorders, the gender dysphoria diagnosis is a good example of the continuum approach, and of how defining and classifying abnormality are inherently affected by social, historical, and cultural contexts (see the chapters "Looking at Abnormality" and "Assessing and Diagnosing Abnormality").

Contributors to Gender Dysphoria

Biological theories of gender dysphoria have focused on the effects of prenatal hormones on brain development (Zucker et al., 2016; Zucker & Wood, 2011). Although several specific mechanisms have been implicated, most theories suggest that people who develop gender dysphoria have been exposed to unusual levels of hormones, which influence later gender identity and sexual orientation by influencing the development of brain structures involved in sexuality. In genetic females, female-to-male gender dysphoria has been associated with hormonal disorders resulting in prenatal exposure to high levels of androgens (Baba et al., 2007), whereas in genetic males, male-to-female gender dysphoria has been associated with prenatal exposure to very low levels of androgens (Hines, Ahmed, & Hughes, 2003; Swaab & Garcia-Filgueras, 2009).

Researchers have identified multiple differences in brain anatomy and function among people with gender dysphoria (Kreukels & Guillamon, 2016; Zucker et al., 2016). In multiple studies, a cluster of cells in the hypothalamus called the bed nucleus of the stria terminalis, which plays a role in sexual behavior, has been implicated in gender dysphoria (Chung, De Vries, & Swaab, 2002; Garcia-Filgueras & Swaab, 2008; see Kreukels & Guillamon, 2016). Typically this cluster of cells is smaller in women's brains than in men's. Studies have found that this cluster of cells is half as large in men with gender dysphoria as in men without the disorder and close to the size usually found in women's brains. Other differences include gray matter volume, white matter structure, and cortical thickness. People with gender dysphoria, compared to people who do not experience gender incongruence, show patterns in these brain areas that are more like those in people of the other biological sex. However, these findings require further investigation. They apply more to natal men with gender dysphoria than to natal women, and also differ depending on sexual orientation (Kreukels & Guillamon, 2016; Zucker et al., 2016).

Hormonal factors and neural factors are closely related; they affect one another. Moreover, both may be tied to genetic factors. Family and twin studies suggest that gender dysphoria may have genetic causes (Coolidge, Thede, & Young, 2002; Heylens et al., 2012), although the specific genetic factors involved are not yet known (Ujike et al., 2009; Zucker et al., 2016).

In general, the evidence in support of psychological contributors to gender dysphoria has been weak (Zucker et al., 2016; Zucker & Wood, 2011). Most psychosocial theories of gender dysphoria focus on the role parents play in shaping their children's gender identity. Parents encourage children to identify with one sex or the other by reinforcing "gender-appropriate" behavior and punishing "gender-inappropriate" behavior. From early infancy, they buy male or female clothes for their children and sex-stereotyped toys (dolls or trucks). They encourage or discourage playing rough-and-tumble games or playing with dolls.

A long-term study of a large sample of boys with gender dysphoria found that their parents were less likely than the parents of boys without gender dysphoria to discourage cross-gender behaviors (Green, 1987). That is, these boys were not punished, either subtly or overtly, for engaging in feminine behavior such as playing with dolls or wearing dresses as much as were boys who did not have gender dysphoria. Further, boys who were highly feminine (although not necessarily with gender dysphoria) tended to have mothers who had wanted a girl rather than a boy, saw their baby sons as girls, and dressed their baby sons as girls. When the boys were older, their mothers tended to prohibit rough-and-tumble play, and the boys had few opportunities to have male playmates. About one-third of these boys had no father in the home, and those who did have a father in the home tended to be very close to their mother. However, conclusions about the role of parenting and psychosocial factors are limited by the design of most studies in this area (see Zucker et al., 2016).

Gender identity tends to be quite stable from childhood into adulthood. However, this stability is less clear among children with gender dysphoria. Many such children grow up to identify with their natal sex. One 24-year longitudinal study found that gender dysphoria in childhood is a better predictor of adult homosexual orientation than of adult gender dysphoria (e.g., Steensma, Van der Ende, Verhulst, & Cohen Ketteni, 2013). Persistence of gender dysphoria from childhood into adolescence is higher among natal girls, children who express more intense dysphoria, and children who have begun taking on a cross-sex social role (Steensma, McGuire, Kreukels, Beekman, & Cohen-Kettenis, 2013). Importantly, research in this area is new, ongoing, and hotly debated, with major social and treatment implications for children (Olson, 2016; Temple Newhook et al., 2018; Zucker, 2018).

Treatments for Gender Dysphoria

Therapists who work with people with gender dysphoria help these individuals clarify their gender identity or experienced gender and their desire for treatment. In addition to psychotherapy, there are three principal treatments for gender dysphoria: (1) cross-sex hormone therapy, (2) full-time real-life experience in the desired gender role, and (3) sex reassignment surgery, which provides the genitalia and secondary sex characteristics (e.g., breasts) of the gender with which the individual identifies (Byne et al., 2012).

Cross-sex hormone therapy stimulates the development of secondary sex characteristics of the preferred sex and suppresses secondary sex characteristics of the birth sex. Estrogens are used in feminizing hormone therapy for male-to-female individuals with gender dysphoria. These hormones cause fatty deposits to develop in the breasts and hips, soften the skin, and inhibit the growth of a beard. Testosterone is used to induce masculinization in female-to-male individuals with gender dysphoria. This hormone causes the voice to deepen, hair to become distributed in a male pattern, fatty tissue in the breast to recede, and muscles to enlarge; the clitoris also may grow larger (Byne et al., 2012). Hormone therapy may be given to individuals regardless of whether they wish to undergo sex reassignment surgery.

Before undergoing sex reassignment surgery, individuals spend up to a year or more living full-time in the gender role they seek. Some choose to live full-time in their desired gender role even if they do not undertake sex reassignment surgery or hormone therapy (Byne et al., 2012).

Sex reassignment requires a series of surgeries and hormone treatments, often over a period of 2 years or longer. In male-to-female surgery, the penis and testicles are removed, and tissue from the penis is used to create an artificial vagina. The construction of male genitals for a female-to-male reassignment is technically more difficult (Byne et al., 2012). First, the internal sex organs (ovaries, fallopian tubes, uterus) and any fatty tissue remaining in the breasts are removed. Then the urethra is rerouted through the enlarged clitoris, or an artificial penis and scrotum are constructed from tissue taken from other parts of the body. This penis allows urination while standing but cannot achieve a natural erection. Other procedures, such as artificial implants, may be used to create an erection.

Sex reassignment surgery is controversial. Follow-up studies suggest that the outcome tends to be positive when patients are carefully selected for gender reassignment procedures based on their motivation for change and their overall psychological health and are given psychological counseling to help them through the change (Byne et al., 2012; Gorin-Lazard et al., 2013). Reviews of outcome studies have found adequate levels of sexual functioning and high sexual satisfaction following sex reassignment surgery (Klein & Gorzalka, 2009; Murad et al., 2010).

Perhaps the most controversial topic in this area is the treatment of children and adolescents. Treatment primarily focuses on psychotherapy to help children clarify their gender identity and deal with interpersonal and psychological issues created by that identity. Most clinicians consider cross-sex hormone therapies and surgeries unacceptable for children and adolescents because of their long-term consequences and children's inability to give fully informed consent for such procedures (Byne et al., 2012). However, current biological treatment options include medications known as gonadotropin-releasing hormone analogues, which delay the progression of puberty. These medications slow the progression of secondary sex characteristics, reducing gender dysphoria and giving children, parents, and clinicians more time to assess gender identity and appropriate treatment for dysphoria (Chew, Anderson, Williams, May, & Pang, 2018; Nahata, Chelvakumar, & Leibowitz, 2017). These drugs have potential side effects, including low bone density.

CHAPTER INTEGRATION

Nowhere is the interplay of biological, psychological, and social forces more apparent than in matters of sexuality (Figure 4). Biological factors influence gender identity, sexual orientation, and sexual functioning. These biological factors can be greatly moderated, however, by psychological and social factors. The meaning people assign to a sexual dysfunction, an unusual sexual practice, or an atypical gender identity is heavily influenced by their attitude toward their sexuality and gender, and by the reactions of people around them. In addition, as we saw with sexual dysfunctions, purely psychological and social conditions can cause a person's body to stop functioning as it normally would.

FIGURE 4 Interplay of Biological, Psychological, and Social Factors in Sexuality.

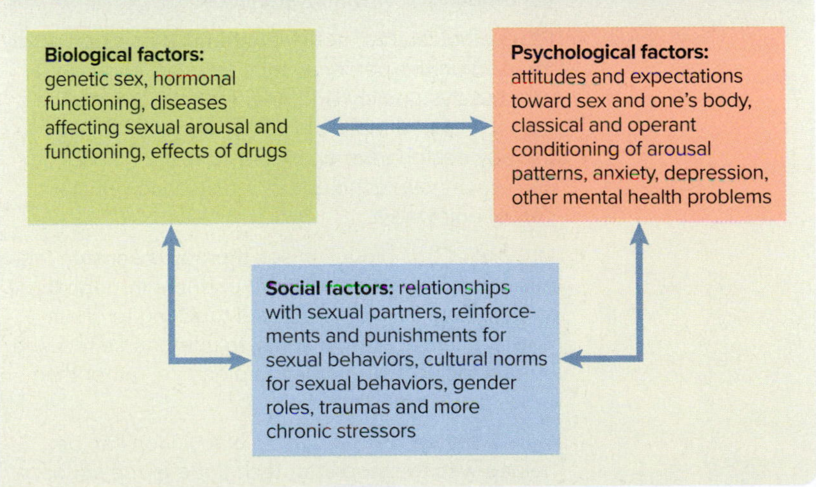

Biological factors: genetic sex, hormonal functioning, diseases affecting sexual arousal and functioning, effects of drugs
Psychological factors: attitudes and expectations toward sex and one's body, classical and operant conditioning of arousal patterns, anxiety, depression, other mental health problems
Social factors: relationships with sexual partners, reinforcements and punishments for sexual behaviors, cultural norms for sexual behaviors, gender roles, traumas and more chronic stressors

CHAPTER SUMMARY

- The sexual response cycle can be divided into the desire, arousal, plateau, orgasm, and resolution phases.
- Disorders of sexual desire/interest and arousal (male hypoactive sexual desire disorder, female sexual interest/arousal disorder, and erectile disorder) are among the most common sexual dysfunctions. People with these disorders experience a chronically lowered or absent desire for sex or deficiencies in sexual arousal.
- Women with female orgasmic disorder experience a persistent or recurrent delay in or the complete absence of orgasm, after having reached the excitement phase of the sexual response cycle.
- Men with early ejaculation persistently experience ejaculation (after minimal sexual stimulation) before, on, or shortly after penetration and before they wish it. Men with delayed ejaculation experience a persistent or recurrent delay in or the absence of ejaculation following the excitement phase of the sexual response cycle.
- Genito-pelvic pain/penetration disorder involves genital pain associated with intercourse or, in women, involuntary contraction of the muscles surrounding the outer third of the vagina when the vagina is penetrated.
- A variety of biological factors, including medical illnesses, the side effects of drugs, nervous system injury, and hormonal deficiencies, can cause sexual dysfunction. The psychological and sociocultural factors leading to sexual dysfunction most commonly involve negative attitudes toward sex, traumatic or stressful experiences, or conflicts with sexual partners.
- Fortunately, most sexual dysfunctions can be treated successfully. Biological treatments include drugs that increase sexual functioning, such as Viagra, and the alleviation of medical conditions that might be contributing to sexual dysfunction.
- Psychological treatments combine (1) psychotherapy focused on the personal concerns of the individual with the dysfunction and on the conflicts between the individual and his or her partner and (2) sex therapy designed to decrease inhibitions about sex and teach new techniques for achieving optimal sexual enjoyment.
- One set of techniques in sex therapy is sensate focus exercises. The exercises lead partners through three stages, from gentle nongenital touching to direct genital stimulation and finally to intercourse focused on enhancing and sustaining pleasure, rather than on orgasm and performance.
- Men experiencing premature ejaculation can be helped with the stop-start technique or the squeeze technique.
- The paraphilic disorders involve recurrent atypical sexual fantasies, urges, and behaviors that cause the individual distress or impairment, or cause harm or risk of harm to others.
- Fetishistic disorder is a paraphilic disorder that involves sexual fantasies, urges, or behaviors focused on nonliving objects or nongenital body parts. A particular form of fetish is transvestism, in which individuals cross-dress in order to become sexually aroused.
- Sexual sadism disorder involves sexual fantasies, urges, or behaviors focused on inflicting pain and humiliation on a sex partner. Sexual masochism disorder involves sexual fantasies, urges, or behaviors focused on experiencing pain or humiliation during sex.
- Voyeuristic disorder involves sexual fantasies, urges, or behaviors focused on secretly watching another person undressing, doing things in the nude, or engaging in sex. Almost all people who engage in voyeurism are men who watch women.
- Exhibitionistic disorder involves sexual fantasies, urges, or behaviors focused on exposing the genitals to involuntary observers, usually strangers.
- Frotteuristic disorder often co-occurs with voyeurism and exhibitionism. The person who engages in frotteurism has sexual fantasies, urges, or behaviors focused on rubbing against and fondling parts of the body of a nonconsenting person. Usually this occurs in a crowded public space.
- People with pedophilic disorder have sexual fantasies, urges, or behaviors focused on prepubescent children.
- Some neurodevelopmental differences are found between people with pedophilic disorder and people without the disorder.
- Behavioral theories suggest that the sexual behaviors of people with paraphilic disorder result from classical and operant conditioning.
- Treatments for the paraphilic disorders include biological interventions to reduce sexual drive, behavioral interventions to decondition arousal due to paraphilic objects, and cognitive-behavioral interventions to combat cognitions supporting paraphilic behavior and increase coping skills.
- Gender dysphoria is diagnosed when an individual believes that he or she was born with the wrong genitals and is fundamentally a person of the other sex. People with this disorder experience a chronic discomfort and sense of inappropriateness with their gender and genitals, wish to be rid of them, and want to live as members of the other sex. Gender dysphoria of childhood is a rare condition in which a child persistently rejects his or her anatomic sex,

desires to be or insists he or she is a member of the other sex, and shows a strong preference for cross-gender roles and activities.

- Biological theories suggest that gender dysphoria is due to prenatal exposure to hormones that affect development of the hypothalamus and other brain structures involved in gender and sexuality.

Socialization theories suggest that the parents of children (primarily boys) with gender dysphoria do not strictly encourage gender-appropriate behaviors.

- Treatment for gender dysphoria includes cross-sex hormone therapy, real-life experience as a member of the desired sex, and sex reassignment surgery.

KEY TERMS

sexual functioning
gender identity
sexual desire
arousal phase
plateau phase
orgasm
resolution
sexual dysfunctions
male hypoactive sexual desire disorder
female sexual interest/arousal disorder
erectile disorder
female orgasmic disorder
early or premature ejaculation
delayed ejaculation
genito-pelvic pain/penetration disorder
substance-induced sexual dysfunction
performance anxiety
sensate focus therapy
stop-start technique
squeeze technique
paraphilic disorder
fetishistic disorder
transvestic disorder
sexual sadism disorder
sexual masochism disorder
sadomasochism
voyeuristic disorder
exhibitionistic disorder
frotteuristic disorder
pedophilic disorder
aversion therapy
gender dysphoria
transgender

Chapter 14

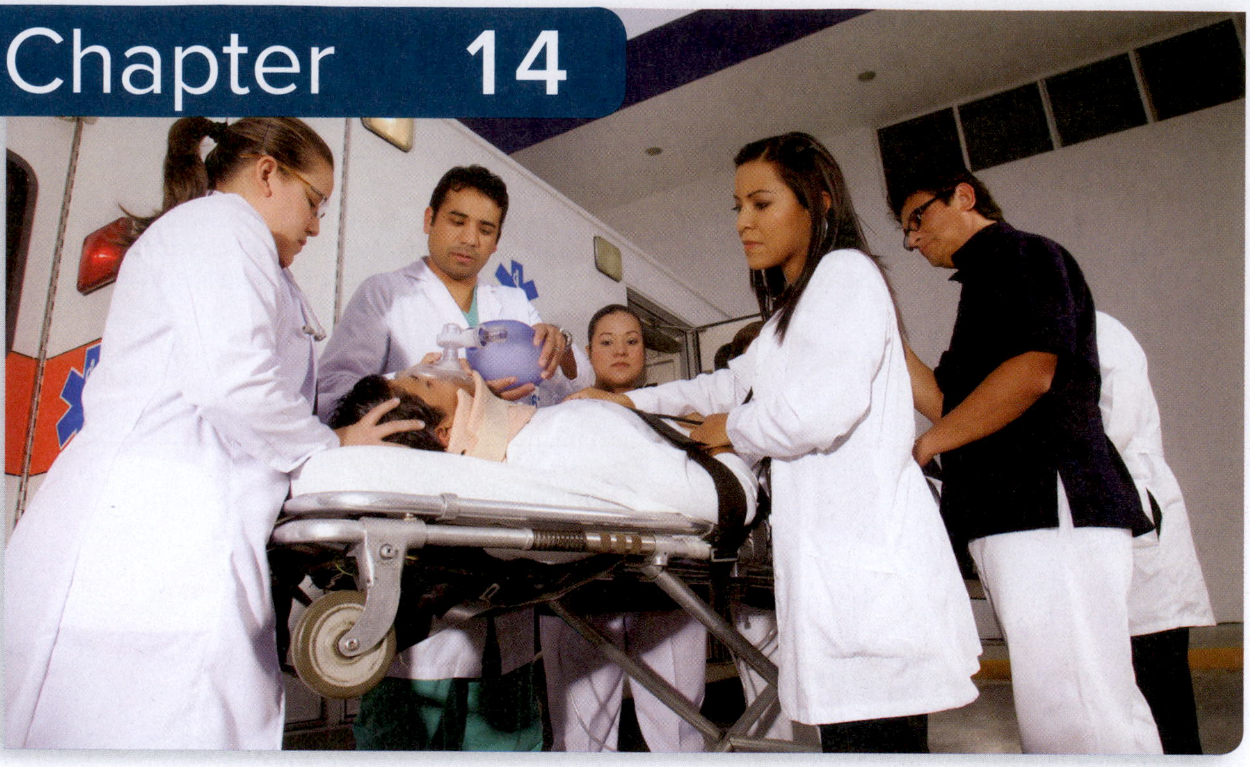

©Jose Girarte/E+/Getty Images

Substance Use and Gambling Disorders

CHAPTER OUTLINE

Substance Use Along the Continuum

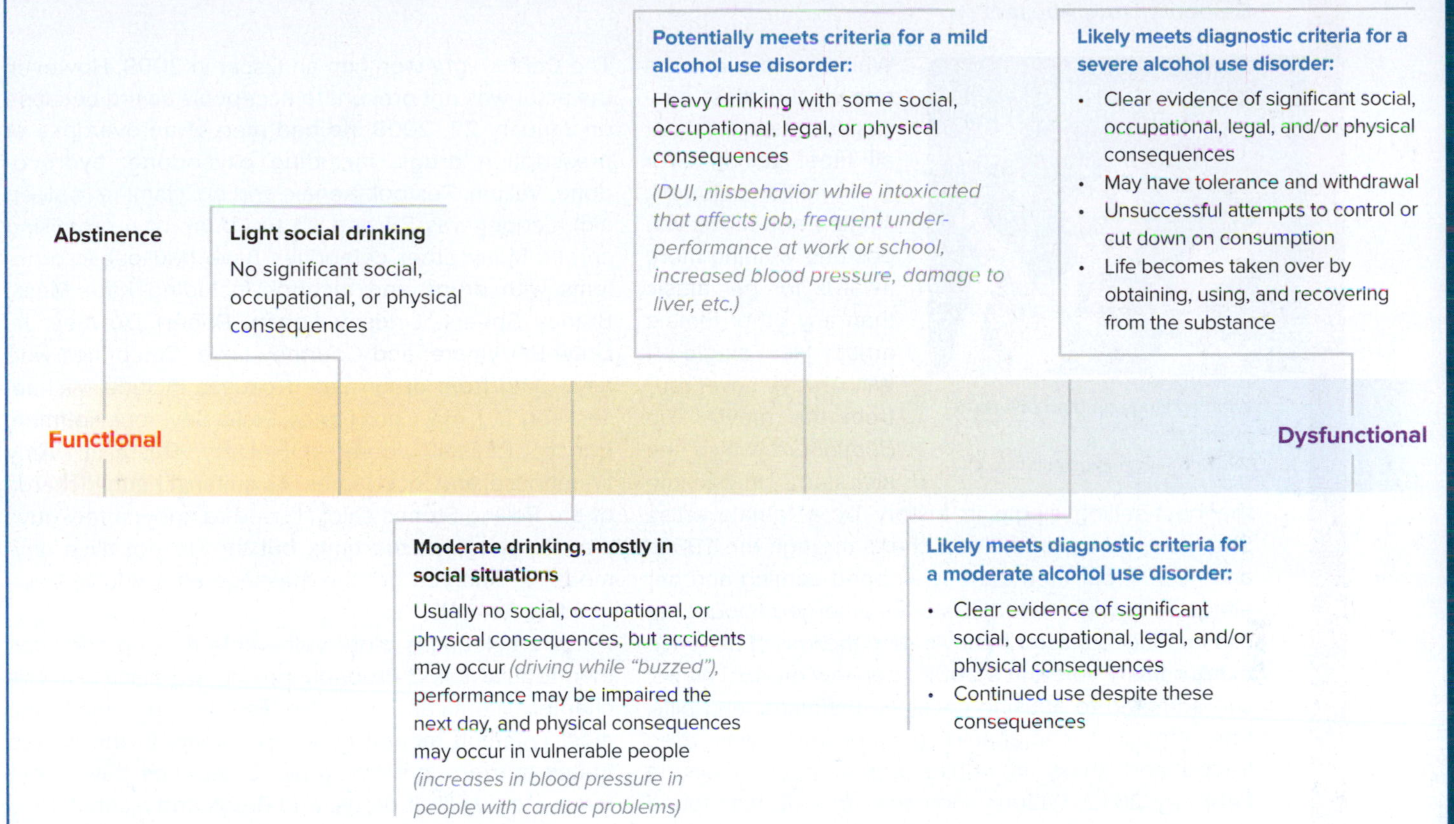

Abstinence
Light social drinking
No significant social, occupational, or physical consequences
Moderate drinking, mostly in social situations
Usually no social, occupational, or physical consequences, but accidents may occur (driving while "buzzed"), performance may be impaired the next day, and physical consequences may occur in vulnerable people (increases in blood pressure in people with cardiac problems)
Potentially meets criteria for a mild alcohol use disorder:
Heavy drinking with some social, occupational, legal, or physical consequences
(DUI, misbehavior while intoxicated that affects job, frequent under-performance at work or school, increased blood pressure, damage to liver, etc.)
Likely meets diagnostic criteria for a moderate alcohol use disorder:
Clear evidence of significant social, occupational, legal, and/or physical consequences
Continued use despite these consequences
Likely meets diagnostic criteria for a severe alcohol use disorder:
Clear evidence of significant social, occupational, legal, and/or physical consequences
May have tolerance and withdrawal
Unsuccessful attempts to control or cut down on consumption
Life becomes taken over by obtaining, using, and recovering from the substance
Functional
Dysfunctional

As a student, you likely know more people along the continuum of substance use than along any continuum in the rest of this book. TV shows and movies often show substance use as a rite of passage into adulthood—think of the college drinking scenes in movies like *Animal House*—and statistics suggest there is some truth in this portrayal. Illegal drug use is highest among young adults (Figure 1; Substance Abuse and Mental Health Services Administration [SAMHSA], 2017), with about 23 percent of college students reporting current use.

At one end of the continuum are people who abstain completely. Some of these do not enjoy the effects of substances; others live in cultures or follow religions that prohibit the use of alcohol or drugs. Globally, 62 percent of people over the age of 15 abstain from alcohol, with abstinence rates much higher among women than men. Most of these people are concentrated in a belt stretching from North Africa across the eastern Mediterranean, south central Asia, and Southeast Asia to the islands of Indonesia (WHO, 2014). In other areas of the world, such as Europe, less than 40 percent of the population abstain from alcohol.

Further along the continuum are people who use drugs and alcohol "recreationally." Nearly half the U.S. population admits to having tried an illegal substance at some time in their life, and approximately 11 percent have used one in the past year (SAMHSA, 2017).

Although movies and TV often make substance use seem cool, the consequences are staggeringly serious. There are more deaths from traffic accidents involving substance-impaired drivers than from all other types of accidents. In 2014, 11 percent of people 16 or over in the United States reported driving under the influence of alcohol, and 4 percent reported driving under the influence of an illicit drug (Lipari, Hughes, & Bose, 2016). About 20 percent of emergency room visits in the United States are related to the misuse of alcohol or of illegal or prescription drugs (SAMHSA, 2013).

At the other end of the continuum are individuals who build their lives around substances. Their immoderate substance use impairs their everyday functioning—they may avoid job and family responsibilities, act impulsively or bizarrely, or endanger their own and others' lives. These people have a substance use disorder.

Extraordinary People

Celebrity Drug Abusers

Whitney Houston died of a drug overdose in 2012.
©Patrick Seeger/Epa/Shutterstock

Whitney Houston was one of the most successful music artists of all time, selling over 170 million albums, singles, and music videos and winning more awards for her music than any other female artist. Her single "I Will Always Love You" from the movie *The Bodyguard,* which she also starred in, became the best-selling single in history by a female artist. She rode the top of the pop charts through the 1980s and 1990s, but then the hits stopped coming and her album sales plummeted as stories emerged about drug use leading to bizarre behavior and the loss of her once extraordinary voice. In a 2002 interview on *ABC News,* she admitted to abusing cocaine, marijuana, and pills. She attempted comebacks, but her voice was often frayed and shaky in public appearances. Then, in February 2012, Whitney Houston, age 48, was found drowned in the bathtub of a Beverly Hills hotel room. A coroner's report ruled the death an accident due to the effects of cocaine, marijuana, and multiple other drugs in her system and to heart damage associated with her long-term drug abuse.

Whitney Houston is only one in a long line of celebrity drug abusers who have died early as a result of their drug use. Heath Ledger's portrayal of the Joker in *The Dark Knight* won him an Oscar in 2009. However, the actor was not present to accept his award because on January 22, 2008, he had died of an overdose of prescription drugs, including oxycodone, hydrocodone, Valium, Restoril, Xanax, and doxylamine (a sleep aid). Ledger was 28 and on the brink of a promising career. Many other celebrities have had public problems with drugs and alcohol, including Kate Moss, Britney Spears, Lindsey Lohan, Robert Downey Jr., Drew Barrymore, and Courtney Love. Celebrities who have died from drug-related causes include Michael Jackson, D.J. AM, Chris Farley, Philip Seymour Hoffman, Prince, Russell Jones (Ol' Dirty Bastard), Amy Winehouse, and Rick James. As guitarist Keith Richards of the Rolling Stones said, "I used to know a few guys that did drugs all the time, but they're not alive anymore. . . . And you get the message after you've been to a few funerals."

Are celebrities more vulnerable to drug addiction than regular folks? Probably not. As we discuss in this chapter, alcohol and drug use disorders are among the most common mental health problems in the United States and around the world. Celebrities have more money to buy illicit drugs, and drugs and alcohol are a big part of the social scene in the entertainment industry. Some celebrities can't handle the pressure to stay on top of their field and may turn to drugs to cope. Also, when celebrities do abuse drugs or alcohol, the media broadcast their missteps widely. But much celebrity drug abuse probably is due to the same biological and psychosocial factors that contribute to drug and alcohol use disorders in noncelebrities.

Everyone has temptations, and some people have more trouble resisting them than others. In this chapter, we consider disorders that involve chronic difficulties in resisting the desire to drink alcohol or take drugs, known in the *DSM-5* as **substance use disorders.** We also consider **gambling disorder,** which involves the inability to resist the impulse to gamble, because the behavioral patterns and causes of this disorder appear to be similar to the behavioral patterns and causes of the substance use disorders (Denis, Fatséas, & Auriacombe, 2012; Petry, Zajac, & Ginley, 2018).

We begin with the substance use disorders. A **substance** is any natural or synthesized product that has psychoactive effects–it changes perceptions, thoughts, emotions, and behaviors. Some of the substances we discuss in this chapter are popularly referred to as drugs (e.g., cocaine and heroin). People who abuse these drugs are often referred to as *drug addicts*. Yet a person need not be physically dependent on a substance, as the term *addict* implies, in order to have a problem with it. For example, some club-goers who are not physically addicted to Ecstasy or Molly still may think they need the drug to have a good time.

Societies differ in their attitudes toward substances with psychoactive effects, with some seeing their use as a matter of individual choice and others seeing it as a grave public health and security concern. Within the United States, attitudes have varied greatly over time and across subgroups (Keyes et al., 2011). U.S. ambivalence toward alcohol use is nicely illustrated in a letter from former congressman Billy Mathews to one of his then-constituents, who wrote:

FIGURE 1 **Illicit Drug Use.** In the United States, ethnic and age groups have different rates of drug use.

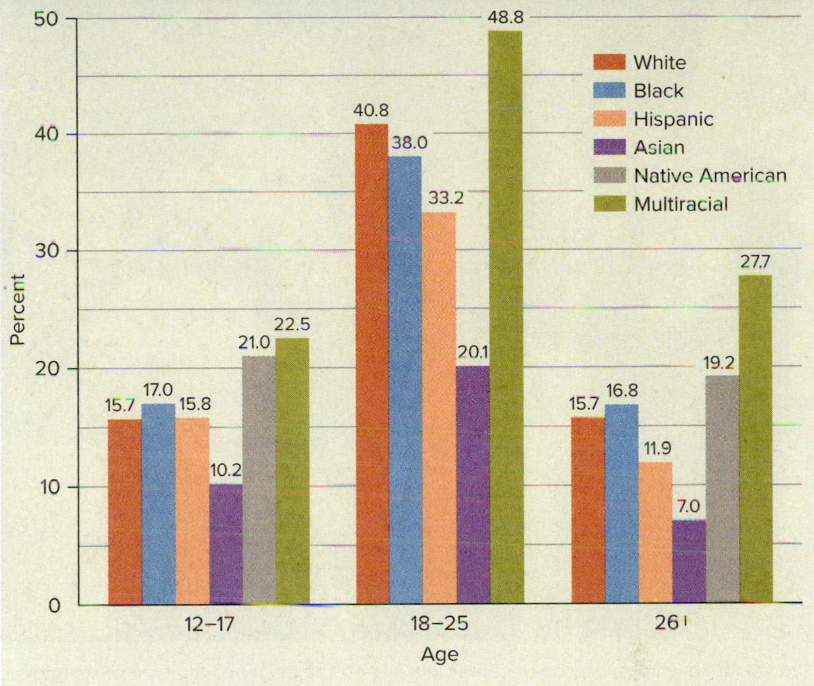

Source: SAMHSA, 2017, Table 1.30B, 226. https://www.samhsa.gov/data/sites/default/files/NSDUH-DetTabs-2016/NSDUH-DetTabs-2016.pdf

Note: Illicit drugs include marijuana, cocaine, heroin, hallucinogens, inhalants, or prescription drugs used nonmedically. No estimate is given for Native Americans 12–17 years old because of a low response rate.

"Dear Congressman, how do you stand on whiskey?" Because the congressman did not know how the constituent stood on alcohol, he fashioned the following safe response:

> My dear friend, I had not intended to discuss this controversial subject at this particular time. However, I want you to know that I do not shun a controversy. On the contrary, I will take a stand on any issue at any time, regardless of how fraught with controversy it may be. You have asked me how I feel about whiskey. Here is how I stand on the issue.
>
> If when you say whiskey, you mean the Devil's brew; the poison scourge; the bloody monster that defiles innocence, dethrones reason, destroys the home, creates misery, poverty, fear; literally takes the bread from the mouths of little children; if you mean the evil drink that topples the Christian man and woman from the pinnacles of righteous, gracious living into the bottomless pit of degradation and despair, shame and helplessness and hopelessness; then certainly, I am against it with all of my power.
>
> But, if when you say whiskey, you mean the oil of conversation, the philosophic wine, the ale that is assumed when great fellows get together, that puts a song in their hearts and laughter on their lips, and the warm glow of contentment in their eyes; if you mean Christmas cheer; if you mean that stimulating drink that puts the spring in the old gentleman's step on a frosty morning; if you mean the drink that enables the man to magnify his joy and his happiness and to forget, if only for a little while, life's great tragedies and heartbreaks and sorrows; if you mean that drink, the sale of which pours into our Treasury untold millions of dollars which are used to provide tender care for little crippled children, our blind, our deaf, our pitiful aged and infirm; to build highways, hospitals, and schools; then certainly, I am in favor of it. This is my stand, and I will not compromise. Your congressman. (Quoted in Marlatt, Larimer, Baer, & Quigley, 1993, p. 462)

Many substances have been used for medicinal purposes for centuries. As long ago as 1500 BCE, people in the Andes highlands chewed coca leaves to increase their endurance (Cocores, Pottash, & Gold, 1991). Coca leaves can be manufactured into cocaine, which was used legally throughout Europe and the United States into the twentieth century to relieve fatigue. It was an ingredient in the original Coca-Cola drink and in more than 50 other widely available beverages and elixirs.

Psychoactive substances also have traditionally appeared in religious ceremonies. When chewed, peyote causes visual hallucinations of colored lights or of geometric forms, animals, or people. Native groups in North America have used it in religious rituals for hundreds of years.

DEFINING SUBSTANCE USE DISORDERS

There are four conditions that have historically been seen as important in defining individuals' use of substances: intoxication, withdrawal, abuse, and dependence. We first define these conditions.

Substance intoxication is a set of behavioral and psychological changes that occur as a result of the physiological effects of a substance on the central nervous system. People become intoxicated soon after they ingest a substance, and the more they ingest, the more intoxicated they become. Intoxication declines as the amount of the substance in blood or tissue declines, but symptoms may last for hours or days after the substance no longer is detectable in the body (Procyshyn, Bezchlibnyk-Butler, & Jeffries, 2017).

The specific symptoms of intoxication depend on what substance is taken, how much of it is taken and

The setting in which a person becomes intoxicated can influence the type of symptoms people develop. People who consume a few alcoholic drinks at a party may become uninhibited and loud, but when they consume the same amount at home alone they may become tired and depressed. ©John Rensten/The Image Bank/Getty Images

when, the user's tolerance, and the context. For example, you may have observed that alcohol makes some people aggressive and others withdrawn. Short-term, or acute, intoxication can produce symptoms different from those of chronic intoxication. The first time people take a moderate dose of cocaine, they may be outgoing and upbeat. With chronic use over days or weeks, they may begin to withdraw socially (Procyshyn et al., 2017). People's expectations about a substance's effects also can influence the types of symptoms they show. People who expect marijuana to make them relaxed may experience relaxation, whereas people who are frightened of disinhibition may experience anxiety (Ruiz & Strain, 2014).

The setting also can influence the types of intoxication symptoms people develop. People who consume a few alcoholic drinks at a party may become uninhibited and loud, but when they consume the same amount at home alone they may become tired and depressed (Brick, 2008). The environment can also influence how maladaptive the intoxication is. People who drink alcohol only at home may be less likely to cause harm to themselves or others than are people who drink at bars and drive home under the influence of alcohol. The diagnosis of intoxication with a substance is given only when the behavioral and psychological changes the person experiences are significantly maladaptive, that is, when they substantially disrupt the person's social and family relationships, cause occupational or financial problems, or place the individual at significant risk for adverse effects, such as a traffic accident, severe medical complications, or legal problems. For example, getting into a fist fight while clearly under the influence of a substance would merit a diagnosis of intoxication. Substance intoxication is common among individuals with a substance use disorder, but also occurs among those without a substance use disorder.

Substance withdrawal is a set of physiological and behavioral symptoms that result when people who have been using substances heavily for prolonged periods of time stop or greatly reduce their use. Symptoms typically are the opposite of those of intoxication. The diagnosis of withdrawal from a substance requires significant distress or impairment in a person's everyday functioning.

The *DSM-IV* distinguished between *substance abuse* and *substance dependence*. The diagnosis of **substance abuse** was given when a person's recurrent use of a substance resulted in significant harmful consequences comprising four categories. First, the individual fails to fulfill important obligations at work, school, or home. He or she may fail to show up at work or for classes, may be unable to concentrate and therefore performs poorly, or may even consume the substance at work or at school. Second, the individual repeatedly uses the substance in situations in which it is physically hazardous to do so, such as while driving. Third, the individual repeatedly has legal problems as a result of substance use, such as arrests for drunk driving or for the possession of illegal substances. Fourth, the individual continues to use the substance despite repeated social or legal problems as a result of use. The *DSM-IV* diagnosis of substance abuse required that the person show repeated problems in at least one of these categories within a 12-month period.

The diagnosis of **substance dependence** in the *DSM-IV* was closest to what people often refer to as *drug addiction*. People who are dependent on, or addicted to, a substance often show **tolerance**—they experience diminished effects from the same dose of a substance and need more and more of it to achieve intoxication. People who have smoked cigarettes for years often smoke more than 20 cigarettes a day, an amount that would have made them violently ill when they first began smoking. A person highly tolerant of a substance may have a very high blood level of it without being aware of its effects. The risk for tolerance varies greatly among substances. Alcohol, opioids, stimulants, and nicotine have high risks for tolerance, whereas cannabis and PCP appear to have lower risks (Brick, 2008). People who are physiologically dependent on a substance often show severe withdrawal symptoms when they stop using it. Sometimes the substance must be withdrawn gradually to prevent the symptoms from becoming overwhelming or dangerous (Brick, 2008). Users may continue to take the substance to relieve or avoid withdrawal symptoms.

Physiological dependence (evidence of tolerance or withdrawal) was not required for a diagnosis of substance dependence in the *DSM-IV*, however. A person needed only to use a substance compulsively despite experiencing significant social, occupational, psychological, or medical problems as a result. The diagnosis of substance dependence preempted the diagnosis of substance abuse. Some individuals abused substances for years, severely disrupting their lives, without qualifying for a diagnosis of substance dependence.

The *DSM-5* combined substance abuse and dependence into one diagnosis, substance use disorder, because of difficulties in distinguishing between abuse and dependence in clinical and research settings and because of the low reliability of the diagnosis of substance abuse (Hasin, Fenton, Beseler, Park, & Wall, 2012). The *DSM-5* diagnostic criteria for substance use disorder include impaired control, the continued use of substances despite negative social, occupational, and health consequences, risky use, as well as evidence of tolerance or withdrawal (see Table 1). Users must show two or more of the symptoms associated with substance use disorder over the course of a year to receive the diagnosis. The criterion in the *DSM-IV* regarding legal problems was dropped because such problems were relatively rare among adults and thus were not very informative, but a criterion of craving was added because it is a common and diagnostically important symptom among people with substance use issues (Hasin et al., 2012). Clinicians also rate the severity of the substance use disorder as mild (two or three of the criteria are met), moderate (four or five criteria are met), or severe (six or more criteria are met).

One study reanalyzed data from a large, nationally representative sample of the United States to determine the effects of changes from the *DSM-IV* to the *DSM-5* criteria for the diagnosis of alcohol-related disorders and found that the 12-month prevalence of alcohol use disorder based on the *DSM-5* criteria (10.8 percent) was quite similar to the combined 12-month prevalence of *DSM-IV* diagnoses of alcohol abuse or alcohol dependence (9.7 percent) (Agrawal, Heath, & Lynskey, 2011). This suggests that the combined prevalences of abuse and dependence diagnoses for each substance based on the *DSM-IV* criteria can be used to estimate the prevalence of substance use disorders for each substance discussed in this chapter.

TABLE 1 Criteria for Substance Use Disorder

Impaired control

1. The substance is taken in increasingly larger amounts or over a longer period of time than originally intended.
2. The substance user craves the substance.
3. The substance user feels an ongoing desire to cut down or control substance abuse, or has made unsuccessful attempts to do so.
4. Much time is spent in obtaining, using, or recovering from the substance.

Social impairment

5. The ongoing use of the substance often results in an inability to meet responsibilities at home, work, or school.
6. Important social, work-related, or recreational activities are abandoned or cut back because of substance use.
7. Ongoing substance use despite recurring social or relationship difficulties caused or made worse by the effects of the substance.

Risky use

8. Ongoing substance use in physically dangerous situations such as driving a car or operating machinery.
9. Substance use continues despite the awareness of ongoing physical or psychological problems that have likely arisen or been made worse by the substance.

Pharmacological

10. Tolerance: the need for increased amounts of the substance to achieve the desired effect or by a diminished experience of intoxication over time with the same amount of the substance.
11. Withdrawal: the substance user experiences the characteristic withdrawal syndrome of the substance and/or takes the same or similar substance to relieve withdrawal symptoms.

Source: *Diagnostic and Statistical Manual of Mental Disorders*, Fifth Edition. American Psychiatric Association, 2013.

Note: Two or more of the above 11 criteria are required to make a diagnosis of substance abuse disorder. Symptoms are organized here by categories for clarity; these categories are not themselves in the *DSM-5*.

DSM-5 recognizes 10 substance classes around which substance use disorders emerge. This chapter organizes these substance use disorders into five categories: (1) central nervous system depressants, including alcohol, barbiturates, benzodiazepines, and inhalants; (2) central nervous system stimulants, including cocaine, amphetamines, nicotine, and caffeine; (3) opioids, including heroin and morphine; (4) hallucinogens and phencyclidine (PCP); and (5) cannabis. We consider the characteristics of the problems people experience from using substances in each category and then discuss certain other drugs commonly misused.

DEPRESSANTS

Depressants slow the central nervous system. In moderate doses, they make people relaxed and somewhat sleepy, reduce concentration, and impair thinking, judgment, and motor skills. In heavy doses, they can induce stupor or even death (see Table 2).

Alcohol

Alcohol's effects on the brain occur in two distinct phases (Brick, 2008). In low doses, alcohol causes many people to feel more self-confident, more relaxed, and perhaps slightly euphoric. They may be less inhibited, and this disinhibitory effect may be what many people find attractive. At increasing doses, however, alcohol induces many of the symptoms of depression, including fatigue and lethargy, decreased motivation, sleep disturbances, depressed mood, and confusion. Also, although many people take alcohol to feel sexier (mainly by reducing their sexual inhibitions), even low doses can impair sexual functioning.

People intoxicated by alcohol slur their words, walk unsteadily, have trouble paying attention or remembering things, and are slow and awkward in their physical reactions. They may act inappropriately, becoming aggressive or belligerent, or saying rude things. Their moods may swing from exuberance to despair. With extreme intoxication, people may fall into a stupor or a coma. Often they do not recognize that they are intoxicated or may flatly deny it. Once sober, they may have amnesia, known as a *blackout,* for the events that occurred while they were intoxicated (Ruiz & Strain, 2014).

One critical determinant of how quickly people become intoxicated with alcohol is whether their stomach is full or empty. An empty stomach speedily delivers alcohol to the small intestine, where it is rapidly absorbed into the body. A person with a full

Drinking alcohol with food leads to a slower absorption rate of the alcohol. ©*Philip Lee Harvey/Stone+/Getty Images*

TABLE 2 Intoxication with and Withdrawal from Depressants

The depressant drugs depress activity in the central nervous system.

Drug	Intoxication Symptoms	Withdrawal Symptoms
Alcohol	Behavioral symptoms (e.g., inappropriate sexual or aggressive behavior, mood lability, impaired judgment)	Autonomic hyperactivity (e.g., sweating, fast pulse)
Benzodiazepines	Sleepiness	Hand tremor
Barbiturates	Slurred speech	Insomnia
	Incoordination	Nausea or vomiting
	Unsteady gait	Transient hallucinations or illusions
	Involuntary eye movement	Psychomotor agitation
	Impairment in attention or memory	Anxiety
	Stupor or coma	Seizures

stomach may ingest significantly more drinks before reaching a dangerous blood-alcohol level or showing clear signs of intoxication (Brick, 2008). People in countries where alcohol is usually consumed with meals, such as France, show lower rates of alcohol use disorders than do people in countries where alcohol often is consumed on an empty stomach.

The legal definition of alcohol intoxication is much narrower than the criteria for a diagnosis of alcohol intoxication. Most U.S. states consider a person to be under the influence of alcohol if his or her blood-alcohol level is 0.08 or above. As Table 3 indicates, it does not take many drinks for most people to reach this level. It takes less alcohol to reach a high blood-alcohol level in women than in men because women generally are smaller and have a lower body water content than men, leading to higher concentrations of alcohol in the blood for a given dose. Deficits in attention, reaction time, and coordination arise even with the first drink and can interfere with the ability to operate a car or machinery safely and to perform other tasks requiring a steady hand, coordination, clear thinking, and clear vision. These deficits are not always readily observable, even to trained eyes. People often leave parties or bars without appearing drunk but having a blood-alcohol level well above the legal limit (Brick, 2008).

Heavy drinking can be part of the culture of a peer group, but it still can lead to alcohol use disorder in some members. Drinking large quantities of alcohol can be fatal, even in people who are not chronic alcohol abusers. About one-third of such deaths result from respiratory paralysis, usually due to a final large dose of alcohol in people who are already intoxicated. Alcohol can also interact fatally with a number of substances, including some antidepressant drugs (Brick, 2008).

Unintentional alcohol-related injuries due to automobile accidents, drowning, burns, poisoning, and falls account for approximately 600,000 deaths per year internationally (WHO, 2014). Nearly half of all fatal automobile accidents and deaths due to falls or fires and over one-third of all drownings are alcohol-related (Fleming & Manwell, 2000; Hunt, 1998). Even being a little "buzzed" (i.e., having a blood alcohol level of 0.02

TABLE 3 Relationships Among Sex, Weight, Oral Alcohol Consumption, and Blood-Alcohol Level

It doesn't take very many drinks for most people to reach a blood-alcohol level of 0.08, which is the legal definition of intoxication in most states.

		Blood-Alcohol Level (Percent)					
Total Alcohol Content (Ounces)	Beverage Intake*	Female (100 lb)	Male (100 lb)	Female (150 lb)	Male (150 lb)	Female (200 lb)	Male (200 lb)
1/2	1 oz spirits† 1 glass wine 1 can beer	0.045	0.037	0.03	0.025	0.022	0.019
1	2 oz spirits 2 glasses wine 2 cans beer	0.090	0.075	0.06	0.050	0.045	0.037
2	4 oz spirits 4 glasses wine 4 cans beer	0.180	0.150	0.12	0.100	0.090	0.070
3	6 oz spirits 6 glasses wine 6 cans beer	0.270	0.220	0.18	0.150	0.130	0.110
4	8 oz spirits 8 glasses wine 8 cans beer	0.360	0.300	0.24	0.200	0.180	0.150
5	10 oz spirits 10 glasses wine 10 cans beer	0.450	0.370	0.30	0.250	0.220	0.180

*In 1 hour
†100-proof spirits (50 percent alcohol)

Source: Data from Ray, O., & Ksir, C., *Drugs, society, and human behavior*. St. Louis: C. V. Mosby, 1993, 194.

percent) is associated with a significantly increased risk of having an automobile accident compared to being completely sober (Phillips & Brewer, 2011). More than half of all murderers and their victims are believed to be intoxicated with alcohol at the time of the murders, and people who attempt or commit suicide often do so under the influence of alcohol.

The symptoms of alcohol withdrawal manifest in three stages (Brick, 2008). The first, which usually begins within a few hours after drinking has been stopped or sharply curtailed, includes tremulousness (the "shakes"), weakness, and profuse perspiration. The person may complain of anxiety (the "jitters"), headache, nausea, and abdominal cramps and may retch and vomit. He or she is flushed, restless, and easily startled but alert. The EEG pattern may be mildly abnormal. The person may begin to see or hear things, at first only with eyes shut but later also with eyes open. Those whose alcohol use disorder is moderate may experience only this first stage of withdrawal, and the symptoms may disappear within a few days.

The second stage includes convulsive seizures, which may begin as soon as 12 hours after drinking stops but more often appear during the second or third day. The third stage of withdrawal is characterized by **delirium tremens,** or **DTs.** Auditory, visual, and tactile hallucinations occur. The person also may develop bizarre, terrifying delusions, such as the belief that monsters are attacking. He or she may sleep little and may become agitated and disoriented. Fever, profuse perspiration, and an irregular heartbeat may develop. Delirium tremens is fatal in approximately 10 percent of cases. Death may occur from hyperthermia (extremely high body temperature) or the collapse of the peripheral vascular system. Fortunately, only about 10 percent of individuals with severe alcohol use disorder ever experience seizures or DTs (Mirijello et al., 2015). These symptoms are more common in people who drink large amounts in a single sitting and have an existing medical illness.

Alcohol Misuse

As noted in Substance Use Along the Continuum, alcohol use and misuse span a broad range from people who completely abstain from drinking alcohol to those who drink alcohol occasionally in social situations, to those who drink more frequently and heavily, and finally to those for whom alcohol use creates significant social, occupational, and health problems. Near the maladaptive end of the continuum are people who engage in binge drinking (five or more drinks within a couple of hours for men, four or more drinks within a couple of hours for women) or heavy drinking (binge drinking on five or more days in a month). Binge drinking and heavy drinking are associated with significant health problems (Paul, Grubaugh, Frueh, Ellis, & Egede, 2011). Large nationwide studies in the United States find that about 24 percent of adults report binge drinking at least once in the last month, and 6 percent of adults are heavy drinkers (Paul et al., 2011; SAMHSA, 2017). Binge drinking on college campuses is common. Nationwide, 35 percent of college students report binge drinking in the past month, compared to 32 percent of 18- to 22-year-olds not in college (Johnston, O'Malley, Bachman, & Schulenberg, 2012). Binge drinking is especially common among members of fraternities and sororities, with 75 percent of members saying they binge drink (Wechsler et al., 2002).

Gender and Age Differences In most nations of the world, men are more likely to drink alcohol than are women, and also are more likely to drink heavily or binge drink (Hughes, Wilsnack, & Kantor, 2016; WHO, 2014). Similarly, across all age groups, males are much more likely to develop alcohol use disorders than are females, as can be seen in Figure 2. The gender gap in alcohol use is much greater among men

FIGURE 2 **Gender Differences in Alcohol.** Men engage in more alcohol use than women do.

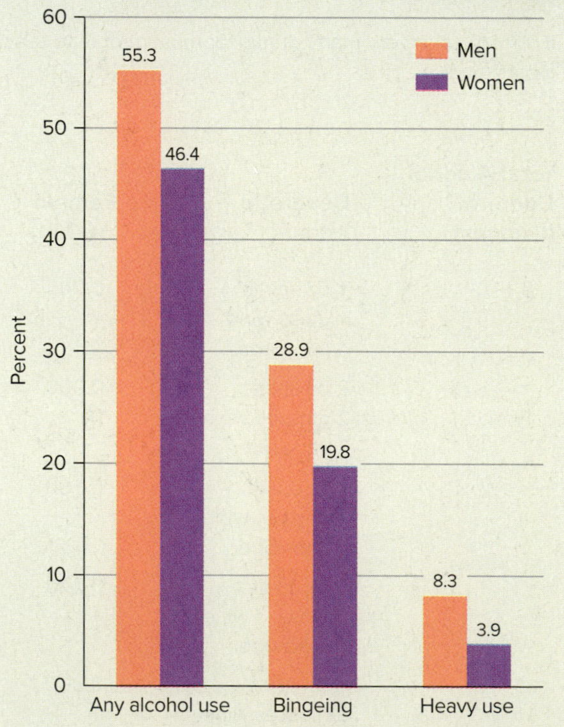

Source: SAMHSA, 2017, Table 2.35B, 816 for any alcohol use, 2.36B, 818 for binge, 2.37B, 820 for heavy use. https://www.samhsa.gov/data/sites/default/files/NSDUH-DetTabs-2016/NSDUH-DetTabs-2016.pdf.

Note: Bingeing is defined as five or more drinks on the same occasion at least once in the past 30 days. Heavy use is defined as five or more drinks on the same occasion on at least 5 different days in the past 30 days.

and women who subscribe to traditional gender roles, which condone drinking for men but not for women (Hughes et al., 2016). Similarly, the gender gap is greater among U.S. ethnic minority groups that more widely accept traditional gender roles, such as Hispanics and recent Asian immigrants, than among European Americans, due largely to high percentages of minority women who completely abstain from alcohol. We discuss other contributors to the gender differences in substance use later in this chapter.

Strong age differences in alcohol use disorders decline with age. There are many reasons for this decline. First, with age the liver metabolizes alcohol at a slower rate, and the lower percentage of body water increases the absorption of alcohol. As a result, older people become intoxicated faster and experience the negative effects of alcohol more severely and more quickly. Second, as people grow older, they may become more mature in their choices, including choices about drinking alcohol to excess. Third, older people have grown up under stronger prohibitions against alcohol use and abuse than have younger people. Fourth, people who have used alcohol excessively for many years may die from alcohol-related diseases before they reach old age (Sher, Grekin, & Williams, 2005).

As people grow older, they may become more mature in their choices, including choices about drinking alcohol to excess.
©Ariel Skelley/DigitalVision/Getty Images

Although alcohol use is illegal for persons under 21 years of age in the United States, one-third of 8th-graders and 70 percent of 12th-graders have tried alcohol (Johnston et al., 2012). Of particular concern, 22 percent of 12th-graders report having engaged in binge drinking in the last year. Several studies suggest that the use of alcohol and the prevalence of alcohol-related problems have been increasing among young people in recent decades and that the age at which alcohol is first consumed is decreasing (e.g., Grucza, Bucholz, Rice, & Bierut, 2008; Keyes, Grant, & Hasin, 2008; Keyes, Martins, Blanco, & Hasin, 2010). The earlier the age of onset of drinking and drinking-related problems, the more likely individuals are to develop alcohol use disorders (Alvanzo, Storr, La Flair, Green, & Wagner, 2011).

Cultural and Ethnic/Racial Differences Cultures differ markedly in their use of alcohol and rates of alcohol-related problems. Consumption in the Russian Federation is high among both men and women, and the rates of negative health consequences due to alcohol are highest in this and surrounding countries (Rehm et al., 2009; WHO, 2014). Low rates of consumption in some African and Middle Eastern countries are tied to Islam's prohibitions against alcohol.

Ethnic groups within the United States differ substantially in their alcohol use. One group at high risk for alcohol-related problems is Native Americans, 43 percent of whom meet the criteria for alcohol abuse or alcohol dependence at some time in their life (Hasin, Stinson, Ogburn, & Grant, 2007). Deaths related to

SHADES OF GRAY

As you may have observed, binge drinking on the weekends is fairly common on college campuses. Read about Nick and his friends, who may resemble people you know.

Nick began drinking in high school, but his drinking escalated when he moved away from home for college. After just a couple of weeks there, Nick became friends with a group that liked to party on the weekends. On Thursday nights, they would drink and get so loud and obnoxious that their neighbors in the dorm would sometimes complain. They would sleep off their hangovers on Friday, miss classes, and then begin drinking again from Friday afternoon through Saturday, finally stopping on Sunday to sleep and recover. Nick was able to keep decent grades through his first year, despite missing many classes. In sophomore year, classes in his major were harder, and he would abstain from drinking from Sunday afternoon until noon on Thursday. But Thursday afternoon he would get the keg of beer for his friends, and the old pattern would kick in.

One night during a drinking game, Nick accidentally punched a hole in the wall of his dorm room and was kicked off campus as a result. Between this incident and his declining grades, his parents threatened to stop paying his college tuition.

Would you diagnose Nick with an alcohol use disorder? (Discussion appears at the end of this chapter.)

alcohol are more than twice as common among Native Americans than in the general U.S. population (Chartier & Caetano, 2010; Landen, Roeber, Naimi, Nielsen, & Sewell, 2014). This higher rate of alcohol-related problems has been tied to excessive rates of poverty and unemployment, lower levels of education, and a greater sense of helplessness and hopelessness.

Long-Term Effects of Alcohol Misuse

Heavy and prolonged use of alcohol can have toxic effects on several systems of the body, including the stomach, esophagus, pancreas, and liver (Paul et al., 2011). One of the most common medical conditions associated with alcohol misuse is low-grade hypertension. This condition, combined with increases in the levels of triglycerides and low-density lipoprotein (or "bad") cholesterol, puts alcohol abusers at increased risk for heart disease. Heavy alcohol use increases the risk of cancer, particularly breast cancer in women (Chen, Rosner, Hankinson, Colditz, & Willett, 2011). People with alcohol use disorders often are malnourished, in part because chronic alcohol ingestion decreases the absorption of critical nutrients from the gastrointestinal system and in part because they tend to "drink their meals." Some show a chronic thiamine (Vitamin B_1) deficiency, which can lead to several disorders of the central nervous system, including numbness and pain in the extremities, deterioration in the muscles, and the loss of visual acuity for both near and far objects (Osiezagha et al., 2013). Heavy prolonged use of alcohol is a risk factor for dementia, a permanent substance-induced major neurocognitive disorder involving loss of intellectual abilities, including memory, abstract thinking, judgment, and problem solving, and often accompanied by personality changes such as increased paranoia (see the chapter "Neurodevelopmental and Neurocognitive Disorders"). Subtler deficits due to central nervous system damage (e.g., substance-induced mild neurocognitive disorder) are observed in many chronic abusers of alcohol, even after they quit drinking.

As noted earlier, binge drinking is relatively common among adolescents and young adults. There is increasing evidence that heavy and prolonged use of alcohol during adolescence and early adulthood may have permanent negative effects on the brain, which is undergoing massive developmental changes during these periods of life (Jacobus & Tapert, 2013). Neuroimaging studies show changes in the structure and functioning of several areas of the brain in adolescents and young adults who binge-drink frequently or are chronic heavy drinkers, changes associated with deficits in performance on a variety of cognitive tests. The few longitudinal studies that have been done suggest that these deleterious effects of alcohol consumption may persist even after people stop drinking.

Some studies indicate that moderate alcohol consumption, particularly of red wine, carries health benefits. Red wine contains antioxidants that can increase good cholesterol, along with other chemicals that can help prevent damage to blood vessels and reduce bad cholesterol, producing positive cardiac effects (Fillmore, Kerr, Stockwell, Chikritzhs, & Bostrom, 2006; Le Strat & Gorwood, 2011). Several studies suggest that individuals who consume one or two drinks a day have better physical health and lower mortality rates than individuals who abstain from alcohol (Corrao, Bagnardi, Zambon, & La Vecchia, 2004; Rehm, Greenfield, & Rogers, 2001). However, abstainers and moderate drinkers differ on many other variables that can affect health. Abstainers are more likely than moderate drinkers to be older, less well educated, physically inactive, and overweight and to have diabetes, hypertension, and high cholesterol (Naimi et al., 2005). Some people classified as abstainers drank heavily earlier in life and have quit due to negative health effects (Fillmore et al., 2006). These factors make the potential health benefits of moderate drinking less clear.

Benzodiazepines and Barbiturates

Like alcohol, benzodiazepines and barbiturates depress the central nervous system. Intoxication with and withdrawal from these substances are similar to alcohol intoxication and withdrawal. Users may initially feel euphoric and become disinhibited but then experience depressed moods, lethargy, perceptual distortions, loss of coordination, and other signs of central nervous system depression.

Benzodiazepines (such as Xanax, Valium, Halcion, Librium, and Klonopin) and **barbiturates** (such as Seconal) are legally manufactured and sold by prescription, usually as sedatives for the treatment of anxiety and insomnia. Benzodiazepines are also used as muscle relaxants and antiseizure medicines. In the United States, approximately 90 percent of people hospitalized for medical care or surgery are prescribed sedatives (Procyshyn et al., 2017). Large quantities of these substances end up on the black market, however. They are especially likely to be abused in combination with other psychoactive substances to produce greater feelings of euphoria or to relieve the agitation created by other substances. Abuse of prescription sedatives and tranquilizers has increased in recent years. Nationwide studies find that about 9 percent of adults, 9.6 percent of college students, and close to 5 percent of teenagers report using prescription sedatives or tranquilizers in the last year for nonmedical purposes (Johnston et al., 2012; McCabe, Cranford, & West, 2008; see also SAMHSA, 2017). *DSM-5* classifies problematic misuse of these drugs as sedative, hypnotic, or anxiolytic use disorders.

Barbiturates and benzodiazepines cause decreases in blood pressure, respiratory rate, and heart rate. In overdose, they can be extremely dangerous and even cause death from respiratory arrest or cardiovascular collapse. Overdose is especially likely when people take these substances (particularly benzodiazepines) with alcohol. These were among the drugs that Heath Ledger overdosed on (see this chapter's Extraordinary People).

STIMULANTS

Stimulants activate the central nervous system, causing feelings of energy, happiness, and power; a decreased desire for sleep; and a diminished appetite (see Table 4). Cocaine and the amphetamines (including the related methamphetamines) are the two types of stimulants associated with severe substance use disorders. Both impart a psychological lift or rush. They cause dangerous increases in blood pressure and heart rate, alter the rhythm and electrical activity of the heart, and constrict the blood vessels, which can lead to heart attacks, respiratory arrest, and seizures. In the United States, over half of drug-related emergency room visits involve use of cocaine or the

TABLE 4 Intoxication with and Withdrawal from Stimulants

The stimulants activate the central nervous system.

Drug	Intoxication Symptoms	Withdrawal Symptoms
Cocaine and amphetamines	Behavioral changes (e.g., euphoria or affective blunting; changes in sociability; hypervigilance; interpersonal sensitivity; anxiety, tension, or anger; impaired judgment) Rapid heartbeat Dilation of pupils Elevated or lowered blood pressure Perspiration or chills Nausea or vomiting Weight loss Psychomotor agitation or retardation Muscular weakness Slowed breathing Chest pain Confusion, seizures, coma	Dysphoric mood Fatigue Vivid, unpleasant dreams Insomnia or hypersomnia Increased appetite Psychomotor retardation or agitation
Nicotine	Not a diagnosis in the *DSM-5*	Dysphoria or depressed mood Insomnia Irritability, frustration, or anger Anxiety Difficulty concentrating Restlessness Decreased heart rate Increased appetite or weight gain
Caffeine	Restlessness Nervousness Excitement Insomnia Flushed face Frequent urination Stomach upset Muscle twitching Rambling flow of thought or speech Rapid or irregular heartbeat Periods of inexhaustibility Psychomotor agitation	Marked fatigue or drowsiness Dysphoric mood or irritability Flulike symptoms (e.g., nausea or vomiting)

amphetamines (SAMHSA, 2013). Prescription stimulants, including Dexedrine and Ritalin, are used to treat asthma and other respiratory problems, obesity, neurological disorders, attention-deficit/hyperactivity disorder (ADHD; see the chapter "Neurodevelopmental and Neurocognitive Disorders"), and a variety of other conditions. Use of these prescription stimulants for nonmedical purposes has increased sharply in recent decades (McCabe et al., 2008). Caffeine and nicotine also are stimulants, and although their psychological effects are not as severe as those of cocaine and amphetamines, these drugs–particularly nicotine–can have long-term negative effects.

Cocaine

Cocaine, a white powder extracted from the coca plant, is one of the most addictive substances known. People snort the powder or inject it intravenously. In the 1970s, even more powerful freebase cocaine appeared when users developed a method for separating the most potent chemicals in cocaine by heating it with ether. Freebase cocaine is usually smoked in a water pipe or mixed in a tobacco or marijuana cigarette. *Crack* is a form of freebase cocaine boiled down into tiny chunks, or rocks, and usually smoked.

Cocaine use causes dangerous increases in blood pressure and heart rate, alterations in the rhythm and electrical activity of the heart, and constricted blood vessels, which can lead to heart attacks, respiratory arrest, and seizures. *©Medioimages/Photodisc/Getty Images*

FIGURE 3 **Effects of Cocaine on Dopamine Systems.** Cocaine blocks transporters for the reuptake of dopamine, resulting in excess dopamine in the synapses.

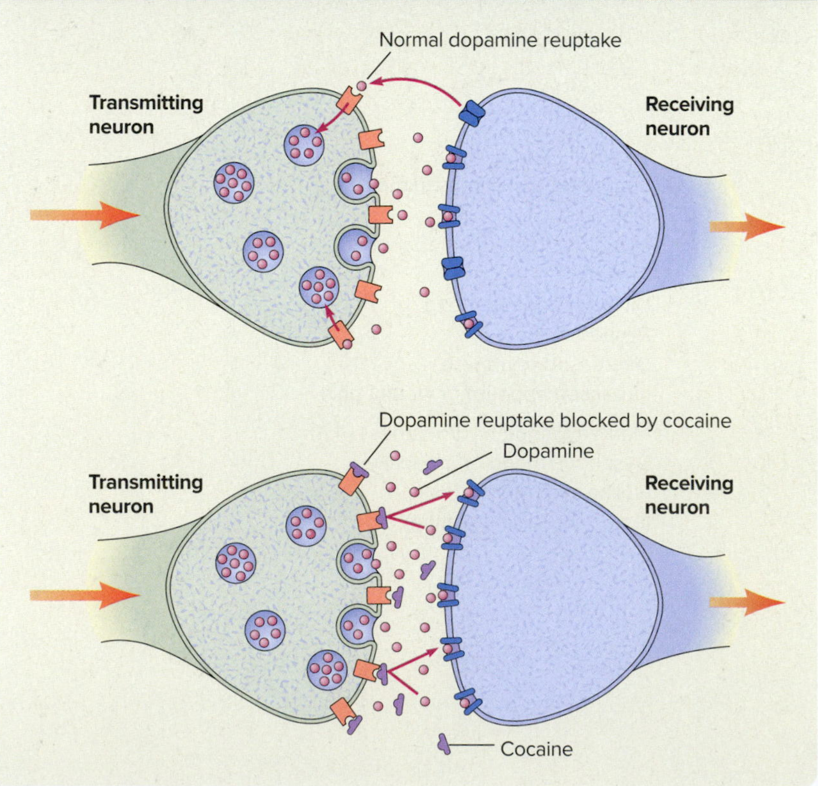

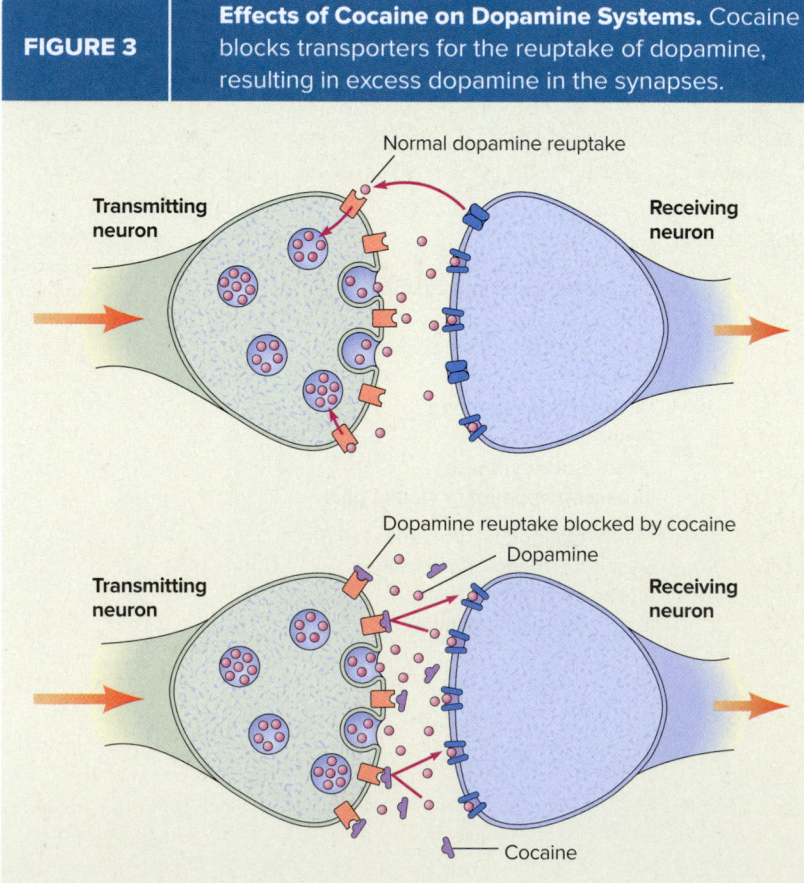

Initially, cocaine produces an instant rush of intense euphoria, followed by heightened self-esteem, alertness, energy, and feelings of competence and creativity. Users crave increasing amounts of the substance, for both its physiological and its psychological effects (Ruiz & Strain, 2014). When taken repeatedly or at high doses, however, it leads to grandiosity, impulsiveness, hypersexuality, compulsive behavior, agitation, and anxiety reaching the point of panic and paranoia. Stopping cocaine use can induce exhaustion and depression.

Cocaine activates those areas of the brain that register reward and pleasure. Normally, a pleasurable event releases dopamine into the synapses in these areas. Dopamine then binds to receptors on neighboring synapses (Figure 3). Cocaine blocks the reuptake of dopamine into the transmitting neuron, causing it to accumulate in the synapse and maintaining the pleasurable feeling (Ruiz & Strain, 2014). The rapid, strong effects of cocaine on the brain's reward centers make this substance more likely than most to lead to a stimulant use disorder. The following case study illustrates this process.

CASE STUDY

Dr. Arnie Rosenthal is a 31-year-old white male dentist, married for 10 years with two children. His wife insisted he see a psychiatrist because of uncontrolled use of cocaine, which over the past year had made it increasingly difficult for him to function as a dentist. During the previous 5 years he used cocaine virtually every day, with only occasional 1- or 2-week periods of abstinence. For the past 4 years Rosenthal wanted to stop, but his desire was overridden by a "compulsion" to take the drug.

He began using marijuana after being married a year, smoking a joint each day after school and spending the evening staring at TV. When he graduated from dental school his wife was pregnant, and he was "scared to death" at the prospect of being a father. His deepening depression was characterized by social isolation, increased loss of interests, and frequent temper outbursts. He needed intoxication with marijuana, or occasionally sedatives, for sex, relaxation, and socialization. Following the birth of the child he "never felt so crazy," and his marijuana and sedative use escalated. Two years later, a second child was born. Dr. Rosenthal was financially successful, had moved to an expensive suburban home with a swimming pool, and had two cars and "everything my parents wanted for me." He was 27 years old, felt he had nothing to look forward to, and felt painfully isolated; drugs were no longer providing relief.

Rosenthal tried cocaine for the first time and immediately felt good. "I was no longer depressed. I used cocaine as often as possible because all my problems seemed to vanish, but I had to keep doing it. The effects were brief and it was very expensive, but I didn't care. When the immediate effects wore off, I'd feel even more miserable and depressed so that I did as much cocaine as I was able to obtain." He is now continuously nervous and irritable. (Spitzer, R. L., Skodol, A. E., Gibbon, M., & Williams, J. B. W., *Psychopathology: A Case Book,* 1983, 81–83. Copyright ©1983 McGraw-Hill Education. Reprinted with permission.)

Cocaine's effects wear off quickly, and the dependent person must take frequent doses to maintain a high. Tolerance also can develop, and the individual must obtain larger and larger amounts to experience a high (Ruiz & Strain, 2014). People with cocaine-related stimulant use disorder spend huge amounts of money on the substance and may engage in theft, prostitution, or drug dealing to obtain enough money to purchase it. Desperation can lead frequent users to participate in extremely dangerous behaviors. Many contract HIV, the virus that causes AIDS, by sharing needles with infected users or by having unprotected sex in exchange for money or cocaine (Ruiz & Strain, 2014).

Other frequent medical complications of cocaine use are heart rhythm disturbances and heart attacks; respiratory failure; neurological effects, including strokes, seizures, and headaches; and gastrointestinal complications, including abdominal pain and nausea. Physical symptoms include chest pain, blurred vision, fever, muscle spasms, convulsions, and coma (Ruiz & Strain, 2014).

A large percentage of people who grew up in the 1960s and 1970s have tried cocaine, but these percentages are much lower in more recent generations: A nationwide study in the United States found that 48 percent of individuals who graduated from high school in 1979 had tried cocaine at some time in their life, compared to about 20 percent of individuals who had graduated from high school between 1980 and 1995 (Johnston et al., 2012). Among U.S. college students, 5.5 percent report ever having used cocaine, whereas 12 percent of 18- to 22-year-olds not in college report ever having used cocaine; among high school students, about 3.5 percent report ever having used cocaine (Johnston et al., 2012).

Amphetamines

Amphetamines and the related *methamphetamines* are stimulants prescribed for the treatment of attention problems (e.g., Ritalin, Adderall), narcolepsy, and chronic fatigue. They also are found in antihistamines (e.g., Sudafed) and diet drugs. Many stimulants are

On the street, amphetamines are known as "speed," "meth," and "chalk." They are most often swallowed as pills but can be injected intravenously, and methamphetamine can be snorted ("crank") or smoked ("crystal meth" or "ice"). Serious health problems can result from their use. ©*The Washington Times/ZUMA Press/ATHENS/TN/USA/Newscom*

used appropriately under the supervision of a physician, but a great many doses are diverted to illegal use and abuse (Ruiz & Strain, 2014). Because of the potential for abuse, most states regulate over-the-counter sales of diet drugs and antihistamines. On the street, amphetamines are known as "speed," "meth," and "chalk." They are most often swallowed as pills but can be injected intravenously, and methamphetamine can be snorted ("crank") or smoked ("crystal meth" or "ice"). Owing in part to the easy and inexpensive manufacture of methamphetamine, its use is widespread in the United States. As of 2016, nearly 700,000 Americans reported using the drug within the last month (SAMHSA, 2017).

Amphetamines release the neurotransmitters dopamine and norepinephrine and block their reuptake. The symptoms of intoxication are similar to those of cocaine intoxication: euphoria, self-confidence, alertness, agitation, and paranoia (Ruiz & Strain, 2014). Like cocaine, amphetamines can produce perceptual illusions. The movement of other people and objects may seem distorted or exaggerated. Users may hear frightening voices making derogatory statements about them, see sores all over their body, or feel snakes crawling on their arms. They may have delusions of being stalked that lead them to act out violently. Some users know that these experiences are not real, but others lose their grip on reality and develop amphetamine-induced psychotic disorders (Ruiz & Strain, 2014).

Legal problems typically arise for amphetamine abusers due to aggressive or inappropriate behavior while intoxicated or as a result of buying the drug illegally. Tolerance develops quickly, as does physical dependence. Users may switch from swallowing pills to injecting amphetamines intravenously. Some go on a *speed run,* in which they inject amphetamines frequently over several days without eating or sleeping. Then they crash into a devastating depression. Acute withdrawal symptoms typically subside within a few days, but chronic users may experience mood instability, memory loss, confusion, paranoid thinking, and perceptual abnormalities for weeks, months, or even years. They often battle the withdrawal symptoms with another speed run (Ruiz & Strain, 2014).

Abuse of amphetamines and methamphetamines can lead to a number of medical issues, particularly cardiovascular problems—including rapid or irregular heartbeat, increased blood pressure, and irreversible, stroke-producing damage to the small blood vessels in the brain. Elevated body temperature and convulsions can occur during overdoses, leading to death. People who share needles to inject amphetamines risk contracting HIV or hepatitis (Brick, 2008). With extended use, people become irritable and hostile and need more stimulants to avoid withdrawal symptoms. Their personal relationships and health decline. Emergency room visits involving amphetamines and methamphetamines increased drastically between 1995 and 2002, and after some decreases in the mid-2000s, began increasing again. Between 2009 and 2011 visits increased by 71 percent (SAMHSA, 2013).

Abuse of these drugs has risen in recent years. In 2011, 8.2 percent of 12th-graders reported using amphetamines or methamphetamines (Johnston et al., 2012). College students trying to stay up late to study may take them; nationwide studies find that 13.4 percent of college students report ever having used amphetamines or methamphetamines, with 9.3 percent reporting their use in the last year (Johnston et al., 2012). Employers may even provide amphetamines to their employees to increase productivity.

Nicotine

All the substances discussed thus far, except alcohol, are illegal for nonprescription use, and many laws regulate the use of alcohol. One of the most addictive substances known, however, is fully legal for use by adults and readily available to adolescents—**nicotine.**

Nicotine is an alkaloid found in tobacco. Cigarettes, the most popular nicotine delivery device, get this substance to the brain within seconds. In the United States, 70 percent of people over age 12 have smoked cigarettes at some time in their life, and about 23 percent currently are smokers (Johnston et al., 2012; SAMHSA, 2017). Smoking usually begins in the early teens. A 2011 survey of 12th-graders found that 40 percent had smoked a cigarette at some time in their life and that 10 percent were smoking daily (Johnston et al., 2012). Rates of cigarette use are much higher in Europe and many developing nations (Danielsson, Wennberg, Hibell, & Romelsjö 2012). Over two-thirds of people who begin smoking become dependent on nicotine, a rate much higher than is found with most other psychoactive substances (Lopez-Quintero et al., 2011).

While the rate of cigarette smoking has decreased in the United States, it is on the rise in many developing countries around the world. ©*KAMBOU SIA/AFP/Getty Images*

Tobacco use has declined in the United States and other industrialized countries over the past few decades, thanks in part to significantly increased taxes on tobacco products, laws restricting their use in public places, and lawsuits limiting tobacco companies' ability to advertise. In contrast, tobacco use is increasing in developing countries.

Nicotine operates on both the central and the peripheral nervous systems. It helps release several biochemicals in the brain, including dopamine, norepinephrine, serotonin, and the endogenous opioids. Although people often say they smoke to reduce stress, nicotine's physiological effects actually resemble the fight-or-flight response (see the chapter "Trauma, Anxiety, Obsessive-Compulsive, and Related Disorders")—several systems in the body are aroused, including the cardiovascular and respiratory systems. The subjective sense that smoking reduces stress actually may reflect the reversal of the tension and irritability that signal nicotine withdrawal. In other words, nicotine addicts need nicotine to feel normal to counteract its effects on the body and the brain (Ruiz & Strain, 2014). *DSM-5* recognizes nicotine dependence as a tobacco use disorder.

In 1964, based on a review of 6,000 empirical studies, the surgeon general of the United States concluded that smoking, particularly cigarette smoking, causes lung cancer, bronchitis, and probably coronary heart disease. Mortality rates for smokers are 70 percent greater than for nonsmokers, meaning that a person between ages 30 and 35 who smokes two packs a day will die 8 to 9 years earlier than a nonsmoker. Each year, an estimated 480,000 people in the United States (about one in five deaths) die prematurely from smoking-related coronary heart disease, lung cancer, emphysema, or chronic bronchitis or from exposure to secondhand smoke. An additional 16 million people have an illness related to smoking (CDC, 2018a). Women who smoke while pregnant give birth to smaller babies. The longer a person smokes and the more he or she smokes each day, the greater the health risks.

When chronic heavy smokers try to quit or are prohibited from smoking for an extended period, such as while at work or on an airplane, they show severe withdrawal symptoms. They become depressed, irritable, angry, anxious, frustrated, restless, and hungry; they have trouble concentrating; and they desperately crave another cigarette. These symptoms are immediately relieved by smoking, another sign of physiological dependence (Ruiz & Strain, 2014).

Because nicotine is relatively cheap and available, dependents tend not to spend much time trying to obtain it. They may panic, however, if they run out of cigarettes and replacements are not available. They also may spend a large part of their day smoking or chewing tobacco, and they continue to use nicotine even though it is damaging their health (e.g., after they have been diagnosed with emphysema). They may skip social activities where smoking is not allowed or recreational activities such as sports because they have trouble breathing.

Electronic cigarettes, also called e-cigarettes, first appeared in 2004 and are now used by millions around the world. The e-cigarette is an electronic device that vaporizes a flavored liquid that is inhaled, a practice called vaping. The fluid usually includes nicotine. Although there is general agreement that e-cigarettes are less harmful to health than cigarettes, long-term health effects are not known. There is some evidence that e-cigarettes can help people to quit smoking, although regulated replacement products and medications are generally viewed as safer (McRobbie, Bullen, Hartmann-Boyce, & Hajek, 2014). The rising popularity of e-cigarettes has been especially noticeable among younger people, just as their rates of cigarette smoking have declined. E-cigarettes are now the most commonly used tobacco product among youth in the United States, with 4 percent of middle school students and 11 percent of high school students reporting using them (CDC, 2018c).

Nearly 70 percent of people who smoke say they want to quit (Babb, Malarcher, Shauer, Asman, & Jamal, 2017), and in fact rates of smoking have decreased consistently since 2005 (CDC, 2018a). Quitting is difficult, however, in part because the withdrawal syndrome is difficult to withstand. Fewer than 10 percent of smokers who try to stop smoking each year are successful, and most relapse within a few days of quitting (Babb et al., 2017). Cravings can remain after a smoker quits, with 50 percent of people who quit smoking reporting they have desired cigarettes in the past 24 hours (Goldstein, 2001). Nicotine patches and gum can help fight this urge.

Caffeine

Caffeine is by far the most heavily used stimulant, with 75 percent of it ingested in coffee (Chou, 1992). A cup of brewed coffee has about 100 milligrams of caffeine, and the average U.S. adult drinks about two cups per day. Other sources include tea (about 40 milligrams of caffeine per 6 ounces), caffeinated soda (45 milligrams per 12 ounces), over-the-counter analgesics and cold remedies (25 to 50 milligrams per tablet), weight-loss drugs (75 to 200 milligrams per tablet), and chocolate and cocoa (5 milligrams per bar).

Caffeine stimulates the central nervous system, increasing the levels of dopamine, norepinephrine, and serotonin. It also increases metabolism, body temperature, and blood pressure. People's appetite wanes, and they feel more alert. But in doses equivalent to just two to three cups of coffee, caffeine can cause unpleasant symptoms, including restlessness, nervousness, and hand tremors. People may experience an upset stomach and feel their heart beating rapidly or irregularly. They may have trouble going to sleep later on and may need to urinate frequently. These are symptoms of caffeine intoxication. Extremely large doses of caffeine can cause extreme agitation, seizures, respiratory failure, and cardiac problems.

The *DSM-5* specifies that a diagnosis of caffeine intoxication should be given only if an individual experiences significant distress or impairment in functioning as a result of the symptoms. Someone who drinks too much coffee for several days in a row during exam week, for example, might be so agitated that she cannot sit through her exams and so shaky that she cannot drive a car; such a person could be given a diagnosis of caffeine intoxication.

Some heavy coffee drinkers who joke that they are "caffeine addicts" actually cannot be diagnosed with caffeine use disorder, according to the *DSM-5*, because dependence on the drug seems not to cause significant social and occupational problems. Still, caffeine users can develop tolerance and undergo withdrawal if they stop ingesting caffeine. They may require several cups of coffee in the morning to feel "normal" and may experience significant headaches, fatigue, and anxiety if they do not get their coffee.

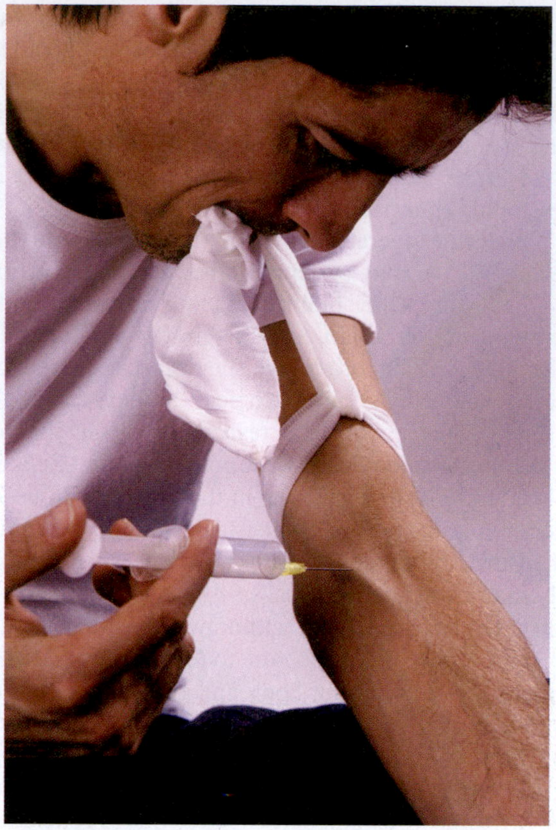

Severe intoxication from heroin use can lead to unconsciousness, coma, and seizures. ©*Michaela Begsteiger/imageBROKER/Getty Images*

OPIOIDS

Morphine, heroin, codeine, and methadone are all **opioids.** They are derived from the sap of the opium poppy, which has been used for thousands of years to relieve pain. Our bodies produce natural opioids, including endorphins and enkephalins, to cope with pain. For example, a sports injury induces the body to produce endorphins to reduce pain and avoid shock. Doctors also may prescribe synthetic opioids, such as hydrocodone (Lorcet, Lortab, Vicodin) or oxycodone (Percodan, Percocet, OxyContin) for pain.

Morphine was widely used as a pain reliever in the nineteenth century, until it was found to be highly addictive. Heroin was developed from morphine in the late nineteenth century and was used for a time for medicinal purposes. By 1917, however, it was clear that heroin and all the opioids have dangerous addictive properties, and Congress passed a law making heroin illegal and banning the other opioids except for specific medical needs. Heroin remained widely available on the street, however (Winger, Hoffmann, & Woods, 2004).

When used illegally, opioids often are injected into the veins (mainlining), snorted, or smoked. The initial symptom of opioid intoxication often is euphoria (see Table 5). People describe a sensation in the abdomen like a sexual orgasm, referring to it as a thrill, kick, or flash. They may have a tingling sensation and a pervasive sense of warmth. They pass into a state of drowsiness, during which they are lethargic, their speech is slurred, and their mind may be clouded. They may experience periods of light sleep with vivid dreams. Pain is reduced (Ruiz & Strain, 2014). A person in this state is referred to as being *on the nod.* Severe intoxication can lead to unconsciousness, coma, and seizures.

Opioids can suppress the respiratory and cardiovascular systems to the point of death. The drugs are especially dangerous when combined with depressants, such as alcohol or sedatives. Withdrawal symptoms include dysphoria, an achy feeling in the back and legs, increased sensitivity to pain, and a craving for more opioids. The person may experience nausea, vomiting, profuse sweating and goose bumps, diarrhea, and fever (Ruiz & Strain, 2014). These symptoms usually appear within 8 to 16 hours of last use and peak within 36 to 72 hours. In chronic or heavy users, they may continue in strong form for 5 to 8 days and in a milder form for weeks to months.

Most street heroin is cut with other substances, so users do not know the actual strength of the drug or its true contents, leaving them at risk for overdose or death. Users also risk contracting HIV through contaminated needles or through unprotected sex, which many opioid abusers exchange for more heroin. In some areas of the United States, up to 60 percent of

TABLE 5 Intoxication with and Withdrawal from Opioids

The opioids include morphine, heroin, codeine, and methadone.

Drug	Intoxication Symptoms	Withdrawal Symptoms
Opioids	Behavioral changes (e.g., initial euphoria followed by apathy, dysphoria, psychomotor agitation or retardation; impaired judgment)	Dysphoric mood Nausea or vomiting Muscle aches
	Constriction of pupils	Tearing or nasal mucus discharge
	Drowsiness or coma	Dilation of pupils
	Slurred speech	Goose bumps
	Attention and memory problems	Sweating
		Diarrhea
		Yawning
		Fever
		Insomnia

chronic heroin users are infected with HIV. Intravenous users also can contract hepatitis, tuberculosis, serious skin abscesses, and deep infections. Women who use heroin during pregnancy risk miscarriage and premature delivery, and children born to mothers with opioid use disorders are at increased risk for sudden infant death syndrome (Brady, Back, & Greenfield, 2009).

One of the biggest developments in the substance abuse area has been an explosion of opioid use and abuse in the United States in recent years, which has been dubbed a national epidemic. The use and misuse of prescription opioid pain relievers such as oxycodone or Vicodin increased significantly in the past two decades. In 2016 alone, 11.5 million people over the age of 12 misused these drugs, a prevalence of over 4 percent (SAMHSA, 2017). The rate among young adults was 7 percent. Opioids are the most common cause of drug overdoses; over 40,000 deaths in the United States in 2016 involved opioids, five times as many as in 1999 (CDC, 2018b). This stunning increase and severity of the opioid epidemic is partially attributable to increased use of illegally made synthetic opioids like fentanyl (CDC, 2018c). The crisis presents severe challenges to local authorities, first responders, state and federal governments, and millions of families.

HALLUCINOGENS AND PCP

Most of the substances discussed so far can produce perceptual illusions and distortions when used in large doses. The **hallucinogens** and *phencyclidine (PCP)* produce perceptual changes even in small doses (see Table 6). The hallucinogens are a mixed group of substances, including lysergic acid diethylamide (LSD), peyote, and psilocybin mushrooms.

TABLE 6 Intoxication with Hallucinogens and PCP

The hallucinogens and PCP cause a variety of perceptual and behavioral changes.

Drug	Intoxication Symptoms
Hallucinogens	Behavioral changes (e.g., marked anxiety or depression, the feeling that others are talking about you, fear of losing your mind, paranoia, impaired judgment)
	Perceptual changes while awake (e.g., intensification of senses, depersonalization, illusions, hallucinations)
	Dilation of pupils
	Rapid heartbeat
	Sweating
	Palpitations
	Blurring of vision
	Tremors
	Incoordination
PCP	Behavioral changes (e.g., belligerence, assaultiveness, impulsiveness, unpredictability, psychomotor agitation, impaired judgment)
	Involuntary rapid eyeball movement
	Hypertension
	Numbness
	Loss of muscle coordination
	Problems speaking due to poor muscle control
	Muscle rigidity
	Seizures or coma
	Exceptionally acute hearing
	Perceptual disturbances

PROFILES

As far as I remember, the following were the most outstanding symptoms: vertigo, visual disturbances; the faces of those around me appeared as grotesque, colored masks; marked motor unrest, alternating with paresis; an intermittent heavy feeling in the head, limbs, and the entire body, as if they were filled with metal; cramps in the legs, coldness, and loss of feeling in the hands; a metallic taste on the tongue; dry constricted sensation in the throat; feeling of choking; confusion alternating between clear recognition of my condition, in which state I sometimes observed, in the manner of an independent, neutral observer, that I shouted half insanely or babbled incoherent words. Occasionally, I felt as if I were out of my body. The doctor found a rather weak pulse but an otherwise normal circulation. Six hours after ingestion of the LSD my condition had already improved considerably. Only the visual disturbances were still pronounced. Everything seemed to sway and the proportions were distorted like the reflections in the surface of moving water. Moreover, all objects appeared in unpleasant, constantly changing colors, the predominant shades being sickly green and blue. When I closed my eyes, an unending series of colorful, very realistic and fantastic images surged in upon me. A remarkable feature was the manner in which all acoustic perceptions (e.g., the noise of a passing car) were transformed into optical effects, every sound causing a corresponding colored hallucination constantly changing in shape and color like pictures in a kaleidoscope. (Source: Hoffman, A., Psychotomimetic agents. In Burger, A. (Ed.), *Drugs affecting the central nervous system,* Vol. 2, 1968, 185–186. New York: Marcel Dekker.)

The psychoactive effects of LSD were first discovered in 1943 when Dr. Albert Hoffman accidentally swallowed a minute amount and experienced visual hallucinations. He later purposefully swallowed a small amount of LSD and reported its effects.

As Hoffman describes, one symptom of intoxication from LSD and other hallucinogens is *synesthesia,* the overflow from one sensory modality to another. People say they hear colors and see sounds. They feel at one with their surroundings, and time seems to pass very slowly. Moods also may shift from depression to elation to fear. Some people become anxious. Others feel a sense of detachment and a great sensitivity for art, music, and feelings. These experiences lent the drugs the label *psychedelic,* from the Greek words for "soul" and "to make manifest." LSD was used in the 1960s as part of the consciousness-expanding movement (Winger et al., 2004).

The hallucinogens are dangerous drugs, however. Although LSD was legal for use in the early 1960s, by 1967 reports of "bad acid trips," or "bummers," had become common, particularly in the Haight-Ashbury district of San Francisco, where many LSD enthusiasts from around the United States congregated (Smith & Seymour, 1994). Symptoms included severe anxiety, paranoia, and loss of control. Some people on bad trips would walk off a roof or jump out a window, believing they could fly, or walk into the sea, believing they were "one with the universe." For some, the anxiety and hallucinations were severe enough to produce psychosis requiring hospitalization and long-term treatment. Some people reexperience their psychedelic experiences, especially visual disturbances, long after the drug has worn off and may develop a distressing or impairing hallucinogen persisting perception disorder.

Phencyclidine (PCP)—also known as angel dust, PeaCePill, Hog, and Tranq—is manufactured as a powder to be snorted or smoked. Although PCP is not classified as a hallucinogen, it has many of the same effects. At lower doses, it produces a sense of intoxication, euphoria or affective dulling, talkativeness, lack of concern, slowed reaction time, vertigo, eye twitching, mild hypertension, abnormal involuntary movements, and weakness. At intermediate doses, it leads to disorganized thinking, distortions of body image (e.g., feeling that one's arms are not part of one's body), depersonalization, and feelings of unreality. A user may become hostile, belligerent, and even violent (Morrison, 1998). At higher doses, PCP produces amnesia and coma, analgesia sufficient to allow surgery, seizures, severe respiratory problems, hypothermia, and hyperthermia. The effects begin immediately after injecting, snorting, or smoking and peak within minutes. Symptoms of severe intoxication can persist for several days; people with PCP intoxication may be misdiagnosed as having a psychotic disorder unrelated to substance use (Morrison, 1998).

Phencyclidine or other hallucinogen use disorder is diagnosed when individuals repeatedly fail to fulfill major role obligations at school, work, or home due to intoxication with these drugs. They may use the drugs in dangerous situations, such as while driving a car, and they may have legal troubles due to their possession of the drugs. Because the drugs can cause paranoia or aggressive behavior, frequent users may find their work and social relationships affected. About 11 percent of the U.S. population reports having tried a hallucinogen or PCP, but only 0.5 percent report having used it in the past month (Johnston et al., 2012; SAMHSA, 2017). Use is higher among teenagers and young adults, however, with 5.8 percent of 12th-graders, 4.1 percent of college students, and 6.4 percent of 18- to 22-year-olds not in college reporting use of a hallucinogen in the past year (Johnston et al., 2012).

CANNABIS

The leaves of the **cannabis** (or hemp) plant can be cut, dried, and rolled into cigarettes or inserted into food and beverages. In North America, the result is known as marijuana, weed, pot, grass, reefer, and Mary Jane. Cannabis is the most commonly used illegal drug, with 42 percent of adults in the United States and 23 percent of Europeans having used the drug (Degenhardt et al., 2008; European Monitoring Centre for Drugs and Drug Action, 2011; Johnston et al., 2012). About half of older adolescents and young adults say they have used cannabis at some time in their life, and about 20 percent have used it in the last year (Johnston et al., 2012).

Intoxication usually begins with a "high" feeling of well-being, relaxation, and tranquility (see Table 7). Users may feel dizzy, sleepy, or dreamy. They may become more aware of their environment, and everything may seem funny. They may become grandiose or lethargic. People who already are very anxious, depressed, or angry may become more so (Ruiz & Strain, 2014). The symptoms of cannabis intoxication may develop within minutes if the drug is smoked but may take a few hours to develop if it is taken orally. The acute symptoms last 3 to 4 hours, but some symptoms may linger or recur for 12 to 24 hours.

Although people often view cannabis as a benign or safe drug, it can significantly affect cognitive and motor functioning. People taking cannabis may believe they are thinking profound thoughts, but their short-term memory is impaired to the point that they cannot remember thoughts long enough to express them in sentences. Motor performance also is impaired. People's reaction times are slower and their concentration and judgment are deficient, putting them at risk for accidents. The cognitive impairments caused by cannabis can last up to a week after heavy use stops (Pope, Gruber, Hudson, Huestis, & Yurgelun-Todd, 2001). These effects appear to be greater in women than in men (Pope, Jacobs, Mialet, Yurgelun-Todd, & Gruber, 1997).

The physiological symptoms of cannabis intoxication include increased or irregular heartbeat, increased appetite, and dry mouth. Cannabis smoke is irritating and increases the risk of chronic cough, sinusitis, bronchitis, and emphysema. It contains even larger amounts of known carcinogens than does tobacco and thus creates a high risk of cancer. The chronic use of cannabis lowers sperm count in men and may cause irregular ovulation in women (Ruiz & Strain, 2014).

At moderate to large doses, cannabis users experience perceptual distortions, feelings of depersonalization, and paranoid thinking. Some find these hallucinogenic effects pleasant, but others become frightened. Some users may have severe anxiety episodes resembling panic attacks. Several studies have found that cannabis use significantly increases the risk of developing a psychotic disorder (e.g., Kuepper et al., 2011; van Winkel & Kuepper, 2014).

Seven to 10 percent of the U.S. population would qualify for a diagnosis of cannabis use disorder. ©belchonock/123RF

TABLE 7 Intoxication and Withdrawal Symptoms with Cannabis

Cannabis is the most commonly used illegal drug in the United States.

Drug	Intoxication Symptoms	Withdrawal Symptoms
Cannabis	Behavioral changes (e.g., impaired motor coordination, euphoria, anxiety, sensation of slowed time, impaired judgment)	Irritability, anger, or aggression Nervousness or anxiety Sleep difficulty Decreased appetite or weight loss
	Red eyes	Restlessness
	Increased appetite	Depressed mood
	Dry mouth	Stomach pain, shakiness, sweating, fever, chills, headache
	Rapid heartbeat	

Physical tolerance to cannabis can develop, with users needing greater amounts to avoid the symptoms of withdrawal, which include irritability, difficulty sleeping, loss of appetite, hot flashes, runny nose, sweating, diarrhea, and hiccups (Schlienz, Budney, Lee, & Vandrey, 2017). About 2 percent of the U.S. population would qualify for a diagnosis of cannabis use disorder (Hasin et al., 2015; SAMHSA, 2017).

In recent years several states have legalized the medicinal and recreational use of cannabis, although it remains illegal at the federal level. The federal government allows exemptions on the basis of mandated regulation. Thirty-one states and the District of Columbia have legalized the use of cannabis in some form for medical reasons (see Pacula & Smart, 2017). As of 2018, recreational cannabis is fully legal in Alaska, California, Colorado, Maine, Massachusetts, Nevada, Oregon, and Washington State and in several smaller jurisdictions. According to a Pew Research Center survey, 61 percent of Americans are in favor of complete or partial legalization of cannabis (Pew Research Center, 2018). As marijuana has come to be perceived to have lower risks over the last decade, the rate and frequency of use has increased (Compton, Han, Jones, Blanco, & Hughes, 2016).

TABLE 8 Intoxication with Inhalants

Inhalants have a variety of effects depending on the specific drug.

Drug	Intoxication Symptoms
Inhalants	Behavioral changes (e.g., belligerence, assaultiveness, apathy, impaired judgment)
	Dizziness
	Nystagmus
	Incoordination
	Slurred speech
	Unsteady gait
	Lethargy
	Depressed reflexes
	Psychomotor retardation
	Tremor
	Generalized muscle weakness
	Blurred vision or diplopia
	Stupor or coma
	Euphoria

INHALANTS

Inhalants are volatile substances that produce chemical vapors, which can be inhaled and which depress the central nervous system (see Table 8; Procyshyn et al., 2017). One group of inhalants is solvents, including gasoline, glue, paint thinners, and spray paints. Users may inhale vapors directly from the can or bottle containing the substance, soak a rag with the substance and hold the rag to their mouth and nose, or place the substance in a paper or plastic bag and inhale the gases from the bag. The chemicals rapidly reach the lungs, bloodstream, and brain. Another group of inhalants is medical anesthetic gases, such as nitrous oxide ("laughing gas"), which also can be found in whipped cream dispensers and products that boost octane levels. Nitrites, another class of inhalants, dilate blood vessels and relax muscles and are used as sex enhancers. Illegally packaged nitrites are called "poppers" or "snappers" on the street. In diagnosing an inhalant use disorder, *DSM-5* recommends specifying the particular substance involved when possible (e.g., solvent use disorder).

A nationwide study of adults found that less than 2 percent reported ever having used inhalants, with about 75 percent of users being male (Howard, Perron, Vaughn, Bender, & Garland, 2010). Adolescents report higher levels of use, with about 10 percent of teenagers reporting ever having used inhalants (Johnston et al., 2012). Some studies find that nearly all the children on some Native American reservations have experimented with inhaling gasoline.

Chronic users of inhalants may have a variety of respiratory irritations and rashes. Inhalants can cause permanent damage to the central nervous system, including degeneration and lesions of the brain; this damage can lead to cognitive deficits, including severe dementia. Recurrent use can also cause hepatitis and other liver and kidney disease. Death can occur from depression of the respiratory or cardiovascular system. Sudden sniffing death is due to acute heartbeat irregularities or loss of oxygen. Users sometimes suffocate when they fall unconscious with an inhalant-filled plastic bag over their nose and mouth. Users also can die or be seriously injured when the inhalants induce the delusion that users can do fantastic things, such as fly, and they then jump off a cliff or a tall building to test their perceived ability (Procyshyn et al., 2017).

OTHER DRUGS OF ABUSE

Drug sellers are creative in coming up with new psychoactive substances. Often these substances initially have legitimate medicinal purposes and then are hijacked or transformed into street drugs. In this section, we discuss ecstasy (3,4-methylenedioxymethamphetamine, or

MDMA), GHB (gamma-hydroxybutyrate), ketamine, and rohypnol (flunitrazepam).

Ecstasy, also known as "Molly," has the stimulant effects of an amphetamine along with occasional hallucinogenic properties. It is fairly popular with young adults; 6.8 percent of college students and 13.0 percent of 18- to 22-year-olds not in college report having used ecstasy at some time (Johnston et al., 2012). Users experience heightened energy and restlessness and claim that their social inhibitions decrease and their affection for others increases. Even short-term use can have long-term negative effects on cognition and health, however. People who use ecstasy score lower on tests related to attention, memory, learning, and general intelligence than do people who do not use the drug. The euphoric effects of ecstasy, and some of the brain damage, may be due to alterations in the functioning of serotonin in the brain—serotonin levels in ecstasy users are half those in people who are not users (Gold, Tabrah, & Frost-Pineda, 2001). Long-term users risk several cardiac problems and liver failure and show increased rates of anxiety, depression, psychotic symptoms, and paranoia (Gold et al., 2001). Another effect of ecstasy is teeth-grinding; some users suck a baby pacifier at parties to relieve this effect.

GHB is a central nervous system depressant approved for the treatment of the sleep disorder narcolepsy. At low doses, it can relieve anxiety and promote relaxation. At higher doses, it can result in sleep, coma, or death. In the 1980s, GHB was widely used by bodybuilders and athletes to lose fat and build muscle and was available over the counter in health food stores. In 1990, it was banned except under the supervision of a physician due to reports of severe side effects, including high blood pressure, wide mood swings, liver tumors, and violent behavior. Other side effects include sweating, headache, decreased heart rate, nausea, vomiting, impaired breathing, loss of reflexes, and tremors (National Institute on Drug Abuse [NIDA], 2018). GHB is also considered a *date-rape drug* because it has been associated with sexual assaults (NIDA, 2018). It goes by the street names Grievous Bodily Harm, G., Liquid Ecstasy, and Georgia Home Boy.

Ketamine is a rapid-acting anesthetic that produces hallucinogenic effects ranging from rapture to paranoia to boredom (NIDA, 2018). Ketamine can elicit an out-of-body or near-death experience. It also can render the user comatose. It has effects similar to those of PCP, including numbness, loss of coordination, a sense of invulnerability, muscle rigidity, aggressive or violent behavior, slurred or blocked speech, an exaggerated sense of strength, and a blank stare. Because ketamine is an anesthetic, users feel no pain, which can lead them to injure themselves (NIDA, 2018).

A ketamine high usually lasts 1 hour but can last as long as 4 to 6 hours, and it takes 24 to 48 hours for users to feel normal again. Large doses can produce vomiting and convulsions and may lead to oxygen starvation in the brain and muscles. One gram can cause death. Ketamine is another date-rape drug used to anesthetize victims (NIDA, 2018).

A widely known date-rape drug is *rohypnol,* which goes by the slang names Roofies, Rophies, Roche, and the Forget-Me Pill, among others. It is a benzodiazepine and has sedative and hypnotic effects (NIDA, 2018). Users may experience a high, as well as muscle relaxation, drowsiness, impaired judgment, blackouts, hallucinations, dizziness, and confusion. Rohypnol tablets can easily be crushed and slipped into someone's drink. Rohypnol is odorless, colorless, and tasteless, so victims often don't notice that their drink has been altered. Side effects can include headaches, muscle pain, and seizures. In combination with alcohol or other depressants, rohypnol can be fatal (NIDA, 2018).

THEORIES OF SUBSTANCE USE DISORDERS

All the substances we have discussed have powerful effects on the brain that determine their rewarding effects. Whether individuals ever use substances, and whether their use progresses into a substance use disorder, depends on a complex interplay of biological, psychological, and social vulnerabilities (Volkow & Boyle, 2018).

Biological Factors

The brain appears to have its own "pleasure pathway" that affects our experience of reward. This pathway begins in the ventral tegmental area in the midbrain, then progresses through an area of the limbic system called the nucleus accumbens and on to the frontal cortex. It is particularly rich in neurons sensitive to the neurotransmitter dopamine (Volkow & Boyle, 2018).

Some drugs, such as amphetamines and cocaine, directly increase the availability of dopamine in this pathway, producing a strong sense of reward or a "high." Cocaine clears out of the brain more rapidly than do amphetamines, which explains why users on a binge need to use cocaine much more frequently to maintain a high than do those using amphetamines (Volkow & Boyle, 2018). Snorting, smoking, or injecting drugs delivers them to the brain much faster than taking them orally and thus produces a quicker, more intense reaction. Other drugs increase the availability of dopamine more indirectly. For example, the

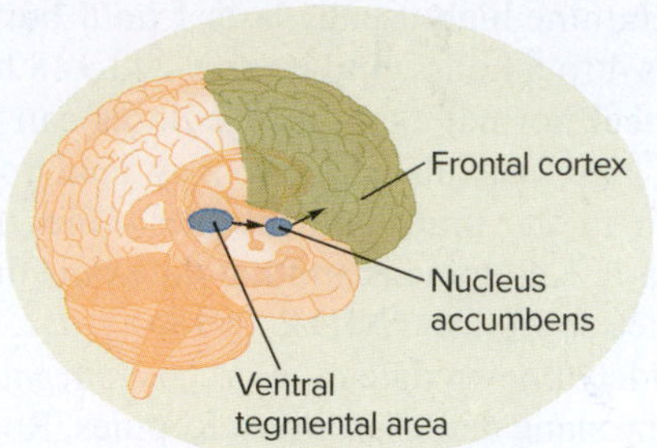

The brain's "pleasure pathway" begins in the ventral tegmental area, then goes through the nucleus accumbens and on to the frontal cortex. It is rich in neurons sensitive to dopamine.

neurons in the ventral tegmental area are inhibited from continuously firing by GABA neurons, so the firing of GABA neurons reduces the high caused by activity in the dopamine neurons. The opiate drugs inhibit GABA, which stops the GABA neurons from inhibiting dopamine, making dopamine available in the reward center (Volkow & Boyle, 2018).

Other areas of the frontal cortex, including the orbitofrontal cortex, the dorsolateral frontal cortex, and the inferior frontal gyrus, play important roles in controlling the urge to drink alcohol or use drugs (Bechara, 2005; Goldstein & Volkow, 2002). Individuals whose reward network overpowers their control network may be more likely to use substances (Goldstein & Volkow, 2002; Hutchison, 2010).

The chronic use of psychoactive substances alters the reward centers, creating a craving for these substances (Berridge & Robinson, 2016). The repeated use of substances such as cocaine, heroin, and amphetamines causes the brain to reduce its production of dopamine, with the result that dopamine receptors in the brain become less sensitive. As the brain produces less dopamine, more of the drug is needed to produce the desired effects. If the individual stops taking the drug, the brain does not immediately compensate for the loss of dopamine, and withdrawal symptoms occur. Also, because the brain is not producing its typical amount of dopamine, the person may feel sad and unmotivated and may have difficulty experiencing pleasure from other sources, such as food or happy events. Craving for the drug sets in because only the drug can produce pleasure (Berridge & Robinson, 2016).

Psychoactive drugs also affect a number of other biochemical (including glutamate) and brain systems. Alcohol produces sedative and antianxiety effects largely by enhancing the activity of the neurotransmitter GABA in the septal/hippocampal system. Alcohol also affects serotonin systems, which are associated with changes in mood (Brick, 2008).

Although individuals who have used a substance for an extended period experience decreased sensitivity to the rewarding aspects of the substance, they become more sensitive to cues associated with their substance use, such as the locations where they typically use the substance or the paraphernalia associated with it. These conditioned responses to drug cues can induce powerful cravings that can lead to relapse (Volkow & Boyle, 2018). Stress also activates reward systems, creating cravings. In addition, chronic use of drugs seems to lead to disrupted activity in frontal regions of the brain involved in impulse control, making it even more difficult for individuals to resist cravings.

Genetic factors regulate the functioning of the neurotransmitter systems involved in the rewarding effects of substance use. Family history, adoption, and twin studies all suggest that genetics plays a substantial role in determining who is at risk for substance use disorders, with about 50 percent of the variation in risk for substance use disorders attributable to genetic factors (see reviews by Urbanoski & Kelly, 2012; Young-Wolff, Kendler, Ericson, & Prescott, 2011). There seems to be a common underlying genetic vulnerability to substance use disorders in general, rather than to use of specific substances, perhaps accounting for the fact that individuals who use one substance are likely to use several.

Much research has focused on the genes that control the dopamine system, given its importance in the reinforcing properties of substances. Genetic variation in the dopamine receptor gene (labeled DRD2) and the dopamine transporter gene (labeled SLC6A3) influences how the brain processes dopamine, thereby affecting how reinforcing a person finds substances such as nicotine (Nemoda, Szekely, & Sasvari-Szekely, 2011). In addition, the genes that control GABA have also been implicated in substance use disorders, particularly alcohol use disorders.

Psychological Factors

Social learning theories (see the chapter "Theories and Treatment of Abnormality") suggest that children and adolescents may learn substance use behaviors from the modeling of their parents and important others in their culture. Even as preschoolers, the children of heavy drinkers are more likely than other children to be able to identify alcoholic drinks and view alcohol use as a part of daily life (Zucker, Kincaid, Fitzgerald, & Bingham, 1995). Children whose parents abuse alcohol by frequently getting drunk or by driving while intoxicated learn that these are acceptable behaviors and thus are more likely to engage in them (Chassin, Pitts, DeLucia, & Todd, 1999; Hussong, Huang, Serrano, Curran, & Chassin, 2012).

Children may learn substance-related behaviors from their parents. ©*Laurence Cartwright Photography/Moment/Getty Images*

Because alcohol-related problems are more common among males than females, most of the adults modeling inappropriate use of alcohol are male. In turn, because children are more likely to learn from adults who are similar to themselves, male children and adolescents may be more likely to learn these behaviors than female children and adolescents. Thus, maladaptive patterns of alcohol use may be passed down through the males in a family through modeling (Chassin et al., 1999; Hussong et al., 2012).

The cognitive theories of alcohol use disorders have focused on people's expectations of alcohol's effects and their beliefs about the appropriateness of using it to cope with stress (Cooper, Kuntsche, Levitt, Barber, & Wolf, 2016). People who expect alcohol to reduce their distress and who do not have more adaptive means of coping (e.g., problem-solving skills or supportive friends or family) are more likely than others to drink alcohol when they are upset and to have social problems related to drinking (Cooper et al., 2016). In long-term studies of the sons of parents with alcohol use disorders, men who used alcohol to cope and relax were more likely to develop alcohol use disorders themselves (Handley & Chassin, 2009; Schuckit, 1998).

One personality characteristic consistently related to an increased risk of substance use disorders is behavioral undercontrol, or the tendency to be impulsive, sensation-seeking, and prone to antisocial behaviors such as violating laws. People with high levels of behavioral undercontrol take psychoactive drugs at an earlier age, ingest more psychoactive drugs, and are more likely to be diagnosed with substance use disorders (McGue, Iacono, Legrand, Malone, & Elkins, 2001; White, Xie, & Thompson, 2001; Zucker, Heitzeg, & Nigg, 2011). Behavioral undercontrol runs strongly in families, and twin studies suggest that this may be due in part to genes (Rutter, Silberg, O'Connor, & Simonoff, 1999). Thus, genetics may influence behavioral undercontrol, which in turn influences the risk that individuals will develop substance use disorders.

Sociocultural Factors

The reinforcing effects of substances—the highs produced by stimulants, the calming and "zoning out" effects of the depressants and the opioids—can be more attractive to people under chronic stress. Thus, rates of substance use disorders are higher among people living in poverty, women in abusive relationships, and adolescents whose parents fight frequently and violently (Hughes, McCabe, Wilsnack, West, & Boyd, 2010; SAMHSA, 2017; Zucker, Chermack, & Curran, 1999). For these people, the effects of substances may be especially reinforcing. They also may think that they have little to lose.

Subtler environmental reinforcements and punishments clearly influence people's substance use habits. Some societies discourage any use of alcohol, often due to religious beliefs, and alcohol abuse and dependence are rare in these societies. Other societies, including many European cultures, allow the drinking of alcohol but strongly discourage excessive drinking and irresponsible behavior while intoxicated. Alcohol-related disorders are less common in these societies than in societies with few restrictions, either legal or cultural, on alcohol use (Sher et al., 2005; WHO, 2014).

Women suffer the effects of excessive alcohol use at lower doses than men do. ©*Gennadiy Poznyakov/123RF*

Gender Differences

Substance use, particularly alcohol use, is more acceptable for men than for women in many societies. Heavy drinking is part of what "masculine" men do and is modeled by heroes and cultural icons. In contrast, until recently heavy drinking in some Western cultures signified that a woman was "not a lady." Societal acceptance of heavy drinking by women has increased in recent generations, as has the rate of alcohol use among young women (Nolen-Hoeksema, 2004; SAMHSA, 2017).

Women tend to be less likely than men to carry risk factors for substance use disorders (Nolen-Hoeksema, 2004). They appear less likely to have personality traits associated with substance use disorder (behavioral undercontrol, sensation seeking). They also appear less motivated to use alcohol to reduce distress and less likely to expect drug consumption to have a positive outcome (Nolen-Hoeksema & Harrell, 2002).

Women suffer alcohol-related physical illnesses at lower levels of exposure to alcohol than men do (Fillmore et al., 1997). In addition, heavy alcohol use is associated with reproductive problems in women. Women may be more likely to experience greater cognitive and motor impairment due to alcohol than do men and to suffer physical harm and sexual assault following alcohol use (Lorenz & Ullman, 2016).

When they do use alcohol, women may notice that they feel intoxicated much sooner than do men, and they may be more likely to find these effects aversive or frightening, leading them to limit their consumption (Nolen-Hoeksema, 2004). This lower consumption, in turn, protects women against developing tolerance to high doses of alcohol and lowers their risk of developing alcohol-related social and occupational problems.

When women become substance abusers, their patterns and reasons for use tend to differ from those of men. Men tend to begin using substances in the context of socializing with male friends, while women most often are initiated by family members, partners, or lovers (McCrady, Epstein, Cook, Jensen, & Hildebrandt, 2009). Perhaps because women's drug use is more closely tied to their intimate relationships, studies have found that treatments that include their partners tend to be more effective in reducing substance use disorders in women (McCrady et al., 2009).

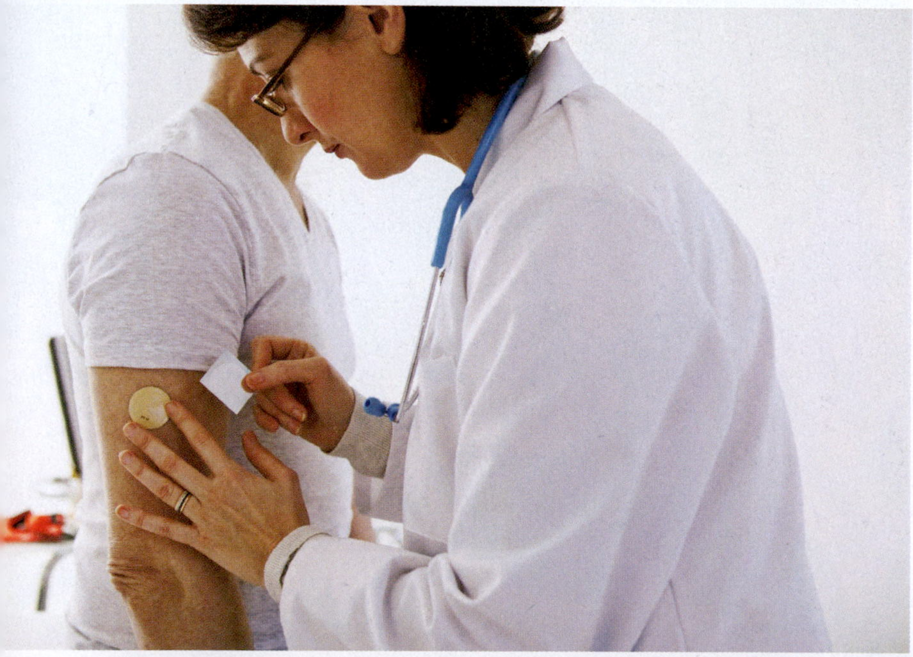

Nicotine replacement therapy aims to decrease substance abuse over time by weaning the user to lower doses, as well as breaking links between the behavior of smoking and its perceived positive physiological consequences. *©Image Point Fr/Shutterstock*

TREATMENTS FOR SUBSTANCE USE DISORDERS

The treatment of substance-related disorders is challenging, and media accounts of celebrity drug abusers who are in rehab one month, out the next, and back a short time later suggest that it seldom is effective. Meta-analyses and reviews of existing treatments suggest that, as a whole, they help only about 17 to 35 percent of people with substance use disorders abstain for up to 1 year (Hutchison, 2010). Here we review the most common and best-supported biological and psychosocial treatments.

Biological Treatments

Medications can help wean individuals off a substance, reduce their desire for it, and maintain their use at a controlled level (Douaihy, Kelly, & Sullivan, 2013).

Antianxiety Drugs, Antidepressants, and Drug Antagonists

Although many people with substance use disorders can withstand withdrawal symptoms if given emotional support, others may require medication. For people dependent on alcohol, a benzodiazepine, which has depressant effects similar to those of alcohol, can reduce tremors and anxiety, decrease pulse and respiration rate, and stabilize blood pressure (Ntais, Pakos, Kyzas, & Ioannidis, 2005). The dosage is decreased each day so that a patient withdraws from the alcohol slowly but does not become dependent on the benzodiazepine.

Antidepressant drugs sometimes are used to treat individuals with substance dependence who are depressed, but their efficacy in treating either alcohol or other drug problems or depression without psychotherapy has not been consistently supported (Nunes & Levin, 2004). People have widely different responses to the SSRIs.

Antagonist drugs block or change the effects of the addictive drug, reducing the desire for it. Naltrexone and naloxone are opioid antagonists—they block the effects of opioids such as heroin. Theoretically, this can reduce the desire for and therefore the use of the addictive drug. The opioid antagonists must be administered very carefully, however, because they can cause severe withdrawal reactions in people addicted to opioids (Douaihy et al., 2013).

Naltrexone has also proven useful in treating alcohol dependents and abusers, possibly because it blocks the effects of endorphins during drinking. People dependent on alcohol who take naltrexone report a diminished craving for alcohol and thus drink less (Douaihy et al., 2013).

The drug acamprosate affects glutamate and GABA receptors in the brain, which are involved in the craving for alcohol. Some clinical trials show that acamprosate can help people maintain abstinence from alcohol better than a placebo, although others do not, suggesting the need for additional research (Douaihy et al., 2013).

A drug that can make alcohol actually punishing is disulfiram, commonly called Antabuse. Just one alcoholic drink can make people taking disulfiram feel sick and dizzy and can make them vomit, blush, and even faint. People must be very motivated to remain on disulfiram, and it works to reduce their alcohol consumption only as long as they continue to take it.

The pharmacological treatment of nicotine dependence uses two general approaches. Most common is nicotine replacement therapy—the use of nicotine gum or a nicotine patch, nasal spray, or inhaler to prevent withdrawal effects. It is hoped that the individual will gradually reduce use of the nicotine replacement while slowly being weaned off nicotine's physiological effects.

The other approach is the use of prescription medication that reduces the craving for nicotine. One drug approved for this use is the antidepressant bupropion (marketed for smoking cessation as Zyban). A drug called varenicline (Chantix), which binds to and partially stimulates nicotine receptors, also has been shown to reduce cravings for nicotine products, decrease their pleasurable effects (Ebbert et al., 2015; Jorenby et al., 2006).

Methadone Maintenance Programs

Gradual withdrawal from heroin can be achieved with **methadone.** This drug is itself an opioid, but it has less potent and less long-lasting effects than heroin when taken orally. The person dependent on heroin takes methadone to reduce extreme negative withdrawal symptoms. Those who take heroin while on methadone do not experience heroin's intense psychological effects, because methadone blocks receptors for heroin (Douaihy et al., 2013).

Although the goal of treatment is for individuals eventually to withdraw from methadone, some patients use it for years under a physician's care. Such methadone maintenance programs are controversial. Some people believe they allow the heroin dependent to simply transfer dependency to another substance that is legal and provided by a physician. Others believe methadone maintenance is the only way to keep some heroin dependents from going back on the street and relapsing. Studies find that patients in such programs are much more likely to remain in psychological treatment than are patients who try to withdraw from heroin without methadone and also are less likely to relapse into heroin use (Mattick, Breen, Kimber, Davoli, & Breen, 2003).

Psychosocial Treatments

Several behavioral and cognitive techniques have proven helpful in the treatment of substance use disorders (Higgins, Sigmon, & Heil, 2014; McCrady, 2014). The techniques have certain goals in common. The first is to motivate the individual to stop using the addictive drug. People who enter treatment often are ambivalent about stopping use and may have been forced into treatment against their will. The second goal is to teach patients new coping skills to replace the use of substances to cope with stress and negative feelings. The third goal is to change the reinforcements for using substances—for example, an individual may need to disengage from social circles that encourage drug use. The fourth is to enhance the individual's support from nonusing friends and family members. The final goal often is to foster adherence to pharmacotherapies in conjunction with psychotherapy.

Behavioral Treatments

Behavioral treatments based on aversive classical conditioning are sometimes used alone or in combination with biological or other psychosocial therapies (Finney & Moos, 1998; Schuckit, 1995). Drugs such as disulfiram (Antabuse) that make the ingestion of alcohol unpleasant or toxic are given to people who are alcohol dependent. Eventually, through classical conditioning, people develop conditioned responses to alcohol—namely, nausea and vomiting. Then, through operant conditioning, they learn to avoid alcohol in order to avoid the aversive response. Aversive conditioning is effective in reducing alcohol consumption, at least in the short term (Schuckit, 1995). "Booster" sessions often are needed to reinforce this conditioning, because its effects tend to weaken with time.

Covert sensitization therapy uses imagery to create associations between thoughts of alcohol use and thoughts of highly unpleasant consequences. An example of a sensitization scene that a therapist might take a client through begins as described in the following profile.

PROFILES

You finish the first sip of beer, and you . . . notice a funny feeling in your stomach. . . . Maybe another drink will help. . . . As you tip back . . . that funny feeling in your stomach is stronger, and you feel like you have to burp. . . . You swallow again, trying to force it down, but it doesn't work. You can feel the gas coming up. . . . You swallow more, but suddenly your mouth is filled with a sour liquid that burns the back of your throat and goes up your nose. . . . [You] spew the liquid all over the counter and sink. (Rimmele, C. T., Miller, W. R., & Dougher, M. J. (1989), "Aversion therapies" in R. K. Hester & W. R. Miller (Eds.), *Handbook of Alcoholism Treatment Approaches: Effective Alternatives* (pp. 128–140). New York: Pergamon Press.)

The imagery gets even more graphic. Covert sensitization techniques seem to be effective in creating conditioned aversive responses to the sight and smell of alcohol and in reducing alcohol consumption.

Contingency management programs provide reinforcements for individuals to curtail their use of substances—for example, employment, housing, or vouchers for purchases at local stores. Studies show that individuals dependent on heroin, cocaine, marijuana, or alcohol will remain in treatment longer and be much more likely to become abstinent when they are provided with incentives contingent on submitting drug-free urine specimens (Higgins et al., 2014; McCrady, 2014).

Cognitive Treatments

Interventions based on the cognitive models of alcohol abuse and dependency help clients identify situations in which they are most likely to drink and lose control over their drinking, as well as their expectations that alcohol will help them cope in those situations (Daley & Marlatt, 2006). Therapists work with clients to challenge these expectations by reviewing alcohol's negative effects on the clients' behavior. Perhaps a client was feeling anxious at a recent party and began to drink heavily. The therapist might have the client recount his embarrassing behavior while intoxicated, challenging the notion that the alcohol helped him cope effectively. Therapists also help clients learn to handle stressful situations in adaptive ways, such as seeking the help of others or engaging in active problem solving. Finally, therapists help clients learn to say "No, thanks" when they are offered a drink and to deal with social pressure by using assertiveness skills.

Following is an excerpt from a discussion between a therapist and a client with alcohol-related problems (adapted from Sobell & Sobell, 1978, pp. 97–98) in which the therapist is helping the client generate strategies for coping with the stress of a possible job promotion. The therapist encourages the client to brainstorm coping strategies and refrains from evaluating them for the moment so the client will feel free to generate as many strategies as possible.

Client: I've been offered the job I've been telling you about. It's a huge promotion. But now I have to make the decision about whether or not to move my entire family across the country to take it. I know my wife and kids don't want to move. And now I am really nervous about whether or not I can even do this new job. I don't have all the skills.

Therapist: Yes, that's a big decision for you and your family. But rather than worrying about the skills problem just now, why don't we explore the different options you have relating to the promotion and move. You know, for now, you don't have to evaluate your options, only list them. The point right now is to come up with as many alternatives as possible. You're not yet acting on anything, only considering your possibilities.

Client: You know, I've been pretty tense and you know what has happened before when I get nervous. I've been drinking quite a lot. My wife is pretty angry about it. And I don't feel so well.

Therapist: Well, in a way, drinking is one option. But what other ways can you think of to deal with the problem of the promotion and move?

Client: I've been thinking that because the new company has an educational benefit, I could take courses to learn more about management. Maybe even get my MBA. But I have no idea about how I could hold down the job, go to school, and be in any way present to my family.

Therapist: Well, remember. Right now we're not talking about how you would do any of this; we're only coming up with options. You're doing really well. Let's keep going.

Client: I could always just stay where I am. The family would be happier, even if I might not be so happy at work. But it means a lot to me that they are happy too. Or I could ask my new boss to give me time to get up to speed with my new responsibilities.

Therapist: Good. Keep going.

Client: What would happen if I take the new job, settle my family in a new state, and then find out that I can't get that kind of support?

Therapist: Well, what do you think would happen? What are your options?

Client: I think I really want the job. Maybe I should just be in touch with the person who hired me and tell her about my concerns. After all, they are willing to move me across the country; they must really want me. I need some time and some more education.

Therapist: You've identified a lot of options today. Why don't we spend some time evaluating each before you make a final decision? (Adapted from Sobell & Sobell, 1978, 97–98)

The therapist helps the client evaluate the effectiveness of each option and anticipate any negative consequences. In this case, the client decides to accept the promotion but to take some courses at the local college to increase his business background. The two discuss the stresses of managing a new job and classes, and they generate ways the client can manage these stresses other than by drinking.

In most cases, therapists using cognitive-behavioral approaches encourage their clients to abstain from alcohol, especially when they have a history of frequent relapses into abuse. When a client's goal is to learn to drink socially and the therapist believes the client can achieve this goal, therapy may focus on teaching the client to engage in social, or controlled, drinking.

Studies have shown that cognitive-behavioral approaches are effective in treating abuse and dependence on alcohol, cannabis, nicotine, heroin, amphetamines, and cocaine (see Higgins et al., 2014; McCrady, 2014; McHugh, Hearon, & Otto, 2010).

Motivational Interviewing

If individuals are not motivated to curtail their substance use, no treatment will be effective. William Miller (1983; Miller & Rollnick, 2012; Miller & Rose, 2009) developed **motivational interviewing** to elicit and solidify clients' motivation and commitment to changing their substance use. Rather than confronting the user, the motivational interviewer adopts an empathic interaction style, drawing out the user's statements of desire, ability, reasons, need, and, ultimately, commitment to change. The interviewer focuses on the client's ambivalence, helping the client voice his or her own arguments for change. Many controlled studies find that just four sessions of motivational interviewing lead to sustained reductions in substance use, particularly alcohol use (e.g., Ball et al., 2007; Carroll et al., 2006; see reviews in Miller & Rollnick, 2012; Miller & Rose, 2009).

Relapse Prevention

Unfortunately, the relapse rate for people undergoing any kind of treatment for an alcohol use disorder is high. The **abstinence violation effect** contributes to relapse. It has two components. The first is a sense of conflict and guilt when an abstinent alcohol abuser or dependent violates abstinence and has a drink. He or she may continue to drink to try to suppress the conflict and guilt. The second component is a tendency to attribute a violation of abstinence to a lack of willpower and self-control rather than to situational factors. Thus, the person may think, "I'm an alcoholic and there's no way I can control my drinking. The fact that I had a drink proves this." This type of thinking may pave the way to continued, uncontrolled drinking.

Relapse prevention programs teach people who abuse alcohol to view slips as temporary and situationally caused (Donovan & Witkiewitz, 2012). Therapists help clients identify high-risk situations, such as parties, and either avoid them or develop effective coping strategies for them. A client who decides to go to a party may first practice with the therapist some assertiveness skills for resisting friends' pressure to drink and write down other coping strategies to use if she feels tempted, such as starting a conversation with a supportive friend or practicing deep-breathing exercises. She also may decide that, if the temptation becomes too great, she will ask a supportive friend to leave the party with her and go somewhere for coffee until the urge to drink passes. Relapse prevention programs have been shown in many studies to reduce the rate of relapse in people with several types of substance use disorders (Donovan & Witkiewitz, 2012).

These cognitive and behavioral interventions have been combined with training in mindfulness meditation, the nonjudgmental acceptance of one's current emotional and physical state, in the treatment of people with substance use disorders (Bowen, Chawla, & Marlatt, 2010; Wilson et al., 2017). People are taught to be aware of their internal states and the external triggers for these states and to accept and "ride out" their negative states rather than reacting to them in a habitual manner (i.e., by using a substance). Studies of people with alcohol and other substance use disorders showed that adding mindfulness meditation training to the usual treatment led to significant reductions in craving and relapse during the follow-up period (e.g., Bowen et al., 2014).

Alcoholics Anonymous

Alcoholics Anonymous (AA) is an organization created by and for people with alcohol-related problems.

PROFILES

I am Duncan. I am an alcoholic. . . . I know that I will always be an alcoholic, that I can never again touch alcohol in any form. It'll kill me if I don't keep away from it. In fact, it almost did. . . . I must have been just past my 15th birthday when I had that first drink everybody talks about. And like so many of them—and you—it was like a miracle. With a little beer in my gut, the world was transformed. I wasn't a weakling anymore, I could lick almost anybody on the block. So, like for so many of you, my friends in the Fellowship, alcohol became the royal road to love, respect, and self-esteem. . . .

Though it's obvious to me now that my drinking even then, in high school, and after I got to college, was a problem, I didn't think so at the time. A couple of minor auto accidents, one conviction for drunken driving, a few fights—nothing out of the ordinary, it seemed to me at the time. True, I was drinking quite a lot, even then, but my friends seemed to be able to down as much beer as I did. I guess the fact that I hadn't really had any blackouts and that I could go for days without having to drink reassured me that things hadn't gotten out of control.

[Later] on, the drinking began to affect both my marriage and my career. With enough booze in me and under the pressures of guilt over my failure to carry out my responsibilities to my wife and children, I sometimes got kind of rough physically with them. I would break furniture, throw things around, then rush out and drive off in the car. I had a couple of wrecks, lost my license for two years because of one of them. Worst of all was when I tried to stop. By then I was totally hooked, so every time I tried to stop drinking, I'd experience withdrawal in all its horrors. I never had DTs, but I came awfully close many times, with the vomiting and the "shakes" and being unable to sit still or to lie down. And that would go on for days at a time. . . . Then, about four years ago, with my life in ruins, my wife given up on me and the kids with her, out of a job, and way down on my luck, the Fellowship and I found each other. Jim, over there, bless his heart, decided to sponsor me—we'd been friends for a long time, and I knew he'd found sobriety through this group. I've been dry now for a little over two years, and with luck and support, I may stay sober. (Spitzer, R. L., Skodol, A. E., Gibbon, M., & Williams, J. B. W., *Psychopathology: A Case Book,* 1983, 81–83. Copyright © 1983 McGraw-Hill Education. Reprinted with permission.)

Its philosophy is based on the disease model of alcoholism, which asserts that, because of biological, psychological, and spiritual deficits, some people will lose all control over their drinking once they have one drink. Therefore, the only way to control alcohol intake is to abstain completely. AA prescribes 12 steps that people dependent on alcohol must take toward recovery. The first step is to admit their dependence on alcohol and their inability to control its effects. AA encourages its members to seek help from a higher power, to admit their weaknesses, and to ask forgiveness. The goal for all members is complete abstinence.

Group members provide moral and social support and make themselves available to one another in times of crisis. Once they are able, they are expected to devote themselves to helping others who are recovering from alcohol dependence. AA members believe that people are never completely cured of alcohol dependence–they are always "recovering alcoholics," with the potential for falling back into uncontrolled drinking after taking only one drink. To motivate others to abstain from alcohol, AA meetings include testimonials from members, as in the following profile.

The practices and philosophies of AA do not appeal to everyone. The emphases on one's powerlessness, need for a higher power, and complete abstinence turn away many. In addition, many people who subscribe to AA's philosophy still find it difficult to maintain complete abstinence, and they "fall off the wagon" throughout their lives. However, many believe that AA has been critical to their recovery from an alcohol use disorder, and it remains the most common source of treatment for people with alcohol-related problems. There are over 100,000 registered AA groups, and meetings take place all over the United States day and night, providing a supportive community as an alternative to drinking. Self-help groups modeled on AA–including Narcotics Anonymous, Cocaine Anonymous, and Marijuana Anonymous–assist people with dependence on other drugs.

Evaluations of AA's effectiveness are complicated by differences between people who might attend and those who would not, the self-help nature of the intervention, and the fact that outcomes often are self-reported (Kelly, 2003). Perhaps as a result, meta-analyses and reviews of studies of AA's effectiveness have produced mixed results, with some analyses suggesting that AA is effective and others suggesting that it is worse than no treatment (Ferri, Amato, & Davoli, 2006; Kaskutas, 2009; Kelly, 2003; Kownacki & Shadish, 1999; Tonigan, Pearson, Magill, & Hagler, 2018; Tonigan, Toscova, & Miller, 1996).

Substance Use Treatment for Older Adults

We tend to think of substance use disorders as problems of the young. Indeed, the use of hard drugs, such as cocaine or heroin, is quite rare among the elderly. Many chronic users of illicit substances die before they reach old age, and others outgrow their use. Certain types of substance abuse and dependence are a frequent problem among older people, however, including alcohol-related problems and the misuse of prescription drugs (Kuerbis, Sacco, Blazer, & Moore, 2014).

Approximately 4 percent of people over age 65 can be diagnosed with an alcohol use disorder, and about 10 percent can be considered heavy drinkers (Kuerbis & Sacco, 2013). One-third to one-half of abusers of alcohol first develop problems after age 65. Moreover, the abuse of and dependence on prescription drugs (e.g., sedative, hypnotic, or anxiolytic use disorders) is a substantial problem among the elderly. Although only 15 percent of the U.S. population is over age 65, this group accounts for one-third of all prescription drug expenditures. Ninety percent of older adults take at least one prescription drug, and 39 percent take at least five (AARP Public Policy Institute, 2018). The most commonly prescribed drugs are diuretics, cardiovascular drugs, and sedatives. Older people also are more likely than younger people to purchase over-the-counter drugs, including analgesics, vitamins, and laxatives.

The abuse of drugs such as the benzodiazepines may begin innocently. Physicians frequently prescribe them for older patients, and as many as one-third of older people take these drugs at least occasionally–for insomnia or after experiencing a loss, for example. As tolerance develops and the withdrawal effects of discontinuing the drug become evident, an individual may try to get more of the drug by copying prescriptions or seeing multiple physicians. Slurred speech and memory problems caused by drug use may be overlooked in the elderly as normal symptoms of old age. Older adults often can hide their drug abuse for a long period of time. Eventually, the side effects of the drugs, the withdrawal symptoms people experience when they try to go off the drugs cold turkey, or the effects of interaction with other medications may land them in a hospital emergency room.

Treatment for older substance abusers is similar to that for younger abusers, although withdrawal symptoms may be more dangerous for older abusers and therefore must be monitored more carefully (Kuerbis et al., 2014). Psychotherapies that have been shown to be useful tend to have the following characteristics (Schonfeld & Dupree, 2002):

- Elders are treated along with people their same age in a supportive, nonconfrontational approach.
- Negative emotional states (such as depression and loneliness) and their relationship to the substance abuse are a focus of the intervention.
- Social skills and social networks are rebuilt.
- Staff members are respectful and are interested in working with older adults.
- Linkages are made with medical facilities and community resources (such as housing services).

Due to increasing longevity and the size of the baby-boomer generation, the proportion of the population that is above age 65 will increase dramatically over the next few decades, and by 2030 all baby boomers will be over age 65 (U.S. Census Bureau, 2018). In addition, older Americans will become much more ethnically diverse in the future, and the proportion of older people who are of Hispanic and Asian descent will increase. Much more research is needed on the psychological health needs of older people, particularly older people in ethnic and racial minority groups with substance use disorders.

Comparing Treatments

A large, multi-site clinical trial called Project MATCH compared three interventions designed to help people with alcohol use disorder: cognitive-behavioral intervention, motivational interviewing and enhancement, and a 12-step program based on the AA model but led by professional counselors (Project MATCH Research Group, 1998). Surprisingly, the study showed that the three interventions were equally effective in reducing drinking behavior and preventing relapse over the following year (Project MATCH Research Group, 1998; Witkiewitz, Van der Maas, Hufford, & Marlatt, 2007).

Another multi-site study of over 1,300 individuals with alcohol use disorder, Project COMBINE, indicated that combining psychosocial intervention with medications did not yield better outcomes than individual therapies (Anton et al., 2006). The psychosocial treatment was a combination of cognitive-behavioral therapy, motivational interviewing, a 12-step program facilitated by a professional, and community support. The medications were either naltrexone, acamprosate, or a combination of the two. Both psychosocial treatment and naltrexone led to significant reductions in drinking, and the combination of the two was not superior to the individual therapies. Acamprosate did not perform better than a placebo either alone or combined with psychosocial treatment (Anton et al., 2006). A similar pattern was found in a 1-year follow-up of the same individuals, with indications that those who received psychosocial treatment were especially likely to have good outcomes whether or not they also received naltrexone (Donovan et al., 2008).

Prevention Programs

Only about 25 percent of people with alcohol use disorder seek treatment (Dawson et al., 2005). About 25 percent may recover on their own, often due to maturation or positive changes in their environment (e.g., getting a good job or marrying a supportive person) that motivate them to control their drinking (Dawson et al., 2005). The remainder of people with significant alcohol problems carry these problems throughout their lives. Some become physically ill or unable to hold a job or maintain a relationship. Others hide or control their alcohol use disorder and may be in relationships with people who facilitate it. Often they have periods of abstinence, sometimes long, but then—perhaps when facing stressful events—they begin drinking again. Therefore, preventing the development of a substance use disorder is very important.

In the United States, young adults between 18 and 24 have the highest rates of alcohol consumption and make up the largest proportion of problem drinkers of any age group. Many colleges have programs to reduce drinking and drinking-related problems. Programs that emphasize alcohol's health-related consequences tend not to impress young people, who are more likely to focus on the short-term gains of alcohol use. Some college counselors refer students with drinking problems to abstinence programs, such as Alcoholics Anonymous, but students often dislike admitting powerlessness and adopting lifelong abstinence. Finally, many colleges provide alternative activities that do not focus on alcohol. In general, however, prevention programs designed to stop drinking have had limited success.

Psychologist Alan Marlatt and his colleagues at the University of Washington (Marlatt, Blume, & Parks, 2001; Marlatt, Larimer, & Witkiewitz, 2011; Marlatt & Witkiewitz, 2010) argued that a more credible approach to college drinking is to recognize it as normative behavior and focus education on the immediate risks of excess (alcohol-related accidents) and the payoffs of moderation (avoidance of hangovers). They view young drinkers as relatively inexperienced in regulating their use of alcohol and in need of skills training to prevent abuse. Learning to drink safely is compared to learning to drive safely in that people must learn to anticipate hazards and avoid "unnecessary accidents."

Based on this **harm reduction model,** the Alcohol Skills Training Program (ASTP) targets heavy-drinking college students for intervention. In eight weekly sessions of 90 minutes each, participants learn to be aware of their drinking habits—including when, where, and with whom they are most likely to overdrink—by keeping daily records of their alcohol consumption and the situations in which they drink. They also are taught to calculate their blood-alcohol level. It often comes as a surprise to them how few drinks it takes to become legally intoxicated.

Next, beliefs about the "magical" effects of drinking on social skills and sexual prowess are challenged. Participants discuss hangovers and alcohol's negative effects on social behaviors, ability to drive, and weight gain. They are encouraged to set personal goals for limiting consumption based on their blood-alcohol level and their desire to avoid drinking's negative effects. They learn skills for limiting consumption, such as alternating alcoholic and nonalcoholic beverages and selecting drinks for quality rather than quantity (e.g., buying two good beers rather than a six-pack of generic). Later, members are taught alternative ways to reduce negative emotional states, such as using relaxation exercises or reducing sources of stress. Finally, via role playing, participants learn skills for resisting peer pressure and avoiding high-risk situations in which they are likely to overdrink.

Evaluations of ASTP have shown that participants decrease their consumption and alcohol-related problems and increase their social skill at resisting alcohol abuse (Fromme, Marlatt, Baer, & Kivlahan, 1994; Marlatt, Baer, & Larimer, 1995; Marlatt et al., 2011). ASTP was designed for a group format, and the use of group pressure to encourage change and allow role playing has many advantages. Adaptations of this program, delivered in person or in written form as a self-help manual, also have shown positive results (Baer, Kivlahan, Blume, McKnight, & Marlatt, 2001; Baer, Marlatt, Kivlahan, & Fromme, 1992).

GAMBLING DISORDER

More than three-quarters of U.S. adults report having gambled in the past year, but most gamble only occasionally and recreationally (Kessler et al., 2008). As noted earlier, *DSM-5* expanded its chapter on substance-related and addictive disorders to include gambling disorder, which some refer to as a behavioral addiction. The *DSM-5* criteria for gambling disorder are given in Table 9. Less than 1 percent of the U.S.

TABLE 9 *DSM-5* Criteria for Gambling Disorder

A. Persistent and recurrent problematic gambling behavior leading to clinically significant impairment or distress, as indicated by the individual exhibiting four (or more) of the following in a 12-month period:

1. Needs to gamble with increasing amounts of money in order to achieve the desired excitement.
2. Is restless or irritable when attempting to cut down or stop gambling.
3. Has made repeated unsuccessful efforts to control, cut back, or stop gambling.
4. Is often preoccupied with gambling (e.g., having persistent thoughts of reliving past gambling experiences, handicapping or planning the next venture, thinking of ways to get money with which to gamble).
5. Often gambles when feeling distressed (e.g., helpless, guilty, anxious, depressed).
6. After losing money gambling, often returns another day to get even ("chasing" one's losses).
7. Lies to conceal the extent of involvement with gambling.
8. Has jeopardized or lost a significant relationship, job, or educational or career opportunity because of gambling.
9. Relies on others to provide money to relieve desperate financial situations caused by gambling.

B. The gambling behavior is not better explained by a manic episode.

Specify if:

Episodic: Meeting diagnostic criteria at more than one time point, with symptoms subsiding between periods of gambling for at least several months.

Persistent: Continuous symptoms for multiple years.

Current Severity: Mild (4–5 criteria met); Moderate (6–7 criteria met); Severe (8–9 criteria met).

population meet these criteria (Kessler et al., 2008; Petry et al., 2018), but for those who do, their gambling frequently leads to serious financial, relationship, and employment problems. The most common criteria are related to preoccupation with gambling and "chasing" losses.

Pathological gamblers also tend to have problems with substance use, depression, and anxiety and a family history of substance abuse and gambling problems (Petry et al., 2018). Gambling disorder is more common among men than women, among non-Hispanic blacks than other racial/ethnic groups, and among people with less than a college education (Dowling et al., 2017; Kessler et al., 2008). Men tend to develop the disorder earlier in life, while women are more likely to show mid- or later life onset gambling disorder.

Gambling disorder appears to be related to the same brain areas (i.e., activation of the brain's reward system) as the substance use disorders and to disruption in systems regulating the neurotransmitter dopamine (Leeman & Potenza, 2012). People with gambling disorder also show high levels of impulsivity, as do people with substance use disorders, as well as poor performance on cognitive tasks assessing control over impulses (Petry et al., 2018; Potenza et al., 2003).

Cognitive-behavioral therapy (CBT) concentrates on changing the individual's distorted beliefs that he or she has more control than the average person over gambling (chance) outcomes, overconfidence, and superstitions and on developing new activities and coping strategies to replace gambling. Some controlled studies of CBT have shown that it can help reduce compulsive gambling, although more research is needed (Casey et al., 2017; Petry, Rash, & Alessi, 2016; Petry et al., 2018). Serotonin reuptake inhibitors and antipsychotic medications have shown only mixed success in treating pathological gambling (Yip & Potenza, 2014). Naltrexone, an opioid antagonist that affects reward sensitivity, shows more promise, but its efficacy is not yet well established (Yip & Potenza, 2014). Very few people with gambling disorder ever seek treatment, however (Kessler et al., 2008), and those that do typically have moderate to severe forms of the disorder.

Gambling disorder is not the only so-called behavioral addiction addressed by the *DSM-5*.

Gambling disorder appears to be related to the same brain areas as the substance use disorders and to disruption in systems regulating the neurotransmitter dopamine. *©Andrew Olney/Exactostock-1672/Superstock*

FIGURE 4 **Integration of Biological and Psychosocial Factors in the Development of Substance-Related Disorders.**

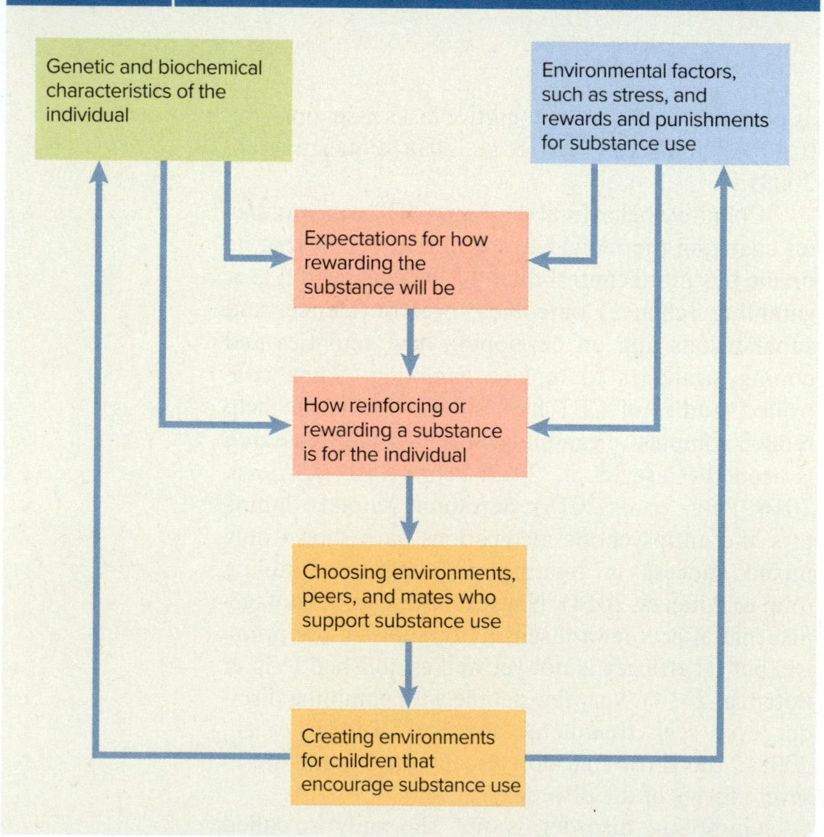
Genetic and biochemical characteristics of the individual
Environmental factors, such as stress, and rewards and punishments for substance use
Expectations for how rewarding the substance will be
How reinforcing or rewarding a substance is for the individual
Choosing environments, peers, and mates who support substance use
Creating environments for children that encourage substance use

Internet gaming disorder, while not listed in the *DSM* as an official disorder, appears in the section listing conditions requiring further study. Video games, including multiplayer games played over the Internet, have become wildly popular across the world (Kuss, Griffiths, & Pontes, 2017). For a minority of people, playing such games can take on a pathological quality, affecting their well-being and occupational and social lives. Criteria for Internet gaming disorder include persistent engagement and preoccupation with gaming, tolerance, withdrawal, loss of interest in other activities, and clinically significant impairment or distress (APA, 2013). Research to define and study Internet gaming disorder is well underway, along with substantial differences of opinion in the field as to whether it is even a true mental disorder (Kuss et al., 2017; Petry et al., 2018). Nevertheless, the World Health Organization announced in 2018 that it would include it, as "gaming disorder," in the addictive disorders section of the *ICD-11*, the newest edition of the international classification system used worldwide (WHO, 2018d).

Some believe other behaviors may also qualify as behavioral addictions when they meet certain criteria and severity. These include Internet addiction, sex addiction, porn addiction, and food addiction (Petry et al., 2018). These are very controversial, not yet well defined, and do not appear in the *DSM-5* as conditions requiring further study. Nevertheless, they are likely to be of greater interest as gambling disorder and gaming disorder attract attention. These issues reflect the challenges in defining "addiction," defining "substance," and distinguishing frequent behavior from pathological abuse or dependence.

CHAPTER INTEGRATION

The substances discussed in this chapter are powerful biological agents. They affect the brain directly, producing changes in mood, thoughts, and perceptions. Some people may be genetically or biochemically predisposed to find these changes more positive or rewarding than other people do (Figure 4). Rewards and punishments in the environment clearly can affect an individual's choice to pursue the effects of substances, however. Even many long-term chronic substance abusers can abstain given strong environmental and social support for abstention.

People who find substances more rewarding, for biological and/or environmental reasons, develop expectations that the substances will be rewarding, which in turn enhance how rewarding they actually are. Likewise, heavy substance users choose friends and situations that support their substance use. They tend to find partners who are also heavy substance users, creating a biological and psychosocial environment for their children that increases vulnerability to substance use disorders. Thus, the cycle of familial transmission of substance misuse has intersecting biological and psychosocial components.

Similar processes may play out in gambling disorder, and potentially Internet gaming disorder as well. For example, biological factors may influence how rewarding an individual finds gambling. The person will then associate with other gamblers, who reinforce the gambling behavior, and eventually the impulse to gamble may become pathological.

SHADES OF GRAY DISCUSSION

Nick's behaviors definitely meet the criteria for an alcohol use disorder. He is failing to fulfill his obligations at school and is continuing to use alcohol despite social problems (ejection from the campus and his parents' threat to withdraw their support). His hangovers are a sign of withdrawal, he spends much time drinking and recovering, and his drinking is hurting his grades. We don't know whether Nick has developed tolerance to alcohol, although the escalation of his drinking suggests that he needs more alcohol to achieve the desired effect. Nick doesn't seem to have any intention of cutting back on his drinking, so the criteria for attempting to control his substance use have not been met.

It may seem odd to think of a college student who drinks with his friends as having a psychiatric diagnosis. Some critics argue that the criteria for alcohol use disorders are too broad and that too many individuals meet them. Others argue that simply because a large percentage of the population meet the criteria for abuse or dependence doesn't mean we should ignore their behavior. What do you think?

CHAPTER SUMMARY

- A substance is any natural or synthesized product that has psychoactive effects. The five groups of substances most often leading to substance disorders are (1) central nervous system depressants, including alcohol, barbiturates, benzodiazepines, and inhalants; (2) central nervous system stimulants, including cocaine, amphetamines, nicotine, and caffeine; (3) opioids; (4) hallucinogens and phencyclidine; and (5) cannabis.
- Substance intoxication is indicated by a set of behavioral and psychological changes that occur as a direct result of the physiological effects of a substance on the central nervous system. Substance withdrawal is a set of physiological and behavioral symptoms that result from the cessation of or reduction in heavy and prolonged use of a substance. The specific symptoms of intoxication and withdrawal depend on the substance being used, the amount ingested, and the method of ingestion.
- Substance use disorders are characterized by a maladaptive pattern of substance use leading to significant problems in a person's life, tolerance to the substance, withdrawal symptoms if it is discontinued, and compulsive substance-taking behavior.
- At low doses, alcohol produces relaxation and mild euphoria. At higher doses, it produces classic signs of depression and cognitive and motor impairment. A large proportion of deaths due to accidents, murders, and suicides are alcohol-related. Withdrawal symptoms can be mild or so severe as to be life-threatening. People with alcohol use disorders experience a wide range of social and interpersonal problems and are at risk for many serious health problems.
- Benzodiazepines and barbiturates can cause an initial rush and a loss of inhibitions, followed by depressed mood, lethargy, and physical signs of central nervous system depression. These substances are dangerous in overdose and when mixed with other substances.
- Cocaine activates those parts of the brain that register reward and pleasure and produces an instant rush of euphoria, followed by increased self-esteem, alertness, and energy and a greater sense of competence, creativity, and social acceptability. The user also may experience frightening perceptual changes. The symptoms of withdrawal from cocaine include exhaustion, a need for sleep, and depression.

Cocaine's extraordinarily rapid and strong effects on the brain's reward centers seem to make it more likely than most illicit substances to lead to abuse and dependence.

- Amphetamines are readily available by prescription to treat certain disorders but often end up available on the black market. They can make people feel euphoric, invigorated, self-confident, and gregarious, but they also can lead to restlessness, hypervigilance, anxiety, aggressiveness, and several dangerous physiological symptoms and changes.
- Nicotine is widely available. Smoking tobacco is legal, but it causes cancer, bronchitis, and coronary heart disease in users and low birth weights in the children of women who smoke when pregnant. People become physiologically dependent on nicotine and undergo withdrawal when they stop smoking.
- The opioids are developed from the juice of the poppy plant. The most commonly used illegal opioid is heroin. The initial symptom of opioid intoxication is euphoria, followed by drowsiness, lethargy, and periods of light sleep. Severe intoxication can lead to respiratory difficulties, unconsciousness, coma, and seizures. Withdrawal symptoms include dysphoria, anxiety, agitation, sensitivity to pain, and a craving for more of the substance.
- The hallucinogens, phencyclidine (PCP), and cannabis produce perceptual changes, including sensory distortions and hallucinations. These experiences are pleasant for some, frightening for others. Some people experience a sense of euphoria or relaxation from using these substances, and others become anxious and agitated.
- The inhalants are volatile agents that people sniff to produce a sense of euphoria, disinhibition, and increased aggressiveness or sexual performance. They are extremely dangerous; even casual use may cause permanent brain damage or serious disease.
- Some additional drugs of abuse are ecstasy (3,4-methylenedioxymethamphetamine, or MDMA), GHB (gamma-hydroxybutyrate), ketamine, and rohypnol (flunitrazepam). These drugs have several euphoric and sedative effects and are used at dance clubs and sometimes by perpetrators of date rape.
- All substances of abuse have powerful effects on areas of the brain involved in the processing of reward. Repeated use of substances can cause alterations in these brain areas that increase the need for more of the substance in order to experience rewarding effects.
- Evidence indicates that genes play a role in vulnerability to substance use disorders through their effects on the synthesis and metabolism of substances.
- Behavioral theories of alcoholism note that people are reinforced or punished for their alcohol-related behaviors and also engage in behaviors modeled by important others. Cognitive theories argue that people who develop alcohol-related problems have expectations that alcohol will help them feel better and cope better with stressful events. One personality characteristic associated with substance use disorders is behavioral undercontrol.
- Men may have more risk factors for substance use than women, and women may be more sensitive to the negative consequences of substance use than men.
- Medications can ease withdrawal symptoms and reduce cravings for many substances. The symptoms of opioid withdrawal can be so severe that dependents are given methadone as they try to discontinue heroin use. Methadone also blocks the effects of subsequent doses of heroin, reducing the desire to obtain heroin. Methadone maintenance programs are controversial.
- People with alcohol use disorder sometimes respond to behavior therapies based on aversive classical conditioning. They use a drug that makes them ill if they ingest alcohol or imagery that makes them develop a conditioned aversive response to the sight and smell of alcohol. Contingency management programs provide incentives for reducing substance use.
- Cognitive therapies focus on training people with alcohol use disorder in developing coping skills and in challenging positive expectations about alcohol's effects.
- Motivational interviewing attempts to empathetically draw out individuals' motivations and their commitment to change their substance use behavior.
- The abstinence violation effect comprises an individual's feeling of guilt over relapse and attribution of relapse to lack of self-control. Relapse prevention programs help identify triggers for relapse.
- The most common treatment for alcohol use disorder is Alcoholics Anonymous (AA), a self-help group that encourages alcoholics to admit their weaknesses and call on a higher power and on other group members to help them abstain from alcohol.
- Prevention programs based on a harm reduction model seek to teach the responsible use of alcohol.
- Gambling disorder is new to *DSM-5* and represents a behavioral addiction. It is characterized by compulsive gambling even in the face of significant social, financial, and psychological consequences. It seems to share many risk factors and clinical patterns with the substance use disorders.

KEY TERMS

substance use disorders
gambling disorder
substance
substance intoxication
substance withdrawal
substance abuse
substance dependence
tolerance
depressants
delirium tremens (DTs)
benzodiazepines
barbiturates
stimulants
cocaine
amphetamines
nicotine
caffeine
opioids
hallucinogens
phencyclidine (PCP)
cannabis
inhalants
antagonist drugs
methadone
motivational interviewing
abstinence violation effect
relapse prevention programs
Alcoholics Anonymous (AA)
harm reduction model
Internet gaming disorder

Chapter 15

©wavebreakmedia/Shutterstock

Health Psychology

CHAPTER OUTLINE

Stress Along the Continuum

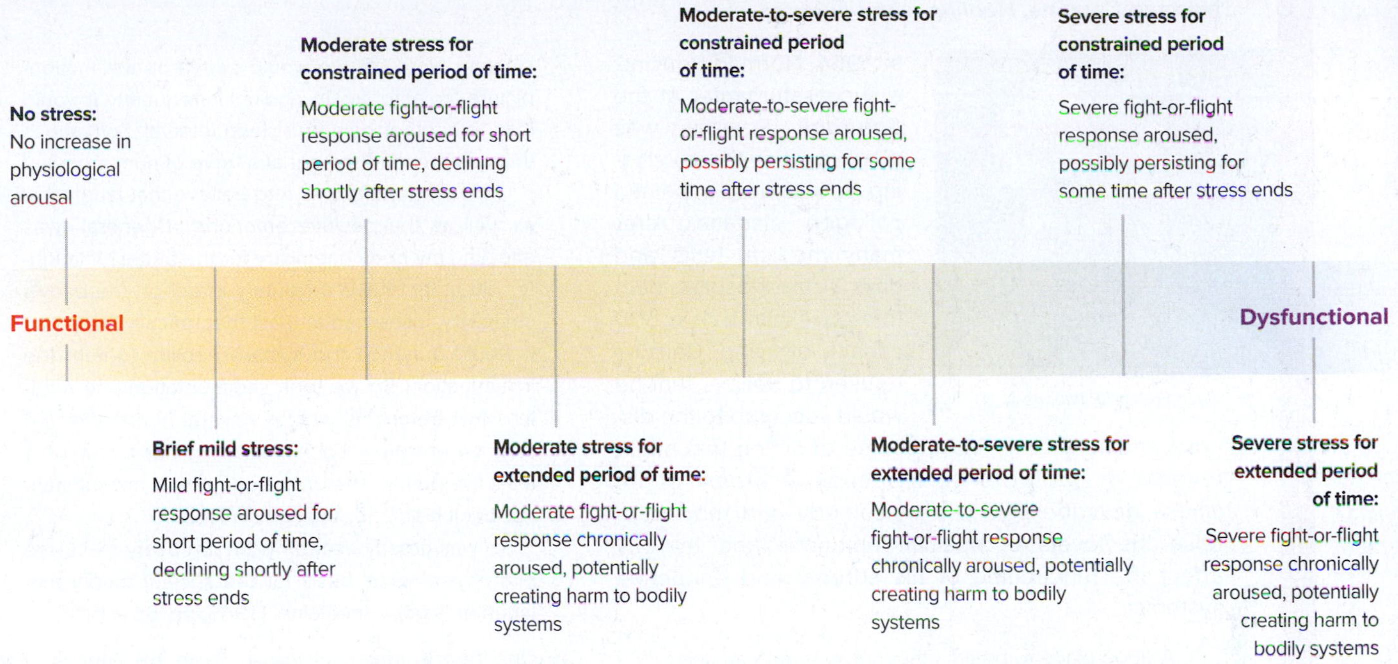

No stress:
No increase in physiological arousal
Brief mild stress:
Mild fight-or-flight response aroused for short period of time, declining shortly after stress ends
Moderate stress for constrained period of time:
Moderate fight-or-flight response aroused for short period of time, declining shortly after stress ends
Moderate stress for extended period of time:
Moderate fight-or-flight response chronically aroused, potentially creating harm to bodily systems
Moderate-to-severe stress for constrained period of time:
Moderate-to-severe fight-or-flight response aroused, possibly persisting for some time after stress ends
Moderate-to-severe stress for extended period of time:
Moderate-to-severe fight-or-flight response chronically aroused, potentially creating harm to bodily systems
Severe stress for constrained period of time:
Severe fight-or-flight response aroused, possibly persisting for some time after stress ends
Severe stress for extended period of time:
Severe fight-or-flight response chronically aroused, potentially creating harm to bodily systems
Functional
Dysfunctional

Anytime we face a stressor, a number of physiological responses kick in, as discussed in the chapter "Trauma, Anxiety, Obsessive-Compulsive, and Related Disorders." Known collectively as the *fight-or-flight response*, bodily changes such as increased heart rate and elevated blood pressure prepare the body to either face the threat or flee from it. The sympathetic system also stimulates the release of a number of hormones—including epinephrine (adrenaline) and norepinephrine—that keep the body ready to react. One of the primary stress hormones is cortisol, which is released by the adrenal cortex. Eventually, when the threatening stimulus has passed, the increase in cortisol signals the body to stop releasing these hormones. This process allows the body to adapt along a continuum of stress.

Even mild stressors trigger the fight-or-flight response. When the stressor is immediate, the response is activated and then subsides. This adaptation is called *allostasis*—the body learns how to react more efficiently to stress when it comes and goes, is not severe, and does not persist for long periods of time (McEwen, 2004). But when a stressor is chronic—that is, when it lasts over a long period of time—and a person or animal cannot fight it or flee from it, then the chronic physiological arousal that results can be severely damaging to the body, a condition known as **allostatic load.**

Persistent uncontrollable and unpredictable stress can create allostatic load. Many factors, including gender, minority status, socioeconomic status, and culture, may affect an individual's exposure to uncontrollable and unpredictable events, perceptions of these events, and reactions to them (Chen & Miller, 2012). For example, many African Americans are exposed to excessive stress due to racism, discrimination, and lower socioeconomic status compared to many European Americans (Mays, Cochran, & Barnes, 2007). In turn, African Americans score higher on a number of indicators of allostatic load, such as persistent high blood pressure (Geronimus, Hicken, Keene, & Bound, 2006).

Culture can alter the very meaning of a stressor, even one as severe as homelessness. A study in Nepal found that homeless street children actually showed lower allostatic load than children living with their families in rural villages (Worthman & Panter-Brick, 2008). The homeless children had formed family groups with other street children, protecting one another and collectively finding food and shelter. The rural village children had stable homes, but these homes had poor sanitation, and the children received only subsistence nutrition and faced heavy physical workloads. In more developed countries such as the United States, in contrast, being a homeless street child is associated with more stress and poorer health than is living with family in a rural small town (Worthman & Panter-Brick, 2008).

Extraordinary People

Norman Cousins, *Healing with Laughter*

©Ron Frehm/AP Images

In 1964, Norman Cousins, a successful writer at the *Saturday Review,* was diagnosed with ankylosing spondylitis, a painful collagen disease. After many medical tests and days in the hospital, doctors gave him a 1 in 500 chance of living. Cousins refused to believe that he would succumb to the disease and set out to find a course of action that might reverse its progression. His book *Anatomy of an Illness* describes his use of comedy and movies to raise his levels of positive emotions and thereby affect the functioning of his adrenal and endocrine systems:

> A good place to begin, I thought, was with amusing movies. Allen Funt, producer of the spoofing television program "Candid Camera," sent films of some of his "CC" classics, along with a motion-picture projector. The nurse was instructed in its use.
>
> It worked. I made the joyous discovery that ten minutes of genuine belly laughter had an anesthetic effect and would give me at least two hours of pain-free sleep. When the painkilling effect of the laughter wore off, we would switch on the motion-picture projector again, and not infrequently, it would lead to another pain-free sleep interval. Sometimes the nurse read to me out of a trove of humor books.
>
> How scientific was it to believe that laughter—as well as the positive emotions in general—was affecting my body chemistry for the better? If laughter did in fact have a salutary effect on the body's chemistry, it seemed at least theoretically likely that it would enhance the system's ability to fight the inflammation. So we took sedimentation-rate readings just before as well as several hours after the laughter episodes. Each time, there was a drop of at least five points. The drop by itself was not substantial, but it held and was cumulative.
>
> I was greatly elated by the discovery that there is a physiological basis for the ancient theory that laughter is good medicine. (1985, pp. 55–66)*

Cousins eventually recovered from his illness. After returning to his career as a writer for several years, Cousins spent the last 12 years of his life at the UCLA Medical School, working with researchers to find scientific proof for his belief that positive emotions have healing properties. One of the leading institutes for the study of the impact of psychological factors on physical health is now named for him: The Cousins Center for Psychoneuroimmunology at UCLA.

*Source: Cousins, N., Anatomy of an Illness as Perceived by the Patient. New York: W.W. Norton & Company, 1985, pp. 55–66.

In the years since Cousins' discovery that laughter was good medicine for him, a considerable number of studies have shown that positive emotions influence physiological functioning (Fredrickson & Joiner, 2002; Fredrickson, Tugade, Waugh, & Larkin, 2003; Dockray & Steptoe, 2010). These findings evoke the ancient mind-body question: Does the mind affect the body, or does the body affect the mind? The answer now is clearly that the mind and the body affect each other reciprocally.

In this chapter, we review the research in *health psychology* (also referred to as *behavioral medicine*), a field that explores how biological, psychological, and social/environmental factors interact to influence physical health. Figure 1 illustrates the components of a biopsychosocial approach to physical health (Baum, Perry, & Tarbell, 2004). First, biological factors, such as genetic makeup, age, and sex, clearly have a major influence on our susceptibility to disease. For example, genetics plays a strong role in susceptibility to cancer, the risk of developing most cancers increases with age, and some forms of cancer, such as breast cancer, are much more common in women than in men. Second, social or environmental factors can directly impact health. The factor most often studied by health psychologists is stress, as we discuss in detail below. Another important social factor is culture, which influences our exposure to diseases and the treatments prescribed for these diseases. For example, the human immunodeficiency virus (HIV) is more widespread in sub-Saharan Africa than anywhere else in the world (UNAIDS, 2018), and cultural stigmas against condom use have played a role in the spread of HIV in this region. Third, a number of psychological factors can impact health. We can engage in behaviors that enhance our health, such as exercising regularly and brushing our teeth, or in behaviors that promote disease, such as smoking and eating fatty foods. When we are ill, we can seek treatment and follow our doctor's orders, or we can avoid treatment or not comply with the doctor's orders.

In addition to their individual direct effects on health, biological, psychological, and social/environmental factors all interact to influence health. Consider a few examples: Genetics not only influences our vulnerability to a particular disease but also influences how much stress we are exposed to in our life and our perceptions of stress (Kendler, Karkowski, & Prescott, 1999; Kendler et al., 2010). In turn, stress can make it more difficult to engage in healthy behaviors such as getting enough exercise. Our personalities influence how much stress we perceive in our lives, which in turn affects our health. What's more, our social experiences in day-to-day life can affect our internal biological functioning and contribute to mental heath problems and physical disease, as in the case of racial and ethnic discrimination (Lewis, Cogburn, & Williams, 2015). Throughout this chapter, we discuss how interactions among biological, psychological, and social/environmental factors promote or damage health.

As a field, health psychology has grown rapidly in recent decades as psychological and social/environmental factors have become increasingly important determinants of both the length and the quality of our lives. At the beginning of the twentieth century, the leading causes of death, in addition to cardiovascular disease, were primarily infectious diseases, including influenza, pneumonia, and tuberculosis (Table 1). Over the past century, advances in medicine have greatly reduced the number of deaths due to these diseases. In the twenty-first century, the five leading causes of death are diseases significantly influenced by psychological and social factors such as smoking, diet, and stress. Thus, understanding how psychological and social/environmental factors interact with each other and with biological vulnerabilities to create disease is a critical part of maintaining people's physical health.

FIGURE 1 **Components in a Biopsychosocial Approach to Physical Health.**

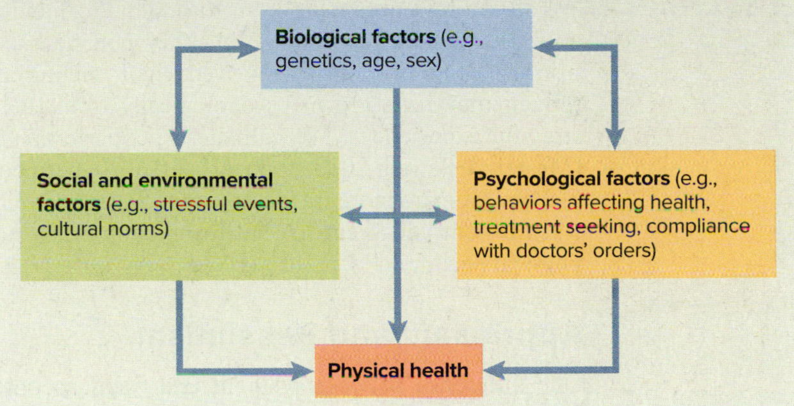

Source: Baum et al., 2004.

TABLE 1 Leading Causes of Death in the United States, 1900 and 2015

1900		2015	
Cause	**Rate (per 100,000)**	**Cause**	**Rate (per 100,000)**
1. Cardiovascular diseases (heart disease, stroke)	345	1. Heart disease	197
2. Influenza and pneumonia	202	2. Cancer	185
3. Tuberculosis	194	3. Chronic lower respiratory diseases	48
4. Gastritis, duodenitis, enteritis, and colitis	143	4. Accidents	46
5. Accidents	72	5. Cerebrovascular diseases	44

Source: Data for 1900: U.S. Bureau of the Census, *Historical Statistics of the United States: Colonial Times to 1970, I.* Washington, DC: U.S. Government Printing Office Table 1, 1975, 429; Data for 2015: Murphy et al., "Deaths: Final data for 2015," *National Vital Statistics Reports*, vol. 66, no. 6, 2017.

PSYCHOLOGICAL FACTORS AND GENERAL HEALTH

We all know people who seem to be able to handle even severe stress extremely well—they bounce back from difficult times with renewed vigor, feeling as though they have grown psychologically from their stressful experiences. We call these people *resilient* (Masten & Powell, 2003; Johnson, 2016). Other people, however, are more fragile—even mild stresses overwhelm them and seem to lead to psychological and physical decline.

Appraisals and Pessimism

One difference between resilient and fragile people is the way they appraise or interpret events. People who tend to have a pessimistic style of interpreting events—seeing negative events as their fault, likely to continue in the future, and having wide consequences—go through life seeing stress around every corner (Carver & Scheier, 2014; Peterson, Seligman, Yurko, Martin, & Friedman, 1998). Pessimism may contribute to poor health by causing chronic arousal of the body's fight-or-flight response, resulting in physiological damage. Several studies have found evidence for this explanation. In one study, the blood pressure of pessimists and optimists was monitored daily for 3 days. The pessimists had chronically higher blood pressure levels than the optimists across the 3 days (Raikkonen, Matthews, Flory, Owens, & Gump, 1999). Other studies find that adults who are pessimistic show poorer immune system functioning than those who are optimistic, even after researchers statistically control for differences between the pessimists and optimists on other measures of current health (see Carver & Scheier, 2014; Rasmussen, Scheier, & Greenhouse, 2009).

A pessimistic outlook also may lead people to engage in unhealthy behaviors. People who are more pessimistic are less likely to practice healthy behaviors, such as maintaining a proper diet, getting enough sleep, abstaining from smoking, and exercising (Carver & Scheier, 2014; Hingle et al., 2014). The effects of pessimism may be lifelong. In a long-term study of men in the Harvard classes of 1939 and 1940, those who were pessimistic in college were more likely to develop physical illness over the subsequent 35 years than were those who were more optimistic in college (Peterson, Seligman, & Vaillant, 1988; see also Peterson et al., 1998).

In short, a pessimistic outlook may affect health directly by causing hyperarousal of the body's physiological response to stress or indirectly by reducing positive coping strategies and healthy behaviors. In contrast, an optimistic outlook, such as the outlook Norman Cousins attempted to create in himself through laughter, may promote physical health by reducing physiological stress responses and promoting positive coping strategies (Carver & Scheier, 2014; Chen & Miller, 2012).

Coping Strategies

The ways people cope with illness and other stressful life circumstances can affect their health (Taylor & Stanton, 2007). One method of coping that can be bad for health is avoidance coping, that is, denying that you are ill or are facing other obvious stresses. Multiple meta-analyses have linked avoidance coping to several health-related problems, including postsurgical pain, poor adherence to medical regimens, and health-risk behaviors, as well as chronic disease progression and mortality for people with cancer, HIV/AIDS, and heart failure (see Kvillemo & Bränström, 2014; Marroquín, Tennen, & Stanton, 2017; McIntosh & Rosselli, 2012; Moskowitz, Hult, Bussolari, & Acree, 2009; Roesch et al., 2005).

In contrast, talking about negative emotions and important issues in one's life appears to have positive effects on health (e.g., Panagopoulou, Maes, Rime, & Montgomery, 2006). In a large series of studies, James Pennebaker (2007) found that encouraging people to reveal personal traumas in diaries or essays improves their health. In one study, 50 healthy college students were randomly assigned to write either about the most traumatic and upsetting events in their lives or about trivial topics for 20 minutes on 4 consecutive days. Blood samples were taken from the students on the day before they began writing, on the last day of writing, and 6 weeks after their writing. The students' blood was tested for several markers of immune system functioning. The number of times the students visited the college health center over the 6 weeks following the writing task was also recorded and was compared with the number of health center visits the students had made before the study. As Figure 2 shows, students who revealed their personal traumas in their essays showed more positive immune system functioning and visited the health center less frequently than did students in the control group (Pennebaker, Kiecolt-Glaser, & Glaser, 1988). In contrast, the group who wrote about trivial events experienced a slight increase in health center visits and a decrease in immune system functioning, for unknown reasons.

Pennebaker (2007) believes that writing helps people understand and find meaning in the events of their lives. Understanding and finding meaning in turn reduce people's negative emotions regarding events and therefore may reduce the physiological strain associated with chronic negative emotions.

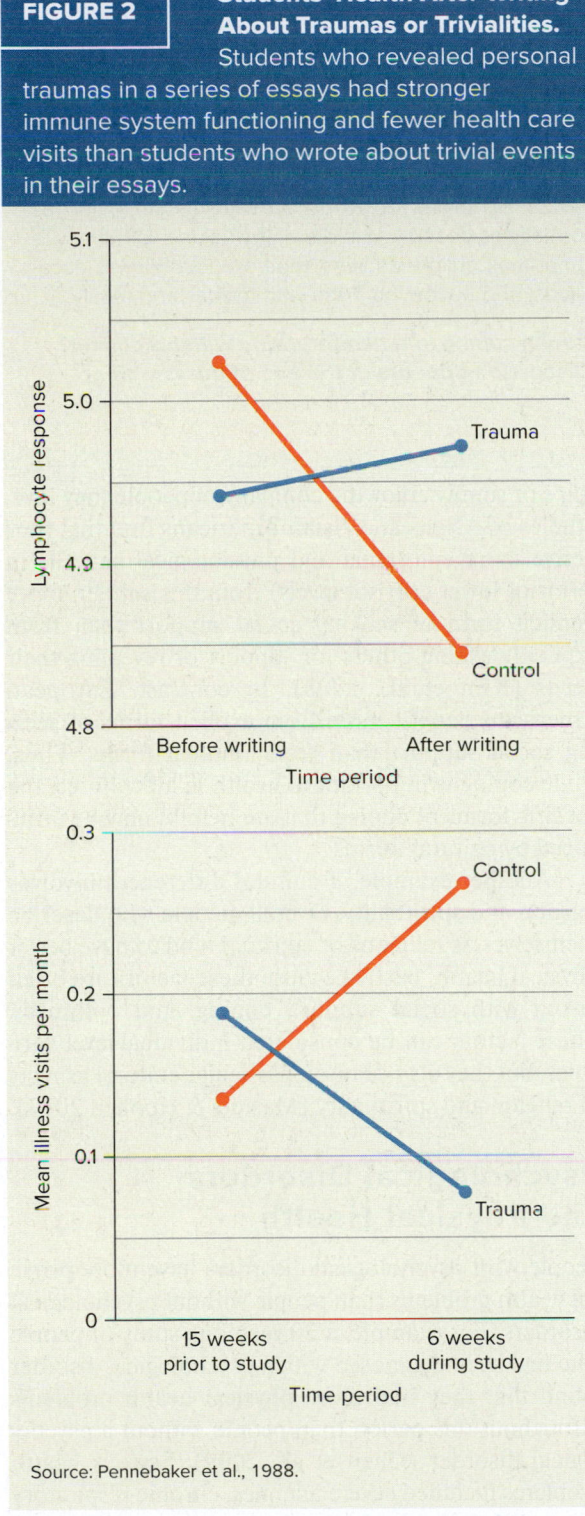

FIGURE 2 **Students' Health After Writing About Traumas or Trivialities.** Students who revealed personal traumas in a series of essays had stronger immune system functioning and fewer health care visits than students who wrote about trivial events in their essays.

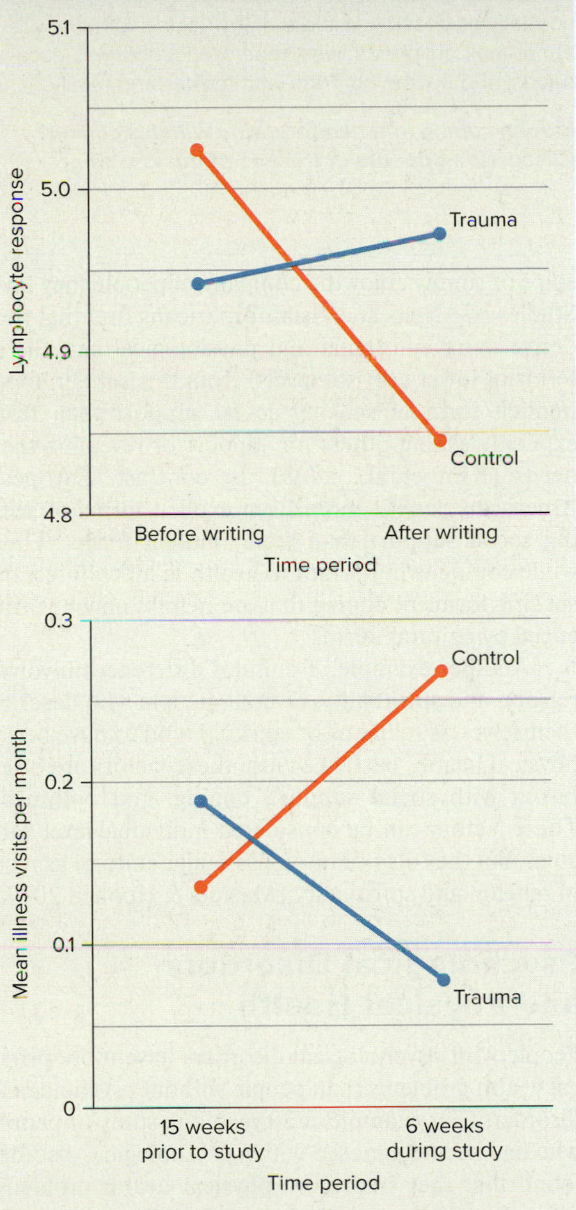

Source: Pennebaker et al., 1988.

Indeed, multiple studies have found that coping by "approaching" one's emotions rather than avoiding them can have psychological and physical benefits, not only for healthy people but also for people coping with illness, including cancer (Moreno, Wiley, & Stanton, 2017; Stanton et al., 2000).

A related positive coping strategy is seeking social support. A wide variety of studies have found that people who seek and receive positive emotional support from others show more positive health outcomes, both on microlevel measures such as immune system activity and on macrolevel outcomes such as the progression of major diseases (Robles, Slatcher, Trombello, & McGinn, 2014; Uchino, 2009). Shelley Taylor and colleagues found that young adults who had grown up in supportive families showed less reactivity in certain areas of the brain to emotionally provocative photos (Taylor, Eisenberger, Saxbe, Lehman, & Lieberman, 2006). This reduced emotional reactivity could reduce physiological reactivity to stress in these individuals. Social support can be soothing in itself, but it can also help facilitate other healthy coping behaviors by encouraging or assisting more effective actions (see Marroquín et al., 2017).

Gender Differences in Coping

Women and men appear to have different responses to stress. Taylor and colleagues (2000; Taylor & Master, 2011) have suggested that women faced with threats engage in a pattern termed *tend and befriend.* Throughout evolutionary history, women have not been as physically capable as men of fighting off aggressors; also, because they have had primary responsibility for their offspring, they have not always been able to run from an aggressor. Instead of attempting to fight a threat or flee from it, women join social groups for protection and resources. Underlying this behavioral response to stress by women is a different neurobiological response to stress: The physiological changes associated with the fight-or-flight response are less prominent in women than in men, but stressed women experience the release of the hormone oxytocin, which is associated with increased affiliative behavior such as seeking out and caring for others.

Women are indeed more likely than men to seek support from others in times of stress and to have larger social networks, including friends and extended family (Kiecolt-Glaser & Newton, 2001; Kiecolt-Glaser, & Wilson, 2017). Men, in contrast, typically have a much smaller network of people they turn to for support and also are less likely than women to share personal issues and concerns with friends and family members. Thus, women may have more opportunity than men to benefit from the positive health effects of social support.

A major source of support is a partner or spouse. Married people have less physical illness and are less likely to die from a variety of conditions, including cancer, heart disease, and surgery, than nonmarried people (see Kiecolt-Glaser & Newton, 2001; Robles et al., 2014). A conflictual marriage, however, can be a major detriment to health (Kiecolt-Glaser & Wilson, 2017; Robles et al., 2014). Experimental studies of

SHADES OF GRAY

As you read the following case study, ask yourself whether it presents a healthful way of coping with a stressful event.

John Park is a 62-year-old engineer, originally from South Korea and now living in Columbus, Ohio. John recently received news from his physician that he has prostate cancer. The urologist John consulted recommended that he undergo radiation therapy to treat it. John told his wife about the diagnosis and treatment, but he did not tell his children, all of whom are grown and living in other cities. John also did not tell any of his co-workers about the cancer. He took vacation time to receive treatment and recover from its aftereffects. John and his wife seldom spoke about the cancer. He preferred to go on with his life, living as normally as possible. He did enjoy talking with his wife about their children's lives, their grandchildren's escapades, and upcoming visits with friends and family.

Is John coping in a healthful way with his cancer? (Discussion appears at the end of this chapter.)

married couples found that those who became hostile and negative toward each other while discussing marital problems showed greater decreases in four indicators of immune system functioning than couples who remained calm and nonhostile while discussing marital problems. Those who became hostile also showed elevated blood pressure for longer periods of time (Kiecolt-Glaser, Malarkey, Chee, & Newton, 1993).

Women are more physiologically reactive than men to marital conflict (Kiecolt-Glaser & Newton, 2001; Kiecolt-Glaser & Wilson, 2017). This may be because women's self-concepts, as well as their financial well-being, tend to be more closely tied to those of their spouse than are men's self-concepts (Cross & Madson, 1997). Women are also more emotionally attuned to their partners, more conscious of conflict in their relationships, and typically occupy a more subordinate societal role (Wanic & Kulik, 2011). For these reasons, women may be more emotionally, cognitively, and physiologically sensitive to marital conflict, and this sensitivity may counteract any positive health effects they might derive from support from their partner (Kiecolt-Glaser & Newton, 2017; Robles et al., 2014). In general, women can benefit physiologically from being in a close relationship, but only if that relationship is a positive one.

Cultural Differences in Coping

Different cultures have different norms for coping with stressful events. People from Asian cultures tend to be more reluctant than European Americans to reach out to others for social support or to express their personal concerns, because they are more concerned about potential harm to their relationships if they do so (Ford & Mauss, 2015; Kim, Sherman, & Taylor, 2008). People from Asian cultures instead may find ways to benefit from their social networks that don't involve revealing personal concerns or weaknesses or potentially burdening others. For example, they may remind themselves of their close relationships or simply enjoy the company of people they love. Studies of Asians and Asian Americans find that they derive more emotional and physiological benefit (in terms of lower cortisol levels) from this subtler, more implicit form of seeking social support than from explicitly asking others for support or revealing their needs (Kim et al., 2008). In contrast, European Americans benefit more from explicit forms of seeking social support than from implicit forms. Thus, while coping is important to health in all cultures, the specific forms of coping that are helpful may be influenced by cultural norms.

Another example of cultural differences involves religion and spirituality. Overall, people who describe themselves as religious or spiritual tend to have better physical health, partly because these factors are often linked with social support, coping, and optimism. These factors can be considered individual-level variables, but they also draw on particular cultural aspects of religion and spirituality (Masters & Hooker, 2013).

Psychological Disorders and Physical Health

People with psychological disorders have more physical health problems than people without psychological disorders. For example, a 20-year-long study of people who had been diagnosed with a psychological disorder found that they had more physical health problems throughout this period than people without a psychological disorder (Chen et al., 2009). Serious health problems included severe allergies, chronic respiratory disease, chronic gastrointestinal disease, cardiovascular disease, cancer, and diabetes. In particular, several studies have found links between depression and a variety of diseases, including cancer, heart disease, diabetes, arthritis, and asthma (Scott et al., 2016).

There may be many mechanisms linking psychological disorders with physical health problems. These include shared genetic causes; medical disorders contributing to psychological disorders; and psychological disorders contributing to medical disorders, elevated stress, impaired coping, or unhealthy behaviors. In some cases, psychopathology and medical illness may share a common genetic cause. For example, depression and cardiovascular disease are both related to genetic factors leading to dysfunction in serotonin systems (McCaffery et al., 2006). In other cases, medical disorders may create psychological disorders. Alzheimer's disease, a neurological disorder leading to dementia, also leads to depression, anxiety, personality changes, and psychotic symptoms such as hallucinations and delusions (see the chapter "Neurodevelopmental and Neurocognitive Disorders"). Thyroid diseases can cause depressive symptoms. Further, the social and psychological stress of having a serious medical illness can cause depression or anxiety (Hammen, 2018).

In still other cases, psychological disorders may contribute to medical disorders. Self-starvation in anorexia nervosa can lead to osteoporosis and loss of bone density as well as to cardiovascular problems (Polivy & Herman, 2002). Substance abuse or dependence can cause many medical diseases, including hypertension and liver and kidney disease (see the chapter "Substance Use and Gambling Disorders").

Living with a psychological disorder is stressful in many ways. An individual may have difficulty holding down a job, face discrimination and social rejection, and have trouble obtaining medical care. People with many psychological disorders show signs of chronic arousal of the fight-or-flight response, including chronically elevated cortisol levels (McEwen, 2004). This excess allostatic load could in turn contribute to physical illness.

Having a psychological disorder also may lead a person to be more pessimistic and to have poorer skills for coping with stress, which could then increase the person's allostatic load. For example, one study found that the greater rate of physical illness in people with depressive disorders than in people with no psychological disorder was explained in part by higher levels of neuroticism in the depressed people (Rhebergen et al., 2010). Neuroticism is a personality trait characterized by hyperreactivity to stress and poor coping skills.

People with psychological disorders also appear to be less likely to engage in positive health-related behaviors (Zvolensky & Smits, 2008). The rate of smoking is two to three times higher in people with psychological disorders than in people without a psychological disorder (Grant, Hasin, Chou, et al., 2004; Lasser et al., 2000). People with psychological disorders also appear to be less likely to exercise (Whooley et al., 2008) or to comply with medical regimens (Chen et al., 2009). These health-related behaviors put the individual at risk for the development or worsening of a medical illness.

PSYCHOSOCIAL FACTORS IN SPECIFIC DISEASES

Health psychologists have intensively studied certain disease processes in which stress and psychological factors are expected to play a role. We consider two groups of diseases here: immune system diseases and cardiovascular diseases.

The Immune System

The **immune system** protects us from disease by identifying and killing pathogens and tumor cells. The immune system is divided into two branches, the *innate immune system* and the *specific immune system,* both of which have a number of cellular mechanisms for attacking invaders. The innate system reacts quickly and nonspecifically to any microorganism or toxin that enters the body, releasing cells that kill and ingest the invaders. The specific immune system is slower to respond, but its response is tailored to the particular type of pathogen present. The specific immune system remembers the pathogen so that if it attacks again the system is able to kill it more quickly and efficiently.

Stress may affect the immune system in several ways. Although short-term stress appears to increase the potency of immune responses, more chronic stress decreases immune functioning, in part because some of the biochemicals released as part of the fight-or-flight response, such as cortisol, suppress the immune system if a stressor persists for long periods (Segerstrom & Miller, 2004; Slavich & Irwin, 2014). The most controlled research linking stress and immune system functioning has been conducted with animals. The animals are experimentally exposed to stressors, and then the functioning of their immune system is measured directly. Studies have shown that immune system cells are suppressed in animals exposed to loud noise, electric shock, separation from their mothers as infants, separation from their peers, and a variety of other stressors (Segerstrom & Miller, 2004).

Animals are most likely to show impairment of their immune system if they are exposed to stressors that are uncontrollable. In one experiment, one group of rats was subjected to an electric shock that the rats could turn off by pressing a lever (Laudenslager, Ryan, Drugan, Hyson, & Maier, 1983). Another group received an identical sequence of shocks but could not control the shock. A third group received no shock. The investigators examined how well the rats' killer T-cells, components of the specific immune system that secrete chemicals that kill harmful cells, multiplied when challenged by invaders. They found that the T-cells in the rats that could control the shock multiplied, as did those in the rats that were not shocked at all (Figure 3). The T-cells in the rats exposed to

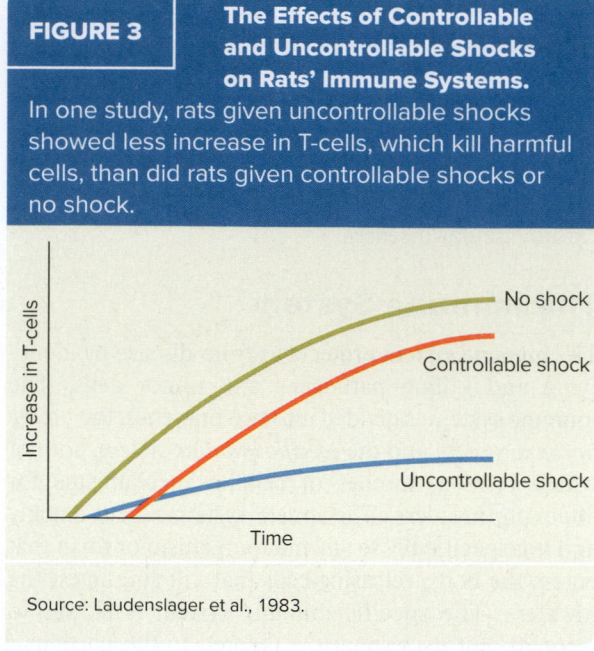

FIGURE 3 **The Effects of Controllable and Uncontrollable Shocks on Rats' Immune Systems.**

In one study, rats given uncontrollable shocks showed less increase in T-cells, which kill harmful cells, than did rats given controllable shocks or no shock.

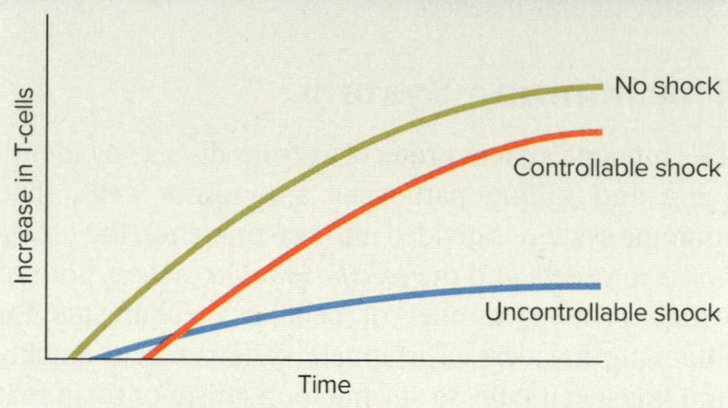

Source: Laudenslager et al., 1983.

uncontrollable shock increased less, however. In another study following the same experimental design, investigators implanted tumor cells into rats, gave them controllable or uncontrollable shocks, and examined whether the rats' natural defenses rejected the tumors. Only 27 percent of the rats given uncontrollable shocks rejected the tumors, whereas 63 percent of the rats given controllable shocks rejected the tumors (Visintainer, Volpicelli, & Seligman, 1982).

People with relatively high levels of stress are more susceptible to coming down with colds. Stress also contributes to higher levels of herpes, mononucleosis, and other infectious diseases. *©wang Tom/123RF*

Uncontrollable stress also impairs immune system functioning in humans (Schneiderman, Ironson, & Siegel, 2005; Slavich & Irwin, 2014). The most common disease in which the immune system plays a role is the cold. You may have observed that you and your friends are more likely to get colds during times of stress. To test this common observation, investigators exposed about 400 healthy volunteers to a nasal wash containing either one of five cold viruses or an innocuous salt solution (Cohen, Tyrrell, & Smith, 1991). Participants received a stress score ranging from 3 (lowest stress) to 12 (highest stress) based on the number of stressful events they had experienced in the past year, the degree to which they felt able to cope with daily demands, and their frequency of negative emotions such as anger or depression. The participants were examined daily for cold symptoms and for the presence of cold viruses in their upper respiratory secretions. About 35 percent of the volunteers who reported the highest stress in their lives developed colds, compared to about 18 percent of those with the lowest stress scores.

Many other studies of humans have compared the functioning of the immune system in persons undergoing particular stressors with that of persons not undergoing these stressors. This research confirms that people show higher rates of infectious diseases, such as colds, herpes, and mononucleosis, during times of stress. For example, following the 1994 Northridge earthquake in the Los Angeles area, people whose lives had been more severely disrupted showed greater declines in immune system functioning than did those who had not experienced as much stress as a result of the earthquake (Solomon, Segerstrom, Grohr, Kemeny, & Fahey, 1997). People who worried more about the impact of the earthquake on their lives were especially likely to show detriments in immune system functioning (Segerstrom, Solomon, Kemeny, & Fahey, 1998).

Negative interpersonal events seem particularly likely to affect immune system functioning. Married couples who argue more show poorer immunological functioning than married couples who have fewer arguments (Kiecolt-Glaser & Wilson, 2017; Robles et al., 2014). Men and women who have recently been separated or divorced show poorer immune system functioning than married control subjects (Robles & Kiecolt-Glaser, 2003). However, the partner who has more control over the divorce or separation—that is, the partner who initiated it—shows better immune system functioning and better health than the other partner. This is another example of how perceptions of the controllability of a stressor can influence the impact of that stressor on health.

Cancer

Can psychosocial factors affect severe immune-related diseases such as cancer? One study of women with breast cancer found that those who felt they had little control over their cancer and other aspects of their lives were more likely to develop new tumors over a 5-year period than were women who felt more in control, even though the two groups of women did not differ in the type or initial seriousness of their cancers (Levy & Heiden, 1991; Watson, Haviland, Greer, Davidson, & Bliss, 1999). Another study found that pessimistic cancer patients are more likely to die during the first few years after their diagnosis than are optimistic cancer patients (Schulz, Bookwala, Knapp, Scheier, & Williamson, 1996). Coping behaviors also may affect cancer: Studies of women with breast cancer have found that those who seek social support from others have greater immune system activity and lower mortality (Helgeson, Snyder, & Seltman, 2004; Kroenke et al., 2012; Turner-Cobb, Sephton, Koopman, Blake-Mortimer, & Spiegel, 2000).

If psychosocial factors such as social support and pessimism do influence the progression of cancer, this raises the possibility that the course of the disease can be affected by psychosocial interventions. Early studies gave hope. In a landmark study of women with advanced breast cancer who were expected to die within 2 years, one group of women participated in a series of weekly support groups and the other group did not (Spiegel, Bollm, Kraemer, & Gottheil, 1989). All the women received standard medical care for their cancer. The support groups focused on facing death and living their remaining days to the fullest. The researchers did not expect to alter the course of the cancer; they wanted only to improve the women's quality of life. To their surprise, 4 years later one-third of the women participating in the support groups had survived, whereas all the women who had not participated in the support groups had died. The average survival time for the women in the support groups was about 40 months, compared to about 19 months for the other women. Because no other differences between the two populations could explain the disparity in average survival times, it seems that the support groups helped prolong the participants' lives. The authors argued that the support groups reduced stress and distress for the women and thus reduced the release of corticosteroids, which can promote tumor growth (Spiegel, 2001). Having greater support also might help cancer patients engage in better health habits and adhere to difficult medical treatments such as chemotherapy.

Some subsequent studies also found that reducing stress can improve health in cancer patients (Fawzy, Kemeny, et al., 1990; Richardson, Shelton, Krailo, & Levine, 1990). In a study of patients with malignant melanoma (skin cancer), some patients were given six weekly treatment sessions in which they were taught stress-management procedures, relaxation, and methods for coping with their illness. Six months after treatment, the group that received the stress-reduction intervention showed better immune system functioning than the control group, whose members received only customary medical care (Fawzy, Cousins, et al., 1990; Fawzy, Kemeny, et al., 1990). At a 5-year follow-up, patients who had received the intervention were less likely to have had recurrences of the cancer and were significantly less likely to have died (Fawzy et al., 1993). At a 10-year follow-up, there were no differences between the intervention group and the control group in recurrences of the cancer, but the intervention group had a higher survival rate than the control group when other risk factors were taken into account (Fawzy, Canada, & Fawzy, 2003).

A controlled trial tested an intervention that targeted stress reduction as well as medication adherence and healthy behaviors, finding that women with breast cancer who received the intervention had a lower risk of death over 11 years than a non-intervention control group (Andersen et al., 2008). Another trial, comparing cognitive-behavioral-based stress management to a psychoeducation-only condition found lower levels of breast cancer recurrence and mortality (Stagl et al., 2015).

However, other studies have failed to find any effects of psychosocial interventions on the progression of cancer. For example, a large clinical trial attempting to replicate the effects in the breast cancer study described above (e.g., Fawzy et al., 2003) failed to find any effects of support groups on health in women with breast cancer (Goodwin et al., 2001; see also Kissane et al., 2007). Meta-analyses and reviews of the effects of psychosocial interventions on survival in cancer patients have found modest or no effects (Chow, Tsao, & Harth, 2004; Coyne, Stefanek, & Palmer, 2007; Edwards, Hulbert-Williams, & Neal, 2008; Mustafa, Carson-Stevens, Gillespie, & Edwards, 2013; Smedslund & Ringdal, 2004). However, psychosocial interventions have been found to improve cancer patients' quality of life and depressive symptoms (e.g., Antoni et al., 2001; Gudenkauf et al., 2015), and this is an important aspect of cancer treatment and survivorship. Researchers continue to hone interventions to target the factors that are most important in psychosocial interventions for cancer, such as cognition and coping strategies (Stanton, Luecken, MacKinnon, & Thompson, 2013).

HIV/AIDS

The Centers for Disease Control estimates that over a million people in the United States have been infected with the human immunodeficiency virus (HIV), which causes AIDS (CDC, 2018f). Worldwide, over 35 million people are infected with HIV (WHO, 2018b). The progression of illness in people infected with HIV varies greatly. Individuals may live for years with no symptoms, then begin to develop relatively minor health problems such as weight loss, fever, and night sweats. Eventually, they may develop a number of serious and potentially fatal diseases, including pneumocystis pneumonia, cancer, dementia, and a wasting syndrome in which the body withers away. When these diseases emerge, a diagnosis of AIDS may be given. Fortunately, antiretroviral drugs appear to suppress the virus in those infected and to slow the development of AIDS. Unfortunately, these drugs do not eliminate the virus, and their side effects lead many people to discontinue their use. Moreover, millions of people around the world who are infected do not have access to these drugs.

Some studies suggest that psychological factors can affect the progression of illness in people infected with HIV (Chida & Vedhara, 2009; Kołodziej, 2016; Leserman, 2008). Much of this research has been conducted with gay men, many of whom have lost their partners and close friends to AIDS, particularly before antiretroviral drugs became available. One study that followed 85 HIV-infected gay men for 3 to 4 years found that those whose partner or close friend had died of AIDS showed a more rapid decline in immune system functioning (Kemeny & Dean, 1995). Another group of investigators followed 96 gay men for over 9 years and found that those who experienced more severe stressors, including the deaths of close friends and partners, showed a faster progression to AIDS (Leserman et al., 1999, 2000, 2002). For every increase of 1 on an index of stress experienced, their risk of developing an AIDS-related clinical condition (e.g., pneumocystis pneumonia) tripled. At the end of the study, 74 percent of the men above the median on the stress index progressed to AIDS, compared to 40 percent below the median.

Experiencing more chronic stressors also appears to affect the progression of HIV in gay men. A study of HIV-positive gay men found that those who felt compelled to conceal their sexual orientation showed a faster progression of disease than those who did not (Cole, Kemeny, Taylor, Visscher, & Fahey, 1995). The differences in health between the men who were "out" and those who were "closeted" did not reflect differences in health-related behaviors (e.g., smoking, exercise). It may be that the stress of chronically hiding one's identity can have direct effects on health (e.g., Hatzenbuehler, 2009). More generally, researchers found that HIV-positive men who experienced declines in social support and increases in loneliness showed poorer immune system control over the virus (Dixon et al., 2001).

Stress also affects the progression of the disease in children and adolescents who have been infected with HIV. In a year-long study of 618 HIV-positive young people, those who experienced two or more stressful life events, such as a parent becoming seriously ill, a death in the family, or the loss of their home, were three times more likely than other participants to show immune system declines (Howland et al., 2000).

Even stressors experienced long before an individual is infected with HIV seem to increase the risk for disease progression. The Coping with HIV/AIDS in the Southeast (CHASE) Study followed 490 HIV-positive adult men and women from five rural southern U.S. states for up to 41 months (Leserman et al., 2007). Those with a history of trauma, including childhood physical or sexual abuse or neglect or the murder of a family member, showed faster development of opportunistic infections and were more likely to die of AIDS-related causes than those without a history of trauma (Mugavero et al., 2007).

Interpretations of stressors appear to be important moderators of their effects. In one study of 412 patients with HIV, those who scored high on questionnaires measuring pessimism at the beginning of the study had a greater load of the virus 18 months later than did those who initially were less pessimistic (Milam, Richardson, Marks, Kemper, & McCutchan, 2004). Similarly, a study of gay men who were HIV-positive found that those who blamed themselves for negative events and those who had more negative expectations showed a greater decline in immune system functioning and a greater development of HIV symptoms over time than did those who had more positive expectations (Reed, Kemeny, Taylor, & Visscher, 1999; Segerstrom, Taylor, Kemeny, Reed, & Visscher, 1996). In fact, a meta-analysis of 37 prospective studies suggests that psychological variables (including coping and personality) were better predictors of HIV progression than stressful events or social support (Chida & Vedhara, 2009).

Coronary Heart Disease and Hypertension

Orrin was having a *myocardial infarction*—a heart attack. A myocardial infarction is one end point of **coronary heart disease,** or **CHD.** CHD occurs when the blood vessels that supply the heart muscles are narrowed or closed by the gradual buildup of a hard, fatty substance called *plaque* and inflammation of the vessel walls, blocking the flow of oxygen and nutrients to the heart. This process is known as *atherosclerosis.* The blockage of vessels can lead to pain, called *angina pectoris,* that radiates across the chest and arm. When oxygen to the heart is completely blocked a myocardial infarction can result.

CASE STUDY

Orrin was so mad he could scream. He had been told at 3:00 that afternoon to prepare a report on the financial status of his division of the company in time for a meeting of the board of directors the next morning. On the way home from work, someone rear-ended him at a stoplight and caused several hundred dollars in damage to his new car. When he got home from work, there was a message from his wife, saying she had been delayed at work and would not be home in time to cook dinner for the children, so Orrin would have to do it. Then, at dinner, Orrin's 12-year-old son revealed that he had flunked his math test that afternoon.

After finishing the dishes, Orrin went to his study to work on the report. The kids had the TV on so loud he couldn't concentrate. Orrin yelled to the kids to turn off the TV but they couldn't hear him. Furious, he stalked into the family room and began yelling at the children about the television and anything else that came to his mind.

Then, suddenly, Orrin began to feel a tremendous pressure on his chest, as if a truck were driving across it. Pain shot through his chest and down his left arm. Orrin felt dizzy and terrified. He collapsed onto the floor. His 7-year-old began screaming. Luckily, his 12-year-old called 911 for an ambulance.

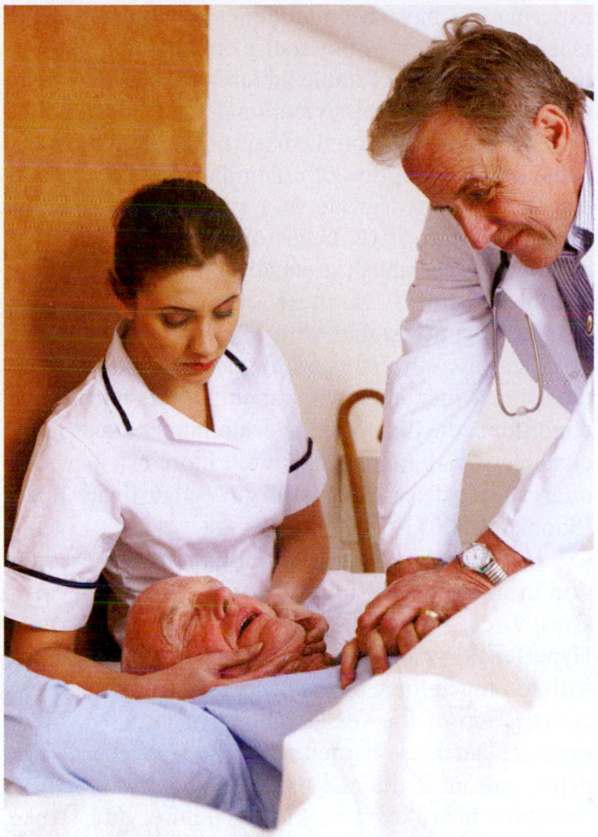

Coronary heart disease occurs when blood vessels supplying the heart are blocked by plaque; complete blockage causes a myocardial infarction—a heart attack. High levels of stress have been shown to increase rates of coronary heart disease.
©Dean Mitchell/iStock/Getty Images

Coronary heart disease is a leading cause of death and chronic illness around the world. Since 1990, more people have died from coronary heart disease than from any other cause (WHO, 2018a). In the United States, CHD accounts for 25 percent of all deaths (CDC, 2018e). CHD is also a chronic disease, and more than 15 million Americans live daily with its symptoms. Men are more prone to CHD than are women, but CHD still is the leading cause of death among women. African Americans and Hispanic Americans have higher rates of CHD than do European Americans. There seems to be a genetic contribution to coronary heart disease–people with family histories of CHD are at increased risk for the disease. However, 80 to 90 percent of people dying from coronary heart disease have one or more major risk factors that are affected by lifestyle choices, such as high blood pressure, high serum cholesterol, diabetes, smoking, and obesity (WHO, 2018a).

People who live in a chronically stressful environment over which they have little control appear to be at increased risk for CHD (Steptoe & Kivimäki, 2013). A study of 30,000 people in 52 countries found that about one-third of the risk for heart disease is connected to the stressfulness of people's environments (Rosengren et al., 2004; Yusuf et al., 2004). People in high-stress jobs are at increased risk for CHD, particularly if their jobs are highly demanding but provide them little control (Hintsanen et al., 2005; Schneiderman et al., 2005). For example, one study followed about 900 middle-aged men and women over 10 years and tracked the emergence of coronary heart disease (Karasek, Russell, & Theorell, 1982). The people in the study worked in a variety of jobs, and the researchers categorized these jobs in terms of how demanding they were and how much control they allowed a worker. Over the 10 years of this study, workers in jobs that were highly demanding but low in control, such as working on a factory production line, had a risk of coronary heart disease 1.5 times greater than that of workers in other occupations.

Experimental studies with animals have shown that disruption of the social environment can induce pathology that resembles coronary artery disease (Crestani, 2016; Sapolsky, 2007). Some of these experiments have been conducted with a type of macaque monkey whose social organization involves the establishment of stable hierarchies of dominance—dominant and submissive animals can be identified within a given group on the basis of the animals' social behavior. Introduction of unfamiliar monkeys into an established social group is a stressor that leads to increased aggressive behavior as group members attempt to reestablish a social dominance hierarchy (Sapolsky, 2007). In these studies, some monkey groups remained stable, with fixed memberships, and other groups were stressed by the repeated introduction of new members. After about 2 years under these conditions, the high-ranking or dominant males in the unstable social condition showed more extensive coronary heart disease than did the subordinate males (Sapolsky, 2007).

Hypertension, or high blood pressure, is a condition in which blood flows through vessels with excessive force, putting pressure on vessel walls. Hypertension can be caused by blood being pushed with too much force by the heart through vessels or by constriction of the vessel walls. Chronic high blood pressure can cause hardening of the arterial walls and deterioration of the cell tissue, leading eventually to coronary heart disease, kidney failure, and stroke. Almost one-third of the population of the United States has hypertension (Merai et al., 2016). As in coronary heart disease, genetics appears to play a role in the predisposition to hypertension, but only about 10 percent of all cases of hypertension can be traced to genetics or to specific organic causes, such as kidney dysfunction. The other 90 percent of cases are known as *essential hypertension,* meaning that the causes are unknown.

Because part of the body's response to stress—the fight-or-flight response—is to increase blood pressure, it is not surprising that people who live in chronically stressful circumstances are more likely to develop hypertension (Schneiderman et al., 2005; Steptoe & Kivimäki, 2013). As an example, people who move from quiet rural settings to crowded, noisy urban settings show increases in their rates of hypertension.

One group that lives in chronically stressful settings and has particularly high rates of hypertension is low-income African Americans (CDC, 2018e). They often lack adequate financial resources for daily living, may be poorly educated and have trouble finding good jobs, live in neighborhoods racked with violence, and frequently experience racism. All these conditions have been linked to higher blood pressure (Chen & Miller, 2012; Lehman, Taylor, Kiefe, & Seeman, 2009).

People with hypertension and the children of parents with hypertension tend to show a stronger blood pressure response to a wide variety of stressors. In experimental situations that have people solve arithmetic problems or immerse their hands in ice water, those with no personal or family history of hypertension show much less blood pressure response than do those with a history of hypertension (Harrell, 1980). In addition, it takes longer for the blood pressure of persons with hypertension to return to normal following exposure to stressors than it does the blood pressure of those without hypertension.

Thus, people with hypertension and people with family or genetic histories of hypertension may have a heightened physiological reactivity to stress. If they are exposed to chronic stress, their chronically elevated blood pressure can lead to hardening and narrowing of the arteries, creating a physiologically based hypertension. Low-income African Americans may have both this physiological predisposition to heightened reactivity to stress and chronic exposure to stressful environments, making them doubly vulnerable to hypertension (Lehman et al., 2009).

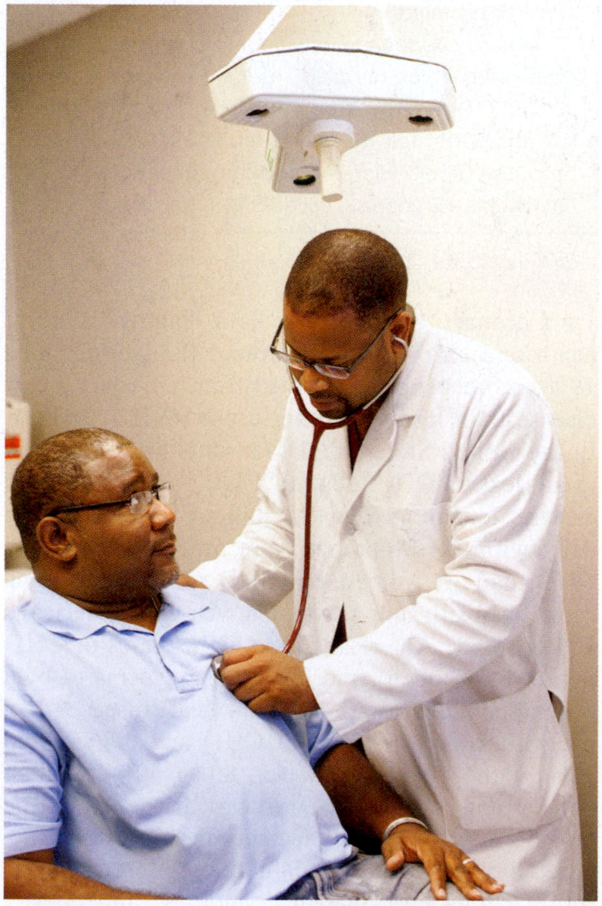

People who live in stressful settings are more likely to experience hypertension than are people who live in quieter and more secure surroundings. One group that disproportionately lives in chronically stressful settings and has particularly high rates of hypertension are low-income African Americans. *©ERproductions Ltd/Blend Images/Getty Images*

Personality and CHD

The personality factor traditionally linked to coronary heart disease is the **Type A behavior pattern.** The three components of the Type A pattern, according to the physicians who identified it (Friedman & Rosenman, 1974), are a sense of time urgency, easily aroused hostility, and competitive striving for achievement. People who are Type A are always in a hurry, setting unnecessary deadlines for themselves and trying to do multiple things at once. They are competitive, even in situations in which being competitive is ridiculous. They also are chronically hostile and will fly into a rage with little provocation.

One of the most compelling studies to demonstrate the relationship between the Type A pattern and coronary heart disease followed more than 3,000 healthy middle-aged men for 8½ years (Rosenman et al., 1976). Over the years of the study, Type A men had twice as many heart attacks or other forms of coronary heart disease as non–Type A men. These results held up even after diet, age, smoking, and other variables associated with coronary heart disease were taken into account. Other studies have confirmed this twofold risk and have linked Type A behavior to heart disease in both men and women (Myrtek, 2007; Schneiderman et al., 2005). In addition, Type A behavior is correlated with the severity of coronary artery blockage as determined at autopsy or in X-ray studies (Friedman, Rosenman, Straus, Wurm, & Kositcheck, 1968; Williams, Barefoot, Haney, & Harrell, 1988). Based on such evidence, in 1981 the American Heart Association classified Type A behavior as a risk factor for coronary heart disease.

Subsequent research suggests that the definition of Type A behavior as originally formulated is too diffuse. The crucial variable in predicting coronary heart disease may be hostility, particularly a cynical form of hostility characterized by suspiciousness, resentment, frequent anger, antagonism, and distrust of others (Chida & Steptoe, 2009; Miller, Smith, Turner, & Guijarro, 1996; Wong, Na, Regan, & Whooley, 2013). Time urgency and competitiveness appear to be less predictive of heart disease.

For example, a 25-year study of 118 male lawyers found that those who scored high on hostility traits on a personality inventory taken in law school were five times more likely to die before age 50 than classmates who scored low on the inventory (Barefoot, Dodge, Peterson, Dahlstrom, & Williams, 1989). Similarly, in a study of physicians, hostility scores obtained in medical school predicted the incidence of coronary heart disease as well as mortality from all causes (Barefoot, Dahlstrom, & Williams, 1983). In both studies, the relationship between hostility and illness was independent of the effects of smoking, age, and high blood pressure.

Individuals with Type A personalities often put heightened stress on themselves, which may put them at risk for coronary heart disease. ©Westend61/Getty Images

How does hostility lead to coronary heart disease? Again, overarousal of the sympathetic nervous system may play a role. Hostile people show greater physiological arousal in the anticipation of stressors and in the early stages of dealing with stressors. Their heart rates and blood pressures are higher, and they have greater secretion of the stress-related biochemicals known as catecholamines. They also return more slowly to baseline levels of sympathetic nervous system activity following stressors than do nonhostile people. This hyperreactivity may cause wear and tear on the coronary arteries, leading to coronary heart disease. Alternately, the excessive secretion of catecholamines in response to stress in hostile people may exert a direct chemical effect on blood vessels. The frequent rise and fall of catecholamine levels may cause frequent changes in blood pressure, reducing the resilience of the blood vessels. Hostile people also tend to engage in behaviors that increase their propensity for heart disease, including smoking, heavy drinking, and high-cholesterol diets (Schneiderman et al., 2005; Wong et al., 2013).

Some research has suggested that men are more likely than women to have the Type A personality pattern. Men also are more likely than women to carry three other risk factors for CHD: smoking, hypertension, and elevated cholesterol. Historically, far more men than women die of cardiovascular disease. In recent years, however, the number of women dying of cardiovascular disease has increased worldwide, while the number of men dying of cardiovascular disease has decreased (Sanchis-Gomar, Perez-Quilis, Leischik, R., & Lucia, 2016).

Contrary to popular belief, women carry as much anger and hostility as men—they just don't express it as readily (Brody, Hall, & Stokes, 2016; Lavoie, Miller, Conway, & Fleet, 2001). Excessive hostility and anger, whether expressed or suppressed, are associated with risk factors for coronary heart disease in both women and men (Matthews, Owens, Kuller, Sutton-Tyrrell, & Jansen-McWilliams, 1998; Wong et al., 2013).

Modifying Hostility to Improve Cardiovascular Functioning

A combination of cognitive and behavioral techniques has been shown to improve cardiovascular health by reducing Type A behavior, particularly hostility (Williams, 2008). One hallmark study included more than 1,000 individuals who had experienced at least one heart attack (Friedman et al., 1994). Treatment helped hostile participants learn to express themselves without exploding and to alter certain behaviors, such as interrupting others or talking or eating hurriedly. This treatment also targeted other aspects of Type A behavior, because the study was done before hostility was identified as the key factor. Participants were taught to overcome their sense of time urgency by practicing standing in line (which Type A individuals find irritating) and using the opportunity to reflect, to watch people, or to strike up a conversation with a stranger. Cognitive techniques helped participants reevaluate certain beliefs (such as the notion that success depends on the quantity of work produced) that might lead to urgent and hostile behavior. Also, participants found ways to make their home and work environments less stressful, such as by reducing unnecessary social engagements. By the end of the study 4½ years later, the intervention group had experienced half as many new heart attacks as the group whose participants were not taught to alter their lifestyles. Some cognitive-behavioral treatments that emphasize stress management and coping show effects on cardiovascular health (e.g., Gulliksson et al., 2011), but others do not. A meta-analysis of studies testing multiple types of psychological intervention found effects on mortality due to cardiac events, but not on other aspects of cardiovascular health (Whalley, Thompson, & Taylor, 2014).

Depression and Coronary Heart Disease

Major depression occurs in 15 to 20 percent of hospitalized patients with coronary heart disease, and up to 50 percent have some depressive symptoms (Steptoe, & Kivimäki, 2013; Whooley & Wong, 2013). There are several other variables that could account for the link between depression and CHD. The blocked arteries that lead to CHD also lead to reduced oxygen in the brain and the marshaling of the immune system, both of which can contribute to mood changes, including depression. Both CHD and depression may be caused by a relative deficiency in the polyunsaturated omega-3 fatty acids, found primarily in fatty fish (Ali et al., 2009). And, as noted earlier, both depression and CHD are linked to genes that alter the functioning of the serotonin system (Whooley & Wong, 2013).

Still, several studies suggest that depression doubles the risk of recurrent heart attacks and mortality in individuals with CHD (Whooley & Wong, 2013). For example, one study of patients with coronary heart disease found that those diagnosed with major depression were more than twice as likely to have a heart attack or some other major cardiac event (e.g., emergency heart surgery) over a 2-year follow-up period, even after taking into account a number of other risk factors for heart disease, such as age and high blood pressure (Frasure-Smith & Lesperance, 2008).

Depression could contribute to CHD through several pathways. Depression is associated with reduced heart rate variability (i.e., less variation from heartbeat to heartbeat), which is an indication of poorer functioning of the autonomic nervous system. In turn, low heart rate variability and other dysfunction of the sympathetic nervous system is a risk factor for CHD. Other pathways include inflammation, activation of the hypothalamic pituitry adrenal (HPA) axis and stress hormones, and effects on blood vessels (Whooley & Wong, 2013).

Depressed people with CHD are less likely than nondepressed people with CHD to engage in behaviors that could reduce their risk of future cardiac events, such as eating a low-fat diet and increasing their exercise (Gehi, Haas, Pipkin, & Whooley, 2005; Whooley & Wong, 2013; Ziegelstein et al., 2000). In one longitudinal study of 1,017 adults with coronary heart disease, those who were depressed were more likely than those who were not depressed to smoke, to be less physically active, to not take prescribed medications, and to have a higher mean body mass index (Whooley et al., 2008). The depressed patients experienced 50 percent more cardiac events (e.g., heart attacks) over the 4-year follow-up than did the nondepressed patients. The depressed patients' poor health behaviors accounted for their increased risk of cardiac events even after controlling for a number of physiological risk factors and possible third variables. In particular, the depressed patients' lower level of physical exercise accounted for 31 percent of the difference in cardiac events between the depressed and the nondepressed patients.

These results suggest that increasing physical exercise is an important target of intervention for depressed patients with coronary heart disease. Exercise is effective in reducing both CHD and depression (Blumenthal et al., 2005, 2007). Attempts to reduce depression in CHD patients through the use of antidepressants or cognitive-behavioral therapy have had success in treating depression, but with limited effects on the CHD (Whalley et al., 2014; Whooley & Wong, 2013). Still, depression likely contributes to CHD and other cardiovascular diseases (such as stroke) through other mechanisms as well, including social isolation, smoking, and medication nonadherence (Whooley & Wong, 2013).

INTERVENTIONS TO IMPROVE HEALTH-RELATED BEHAVIORS

We know that our behaviors have a large influence on our health, yet most of us do not follow the recommendations of experts. Why? According to health psychologists, it takes more than information to change people's actions. People must have the motivation to change their behavior, believe they can change it, and have the skills to do so (Ajzen, 1991; Bandura, 2006; Leventhal, Weinman, Leventhal, & Phillips, 2008). Here we consider some attempts to give people the tools they need to change their health-related behaviors.

Guided Mastery Techniques

Guided mastery techniques provide people with explicit information about how to engage in positive health-related behaviors and with opportunities to do so in increasingly challenging situations. The goals are to increase people's skills as well as their beliefs that they can engage in the behaviors, known as *self-efficacy beliefs* (Bandura, 2006). The kinds of actions that might be targeted include using condoms during sex in order to prevent the spread of HIV and other sexually transmitted diseases, refusing alcohol when being pressured to drink, and starting an exercise program.

A guided mastery program for teaching women how to negotiate safe sexual practices might begin with information on condom use. A counselor then might model how a woman can ask a man to use a condom. The women would watch the counselor and then practice insisting on condom use in role-plays with the counselor or other group participants. In this role playing, the women would face increasingly difficult challenges to their insistence on condom use, learn strategies for meeting these challenges, and practice using those strategies. The women might also be taught to determine when it is useless to argue any longer and skills for removing themselves from unsafe sexual encounters.

Guided mastery techniques were used successfully in a program with African American women called Sister-to-Sister: The Black Women's Health Project Intervention (Jemmott, Jemmott, & O'Leary, 2007). In five short interventions, nurses gave women information about the cause, transmission, and prevention of sexually transmitted diseases (STDs). The women then participated in guided mastery exercises to increase their skills and self-confidence for negotiating condom use by their male partners. The women also learned to eroticize condom use by incorporating putting on condoms into foreplay and intercourse in ways that increase positive attitudes toward their use. Compared to women who received only information, without guided mastery exercises, these women showed greater confidence in negotiating condom use and a stronger intention to use condoms (O'Leary, Jemmott, & Jemmott, 2008). Most important, the program resulted in lower sexual risk behavior and lower incidence of STDs over the 12 months following it.

Cultural norms regarding health behaviors can affect people's willingness to engage in them (Ajzen, 1991). Programs like the guided mastery program described above have been adapted to address cultural norms that might encourage or interfere with targeted health behaviors (Bandura, 2006). For example, a strong cultural value in many Hispanic groups is *familism,* or prioritizing the respect and care of one's family over one's individual needs. One study of Hispanic adolescents adapted a guided mastery program to include discussions of the impact of risky sexual behaviors on the loved ones of the adolescents (Koniak-Griffin et al., 2008). The adolescents in this program were all teen parents, so the program materials focused on cultural values of parental protectiveness, using traditional teachings of Chicano, Latino, and Native American ancestors. The adolescents who received this culturally adapted intervention showed greater increases in condom use than a comparison group of adolescents who received only general information about HIV prevention. This is an example of how culturally modified interventions and cultural sensitivity, as discussed in the chapter "Theories and Treatment of Abnormality," can also be important in interventions targeting physical health.

Internet-Based Health Interventions

Millions of people around the world get health information from the Internet every day. The Web can deliver high-quality health information and interventions to promote behaviors that improve health. Moreover, online interventions can be delivered to individuals who might not have access to in-person programs, either because none are available in their area or because they cannot afford them. More than half the world population has access to the Internet, and the majority of Internet users say they get health

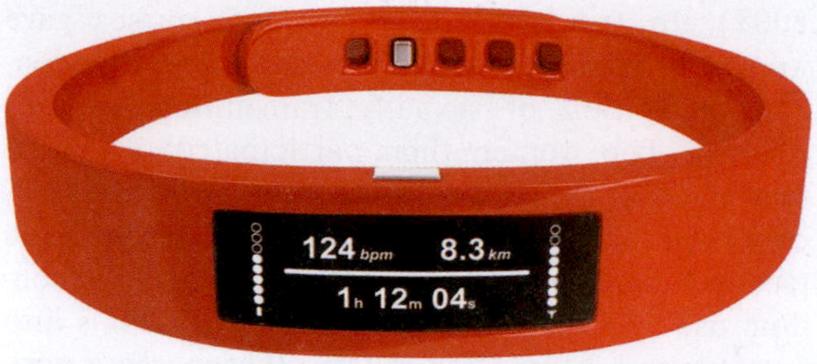

Fitness trackers, which are wearable electronic devices or computer applications that record an individual's daily physical activity, are used by many to motivate healthy lifestyle choices. ©Mile Atanasov/123RF RF

information off the Web (Vandelanotte et al., 2016; Vandelanotte, Spathonis, Eakin, & Owen, 2007). Controlled studies of the effectiveness of these interventions offer hope that they can be effective in helping people change their behaviors and improve their health.

Many Internet-based behavioral interventions aim to increase people's exercise and improve their diet. Regular physical exercise significantly decreases the risk of cardiovascular disease, diabetes, and several forms of cancer (Ehrman, Gordon, Visich, & Keteyian, 2009). Yet most people do not exercise regularly. Similarly, while eating fresh fruits and vegetables every day reduces the risk of developing several major illnesses, the diets of people around the world increasingly are filled with high-fat, high-sugar, low-nutrition foods (Brownell & Walsh, 2017). As a result, obesity rates are skyrocketing, especially in developed countries. Intensive, in-person programs can spur people to increase their exercise and improve their diet. However, these programs are expensive, time-consuming, and unavailable to many people. The Internet provides the opportunity to deliver exercise and nutrition programs to large segments of the population for a relatively low cost.

One such program was designed by General Electric to improve the health of its workforce (Pratt, Jandzio, Tomlinson, Kang, & Smith, 2006). Employees were invited by e-mail to participate in the program, which involved increasing their daily exercise to 10,000 steps or 30 minutes of moderate-intensity physical exercise, eating five servings of fruits and vegetables a day, and losing weight if significantly overweight. Participating employees completed an online assessment of their current behaviors and physical needs. Based on their profile, they received regular e-mails about their progress in the program, as well as e-newsletters with health tips and case studies of employees who had made major lifestyle changes. They were given phone and e-mail access to nutrition and fitness coaches who could answer their questions and provide personalized advice. Participants discussed exercise and diet in chat rooms. The Weight Watchers program was made available online. The company even created a "video reality series" that followed two employees who were participating in the program.

An evaluation of 2,498 employees across 53 nations who participated in the program for about 8 months showed that these employees significantly increased their physical activity and their consumption of fruits and vegetables (Pratt et al., 2006). They also lost an average of 4 to 5 pounds over the duration of the program.

Reviews of Internet-based programs designed to improve physical activity and diet found that the majority resulted in positive outcomes for participants compared to control groups (Vandelanotte et al., 2016; Vandelanotte et al., 2007). Gains tend to be relatively modest, and they are short-lived if the programs are not continued. Across thousands or even millions of people, however, the potential public health impact of these programs is great. In addition to these interventions focused on health behaviors, other Internet-based self-help interventions are targeted toward people coping with chronic health conditions, like irritable bowel syndrome and chronic pain. A review of such interventions, which largely emphasize cognitive-behavioral techniques, showed that they can be effective in reducing physical symptoms and, to a lesser degree, psychological distress (Beatty & Lambert, 2013).

The new frontier in Internet-based health interventions capitalizes on the increased use of mobile devices, like smartphones and tablets. Such devices allow people to carry the tool with them, engage with social networks, and in some cases, record diet and physical activity data more accurately (Vandelanotte et al., 2016). Some trials suggest that interventions incorporating apps and social network components are more effective than traditional Internet-delivered interventions (Vandelanotte et al., 2017), although attrition tends to be high, and meta-analyses have found only small effects on health behavior (e.g., Maher et al., 2014). Vandelanotte and colleagues (2016) note that empirically based techniques for behavior change are currently not used in most popular apps, and that future development in this area may improve outcomes.

SLEEP AND HEALTH

Getting enough sleep is critically important to health. People who sleep fewer than 6 hours each night have a 70 percent higher mortality rate than those who sleep at least 7 or 8 hours each night (Ikehara et al., 2009; Kryger, Roth, & Dement, 2017). This is true for both men and women, for people of many ethnicities, and for people with many different health backgrounds.

Lack of sleep weakens the immune system (Irwin, 2015; Irwin & Opp, 2017). Among middle-aged adults, those who sleep less show greater development of heart disease over time (King et al., 2008). People who work rotating shifts have higher rates of illness, including cardiovascular and gastrointestinal disease, than other people (Ohayon, Smolensky, & Roth, 2010).

Sleep deprivation also has many psychological effects: It impairs memory, learning, logical reasoning, arithmetic skills, complex verbal processing, and decision making. For example, reducing your amount of sleep to 5 hours each night for only 2 nights significantly reduces performance on math problems and creative-thinking tasks. This means that staying up to study for exams for only a couple of nights can significantly impair the ability to do well on those exams (Wolfson, 2010). Sleep deprivation also causes irritability, emotional ups and downs, and perceptual distortions, such as mild hallucinations (Harvey, 2008a). Sleep-deprived individuals are more reactive to both positive and negative emotional stimuli, but their emotional expressions and abilities to perceive others' emotions are blunted, which can cause problems during the day (Goldstein & Walker, 2014).

Sleep deprivation can literally kill. Each year in the United States, 7 percent of all car crashes and 16 percent of all car-crash deaths are due to driver sleepiness (National Transportation Safety Board, 2018). Over half of automobile drivers admit to having driven when drowsy at least once in the past year, and 28 percent say they have fallen asleep at the wheel (National Sleep Foundation, 2009). Medical professionals work longer hours than members of almost any other profession, and as many as 98,000 deaths occur annually in the United States due to medical errors—many associated with sleep deprivation. Some of the most serious disasters in modern history have been the result of mistakes made by sleepy people (Mitler & Miller, 1995). In 1979, the worst nuclear plant accident in the United States occurred when fatigued workers at Three Mile Island failed to respond to a mechanical problem at the plant. In 1986, the world's worst nuclear disaster happened in Chernobyl in Ukraine (then part of the Soviet Union) during a test conducted by an exhausted team of engineers. In 2008, a Boston trolley car crashed into a stopped trolley after the driver of the first vehicle ran a red light; the National Transportation Safety Board concluded that the driver went into a "microsleep"—falling asleep for only a few seconds—resulting in the crash and her death (Ahlers, 2009).

It is frightening to realize that sleep deprivation is so widespread. Over half of Americans say they chronically feel sleep deprived (Hirshkowitz et al., 2015; National Sleep Foundation, 2009); about 9 percent of men and 13 percent of women say they are chronically severely sleepy (Ohayon, 2012). Young adults need, on average, 9.2 hours of sleep each day. Yet most young adults sleep 7.5 or fewer hours each day (National Sleep Foundation, 2009). Similarly, most middle-aged adults need at least 7 or 8 hours of sleep each day, but most get fewer than 7 hours. People who work rotating shifts or in jobs demanding long periods of activity, such as nurses, doctors, firefighters, police, and rescue personnel, often are chronically sleep deprived (Chatzitheochari & Arber, 2009). Even when they have time to sleep, they have trouble falling asleep because their body's natural rhythms have been disrupted by their irregular schedule. The effects of sleep deprivation are cumulative. A person builds up an increasing "sleep debt" for every 24-hour period in which he or she does not get adequate sleep, and on average, Americans incur 26 minutes of sleep debt per day (Kryger et al., 2017; National Sleep Foundation, 2015).

Stress is a frequent contributor to sleep problems. A 2009 poll taken during a period of economic crisis found that one-third of Americans were losing sleep over the state of the U.S. economy and personal financial matters (National Sleep Foundation, 2009). A 2015 poll showed that 43 percent reported moderate, severe, or very severe stress, and the more stress people experienced, the shorter the duration and poorer the quality of their sleep (National Sleep Foundation, 2015). In general, Americans are sleeping less while trying to cram more and more into the day, including multiple jobs, exercise, socializing, and school. Similar patterns are found in other developed countries, including Great Britain (Chatzitheochari & Arber, 2009). Over the past century, the average night's sleep time in these societies has declined more than 20 percent (National Sleep Foundation, 2009).

Assessing Sleep

What is sleep? Analysis of brain-wave activity suggests that there are five stages of sleep: four differing depths of sleep and a fifth stage known as rapid eye movement (or REM) sleep (Figure 4). When a person closes his or her eyes and relaxes, the brain waves characteristically show a regular pattern of 8 to 12 hertz (cycles per second); these are known as *alpha waves.* As the individual drifts into Stage 1 sleep, the brain waves become less regular and have lower amplitude (in other words, they go up and down less, reflecting less electrical activity). Stage 2 includes spindles—short runs of higher-frequency activity of 12 to 16 hertz—and an occasional sudden sharp rise and fall in the amplitude of the entire EEG (this is referred to as a K-complex). The still deeper Stage 3 and Stage 4 are characterized by slow waves of 1 to 2 hertz, known as *delta waves.*

FIGURE 4 **EEG Recordings During Various Stages of Sleep.** The awake stage (relaxed with eyes closed) is characterized by alpha waves (8 to 12 hertz). Stage 1 is basically a transition from wakefulness to the deeper stages of sleep. Stage 2 is defined by the presence of sleep spindles (brief bursts of 12- to 16-hertz waves) and K-complexes (a sharp rise and fall in the brainwave pattern). Stages 3 and 4 are marked by the presence of delta waves (1 to 12 hertz), and the only difference between these two stages is the amount of delta waves found. Stage 3 is scored when 20 to 50 percent of the record contains delta waves, and Stage 4 when the percentage of delta waves is 50 percent or more.

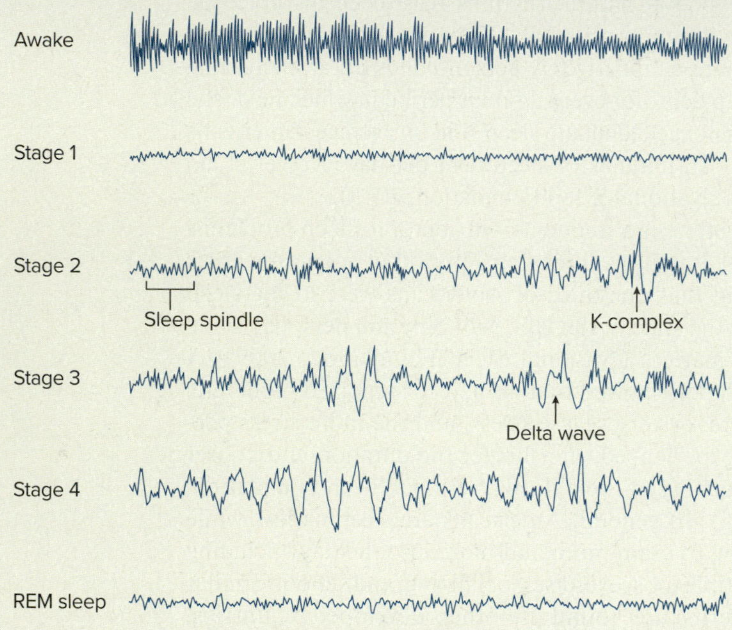

Busy students are often sleep deprived. ©*Yellow Dog Productions/The Image Bank/Getty Images*

After an adult has been asleep for an hour or so, the EEG becomes very active. Electrodes near the person's eyes detect pronounced rapid eye movements. This stage is known as *REM sleep;* the other four stages are known as *non-REM* (or *NREM*) *sleep.* The stages alternate throughout the night, beginning with the NREM stages. Several sleep cycles occur, each containing some REM and some NREM sleep. There usually are four or five distinct REM periods over the course of an 8-hour night's sleep, with an occasional brief awakening as morning arrives. Dreaming occurs during REM sleep.

The pattern of the sleep cycles varies with a person's age. Newborn infants, for instance, spend about half their sleeping time in REM sleep. This drops to 20 to 25 percent of total sleep time by age 5 and remains fairly constant until old age, when it drops to 18 percent of total sleep time or less. Older people tend to experience less Stage 3 and Stage 4 sleep (sometimes these stages disappear) and more frequent and longer nighttime awakenings (Zdanys & Steffens, 2015).

A comprehensive assessment of how people sleep can be obtained by a *polysomnographic* (*PSG*) evaluation. This requires individuals to spend one or more nights in a sleep lab, connected to instruments that measure respiration and oxygen desaturation (a measure of airflow), leg movements, eye movements, brain-wave activity, and heart activity (Buysse, Ancoli-Israel, Edinger, Lichstein, & Morin, 2006). This evaluation gives the sleep specialist the data to determine what aspects of sleep may be irregular (for example, if a person is waking during REM of NREM sleep, or whether awakenings are related to low oxygen levels). An alternative is for individuals to wear a wristwatch-like device called an *actigraph,* which records movement (Morgenthaler et al., 2007; see Irwin, 2015). The data it gathers can be compared to known patterns of movement during sleep to determine when individuals are awake or asleep.

These methods of assessing sleep are objective and detailed, but they also are expensive and require special equipment. More frequently, people are asked to keep a detailed diary of their sleep patterns (what time they go to bed, when they awaken during the night, and when they get up in the morning). Questionnaires may be used to assess people's sleep patterns even more quickly.

Sleep Disorders

Some people experience so much difficulty sleeping that they may be diagnosed with a sleep-wake disorder. Disturbances in sleeping or staying awake can occur for many reasons. They may be the result of another psychological disorder. In particular, insomnia is a symptom of unipolar depression and co-occurs at high rates in bipolar disorder, schizophrenia, attention-deficit/hyperactivity disorder, the anxiety disorders, and substance use disorder (Harvey, 2008a). The symptoms of these disorders, such as anxiety, can make it difficult to sleep. In turn, insomnia can worsen the symptoms of these other disorders, perhaps in part because people who are sleep deprived are more emotionally reactive and have more difficulty regulating their emotions. They also have more difficulty functioning in their daily life due to decreased concentration and performance, leading to the further accumulation of stressors (Harvey, 2008b). Sleep plays a key role in maintaining healthy functioning of the emotional parts of the brain for people in general, but a vicious cycle of psychological symptoms and insomnia among people with psychiatric conditions can make healthy sleep especially important (Goldstein & Walker, 2014).

Sleep disorders also often result from the physiological effects of a medical condition. Many medical conditions can disturb sleep, including degenerative neurological illnesses, such as Parkinson's disease; cerebrovascular disease, including strokes; endocrine conditions, such as hypo- or hyperthyroidism; viral and bacterial infections, such as viral encephalitis; pulmonary diseases, such as chronic bronchitis; and pain from musculoskeletal diseases, such as rheumatoid arthritis or fibromyalgia (Pack & Pien, 2011). In addition, substances such as illicit drugs, alcohol, or prescription drugs can lead to many sleep disturbances; in such cases, the diagnosis is **substance-induced sleep disorder.**

Insomnia

Probably the most familiar sleep-wake disorder is **insomnia disorder**—chronic difficulty initiating or maintaining sleep or sleep that does not restore energy and alertness. People with insomnia usually report a combination of difficulty falling asleep and intermittent wakefulness during the night.

Occasional problems with insomnia are extremely common, with up to 50 percent of adults reporting they have had insomnia at some time in their life and one in three adults complaining they have had insomnia in the past year (National Sleep Foundation, 2015). Episodic insomnia is defined as difficulty falling asleep or staying asleep that lasts only a few days and is an isolated occurrence (Pack & Pien, 2011). This difficulty is often tied to a specific stressor, such as facing a major exam or being in an unfamiliar place, and it stops once the stressor has passed.

To receive the diagnosis of insomnia disorder, the symptoms of insomnia must occur at least three nights per week for at least 3 months, and the sleep disturbance must cause significant distress or impairment in functioning (Table 2). Chronic insomnia affects 10 to 15 percent of adults and is more frequent in women than in men and more common in older adults than in younger adults (Riemann et al., 2015; Zhang & Wing, 2006).

When we fall asleep and when we awaken are strongly influenced by our biological rhythms, particularly body temperature rhythms (Lack, Gradisar, Van Someren, Wright, & Lushington, 2008; Riemann et al., 2015). When we are on a schedule of sleeping at night and being awake and active during the day,

A familiar sleep-wake order is insomnia, which usually involves a combination of falling asleep and intermittent wakefulness during the night. *©Katarzyna Białasiewicz/123RF*

TABLE 2 *DSM-5* Criteria for Insomnia Disorder

A. A predominant complaint of dissatisfaction with sleep quantity or quality associated with one (or more) of the following symptoms:
   1. Difficulty initiating sleep. (In children, this may be manifested as difficulty initiating sleep without caregiver intervention.)
   2. Difficulty maintaining sleep, characterized by frequent awakenings or problems returning to sleep after awakenings. (In children this may be manifested as difficulty returning to sleep without caregiver intervention.)
   3. Early-morning awakening with inability to return to sleep.

B. The sleep disturbance causes clinically significant distress or impairment in social, occupational, educational, academic, behavioral, or other important areas of functioning.

C. The sleep difficulty occurs at least 3 nights per week.

D. The sleep difficulty is present for at least 3 months.

E. The sleep difficulty occurs despite adequate opportunity to sleep.

F. The insomnia is not better explained by and does not occur exclusively during the course of another sleep-wake disorder (a parasomnia).

G. The insomnia is not attributable to the physiological effects of a substance (e.g., a drug of abuse, a medication).

H. Coexisting mental disorders and medical conditions do not adequately explain the predominant complaint of insomnia.

Specify if:

With non-sleep disorder mental comorbidity, including substance use disorders

With other medical comorbidity

With other sleep disorder

our core body temperature typically reaches its minimum between 4 and 6 A.M.; falling asleep is easiest 5 to 6 hours before that minimum is reached (between about 11 P.M. and 1 A.M.). Awakening usually occurs 1 to 3 hours after the minimum core body temperature is reached. Some people have disruptions in this body temperature rhythm that interfere with their ability to fall asleep in the late evening or to stay asleep in the early morning (Lack et al., 2008).

Any major stressor can trigger an episode of insomnia, including relationship difficulties, job loss, the death of a loved one, and financial problems. In a vicious cycle, this episodic insomnia can become chronic insomnia. The longer the person lies in bed unable to go to sleep, the more distressed and restless he or she becomes. The person's wakefulness then becomes conditioned to the environment—to the bed and bedroom—leading to even more difficulty sleeping the next night.

Cognitive factors help maintain insomnia (Harvey, 2005). First, during the day and when trying to sleep, individuals with insomnia worry about whether they will sleep. They may monitor the clock while trying to fall asleep, worrying more as time passes (Tang, Schmidt, & Harvey, 2007). This worry creates a cognitive and physiological arousal that keeps them awake. Second, they are hypervigilant for things that might keep them awake, such as noises in the environment or bodily aches and pains (Semler & Harvey, 2007). Third, they believe they get less sleep than they do and attribute daytime problems to their insomnia. This cognition feeds their anxiety about their insomnia. Fourth, they engage in counterproductive behaviors to try to help themselves sleep. They may drink alcohol, which can exacerbate insomnia, or avoid social engagements at night, which leaves them with more time alone to worry.

Cognitive-behavioral interventions for insomnia can be highly effective (Harvey et al., 2014; Harvey & Buysse, 2017; Trauer, Qian, Doyle, Rajaratnam, & Cunnington, 2015). Cognitive techniques aim to reduce worries about sleep ("I wonder if I'm going to have a bad night again tonight!"), unhelpful beliefs about sleep ("Waking up during the night means I haven't slept well at all"), and misperceptions about the effects of sleep loss ("If I don't get 8 hours, I'll be a wreck tomorrow!"). The behavioral techniques include stimulus control, that is, controlling conditions around the person, the ways they prepare for sleep, that might interfere with sleep (Morin et al.,

2006). A person experiencing insomnia would be told to do the following:

1. Go to bed only when sleepy.
2. Use the bed and bedroom only for sleep and sex, not for reading, television watching, eating, or working.
3. Get out of bed and go to another room if you are unable to sleep for 15 to 20 minutes, and do not return to bed until you are sleepy.
4. Get out of bed at the same time each morning.
5. Don't nap during the day.

Sleep restriction therapy involves initially restricting the amount of time insomniacs can try to sleep in the night, and is typically part of cognitive-behavioral treatment (Morin et al., 2006). Once they are able to sleep when they are in bed, they are gradually allowed to spend more time in bed. In addition, people often are taught relaxation exercises and are given information about the effects of diet, exercise, and substance use on sleep.

Various medications are used in the treatment of insomnia, including antidepressants, antihistamines, tryptophan, delta-sleep-inducing peptide (DSIP), melatonin, and benzodiazepines (Buysse, Rush, & Reynolds, 2017; Neubauer, Pandi-Perumal, Spence, Buttoo, & Monti, 2018). All these have proven effective in at least some studies, although the number of studies done on most of these agents is small. Those that have the least clear benefit are antihistamines and tryptophan. Those that have proven most reliably effective are benzodiazepines and zolpidem (trade name Ambien). Individuals can become dependent on these sleep aids, however, and may experience withdrawal when they try to stop using them. Rare cases of sleep-eating have been reported among users of Ambien—these users get up during the night and consume large quantities of food, then don't remember doing so in the morning. Insomnia often returns after individuals stop taking the medications, and can even get worse. In contrast, the behavioral and cognitive interventions tend to have long-lasting positive effects (Buysse et al., 2017).

Hypersomnolence Disorders and Narcolepsy

Hypersomnolence disorders are characterized by excessive sleepiness, which can be expressed as an excessive quantity of sleep (also referred to as *hypersomnia*) or a low quality of wakefulness (see Table 3). People with a hypersomnolence disorder are chronically sleepy and sleep for long periods. They may sleep 12 hours at a stretch and still wake up sleepy. A nap during the day may last an hour or more, and they may wake up unrefreshed. If their environment is not stimulating (e.g., during a boring lecture), they are sure to fall asleep. They may even fall asleep while driving. To qualify for a diagnosis, the hypersomnolence must be present at least three times per week for at least 3 months and must cause significant distress or impairment in functioning. Hypersomnolence is a chronic condition that most often begins in early adulthood (Barateau, Lopes, Franchi, & Dauvilliers, 2017; Lee & Kazaglis, 2015). It is estimated that only 1 percent of the population meet the full criteria for a hypersomnolence disorder, but its prevalence is much higher among people with mood disorders (Barateau et al., 2017; Ohayon, Dauvilliers, & Reynolds, 2012).

TABLE 3 *DSM-5* Criteria for Hypersomnolence Disorder

A. Self-reported excessive sleepiness (hypersomnolence) despite a main sleep period lasting at least 7 hours, with at least one of the following symptoms:
   1. Recurrent periods of sleep or lapses into sleep within the same day
   2. A prolonged main sleep episode of more than 9 hours per day that is nonrestorative (i.e., unrefreshing)
   3. Difficulty being fully awake after abrupt awakening.

B. The hypersomnolence occurs at least three times per week, for at least 3 months.

C. The hypersomnolence is accompanied by significant distress or impairment in cognitive, social, occupational, or other important areas of functioning.

D. The hypersomnolence is not better explained by and does not occur exclusively during the course of another sleep disorder (e.g., narcolepsy, breathing-related sleep disorder, circadian rhythm sleep-wake disorder, or a parasomnia).

E. The hypersomnolence is not attributable to the physiological effects of a substance (e.g., a drug of abuse, a medication).

F. Coexisting mental and medical disorders do not adequately explain the predominant complaint of hypersomnolence.

Narcolepsy involves recurrent attacks of an irrepressible need to sleep, lapses into sleep, or naps occurring within the same day. Sleep episodes generally last 10 to 20 minutes but can last up to 1 hour, and people with narcolepsy move into REM sleep within a few minutes. Most people with narcolepsy experience **cataplexy,** usually characterized by episodes of sudden loss of muscle tone lasting under 2 minutes, triggered by laughter or joking in people who have had narcolepsy for a long time. People with cataplexy may suddenly drop objects, buckle at the knees, or even fall to the ground, but they are not asleep—their hearing and awareness may be normal. More rarely, cataplexy may be characterized by spontaneous grimacing or jaw-opening episodes with tongue thrusting and by low muscle tone. These symptoms tend to occur in children who then go on to develop the more common characteristics of cataplexy (Plazzi et al., 2011). When people with narcolepsy awaken, they may experience brief periods when they can't move or speak, referred to as *sleep paralysis*.

There are two types of narcolepsy. The vast majority of people with symptoms of narcolepsy with cataplexy lack cells in the hypothalamus that secrete the neurotransmitter hypocretin, which promotes wakefulness (Mignot et al., 2002; Pack & Pien, 2011). In contrast, only a minority of people with symptoms of narcolepsy without cataplexy show low levels of hypocretin (Dauvilliers et al., 2003). The *DSM-5* defines narcolepsy as a disorder (see criteria in Table 4) and allows for the specification of whether hypocretin deficiency is involved as a subtype diagnosis. Researchers now believe that deficiencies in hypocretin in the hypothalamus may be due to autoimmune mechanisms—that is, the body's immune system acting against itself (Partinen et al., 2014).

Other biological factors have been implicated in hypersomnia and narcolepsy without cataplexy. Low levels of histamine, another neurotransmitter that promotes wakefulness, have been found in people with these disorders (Kanbayashi et al., 2009; Nishino et al., 2009). Also, hypersomnia and narcolepsy run in families. Specific genes have been implicated in narcolepsy, including genes linked to autoimmune functioning (Partinen et al., 2014). Hypersomnia often is related to other mental disorders, particularly depression (Barateau et al., 2017; Plante, 2017).

The stimulant modafinil is consistently effective in the treatment of daytime sleepiness in individuals with narcolepsy or hypersomnia (Kallweit & Bassetti, 2017). Other stimulants, including amphetamines, methamphetamine, and methylphenidate, are also used as treatments for daytime sleepiness due to narcolepsy or hypersomnia. Sodium oxybate and selegiline can reduce cataplexy, hallucinations, and sleep paralysis in narcolepsy. In addition, some physicians prescribe antidepressants, although their effectiveness in treating narcolepsy or hypersomnia is less clear (Kallweit & Bassetti, 2017).

Sleep-Related Breathing Disorders

It's difficult to sleep well if you can't breathe well. The *DSM-5* recognizes three sleep disorders related to problems in breathing: central sleep apnea, sleep-

TABLE 4 *DSM-5* Criteria for Narcolepsy

A. Recurrent periods of irrepressible need to sleep, lapsing into sleep, or napping occurring within the same day. These must have been occurring at least three times per week over the last 3 months.

B. The presence of at least one of the following:

1. Episodes of cataplexy, defined as either (a) or (b), occurring at least a few times per month:
    a. In individuals with long-standing disease, brief (seconds to minutes) episodes of sudden bilateral loss of muscle tone with maintained consciousness that are precipitated by laughter or joking.
    b. In children or in individuals within six months of onset, spontaneous grimaces or jaw-opening episodes with tongue thrusting or a global hypotonia, without any obvious emotional triggers.
2. Hypocretin deficiency, as measured using cerebrospinal fluid (CSF) hypocretin-1 immunoreactivity values (less than or equal to one-third of values obtained in healthy subjects tested using the same assay, or less than or equal to 110 pgmL). Low CSF of hypocretin-1 must not be observed in the context of acute brain injury, inflammation, or infection.
3. Nocturnal sleep polysomnography showing rapid eye movement (REM) sleep latency less than or equal to 15 minutes, or a multiple sleep latency test showing a mean sleep latency less than or equal to 8 minutes and two or more sleep-onset REM periods.

related hypoventilation, and obstructive sleep apnea/hypopnea (see Table 5). People with **central sleep apnea** experience complete cessation of respiratory activity for brief periods of time (20 seconds or more) yet do not have frequent awakenings and do not tend to feel tired during the day. Central sleep apnea occurs when the brain does not send the signal to breathe to the respiratory system. It can be caused by central nervous system disorders, including cerebral vascular disease and head trauma; heart disease; and chronic opioid use (Muza, 2015). It also occurs in premature infants. The first line of treatment is to treat the underlying disorder leading to central sleep apnea. **Sleep-related hypoventilation,** a new disorder in the *DSM-5*, is characterized by episodes of decreased breathing associated with high carbon dioxide levels. Unlike hyperventilation, which is breathing too much or too quickly, hypoventilation refers to breathing too little. It is frequently associated with lung disease or diseases of the chest wall (Böing & Randerath, 2015).

By far, the most common **breathing-related sleep disorder** is **obstructive sleep apnea/hypopnea syndrome.** You have probably heard it referred to simply as sleep apnea. As noted above, apneas are brief episodes of complete cessation of breathing. Hypopneas are episodes of abnormally shallow breathing or a low respiratory rate. To meet the criteria for this diagnosis, an individual has to have evidence from polysomnograph tests showing frequent apneas or hypopneas (see Table 5 for frequencies). People with this disorder may snore loudly, go silent and stop breathing for several seconds at a time, and then gasp for air. Obstructive sleep apnea/hypopnea occurs when airflow is stopped due to a narrow airway or an obstruction (an abnormality or damage) in the airway. Although it is associated with obesity, hypertension, and diabetes, it also can occur in tonsillitis and other disorders that cause inflammation in the airway. Estimates of prevalence vary widely worldwide, from 9 percent to 38 percent (Lim & Pack, 2017; Senaratna et al., 2017). Higher rates are seen in men than women and at older ages (Senaratna et al., 2017). The dramatic increase in overweight and obesity in recent decades (see the chapter "Eating Disorders") is associated with a major increase in obstructive sleep apnea.

Obstructive sleep apnea/hypopnea syndrome can be treated with a device called a continuous positive air pressure (CPAP) machine. The CPAP machine delivers a stream of compressed air via a hose to a

TABLE 5 *DSM-5* Criteria for Sleep-Related Breathing Disorders

Disorder	*DSM-5* Criteria
Central Sleep Apnea	A. Evidence by polysomnography of five or more central apneas per hour of sleep. B. The disorder is not better explained by another current sleep disorder.
Sleep-Related Hypoventilation	A. Polysomnography demonstrates episodes of decreased respiration associated with elevated CO_2 levels. (Note: In the absence of objective measurement of CO_2, persistent low levels of hemoglobin oxygen saturation unassociated with apneic/hypopneic events may indicate hypoventilation.) B. The disturbance is not better explained by another current sleep disorder.
Obstructive Sleep Apnea/Hypopnea	Either (1) or (2): 1. Evidence by polysomnography of at least five obstructive apneas or hypopneas per hour of sleep and either of the following sleep symptoms: a. Nocturnal breathing disturbances: snoring, snorting/gasping, or breathing pauses during sleep. b. Daytime sleepiness, fatigue or unrefreshing sleep despite sufficient opportunities to sleep that is not better explained by another mental disorder (including a sleep disorder) and is not attributable to another medical condition. 2. Evidence by polysomnography of 15 or more obstructive apneas and/or hypopneas per hour of sleep regardless of accompanying symptoms. *Specify current severity:* **Mild:** Apnea hypopnea index is less than 15. **Moderate:** Apnea hypopnea index is 15–30. **Severe:** Apnea hypopnea index is greater than 30.

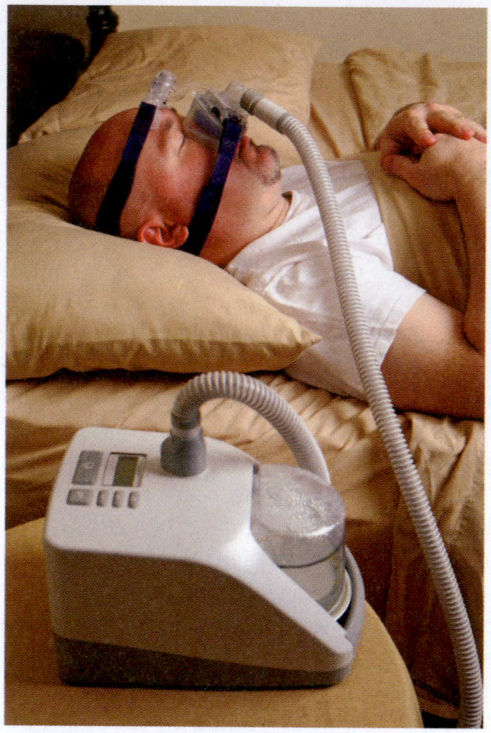

The CPAP machine helps people with breathing-related sleep patterns. ©*Amy Walters/Shutterstock*

nasal mask, keeping the airway open under air pressure so that unobstructed breathing is possible. CPAP is an effective treatment for obstructive sleep apnea and hypopnea, but 25 to 50 percent of people reject it because it makes them uncomfortable or does not offer sufficient relief from their breathing problems (Veasey et al., 2006). CPAP also is sometimes used to treat central sleep apnea.

Other treatment options include medication and surgery. Drugs that affect the serotonin system, including the serotonin reuptake inhibitors, have shown mixed effects in the treatment of obstructive sleep apnea/hypopnea; stimulants such as modafinil can reduce the daytime sleepiness associated with the disorder (Veasey et al., 2006). Surgery to remove obstructive tissue blocking the airway or to increase the upper airway area can be done in extreme cases, but meta-analyses of the small number of studies on the effectiveness of such surgeries do not show them to be consistently effective in treating the disorder (Franklin et al., 2009).

Circadian Rhythm Sleep-Wake Disorders

As noted, insomnia can be caused by disruptions in biological rhythms, especially core body temperature. These biological rhythms, also known as *circadian rhythms,* are driven by mechanisms in the brain that keep people in sync with the regular patterns of light and dark over the course of the day. These mechanisms are located in a part of the hypothalamus called the superchiasmatic nucleus and modulate daily rhythms in many systems of the body, including sleep and alertness (Riemann et al., 2015; Sack et al., 2007). Circadian rhythms are on a roughly 24-hour clock but can be affected by environmental time signals, especially the solar light/dark signal. Some people have more difficulty than others in adjusting their circadian rhythms after a disruption. Individual differences appear to have genetic roots (Riemann et al., 2015; Sack et al., 2007). If sustained and distressing, such difficulty can be diagnosed as a **circadian rhythm sleep-wake disorder** (Table 6).

The *DSM-5* recognizes five circadian rhythm sleep-wake disorders, each defined by the unique pattern of disturbance. These types are referred to as delayed sleep phase type, advanced sleep phase type, irregular sleep-wake type, non-24-hour type, and shift-work type. *Delayed sleep phase type* involves a persistent pattern of delayed sleep onset and awakenings and an inability to go to sleep or wake up earlier if desired. Adolescents typically experience a phase in their biological clock that makes them want to stay up late and sleep late. Delayed sleep phase type circadian rhythm disorder is diagnosed only when it seriously interferes with the person's functioning and causes distress. It is the most common circadian rhythm disorder diagnosed in clinical settings.

In contrast, *advanced sleep phase type* involves a persistent pattern of sleep onset and awakenings that are 2 or more hours earlier than desired (i.e., they are "advanced" to an earlier time than preferred). This pattern results in symptoms of early-morning insomnia and excessive sleepiness during the day. Individuals with this disorder show evidence of earlier timing of circadian biomarkers, including melatonin and core body temperature changes (Abbott, Reid, & Zee, 2015).

People with *irregular sleep-wake type* do not have a discernable sleep-wake rhythm. Their sleep tends to be fragmented into at least three periods per 24 hours; they may have insomnia during the night but be very sleepy during periods of the day. This disorder can be associated with neurological disorders (Abbott et al., 2015). People with *non-24-hour type* circadian rhythm sleep-wake disorder appear to have a free-running sleep-wake cycle that is not calibrated with the light-dark cycle of the day. The disorder has been most frequently documented in people who cannot see—particularly those who perceive no light at all—but it also has been documented in sighted individuals (Flynn-Evans, Tabandeh, Skene, & Lockley, 2014). It may begin with a gradual movement of the onset of sleep to later and later at night until the individual sleeps during the day and is awake at night. Individuals with this disorder complain of sleepiness during daylight and show deficits in cognition and functioning.

TABLE 6 *DSM-5* Criteria for Circadian Rhythm Sleep-Wake Disorders

A. A persistent or recurrent pattern of sleep disruption that is primarily due to an alteration of the circadian system or to a misalignment between the endogenous circadian rhythm and the sleep-wake schedule required by an individual's physical environment, social or professional.

B. The sleep disruption leads to excessive sleepiness or insomnia, or both.

C. The sleep disturbance causes clinically significant distress or impairment in social, occupational, or other important areas of functioning.

Specify whether:

Delayed Sleep Phase Type: A pattern of delayed sleep onset and awakening times, with an inability to fall asleep and awaken at a desired or conventionally acceptable earlier time.

Specify if:

Familial: A family history of delayed sleep phase is present.

Specify if:

Overlapping with non-24-hour sleep-wake type: Delayed sleep phase type may overlap with another circadian rhythm sleep-wake disorder, non-24-hour sleep-wake type.

Advanced Sleep Phase Type: A pattern of advanced sleep onset and awakening times, with an inability to remain awake or asleep until the desired or conventionally acceptable later sleep or wake times.

Specify if:

Familial: A family history of advanced sleep phase is present.

Irregular Sleep-Wake Type: A temporally disorganized sleep and wake pattern, such that the timing of sleep and wake periods is variable throughout the 24-hour period.

Non-24-Hour Sleep-Wake Type: A pattern of sleep and wake cycles that is not synchronized to the 24-hour environment, with a consistent daily drift (usually to later and later times) of sleep onset and times.

Shift Work Type: Insomnia during the major sleep period and/or excessive sleepiness (including inadvertent sleep) during the major awake period associated with shift work schedule (i.e., requiring unconventional work hours).

Unspecified type

Specify if:

Episodic: Symptoms last at least 1 month but less than 3 months.

Persistent: Symptoms last 3 months or longer.

Recurrent: Two or more episodes occur within the space of 1 year.

Finally, *shift work type* circadian rhythm sleep-wake disorder is caused by working rotating shifts or irregular hours. In one study, 31 percent of night workers and 26 percent of rotating shift workers met the criteria for this disorder (Drake, Roehrs, Richardson, Walsh, & Roth, 2004).

Behavioral interventions can help treat circadian rhythm sleep-wake disorders. It is easier to stay up late than to go to sleep early, so rotating shift workers can more easily move their shifts clockwise than counterclockwise (Sack et al., 2007). Planned napping during night shifts also can help reduce worker sleepiness and associated accidents (Sallinen, Harma, Akerstedt, Rosa, & Lillqvist, 1998). Exposing shift workers to bright light during night shifts can help shift their circadian rhythms (Sack et al., 2007). Similarly, exposing individuals with the delayed sleep phase type disorder to bright lights early in the morning can help shift their circadian rhythms.

Administering melatonin at prescribed times during the day has been shown to enhance the shifting of circadian rhythms in individuals with the delayed sleep phase type, blind adults with non-24-hour type, and the shift work type circadian rhythm sleep-wake disorders (Auger et al., 2015). The dosage and timing of melatonin administration are tricky, however, and can vary from one individual to another. Stimulants, such as modafinil, can improve alertness during night shifts and after crossing time zones, as can caffeine.

Disorders of Arousal

Disorders of arousal involve recurrent episodes of incomplete awakening from sleep that seem to mix elements of wakefulness and NREM sleep (see Table 7). "Arousal" in this case does not mean sexual arousal, as in the sexual disorders, or physiological arousal, as in the anxiety disorders. It refers to being more awake than during normal sleep, but not really quite awake. There are three types: sleep terrors, sleepwalking, and confusional arousals. **Sleep terror disorder** occurs most often in children (Neylan, Reynolds, & Kupfer, 2007). The sleeping child screams, sweating and with heart racing. Unlike nightmares, which occur during REM sleep, sleep terrors occur during NREM sleep. Children experiencing a sleep terror cannot be easily awakened and usually do not remember their sleep terrors on awakening. Adults can experience sleep terrors as well. One large epidemiological study in Norway found that 2.7 percent of adults had experienced sleep terrors at least once in the last 3 months and that 1.0 percent experienced sleep terrors at least once per week (Bjorvatn, Grønli, & Pallesen, 2010).

Like sleep terrors, **sleepwalking disorder** is relatively common in children, with 15 to 30 percent having experienced at least one episode (Neylan et al., 2007). In the study in Norway, about 22 percent of adults reported having sleepwalked at some time in their lives, but only 1.7 percent reported sleepwalking in the previous 3 months (Bjorvatn et al., 2010). Sleepwalking occurs during NREM sleep, so the person sleepwalking is not acting out a dream. Sleepwalkers may respond to others' questions or commands but cannot hold a conversation. They may engage in nocturnal eating, going to the kitchen and eating food while asleep. They can injure themselves by running into furniture or thrashing about, especially if they are also experiencing a sleep terror (American Psychiatric Association, 2013). Sleepwalkers are difficult to wake (although doing so is not dangerous, as popularly believed). People sometimes do not remember their sleepwalking activity, but some do (Zadra, Desautels, Petit, & Montplaisir, 2013).

Confusional arousals are episodes of incomplete awakening during NREM sleep that do not involve sleep terrors or sleepwalking. They involve foggy thinking, slow speech, and sometimes disorientation, and occur most commonly when a person is awoken by someone else. These episodes are relatively common in adults, and are typically of relatively brief duration before the person fully awakens. The study in Norway found that nearly 7 percent reported episodes of confusional arousal occurring in the previous 3 months, with nearly 2 percent having had an episode at least once per week (Bjorvatn et al., 2010).

Sleepwalking and sleep terrors tend to run in families (Petit et al., 2015). Twin studies of sleep terrors show higher concordance rates among monozygotic twins than among dizygotic twins, suggesting a genetic influence on sleep terrors (Hublin, Kaprio, Partinen, Heikkilä, & Koskenvuo, 1997; Nguyen et al., 2008). Stress, previous sleep deprivation, extreme fatigue, and the use of sedative or hypnotic drugs have been associated with both sleep terrors and sleepwalking.

Antidepressants are sometimes used to treat sleep terrors, with mixed results (Neylan et al., 2007). A behavioral treatment involves waking a child 30

TABLE 7 *DSM-5* Criteria for Non-Rapid Eye Movement Sleep Arousal Disorders

A. Recurrent episodes of incomplete awakening from sleep, usually occurring during the first third of the major sleep episode accompanied by either one of the following:
   1. **Sleepwalking:** Repeated episodes of rising from bed during sleep and walking about. While sleepwalking, the person has a blank, staring face, is relatively unresponsive to the efforts of others to communicate with him or her, and can be awakened only with great difficulty.
   2. **Sleep terrors:** Recurrent episodes of abrupt terror arousals from sleep, usually beginning with a panicky scream. There is intense fear and signs of autonomic arousal, such as mydriasis, tachycardia, rapid breathing, and sweating, during each episode. There is relative unresponsiveness to efforts of others to comfort the person during the episode.

B. No or little (e.g., only a single visual scene) dream imagery is recalled.

C. Amnesia for the episode is present.

D. The episodes cause clinically significant distress or impairment in social, occupational, or other important areas of functioning.

E. The disturbance is not attributable to the physiological effects of a substance (e.g., a drug of abuse, a medication).

F. Coexisting mental and medical disorders do not explain the episodes of sleepwalking or sleep terrors.

minutes before the time of night he or she typically would have a sleep terror or sleepwalking episode; after the child can go at least a week without a night terror, the scheduled wakenings are gradually ended. One study showed that such scheduled wakenings quickly reduced the frequency of children's night terrors; in a 1-year follow-up after the scheduled wakenings ended, the reductions in sleep terror episodes were maintained (Durand & Mindell, 1999).

Rapid Eye Movement Sleep Behavior Disorder

Whereas sleepwalking, sleep terrors, and confusional arousals occur during NREM sleep, other people become active during REM sleep. When this happens, they may engage in complex and often dangerous or violent behaviors, such as thrashing or fighting while asleep. They may appear to be acting out dreams and engaging in conversations with people in their dreams. Most people engaging in violent behaviors report having vivid dreams at the time, often involving being attacked by a person or an animal or protecting a loved one from harm (Ohayon, Guilleminault, & Chokroverty, 2010). They may actually injure themselves or their bed partner with their behaviors. About 4 percent of adults report ever having injured themselves or another during sleep (Bjorvatn et al., 2010). When behaviors during REM sleep are frequent and impairing, the individual may be diagnosed with **rapid eye movement (REM) sleep behavior disorder** (Table 8).

A substantial percentage of people with REM sleep behavior disorder develop neurodegenerative diseases such as Parkinson's disease (Barber et al., 2017; Iranzo, Santamaria, & Tolosa, 2016). For example, one study found that the risk of developing Parkinson's disease or a related neurodegenerative disease among people with REM sleep behavior disorder was 65 percent over a 10-year period (Schenck & Mahowald, 2003). Individuals with REM sleep behavior disorder show abnormalities in dopamine functioning in the brain similar to those shown by people with Parkinson's disease (see the chapter "Neurodevelopmental and Neurocognitive Disorders"), even when they have not yet developed any neurological symptoms. In addition, the violent behaviors characteristic of REM sleep behavior disorder are comorbid with other sleep-wake disorders, including sleepwalking, sleep terrors, confusional arousals, and obstructive sleep apnea (Ohayon et al., 2010), suggesting that these disorders share some common causes.

The drug most often used to treat REM sleep behavior disorder is clonazepam, a benzodiazepine also commonly used to treat anxiety disorders (Jung & Louis, 2016). Melatonin also shows some efficacy in treating the disorder, alone or in combination with clonazepam. In contrast, some antidepressants that influence levels of norepinephrine and serotonin, including venlaxafine and mirtazapine, have been shown to worsen REM sleep behavior disorder, as can caffeine and chocolate when consumed in excess.

Nightmare Disorder

Over two-thirds of adults have had nightmares, or terrifying dreams (Bjorvatn et al., 2010). People often awaken from nightmares frightened, sweating, and with their heart racing. They may have vivid memo-

TABLE 8 *DSM-5* Diagnostic Criteria for Rapid Eye Movement Sleep Behavior Disorder

A. Repeated episodes of arousal during sleep associated with vocalization and/or complex motor behaviors.

B. These behaviors arise during rapid eye movement (REM) sleep and therefore usually occur more than 90 minutes after sleep onset, are more frequent during the later portions of the sleep period, and uncommonly occur during daytime naps.

C. Upon awakening from these episodes, the individual is completely awake, alert, and not confused or disoriented.

D. Either of the following:

1. REM sleep without atonia on polysomnographic recording.
2. A history suggestive of REM sleep behavior disorder and an established synucleinopathy diagnosis (e.g., Parkinson's disease, multiple system atrophy).

E. The behaviors cause clinically significant distress or impairment in social, occupational, or other important areas of functioning (which may include injury to self or the bed partner).

F. The disturbance is not attributable to the physiological effects of a substance (e.g., a drug of abuse, a medication) or another medical condition.

G. Coexisting mental and medical disorders do not explain the episodes.

ries of the dream, which often involves physical danger. Nightmares are common among people who have recently experienced a traumatic event (Nadorff, Lambdin, & Germain, 2014). Nightmares are more common in children than in adults, with 10 to 50 percent of children having a sufficient number of nightmares to disturb their parents (Neylan et al., 2007). For a diagnosis of **nightmare disorder,** the nightmares must be frequent enough to cause significant distress or impairment in functioning (Table 9). The epidemiologic study in Norway found that 2.8 percent of adults have nightmares at least once per week (Bjorvatn et al., 2010), and worldwide between 2 to 6 percent of people meet criteria for nightmare disorder (Nadorff et al., 2014). Cognitive-behavioral interventions for nightmare disorder include exposure-based techniques that desensitize individuals to their nightmares. The person records the content of the nightmare in detail and then reads it repeatedly while doing relaxation exercises. Such interventions have been shown in small controlled trials to reduce the frequency of nightmares as well as the anxiety, depression, and sleeplessness associated with them. These gains persisted in a 4-year follow-up (Grandi, Fabbri, Panatoni, Gonnella, & Marks, 2006). A medication called prazosin, which affects sympathetic nervous system activity, has been shown to be effective in multiple randomized controlled trials among people whose nightmares are related to posttraumatic stress disorder (Nadorff et al., 2014).

TABLE 9 *DSM-5* Criteria for Nightmare Disorder

A. Repeated occurrences of extended, extremely dysphoric, and well-remembered dreams that usually involve efforts to avoid threats to survival, security, or physical integrity and that generally occur during the second half of the major sleep episode.

B. On awakening from the dysphoric dreams, the individual rapidly becomes oriented and alert.

C. The sleep disturbance causes clinically significant distress or impairment in social, occupational, or other important areas of functioning.

D. The nightmare symptoms are not attributable to the physiological effects of a substance (e.g., a drug of abuse, a medication).

E. Coexisting mental and medical disorders do not adequately explain the predominant complaint of dysphoric dreams.

Restless Legs Syndrome

Imagine that you are lying in bed and having creeping, crawling, tingling, itching sensations in your legs that are prominent enough to keep you awake. You feel as though you just have to move your legs. You get up and walk around and shake out your legs, and the sensations go away. But then, when you go back to bed, if you don't soon go to sleep the creeping, crawling sensations are back, and you just have to move again. This is the nature of **restless legs syndrome (RLS).**

Many people experience restless legs syndrome occasionally, usually or only at night. In order to be diagnosed with RLS, the *DSM-5* stipulates that the symptoms must be frequent and severe enough to significantly interfere with sleep and cause fatigue, mental health problems, and difficulty functioning (Table 10). About 2 to 3 percent of the population have RLS to this degree (see Allen et al., 2014). People with this syndrome have significantly higher

TABLE 10 *DSM-5* Diagnostic Criteria for Restless Legs Syndrome

A. An urge to move the legs, usually accompanied by or in response to uncomfortable and unpleasant sensations in the legs, characterized by all of the following:

1. The urge to move the legs begins or worsens during periods of rest or inactivity.
2. The urge to move the legs is partially or totally relieved by movement.
3. The urge to move the legs is worse in the evening or at night than during the day, or occurs only in the evening or at night.

B. The symptoms in Criterion A occur at least three times per week and have persisted for at least 3 months.

C. The symptoms in Criterion A are accompanied by significant distress or impairment in social, occupational, educational, academic, behavioral, or other important areas of functioning.

D. The symptoms in Criterion A are not attributable to another mental disorder or medical condition (e.g., arthritis, leg edema, peripheral ischemia, leg cramps) and are not better explained by a behavioral condition (e.g., positional discomfort, habitual foot tapping).

E. The symptoms are not attributable to the physiological effects of a drug of abuse or medication (e.g., akathisia).

rates of depression and anxiety disorders than do people in the general population, as well as more physical comorbidities (Szentkirályi, Völzke, Hoffmann, Trenkwalder, & Berger, 2014).

Specific genetic loci have been associated with RLS (Winkelmann et al., 2007). Abnormalities in the dopamine system also are associated with the disorder, and treatment with drugs that alter dopamine levels can be effective in treating it (Zintzaras et al., 2010). Iron deficiencies also are associated with the disorder, and reversal of iron deficiencies reduces symptoms (Trotti & Rye, 2011).

CHAPTER INTEGRATION

This chapter amply illustrates the effects of the body, the mind, and the environment on one another (Figure 5). Psychological and social factors can have direct effects on the physiology of the body and indirect effects on health by leading people to engage in behaviors that either promote or impair health. In turn, physical health affects people's emotional health and self-concept. People with a life-threatening or debilitating physical illness are at a greatly increased risk for depression and other emotional problems. For these reasons, health psychologists begin with the assumption that biology, psychology, and the social environment have reciprocal influences on one another. They then attempt to characterize these influences and determine their relative importance. Health psychologists also study how physical health problems impact other people—for example, caregivers of people with cancer, who are themselves at risk for stress and mental health problems like depression because of their caregiving role (e.g., Kim, Shaffer, Carver, & Cannady, 2014). Health psychologists also examine larger systems from a behavioral perspective, including doctor-patient communication, hospital systems, prevention programs, and public policies.

FIGURE 5 **Reciprocal Effects of Psychological, Social, and Biological Factors in Stress-Related Disorders.**

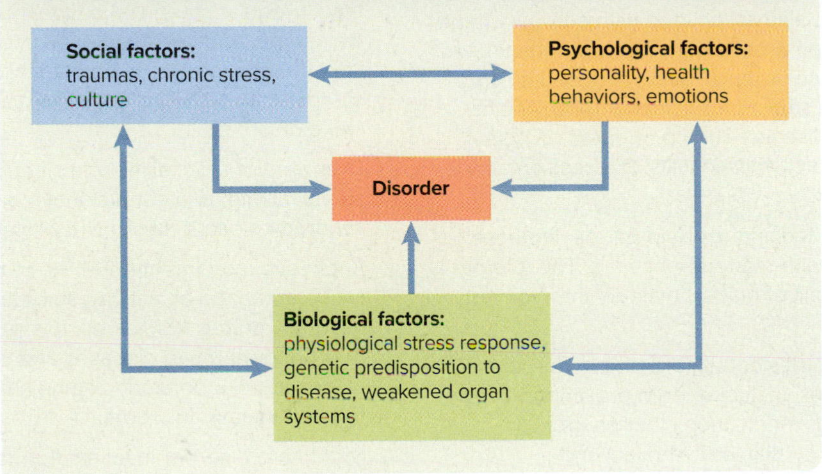

SHADES OF GRAY DISCUSSION

At first glance you might think that John's avoidance of thinking or talking about his cancer is an unhealthy way of coping. He is not drawing on social support from his children or his co-workers. You might even wonder if he is living in denial of his serious illness. But look closer. John appears to be engaging in a subtler form of social support characteristic of Asian cultures. He enjoys talking with his wife about their children and grandchildren and about visiting friends and family. For John, this may be a more acceptable means of coping than overtly asking for support from people other than his wife.

CHAPTER SUMMARY

- Three dimensions that affect the level of stress in situations are uncontrollability, unpredictability, and duration.
- The fight-or-flight response is a set of physiological changes the body undergoes when it faces a threat. In the short term it is adaptive, but if it persists for a long time it can cause damage to the body, a condition called allostatic load.
- Psychological factors associated with poorer health include pessimism and avoidance coping, while expressive writing and seeking social support are associated with better health. People with psychological disorders, especially depression, are at increased risk for a number of physical health problems.
- The immune system protects us from disease by identifying and killing pathogens and tumor cells. Chronic, uncontrollable stress; pessimism; and avoidance coping are associated with impaired immune system functioning, and with worse health in individuals with cancer or HIV/AIDS. Whether interventions to reduce stress or improve cognitions about stress affect the progression of cancer is not clear, however.
- Chronic stress is also associated with coronary heart disease. The Type A behavior pattern, characterized by a sense of time urgency, easily aroused hostility, and competitive striving for achievement, predicts coronary heart disease. The component of Type A that is most predictive is hostility. Depression also is predictive of CHD.
- Guided mastery techniques help people increase their positive health-related behaviors. The Internet is being used to deliver guided mastery interventions worldwide.
- Substance-induced sleep disorders are due to the use of substances, including both prescription medications (e.g., medications that control hypertension or cardiac arrhythmias) and nonprescription substances (e.g., alcohol and caffeine).
- Insomnia is difficulty initiating or maintaining sleep or sleep that chronically does not restore energy and alertness. It can be caused by disruptions in body temperature rhythms, stress, and faulty cognitions and habits concerning sleep. Cognitive-behavioral therapy is effective in treating insomnia. A variety of medications also are prescribed for insomnia, but cognitive-behavioral therapy is the most effective treatment.
- Hypersomnolence is chronic excessive sleepiness as evidenced by either prolonged sleep episodes or daytime sleep episodes that occur almost daily. Narcolepsy involves irresistible attacks of sleep; people with narcolepsy also have (1) cataplexy or (2) recurrent intrusions of elements of rapid eye movement (REM) sleep into the transition between sleep and wakefulness. Stimulants are prescribed for people with hypersomnia or narcolepsy.
- Sleep-related breathing disorders (central sleep apnea, obstructive sleep apnea/hypopnea syndrome, sleep-related hypoventilation) involve numerous brief sleep disturbances due to breathing problems. Continuous positive airway pressure (CPAP) machines are used to treat obstructive sleep apnea. Obstructive sleep apnea also is sometimes treated with weight loss and/or surgery. Serotonin reuptake inhibitors and stimulants are sometimes prescribed.
- Circadian rhythm sleep-wake disorder includes delayed sleep phase type, advanced sleep phase type, irregular sleep-wake type, non-24-hour sleep-wake type, and shift work type. Melatonin, stimulants, light therapy, and behavioral techniques to change sleep habits are used to treat circadian rhythm sleep-wake disorders.
- Disorders of arousal include sleep terrors, sleepwalking, and confusional arousal. These syndromes occur during NREM sleep.
- Rapid eye movement (REM) sleep behavior disorder is characterized by activity, sometimes violent or injurious, during REM sleep. It is associated with neurodegenerative diseases and can be treated with clonazepam, a benzodiazepine also commonly used to treat anxiety disorders.
- Nightmare disorder involves frequent experiences of nightmares during REM sleep.
- Restless legs syndrome is characterized by evening or nighttime feelings of creeping, crawling, and itching in the legs accompanied by a desire to move the legs. It can be caused by abnormalities in the dopamine system and by iron deficiencies, and treatment with drugs designed to reverse these factors can be effective.

KEY TERMS

allostatic load
immune system
coronary heart disease (CHD)
hypertension
Type A behavior pattern
guided mastery techniques
sleep disorders
substance-induced sleep disorder
insomnia disorder
hypersomnolence disorders
narcolepsy
cataplexy
central sleep apnea
sleep-related hypoventilation
breathing-related sleep disorder
obstructive sleep apnea hypopnea syndrome
circadian rhythm sleep-wake disorder
disorders of arousal
sleep terror disorder
sleepwalking
rapid eye movement (REM) sleep behavior disorder
nightmare disorder
restless legs syndrome (RLS)

Chapter 16

©Rich Legg/Getty Images

Mental Health and the Law

CHAPTER OUTLINE

Mental Health Law Along the Continuum

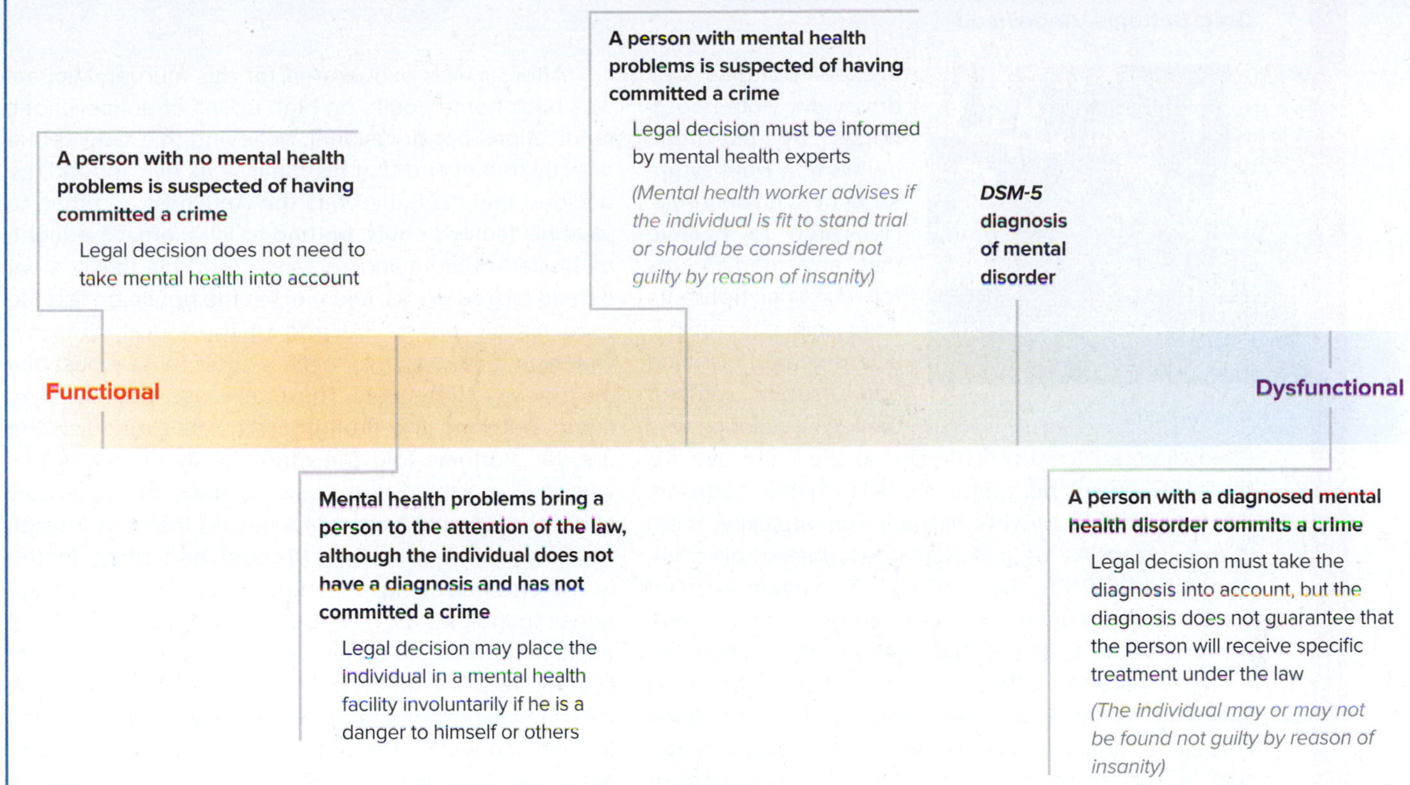
A person with no mental health problems is suspected of having committed a crime
Legal decision does not need to take mental health into account
A person with mental health problems is suspected of having committed a crime
Legal decision must be informed by mental health experts
(Mental health worker advises if the individual is fit to stand trial or should be considered not guilty by reason of insanity)
DSM-5 diagnosis of mental disorder
Functional
Dysfunctional
Mental health problems bring a person to the attention of the law, although the individual does not have a diagnosis and has not committed a crime
Legal decision may place the individual in a mental health facility involuntarily if he is a danger to himself or others
A person with a diagnosed mental health disorder commits a crime
Legal decision must take the diagnosis into account, but the diagnosis does not guarantee that the person will receive specific treatment under the law
(The individual may or may not be found not guilty by reason of insanity)

Think back to before you took this course, before you had a sense of how fuzzy our definitions and understanding of mental disorders can be. Imagine yourself hearing a report on the news about a college student who posted videos of himself on YouTube ranting about injustices done to him and then went on a shooting rampage on his college campus and was subsequently caught and jailed. Back then, you might have thought that it should have been obvious to campus authorities that there was something seriously wrong with this person. Once the person was incarcerated, you might have thought the authorities should simply determine whether he had a mental disorder that caused him to be violent and then take appropriate action. If his violence was the result of a mental disorder, he should be given treatment to overcome the mental disorder; if his violence was not due to a mental disorder but was voluntary and intentional, he should be incarcerated.

Now you understand that the situation is not that clear-cut. The *DSM* provides criteria for diagnosing mental disorders, but whether a particular individual's behaviors meet those criteria is often a judgment call. Furthermore, we are limited in our ability to generalize from the research literature to individual cases. For example, just because a person has a mental disorder that may be associated with an increased risk of aggression or violence, we cannot know for certain whether this particular individual will be violent in the future.

When someone who appears to have mental health problems interacts with the judicial system, these judgment calls become even more complex. The fuzziness in our diagnostic criteria and in our understanding of mental disorders combines with the difficult ethical and social issues these cases involve. A *DSM-5* diagnosis of a mental disorder does not ensure that an individual will be treated in a particular way by the law. For example, a diagnosed mental disorder is not enough to ensure that an individual receives needed treatment and may not exonerate an individual who has committed a crime. Mental health law is further complicated by the fact that the laws concerning people with mental health problems vary from region to region and have changed dramatically over the past 50 years.

Thus, the fuzziness in our diagnostic systems that is inherent in the fact that psychological problems fall along a continuum, combined with the fuzziness in laws and their application to people with mental health problems, means that a great deal of subjective judgment is involved in mental health law.

Extraordinary People

Greg Bottoms, *Angelhead*

©William DiLillo

Michael Bottoms was driven to violent outbursts by psychotic beliefs that were symptoms of schizophrenia. He came to believe that any medications for his schizophrenia were part of a conspiracy to control his mind and usually refused them. His violence was often directed toward his family, to the point that his brother Greg and his parents would lock their bedroom doors at night to prevent Michael from attacking them in their sleep. As Greg Bottoms describes in his book *Angelhead* (2000), the family tried to have Michael institutionalized but was told they could not unless they proved he was an imminent danger to himself or others.

Eventually the family found an institution that would take their insurance and placed Michael there. He hated the place, though, refused his medications, and attempted suicide. This landed him in a state psychiatric hospital for a while. Later he "confessed" to a murder he had not committed, having been convinced by the voices in his head that he was guilty. He was jailed, but DNA evidence proved Michael couldn't have committed the murder.

After he was exonerated for this murder, Michael was back home again, on high doses of antipsychotic medications but delusional, believing that God spoke directly to him and that his family was evil. Indeed, he decided that his father was the Antichrist and that, to save his family's souls, he had to kill them. One night, as his father lay dying of cancer and his family slept behind locked doors, Michael set the house on fire. He rode his bicycle to the end of the street, then sat watching, expecting his family's souls to float past him on the way to heaven. The family escaped. As they stood watching the firefighters try to extinguish the fire, Mr. Bottoms told the other family members this was the best thing that could happen, because now Michael could really be put away. In the next instant, however, he feared that Michael had been in the house and was dying in the fire. He tried to run into the house to look for Michael, but the firefighters held him back. Meanwhile, Michael rode up on his bicycle, nonchalant. A police officer asked Michael if he could ask him some questions, and Michael held out his hands for the handcuffs. Then he turned to his mother and asked her casually what she was going to make for breakfast. Michael confessed to setting the fire with the purpose of killing his family. He was convicted for attempted murder and arson and was sent to prison for 30 years.

Mental health professionals are asked regularly to help families such as the Bottoms family deal with the laws and social systems that guide the treatment of people with psychological disorders. Fundamental questions about society's values confront the personal wishes of people with mental disorders and their families: Does society have a right to impose treatment on an individual who doesn't want it? Under what conditions should people be absolved of responsibility for behaviors that harm others? Should the diagnosis of a psychological disorder entitle a person to special services and protection against discrimination?

This chapter explores how the law becomes involved in the lives of people with mental health problems, focusing first on when a person can be committed to a mental health facility against his or her will. Then we examine how the law regards a person charged with a crime who might have a mental disorder. Finally, we discuss how society treats a person who has a mental disorder and is convicted of a crime.

CIVIL COMMITMENT

In the best circumstances, people who need treatment for a psychological disorder seek it themselves. They work with mental health professionals to find medication and/or psychotherapy to reduce their symptoms and keep their disorder under control. Many people who have serious psychological problems, however, do not recognize their need for treatment or may refuse treatment for a variety of reasons. For example, Michael Bottoms believed the doctors treating him were part of a conspiracy and refused to follow their prescriptions. A man experiencing a manic episode may enjoy many of the symptoms—the high energy, inflated self-esteem, and grandiose thoughts—and not want to take medication that would reduce those symptoms. A teenager who is abusing illegal drugs may believe that it is her right to do so and that there is nothing wrong with her abuse. Can these people be forced to enter mental institutions and to undergo treatment against their will? These are the questions we address in this section.

Criteria for Civil Commitment

Prior to the mid-twentieth century, in the United States the **need for treatment** was sufficient cause to hospitalize people against their will and force them to undergo treatment. Such involuntary hospitalization is called **civil commitment.** All that was needed for civil commitment was a certificate signed by two physicians stating that a person needed treatment and was not agreeing to it voluntarily. The person could then be confined, often indefinitely, without recourse to an attorney, a hearing, or an appeal (Meyer & Weaver, 2006).

The need for treatment alone is no longer sufficient legal cause for civil commitment in most states in the United States. This change came about as part of the patients' rights movement of the 1960s, which raised concerns about violations of the personal freedoms and civil liberties of mental patients. Opponents of the civil commitment process argued that it allowed people to be incarcerated simply for having alternative lifestyles or different political or moral values (Szasz, 1963, 1977). Certainly, there were many cases in the former Soviet Union and other countries of political dissidents being labeled mentally ill and in need of treatment and then being incarcerated in prisons for years. There also were disturbing cases of the misuse of civil commitment proceedings in the United States. In the 1860s, for example, Illinois law allowed a husband to have his wife involuntarily committed without evidence that she had lost touch with reality or was dangerous. For example, Mrs. E. P. W. Packard was committed by her husband for holding "unacceptable" and "sick" political or moral views (Weiner & Wettstein, 1993). Mrs. Packard remained hospitalized for 3 years before winning her release; she then began crusading against civil commitment.

Procedurally, most states now mandate that persons being considered for involuntary commitment have the right to a public hearing, the right to counsel, the right to call and confront witnesses, the right to appeal decisions, and the right to be placed in the least restrictive treatment setting. In practice, however, judges typically defer to the judgment of mental health professionals about a person's mental health and whether the criteria for commitment are met (Melton et al., 2017; Meyer & Weaver, 2006). Even attorneys who are supposed to be upholding an individual's rights tend to acquiesce to the judgment of mental health professionals, particularly if the attorney is court-appointed, as is often the case.

In the United States and many other countries, individuals must be judged to meet one of the following criteria in order to be committed to a psychiatric facility against their will: (1) grave disability, (2) dangerousness to self, or (3) dangerousness to others. In addition, most states require that the danger people pose to themselves or to others be imminent—in other words, if they are not immediately incarcerated, they or someone else will likely be harmed in the very near future. Finally, all persons committed to psychiatric facilities must be diagnosed with a mental disorder, although the definition of mental disorders or mental illnesses varies from state to state (Meyer & Weaver, 2006). In particular, some states exclude substance abuse or dependence and mental retardation from their list of mental disorders or mental illnesses.

Grave Disability

The **grave disability** criterion requires that people be so incapacitated by a mental disorder that they cannot provide for their basic needs of food, clothing, and shelter. This criterion is, in theory, much more severe than the need for treatment criterion because it requires that the person's survival be in immediate danger because of a mental disorder.

You might think that the grave disability criterion could be used to hospitalize homeless people living on the streets who appear to be psychotic and unable to take care of their basic needs. In the winter of 1988, New York City Mayor Ed Koch invoked the legal principle of *parens patriae* (sovereign as parent) to have mentally ill homeless people taken to mental health facilities. Mayor Koch argued that it was the city's duty to protect these mentally ill homeless people from the ravages of the winter weather because they were unable to protect themselves. One of the homeless people who was involuntarily hospitalized was 40-year-old Joyce Brown, who subsequently was diagnosed with paranoid schizophrenia. Brown had been living on the streets on and off for years, resisting efforts by her family to get her into psychiatric treatment. Brown and the American Civil Liberties Union contested her commitment and won her release on the grounds that the city had no right to incarcerate Brown if she had no intention of being treated (Kasindorf, 1988).

One legal precedent relevant to Joyce Brown's release was *O'Connor v. Donaldson* (1975). Kenneth Donaldson had been committed to a Florida state hospital for 14 years. Donaldson's father originally had him committed, believing that Donaldson was delusional and therefore a danger to himself. At the time, Florida law allowed people to be committed if their mental disorder might impair their ability to manage their finances or to protect themselves against being cheated by others. Throughout his hospitalization, Donaldson refused medication because it violated his Christian Science beliefs. The superintendent, Dr. J. B. O'Connor, considered this refusal to be a symptom of Donaldson's mental disorder. Even though Donaldson had been caring for himself adequately before his hospitalization and had friends who offered to help care for him if he was released from the hospital, O'Connor and the hospital continually refused Donaldson's requests for release. Donaldson sued on the grounds that he had received only custodial care during his hospitalization and was not a danger to himself. He requested to be released to the care of his friends and family. The Supreme Court agreed, ruling that "a State cannot constitutionally confine . . . a nondangerous individual, who is capable of surviving safely in freedom by himself or with the help of willing and responsible family and friends" (*O'Connor v. Donaldson*, 1975, p. 4).

In practice, however, most people involuntarily committed because of grave disability do not have the ACLU championing their rights or the personal ability to file suit. Often, they are people with few financial resources or friends. Their family members may also have serious mental disorders. The elderly mentally ill are especially likely to be committed because of grave disability (Turkheimer & Parry, 1992). Often, these people are committed to psychiatric facilities because their families are unable to care for them and there are not enough less restrictive treatment facilities available in their communities.

Dangerousness to Self

The criterion **dangerousness to self** is most often invoked when it is believed that a person is imminently suicidal. In such cases, the person often is held in an inpatient psychiatric facility for a few days while undergoing further evaluation and possibly treatment. Most states allow short-term commitments without a court hearing in emergency situations such as this. All that is needed is a certification by the attending mental health professionals that the individual is in imminent danger to him- or herself. If the mental health professionals judge that the person needs further treatment but the person does not voluntarily agree to treatment, they can go to court to request that the person be committed for a longer period of time.

Dangerousness to Others

Dangerousness to others is the third criterion under which people can be committed involuntarily. If a person with a mental disorder is going to hurt another person if set free, then society has claimed the right to protect itself. While this action may seem justified, the appropriateness of this criterion rests on predictions of who will be dangerous and who will not. It is exceedingly difficult to make such predictions accurately (Monahan & Walker, 2014). We can all recall incidents in which individuals with severe mental health problems became violent and the media and public cried "How could we not have seen this coming?" In 2007, college student Seung-Hui Cho, who had been diagnosed with multiple mental disorders, shot and killed 32 people and wounded 17 others on the campus of Virginia Polytechnic University (also known as Virginia Tech). Professors and students had raised alarms with university officials because of Cho's disturbing writings and behaviors, and Cho had been investigated for stalking a woman student. He was ordered by a court to undergo outpatient treatment for his behaviors but did not comply and was not forced to do so. In 2009, U.S. Army psychiatrist Major Nidal Hasan shot and killed 13 people at Fort Hood, Texas. Students and faculty at Walter Reed Hospital, where Hasan trained, called Hasan's behavior "disconnected, aloof, paranoid, belligerent, and schizoid" (Zwerdling, 2009). Still, no one connected the dots to predict that Hasan could be a danger to others, and no action was taken to remove him from his post.

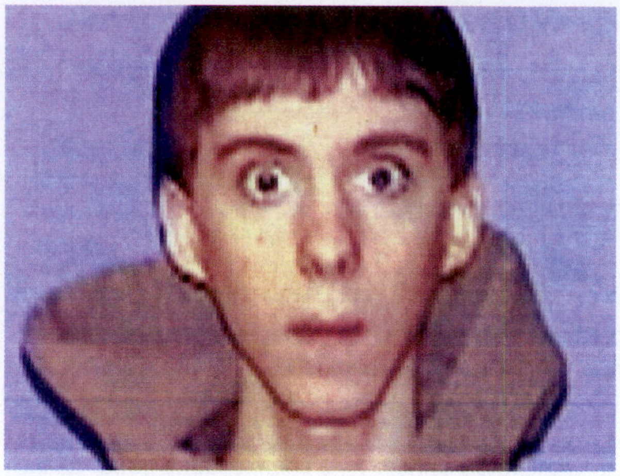

Adam Lanza, who had previously exhibited behavior potentially indicative of a mental disorder, killed 20 children and 6 adults before fatally shooting himself at the Sandy Hook Elementary School in Newtown, Connecticut. ©*Uncredited/AP Images*

If mental health professionals believe that an individual may harm another person, they have a duty to warn that person, even if this violates a client's confidentiality. This duty to warn was established in a decision in the case of *Tarasoff v. Regents of the University of California* (1974). Tatiana Tarasoff was a student at the University of California at Berkeley in the late 1960s. A graduate student named Prosenjit Poddar was infatuated with Tarasoff, who had rejected him. Poddar told his therapist in the student counseling service that he planned to kill Tarasoff when she returned to campus from vacation. The therapist informed the campus police, who picked up Poddar for questioning. Poddar agreed to leave Tarasoff alone, and the campus police released him. Two months later, Poddar killed Tarasoff. Tarasoff's parents sued the university, arguing that the therapist should have protected Tarasoff from Poddar. The California courts agreed and established the precedent that therapists have a duty to warn persons who are threatened by their clients during therapy sessions and to take actions to protect those persons (Meyer & Weaver, 2006).

After Seung-Hui Cho's shooting rampage, officials at Virginia Tech reevaluated their interpretation of federal privacy laws that had led them not to share information about Cho's behavior or diagnoses with concerned faculty and administrators prior to the shooting. In 2008, the U.S. Department of Education proposed changes in the regulations governing the balance between protecting students' privacy rights and public safety in light of the Cho incident. Virginia Tech also was criticized for delays in warning the campus of danger once the shooting rampage began. Since this incident, many universities have instituted new policies and alarm systems to alert students, faculty, and staff when a violent incident is erupting.

Tragedies like the shootings by Seung-Hui Cho at Virginia Tech University (pictured) and Adam Lanza at Sandy Hook Elementary School have led the public to call for more intervention for troubled, potentially violent youth. *©MSNBC/ZUMA Press/Blacksburg/Virginia/USA/Newscom*

Violence by People with Mental Disorders

Incidents such as the shootings discussed above lead the public to believe that people with a mental disorder are much more prone to violence than people without a mental disorder. They also lead to public demands for more intervention with troubled youth, regardless of whether they and their parents want it. One group of researchers examined the public's beliefs about the potential for harm to self or others by youth with mental health problems and the public's willingness to coerce these youth to get treatment (Pescosolido, Fettes, Martin, Monahan, & McLeod, 2007). They asked over 1,100 adults to read vignettes depicting youth with attention-deficit/hyperactivity disorder (ADHD), major depression, asthma, or "daily troubles." Many more youth with ADHD or major depression were perceived as somewhat likely or very likely to be dangerous to themselves or others (33 percent for ADHD, 81 percent for major depression), compared to youth with asthma (15 percent) or "daily troubles" (13 percent). Over one-third of the adults in the study were willing to use legal means to force the youth with major depression to get mental health treatment. Adults who labeled the youth with ADHD or major depression "mentally ill" were twice as likely to see a potential for violence in these youth and five times more likely to support forced treatment, compared to adults who didn't apply the label "mentally ill" to the youth. These results suggest that the public associates diagnoses of mental disorders in youth with dangerousness and that a substantial portion of the public is ready to use the legal system to force youth with mental disorders into treatment (see Pescosolido, 2013).

Are people with a mental disorder actually more prone to violence than those without a mental disorder? Research suggests that the answer is complex (Monahan & Skeem, 2014). In one major study, researchers followed 1,136 men and women with mental disorders for 1 year after they were discharged from a psychiatric hospital, monitoring their self-reports of violent behaviors, reports in police and hospital records, and reports by other informants, such as family members (Steadman et al., 1998). Serious violent acts were defined as battery that resulted in physical injury, sexual assaults, assaultive acts that involved the use of a weapon, and threats made with a weapon in hand. The former psychiatric patients' records of violent activity were compared to those of 519 people living in the same neighborhoods the patients lived in after their hospital discharge. This community group was interviewed only once, at the end of the year-long study, and was asked about violent behavior in the past 10 weeks.

The likelihood that the former patients would commit a violent act was strongly related to their specific diagnosis and whether they had a substance abuse problem. About 18 percent of the former patients who had a diagnosis of a major mental disorder (e.g., schizophrenia, major depression, some other psychotic disorder) without a history of substance abuse committed a serious violent act in the year following discharge, compared to 31 percent of those with a major mental disorder and a history of substance abuse and 43 percent of those with a diagnosis of "other" mental disorder (i.e., a personality or adjustment disorder) and a co-occurring substance abuse problem (Steadman et al., 1998). The researchers were somewhat surprised to find that the former patients were most likely to commit a violent act in the first couple of months following their discharge and less likely to do so as the year wore on (Figure 1). They suggested that patients might still be in crisis shortly after their hospitalization and that it may take some months for social support systems and treatment to begin to affect their behavior (Steadman et al., 1998).

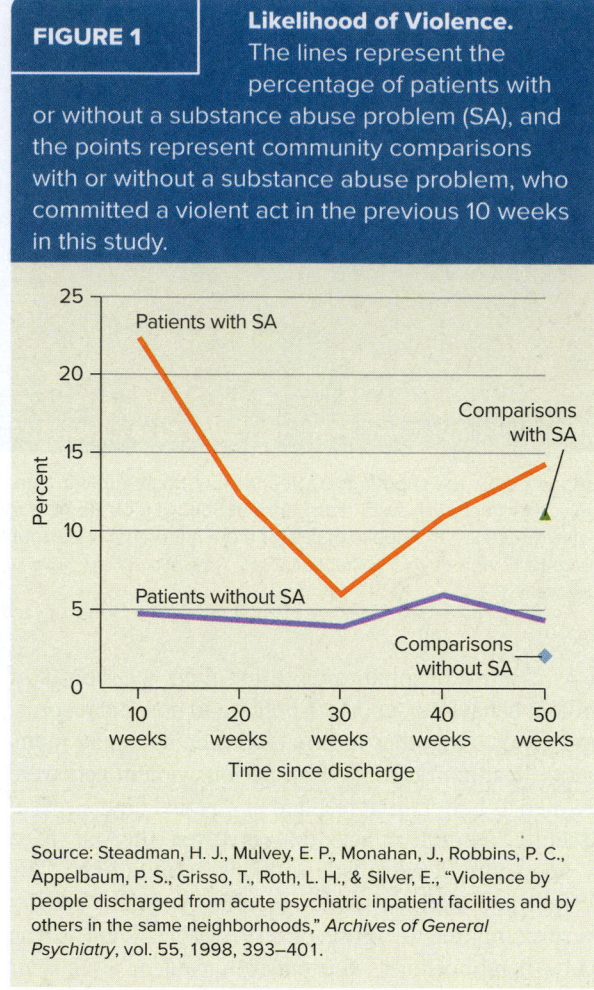

FIGURE 1 **Likelihood of Violence.** The lines represent the percentage of patients with or without a substance abuse problem (SA), and the points represent community comparisons with or without a substance abuse problem, who committed a violent act in the previous 10 weeks in this study.

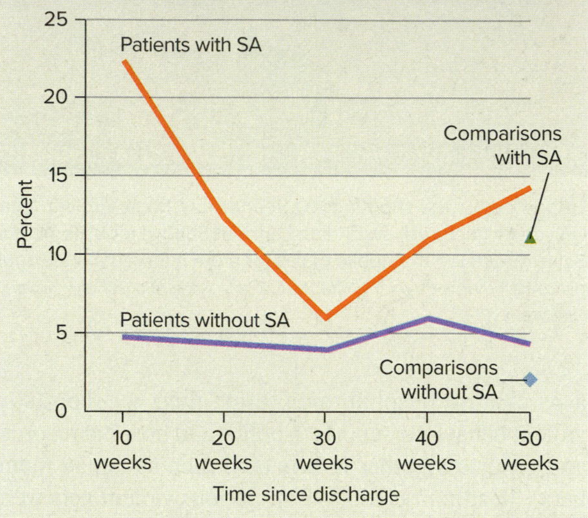

Source: Steadman, H. J., Mulvey, E. P., Monahan, J., Robbins, P. C., Appelbaum, P. S., Grisso, T., Roth, L. H., & Silver, E., "Violence by people discharged from acute psychiatric inpatient facilities and by others in the same neighborhoods," *Archives of General Psychiatry*, vol. 55, 1998, 393–401.

The rate of violence in the community sample was also strongly related to whether individuals had a history of substance abuse. Eleven percent of those with a substance abuse problem committed a violent act during the year of the study, compared to 3 percent of those with no substance abuse problem (Steadman et al., 1998). Although the overall rate of violence in the community sample was lower than in the patient sample, this difference was statistically significant only when the researchers considered violence committed by the former patients shortly after their discharge. By the end of that year, the former patients were no more likely to commit a violent act than were the people in the community comparison group.

The targets of violence by both the former patients and the community members most often were family members, followed by friends and acquaintances. The former patients actually were somewhat less likely than the comparison group to commit a violent act against a stranger (13.8 percent of the acts committed by former patients compared to 22.2 percent of the acts committed by the comparison group).

The rates of violence recorded in this study may seem high, for both the patient group and the comparison group. The patient group probably represented people with more serious psychological disorders who were facing acute crises in their lives. The comparison group consisted largely of people with low socioeconomic status living in impoverished neighborhoods. These contextual factors may account for the relatively high rates of violence in both groups.

The researchers who conducted this study emphasized that their data show how inappropriate it is to consider "former mental patients" to be a homogeneous group of people all prone to violence. The presence of substance abuse problems was a strong predictor of violent behavior both in this group and in the group of people who had not been mental patients; subsequent studies have also emphasized substance use as a key factor (see Swanson, McGinty, Fazel, & Mays, 2015). Moreover, the majority of people with serious mental disorders did not commit any violent acts in the year after their discharge, especially against random strangers, contrary to what media depictions of former mental patients often suggest.

Other research has suggested that violence by mentally ill women tends to be underestimated by clinicians (Coontz, Lidz, & Mulvey, 1994; Robbins, Monahan, & Silver, 2003). Clinicians do not expect mentally ill women to be violent to the same degree that they expect mentally ill men to be violent. As a result, they do not probe mentally ill women for evidence of a tendency toward violence as much as they do mentally ill men. In reality, however, mentally ill women and mentally ill men are equally likely to commit violent acts against others (Robbins et al., 2003; Sturup, Monahan, & Kristiansson, 2013). The victims of mentally ill women's violent acts are most likely to be family members; mentally ill men also are most often violent toward family members, but they commit violent acts against strangers more often than do mentally ill women (Newhill, Mulvey, & Lidz, 1995). Mentally ill men who commit violence are more likely to have been drinking before the violence and to be arrested following it than are mentally ill women who commit violence (Robbins et al., 2003).

Racial stereotypes lead people to expect mentally ill persons from ethnic minority groups to be more likely to commit acts of violence than white mentally ill people. However, there are no differences between ethnic groups in the rates of violence among mentally ill people (see Rueve & Welton, 2008).

Multiple meta-analyses and reviews have found that people with a mental disorder on average are more likely to commit violent acts than are those without a mental disorder, with rates varying depending on a number of factors (Choe, Teplin, & Abram, 2008; Fazel, Långström, Hjern, Grann, & Lichtenstein,

2009; Fazel, Lichtenstein, Grann, Goodwin, & Långström, 2010). Risk of violence is heightened with specific symptoms like hallucinations, delusions, and uncontrolled anger, but the most important factor is substance abuse (Swanson et al., 2015). It is important to note that people with mental disorders are much more likely to be the *victims* of violence than they are to be the perpetrators. They are also more likely to be victimized than people without a mental disorder.

Prevalence of Involuntary Commitment

How often are people involuntarily committed to a psychiatric facility? The data necessary to answer this question are sparse, but the available studies suggest that about 25 percent of admissions to inpatient psychiatric facilities in the United States are involuntary and that about 15 to 20 percent of inpatient admissions in European countries are involuntary (Monahan et al., 2001). Admissions to state and county mental hospitals are much more likely to be involuntary than are admissions to other types of hospitals (Table 1). In addition, 12 to 20 percent of patients of outpatient psychiatric facilities report having been ordered by civil courts to participate in outpatient treatment (Monahan et al., 2005). Court orders for outpatient care were more common among individuals who lived in residential psychiatric facilities and who had poor social support and poor psychosocial functioning, a recent history of violent behavior, recent police encounters, substance abuse problems, and higher rates of lifetime hospitalizations and involuntary hospitalizations (Swartz, Swanson, Kim, & Petrila, 2006). Involuntary commitment and court-ordered treatment rates also vary widely from state to state (Swartz, Bhattacharya, Robertson, & Swanson, 2017; Testa & West, 2010).

TABLE 1 Frequency of Involuntary Admissions to Psychiatric Facilities

These data indicate the percent of all admissions to various types of psychiatric facilities that involve involuntary commitments. Data are from the United States in 1986.

Type of Facility	Percent of All Admissions That Are Involuntary
State and county hospitals	61.6%
Multiservice mental health organizations (e.g., community mental health centers)	46.1
Private psychiatric hospitals	15.6
Nonfederal general hospitals	14.8
Veterans Administration hospitals	5.6

Source: Monahan, J., Bonnie, R. J., Appelbaum, P. S., Hyde, P. S., Steadman, H. J., & Swartz, M. S., "Mandated community treatment: Beyond outpatient commitment," *Psychiatric Services*, vol. 52, 2001, 1198–1205.

The numbers in Table 1 probably underestimate the number of people coerced into mental health care treatment, because parents and legal guardians often "volunteer" a protesting child or incompetent adult for admission (Monahan et al., 2001). In one study, nearly 50 percent of the adults admitted voluntarily to inpatient psychiatric facilities reported that someone other than themselves had initiated their going to the hospital, and 14 percent of the patients were under the custody of someone else at the time of admission (Hoge, Poythress, et al., 1997; Segal, Laurie, & Franskoviak, 2004). Nearly 40 percent of the voluntary patients believed they would have been involuntarily committed if they had not agreed to be hospitalized. Some of the patients felt they had been coerced by their therapists, who did not include them in the admissions process. Patients involuntarily committed often may need treatment that they cannot acknowledge they need. About half of those patients who felt they were coerced into treatment eventually acknowledge that they needed treatment, but about half continue to believe treatment was unnecessary (Gardner et al., 1999).

Marvin Swartz and colleagues (2010) evaluated the outcomes for individuals involuntarily committed to outpatient mental health care in New York over an 8-year period. Compared to the period before they were ordered to receive treatment, the involuntarily committed individuals had fewer hospitalizations, were more likely to have an adequate supply of medication appropriate for their diagnosis, and were more likely to be receiving intensive management of their condition. In addition, they had fewer hospitalizations than individuals with similar mental health problems who were receiving treatment voluntarily. Thus, it seems that involuntary treatment can result in several positive outcomes for individuals with serious mental health problems (Swartz et al., 2017)

PATIENTS' RIGHTS

Numerous court cases over the years have established that people committed to mental health institutions retain most of their civil rights. They also have certain additional rights, which we discuss in this section.

Right to Treatment

One basic right of people who have been committed is the **right to treatment.** In the past, mental patients, including both those involuntarily committed and

One fundamental right of people committed to a mental health facility is the right to be treated rather than simply warehoused. *©Oleksandr Rupeta/Alamy Stock Photo*

those seeking treatment voluntarily, were often only warehoused. The conditions in which they lived were appalling, with little stimulation and few pleasantries, let alone treatment for their disorders. In *Wyatt v. Stickney* (1971), patient Ricky Wyatt and others filed a class action suit against a custodial facility in Alabama, charging that they received no useful treatment and lived in minimally acceptable living conditions. After 33 years in the courts, the case finally was settled in 2003. From the court ruling came four standards, known as the "Wyatt Standards," for the evaluation of care of psychiatric patients: (1) They must be provided with a humane psychological and physical environment, (2) there must be qualified and sufficient staff for the administration of treatment, (3) there must be individualized treatment plans, and (4) restrictions of patient freedoms must be kept to a minimum (Sundram, 2009).

Right to Refuse Treatment

Another basic right is the **right to refuse treatment.** One of the greatest fears of people committed against their will is that they will be given drugs or other treatments that rob them of their consciousness and their free will. Many states now do not allow mental institutions or prisons to administer treatments without the informed consent of patients. **Informed consent** means that a patient accepts treatment after receiving a full and understandable explanation of the treatment being offered and making a decision based on his or her judgment of the risks and benefits of that treatment (Meyer & Weaver, 2006).

The right to refuse treatment is not recognized in some states, however, and in most states this right can be overruled in many circumstances (Monahan et al., 2001; Testa & West, 2010). Particularly if a patient is psychotic or manic, it may be judged that he or she cannot make a reasonable decision about treatment. Up to 45 percent of psychiatric inpatients may be incompetent to make decisions about their own treatment (Lepping, Stanly, & Turner, 2015). In some jurisdictions, the simple fact that patients have a psychiatric diagnosis is enough to have them declared incompetent to make decisions, especially if the diagnosis is schizophrenia (Appelbaum, Appelbaum, & Grisso, 1998). Yet studies using reliable measures of patients' ability to make rational decisions suggest that as many as 75 percent of those with schizophrenia and 90 percent of those with depression have adequate decision-making capacity (Grisso & Appelbaum, 1995; Larkin & Hutton, 2017).

Patients' psychiatrists or families may seek court rulings allowing them to administer treatment even if the patients refuse treatment. Judges most often agree with the psychiatrists' or families' requests to force treatment on patients. Most cases in which patients refuse treatment never go to court, however. Instead, clinicians and family members pressure patients to accept treatment, and most patients eventually agree to treatment after initially refusing (Griffin, Steadman, & Petrila, 2002; Monahan et al., 2001).

COMPETENCE TO STAND TRIAL

One fundamental principle of law is that, in order to stand trial, accused individuals must have a rational understanding of both the charges against them and the proceedings of the trial and must be able to participate in their defense. People who do not have an understanding of what is happening to them in a courtroom and who cannot participate in their defense are said to be **incompetent to stand trial.** Incompetence may involve impairment in several capacities, including the capacity to understand information, to think rationally about alternative courses of action, to make good choices, and to appreciate one's situation as a criminal defendant (Hoge, Bonnie, et al., 1997; Stafford & Sadoff, 2011).

Impaired competence may be a common problem. Defense attorneys suspect impaired competence in their clients in up to 10 percent of cases. Although only a handful of these clients are referred for formal evaluation, about 60,000 evaluations of criminal defendants for competence to stand trial are performed every year in the United States (Bonnie & Grisso, 2000). Competence judgments are one of the

Competence to stand trial is one of the most common judgments psychologists are asked to help courts make.
©Rich Legg/E+ /Getty Images

most frequent types of judgments that mental health professionals are asked to make for the courts. Judges appear to value the testimony of mental health experts concerning defendants' competence and rarely rule against these experts' recommendations.

The consequences of competence judgments for defendants are great. If defendants are judged incompetent, trials are postponed as long as there is reason to believe they will become competent in the foreseeable future, and defendants may be forced to receive treatment. On the other hand, incompetent defendants who are wrongly judged competent may not contribute adequately to their defense and may be wrongly convicted and incarcerated. Defendants who are suspected of being incompetent are described by their attorneys as much less helpful in establishing the facts of their case and much less actively involved in making decisions about their defense (MacArthur Research Network on Mental Health and the Law, 1998).

Not surprisingly, defendants with a long history of psychiatric problems, particularly schizophrenia or psychotic symptoms, are more likely than those without such a history to be referred for competence evaluations (Pirelli, Gottdiener, & Zapf, 2011). Defendants referred for competence evaluations also tend to have less education and to be poor, unemployed, and unmarried, compared to those not referred for evaluation. There is also some evidence that ethnic/racial minority individuals are more likely than whites to be judged incompetent to stand trial (Pirelli et al., 2011).

Psychologists have developed tests of those cognitive attributes important to the ability to follow legal proceedings, and people who perform poorly on these tests are more likely to be judged incompetent to stand trial. These tests have not been widely used, however (Appelbaum, 2007). Instead, judgments of incompetence usually are made for people who have existing diagnoses of psychotic disorders or who have symptoms indicating severe psychopathology, such as gross disorientation, delusions, hallucinations, and formal thought disorder (Cochrane, Grisso, & Frederick, 2001; Pirelli et al., 2011; Larkin & Hutton, 2017).

THE INSANITY DEFENSE

Insanity is a legal term rather than a psychological or medical term, and it has been defined in various ways. The **insanity defense** is based on the belief that people cannot be held fully responsible for illegal acts if they were so mentally incapacitated at the time of committing the acts that they could not conform to the rules of society (Kimonis, 2015; Meyer & Weaver, 2006). Note that people do not

John Hinckley was judged not guilty by reason of insanity in the shooting of President Ronald Reagan. This judgment inspired a reappraisal of the insanity defense. *©FBI/ZUMA Press/ Washington/District of Columbia/U.S./Newscom*

have to be chronically mentally incapacitated for the insanity defense to apply. They only have to be judged to have been incapacitated at the time they committed the illegal acts. This judgment can be difficult to make.

The insanity defense has been one of the most controversial applications of psychology to the law. The lay public often thinks of the insanity defense as a means by which guilty people "get off." When the insanity defense has been used successfully in celebrated cases—as when John Hinckley successfully used this defense after shooting President Ronald Reagan and the president's press secretary, Jim Brady, in 1981—there have been calls to eliminate it altogether (Kimonis, 2015). Indeed, these celebrated cases have often led to reappraisals of the insanity defense and redefinitions of the legal meaning of insanity.

The insanity defense actually is used much less often than the public tends to think. As shown in Table 2, fewer than 1 in 100 defendants in felony cases files an insanity plea, and only 26 percent of these cases result in acquittal (Melton et al., 2017; Silver, Cirincione, & Steadman, 1994). This means that only about 1 in 400 people charged with a felony are judged not guilty by reason of insanity. About 265 of these people have diagnoses of schizophrenia, and most have a history of psychiatric hospitalizations and previous crimes (McGreevy, Steadman, & Callahan, 1991; Melton et al., 2017).

TABLE 2 Comparison of Public Perceptions of the Insanity Defense with Actual Use and Results

The public has the perception that many more accused persons use the insanity defense successfully than is actually the case.

	Public Perception	Reality
Percent of felony indictments for which an insanity plea is made	37%	1%
Percent of insanity pleas resulting in "not guilty by reason of insanity"	44%	26%
Percent of persons "not guilty by reason of insanity" sent to mental hospitals	51%	85%
Percent of persons "not guilty by reason of insanity" set free	26%	15%
Percent given conditional release		12%
Percent assigned to outpatient treatment		3%
Percent given unconditional release		1%
Length of confinement of persons "not guilty by reason of insanity":		
All crimes		21.8 months
Murder		32.5 months

Source: Silver, E., Cirincione, C., & Steadman, H. J., "Demythologizing inaccurate perceptions of the insanity defense," *Law & Human Behavior*, vol. 18, 1994, 63–70.

Almost 90 percent of the people who are acquitted after pleading the insanity defense are male, and 66 percent are white (McGreevy et al., 1991; Warren, Murrie, Chauhan, Dietz, & Morris, 2004). The reasons why men and whites are more likely to successfully plead the insanity defense are unclear but may have to do with their greater access to competent attorneys who can effectively argue the insanity defense. In the past decade or two, as society has become more aware of the plight of abused and battered women, increasing numbers of women are pleading the insanity defense after injuring or killing a partner who had been abusing them.

One such case is that of Lorena Bobbitt. According to Bobbitt, her husband, John, had sexually and emotionally abused her for years. One night in 1994, John returned home drunk and raped Lorena. In what her attorneys described as a brief psychotic episode, Lorena cut off her husband's penis and threw it away. She was acquitted of charges of malicious injury by reason of temporary insanity. She was referred to a mental institution for further evaluation and was released a few months later.

Even when a defendant is judged not guilty by reason of insanity, he or she usually is not set free. Of those people acquitted because of insanity, about 85 percent are sent to mental hospitals, and all but 1 percent are put under some type of supervision and care. Of those who are sent to mental hospitals, the average length of stay (or incarceration) in the hospital is almost 3 years when all types of crimes are considered, and over 6 years for those who have been accused of murder (and acquitted by reason of insanity) (McGreevy et al., 1991; Silver et al., 1994). Some states stipulate that people judged not guilty by reason of insanity cannot be incarcerated in mental institutions for longer than they would have served in prison had they been judged guilty of their crimes, but not all states have this rule. In short, there is little evidence that the insanity defense is widely used to help people avoid incarceration for their crimes.

Insanity Defense Rules

Five rules have been used in modern history to evaluate defendants' pleas that they be judged not guilty by reason of insanity. These rules are listed in Table 3.

M'Naghten Rule

The first insanity defense rule was the **M'Naghten rule** (Kimonis, 2015; Melton et al., 2017). Daniel M'Naghten lived in England in the mid-1800s and believed that the English Tory party was persecuting him. He set out to kill the Tory prime minister but mistakenly shot the prime minister's secretary. At his trial in 1843, the jury judged M'Naghten not guilty by reason of insanity. There was a public outcry at this verdict, leading the House of Lords to establish a rule formalizing when a person could be absolved from responsibility for his or her acts because of a mental disorder. This rule, known as the M'Naghten rule, still is used in many jurisdictions today:

> To establish a defense on the ground of insanity, it must be clearly proved that at the time of committing the act, the party accused was labouring under such a defect of reason, from disease of the mind, as not to know the nature and quality of the act he was doing, or if he did know it, that he did not know he was doing what was wrong.

TABLE 3 Insanity Defense Rules

Five rules have been used in determining whether an individual was insane at the time he or she committed a crime and therefore should not be held responsible for the crime.

Rule	The Individual Is Not Held Responsible for a Crime If . . .
M'Naghten rule	At the time of the crime, the individual was so affected by a disease of the mind that he or she did not know the nature of the act he or she was committing or did not know it was wrong.
Irresistible impulse rule	At the time of the crime, the individual was driven by an irresistible impulse to perform the act or had a diminished capacity to resist performing the act.
Durham rule	The crime was a product of a mental disease or defect.
ALI rule	At the time of the crime, as a result of a mental disease or defect, the person lacked substantial capacity either to appreciate the criminality (wrongfulness) of the act or to conform his or her conduct to the law.
Insanity Defense Reform Act	At the time of the crime, as a result of mental disease or mental retardation, the person was unable to appreciate the wrongfulness of his or her conduct.

The M'Naghten rule reflects the doctrine that a person must have a "guilty mind"—in Latin, *mens rea*—or the intention to commit the illegal act in order to be held responsible for the act.

Applying the M'Naghten rule might seem to be a straightforward matter—one simply determines whether a person suffers from a disease of the mind and whether during the crime he or she understood that his or her actions were wrong. Unfortunately, it is not that simple. A major problem in applying the M'Naghten rule is determining what is meant by a "disease of the mind." The law has been unclear and inconsistent in what disorders it recognizes as diseases of the mind. The most consistently recognized diseases are psychoses. It has been relatively easy for the courts and the public to accept that someone experiencing severe delusions and hallucinations is suffering from a disease and, at times, may not know right from wrong. However, defendants have argued that several other disorders, including alcohol abuse, severe depression, and posttraumatic stress disorder, are diseases of the mind that impair judgments of right and wrong. It is much more difficult for courts, the lay public, and mental health professionals to agree on the validity of such claims (Meyer & Weaver, 2006; Kimonis, 2015).

Another major problem is that the M'Naghten rule requires that a person not know right from wrong at the time of the crime in order to be judged not guilty by reason of insanity (Meyer & Weaver, 2006). This is a difficult judgment to make because it is retrospective. Even when everyone agrees that a defendant suffers from a severe psychological disorder, it does not necessarily follow that at the time of the crime the person was incapable of knowing "right from wrong," as the M'Naghten rule requires. For example, serial killer Jeffrey Dahmer, who tortured, killed, dismembered, and ate his victims, clearly seemed to have a psychological disorder. Nevertheless, the jury denied his insanity defense in part because he took great care to hide his crimes from the local police, suggesting that he knew that what he was doing was wrong or against the law.

Irresistible Impulse Rule

The second rule used to judge the acceptability of the insanity defense is the **irresistible impulse rule.** First applied in Ohio in 1934, the irresistible impulse rule broadened the conditions under which a criminal act could be considered the product of insanity to include "acts of passion." Even if a person knew that the act he or she was committing was wrong, the person could be absolved of responsibility for performing the act if he or she was driven by an irresistible impulse to perform the act or had a diminished capacity to resist performing it (Kimonis, 2015).

One of the most celebrated applications of the notion of diminished capacity was the "Twinkie Defense" of Dan White. As depicted in the 2008 movie *Milk,* in 1979 Dan White assassinated San Francisco Board of Supervisors member Harvey Milk and mayor George Moscone. White argued that he had had diminished capacity to resist the impulse to shoot Moscone and Milk due to the psychological effects of extreme stress and the consumption of large amounts of junk food. Using a particularly broad definition of diminished capacity in force in California law at the time, the jury convicted White of manslaughter instead of first-degree murder. Variations of the "Twinkie Defense" have rarely been attempted since White's trial.

After Dan White (pictured) killed San Francisco supervisor and gay rights activist Harvey Milk and mayor George Moscone, his lawyers argued that he had diminished capacity due to the psychological effects of extreme stress and the consumption of large quantities of junk food. ©*AP Images*

Durham Rule

In 1954, Judge David Bazelon further broadened the criteria for the legal definition of insanity in his ruling on the case *Durham v. United States,* which produced the third rule for defining insanity–the **Durham rule.** According to the Durham rule, the insanity defense could be accepted for any crimes that were the "product of mental disease or mental defect." This rule allowed defendants to claim that the presence of any disorder recognized by mental health professionals was the "cause" of their crimes. The Durham rule did not require that defendants show they were incapacitated by their disorders or did not understand that their acts were illegal. The rule eventually was dropped by almost all jurisdictions by the early 1970s (Kimonis, 2015).

ALI Rule

The fourth rule for deciding the acceptability of the insanity defense was proposed by the American Law Institute in 1962. Motivated by dissatisfaction with the existing legal definitions of insanity, a group of lawyers, judges, and scholars associated with the American Law Institute (ALI) worked to formulate a better definition, which eventually resulted in what is known as the **ALI rule:**

> A person is not responsible for criminal conduct if at the time of such conduct as the result of mental disease or defect he lacks substantial capacity either to appreciate the criminality (wrongfulness) of his conduct or to conform his conduct to the requirements of the law.

This rule is broader than the M'Naghten rule because it requires only that the defendant have a lack of appreciation of the criminality of his or her act, not an absence of understanding of the criminality of the act. The defendant's inability to conform his or her conduct to the requirements of the law can result from the emotional symptoms of a psychological disorder as well as from the cognitive deficits caused by the disorder. This expanded understanding incorporates some of the crimes recognized by the irresistible impulse rule. The ALI rule clearly is more restrictive than the Durham rule, however, because it requires some lack of appreciation of the criminality of an act, rather than the mere presence of a mental disorder (Kimonis, 2015). The ALI rule further restricts the types of mental disorders that can contribute to a successful insanity defense:

> As used in this Article, the term "mental disease or defect" does not include an abnormality manifested only by repeated criminal or otherwise antisocial conduct.

This restriction prohibits defense attorneys from arguing that a defendant's long history of antisocial acts is itself evidence of the presence of a mental disease or defect. Further, in 1977, in *Barrett v. United States,* it was ruled that "temporary insanity created by voluntary use of alcohol or drugs" also does not qualify a defendant for acquittal by reason of insanity.

The ALI rule was widely adopted in the United States, including in the jurisdiction in which John Hinckley was tried for shooting Ronald Reagan. Hinckley had a long-standing diagnosis of schizophrenia and an obsession with the actress Jodie Foster. Letters he wrote to Foster before shooting Reagan indicated that he committed the act under the delusion that it would impress Foster and cause her to return his love. Hinckley's defense attorneys successfully argued that he had a diminished capacity to understand the wrongfulness of shooting Reagan or to conform his behaviors to the requirements of the law. The public outcry over the judgment that Hinckley was "not guilty by reason of insanity" initiated another reappraisal of the legal definition of insanity and the use of the insanity defense (Kimonis, 2015).

Insanity Defense Reform Act

The reappraisal of the insanity defense after John Hinckley's shooting of President Reagan led to the fifth rule for defining legal insanity, codified in the **Insanity Defense Reform Act,** enacted by Congress in 1984. The Insanity Defense Reform Act adopted the 1983 **American Psychiatric Association definition of insanity.** This definition dropped the provision in the ALI rule that absolved people of responsibility for criminal acts if they were unable to conform their behavior to the law and retained the wrongfulness criterion initially proposed in the M'Naghten rule (Kimonis, 2015). The definition reads as follows:

> A person charged with a criminal offense should be found not guilty by reason of insanity if it is shown that, as a result of mental disease or mental retardation, he was unable to appreciate the wrongfulness of his conduct at the time of his offense.

This definition now applies in all cases tried in U.S. federal courts and in the courts of about half the states. Also following the Hinckley verdict, most states now require that a defendant pleading not guilty by reason of insanity prove that he or she was insane at the time of the crime. Previously, the burden of proof had been on the prosecution to prove that the defendant was sane at the time the crime was committed (Kimonis, 2015). The specific rules that are applied vary state to state, but some version of the M'Naghten, ALI, or federal rules is most common. As of 2018, all of the states except Kansas, Idaho, Montana, and Utah have some form of the insanity defense.

Problems with the Insanity Defense

Cases in which the insanity defense is pled often use mental health professionals to provide expert opinions. Despite their expertise, mental health professionals often disagree about the nature and causes of psychological disorders, the presence or absence of a psychological disorder, and the evaluation of defendants' states of mind at the time crimes were committed (Melton et al., 2017; Warren et al., 2004). Usually, lawyers on both sides of the case find a mental health professional who supports their point of view, and the two professionals inevitably are in disagreement with each other. This disagreement leads to confusion on the part of judges, juries, and the public.

Mental health professionals also have raised concerns about the rules used to determine the acceptability of the insanity defense (Meyer & Weaver, 2006). Behind these rules is the assumption that most people, including most people with a psychological disorder, have free will and usually can choose how they will act in any given situation. Many current models of both normal and abnormal behavior suggest that people do not have that much control over their behaviors. Biological predispositions, early life experiences, or disordered patterns of thinking can make people act in irrational and perhaps uncontrolled ways. This view makes it more difficult to determine when individuals should or should not be held responsible for their behaviors.

Andrea Yates argued that severe psychosis and postpartum depression led her to drown her five young children in 2001.
©8708/Gamma-Rapho/Getty Images

SHADES OF GRAY

Read the following case study.

On June 20, 2001, after her husband Rusty left for work, Andrea Yates methodically drowned all five of her young children in the bathtub. She then called 911 and asked that a police officer come to her house. She also called her husband at work and told him he needed to come home.

Andrea had a long history of psychotic depression. In the summer of 1999, she had tried to commit suicide and had been hospitalized twice. She had hallucinations and delusions that led her to believe she was evil and that her children were irreparably damaged and doomed to hell. Her psychiatrist diagnosed her with postpartum psychosis and successfully treated her but urged the couple not to have any more children, saying future episodes of psychotic depression were inevitable. The Yates conceived their fifth child approximately 7 weeks after her discharge from the hospital.

Three months after the birth of her fifth child, Andrea's father died, and her condition worsened, leading her to be hospitalized. When she was discharged, her psychiatrist gave instructions that she be watched around the clock. On the day of the drowning, her husband left for work expecting his mother to arrive at the house soon to supervise Andrea and the children. It was then that Andrea drowned the children. She later told a psychiatrist, "My children weren't righteous. They stumbled because I was evil. The way I was raising them, they could never be saved. They were doomed to perish in the fires of hell." (*Houston Chronicle,* March 5, 2002)

Would you judge Andrea Yates "not guilty by reason of insanity"? Why or why not? (Discussion appears at the end of this chapter.)

Guilty but Mentally Ill

In a sixth and most recent reform of the insanity defense, some states have adopted as an alternative to the verdict "not guilty by reason of insanity" the verdict **guilty but mentally ill (GBMI).** Defendants convicted as guilty but mentally ill are incarcerated for the normal term designated for their crimes, with the expectation that they also will receive treatment for their mental illness (Kimonis, 2015). Proponents of the GBMI verdict argue that it recognizes the mental illness of defendants while still holding them responsible for their actions. Critics argue that the GBMI verdict is essentially a guilty verdict and a means of eliminating the insanity defense (Tanay, 1992). Juries may believe they are ensuring that a person gets treatment by judging him or her guilty but mentally ill, but there is no guarantee that a person convicted under GBMI will receive treatment. In most states, it is left to legal authorities to decide whether to incarcerate people judged guilty but mentally ill in mental institutions or in prisons and, if they are sent to prisons, whether to provide them with treatment for their mental illness. As we discuss in the next section, people with mental disorders usually do not receive adequate–if any–treatment when they are incarcerated.

MENTAL HEALTH CARE IN THE JUSTICE SYSTEM

Since the 1970s, the number of prisoners in U.S. prisons has quadrupled. Nearly one out of 100 Americans is in prison, a rate 5 to 10 times that of other industrialized democracies (National Research Council [NRC], 2014). This increase has largely to do with tougher enforcement of drug possession laws beginning in the 1980s and anti-crime initiatives in the 1990s, and disproportionately affects lower-income and ethnic minority individuals (Alexander, 2012; NRC, 2014). At the same time, the deinstitutionalization movement (see the chapter "Looking at Abnormality") has led to mentally ill and at-risk individuals living in their communities without adequate care. It is not surprising that these social and historical factors combine to affect mental health and the justice system for the worse.

Men with a mental disorder are four times likelier to be incarcerated than men without a mental disorder, and women with a mental disorder are eight times likelier to be incarcerated than women without a mental disorder (Teplin, Abram, & McClelland, 1996). Although a subset of the crimes committed by people with mental disorders involve violence or theft, many of their crimes involve drug possession and use (Osher & Steadman, 2007). Many of these individuals are repeat offenders, going through a revolving door between prison and a freedom characterized by joblessness, homelessness, and poverty.

As a result, the jail and prison systems have become the de facto mental health system for millions of people with mental disorders (NRC, 2014; Osher & Steadman, 2007). Multiple studies show very high rates of mental disorders in incarcerated populations, up to three times the rates in the general population (NRC, 2014; Prins, 2014). Rates are especially high for serious mental illnesses like bipolar disorder and psychotic disorders (Steadman, Osher, Robbins, Case, & Samuels, 2009). Studies of detained youth find that 60 percent of boys and two-thirds of girls have a diagnosable mental disorder, even when conduct disorder is excluded (Teplin, Abram, McClelland, Dulcan, & Mericle, 2002). Over 50 percent of incarcerated adult males can be diagnosed with a mental disorder, most often a substance use disorder or antisocial personality disorder (James & Glaze, 2006; NRC, 2014). A study of women prison inmates found that 64 percent had a lifetime history of a major psychiatric disorder such as major depression, an anxiety disorder, a substance use disorder, or a personality disorder and that 46 percent had had symptoms of a major psychiatric disorder in the previous 6 months (Jordan, Schlenger, Fairbank, & Caddell, 1996). In addition, nearly 80 percent of these women had been exposed to an extreme trauma, such as sexual abuse, sometime in their life. Another study of 1,272 women jail detainees awaiting trial in Chicago found that over 80 percent had a lifetime history of a psychiatric disorder and that 70 percent had been symptomatic within the previous 6 months (Teplin et al., 1996). In these studies, the most common diagnosis the women received was substance abuse or dependence, but substantial percentages of the women also had been diagnosed with major depression and/or a borderline or antisocial personality disorder.

Numerous court decisions have mandated that prison inmates receive necessary mental health services, just as they should receive necessary medical services. Most inmates with mental disorders do not receive these services, however. About one-third of prison and jail inmates with significant mental health problems receive treatment while incarcerated, according to federal statistics (Bronson & Berzofsky, 2017). A study of male inmates found that only 37 percent of those with schizophrenia or a major mood disorder received treatment while in jail (Teplin, 1990), and a study of female inmates found that only 23.5 percent of these with schizophrenia or a major mood disorder received treatment in jail (Teplin, Abram, & McClelland, 1997). Only 15.4 percent of youth in detention facilities who have a mental disorder receive treatment (Teplin et al., 2002). Depression in inmates is particularly likely to go unnoticed and untreated, even though suicide is one of the leading causes of death among incarcerated people.

The services inmates do receive often are minimal. Substance abuse treatments may involve only the provision of information about drugs and perhaps Alcoholics Anonymous or Narcotics Anonymous meetings held in the prison. Treatment for schizophrenia or depression may involve only occasional visits with a prison physician who prescribes a standard drug treatment but has neither the time nor the expertise to follow individuals closely.

Comprehensive treatment programs focusing on the special needs of prison inmates with mental disorders can successfully reduce their symptoms of mental disorder, their substance abuse, and their repeat offense rates. Many of these treatment programs focus on male inmates, who greatly outnumber female inmates.

Female inmates may have different needs for services than male inmates (Teplin et al., 1997). Female inmates may be more likely than male inmates to have a history of sexual and physical abuse, which needs to be addressed in treatment. Also, female inmates are more likely than male inmates to be suffering from depression or anxiety and to have children for whom they will become caregivers after they are released from prison.

Increasingly, communities are developing systems to divert criminal offenders with mental disorders into community-based treatment programs rather than incarceration (Redlich, Steadman, Monahan, Robbins, & Petrila, 2006). The hope is that providing these individuals with comprehensive mental health treatment combined with occupational rehabilitation and social services will enable them to live in the community as healthy and productive citizens. Diversion from jail into community services is especially likely to be a goal when the offender is a youth (Steinberg, 2009).

Some states have developed mental health courts, in which the cases of offenders with mental disorders are reviewed by judges who specialize in working with mental health and social service professionals to divert offenders into treatment and rehabilitation. Courts that focus specifically on drug offenders often are called *drug courts*. Offenders diverted by mental health courts or drug courts into community treatment are still under the watchful eye of the court. If they do not cooperate with the plan developed by the mental health court for their treatment and rehabilitation, they can be diverted back into jail. This feature of mental health courts is controversial because it amounts to coercing offenders into treatment. Most courts attempt to avoid reincarceration and instead use milder sanctions, such as requiring offenders to reappear before the judge, to motivate them to cooperate with their treatment plan (Redlich et al., 2006). The effectiveness of mental health courts and drug courts in reducing recidivism and rehabilitating offenders into the community relies heavily on the availability of high-quality community services, services sorely lacking in many communities (Boothroyd, Mercado, Poythress, Christy, & Petrila, 2005).

CHAPTER INTEGRATION

There has perhaps been less integration of biological, social, and psychological viewpoints in the law's approach to issues of mental health than in the mental health field itself. The rules governing the insanity defense suggest that the law takes a biological perspective on psychological disorders, conforming to the belief that mental disorders are like medical diseases (Figure 2). Similarly, civil commitment rules require certification that a person has a mental disorder or disease before he or she can be committed, further legitimating psychiatric diagnostic systems based on medical models.

In each area discussed in this chapter, however, there are mental health professionals advocating a more integrated and complex view of mental disorders than that traditionally held by the legal system. These professionals are trying to educate judges, juries, and laypeople to help them understand that some people have biological, psychological, or social predispositions to disorders and that other biological,

FIGURE 2 **Differences Between the Perspective of the Law and That of the Mental Health Profession.**

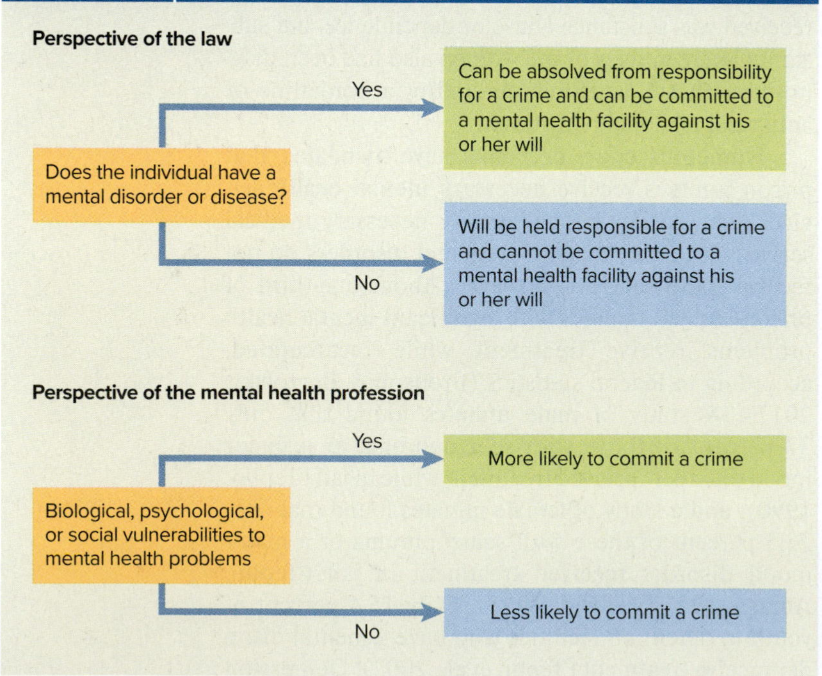

Perspective of the law
Does the individual have a mental disorder or disease?
Yes
Can be absolved from responsibility for a crime and can be committed to a mental health facility against his or her will
No
Will be held responsible for a crime and cannot be committed to a mental health facility against his or her will
Perspective of the mental health profession
Biological, psychological, or social vulnerabilities to mental health problems
Yes
More likely to commit a crime
No
Less likely to commit a crime

psychological, or social factors can interact with these predispositions to trigger the onset of mental disorders or certain manifestations of mental disorders. What is most difficult to explain is the probabilistic nature of the predictions that can be made about mental disorders and about the behavior of people with these disorders. While a predisposition or certain recent life experiences may make a person more likely to develop a disorder or to engage in a specific behavior (such as a violent behavior), they do not determine the disorder or the specific behavior.

We all prefer to have predictions about the future that are definite, especially when we are making decisions that will determine a person's freedom or confinement. That kind of definitiveness is not possible, however, given our present knowledge of the ways biological, psychological, and social forces interact to influence people's behavior.

SHADES OF GRAY DISCUSSION

The first point you might note in making your decision is that Andrea Yates had a well-documented history of psychotic depressions—in fact, the psychiatrist who treated her in 1999 warned that she could harm her children as a result of her psychosis. Yates testified that on the morning of the drownings, her delusions and hallucinations led her to believe that she had to kill her children to "save" them. But consider the fact that Yates called 911 and her husband after the drownings. Would this affect your decision? For the jury in Yates' 2002 murder trial, it did. They rejected the insanity defense, accepting the assertion by the State of Texas that the fact that Yates called 911 proved she knew her actions were wrong despite her mental defect. Yates was convicted of murder and sentenced to life in prison. In 2005, Yates' conviction was overturned due to false testimony by one of the prosecution witnesses. In 2006, Yates was retried, and this time she was found not guilty by reason of insanity and committed to a Texas state mental hospital.

In making your judgment, you likely found yourself struggling with emotions related to accepting the killing of children by a parent. You are not alone. The public often cannot accept any excuse for such a crime, and therefore the plea of "not guilty by reason of insanity," supposedly as the result of psychotic postpartum depression, is highly controversial in such cases (Williamson, 1993). Severe postpartum depression with psychotic symptoms is very rare, and violence by these women against their newborns is even rarer (Nolen-Hoeksema, 1990). When such violence does occur, some courts have accepted that the mothers' behaviors are the result of the postpartum psychosis and have judged these women not guilty by reason of insanity, as the Texas courts finally did in Andrea Yates' case. At other times, however, even though the law is intended to be objective, its application can be influenced by people's emotional reactions to the behaviors of people with mental disorders.

CHAPTER SUMMARY

- Civil commitment is the procedure through which a person may be committed for treatment in a mental institution against his or her will. In most jurisdictions, three criteria are used to determine whether individuals may be committed: if they suffer from grave disability that impairs their ability to provide for their own basic needs, if they are an imminent danger to themselves, or if they pose an imminent danger to others. Each of these criteria requires a subjective judgment on the part of clinicians and, often, predictions about the future that clinicians may not be competent to make. In particular, the prediction of who will pose a danger to others in the future is difficult to make and often is made incorrectly.
- When being considered for commitment, patients have the right to have an attorney, to have a public hearing, to call and confront witnesses, to appeal decisions, and to be placed in the least restrictive treatment setting. (The right to a hearing is often waived for short-term commitments in emergency settings.) Once committed, patients have the right to be treated and the right to refuse treatment.
- People with mental disorders, particularly those who also have a history of substance abuse, are somewhat more likely to commit violent acts, especially against family members and friends, than are people without a mental disorder. The prevalence of violence among people with mental disorders is not as great as is often perceived by the public and the media, however.

- One fundamental principle of law is that, in order to stand trial, an accused individual must have a reasonable degree of rational understanding both of the charges against him or her and of the proceedings of the trial and must be able to participate in his or her defense. People who do not have an understanding of what is happening to them in a courtroom and who cannot participate in their defense are said to be incompetent to stand trial. Defendants who have a history of a psychotic disorder, who have current symptoms of psychosis, or who perform poorly on tests of important cognitive skills may be judged incompetent to stand trial.
- Five rules for judging the acceptability of the insanity defense have been used in recent history: the M'Naghten rule, the irresistible impulse rule, the Durham rule, the ALI rule, and the Insanity Defense Reform Act. Each of these rules requires that the defendant be diagnosed with a mental disorder, and most of them require that it be shown that the defendant did not appreciate the criminality of his or her act or could not control his or her behaviors at the time of the crime.
- The verdict "guilty but mentally ill" was introduced following public uproar over uses of the insanity defense in high-profile cases. Persons judged guilty but mentally ill are confined for the duration of a regular prison term but with the assumption that they will receive psychiatric treatment while incarcerated.
- Mental health professionals have raised a number of concerns about the insanity defense. For one thing, it requires after-the-fact judgments of a defendant's state of mind at the time of the crime. In addition, the rules governing the insanity defense presume that people have free will and usually can control their actions. These presumptions contradict some models of normal and abnormal behavior that suggest that behavior is strongly influenced by biological, psychological, and social forces.
- Communities are increasingly attempting to divert persons with mental disorders who commit crimes away from jail and into community-based treatment programs. Mental health courts and drug courts have been established specifically for this purpose.

KEY TERMS

need for treatment
civil commitment
grave disability
dangerousness to self
dangerousness to others
right to treatment
right to refuse treatment
informed consent
incompetent to stand trial
insanity
insanity defense
M'Naghten rule
irresistible impulse rule
Durham rule
ALI rule
Insanity Defense Reform Act
American Psychiatric Association definition of insanity
guilty but mentally ill (GBMI)

GLOSSARY

A

ABAB (reversal) design type of experimental design in which an intervention is introduced, withdrawn, and then reinstated, and the behavior of a participant is examined on and off the treatment

abstinence violation effect what happens when a person attempting to abstain from alcohol use ingests alcohol and then endures conflict and guilt by making an internal attribution to explain why he or she drank, thereby making him or her more likely to continue drinking in order to cope with the self-blame and guilt

acute stress disorder disorder similar to posttraumatic stress disorder but occurs within 1 month of exposure to the stressor and does not last more than 4 weeks; often involves dissociative symptoms

adjustment disorder stress-related disorder that involves emotional and behavioral symptoms (depressive symptoms, anxiety symptoms, and/or antisocial behaviors) that arise within 3 months of the onset of a stressor

adolescent-onset conduct disorder a conduct disorder characterized by aggression, destructiveness, deceitfulness, and rules violation beginning after age 10

adoption study study of the heritability of a disorder by finding adopted people with a disorder and then determining the prevalence of the disorder among their biological and adoptive relatives, in order to separate out contributing genetic and environmental factors

adrenal-cortical system the hormonal system situated in the adrenal cortex and activated by the hypothalamus, that responds to stress to determine fight- or-flight reactions

agnosia impaired ability to recognize objects or people

agoraphobia anxiety disorder characterized by fear of places and situations in which it would be difficult to escape, such as enclosed places, open spaces, and crowds

Alcoholics Anonymous (AA) an organization created by and for people with alcoholism involving a 12-step treatment program

ALI rule legal principle stating that a person is not responsible for criminal conduct if he or she lacks the capacity to appreciate the criminality (wrongfulness) of the act or to conform his or her conduct to the requirements of the law as a result of mental disease

allostatic load physiological condition resulting from chronic arousal of the fight-or-flight response to stress

altruistic suicide suicide committed by people who believe that taking their own life will benefit society

Alzheimer's disease progressive neurological disease that is the most common cause of dementia

amenorrhea cessation of the menses

American Psychiatric Association definition of insanity definition of insanity stating that people cannot be held responsible for their conduct if, at the time they commit crimes, as the result of mental disease or mental retardation they are unable to appreciate the wrongfulness of their conduct

amphetamines stimulant drugs that can produce symptoms of euphoria, self-confidence, alertness, agitation, paranoia, perceptual illusions, and depression

amygdala structure of the limbic system critical in emotions such as fear

animal studies studies that attempt to test theories of psychopathology using animals

animal-type phobias extreme fears of specific animals that may induce immediate and intense panic attacks and cause the individual to go to great lengths to avoid the animals

anomic suicide suicide committed by people who experience a severe disorientation and role confusion because of a large change in their relationship to society

anorexia nervosa eating disorder in which people fail to maintain body weights that are normal for their age and height and have fears of becoming fat, distorted body images, and amenorrhea

antagonism hostility toward others

antagonist drugs drugs that block or change the effects of an addictive drug, reducing desire for the drug

anterograde amnesia deficit in the ability to learn new information

antianxiety drugs drugs used to treat anxiety, insomnia, and other psychological symptoms

anticonvulsants drugs used to treat mania and depression

antidepressant drugs drugs used to treat the symptoms of depression, such as sad mood, negative thinking, and disturbances of sleep and appetite; common types are tricyclics, selective serotonin reuptake inhibitors, and serotonin-norepinephrine reuptake inhibitors

antipsychotic drugs drugs used to treat psychotic symptoms, such as delusions, hallucinations, and disorganized thinking

antisocial personality disorder (ASPD) pervasive pattern of criminal, impulsive, callous, and/or ruthless behavior, predicated on disregard for the rights of others and an absence of respect for social norms

anxiety state of apprehension, tension, and worry

anxiety sensitivity belief that bodily symptoms have harmful consequences

aphasia impaired ability to produce and comprehend language

applied tension technique technique used to treat blood-injection-injury type phobias in which the therapist teaches the client to increase his or her blood pressure and heart rate, thus preventing the client from fainting

apraxia impaired ability to initiate common voluntary behaviors

arousal phase in the sexual response cycle, psychological experience of arousal and pleasure as well as physiological changes, such as the tensing of muscles and enlargement of blood vessels and tissues (also called the excitement phase)

assertive community treatment programs system of treatment that provides comprehensive services to people with schizophrenia, employing the expertise of medical professionals, social workers, and psychologists to meet the variety of patients' needs 24 hours a day

assessment process of gathering information about a person's symptoms and their possible causes

association studies genetic studies in which researchers identify physical disorders associated with a target psychological disorder for which genetic abnormalities or markers are known; the DNA of individuals with the psychological disorder and their first-degree relatives is then examined to determine if they also have this genetic marker (one form of molecular genetic studies)

attention-deficit/hyperactivity disorder (ADHD) syndrome marked by deficits in controlling attention, inhibiting impulses, and organizing behavior to accomplish long-term goals

atypical anorexia nervosa disorder characterized by all the criteria for anorexia nervosa except that despite significant weight loss, the weight of the affected individual remains within or above the normal range

atypical antipsychotics drugs that seem to be even more effective in treating schizophrenia than phenothiazines without the same neurological side effects; they bind to a different type of dopamine receptor than other neuroleptic drugs

autism childhood disorder marked by deficits in social interaction (such as a lack of interest in one's family or other children), communication (such as failing to modulate one's voice to signify emotional expression), and activities and interests (such as engaging in bizarre, repetitive behaviors)

autism spectrum disorder (ASD) a spectrum of neurodevelopmental disorders characterized by disrupted social and language development (formerly referred to as autism)

autonomic nervous system the part of the nervous system that controls bodily functions not consciously directed, such as breathing, the heartbeat, and digestive processes

aversion therapy treatment that involves the pairing of unpleasant stimuli with deviant or maladaptive sources of pleasure in order to induce an aversive reaction to the formerly pleasurable stimulus

avoidant personality disorder pervasive anxiety, sense of inadequacy, and fear of being criticized that lead to the avoidance of most social interactions with others and to restraint and nervousness in social interactions

avolition inability to persist at common goal-directed activities

B

barbiturates drugs used to treat anxiety and insomnia that work by suppressing the central nervous system and decreasing the activity level of certain neurons

behavioral approaches approaches to psychopathology that focus on the influence of reinforcements and punishments in producing behavior; the two core principles or processes of learning according to behaviorism are *classical conditioning* and *operant conditioning*

behavioral genetics study of the processes by which genes affect behavior and the extent to which personality and abnormality are genetically inherited

behavioral inhibition set of behavioral traits including shyness, fearfulness, irritability, cautiousness, and introversion; behaviorally inhibited children tend to avoid or withdraw from novel situations, are clingy with parents, and become excessively aroused when exposed to unfamiliar situations

behavioral observation method for assessing the frequency of a client's behaviors and the specific situations in which they occur

behavioral theories of depression theories that view depression as resulting from negative life events that represent a reduction in positive reinforcement; sympathetic responses to depressive behavior then serve as positive reinforcement for the depression itself

behavioral therapies psychotherapeutic approaches that focus on identifying the reinforcements and punishments contributing to a person's maladaptive behaviors and on changing specific behaviors

behavioral therapy therapy that focuses on changing a person's specific behaviors by replacing unwanted behaviors with desired behaviors

behaviorism study of the impact of reinforcements and punishments on behavior

benzodiazepines drugs that reduce anxiety and insomnia

beta-amyloid class of proteins that accumulates in the spaces between neurons in the brain, contributing to Alzheimer's disease

binge-eating disorder eating disorder in which people compulsively overeat either continuously or on discrete binges but do not behave in ways to compensate for the overeating

bingeing eating a large amount of food in one sitting

binge/purge type of anorexia nervosa type of anorexia nervosa in which periodic bingeing or purging behaviors occur along with behaviors that meet the criteria for anorexia nervosa

biological approach view that biological factors cause and should be used to treat abnormality

biological theories theories of abnormality that focus on biological causes of abnormal behaviors

biopsychosocial approach approach to psychopathology that seeks to integrate biological, psychological, and social factors in understanding and treating psychopathology

bipolar disorder disorder marked by cycles between manic episodes and depressive episodes; also called manic-depression

bipolar I disorder form of bipolar disorder in which the full symptoms of mania are experienced; depressive aspects may be more infrequent or mild

bipolar II disorder form of bipolar disorder in which only hypomanic episodes are experienced and the depressive component is more pronounced

blood-injection-injury type phobias extreme fears of seeing blood or an injury or of receiving an injection or another invasive medical procedure, which cause a drop in heart rate and blood pressure and fainting

body dysmorphic disorder syndrome involving obsessive concern over a part of the body the individual believes is defective

borderline personality disorder syndrome characterized by rapidly shifting and unstable mood, self-concept, and interpersonal relationships, as well as impulsive behavior and transient dissociative states

breathing-related sleep disorder group of sleep disorders characterized by numerous brief sleep disturbances due to problems breathing

brief psychotic disorder disorder characterized by the sudden onset of delusions, hallucinations, disorganized speech, and/or disorganized behavior that lasts only between 1 day and 1 month, after which the symptoms vanish completely

bulimia nervosa eating disorder in which people engage in bingeing and behave in ways to prevent weight gain from the binges, such as self-induced vomiting, excessive exercise, and abuse of purging drugs (such as laxatives)

C

caffeine chemical compound with stimulant effects

cannabis substance that causes feelings of well-being, perceptual distortions, and paranoid thinking

case studies in-depth analyses of individuals

cataplexy episodes of sudden loss of muscle tone lasting under 2 minutes, triggered by laughter or joking in people who have had narcolepsy for a long time

catatonia group of disorganized behaviors that reflect an extreme lack of responsiveness to the outside world

catharsis expression of emotions connected to memories and conflicts, which, according to Freud, leads to the release of energy used to keep these memories in the unconscious

causal attribution explanation for why an event occurred

central sleep apnea sleep disorder characterized by complete cessation of respiratory activity for brief periods of time (20 seconds or more); sufferers do not have frequent awakenings and do not tend to feel tired during the day; occurs when the brain does not send the signal to breathe to the respiratory system

cerebral cortex part of the brain that regulates complex activities, such as speech and analytical thinking

cerebrovascular disease disease that occurs when the blood supply to the brain is blocked, causing tissue damage to the brain

childhood-onset conduct disorder a conduct disorder characterized by aggression, destructiveness, deceitfulness, and rules violation beginning before age 10 that tends to worsen with age

childhood-onset fluency disorder disturbances of the normal fluency and motor production of speech, including repetitive sounds or syllables, prolongation of consonants or vowel sounds, broken words, blocking or words produced with an excess of physical tension; also known as stuttering

chlorpromazine antipsychotic drug

circadian rhythm sleep-wake disorder sleep disorder characterized by insomnia, excessive sleepiness, or both due to disruptions in circadian rhythms

civil commitment forcing of a person into a mental health facility against his or her will

classical conditioning form of learning in which a neutral stimulus becomes associated with a stimulus that naturally elicits a response, thereby making the neutral stimulus itself sufficient to elicit the same response

classification system set of syndromes and the rules for determining whether an individual's symptoms are part of one of these syndromes

client-centered therapy (CCT) Carl Rogers' form of psychotherapy, which consists of an equal relationship between therapist and client as the client searches for his or her inner self, receiving unconditional positive regard and an empathic understanding from the therapist

cocaine central nervous system stimulant that causes a rush of positive feelings initially but that can lead to impulsiveness, agitation, and anxiety and can cause withdrawal symptoms of exhaustion and depression

cognitions thoughts or beliefs

cognitive-behavioral therapy (CBT) treatment focused on changing negative patterns of thinking and solving concrete problems through brief sessions in which a therapist helps a client challenge negative thoughts, consider alternative perspectives, and take effective actions

cognitive theories theories that focus on belief systems and ways of thinking as the causes of abnormal behavior

cognitive therapies therapeutic approaches that focus on changing people's maladaptive thought patterns

cohort effect effect that occurs when people born in one historical period are at different risk for a disorder than are people born in another historical period

collective unconscious according to Carl Jung, the wisdom accumulated by a society over hundreds of years of human existence and stored in the memories of individuals

communication disorders disorders characterized by persistent difficulties in the acquisition and use of language and other means of communicating

community mental health centers institutions for the treatment of people with mental health problems in the community; may include teams of social workers, therapists, and physicians who coordinate care

community mental health movement movement launched in 1963 that attempted to provide coordinated mental health services to people in community-based treatment centers

comorbidity meeting the criteria for two or more diagnostic categories simultaneously

compulsions repetitive behaviors or mental acts that an individual feels he or she must perform

computerized tomography (CT) method of analyzing brain structure by passing narrow X-ray beams through a person's head from several angles to produce measurements from which a computer can construct an image of the brain

concordance rate probability that both twins will develop a disorder if one twin has the disorder

conditioned avoidance response behavior that is reinforced because it allows individuals to avoid situations that cause anxiety

conditioned response (CR) in classical conditioning, response that first followed a natural stimulus but that now follows a conditioned stimulus

conditioned stimulus (CS) in classical conditioning, previously neutral stimulus that, through pairing with a natural stimulus, becomes sufficient to elicit a response

conduct disorder syndrome marked by chronic disregard for the rights of others, including specific behaviors such as stealing, lying, and engaging in acts of violence

conscious refers to mental contents and processes of which we are actively aware

continuous variable factor that is measured along a continuum (such as 0–100) rather than falling into a discrete category (such as "diagnosed with depression")

continuum model of abnormality model of abnormality that views mental disorders not as categorically different from "normal" experiences but as lying somewhere along a continuum from healthy, functional behaviors, thoughts, and feelings to unhealthy, dysfunctional behaviors, thoughts, and feelings

control group in an experimental study, group of subjects whose experience resembles that of the experimental group in all ways except that they do not receive the key manipulation

conversion disorder (functional neurological symptom disorder) syndrome marked by a sudden loss of functioning in a part of the body, usually following an extreme psychological stressor

coronary heart disease (CHD) chronic illness that is a leading cause of death in the United States, occurring when the blood vessels that supply the heart with oxygen and nutrients are narrowed or closed by plaque, resulting in a myocardial infarction (heart attack) when closed completely

correlational studies method in which researchers assess only the relationship between two variables and do not manipulate one variable to determine its effects on another variable

correlation coefficient statistic used to indicate the degree of relationship between two variables

cortisol hormone that helps the body respond to stressors, inducing the fight-or-flight response

cross-sectional type of research examining people at one point in time but not following them over time

cultural relativism view that norms among cultures set the standard for what counts as normal behavior, which implies that abnormal behavior can only be defined relative to these norms and that no universal definition of abnormality is therefore possible; only definitions of abnormality relative to a specific culture are possible

cyclothymic disorder milder but more chronic form of bipolar disorder that consists of alternation between hypomanic episodes and mild depressive episodes over a period of at least 2 years

D

dangerousness to others legal criterion for involuntary commitment that is met when a person would pose a threat or danger to other people if not incarcerated

dangerousness to self legal criterion for involuntary commitment that is met when a person is imminently suicidal or a danger to him- or herself as judged by a mental health professional

day treatment centers mental health facilities that allow people to obtain treatment, along with occupational and rehabilitative therapies, during the day but to live at home at night

deep brain stimulation procedure to treat depression in which electrodes are surgically implanted in specific areas of the brain and connected to a pulse generator that is placed under the skin and stimulates these brain areas

defense mechanisms strategies the ego uses to disguise or transform unconscious wishes

degradation process in which a receiving neuron releases an enzyme into the synapse, breaking down neurotransmitters into other biochemicals

deinstitutionalization movement in which thousands of mental patients were released from mental institutions; a result of the patients' rights movement, which was aimed at stopping the dehumanization of mental patients and at restoring their basic legal rights

delayed ejaculation marked delay, infrequency, or absence of ejaculation during sexual encounters

delirium cognitive disorder including disorientation and memory loss that is acute and usually transient

delirium tremens (DTs) symptoms that result during severe alcohol withdrawal, including hallucinations, delusions, agitation, and disorientation

delusional disorder disorder characterized by delusions lasting at least 1 month regarding situations that occur in real life, such as being followed, poisoned, or deceived by a spouse or having a disease; people with this disorder do not show any other symptoms of schizophrenia

delusion of reference false belief that external events, such as other people's actions or natural disasters, relate somehow to oneself

delusions fixed beliefs with no basis in reality

delusions of thought insertion beliefs that one's thoughts are being controlled by outside forces

demand characteristics factors in an experiment that suggest to participants how the experimenter would like them to behave

dementia cognitive disorder in which a gradual and usually permanent decline of intellectual functioning occurs; can be caused by a medical condition, substance intoxication, or withdrawal; also known as *major neurocognitive disorder*

dependent personality disorder people suffering from this disorder are anxious about interpersonal interactions, but their anxiety stems from a deep need to be cared for by others, rather than from a concern that they will be criticized

dependent variable factor that an experimenter seeks to predict

depersonalization/derealization disorder syndrome marked by frequent episodes of feeling detached from one's own body and mental processes, as if one were an outside observer of oneself; symptoms must cause significant distress or interference with one's ability to function

depressants drugs that slow the nervous system

depression state marked by either a sad mood or a loss of interest in one's usual activities, as well as feelings of hopelessness, suicidal ideation, psychomotor agitation or retardation, and trouble concentrating

depressive disorders a set of disorders characterized by depressed mood and/or anhedonia (and not mania)

detachment the inability to connect with others

developmental coordination disorder disorder involving deficits in the ability to walk, run, or hold on to objects

diagnosis label given to a set of symptoms that tend to occur together

Diagnostic and Statistical Manual of Mental Disorders (DSM) official manual for diagnosing mental disorders in the United States, containing a list of specific criteria for each disorder, how long a person's symptoms must be present to qualify for a diagnosis, and requirements that the symptoms interfere with daily functioning in order to be called disorders

dialectical behavior therapy cognitive-behavioral intervention aimed at teaching problem-solving skills, interpersonal skills, and skill at managing negative emotions

diathesis-stress model model that asserts that only when a diathesis or vulnerability interacts with a stress or trigger will a disorder emerge

disinhibition lack of restraint

disorders of arousal sleep disorders that involve recurrent episodes of incomplete awakening from sleep that seem to mix elements of wakefulness and NREM sleep

disruptive mood dysregulation disorder a disorder in children characterized by immature and inappropriate temper outbursts that are grossly out of proportion to a situation in intensity and duration

dissociation process whereby different facets of an individual's sense of self, memories, or consciousness become split off from one another

dissociative amnesia loss of memory for important facts about a person's own life and personal identity, usually including the awareness of this memory loss

dissociative fugue disorder in which a person moves away and assumes a new identity, with amnesia for the previous identity

dissociative identity disorder (DID) syndrome in which a person develops more than one distinct identity or personality, each of which can have distinct facial and verbal expressions, gestures, interpersonal styles, attitudes, and even physiological responses

dizygotic (DZ) twins twins who average only 50 percent of their genes in common because they developed from two separate fertilized eggs

dopamine neurotransmitter in the brain, excess amounts of which have been thought to cause schizophrenia

double-blind experiment study in which both the researchers and the participants are unaware of which experimental condition the participants are in, in order to prevent demand effects

Durham rule legal principle stating that the presence of a mental disorder is sufficient to absolve an individual of responsibility for a crime

E

early or premature ejaculation recurrent ejaculation within 1 minute of initiation of partnered sexual activity when not desired

echolalia communication abnormality in which an individual simply repeats back what he or she hears rather than generating his or her own speech

effectiveness in therapy outcome research, how well a therapy works in real-world settings

efficacy in therapy outcome research, how well a therapy works in highly controlled settings with a narrowly defined group of people

ego part of the psyche that channels libido to be acceptable to the superego and within the constraints of reality

egoistic suicide suicide committed by people who feel alienated from others and who lack social support

ego psychology branch of psychodynamic theory emphasizing the importance of the individual's ability to regulate defenses in ways that allow healthy functioning within the realities of society

electroconvulsive therapy (ECT) treatment for depression that involves the induction of a brain seizure by passing electrical current through the patient's brain while he or she is anesthetized

electroencephalogram (EEG) procedure in which multiple electrodes are placed on the scalp to detect low-voltage electrical current produced by the firing of specific neurons in the brain

endocrine system system of glands that produces many different hormones

epidemiology study of the frequency and distribution of a disorder, or a group of disorders, in a population

epigenetics study of how environmental conditions can change the expression of genes without changing the gene sequence

erectile disorder in men, recurrent inability to attain or maintain an erection until the completion of sexual activity

executive functions functions of the brain that involve the ability to sustain concentration; use abstract reasoning and concept formation; anticipate, plan, and program; initiate purposeful behavior; self–monitor; and shift from maladaptive patterns of behavior to more adaptive ones

exhibitionist disorder obtainment of sexual gratification by exposing one's genitals to involuntary observers

experimental group in an experimental study, group of participants that receive the key manipulation

experimental studies studies in which the independent variables are directly manipulated and the effects on the dependent variable are examined

exposure and response prevention type of therapy in which individuals with anxiety symptoms are exposed repeatedly to the focus of their anxiety but prevented from avoiding it or engaging in compulsive responses to the anxiety

expressed emotion family interaction style in which families are overinvolved with each other, are overprotective of the disturbed family member, voice self-sacrificing attitudes to the disturbed family member, and simultaneously are critical, hostile, and resentful of this member

external validity extent to which a study's results can be generalized to phenomena in real life

F

factitious disorder disorder marked by deliberately faking physical or mental illness to gain medical attention

factitious disorder imposed on another disorder in which the individual creates an illness in another individual in order to gain attention

family-focused therapy (FFT) treatment for people with bipolar disorder in which patients and their families are given education about bipolar disorder and training in communication and problem-solving skills

family history study study of the heritability of a disorder involving identifying people with the disorder and people without the disorder and then determining the disorder's frequency within each person's family

family systems theories theories that see the family as a complex system that works to maintain the status quo

family systems therapy psychotherapy that focuses on the family, rather than the individual, as the source of problems; family therapists challenge communication styles, disrupt pathological family dynamics, and challenge defensive conceptions in order to harmonize relationships among all members and within each member

female orgasmic disorder in women, recurrent delay in or absence of orgasm after having reached the excitement phase of the sexual response cycle (also called anorgasmia)

female sexual interest/arousal disorder in women, recurrent inability to attain or maintain the swelling-lubrication response of sexual excitement

fetal alcohol syndrome (FAS) syndrome that occurs when a mother abuses alcohol during pregnancy, causing the baby to have lowered IQ, increased risk for mental retardation, distractibility, and difficulties with learning from experience

fetishistic disorder paraphilic disorder in which a person uses inanimate objects as the preferred or exclusive source of sexual arousal

fight-or-flight response physiological changes in the human body that occur in response to a perceived threat, including the secretion of glucose, endorphins, and hormones as well as the elevation of heart rate, metabolism, blood pressure, breathing, and muscle tension

five-factor model a dimensional perspective that posits that everyone's personality is organized along five broad personality traits: negative emotionality, extraversion, openness to experience, agreeableness, and conscientiousness

formal thought disorder state of highly disorganized thinking (also known as loosening of associations)

free association method of uncovering unconscious conflicts in which the client is taught to talk about whatever comes to mind, without censoring any thoughts

frotteuristic disorder disorder characterized by obtainment of sexual gratification by rubbing one's genitals against or fondling the body parts of a nonconsenting person

G

gambling disorder a disorder, similar to substance abuse, characterized by the inability to resist the impulse to gamble

gender dysphoria condition in which a person believes that he or she was born with the wrong sex's genitals and is fundamentally a person of the opposite sex

gender identity one's perception of oneself as male or female

generalizability extent to which the results of a study generalize to, or inform us about, people other than those who were studied

generalized anxiety disorder (GAD) anxiety disorder characterized by chronic anxiety in daily life

general paresis disease that leads to paralysis, insanity, and eventually death; discovery of this disease helped establish a connection between biological diseases and mental disorders

genito-pelvic pain/penetration disorder marked difficulty having vaginal penetration; pain or tightening of pelvic floor muscles during penetration

global assumptions fundamental beliefs that encompass all types of situations

grandiose delusions false, persistent beliefs that one has superior talents and traits

grave disability legal criterion for involuntary commitment that is met when a person is so incapacitated by a mental disorder that he or she cannot provide his or her own basic needs, such as food, clothing, or shelter, and his or her survival is threatened as a result

group comparison study study that compares two or more distinct groups on a variable of interest

guided mastery techniques interventions designed to increase health-promoting behaviors by providing explicit information about how to engage in these behaviors, as well as opportunities to engage in the behaviors in increasingly challenging situations

guilty but mentally ill (GBMI) verdict that requires a convicted criminal to serve the full sentence designated for his or her crime, with the expectation that he or she will also receive treatment for mental illness

H

hair-pulling disorder (trichotillomania) disorder characterized by recurrent pulling out of the hair resulting in noticeable hair loss; these individuals report tension immediately before or while attempting to resist the impulse, and pleasure or relief when they are pulling out their hair (also known as trichotillomania)

halfway houses living facilities that offer people with long-term mental health problems the opportunity to live in a structured, supportive environment while they are trying to reestablish employment and ties to family and friends

hallucinations perceptual experiences that are not real

hallucinogens substances, including LSD and MDMA (ecstasy), that produce perceptual illusions and distortions even in small doses

harm reduction model approach to treating substance use disorders that views alcohol use as normative behavior and focuses education on the immediate risks of the excessive use of alcohol (such as alcohol-related accidents) and on the payoffs of moderation (such as avoidance of hangovers)

hippocampus structure of the brain involved in memory and in the stress response

histrionic personality disorder sharing features with borderline personality disorder, including rapidly shifting emotions and intense, unstable relationships, people with this disorder also behave in ways to draw attention to themselves across situations

hoarding a compulsive disorder characterized by the inability to throw away unneeded possessions (such as trash)

hopelessness sense that the future is bleak and there is no way to make it more positive

hormone chemical that carries messages throughout the body, potentially affecting a person's mood, level of energy, and reaction to stress

humanistic theories views that people strive to develop their innate potential for goodness and self-actualization; abnormality arises as a result of societal pressures to conform to unchosen dictates that clash with a person's self-actualization needs and from an inability to satisfy more basic needs, such as hunger

humanistic therapy type of therapy in which the goal is to help the client discover his or her place in the world and to accomplish self-actualization through self-exploration; based on the assumption that the natural tendency for humans is toward growth (also called person-centered therapy)

human laboratory study experimental study involving human participants

hypersomnolence disorders disorders characterized by excessive sleepiness, which can be expressed as either an excessive quantity of sleep (also referred to as hypersomnia) or a low quality of wakefulness

hypertension condition in which the blood supply through the blood vessels is excessive and can lead to deterioration of the cell tissue and hardening of the arterial walls

hypomania state in which an individual shows mild symptoms of mania

hypothalamic-pituitary-adrenal axis (HPA axis) three key components of the neuroendocrine system that work together in a feedback system interconnected with the limbic system and the cerebral cortex

hypothalamus component of the brain that regulates eating, drinking, sex, and basic emotions; abnormal behaviors involving any of these activities may be the result of dysfunction in the hypothalamus

hypothesis testable statement about two or more variables and the relationship between them

I

id according to Freud, the most primitive part of the unconscious; consists of drives and impulses seeking immediate gratification

illness anxiety disorder a form of anxiety characterized by a preoccupation with fears of having a serious medical illness based on misinterpretations of bodily sensations (formerly called hypochondriasis)

immune system system that protects the body from disease-causing microorganisms and affects susceptibility to diseases

impulsivity difficulty controlling behaviors; acting without thinking first

incidence number of new cases of a specific disorder that develop during a specific period of time

incompetent to stand trial legal status of an individual who lacks a rational understanding of the charges against him or her, an understanding of the proceedings of his or her trial, or the ability to participate in his or her defense

independent variable factor that is manipulated by an experimenter or used to predict the dependent variable

informed consent procedure (often legally required prior to treatment administration) in which a patient receives a full and understandable explanation of the treatment being offered and makes a decision about whether to accept or refuse the treatment

inhalants solvents, such as gasoline, glue, or paint thinner, that one inhales to produce a high and that can cause permanent central nervous system damage as well as liver and kidney disease

insanity legal term denoting a state of mental incapacitation during the time a crime was committed

insanity defense defense used by people accused of a crime in which they state that they cannot be held responsible for their illegal acts because they were mentally incapacitated at the time of the act

Insanity Defense Reform Act 1984 law, affecting all federal courts and about half the state courts, that finds a person not guilty by reason of insanity if it is shown that, as a result of mental disease or mental retardation, the accused was unable to appreciate the wrongfulness of his or her conduct at the time of the offense

insomnia disorder a disorder characterized by chronic difficulty initiating or maintaining sleep or by sleep that does not restore energy and alertness

intellectual disability (ID) a spectrum of neurodevelopmental disorders characterized by impaired general intellectual functioning (formerly referred to as mental retardation)

intelligence tests tests that assess a person's intellectual strengths and weaknesses

intermittent explosive disorder disorder characterized by (a) several episodes of failure to resist aggressive impulses that result in serious assaultive acts or destruction of property, (b) a degree of aggressiveness grossly out of proportion to the situation, and (c) symptoms not better explained by another mental disorder (such as antisocial personality disorder), the effects of substances, or a medical condition (e.g., a head trauma)

internal validity extent to which all factors that could extraneously affect a study's results are controlled within a laboratory study

Internet gaming disorder Persistent engagement and preoccupation with Internet and video gaming, with symptoms of tolerance, withdrawal, loss of interest in other activities, and clinically significant impairment or distress

interoceptive awareness sensitivity to stimuli arising from within the body, such as heart rate

interoceptive conditioning process by which symptoms of anxiety that have preceded panic attacks become the signals for new panic attacks

interpersonal and social rhythm therapy (ISRT) treatment for people with bipolar disorder that helps them manage their social relationships and daily rhythms to try to prevent relapse

interpersonal theories of depression theories that view the causes of depression as rooted in interpersonal relationships

interpersonal therapy (IPT) more structured, short-term version of psychodynamic therapies

irresistible impulse rule legal principle stating that even a person who knowingly performs a wrongful act can be absolved of responsibility if he or she was driven by an irresistible impulse to perform the act or had a diminished capacity to resist performing the act

L

language disorder a communication disorder characterized by difficulties with spoken and written language and other language modalities (e.g., sign language)

learned helplessness theory view that exposure to uncontrollable negative events leads to a belief in one's inability to control important outcomes and a subsequent loss of motivation, indecisiveness, and failure of action

libido according to Freud, psychical energy derived from physiological drives

life-course-persistent antisocial behavior a form of conduct disorder involving aggression, destructiveness, deceitfulness, and rules violation that persists into adulthood

light therapy treatment for seasonal affective disorder that involves exposure to bright lights during the winter months

limbic system part of the brain that relays information from the primitive brain stem about changes in bodily functions to the cortex, where the information is interpreted

linkage analysis genetic study that looks for associations between psychological disorders and physical disorders for which genetic causes are known

lithium drug used to treat manic and depressive symptoms

locus ceruleus area of the brain stem that plays a part in the emergency response and may be involved in panic attacks

longitudinal type of research evaluating the same group(s) of people for an extended period of time

M

magnetic resonance imaging (MRI) method of measuring both brain structure and brain function through the construction of a magnetic field that affects hydrogen atoms in the brain, emitting signals that a computer then records and uses to produce a three-dimensional image of the brain

major depressive disorder disorder involving a sad mood or anhedonia plus four or more of the following symptoms: weight loss or a decrease in appetite, insomnia or hypersomnia, psychomotor agitation or retardation, fatigue, feelings of worthlessness or severe guilt, trouble concentrating, and suicidal ideation; these symptoms must be present for at least 2 weeks and must produce marked impairments in normal functioning

major neurocognitive disorder a brain disorder characterized by a deteriorating course of deficits in neurocognitive functioning (e.g., memory, attention) that interferes significantly with independent living

male hypoactive sexual desire disorder condition in which a man's desire for sex is diminished to the point that it causes him significant distress or interpersonal difficulties and is not due to transient life circumstances or another sexual dysfunction

malingering feigning of a symptom or a disorder for the purpose of avoiding an unwanted situation, such as military service

managed care health care system in which all necessary services for an individual patient are supposed to be coordinated by a primary care provider; the goals are to coordinate services for an existing medical problem and to prevent future medical problems

mania state of persistently elevated mood, feelings of grandiosity, overenthusiasm, racing thoughts, rapid speech, and impulsive actions

mental hygiene movement movement to treat mental patients more humanely and to view mental disorders as medical diseases

mentalization-based treatment a form of psychodynamic treatment for borderline personality disorder based on attachment

mesmerism treatment for hysterical patients based on the idea that magnetic fluids in the patients' bodies are affected by the magnetic forces of other people and objects; the patients' magnetic forces are thought to be realigned by the practitioner through his or her own magnetic force

mesolimbic pathway subcortical part of the brain involved in cognition and emotion

meta-analysis statistical technique for summarizing results across several studies

methadone opioid that is less potent and longer-lasting than heroin; taken by heroin users to decrease their cravings and help them cope with negative withdrawal symptoms

mild neurocognitive disorder a mental disorder manifesting a slight abnormal decrease in mental function involving memory, thought, communication, behavior, or the completion of tasks

M'Naghten rule legal principle stating that, in order to claim a defense of insanity, accused persons must have been burdened by such a defect of reason, from disease of the mind, as not to know the nature and quality of the act they were doing or, if they did know it, as not to know what they were doing was wrong

modeling process of learning behaviors by imitating others, especially authority figures or people like oneself

molecular genetic studies studies of the structure and function of genes that help in understanding how genetic mutations can lead to disease

monoamine oxidase inhibitors (MAOIs) class of antidepressant drugs

monoamines neurotransmitters, including catecholamines (epinephrine, norepinephrine, and dopamine) and serotonin, that have been implicated in the mood disorders

monozygotic (MZ) twins twins who share 100 percent of their genes because they developed from a single fertilized egg

moral treatment type of treatment delivered in mental hospitals in which patients were treated with respect and dignity and were encouraged to exercise self-control

motivational interviewing intervention for sufferers of substance use disorders to elicit and solidify individuals' motivation and commitment to changing their substance use; rather than confronting the user, the motivational interviewer adopts an empathic interaction style, drawing out the user's own statements of desire, ability, reasons, need, and, ultimately, commitment to change

motor disorders a group of disorders characterized by motor symptoms such as tics, stereotypic movements, or dyscoordination

multiple baseline design type of study in which an intervention is given to the same individual but begun in different settings or is given to different individuals but at different points in time and in which the effects of the intervention are systematically observed

N

narcissistic personality disorder syndrome marked by grandiose thoughts and feelings of one's own worth as well as an obliviousness to others' needs and an exploitative, arrogant demeanor

narcolepsy sleep disorder characterized by irresistible attacks of sleep plus (1) cataplexy or (2) recurrent intrusions of elements of rapid eye movement (REM) sleep into the transition between sleep and wakefulness

natural environment type phobias extreme fears of events or situations in the natural environment that cause impairment in one's ability to function normally

need for treatment legal criterion operationalized as a signed certificate by two physicians stating that a person requires treatment but will not agree to it voluntarily; formerly a sufficient cause to hospitalize the person involuntarily and force him or her to undergo treatment

negative affectivity a dimension of personality characterized by negative mood states

negative cognitive triad perspective seen in depressed people in which they have negative views of themselves, of the world, and of the future

negative reinforcement process in which people avoid being exposed to feared objects and their avoidance is reinforced by the subsequent reduction of their anxiety

negative symptoms in schizophrenia, deficits in functioning that indicate the absence of a capacity present in people without schizophrenia, such as restricted affect

neurocognitive disorders behavioral disorders known or presumed to result from disruptions of brain structure and functioning

neurodevelopmental disorders behavioral disorders with onset during childhood known or presumed to result at least in part from disruption of brain development

neurofibrillary tangles twists or tangles of filaments within nerve cells, especially prominent in the cerebral cortex and hippocampus, common in the brains of Alzheimer's disease patients

neuroleptics drugs used to treat psychotic symptoms

neuropsychological tests tests of cognitive, sensory, and/or motor skills that attempt to differentiate people with deficits in these areas from normal subjects

neurotransmitters biochemicals, released from a sending neuron, that transmit messages to a receiving neuron in the brain and nervous system

nicotine alkaloid found in tobacco; operates on both the central and peripheral nervous systems, resulting in the release of biochemicals, including dopamine, norepinephrine, serotonin, and the endogenous opioids

night eating disorder an eating disorder characterized by the regular intake of excessive amounts of food after dinner and into the night

nightmare disorder sleep disorder characterized by nightmares frequent enough to cause significant distress or impairment in functioning

nonsuicidal self-injury (NSSI) act of deliberately cutting, burning, puncturing, or otherwise significantly injuring one's skin with no intent to die

norepinephrine neurotransmitter that is involved in the regulation of mood

norepinephrine-dopamine reuptake inhibitors drugs used to treat depression; inhibit the reuptake of both norepinephrine and dopamine

null hypothesis alternative to a primary hypothesis, stating that there is no relationship between the independent variable and the dependent variable

O

obesity condition of being significantly overweight, defined by the Centers for Disease Control as a body mass index (BMI) of 30 or over, where BMI is calculated as weight in pounds multiplied by 703, then divided by the square of height in inches

object relations view held by a group of modern psychodynamic theorists that one develops a self-concept and appraisals of others in a four-stage process during childhood and retains them throughout adulthood; psychopathology consists of an incomplete progression through these stages or an acquisition of poor self- and other concepts

observational learning learning that occurs when a person observes the rewards and punishments of another's behavior and then behaves in accordance with the same rewards and punishments

obsessions uncontrollable, persistent thoughts, images, ideas, or impulses that an individual feels intrude on his or her consciousness and that cause significant anxiety or distress

obsessive-compulsive disorder (OCD) anxiety disorder characterized by obsessions (persistent thoughts) and compulsions (rituals)

obsessive-compulsive personality disorder pervasive rigidity in one's activities and interpersonal relationships; includes qualities such as emotional constriction, extreme perfectionism, and anxiety resulting from even slight disruptions in one's routine

obstructive sleep apnea hypopnea syndrome sleep disorder characterized by repeated episodes of upper-airway obstruction during sleep

operant conditioning form of learning in which behaviors lead to consequences that either reinforce or punish the organism, leading to an increased or a decreased probability of a future response

operationalization specific manner in which variables in a study are measured or manipulated

opioids substances, including morphine and heroin, that produce euphoria followed by a tranquil state; in severe intoxication, can lead to unconsciousness, coma, and seizures; can cause withdrawal symptoms of emotional distress, severe nausea, sweating, diarrhea, and fever

oppositional defiant disorder syndrome of chronic misbehavior in childhood marked by belligerence, irritability, and defiance, although not to the extent found in a diagnosis of conduct disorder

organic amnesia loss of memory caused by brain injury resulting from disease, drugs, accidents (blows to head), or surgery

orgasm discharge of neuromuscular tension built up during sexual activity; in men, entails rhythmic contractions of the prostate, seminal vesicles, vas deferens, and penis and seminal discharge; in women, entails contractions of the orgasmic platform and uterus

other specified feeding or eating disorder presentations of an eating disorder that cause clinically significant distress or impairment but do not meet the full diagnostic criteria for any of the eating disorders otherwise identified

P

palilalia continuous repetition of sounds and words

panic attacks short, intense periods during which an individual experiences physiological and cognitive symptoms of anxiety, characterized by intense fear and discomfort

panic disorder disorder characterized by recurrent, unexpected panic attacks

paranoid personality disorder personality disorder characterized by a pervasive pattern of mistrust and suspiciousness of others' motives

paraphilic disorder disorder characterized by atypical sexual activity that involves one of the following: (1) nonhuman objects, (2) nonconsenting adults, (3) the suffering or humiliation of oneself or one's partner, or (4) children

patients' rights movement movement to ensure that mental patients retain their basic rights and to remove them from institutions and care for them in the community

pedophilic disorder disorder characterized by adult obtainment of sexual gratification by engaging in sexual activities with young children

performance anxiety anxiety over sexual performance that interferes with sexual functioning

peripartum onset subtype of major depressive or manic episode used when the episode occurs during pregnancy or in the 4 weeks after childbirth

persecutory delusions false, persistent beliefs that one is being pursued by other people

persistent depressive disorder a chronic form of depression with symptoms lasting for at least 2 years

persistent motor or vocal tic disorder (PMVTD) a condition involving quick and uncontrollable movements or vocal outbursts (but not both)

personality patterns of thinking, emotions, and behavior that tend to be enduring

personality disorder chronic pattern of maladaptive cognition, emotion, and behavior that begins by adolescence or early adulthood and continues into later adulthood

personality inventories questionnaires that assess people's typical ways of thinking, feeling, and behaving; used to obtain information about people's well-being, self-concept, attitudes, and beliefs

personality trait a facet of personality on which people differ from one another

pervasive developmental disorders disorders characterized by severe and persisting impairment in several areas of development

phencyclidine (PCP) substance that produces euphoria, slowed reaction times, and involuntary movements at low doses; disorganized thinking, feelings of unreality, and hostility at intermediate doses; and amnesia, analgesia, respiratory problems, and changes in body temperature at high doses

phenothiazines drugs that reduce the functional level of dopamine in the brain and tend to reduce the symptoms of schizophrenia

pituitary major endocrine gland that lies partly on the outgrowth of the brain and just below the hypothalamus; produces the largest number of different hormones and controls the secretions of other endocrine glands

placebo control group in a therapy outcome study, group of people whose treatment is an inactive substance (to compare with the effects of a drug) or a nontheory-based therapy providing social support (to compare with the effects of psychotherapy)

plaques deposits of amyloid protein that accumulate in the extracellular spaces of the cerebral cortex, hippocampus, and other forebrain structures in people with Alzheimer's disease

plateau phase in the sexual response cycle, period between arousal and orgasm, during which excitement remains high but stable

polygenic combination of many genes, each of which makes a small contribution to an inherited trait

positive symptoms in schizophrenia, hallucinations, delusions, and disorganization in thought and behavior

positron-emission tomography (PET) method of localizing and measuring brain activity by detecting photons that result from the metabolization of an injected isotope

posttraumatic stress disorder (PTSD) anxiety disorder characterized by (1) repeated mental images of experiencing a traumatic event, (2) emotional numbing and detachment, and (3) hypervigilance and chronic arousal

preconscious according to Freud, area of the psyche that contains material from the unconscious before it reaches the conscious mind

premenstrual dysphoric disorder a set of symptoms occurring immediately prior to onset of menses characterized by a mixture of depression, anxiety and tension, and irritability and anger; may occur in mood swings during the week before onset of menses and subside once menses has begun

prepared classical conditioning theory that evolution has prepared people to be easily conditioned to fear objects or situations that were dangerous in ancient times

prevalence proportion of the population who have a specific disorder at a given point or period in time

primary prevention prevention of the development of psychological disorders before they start

prodromal symptoms in schizophrenia, milder symptoms prior to an acute phase of the disorder, during which behaviors are unusual and peculiar but not yet psychotic or completely disorganized

projective test presentation of an ambiguous stimulus, such as an inkblot, to a client, who then projects unconscious motives and issues onto the stimulus in his or her interpretation of its content

psychic epidemics phenomena in which large numbers of people begin to engage in unusual behaviors that appear to have a psychological origin

psychoanalysis form of treatment for psychopathology involving alleviating unconscious conflicts driving psychological symptoms by helping people gain insight into their conflicts and finding ways of resolving these conflicts

psychodynamic theories theories developed by Freud's followers but usually differing somewhat from Freud's original theories

psychodynamic therapies therapies focused on uncovering and resolving unconscious conflicts that drive psychological symptoms

psychogenic amnesia loss of memory in the absence of any brain injury or disease and thought to have psychological causes

psychological approach approach to abnormality that focuses on personality, behavior, and ways of thinking as possible causes of abnormality

psychological theories theories that view mental disorders as caused by psychological processes, such as beliefs, thinking styles, and coping styles

psychopathology symptoms that cause mental, emotional, and/or physical pain

psychopathy set of broad personality traits including superficial charm, a grandiose sense of self-worth, a tendency toward boredom and need for stimulation, pathological lying, an ability to be cunning and manipulative, and a lack of remorse

psychophysiological tests tests in which instruments are attached to the periphery of the body to record changes due to activity in the nervous system

psychosexual stages according to Freud, stages in the developmental process children pass through; in each stage, sex drives are focused on the stimulation of certain areas of the body, and particular psychological issues can arouse anxiety

psychosis state involving a loss of contact with reality as well as an inability to differentiate between reality and one's subjective state

psychosurgery rare treatment for mental disorders in which a neurosurgeon attempts to destroy small areas of the brain thought to be involved in a patient's symptoms

psychoticism proneness to psychotic-like symptoms, such as illusions

PTSD with prominent dissociative (depersonalization/derealization) symptoms a form of posttraumatic stress disorder in which the individual experiences feelings of being detached from his or her mental processes or body and of the unreality of the surroundings

R

random assignment assignment of participants in an experiment to groups based on a random process

rapid cycling bipolar disorder diagnosis given when a person has four or more cycles of mania and depression within 1 year

rapid eye movement (REM) sleep behavior disorder frequent and impairing behaviors such as sleepwalking, sleep terrors, and confusional episodes during REM sleep

receptors molecules on the membranes of neurons to which neurotransmitters bind

reflection method of responding in which a therapist expresses his or her attempt to understand what the client is experiencing and trying to communicate

reformulated learned helplessness theory view that people who attribute negative events to internal, stable, and global causes are more likely than other people to experience learned helplessness deficits following such events and thus are predisposed to depression

rejection sensitivity tendency to be hypervigilant and overreactive to signs of rejection from others

relapse prevention programs treatments that seek to offset continued alcohol use by identifying high-risk situations for those attempting to stop or cut down on drinking and teaching them either to avoid those situations or to use assertiveness skills when in them, while viewing setbacks as temporary

relational psychoanalysis a subfield of psychoanalysis that emphasizes internalized relationships with other people based on the influences of early formative relationships with parents and other attachment figures

reliability degree of consistency in a measurement—that is, the extent to which it yields accurate measurements of a phenomenon across several trials, across different populations, and in different forms

repetitive transcranial magnetic stimulation (rTMS) biological treatment that exposes patients to repeated, high-intensity magnetic pulses that are focused on particular brain structures in order to stimulate those structures

repression defense mechanism in which the ego pushes anxiety-provoking material back into the unconscious

residual symptoms symptoms associated with schizophrenia, such as unusual beliefs or strange perceptual experiences, that are present for at least six months

resistance in psychodynamic therapy, when a client finds it difficult or impossible to address certain material; the client's resistance signals an unconscious conflict, which the therapist then tries to interpret

resolution in the sexual response cycle, state of deep relaxation following orgasm in which a man loses his erection and a woman's orgasmic platform subsides

restless legs syndrome (RLS) creeping, crawling, tingling, itching sensations in the legs that are prominent enough to interfere with sleep

restricted affect a symptom in which emotional expression is reduced or absent

restricting type of anorexia nervosa type of anorexia nervosa in which weight gain is prevented by refusal to eat

retrograde amnesia deficit in the ability to recall previously learned information or past events

reuptake process in which a sending neuron reabsorbs some of the neurotransmitter in the synapse, decreasing the amount left in the synapse

right to refuse treatment right, not recognized by all states, of involuntarily committed people to refuse drugs or other treatment

right to treatment fundamental right of involuntarily committed people to receive active treatment for their disorders rather than shelter alone

risk factors conditions or variables associated with a higher risk of having a disorder

rumination focusing on one's personal concerns and feelings of distress repetitively and passively

S

sadomasochism pattern of sexual rituals between a sexually sadistic "giver" and a sexually masochistic "receiver"

sample group of people taken from a population of interest to participate in a study

schizoaffective disorder disorder in which individuals simultaneously experience schizophrenic symptoms (i.e., delusions, hallucinations, disorganized speech and behavior, and/or negative symptoms) and mood symptoms meeting the criteria for a major depressive episode, a manic episode, or an episode of mixed mania/depression

schizoid personality disorder personality disorder characterized by pervasive detachment from social relationships and a restricted range of emotional expression

schizophrenia disorder consisting of unreal or disorganized thoughts and perceptions as well as verbal, cognitive, and behavioral deficits

schizophrenia spectrum the set of psychiatric disorders related to schizophrenia that vary along a severity continuum

schizophreniform disorder disorder in which individuals meet the primary criteria for schizophrenia but show symptoms lasting only 1 to 6 months

schizotypal personality disorder chronic pattern of inhibited or inappropriate emotion and social behavior as well as aberrant cognitions and disorganized speech

scientific method systematic method of obtaining and evaluating information relevant to a problem

seasonal affective disorder (SAD) disorder identified by a 2-year period in which a person experiences major depression during winter months and then recovers fully during the summer; some people with this disorder also experience mild mania during summer months

secondary prevention detection of psychological disorders in their earliest stages and treatment designed to reduce their development

selective serotonin-norepinephrine reuptake inhibitors (SNRIs) drugs that affect both the serotonin system and the norepinephrine system and are used to treat anxiety and depression

selective serotonin reuptake inhibitors (SSRIs) class of antidepressant drugs

self-actualization fulfillment of one's potential for love, creativity, and meaning

self-efficacy beliefs beliefs that one can engage in the behaviors necessary to overcome a situation

self-monitoring method of assessment in which a client records the number of times per day that he or she engages in a specific behavior and the conditions surrounding the behavior

self psychology a form of psychoanalytic theory and therapy developed by Heinz Kohut in which psychopathology is viewed as being the result of disrupted or unmet developmental needs

sensate focus therapy treatment for sexual dysfunction in which partners alternate between giving and receiving stimulation in a relaxed, openly communicative atmosphere in order to reduce performance anxiety and concern over achieving orgasm by learning each partner's sexual fulfillment needs

separation anxiety disorder syndrome of childhood and adolescence marked by the presence of abnormal fear or worry over becoming separated from one's caregiver(s) as well as clinging behaviors in the presence of the caregiver(s)

serotonin neurotransmitter involved in the regulation of mood and impulsive responses

sexual desire in the sexual response cycle, an urge or inclination to engage in sexual activity

sexual dysfunctions problems in experiencing sexual arousal or carrying through with sexual acts to the point of sexual arousal

sexual functioning the ability and capacity to engage in sexual behavior

sexual masochism disorder disorder characterized by obtaining sexual gratification through experiencing pain and humiliation at the hands of one's partner

sexual sadism disorder disorder characterized by obtaining sexual gratification through inflicting pain and humiliation on one's partner

simple control group consists of participants who do not receive the experimental therapy but are tracked for the same period of time as the participants who do receive the therapy

single-case experimental design experimental design in which an individual or a small number of individuals are studied intensively; the individual is put through some sort of manipulation or intervention, and his or her behavior is examined before and after this manipulation to determine the effects

single photon emission computed tomography (SPECT) procedure to assess brain functioning in which a tracer substance is injected into the bloodstream and then travels to the brain, where it can indicate the activity level of specific areas of the brain when viewed through a SPECT scanner

situational type phobias extreme fears of situations such as public transportation, tunnels, bridges, elevators, flying, driving, or enclosed spaces

skin-picking disorder a disorder characterized by recurrent picking at scabs or places on the skin, creating significant lesions that often become infected and cause scars

sleep disorders disturbances in sleeping or staying awake, such as insomnia and narcolepsy

sleep-related hypoventilation episodes of decreased breathing associated with high carbon dioxide levels

sleep terror disorder disorder of arousal in which the individual screams, sweats, and has a racing heart during NREM sleep; the person cannot be easily wakened and usually does not remember the episode on awakening

sleepwalking disorder of arousal characterized by repeated episodes of walking during NREM sleep

social anxiety disorder an anxiety disorder in which the individual experiences intense fear of public humiliation or rejection and therefore tends to avoid social situations

social communication disorder a communication disorder characterized by difficulty using language and other modalities for communicating in social situations

social drift explanation for the association between schizophrenia and low social status that says that because schizophrenia symptoms interfere with a person's ability to complete an education and hold a job, people with schizophrenia tend to drift downward in social class compared to their family of origin

sociocultural approach approach to psychopathology focusing on the role of the environment, stress, and culture in producing psychopathology

somatic symptom disorder syndrome marked by health concerns that are excessive given actual physical health, that persist despite contrary evidence, and that interfere with daily functioning

specific learning disorder disrupted or delayed development in a specific domain of cognition, such as reading

specific phobias extreme fears of specific objects or situations that cause an individual to routinely avoid those objects or situations

speech sound disorder a communication disorder characterized by difficulties in producing speech

squeeze technique sex therapy technique used for premature ejaculation; the man's partner stimulates him to an erection, and then when he signals that ejaculation is imminent, the partner applies a firm but gentle squeeze to his penis, either at the glans or at the base, for 3 or 4 seconds; the goal of this technique is for the man to learn to identify the point of ejaculatory inevitability and to control his arousal level at that point

statistical significance likelihood that a study's results have occurred only by chance

stereotypic movement disorder a motor disorder characterized by repetitive, seemingly driven, and apparently purposeless motor behavior, such as hand waving or head banging

stimulants drugs that activate the nervous system

stop-start technique sex therapy technique used for premature ejaculation; the man or his partner stimulates his penis until he is about to ejaculate; the man then relaxes and concentrates on the sensations in his body until his level of arousal declines; the goal of this technique is for the man to learn to identify the point of ejaculatory inevitability and to control his arousal level at that point

stress-inoculation therapy a form of cognitive-behavior therapy that focuses on developing skills that allow the individual to cope with stress

stroke sudden damage to the brain due to blockage of blood flow or hemorrhaging

structured interview meeting between a clinician and a client or a client's associate(s) in which the clinician asks questions that are standardized and are usually designed to determine whether a diagnosis is warranted

substance naturally occurring or synthetically produced product that alters perceptions, thoughts, emotions, and behaviors when ingested, smoked, or injected

substance abuse diagnosis given in the *DSM-IV* when a person's recurrent substance use leads to significant harmful consequences, as manifested by a failure to fulfill obligations at work, school, or home; the use of substances in physically hazardous situations; legal problems; and continued use despite social and legal problems

substance dependence diagnosis given in the *DSM-IV* when a person's substance use leads to physiological dependence or significant impairment or distress, as manifested by an inability to use the substance in moderation; a decline in social, occupational, or recreational activities; or the spending of large amounts of time obtaining substances or recovering from their effects

substance-induced sexual dysfunction problems in sexual functioning caused by substance use

substance-induced sleep disorder sleep disturbance due to the use of substances, including prescription medications (e.g., medications that control hypertension or cardiac arrhythmias) and nonprescription substances (e.g., alcohol and caffeine)

substance intoxication experience of significantly maladaptive behavioral and psychological symptoms due to the effect of a substance on the central nervous system that develops during or shortly after use of the substance

substance use disorders disorders characterized by inability to use a substance in moderation and/or the intentional use of a substance to change one's thoughts, feelings, and/or behaviors, leading to impairment in work, academic, personal, or social endeavors

substance withdrawal experience of clinically significant distress in social, occupational, or other areas of functioning due to the cessation or reduction of substance use

suicidal ideation thoughts about killing oneself

suicide purposeful taking of one's own life

suicide attempts behaviors engaged in with some intent to kill oneself

suicide cluster when two or more suicides or attempted suicides nonrandomly occur closely together in space or time

suicide contagion phenomenon in which the suicide of a well-known person is linked to the acceptance of suicide by people who closely identify with that person

superego part of the unconscious that consists of absolute moral standards internalized from one's parents during childhood and from one's culture

supernatural theories theories that see mental disorders as the result of supernatural forces, such as divine intervention, curses, demonic possession, and/or personal sins; mental disorders then can be cured through religious rituals, exorcisms, confessions, and/or death

symptom questionnaire questionnaire that assesses what symptoms a person is experiencing

synapse space between a sending neuron and a receiving neuron into which neurotransmitters are first released (also known as the synaptic gap)

syndrome set of symptoms that tend to occur together

systematic desensitization therapy type of behavior therapy that attempts to reduce client anxiety through relaxation techniques and progressive exposure to feared stimuli

T

tardive dyskinesia neurological disorder marked by involuntary movements of the tongue, face, mouth, or jaw, resulting from taking neuroleptic drugs

tertiary prevention program focusing on people who already have a disease with the aim of preventing relapse and reducing the impact of the disease on the person's quality of life

thalamus structure of the brain that directs incoming information from sense receptors (such as vision and hearing) to the cerebrum

theory set of assumptions about the likely causes of abnormality and appropriate treatments

therapy outcome studies experimental studies that assess the effects of an intervention designed to reduce psychopathology in an experimental group, while performing no intervention or a different type of intervention on another group

third variable problem possibility that variables not measured in a study are the real cause of the relationship between the variables measured in the study

third-wave approaches modern psychotherapeutic techniques that combine elements of the first- and second-wave approaches—behavioral therapy and cognitive therapy, respectively—with mindfulness meditation practices derived from Zen Buddhism to help people accept, understand, and better regulate their emotions

tolerance condition of experiencing less and less effect from the same dose of a substance

Tourette's disorder a motor disorder characterized by multiple motor tics and one or more vocal tics

transference in psychodynamic therapies, the client's reaction to the therapist as if the therapist were an important person in his or her early development; the client's feelings and beliefs about this other person are transferred onto the therapist

transference-focused therapy a highly structured psychodynamic treatment for borderline personality disorder that uses the relationship between patient and therapist to help patients develop a more realistic and healthier understanding of their interpersonal relationships

transgender a term for the broad spectrum of individuals who identify with a gender different from their natal (born) biological sex.

transvestic disorder paraphilic disorder in which a heterosexual man dresses in women's clothing as his primary means of becoming sexually aroused

traumatic brain injury injury to the brain resulting from traumatic force; often associated with loss of consciousness

trephination procedure in which holes were drilled in the skulls of people displaying abnormal behavior, presumably to allow evil spirits to depart their bodies; performed in the Stone Age

tricyclic antidepressants class of antidepressant drugs

twin studies studies of the heritability of a disorder by comparing concordance rates between monozygotic and dizygotic twins

Type A behavior pattern personality pattern characterized by time urgency, hostility, and competitiveness

U

unconditioned response (UR) in classical conditioning, response that naturally follows when a certain stimulus appears, such as a dog salivating when it smells food

unconditioned stimulus (US) in classical conditioning, stimulus that naturally elicits a reaction, as food elicits salivation in dogs

unconscious according to Freud, an area of the psyche where memories, wishes, and needs are stored and where conflicts among the id, ego, and superego are played out

V

vagus nerve stimulation (VNS) treatment in which the vagus nerve—the part of the autonomic nervous system that carries information from the head, neck, thorax, and abdomen to several areas of the brain, including the hypothalamus and amygdala—is stimulated by a small electronic device much like a cardiac pacemaker, which is surgically implanted under a patient's skin in the left chest wall

validity degree of correspondence between a measurement and the phenomenon under study

variable measurable factor or characteristic that can vary within an individual, between individuals, or both

vascular neurocognitive disorder a form of dementia resulting from multiple strokes and/or ischemic events

voyeuristic disorder disorder characterized by obtainment of sexual arousal by compulsively and secretly watching another person undressing, bathing, engaging in sex, or being naked

W

wait list control group in a therapy outcome study, group of people that functions as a control group while an experimental group receives an intervention and then receives the intervention itself after a waiting period

working through method used in psychodynamic therapies in which the client repeatedly goes over and over painful memories and difficult issues as a way to understand and accept them

REFERENCES

A

AARP Public Policy Institute. (2018). Prescription drug abuse among older adults. https://www.aarp.org/ppi/info-2017/prescription-drug-abuse-among-older-adults.html. Retrieved July 4, 2018.

Aarsland, D., & Kurz, M. W. (2009). The epidemiology of dementia associated with Parkinson disease. *Journal of the Neurological Sciences, 289,* 18–22.

Abbott, S. M., Reid, K. J., & Zee, P. C. (2015). Circadian rhythm sleep-wake disorders. *Psychiatric Clinics, 38*(4), 805–823.

Abi-Dargham, A., Kegeles, L. S., Zea-Ponce, Y., Mawlawi, O., Martinez, D., Mitropoulou, V., O'Flynn, K., Koenigsberg, H. W., van Heertum, R., Cooper, T., Laruelle, M., & Siever, L. J. (2004). Striatal amphetamine-induced dopamine release in patients with schizotypal personality disorder studied with single photon emission computed tomography and [123I]Iodobenzamide. *Biological Psychiatry, 55,* 1001–1006.

Abramowitz, J. S., & Jacoby, R. J. (2015). Obsessive-compulsive and related disorders: A critical review of the new diagnostic class. *Annual Review of Clinical Psychology, 11,* 165–186.

Abramson, L. Y., Alloy, L. B., Hankin, B. L., Haeffel, G. J., MacCoon, D. G., & Gibb, B. E. (2002). Cognitive vulnerability-stress models of depression in a self-regulatory and psychobiological context. In I. H. Gotlib & C. L. Hammen (Eds.), *Handbook of depression* (pp. 268–294). New York: Guilford Press.

Abramson, L. Y., Bardone-Cone, A. M., Vohs, K. D., Joiner, T. E., Jr., & Heatherton, T. F. (2006). Cognitive vulnerability to bulimia. In L. B. Alloy & J. H. Riskind (Eds.), *Cognitive vulnerability to emotional disorders* (pp. 329–364). Mahwah, NJ: Erlbaum.

Abramson, L. Y., Metalsky, G. I., & Alloy, L. B. (1989). Hopelessness depression: A theory-based subtype of depression. *Psychological Review, 96,* 358–372.

Abramson, L. Y., Seligman, M. E. P., & Teasdale, J. (1978). Learned helplessness in humans: Critique and reformulation. *Journal of Abnormal Psychology, 87,* 49–74.

Achilli, C., Pundir, J., Ramanathan, P., Sabatini, L., Hamoda, H., & Panay, N. (2017). Efficacy and safety of transdermal testosterone in postmenopausal women with hypoactive sexual desire disorder: A systematic review and meta-analysis. *Fertility and Sterility, 107*(2), 475–482.

Adams, C. E., Awad, G., Rathbone, J., & Thornley, B. (2007). Chlorpromazine versus placebo for schizophrenia. *Cochrane Database of Systematic Reviews, 2,* CD000284.

Addis, M. E. (2008). Gender and depression in men. *Clinical Psychology: Science and Practice, 15,* 153–168.

Aderibigbe, Y. A., Bloch, R. M., & Walker, W. R. (2001). Prevalence of depersonalization and derealization experiences in a rural population. *Social Psychiatry & Psychiatric Epidemiology, 36,* 63–69.

Adler, C. M., Adams, J., DelBello, M. P., Holland, S. K., Schmithorst, V., Levine, A., Jarvis, K., & Strakowski, S. M. (2006). Evidence of white matter pathology in bipolar disorder adolescents experiencing their first episode of mania: A diffusion tensor imaging study. *American Journal of Psychiatry, 163,* 322–324.

Afifi, T. O., Mather, A., Boman, J., Fleisher, W., Enns, M. W., MacMillan, H., & Sareen, J. (2011). Childhood adversity and personality disorders: Results from a nationally representative population-based study. *Journal of Psychiatric Research, 45,* 814–822.

Ágh, T., Kovács, G., Pawaskar, M., Supina, D., Inotai, A., & Vokó, Z. (2015). Epidemiology, health-related quality of life and economic burden of binge eating disorder: A systematic literature review. *Eating and Weight Disorders—Studies on Anorexia, Bulimia and Obesity, 20*(1), 1–12.

Agras, W. S., Fitzsimmons-Craft, E. E., & Wilfley, D. E. (2017). Evolution of cognitive-behavioral therapy for eating disorders. *Behaviour Research and Therapy, 88,* 26–36.

Agras, W. S., Walsh, B. T., Fairburn, C. C., Wilson, G. T., & Kraemer, H. C. (2000). A multicenter comparison of cognitive-behavioral therapy and interpersonal psychotherapy for bulimia nervosa. *Archives of General Psychiatry, 57,* 459–466.

Agrawal, A., Heath, A. C., & Lynskey, M. T. (2011). *DSM-IV* to *DSM-5*: The impact of proposed revisions on diagnosis of alcohol use disorders. *Addiction, 106,* 1935–1943.

Ahlers, M. M. (2009, July 14). NTSB: Sleep disorder may have contributed to Boston train crash. http://www.cnn.com/2009/US/07/14/ntsb.train.crash/index.html (accessed July 23, 2009).

Ahmad, S. I., & Hinshaw, S. P. (2016). Attention-deficit/hyperactivity disorder: Similarities to and differences from other externalizing disorders. In T. P. Beauchaine & S. P. Hinshaw (Eds.), *The Oxford handbook of externalizing spectrum disorders* (pp. 19–37). New York: Oxford University Press.

Ahmed, A. O., Buckley, P. F., & Mabe, P. A. (2012). Latent structure of psychotic experiences in the general population. *Acta Psychiatrica Scandinavica, 125,* 54–65.

Ajdacic-Gross, V., Killias, M., Hepp, U., Gadola, E., Bopp, M., Lauber, C., Schnyder, U., Gutzwiller, F., & Rossler, W. (2006). Changing times: A longitudinal analysis of international firearm suicide data. *American Journal of Public Health, 96,* 1752–1755.

Ajzen, I. (1991). The theory of planned behavior. *Organizational Behavior and Human Decision Processes, 50,* 179–211.

Alarcon, R. D., Becker, A. E., Lewis-Fernandez, R., Like, R. C., Desai, P., Foulks, E., Gonzales, J., Hansen, H., Kopelowicz, A., Lu, F. G., Oquendo, M. A., & Primm, A. (2009). Issues for *DSM-V:* The role of culture in psychiatric diagnosis. *Journal of Nervous and Mental Disease, 197,* 559–560.

Albert, P. R., Benkelfat, C., & Descarries, L. (2012). The neurobiology of depression—revisiting the serotonin hypothesis. I. Cellular and molecular mechanisms. *Philosophical Transactions of the Royal Society, 367,* 2378–2381.

Albuquerque, D., Stice, E., Rodríguez-López, R., Manco, L., & Nóbrega, C. (2015). Current review of genetics of human obesity: From molecular mechanisms to an evolutionary perspective. *Molecular Genetics and Genomics, 290*(4), 1191–1221

Aldao, A., Mennin, D. S., Linardatos, E., & Fresco, D. M. (2010). Differential patterns of physical symptoms and subjective processes in generalized anxiety disorder and unipolar depression. *Journal of Anxiety Disorders, 24,* 250–259.

Alegría, M., Álvarez, K., & DiMarzio, K. (2017). Immigration and mental health. *Current Epidemiology Reports, 4*(2), 145–155.

Alegría, M., Canino, G., Shrout, P. E., Woo, M., Duan, N., Vila, D., et al. (2008). Prevalence of mental illness in immigrant and nonimmigrant U.S. Latino groups. *American Journal of Psychiatry, 165,* 359–369.

Alexander, M. (2012). *The new Jim Crow: Mass incarceration in the age of colorblindness.* New York: New Press.

Ali, S., Garg, S., Cohen, B. E., Bhave, P., Harris, W. S., & Whooley, M. A. (2009). Association between omega-3 fatty acids and depressive symptoms among patients with established coronary artery disease: Data from the Heart and Soul Study. *Psychotherapy and Psychosomatics, 78,* 125–127.

Allderidge, P. (1979). Hospitals, madhouses and asylums: Cycles in the care of the insane. *British Journal of Psychiatry, 134,* 321–334.

Allen, N. C., Bagade, S., McQueen, M. B., Ioannidis, J. P., Kavvoura, F. K., Khoury, M. J., Tanzi, R. E., & Bertram, L. (2008). Systematic meta-analyses and field synopsis of genetic association studies in schizophrenia: The SzGene database. *Nature Genetics, 40,* 827–834.

Allen, R. P., Picchietti, D. L., Garcia-Borreguero, D., Ondo, W. G., Walters, A. S., Winkelman, J. W., & International Restless Legs Syndrome Study Group. (2014). Restless legs syndrome/Willis-Ekbom disease diagnostic criteria: Updated International Restless Legs Syndrome Study Group (IRLSSG) consensus criteria—history, rationale, description, and significance. *Sleep Medicine, 15*(8), 860–873.

Allison, K. C. (2017). Night eating syndrome. In K. D. Brownell & B. T. Walsh (Eds.), *Eating disorders and obesity: A comprehensive handbook* (3rd ed., pp. 203–208). New York: Guilford.

Alloy, L. B., Abramson, L. Y., & Francis, E. L. (1999). Do negative cognitive styles confer vulnerability to depression? *Current Directions in Psychological Science, 8,* 128–132.

Alloy, L. B., Abramson, L. Y., Walshaw, P. D., Cogswell, A., Grandin, L. D., Hughes, M. E., Iacoviello, B. M., Whitehouse, W. G., Urosevic, S., Nusslock, R., & Hogan, M. E. (2008). Inhibition system sensitivities and bipolar spectrum disorders: Prospective prediction of bipolar mood episodes. *Bipolar Disorders, 10,* 310–322.

Alloy, L. B., Hamilton, J. L., Hamlat, E. J., & Abramson, L. Y. (2016). Pubertal development, emotion regulatory styles, and the emergence of sex differences in internalizing disorders and symptoms in adolescence. *Clinical Psychological Science, 4*(5), 867–881.

Alloy, L. B., Nusslock, R., & Boland, E. M. (2015). The development and course of bipolar spectrum disorders: An integrated reward and circadian rhythm dysregulation model. *Annual Review of Clinical Psychology, 11,* 213.

Althof, S. E. (1995). Pharmacologic treatment of rapid ejaculation. *Psychiatric Clinics of North America, 18,* 85–94.

Althof, S. E. (2000). Erectile dysfunction: Psychotherapy with men and couples. In S. R. Leiblum & R. C. Rosen (Eds.), *Principles and practice of sex therapy* (3rd ed., pp. 242–275). New York: Guilford Press.

Altman, S., Haeri, S., Cohen, L. J., Ten, A., Harron, E., Galynker, I. I., et al. (2006). Predictors of relapse in bipolar disorder: A review. *Journal of Psychiatric Practice, 12,* 269–282.

Alvanzo, A. A. H., Storr, C. L., La Flair, L., Green, K. G., & Wagner, F. A. (2011). Race/ethnicity and sex differences in progression from drinking initiation to the development of alcohol dependence. *Drug and Alcohol Dependence, 118,* 375–382.

Alzheimer's Association. (2018). Alzheimer's disease facts and figures. *Alzheimer's & Dementia, 14*(3), 367–429.

American Psychiatric Association (APA). (2000). *Diagnostic and statistical manual of mental disorders* (4th ed., Text Revision). Washington, DC: American Psychiatric Association.

American Psychiatric Association (APA). (2013). *Diagnostic and statistical manual of mental disorders* (5th ed.). Washington, DC: Author.

American Psychological Association. (2009). *Report of the American Psychological Association task force on appropriate therapeutic responses to sexual orientation.* Washington, DC: Author.

American Psychological Association. (2015). Guidelines for psychological practice with transgender and gender nonconforming people. *American Psychologist, 70*(9), 832–864.

Andersen, A. E., & DiDomenico, L. (1992). Diet vs. shape content of popular male and female magazines: A dose-response relationship to the incidence of eating disorders? *International Journal of Eating Disorders, 11,* 283–287.

Andersen, B. L., Yang, H. C., Farrar, W. B., Golden-Kreutz, D. M., Emery, C. F., Thornton, L. M., et al. (2008). Psychologic intervention improves survival for breast cancer patients: A randomized clinical trial. *Cancer, 113,* 3450–3458.

Anderson, D. K., Liang, J. W., & Lord, C. (2014). Predicting young adult outcome among more and less cognitively able individuals with autism spectrum disorders. *Journal of Child Psychology and Psychiatry, 55*(5), 485–494.

Anderson, E. R., & Mayes, L. C. (2010). Race/ethnicity and internalizing disorders in youth: A review. *Clinical Psychology Review, 30,* 338–348.

Anderson, P. L., Price, M., Edwards, S. M., Obasaju, M. A., Schmertz, S. K., Zimand, E., & Calamaras, M. R. (2013). Virtual reality exposure therapy for social anxiety disorder: A randomized controlled trial. *Journal of Consulting and Clinical Psychology, 81,* 751–760.

Anderson, R. E., Bartlett, S. J., Morgan, G. D., & Brownell, K. D. (1995). Weight loss, psychological, and nutritional patterns in competitive male body builders. *International Journal of Eating Disorders, 18,* 49–57.

Andersson, G. (2016). Internet-delivered psychological treatments. *Annual Review of Clinical Psychology, 12,* 157–179.

Andrade, L., Caraveo-Anduaga, J. J., Berglund, P., Bijl, R. V., DeGraaf, R., Volbergh, W., et al. (2003). The epidemiology of major depressive episodes: Results from the International Consortium of Psychiatric Epidemiology (ICPE) surveys. *International Journal of Methods in Psychiatric Research, 12,* 3–21.

Andreasen, N. C. (1998). Jeff: A difficult case of schizophrenia. In R. P. Halgin & S. K. Whitbourne (Eds.), *A casebook in abnormal psychology from the files of experts* (pp. 197–210). New York: Oxford University Press.

Andreasen, N. C., Flaum, M., Swayze, V. W., Tyrrell, G., & Arndt, S. (1990). Positive and negative symptoms in schizophrenia: A critical reappraisal. *Archives of General Psychiatry, 47,* 615–621.

Andrews, G., Hobbs, M. J., Borkovec, T. D., Beesdo, K., Craske, M. G., Heimberg, R. G., Rapee, R. M., Ruscio, A. M., & Stanley, M. A. (2010). Generalized worry disorder: A review of *DSM-IV* generalized anxiety disorder and options for *DSM-V. Depression and Anxiety, 0,* 1–14.

Anestis, M. D., & Anestis, J. C. (2015). Suicide rates and state laws regulating access and exposure to handguns. *American Journal of Public Health, 105*(10), 2049–2058.

Anestis, M. D., Soberay, K. A., Gutierrez, P. M., Hernández, T. D., & Joiner, T. E. (2014). Reconsidering the link between impulsivity and suicidal behavior. *Personality and Social Psychology Review, 18*(4), 366–386.

Angold, A., Costello, E. J., & Worthman, C. M. (1998). Puberty and depression: The roles of age, pubertal status, and pubertal timing. *Psychological Medicine, 28,* 51–61.

Angold, A., Erkanli, A., Egger, H. L., & Costello, J. (2000). Stimulant treatment for children: A community perspective. *Journal of the American Academy of Child & Adolescent Psychiatry, 39,* 975–994.

Angst, J., Gamma, A., Endrass, J., Goodwin, R., Ajdacic, V., Eich, D., & Rossler, W. (2004). Obsessive-compulsive severity spectrum in the community: Prevalence, comorbidity, and course. *European Archives of Psychiatry & Clinical Neuroscience, 254,* 156–164.

Angst, J., Gamma, A., Pezawas, L., Ajdacic-Gross, V., Eich, D., Rossler, W., & Altamura, C. (2007). Parsing the clinical phenotype of depression: The need to integrate brief depressive episodes. *Acta Psychiatrica Scandinavica, 115,* 221–228.

Anonymous. (1992). First-person account: Portrait of a schizophrenic. *Schizophrenia Bulletin, 18,* 333–334.

Anton, R. F., O'Malley, S. S., Ciraulo, D. A., Cisler, R. A., Couper, D., Donovan, D. M., Gastfriend, D. R., Hosking, J. D., Johnson, B. A., LoCastro, J. S., Longabaugh, R., Mason, B. J., Mattson, M. E., Miller, W. R., Pettinati, H. M., Randall, C. L., Swift, R., Weiss, R. D., Williams, L. D., & Zweben, A. (2006). Combined pharmacotherapies and behavioral interventions for alcohol dependence: The COMBINE study: A randomized controlled trial. *JAMA, 295,* 2003-2017.

Antoni, M. H., Lehman, J. M., Kilbourn, K. M., Boyers, A. E., Culver, J. L., Alferi, S. M., Young, S. E., McGregor, B. A., Arena, P. L., Harris, S. D., Price, A. A., & Carver, C. S. (2001). Cognitive-behavioral stress management intervention decreases the prevalence of depression and enhances benefit finding among women under treatment for early-stage breast cancer. *Health Psychology, 20,* 20–32.

Antypa, N., Serretti, A., & Rujescu, D. (2013). Serotonergic genes and suicide: A systematic review. *European Neuropsychopharmacology, 23*(10), 1125–1142.

Appelbaum, B. C., Appelbaum, P. S., & Grisso, T. (1998). Competence to consent to voluntary psychiatric hospitalization: A test of a standard proposed by APA. *Psychiatric Services, 49,* 1193–1196.

Appelbaum, P. S. (2007). Assessment of patients' competence to consent to treatment. *New England Journal of Medicine, 357*(18), 1834–1840.

Arcelus, J., Bouman, W. P., Van Den Noortgate, W., Claes, L., Witcomb, G., & Fernandez-Aranda, F. (2015). Systematic review and meta-analysis of prevalence studies in transsexualism. *European Psychiatry, 30*(6), 807–815.

Arcelus, J., Mitchell, A. J., Wales, J., & Nielson, S. (2011). Mortality rates in patients with anorexia nervosa and other eating disorders. *Archives of General Psychiatry, 68,* 724–731.

Arias, J. M. C., Palacio Acosta, C. A., Valencia, J. G., Montoya, G. J., Arango Viana, J. C., Nieto, O. C., Florez, A. F., Camarena Medellind, B. E., Montoya, R. M., Lopez Jaramilloa C. A., Achury, J. G., Fuentes, C. C., Berrio, G. B., & Andres Ruiz-Linares, A. (2011). Exploring epistasis in candidate genes for antisocial personality disorder. *Psychiatric Genetics, 21,* 115–124.

Arntz, A., Weertman, A., & Salet, S. (2011). Interpretation bias in Cluster-C and borderline personality disorders. *Behaviour Research and Therapy, 49,* 472–481.

Arroyo, A., Segrin, C., & Andersen, K. K. (2017). Intergenerational transmission of disordered eating: Direct and indirect maternal communication among grandmothers, mothers, and daughters. *Body Image, 20,* 107–115.

Asarnow, J. R., Hughes, J. L., Babeva, K. N., & Sugar, C. A. (2017). Cognitive-behavioral family treatment for suicide attempt prevention: A randomized controlled trial. *Journal of the American Academy of Child & Adolescent Psychiatry, 56*(6), 506–514.

Asher, M., Asnaani, A., & Aderka, I. M. (2017). Gender differences in social anxiety disorder: A review. *Clinical Psychology Review, 56,* 1–12.

Asherson, P., Buitelaar, J., Faraone, S. V., & Rohde, L. A. (2016). Adult attention-deficit hyperactivity disorder: Key conceptual issues. *Lancet Psychiatry, 3*(6), 568–578.

Ashok, A. H., Marques, T. R., Jauhar, S., Nour, M. M., Goodwin, G. M., Young, A. H., & Howes, O. D. (2017). The dopamine hypothesis of bipolar affective disorder: The state of the art and implications for treatment. *Molecular Psychiatry, 22*(5), 666–679.

A-Tjak, J. G., Davis, M. L., Morina, N., Powers, M. B., Smits, J. A., & Emmelkamp, P. M. (2015). A meta-analysis of the efficacy of acceptance and commitment therapy for clinically relevant mental and physical health problems. *Psychotherapy and Psychosomatics, 84*(1), 30–36.

Attia, E., & Roberto, C. A. (2009). Should amenorrhea be a diagnostic criterion for anorexia nervosa? *International Journal of Eating Disorders, 42,* 581–589.

Attia, E., & Walsh, B. T. (2007). Anorexia nervosa. *American Journal of Psychiatry, 164,* 1805–1810.

Auger, R. R., Burgess, H. J., Emens, J. S., Deriy, L. V., Thomas, S. M., & Sharkey, K. M. (2015). Clinical practice guideline for the treatment of intrinsic circadian rhythm sleep-wake disorders: advanced sleep-wake phase disorder (ASWPD), delayed sleep-wake phase disorder (DSWPD), non-24-hour sleep-wake rhythm disorder (N24SWD), and irregular sleep-wake rhythm disorder (ISWRD). An update for 2015. *Journal of Clinical Sleep Medicine, 11*(10), 1199–1236.

Aybek, S., & Vuilleumier, P. (2016). Imaging studies of functional neurologic disorders. *Handbook of Clinical Neurology, 139,* 73–84.

Ayers, C. R., Saxena, S., Golshan, S., & Wetherell, J. L. (2009). Age at onset and clinical features of late life compulsive hoarding. *International Journal of Geriatric Psychiatry, 25,* 142–149.

Azrin, N. H., & Nunn, R. G. (1973). Habit-reversal: A method of eliminating nervous habits and tics. *Behaviour Research and Therapy, 11,* 619–628.

Azrin, N. H., Nunn, R. G., & Frantz, S. E. (1980). Treatment of hair-pulling (trichotillomania): A comparative study of habit reversal and negative practice training. *Journal of Behavior Therapy and Experimental Psychiatry, 11,* 13–20.

B

Baba, T., Endo, T., Honnma, H., Kitajima, Y., Hayashi, T., Ikeda, H., et al. (2007). Association between polycystic ovary syndrome and female-to-male transsexuality. *Human Reproduction, 22,* 1011–1016.

Babb, S., Malarcher, A., Shauer, G., Asman, K., & Jamal, A. (2017). Quitting smoking among adults—United States, 2000–2015. *Morbidity and Mortality Weekly Report, 65,* 1457–1464.

Bachhuber, M. A., Hennessy, S., Cunningham, C. O., & Starrels, J. L. (2016). Increasing benzodiazepine prescriptions and overdose mortality in the United States, 1996–2013. *American Journal of Public Health, 106*(4), 686–688.

Baer, J. S., Kivlahan, D. R., Blume, A. W., McKnight, P., & Marlatt, G. A. (2001). Brief intervention for heavy-drinking college students: 4-year follow-up and natural history. *American Journal of Public Health, 91,* 1310-1316.

Baer, J. S., Marlatt, G. A., Kivlahan, D. R., & Fromme, K. (1992). An experimental test of three methods of alcohol risk reduction with young adults. *Journal of Consulting & Clinical Psychology, 60,* 974–979.

Baer, R. A., Peters, J. R., Eisenlohr-Moul, T. A., Geider, P. J., & Sauer, S. E. (2012). Emotion-related cognitive processes in borderline personality disorder: A review of the empirical literature. *Clinical Psychology, 32,* 359–369.

Baird, G., Simonoff, E., Pickles, A., Chandler, S., Loucas, T., Meldrum, D., & Charman, T. (2006). Prevalence of disorders of the autism spectrum in a population cohort of children in South Thames: The Special Needs and Autism Project (SNAP). *Lancet, 368*(9531), 210–215.

Baker, D., Hunter, E., Lawrence, E., Medford, N., Patel, M., Senior, C., Sierra, M., Lambert, M. V., Phillips, M. L., & David, A. S. (2003). Depersonalisation disorder: Clinical features of 204 cases. *British Journal of Psychiatry, 182,* 428–433.

Baker, L. A., Jacobson, K. C., Raine, A., Lozano, D. I., & Bezdjian, S. (2007). Genetic and environmental bases of childhood antisocial behavior: A multi-informant twin study. *Journal of Abnormal Psychology, 116,* 219–235.

Baldessarini, R. J., Tondo, L., & Hennen, J. (2001). Treating the suicidal patient with bipolar disorder: Reducing suicide risk with lithium. *Annals of the New York Academy of Sciences, 932,* 24–38.

Balia, C., Carucci, S., Coghill, D., & Zuddas, A. (2018). The pharmacological treatment of aggression in children and adolescents with conduct disorder: Do callous-unemotional traits modulate the efficacy of medication? *Neuroscience & Biobehavioral Reviews, 91,* 218–238.

Ball, S. A., Martino, S., Nich, C., Frankforter, T. L., Van Horn, D., Crits-Christoph, P., Woody, G. E., Obert, J. L., Farentinos, C., & Carroll, K. M. (2007). Site matters: Multisite randomized trial of motivational enhancement therapy in community drug abuse clinics. *Journal of Consulting and Clinical Psychology, 75,* 556–567.

Ballenger, J. C., Davidson, J. R. T., Lecrubier, Y., Nutt, D. J., Marshall, R. D., Nemeroff, C. B., Shalev, A. Y., & Yehuda, R. (2004). Consensus statement update on posttraumatic stress disorder from the International Consensus Group on Depression and Anxiety. *Journal of Clinical Psychiatry, 65*(Suppl. 1), 55–62.

Balon, R., Segraves, R. T., & Clayton, A. (2007). Issues for *DSM-V*: Sexual dysfunction, disorder, or variation along normal distribution: Toward rethinking *DSM* criteria of sexual dysfunctions. *American Journal of Psychiatry, 164,* 198–200.

Bandura, A. (1969). *Principles of behavior modification.* New York: Holt, Rinehart & Winston.

Bandura, A. (2006). Going global with social cognitive theory: From prospect to paydirt. In S. I. Donaldson, D. E. Berger, & K. Pezdek (Eds.), *Applied psychology: New frontiers and rewarding careers* (pp. 53–79). Mahwah, NJ: Erlbaum.

Barateau, L., Lopez, R., Franchi, J. A. M., & Dauvilliers, Y. (2017). Hypersomnolence, hypersomnia, and mood disorders. *Current Psychiatry Reports, 19*(2), 13.

Barber, T. R., Lawton, M., Rolinski, M., Evetts, S., Baig, F., Ruffmann, C., et al. (2017). Prodromal Parkinsonism and neurodegenerative risk stratification in REM sleep behavior disorder. *Sleep, 40*(8).

Barch, D. M., Csernansky, J. G., Conturo, T., & Snyder, A. Z. (2002). Working and long-term memory deficits in schizophrenia: Is there a common prefrontal mechanism? *Journal of Abnormal Psychology, 111,* 478–494.

Barch, D. M., & Sheffield, J. M. (2017). Cognitive control in schizophrenia. In T. Egner (Ed.), *Wiley handbook of cognitive control* (pp. 556–580). Chichester, UK: Wiley.

Barefoot, J. C., Dahlstrom, W. G., & Williams, R. B. (1983). Hostility, CHD incidence, and total mortality: A 25-yr follow-up study of 255 physicians. *Psychosomatic Medicine, 45,* 59–63.

Barefoot, J. C., Dodge, K. A., Peterson, B. L., Dahlstrom, W. G., & Williams, R. B., Jr. (1989). The Cook-Medley Hostility Scale: Item content and ability to predict survival. *Psychosomatic Medicine, 51,* 46–57.

Barker, E. D., Walton, E., & Cecil, C. A. (2018). Annual research review: DNA methylation as a mediator in the association between risk exposure and child and adolescent psychopathology. *Journal of Child Psychology and Psychiatry, 59*(4), 303–322.

Barkhof, E., Meijer, C. J., de Sonneville, L. M. J., Linszen, D. H., & de Haan, L. (2012). Interventions to improve adherence to antipsychotic medication in patients with schizophrenia: A review of the past decade. *European Psychiatry, 27,* 9–18.

Barkley, R. A. (2014). *Attention-deficit hyperactivity disorder: A handbook for diagnosis and treatment* (4th ed.). New York: Guilford Press.

Barlow, D. H. (1986). Causes of sexual dysfunction: The role of anxiety and cognitive interference. *Journal of Consulting & Clinical Psychology, 54,* 140–148.

Barlow, D. H. (2011). The development and evaluation of psychological treatments for panic disorder. In M. Gernsbacher, D. Pew, & L. Hough (Eds.), *Psychology and the real world: Essays illustrating fundamental contributors to society* (pp. 198–204). New York: Worth.

Barlow, D. H., Farchione, T. J., Bullis, J. R., Gallagher, M. W., Murray-Latin, H., Sauer-Zavala, S., et al. (2017). The Unified protocol for transdiagnostic treatment of emotional disorders compared with diagnosis-specific protocols for anxiety disorders: A randomized clinical trial. *JAMA Psychiatry,* 74, 875–884.

Barlow, D. H., Farchione, T. J., Sauer-Zavala, S., Latin, H. M., Ellard, K. K., Bullis, J. R., et al. (2018). *Unified protocol for transdiagnostic treatment of emotional disorders: Therapist guide.* New York: Oxford University Press.

Barlow, D. H., Gorman, J. M., Shear, M. K., & Woods, S. W. (2000). Cognitive-behavioral therapy, imipramine, or their combination for panic disorder: A randomized controlled trial. *JAMA, 283,* 2529–2536.

Barlow, D. H., Sakheim, D. K., & Beck, J. G. (1983). Anxiety increases sexual arousal. *Journal of Abnormal Psychology, 92,* 49–54.

Barnes, L. L., Wilson, R. S., Bienias, J. L., Schneider, J. A., Evans, D. A., & Bennett, D. A. (2005). Sex differences in the clinical manifestations of Alzheimer disease pathology. *Archives of General Psychiatry, 62,* 685–691.

Barrio, C., & Yamada, A. M. (2010). Culturally based intervention development: The case of Latino families dealing with schizophrenia. *Research on Social Work Practice, 20*(5), 483–492.

Barsaglini, A., Sartori, G., Benetti, S., Pettersson-Yeo, W., & Mechelli, A. (2014). The effects of psychotherapy on brain function: A systematic and critical review. *Progress in Neurobiology, 114,* 1–14.

Bas-Hoogendam, J. M., Blackford, J. U., Brühl, A. B., Blair, K. S., van der Wee, N. J., & Westenberg, P. M. (2016). Neurobiological candidate endophenotypes of social anxiety disorder. *Neuroscience & Biobehavioral Reviews, 71,* 362–378.

Basson, R., Berman, J., Burnett, A., Derogatis, L., Ferguson, D., Fourcroy, J., Goldstein, I., Graziottin, A., Heiman, J., Laan, E., Leiblum, S., Padma-Nathan, H., Rosen, R., Segraves, K., Segraves, R. T., Shabsigh, R., Sipski, M., Wagner, G., & Whippie, B. (2001). Report of the international consensus development conference on female sexual dysfunction: Definitions and classifications. *Journal of Sex & Marital Therapy, 27,* 83–94.

Batelaan, N. M., Van Balkom, A. J. L. M., & Stein, D. J. (2012). Evidence-based pharmacotherapy of panic disorder: An update. *International Journal of Neuropsychopharmacology, 15,* 403–415.

Bateman, A., & Fonagy, P. (2008). 8-year follow-up of patients treated for borderline personality disorder: Mentalization-based treatment versus treatment as usual. *American Journal of Psychiatry, 165,* 631–638.

Bateson, G., Jackson, D. D., Haley, J., & Weakland, J. (1956). Toward a theory of schizophrenia. *Behavioral Science, 1,* 251–264.

Baum, A., Perry, N. W., Jr., & Tarbell, S. (2004). The development of psychology as a health science. In T. J. Ball, R. G. Frank, A. Baum, & J. L. Wallander (Eds.), *Handbook of clinical health psychology: Volume 3. Models and perspectives in health psychology* (pp. 9–28). Washington, DC: American Psychological Association.

Baxter, L., Schwartz, J., Bergman, K., & Szuba, M. (1992). Caudate glucose metabolic rate changes with both drug and behavior therapy for obsessive-compulsive disorder. *Archives of General Psychiatry, 49,* 681–689.

Beards, S., Gayer-Anderson, C., Borges, S., Dewey, M. E., Fisher, H. L., & Morgan, C. (2013). Life events and psychosis: A review and meta-analysis. *Schizophrenia Bulletin, 39*(4), 740–747.

Beatty, L., & Lambert, S. (2013). A systematic review of Internet-based self-help therapeutic interventions to improve distress and disease-control among adults with chronic health conditions. *Clinical Psychology Review, 33,* 609–622.

Beauchaine, T. P., & Constantino, J. N. (2017). Redefining the endophenotype concept to accommodate transdiagnostic vulnerabilities and etiological complexity. *Biomarkers in Medicine, 11*(9), 769–780.

Beauchaine, T. P., Hinshaw, S. P., & Pang, K. L. (2010). Comorbidity of attention-deficit/hyperactivity disorder and early-onset conduct disorder: Biological, environmental, and developmental mechanisms. *Clinical Psychology: Science and Practice, 17,* 327–336.

Bechara, A. (2005). Decision making, impulse control and loss of willpower to resist drugs: A neurocognitive perspective. *Nature Neuroscience, 8,* 1458–1463.

Beck, A. T. (1967). *Depression: Clinical, experimental, and theoretical aspects.* New York: Harper & Row.

Beck, A. T. (1976). *Cognitive therapy and the emotional disorders.* New York: International Universities Press.

Beck, A. T., & Beck, R. W. (1972). Screening depressed patients in family practice: A rapid technique. *Postgraduate Medicine, 52,* 81–85.

Beck, A. T., & Bredemeier, K. (2016). A unified model of depression: Integrating clinical, cognitive, biological, and evolutionary perspectives. *Clinical Psychological Science, 4*(4), 596–619.

Beck, A. T., Butler, A. C., Brown, G. K., Dahlsgaard, K. K., Newman, C. F., & Beck, J. S. (2001). Dysfunctional beliefs discriminate personality disorders. *Behaviour Research & Therapy, 39,* 1213–1225.

Beck, A. T., Davis, D. D., & Freeman, A. (Eds.). (2015). *Cognitive therapy of personality disorders* (3rd ed.). New York: Guilford.

Beck, A. T., & Emery, G. (1985). *Anxiety disorders and phobias: A cognitive perspective.* New York: Basic Books.

Beck, A. T., & Freeman, A. M. (1990). *Cognitive therapy of personality disorders.* New York: Guilford Press.

Beck, A. T., & Rector, N. A. (2005). Cognitive approaches to schizophrenia: Theory and therapy. *Annual Review of Clinical Psychology, 1,* 577–606.

Beck, A. T., Rush, A. J., Shaw, B. F., & Emery, G. (1979). *Cognitive therapy of depression.* New York: Guilford Press.

Beck, A. T., Steer, R. A., Kovacs, M., & Garrison, B. (1985). Hopelessness and eventual suicide: A 10-year prospective study of patients hospitalized with suicidal ideation. *American Journal of Psychiatry, 142,* 559–563.

Beck, A. T., Ward, C. H., Mendelson, M., Moch, J. E., & Erbaugh, J. (1962). Reliability of psychiatric diagnosis: II. A study of consistency of clinical judgments and ratings. *American Journal of Psychiatry, 119,* 351–357.

Beck, A. T., Weissman, A., Lester, D., & Trexler, L. (1974). The measurement of pessimism: The Hopelessness Scale. *Journal of Consulting & Clinical Psychology, 42,* 861–865.

Becker, A. E., Fay, K. E., Agnew-Blais, J., Kahn, A. N., Striegel-Moore, R. H., & Gilman, S. E. (2011). Social network media exposure and adolescent eating pathology in Fiji. *British Journal of Psychiatry 198,* 43–50.

Becker, C. B., & Stice, E. (2017). From efficacy to effectiveness to broad implementation: Evolution of the Body Project. *Journal of Consulting and Clinical Psychology, 85*(8), 767.

Becker-Blease, K. A., Deater-Deckard, K., Eley, T., Freyd, J. J., Stevenson, J., & Plomin, R. (2004). A genetic analysis of individual differences in dissociative behaviors in childhood and adolescence. *Journal of Child Psychology & Psychiatry, 45,* 522–532.

Bednarchik, C. L., Kottwitz, M., & Geiger, S. W. (2016). Self-injection, transurethral, and topical therapy in erectile dysfunction. In T. S. Köhler & K. T. McVary (Eds.), *Contemporary treatment of erectile dysfunction: A clinical guide* (pp. 187–207). Cham: Springer.

Beech, A. R., Miner, M. H., & Thornton, D. (2016). Paraphilias in the DSM-5. *Annual Review of Clinical Psychology, 12,* 383–406.

Bekhuis, E., Schoevers, R. A., van Borkulo, C. D., Rosmalen, J. G. M., & Boschloo, L. (2016). The network structure of major depressive disorder, generalized anxiety disorder and somatic symptomatology. *Psychological Medicine, 46*(14), 2989–2998.

Belle, D., & Doucet, J. (2003). Poverty, inequality, and discrimination as sources of depression among U.S. women. *Psychology of Women Quarterly, 27,* 101–113.

Bender, D. S. (2012). Mirror, mirror on the wall: Reflecting on narcissism. *Journal of Psychology, 68,* 877–885.

Bender, L. (1938). *A visual motor gestalt test and its clinical use.* New York: American Orthopsychiatric Association.

Benet-Martinez, V., & John, O. P. (1998). Los Cinco Grandes across cultures and ethnic groups: Multitrait-multimethod analyses of the Big Five in Spanish and English. *Journal of Personality & Social Psychology, 75,* 729–750.

Bennett, N. E. (2016). Oral prescription therapy for erectile dysfunction. In T. S. Köhler & K. T. McVary (Eds.), *Contemporary treatment of erectile dysfunction: A clinical guide* (pp. 163–173). Cham: Springer.

Benson, L., & Christensen, A. (2016). Empirically supported couple therapies. In K. T. Sullivan & E. Lawrence (Eds.), *The Oxford handbook of relationship science and couple interventions* (pp. 177–192). New York: Oxford University Press.

Bentall, R. P., Rouse, G., Kinderman, P., Blackwood, N., Howard, R., Moore, R., et al. (2008). Paranoid delusions in schizophrenia spectrum disorders and depression: The transdiagnostic role of expectations of negative events and negative self-esteem. *Journal of Nervous and Mental Disease, 196,* 375–383.

Bentley, K. H., Cassiello-Robbins, C. F., Vittorio, L., Sauer-Zavala, S., & Barlow, D. H. (2015). The association between nonsuicidal self-injury and the emotional disorders: A meta-analytic review. *Clinical Psychology Review, 37,* 72–88.

Bentley, K. H., Franklin, J. C., Ribeiro, J. D., Kleiman, E. M., Fox, K. R., & Nock, M. K. (2016). Anxiety and its disorders as risk factors for suicidal thoughts and behaviors: A meta-analytic review. *Clinical Psychology Review, 43,* 30–46.

Berger, W., Coutinho, E. S. F., Figueira, I., Marques-Portella, C., Luz, M. P., Neylan, T. C., . . . & Mendlowicz, M. V. (2012). Rescuers at risk: A systematic review and meta-regression analysis of the worldwide current prevalence and correlates of PTSD in rescue workers. *Social Psychiatry and Psychiatric Epidemiology, 47*(6), 1001–1011.

Berkowitz, R. I., Wadden, T. A., Gehrman, C. A., Bishop-Gilyard, C. T., Moore, R. H., Womble, L. G., Cronquist, J. L., Trumpikas, N. L., Levitt-Katz, L. E., & Xanthopoulos, M. S. (2011). Meal replacements in the treatment of adolescent obesity: A randomized control trial. *Obesity, 19,* 1193–1199.

Berlin, L. J., Brooks-Gunn, J., McCartoon, C., & McCormick, M. C. (1998). The effectiveness of early intervention: Examining risk factors and pathways to enhanced development. *Preventive Medicine, 27,* 238–245.

Berridge, K. C., & Robinson, T. E. (2016). Liking, wanting, and the incentive-sensitization theory of addiction. *American Psychologist, 71*(8), 670–679.

Berthoud, H. R., & Morrison, C. (2008). The brain, appetite, and obesity. *Annual Review of Psychology, 59,* 55–92.

Bettelheim, B. (1967). *The empty fortress: Infantile autism and the birth of the self.* New York: Free Press.

Bhati, K. S. (2014). Effect of client-therapist gender match on the therapeutic relationship: An exploratory analysis. *Psychological Reports, 115*(2), 565–583.

Biederman, J., Faraone, S. V., Hirschfeld-Becker, D. R., Friedman, D., Robin, J. A., & Rosenbaum, J. F. (2001). Patterns of psychopathology and dysfunction in high-risk children of parents with panic disorder and major depression. *American Journal of Psychiatry, 158,* 49–57.

Biederman, J., Mick, E., Faraone, S. V., Braaten, E., Doyle, A., Spencer, T., Wilens, T. E., Frazier, E., & Johnson, M. (2002). Influence of gender on attention deficit hyperactivity disorder in children referred to a psychiatric clinic. *American Journal of Psychiatry, 159,* 36–42.

Birmaher, B., Axelson, D., Strober, M., Gill, M. K., Valeri, S., Chiappetta, L., Ryan, N., Leonard, H., Junt, J., Iyengar, S., & Keller, M. (2006). Clinical course of children and adolescents with bipolar spectrum disorders. *Archive of General Psychiatry, 63,* 175–183.

Biron, M., Risch, N., Hamburger, R., Mandel, B., Kushner, S., Newman, M., Drumer, D., & Belmaker, R. H. (1987). Genetic linkage between X-chromosome markers and bipolar affective illness. *Nature, 326,* 289–292.

Bjorvatn, B., Grønli, J., & Pallesen, S. (2010). Prevalence of different parasomnias in the general population. *Sleep Medicine Reviews, 11,* 1031–1034.

Blacher, J. B., Hanneman, R. A., & Rousey, A. B. (1992). Out-of-home placement of children with severe handicaps: A comparison of approaches. *American Journal on Mental Retardation, 96,* 607–616.

Black, D. W., Zanarini, M. C., Romine, A., Shaw, M., Allen, J., & Schulz, S. C. (2014). Comparison of low and moderate dosages of extended-release quetiapine in borderline personality disorder: A randomized, double-blind, placebo-controlled trial. *American Journal of psychiatry, 171*(11), 1174–1182.

Blaney, P. H. (1986). Affect and memory: A review. *Psychological Bulletin, 99,* 229–246.

Blank, R., Smits-Engelsman, B., Polatajko, H., & Wilson, P. (2012). European Academy for Childhood Disability (EACD): Recommendations on the definition, diagnosis and intervention of developmental coordination disorder (long version). *Developmental Medicine and Child Neurology, 54,* 54–93.

Blashfield, R. K., Reynolds, S. M., & Stennett, B. (2012). The death of histrionic personality disorder. In T. A. Widiger (Ed.), *The Oxford handbook of personality disorders* (pp. 603–627). New York: Oxford University Press.

Bloch, M. H., Landeros-Weisenberger, A., Rosario, M. C., Pittenger, C., & Leckman, J. F. (2008). Meta-analysis of the symptom structure of obsessive-compulsive disorder. *American Journal of Psychiatry, 165,* 532–542.

Blond, A. (2008). Impacts of exposure to images of ideal bodies on male body dissatisfaction: A review. *Body Image, 5,* 244–250.

Blöte, A. W., Miers, A. C., Heyne, D. A., & Westenberg, P. M. (2015). Social anxiety and the school environment of adolescents. In K. Ranta, A. M. La Greca, L.-J. Garcia-Lopez, & M. Marttunen (Eds.), *Social anxiety and phobia in adolescents* (pp. 151–181). Cham: Springer.

Blum, N., St. John, D., Pfohl, B., Stuart, S., McCormick, B., Allen, J., Arndt, S., & Black, D. W. (2008). Systems training for emotional predictability and problem solving (STEPPS) for outpatients with borderline personality disorder: A randomized controlled trial and 1-year follow-up. *American Journal of Psychiatry, 165,* 468–478.

Blumenthal, J. A., Babyak, M. A., Doraiswamy, P. M., Watkins, L., Hoffman, B. M., Barbour, K. A., Herman, S., Craighead, W. E., Brosse, A. L., Waugh, R., Hinderliter, A., & Sherwood, A. (2007). Exercise and pharmacotherapy in the treatment of major depressive disorder. *Psychosomatic Medicine, 69,* 587–596.

Blumenthal, J. A., Sherwood, A., Babyak, M. A., Watkins, L. L., Waugh, R., Georgiades, A., Bacon, S. L., Hayano, J., Coleman, R. E., & Hinderliter, A. (2005). Effects of exercise and stress management training on markers of cardiovascular risk in patients with ischemic heart disease: A randomized controlled trial. *JAMA, 293,* 1626–1634.

Bockting, C. L., Hollon, S. D., Jarrett, R. B., Kuyken, W., & Dobson, K. (2015). A lifetime approach to major depressive disorder: The contributions of psychological interventions in preventing relapse and recurrence. *Clinical Psychology Review, 41,* 16–26.

Bögels, S. M., Alden, L., Beidel, D. C., Clark, L. A., Pine, D. S., Stein, M. B., & Voncken, M. (2010). Social anxiety disorder: Questions and answers for the *DSM-V. Depression and Anxiety, 27,* 168–189.

Bögels, S. M., Knappe, S., & Clark, L. A. (2013). Adult separation anxiety disorder in *DSM-5. Clinical Psychology Review, 33,* 663–674.

Bohart, A. C. (1995). The person-centered psychotherapies. In A. S. Gurman (Ed.), *Essential psychotherapies: Theory and practice* (pp. 55–84). New York: Guilford Press.

Bohus, M., Haaf, B., Simms, T., Limberger, M. F., Schmahl, C., Unckel, C., Lieb, K., & Linehan, M. M. (2004). Effectiveness of inpatient dialectical behavioral therapy for borderline personality disorder: A controlled trial. *Behaviour Research & Therapy, 42,* 487–499.

Böing, S., & Randerath, W. J. (2015). Chronic hypoventilation syndromes and sleep-related hypoventilation. *Journal of Thoracic Disease, 7*(8), 1273–1285.

Bölte, S., & Poustka, F. (2004). Comparing the intelligence profiles of savant and nonsavant individuals with autistic disorder. *Intelligence, 32,* 121–131.

Bonanno, G. A., Neria, Y., Mancini, A., Coifman, K. G., Litz, B., & Insel, B. (2007). Is there more to complicated grief than depression and posttraumatic stress disorder? A test of incremental validity. *Journal of Abnormal Psychology, 116,* 342–351.

Bonanno, G. A., Westphal, M., & Mancini, A. D. (2011). Resilience to loss and potential trauma. *Annual Review of Clinical Psychology, 7,* 511–535.

Bond, G. R., & Drake, R. E. (2015). The critical ingredients of assertive community treatment. *World Psychiatry, 14*(2), 240–242.

Bonnie, R. J., & Grisso, T. (2000). Adjudicative competence and youthful offenders. In T. Grisso & R. G. Schwartz (Eds.), *Youth on trial: A developmental perspective on juvenile justice.* Chicago: University of Chicago Press.

Book, A. S., Starzyk, K. B., & Quinsey, V. L. (2001). The relationship between testosterone and aggression: A meta-analysis. *Aggression & Violent Behavior, 6,* 579–599.

Boone, L., Soenens, B., & Luyten, P. (2014). When or why does perfectionism translate into eating disorder pathology? A longitudinal examination of the moderating and mediating role of body dissatisfaction. *Journal of Abnormal Psychology, 123*(2), 412.

Boothroyd, R. A., Mercado, C. C., Poythress, N. G., Christy, A., & Petrila, J. (2005). Clinical outcomes of defendants in mental health court. *Psychiatric Services, 56,* 829–834.

Borges, G., Angst, J., Nock, M. K., Ruscio, A. M., & Kessler, R. C. (2008). Risk factors for the incidence and persistence of suicide-related outcomes: A 10-year follow-up study using the national comorbidity surveys. *Journal of Affective Disorders, 105,* 25–33.

Borges, G., Nock, M. K., Haro Abad, J. M., Hwang, I., Sampson, N. A., Alonso, J., Andrade, L. H., et al. (2010). Twelve-month prevalence of and risk factors for suicide attempts in the World Health Organization World Mental Health Surveys. *Journal of Clinical Psychiatry, 71,* 1617–1628.

Borkovec, T. D., Alcaine, O., & Behar, E. (2004). Avoidance theory of worry and generalized anxiety disorder. In R. G. Heimberg, C. L. Turk, & D. S. Mennin (Eds.), *Generalized anxiety disorder: Advances in research and practice* (pp. 77–108). New York: Guilford Press.

Borkovec, T. D., Newman, M. G., & Castonguay, L. G. (2003). Cognitive-behavioral therapy for generalized anxiety disorder with integrations from interpersonal and experiential therapies. *CNS Spectrums, 8,* 382–389.

Borkovec, T. D., Newman, M. G., Pincus, A. L., & Lytle, R. (2002). A component analysis of cognitive-behavioral therapy for generalized anxiety disorder and the role of interpersonal problems. *Journal of Consulting & Clinical Psychology, 70,* 288–298.

Borkovec, T. D., & Roemer, L. (1995). Perceived functions of worry among generalized anxiety disorder subjects: Distraction from more emotionally distressing topics? *Journal of Behavior Therapy and Experimental Psychiatry, 26,* 25–30.

Borkovec, T. D., & Ruscio, A. M. (2001). Psychotherapy for generalized anxiety disorder. *Journal of Clinical Psychiatry, 62*(Suppl. 11), 37–42.

Bornstein, R. F. (2012). Illuminating a neglected clinical issue: Societal costs of interpersonal dependency and dependent personality disorder. *Journal of Clinical Psychology, 68,* 766–781.

Bottoms, G. (2000). *Angelhead.* New York: Three Rivers Press.

Bouton, M. E., Mineka, S., & Barlow, D. H. (2001). A modern learning theory perspective on the etiology of panic disorder. *Psychological Review, 108,* 4–32.

Bowen, S., Chawla, N., & Marlatt, G. A. (2010). *Mindfulness-based relapse prevention for the treatment of substance-use disorders: A clinician's guide.* New York: Guilford Press.

Bowen, S., Witkiewitz, K., Clifasefi, S. L., Grow, J., Chawla, N., Hsu, S. H., et al. (2014). Relative efficacy of mindfulness-based relapse prevention, standard relapse prevention, and treatment as usual for substance use disorders: A randomized clinical trial. *JAMA Psychiatry, 71*(5), 547–556.

Bowie, C. R., Leung, W. W., Reichenberg, A., McClure, M. M., Patterson, T., Heaton, R. K., & Harvey, P. D. (2008). Predicting schizophrenia patients' real-world behavior with specific neuropsychological and functional capacity measures. *Biological Psychiatry, 63,* 505–511.

Braden, A., Rhee, K., Peterson, C. B., Rydell, S. A., Zucker, N., & Boutelle, K. (2014). Associations between child emotional eating and general parenting style, feeding practices, and parent psychopathology. *Appetite, 80,* 35–40.

Brady, K. T., Back, S. E., & Greenfield, S. F. (Eds.). (2009). *Women and addiction: A comprehensive handbook.* New York: Guilford Press.

Brady, R. O., Jr., Tandon, N., Masters, G. A., Margolis, A., Cohen, B. M., Keshavan, M., & Öngür, D. (2017). Differential brain network activity across mood states in bipolar disorder. *Journal of Affective Disorders, 207,* 367–376.

Brand, B. L., Loewenstein, R. J., & Spiegel, D. (2014). Dispelling myths about dissociative identity disorder treatment: An empirically based approach. *Psychiatry: Interpersonal and Biological Processes, 77*(2), 169–189.

Brent, D. A., & Bridge, J. (2003). Firearms availability and suicide. *American Behavioral Scientist, 46*(9), 1192–1210.

Brent, D. A., Kerr, M. M., Goldstein, C., Bozigar, J., Wartella, M., & Allan, M. J. (1989). An outbreak of suicide and suicidal behavior in a high school. *Journal of the American Academy of Child & Adolescent Psychiatry, 28,* 918–924.

Brent, D. A., Oquendo, M., Birmaher, B., Greenhill, L., Kolko, D., Stanley, B., Zelazny, J., Brodsky, B., Bridge, J., Ellis, S., Salazer, J. O., & Mann, J. J. (2002). Familial pathways to early-onset suicide attempt. *Archives of General Psychiatry, 59,* 801–807.

Brent, D. A., Oquendo, M., Birmaher, B., Greenhill, L., Kolko, D., Stanley, B., Zelazny, J., Brodsky, B., Firinciogullari, S., Ellis, S. P., & Mann, J. J. (2003). Peripubertal suicide attempts in offspring of suicide attempters with siblings concordant for suicidal behavior. *American Journal of Psychiatry, 160,* 1486–1493.

Brewin, C. R., & Andrews, B. (2017). Creating memories for false autobiographical events in childhood: A systematic review. *Applied Cognitive Psychology, 31*(1), 2–23.

Brick, J. (Ed.). (2008). *Handbook of the medical consequences of alcohol and drug abuse* (2nd ed.). New York: Haworth Press/Taylor & Francis Group.

Briere, J., & Conte, J. R. (1993). Self-reported amnesia for abuse in adults molested as children. *Journal of Traumatic Stress, 6,* 21–31.

Briley, D. A., & Tucker-Drob, E. M. (2012). Broad bandwidth or high fidelity? Evidence from the structure of genetic and environmental effects on the facets of the five factor model. *Behavior Genetics, 42,* 743–763.

Britton, J. C., & Rauch, S. L. (2009). Neuroanatomy and neuroimaging of anxiety disorders. In M. M. Antony & M. B. Stein (Eds.), *Oxford handbook of anxiety and related disorders* (pp. 97–110). New York: Oxford University Press.

Brody, L. R., Hall, J. A., & Stokes, L. R. (2016). Gender and emotion: Theory, findings, and context. In L. F. Barrett, M. Lewis, & J. M. Haviland-Jones (Eds.), *Handbook of emotions,* 4th ed. (pp. 369–392). New York: Guilford.

Bronson, J., & Berzofsky, M. (2017). *Indicators of mental health problems reported by prisoners and jail inmates, 2011–12.* Washington, DC: Bureau of Justice Statistics.

Brosschot, J. F., Van Dijk, E., & Thayer, J. F. (2007). Daily worry is related to low heart rate variability during waking and the subsequent nocturnal sleep period. *International Journal of Psychophysiology, 63,* 39–47.

Brotman, M. A., Sharif-Askary, B., Dickstein, D. P., & Leibenluft, E. (2016). Biological factors in bipolar disorder in childhood and adolescence. In J. C. Soares & A. H. Young (Eds.), *Bipolar disorders: Basic mechanisms and therapeutic implications* (pp. 219–233). Cambridge: Cambridge University Press.

Brotto, L. A. (2017). Evidence-based treatments for low sexual desire in women. *Frontiers in Neuroendocrinology, 45,* 11–17.

Brown, C. H., IV. (2014). Delirium in the cardiac surgical intensive care unit. *Current Opinion in Anaesthesiology, 27*(2), 117–122.

Brown, C. W., Olson, H. C., & Croninger, R. G. (2010). Maternal alcohol consumption during pregnancy and infant social, mental, and motor development. *Journal of Early Intervention, 32,* 110–126.

Brown, J. E., Ayowa, O. B., & Brown, R. C. (1993). Dry and tight: Sexual practices and potential risks in Zaire. *Social Science & Medicine, 37,* 989–994.

Brown, T. A., O'Leary, T. A., & Barlow, D. H. (2001). Generalized anxiety disorder. *Clinical handbook of psychological disorders: A step-by-step treatment manual* (3rd ed., pp. 154–208). New York: Guilford Press.

Browne, K. O. (2001). Cultural formulation of psychiatric diagnoses. *Culture, Medicine, & Psychiatry, 25,* 411–425.

Brownell, K. D., & Horgen, K. B. (2004). *Food fight: The inside story of the food industry, America's obesity crisis, and what we can do about it.* New York: McGraw-Hill.

Brownell, K. D., & Walsh, B. T. (2017). *Eating disorders and obesity: A comprehensive handbook* (3rd ed.). New York: Guilford.

Brownley, K. A., Berkman, N. D., Peat, C. M., Lohr, K. N., Cullen, K. E., Bann, C. M., & Bulik, C. M. (2016). Binge-eating disorder in adults: A systematic review and meta-analysis. *Annals of Internal Medicine, 165*(6), 409–420.

Bruch, H. (1973). *Eating disorders: Obesity, anorexia nervosa, and the person within.* New York: Basic Books.

Bruch, H. (1982). Anorexia nervosa: Therapy and theory. *American Journal of Psychiatry, 139,* 1531–1538.

Bruffaerts, R., Demyttenaere, K., Borges, G., Haro, J. M., Chiu, W. T., Hwang, I., et al. (2010). Childhood adversities as risk factors for onset and persistence of suicidal behaviour. *British Journal of Psychiatry, 197*(1), 20–27.

Bruffaerts, R., Demyttenaere, K., Hwang, I., Chiu, W. T., Sampson, N., Kessler, R. C., et al. (2011). Treatment of suicidal people around the world. *British Journal of Psychiatry, 199*(1), 64–70.

Bryant, C., Jackson, H., & Ames, D. (2008). The prevalence of anxiety in older adults: Methodological issues and a review of the literature. *Journal of Affective Disorders, 109,* 233–250.

Bryant, R. A., & Das, P. (2012). The neural circuitry of conversion disorder and its recovery. *Journal of Abnormal Psychology, 121,* 289–296.

Bryant, R. A., Friedman, M. J., Spiegel, D., Ursano, R., & Strain, J. (2011). A review of acute stress disorder in *DSM-5. Depression and Anxiety, 28,* 802–817.

Buka, S. L., Cannon, T. D., Torrey, E. F., Yolken, R. H., and the Collaborative Study Group on the Perinatal Origins of Severe Psychotic Disorders. (2008). Maternal exposure to herpes simplex virus and risk of psychosis among adult offspring. *Biological Psychiatry, 63,* 809–815.

Bulik, C. M., Sullivan, P. F., & Kendler, K. S. (2003). Genetic and environmental contributions to obesity and binge eating. *International Journal of Eating Disorders, 33,* 293–298.

Bulik, C. M., Sullivan, P. F., Tozzi, F., Furberg, H., Lichtenstein, P., & Pedersen, N. L. (2006). Prevalence, heritability, and prospective risk factors for anorexia nervosa. *Archives of General Psychiatry, 63,* 305–312.

Bulik, C. M., Thornton, L. M., Root, T. L., Pisetsky, E. M., Lichtenstein, P., & Pedersen, N. L. (2010). Understanding the relation between anorexia nervosa and bulimia nervosa in a Swedish national twin sample. *Biological Psychiatry, 67,* 71–77.

Burhan, A. M., Moradizadeh, M., & Marlatt, N. E. (2018). Major or mild vascular neurocognitive disorder. In A. Hategan, J. Bourgeois, C. Hirsch, & C. Giroux (Eds.), *Geriatric psychiatry* (pp. 445–466). New York: Springer International.

Burnam, M. A., Stein, J. A., Golding, J. M., & Siegel, J. M. (1988). Sexual assault and mental disorders in a community population. *Journal of Consulting & Clinical Psychology, 56,* 843–850.

Busfield, J. (1986). *Managing madness: Changing ideas and practice.* London: Unwin Hyman.

Bustillo, J. R., Lauriello, J., Horan, W. P., & Keith, S. J. (2001). The psychosocial treatment of schizophrenia: An update. *American Journal of Psychiatry, 158,* 163–175.

Buysse, D. J., Ancoli-Israel, S., Edinger, J. D., Lichstein, K. L., & Morin, C. M. (2006). Recommendations for a standard research assessment of insomnia. *Sleep, 29,* 1155–1173.

Buysse, D. J., Rush, A. J., & Reynolds, C. F. (2017). Clinical management of insomnia disorder. *JAMA, 318*(20), 1973–1974.

Byne, W., Bradley, S. J., Coleman, E., Eyler, A. E., Green, R., Menvielle, E., Meyer-Bahlburg, H. F., Pleak, R. R., & Tompkins, D. A. (2012). Treatment of gender identity disorder. *American Journal of Psychiatry, 169,* 875–876.

Byrne, S., Wade, T., Hay, P., Touyz, S., Fairburn, C. G., Treasure, J., et al. (2017). A randomised controlled trial of three psychological treatments for anorexia nervosa. *Psychological Medicine, 47*(16), 2823–2833.

Bystritsky, A., Ackerman, D. L., Rosen, R. M., Vapnik, T., Gorvis, E., Maidment, K. M., & Saxena, S. (2004). Augmentation of serotonin reuptake inhibitors in refractory obsessive-compulsive disorder using adjunctive olanzapine: A placebo-controlled trial. *Journal of Clinical Psychiatry, 65,* 565–568.

C

Cale, E. M., & Lilienfeld, S. O. (2002). Sex differences in psychopathy and antisocial personality disorder: A review and integration. *Clinical Psychology Review, 22,* 1179–1207.

Calear, A. L., Christensen, H., Freeman, A., Fenton, K., Grant, J. B., Van Spijker, B., & Donker, T. (2016). A systematic review of psychosocial suicide prevention interventions for youth. *European Child & Adolescent Psychiatry, 25*(5), 467–482.

Callaghan, G. M., Summers, C. J., & Weidman, M. (2003). The treatment of histrionic and narcissistic personality disorder behaviors: A single-subject demonstration of clinical improvement using functional-analytic psychotherapy. *Journal of Contemporary Psychotherapy, 33,* 321–339.

Cameron, N., & Rychlak, J. F. (1985). *Personality development and psychopathology: A dynamic approach.* Boston: Houghton Mifflin.

Canino, G., Polanczyk, G., Bauermeister, J. J., Rohde, L. A., Frick, P. J. (2010). Does the prevalence of CD and ODD vary across cultures? *Social Psychiatry and Psychiatric Epidemiology, 45,* 695–704.

Cannon, B. J., & Kramer, L. M. (2012). Delusion content across the 20th century in an American psychiatric hospital. *International Journal of Social Psychiatry, 58*(3), 323–327.

Cannon, T. D. (2009). What is the role of theories in the study of schizophrenia? *Schizophrenia Bulletin, 35,* 563–567.

Cannon, T. D., Hennah, W., van Erp, T. G., Thompson, P. M., Lonnqvist, J., Huttunen, M., Gasperoni, T., Tuulio-Henriksson, A., Pirkola, T., Toga, A. W., Kaprio, J., Mazziotta, J., & Peltonen, L. (2005). Association of DISC1/TRAX haplotypes with schizophrenia, reduced prefrontal gray matter, and impaired short- and long-term memory. *Archives of General Psychiatry, 62,* 1205–1213.

Cannon, T. D., Kapiro, J., Lonnqvist, J., Huttunen, M., & Koskenvuo, M. (1998). The genetic epidemiology of schizophrenia in a Finnish twin cohort. *Archives of General Psychiatry, 55,* 67–74.

Cannon, T. D., Rosso, I. M., Bearden, C. E., Sanchez, L. E., & Hadley, T. (1999). A prospective cohort study of neurodevelopmental processes in the genesis and epigenesis of schizophrenia. *Development & Psychopathology, 11,* 467–485.

Cannon, T. D., van Erp, T. G. M., Bearden, C. E., Loewy, R., Thompson, P., Toga, A. W., Huttunen, M. O., Keshavan, M. S., Seidman, L. J., & Tsuang, M. T. (2003). Early and late neurodevelopmental influences in the prodrome to schizophrenia: Contributions of genes, environment, and their interactions. *Schizophrenia Bulletin, 29,* 653–669.

Cannon, T. D., van Erp, T. G. M., & Glahn, D. C. (2002). Elucidating continuities and discontinuities between schizotypy and schizophrenia in the nervous system. *Schizophrenia Research, 54,* 151–156.

Cantor, J. M., Kabani, N., Christensen, B. K., Zipursky, R. B., Barbaree, H. E., Dickey, R., Klassen, P. E., Mikulis, D. J., Kuban, M. E., Blak, T., Richards, B. A., Hanratty, M. K., & Blanchard, R. (2008). Cerebral white matter deficiencies in pedophilic men. *Journal of Psychiatric Research, 42,* 167–183.

Cantor-Graae, E., & Selten, J. P. (2005). Schizophrenia and migration: A meta-analysis and review. *American Journal of Psychiatry, 162,* 12–24.

Cardeña, E., & Carlson, E. (2011). Acute stress disorder revisited. *Annual Review of Clinical Psychology, 7,* 245–267.

Cardeña, E., van Duijl, M., Weiner, L. A., & Terhune, D. B. (2009). Possession/trance phenomena. In P. F. Dell & J. A. O'Neil (Eds.), *Dissociation and the dissociative disorders: DSM-V and beyond* (pp. 171–184). New York: Routledge.

Cardozo, B. L., Bilukha, O. O., Gotway Crawford, C. A., et al. (2004). Mental health, social functioning, and disability in postwar Afghanistan. *JAMA, 292,* 575–584.

Cardozo, B. L., Kaiser, R., Gotway, C. A., & Agani, F. (2003). Mental health, social functioning, and feelings of hatred and revenge in Kosovar Albanians one year after the war in Kosovo. *Journal of Traumatic Stress, 16,* 351–360.

Cardozo, B. L., Vergara, A., Agani, F., & Gotway, C. A. (2000). Mental health, social functioning, and attitudes of Kosovar Albanians following the war in Kosovo. *JAMA, 284,* 569–577.

Carlo, G., Knight, G. P., Roesch, S. C., Opal, D., & Davis, A. (2014). Personality across cultures: A critical analysis of Big Five research and current directions. In F. T. L. Leong, L. Comas-Díaz, G. C. Nagayama Hall, V. C. McLoyd, & J. E. Trimble (Eds.), *APA handbook of multicultural psychology: Vol. 1. Theory and research* (pp. 285–298). Washington, DC: American Psychological Association.

Carpenter, K. M., Williams, K., & Worly, B. (2017). Treating women's orgasmic difficulties. In Z. D. Peterson (Ed.), *The Wiley handbook of sex therapy* (pp. 57–71). Oxford: Wiley.

Carpenter, R. W., & Trull, T. J. (2013). Components of emotion dysregulation in borderline personality disorder: A review. *Current Psychiatry Reports, 15*(1), 335.

Carr, A. (2014). The evidence base for family therapy and systemic interventions for child-focused problems. *Journal of Family Therapy, 36*(2), 107–157.

Carrion-Castillo, A., Franke, B., & Fisher, S. E. (2013). Molecular genetics of dyslexia: An overview. *Dyslexia, 19*(4), 214–240.

Carroll, K. M., Ball, S. A., Nich, C., Martino, S., Frankforter, T. L., Farentinos, C., Kunkel, L. E., Mikulich-Gilbertson, S. K., Morgenstern, J., Obert, J. L., Polcin, D., Snead, N., & Woody, G. E. (2006). Motivational interviewing to improve treatment engagement and outcome in individuals seeking treatment for substance abuse: A multisite effectiveness study. *Drug and Alcohol Dependence, 81,* 301–312.

Carter, J. C., Mercer-Lynn, K. B., Norwood, S. J., Bewll-Weiss, C. V., Crosby, R. D., Woodside, D. B., & Olmstead, M. P. (2012). A prospective study of predictors of relapse in anorexia nervosa: Implications for relapse prevention. *Psychiatry Research, 200,* 518–523.

Carver, C. S., & Scheier, M. F. (2014). Dispositional optimism. *Trends in Cognitive Sciences, 18*(6), 293–299.

Casey, B. J., Tottenham, N., Liston, C., & Durston, S. (2005). Imaging the developing brain: What have we learned about cognitive development? *Trends in Cognitive Sciences, 9,* 104–110.

Casey, L. M., Oei, T. P., Raylu, N., Horrigan, K., Day, J., Ireland, M., & Clough, B. A. (2017). Internet-based delivery of cognitive behaviour therapy compared to monitoring, feedback and support for problem gambling: A randomised controlled trial. *Journal of Gambling Studies, 33*(3), 993–1010.

Caspi, A., Harrington, H., Milne, B., Amell, J. W., Theodore, R. F., & Moffitt, T. E. (2003). Children's behavioral styles at age 3 are linked to their adult personality traits at age 26. *Journal of Personality, 71,* 495–513.

Caspi, A., McClay, J., Moffitt, T. E., Mill, J., Martin, J., Craig, I. W., et al. (2002). Role of genotype in the cycle of violence in maltreated children. *Science, 297,* 851–854.

Caspi, A., Sugden, K., Moffitt, T. E., Taylor, A., Craig, I. W., et al. (2003). Influence of life stress on depression: Moderation by a polymorphism in the 5-HTT gene. *Science, 301,* 386–389.

Castiglioni, A. (1946). *Adventures of the mind* (1st American ed.). New York: Knopf.

Catala-Lopez, F., Hutton, B., Núñez-Beltrán, A., Page, M. J., Ridao, M., Saint-Gerons, D. M., et al. (2017). The pharmacological and non-pharmacological treatment of attention deficit hyperactivity disorder in children and adolescents: A systematic review with network meta-analyses of randomised trials. *PLoS One, 12*(7), e0180355.

Catty, J., Burns, T., Knapp, M., Watt, H., Wright, C., Henderson, J., et al. (2002). Home treatment for mental health problems: A systematic review. *Psychological Medicine, 32,* 383–401.

Ceci, S. J., & Bruck, M. (1995). *Jeopardy in the courtroom.* Washington, DC: American Psychological Association.

Centers for Disease Control (CDC). (2008a). HIV/AIDS in the United States. http://www.cdc.gov (accessed March 13, 2009).

Centers for Disease Control (CDC). (2008b). Tracking fetal alcohol syndrome. http://www.cdc.gov/ncbddd/fas/fassurv.htm (accessed December 5, 2008).

Centers for Disease Control (CDC). (2015). Suicide: Facts at a glance. www.cdc.gov/ncipc/dvp/suicide/SuicideDataSheet.pdf (accessed May 14, 2018).

Centers for Disease Control (CDC). (2018a). Current cigarette smoking among adults in the United States.

https://www.cdc.gov/tobacco/data_statistics/fact_sheets/adult_data/cig_smoking/index.htm. Retrieved July 3, 2018.

Centers for Disease Control (CDC). (2018b). Drug overdose death data. https://www.cdc.gov/drugoverdose/data/statedeaths.html. Retrieved July 4, 2018.

Centers for Disease Control (CDC). (2018c). Electronic cigarettes. https://www.cdc.gov/tobacco/basic_information/e-cigarettes/index.htm. Retrieved July 3, 2018.

Centers for Disease Control (CDC). (2018d). Fetal alcohol spectrum disorders (FASDs). https://www.cdc.gov/ncbddd/fasd/facts.html (accessed June 11, 2018).

Centers for Disease Control (CDC). (2018e). Heart disease fact sheet. https://www.cdc.gov/dhdsp/data_statistics/fact_sheets/fs_heart_disease.htm. Retrieved July 5, 2018.

Centers for Disease Control (CDC). (2018f). HIV/AIDS Basic Statistics. https://www.cdc.gov/hiv/basics/statistics.html. Retrieved July 5, 2018.

Centers for Disease Control (CDC). (2018g). Obesity. Retrieved June 21, 2018, from http://www.cdc.gov/obesity.

Cervantes, R. C., Salgado de Snyder, V. N., & Padilla, A. M. (1989). Posttraumatic stress in immigrants from Central America and Mexico. *Hospital & Community Psychiatry, 40,* 615–619.

Chan, E., Fogler, J. M., & Hammerness, P. G. (2016). Treatment of attention-deficit/hyperactivity disorder in adolescents: A systematic review. *JAMA, 315*(18), 1997–2008.

Chang, S. H., Stoll, C. R., Song, J., Varela, J. E., Eagon, C. J., & Colditz, G. A. (2014). The effectiveness and risks of bariatric surgery: An updated systematic review and meta-analysis, 2003–2012. *JAMA Surgery, 149*(3), 275–287.

Chapman, L. J., Edell, W. S., & Chapman, J. P. (1980). Physical anhedonia, perceptual aberration, and psychosis proneness. *Schizophrenia Bulletin, 6,* 639–653.

Chard, K. M., Schuster, J. L., & Resick, P., A. (2012). Empirically supported psychological treatments: Cognitive processing therapy. In J. G. Beck & D. M. Sloan (Eds.), *The Oxford handbook of traumatic stress disorders* (pp. 439–448). New York: Oxford University Press.

Charney, D. S. (2004). Psychobiological mechanisms of resilience and vulnerability: Implications for successful adaptation to extreme stress. *American Journal of Psychiatry, 161,* 195–216.

Charney, D. S., Nagy, L. M., Bremner, J. D., Goddard, A. W., Yehuda, R., & Southwick, S. M. (2000). Neurobiologic mechanisms of human anxiety. In B. S. Fogel (Ed.), *Synopsis of neuropsychiatry* (pp. 273–288). Philadelphia: Lippincott Williams & Wilkins.

Chartier, K., & Caetano, R. (2010). Ethnicity and health disparities in alcohol research. *Alcohol Research & Health, 33*(1-2), 152–160.

Chassin, L., Pitts, S. C., DeLucia, C., & Todd, M. (1999). A longitudinal study of children of alcoholics: Predicting young adult substance use disorders, anxiety, and depression. *Journal of Abnormal Psychology, 108,* 106–119.

Chatzitheochari, S., & Arber, S. (2009). Lack of sleep, work and the long hours culture: Evidence from the UK time use survey. *Work, Employment and Society, 23,* 30–48.

Chavira, D. A., Grilo, C. M., Shea, M. T., Yen, S., Gunderson, J. G., Morey, L. C., et al. (2003). Ethnicity and four personality disorders. *Comprehensive Psychiatry, 44,* 483–491.

Checknita, D., Maussion, G., Labonté, B., Comai, S., Tremblay, R. E., Vitaro, F., et al. (2015). Monoamine oxidase: A gene promoter methylation and transcriptional downregulation in an offender population with antisocial personality disorder. *British Journal of Psychiatry, 206*(3), 216–222.

Chen, E., & Miller, G. E. (2012). "Shift-and-persist" strategies: Why being low in socioeconomic status isn't always bad for health. *Perspectives on Psychological Science, 7,* 135–158.

Chen, H., Cohen, P., Crawford, T. N., Kasen, S., Guan, B., & Gordon, K. (2009). Impact of early adolescent psychiatric and personality disorder on long-term physical health: A 20-year longitudinal follow-up study. *Psychological Medicine, 39,* 865–874.

Chen, J. A., Peñagarikano, O., Belgard, T. G., Swarup, V., & Geschwind, D. H. (2015). The emerging picture of autism spectrum disorder: Genetics and pathology. *Annual Review of Pathology: Mechanisms of Disease, 10,* 111–144.

Chen, L., Staubli, S. E., Schneider, M. P., Kessels, A. G., Ivic, S., Bachmann, L. M., & Kessler, T. M. (2015). Phosphodiesterase 5 inhibitors for the treatment of erectile dysfunction: a trade-off network meta-analysis. *European Urology, 68*(4), 674–680.

Chen, R., Ma, Y., Wilson, K., Hu, Z., Sallah, D., Wang, J., Fan, L., Chen, R. L., & Copeland, J. R. (2012). A multicentre community-based study of dementia cases and subcases in older people in China—the GMS-AGECAT prevalence and socio-economic correlates. *International Journal of Geriatric Psychiatry, 27,* 692–702.

Chen, W. Y., Rosner, B., Hankinson, S. F., Colditz, G. A., & Willett, W. C. (2011). Moderate alcohol consumption during adult life, drinking patterns, and breast cancer risk. *JAMA, 306,* 1884–1890.

Cheng, A. T., Hawton, K., Lee, C. T., & Chen, T. H. (2007). The influence of media reporting of the suicide of a celebrity on suicide rates: A population-based study. *International Journal of Epidemiology, 36,* 1229–1234.

Chew, D., Anderson, J., Williams, K., May, T., & Pang, K. (2018). Hormonal treatment in young people with gender dysphoria: A systematic review. *Pediatrics, 141*(4), e20173742.

Chida, Y., & Steptoe, A. (2009). The association of anger and hostility with future coronary heart disease: A meta-analytic review of prospective evidence. *Journal of the American College of Cardiology, 53*(11), 936–946.

Chida, Y., & Vedhara, K. (2009). Adverse psychosocial factors predict poorer prognosis in HIV disease: A meta-analytic review of prospective investigations. *Brain, Behavior, and Immunity, 23*(4), 434–445.

Chilvers, R., Macdonald, G. M., & Hayes, A. A. (2006). Supported housing for people with severe mental disorders. *Cochrane Database of Systematic Reviews, 4,* CD000453.

Chin, A. L., Negash, S., & Hamilton, R. (2011). Diversity and disparity in dementia: The impact of ethnoracial differences in Alzheimer's disease. *Alzheimer's Disease and Associated Disorders, 25,* 187–195.

Chmielewski, M., Clark, L. A., Bagby, R. M., & Watson, D. (2015). Method matters: Understanding diagnostic reliability in DSM-IV and DSM-5. *Journal of Abnormal Psychology, 124,* 764–769.

Choe, J. Y., Teplin, L. A., & Abram, K. M. (2008). Perpetration of violence, violent victimization, and severe mental illness: Balancing public health concerns. *Psychiatric Services, 59,* 153–164.

Choi-Kain, L. W., Finch, E. F., Masland, S. R., Jenkins, J. A., & Unruh, B. T. (2017). What works in the treatment of borderline personality disorder. *Current Behavioral Neuroscience Reports, 4*(1), 21–30.

Chou, T. (1992). Wake up and smell the coffee: Caffeine, coffee, and the medical consequences. *Western Journal of Medicine, 157,* 544–553.

Chow, E., Tsao, M. N., & Harth, T. (2004). Does psychosocial intervention improve survival in cancer? A meta-analysis. *Palliative Medicine, 18,* 25–31.

Christenson, G. A., & Mansueto, C. S. (1999). Trichotillomania: Descriptive characteristics and phenomenology. In D. J. Stein, G. A. Christenson, & E. Hollander (Eds.), *Trichotillomania* (pp. 1–42). Washington, DC: American Psychiatric Publishing.

Christenson, G. A., Pyle, R. L., & Mitchell, J. E. (1991). Estimated lifetime prevalence of trichotillomania in college students. *Journal of Clinical Psychiatry, 52,* 415–417.

Chu, C., Buchman-Schmitt, J. M., Stanley, I. H., Hom, M. A., Tucker, R. P., Hagan, C. R., et al. (2017). The interpersonal theory of suicide: A systematic review and meta-analysis of a decade of cross-national research. *Psychological Bulletin, 143*(12), 1313–1345.

Chu, J., & Leino, A. (2017). Advancement in the maturing science of cultural adaptations of evidence-based interventions. *Journal of Consulting and Clinical Psychology, 85,* 45–57.

Chu, J., Leino, A., Pflum, S., & Sue, S. (2016). A model for the theoretical basis of cultural competency to guide psychotherapy. *Professional Psychology: Research and Practice, 47*(1), 18–29.

Chui, H. C., & Gatz, M. (2005). Cultural diversity in Alzheimer disease: The interface between biology, belief, and behavior. *Alzheimer Disease and Associated Disorders, 19,* 250–255.

Chung, W. C., De Vries, G. J., & Swaab, D. F. (2002). Sexual differentiation of the bed nucleus of the striaterminalis in humans may extend into adulthood. *Journal of Neuroscience, 22,* 1027–1033.

Cicchetti, D., & Rogosch, F. A. (2001). Diverse patterns of neuroendocrine activity in maltreated children. *Development & Psychopathology, 13,* 677–694.

Cicchetti, D., & Toth, S. L. (2005). Child maltreatment. *Annual Review of Clinical Psychology, 1,* 409–438.

Cicchetti, D., & Toth, S. L. (2016). Child maltreatment and developmental psychopathology: A multilevel perspective. In Cicchetti, D. (Ed.), *Developmental psychopathology: Vol. 3. Maladaptation and psychopathology* (3rd ed., pp. 457–512). Hoboken, NJ: Wiley.

Clancy, S. A., McNally, R. J., Schacter, D. L., Lenzenweger, M. F., & Pitman, R. K. (2002). Memory distortion in people reporting abduction by aliens. *Journal of Abnormal Psychology, 111,* 455–461.

Clancy, S. A., Schacter, D. L., McNally, R. J., & Pitman, R. (2000). False recognition in women reporting recovered memories of sexual abuse. *Psychological Science, 11,* 26–31.

Clark, D. A., & Purdon, C. (1993). New perspectives for a cognitive theory of obsessions. *Australian Psychologist, 28,* 161–167.

Clark, D. M. (1988). A cognitive model of panic attacks. In S. Rachman & J. D. Maser (Eds.), *Panic: Psychological perspectives* (pp. 71–89). Hillsdale, NJ: Erlbaum.

Clark, D. M., & Wells, A. (1995). A cognitive model of social phobia. In R. G. Heimberg, M. R. Liebowitz, D. A. Hope, & F. R. Schneier (Eds.), *Social phobia: Diagnosis, assessment and treatment* (pp. 69–93). New York: Guilford Press.

Clark, L. A., Cuthbert, B., Lewis-Fernández, R., Narrow, W. E., & Reed, G. M. (2017). Three approaches to understanding and classifying mental disorder: *ICD-11, DSM-5*, and the National Institute of Mental Health's Research Domain Criteria (RDoC). *Psychological Science in the Public Interest, 18*(2), 72–145.

Clark, L. A., Vanderbleek, E. N., Shapiro, J. L., Nuzum, H., Allen, X., Daly, E., et al. (2015). The brave new world of personality disorder-trait specified: Effects of additional definitions on coverage, prevalence, and comorbidity. *Psychopathology Review, 2*(1), 52–82.

Clarkin, J. F., Levy, K. N., Lenzenweger, M. F., & Kernberg, O. F. (2007). Evaluating three treatments for borderline personality disorder: A multiwave study. *American Journal of Psychiatry, 164,* 922–928.

Clayton, A. H. (2007). Epidemiology and neurobiology of female sexual dysfunction. *Journal of Sexual Medicine, 4,* 260–268.

Cleckley, H. M. (1941/1982). *The mask of sanity: An attempt to reinterpret the so-called psychopathic personality.* St. Louis: Mosby.

Cloninger, C. R., & Gottesman, I. I. (1987). Genetic and environmental factors in antisocial behavior disorders. In S. A. Mednick, T. E. Moffitt, & S. A. Stack (Eds.), *The causes of crime: New biological approaches* (pp. 92–109). New York: Cambridge University Press.

Coccaro, E. F. (2012). Intermittent explosive disorder as a disorder of impulsive aggression for DSM-5. *American Journal of Psychiatry, 169*(6), 577–588.

Coccaro, E. F., Fanning, J. R., & Lee, R. (2017). Intermittent explosive disorder and substance use disorder: Analysis of the National Comorbidity Survey Replication sample. *Journal of Clinical Psychiatry, 78*(6), 697–702.

Coccaro, E. F., Lee, R., & Kavoussi, R. J. (2010). Aggression, suicidality, and intermittent explosive disorder: Serotonergic correlates in personality disorder and healthy control subjects. *Neuropsychopharmacology, 35,* 435–444.

Cochrane, M., Petch, I., & Pickering, A. D. (2012). Aspects of cognitive functioning in shizotypy and schizophrenia: Evidence for a continuum model. *Psychiatry Research, 196,* 230–234.

Cochrane, R. E., Grisso, T., & Frederick, R. I. (2001). The relationship between criminal charges, diagnoses, and psycholegal opinions among federal pretrial defendants. *Behavioral Sciences & the Law, 19,* 565–582.

Cocores, J., Pottash, A. C., & Gold, M. S. (1991). Cocaine. In N. S. Miller (Ed.), *Comprehensive handbook of drug and alcohol addiction* (pp. 341–352). New York: Marcel Dekker.

Cohen, K. M., & Savin-Williams, R. C. (2017). Treating sexual problems in lesbian, gay, and bisexual clients. In Z. D. Peterson (Ed.), *The Wiley handbook of sex therapy* (pp. 269–290). Oxford: Wiley.

Cohen, S., Tyrrell, D. A., & Smith, A. P. (1991). Psychological stress and susceptibility to the common cold. *New England Journal of Medicine, 325,* 606–612.

Coid, J. W., Kirkbride, J. B., Barker, D., Cowden, F., Stamps, R., Yang, M., et al. (2008). Raised incidence rates of all psychoses among migrant groups. *Archives of General Psychiatry, 65,* 1250–1258.

Colapinto, J. (2000). *As nature made him: The boy who was raised as a girl.* New York: HarperCollins.

Colapinto, J. (2004, June 3). Gender gap: What were the real reasons behind David Reimer's suicide? *Slate.* http://www.slate.com/articles/health_and_science/medical_examiner/2004/06/gender_gap.html.

Cole, J., Costafreda, S. G., McGuffin, P., & Fu, C. H. (2011). Hippocampal atrophy in first episode depression: A meta-analysis of magnetic resonance imaging studies. *Journal of Affective Disorders, 134*(1), 483–487.

Cole, M. G., Ciampi, A., Belzile, E., & Zhong, L. (2009). Persistent delirium in older hospital patients: A systematic review of frequency and prognosis. *Age Ageing, 38,* 19–26.

Cole, S. W., Kemeny, M. E., Taylor, S. E., Visscher, B. R., & Fahey, J. L. (1995). Accelerated course of human immunodeficiency virus infection in gay men who conceal their homosexual identity. *Psychosomatic Medicine, 58,* 219–238.

Coles, A. S., Kozak, K., & George, T. P. (2018). A review of brain stimulation methods to treat substance use disorders. *American Journal on Addictions, 27,* 71–91.

Coltheart, M., Langdon, R., & McKay, R. (2011). Delusional belief. *Annual Review of Psychology, 62,* 271–298.

Committee on Gulf War and Health. (2008). *Gulf War and health: Vol. 7. Long-term consequences of traumatic brain injury.* Washington, DC: National Academies Press.

Compton, W. M., Han, B., Jones, C. M., Blanco, C., & Hughes, A. (2016). Marijuana use and use disorders in adults in the USA, 2002–14: Analysis of annual cross-sectional surveys. *Lancet Psychiatry, 3*(10), 954–964.

Conduct Problems Prevention Research Group. (2002). Evaluation of the first 3 years of the Fast Track Prevention Trial with children at high risk for adolescent conduct problems. *Journal of Abnormal Child Psychology, 30,* 19–35.

Conduct Problems Prevention Research Group. (2007). The Fast Track randomized controlled trial to prevent externalizing psychiatric disorders: Findings from grades 3 to 9. *Journal of the American Academy of Child and Adolescent Psychiatry, 46,* 1250–1262.

Conduct Problems Prevention Research Group. (2015). Impact of early intervention on psychopathology, crime, and well-being at age 25. *American Journal of Psychiatry, 172,* 59–70.

Conwell, Y., & Thompson, C. (2008). Suicidal behavior in elders. *Psychiatric Clinics of North America, 31,* 333–356.

Cook, B. L., Zuvekas, S. H., Carson, N., Wayne, G. F., Vesper, A., & McGuire, T. G. (2014). Assessing racial/ethnic disparities in treatment across episodes of mental health care. *Health Services Research, 49*(1), 206–229.

Coolidge, F. L., Thede, L., & Jang, K. L. (2004). Are personality disorders psychological manifestations of executive function deficits? Bivariate heritability evidence from a twin study. *Behavior Genetics, 34,* 75–84.

Coolidge, F. L., Thede, L. L., & Young, S. E. (2002). The heritability of gender identity disorder in a child and adolescent twin sample. *Behavior Genetics, 32,* 251–257.

Coon, K. D., Myers, A. J., Craig, D. W., Webster, J. A., Pearson, J. V., Lince, D. H., Zismann, V. L., Beach, T. G., Leung, D., Bryden, L., Halperin, R. F., Marlowe, L., Kaleem, M., Walker, D. G., Ravid, R., Heward, C. B., Rogers, J., Papassotiropoulos, A., Reiman, E. M., Hardy, J., & Stephan, D. A. (2007). A high-density whole-genome association study reveals that APOE is the major susceptibility gene for sporadic late-onset Alzheimer's disease. *Journal of Clinical Psychiatry, 68,* 613–618.

Coons, P. M. (1980). Multiple personality: Diagnostic considerations. *Journal of Clinical Psychiatry, 41,* 330–336.

Coons, P. M. (1984). *Childhood antecedents of multiple personality.* Paper presented at the Meeting of the American Psychiatric Association, Los Angeles.

Coons, P. M. (1994). Confirmation of childhood abuse in child and adolescent cases of multiple personality disorder and dissociative disorder not otherwise specified. *Journal of Nervous & Mental Disease, 182,* 461–464.

Coons, P. M., Cole, C., Pellow, T. A., & Milstein, V. (1990). Symptoms of posttraumatic stress disorder and dissociation in women victims of abuse. In R. P. Kluft (Ed.), *Incest-related syndromes of adult psychopathology* (pp. 205–226). Washington, DC: American Psychiatric Press.

Coons, P. M., & Milstein, V. (1986). Psychosexual disturbances in multiple personality: Characteristics, etiology, and treatment. *Journal of Clinical Psychiatry, 47,* 106–110.

Coons, P. M., & Milstein, V. (1990). Self-mutilation associated with dissociative disorders. *Dissociation: Progress in the Dissociative Disorders, 3,* 81–87.

Coontz, P. D., Lidz, C. W., & Mulvey, E. P. (1994). Gender and the assessment of dangerousness in the psychiatric emergency room. *International Journal of Law & Psychiatry, 17,* 369–376.

Cooper, M. L., Kuntsche, E., Levitt, A., Barber, L. L., & Wolf, S. (2016). Motivational models of substance use: A review of theory and research on motives for using alcohol, marijuana, and tobacco. In K. Sher (Ed.), *The Oxford handbook of substance use and substance use disorders,* vol. 1 (pp. 375–421). Oxford: Oxford University Press.

Cornelius, M. D., Goldschmidt, L., Day, N. L., & Larkby, C. (2002). Alcohol, tobacco and marijuana use among pregnant teenagers: 6-year follow-up of offspring growth effects. *Neurotoxicology & Teratology, 24,* 703–710.

Coronado, V. G., Haileyesus, T., Cheng, T. A., Bell, J. M., Haarbauer-Krupa, J., Lionbarger, M. R., et al. (2015). Trends in sports- and recreation-related traumatic brain injuries treated in US emergency departments: The National Electronic Injury Surveillance System-All Injury Program (NEISS-AIP) 2001–2012. *Journal of Head Trauma Rehabilitation, 30*(3), 185–197.

Corrao, G., Bagnardi, V., Zambon, A., & La Vecchia, C. (2004). A meta-analysis of alcohol consumption and the risk of 15 diseases. *Prevention by Medicine, 38,* 613–619.

Costanza, A., D'Orta, I., Perroud, N., Burkhardt, S., Malafosse, A., Mangin, P., & La Harpe, R. (2014). Neurobiology of suicide: Do biomarkers exist? *International Journal of Legal Medicine, 128*(1), 73–82.

Costello, E. J., Compton, S. N., Keeler, G., & Angold, A. (2003). Relationships between poverty and psychopathology: A natural experiment. *JAMA, 290,* 2023–2029.

Courtet, P., Picot, M.-C., Bellivier, F., Torres, S., Jollant, F., Michelon, C., Castelnau, D., Astruc, B., Buresi, C., & Malafosse, A. (2004). Serotonin transporter gene may be involved in short-term risk of subsequent suicide attempts. *Biological Psychiatry, 55,* 46–51.

Cousins, N. (1985). Therapeutic value of laughter. *Integrative Psychiatry, 3,* 112.

Cox, B. J., Turnbull, D. L., Robinson, J. A., Grant, B. F., & Stein, M. B. (2011). The effect of avoidant personality disorder on the persistence of generalized social anxiety disorder in the general population: Results from a longitudinal, nationally representative mental health survey. *Depression and Anxiety, 28,* 250–255.

Coyne, J. C. (1976). Toward an interactional description of depression. *Psychiatry, 39,* 28–40.

Coyne, J. C., Stefanek, M., & Palmer, S. C. (2007). Psychotherapy and survival in cancer: The conflict between hope and evidence. *Psychological Bulletin, 133,* 367–394.

Craddock, N., & Sklar, P. (2013). Genetics of bipolar disorder. *Lancet, 381*(9878), 1654–1662.

Craske, M. G. (2017). *Cognitive-behavioral therapy.* Washington, D.C.: American Psychological Association.

Craske, M. G., & Barlow, D. H. (2014). Panic disorder and agoraphobia. In D. H. Barlow (Ed.), *Clinical handbook of psychological disorders: A step-by-step treatment manual* (pp. 1–61). New York: Guilford.

Craske, M. G., Kircanski, K., Epstein, A., Wittchen, H.-U., Pine, D. S., Lewis-Fernández, R., Hinton, D., & *DSM-V* OC Spectrum, Posttraumatic and Dissociative Disorder Work Group. (2010). Panic disorder: A review of *DSM-IV* panic disorder and proposals for *DSM-V. Depression and Anxiety, 27,* 93–112.

Craske, M. G., Niles, A. N., Burklund, L. J., Wolitzky-Taylor, K. B., Vilardaga, J. C. P., Arch, J. J., et al. (2014). Randomized controlled trial of cognitive behavioral therapy and acceptance and commitment therapy for social phobia: Outcomes and moderators. *Journal of Consulting and Clinical Psychology, 82,* 1034–1048.

Craske, M. G., Treanor, M., Conway, C. C., Zbozinek, T., & Vervliet, B. (2014). Maximizing exposure therapy: An inhibitory learning approach. *Behaviour Research and Therapy, 58,* 10–23.

Craske, M. G., & Waters, A. M. (2005). Panic disorder, phobias, and generalized anxiety disorder. *Annual Review of Clinical Psychology, 1,* 197–226.

Crepault, C., & Couture, M. (1980). Men's erotic fantasies. *Archives of Sexual Behavior, 9,* 565–581.

Crestani, C. C. (2016). Emotional stress and cardiovascular complications in animal models: A review of the influence of stress type. *Frontiers in Physiology, 7,* 251.

Crick, N. R., & Ladd, G. W. (1990). Children's perceptions of the outcomes of social strategies: Do the ends justify being mean? *Developmental Psychology, 26,* 612–620.

Crick, N. R., Ostrov, J. M., & Kawabata, Y. (2007). Relational aggression and gender: An overview. In D. J. Flannery, A. T. Vazsonyi, & I. D. Waldman (Eds.), *The Cambridge handbook of violent behavior and aggression* (pp. 245–259). New York, NY: Cambridge University Press.

Cromby, J., Chung, E., Papadopoulos, D., & Talbot, C. (2016). Reviewing the epigenetics of schizophrenia. *Journal of Mental Health,* 1-9.

Cronbach, L. J., & Meehl, P. E. (1955). Construct validity in psychological tests. *Psychological Bulletin, 52,* 281–302.

Cross, S. E., & Madson, L. (1997). Models of the self: Self-construals and gender. *Psychological Bulletin, 122,* 5–37.

Crowther, J. H., Armey, M., Luce, K. H., Dalton, G. R., & Leahey, T. (2008). The point prevalence of bulimic disorders from 1990 to 2004. *International Journal of Eating Disorders, 41,* 491–497.

Cubillo, A., Halari, R., Smith, A., Taylor, E., & Rubia, K. (2012). A review of fronto-cortico brain abnormalities in children and adults with attention deficit hyperactivity disorder (ADHD) and new evidence for dysfunction in adults with ADHD during motivation and attention. *Cortex, 8,* 194–215.

Cuijpers, P., Dekker, J., Hollon, S. D., & Andersson, G. (2009). Adding psychotherapy to pharmacotherapy in the treatment of depressive disorders in adults: A meta-analysis. *Journal of Clinical Psychiatry, 70,* 1219–1229.

Cuijpers, P., Donker, T., Weissman, M. M., Ravitz, P., & Cristea, I. A. (2016). Interpersonal psychotherapy for mental health problems: A comprehensive meta-analysis. *American Journal of Psychiatry.*

Cuijpers, P., Sijbrandij, M., Koole, S., Huibers, M., Berking, M., & Andersson, G. (2014). Psychological treatment of generalized anxiety disorder: A meta-analysis. *Clinical Psychology Review, 34,* 130–140.

Cuijpers, P., van Straten, A., van Oppen, P., & Andersson, G. (2008). Are psychological and pharmacological interventions equally effective in the treatment of adult depressive disorders? A meta-analysis of comparative studies. *Journal of Clinical Psychiatry, 69,* 1675–1685.

Cuijpers, P., van Straten, A., Warmerdam, L., & Andersson, G. (2009). Psychological treatment versus combined treatment of depression: A meta-analysis. *Depression & Anxiety, 26,* 279–288.

Culbert, K. M., Racine, S. E., & Klump, K. L. (2015). Research review: What we have learned about the causes of eating disorders—a synthesis of sociocultural, psychological, and biological research. *Journal of Child Psychology and Psychiatry, 56*(11), 1141–1164.

Cummings, J., Aisen, P. S., DuBois, B., Frölich, L., Jack, C. R., Jones, R. W., et al. (2016). Drug development in Alzheimer's disease: The path to 2025. *Alzheimer's Research & Therapy, 8*(1), 39.

Cusack, K., Jonas, D. E., Forneris, C. A., Wines, C., Sonis, J., Middleton, J. C., et al. (2016). Psychological treatments for adults with posttraumatic stress disorder: A systematic review and meta-analysis. *Clinical Psychology Review, 43,* 128–141.

Cuthbert, B. N., & Insel, T. R. (2013). Toward the future of psychiatric diagnosis: The seven pillars of RDoC. *BMC Medicine, 11*(1), 126.

D

Daley, D. C., & Marlatt, G. A. (2006). *Overcoming your alcohol or drug problem: Effective recovery strategies: Therapist guide* (2nd ed.). New York: Oxford University Press.

Damasio, H., Grabowski, T., Frank, R., Galaburda, A. M., & Damasio, A. R. (1994). The return of Phineas Gage: Clues about the brain from the skull of a famous patient. *Science, 264,* 1102–1105.

Dana, R. H. (2005). *Multicultural assessment: Principles, applications, and examples.* Mahwah, NJ: Routledge.

Danielsson, A. K., Wennberg, P., Hibell, B., & Romelsjö, A. (2012). Alcohol use, heavy episodic drinking and subsequent problems among adolescents in 23 European countries: Does the prevention paradox apply? *Addiction, 107,* 71–80.

Dansinger, M. L., Gleason, J. A., Griffith, J. L., Selker, H. P., & Schaefer, E. J. (2005). Comparison of the Atkins, Ornish, Weight Watchers, and Zone diets for weight loss and heart disease risk reduction: A randomized trial. *JAMA, 293,* 43–53.

Darcangelo, S. (2008). Fetishism: Psychopathology and treatment. In D. R. Laws & W. T. O'Donohue (Eds.), *Sexual deviance: Theory, assessment, and treatment* (pp. 108–119). New York: Guilford Press.

Darcangelo, S., Hollings, A., & Paladino, G. (2008). Fetishism: Assessment and treatment. In D. R. Laws & W. T. O'Donohue (Eds.), *Sexual deviance: Theory, assessment, and treatment* (pp. 119–131). New York: Guilford Press.

Dauvilliers, Y., Baumann, C. R., Carlander, B., Bischof, M., Blatter, T., Lecendreux, M., et al. (2003). CSF hypocretin-1 levels in narcolepsy, Kleine-Levin syndrome, and other hypersomnias and neurological conditions. *Journal of Neurology, Neurosurgery, and Psychiatry, 74,* 1667.

Davidson, J., Allgulander, C., Pollack, M. H., Hartford, J., Erickson, J. S., Russell, J. M., Perahia, D., Wohlreich, M. M., Carlson, J., & Raskin, J. (2008). Efficacy and tolerability of duloxetine in elderly patients with generalized anxiety disorder: A pooled analysis of four randomized, double-blind, placebo-controlled studies. *Human Psychopharmacology, 23,* 519–526.

Davidson, J. R. T. (2001). Pharmacotherapy of generalized anxiety disorder. *Journal of Clinical Psychiatry, 62*(Suppl. 11), 46–50.

Davidson, K., Norrie, J., Tyrer, P., Gumley, A., Tata, P., Murray, H., & Palmer, S. (2006). The effectiveness of cognitive behavior therapy for borderline personality disorder: Results from the borderline personality disorder of cognitive therapy (BOSCOT) trial. *Journal of Personality Disorders, 20,* 450–465.

Davidson, R. J., Pizzagalli, D. A., & Nitschke, J. B. (2009). Representation and regulation of emotion in depression: Perspectives from affective neuroscience. In

I. H. Gotlib & C. L. Hammen (Eds.), *Handbook of depression* (2nd ed., pp. 218–248). New York: Guilford Press.

Davidson, R. J., Pizzagalli, D., Nitschke, J. B., & Putnam, K. (2002). Depression: Perspectives from affective neuroscience. *Annual Review of Psychology, 53,* 545–574.

Davis, K. L., Kahn, R. S., Ko, G., & Davidson, M. (1991). Dopamine in schizophrenia: A review and conceptualization. *American Journal of Psychiatry, 148,* 1474–1486.

Davis, O. S. P., Haworth, C. M. A., & Plomin, R. (2009). Learning abilities and disabilities: Generalist genes in early adolescence. *Cognitive Neuropsychiatry, 14,* 312–331.

Davis, T. E., III, Ollendick, T. H., & Öst, L. G. (2009). Intensive treatment of specific phobias in children and adolescents. *Cognitive and Behavioral Practice, 16,* 294–303.

Davis, T. S., Mauss, I. B., Lumian, D., Troy, A. S., Shallcross, A. J., Zarolia, P., et al. (2014). Emotional reactivity and emotion regulation among adults with a history of self-harm: Laboratory self-report and functional MRI evidence. *Journal of Abnormal Psychology, 123,* 499–509.

Dawson, D. A., Grant, B. F., Stinson, F. S., Chou, P. S., Huang, B., & Ruan, W. J. (2005). Recovery from *DSM-IV* alcohol dependence: United States, 2001–2002. *Addiction, 100,* 281–292.

Deary, V., Chalder, T., & Sharpe, M. (2007). The cognitive behavioural model of medically unexplained symptoms: A theoretical and empirical review. *Clinical Psychology Review, 27,* 781–797.

Deeny, S. P., Poeppel, D., Zimmerman, J. B., Roth, S. M., Brandauer, J., Witkoswki, S., Hearn, J. W., Ludlow, A. T., Contreras-Vital, J. L., Brandt, J., & Hatfield, B. D. (2008). Exercise, APOE, and working memory: MEG and behavioral evidence for benefit of exercise in epsilon4 carriers. *Biological Psychology, 78,* 179–187.

De Fruyt, F., & De Clercq, B. (2014). Antecedents of personality disorder in childhood and adolescence: Toward an integrative developmental model. *Annual Review of Clinical Psychology, 10,* 449–476.

Degenhardt, L., Chiu, W. T., Sampson, N., Kessler, R. C., Anthony, J. C., Angermeyer, M., Bruffaerts, R., de Girolamo, G., Gureje, O., Huang, Y., Karam, A., Kostyuchenko, S., Lepine, J. P., Mora, M. E., Neumark, Y., Ormel, J. H., Pinto-Meza, A., Posada-Villa, J., Stein, D. J., Takeshima, T., & Wells, J. E. (2008). Toward a global view of alcohol, tobacco, cannabis, and cocaine use: Findings from the WHO World Mental Health Surveys. *PLoS Med., 5,* e141.

De Genna, N. M., & Feske, U. (2013). Phenomenology of borderline personality disorder: The role of race and socioeconomic status. *Journal of Nervous and Mental Disease, 201*(12), 1027–1034.

de Gusmão, C. M., Guerriero, R. M., Bernson-Leung, M. E., Pier, D., Ibeziako, P. I., Bujoreanu, S., et al. (2014). Functional neurological symptom disorders in a pediatric emergency room: Diagnostic accuracy, features, and outcome. *Pediatric Neurology, 51*(2), 233–238.

del Campo, N., Chamberlain, S. R., Sahakian, B. J., & Robbins, T. W. (2011). The roles of dopamine and noradrenaline in the pathophysiology and treatment of attention-deficit/hyperactivity disorder. *Biological Psychiatry, 69,* e146–e157.

Dell, P. F. (2018). Reconsidering the autohypnotic model of the dissociative disorders. *Journal of Trauma & Dissociation,* 1–31.

Dell, P. F., & Eisenhower, J. W. (1990). Adolescent multiple personality disorder: A preliminary study of eleven cases. *Journal of the American Academy of Child & Adolescent Psychiatry, 29,* 359–366.

De Los Reyes, A., Augenstein, T. M., Wang, M., Thomas, S. A., Drabick, D. A., Burgers, D. E., & Rabinowitz, J. (2015). The validity of the multi-informant approach to assessing child and adolescent mental health. *Psychological Bulletin, 141*(4), 858–900.

Denis, C., Fatséas, M., & Auriacombe, M. (2012). Analyses related to the development of *DSM-5* criteria for substance use related disorders: 3. An assessment of pathological gambling criteria. *Drug and Alcohol Dependence, 122,* 22–27.

Depression and Bipolar Support Alliance. (2008). Suicide prevention: Responding to an emergency situation. http://www.ndma.org (accessed May 15, 2008).

DePrince, A. P. & Freyd, J. J. (2014). Trauma-induced dissociation. In M. J. Friedman, T. M. Keane, & P. A. Resick (Eds.), *Handbook of PTSD: Science and practice* (2nd ed., pp 219–233). New York: Guilford Press.

De Raedt, R., Vanderhasselt, M.-A., & Baeken, C. (2015). Neurostimulation as an intervention for treatment resistant depression: From research on mechanisms towards targeted neurocognitive strategies. *Clinical Psychology Review, 41,* 61–69.

DeRubeis, R. J., Gelfand, L. A., Tang, T. Z., & Simons, A. D. (1999). Medications versus cognitive behavior therapy for severely depressed outpatients: Mega-analysis of four randomized comparisons. *American Journal of Psychiatry, 156,* 1001–1013.

DeRubeis, R. J., Hollon, S. D., Amsterdam, J. D., Shelton, R. C., Young, P. R., Salomon, R. M., et al. (2005). Cognitive therapy vs. medications in the treatment of moderate to severe depression. *Archives of General Psychiatry, 62,* 409–416.

deSilva, P., Rachman, S., & Seligman, M. (1977). Prepared phobias and obsessions. *Behaviour Research & Therapy, 15,* 65–77.

de Snyder, V. N. S., Diaz-Perez, M. D., & Ojeda, V. D. (2000). The prevalence of nervios and associated symptomatology among inhabitants of Mexican rural communities. *Culture, Medicine & Psychiatry, 24,* 453–470.

Dessemontet, R. S., Bless, G., & Morin, D. (2012). Effects of inclusion on the academic achievement and adaptive behavior of children with intellectual disabilities. *Journal of Intellectual and Disability Research, 56,* 579–587.

Deutsch, Albert. 1937. *The mentally ill in America* (1st ed.). New York: Doubleday.

Dewaraja, R., & Sasaki, Y. (1991). Semen-loss syndrome: A comparison between Sri Lanka and Japan. *American Journal of Psychotherapy, 45,* 14–20.

Dhawan, N., Kunik, M. E., Oldham, J., & Coverdale, J. (2010). Prevalence and treatment of narcissistic personality disorder in the community: a systematic review. *Comprehensive Psychiatry, 51,* 333–339.

Dick, D. M., Agrawal, A., Keller, M. C., Adkins, A., Aliev, F., Monroe, S., et al. (2015). Candidate gene–environment interaction research: Reflections and recommendations. *Perspectives on Psychological Science, 10*(1), 37–59.

Dickey, R., & Stephens, J. (1995). Female-to-male transsexualism, heterosexual type: Two cases. *Archives of Sexual Behavior, 24,* 439–445.

Diedrich, A., & Voderholzer, U. (2015). Obsessive–compulsive personality disorder: A current review. *Current Psychiatry Reports, 17*(2), 2.

Dimidjian, S., Arch, J. J., Schneider, R. L., Desormeau, P., Felder, J. N., & Segal, Z. V. (2016). Considering meta-analysis, meaning, and metaphor: A systematic review and critical examination of "third wave" cognitive and behavioral therapies. *Behavior Therapy, 47(6),* 886–905.

Dimidjian, S., Barrera, M., Jr., Martell, C., Muñoz, R. F., & Lewinsohn, P. M. (2011). The origins and current status of behavioral activation treatments for depression. *Annual Review of Clinical Psychology, 7,* 1–38.

Dimidjian, S., Hollon, S. D., Dobson, K. S., Schmaling, K. B., Kohlenberg, R. J., Addis, M. E., Gallop, R., McGlinchey, J. B., Markley, D. K., Gollan, J. K., Atkins, D. C., Dunner, D. L., & Jacobson, N. S. (2006). Randomized trial of behavioral activation, cognitive therapy, and antidepressant medication in the acute treatment of adults with major depression. *Journal of Consulting and Clinical Psychology, 74,* 658–670.

Dishion, T. J., & Patterson, G. R. (1997). The timing and severity of antisocial behavior: Three hypotheses within an ecological framework. In D. M. Stoff, J. Breiling, & J. D. Maser (Eds.), *Handbook of antisocial personality disorder* (pp. 205–217). New York: Wiley.

Disney, K. L., Weinstein, Y., & Oltmanns, T. F. (2012). Personality disorder symptoms are differentially related to divorce frequency. *Journal of Family Psychology, 26,* 959–965.

Distel, M. A., Rebollo-Mesa, I., Willemsen, G., Derom, C. A., Trull, T. J., Martin, N. G., & Boomsma, D. I. (2009). Familial resemblance of borderline personality disorder features: Genetic or cultural transmission? *PLoS One, 4,* e5334.

Diwadkar, V. A., Bustamante, A., Rai, H., & Uddin, M. (2014). Epigenetics, stress, and their potential impact on brain network function: A focus on the schizophrenia diatheses. *Frontiers in Psychiatry, 5,* 71.

Dixon, D., Cruess, S., Kilbourn, K., Klimas, N., Fletcher, M. A., Ironson, G., Baum, A., Schneiderman, N., & Antoni, M. H. (2001). Social support mediates loneliness and human herpes virus Type 6 (HHV-6) antibody titers. *Journal of Applied Social Psychology, 31,* 1111–1132.

Dockray, S., & Steptoe, A. (2010). Positive affect and psychobiological processes. *Neuroscience & Biobehavioral Reviews, 35*(1), 69–75.

Dodge, K. A. (2009). Mechanisms of gene-environment interaction effects in the development of conduct disorder. *Perspectives on Psychological Science, 4,* 408–414.

Dodge, K. A., & Pettit, G. S. (2003). A biopsychosocial model of the development of chronic conduct problems in adolescence. *Developmental Psychology, 39,* 349–371.

Dohrenwend, B. P. (2000). The role of adversity and stress in psychopathology: Some evidence and its implications for theory and research. *Journal of Health and Social Behavior, 41,* 1–19.

Dohrenwend, B. P., Shrout, P. E., Link, B. G., Martin, J. L., & Skodol, A. E. (1987). Overview and initial results of a risk factor study of depression and schizophrenia. In *From social class to social stress* (pp. 210–234). Berlin, Heidelberg: Springer.

Dohrenwend, B. P., Turner, J. B., Turse, N. A., Adams, B. G., Koenen, K. C., & Marshall, R. (2006). The psychological risks of Vietnam for U.S. veterans: A revisit with new data and methods. *Science, 313,* 979–982.

Dolan, A. (2006). The obsessive disorder that haunts my life. www.dailymail.co.uk (accessed February 26, 2009).

Donegan, N. H., Sanislow, C. A., Blumberg, H. P., Fulbright, R. K., Lacadie, C., Skudlarski, P., Gore, J. C., Olson, I. R., McGlashan, T. H., & Wexler, B. E. (2003). Amygdala hyperreactivity in borderline personality disorder: Implications for emotional dysregulation. *Biological Psychiatry, 54,* 1284–1293.

Donovan, D., & Witkiewitz, K. (2012). Relapse prevention: From radical idea to common practice. *Addiction Research & Theory, 20,* 204–217.

Donovan, D. M., Anton, R. F., Miller, W. R., Longabaugh, R., Hosking, J. D., & Youngblood, M. (2008). Combined pharmacotherapies and behavioral interventions for alcohol dependence (the COMBINE study): Examination of posttreatment drinking outcomes. *Journal of Studies on Alcohol and Drugs, 69,* 5–13.

Dorahy, M. J., Brand, B. L., Şar, V., Krüger, C., Stavropoulos, P., Martínez-Taboas, A., et al. (2014). Dissociative identity disorder: An empirical overview. *Australian & New Zealand Journal of Psychiatry, 48*(5), 402–417.

Dorris, M. (1989). *The unbroken cord.* New York: Harper & Row.

Douaihy, A. B., Kelly, T. M., & Sullivan, C. (2013). Medications for substance use disorders. *Social Work in Public Health, 28*(3–4), 264–278.

Dougherty, D. D., & Rauch, S. L. (2007). Brain correlates of antidepressant treatment outcome from neuroimaging studies in depression. *Psychiatric Clinics of North America, 30,* 91–103.

Dowling, N. A., Merkouris, S. S., Greenwood, C. J., Oldenhof, E., Toumbourou, J. W., & Youssef, G. J. (2017). Early risk and protective factors for problem gambling: A systematic review and meta-analysis of longitudinal studies. *Clinical Psychology Review, 51,* 109–124.

Downey, G., & Feldman, S. I. (1996). Implications of rejection sensitivity for intimate relationships. *Journal of Personality and Social Psychology, 70,* 1327–1343.

Drake, C. L., Roehrs, T., Richardson, G., Walsh, J. K., & Roth, T. (2004). Shift work sleep disorder: Prevalence and consequences beyond that of symptomatic day workers. *Sleep, 27,* 1453–1462.

Drake, K. L., & Ginsburg, G. S. (2012). Family factors in the development, treatment, and prevention of childhood anxiety disorders. *Clinical Child and Family Psychology Review, 15*(2), 144–162.

Drayna, D., & Kang, C. (2011). Genetic approaches to understanding the causes of stuttering. *Journal of Neurodevelopment Disorders, 3,* 374–380.

Driessen, E., Van, H. L., Peen, J., Don, F. J., Twisk, J. W., Cuijpers, P., & Dekker, J. J. (2017). Cognitive-behavioral versus psychodynamic therapy for major depression: Secondary outcomes of a randomized clinical trial. *Journal of Consulting and Clinical Psychology, 85*(7), 653.

Duffy, J. D. (1995). General paralysis of the insane: Neuropsychiatry's first challenge. *Journal of Neuropsychiatry, 7,* 243–249.

Dukart, J., Regen, F., Kherif, F., Colla, M., Bajbouj, M., Heuser, I., et al. (2014). Electroconvulsive therapy-induced brain plasticity determines therapeutic outcome in mood disorders. *Proceedings of the National Academy of Sciences, 111*(3), 1156–1161.

Dunn, E. C., Brown, R. C., Dai, Y., Rosand, J., Nugent, N. R., Amstadter, A. B., & Smoller, J. W. (2015). Genetic determinants of depression: Recent findings and future directions. *Harvard Review of Psychiatry, 23*(1), 1–18.

Durand, V. M., & Mindell, J. A. (1999). Behavioral intervention for childhood sleep terrors. *Behavior Therapy, 30,* 705–715.

Durkheim, E. (1897). *Le suicide: Étude de sociologie.* Paris: F. Alcan.

Dutra, S. J., Cunningham, W. A., Kober, H., & Gruber, J. (2015). Elevated striatal reactivity across monetary and social rewards in bipolar I disorder. *Journal of Abnormal Psychology, 124,* 890–904.

Duval, E. R., Javanbakht, A., & Liberzon, I. (2015). Neural circuits in anxiety and stress disorders: a focused review. *Therapeutics and Clinical Risk Management, 11,* 115–126.

E

Eaton, N. R., Krueger, R. F., Keyes, K. M., Skodol, A. E., Markon, K. E., Grant, B. F., & Hasin, D. S. (2011). Borderline personality disorder co-morbidity: Relationship to the internalizing-externalizing structure of common mental disorders. *Psychological Medicine, 41,* 1041–1050.

Eaton, W. W., Moortensenk, P. B., Herrman, H., & Freeman, H. (1992). Long-term course of hospitalization for schizophrenia: I. Risk for rehospitalization. *Schizophrenia Bulletin, 18,* 217–228.

Eaton, W. W., Thara, R., Federman, E., & Tien, A. (1998). Remission and relapse in schizophrenia: The Madras longitudinal study. *Journal of Nervous & Mental Disease, 186,* 357–363.

Ebbert, J. O., Hughes, J. R., West, R. J., Rennard, S. I., Russ, C., McRae, T. D., et al. (2015). Effect of varenicline on smoking cessation through smoking reduction: A randomized clinical trial. *JAMA, 313*(7), 687–694.

Ebner-Priemer, U. W., Houben, M., Santangelo, P., Kleindienst, N., Tuerlinckx, F., Oravecz, Z., et al. (2015). Unraveling affective dysregulation in borderline personality disorder: A theoretical model and empirical evidence. *Journal of Abnormal Psychology, 124,* 186–198.

Edelmann, R. J. (1992). *Anxiety: Theory, research, and intervention in clinical and health psychology.* Chichester, NY: Wiley.

Edinger, D. (1963). *Bertha Pappenheim–Freud's Anna O.* Highland Park, IL: Congregation Solel.

Edwards, A. G. K., Hulbert-Williams, S., & Neal, R. D. (2008). Psychological interventions for women with metastatic breast cancer. *Cochrane Database of Systematic Reviews, 3,* CD004253.

Egeland, J. A. (1986). Cultural factors and social stigma for manic-depression: The Amish Study. *American Journal of Social Psychiatry, 6,* 279–286.

Egeland, J. A. (1994). An epidemiologic and genetic study of affective disorders among the Old Order Amish. In D. F. Papolos & H. M. Lachman (Eds.), *Genetic studies in affective disorders: Overview of basic methods, current directions, and critical research issues* (pp. 70–90). Oxford, UK: Wiley.

Egeland, J. A., & Hostetter, A. M. (1983). Amish study: I. Affective disorders among the Amish, 1976–1980. *American Journal of Psychiatry, 140,* 56–61.

Ehlers, A., Clark, D. M., Dunmore, E., Jaycox, L., Meadows, E., & Foa, E. (1998). Predicating response to exposure treatment in PTSD: The role of mental defeat and alienation. *Journal of Traumatic Stress, 11,* 457–471.

Ehlers, A., Clark, D. M., Hackmann, A., Grey, N., Liness, S., Wild, J., et al. (2010). Intensive cognitive therapy for PTSD: A feasibility study. *Behavioural and Cognitive Psychotherapy, 38,* 383–398.

Ehring, T., Ehlers, A., Cleare, A., & Glucksman, E. (2008). Do acute psychological and psychobiological responses to trauma predict subsequent symptom severities and PTSD and depression? *Psychiatry Research, 161,* 67–75.

Ehrman, J. K., Gordon, P. M., Visich, P. S., & Keteyian, S. J. (Eds.). (2009). *Clinical exercise physiology* (2nd ed.). Champaign, IL: Human Kinetics.

Eilenberg, T., Fink, P., Jensen, J. S., Rief, W., & Frostholm, L. (2016). Acceptance and commitment group therapy (ACT-G) for health anxiety: A randomized controlled trial. *Psychological Medicine, 46*(1), 103–115.

Eisenberg, N., Spinrad, T. L., & Eggum, N. D. (2010). Emotion-related self-regulation and its relation to children's maladjustment. *Annual Review of Clinical Psychology, 6,* 495–525.

Elder, G. H., & Clipp, E. C. (1989). Combat experience and emotional health: Impairment and resilience in later life. *Journal of Personality, 57,* 311–341.

Eldevik, S., Hastings, R. P., Hughes, J. C., Jahr, E., Eikeseth, S., & Cross, S. (2009). Meta-analysis of early intensive behavioral intervention for children with autism. *Journal of Clinical Child & Adolescent Psychology, 38,* 439–450.

Eley, T. C., Bolton, D., O'Connor, T. G., Perrin, S., Smith, P., & Plomin, R. (2003). A twin study of anxiety-related behaviours in pre-school children. *Journal of Child Psychology & Psychiatry, 44,* 945–960.

Ellason, J. W., & Ross, C. A. (1997). Two-year follow-up of inpatients with dissociative identity disorder. *American Journal of Psychiatry, 154,* 832–839.

Ellason, J. W., Ross, C. A., & Fuchs, D. L. (1996). Lifetime Axis I and II comorbidity and childhood trauma history in dissociative identity disorder. *Psychiatry, 59,* 255–266.

Elliott, R., Greenberg, L. S., Lietaer, G. (2004). Research on experiential therapies. In M. J. Lambert (Ed.), *Bergin and Garfield's handbook of psychotherapy and behavior change* (5th ed.), pp. 493–539. New York: John Wiley.

Ellis, A. (1997). The evolution of Albert Ellis and emotive behavior therapy. In J. K. Zeig (Ed.), *The rational evolution of psychotherapy: The third conference* (pp. 69–78). New York: Brunner/Mazel.

Ellis, A., & Harper, R. A. (1961). *A guide to rational living.* Englewood Cliffs, NJ: Prentice Hall.

Ellison, J. W., Rosenfeld, J. A., & Shaffer, L. G. (2013). Genetic basis of intellectual disability. *Annual Review of Medicine, 64,* 441–450.

Ellman, L. M., & Cannon, T. D. (2008). Environmental pre- and perinatal influences on etiology. In K. T. Mueser & D. V. Jeste (Eds.), *Clinical handbook of schizophrenia* (pp. 65–73). New York: Guilford Press.

Emerson, E., Shahtahmasebi, S., Lancaster, G., & Berridge, D. (2010). Poverty transitions among families supporting a child with intellectual disability. *Journal of Intellectual & Developmental Disability, 35,* 224–234.

Emmelkamp, P. M. G., Benner, A., Kuipers, A., Feiertag, G. A., Koster, H. C., & van Apeldoorn, F. J. (2006). Comparison of brief dynamic and cognitive-behavioural therapies in avoidant personality disorder. *British Journal of Psychiatry, 189,* 60–64.

Epperson, C. N., Steiner, M., Hartlage, S. A., Eriksson, E., Schmidt, P. J., Jones, I., & Yonkers, K. A. (2012). Premenstrual dysphoric disorder: Evidence for a new category for *DSM-5. American Journal of Psychiatry, 169,* 465–475.

Epstein, J., Saunders, B. E., & Kilpatrick, D. G. (1997). Predicting PTSD in women with a history of childhood rape. *Journal of Traumatic Stress, 10,* 573–588.

Erbes, C., Westermeyer, J., Engdahl, B., & Johnsen, E. (2007). Post-traumatic stress disorder and service utilization in a sample of service members from Iraq and Afghanistan. *Military Medicine, 172,* 359–363.

Erdelyi, M. H. (1992). Psychodynamics and the unconscious. *American Psychologist, 47,* 784–787.

Erdur, L., Kallenbach-Dermutz, B., Lehmann, V., Zimmermann-Viehoff, F., Koepp, W., Weber, C., & Deter, H.-C. (2012). Somatic comorbidity in anorexia nervosa: First results of a 21-year follow-up study on female inpatients. *Biopsychosocial Medicine, 6,* 4.

Erlenmeyer-Kimling, L., Rock, D., Squires-Wheeler, E., & Roberts, S. (1991). Early life precursors of psychiatric outcomes in adulthood in subjects at risk for schizophrenia or affective disorders. *Psychiatry Research, 39,* 239–256.

Erskine, H. E., Norman, R. E., Ferrari, A. J., Chan, G. C., Copeland, W. E., Whiteford, H. A., & Scott, J. G. (2016). Long-term outcomes of attention-deficit/hyperactivity disorder and conduct disorder: A systematic review and meta-analysis. *Journal of the American Academy of Child & Adolescent Psychiatry, 55*(10), 841–850.

Escobar, J. I. (1993). Psychiatric epidemiology. In A. C. Gaw (Ed.), *Culture, ethnicity, and mental illness* (pp. 43–73). Washington, DC: American Psychiatric Press.

European Monitoring Centre for Drugs and Drug Addiction (EMCDDA). (2011, November). *2011 Annual report on the state of the drugs problem in Europe.* Lisbon, Portugal: Author.

Evans, S. W., Owens, J. S., Wymbs, B. T., & Ray, A. R. (2018). Evidence-based psychosocial treatments for children and adolescents with attention deficit/hyperactivity disorder. *Journal of Clinical Child & Adolescent Psychology, 47*(2), 157–198.

Everson-Rose, S. A., & Lewis, T. T. (2005). Psychosocial factors and cardiovascular diseases. *Annual Review of Public Health, 26,* 469–500.

Exner, J., Exner, J., Levy, A., Exner, J., Groth-Marnat, G., Wood, J. M., & Garb, H. N. (2008). *The Rorschach: A comprehensive system. Volume 1: The Rorschach, basic foundations and principles of interpretation.* New York: Wiley.

Eysenck, H. J. (1994). The biology of morality. In B. Puka (Ed.), *Defining perspectives in moral development* (pp. 212–229). New York: Garland.

F

Fabiano, G. A., Pelham Jr, W. E., Coles, E. K., Gnagy, E. M., Chronis-Tuscano, A., & O'Connor, B. C. (2009). A meta-analysis of behavioral treatments for attention-deficit/hyperactivity disorder. *Clinical Psychology Review, 29*(2), 129–140.

Fabrega, H. (1993). Toward a social theory of psychiatric phenomena. *Behavioral Science, 38,* 75–100.

Fabrega, H., Ulrich, R., Pilkonis, P., & Mezzich, J. (1991). On the homogeneity of personality disorder clusters. *Comprehensive Psychiatry, 32,* 373–386.

Fahy, T. A. (1988). The diagnosis of multiple personality disorder: A critical review. *British Journal of Psychiatry, 153,* 597–606.

Fairburn, C. G. (1997). Eating disorders. In D. M. Clark & C. G. Fairburn (Eds.), *Science and practice of cognitive behaviour therapy* (pp. 209–241). Oxford: Oxford University Press.

Fairburn, C. G. (2005). Evidence-based treatment of anorexia nervosa. *International Journal of Eating Disorders, 37,* 526–530.

Fairburn, C. G., Bailey-Straebler, S., Basden, S., Doll, H. A., Jones, R., Murphy, R., et al. (2015). A transdiagnostic comparison of enhanced cognitive behaviour therapy (CBT-E) and interpersonal psychotherapy in the treatment of eating disorders. *Behaviour Research and Therapy, 70,* 64–71.

Fairburn, C. G., Cooper, Z., Bohn, K., O'Connor, M. E., Doll, H. A., & Palmer, R. L. (2007). The severity and status of eating disorder NOS: Implications for *DSM-V. Behaviour Research and Therapy, 45,* 1705–1715.

Fairburn, C. G., Cooper, Z., Doll, H. A., O'Connor, M. E., Bohn, K., Hawker, D. H., Wales, J. A., & Palmer, R. L. (2009). Transdiagnostic cognitive-behavioral therapy for patients with eating disorders: A two-site trial with 60-week follow-up. *American Journal of Psychiatry, 166,* 311–319.

Fairburn, C. G., Cooper, Z., Shafra, R., Bohn, K., & Hawker, D. M. (2008). Clinical perfectionism, core low self-esteem and interpersonal problems. In C. G. Fairburn (Ed.), *Cognitive behavior therapy and eating disorders* (pp. 197–220). New York: Guilford Press.

Fairburn, C. G., Jones, R., Peveler, R. C., & Carr, S. J. (1991). Three psychological treatments for bulimia nervosa: A comparative trial. *Archives of General Psychiatry, 48,* 463–469.

Fairburn, C. G., Norman, P. A., Welch, S. L., O'Connor, M. E., Doll, H. A., & Peveler, R. C. (1995). A prospective study of outcome in bulimia nervosa and the long-term effects of three psychological treatments. *Archives of General Psychiatry, 52,* 304–312.

Fairweather, G. W., Sanders, D. H., Maynard, H., & Cressler, D. L. (1969). *Community life for the mentally ill: An alternative to institutional care.* Chicago: Aldine.

Fang, A., & Wilhelm, S. (2015). Clinical features, cognitive biases, and treatment of body dysmorphic disorder. *Annual Review of Clinical Psychology, 11,* 187–212.

Fanous, A. H., Prescott, C. A., & Kendler, K. S. (2004). The prediction of thoughts of death or self-harm in a population-based sample of female twins. *Psychological Medicine, 34,* 301–312.

Fanti, K. A. (2018). Understanding heterogeneity in conduct disorder: A review of psychophysiological studies. *Neuroscience & Biobehavioral Reviews, 91,* 4–20.

Faraone, S. V., Biederman, J., Keenan, K., & Tsuang, M. T. (1991). A family-genetic study of girls with *DSM-III* attention deficit disorder. *American Journal of Psychiatry, 148,* 112–117.

Faravelli, C., Giugni, A., Salvatori, S., & Ricca, V. (2004). Psychopathology after rape. *American Journal of Psychiatry, 161,* 1483–1485.

Farmer, M. A., Kao, A., & Binik, Y. M. (2009). Dyspareunia and vaginismus. In R. Balon & E. R. Segraves (Eds.), *Clinical manual of sexual disorders* (pp. 305–334). Arlington, VA: American Psychiatric Publishing.

Farmer, M. A., Kukkonen, T., & Binik, Y. M. (2008). Female genital pain and its treatment. In D. L. Rowland & L. Incrocci (Eds.), *Handbook of sexual and gender identity disorders* (pp. 220–250). Hoboken, NJ: Wiley.

Fawzy, F. I., Canada, A. L., & Fawzy, N. W. (2003). Malignant melanoma: Effects of a brief, structured psychiatric intervention on survival and recurrence at 10-year follow-up. *Archives of General Psychiatry, 60,* 100–103.

Fawzy, F. I., Cousins, N., Fawzy, N. W., Kemeny, M. E., Elashoff, R., & Morton, D. (1990). A structured psychiatric intervention for cancer patients: I. Changes over time in methods of coping and affective disturbance. *Archives of General Psychiatry, 47,* 720–725.

Fawzy, F. I., Fawzy, N. W., Huyn, C. S., Elashoff, R., Morton, D., Cousins, N., & Fahey, J. L. (1993). Effects of an early structured psychiatric intervention, coping and affective state on recurrence and survival 6 years later. *Archives of General Psychiatry, 50,* 681–689.

Fawzy, F. I., Kemeny, M. E., Fawzy, N. W., Elashoff, R., et al. (1990). A structured psychiatric intervention for cancer patients: II. Changes over time in immunological measures. *Archives of General Psychiatry, 47,* 729–735.

Fazel, S., & Danesh, J. (2002). Serious mental disorder in 23,000 prisoners: A systematic review of 62 surveys. *Lancet, 359,* 545–550.

Fazel, S., Långström, N., Hjern, A., Grann, M., & Lichtenstein, P. (2009). Schizophrenia, substance abuse, and violent crime. *JAMA, 301*(19), 2016–2023.

Fazel, S., Lichtenstein, P., Grann, M., Goodwin, G. M., & Långström, N. (2010). Bipolar disorder and violent crime: New evidence from population-based longitudinal studies and systematic review. *Archives of General Psychiatry, 67*(9), 931–938.

Feder, A., Olfson, M., Fuentes, M., Shea, S., Lantigua, R. A., & Weissman, M. M. (2001). Medically unexplained symptoms in an urban general medicine practice. *Psychosomatics, 42,* 261–268.

Feingold, A. (1994). Gender differences in personality: A meta-analysis. *Psychological Bulletin, 116,* 429–456.

Feinstein, A. (2011). Conversion disorder: Advances in our understanding. *Canadian Medical Association Journal, 183,* 915–920.

Feldman, M. A. (Ed.). (2004). *Early intervention: The essential readings.* Malden, MA: Blackwell.

Feldman, R. P., & Goodrich, J. T. (2001). Psychosurgery: A historical overview. *Neurosurgery, 48,* 647–659.

Fennell, M. J. V., & Teasdale, J. D. (1987). Cognitive therapy for depression: Individual differences and the process of change. *Cognitive Therapy & Research, 11,* 253–271.

Ferguson, C. J. (2010). Genetic contributions to antisocial personality and behavior: A meta-analytic review from an evolutionary perspective. *Journal of Social Psychology, 150*(2), 160–180.

Ferri, C. P., Prince, M., Brayne, C., Brodaty, H., Fratiglioni, L., Ganguli, M., et al. (2005). Global prevalence of dementia: A Delphi consensus study. *Lancet, 366,* 2112–2117.

Ferri, M., Amato, L., & Davoli, M. (2006). Alcoholics Anonymous and other 12-step programmes for alcohol dependence. *Cochrane Database of Systematic Reviews 2006,* Issue 3.

Ficks, C. A., & Waldman, I. D. (2014). Candidate genes for aggression and antisocial behavior: A meta-analysis of association studies of the 5HTTLPR and MAOA-uVNTR. *Behavior Genetics, 44*(5), 427–444.

Fillmore, K. M., Golding, J. M., Leino, E. V., Motoyoshi, M., Shoemaker, C., Terry, H., et al. (1997). Patterns and trends in women's and men's drinking. In R. W. Wilsnack & S. C. Wilsnack (Eds.), *Gender and alcohol: Individual and social perspectives* (pp. 21–48). Piscataway, NJ: Rutgers Center of Alcohol Studies.

Fillmore, K. M., Kerr, W. C., Stockwell, T., Chikritzhs, T., & Bostrom, A. (2006). Moderate alcohol use and reduced mortality risk: Systematic error in prospective studies. *Addiction Research and Theory, 14,* 101–132.

Fink, M. (2001). Convulsive therapy: A review of the first 55 years. *Journal of Affective Disorders, 63,* 1–15.

Finney, J. W., & Moos, R. H. (1998). Psychosocial treatments for alcohol use disorders. In P. E. Nathan (Ed.), *A guide to treatments that work* (pp. 156–166). New York: Oxford University Press.

First, M. B. (2010). Paradigm shifts and the development of the *Diagnostic and Statistical Manual of Mental Disorders*: Past experiences and future aspirations. *Canadian Journal of Psychiatry, 55,* 692–700.

First, M. B., Spitzer, R. L., Gibbon, M., & Williams, J. B. W. (1997). *Structured Clinical Interview for* DSM-IV *Axis I Disorders–non-patient edition* (version 2.0). New York: New York State Psychiatric Institute, Biometrics Research Department.

Fischer, M., & Barkley, R. (2006). Young adult outcomes of children with hyperactivity: Leisure, financial, and social activities. *International Journal of Disability, Development and Education, 53,* 229–245.

Fiske, A., Wetherell, J. L., & Gatz, M. (2009). Depression in older adults. *Annual Review of Clinical Psychology, 9,* 363–391.

Fitzsimmons, S., & Buettner, L. L. (2002). Therapeutic recreation interventions for need-driven dementia-compromised behaviors in community-dwelling elders. *American Journal of Alzheimer's Disorder and Other Dementias, 17,* 367–381.

Flakierska-Praquin, N., Lindstrom, M., & Gilberg, C. (1997). School phobia with separation anxiety disorder: A comparative 20- to 29-year follow up study of 35 school refusers. *Comprehensive Psychology, 38,* 17–22.

Flament, M. F., Bissada, H., & Spettigue, W. (2012). Evidence-based pharmacotherapy of eating disorders. *International Journal of Neuropsychopharmacology, 15,* 189–207.

Flegal, K. M., Carroll, M. D., Ogden, C. L., & Johnson, C. L. (2002). Prevalence and trends in obesity among U.S. adults, 1999–2000. *JAMA, 288,* 1723–1727.

Fleming, M., & Manwell, L. B. (2000). Epidemiology. In G. Zernig (Ed.), *Handbook of alcoholism* (pp. 271–286). Boca Raton, FL: CRC Press.

Flessner, C. A. (2011). Cognitive-behavioral therapy for childhood repetitive behavior disorders: Tic disorders and trichotillomania. *Child and Adolescent Psychiatric Clinics of North America, 20,* 319–328.

Fletcher, J. M., Lyon, G. R., Fuchs, L. S., & Barnes, M. A. (2018). *Learning disabilities: From identification to intervention* (2nd ed.). New York: Guilford Press.

Flint, J., & Kendler, K. S. (2014). The genetics of major depression. *Neuron, 81*(3), 484–503.

Flores, A. R., Herman, J. L., Gates, G. J., & Brown, T. N. T. (2016). *How many adults identify as transgender in the United States?* Los Angeles: Williams Institute.

Flynn-Evans, E. E., Tabandeh, H., Skene, D. J., & Lockley, S. W. (2014). Circadian rhythm disorders and melatonin production in 127 blind women with and without light perception. *Journal of Biological Rhythms, 29*(3), 215–224.

Foa, E. B., & McLean, C. P. (2016). The efficacy of exposure therapy for anxiety-related disorders and its underlying mechanisms: The case of OCD and PTSD. *Annual Review of Clinical Psychology, 12,* 1–28.

Foa, E. D., & Riggs, D. S. (1995). Posttraumatic stress disorder following assault: Theoretical considerations and empirical findings. *Current Directions in Psychological Science, 4,* 61–65.

Fombonne, E. (1999). The epidemiology of autism: A review. *Psychological Medicine, 29,* 769–786.

Fombonne, E. (2009). Epidemiology of pervasive developmental disorders. *Pediatric Research, 65,* 591–598.

Fonagy, P., & Bateman, A. (2008). The development of borderline personality disorder: A mentalizing model. *Journal of Personality Disorders, 22,* 4–21.

Fontaine, R. G., & Dodge, K. A. (2006). Real-time decision making and aggressive behavior in youth: A heuristic model of response evaluation and decision (RED). *Aggressive Behavior, 32*(6), 604–624.

Foote, B., Smolin, Y., Kaplan, M., Legatt, M. E., & Lipschitz, D. (2006). Prevalence of dissociative disorders in psychiatric outpatients. *American Journal of Psychiatry, 163,* 623–629.

Forbes, M. K., Rapee, R. M., Camberis, A. L., & McMahon, C. A. (2017). Unique associations between childhood temperament characteristics and subsequent psychopathology symptom trajectories from childhood to early adolescence. *Journal of Abnormal Child Psychology, 45*(6), 1221–1233.

Ford, B. Q., & Mauss, I. B. (2015). Culture and emotion regulation. *Current Opinion in Psychology, 3,* 1–5.

Forslund, T., Brocki, K. C., Bohlin, G., Granqvist, P., & Eninger, L. (2016). The heterogeneity of attention-deficit/hyperactivity disorder symptoms and conduct problems: Cognitive inhibition, emotion regulation, emotionality, and disorganized attachment. *British Journal of Developmental Psychology, 34*(3), 371–387.

Fournier, J. C., DeRubeis, R. J., Hollon, S. D., et al. (2010). Antidepressant drug effect and depression severity: A patient-level meta-analysis. *JAMA, 303,* 47–53.

Fox, K. R., Franklin, J. C., Ribeiro, J. D., Kleiman, E. M., Bentley, K. H., & Nock, M. K. (2015). Meta-analysis of risk factors for nonsuicidal self-injury. *Clinical Psychology Review, 42,* 156–167.

Fox, K. R., Toole, K. E., Franklin, J. C., & Hooley, J. M. (2017). Why does nonsuicidal self-injury improve mood? A preliminary test of three hypotheses. *Clinical Psychological Science, 5*(1), 111–121.

Frances, A. (2013). The new somatic symptom disorder in DSM-5 risks mislabeling many people as mentally ill. *BMJ: British Medical Journal (Online), 346.*

Frances, A., & First, M. B. (2011). Paraphilia NOS, nonconsent: Not ready for the courtroom. *Journal of the American Academy of Psychiatry and the Law, 39,* 555–561.

Frances, A. J., & Widiger, T. (2012). Psychiatric diagnosis: Lessons from the *DSM-IV* past and cautions for the *DSM-5* future. *Clinical Psychology, 8,* 109–130.

Frank, E., Kupfer, D. J., Thase, M. E., Mallinger, A. G., Swartz, H. A., Fagiolini, A. M., Grochocinski, V., Houck, P., Scott, J., Thompson, W., & Monk, T. (2005). Two-year outcomes for interpersonal and social rhythm therapy in individuals with bipolar I disorder. *Archives of General Psychiatry, 62,* 996–1004.

Frank, E., Swartz, H. A., & Kupfer, D. J. (2000). Interpersonal and social rhythm therapy: Managing the chaos of bipolar disorder. *Biological Psychiatry, 48,* 593–604.

Frank, J. D. (1978). *Effective ingredients of successful psychotherapy*. New York: Brunner/Mazel.

Franklin, J. C., Fox, K. R., Franklin, C. R., Kleiman, E. M., Ribeiro, J. D., Jaroszewski, A. C., et al. (2016). A brief mobile app reduces nonsuicidal and suicidal self-injury: Evidence from three randomized controlled trials. *Journal of Consulting and Clinical Psychology, 84*(6), 544–557.

Franklin, K. A., Anttila, H., Axelsson, S., Gislason, T., Maasita, P., Myhre, K. I., & Rehnqvist, N. (2009). Effects and side-effects of surgery for snoring and obstructive sleep apnea—a systematic review. *Sleep, 32,* 27–36.

Frasure-Smith, N., & Lesperance, F. (2008). Depression and anxiety as predictors of 2-year cardiac events in patients with stable coronary artery disease. *Archives of General Psychiatry, 65,* 62–71.

Frazier, J. A., Breeze, J. L., Papadimitriou, G., Kennedy, D. M., Hodge, S. M., Moore, C. M., Howard, J. D., Rohan, M. P., Caviness, V. S., & Makris, N. (2007). White matter abnormalities in children with and at risk for bipolar disorder. *Bipolar Disorders, 9,* 799–809.

Fredrickson, B. L., & Joiner, T. (2002). Positive emotions trigger upward spirals toward emotional well-being. *Psychological Science, 13,* 172–175.

Fredrickson, B. L., Tugade, M. M., Waugh, C. E., & Larkin, G. R. (2003). What good are positive emotions in crisis? A prospective study of resilience and emotions following the terrorist attacks on the United States on September 11th, 2001. *Journal of Personality & Social Psychology, 84,* 365–376.

Freeman, A., & Reinecke, M. A. (1995). Cognitive therapy. In A. S. Gurman (Ed.), *Essential psychotherapies: Theory and practice* (pp. 182–225). New York: Guilford Press.

Freeman, S. F. N., & Alkin, M. C. (2000). Academic and social attainments of children with mental retardation in general education and special education settings. *Remedial and Special Education, 21,* 2–18.

Frenda, S. J., Nichols, R. M., & Loftus, E. F. (2011). Current issues and advances in misinformation research. *Current Directions in Psychological Science, 20,* 20–23.

Freud, S. (1909). *Analysis of a phobia of a five-year-old boy* (Vol. III). New York: Basic Books.

Freyd, J. J. (1996). *Betrayal trauma: The logic of forgetting childhood abuse.* Cambridge, MA: Harvard University Press.

Freyd, J. J., Martorella, S. R., Alvarado, J. S., Hayes, A. E., & Christman, J. C. (1998). Cognitive environments and dissociative tendencies: Performance on the standard Stroop task for high versus low dissociators. *Applied Cognitive Psychology, 12,* S91–S103.

Frías, Á., Palma, C., Farriols, N., & González, L. (2015). Comorbidity between obsessive-compulsive disorder and body dysmorphic disorder: Prevalence, explanatory theories, and clinical characterization. *Neuropsychiatric Disease and Treatment, 11,* 2233–2244.

Frick, P. J. (2012). Developmental pathways to conduct disorder: Implications for future directions in research, assessment, and treatment. *Journal of Clinical Child and Adolescent Psychology, 41,* 378–389.

Frick, P. J. (2016). Current research on conduct disorder in children and adolescents. *South African Journal of Psychology, 46*(2), 160–174.

Frick, P. J., & Nigg, J. T. (2012). Current issues in the diagnosis of attention deficit hyperactivity disorder, oppositional defiant disorder, and conduct disorder. *Clinical Psychology, 8,* 77–107.

Friedman, M., & Rosenman, R. H. (1974). *Type A behavior and your heart.* New York: Knopf.

Friedman, M., Rosenman, R. H., Straus, R., Wurm, M., & Kositcheck, R. (1968). The relationship of behavior pattern A to the state of coronary vasculature. *American Journal of Medicine, 44,* 525–537.

Friedman, M., Thoresen, C. E., Gill, J. J., Ulmer, D., Powell, L. H., Price, V., Brown, B., Thompson, L., Rabin, D. D., et al. (1994). Alteration of Type A behavior and its effect on cardiac recurrences in post myocardial infarction patients: Summary results of the recurrent coronary prevention project. In A. Steptoe (Ed.), *Psychosocial processes and health: A reader.* Cambridge, England: Cambridge University Press.

Friedman, M. J., Resik, P. A., Bryant, R. A., Strain, J., Horowitz, M., & Spiegel, D. (2011). Classification of trauma and stressor-related disorders in *DSM-5. Depression and Anxiety, 28,* 737–749.

Frith, M. (2006, April 3). Beckham reveals his battle with obsessive disorder. http://www.independent.co.uk/news/uk/this-britain/beckham-reveals-his-battle-with-obsessive-disorder-472573.html (accessed October 15, 2009).

Fromme, K., Marlatt, G. A., Baer, J. S., & Kivlahan, D. R. (1994). The Alcohol Skills Training Program: A group intervention for young adult drinkers. *Journal of Substance Abuse Treatment, 11,* 143–154.

Fromm-Reichmann, F. (1948). Notes on the development of treatments of schizophrenia by psychoanalytic psychotherapy. *Psychiatry, 2,* 263–273.

Frost, R. O., & Steketee, G. (2010). *Stuff: Compulsive hoarding and the meaning of things.* Boston: Mariner Books.

Frost, R. O., Steketee, G., & Tolin, D. F. (2012). Diagnosis and assessment of hoarding disorder. *Annual Review of Clinical Psychology, 8,* 219–242.

Frühauf, S., Gerger, H., Schmidt, H. M., Munder, T., & Barth, J. (2013). Efficacy of psychological interventions for sexual dysfunction: A systematic review and meta-analysis. *Archives of Sexual Behavior, 42*(6), 915–933.

Fuller, D. A., Sinclair, E., Geller, J., Quanbeck, C., & Snook, J. (2016). *Going, going, gone: Trends and consequences of* *eliminating state psychiatric beds*. Arlington, VA: Treatment Advocacy Center.

Furr, S. R., Westefeld, J. S., McConnell, G. N., & Jenkins, J. M. (2001). Suicide and depression among college students: A decade later. *Professional Psychology: Research & Practice, 32,* 97–100.

G

Gabrieli, J. D. (2009). Dyslexia: A new synergy between education and cognitive neuroscience. *Science, 325*(5938), 280–283.

Gajilan, A. C. (2008). Iraq vets and post-traumatic stress: No easy answers. Retrieved from cnnhealth.com, February 26, 2009.

Galderisi, S., Mucci, A., Bitter, I., Libiger, J., Bucci, P., Fleischhacker, W. W., & Kahn, R. S. (2012). Persistent negative symptoms in first episode patients with schizophrenia: Results from the European First Episode Schizophrenia Trial. *European Neuropsychopharmacology, 23,* 196–204.

Galea, S., Ahern, J., Resnick, H., Kilpatrick, D., Bucuvalas, M., Gold, J., & Vlahov, D. (2002). Psychological sequelae of the September 11 terrorist attacks in New York City. *New England Journal of Medicine, 346,* 982–987.

Galea, S., Brewin, C. R., Gruber, M., Jones, R. T., King, D. W., King, L. A., McNally, R. J., Ursano, R. J., Petukhova, M., & Kessler, R. C. (2007). Exposure to hurricane-related stressors and mental illness after Hurricane Katrina. *Archives of General Psychiatry, 64,* 1427–1434.

Galea, S., Tracy, M., Norris, F., & Coffey, S. F. (2008). Financial and social circumstances and the incidence and course of PTSD in Mississippi during the first two years after Hurricane Katrina. *Journal of Traumatic Stress, 21,* 357–368.

Gallegos, A. M., Crean, H. F., Pigeon, W. R., & Heffner, K. L. (2017). Meditation and yoga for posttraumatic stress disorder: A meta-analytic review of randomized controlled trials. *Clinical Psychology Review, 15,* 115–124.

Galván, A., & Tottenham, N. (2016). Adolescent brain development. In Cicchetti, D. (Ed.), *Developmental psychopathology: Vol. 2. Developmental neuroscience* (3rd ed., pp. 684–719). Hoboken, NJ: Wiley

Garber, J., & Horowitz, J. L. (2002). Depression in children. In I. H. Gotlib & C. L. Hammen (Eds.), *Handbook of depression* (pp. 510–540). New York: Guilford Press.

Garber, J., Walker, L. S., & Zeman, J. (1991). Somatization symptoms in a community sample of children and adolescents: Further validation of the Children's Somatization Inventory. *Psychological Assessment, 3,* 588–595.

Garcia, F. D., Delavenne, H. G., Assumpção, A. D. F. A., & Thibaut, F. (2013). Pharmacologic treatment of sex offenders with paraphilic disorder. *Current Psychiatry Reports, 15*(5), 356.

Garcia-Falgueras, A., & Swaab, D. F. (2008). A sex difference in the hypothalamic uncinate nucleus: Relationship to gender identity. *Brain, 131*(12), 3132–3146.

Gardner, C. D., Kiazand, A., Alhassan, S., Kim, S., Stafford, R. S., Balise, R. R., et al. (2007). Comparison of the Atkins, Zone, Ornish, and LEARN diets for change in weight and related risk factors among overweight premenopausal women, the A to Z weight loss story: A randomized trial. *JAMA, 297,* 969–977.

Gardner, H. (2008). *Multiple intelligences: New horizons in theory and practice.* New York: Basic Books.

Gardner, W., Lidz, C. W., Hoge, S. K., Monahan, J., Eisenberg, M. M., Bennett, N. S., Mulvey, E. P., & Roth, L. H. (1999). Patients' revisions of their beliefs about the need for hospitalization. *American Journal of Psychiatry, 156,* 1385–1391.

Garety, P. A., & Freeman, D. (2013). The past and future of delusions research: From the inexplicable to the treatable. *British Journal of Psychiatry, 203*(5), 327–333.

Garland, E. J., Kutcher, S., Virani, A., & Elbe, D. (2016). Update on the use of SSRIs and SNRIs with children and adolescents in clinical practice. *Journal of the Canadian Academy of Child and Adolescent Psychiatry, 25*(1), 4–10.

Garner, D. M., & Garfinkel, P. E. (1980). Sociocultural factors in the development of anorexia nervosa. *Psychological Medicine, 10,* 647–656.

Garner, D. M., Rockert, W., Davis, R., & Garner, M. V. (1993). Comparison of cognitive-behavioral and supportive-expressive therapy for bulimia nervosa. *American Journal of Psychiatry, 150,* 37–46.

Garrett, A. S., Reiss, A. L., Howe, M. E., Kelley, R. G., Singh, M. K., Adleman, N. E., et al. (2012). Abnormal amygdala and prefrontal cortex activation to facial expressions in pediatric bipolar disorder. *Journal of the American Academy of Child & Adolescent Psychiatry, 51*(8), 821–831.

Gatz, M. (2007). Genetics, dementia, and the elderly. *Current Directions in Psychological Science, 16,* 123–127.

Gatz, M., Prescott, C. A., & Pedersen, N. L. (2006). Lifestyle risk and delaying factors. *Alzheimer Disease and Associated Disorders, 20,* S84–S88.

Gatz, M., Reynolds, C. A., Fratiglioni, L., Johansson, B., Mortimer, J. A., Berg, S., Fiske, A., & Pedersen, N. L. (2006). Role of genes and environments for explaining Alzheimer disease. *Archives of General Psychiatry, 63,* 168–174.

Gauntlett-Gilbert, J., & Kuipers, E. (2003). Phenomenology of visual hallucinations in psychiatric conditions. *Journal of Nervous and Mental Disease, 191,* 203–205.

Gearhardt, A. N., Bragg, M. A., Pearl, R. L., Schvey, N. A., Roberto, C. A., & Brownell, K. D. (2012). Obesity and public policy. *Annual Review of Clinical Psychology, 8,* 405–430.

Gearhardt, A. N., Davis, C., Kuschner, R., & Brownell, K. D. (2011). The addiction potential of hyperpalatable foods. *Current Drug Abuse Review, 4,* 140–145.

Gearhardt, A. N., Yokum, S., Orr, P., Stice, E., Corbin, W., & Brownell, K. (2011). Neural correlates of food addiction. *Archive of General Psychiatry, 68,* 808–816.

Gearing, R. E., & Alonzo, D. (2018). Religion and suicide: New findings. *Journal of Religion and Health,* 1–22.

Geddes, J. R., Burgess, S., Hawton, K., Jamison, K., & Goodwin, G. M. (2004). Long-term lithium therapy for bipolar disorder: Systematic review and meta-analysis of randomized controlled trials. *American Journal of Psychiatry, 161,* 217–222.

Gehi, A., Haas, D., Pipkin, S., & Whooley, M. A. (2005). Depression and medication adherence in outpatients with coronary heart disease: Findings from the Heart and Soul Study. *Archives of Internal Medicine, 165,* 2508–2513.

Gelauff, J., & Stone, J. (2016). Prognosis of functional neurologic disorders. *Handbook of Clinical Neurology, 139,* 523–541.

Geoffroy, P. A., Bellivier, F., Scott, J., Boudebesse, C., Lajnef, M., Gard, S., et al. (2013). Bipolar disorder with seasonal pattern: Clinical characteristics and gender influences. *Chronobiology International, 30*(9), 1101–1107.

Gerardin, P., & Thibaut, F. (2004). Epidemiology and treatment of juvenile sexual offending. *Pediatric Drugs, 6,* 79–91.

Geronimus, A. T., Hicken, M., Keene, D., & Bound, J. (2006). "Weathering" and age patterns of allostatic load scored among blacks and whites in the United States. *American Journal of Public Health, 96,* 826–833.

Geschwind, D. H., & Flint, J. (2015). Genetics and genomics of psychiatric disease. *Science, 349*(6255), 1489–1494.

Ghasemi, A., Seifi, M., Baybordi, F., Danaei, N., & Rad, B. S. (2018). Association between serotonin 2A receptor genetic variations, stressful life events and suicide. *Gene, 658,* 191–197.

Gibbons, R. D., Weiss, D. J., Frank, E., & Kupfer, D. (2016). Computerized adaptive diagnosis and testing of mental health disorders. *Annual Review of Clinical Psychology, 12,* 83–104.

Giesen-Bloo, J., van Dyck, R., Spinhoven, P., van Tilburg, W., Dirksen, C., van Asselt, T., Kremers, I., Nadort, M., & Arntz, A. (2006). Outpatient psychotherapy for borderline personality disorder: Randomized trial of schema-focused therapy vs. transference-focused psychotherapy. *Archives of General Psychiatry, 63,* 649–658.

Gillespie, N. A., Zhu, G., Heath, A. C., Hickie, I. B., & Martin, N. G. (2000). The genetic aetiology of somatic distress. *Psychological Medicine, 30,* 1051–1061.

Gilman, S. E., Cochran, S. D., Mays, V. M., Hughes, M., Ostrow, D., & Kessler, R. C. (2001). Risk of psychiatric disorders among individuals reporting same-sex sexual partners in the National Comorbidity Survey. *American Journal of Public Health, 91,* 933–939.

Giraldi, A., Kristensen, E., & Sand, M. (2015). Endorsement of models describing sexual response of men and women with a sexual partner: An online survey in a population sample of Danish adults ages 20–65 years. *Journal of Sexual Medicine, 12*(1), 116–128.

Gitlin, M. J. (2015). Pharmacotherapy and other somatic treatments for depression. In I. H. Gotlib & C. L. Hammen (Eds.), *Handbook of depression* (3rd ed., pp. 492–512). New York: Guilford.

Gitlin, M., Nuechterlein, K., Subotnik, K. L., Ventura, J., Mintz, J., Fogelson, D. L., Bartzokis, G., & Aravagiri, M. (2001). Clinical outcome following neuroleptic discontinuation in patients with remitted recent-onset schizophrenia. *American Journal of Psychiatry, 158,* 1835–1842.

Glassman, A. (1969). Indoleamines and affective disorders. *Psychosomatic Medicine, 31,* 107–114.

Gleaves, D. H., Hernandez, E., & Warner, M. S. (2003). The etiology of dissociative identity disorder: Reply to Gee, Allen, and Powell (2003). *Professional Psychology: Research & Practice, 34,* 116–118.

Gleaves, D. H., Smith, S. M., Butler, L. D., & Spiegel, D. (2004). False and recovered memories in the laboratory and clinic: A review of experimental and clinical evidence. *Clinical Psychology: Science & Practice, 11,* 3–28.

Glenn, A. L., Johnson, A. K., & Raine, A. (2013). Antisocial personality disorder: A current review. *Current Psychiatry Reports, 15*(12), 427.

Glenn, C. R., Franklin, J. C., & Nock, M. K. (2015). Evidence-based psychosocial treatments for self-injurious thoughts and behaviors in youth. *Journal of Clinical Child and Adolescent Psychology, 44,* 1–29.

Glowinski, A. L., Bucholz, K. K., Nelson, E. C., Fu, Q., Madden, P. A. F., Reich, W., & Heath, A. C. (2001). Suicide attempts in an adolescent female twin sample. *Journal of the American Academy of Child & Adolescent Psychiatry, 40,* 1300–1307.

Go, G. (2017). Amnesia and criminal responsibility. *Journal of Law and the Biosciences, 4*(1), 194–204.

Godfrey, J. R., & Brownell, K. (2008). Toward optimal health: The influence of the environment on obesity. *Journal of Women's Health, 17,* 325–330.

Goikolea, J. M., Colom, F., Martinez-Aran, A., Sanchez-Moreno, J., Giordano, A., Bulbena, A., & Vieta, E. (2007). Clinical and prognostic implications of seasonal pattern in bipolar disorder: A 10-year follow-up of 302 patients. *Psychological Medicine, 37,* 1595–1599.

Gold, M. S., Tabrah, H., & Frost-Pineda, K. (2001). Psychopharmacology of MDMA (ecstasy). *Psychiatric Annals, 31,* 675–681.

Goldberg, E. M., & Morrison, S. L. (1963). Schizophrenia and social class. *British Journal of Psychiatry, 109,* 785–802.

Goldin, P. R., & Gross, J. J. (2010). Effects of mindfulness-based stress reduction (MBSR) on emotion regulation in social anxiety disorder. *Emotion, 10,* 83–91.

Goldschmidt, A. B., Conceição, E. M., Thomas, J. G., Mitchell, J. E., Raynor, H. A., & Bond, D. S. (2016). Conceptualizing and studying binge and loss of control eating in bariatric surgery patients—time for a paradigm shift? *Surgery for Obesity and Related Diseases, 12*(8), 1622–1625.

Goldstein, A. (2001). *Addiction: From biology to drug policy* (2nd ed.). New York: W. H. Freeman.

Goldstein, A. N., & Walker, M. P. (2014). The role of sleep in emotional brain function. *Annual Review of Clinical Psychology, 10,* 679–708.

Goldstein, J. M., Seidman, L. J., Buka, S. L., Horton, N. J., Donatelli, J. L., Rieder, R. O., & Tsuang, M. T. (2000). Impact of genetic vulnerability and hypoxia on overall intelligence by age 7 in offspring at high risk for schizophrenia compared with affective psychoses. *Schizophrenia Bulletin, 26,* 323–334.

Goldstein, M. J., Talovic, S. A., Nuechterlein, K. H., & Fogelson, D. L. (1992). Family interaction versus individual psychopathology: Do they indicate the same processes in the families of schizophrenia? *British Journal of Psychiatry, 161,* 97–102.

Goldstein, R. Z., & Volkow, N. D. (2002). Drug addiction and its underlying neurobiological basis: Neuroimaging evidence for the involvement of the frontal cortex. *American Journal of Psychiatry,* 159, 1642–1652.

Goldston, D. B., Daniel, S. S., Erkanli, A., Heilbron, N., Doyle, O., Weller, B., et al. (2015). Suicide attempts in a longitudinal sample of adolescents followed through adulthood: Evidence of escalation. *Journal of Consulting and Clinical Psychology, 83,* 253–264.

Gone, J. P. (2010). Psychotherapy and traditional healing for American Indians: Exploring the prospects for therapeutic integration. *Counseling Psychologist, 38,* 166–235.

González, H. M., Tarraf, W., Whitfield, K. E., & Vega, W. A. (2010). The epidemiology of major depression and ethnicity in the United States. *Journal of Psychiatric Research, 44*(15), 1043–1051.

Goodlad, J. K., Marcus, D. K., & Fulton, J. J. (2013). Lead and attention-deficit/hyperactivity disorder (ADHD) symptoms: A meta-analysis. *Clinical Psychology Review, 33*(3), 417–425.

Goodwin, F. K., & Jamison, K. R. (1990). *Manic-depressive illness.* New York: Oxford University Press.

Goodwin, F. K., & Jamison, K. R. (Eds.). (2007). *Manic depressive illness: Bipolar disorders and recurrent depression* (2nd ed.). New York: Oxford University Press.

Goodwin, P. J., Leszcz, M., Ennis, M., et al. (2001). The effect of group psychosocial support on survival in metastatic breast cancer. *New England Journal of Medicine, 345,* 1719–1726.

Gordon, O. M., Salkovskis, P. M., Oldfield, V. B., & Carter, N. (2013). The association between obsessive compulsive disorder and obsessive compulsive personality disorder: Prevalence and clinical presentation. *British Journal of Clinical Psychology, 52,* 300–315.

Gordon, R. A. (2017). The history of eating disorders. In K. D. Brownell & B. T. Walsh (Eds.), *Eating disorders and obesity: A comprehensive handbook* (3rd ed., pp. 163–168). New York: Guilford.

Gorin-Lazard, A., Baumstarck, K., Boyer, L., Maquigneau, A., Penochet, J. C., Pringuey, D., et al. (2013). Hormonal therapy is associated with better self-esteem, mood, and quality of life in transsexuals. *Journal of nervous and mental disease, 201*(11), 996–1000.

Gorman, J. M. (2003). Treating generalized anxiety disorder. *Journal of Clinical Psychiatry, 64*(Suppl. 2), 24–29.

Gorman, J. M., Papp, L. A., & Coplan, J. D. (1995). Neuroanatomy and neurotransmitter function in panic disorder. In S. P. Roose & R. A. Glick (Eds.), *Anxiety as symptom and signal* (pp. 39–56). Hillsdale, NJ: Analytic Press.

Gotlib, I. H., Krasnoperova, E., Yue, D. L., & Joormann, J. (2004). Attentional biases for negative interpersonal stimuli in clinical depression. *Journal of Abnormal Psychology, 113,* 127–135.

Gotlib, I. H., Lewinsohn, P. M., & Seeley, J. R. (1995). Symptoms versus a diagnosis of depression: Differences in psychosocial functioning. *Journal of Consulting and Clinical Psychology, 63,* 90–100.

Gottesman, I. I. (1991). *Schizophrenia genesis: The origins of madness.* New York: W. H. Freeman.

Gottesman, I. I., & Erlenmeyer-Kimling, L. (2001). Family and twin strategies as a head start in defining prodromes and endophenotypes for hypothetical early-interventions in schizophrenia. *Schizophrenia Research, 51,* 93–102.

Gottesman, I. I., & Shields, J. (1976). A critical review of recent adoption, twin, and family studies of schizophrenia: Behavioral genetics perspectives. *Schizophrenia Bulletin, 2*(3), 360.

Gould, M. S., Greenberg, T., Velting, D. M., & Shaffer, D. (2003). Youth suicide risk and preventive interventions: A review of the past 10 years. *Journal of the American Academy of Child & Adolescent Psychiatry, 42,* 386–405.

Gould, M. S., Jamieson, P., & Romer, D. (2003). Media contagion and suicide among the young. *American Behavioral Scientist, 46,* 1269–1284.

Gould, M. S., Marrocco, F., Kleinman, M., Thomas, J. G., Mostkoff, K., Cote, J., & Davies, M. (2005). Evaluating iatrogenic risk of youth suicide screening programs: A randomized controlled trial. *JAMA, 293,* 1635–1643.

Grabe, S., Ward, L. M., & Hyde, J. S. (2008). The role of the media in body image concerns among women: A meta-analysis of experimental and correlational studies. *Psychological Bulletin, 134,* 460–476.

Grandi, S., Fabbri, S., Panatoni, N., Gonnella, E., & Marks, I. (2006). Self-exposure treatment of recurrent nightmares: Waiting-list-controlled trial and 4-year follow-up. *Psychotherapy and Psychosomatics, 75,* 384–388.

Grandin, T. (1995). *Thinking in pictures and my other reports from my life with autism.* New York: Vintage Books.

Grant, B. F., Hasin, D. S., Chou, S. P., Stinson, F. S., & Dawson, D. A. (2004). Nicotine dependence and psychiatric disorders in the United States: Results from the National Epidemiologic Survey on Alcohol and Related Conditions. *Archives of General Psychiatry, 61,* 1107–1115.

Grant, B. F., Hasin, D. S., Stinson, F. S., Dawson, D. A., Chou, S. P., Ruan, W. J., & Pickering, R. P. (2004). Prevalence, correlates, and disability of personality disorders in the United States: Results from the National Epidemiologic Survey on Alcohol and Related Conditions. *Journal of Clinical Psychiatry, 65,* 948–958.

Grant, B. F., Stinson, F., Dawson, D., Chou, P., Dufour, M., Compton, W., Pickering, R., & Kaplan, K. (2004). Prevalence and co-occurrence of substance use disorders and independent mood and anxiety disorders: Results from the National Epidemiologic Survey on Alcohol and Related Conditions. *Archives of General Psychiatry, 61,* 807–816.

Grant, B. F., Stinson, F. S., Dawson, D. A., Chou, S. P., & Ruan, W. J. (2005). Co-occurrence of *DSM-IV* personality disorders in the United States: Results from the National Epidemiologic Survey on Alcohol and Related Conditions. *Comprehensive Psychiatry, 46,* 1–5.

Gratz, K. L., Moore, K. E., & Tull, M. T. (2016). The role of emotion dysregulation in the presence, associated difficulties, and treatment of borderline personality disorder. *Personality Disorders: Theory, Research, and Treatment, 7*(4), 344–353.

Gratz, K. L., Rosenthal, M. Z., Tull, M. T., Lejuez, C. W., & Gunderson, J. G. (2010). An experimental investigation of emotional reactivity and delayed emotional recovery in borderline personality disorder: The role of shame. *Comprehensive Psychiatry, 51,* 275–285.

Greaves, G. B. (1980). Multiple personality: 165 years after Mary Reynolds. *Journal of Nervous & Mental Disease, 168,* 577–596.

Green, M., Kern, R. S., Braff, D. L., & Mintz, J. (2000). Neurocognitive deficits and functional outcome in Schizophrenia: Are we measuring the "right stuff?" *Schizophrenia Bulletin, 18,* 119–136.

Green, R. (1987). *The "Sissy boy syndrome" and the development of homosexuality.* New Haven, CT: Yale University Press.

Grieve, F. G., & Bonneau-Kaya, C. M. (2007). Weight loss and muscle building content in popular magazines oriented toward women and men. *North American Journal of Psychology, 9*(1), 97–102.

Griffin, P. A., Steadman, H. J., & Petrila, J. (2002). The use of criminal charges and sanctions in mental health courts. *Psychiatric Services, 53,* 1285–1289.

Grisso, T., & Appelbaum, P. S. (1995). The MacArthur Treatment Competence Study: III. Abilities of patients to consent to psychiatric and medical treatments. *Law & Human Behavior, 19,* 149–174.

Grob, G. N. (1994). *The mad among us: A history of the care of America's mentally ill.* Cambridge, MA: Harvard University Press.

Groesz, L. M., Levine, M. P., & Murnen, S. K. (2002). The effect of experimental presentation of thin media images on body satisfaction: A meta-analytic review. *International Journal of Eating Disorders, 31,* 1–16.

Gross, R. T., Brooks-Gunn, J., & Spiker, D. (1992). Efficacy of educational interventions for low birth weight infants: The Infant Health and Development Program. In S. L. Friedman & M. D. Sigman (Eds.), *The psychological development of low birth weight children: Advances in applied developmental psychology* (Vol. 6, pp. 411–433). Norwood, NJ: Ablex.

Gross-Isseroff, R., Biegon, A., Voet, H., & Weizman, A. (1998). The suicide brain: A review of postmortem receptor/transporter binding studies. *Neuroscience & Biobehavioral Reviews, 22,* 653–661.

Grossman, L. S., Harrow, M., Rosen, C., Faull, R., & Strauss, G. P. (2008). Sex differences in schizophrenia and other psychotic disorders: A 20-year longitudinal study of psychosis and recovery. *Comprehensive Psychiatry, 49,* 523–529.

Groth-Marnat, G., & Wright, A. J. (2016). *Handbook of psychological assessment* (6th ed.). Hoboken, NJ: Wiley.

Gruber, A. J., & Pope, H. G. (1998). Ephedrine abuse among 36 female weightlifters. *American Journal of Addiction, 7,* 256–261.

Grucza, R. A., Bucholz, K. K., Rice, J. P., & Bierut, L. J. (2008). Secular trends in the lifetime prevalence of alcohol dependence in the United States: A re-evaluation. *Alcoholism: Clinical and Experimental Research, 32,* 763–770.

Guarnaccia, P. J., Guevara-Ramos, L. M., Gonzales, G., Canino, G. J., & Bird, H. (1992). Cross-cultural aspects of psychiatric symptoms in Puerto Rico. *Community & Mental Health, 7,* 99–110.

Guarnaccia, P. J., Rivera, M., Franco, F., Neighbors, C., & Allende-Ramos, C. (1996). The experiences of *ataques de nervios:* Toward an anthropology of emotions in Puerto Rico. *Culture, Medicine, & Psychiatry, 15,* 139–165.

Gudenkauf, L. M., Antoni, M. H., Stagl, J. M., Lechner, S. C., Jutagir, D. R., Bouchard, L. C., et al. (2015). Brief cognitive-behavioral and relaxation training interventions for breast cancer: A randomized controlled trial. *Journal of Consulting and Clinical Psychology, 83,* 677–688.

Gulliksson, M., Burell, G., Vessby, B., Lundin, L., Toss, H., & Svärdsudd, K. (2011). Randomized controlled trial of cognitive behavioral therapy vs standard treatment to prevent recurrent cardiovascular events in patients with coronary heart disease: Secondary Prevention in Uppsala Primary Health Care project (SUPRIM). *Archives of Internal Medicine, 171*(2), 134–140.

Gunderson, J. G., Stout, R. L., McGlashan, T. H., Shea, T., Morey, L. C., Grilo, C. M., Zanarini, M. C., Yen, S., Markowitz, J. C., Sanislow, C., Ansell, E., Pinto, A., & Skodol, A. E. (2011). Ten-year course of borderline personality disorder: Psychopathology and function from the Collaborative Longitudinal Personality Disorders Study. *Archive of General Psychiatry, 68,* 827–837.

Gunderson, J. G., Zanarini, M. C., Choi-Kain, L. W.; Mitchell, K. S., Jang, K. L., & Hudson, J. I. (2011). Family study of borderline personality disorder and its sectors of psychopathology. *Archives of General Psychiatry, 68,* 753–762.

Guo, X., et al. (2010). Effect of antipsychotic medication alone vs. combined with psychosocial intervention on outcomes of early-stage schizophrenia. *Archive of General Psychiatry, 67*(9): 895–904.

Gur, R. E., Calkins, M. E., Gur, R. C., Horan, W. P., Nuechterlein, K. H., Seidman, L. J., & Stone, W. S. (2007). The Consortium on the Genetics of Schizophrenia: Neurocognitive endophenotypes. *Schizophrenia Bulletin, 33,* 49–68.

Gustavsson, A., Svensson, M., Jacobi, F., Allgulander, C., Alonso, J., Beghi, E., Dodel, R., Ekman, M., et al., (2011). Cost of disorders of the brain in Europe 2010. *European Neuropsychopharmacology, 21,* 718–779.

H

Hachinski, V. (2008). World Stroke Day 2008: "Little strokes, big trouble." *Stroke, 39,* 2407–2420.

Hall, G. C. N. (2001). Psychotherapy research with ethnic minorities: Empirical, ethical, and conceptual issues. *Journal of Consulting & Clinical Psychology, 69,* 502–510.

Hall, K. S. K. (2016). Multicultural sensitivity in the treatment of sexual dysfunction. In L. Lipshultz, A. Pastuszak, A. Goldstein, A. Giraldi, & M. Perelman (Eds.), *Management of sexual dysfunction in men and women* (pp. 25–29). New York: Springer.

Hall, K. S. K., & Graham, C. A. (2013). *The cultural context of sexual pleasure and problems: Psychotherapy with diverse clients.* New York: Routledge.

Halldorsdottir, T., & Binder, E. B. (2017). Gene × environment interactions: From molecular mechanisms to behavior. *Annual Review of Psychology, 68,* 215–241.

Hallmayer, J., Cleveland, S., Torres, A., Phillips, J., Cohen, B., Torigoe, T., et al. (2011). Genetic heritability and shared environmental factors among twin pairs with autism. *Archives of General Psychiatry, 68*(11), 1095–1102.

Halpern, A. L. (2011). The proposed diagnosis of hypersexual disorder for inclusion in *DSM-5*: Unnecessary and harmful. *Archives of Sexual Behavior, 40,* 487–488, author reply 489–490.

Hames, J. L., Hagan, C. R., & Joiner, T. E. (2013). Interpersonal processes in depression. *Annual Review of Clinical Psychology, 9,* 355–377.

Hammen, C. (2003). Social stress and women's risk for recurrent depression. *Archives of Women's Mental Health, 6,* 9–13.

Hammen, C. (2018). Risk factors for depression: An autobiographical review. *Annual Review of Clinical Psychology, 14.*

Handley, E. D., & Chassin, L. (2009). Intergenerational transmission of alcohol expectancies in a high-risk sample. *Journal of Studies on Alcohol and Drugs, 70*(5), 675–682.

Hanson, R. F., Borntrager, C., Self-Brown, S., et al. (2008). Relations among gender, violence exposure, and mental health: The National Survey of Adolescents. *American Journal of Orthopsychiatry, 78,* 313–321.

Hare, R. D., & Hart, S. D. (1993). Psychopathy, mental disorder, and crime. In S. Hodgins (Ed.), *Mental disorder and crime* (pp. 104–115). Thousand Oaks, CA: Sage.

Hare, R. D., & Neumann, C. S. (2008). Psychopathy as a clinical and empirical construct. *Annual Review of Clinical Psychology, 4,* 217–246.

Harold, G. T., Leve, L. D., Barrett, D., Elam, K., Neiderhiser, J. M., Natsuaki, M. N., et al. (2013). Biological and rearing mother influences on child ADHD symptoms: Revisiting the developmental interface between nature and nurture. *Journal of Child Psychology and Psychiatry, 54*(10), 1038–1046.

Harrell, J. P. (1980). Psychological factors and hypertension: A status report. *Psychological Bulletin, 87,* 482–501.

Harris, K., & Singer, H. S. (2006). Tic disorders: Neural circuits, neurochemistry, and neuroimmunology. *Journal of Child Neurology, 21,* 678–689.

Harris, M. J., Milich, R., Corbitt, E. M., & Hoover, D. W. (1992). Self-fulfilling effects of stigmatizing information on children's social interactions. *Journal of Personality & Social Psychology, 63,* 41–50.

Harrow, M., Grossman, L. S., Jobe, T. H., & Herbener, E. S. (2005). Do patients with schizophrenia ever show periods of recovery? A 15-year multi-follow-up study. *Schizophrenia Bulletin, 31,* 723–734.

Harrow, M., & Jobe, T. H. (2013). Does long-term treatment of schizophrenia with antipsychotic medications facilitate recovery? *Schizophrenia Bulletin, 39*(5), 962–965.

Harter, S. (1983). Developmental perspectives on the self-system. In P. H. Mussen (Ed.), *Handbook of child development* (pp. 275–385). New York: Wiley.

Harvey, A. G. (2005). A cognitive theory and therapy for chronic insomnia. *Journal of Cognitive Psychotherapy, 19,* 41–59.

Harvey, A. G. (2008a). Insomnia, psychiatric disorders, and the transdiagnostic perspective. *Current Directions in Psychological Science, 17,* 299–303.

Harvey, A. G. (2008b). Sleep and circadian rhythms in bipolar disorder: Seeking synchrony, harmony, and regulation. *American Journal of Psychiatry, 165,* 820–829.

Harvey, A. G., Bélanger, L., Talbot, L., Eidelman, P., Beaulieu-Bonneau, S., Fortier-Brochu, É., et al. (2014). Comparative efficacy of behavior therapy, cognitive therapy, and cognitive behavior therapy for chronic insomnia: A randomized controlled trial. *Journal of Consulting and Clinical Psychology, 82*(4), 670–683.

Harvey, A. G., & Buysse, D. J. (2017). *Treating sleep problems: A transdiagnostic approach.* New York: Guilford.

Harvey, A. G., Soehner, A. M., Kaplan, K. A., Hein, K., Lee, J., Kanady, J. L., et al. (2015). Treating insomnia improves mood state, sleep, and functioning in bipolar disorder: A pilot randomized controlled trial. *Journal of Consulting and Clinical Psychology, 83,* 564–577.

Harvey, A. G., Watkins, E., Mansell, W., & Shafran, R. (2004). *Cognitive behavioural processes across psychological disorders: A transdiagnostic approach to research and treatment.* Oxford: Oxford University Press.

Harwood, D. M. J., Hawton, K., Hope, T., & Jacoby, R. (2000). Suicide in older people: Mode of death, demographic factors, and medical contact before death. *International Journal of Geriatric Psychiatry, 15,* 736–743.

Hasin, D. S., Fenton, M. C., Beseler, C., Park, J. Y., & Wall, M. M. (2012). Analysis related to the development of *DSM-5* criteria for substance use related disorders: 2. Proposed *DSM-5* criteria for alcohol, cannabis, cocaine, and heroin disorders in 663 substance abuse patients. *Drug and Alcohol Dependence, 122,* 28–37.

Hasin, D. S., Fenton, M. C., Skodol, A., Krueger, R., Keyes, K., Geier, T., Greenstein, E., Blanco, C., & Grant, B. (2011). Personality disorders and the 3-year course of alcohol, drug, and nicotine use disorders. *Archives of General Psychiatry, 68,* 1158–1167.

Hasin, D. S., Saha, T. D., Kerridge, B. T., Goldstein, R. B., Chou, S. P., Zhang, H., et al. (2015). Prevalence of marijuana use disorders in the United States between 2001–2002 and 2012–2013. *JAMA Psychiatry, 72*(12), 1235–1242.

Hasin, D. S., Stinson, F. S., Ogburn, E., & Grant, B. F. (2007). Prevalence, correlates, disability and comorbidity of *DSM-IV* alcohol abuse and dependence in the United States: Results from the National Epidemiologic Survey on alcohol and related conditions. *Archives of General Psychiatry, 64,* 830–842.

Hatzenbuehler, M. L. (2009). How does sexual minority stigma "get under the skin"? A psychological mediation framework. *Psychological Bulletin, 135,* 707–730.

Hatzenbuehler, M. L. (2016). Structural stigma: Research evidence and implications for psychological science. *American Psychologist, 71*(8), 742–751.

Hatzenbuehler, M. L., Keyes, K. M., & Hasin, D. S. (2009). State-level policies and psychiatric morbidity in LGB populations. *American Journal of Public Health, 99,* 2275–2281.

Hatzenbuehler, M. L., McLaughlin, K. A., Keyes, K. M., & Hasin, D. S. (2010). The impact of institutional discrimination on psychopathology in LGB populations: A prospective study. *American Journal of Public Health, 100,* 452–459.

Hausenblas, H. A., Campbell, A., Menzel, J. E., Doughty, J., Levine, M., & Thompson, J. K. (2013). Media effects of experimental presentation of the ideal physique on eating disorder symptoms: A meta-analysis of laboratory studies. *Clinical Psychology Review, 33*(1), 168–181.

Haw, C., Hawton, K., Niedzwiedz, C., & Platt, S. (2013). Suicide clusters: A review of risk factors and mechanisms. *Suicide and Life-Threatening Behavior, 43*(1), 97–108.

Hawton, K., Saunders, K. E., & O'Connor, R. C. (2012). Self-harm and suicide in adolescents. *Lancet, 379*(9834), 2373–2382.

Haynes, P. L., Gengler, D., & Kelly, M. (2016). Social rhythm therapies for mood disorders: An update. *Current Psychiatry Reports, 18*(8), 75.

Hayes, S. C., Luoma, J. B., Bond, F. W., Masuda, A., & Lillis, J. (2006). Acceptance and commitment therapy: Model, processes, and outcomes. *Behaviour Research and Therapy, 44,* 1–25.

Hayward, C., Killen, J. D., Kraemer, H. C., & Taylor, C. B. (2000). Predictors of panic attacks in adolescents. *Journal of the American Academy of Child & Adolescent Psychiatry, 39,* 207–214.

Hebert, L. E., Weuve, J., Scherr, P. A., & Evans, D. A. (2013). Alzheimer disease in the United States (2010–2050) estimated using the 2010 census. *Neurology, 80*(19), 1778–1783.

Heckers, S., Barch, D. M., Bustillo, J., Gaebel, W., Gur, R., Malaspina, D., Owen, M. J., Schultz, S., Tandon, R., Tsuang, M., Van Os, J., & Carpenter, W. (2013). Structure of the psychotic disorders classification in *DSM 5. Schizophrenia Research, 13,* 255–257.

Hedley, A. A., Ogden, C. L., Johnson, C. L., Carroll, M. D., Curtin, L. R., & Flegal, K. M. (2004). Prevalence of overweight and obesity among U.S. children, adolescents, and adults, 1999–2002. *JAMA, 291,* 2847–2850.

Hedman, E., & Axelsson, E. (2017). Severe health anxiety in the somatic symptom and related disorders. Treatments for psychological problems and syndromes. In D. McKay, J. S. Abramowitz, & E. A. Storch (Eds.), *Treatments for psychological problems and syndromes* (pp. 345–359). Hoboken, NJ: Wiley & Sons.

Heim, C., Meinlschmidt, G., & Nemeroff, C. B. (2003). Neurobiology of early-life stress. *Psychiatric Annals, 33,* 18–26.

Heim, C., & Nemeroff, C. B. (2001). The role of childhood trauma in the neurobiology of mood and anxiety disorders: Preclinical and clinical studies. *Biological Psychiatry, 49,* 1023–1039.

Heim, C., Plotsky, P. M., & Nemeroff, C. B. (2004). Importance of studying the contributions of early adverse experience to neurobiological findings in depression. *Neuropsychopharmacology, 29,* 641–648.

Heiman, J. R. (2000). Orgasmic disorders in women. In S. R. Leiblum & R. C. Rosen (Eds.), *Principles and practice of sex therapy* (3rd ed., pp. 118–153). New York: Guilford Press.

Heimberg, R. G., Brozovich, F. A., & Rapee, R. M. (2010). A cognitive-behavioral model of social anxiety disorder: Update and extension. In S. G. Hofmann & P. M. DiBartolo (Eds.), *Social anxiety: Clinical, developmental, and social perspectives* (2nd ed., pp. 395–422). New York: Academic Press.

Heinz, A., Deserno, L., & Reininghaus, U. (2013). Urbanicity, social adversity and psychosis. *World Psychiatry, 12*(3), 187–197.

Heiser, N. A., Turner, S. M., & Beidel, D. C. (2003). Shyness: Relationship to social phobia and other psychiatric disorders. *Behaviour Research & Therapy, 41,* 209–221.

Helgeland, M. I., & Torgersen, S. (2004). Developmental antecedents of borderline personality disorder. *Comprehensive Psychiatry, 45,* 138–147.

Helgeson, V. S., Snyder, P., & Seltman, H. (2004). Psychological and physical adjustment to breast cancer over 4 years: Identifying distinct trajectories of change. *Health Psychology, 23,* 3–15.

Hellstrom, I. C., & Meaney, M. (2010). Epigenetics and the environmental regulation of the brain's genome and its function. *Current Psychiatry Reviews, 6,* 145–158.

Helseth, S. A., Waschbusch, D. A., King, S., & Willoughby, M. T. (2015). Aggression in children with conduct problems and callous-unemotional traits: Social information processing and response to peer provocation. *Journal of Abnormal Child Psychology, 43*(8), 1503–1514.

Helzer, J. E., Kraemer, H. C., Krueger, R. F., Wittchen, H.-U., Sirovatka, P. J., & Regier, D. A. (2008). *Dimensional* *approaches in diagnostic classification: Refining the research agenda for* DSM-V. Arlington, VA: American Psychiatric Association.

Hengartner, M. P., & Moncrieff, J. (2018). Inconclusive evidence in support of the dopamine hypothesis of psychosis: Why neurobiological research must consider medication use, adjust for important confounders, choose stringent comparators, and use larger samples. *Frontiers in Psychiatry, 9,* 174.

Henry, M. E., Schmidt, M. E., Matochik, J. A., Stoddard, E. P., & Potter, W. Z. (2001). The effects of ECT on brain glucose: A pilot FDG PET study. *Journal of ECT, 17,* 33–40.

Herbert, J. D., Gaudiano, B. A., Rheingold, A. A., Myers, V. H., Dalrymple, K., & Nolan, E. M. (2005). Social skills training augments the effectiveness of cognitive behavioral group therapy for social anxiety disorder. *Behavior Therapy, 36,* 125–138.

Herman, J. L., & Harvey, M. R. (1997). Adult memories of childhood trauma: A naturalistic clinical study. *Journal of Traumatic Stress, 10,* 557–571.

Hettema, J. M., Neale, M. C., & Kendler, K. S. (2001). A review and meta-analysis of the genetic epidemiology of anxiety disorders. *American Journal of Psychiatry, 158,* 1568–1578.

Heylens, G., De Cuypere, G., Zucker, K. J., Schelfaut, C., Elaut, E., VandenBossche, H., De Baere, E., & T'Sjoen, G. (2012). Gender identity disorder in twins: A review of the case report literature. *Journal of Sexual Medicine, 9,* 751–757.

Higgins, S. T., Sigmon, S. C., & Heil, S. H. (2014). Drug use disorders. In D. H. Barlow (Ed.), *Clinical handbook of psychological disorders: A step-by-step treatment manual* (pp. 588–616). New York: Guilford.

Hilbert, A., Pike, K. M., Goldschmidt, A. B., Wilfley, D. E., Fairburn, C. G., Dohm, F. A., et al. (2014). Risk factors across the eating disorders. *Psychiatry Research, 220*(1), 500–506.

Hilbert, A., Wilfley, D. E., Dohm, F.-A., & Striegel-Moore, R. H. (2011). Characterization, significance, and predictive validity of binge size in binge eating disorder. In R. H. Striegel-Moore, S. A. Wonderlich, B. T. Walsh, & J. E. Mitchell (Eds.), *Developing an evidence-based classification of eating disorders: Scientific findings for DSM-5* (pp. 47–66). Washington, DC: American Psychiatric Association.

Hilgard, E. R. (1977/1986). *Divided consciousness: Multiple controls in human thought and action.* New York: Wiley.

Hilgard, E. R. (1992). Divided consciousness and dissociation. *Consciousness & Cognition: An International Journal, 1,* 16–31.

Hill, A. J., & Franklin, J. A. (1998). Mothers, daughters, and dieting: Investigating the transmission of weight control. *British Journal of Clinical Psychology, 37,* 3–13.

Hillman, J. (2017). Treating sexual problems in aging adults. In Z. D. Peterson (Ed.), *The Wiley handbook of sex therapy* (pp. 324–344). Oxford: Wiley.

Hines, M., Ahmed, S. F., & Hughes, I. A. (2003). Psychological outcomes and gender-related development in complete androgen insensitivity syndrome. *Archives of Sexual Behavior, 32,* 93–101.

Hingle, M. D., Wertheim, B. C., Tindle, H. A., Tinker, L., Seguin, R. A., Rosal, M. C., & Thomson, C. A. (2014). Optimism and diet quality in the Women's Health Initiative. *Journal of the Academy of Nutrition and Dietetics, 114*(7), 1036–1045.

Hinshaw, S. P. (2018). Attention deficit hyperactivity disorder (ADHD): Controversy, developmental mechanisms, and multiple levels of analysis. *Annual Review of Clinical Psychology, 14,* 291–316.

Hintsanen, M., Kivimaki, M., Elovainio, M., Pulkki-Raback, L., Keskivaara, P., Juonala, M., Raitakari, O. Y., & Keltikangas-Jarvinen, L. (2005). Job strain and early atherosclerosis: The Cardiovascular Risk in Young Finns Study. *Psychosomatic Medicine, 67,* 740–747.

Hirshkowitz, M., Whiton, K., Albert, S. M., Alessi, C., Bruni, O., DonCarlos, L., et al. (2015). National Sleep Foundation's sleep time duration recommendations: Methodology and results summary. *Sleep Health, 1*(1), 40–43.

Hirschtritt, M. E., Bloch, M. H., & Mathews, C. A. (2017). Obsessive-compulsive disorder: Advances in diagnosis and treatment. *JAMA,* 317(13), 1358–1367.

Hlastala, S. A., Frank, E., Kowalski, J., Sherrill, J. T., & Tu, X. M. (2000). Stressful life events, bipolar disorder, and the "kindling model." *Journal of Abnormal Psychology, 109,* 777–787.

Hobfoll, S. E., Blais, R. K., Stevens, N. R., Walt, L., & Gengler, R. (2016). Vets prevail online intervention reduces PTSD and depression in veterans with mild-to-moderate symptoms. *Journal of Consulting and Clinical Psychology, 84,* 31–42.

Hobson, C. W., Scott, S., & Rubia, K. (2011). Investigation of cool and hot executive function in ODD/CD independently of ADHD. *Journal of Child Psychology and Psychiatry, 52*(10), 1035–1043.

Hockenberry, M. S., & Masson P. (2016). Hormonal evaluation and therapy of erectile dysfunction. In T. S. Köhler & K. T. McVary (Eds.), *Contemporary treatment of erectile dysfunction: A clinical guide* (pp. 85–100). Cham: Springer.

Hoek, H. W., van Harten, P. N., Hermans, K. M. E., Katzman, M. A., Matroos, G. E., & Susser, E. S. (2005). The incidence of anorexia nervosa on Curaçao. *American Journal of Psychiatry, 162,* 748–752.

Hoffman, A. (1968). Psychotomimetic agents. In A. Burger (Ed.), *Drugs affecting the central nervous system* (Vol. 2, pp. 184–185). New York: Marcel Dekker.

Hogarty, G. E., Anderson, C. M., Reiss, D. J., Kornblith, S. J., Greenwald, D. P., Ulrich, R. F., & Carter, M. (1991). Family psychoeducation, social skills training, and maintenance chemotherapy in the aftercare treatment of schizophrenia: II. Two-year effects of a controlled study on relapse and adjustment. *Archives of General Psychiatry, 48,* 340–347.

Hoge, C. W., Auchterlonie, J. L., & Milliken, C. S. (2006). Mental health problems, use of mental health services, and attrition from military service after returning from deployment to Iraq or Afghanistan. *JAMA, 295,* 1023–1032.

Hoge, C. W., Castro, C. A., Messer, S. C., McGurk, D., Cotting, D. I., & Koffman, R. L. (2004). Combat duty in Iraq and Afghanistan, mental health problems, and barriers to care. *New England Journal of Medicine, 351,* 13–22.

Hoge, S. K., Bonnie, R. J., Poythress, N., Monahan, J., Eisenberg, M., & Feucht-Haviar, T. (1997). The MacArthur Adjudicative Competence Study: Development and validation of a research instrument. *Law & Human Behavior, 21,* 141–179.

Hoge, S. K., Poythress, N., Bonnie, R. J., Monahan, J., Eisenberg, M., & Feucht-Haviar, T. (1997). The MacArthur Adjudicative Competence Study: Diagnosis, psychopathology, and competence-related abilities. *Behavioral Sciences & the Law, 15,* 329–345.

Holden, C. (1980). Identical twins reared apart. *Science, 207*(4437), 1323–1328.

Hollon, S. D., DeRubeis, R. J., Shelton, R. C., Amsterdam, J. D., Salomon, R. M., O'Reardon, J. P., et al. (2005). Prevention or relapse following cognitive therapy versus medications in moderate to severe depression. *Archives of General Psychiatry, 62,* 417–422.

Hollon, S. D., & Dimidjian, S. (2015). Cognitive and behavioral treatment of depression. In I. H. Gotlib & C. L. Hammen

(Eds.), *Handbook of depression* (3rd ed., pp. 513–531). New York: Guilford.

Holm-Denoma, J. M., Scaringi, V., Gordon, K. H., van Orden, K. A., & Joiner, T. E., Jr. (2009). Eating disorder symptoms among undergraduate varsity athletes, club athletes, independent exercisers, and nonexercisers. *International Journal of Eating Disorders, 42,* 47–53.

Holoyda, B. J., & Kellaher, D. C. (2016). The biological treatment of paraphilic disorders: An updated review. *Current Psychiatry Reports, 18*(2), 19.

Holtom-Viesel, A., & Allan, S. (2014). A systematic review of the literature on family functioning across all eating disorder diagnoses in comparison to control families. *Clinical Psychology Review, 34*(1), 29–43.

Hoogman, M., Bralten, J., Hibar, D. P., Mennes, M., Zwiers, M. P., Schweren, L. S., et al. (2017). Subcortical brain volume differences in participants with attention deficit hyperactivity disorder in children and adults: A cross-sectional mega-analysis. *Lancet Psychiatry, 4*(4), 310–319.

Hooley, J. M. (2007). Expressed emotion and relapse of psychopathology. *Annual Review of Clinical Psychology, 3,* 329–352.

Hooley, J. M., & Campbell, C. (2002). Control and controllability: Beliefs and behaviour in high and low expressed emotion relatives. *Psychological Medicine, 32,* 1091–1099.

Hopko, D. R., Robertson, S. M. C., Widman, L., & Lejuez, C. W. (2008). Specific phobias. In M. Hersenand & J. Rosqvist (Eds.), *The handbook of assessment, conceptualization, and treatment (HACT)* (pp. 139–170). New York: John Wiley.

Hopper, K. (2008). Outcomes elsewhere: Course of psychosis in “other cultures.” In C. Morgan, K. McKenzie, & P. Fearon (Eds.), *Society and psychosis* (pp. 198–216). Cambridge: Cambridge University Press.

Hopwood, T. L., & Schutte, N. S. (2017). A meta-analytic investigation of the impact of mindfulness-based interventions on post traumatic stress. *Clinical Psychology Review, 57,* 12–20.

Hornbacher, M. (1998). *Wasted.* New York: HarperPerennial.

Hornbacher, M. (2008). *Madness: A bipolar life.* New York: Houghton Mifflin.

Hornstein, N. L., & Putnam, F. W. (1992). Clinical phenomenology of child and adolescent dissociative disorders. *Journal of the American Academy of Child & Adolescent Psychiatry, 31,* 1077–1085.

Horowitz, M. J., Siegel, B., Holen, A., Bonanno, G. A., Milbrath, C., & Stinson, C. H. (1997). Diagnostic criteria for complicated grief disorder. *American Journal of Psychiatry, 154,* 904–910.

Houtsma, C., Butterworth, S. E., & Anestis, M. D. (2018). Firearm suicide: Pathways to risk and methods of prevention. *Current Opinion in Psychology, 22,* 7–11.

Howard, A. L., Robinson, M., Smith, G. J., Ambrosini, G. L., Piek, J. P., & Oddy, W. H. (2011). ADHD is associated with a “western” dietary pattern in adolescents. *Journal of Attention Disorders, 15,* 403–411.

Howard, M. O., Perron, B. E., Vaughn, M. G., Bender, K. A., & Garland, E. (2010). Inhalant use, inhalant-use disorders, and antisocial behavior: Findings from the National Epidemiologic Survey on Alcohol and Related Conditions (NESARC). *Journal of Studies on Alcohol and Drugs, 71,* 201–209.

Howell, P. (2007). Signs of developmental stuttering up to age eight and at 12 plus. *Clinical Psychology Review, 27,* 287–306.

Howes, O. D., McCutcheon, R., Owen, M. J., & Murray, R. M. (2017). The role of genes, stress, and dopamine in the development of schizophrenia. *Biological Psychiatry, 81*(1), 9–20.

Howes, O., McCutcheon, R., & Stone, J. (2015). Glutamate and dopamine in schizophrenia: An update for the 21st century. *Journal of Psychopharmacology, 29*(2), 97–115.

Howes, O. D., & Murray, R. M. (2014). Schizophrenia: An integrated sociodevelopmental-cognitive model. *Lancet, 383*(9929), 1677–1687.

Howland, L. C., Gortmaker, S. L., Mofenson, L. M., Spino, C., Gardner, J. D., Gorski, H., Fowler, M. G., & Oleske, J. (2000). Effects of negative life events on immune suppression in children and youth infected with human immunodeficiency virus type 1. *Pediatrics, 106,* 540–546.

Howlin, P., Goode, S., Hutton, J., & Rutter, M. (2004). Adult outcome for children with autism. *Journal of Child Psychology & Psychiatry, 45,* 212–229.

Hoza, B., Mrug, S., Verdes, A. C., Hinshaw, S. P., Bukowski, W. M., Gold, J. A., Kraemer, H. C., Pelma, W. E., Jr., Wigal, T., & Arnold, L. E. (2005). What aspects of peer relationships are impaired in children with attention-deficit/hyperactivity disorder? *Journal of Consulting and Clinical Psychology, 73,* 411–423.

Hublin, C., Kaprio, J., Partinen, M., Heikkilä, K., & Koskenvuo, M. (1997). Prevalence and genetics of sleepwalking: A population-based twin study. *Neurology, 48,* 177–181.

Hucker, S. J. (2008). Sexual masochism: Psychopathology and theory. In D. R. Laws & W. T. O’Donohue (Eds.), *Sexual deviance: Theory, assessment, and treatment* (pp. 250–264). New York: Guilford Press.

Hudson, J. I., Hiripi, E., Pope, H. G., & Kessler, R. C. (2007). The prevalence and correlates of eating disorders in the National Comorbidity Survey Replication. *Biological Psychiatry, 61,* 348–358.

Hudziak, J. J., van Beijsterveldt, C. E. M., Althoff, R. R., Stanger, C., Rettew, D. C., Nelson, E. C., Todd, R. D., Bartels, M., & Boomsma, D. I. (2004). Genetic and environmental contributions to the Child Behavior Checklist Obsessive-Compulsive Scale: A cross-cultural twin study. *Archives of General Psychiatry, 61,* 608–616.

Huerta, M., Bishop, S. L., Duncan, A., Hus, V., & Lord, C. (2012). Application of *DSM-5* criteria for autism spectrum disorder to three samples of children with *DSM-IV* diagnoses of pervasive developmental disorders. *American Journal of Psychiatry, 169* (10), 1056–1064.

Hugdahl, K., & Ohman, A. (1977). Effects of instruction on acquisition and extinction of electrodermal response to fear-relevant stimuli. *Journal of Experimental Psychiatry: Human Learning & Memory, 3,* 608–618.

Hughes, T., McCabe, S. E., Wilsnack, S. C., West, B. T., & Boyd, C. J. (2010). Victimization and substance use disorders in a national sample of heterosexual and sexual minority women and men. *Addiction, 105,* 2130–2140.

Hughes, T. L., Wilsnack, S. C., & Kantor, L. W. (2016). The influence of gender and sexual orientation on alcohol use and alcohol-related problems: Toward a global perspective. *Alcohol Research: Current Reviews, 38*(1), 121–132.

Hultman, C. M., Sandin, S., Levine, S. Z., Lichtenstein, P., & Reichenberg, A. (2011). Advancing paternal age and risk of autism: New evidence from a population-based study and a meta-analysis of epidemiological studies. *Molecular Psychiatry, 16*(12), 1203–1212.

Humeau, Y., Gambino, F., Chelly, J., & Vitale, N. (2009). X-linked mental retardation: Focus on synaptic function and plasticity. *Neurochemistry, 109,* 1–14.

Hunt, W. A. (1998). Pharmacology of alcohol. In R. E. Tarter, R. T. Ammerman, & P. J. Ott (Eds.), *Handbook of substance abuse: Neurobehavioral pharmacology* (pp. 7–21). New York: Plenum Press.

Hurley, R. A., Saxena, S., Rauch, S. L., Hoehn-Saric, R., & Taber, K. H. (2008). Predicting treatment response in obsessive-compulsive disorder. In R. A. Hurley & K. H. Taber (Eds.), *Windows to the brain: Insights from neuroimaging* (pp. 213-219). Arlington, VA: American Psychiatric Publishing.

Hussong, A. M., Huang, W., Serrano, D., Curran, P. J., & Chassin, L. (2012). Testing whether and when parent alcoholism uniquely affects various forms of adolescent substance use. *Journal of Abnormal Child Psychology, 40*(8), 1265–1276.

Hutchison, K. E. (2010). Realizing the promise of pharmacogenomics and personalized medicine. *Annual Review of Clinical Psychology, 6,* 577–589.

Hyman, S. E. (2010). The diagnosis of mental disorders: The problem of reification. *Clinical Psychology, 6,* 155–179.

I

Iacovino, J. M., Jackson, J. J., & Oltmanns, T. F. (2014). The relative impact of socioeconomic status and childhood trauma on Black-White differences in paranoid personality disorder symptoms. *Journal of Abnormal Psychology, 123,* 225–230.

Iervolino, A. C., Perroud, N., Rullana, M. A., Guipponi, M., Cherkas, L., Collier, D. A., & Mataix-Cols, D. (2009). Prevalence and heritability of compulsive hoarding: A twin study. *American Journal of Psychiatry, 166,* 1156–1161.

Ikehara, S., Iso, H., Date, C., Kikuchi, S., Watanabe, Y., Wada, Y., Inaba, Y., Tamakoshi, A., & JACC Study Group. (2009). Association of sleep duration with mortality from cardiovascular disease and other causes for Japanese men and women: The JACC Study. *Sleep, 32,* 259–301.

Infant Health and Development Program. (1990). Enhancing the outcome of low-birth-weight, premature infants: A multisite randomized trial. *JAMA, 263,* 3035–3042.

Ingram, R. E., Hayes, A., & Scott, W. (2000). Empirically supported treatments: A critical analysis. In C. R. Snyder & R. E. Ingram (Eds.), *Handbook of psychological change: Psychotherapy processes and practices for the 21st century* (pp. 40–60). New York: Wiley.

Inouye, S. K., Westendorp, R. G., & Saczynski, J. S. (2014). Delirium in elderly people. *Lancet, 383*(9920), 911–922.

Insel, T. R. (Ed.). (1984). *New findings in obsessive-compulsive disorder.* Washington, DC: American Psychiatric Press.

Institute of Medicine. (2008). *Treatment of posttraumatic stress disorder: An assessment of the evidence.* Washington, DC: National Academies Press.

International Society for the Study of Trauma and Dissociation (ISSTD). (2011). Guidelines for treating dissociative identity disorder in adults (3rd Rev.: Summary version). *Journal of Trauma & Dissociation, 12,* 188–212.

Iranzo, A., Santamaria, J., & Tolosa, E. (2016). Idiopathic rapid eye movement sleep behaviour disorder: Diagnosis, management, and the need for neuroprotective interventions. *Lancet Neurology, 15*(4), 405–419.

Ironside, R. N., & Batchelor, I. R. C. (1945). *Aviation neuro-psychiatry.* Baltimore: Williams & Wilkins.

Irwin, M. R. (2015). Why sleep is important for health: A psychoneuroimmunology perspective. *Annual Review of Psychology, 66,* 143–172.

Irwin, M. R., & Opp, M. R. (2017). Sleep health: Reciprocal regulation of sleep and innate immunity. *Neuropsychopharmacology, 42*(1), 129–155.

Isidori, A. M., Buvat, J., Corona, G., Goldstein, I., Jannini, E. A., Lenzi, A., et al. (2014). A critical analysis of the role of testosterone in erectile function: From pathophysiology to treatment—a systematic review. *European Urology, 65*(1), 99–112.

Iversen, A. C., Fear, N. T., Ehlers, A., Hacker Hughes, J., Hull, L., Earnshaw, M., Greenberg, N., Rona, R., Wessely, S., & Hotopf, M. (2008). Risk factors for post-traumatic stress disorder among UK Armed Forces personnel. *Psychological Medicine, 38,* 511–522.

J

Jablensky, A. (2000). Epidemiology of schizophrenia: The global burden of disease and disability. *European Archives of Psychiatry & Clinical Neuroscience, 250,* 274–285.

Jack, C. R., Jr., Petersen, R. C., Grundman, M., Jin, S., Gamst, A., Ward, C. P., Sencakova, D., Doody, R. S., & Thal, L. J. (2007). Longitudinal MRI findings from the vitamin E and donepezil treatment study for MCI. *Neurobiology of Aging, 29,* 1285–1295.

Jack, D. C. (1991). *Silencing the self: Women and depression.* New York: HarperPerennial.

Jack, R. (1992). *Women and attempted suicide.* Hillsdale, NJ: Erlbaum.

Jacobi, F., Wittchen, H.-U., Hölting, C., Höfler, M., Pfister, H., Muller, N., et al. (2004). Prevalence, co-morbidity and correlates of mental disorders in the general population: Results from the German Health Interview and Examination Survey (GHS). *Psychological Medicine, 34,* 597–611.

Jacobson, C. M., & Gould, M. (2009). Suicide and nonsuicidal self-injurious behaviors among youth: Risk and protective factors. In S. Nolen-Hoeksema & L. Hilt (Eds.), *Handbook of depression in adolescents* (pp. 207–236). New York: Routledge.

Jacobson, E. (1964). *The self and the object world.* New York: International Universities Press.

Jacobson, S. W., & Jacobson, J. L. (2000). Teratogenic insult and neurobehavioral function in infancy and childhood. In C. A. Nelson (Ed.), *The Minnesota symposia on child psychology: Vol. 31. The effects of early adversity on neurobehavioral development* (pp. 61–112). Mahwah, NJ: Erlbaum.

Jacobus, J., & Tapert, S. F. (2013). Neurotoxic effects of alcohol in adolescence. *Annual Review of Clinical Psychology, 9,* 703–721.

Jacoby, R. J., & Abramowitz, J. S. (2016). Inhibitory learning approaches to exposure therapy: A critical review and translation to obsessive-compulsive disorder. *Clinical Psychology Review, 49,* 28–40.

James, D. J., & Glaze, L. E. (2006). *Mental health problems of prison and jail inmates.* Washington, DC: Bureau of Justice Statistics (BJS), U.S. Dept. of Justice, Office of Justice Programs.

Jamison, K. R. (1993). *Touched with fire: Manic-depressive illness and the artistic temperament.* New York: Free Press.

Jamison, K. R. (1995). *An unquiet mind: A memoir of moods and madness.* New York: Knopf.

Jang, K. L., Livesley, W. J., Ando, J., Yamagata, S., Suzuki, A., Angleitner, A., Ostendorf, F., Riemann, R., & Spinath, F. (2006). Behavioral genetics of the higher-order factors of the Big Five. *Personality and Individual Differences, 41,* 261–272

Jauhar, S., McKenna, P. J., Radua, J., Fung, E., Salvador, R., & Laws, K. R. (2014). Cognitive-behavioural therapy for the symptoms of schizophrenia: Systematic review and meta-analysis with examination of potential bias. *British Journal of Psychiatry, 204*(1), 20–29.

Jefferson, J. W. (2001). Benzodiazepines and anticonvulsants for social phobia (social anxiety disorder). *Journal of Clinical Psychiatry, 62*(Suppl. 1), 50–53.

Jelovac, A., Kolshus, E., & McLoughlin, D. M. (2013). Relapse following successful electroconvulsive therapy for major depression: A meta-analysis. *Neuropsychopharmacology, 38,* 2467–2474.

Jemmott, L. S., Jemmott, J. B., III, & O'Leary, A. (2007). A randomized controlled trial of brief HIV/STD prevention interventions for African American women in primary care settings: Effects on sexual risk behavior and STD incidence. *American Journal of Public Health, 97,* 1034–1040.

Jenkins, J. H., & Karno, M. (1992). The meaning of expressed emotion: Theoretical issues raised by cross-cultural research. *American Journal of Psychiatry, 149,* 9–21.

Jenkins, J. H., Kleinman, A., & Good, B. J. (1991). Cross-cultural studies of depression. In J. Becker (Ed.), *Psychosocial aspects of depression* (pp. 67–99). Hillsdale, NJ: Erlbaum.

Jenkins, R. L. (1973). *Behavior disorders of childhood and adolescence.* Springfield, IL: Charles C. Thomas.

Jennings, W. G., Perez, N. M., & Reingle Gonzalez, J. M. (2018). Conduct disorders and neighborhood effects. *Annual Review of Clinical Psychology, 14,* 317–341.

Jensen, P. S., Arnold, E., Swanson, J. M., Vitiello, B., Abikoff, H. B., Greenhill, L. L., Hechtman, L., Hinshaw, S. P., Pelma, W. E., Wells, K. C., Conners, C. K., Elliott, G. R., Epstein, J. N., Hoza, B., March, J. S., Molina, B. S. G., Newcorn, J. H., Severe, J. B., Wigal, T., Gibbons, R. D., & Hur, K. (2007). Three-year follow-up of the NIMH MTA study. *Journal of the American Academy of Child and Adolescent Psychiatry, 46,* 989–1002.

Jensen, P. S., Hinshaw, S. P., Swanson, J. M., Greenhill, L. L., Conners, C. K., Arnold, L. E., Abikoff, H. B., Elliott, G., Hechtman, L., Hoza, B., March, J. S., Newcorn, J. H., Severe, J. B., Vitiello, B., Wells, K., & Wigal, T. (2001). Findings from the NIMH Multimodal Treatment Study of ADHD (MTA): Implications and applications for primary care providers. *Journal of Developmental & Behavioral Pediatrics, 22,* 60–73.

Jin, H., & Mosweu, I. (2017). The societal cost of schizophrenia: A systematic review. *Pharmacoeconomics, 35*(1), 25–42.

Jobe, T. H., & Harrow, M. (2010). Schizophrenia course, long-term outcome, recovery, and prognosis. *Current Directions in Psychological Science, 19*(4), 220–225.

Joe, S., & Kaplan, M. S. (2001). Suicide among African American men. *Suicide & Life-Threatening Behavior, 31*(Suppl.), 106–121.

Johns, L. C., Cannon, M., Singleton, N., Murray, R. M., Farrell, M., Brugha, T., et al. (2004). Prevalence and correlates of self-reported psychotic symptoms in the British population. *British Journal of Psychiatry, 185,* 298–305.

Johns, L. C., Kompus, K., Connell, M., Humpston, C., Lincoln, T. M., Longden, E., et al., (2014). Auditory verbal hallucinations in persons with and without a need for care. *Schizophrenia Bulletin, 40*(Suppl. 4), S255–S264.

Johnson, J. (2016). Resilience: The bi-dimensional framework. In E. M. Wood & J. Johnson (Eds.), *Wiley handbook of positive clinical psychology* (pp. 73–88). Oxford: Wiley.

Johnson, P. M., & Kenny, P. J. (2010). Dopamine D2 receptors in addiction-like reward dysfunction and compulsive eating in obese rats. *Nature Neuroscience, 13,* 635–641.

Johnson, S. L., Fulford, D., & Carver, C. S. (2012). The double-edged sword of goal engagement: Consequences of goal pursuit in bipolar disorder. *Clinical Psychology and Psychotherapy, 19,* 352–362.

Johnson, S. M., Simakhodskaya, Z. & Moran, M. (2018). Addressing issues of sexuality in in couples therapy: Emotionally focused therapy meets sex therapy. *Current Sexual Health Reports, 10,* 65–71.

Johnston, L. D., O'Malley, P. M., Bachman, J. G., & Schulenberg, J. E. (2012). *Monitoring the Future national survey results on drug use, 1975–2011. Volume 2. College students and adults ages 19–50.* Ann Arbor: Institute for Social Research, University of Michigan.

Joiner, T. E. (2005). *Why people die by suicide.* Cambridge, MA: Harvard University Press.

Joiner, T. E., Brown, J. S., & Wingate, L. R. (2005). The psychology and neurobiology of suicidal behavior. *Annual Review of Psychology, 56,* 287–314.

Joiner, T. E., & Timmons, K. A. (2009). Depression in its interpersonal context. In I. H. Gotlib & C. L. Hammen (Eds.), *Handbook of depression* (2nd ed., pp. 322–339). New York: Guilford Press.

Jones, D., Godwin, J., Dodge, K. A., Bierman, K. L., Coie, J. D., Greenberg, M. T., Lochman, J. E., McMahon, R. J., & Pinderhughes, E. E. (2010). Impact of the fast track program on health services use by conduct-problem youth. *Pediatrics, 125,* 130–136.

Joormann, J. (2004). Attentional bias in dysphoria: The role of inhibitory processes. *Cognition and Emotion, 18,* 125–147.

Joormann, J., & Vanderlind, W. M. (2014). Emotion regulation in depression: The role of biased cognition and reduced cognitive control. *Clinical Psychological Science, 2*(4), 402–421.

Jordan, B. K., Schlenger, W. E., Fairbank, J. A., & Caddell, J. M. (1996). Prevalence of psychiatric disorders among incarcerated women: II. Convicted felons entering prison. *Archives of General Psychiatry, 53,* 513–519.

Jordan, K., Fromberger, P., Stolpmann, G., & Müller, J. L. (2011). The role of testosterone in sexuality and paraphilia—a neurobiological approach. Part II: Testosterone and paraphilia. *Journal of Sexual Medicine, 8,* 3008–3029.

Jorenby, D. E., Hays, J. T., Rigotti, N. A., Azoulay, S., Watsky, E. J., Williams, K. E., Billing, C. B., Gong, J., & Reeves, K. R. (2006). Efficacy of varenicline, an alpha 4 beta 2 nicotinic acetylcholine receptor partial agonist, vs. placebo or sustained-release bupropion for smoking cessation: A randomized controlled trial. *JAMA, 296,* 56–63.

Joy, E., Kussman, A., & Nattiv, A. (2016). 2016 update on eating disorders in athletes: A comprehensive narrative review with a focus on clinical assessment and management. *British Journal of Sports Medicine, 50*(3), 154–162.

Joyner, M. A., Kim, S., & Gearhardt, A. N. (2017). Investigating an incentive-sensitization model of eating behavior: Impact of a simulated fast-food laboratory. *Clinical Psychological Science, 5*(6), 1014–1026.

Jung, Y., & Louis, E. K. S. (2016). Treatment of REM sleep behavior disorder. *Current Treatment Options in Neurology, 18*(11), 50.

K

Kafantaris, V., Kingsley, P., Ardekani, B., Saito, E., Lencz, T., Lim, K., & Szeszko, P. (2009). Lower orbital frontal white matter integrity in adolescents with bipolar I disorder. *Journal of the American Academy of Child & Adolescent Psychiatry, 48*(1), 79–86.

Kafka, M. P. (2010). Hypersexual disorder: A proposed diagnosis for *DSM-V. Archives of Sexual Behavior, 39,* 377–400.

Kafka, M. P., & Hennen, J. (2003). Hypersexual desire in males: Are males with paraphilias different from males with paraphilia-related disorders? *Sexual Abuse: A Journal of Research and Treatment, 15,* 307–321.

Kagan, J., Reznick, J. S., & Snidman, M. (1987). The physiology and psychology of behavioral inhibition in children. *Child Development, 58,* 1459–1473.

Kallweit, U., & Bassetti, C. L. (2017). Pharmacological management of narcolepsy with and without cataplexy. *Expert Opinion on Pharmacotherapy, 18*(8), 809–817.

Kanbayashi, T., Kodama, T., Kondo, H., Satoh, S., Inoue, U., Chiba, S., Shimizu, T., & Nishino, S. (2009). CSF histamine contents in narcolepsy, idiopathic hypersomnia and obstructive sleep apnea syndrome. *Sleep, 32,* 181–187.

Kanner, L. (1943). Autistic disturbances of affective contact. *Nervous Child, 21,* 217–250.

Kaplan, M. S., & Krueger, R. B. (2012). Cognitive-behavioral treatment of the paraphilias. *Israeli Journal of Psychiatry and Relationship Science, 49*(4), 291–296.

Karasek, R. A., Russell, R. S., & Theorell, T. (1982). Physiology of stress and regeneration in job related cardiovascular illness. *Journal of Human Stress, 8,* 29–42.

Karazsia, B. T., Murnen, S. K., & Tylka, T. L. (2017). Is body dissatisfaction changing across time? A cross-temporal meta-analysis. *Psychological Bulletin, 143*(3), 293–320.

Karg, K., Burmeister, M., Shedden, K., & Sen, S. (2011). The serotonin transporter promoter variant (5-HTTLPR), stress and depression meta-analysis revisited. *Archives of General Psychiatry, 68,* 444–454.

Karlsgodt, K. H., Niendam, T. A., Bearden, C. E., & Cannon, T. D. (2009). White matter integrity and prediction of social and role functioning in subjects at ultra-high risk for psychosis. *Biological Psychiatry, 66,* 562–569.

Karlsgodt, K. H., Sun, D., & Cannon, T. D. (2010). Structural and functional brain abnormalities in schizophrenia. *Current Directions in Psychological Science, 19*(4), 226–231.

Karlsgodt, K. H., van Erp, T. G., Poldrack, R. A., Bearden, C. E., Nuechterlein, K. H., & Cannon, T. D. (2008). Diffusion tensor imaging of the superior longitudinal fasciculus and working memory in recent-onset schizophrenia. *Biological Psychiatry, 63,* 512–518.

Karno, M., & Golding, J. M. (1991). Obsessive compulsive disorder. In L. R. Robins & D. A. Regier (Eds.), *Psychiatric disorders in America: The Epidemiologic Catchment Area study* (pp. 204–219). New York: Maxwell Macmillan International.

Karno, M., Hough, R., Burnam, A., Escobar, J. I., Timbers, D. M., Santana, F., & Boyd, J. H. (1987). Lifetime prevalence of specific psychiatric disorders among Mexican Americans and non-Hispanic whites in Los Angeles. *Archives of General Psychiatry, 44,* 695–701.

Karno, M., & Jenkins, J. H. (1993). Cross-cultural issues in the course and treatment of schizophrenia. *Psychiatric Clinics of North America, 16,* 339–350.

Kartheiser, P. H., Ursano, A. M., & Barnhill, L. J. (2007). Communication disorders. In R. Fletcher, E. Loschen, C. Stavrakaki, & M. First (Eds.), *Diagnostic manual of intellectual disability: A textbook of diagnosis of mental disorders in persons with intellectual disability* (pp. 97–106). Kingston, NY: National Association for the Dually Diagnosed.

Kasindorf, J. (1988, May 2). *The real story of Billie Boggs: Was Koch right–or the civil libertarians? New York,* pp. 35–44. https://clantilyscad.com/2013/08/25/joyce-brown-billie-bogs-and-nycs-forgotten-involuntary-confinement-program/

Kaskutas, L. A. (2009). Alcoholics Anonymous effectiveness: Faith meets science. *Journal of Addictive Diseases, 28,* 145–157.

Katon, W. (2003). Clinical and health services relationships between major depression, depressive symptoms, and general medical illness. *Biological Psychiatry, 54,* 216–226.

Katon, W., Sullivan, M., & Walker, E. (2001). Medical symptoms without identified pathology: Relationship to psychiatric disorders, childhood and adult trauma, and personality traits. *Annals of International Medicine, 134,* 917–925.

Katzman, R. (1993). Education and the prevalence of dementia and Alzheimer's disease. *Neurology, 43,* 13–20.

Kaufman, J., Yang, B. Z., Douglas-Palumberi, H., Grasso, D., Lipschitz, D., et al. (2006). Brain-derived neurotrophic factor-5-HTTLPR gene interactions and environmental modifiers of depression in children. *Biological Psychiatry, 59,* 673–680.

Kaufman, J., Yang, B. Z., Douglas-Palumberi, H., Houshyar, S., Lipschitz, D., et al. (2004). Social supports and serotonin transporter gene moderate depression in maltreated children. *Proceedings of the National Academy of Sciences, 101,* 17316–17321.

Kaysen, S. (1993). *Girl, interrupted*. New York: Turtle Bay.

Kazdin, A. E. (2015). Psychosocial treatments for conduct disorder in children and adolescents. In P. E. Nathan & J. M. Gorman (Eds.), *A guide to treatments that work* (4th ed., pp. 141–173). New York: Oxford University Press.

Kazdin, A. E. (2017). Parent management training and problem-solving skills training for child and adolescent conduct problems. In J. R. Weisz & A. E. Kazdin (Eds.), *Evidence-based psychotherapies for children and adolescents,* 3rd ed. (pp. 142–158). New York: Guilford.

Kazdin, A. E. (2018). Implementation and evaluation of treatments for children and adolescents with conduct problems: Findings, challenges, and future directions. *Psychotherapy Research, 28*(1), 3–17.

Kazdin, A. E., & Blase, S. L. (2011). Rebooting psychotherapy research and practice to reduce the burden of mental illness. *Perspectives on Psychological Science, 6,* 21–37.

Kazdin, A. E., Fitzsimmons-Craft, E. E., & Wilfley, D. E. (2017). Addressing critical gaps in the treatment of eating disorders. *International Journal of Eating Disorders, 50,* 170–189.

Keel, P. K., Brown, T. A., Holland, L. A., & Bodell, L. P. (2012). Empirical classification of eating disorders. In *Annual Review of Clinical Psychology, 8,* 381–404.

Keel, P. K., & Forney, K. J. (2013). Psychosocial risk factors for eating disorders. *International Journal of Eating Disorders, 46*(5), 433–439.

Keel, P. K., Heatherton, T. F., Dorer, D. J., Joiner, T. E., & Zalta, A. K. (2006). Point prevalence of bulimia nervosa in 1982, 1992, and 2002. *Psychological Medicine, 36,* 119–127.

Keel, P. K., & Klump, K. L. (2003). Are eating disorders culture-bound syndromes? Implications for conceptualizing their etiology. *Psychological Bulletin, 129,* 747–769.

Kegel, M., Dam, H., Ali, F., & Bjerregaard, P. (2009). The prevalence of seasonal affective disorder (SAD) in Greenland is related to latitude. *Nordic Journal of Psychiatry, 63*(4), 331–335.

Keller, M. B., McCullough, J. P., Klein, D. N., Arnow, B., Dunner, D. L., Gelenberg, A. J., Markowitz, J. C., Nemeroff, C. B., Russell, J. M., Thase, M. E., Trivedi, M. H., & Zajecka, J. (2000). A comparison of nefazodone, the cognitive behavioral analysis system of psychotherapy, and their combination for the treatment of chronic depression. *New England Journal of Medicine, 342,* 1462–1470.

Kellermann, A. L., Rivara, F. P., Somes, G., & Reay, D. T. (1992). Suicide in the home in relation to gun ownership. *New England Journal of Medicine, 327,* 467–472.

Kellett, S. (2007). A time series evaluation of the treatment of histrionic personality disorder with cognitive analytic therapy. *Psychology and Psychotherapy: Theory, Research, and Practice, 80,* 389–405.

Kelly, J. F. (2003). Self-help for substance-use disorders: History, effectiveness, knowledge gaps, and research opportunities. *Clinical Psychological Revue, 23,* 639–663.

Kelly, S. J., Day, N., & Streissguth, A. P. (2000). Effects of prenatal alcohol exposure on social behavior in humans and other species. *Neurotoxicology & Teratology, 22,* 143–149.

Kemeny, M. E., & Dean, L. (1995). Effects of AIDS-related bereavement on HIV progression among New York City gay men. *AIDS Education and Prevention, 7,* 36–47.

Kendall, P. C., Crawford. E. A., Kagan, E. R., Furr, J. M., & Podell, J. L. (2017). Child-focused treatment for anxiety. In A. E. Kazdin & J. R. Weisz (Eds.), *Evidence-based psychotherapies for children and adolescents* (pp. 17–34). New York: Guilford.

Kendall, P. C., Hollon, S. D., Beck, A. T., Hammen, C. L., & Ingram, R. E. (1987). Issues and recommendations regarding use of the Beck Depression Inventory. *Cognitive Therapy & Research, 11,* 289–299.

Kendall, P. C., Hudson, J. L., Gosch, E., Flannery-Schroeder, E., & Suveg, C. (2008). Cognitive-behavioral therapy for anxiety disordered youth: A randomized clinical trial evaluating child and family modalities. *Journal of Consulting and Clinical Psychology, 76,* 282–297.

Kendall-Tackett, K. A., Williams, L. M., & Finkelhor, D. (1993). Impact of sexual abuse on children: A review and synthesis of recent empirical studies. *Psychological Bulletin, 113,* 164–180.

Kendler, K. S., & Engstrom, E. J. (2016). Kahlbaum, Hecker, and Kraepelin and the transition from psychiatric symptom complexes to empirical disease forms. *American Journal of Psychiatry, 174(2),* 102–109.

Kendler, K. S., Karkowski, L. M., & Prescott, C. A. (1999). Causal relationship between stressful life events and the onset of major depression. *American Journal of Psychiatry, 156,* 837–848.

Kendler, K. S., Kessler, R. C., Walters, E. E., MacLean, C., Neale, M. C., Heath, A. C., & Eaves, L. J. (2010). Stressful life events, genetic liability, and onset of an episode of major depression in women. *Focus, 8*(3), 459–470.

Kendler, K. S., Myers, J., Prescott, C. A., & Neale, M. C. (2001). The genetic epidemiology of irrational fears and phobias in men. *Archives of General Psychiatry, 58,* 257–265.

Kendler, K. S., Neale, M. C., Kessler, R. C., Heath, A. C., & Eaves, L. J. (1993). A test of the equal-environment assumption in twin studies of psychiatric illness. *Behavior Genetics, 23,* 21–28.

Kennedy, S. H., Evans, K. R., Kruger, S., Mayberg, H. S., Meyer, J. H., et al. (2001). Changes in regional brain glucose metabolism measured with positron emission tomography after paroxetine treatment of major depression. *American Journal of Psychiatry, 158,* 899–905.

Kernberg, O. F. (1979). Psychoanalytic profile of the borderline adolescent. *Adolescent Psychiatry, 7,* 234–256.

Kernberg, O. F. (1993). *Severe personality disorders: Psychotherapeutic strategies.* New Haven, CT: Yale University Press.

Kessing, L. V., Hansen, M. G., & Andersen, P. K. (2004). Course of illness in depressive and bipolar disorders: Naturalistic study, 1994–1999. *British Journal of Psychiatry, 185,* 372–377.

Kessler, R. C. (2003). The impairments caused by social phobia in the general population: Implications for intervention. *Acta Psychiatrica Scandinavica, 108*(Suppl. 417), 19–27.

Kessler, R. C., Adler, L., Barkley, R., Biederman, J., Conners, C. K., Demler, O., Faraone, S. V., Greenhill, L. L., Howes, M. J., Secnik, K., Spencer, T., Ustun, T. B., Walters, E. E., & Zaslavsky, A. M. (2006). The prevalence and correlates of adult ADHD in the United States: Results from the National Comorbidity Survey Replication. *American Journal of Psychiatry, 163,* 716–723.

Kessler, R. C., Aguilar-Gaxiola, S., Alonso, J., Chatterji, S., Lee, S., Ormel, J., et al. (2009). The global burden of mental disorders: An update from the WHO World Mental Health (WMH) Surveys. *Epidemiologia e Psichiatria Sociale, 18,* 23–33.

Kessler, R. C., Andrade, L. H., Bijl, R. V., Offord, D. R., Demler, O. V., & Stein, D. J. (2002). The effects of co-morbidity on the onset and persistence of generalized anxiety disorder in the ICPE surveys. *Psychological Medicine, 32,* 1213–1225.

Kessler, R. C., Avenevoli, S., Costello, E. J., Georgiades, K., Green, J. G., Gruber, M. J., He, J. P., Koretz, D., McLaughlin, K. A., Petukhova, M., Sampson, N. A., Zaslavsky, A. M., & Merikangas, K. R. (2012). Prevalence, persistence, and sociodemographic correlates of *DSM-IV* disorders in the National Comorbidity Survey Replication Adolescent Supplement. *Archives of General Psychiatry, 69,* 372–380.

Kessler, R. C., Berglund, P. A., Bruce, M. L., Koch, J. R., et al. (2001). The prevalence and correlates of untreated serious mental illness. *Health Services Research, 36,* 987–1007.

Kessler, R. C., Berglund, P. A., Chiu, W. T., Deitz, A. C., Hudson, J. I., Shahly, V., et al. (2013). The prevalence and correlates of binge eating disorder in the World Health Organization World Mental Health Surveys. *Biological Psychiatry, 73*(9), 904–914.

Kessler, R. C., Berglund, P., Demler, O., Jin, R., Koretz, D., Merikangas, K. R., Rush, A. J., Walters, E. E., & Wang, P. S. (2003). The epidemiology of major depressive disorder: Results from the national comorbidity survey replication (NCS-R). *JAMA, 289,* 3095–3105.

Kessler, R. C., Berglund, P., Demler, O., Jin, R., Merikangas, M. R., & Walters, E. E. (2005). Lifetime prevalence and age-of-onset distributions of *DSM-IV* disorders in the National Comorbidity Survey Replication. *Archives of General Psychiatry, 62,* 593–602.

Kessler, R. C., Birnbaum, H., Bromet, E., Hwang, I., Sampson, N., & Shahly, V. (2010). Age differences in major depression: Results from the National Comorbidity Survey Replication (NCS-R). *Psychological Medicine, 40,* 225–237.

Kessler, R. C., Chiu, W. T., Jin, R., Ruscio, A. M., Shear, K., & Walters, E. E. (2006). The epidemiology of panic attacks, panic disorder, and agoraphobia in the National Comorbidity Survey Replication. *Archives of General Psychiatry, 63,* 415–424.

Kessler, R. C., Coccaro, E. F., Fava, M., Jaeger, S., Jin, R., & Walters, E. (2006). The prevalence and correlates of *DSM-IV* intermittent explosive disorder in the National Comorbidity Survey Replication. *Archives of General Psychiatry, 63,* 669–678.

Kessler, R. C., Heeringa, S., Lakoma, M. D., Petukhova, M., Rupp, A. E., Schoenbaum, M., et al. (2008). Individual and societal effects of mental disorders on earnings in the United States: Results from the National Comorbidity Survey Replication. *American Journal of Psychiatry, 165,* 703–711.

Kessler, R. C., Merikangas, K. R., & Wang, P. S. (2007). Prevalence, comorbidity, and service utilization for mood disorders in the United States at the beginning of the twenty-first century. *Annual Review of Clinical Psychology, 3,* 137–158.

Kessler, R. C., Sonnega, A., Bromet, E., Hughes, M., & Nelson, C. B. (1995). Posttraumatic stress disorder in the National Comorbidity Survey. *Archives of General Psychiatry, 52,* 1048–1060.

Kessler, R. C., Stein, M. B., & Berglund, P. (1998). Social phobia subtypes in the National Comorbidity Survey. *American Journal of Psychiatry, 155,* 613–619.

Kessler, R. C., & Wang, P. S. (2008). The descriptive epidemiology of commonly occurring mental disorders in the United States. *Public Health, 29,* 115–129.

Ketter, T. A., Miller, S., Dell'Osso, B., & Wang, P. W. (2016). Treatment of bipolar disorder: Review of evidence regarding quetiapine and lithium. *Journal of Affective Disorders, 191,* 256–273.

Kety, S. S., Wender, P. H., Jacobsen, B., Ingraham, L. J., Jansson, L., Faber, B., & Kinney, D. K. (1994). Mental illness in the biological and adoptive relative of schizophrenic adoptees: Replication of the Copenhagen study in the rest of Denmark. *Archives of General Psychiatry, 51,* 442–455.

Keyes, K. M., Eaton, N. R., Krueger, R. F., McLaughlin, K. A., Wall, M. M., Grant, B. F., & Hasin, D. S. (2012). Childhood maltreatment and the structure of common psychiatric disorders. *British Journal of Psychiatry, 200*(2), 107–115.

Keyes, K. M., Grant, B. F., & Hasin, D. S. (2008). Evidence for a closing gender gap in alcohol use, abuse, and dependence in the United States population. *Drug and Alcohol Dependence, 93,* 21–29.

Keyes, K. M., Martins, S. S., Blanco, C., & Hasin, D. S. (2010). Telescoping and gender differences in alcohol dependence: New evidence from two national surveys. *American Journal of Psychiatry, 167,* 969–976.

Keyes, K. M., Schulenberg, J. E., O'Malley, M., Johnston, L. D., Bachman, J. G., Li, G., & Hasin, D. (2011). The social norms of birth cohorts and adolescent marijuana use in the United States, 1976–2007. *Addiction, 106,* 1790–1800.

Khan, A., Leventhal, R. M., Khan, S. R., & Brown, W. A. (2002). Severity of depression and response to antidepressants and placebo: An analysis of the Food and Drug Administration database. *Journal of Clinical Psychopharmacology, 22,* 40–45.

Kiecolt-Glaser, J. K., Malarkey, W. B., Chee, M., & Newton, T. (1993). Negative behavior during marital conflict is associated with immunological down-regulation. *Psychosomatic Medicine, 55,* 395–409.

Kiecolt-Glaser, J. K., & Newton, T. L. (2001). Marriage and health: His and hers. *Psychological Bulletin, 127,* 472–503.

Kiecolt-Glaser, J. K., & Wilson, S. J. (2017). Lovesick: How couples' relationships influence health. *Annual Review of Clinical Psychology, 13,* 421–443.

Kieling, C., Kieling, R. R., Rohde, L. A., Frick, P. J., Moffitt, T., Nigg, J. T., Tannock, R., & Castellanos, F. X. (2010). The age at onset of attention deficit hyperactivity disorder. *American Journal of Psychiatry, 167,* 14–16.

Kihlstrom, J. F. (2001). Dissociative disorders. In P. B. Sutker (Ed.), *Comprehensive handbook of psychopathology* (3rd ed., pp. 259–276). New York: Kluwer Academic/Plenum.

Kihlstrom, J. F. (2005). Dissociative disorders. *Annual Review of Clinical Psychology, 1,* 227–254.

Kihlstrom, J. F., & Couture, L. J. (1992). Awareness and information processing in general anesthesia. *Journal of Psychopharmacology, 6,* 410–417.

Kihlstrom, J. F., Glisky, M. L., & Angiulo, M. J. (1994). Dissociative tendencies and dissociative disorders. *Journal of Abnormal Psychology, 103,* 117–124.

Kim, H. S., Sherman, D. K., & Taylor, S. E. (2008). Culture and social support. *American Psychologist, 63,* 518–526.

Kim, J., & Lopez, S. R. (2014). The expression of depression in Asian Americans and European Americans. *Journal of Abnormal Psychology, 123,* 754–763.

Kim, L. I. C. (1993). Psychiatric care of Korean Americans. In A. C. Gaw (Ed.), *Culture, ethnicity, and mental illness* (pp. 347–375). Washington, DC: American Psychiatric Press.

Kim, Y., Shaffer, K. M., Carver, C. S., & Cannady, R. S. (2014). Prevalence and predictors of depressive symptoms among cancer caregivers 5 years after the relative's cancer diagnosis. *Journal of Consulting and Clinical Psychology, 82,* 1–8.

Kim, Y. S., Leventhal, B. L., Koh, Y.-J., Fombonne, E., Laska, E., Lim, E.-C., Cheon, K.-A., Kim, S.-J., Kim, Y.-Y., Lee, H., Song, D.-H., & Grinker, R.-R. (2011). Prevalence of autism spectrum disorders in a total population sample. *American Journal of Psychiatry, 168,* 904–912.

Kim-Cohen, J., Caspi, A., Rutter, M., Polo Tomas, M., & Moffitt, T. E. (2006). The caregiving environments provided to children by depressed mothers with or without an antisocial history. *American Journal of Psychiatry, 163,* 1009–1018.

Kimonis, E. R. (2015). Insanity defense/guilty but mentally ill. In *The encyclopedia of clinical psychology* (pp. 1–6). Chichester, UK: Wiley Blackwell.

Kimonis, E. R., Fanti, K. A., Frick, P. J., Moffitt, T. E., Essau, C., Bijjtebier, P., & Marsee M. A. (2015). Using self-reported callous-unemotional traits to cross-nationally assess the DSM-5 "With Limited Prosocial Emotions" specifier. *Journal of Child Psychology and Psychiatry, 56,* 1249–1261.

King, B. H., Hodapp, R. M., & Dykens, E. M. (2005). Mental retardation. In B. J. Sadock & V. A. Sadock (Eds.), *Kaplan & Sadock's comprehensive textbook of psychiatry* (pp. 3076–3206). Philadelphia: Lippincott Williams & Wilkins.

King, C. R., Knutson, K. L., Rathouz, P. J., Sidney, S., Liu, K., & Lauderdale, D. S. (2008). Short sleep duration and incident coronary artery calcification. *Jama, 300*(24), 2859–2866.

Kirk, S. A., & Kutchins, H. (1992). *The selling of DSM: The rhetoric of science in psychiatry.* New York: A. de Gruyter.

Kirkbride, J. B., Fearon, P., Morgan, C., Dazzan, P., Morgan, K., Tarrant, J., Lloyd, T., Holloway, J., Hutchinson, G., Leff, J. P., Mallett, R. M., Harrison, G. L., Murray, R. M., & Jones, P. B. (2006). Heterogeneity in incidence rates of schizophrenia and other psychotic syndromes: Findings from the 3-center ÆSOP study. *Archives of General Psychiatry, 63,* 250–258.

Kirmayer, L. J. (2001). Cultural variations in the clinical presentation of depression and anxiety: Implications for diagnosis and treatment. *Journal of Clinical Psychiatry, 62*(Suppl. 13), 22–30.

Kirsch, I., Deacon, B. J., Huedo-Medina, T. B., Scoboria, A., Moore, T. J., & Johnson, B. T. (2008). Initial severity and antidepressant benefits: A meta-analysis of data submitted to the Food and Drug Administration. *PLoS Medicine, 5,* e45.

Kisiel, C. L., & Lyons, J. S. (2001). Dissociation as a mediator of psychopathology among sexually abused children and adolescents. *American Journal of Psychiatry, 158,* 1034–1039.

Kissane, D. W., Grabsch, B., Clarke, D. M., Smith, G. C., Love, A. W., Bloch, S., Snyder, R. D., & Li, Y. (2007). Supportive-expressive group therapy for women with metastatic breast cancer: Survival and psychosocial outcome from a randomized controlled trial. *Psycho-Oncology, 16,* 277–286.

Klassen, L. J., Katzman, M. A., & Chokka, P. (2010). Adult ADHD and its comorbidities, with a focus on bipolar disorder. *Journal of Affective Disorders, 124,* 1–8.

Klein, C., & Gorzalka, B. B. (2009). Sexual functioning in transsexuals following hormone therapy and genital surgery: A review. *Journal of Sexual Medicine, 6,* 2922–2939.

Klein, M. (1952). Notes on some schizoid mechanisms. In M. Klein, P. Heimann, S. Isaacs, & J. Riviere (Eds.), *Developments in psychoanalysis* (pp. 292–320). London: Hogarth Press.

Klerman, G. L., & Weissman, M. M. (1989). Increasing rates of depression. *JAMA, 261,* 2229–2235.

Klerman, G. L., Weissman, M. M., Rounsaville, B., & Chevron, E. (1984). *Interpersonal psychotherapy of depression.* New York: Basic Books.

Klonsky, E. D., May, A. M., & Saffer, B. Y. (2016). Suicide, suicide attempts, and suicidal ideation. *Annual Review of Clinical Psychology, 12,* 307–330.

Klorman, R., Cicchetti, D., Thatcher, J. E., & Ison, J. R. (2003). Acoustic startle in maltreated children. *Journal of Abnormal Child Psychology, 31,* 359–370.

Klump, K. L., Culbert, K. M., Slane, J. D., Burt, S. A., Sisk, C. L., & Nigg, J. T. (2012). The effects of puberty on genetic risk for disordered eating: Evidence for a sex difference. *Psychological Medicine, 42,* 627–637.

Knable, M. B., Barci, B. M., Webster, M. J., Meador-Woodruff, J., & Torrey, E. F. (2004). Molecular abnormalities of the hippocampus in severe psychiatric illness: Postmortem findings from the Stanley Neuropathology Consortium. *Molecular Psychiatry, 9,* 609–620.

Kneeland, R. E., & Fatemi, S. H. (2013). Viral infection, inflammation and schizophrenia. *Progress in Neuro-Psychopharmacology and Biological Psychiatry, 42,* 35–48.

Knight, R. A. (2010). Is a diagnostic category for paraphilic coercive disorder defensible? *Archives of Sexual Behavior, 39,* 419–426.

Knouse, L. E., Teller, J., & Brooks, M. A. (2017). Meta-analysis of cognitive-behavioral treatments for adult ADHD. *Journal of Consulting and Clinical Psychology, 85*(7), 737–750.

Knowles, R., McCarthy-Jones, S., & Rowse, G. (2011). Grandiose delusions: A review and theoretical integration of cognitive and affective perspectives. *Clinical Psychology Review, 31*(4), 684–696.

Kober, H., & Boswell, R. G. (2018). Potential psychological and neural mechanisms in binge eating disorder: Implications for treatment. *Clinical Psychology Review, 60,* 32–44.

Koenen, K. C., Harley, R., Lyons, M. J., Wolfe, J., Simpson, J. C., Goldberg, J., et al. (2002). A twin registry study of familial and individual risk factors for trauma exposure and posttraumatic stress disorder. *Journal of Nervous and Mental Disease, 190,* 209–218.

Köhler, T. S., & McVary, K. T. (2016). *Contemporary treatment of erectile dysfunction: A clinical guide.* Cham: Springer.

Kohut, H. (1977). *The restoration of the self.* New York: International Universities Press.

Kolodziej, J. (2016). Effects of stress on HIV infection progression. *HIV & AIDS Review, 15,* 13–16.

Kong, L. L., Allen, J. J. B., & Glisky, E. L. (2008). Interidentity memory transfer in dissociative identity disorder. *Journal of Abnormal Psychology, 117,* 686–692.

Koniak-Griffin, D., Lesser, J., Henneman, T., Huang, R., Huang, X., Kappos, B., et al. (2008). HIV prevention for Latino adolescent mothers and their partners. *Western Journal of Nurse Research, 30,* 724.

Koopman, C., Drescher, K., Bowles, S., Gusman, F., Blake, D., Dondershine, H., Chang, V., Butler, L. D., & Spiegel, D. (2001). Acute, dissociative reactions in veterans with PTSD. *Journal of Trauma & Dissociation, 2,* 91–111.

Koss, J. D. (1990). Somatization and somatic complaint syndromes among Hispanics: Overview and ethnopsychological perspectives. *Transcultural Psychiatric Research Review, 27,* 5–29.

Koss, M. P., & Kilpatrick, D. G. (2001). Rape and sexual assault. In E. Gerrity (Ed.), *The mental health consequences of torture* (pp. 177–193). New York: Kluwer Academic/Plenum.

Koss-Chioino, J. D. (2000). Traditional and folk approaches among ethnic minorities. In J. F. Aponte & J. Wohl (Eds.), *Psychological intervention and cultural diversity* (2nd ed., pp. 149–166). Needham Heights, MA: Allyn & Bacon.

Kotlicka-Antczak, M., Pawełczyk, A., Pawełczyk, T., Strzelecki, D., Żurner, N., & Karbownik, M. S. (2017). A history of obstetric complications is associated with the risk of progression from an at risk mental state to psychosis. *Schizophrenia Research.*

Koukoui, S. D., & Chaudhuri, A. (2007). Neuroanatomical, molecular, genetic, and behavioral correlates of fragile X syndrome. *Brain Research Reviews, 53,* 27–38.

Kownacki, R. J., & Shadish, W. R. (1999). Does Alcoholics Anonymous work? The results from a meta-analysis of controlled experiments. *Substance Use and Misuse, 34,* 1897–1916.

Krakowsky, Y., & Grober, E. D. (2016). Hypoactive sexual desire in men. In L. Lipshultz, A. Pastuszak, A. Goldstein, A. Giraldi, & M. Perelman (Eds.). *Management of sexual dysfunction in men and women* (pp. 171–187). New York: Springer.

Kratochvil, C. J., Michelson, D., Newcorn, J. H., Weiss, M. D., Busner, J., Moore, R. J., Ruff, D. D., Ramsey, J., Dickson, R., Turgay, A., Saylor, K. E., Luber, S., Vaughan, B., Allen, A. J., & the Atomoxetine High-Dose Study Group. (2007). High-dose atomoxetine treatment of ADHD in youths with limited response to standard doses. *Journal of the American Academy of Child and Adolescent Psychiatry, 46,* 1128–1137.

Kraus, G., & Reynolds, D. J. (2001). The "A-B-C's" of the Cluster B's: Identifying, understanding, and treating Cluster B personality disorders. *Clinical Psychology Review, 21,* 345–373.

Krentz, E. M., & Warschburger, P. (2011). Sport-related correlates of disordered eating: A comparison between aesthetic and ballgame sports. *International Journal of Sport Psychology, 42,* 548–564.

Kreukels, B. P., & Guillamon, A. (2016). Neuroimaging studies in people with gender incongruence. *International Review of Psychiatry, 28*(1), 120–128.

Kring, A. M., & Elis, O. (2013). Emotion deficits in people with schizophrenia. *Annual Review of Clinical Psychology, 9,* 409–433.

Kring, A. M., & Moran, E. K. (2008). Emotional response deficits in schizophrenia: Insights from affective science. *Schizophrenia Bulletin, 34,* 819–834.

Kring, A. M., & Neale, J. M. (1996). Do schizophrenic patients show a disjunctive relationship among expressive, experiential, and psychophysiological components of emotion? *Journal of Abnormal Psychology, 105,* 249–257.

Kring, A. M., & Sloan, D. S. (Eds.). (2009). *Emotion regulation and psycho-pathology: A transdiagnostic approach to etiology and treatment.* New York: Guilford Press.

Kroenke, C. H., Kwan, M. L., Neugut, A. I., Ergas, I. J., Wright, J. D., Caan, B. J., et al. (2012). Social networks, social support mechanisms, and quality of life after breast cancer diagnosis. *Breast Cancer Research and Treatment, 139*(2), 515–527.

Kroll, J. (1973). A reappraisal of psychiatry in the Middle Ages. *Archives of General Psychiatry, 29,* 276–283.

Krueger, R. B., and Kaplan, M. S. (2008). Frotteurism: Assessment and treatment. In D. R. Laws & W. T. O'Donohue (Eds.), *Sexual deviance: Theory, assessment, and treatment* (pp. 150–164). New York: Guilford Press.

Krueger, R. F., & Markon, K. E. (2014). The role of the DSM-5 personality trait model in moving toward a quantitative and empirically based approach to classifying personality and psychopathology. *Annual Review of Clinical Psychology, 10,* 477–501.

Krug, O. (2016). Existential, humanistic, experiential psychotherapies in historical perspective. In A. J. Consoli, L. E. Beutler, & B. Bongar (Eds.), *Comprehensive textbook of psychotherapy: Theory and practice* (2nd ed.), pp. 91–105. New York: Oxford University Press.

Kryger, M. H., Roth, T., & Dement, W. C. (Eds.). (2017). *Principles and practice of sleep medicine* (6th ed.). Philadelphia: Elsevier.

Kuepper, R., van Os, J., Lieb, R., Wittchen, H. U., Höfler, M., & Henquet, C. (2011). Continued cannabis use and risk of incidence and persistence of psychotic symptoms: 10 year follow-up cohort study. *British Medical Journal, 342,* d738.

Kuerbis, A., & Sacco, P. (2013). A review of existing treatments for substance abuse among the elderly and recommendations for future directions. *Substance Abuse: Research and Treatment, 7,* 13–37.

Kuerbis, A., Sacco, P., Blazer, D. G., & Moore, A. A. (2014). Substance abuse among older adults. *Clinics in Geriatric Medicine, 30*(3), 629–654.

Kuester, A., Niemeyer, H., & Knaevelsrud, C. (2016). Internet-based interventions for posttraumatic stress: A meta-analysis of randomized controlled trials. *Clinical Psychology Review, 43,* 1–16.

Kujawa, A., Proudfit, G. H., & Klein, D. N. (2014). Neural reactivity to rewards and losses in offspring of mothers and fathers with histories of depressive and anxiety disorders. *Journal of Abnormal Psychology, 123,* 287–297.

Kumar, M. S., Murhekar, M. V., Hutin, Y., Subramanian, T., Ramachandran, V., & Gupte, M. D. (2007). Prevalence of posttraumatic stress disorder in a coastal fishing village in Tamil Nadu, India, after the December 2004 tsunami. *American Journal of Public Health, 97,* 99–101.

Kuss, D. J., Griffiths, M. D., & Pontes, H. M. (2017). Chaos and confusion in DSM-5 diagnosis of Internet Gaming Disorder: Issues, concerns, and recommendations for clarity in the field. *Journal of Behavioral Addictions, 6*(2), 103–109.

Kvillemo, P., & Bränström, R. (2014). Coping with breast cancer: A meta-analysis. *PLoS One, 9,* e112733.

Kwapil, T. R., & Barrantes-Vidal, N. (2012). Schizotypal personality disorder: an integrative review. In T. A. Widiger (Ed.), *The Oxford handbook of personality disorders* (pp. 437–477). New York: Oxford University Press.

L

Lack, L. C., Gradisar, M., Van Someren, E. J. W., Wright, H. R., & Lushington, K. (2008). The relationship between insomnia and body temperatures. *Sleep Medicine Reviews, 12,* 307–317.

Ladwig, K. H., Martin-Mittag, B., Lacruz, M. E., Henningsen, P., & Creed, F. (2010). Screening for multiple somatic complaints in a population-based survey: Does excessive symptom reporting capture the concept of somatic symptom disorders? *Journal of Psychosomatic Research, 68,* 427–437.

LaGreca, A. M., Silverman, W. K., Vernberg, E. M., & Prinstein, M. J. (1996). Symptoms of posttraumatic stress in children after Hurricane Andrew: A prospective study. *Journal of Consulting & Clinical Psychology, 64,* 712–723.

Lalonde, J. K., Hudson, J. I., Gigante, R. A., & Pope, H. G. (2001). Canadian and American psychiatrists' attitudes towards dissociative disorders diagnoses. *Canadian Journal of Psychiatry, 46,* 407–412.

Lamb, H. R., & Weinberger, L. E. (2016). Rediscovering the concept of asylum for persons with serious mental illness. *Journal of the American Academy of Psychiatry and the Law, 44*(1), 106–110.

Lamb, H. R., & Weinberger, L. E. (2017). Understanding and treating offenders with serious mental illness in public sector mental health. *Behavioral Sciences & the Law, 35*(4), 303–318.

Lambert, M. C., Knight, F., Overly, K., Weisz, J. R., Desrosiers, M., & Thesiger, C. (1992). Jamaican and American adult perspectives on child psychopathology: Further exploration of the threshold model. *Journal of Consulting & Clinical Psychology, 60,* 146–149.

Landen, M., Roeber, J., Naimi, T., Nielsen, L., & Sewell, M. (2014). Alcohol-attributable mortality among American Indians and Alaska natives in the United States, 1999–2009. *American Journal of Public Health, 104*(S3), S343-S349.

Laney, C., & Loftus, E. F. (2013). Recent advances in false memory research. *South African Journal of Psychology, 43*(2), 137–146.

Langberg, J. M., Molina, B. S. G., Arnold, L. E., Epstein, J. N., Altaye, M., Hinshaw, S. P., Swanson, J. M., Wigal, T., & Hechtman, L. (2012). Patterns and predictors of adolescent academic achievement and performance in a sample of children with attention-deficit/hyperactivity disorder. *Journal of Clinical Child & Adolescent Psychology, 40,* 519–531.

Langlois, J. A., Rutland-Brown, W., & Wald, M. M. (2006). The epidemiology and impact of traumatic brain injury: A brief overview. *Journal of Head Trauma Rehabilitation 21,* 375–378.

Langstrom, N. (2009, November 19). The *DSM* diagnostic criteria for exhibitionism, voyeurism, and frotteurism. *Archives of Sexual Behavior.* Doi: 10.1007/s10508-009-9577-4

Langstrom, N., & Seto, M. C. (2006). Exhibitionistic and voyeuristic behavior in a Swedish national population survey. *Archives of Sexual Behavior, 35,* 427–435.

Langstrom, N., & Zucker, K. J. (2005). Transvestic fetishism in the general population: Prevalence and correlates. *Journal of Sex and Marital Therapy, 31,* 87–95.

Larkin, A., & Hutton, P. (2017). Systematic review and meta-analysis of factors that help or hinder treatment decision-making capacity in psychosis. *British Journal of Psychiatry, 211*(4), 205–215.

Larøi, F., Luhrmann, T. M., Bell, V., Christian W. A., Jr., Deshpande, S., Fernyhough, C., et al. (2014). Culture and hallucinations: Overview and future directions. *Schizophrenia Bulletin, 40*(Suppl. 4), S213–S220.

Larsson, H., Chang, Z., D'Onofrio, B. M., & Lichtenstein, P. (2014). The heritability of clinically diagnosed attention deficit hyperactivity disorder across the lifespan. *Psychological Medicine, 44*(10), 2223–2229.

Larsson, H., Tuvblad, C., Rijsdijk, F. V., Andershed, H., Grann, M., & Lichtenstein, P. (2007). A common genetic factor explains the association between psychopathic personality and antisocial behavior. *Psychological Medicine, 37,* 15–26.

Lasser, K., Boyd, J. W., Woolhandler, S., Himmelstein, D. U., McCormick, D., & Bor, D. H. (2000). Smoking and mental illness: A population-based prevalence study. *JAMA, 284,* 2606–2610.

Lataster, J., Myin-Germeys, I., Lieb, R., Wittchen, H. U., & van Os, J. (2011). Adversity and psychosis: A 10-year prospective study investigating synergism between early and recent adversity in psychosis. *Acta Psychiatrica Scandinavica, 125*(5), 388–399.

Latvala, A., Kuja-Halkola, R., Almqvist, C., Larsson, H., & Lichtenstein, P. (2015). A longitudinal study of resting heart rate and violent criminality in more than 700,000 men. *JAMA Psychiatry, 72*(10), 971–978.

Laudenslager, M. L., Ryan, S. M., Drugan, R. C., Hyson, R. L., & Maier, S. F. (1983). Coping and immunosuppression: Inescapable but not escapable shock suppresses lymphocyte proliferation. *Science, 221,* 569–570.

Laumann, E. O., Gagnon, J. H., Michael, R. T., & Michaels, S. (1994). *The social organization of sexuality: Sexual practices in the United States.* Chicago: University of Chicago Press.

Laumann, E. O., Paik, A., & Rosen, R. C. (1999). Sexual dysfunction in the United States. *JAMA, 281,* 537–544.

Laursen, T. M., Nordentoft, M., & Mortensen, P. B. (2014). Excess early mortality in schizophrenia. *Annual Review of Clinical Psychology, 10,* 425–448.

Lavin, M. (2008). Voyeurism: Psychopathology and theory. In D. R. Laws & W. T. O'Donohue (Eds.), *Sexual deviance: Theory, assessment, and treatment* (pp. 305–320). New York: Guilford Press.

Lavoie, K. L., Miller, S. B., Conway, M., & Fleet, R. P. (2001). Anger, negative emotions, and cardiovascular reactivity during interpersonal conflict in women. *Journal of Psychosomatic Research, 51,* 503–512.

Lavretsky, H. (2008). History of schizophrenia as a psychiatric disorder. In K. T. Mueser & D. V. Jeste (Eds.), *Clinical handbook of schizophrenia* (pp. 3–13). New York: Guilford Press.

Lawrence, A. A. (2008). Gender identity disorders in adults: Diagnosis and treatment. In D. L. Rowland & L. Incrocci (Eds.), *Handbook of sexual and gender identity disorders* (pp. 423–456). Hoboken, NJ: Wiley.

Lawrie, S. M., McIntosh, A. M., Hall, J., Owens, D. G. C., & Johnstone, E. C. (2008). Brain structure and function changes during the development of schizophrenia: The evidence from studies of subjects at increased genetic risk. *Schizophrenia Bulletin, 34,* 330–340.

Lazarus, S. A., Cheavens, J. S., Festa, F., & Rosenthal, M. Z. (2014). Interpersonal functioning in borderline personality disorder: A systematic review of behavioral and laboratory-based assessments. *Clinical Psychology Review, 34,* 193–205.

Le, L. K. D., Barendregt, J. J., Hay, P., & Mihalopoulos, C. (2017). Prevention of eating disorders: A systematic review and meta-analysis. *Clinical Psychology Review, 53,* 46–58.

Leadbeater, B. J., Kuperminc, G. P., Blatt, S. J., & Herzog, C. (1999). A multivariate model of gender differences in adolescents' internalizing and externalizing problems. *Developmental Psychology, 35,* 1268–1282.

LeBeau, R. T., Glenn, D., Liao, B., Wittchen, H.-U., Beesdo-Baum, K., Ollendick, T., & Craske, M. G. (2010). Specific phobia: A review of *DSM-IV* specific phobia and preliminary recommendations for *DSM-V. Depression and Anxiety, 27,* 148–167.

Lebowitz, M. S., & Ahn, W. K. (2012). Combining biomedical accounts of mental disorders with treatability information to reduce mental illness stigma. *Psychiatric Services, 63,* 496–499.

Leckman, J. F., Denys, D., Simpson, H. B., Mataix-Cols, D., Hollander, E., Saxena, S., Miguel, E. C., Rauch, S. L., Goodman, W. K., Phillips, K. A., & Stein, D. S. (2010). Obsessive-compulsive disorder: A review of the diagnostic criteria and possible subtypes and dimensional signifiers for *DSM-V. Depression and Anxiety, 27,* 507–527.

LeDoux, J. E. (1996). *The emotional brain: The mysterious underpinnings of emotional life.* New York: Simon & Schuster.

Lee, E. K., & Kazaglis, L. (2015). Hypersomnolence disorders in DSM-5: A review for clinicians. *Psychiatric Annals, 45*(1), 25–29.

Lee, J. K. P., Jackson, H. J., Pattison, P., & Ward, T. (2002). Developmental risk factors for sexual offending. *Child Abuse & Neglect, 26,* 73–92.

Leehr, E. J., Krohmer, K., Schag, K., Dresler, T., Zipfel, S., & Giel, K. E. (2015). Emotion regulation model in binge eating disorder and obesity—a systematic review. *Neuroscience & Biobehavioral Reviews, 49,* 125–134.

Leeman, R. F., & Potenza, M. N. (2012). Similarities and differences between pathological gambling and substance use disorders: A focus on impulsivity and compulsivity. *Psychopharmacology, 219,* 469–490.

Lehman, B. J., Taylor, S. E., Kiefe, C., & Seeman, T. E. (2009). Relationship of early life stress and psychological functioning to blood pressure in the CARDIA study. *Health Psychology, 28,* 338–346.

Lehn, A., Gelauff, J., Hoeritzauer, I., Ludwig, L., McWhirter, L., Williams, S., et al. (2016). Functional neurological disorders: Mechanisms and treatment. *Journal of Neurology, 263*(3), 611–620.

Leiblum, S. R. (Ed.). (2010). *Treating sexual desire disorders: A clinical casebook.* New York: Guilford Press.

Leiblum, S. R., Koochaki, P. E., Rodenberg, C. A., Barton, I. P., & Rosen, R. C. (2006). Hypoactive sexual desire disorder in postmenopausal women: U.S. results from the Women's International Study of Health and Sexuality (WISHeS). *Menopause, 13,* 46–56.

Leiblum, S. R., & Rosen, R. C. (2000). *Principles and practice of sex therapy* (3rd ed.). New York: Guilford Press.

Leichsenring, F., & Steinert, C. (2018). Towards an evidence-based unified psychodynamic protocol for emotional disorders. *Journal of Affective Disorders, 232,* 400–416.

Lemmens, L. H., Galindo-Garre, F., Arntz, A., Peeters, F., Hollon, S. D., DeRubeis, R. J., & Huibers, M. J. (2017). Exploring mechanisms of change in cognitive therapy and interpersonal psychotherapy for adult depression. *Behaviour Research and Therapy, 94,* 81–92.

Lenzenweger, M. F. (2008). Epidemiology of personality disorders. *Psychiatric Clinics of North America, 31,* 395–403.

Leon, G. R., Fulkerson, J. A., Perry, C. L., & Early-Zald, M. B. (1995). Prospective analysis of personality and behavioral vulnerabilities and gender influences in the later development of disordered eating. *Journal of Abnormal Psychology, 104,* 140–149.

Lepping, P., Stanly, T., & Turner, J. (2015). Systematic review on the prevalence of lack of capacity in medical and psychiatric settings. *Clinical Medicine, 15*(4), 337–343.

Leserman J. (2008). Role of depression, stress, and trauma in HIV disease progression. *Psychosomatic Medicine, 70,* 539–545.

Leserman, J., Jackson, E. D., Petitto, J. M., Golden, R. N., Silva, S. G., Perkins, D. O., Cai, J., Folds, J. D., & Evans, D. L. (1999). Progression to AIDS: The effects of stress, depressive symptoms, and social support. *Psychosomatic Medicine, 61,* 397–406.

Leserman, J., Pence, B. W., Whetten, K., Mugavero, M. J., Thielman, N. M., Swartz, M. S., & Stangl, D. (2007). Relation of lifetime trauma and depressive symptoms to mortality in HIV. *American Journal of Psychiatry, 164,* 1707–1713.

Leserman, J., Petitto, J. M., Golden, R. N., Gaynes, B. N., Gu, H., et al. (2000). Impact of stressful life events, depression, social support, coping, and cortisol on progression to AIDS. *American Journal of Psychiatry, 157,* 1221–1228.

Leserman, J., Petitto, J. M., Gu, H., Gaynes, B. N., Barroso, J., Golden, R. N., Perkins, D. O., Folds, J. D., & Evans, D. L. (2002). Progression to AIDS, a clinical AIDS condition, and mortality: Psychosocial and physiological predictors. *Psychological Medicine, 32,* 1059–1073.

Le Strat, Y., & Gorwood, P. (2011). Hazardous drinking is associated with lower risk of coronary heart disease: Results from a national representative sample. *American Journal on Addictions, 20*(3), 257–263.

Leventhal, H., Weinman, J., Leventhal, E. A., & Phillips, L. A. (2008). Health psychology: The search for pathways between behavior and health. *Annual Review of Psychology, 59,* 477–506.

Levine, S., Rabinowitz, J., Ascher-Svanum, H., Faries, D. E., & Lawson, A. H. (2011). Extent of attaining and maintaining symptom remission by antipsychotic medication in the treatment of chronic schizophrenia: Evidence from the CATIE study. *Schizophrenia Research, 133,* 42–46.

Levinson, D. F. (2006). The genetics of depression: A review. *Biological Psychiatry 60,* 84–92.

Levy, S. M., & Heiden, L. (1991). Depression, distress, and immunity: Risk factors for infectious disease. *Stress Medicine, 7,* 45–51.

Lewinsohn, P. M. (1974). A behavioral approach to depression. In R. J. Friedman & M. M. Katz (Eds.), *The psychology of depression: Contemporary theory and research* (pp. 157–178). Washington, DC: Winston-Wiley.

Lewinsohn, P. M., & Gotlib, I. H. (1995). Behavioral therapy and treatment of depression. In E. E. Beckham & W. R. Leber (Eds.), *Handbook of depression* (2nd ed., pp. 352–375). New York: Guilford Press.

Lewinsohn, P. M., Muñoz, R. F., Youngren, M. A., & Zeiss, A. M. (1986). *Control your depression.* Englewood Cliffs, NJ: Prentice Hall.

Lewinsohn, P. M., Striegel-Moore, R. H., & Seeley, J. R. (2000). Epidemiology and natural course of eating disorders in young women from adolescence to young adulthood. *Journal of the American Academy of Child & Adolescent Psychiatry, 39,* 1284–1292.

Lewis, G., David, A., Andreasson, S., & Allebeck, P. (1992). Schizophrenia and city life. *Lancet, 340,* 137–140.

Lewis, R. W., Fugl-Meyer, K. S., Corona, G., Hayes, R. D., Laumann, E. O., Moreira, E. D., Jr., Rellini, A. H., & Segraves, T. (2010). Definitions/epidemiology/risk factors for sexual dysfunction. *Journal of Sexual Medicine, 7* (4, pt. 2), 1598–1607.

Lewis, R. W., Yuan, J., & Wangt, R. (2008). Male sexual arousal disorder. In D. L. Rowland & L. Incrocci (Eds.), *Handbook of sexual and gender identity disorders* (pp. 32–67). Hoboken, NJ: Wiley.

Lewis, T. T., Cogburn, C. D., & Williams, D. R. (2015). Self-reported experiences of discrimination and health: Scientific advances, ongoing controversies, and emerging issues. *Annual Review of Clinical Psychology, 11,* 407–440.

Lewis-Fernandez, R., Hinton, D. E., Laria, A. J., Patterson, E. H., Hofmann, S. G., Craske, M. G., Stein, D. J., Asnaani, A., & Liao, B. (2010). Culture and the anxiety disorders: Recommendations for the *DSM-V. Depression and Anxiety, 27,* 212–229.

Li, Z., Chang, S. H., Zhang, L. Y., Gao, L., & Wang, J. (2014). Molecular genetic studies of ADHD and its candidate genes: A review. *Psychiatry Research, 219,* 10–24.

Liberman, R. P. (2008). *Recovery from disability: Manual of psychiatric rehabilitation.* Washington, DC: American Psychiatric Publishing.

Liberman, R. P., Glynn, S., Blair, K. E., Ross, D., & Marder, S. R. (2002). In vivo amplified skills training: Promoting generalization of independent living skills for clients with schizophrenia. *Psychiatry: Interpersonal & Biological Processes, 65,* 137–155.

Lichtenstein, P., Yip, B. H., Björk, C., Pawitan, Y., Cannon, T. D., Sullivan, P. F., & Hultman, C. M. (2009). Common genetic determinants of schizophrenia and bipolar disorder in Swedish families: A population-based study. *Lancet, 373*(9659), 234–239.

Lieberman, J. A., Girgis, R. R., Brucato, G., Moore, H., Provenzano, F., Kegeles, L., et al. (2018). Hippocampal dysfunction in the pathophysiology of schizophrenia: A selective review and hypothesis for early detection and intervention. *Molecular Psychiatry,* 1-9

Lieberman, J. A., Stroup, T. S., & Perkins, D. O. (2012). *Essentials of schizophrenia.* Arlington, VA: American Psychiatric Publishing.

Lilienfeld, S. O., & Treadway, M. T. (2016). Clashing diagnostic approaches: DSM-ICD versus RDoC. *Annual Review of Clinical Psychology, 12,* 435–463.

Lim, D. C., & Pack, A. I. (2017). Obstructive sleep apnea: Update and future. *Annual Review of Medicine, 68,* 99–112.

Linardon, J., Wade, T. D., de la Piedad Garcia, X., & Brennan, L. (2017). The efficacy of cognitive-behavioral therapy for eating disorders: A systematic review and meta-analysis. *Journal of Consulting and Clinical Psychology, 85(11),* 1080–1094.

Lindau, S. T., Schumm, L. P., Laumann, E. O., Levinson, W., O'Muircheartaigh, C. A., & Waite, L. J. (2007). A study of sexuality and health among older adults in the United States. *New England Journal of Medicine, 357*(8), 762–774.

Lindsay, S. D., Hagen, L., Read, J. D., Wade, K. A., & Garry, M. (2004). True photographs and false memories. *Psychological Science, 15,* 149–154.

Linehan, M. M. (1973). Suicide and attempted suicide: Study of perceived sex differences. *Perceptual & Motor Skills, 37,* 31–34.

Linehan, M. M. (1999). Standard protocol for assessing and treating suicidal behaviors for patients in treatment. In D. G. Jacobs (Ed.), *The Harvard Medical School guide to suicide assessment and intervention* (pp. 146–187). San Francisco: Jossey-Bass.

Linehan, M. M., Cochran, B. N., & Kehrer, C. A. (2001). Dialectical behavior therapy for borderline personality disorder. In D. H. Barlow (Ed.), *Clinical handbook of psychological disorders: A step-by-step treatment manual* (pp. 470–522). New York: Guilford Press.

Linehan, M. M., Comtois, K. A., Murray, A. M., Brown, M. Z., Gallop, R. J., Heard, H. L., et al. (2006). Two-year randomized controlled trial and follow-up of dialectical behavior therapy vs therapy by experts for suicidal behaviors and borderline personality disorder. *Archives of General Psychiatry, 63*(7), 757–766.

Links, P. S., & Eynan, R. (2013). The relationship between personality disorders and Axis I psychopathology: Deconstructing comorbidity. *Annual Review of Clinical Psychology, 9,* 529–554.

Linschoten, M., Weiner, L., & Avery-Clark, C. (2016). Sensate focus: A critical literature review. *Sexual and Relationship Therapy, 31*(2), 230–247.

Linscott, R. J., Allardyce, J., & van Os, J. (2009). Seeking verisimilitude in a class: A systematic review of evidence that the criterial clinical symptoms of schizophrenia are taxonic. *Schizophrenia Bulletin*. doi:10.1093

Linscott, R. J., & van Os, J. (2010). Systematic reviews of categorical versus continuum models in psychosis: Evidence for discontinuous subpopulations underlying a psychometric continuum. Implications for *DSM-V, DSM-VI,* and *DSM-VII. Annual Review of Clinical Psychology,* 6. 391–419.

Lipari, R. N., Hughes, A., & Bose, J. (2016). *Driving under the influence of alcohol and illicit drugs. The CBHSQ Report: December 27, 2016.* Rockville, MD: Center for Behavioral Health Statistics and Quality, Substance Abuse and Mental Health Services Administration.

Little, K., Olsson, C. A., Youssef, G. J., Whittle, S., Simmons, J. G., Yücel, M., et al. (2015). Linking the serotonin transporter gene, family environments, hippocampal volume and depression onset: A prospective imaging gene × environment analysis. *Journal of Abnormal Psychology, 124,* 834–849.

Liu, H. Y., Potter, M. P., Woodsworth, K. Y., Yorks, D. M., Petty, C. R., Wozniak, J. R., Faraone, S. V., & Biederman, J. (2011). Pharmacologic treatments for pediatric bipolar disorder: A review and meta-analysis. *Journal of the American Academy of Child & Adolescent Psychiatry, 50,* 749–762.

Liu, R. T. (2013). Stress generation: Future directions and clinical implications. *Clinical Psychology Review, 33,* 406–416.

Loas, G., Cormier, J., & Perez-Diaz, F. (2011). Dependent personality disorder and physical abuse. *Psychiatry Research, 185,* 167–170.

Lochner, C., Roos, A., & Stein, D. J. (2017). Excoriation (skin-picking) disorder: A systematic review of treatment options. *Neuropsychiatric Disease and Treatment, 13,* 1867–1872.

Lochner, C., Serebro, P., van der Merwe, L., Hemmings, S., Kinnear, C., Seedat, S., & Stein, D. J. (2011). Comorbid obsessive-compulsive personality disorder in obsessive-compulsive disorder (OCD): A marker of severity. *Progress in Neuropsychopharmacology & Biological Psychiatry, 35,* 1087–1092.

Lock, J., Agras, W. S., Bryson, S., & Kraemer, H. C. (2005). A comparison of short- and long-term family therapy for adolescent anorexia nervosa. *Journal of the American Academy of Child and Adolescent Psychiatry, 44,* 632–639.

Lock, J., & le Grange D. (2013). *Treatment manual for anorexia nervosa: A family-based approach* (2nd ed.). New York: Guilford.

Loebel, J. P., Loebel, J. S., Dager, S. R., Centerwall, B. S., & Reay, D. T. (1991). Anticipation of nursing home placement may be a precipitant of suicide among the elderly. *Journal of the American Geriatric Society, 39,* 407–408.

Loeber, R., & Burke, J. D. (2011). Developmental pathways in juvenile externalizing and internalizing problems. *Journal of Research on Adolescence, 21,* 34–46.

Loeber, R., Burke, J., & Pardini, D. A. (2009a). Development and etiology of disruptive and delinquent behavior. *Clinical Psychology, 5,* 291–310.

Loeber, R., Burke, J., & Pardini, D. A. (2009b). Perspectives on oppositional defiant disorder, conduct disorder, and psychopathic features. *Journal of Child Psychology and Psychiatry, 50,* 133–142.

Loehlin, J. C. (2009). History of behavior genetics. In Y.-K. Kim (Ed.), *Handbook of behavior genetics* (pp. 3–11). New York: Spring Science & Business Media.

Loftus, E. F. (1993). The reality of repressed memories. *American Psychologist, 48,* 518–537.

Loftus, E. F. (2003). Make-believe memories. *American Psychologist, 58,* 867–873.

Loftus, E. F. (2011). Crimes of memory: False memories and societal justice. In M. A. Gernsbacher, R. W. Pew, L. M. Hough, & J. R. Pomerantz (Eds., FABBS Foundation), *Psychology and the real world: Essays illustrating fundamental contributions to society* (pp. 83–88). New York: Worth.

Long, P. W. (1996). Internet mental health. http://www.mentalhealth.com/ (accessed June 1, 2006).

Lopez, S. R., & Guarnaccia, P. J. J. (2000). Cultural psychopathology: Uncovering the social world of mental illness. *Annual Review of Psychology, 51,* 571–598.

Lopez, S. R., Kopelowicz, A., & Canive, J. M. (2002). Strategies in developing culturally congruent family interventions for schizophrenia: The case of Hispanics. In H. P. Lefley & D. L. Johnson (Eds.), *Family interventions in mental illness: International perspectives* (pp. 61–90). Westport, CT: Praeger.

Lopez-Quintero, C., Pérez de los Cobos, J., Hasin, D. S., Okuda, M., Wang, S., Grant, B. F., & Blanco, C. (2011). Probability and predictors of transition from first use to dependence on nicotine, alcohol, cannabis, and cocaine: Results of the National Epidemiologic Survey on Alcohol and Related Conditions (NESARC). *Drug and Alcohol Dependence, 115*(1–2), 120–130.

Lord, C., & Bishop, S. L. (2015). Recent advances in autism research as reflected in DSM-5 criteria for autism spectrum disorder. *Annual Review of Clinical Psychology, 11,* 53–70.

Lorenz, K., & Ullman, S. E. (2016). Alcohol and sexual assault victimization: Research findings and future directions. *Aggression and Violent Behavior, 31,* 82–94.

Lotspeich, L. J., Kwon, H., Schumann, C. M., Fryer, S. L., Goodlin-Jones, B. L., Buonocore, M. H., Lammers, C. R., Amaral, D. G., & Reiss, A. L. (2004). Investigation of neuroanatomical differences between autism and Asperger syndrome. *Archives of General Psychiatry, 61,* 291–298.

Lovaas, O. I. (1987). Behavioral treatment and normal educational and intellectual functioning in young autistic children. *Journal of Consulting & Clinical Psychology, 55,* 3–9.

Löwe, B., Spitzer, R. L., Williams, J. B., Mussell, M., Schellberg, D., & Kroenke, K. (2008). Depression, anxiety and somatization in primary care: Syndrome overlap and functional impairment. *General Hospital Psychiatry, 30*(3), 191–199.

Luborsky, L., & Barrett, M. S. (2006). The historical and empirical status of key psychoanalytic concepts. *Annual Review of Clinical Psychology, 2,* 1–20.

Ludwig, A. M. (1992). Creative achievement and psychopathology: Comparison among professions. *American Journal of Psychotherapy, 46,* 330–356.

Ludwig, L., Pasman, J. A., Nicholson, T., Aybek, S., David, A. S., Tuck, S., et al. (2018). Stressful life events and maltreatment in conversion (functional neurological) disorder: Systematic review and meta-analysis of case-control studies. *Lancet Psychiatry, 5*(4), 307–320.

Lund, C., & Cois, A. (2018). Simultaneous social causation and social drift: Longitudinal analysis of depression and poverty in South Africa. *Journal of Affective Disorders, 229,* 396–402.

Luria, A. (1973). *The working brain.* New York: Basic Books.

Lussier, P., & Piché, L. (2008). Frotteurism: Psychopathology and theory. In D. R. Laws & W. T. O'Donohue (Eds.), *Sexual deviance: Theory, assessment, and treatment* (pp. 131–150). New York: Guilford Press.

Lyketsos, C. G., & Miller, D. S., & Neuropsychiatric Syndromes Professional Interest Area of the International Society to Advance Alzheimer's Research and Treatment. (2012). Addressing the Alzheimer's disease crisis through better understanding, treatment, and eventual prevention of associated neuropsychiatric syndromes. *Alzheimer's & Dementia: The Journal of the Alzheimer's Association, 8,* 60–64.

Lyman, R. (1997, April 15). Michael Dorris dies at 52: Wrote of his son's suffering. *New York Times,* p. 24.

Lynam, D. R., Caspi, A., Moffitt, T. E., Wikstrom, P. H., Loeber, R., & Novak, S. (2000). The interaction between impulsivity and neighborhood context on offending: The effects of impulsivity are stronger in poorer neighborhoods. *Journal of Abnormal Psychology, 109,* 563–574.

Lyness, J. M. (2004). Treatment of depressive conditions in later life: Real-world light for dark (or dim) tunnels. *JAMA, 291,* 1626–1628.

Lynn, S. J., Lilienfeld, S. O., Merckelbach, H., Giesbrecht, T., & van der Kloet, D. (2012). Dissociation and dissociative disorders: Challenging conventional wisdom. *Current Directions in Psychological Science, 21*(1), 48–53.

Lyons-Ruth, K., Holmes, B. M., Sasvari-Szekely, M., Ronai, Z., Nemoda, Z., & Pauls, D. (2007). Serotonin transporter polymorphism and borderline or antisocial traits among low-income young adults. *Psychiatric Genetics, 17,* 339–343.

M

MacArthur Research Network on Mental Health and the Law. (1998). Executive summary. http://ness.sys.Virginia.EDU/macarthur/violence.html (accessed June 1, 2006).

Madden, J. M., Lakoma, M. D., Lynch, F. L., Rusinak, D., Owen-Smith, A. A., Coleman, K. J., et al. (2017). Psychotropic medication use among insured children with autism spectrum disorder. *Journal of Autism and Developmental Disorders, 47*(1), 144–154.

Maeng, L. Y., & Milad, M. R. (2015). Sex differences in anxiety disorders: Interactions between fear, stress, and gonadal hormones. *Hormones and Behavior, 76,* 106–117.

Maher, B. A. (1966). *Principles of psychotherapy: An experimental approach.* New York: McGraw-Hill.

Maher, C. A., Lewis, L. K., Ferrar, K., Marshall, S., De Bourdeaudhuij, I., & Vandelanotte, C. (2014). Are health behavior change interventions that use online social networks effective? A systematic review. *Journal of Medical Internet Research, 16*(2), e40.

Maher, W. B., & Maher, B. A. (1985). Psychopathology: I. From ancient times to eighteenth century. In G. A. Kimble & K. Schlesinger (Eds.), *Topics in the history of psychology* (Vol. 2). Hillsdale, NJ: Erlbaum.

Mahler, M. (1968). *On human symbiosis and the vicissitudes of individuation: Vol. 1. Infantile psychosis.* New York: International Universities Press.

Maiorino, M. I., Bellastella, G., & Esposito, K. (2014). Diabetes and sexual dysfunction: Current perspectives. *Diabetes, Metabolic Syndrome and Obesity: Targets and Therapy, 7,* 95–105.

Maletzky, B. (1998). The paraphilias: Research and treatment. In P. E. Nathan (Ed.), *A guide to treatments that work* (pp. 472–500). New York: Oxford University Press.

Maletzky, B. M., & Field, G. (2003). The biological treatment of dangerous sexual offenders, a review and preliminary report of the Oregon pilot depo-Provera program. *Aggression and Violent Behavior, 8,* 391–412.

Malhi, G. S., Tanious, M., Das, P., Coulston, C. M., & Berk, M. (2013). Potential mechanisms of action of lithium in bipolar disorder. *CNS drugs, 27*(2), 135–153.

Mandel, H. (2009). *Here's the deal: Don't touch me.* New York: Bantam Books

Mandell, D., Siegle, G. J., Shutt, L., Feldmiller, J., & Thase, M. E. (2014). Neural substrates of trait ruminations in depression. *Journal of Abnormal Psychology, 123,* 35–48.

Manicavasagar, V., Silove, D., Rapee, R., Waters, F., & Momartin, S. (2001). Parent-child concordance for separation anxiety: A clinical study. *Journal of Affective Disorders, 65,* 81–84.

Mann, J. J. (2013). The serotonergic system in mood disorders and suicidal behaviour. *Philosophical Transactions of the Royal Society B, 368*(1615), 20120537.

Mannino, J. D. (1999). *Sexually speaking.* New York: McGraw-Hill.

Marangell, L. B. (2004). The importance of subsyndromal symptoms in bipolar disorder. *Journal of Clinical Psychiatry, 65*(Suppl. 10), 24–27.

Marazziti, D., Catena, M., & Pallanti, S. (2006). Pharmacologic treatment of obsessive-compulsive disorder. *Psychiatric Annals, 36,* 454–462.

March, D., Hatch, S. L., Morgan, C., Kirkbride, J. B., Bresnahan, M., Fearon, P., & Susser, E. (2008). Psychosis and place. *Epidemiologic Reviews, 30*(1), 84–100.

Marcos, L. R. (1979). Effects of interpreters on the evaluation of psychopathology in non-English-speaking patients. *American Journal of Psychiatry, 136,* 171–174.

Marder, S. R., & Galderisi, S. (2017). The current conceptualization of negative symptoms in schizophrenia. *World Psychiatry, 16*(1), 14–24.

Markovitz, P. J. (2004). Recent trends in the pharmacotherapy of personality disorders. *Journal of Personality Disorders, 18,* 99–101.

Marlatt, G. A., Baer, J. S., & Larimer, M. (1995). Preventing alcohol abuse in college students: A harm reduction approach. In G. M. Boyd, J. Howard, & R. A. Zucker (Eds.), *Alcohol problems among adolescents: Current directions in prevention research* (pp. 147–172). Hillsdale, NJ: Erlbaum.

Marlatt, G. A., Blume, A. W., & Parks, G. A. (2001). Integrating harm reduction therapy and traditional substance abuse treatment. *Journal of Psychoactive Drugs, 33,* 13–21.

Marlatt, G. A., Larimer, M. E., Baer, J. S., & Quigley, L. A. (1993). Harm reduction for alcohol problems: Moving beyond the controlled drinking economy. *Behavior Therapy, 24,* 461–503.

Marlatt, G. A., Larimer, M. E., & Witkiewitz, K. (Eds.). (2011). *Harm reduction: Pragmatic strategies for managing high-risk behaviors.* New York: Guilford.

Marlatt, G. A., & Witkiewitz, K. (2010). Update on harm reduction policy and intervention research. *Annual Review of Clinical Psychology, 6,* 591–606.

Marques, J. K., Wiederanders, M., Day, M., Nelson, C., & van Ommeren, A. (2005). Effects of a relapse prevention program on sexual recidivism: Final results from California's Sex Offender Treatment Evaluation Project (SOTEP). *Sex Abuse, 17,* 79–107.

Marroquín, B., & Nolen-Hoeksema, S. (2015). Emotion regulation and depressive symptoms: Close relationships as context and influence. *Journal of Personality and Social Psychology, 109,* 836–855.

Marroquín, B., Tennen, H., & Stanton, A. L. (2017). Coping, emotion regulation, and well-being: Intrapersonal and interpersonal processes. In M. D. Robinson & M. Eid (Eds.), *The happy mind: Cognitive contributions to well-being* (pp. 253–274). Cham: Springer.

Marshall, G. N., & Orlando, M. (2002). Acculturation and peritraumatic dissociation in young adult Latino survivors of community violence. *Journal of Abnormal Psychology, 111,* 166–174.

Marshall, T., Jones, D. P. H., Ramchandrani, P. G., Stein, A., & Bass, C. (2007). Intergenerational transmission of health beliefs in somatoform disorders. *British Journal of Psychiatry, 191,* 449–450.

Marshall, W. L., & Marshall, L. E. (2015). Psychological treatment of the paraphilias: A review and an appraisal of effectiveness. *Current Psychiatry Reports, 17*(6), 47.

Martins, C. M. S., de Carvalho Tofoli, S. M., Von Werne Baes, C., & Juruena, M. (2011). Analysis of the occurrence of early life stress in adult psychiatric patients: A systematic review. *Psychology & Neuroscience, 4,* 219–227.

Martínez-Taboas, A. (2005). Psychogenic seizures in an espiritismo context: The role of culturally sensitive psychotherapy. *Psychotherapy: Theory, Research, Practice, Training, 42,* 6–13.

Martorana, A., Esposito, Z., & Koch, G. (2010). Beyond the cholinergic hypothesis: Do current drugs work in Alzheimer's disease? *CNS Neuroscience & Therapeutics, 16,* 235–245.

Masheb, R. M., Grilo, C. M., & White, M. A. (2011). An examination of eating patterns in community women with bulimia nervosa and binge eating disorder. *International Journal of Eating Disorders, 44,* 618–624.

Masten, A. S., & Powell, J. L. (2003). A resilience framework for research, policy, and practice. In S. E. Luthar (Ed.), *Resilience and vulnerability: Adaptation in the context of childhood adversities* (pp. 1-25). New York: Cambridge University Press.

Masters, K. S., & Hooker, S. A. (2013). Religiousness/spirituality, cardiovascular disease, and cancer: Cultural integration for health research and intervention. *Journal of Consulting and Clinical Psychology, 81,* 206–216.

Masters, W. H., & Johnson, V. E. (1970). *Human sexual inadequacy.* Boston: Little, Brown.

Mataix-Cols, D., Frost, R. O., Pertusa, A., Clark, L. A., Saxena, S., Leckman, J. F., Stein, D. J., Matsunaga, H., & Wilhelm, S. (2010). Hoarding disorder: A new diagnosis for *DSM-V*? *Depression and Anxiety, 27,* 556–572.

Matarazzo, J. D. (1985). Psychotherapy. In G. A. Kimble & K. Schlesinger (Eds.), *Topics in the history of psychology* (pp. 219–250). Hillsdale, NJ: Erlbaum.

Mathews, A., & MacLeod, C. (2005). Cognitive vulnerability to emotional disorders. *Annual Review of Clinical Psychology, 1,* 167–196.

Matson, J. L., & Neal, D. (2009). Psychotropic medication use for challenging behaviors in persons with intellectual disabilities: An overview. *Research in Developmental Disabilities, 30,* 572–586.

Matt, G. E., Vasquez, C., & Campbell, W. K. (1992). Mood-congruent recall of affectively toned stimuli: A meta-analytic review. *Clinical Psychology Review, 12,* 227–255.

Matthews, K. A., Owens, J. F., Kuller, L. H., Sutton-Tyrrell, K., & Jansen-McWilliams, L. (1998). Are hostility and anxiety associated with carotid atherosclerosis in healthy postmenopausal women? *Psychosomatic Medicine, 5,* 633–638.

Matthiasdottir, E., Jonsson, S. H., & Kristjansson, A. L. (2012). Body weight dissatisfaction in the Icelandic adult population: A normative discontent? *European Journal of Public Health, 22,* 116–121.

Matthys, W., Vanderschuren, L. J., & Schutter, D. J. (2013). The neurobiology of oppositional defiant disorder and conduct disorder: Altered functioning in three mental domains. *Development and Psychopathology, 25*(1), 193–207.

Mattick, R. P., Breen, C., Kimber, J., Davoli, M., & Breen, R. (2003). Methadone maintenance therapy versus no opioid replacement therapy for opioid dependence. *Cochrane Database of Systematic Reviews, 2,* CD002209.

Mattila, M.-L., Kielinen, M., Linna, S.-S., Jussila, K., Ebeling, H., Bloigu, R., Joseph, R. M., & Moilanen, I. (2011). Autism spectrum disorders according to *DSM-IV-TR* and comparison with *DSM-5* draft criteria: An epidemiological study. *Journal of the American Academy of Child and Adolescent Psychiatry, 50,* 583–592.

Maughan, B., Pickles, A., Rowe, R., Costello, E. J., & Angold, A. (2000). Developmental trajectories of aggressive and non-aggressive conduct problems. *Journal of Quantitative Criminology, 16,* 199–221.

Maughan, B., Rowe, R., Messer, J., Goodman, R., & Meltzer, H. (2004). Conduct disorder and oppositional defiant disorder in a national sample: Developmental epidemiology. *Journal of Child Psychology & Psychiatry, 45,* 609–621.

Mausbach, B. T., Coon, D. W., Depp, C., Rabinowitz, Y. G., Wilson-Arias, E., Kraemer, H. C., Thompson, L. W., Lane, G., & Gallagher-Thompson, D. (2004). Ethnicity and time to institutionalization of dementia patients: A comparison of Latina and Caucasian female family caregivers. *Journal of the American Geriatrics Society, 52,* 1077–1084.

Mayberg, H. S., Lozano, A. M., Voon, V., et al. (2005). Deep brain stimulation for treatment-resistant depression. *Neuron, 45,* 651–660.

Mayou, R., Bryant, B., & Ehlers, A. (2001). Prediction of psychological outcomes one year after a motor vehicle accident. *American Journal of Psychiatry, 158,* 1231–1238.

Mayo-Wilson, E., Dias, S., Mavranezouli, I., Kew, K., Clark, D. M., Ades, A. E., & Pilling, S. (2014). Psychological and pharmacological interventions for social anxiety disorder in adults: A systematic review and network meta-analysis. *Lancet Psychiatry, 1*(5), 368–376.

Mays, V. M., Cochran, S. D., & Barnes, N. W. (2007). Race, race-based discrimination, and health outcomes among African Americans. *Annual Review of Psychology, 58,* 201–225.

Mazure, C. M. (1998). Life stressors as risk factors in depression. *Clinical Psychology: Science & Practice, 5,* 291–313.

Mazzoni, G., & Loftus, E. F. (1998). Dream interpretations can change beliefs about the past. *Psychotherapy, 35,* 177–187.

McCabe, M. P., Sharlip, I. D., Lewis, R., Atalla, E., Balon, R., Fisher, A. D., et al. (2016). Incidence and prevalence of sexual dysfunction in women and men: A consensus statement from the Fourth International Consultation on Sexual Medicine 2015. *Journal of Sexual Medicine, 13*(2), 144–152.

McCabe, R., Antony, M., Summerfeldt, L., Liss, A., & Swinson, R. (2003). Preliminary examination of the relationship between anxiety disorders in adults and self-reported history of teasing or bullying experiences. *Cognitive Behaviour Therapy, 32,* 187–193.

McCabe, S. E., Cranford, J. A., & West, B. T. (2008). Trends in prescription drug abuse and dependence, co-occurrence with other substance use disorders, and treatment utilization: Results from two national surveys. *Addictive Behaviors, 33,* 1297–1305.

McCaffery, J. M., Frasure-Smith, N., Dubé, M. P., Théroux, P., Rouleau, G. A., Duan, Q., & Lesperance, F. (2006). Common genetic vulnerability to depressive symptoms and coronary artery disease: A review and development of candidate genes related to inflammation and serotonin. *Psychosomatic Medicine, 68,* 187–200.

McCarthy, B. W. (1989). Cognitive-behavioral strategies and techniques in the treatment of early ejaculation. In S. R. Leiblum & R. C. Rosen (Eds.), *Principles and practice of* *sex therapy: Update for the 1990s* (pp. 141–167). New York: Guilford Press.

McCarthy, B. W. (2001). Relapse prevention strategies and techniques with erectile dysfunction. *Journal of Sex & Marital Therapy, 27,* 1–8.

McCarthy, B. W., & Ross, L. W. (2017). Integrating sexual concepts and interventions into couple therapy. In J. Fitzgerald (Ed.), *Foundations for couples' therapy: Research for the real world* (pp. 355–364). New York: Routledge.

McCarthy, B., & Ross, L. W. (2018). Maintaining sexual desire and satisfaction in securely bonded couples. *Family Journal: Counseling and Therapy for Couples and Families.*

McCarthy, M. (1990). The thin ideal, depression and eating disorders in women. *Behaviour Research & Therapy, 28,* 205–215.

McCloskey, M. S., Noblett, K. L., Deffenbacher, J. L., Gollan, J. K., & Coccaro, E. F. (2008). Cognitive-behavioral therapy for intermittent explosive disorder: A pilot randomized clinical trial. *Journal of Consulting and Clinical Psychology, 76,* 876–886.

McConaghy, N. (1998). Paedophilia: A review of the evidence. *Australian & New Zealand Journal of Psychiatry, 32,* 252–265.

McCormick, M. C., McCarton, C., Brooks-Gunn, J., Belt, P., & Gross, R. T. (1998). The Infant Health and Development Program: Interim summary. *Developmental & Behavioral Pediatrics, 19,* 359–370.

McCrady, B. S. (2014). Alcohol use disorders. In D. H. Barlow (Ed.), *Clinical handbook of psychological disorders: A step-by-step treatment manual* (pp. 533–587). New York: Guilford.

McCrady, B. S., Epstein, E. E., Cook, S., Jensen, N., & Hildebrandt, T. (2009). A randomized trial of individual and couple behavioral alcohol treatment for women. *Journal of Consulting and Clinical Psychology, 77,* 243–256.

McCrae, R. R., & Costa, P. T. (1999). A five-factor theory of personality. In L. A. Pervin (Ed.), *Handbook of personality: Theory and research* (2nd ed., pp. 139–153). New York: Guilford Press.

McCrae, R. R., & Costa, P. T. (2013). Introduction to the empirical and theoretical status of the five-factor model of personality traits. In T. A. Widiger & P. T. Costa (Ed.), *Personality disorders and the five-factor model of personality* (3rd ed., pp. 15–27). Washington, DC: American Psychological Association.

McCrae, R. R., & Terracciano, A. (2005). Universal features of personality traits from the observer's perspective: Data from 50 cultures. *Journal of Personality and Social Psychology, 88,* 547–561.

McEwen, B. S. (2004). Protection and damage from acute and chronic stress: Allostasis and allostatic overload and relevance to the pathophysiology of psychiatric disorders. *Annals of the New York Academy of Sciences, 1032*(1), 1–7.

McFarlane, A. C., Barton, C. A., Yehuda, R., & Wittert, G. (2011). Cortisol response to acute trauma and risk of posttraumatic stress disorder. *Psychoneuroendocrinology, 36,* 720–727.

McGovern, C. M. (1985). *Masters of madness.* Hanover, NH: University Press of New England.

McGreevy, M. A., Steadman, H. J., & Callahan, L. A. (1991). The negligible effects of California's 1982 reform of the insanity defense test. *American Journal of Psychiatry, 148,* 744–750.

McGue, M., Iacono, W. G., Legrand, L. N., Malone, S., & Elkins, I. (2001). Origins and consequences of age at first drink: I. Associations with substance-use disorders, disinhibitory behavior and psychopathology, and P3 amplitude. *Alcoholism: Clinical & Experimental Research, 25,* 1156–1165.

McGuffin, P., Rijsdijk, F., Andrew, M., Sham, P., Katz, R., & Cardno, A. (2003). The heritability of bipolar affective disorder and the genetic relationship to unipolar depression. *Archives of General Psychiatry, 60,* 497–502.

McGuire, J. F., Piacentini, J., Brennan, E. A., Lewin, A. B., Murphy, T. K., Small, B. J., & Storch, E. A. (2014). A meta-analysis of behavior therapy for Tourette syndrome. *Journal of Psychiatric Research, 50,* 106–112.

McGurk, S. R., Mueser, K. T., Mischel, R., Adams, R., Harvey, P. D., McClure, M. M., Look, A. E., Leung, W. W., & Siever, L. J. (2013). Vocational functioning in schizotypal and paranoid personality disorders. *Psychiatry Research.*

McHugh, R. K., Hearon, B. A., & Otto, M. W. (2010). Cognitive behavioral therapy for substance use disorders. *Psychiatric Clinics, 33*(3), 511–525.

McIntosh, J. L. (1995). Suicide prevention in the elderly (age 65–99). *Suicide & Life-Threatening Behaviors, 25,* 180–192.

McIntosh, R. C., & Rosselli, M. (2012). Stress and coping in women living with HIV: A meta-analytic review. *AIDS and Behavior, 16,* 2144–2159.

McKinnon, D. H., McLeod, S., & Reilly, S. (2008). The prevalence of stuttering, voice, and speech-sound disorders in primary school students in Australia. *Language, Speech, and Hearing Services in Schools, 38,* 5–15.

McLaughlin, J., O'Carroll, R. E., & O'Connor, R. C. (2012). Intimate partner abuse and suicidality: A systematic review. *Clinical Psychology Review, 32*(8), 677–689.

McMillan, T. M., & Rachman, S. J. (1987). Fearlessness and courage: A laboratory study of paratrooper veterans of the Falklands War. *British Journal of Psychology, 78,* 375–383.

McNally, R. J. (2002). Anxiety sensitivity and panic disorder. *Biological Psychiatry, 52*(10), 938–946.

McNally, R. J. (2003). Recovering memories of trauma: A view from the laboratory. *Current Directions in Psychological Science, 12,* 32–35.

McNally, R. J. (2017). False memories in the laboratory and in life: Commentary on Brewin and Andrews (2016). *Applied Cognitive Psychology, 31*(1), 40–41.

McNally, R. J., Clancy, S. A., & Schacter, D. L. (2001). Directed forgetting of trauma cues in adults reporting repressed or recovered memories of childhood sexual abuse. *Journal of Abnormal Psychology, 110,* 151–156.

McNally, R. J., Clancy, S. A., Schacter, D. L., & Pitman, R. K. (2000a). Cognitive processing of trauma cues in adults reporting repressed, recovered, or continuous memories of childhood sexual abuse. *Journal of Abnormal Psychology, 109,* 355–359.

McNally, R. J., Clancy, S. A., Schacter, D. L., & Pitman, R. K. (2000b). Personality profiles, dissociation, and absorption in women reporting repressed, recovered, or continuous memories of childhood sexual abuse. *Journal of Consulting Clinical Psychology, 68,* 1033–1037.

McPartland, J., Reichow, B., & Volkmar, F. R. (2012). Sensitivity and specificity of proposed *DSM-5* diagnostic criteria for autism spectrum disorder. *Journal of the American Academy of Child & Adolescent Psychiatry, 51,* 368–383.

McRobbie, H., Bullen, C., Hartmann-Boyce, J., & Hajek, P. (2014). Electronic cigarettes for smoking cessation and reduction. Cochrane Library 12: CD010216.

McWilliams, N. (2011). *Psychoanalytic diagnosis: Understanding personality structure in the clinical process.* Guilford Press.

Meaney, M. (2010). Epigenetics and the biological definition of gene x environment interactions. *Child Development, 81,* 41–79.

Mechanic, D., & Olfson, M. (2016). The relevance of the Affordable Care Act for improving mental health care. *Annual Review of Clinical Psychology, 12,* 515–542.

Mednick, B., Reznick, C., Hocevar, D., & Baker, R. (1987). Long-term effects of parental divorce on young adult male crime. *Journal of Youth & Adolescence, 16,* 31–45.

Mednick, S. A., Machon, R. A., Huttunen, M. O., & Bonett, D. (1988). Adult schizophrenia following prenatal exposure to an influenza epidemic. *Archives of General Psychiatry, 45,* 189–192.

Mednick, S. A., Watson, J. B., Huttunen, M., Cannon, T. D., Katila, H., Machon, R., Mednick, B., Hollister, M., Parnas, J., Schulsinger, F., Sajaniemi, N., Voldsgaard, P., Pyhala, R., Gutkind, D., & Wang, X. (1998). A two-hit working model of the etiology of schizophrenia. In M. F. Lenzenweger & R. H. Dworkin (Eds.), *Origins of the development of schizophrenia* (pp. 27–66). Washington, DC: American Psychological Association.

Melton, G. B., Petrila, J., Poythress, N. G., Slobogin, C., Otto, R. K., Mossman, D., & Condie, L. O. (2017). *Psychological evaluations for the courts: A handbook for mental health professionals and lawyers.* New York: Guilford.

Mendrek, A., & Mancini-Marie, A. (2016). Sex/gender differences in the brain and cognition in schizophrenia. *Neuroscience & Biobehavioral Reviews, 67,* 57–78.

Menezes, N. M., Arenovich, T., & Zipursky, R. B. (2006). A systematic review of longitudinal outcomes studies of first-episode psychosis. *Psychological Medicine, 36,* 1349–1362.

Mennin, D. S., Fresco, D. M., O'Toole, M. S., & Heimberg, R. G. (2018). A randomized controlled trial of emotion regulation therapy for generalized anxiety disorder with and without co-occurring depression. *Journal of Consulting and Clinical Psychology, 86*(3), 268–281.

Merai, R., Siegel, C., Rakotz, M., Basch, P., Wright, J., Wong, B., & Thorpe, P. (2016). CDC grand rounds: A public health approach to detect and control hypertension. *Morbidity and Mortality Weekly Report, 65*(45), 1261–1264.

Merikangas, K. R., Akiskal, H. S., Angst, J., Greenberg, P. E., Hirschfield, R. M. A., Petukhova, M., & Kessler, R. C. (2007). Lifetime and 12-month prevalence of bipolar spectrum disorder in the national comorbidity survey replication. *Archives of General Psychiatry, 64,* 543–552.

Merikangas, K. R., Jin, R., He, J.-P., Kessler, R. C., Lee, S., Sampson, N. A., Vianna, M. C., Andrade, L. H., Hu, C., Karam, E. G., Ladea, M., Medina-Mora, M. E., Ono, Y., Posada-Villa, J., Sagar, R., Wells, J. E., & Zarkov, Z. (2011). Prevalence and correlates of bipolar spectrum disorder in the World Mental Health Survey Initiative. *Archive of General Psychiatry, 68*(3), 241–251.

Merikangas, K. R., & Knight, E. (2009). Epidemiology of adolescent depression. In S. Nolen-Hoeksema & L. Hilt (Eds.), *Handbook of depression in adolescents* (pp. 53–74). New York: Routledge.

Merikangas, K. R., Lieb, R., Wittchen, H.-U., & Avenevoli, S. (2003). Family and high-risk studies of social anxiety disorder. *Acta Psychiatrica Scandinavica, 108*(Suppl. 417), 28–37.

Merrill, L. L., Thomsen, C. J., Sinclair, B. B., Gold, S. R., & Milner, J. S. (2001). Predicting the impact of child sexual abuse on women: The role of abuse severity, parental support, and coping strategies. *Journal of Consulting & Clinical Psychology, 69,* 992–1006.

Meston, C. M., & Bradford, A. (2007). Sexual dysfunctions in women. *Annual Review of Clinical Psychology, 3,* 233–256.

Meuret, A. E., Kroll, J., & Ritz, T. (2017). Panic disorder comorbidity with medical conditions and treatment implications. *Annual Review of Clinical Psychology, 13,* 209–240.

Meyer, I. H. (2003). Prejudice, social stress, and mental health in lesbian, gay, and bisexual populations: Conceptual issues and research evidence. *Psychological Bulletin, 129,* 674–697.

Meyer, R. G., & Weaver, C. M. (2006). *Law and mental health: A case-based approach.* New York: Guilford Press.

Mian, M., Shah, J., Dalpiaz, A., Schwamb, R., Miao, Y., Warren, K., & Khan, S. (2015). Shaken baby syndrome: A review. *Fetal and Pediatric Pathology, 34*(3), 169–175.

Micallef, J., & Blin, O. (2001). Neurobiology and clinical pharmacology of obsessive-compulsive disorder. *Clinical Neuropharmacology, 24,* 191–207.

Michael, R. T., Gagnon, J. H., Laumann, E., & Kolata, G. (1994). *Sex in America: A definitive survey.* Boston: Little, Brown.

Micheau, J., & Marighetto, A. (2011). Acetylcholine and memory: A long, complex and chaotic but still living relationship. *Behavioural Brain Research, 221,* 24–29.

Mier, D., Lis, S., Esslinger, C., Sauer, C., Hagenhoff, M., Ulferts, J., et al. (2012). Neuronal correlates of social cognition in borderline personality disorder. *Social Cognitive and Affective Neuroscience, 8*(5), 531–537.

Mignot, E., Lammers, G. J., Ripley, B., Okun, M., Nevsimalova, S., Overeem, S., et al. (2002). The role of cerebrospinal fluid hypocretin measurement in the diagnosis of narcolepsy and other hypersomnias. *Archives of Neurology, 59,* 1553.

Mihura, J. L., Meyer, G. J., Dumitrascu, N., & Bombel, G. (2013). The validity of individual Rorschach variables: Systematic reviews and meta-analyses of the comprehensive system. *Psychological Bulletin, 139*(3), 548–605.

Miklowitz, D. J. (2010). *The bipolar disorder survival guide* (2nd ed.). New York: Guilford Press.

Miklowitz, D. J., & Chung, B. (2016). Family-focused therapy for bipolar disorder: Reflections on 30 years of research. *Family Process, 55*(3), 483–499.

Miklowitz, D. J., Schneck, C. D., Singh, M. K., Taylor, D. O., George, E. L., Cosgrove, V. E., et al. (2013). Early intervention for symptomatic youth at risk for bipolar disorder: A randomized trial of family-focused therapy. *Journal of the American Academy of Child & Adolescent Psychiatry, 52*(2), 121–131.

Milad, M. R., & Rauch, S. L. (2012). Obsessive-compulsive disorder: Beyond segregated cortico-striatal pathways. *Trends in Cognitive Sciences, 16,* 43–51.

Milam, J. E., Richardson, J. L., Marks, G., Kemper, C. A., & McCutchan, A. J. (2004). The roles of dispositional optimism and pessimism in HIV disease progression. *Psychology & Health, 19,* 167–181.

Miller, J. D., Campbell, W. K., & Pilkonis, P. A. (2007). Narcissistic Personality Disorder: Relations with distress and functional impairment. *Comprehensive Psychiatry, 48,* 170–177.

Miller, J. D., Lynam, D. R., Hyatt, C. S., & Campbell, W. K. (2017). Controversies in narcissism. *Annual Review of Clinical Psychology, 13,* 291–315.

Miller, M., & Hemenway, D. (2008). Guns and suicide in the United States. *New England Journal of Medicine, 359,* 989–991.

Miller, T. Q., Smith, T. W., Turner, C. W., & Guijarro, M. L. (1996). Meta-analytic review of research on hostility and physical health. *Psychological Bulletin, 119,* 322–348.

Miller, W. R. (1983). Motivational interviewing with problem drinkers. *Behavioural Psychotherapy, 11,* 147–172.

Miller, W. R., & Rollnick, S. (2012). *Motivational interviewing: Helping people change* (3rd ed.). New York: Guilford.

Miller, W. R., & Rose, G. S. (2009). Toward a theory of motivational interviewing. *American Psychologist, 64,* 527–537.

Milliken, C. S., Auchterlonie, J. L., & Hoge, C. W. (2007). Longitudinal assessment of mental health problems among active and reserve component soldiers returning from the Iraq war. *JAMA, 298,* 2141–2148.

Millon, T. (1969). *Modern psychopathology: A biosocial approach to maladaptive learning and functioning.* Philadelphia: Saunders.

Millon, T., Grossman, S., Millon, C., Meagher, S., & Ramnath, R. (2004). *Personality disorders in modern life* (2nd ed.). Hoboken, NJ: Wiley.

Mineka, S. (1985). Animal models of anxiety based disorders: Their usefulness and limitations. In A. H. Tuma & J. Maser (Eds.), *Anxiety and the anxiety disorders* (pp. 199–244). Hillsdale, NJ: Erlbaum.

Mineka, S., Davidson, M., Cook, M., & Keir, R. (1984). Observational conditioning of snake fear in rhesus monkeys. *Journal of Abnormal Psychology, 93,* 355–372.

Mineka, S., Gunnar, M., & Champoux, M. (1986). Control and early socioemotional development: Infant rhesus monkeys reared in controllable versus uncontrollable environments. *Child Development, 57,* 1241–1256.

Mineka, S., & Zinbarg, R. (2006). A contemporary learning theory perspective on the etiology of anxiety disorders: It's not what you thought it was. *American Psychologist, 61,* 10–26.

Minor, K. S., & Cohen, A. S. (2010). Affective reactivity of speech disturbances in schizotypy. *Journal of Psychiatric Research, 44,* 99–105.

Minuchin, S., Rosman, B. L., & Baker, L. (1978). *Psychosomatic families: Anorexia nervosa in context.* Cambridge, MA: Harvard University Press.

Miranda, J., Bernal, G., Lau, A., Kohn, L., Hwang, W. C., & La Fromboise, T. (2005). State of the science on psychosocial interventions for ethnic minorities. *Annual Review of Clinical Psychology, 1,* 113–142.

Mirijello, A., D'Angelo, C., Ferrulli, A., Vassallo, G., Antonelli, M., Caputo, F., et al. (2015). Identification and management of alcohol withdrawal syndrome. *Drugs, 75,* 353–365.

Mirsky, A. E., Bieliauskas, L. A., French, L. M., Van Kammen, D. P., Joensson, E., & Sedvall, S. (2000). A 39-year follow-up on the Genain quadruplets. *Schizophrenia Bulletin, 26,* 699–708.

Mitler, M. M., & Miller, J. C. (1995). Some practical considerations and policy implications of studies and sleep patterns. *Behavioral Medicine, 21,* 184–185.

Mitropoulou, V., Barch, D., Harvey, P., Maldari, L., New, B., Cornblatt, B., & Siever, L. (2003). Two studies of attentional processing in schizotypal personality disorder. *Schizophrenia Research, 60,* S148.

Mittal, V. A., Willhite, R., Daley, M., Bearden, C. E., Niendam, T., Ellman, L. M., & Cannon, T. D. (2009). Obstetric complications and risk for conversion to psychosis among individuals at high clinical risk. *Early Intervention in Psychiatry, 3,* 226–230.

Moffitt, T. E. (1993). The neuropsychology of conduct disorder. *Development & Psychopathology, 5,* 135–151.

Moffitt, T. E. (2006). Life-course persistent versus adolescence-limited antisocial behavior. In D. Cicchetti & D. J. Cohen (Eds.), *Developmental psychopathology: Vol. 3. Risk, disorder, and adaptation* (2nd ed., pp. 570–598). New York: Wiley.

Moffitt, T. E., Arseneault, L., Jaffee, S. R., Kim-Cohen, J., Koenen, K. C., Odgers, C. L., Slutske, W. S., & Viding, E. (2008). Research review: *DSM-V* conduct disorder: Research needs for an evidence base. *Journal of Child Psychology and Psychiatry, 49,* 3–33.

Moffitt, T. E., Brammer, G. L., Caspi, A., Fawcet, J. P., Raleigh, M., Yuwiler, A., & Silva, P. A. (1998). Whole blood serotonin relates to violence in an epidemiological study. *Biological Psychiatry, 43,* 446–457.

Moffitt, T. E., & Caspi, A. (2001). Childhood predictors differentiate life-course persistent and adolescence-limited antisocial pathways among males and females. *Development & Psychopathology, 13,* 355–375.

Moffitt, T. E., Caspi, A., Harrington, H., & Milne, B. J. (2002). Males on the life-course-persistent and adolescence-limited antisocial pathways: Follow-up at age 26 years. *Development and Psychopathology, 14,* 179–207.

Moffitt, T. E., Caspi, A., Rutter, M., & Silva, P. A. (2001). *Sex differences in antisocial behaviour: Conduct disorder, delinquency, and violence in the Dunedin Longitudinal Study.* Cambridge: Cambridge University Press.

Moffitt, T. E., Caspi, A., Taylor, A., Kokaua, J., Milne, B. J., Polanczyk, G., & Poulton, R. (2010). How common are common mental disorders? Evidence that lifetime prevalence rates are doubled by prospective versus retrospective ascertainment. *Psychological Medicine, 40,* 899–909.

Molina, B. S., Hinshaw, S. P., Swanson, J. M., Arnold, L. E., Vitiello, B., Jensen, P. S., Epstein, J. N., Hoza, B., Hechtman, L., Abikoff, H. B., Elliott, G. R., Greenhill, L. L., Newcorn, J. H., Wells, K. C., Wigal, T., Gibbons, R. D., Hur, K., & Houck, P. R. (2009). The MTA at 8 years: Prospective follow-up of children treated for combined-type ADHD in a multisite study. *Journal of the American Academy of Child and Adolescent Psychiatry, 48,* 484–500.

Molnar, B. E., Berkman, L. F., & Buka, S. L. (2001). Psychopathology, childhood sexual abuse and other childhood adversities: Relative links to subsequent suicidal behavior in the U.S. *Psychological Medicine, 31,* 965–977.

Monahan, J., Bonnie, R. J., Appelbaum, P. S., Hyde, P. S., Steadman, H. J., & Swartz, M. S. (2001). Mandated community treatment: Beyond outpatient commitment. *Psychiatric Services, 52,* 1198–1205.

Monahan, J., Redlich, A. D., Swanson, J., Robbins, P. C., Appelbaum, P. S., Petrila, J., . . . & McNiel, D. E. (2005). Use of leverage to improve adherence to psychiatric treatment in the community. *Psychiatric Services, 56*(1), 37–44.

Monahan, J., & Skeem, J. L. (2014). The evolution of violence risk assessment. *CNS Spectrums, 19*(5), 419–424.

Monahan, J., & Walker, L. (2014). *Social science in law: Cases and materials* (8th ed.). Westbury, NY: Foundation Press.

Monroe, S. M. (2010). Recurrence in major depression: Assessing risk indicators in the context of risk estimates. In C. S. Richards & M. G. Perri (Eds.), *Relapse prevention for depression* (pp. 27–49). Washington, DC: American Psychological Association.

Montejo, A. L., Montejo, L., & Navarro-Cremades, F. (2015). Sexual side-effects of antidepressant and antipsychotic drugs. *Current Opinion in Psychiatry, 28*(6), 418–423.

Mora, G. (2008). Renaissance conceptions and treatments of madness. In E. Wallace, IV, & J. Gach (Eds.), *History of psychiatry and medical psychology: With an epilogue on psychiatry and the mind-body relation* (pp. 199–226). New York: Springer Science.

Moran, E. K., & Kring, A. M. (2018). Anticipatory emotion in schizophrenia. *Clinical Psychological Science, 6*(1), 63–75.

Moreno, P. I., Wiley, J. F., & Stanton, A. L. (2017). Coping through emotional approach: The utility of processing and expressing emotions in responding to stressors. In

Prins, S. J. (2014). Prevalence of mental illnesses in US state prisons: A systematic review. *Psychiatric Services, 65*(7), 862–872.

Prochaska, J. O. (1995). Common problems: Common solutions. *Clinical Psychology: Science & Practice, 2,* 101–105.

Prochaska, J. O., & Norcross, J. C. (2014). Systemic therapies. In J. O. Prochaska & J. C. Norcross (Eds.), *Systems of psychotherapy: A transtheoretical analysis* (9th ed., pp. 289–321). New York: Oxford University Press.

Proctor, A., Yairi, E., Duff, M. C., & Zhang, J. (2008). Prevalence of stuttering in African American preschoolers. *Journal of Speech, Language and Hearing Research, 51,* 1465–1479.

Procyshyn, R. M., Bezchlibnyk-Butler, K. Z., & Jeffries, J. J. (Eds.). (2017). *Clinical handbook of psychotropic drugs.* Boston: Hogrefe.

Project MATCH Research Group. (1998). Matching alcoholism treatments to client heterogeneity: Treatment main effects and matching effects on drinking during treatment. *Journal of Studies on Alcohol, 59,* 631–639.

Przeworski, A., Newman, M. G., Pincus, A. L., Kasoff, M. B., Yamasaki, A. S., Castonguay, L. G., & Berlin, K. S. (2011). Interpersonal pathoplasticity in individuals with generalized anxiety disorder. *Journal of Abnormal Psychology, 120,* 286–298.

Pulay, A. J., Stinson, F. S., Dawson, D. A., Goldstein, R. B., Chou, S. P., et al. (2009). Prevalence, correlates, disability, and comorbidity of *DSM-IV* schizotypal personality disorder: Results from the wave 2 National Epidemiologic Survey on Alcohol and Related Conditions. *Primary Care Companion, Journal of Clinical Psychiatry, 11,* 53–67.

Putnam, F., Zahn, T., & Post, R. (1990). Differential autonomic nervous system activity in multiple personality disorder. *Physical Review, 31,* 251–260.

Putnam, F. W., Guroff, J. J., Silberman, E. K., & Barban, L. (1986). The clinical phenomenology of multiple personality disorder: Review of 100 recent cases. *Journal of Clinical Psychiatry, 47,* 285–293.

Putnam, F. W., & Lowenstein, R. J. (1993). Treatment of multiple personality disorder: A survey of current practices. *American Journal of Psychiatry, 150,* 1048–1052.

R

Rabin, L. A., Smart, C. M., & Amariglio, R. E. (2017). Subjective cognitive decline in preclinical Alzheimer's disease. *Annual Review of Clinical Psychology, 13,* 369–396.

Rachman, S. (1993). Obsessions, responsibility and guilt. *Behaviour Research & Therapy, 31,* 149–154.

Rachman, S. (1997). A cognitive theory of obsessions. *Behaviour Research & Therapy, 35,* 667–682.

Rachman, S., & deSilva, P. (1978). Abnormal and normal obsessions. *Behaviour Research & Therapy, 16,* 233–248.

Raikkonen, K., Matthews, K. A., Flory, J. D., Owens, J. F., & Gump, B. B. (1999). Effects of optimism, pessimism, and trait anxiety on ambulatory blood pressure and mood during everyday life. *Journal of Personality & Social Psychology, 76,* 104–113.

Raine, A. (2018). Antisocial personality as a neurodevelopmental disorder. *Annual Review of Clinical Psychology, 14,* 259–289

Raine, A., Lencz, T., Bihrle, S., LaCasse, L., & Colletti, P. (2000). Reduced prefrontal gray matter volume and reduced autonomic activity in antisocial personality disorder. *Archives of General Psychiatry, 57*(2), 119–127.

Raine, A., Yang, Y., Narr, K. L., & Toga, A. W. (2011). Sex differences in orbitofrontal gray as a partial explanation for sex differences in antisocial personality. *Molecular Psychiatry, 16,* 227–236.

Rapee, R. M., Schniering, C. A., & Hudson, J. L. (2009). Anxiety disorders during childhood and adolescence: Origins and treatment. *Annual Review of Clinical Psychology, 5,* 311–341.

Rapoport, J. L. (1989). The biology of obsessions and compulsions. *Scientific American,* 83–89.

Rapoport, J. L. (1990). *The boy who couldn't stop washing.* New York: Plume.

Rapoport, J. L. (1991). Recent advances in obsessive-compulsive disorder. *Neuropsychopharmacology, 5,* 1–10.

Rapoport, J. L., Jensen, P. S., Inoff-Germain, G., Weissman, M. M., Greenwald, S., Narrow, W. E., Lahey, B. B., & Canino, G. (2000). Childhood obsessive-compulsive disorder in the NIMH MECA study: Parent versus child identification of cases. *Journal of Anxiety Disorders, 14,* 535–548.

Rasmussen, H. N., Scheier, M. F., & Greenhouse, J. B. (2009). Optimism and physical health: A meta-analytic review. *Annals of Behavioral Medicine, 37*(3), 239–256.

Rauch, S. L., Phillips, K. A., Segal, E., Makris, N., Shin, L. M., Whalen, P. J., Jenike, M. A., Caviness, V. S., Jr., & Kennedy, D. N. (2003). A preliminary morphometric magnetic resonance imaging study of regional brain volumes in body dysmorphic disorder. *Psychiatry Research: Neuroimaging, 122,* 13–19.

Ravussin, E., Valencia, M. E., Esparza, J., Bennett, P. H., & Schulz, L. O. (1994). Effects of a traditional lifestyle on obesity in Pima Indians. *Diabetes Care, 17,* 1067–1074.

Ray, O., & Ksir, C. (1993). *Drugs, society, and human behavior.* St. Louis: C. V. Mosby.

Razran, G. (1961). The observable unconscious and the inferable conscious in current Soviet psychophysiology: Interoceptive conditioning, semantic conditioning, and the orienting reflex. *Psychological Review, 68,* 81–150.

Reas, D. L., & Grilo, C. M. (2008). Review and meta-analysis of pharmacotherapy for binge-eating disorder. *Obesity, 16,* 2024–2038.

Redlich, A. D., Steadman, H. J., Monahan, J., Robbins, P. C., & Petrila, J. (2006). Patterns of practice in mental health courts: A national survey. *Law and Human Behavior, 30,* 347–362.

Reed, G. M., Kemeny, M. E., Taylor, S. E., & Visscher, B. R. (1999). Negative HIV-specific expectancies and AIDS-related bereavement as predictors of symptom onset in asymptomatic HIV-positive gay men. *Health Psychology, 18,* 354–363.

Regier, D. A., Narrow, W. E., Rae, D. S., Manderscheid, R. W., Locke, B. Z., & Goodwin, F. K. (1993). The de facto U.S. mental and addictive disorders service system. *Archives of General Psychiatry, 50,* 85–94.

Rehm, J., Greenfield, T. K., & Rogers, J. D. (2001). Average volume of alcohol consumption, patterns of drinking, and all-cause mortality: Results from the U.S. National Alcohol Survey. *American Journal of Epidemiology, 153,* 64–71.

Rehm, J., Samokhvalov, A. V., Neuman, M. G., Room, R., Parry, C., Lönnroth, K., Patra, J., Poznyak, V., & Popova, S. (2009). The association between alcohol use, alcohol use disorders and tuberculosis (TB). A systematic review. *BMC Public Health, 9,* 450.

Rehm, L. P. (1977). A self-control model of depression. *Behavior Therapy, 8,* 787–804.

Reichow, B., Barton, E. E., Boyd, B. A., & Hume, K. (2012). Early intensive behavioral intervention (EIBI) for young children with autism spectrum disorders (ASD). *Cochrane Database of Systematic Reviews, 10,* CD009260.

Reid, R. C., Carpenter, B. N., Hook, J. N., Garos, S., Manning, J. C., Gilliland, R., et al. (2012). Report of findings in a *DSM-5* field trial for hypersexual disorder. *Journal of Sexual Medicine, 9,* 2868–2877.

Reinares, M., Bonnin, C. M., Hidalgo-Mazzei, D., Sánchez-Moreno, J., Colom, F., & Vieta, E. (2016). The role of family interventions in bipolar disorder: A systematic review. *Clinical Psychology Review, 43,* 47–57.

Reitan, R. M., & Davidson, L. A. (1974). *Clinical neuropsychology: Current status and applications.* Washington, DC: V. H. Winston.

Resick, P. A., Wachen, J. S., Dondanville, K. A., Pruiksma, K. E., Yarvis, J. S., Peterson, A. L., et al. (2017). Effect of group vs individual cognitive processing therapy in active-duty military seeking treatment for posttraumatic stress disorder: A randomized clinical trial. *JAMA Psychiatry, 74*(1), 28–36.

Resick, P. A., Williams, L. F., Suvak, M. K., Monson, C. M., & Gradus, J. L. (2012). Long-term outcomes of cognitive-behavioral treatments for posttraumatic stress disorder among female rape survivors. *Journal of Consulting and Clinical Psychology, 80*(2), 201–210.

Resnick, H. S., Kilpatrick, D. G., Dansky, B. S., & Saunders, B. E. (1993). Prevalence of civilian trauma and posttraumatic stress disorder in a representative national sample of women. *Journal of Consulting & Clinical Psychology, 61,* 984–991.

Reynolds, K., Pietrzak, R. H., El-Gabalawy, R., Mackenzie, C. S., & Sareen, J. (2015). Prevalence of psychiatric disorders in US older adults: Findings from a nationally representative survey. *World Psychiatry, 14*(1), 74–81.

Rhebergen, D., Beekman, A. T. F., de Graaf, R., Nolen, W. A., Spijker, J., Hoogendijk, W. J., & Pennix, B. W. J. H. (2010). Trajectories of recovery of social and physical functioning in major depression, dysthymic disorder, and double depression: A 3-year follow-up. *Journal of Affective Disorders, 124,* 148–156.

Richardson, J. L., Shelton, D. R., Krailo, M., & Levine, A. M. (1990). The effect of compliance with treatment in survival among patients with hematologic malignancies. *Journal of Clinical Oncology, 8,* 356.

Ridley, N. J., Draper, B., & Withall, A. (2013). Alcohol-related dementia: An update of the evidence. *Alzheimer's Research & Therapy, 5*(1), 3.

Rief, W., Glaesmer, H., Baehr, V., Broadbent, E., Brahler, E., & Petrie, K. J. (2012). The relationship of modern health worries to depression, symptom reporting and quality of life in a general population survey. *Journal of Psychosomatic Research, 72,* 318–320.

Rief, W., & Martin, A. (2014). How to use the new DSM-5 somatic symptom disorder diagnosis in research and practice: A critical evaluation and a proposal for modifications. *Annual Review of Clinical Psychology, 10,* 339–367.

Riemann, D., Nissen, C., Palagini, L., Otte, A., Perlis, M. L., & Spiegelhalder, K. (2015). The neurobiology, investigation, and treatment of chronic insomnia. *Lancet Neurology, 14*(5), 547–558.

Rienecke, R. D. (2017). Family-based treatment of eating disorders in adolescents: Current insights. *Adolescent Health, Medicine and Therapeutics, 8,* 69–79

Rimmele, C. T., Miller, W. R., & Dougher, M. J. (1989). Aversion therapies. In R. K. Hester & W. R. Miller (Eds.), *Handbook of alcoholism treatment approaches: Effective alternatives* (pp. 128–140). New York: Pergamon Press.

Ripoll, L. H., Triebwasser, J., & Siever, L. J. (2011). Evidence-based pharmacotherapy for personality disorders. *International Journal of Neuropsychopharmacology, 14,* 1257–1288.

Risch, N., Herrell, R., Lehner, T., Liang, K. Y., Eaves, L., Hoh, J., Griem, A., Kovacs, M., Ott, J., & Merikangas, K. R. (2009). Interaction between the serotonin transporter gene (5-HTTLPR), stressful life events, and risk of depression: A meta-analysis. *JAMA, 301,* 2462–2471.

Rizzo, A., Roy, M. J., Hartholt, A., Costanzo, M., Highland, K. B., Jovanovic, T., et al. (2017). Virtual reality applications for the assessment and treatment of PTSD. In S. Bowles & Bartone, P. (Eds.) *Handbook of military psychology* (pp. 453–471). Cham: Springer.

Robbins, P. C., Monahan, J., & Silver, E. (2003). Mental disorder, violence, and gender. *Law and Human Behavior, 27,* 561–571.

Roberts, A. L., Gilman, S. E., Brelau, J., & Koenen, K. C. (2011). Race/ethnic differences in exposure to traumatic events, development of post-traumatic stress disorder, and treatment-seeking for post-traumatic stress disorder in the United States. *Psychological Medicine, 41,* 71–83.

Robles, T. F., & Kiecolt-Glaser, J. K. (2003). The physiology of marriage: Pathways to health. *Physiology & Behavior, 79,* 409–416.

Robles, T. F., Slatcher, R. B., Trombello, J. M., & McGinn, M. M. (2014). Marital quality and health: A meta-analytic review. *Psychological Bulletin, 140,* 140–187.

Rockney, R. M., & Lemke, T. (1992). Casualties from a junior-senior high school during the Persian Gulf War: Toxic poisoning or mass hysteria? *Journal of Developmental & Behavioral Pediatrics, 13,* 339–342.

Rodin, J., Silberstein, L. R., & Striegel-Moore, R. H. (1984). Women and weight: A normative discontent. In T. B. Sonderegger (Ed.), *Nebraska symposium on motivation.* Lincoln: University of Nebraska Press.

Roehling, M. V., Pichler, S., & Bruce, T. A. (2013). Moderators of the effect of weight on job-related outcomes: A meta-analysis of experimental studies. *Journal of Applied Social Psychology, 43(2),* 237–252.

Roehling, M. V., Pichler, S., Oswald, F., & Bruce, T. (2008). *The effects of weight bias on job-related outcomes: A meta-analysis of experimental studies.* Paper presented at the Academy of Management Annual Meeting, Anaheim, CA.

Roelofs, K., Hoogduin, K. A. L., Keijsers, G. P. J., Naring, G. W. B., Moene, F. C., & Sandijck, P. (2002). Hypnotic susceptibility in patients with conversion disorder. *Journal of Abnormal Psychology, 111,* 390–395.

Roesch, S. C., Adams, L., Hines, A., Palmores, A., Vyas, P., Tran, C., et al. (2005). Coping with prostate cancer: A meta-analytic review. *Journal of Behavioral Medicine, 28*(3), 281–293

Roessner, V., Hoekstra, P. J., & Rothenberger, A. (2011). Tourette's disorder and other tic disorders in *DSM-5*: A comment. *European Child and Adolescent Psychiatry, 20,* 71–74.

Roessner, V., Schoenefeld, K., Buse, J., Bender, S., Ehrlich, S., & Münchau, A. (2013). Pharmacological treatment of tic disorders and Tourette syndrome. *Neuropharmacology, 68,* 143–149.

Rogers, C. R. (1951). *Client-centered therapy, its current practice, implications, and theory.* Boston: Houghton Mifflin.

Rogler, L. H. (1989). The meaning of culturally sensitive research in mental health. *American Journal of Psychiatry, 146,* 296–303.

Rohan, K. J., Mahon, J. N., Evans, M., Ho, S. Y., Meyerhoff, J., Postolache, T. T., & Vacek, P. M. (2015). Randomized trial of cognitive-behavioral therapy versus light therapy for seasonal affective disorder: Acute outcomes. *American Journal of Psychiatry, 172*(9), 862–869.

Rohan, K. J., Roecklein, K. A., & Haaga, D. A. F. (2009). Biological and psychological mechanisms of seasonal affective disorder: A review and integration. *Current Psychiatry Reviews, 5,* 37–47.

Rohan, K. J., Roecklein, K. A., Lacy, T. J., & Vacek, P. M. (2009). Winter depression recurrence one year after cognitive-behavioral therapy, light therapy, or combination treatment. *Behavior Therapy, 40,* 225–238.

Rohan, K. J., Roecklein, K. A., Lindsey, K. T., Johnson, L. G., Lippy, R. D., Lacy, T. J., & Barton, F. B. (2007). A randomized controlled trial of cognitive-behavioral therapy, light therapy, and their combination for seasonal affective disorder. *Journal of Consulting and Clinical Psychology, 75,* 489–500.

Romanelli, R. J., Wu, F. M., Gamba, R., Mojtabai, R., & Segal, J. B. (2014). Behavioral therapy and serotonin reuptake inhibitor pharmacotherapy in the treatment of obsessive-compulsive disorder: A systematic review and meta-analysis of head-to-head randomized controlled trials. *Depression and Anxiety, 31,* 641–652.

Ronningstam, E. (2011a). Narcissistic personality disorder: A clinical perspective. *Journal of Psychiatric Practice, 17,* 89–99.

Ronningstam, E. (2011b). Narcissistic personality disorder in *DSM-V*–In support of retaining a significant diagnosis. *Journal of Personality Disorders, 25,* 248–259.

Rosen, G. (1968). *Madness in society: Chapters in the historical sociology of mental illness.* Chicago: University of Chicago Press.

Rosenbaum, M. (1980). The role of the term schizophrenia in the decline of the diagnoses of multiple personality. *Archives of General Psychiatry, 37,* 1383–1385.

Rosenblatt, P. C. (2008). Grief across cultures: A review and research agenda. In M. S. Stroebe, R. O. Hansson, H. Schut, & W. Stroebe (Eds.), *Handbook of bereavement research and practice: Advances in theory and intervention* (pp. 207–222). Washington, DC, US: American Psychological Association.

Rosengren, A., Hawken, S., Ounpuu, S., Sliwa, K., Zubaid, M., et al. (2004). Association of psychosocial risk factors with risk of acute myocardial infarction in 11,119 cases and 13,648 controls from 52 countries (the INTERHEART study): Case-control study. *Lancet, 364,* 953–962.

Rosenhan, D. L. (1973). On being sane in insane places. *Science, 179,* 250–258.

Rosenman, R. H., Brand, R. J., Jenkins, C. D., Friedman, M., Straus, R., & Wrum, M. (1976). Coronary heart disease in the Western Collaborative Group Study: Final follow-up experience of 8 years. *JAMA, 233,* 877–878.

Rosenstein, M. J., Milazzo-Sayre, L. J., & Manderscheid, R. W. (1989). Care of persons with schizophrenia: A statistical profile. *Schizophrenia Bulletin, 15,* 45–58.

Rosenström, T., Ystrom, E., Torvik, F. A., Czajkowski, N. O., Gillespie, N. A., Aggen, S. H., et al. (2017). Genetic and environmental structure of DSM-IV criteria for antisocial personality disorder: A twin study. *Behavior Genetics, 47*(3), 265–277.

Ross, C. A. (1997). *Dissociative identity disorder: Diagnosis, clinical features, and treatment of multiple personality.* Toronto: Wiley.

Ross, C. A. (1999). Dissociative disorders. In T. Millon (Ed.), *Oxford textbook of psychopathology* (pp. 466–481). New York: Oxford University Press.

Ross, C. A. (2011). Possession experiences in dissociative identity disorder: A preliminary study. *Journal of Trauma and Dissociation, 12,* 393–400.

Ross, C. A., & Ness, L. (2010). Symptom patterns in dissociative identity disorder patients and the general population. *Journal of Trauma and Dissociation, 11,* 458–468.

Ross, C. A., Aylward, E. H., Wild, E. J., Langbehn, D. R., Long, J. D., Warner, J. H., et al. (2014). Huntington disease: Natural history, biomarkers and prospects for therapeutics. *Nature Reviews Neurology, 10*(4), 204.

Ross, C. E., & Mirowsky, J. (1984). Socially-desirable response and acquiescence in a cross-cultural survey of mental health. *Journal of Health & Social Behavior, 25,* 189–197.

Ross, L., Lepper, M. R., & Hubbard, M. (1975). Perseverance in self-perception and social perception: Biased attributional processes in the debriefing paradigm. *Journal of Personality and Social Psychology, 32*(5), 880–892.

Rosselló, J., & Bernal, G. (2005). New developments in cognitive-behavioral and interpersonal treatments for depressed Puerto Rican adolescents. In E. D. Hibbs & P. S. Jensen (Eds.), *Psychosocial treatments for child and adolescent disorders: Empirically based strategies for clinical practice* (2nd ed., pp. 187–217). Washington, DC: American Psychological Association.

Rothbaum, B. O., & Foa, E. B. (1991). Exposure treatment of PTSD concomitant with conversion mutism: A case study. *Behavior Therapy, 22,* 449–456.

Rothbaum, B. O., Foa, E. D., Riggs, D. S., & Murdock, T. (1992). A prospective examination of post-traumatic stress disorder in rape victims. *Journal of Traumatic Stress, 5,* 455–475.

Rothemund, Y., Preuschhof, C., Bohner, G., Bauknecht, H. C., Klingebiel, R., Flor, H., & Klapp, B. F. (2007). Differential activation of the dorsal striatum by high-calorie visual food stimuli in obese individuals. *NeuroImage, 37,* 410–421.

Rowe, R., Maughan, B., Worthman, C. M., Costello, E. J., & Angold, A. (2004). Testosterone, antisocial behavior, and social dominance in boys: Pubertal development and biosocial interaction. *Biological Psychiatry, 55,* 546–552.

Rowland, D. L., & Cooper, S. E. (2017). Treating men's orgasmic difficulties. In Z. D. Peterson (Ed.), *The Wiley handbook of sex therapy* (pp. 72–97). Oxford: Wiley.

Rozin, P., Bauer, R., & Catanese, D. (2003). Food and life, pleasure and worry, among American college students: Gender differences and regional similarities. *Journal of Personality & Social Psychology, 85,* 132–141.

Rudolph, K. D. (2008). The interpersonal context of adolescent depression. In S. Nolen-Hoeksema & L. M. Hilt (Eds.), *Handbook of depression in adolescents* (pp. 377–417). New York: Routledge.

Rudolph, K. D., & Conley, C. S. (2005). The socioeconomic costs and benefits of social-evaluative concerns: Do girls care too much? *Journal of Personality, 73,* 115–137.

Rueve, M. E., & Welton, R. S. (2008). Violence and mental illness. *Psychiatry (Edgmont), 5*(5), 34–48.

Ruiz, P., & Strain, E. C. (2014). *The substance abuse handbook.* Philadelphia: Lippincott Williams & Wilkins.

Ruocco, A. C., Amirthavasagam, S., & Zakzanis, K. K. (2012). Amygdala and hippocampal volume reductions as candidate endophenotypes for borderline personality disorder: A meta-analysis of magnetic resonance imaging studies. *Psychiatric Research: Neuroimaging, 201,* 245–252.

Ruscio, A. M., Gentes, E. L., Jones, J. D., Hallion, L. S., Coleman, E. S., & Swendsen, J. (2015). Rumination predicts heightened responding to stressful life events in major depressive disorder and generalized anxiety disorder. *Journal of Abnormal Psychology, 124,* 17–26.

Rutter, M., Caspi, A., Fergusson, D., Horwood, L. J., Goodman, R., Maughan, B., Moffitt, T. E., Meltzer, H., & Carroll, J. (2004). Sex differences in developmental reading disability: New findings from 4 epidemiological studies. *JAMA, 291,* 2007–2012.

Rutter, M., Silberg, J., O'Connor, T., & Simonoff, E. (1999). Genetics and child psychiatry: II. Empirical research findings. *Journal of Child Psychology & Psychiatry, 40,* 19–55.

Ryan, J. J., & Lopez, S. J. (2001). Wechsler Adult Intelligence Scale-III. In W. I. Dorfman & S. M. Freshwater (Eds.), *Understanding psychological assessment* (pp. 19–42). Dordrecht, Netherlands: Kluwer Academic.

Ryder, A. G., Yang, J., Zhu, X., Yao, S., Yi, J., Heine, S., & Bagby, R. M. (2008). The cultural shaping of depression: Somatic symptoms in China, psychological symptoms in North America? *Journal of Abnormal Psychology, 117,* 300–313.

S

Sack, R. L., Auckley, D., Auger, R. R., Carskadon, M. A., Wright, K. P., Jr., Vitiello, M. V., & Zhdanova, I. V. (2007). Circadian rhythm sleep disorders: Part I, Basic principles, shift work and jet lag disorders. *Sleep, 30,* 1460–1483.

Sackeim, H. A., Prudic, J., Fuller, R., Keilp, J., Lavori, P. W., & Olfson, M. (2007). The cognitive effects of electroconvulsive therapy in community settings. *Neuropsychopharmacology, 32,* 244–254.

Safer, D. J. (2016). Recent trends in stimulant usage. *Journal of Attention Disorders, 20*(6), 471–477.

Safer, D. L., Telch, C. F., & Chen, E. Y. (2009). *Dialectical behavior therapy for binge eating and bulimia.* New York: Guilford Press.

Safran, J. D. (2012). *Psychoanalysis and psychoanalytic therapies.* Washington DC: American Psychological Association.

Saigal, C. S., Wessells, H., Pace, J., Schonlau, M., Wilt, T. J., & The Urologic Diseases in America Project. (2006). Predictors and prevalence of erectile dysfunction in a racially diverse population. *Archives of Internal Medicine, 166,* 207–212.

Sajatovic, M., Madhusoodanan, S., & Fuller, M. A. (2008). Clozapine. In K. T. Mueser & D. V. Jeste (Eds.), *Clinical handbook of schizophrenia* (pp. 178–185). New York: Guilford Press.

Salkovskis, P. M. (1998). Psychological approaches to the understanding of obsessional problems. In R. Swinson (Ed.), *Obsessive-compulsive disorder: Theory, research, and treatment* (pp. 33–50). New York: Guilford Press.

Salkovskis, P. M., & Millar, J. F. (2016). Still cognitive after all these years? Perspectives for a cognitive behavioural theory of obsessions and where we are 30 years later. *Australian Psychologist, 51*(1), 3–13.

Sallinen, M., Harma, M., Akerstedt, T., Rosa, R., & Lillqvist, O. (1998). Promoting alertness with a short nap during a night shift. *Journal of Sleep Research, 7,* 240–247.

Saluja, G., Iachan, R., Scheidt, P. C., Overpeck, M. D., Sun, W., & Giedd, J. N. (2004). Prevalence of and risk factors for depressive symptoms among young adolescents. *Archives of Pediatrics & Adolescent Medicine, 158,* 760–765.

Salvatore, J. E., & Dick, D. M. (2016). Genetic influences on conduct disorder. *Neuroscience & Biobehavioral Reviews, 91,* 91–101.

Salvatore, S., Redaelli, A., Baini, I., & Candiani, M. (2016). Sexual function after delivery. In D. Riva & G. Minini (Eds.), *Childbirth-related pelvic floor dysfunction: Risk factors, prevention, evaluation, and treatment* (pp. 101–104). Springer: Cham.

Samara, M. T., Dold, M., Gianatsi, M., Nikolakopoulou, A., Helfer, B., Salanti, G., & Leucht, S. (2016). Efficacy, acceptability, and tolerability of antipsychotics in treatment-resistant schizophrenia: A network meta-analysis. *JAMA Psychiatry, 73*(3), 199–210.

Sampson, R. J., & Laub, J. H. (1992). Crime and deviance in the life course. *Annual Review of Sociology, 18,* 63–84.

Samuels, J. F., Bienvenu, O. J., Grados, M. A., Cullen, B., Riddle, M. A., Liang, K. Y., Eaton, W. W., & Nestadt, G. (2008). Prevalence and correlates of hoarding behavior in a community-based sample. *Behaviour Research and Therapy, 46,* 836–844.

Sanchez-Roige, S., Gray, J. C., MacKillop, J., Chen, C. H., & Palmer, A. A. (2018). The genetics of human personality. *Genes, Brain and Behavior, 17*(3), e12439.

Sanchis-Gomar, F., Perez-Quilis, C., Leischik, R., & Lucia, A. (2016). Epidemiology of coronary heart disease and acute coronary syndrome. *Annals of Translational Medicine, 4*(13), 256.

Sand, M., & Fisher, W. A. (2007). Women's endorsement of models of female sexual response: The nurses' sexuality study. *Journal of Sexual Medicine, 4,* 708–719.

Sanderson, W. C., Rapee, R. M., & Barlow, D. H. (1989). The influence of an illusion of control on panic attacks induced via inhalation of 5.5% carbon dioxide-enriched air. *Archives of General Psychiatry, 46*(2), 157–162.

Sandnabba, N. K., Santtila, P., Alison, L., & Nordling, N. (2002). Demographics, sexual behaviour, family background and abuse experiences of practitioners of sadomasochistic sex: A review of recent research. *Sexual & Relationship Therapy, 17,* 39–55.

Sanislow, C. A., da Cruz, K., Gianoli, M. O., & Reagan, E. (2012). Avoidant personality disorder, traits, and type. In T. A. Widiger (Ed.), *The Oxford handbook of personality disorders* (pp. 549–565). New York: Oxford University Press.

Sanislow, C. A., Pine, D. S., Quinn, K. J., Kozak, M. J., Garvey, M. A., Heinssen, R. K., Wang, P. S., & Cuthbert, B. N. (2011). Developing constructs for psychopathology research: Research domain criteria. *Journal of Abnormal Psychology, 119,* 631–639.

Sapolsky, R. M. (2007). Why zebras don't get ulcers: Stress, metabolism, and liquidating your assets. In A. Monat, R. S. Lazarus, & G. Reevy (Eds.). *The Praeger handbook on stress and coping:* Vol. 1 (pp. 181–197). Westport, CT: Praeger.

Sar, V., Krüger, C., Martínez-Taboas, A., Middleton, W., & Dorahy, M. (2013). Sociocognitive and posttraumatic models of dissociation are not opposed. *The Journal of Nervous and Mental Disease, 201*(5), 439–440.

Sarbin, T. R., & Juhasz, J. B. (1967). The historical background of the concept of hallucination. *Journal of the History of the Behavioral Sciences, 3,* 339–358.

Sariaslan, A., Fazel, S., D'Onofrio, B. M., Långström, N., Larsson, H., Bergen, S. E., et al. (2016). Schizophrenia and subsequent neighborhood deprivation: Revisiting the social drift hypothesis using population, twin and molecular genetic data. *Translational Psychiatry, 6*(5), e796.

Saveanu, R. V., & Nemeroff, C. B. (2012). Etiology of depression: Genetic and environmental factors. *Psychiatric Clinics of North America, 35,* 51–71.

Savill, N. C., Buitelaar, J. K., Anand, E., Day, K. A., Treuer, T., Upadhyaya, H. P., & Coghill, D. (2015). The efficacy of atomoxetine for the treatment of children and adolescents with attention-deficit/hyperactivity disorder: A comprehensive review of over a decade of clinical research. *CNS Drugs, 29*(2), 131–151.

Savla, G. N., Moore, D. J., & Palmer, B. W. (2008). Cognitive functioning in K. T. Mueser & Dilip V. Jeste (Eds.), *Clinical handbook of schizophrenia* (pp. 91–99). New York: Guilford Press.

Saxena, S. (2008). Neurobiology and treatment of compulsive hoarding. *CNS Spectrums, 13* (9, Suppl. 14), 29–36.

Saxena, S., Brody, A. L., Ho, M. L., Zohrabi, N., Maidment, K. M., & Baxter, L. R., Jr. (2003). Differential brain metabolic predictors of response to paroxetine in obsessive-compulsive disorder versus major depression. *American Journal of Psychiatry, 160,* 522–532.

Saxena, S., Brody, A. L., Maidment, K. M., Dunkin, J. J., Colgan, M., Alborzian, S., Phelps, M. E., & Baxter, L. R. (1999). Localized orbitofrontal and subcortical metabolic changes and predictors of response to paroxetine treatment in obsessive-compulsive disorder. *Neuropsychopharmacology, 21,* 683–693.

Saxena, S., & Prasad, K. V. (1989). *DSMIII* subclassification of dissociative disorders applied to psychiatric outpatients in India. *American Journal of Psychiatry, 146,* 261–262.

Scaini, S., Belotti, R., & Ogliari, A. (2014). Genetic and environmental contributions to social anxiety across different ages: A meta-analytic approach to twin data. *Journal of Anxiety Disorders, 28*(7), 650–656.

Scammacca, N. K., Roberts, G. J., Cho, E., Williams, K. J., Roberts, G., Vaughn, S. R., & Carroll, M. (2016). A century of progress: Reading interventions for students in grades 4–12, 1914–2014. *Review of Educational Research, 86*(3), 756–800.

Schacter, D. L., Chiao, J. Y., & Mitchell, J. P. (2003). The seven sins of memory: Implications for the self. In J. LeDoux, J. Debiece, & H. Moss (Eds.), The self: From soul to brain. *Annals of the New York Academy of Sciences, 1001,* 226–239.

Scheltens, P., Blennow, K., Breteler, M., de Strooper, B., Frisoni, G., Salloway, S., & der Flier, W. (2016). Alzheimer's disease. *Lancet, 388,* 505–517.

Schenck, C. H., & Mahowald, M. W. (2003). REM behavior disorder (RBD): Delayed emergence of Parkinsonism and/or dementia in 65% of older men initially diagnosed with idiopathic RBD, and an analysis of the minimum & maximum tonic and/or phasic electromyographic abnormalities found during REM sleep. *Sleep, 26,* A316Abs.

Schienle, A., Hettema, J. M., Caceda, R., & Nemeroff, C. B. (2011). Neurobiology and genetics of generalized anxiety disorder. *Psychiatric Annals, 41*(2), 113–123.

Schildkraut, J. J. (1965). The catecholamine hypothesis of affective disorder: A review of supporting evidence. *American Journal of Psychiatry, 122,* 509–522.

Schilling, E. A., Lawless, M., Buchanan, L., & Aseltine, R. H. (2014). "Signs of Suicide" shows promise as a middle school suicide prevention program. *Suicide and Life-Threatening Behavior, 44*(6), 653–667.

Schimmenti, A., & Caretti, V. (2016). Linking the overwhelming with the unbearable: Developmental trauma, dissociation, and the disconnected self. *Psychoanalytic Psychology, 33*(1), 106–128.

Schlienz, N. J., Budney, A. J., Lee, D. C., & Vandrey, R. (2017). Cannabis withdrawal: A review of neurobiological mechanisms and sex differences. *Current Addiction Reports, 4,* 75–81.

Schlosser, D. A., Zinberg, J. L., Loewy, R. L., Casey-Cannon, S., O'Brien, M. P., Bearden, C. E., Vinogradov, S., & Cannon, T. D. (2010). Predicting the longitudinal effects of the family environment on prodromal symptoms and functioning in patients at-risk for psychosis. *Schizophrenia Research, 118,* 69–75.

Schmidt, N. B., & Keough, M. E. (2010). Treatment of panic. *Annual Review of Clinical Psychology, 6,* 241–256.

Schneiderman, N., Ironson, G., & Siegel, S. D. (2005). Stress and health: Psychological, behavioral, and biological determinants. *Annual Review of Clinical Psychology, 1,* 607–628.

Scholte, W. F., Olff, M., Ventevogel, P., de Vries, G.-J., Jansveld, E., Cardozo, B. L., & Crawford, C. A. G. (2004). Mental health symptoms following war and repression in eastern Afghanistan. *JAMA, 292,* 585–593.

Schonfeld, L., & Dupree, L. W. (2002). Age-specific cognitive-behavioral and self-management treatment approaches. In A. M. Gurnack, R. Atkinson, & N. J. Osgood (Eds.), *Treating alcohol and drug abuse in the elderly* (pp. 109–130). New York: Springer.

Schuckit, M. A. (1995). *Drug and alcohol abuse: A clinical guide to diagnosis and treatment.* New York: Plenum Medical.

Schuckit, M. A. (1998). Biological, psychological, and environmental predictors of the alcoholism risk: A longitudinal study. *Journal of Studies on Alcohol, 59,* 485–494.

Schulte, E. M., Grilo, C. M., & Gearhardt, A. N. (2016). Shared and unique mechanisms underlying binge eating disorder and addictive disorders. *Clinical Psychology Review, 44,* 125–139.

Schulz, R., Bookwala, J., Knapp, J. E., Scheier, M., & Williamson, G. M. (1996). Pessimism, age, and cancer mortality. *Psychology & Aging, 11,* 304–309.

Schultz, R. T. (2005). Developmental deficits in social perception in autism: The role of the amygdala and fusiform face area. *International Journal of Developmental Neuroscience, 23,* 125–141.

Schumm, J. A., Dickstein, B. D., Walter, K. H., Owens, G. P., & Chard, K. M. (2015). Changes in posttraumatic cognitions predict changes in posttraumatic stress disorder symptoms during cognitive processing therapy. *Journal of Consulting and Clinical Psychology, 83,* 1161–1166.

Schuster, M. A., Stein, B. D., Jaycox, L. H., Collins, R. L., Marshall, G. N., Elliott, M. N., Zhou, A. J., Kanouse, D. E., Morrison, J. L., & Berry, S. H. (2001). A national survey of stress reactions after the September 11, 2001, terrorist attacks. *New England Journal of Medicine, 345,* 1507–1512.

Schwartz, J., Stoessel, P. W., Baxter, L. R., Martin, K. M., & Phelps, M. C. (1996). Systemic changes in cerebral glucose metabolic rate after successful behavior modification treatment of obsessive-compulsive disorder. *Archives of General Psychiatry, 53,* 109–113.

Schwartz, R. C., & Blankenship, D. M. (2014). Racial disparities in psychotic disorder diagnosis: A review of empirical literature. *World Journal of Psychiatry, 4*(4), 133–140.

Sciberras, E., Mulraney, M., Silva, D., & Coghill, D. (2017). Prenatal risk factors and the etiology of ADHD: Review of existing evidence. *Current Psychiatry Reports, 19*(1), 1.

Scoboria, A., Wade, K. A., Lindsay, D. S., Azad, T., Strange, D., Ost, J., & Hyman, I. E. (2017). A mega-analysis of memory reports from eight peer-reviewed false memory implantation studies. *Memory, 25*(2), 146–163.

Scogin, F., Floyd, M., & Forde, J. (2000). Anxiety in older adults. In S. K. Whitbourne (Ed.), *Psychopathology in later adulthood* (pp. 117–140). New York: Wiley.

Scott, K. M., Hwang, I., Chiu, W.-T., Kessler, R. C., Sampson, N. A., Angermeyer, M., et al. (2010). Chronic physical conditions and their association with first onset of suicidal behavior in the World Mental Health Surveys. *Psychosomatic Medicine, 72,* 712–719.

Scott, K. M., Lim, C., Al-Hamzawi, A., Alonso, J., Bruffaerts, R., Caldas-de-Almeida, J. M., et al. (2016). Association of mental disorders with subsequent chronic physical conditions: World mental health surveys from 17 countries. *JAMA Psychiatry, 73*(2), 150–158.

Scull, A. (1993). *The most solitary of afflictions.* New Haven: Yale University Press.

Sears, C. S., Robinson, J. W., & Walker, L. M. (2018). A comprehensive review of sexual health concerns after cancer treatment and the biopsychosocial treatment options available to female patients. *European Journal of Cancer Care, 27*(2), e12738.

Seedat, S., Stein, M. B., & Forde, D. R. (2003). Prevalence of dissociative experiences in a community sample. *Journal of Nervous & Mental Disorders, 191,* 115–120.

Seeman, M. V. (2008). Gender. In K. T. Mueser & Dilip V. Jeste (Eds.), *Clinical handbook of schizophrenia* (pp. 575–580). New York: Guilford Press.

Segal, S. P., Laurie, T. A., & Franskoviak, P. (2004). Ambivalence of PES patients toward hospitalization and factors in their disposition. *International Journal of Law & Psychiatry, 27,* 87–99.

Segerstrom, S. C., & Miller, G. E. (2004). Psychological stress and the human immune system: A meta-analytic study of 30 years of inquiry. *Psychological Bulletin, 130,* 601–630.

Segerstrom, S. C., Solomon, G. F., Kemeny, M. E., & Fahey, J. L. (1998). Relationship of worry to immune sequelae of the Northridge earthquake. *Journal of Behavioral Medicine, 21,* 433–450.

Segerstrom, S. C., Taylor, S. E., Kemeny, M. E., Reed, G. M., & Visscher, B. R. (1996). Causal attributions predict rate of immune decline in HIV seropositive gay men. *Health Psychology, 15,* 485–493.

Seidman, L. J., Faraone, S. V., Goldstein, J. M., Kremen, W. S., Horton, N. J., Makris, N., Toomey, R., Kennedy, D., Caviness, V. S., & Tsuang, M. T. (2002). Left hippocampal volume as a vulnerability indicator for schizophrenia. *Archives of General Psychiatry, 59,* 839–849.

Selby, E. A., Anestis, M., Bender, T., & Joiner, T. (2009). An exploration of the emotional cascade model in borderline personality disorder. *Journal of Abnormal Psychology, 118,* 375–387.

Seligman, M. E. (1970). On the generality of the laws of learning. *Psychological Review, 77,* 406–418.

Seligman, M. E. (1975). *Helplessness: On depression, development, and death.* San Francisco: Freeman, Cooper.

Seligman, M. E. (1993). *What you can change and what you can't: The complete guide to self-improvement.* New York: Knopf.

Seligman, M. E., & Maier, S. F. (1967). Failure to escape traumatic shock. *Journal of Experimental Psychology, 74,* 1–9.

Selling, L. H. (1940). *Men against madness.* New York: Greenberg.

Semans, J. H. (1956). Premature ejaculation: A new approach. *Southern Medical Journal, 49,* 353–357.

Semler, C. N., & Harvey, A. G. (2007). An experimental investigation of daytime monitoring for sleep-related threat in primary insomnia. *Cognition and Emotion, 21,* 146–161.

Sempertegui, G. A., Karreman, A., Arntz, A., & Bekker, M. H. (2013). Schema therapy for borderline personality disorder: A comprehensive review of its empirical foundations, effectiveness and implementation possibilities. *Clinical Psychology Review, 33*(3), 426–447.

Semrau, M., Barley, E. A., Law, A., & Thornicroft, G. (2011). Lessons learned in developing community mental health care in Europe. *World Psychiatry, 10,* 217–225.

Senaratna, C. V., Perret, J. L., Lodge, C. J., Lowe, A. J., Campbell, B. E., Matheson, M. C., et al. (2017). Prevalence of obstructive sleep apnea in the general population: A systematic review. *Sleep Medicine Reviews, 34,* 70–81.

Seto, M. C. (2008). Pedophilia: Psychopathology and theory. In D. R. Laws & W. T. O'Donohue (Eds.), *Sexual deviance: Theory, assessment, and treatment* (pp. 164–183). New York: Guilford Press.

Seto, M. C. (2009). Pedophilia. *Annual Review of Clinical Psychology, 5,* 391–407.

Shaffer, D., & Gould, M. S. (2000). Suicide prevention in the schools. In K. Hawton (Ed.), *The international handbook of suicide and attempted suicide* (pp. 585–724). New York: Wiley.

Shaffer, D., Gould, M. S., Fisher, P., Trautman, P., Moreau, D., Kleinman, M., & Flory, M. (1996). Psychiatric diagnosis in child and adolescent suicide. *Archives of General Psychiatry, 53,* 339–348.

Shapiro, J. R., Berkman, N. D., Brownley, K. A., Sedway, J. A., Lohr, K. N., & Bulik, C. M. (2007). Bulimia nervosa treatment: A systematic review of randomized controlled trials. *International Journal of Eating Disorders, 40,* 321–336.

Sharif, Z. A., Raza, A., & Ratakonda, S. S. (2000). Comparative efficacy of risperidone and clozapine in the treatment of patients with refractory schizophrenia or schizoaffective disorder: A retrospective analysis. *Journal of Clinical Psychiatry, 61,* 498–504.

Sharp, C., Kim, S., Herman, L., Pane, H., Reuter, T., & Strathearn, L. (2014). Major depression in mothers predicts reduced ventral striatum activation in adolescent female offspring with and without depression. *Journal of Abnormal Psychology, 123,* 298–309.

Sharp, C., Wright, A. G. C., Fowler, J. C., Frueh, B. C., Allen, J. G., Oldham, J., & Clark, L. A. (2015). The structure of personality pathology: Both general ('g') and specific ('s') factors? *Journal of Abnormal Psychology, 124,* 387–398.

Shaw, D. S., & Shelleby, E. C. (2014). Early-starting conduct problems: Intersection of conduct problems and poverty. *Annual Review of Clinical Psychology, 10,* 503–528.

Shaw, P., Lerch, J. P., Pruessner, J. C., Taylor, K. N., Rose, A. B., et al. (2007). Cortical morphology in children and adolescents with different apolipoprotein E gene polymorphisms: An observational study. *Lancet Neurology, 6,* 494–500.

Shaywitz, B., Shaywitz, S., Blachman, B., Pugh, K., Fulbright, R., Skudlarski, P., et al. (2004). Development of left occipito-temporal systems for skilled reading in children after a phonologically-based intervention. *Biological Psychiatry, 55,* 926–933.

Shaywitz, S. (2003). *Overcoming dyslexia: A new and complete science-based program for reading problems at any level.* New York: Knopf.

Shaywitz, S. E., & Shaywitz, B. A. (2008). Paying attention to reading: The neurobiology of reading and dyslexia. *Development and Psychopathology, 20,* 1329–1349.

Shea, M. T., Stout, R., Gunderson, J., Morey, L. C., Grilo, C. M., McGlashan, T., Skodol, A. E., Dolan-Sewell, R., Dyck, I., Zanarini, M. C., & Keller, M. B. (2002). Short-term diagnostic stability of schizotypal, borderline, avoidant, and obsessive-compulsive personality disorders. *American Journal of Psychiatry, 159,* 2036–2041.

Shedler, J. (2010). The efficacy of psychodynamic psychotherapy. *American Psychologist, 65*(2), 98–109.

Sher, K. J., Grekin, E. R., & Williams, N. A. (2005). The development of alcohol use disorders. In S. Nolen-Hoeksema, T. D. Cannon, & T. A. Widiger (Eds.), *Annual review of clinical psychology* (Vol. 1, pp. 493–523). Palo Alto, CA: Annual Reviews.

Shimada-Sugimoto, M., Otowa, T., & Hettema, J. M. (2015). Genetics of anxiety disorders: Genetic epidemiological and molecular studies in humans. *Psychiatry and Clinical Neurosciences, 69*(7), 388–401.

Shin, L. M., Bush, G., Milad, M. R., Lasko, N. B., Brohawn, K. H., Hughes, K. C., Macklin, M. L., Gold, A. L., Karpf, R. D., Orr, S. P., Rauch, S. L., & Pitman, R. K. (2011). Exaggerated activation of dorsal anterior cingulate cortex during cognitive interference: A monozygotic twin study of posttraumatic stress disorder. *American Journal of Psychiatry, 168,* 979–985.

Shirk, C. (2008). *Medicaid and mental health services.* Washington, DC: National Health Policy Forum.

Shortt, A. L., Barrett, P. M., & Fox, T. L. (2001). Evaluating the FRIENDS program: A cognitive-behavioral group treatment for anxious children and their parents. *Journal of Clinical Child Psychology, 30,* 525–535.

Sibrava, N. J., Beard, C., Bjornsson, A. S., Moitra, E., Weisberg, R. B., & Keller, M. B. (2013). Two-year course of generalized anxiety disorder, social anxiety disorder, and panic disorder in a longitudinal sample of African American adults. *Journal of Consulting and Clinical Psychology, 81,* 1052–1062.

Siev, J., & Chambless, D. L. (2007). Specificity of treatment effects: Cognitive therapy and relaxation for generalized anxiety and panic disorders. *Journal of Consulting and Clinical Psychology, 75,* 513–522.

Siever, L. J. (2008). Neurobiology of aggression and violence. *American Journal of Psychiatry, 165,* 429–442.

Sigman, M., Spence, S. J., & Wang, A. T. (2006). Autism from developmental and neuropsychological perspectives. *Annual Review of Clinical Psychology, 2,* 327–355.

Sigurdsson, E., Van Os, J., & Fombonne, E. (2002). Are impaired childhood motor skills a risk factor for adolescent anxiety? Results from the 1958 U.K. birth cohort and the National Child Development Study. *American Journal of Psychiatry, 159,* 1044–1046.

Silberg, J. L. (2014). Dissociative disorders in children and adolescents. *Handbook of Developmental Psychopathology* (pp. 761–775). Springer: Boston, MA.

Silberg, J. L., Maes, H., & Eaves, L. J. (2012). Unraveling the effect of genes and environment in the transmission of parental antisocial behavior to children's conduct disturbance, depression, and hyperactivity. *Journal of Child Psychology and Psychiatry, 53,* 668–677.

Silberg, J. L., Parr, T., Neale, M. C., Rutter, M., Angold, A., & Eaves, L. J. (2003). Maternal smoking during pregnancy and risk to boys' conduct disturbance: An examination of the causal hypothesis. *Biological Psychiatry, 53,* 130–135.

Silk, K. R., & Feurino, L., III (2012). Psychopharmacology of personality disorders. In T. A. Widiger (Ed.), *The Oxford handbook of personality disorders* (pp. 713–726). New York: Oxford University Press.

Silva, C., & Van Orden, K. A. (2018). Suicide among Hispanics in the United States. *Current Opinion in Psychology, 22,* 44–49.

Silver, E., Cirincione, C., & Steadman, H. J. (1994). Demythologizing inaccurate perceptions of the insanity defense. *Law & Human Behavior, 18,* 63–70.

Silvers, J. A., Hubbard, A. D., Biggs, E., Shu, J., Fertuck, E., Chaudhury, S., et al. (2016). Affective lability and difficulties with regulation are differentially associated with amygdala and prefrontal response in women with borderline personality disorder. *Psychiatry Research: Neuroimaging, 254,* 74–82.

Simeon, D., Guralnik, O., Schmeidler, J., Sirof, B., & Knutelska, M. (2001). The role of childhood interpersonal trauma in depersonalization disorder. *American Journal of Psychiatry, 158,* 1027–1033.

Simpson, E. B., Yen, S., Costello, E., Rosen, K., Begin, A., Pistorello, J., & Pearlstein, T. (2004). Combined dialectical behavior therapy and fluoxetine in the treatment of borderline personality disorder. *Journal of Clinical Psychiatry, 65,* 379–385.

Sing, L. (1995). Self-starvation in context: Towards a culturally sensitive understanding of anorexia nervosa. *Social Science & Medicine, 41,* 25–36.

Singer, H. S. (2005). Tourette's syndrome: From behaviour to biology. *Lancet Neurology, 4,* 149–159.

Singh, M. K., & Gotlib, I. H. (2014). The neuroscience of depression: Implications for assessment and intervention. *Behaviour Research and Therapy, 62,* 60–73.

Singh, N. N. (2016). *Handbook of evidence-based practices in intellectual and developmental disabilities.* Cham: Springer.

Slavich, G. M., & Irwin, M. R. (2014). From stress to inflammation and major depressive disorder: A social signal transduction theory of depression. *Psychological Bulletin, 140*(3), 774.

Slotema, C. W., Blom, J. D., Hoek, H. W., & Sommer, I. E. (2010). Should we expand the toolbox of psychiatric treatment methods to include repetitive transcranial magnetic stimulation (rTMS)? A meta-analysis of the efficacy of rTMS in psychiatric disorders. *Journal of Clinical Psychiatry, 71,* 873–884.

Smart, C. M., Karr, J. E., Areshenkoff, C. N., Rabin, L. A., Hudon, C., Gates, N., et al. (2017). Non-pharmacologic interventions for older adults with subjective cognitive decline: Systematic review, meta-analysis, and preliminary recommendations. *Neuropsychology Review, 27*(3), 245–257.

Smedslund, G., & Ringdal, G. I. (2004). Meta-analysis of the effects of psychosocial interventions on survival time in cancer patients. *Journal of Psychosomatic Research, 57,* 123–131.

Smink, F. R., van Hoeken, D., Donker, G. A., Susser, E. S., Oldehinkel, A. J., & Hoek, H. W. (2016). Three decades of eating disorders in Dutch primary care: Decreasing incidence of bulimia nervosa but not of anorexia nervosa. *Psychological Medicine, 46*(6), 1189–1196.

Smink, F. R., van Hoeken, D., & Hoek, H. W. (2013). Epidemiology, course, and outcome of eating disorders. *Current Opinion in Psychiatry, 26,* 543–548.

Smith, C. A., & Farrington, D. P. (2004). Continuities in antisocial behavior and parenting across three generations. *Journal of Child Psychology & Psychiatry, 45,* 230–247.

Smith, D. E., & Seymour, R. B. (1994). LSD: History and toxicity. *Psychiatric Annals, 24,* 145–147.

Smolak, L., Murnen, S. K., & Ruble, A. E. (2000). Female athletes and eating problems: A meta-analysis. *International Journal of Eating Disorders, 27,* 371–380.

Smolak, L., & Striegel-Moore, R. H. (2001). Challenging the myth of the golden girl: Ethnicity and eating disorders. In R. H. Striegel-Moore & L. Smolak (Eds.), *Eating disorders: Innovative directions in research and practice* (pp. 111–132). Washington, DC: American Psychological Association.

Smoller, J. (2016). The genetics of stress-related disorders: PTSD, depression, and anxiety disorders. *Neuropsychopharmacology, 41*(1), 297–319.

Smoller, J., Cerrato, F., & Weatherall, S. (2015). The genetics of anxiety disorders. In K. Ressler, D. S. Pine, & B. O. Rothbaum (Eds.), *Anxiety disorders: Translational perspectives on diagnosis and treatment* (pp. 47–61). Oxford: Oxford University Press.

Snitz, B. E., MacDonald, A. W., III, & Carter, C. S. (2006). Cognitive deficits in unaffected first-degree relatives of schizophrenia patients: A meta-analytic review of putative endophenotypes. *Schizophrenia Bulletin, 32,* 179–194.

Snowden, L. R. (2014). Poverty, safety net programs, and African Americans' mental health. *American Psychologist, 69*(8), 773–781.

Snowden, L. R., & Cheung, F. K. (1990). Use of inpatient mental health services by members of ethnic minority groups. *American Psychologist, 45,* 347–355.

Snowden, L. R., & Yamada, A. M. (2005). Cultural differences in access to care. *Annual Review of Clinical Psychology, 1,* 143–166.

Snowdon, D. A. (1997). Aging and Alzheimer's disease: Lessons from the Nun Study. *Gerontologist, 37,* 150–156.

Snowdon, D. A. (2003). Healthy aging and dementia: Findings from the Nun Study. *Annals of Internal Medicine, 139,* 450–454.

Snowdon, D. A., Greiner, L. H., Mortimer, J. A., Riley, K. P., Greiner, P. A., & Markesbery, W. R. (1997). Brain infarction and the clinical expression of Alzheimer disease. The Nun Study. *JAMA, 277,* 813–817.

Snowdon, D. A., Kemper, S. J., Mortimer, J. A., Greiner, L. H., Wekstein, D. R., & Markesbery, W. R. (1996). Linguistic ability in early life and cognitive function and Alzheimer's disease in late life: Findings from the Nun Study. *JAMA, 275,* 528–532.

Sobal, J., & Stunkard, A. J. (1989). Socioeconomic status and obesity: A review of the literature. *Psychological Bulletin, 105,* 260–275.

Sobell, M. B., & Sobell, L. C. (1978). *Behavioral treatment of alcohol problems.* New York: Plenum Press.

Sockol, L. E., Epperson, C. N., & Barber, J. P. (2013). Preventing postpartum depression: A meta-analytic review. *Clinical Psychology Review, 33,* 1205–1217.

Soloff, P. H., & Chiappetta, L. (2012). Prospective predictors of suicidal behavior in borderline personality disorder at 6-year follow-up. *American Journal of Psychiatry, 169,* 484–490.

Soloff, P. H., Pruitt, P., Sharma, M., Radwan, J., White, R., & Diwadkar, V. A. (2012). Structural brain abnormalities and suicidal behavior in borderline personality disorder. *Journal of Psychiatric Research, 46,* 516–525.

Solomon, D. A., Keller, M. B., Leon, A. C., Mueller, T. I., Lavori, D. W., Shea, M. T., et al. (2000). Multiple recurrences of major depressive disorder. *American Journal of Psychiatry, 157,* 229–233.

Solomon, G. F., Segerstrom, S. C., Grohr, P., Kemeny, M., & Fahey, J. (1997). Shaking up immunity: Psychological and immunologic changes following a natural disaster. *Psychosomatic Medicine, 59,* 114–127.

Southwick, S. M., Vythilingam, M., & Charney, D. S. (2005). The psychobiology of depression and resilience to stress: Implications for prevention and treatment. *Annual Review of Clinical Psychology, 1,* 255–292.

Sowell, E. R., Peterson, B. S., Thompson, P. M., Welcome, S. E., Henkenius, A., & Toga, A. W. (2003). Mapping cortical change across the human life span. *Nature Neuroscience, 6,* 309–315.

Spanos, N. (1994). Multiple identity enactments and multiple personality disorder: A sociocognitive perspective. *Psychological Bulletin, 120,* 42–59.

Spanos, N. P. (1978). Witchcraft in histories of psychiatry: A critical analysis and an alternative conceptualization. *Psychological Bulletin, 85,* 417–439.

Spence, S. H., & Rapee, R. M. (2016). The etiology of social anxiety disorder: An evidence-based model. *Behaviour Research and Therapy, 86,* 50–67.

Spiegel, D. (2001). Mind matters—group therapy and survival in breast cancer. *New England Journal of Medicine, 345,* 1767–1768.

Spiegel, D., Bollm, J. R., Kraemer, H. C., & Gottheil, E. (1989). Psychological support for cancer patients. *Lancet, 2,* 1447.

Spiegel, D., Lewis-Fernández, R., Lanius, R., Vermetten, E., Simeon, D., & Friedman, M. (2013). Dissociative disorders in DSM-5. *Annual Review of Clinical Psychology, 9,* 299–326.

Spierings, C., Poels, P. J., Sijben, N., Gabreels, F. J., & Renier, W. O. (1990). Conversion disorders in childhood: A retrospective follow-up study of 84 inpatients. *Developmental Medicine & Child Neurology, 32,* 865–871.

Spitzer, R. L. (1981). The diagnostic status of homosexuality in *DSM-III*: A reformulation of the issues. *American Journal of Psychiatry, 138,* 210–215.

Spitzer, R. L., Skodol, A. E., Gibbon, M., & Williams, J. B. W. (1983). *Psychopathology, a case book.* New York: McGraw-Hill.

Stadler, C., Sterzer, P., Schmeck, K., Krebs, A., Kleinschmidt, A., & Poustka, F. (2007). Reduced anterior cingulate activation in aggressive children and adolescents during affective stimulation: Association with temperament traits. *Journal of Psychiatric Research, 41*(5), 410–417.

Stafford, K. P., & Sadoff, R. L. (2011). Competence to stand trial. In E. Y. Drogin, F. M. Dattilio, R. L. Sadoff, & T. G. Gutheil (Eds.), *Handbook of forensic assessment: Psychological and psychiatric perspectives* (pp. 3–23). New York: Wiley.

Stagl, J. M., Lechner, S. C., Carver, C. S., Bouchard, L. C., Gudenkauf, L. M., Jutagir, D. R., et al. (2015). A randomized controlled trial of cognitive-behavioral stress management in breast cancer: Survival and recurrence at 11-year follow-up. *Breast Cancer Research and Treatment, 154,* 319–328.

Staniloiu, A., & Markowitsch, H. J. (2014). Dissociative amnesia. *The Lancet Psychiatry, 1*(3), 226–241.

Stanton, A. L., Danoff-Burg, S., Cameron, C. L., Bishop, M., Collins, C. A., Kirk, S. B., & Twillman, R. (2000). Emotionally expressive coping predicts psychological and physical adjustment to breast cancer. *Journal of Consulting and Clinical Psychology, 68,* 875–882.

Stanton, A. L., Luecken, L. J., MacKinnon, D. P., & Thompson, E. H. (2013). Mechanisms in psychosocial interventions for adults living with cancer: Opportunity for integration of theory, research, and practice. *Journal of Consulting and Clinical Psychology, 81,* 318–335.

Steadman, H. J., Mulvey, E. P., Monahan, J., Robbins, P. C., Appelbaum, P. S., Grisso, T., Roth, L. H., & Silver, E. (1998). Violence by people discharged from acute psychiatric inpatient facilities and by others in the same neighborhoods. *Archives of General Psychiatry, 55,* 393–401.

Steadman, H. J., Osher, F. C., Robbins, P. C., Case, B., & Samuels, S. (2009). Prevalence of serious mental illness among jail inmates. *Psychiatric Services, 60*(6), 761–765.

Steensma, T. D., McGuire, J. K., Kreukels, B. P., Beekman, A. J., & Cohen-Kettenis, P. T. (2013). Factors associated with desistence and persistence of childhood gender dysphoria: A quantitative follow-up study. *Journal of the American Academy of Child & Adolescent Psychiatry, 52*(6), 582–590.

Steensma, T. D., Van der Ende, J., Verhulst, F. C., & Cohen-Kettenis, P. T. (2013). Gender variance in childhood and sexual orientation in adulthood: A prospective study. *Journal of Sexual Medicine, 10*(11), 2723–2733.

Stein, A. (2016). Pelvic floor physical therapy in the treatment of sexual dysfunctions. In L. Lipshultz, A. Pastuszak, A. Goldstein, A. Giraldi, & M. Perelman (Eds.). *Management of sexual dysfunction in men and women* (pp. 189–195). New York: Springer.

Stein, A., Woolley, H., Cooper, S., Winterbottom, J., Fairburn, C. G., & Cortina-Borja, M. (2006). Eating habits and attitudes among 10-year-old children of mothers with eating disorders. *British Journal of Psychiatry, 189,* 324–329.

Stein, B. D., Elliott, M. N., Jaycox, L. H., Collins, R. L., Berry, S. H., Klein, D. J., & Schuster, M. A. (2004). A national longitudinal study of the psychological consequences of the September 11, 2001 terrorist attacks: Reactions, impairments, and help-seeking. *Psychiatry, 67,* 105–117.

Stein, D. J., Chiu, W. T., Hwang, I., Kessler, R. C., Sampson, N., et al. (2010). Cross-national analysis of the associations between traumatic events and suicidal behavior: Findings from the WHO World Mental Health Surveys. *PLoS ONE, 5,* e10574.

Stein, D. J., Grant, J. E., Franklin, M. E., Keuthen, N., Lochner, C., Singer, H. S., & Woods, D. W. (2010). Trichotillomania (hair pulling disorder), skin picking disorder, and stereotypic movement disorder: Toward DSM-V. *Depression and Anxiety, 27*(6), 611–626.

Stein, D. J., Lim, C. C., Roest, A. M., de Jonge, P., Aguilar-Gaxiola, S., Al-Hamzawi, A., et al. (2017). The cross-national epidemiology of social anxiety disorder: Data from the World Mental Health Survey Initiative. *BMC Medicine, 15(*1), 143.

Stein, M. B., Jang, K. J., Taylor, S., Vernon, P. A., & Livesley, W. J. (2002). Genetic and environmental influences on trauma exposure and posttraumatic stress disorder: A twin study. *American Journal of Psychiatry 159,* 1675–1681.

Steinberg, L. (2009). Adolescent development and juvenile justice. *Annual Review of Clinical Psychology, 5,* 459–486.

Steiner, M., Dunn, E., & Born, L. (2003). Hormones and mood: From menarche to menopause and beyond. *Journal of Affective Disorders, 74,* 67–83.

Stepanova, E., Dowling, S., Phelps, M., & Findling, R. L. (2017). Pharmacotherapy of emotional and behavioral symptoms associated with autism spectrum disorder in children and adolescents. *Dialogues in Clinical Neuroscience, 19*(4), 395–402.

Stephens, S., Kenny, R. A., Rowan, E., Allan, L., Kalaria, R. N., Bradbury, M., & Ballard, C. G. (2004). Neuropsychological characteristics of mild vascular cognitive impairment and dementia after stroke. *International Journal of Geriatric Psychiatry, 19,* 1053–1057.

Steptoe, A., & Kivimäki, M. (2013). Stress and cardiovascular disease: An update on current knowledge. *Annual Review of Public Health, 34,* 337–354.

Stern, Y., Gurland, B., Tatemichi, T. K., & Tang, M. X. (1994). Influence of education and occupation on the incidence of Alzheimer's disease. *JAMA, 271,* 1004–1010.

Sternberg R. J. (2015) Multiple intelligences in the new age of thinking. In S. Goldstein, D. Princiotta, & J. Naglieri (Eds.), *Handbook of intelligence.* New York: Springer.

Sterzer, P., Stadler, C., Krebs, A., Kleinschmidt, A., & Poustka, F. (2005). Abnormal neural responses to emotional visual stimuli in adolescents with conduct disorder. *Biological Psychiatry, 57,* 7–15.

Stevens, J. S., Almli, L. M., Fani, N., Gutman, D. A., Bradley, B., Norrholm, S. D., et al. (2014). PACAP receptor gene polymorphism impacts fear responses in the amygdala and hippocampus. *Proceedings of the National Academy of Sciences, 111*(8), 3158–3163.

Stice, E. (2016). Interactive and mediational etiologic models of eating disorder onset: Evidence from prospective studies. *Annual Review of Clinical Psychology, 12,* 359–381.

Stice, E. (2002). Risk and maintenance factors for eating pathology: A meta-analytic review. *Psychological Bulletin, 128,* 825–848.

Stice, E., Bohon, C., Marti, C. N., & Fischer, K. (2008). Subtyping women with bulimia nervosa along dietary and negative affect dimensions: Further evidence of reliability and validity. *Journal of Counseling and Clinical Psychology, 76,* 1022–1033.

Stice, E., Burton, E. M., & Shaw, H. (2004). Prospective relations between bulimic pathology, depression, and substance abuse: Unpacking comorbidity in adolescent girls. *Journal of Consulting & Clinical Psychology, 72,* 62–71.

Stice, E., & Fairburn, C. G. (2003). Dietary and dietary-depressive subtypes of bulimia nervosa show differential symptom presentation, social impairment, comorbidity, and course of illness. *Journal of Consulting & Clinical Psychology, 71,* 1090–1094.

Stice, E., Marti, C. N., & Durant, S. (2011). Risk factors for onset of eating disorders: Evidence of multiple risk pathways from an 8-year prospective study. *Behavior Research and Therapy, 49,* 622–627.

Stice, E., Marti, C. N., & Rohde, P. (2013). Prevalence, incidence, impairment, and course of the proposed *DSM-5* eating disorder diagnoses in an 8-year prospective community study of young women. *Journal of Abnormal Psychology, 122*(2), 445–457.

Stice, E., Maxfield, J., & Wells, T. (2003). Adverse effects of social pressure to be thin on young women: An experimental investigation of the effects of "fat talk." *International Journal of Eating Disorders, 34,* 108–117.

Stice, E., Presnell, K., & Spangler, D. (2002). Risk factors for binge eating onset in adolescent girls: A 2-year prospective investigation. *Health Psychology, 21,* 131–138.

Stice, E., & Shaw, H. (2017). Eating disorders: Insights from imaging and behavioral approaches to treatment. *Journal of Psychopharmacology, 31*(11), 1485–1495.

Stice, E., & Shaw, H. E. (1994). Adverse effects of the media-portrayed thin-ideal on women and linkages to bulimic symptomatology. *Journal of Social & Clinical Psychology, 13,* 288–308.

Stice, E., Spangler, D., & Agras, W. S. (2001). Exposure to media-portrayed thin-ideal images adversely affects vulnerable girls: A longitudinal experiment. *Journal of Social & Clinical Psychology, 20,* 270–288.

Stice, E., Spoor, S., Bohon, C., Veldhuizen, M. G., & Small, D. M. (2008). Relation of reward from food intake and anticipated food intake to obesity: A functional magnetic resonance imaging study. *Journal of Abnormal Psychology, 117,* 924–935.

Stice, E., Spoor, S., Ng, J., & Zald, D. H. (2009). Relation of obesity to consummatory and anticipatory food reward. *Physiology & Behavior, 97*(5), 551–560.

Stice, E., Yokum, S., Bohon, C., Marti, N., & Smolen, A. (2010). Reward circuitry responsivity to food predicts future increases in body mass: Moderating effects of DRD2 and DRD4. *NeuroImage, 50,* 1618–1625.

Stinson, F. S., Dawson, D. A., Goldstein, R. B., Chou, S. P., Huang, B., Smith, S. M., Ruan, W. J., Pulay, A. J., Saha, T. D., Pickering, R. P., & Grant, B. F. (2008). Prevalence, correlates, disability, and comorbidity of *DSM-IV* narcissistic personality disorder: Results from the Wave 2 National Epidemiologic Survey on Alcohol and Related Conditions. *Journal of Clinical Psychiatry, 69,* 1033–1045.

Stoeckel, L. E., Weller, R. E., Cook, E. W., 3rd, Twieg, D. B., Knowlton, R. C., & Cox, J. E. (2008). Widespread reward-system activation in obese women in response to pictures of high-calorie foods. *NeuroImage, 41,* 636–647.

Stoffers, J. M., Ferriter, M., Vollm, B. A., Gibbon, S., Jones, H., et al. (2011). Pharmacological interventions for people with narcissistic personality disorder (protocol). *Cochrane Database Systematic Review,* 10:CD009399.

Stoffers, J. M., & Lieb, K. (2015). Pharmacotherapy for borderline personality disorder: Current evidence and recent trends. *Current Psychiatry Reports, 17*(1), 534.

Stone, J., LaFrance, W. C., Brown, R., Spiegel, D., Levenson, J. L., & Sharpe, M. (2011). Conversion disorder:

Current problems and potential solutions for *DSM-5*. *Journal of Psychosomatic Research, 71,* 369–376.

Story, M., Nanney, M. S., & Schwartz, M. B. (2009). Schools and obesity prevention: Creating school environments and policies to promote healthy eating and physical activity. *Milbank Quarterly, 87,* 71–100.

Stouthamer-Loeber, M., Loeber, R., Homish, D. L., & Wei, E. (2001). Maltreatment of boys and the development of disruptive and delinquent behavior. *Development & Psychopathology, 13,* 941–955.

Stoving, R. K., Andries, A., Brixen, K., Bilenberg, N., & Horder, K. (2011). Gender differences in outcome of eating disorders: A retrospective cohort study. *Psychiatric Research, 186,* 362–366.

Stoving, R. K., Andries, A., Brixen, K. T., Bilenberg, N., Lichtenstein, M. B., & Horder, K. (2012). Purging behavior in anorexia nervosa and eating disorder not otherwise specified: A retrospective cohort study. *Psychiatry Research, 198,* 253–258.

Strauss, G. P., Harrow, M., Grossman, L. S., & Rosen, C. (2010). Periods of recovery in deficit syndrome schizophrenia: A 20-year multi-follow-up longitudinal study. *Schizophrenia Bulletin, 36,* 788–799.

Strauss, J. S. (1969). Hallucinations and delusions as points on continua function: Rating scale evidence. *Archives of General Psychiatry, 21,* 581–586.

Strawn, J. R., Welge, J. A., Wehry, A. M., Keeshin, B., & Rynn, M. A. (2015). Efficacy and tolerability of antidepressants in pediatric anxiety disorders: A systematic review and meta-analysis. *Depression and Anxiety, 32*(3), 149–157.

Striegel-Moore, R. H., Fairburn, C. G., Wilfley, D. E., Pike, K. M., Dohm, F.-A., & Kraemer, H. C. (2005). Toward an understanding of risk factors for binge-eating disorder in black and white women: A community-based case-control study. *Psychological Medicine, 35,* 907–917.

Striegel-Moore, R. H., & Franko, D. L. (2008). Should binge eating disorder be included in the *DSM-V*? A critical review of the state of the evidence. *Annual Review of Clinical Psychology, 4,* 305–324.

Striegel-Moore, R. H., Seeley, J. R., & Lewinsohn, P. M. (2003). Psychosocial adjustment in young adulthood of women who experienced an eating disorder during adolescence. *Journal of the American Academy of Child & Adolescent Psychiatry, 42,* 587–593.

Stringaris, A., Cohen, P., Pine, D. S., & Leibenluft, E. (2009). Adult outcomes of youth irritability: A 20-year prospective community-based study. *American Journal of Psychiatry, 166*(9), 1048–1054.

Stunkard, A. J. (1993). A history of binge eating. In C. G. Fairburn & G. T. Wilson (Eds.), *Binge eating: Nature, assessment, and treatment* (pp. 15–34). New York: Guilford Press.

Stunkard, A. J. (2011). Eating disorders and obesity. *Psychiatric Clinic North America, 34,* 765–771.

Sturup, J., Monahan, J., & Kristiansson, M. (2013). Violent behavior and gender of Swedish psychiatric patients: A prospective clinical study. *Psychiatric Services, 64*(7), 688–693.

Substance Abuse and Mental Health Services Administration (SAMHSA). (2013). *Drug Abuse Warning Network, 2011: National Estimates of Drug-Related Emergency Department Visits.* HHS Publication No. (SMA) 13-4760, DAWN Series D-39. Rockville, MD.

Substance Abuse and Mental Health Services Administration (SAMHSA). (2017). *Key substance use and mental health indicators in the United States: Results from the 2016 National Survey on Drug Use and Health* (HHS Publication No. SMA 17-5044, NSDUH Series H-52). Rockville, MD: Center for Behavioral Health Statistics and Quality, Substance Abuse and Mental Health Services Administration. Retrieved from https://www. samhsa.gov/data/.

Sue, D. W., & Sue, D. (2003). *Counseling the culturally diverse: Theory and practice* (4th ed.). New York: Wiley.

Sue, S., & Lam, A. G. (2002). Cultural and demographic diversity. In J. C. Norcross (Ed.), *Psychotherapy relationships that work: Therapist contributions and responsiveness to patients* (pp. 401–421). London: Oxford University Press.

Sue, S., & Zane, N. (1987). The role of culture and cultural techniques in psychotherapy: A critique and reformulation. *American Psychologist, 42,* 37–51.

Suhail, K., & Cochrane, R. (2002). Effect of culture and environment on the phenomenology of delusions and hallucinations. *International Journal of Social Psychiatry, 48,* 126–138.

Sultzer, D. L., Davis, S. M., Tariot, P. N., Dagerman, K. S., Lebowitz, B. D., Lyketsos, C. G., Rosenheck, R. A., Hsiao, J. K., Lieberman, J. A., & Schneider, L. S. (2008). Clinical symptom responses to atypical antipsychotic medications in Alzheimer's disease: Phase 1 outcomes from the CATIE-AD effectiveness trial. *American Journal of Psychiatry, 165,* 844–854.

Sun, D., Stuart, G. W., Jenkinson, M., Wood, S. J., McGorry, P. D., Velakoulis, D., van Erp, T. G., Thompson, P. M., Toga, A. W., Smith, D. J., Cannon, T. D., & Pantelis, C. (2009). Brain surface contraction mapped in first-episode schizophrenia: A longitudinal magnetic resonance imaging study. *Molecular Psychiatry, 14,* 976–986.

Sundgot-Borgen, J. (1994). Risk and trigger factors for the development of eating disorders in female elite athletes. *Medicine & Science in Sports & Exercise, 26,* 414–419.

Sundin, J., Fear, N. T., Iversen, A., Rona, R. J., & Wessely, S. (2010). PTSD after deployment to Iraq: Conflicting rates, conflicting claims. *Psychological Medicine, 40,* 367–382.

Sundram, C. J. (2009). *Wyatt v. Stickney*–a long odyssey reaches an end. http://www.cqcapd.state.ny.us/pressreleases/ wyattclarence.htm (accessed September 29, 2009).

Suomi, S. J. (1999). Developmental trajectories, early experiences, and community consequences: Lessons from studies with rhesus monkeys. In D. P. Keating (Ed.), *Developmental health and the wealth of nations: Social, biological, and educational dynamics* (pp. 185–200). New York: Guilford Press.

Susman, J., & Klee, B. (2005). The role of high-potency benzodiazepines in the treatment of panic disorder. *Primary Care Companion to the Journal of Clinical Psychiatry, 7(1), 5–11.*

Sutker, P. B., Allain, A. N., & Winstead, D. K. (1993). Psychopathology and psychiatric diagnoses of World War II Pacific theater prisoners of war and combat veterans. *American Journal of Psychiatry, 150,* 240–245.

Sutker, P. B., Davis, J. M., Uddo, M., & Ditta, S. R. (1995). Assessment of psychological distress in Persian Gulf troops: Ethnicity and gender comparisons. *Journal of Personality Assessment, 64,* 415–427.

Suzuki, M., Zhou, S. Y., Takahashi, T., Hagino, H., Kawasaki, Y., Niu, L., et al. (2005). Differential contributions of prefrontal and temporolimbic pathology to mechanisms of psychosis. *Brain, 128,* 2109–2122.

Suzuki, T., Griffin, S. A., & Samuel, D. B. (2017). Capturing the *DSM-5* alternative personality disorder model traits in the five-factor model's nomological net. *Journal of Personality, 85*(2), 220–231.

article/0,9171,984465,00.html (accessed October 29, 2009).

Trace, S. E., Baker, J. H., Peñas-Lledó, E., & Bulik, C. M. (2013). The genetics of eating disorders. *Annual Review of Clinical Psychology, 9,* 589–620.

Trauer, J. M., Qian, M. Y., Doyle, J. S., Rajaratnam, S. M., & Cunnington, D. (2015). Cognitive behavioral therapy for chronic insomnia: A systematic review and meta-analysis. *Annals of Internal Medicine, 163*(3), 191–204.

Treasure, J., & Cardi, V. (2017). Anorexia nervosa, theory and treatment: Where are we 35 years on from Hilde Bruch's foundation lecture? *European Eating Disorders Review, 25*(3), 139–147.

Trestman, R. L., Ford, J., Zhang, W., & Wiesbrock, V. (2007). Current and lifetime psychiatric illness among inmates not identified as acutely mentally ill at intake in Connecticut's jails. *Journal of the American Academy of Psychiatry and Law, 35,* 490–500.

Trotti, L. M., & Rye, D. B. (2011). Restless legs syndrome. *Handbook of Clinical Neurology, 100,* 661–673.

True, W. R., Rice, J., Eisen, S. A., Heath, A. C., Goldberg, J., Lyons, M. J., & Nowak, J. (1993). A twin study of genetic and environmental contributions to liability for posttraumatic stress symptoms. *Archives of General Psychiatry, 50,* 257–264.

Trull, T. J., Jahng, S., Tomko, R. L., Wood, P. K., & Sher, K. J. (2010). Revised NESARC personality disorder diagnoses: Gender, prevalence, and comorbidity with substance dependence disorders. *Journal of Personality Disorders, 24*(4), 412–426.

Trull, T. J., Solhan, M. B., Tragesser, S. L., Jahng, S., Wood, P. K., Paisecki, T. M., & Watson, D. (2008). Affective instability: Measuring a core feature of borderline personality disorder with ecological momentary assessment. *Journal of Abnormal Psychology, 117,* 647–661.

Tseng, W. (1973). The development of psychiatric concepts in traditional Chinese medicine. *Archives of General Psychiatry, 29,* 569–575.

Ttofi, M. M., Farrington, D. P., & Lösel, F. (2012). School bullying as a predictor of violence later in life: A systematic review and meta-analysis of prospective longitudinal studies. *Aggression and Violent Behavior, 17*(5), 405–418.

Turk, C. L., Heimberg, R. G., & Hope, D. A. (2001). Social anxiety disorder. *Clinical handbook of psychological disorders: A step-by-step treatment manual* (3rd ed., pp. 114–153). New York: Guilford Press.

Turk, D. C., & Ruby, T. E. (1992). Cognitive factors and persistent pain: A glimpse into Pandora's box. *Cognitive Therapy & Research, 16,* 99–122.

Turk, J. (2011). Fragile X syndrome: Lifespan developmental implications for those without as well as with intellectual disability. *Current Opinion in Psychiatry, 24,* 387–397.

Turkheimer, E., & Parry, C. D. (1992). Why the gap? Practice and policy in civil commitment hearings. *American Psychologist, 47,* 646–655.

Turner, D. T., van der Gaag, M., Karyotaki, E., & Cuijpers, P. (2014). Psychological interventions for psychosis: A meta-analysis of comparative outcome studies. *American Journal of Psychiatry, 171*(5), 523–538.

Turner-Cobb, J. M., Sephton, S. E., Koopman, C., Blake-Mortimer, J., & Spiegel, D. (2000). Social support and salivary cortisol in women with metastatic breast cancer. *Psychosomatic Medicine, 62,* 337–345.

Twenge, J. M., Joiner, T. E., Rogers, M. L., & Martin, G. N. (2018). Increases in depressive symptoms, suicide-related outcomes, and suicide rates among US adolescents after 2010 and links to increased new media screen time. *Clinical Psychological Science, 6*(1), 3–17.

Twenge, J. M., & Nolen-Hoeksema, S. (2002). Age, gender, race, SES, and birth cohort differences on the Children's Depression Inventory: A meta-analysis. *Journal of Abnormal Psychology, 111,* 578–588.

Tyrer, P., Cooper, S., Crawford, M., Dupont, S., Green, J., Murphy, D., Salkovskis, P., Smith, G., Wang, D., Bhogal, S., et al. (2011). Prevalence of health anxiety problems in medical clinics. *Journal of Psychosomatic Research, 71,* 392–394.

U

Uchino, B. N. (2009). Understanding the links between social support and physical health: A life-span perspective with emphasis on the separability of perceived and received support. *Perspectives on Psychological Science, 4,* 236–255.

Ujike, H., Otani, K., Nakatsuka, M., Ishii, K., Sasaki, A., Oishi, T., Sato, T., Okahisa, Y., Matsumoto, Y., Namba, Y., Kimata, Y., & Kuroda, S. (2009). Association study of gender identity disorder and sex hormone–related genes. *Progress in Neuro-Psychopharmacology & Biological Psychiatry, 3,* 1241–1244.

Ullman, L. P., & Krasner, L. (1975). *A psychological approach to abnormal behavior* (2nd ed.). Oxford: Prentice Hall.

UNAIDS. (2018). Fact sheet–Latest statistics on the status of the AIDS epidemic. http://www.unaids.org/en/resources/fact-sheet. Retrieved July 5, 2018.

Unwin, G. L., & Deb, S. (2011). Efficacy of atypical antipsychotic medication in the management of behaviour problems in children with intellectual disabilities and borderline intelligence: A systematic review. *Research in Developmental Disabilities, 32,* 2121–2133.

Urbanoski, K. A., & Kelly, J. F. (2012). Understanding genetic risk for substance use and addiction: A guide for non-geneticists. *Clinical Psychology Review, 32,* 60–70.

U.S. Census Bureau. (2018). Older people projected to outnumber younger people for first time in U.S. history. https://www.census.gov/newsroom/press-releases/2018/cb18-41-population-projections.html. Retrieved July 4, 2018.

V

Valdez, J. N. (2014). Curanderismo: A complementary and alternative approach to Mexican American health psychology. In Gurung, R. A. R (Ed.), *Multicultural approaches to health and wellness in America* (pp. 227–258). Santa Barbara, CA: Praeger.

Valenzuela, M. J. (2008). Brain reserve and the prevention of dementia. *Current Opinion in Psychiatry 21,* 296–302.

Vandelanotte, C., Kolt, G. S., Caperchione, C. M., Savage, T. N., Rosenkranz, R. R., et al. (2017). Effectiveness of a Web 2.0 intervention to increase physical activity in real-world settings: Randomized ecological trial. *Journal of Medical Internet Research, 19*(11): e390.

Vandelanotte, C., Müller, A. M., Short, C. E., Hingle, M., Nathan, N., Williams, S. L., et al. (2016). Past, present, and future of eHealth and mHealth research to improve physical activity and dietary behaviors. *Journal of Nutrition Education and Behavior, 48*(3), 219–228.

Vandelanotte, C., Spathonis, K. M., Eakin, E. G., & Owen, N. (2007). Website-delivered physical activity interventions: A review of the literature. *American Journal of Preventative Medicine, 33,* 54–64.

VanderKruik, R., Barreix, M., Chou, D., Allen, T., Say, L., & Cohen, L. S. (2017). The global prevalence of postpartum psychosis: A systematic review. *BMC Psychiatry, 17*(1), 272.

van der Velden, P. G., van Loon, P., Benight, C. C., & Eckardt, T. (2012). Mental health problems among search and rescue workers deployed in the Haiti earthquake 2010: A pre-post comparison. *Psychiatry Research, 198*, 100–105.

Van Dijk, S., Jeffrey, J., & Katz, M. R. (2013). A randomized, controlled, pilot study of dialectical behavior therapy skills in a psychoeducational group for individuals with bipolar disorder. *Journal of Affective Disorders, 145*, 386–393.

Van Geel, M., Vedder, P., & Tanilon, J. (2014). Are overweight and obese youths more often bullied by their peers? A meta-analysis on the relation between weight status and bullying. *International Journal of Obesity, 38*(10), 1263–1267.

van Ommeren, M., De Jong, J. T. V. M., Bhogendra, S., Komproe, I., Thapa, S. B., & Cardena, E. (2001). Psychiatric disorders among tortured Bhutanese refugees in Nepal. *Archives of General Psychiatry, 58*, 475–482.

van Os, J., Hanssen, M., Bijl, R. V., & Vollebergh, W. (2001). Prevalence of psychotic disorder and community level of psychotic symptoms. *Archives of General Psychiatry, 58*, 663–668.

Van Winkel, R., & Kuepper, R. (2014). Epidemiological, neurobiological, and genetic clues to the mechanisms linking cannabis use to risk for nonaffective psychosis. *Annual Review of Clinical Psychology, 10*, 767–791.

Vassos, E., Collier, D. A., & Fazel, S. (2014). Systematic meta-analyses and field synopsis of genetic association studies of violence and aggression. *Molecular Psychiatry, 19*(4), 471–477.

Vaughn, M. G., Fu, Q., Bender, K., DeLisi, M., Beaver, K. M., Perron, B. E., & Howard, M. O. (2010). Psychiatric correlates of bullying in the United States: Findings from a national sample. *Psychiatric Quarterly, 81*(3), 183–195.

Veasey, S. C., Guilleminault, C., Strohl, K. P., Sanders, M. H., Ballard, R. D., & Magalang, U. J. (2006). Medical therapy for obstructive sleep apnea: A review by the Medical Therapy for Obstructive Sleep Apnea Task Force of the Standards of Practice Committee of the American Academy of Sleep Medicine. *Sleep, 29*, 1036–1044.

Veith, I. (1965). *Hysteria: The history of a disease.* Chicago: University of Chicago Press.

Velting, O. N., Setzer, N. J., & Albano, A. M. (2004). Update on and advances in assessment and cognitive-behavioral treatment of anxiety disorders in children and adolescents. *Professional Psychology: Research & Practice, 35*, 42–54.

Ventriglio, A., Gentile, A., Bonfitto, I., Stella, E., Mari, M., Steardo, L., & Bellomo, A. (2016). Suicide in the early stage of schizophrenia. *Frontiers in Psychiatry, 7*, 116.

Ventura, J., Neuchterlein, K. H., Lukoff, D., & Hardesty, J. P. (1989). A prospective study of stressful life events and schizophrenic relapse. *Journal of Abnormal Psychology, 98*, 407–411.

Verheul, R., & Widiger, T. A. (2004). A meta-analysis of the prevalence and usage of the personality disorder not otherwise specified (PDNOS) diagnosis. *Journal of Personality Disorders, 18*, 309–319.

Verma, K. K., Khaitan, B. K., & Singh, O. P. (1998). The frequency of sexual dysfunctions in patients attending a sex therapy clinic in north India. *Archives of Sexual Behavior, 27*, 309–314.

Vervliet, B., Craske, M. G., & Hermans, D. (2013). Fear extinction and relapse: State of the art. *Annual Review of Clinical Psychology, 9*, 215–248.

Vesga-López, O., Schneier, F., Wang, S., Heimberg, R., Liu, S. M., Hasin, D. S., & Blanco, C. (2008). Gender differences in generalized anxiety disorder: Results from the National Epidemiologic Survey on Alcohol and Related Conditions (NESARC). *The Journal of Clinical Psychiatry, 69*(10), 1606–1616.

Via, E., Radua, J., Cardoner, N., Happé, F., & Mataix-Cols, D. (2011). Meta-analysis of gray matter abnormalities in autism spectrum disorder: Should Asperger disorder be subsumed under a broader umbrella of autistic spectrum disorder? *Archive of General Psychiatry, 68*, 409–418.

Vigerland, S., Lenhard, F., Bonnert, M., Lalouni, M., Hedman, E., Ahlen, J., et al. (2016). Internet-delivered cognitive behavior therapy for children and adolescents: A systematic review and meta-analysis. *Clinical Psychology Review, 50*, 1–10.

Viken, R. J., Treat, T. A., Nosofsky, R. M., McFall, R. M., & Palmeri, T. J. (2002). Modeling individual differences in perceptual and attentional processes. *Journal of Abnormal Psychology, 111*, 598–609.

Villemagne, V. L., Doré, V., Burnham, S. C., Masters, C. L., & Rowe, C. C. (2018). Imaging tau and amyloid- proteinopathies in Alzheimer disease and other conditions. *Nature Reviews Neurology, 14*(4), 225–236.

Visintainer, M. A., Volpicelli, J. R., & Seligman, M. E. (1982). Tumor rejection in rats after inescapable or escapable shock. *Science, 216*, 437–439.

Vismara, L. A., & Rogers, S. J. (2010). Behavioral treatments in autism spectrum disorder: What do we know? *Annual Review of Clinical Psychology, 6*, 447–468.

Visser, F. E., Aldenkamp, A. P., van Huffelen, A. C., Kuilman, M., Overweg, J., & van Wijk, J. (1997). Prospective study of the prevalence of Alzheimer-type dementia in institutionalized individuals with Down syndrome. *American Journal on Mental Retardation, 101*, 400–412.

Vitkus, J. (2004). *Casebook in abnormal psychology*. New York: McGraw-Hill.

Vohs, K. D., Voelz, Z. R., Pettit, J. W., Bardone, A. M., Katz, J., Abramson, L. Y., Heatherton, T. F., & Joiner, T. E. (2001). Perfectionism, body dissatisfaction, and self-esteem: An interactive model of bulimic symptom development. *Journal of Social & Clinical Psychology, 20*, 476–497.

Volkmar, F. R., State, M., & Klin, A. (2009). Autism and autism spectrum disorders: Diagnostic issues for the coming decade. *Journal of Child Psychology and Psychiatry, 50*, 108–115.

Volkow, N. D., & Boyle, M. (2018). Neuroscience of addiction: Relevance to prevention and treatment. *American Journal of Psychiatry.* Doi: 10.1176/appi.ajp.2018.17101174.

Volkow, N. D., Wise, R. A., & Baler, R. (2017). The dopamine motive system: Implications for drug and food addiction. *Nature Reviews Neuroscience, 18*(12), 741.

Vonderlin, R., Kleindienst, N., Alpers, G. W., Bohus, M., Lyssenko, L., & Schmahl, C. (2018). Dissociation in victims of childhood abuse or neglect: A meta-analytic review. *Psychological Medicine*, 1–10.

Voort, J. L. V., He, J. P., Jameson, N. D., & Merikangas, K. R. (2014). Impact of the DSM-5 attention-deficit/hyperactivity disorder age-of-onset criterion in the US adolescent population. *Journal of the American Academy of Child & Adolescent Psychiatry, 53*(7), 736–744.

Vukasović, T., & Bratko, D. (2015). Heritability of personality: A meta-analysis of behavior genetic studies. *Psychological Bulletin, 141*(4), 769–785.

Vythilingam, M., Heim, C., Newport, J., Miller, A. H., Anderson, E., Bronen, R., Brummer, M., Staib, L., Vermetten, E., Charney, D. S., Nemeroff, C. B., & Bremner, J. D. (2002). Childhood trauma associated with smaller hippocampal volume in women with major depression. *American Journal of Psychiatry, 159*, 2072–2080.

W

Wadden, T. A., Neiberg, R. H., Wing, R. R., Clark, J. M., Delahanty, L. M., Hill, J. O., Krakoff, J., Otto, A., Ryan, D. H., & Vitolins, M. Z. (2011). Four-year weight losses in the Look AHEAD study: Factors associated with long-term success. *Obesity, 19,* 1987–1998.

Wadden, T. A., Wilson, G. T., Stunkard, A. J., & Berkowitz, R. I. (2011). Obesity and associated eating disorders: A guide for mental health professionals. *Psychiatric Clinics of North America, 34,* xiii–xvi.

Wade, T. D., Bergin, J. L., Tiggemann, M., Bulik, C. M., & Fairburn, C. G. (2006). Prevalence and long-term course of lifetime eating disorders in an adult Australian twin cohort. *Australian and New Zealand Journal of Psychiatry, 40,* 121–128.

Wade, T. D., Gillespie, N., & Martin, N. G. (2007). A comparison of early family life events amongst monozygotic twin women with lifetime anorexia nervosa, bulimia nervosa, or major depression. *International Journal of Eating Disorders, 40,* 679–686.

Wade, T. D., Tiggemann, M., Bulik, C. M., Fairburn, C. G., Wray, N. R., & Martin, N. G. (2008). Shared temperament risk factors for anorexia nervosa: A twin study. *Psychosomatic Medicine, 70,* 239–244.

Wade, T. D., & Watson, H. J. (2012). Psychotherapies in eating disorders. In J. Alexander & J. Treasure (Eds.), *A collaborative approach to eating disorders* (pp. 125–135). New York: Routledge/Taylor & Francis Group.

Wagner, P. S., & Spiro, C. (2005). *Divided minds: Twin sisters and their journey through schizophrenia.* New York: St. Martin's Press.

Wakschlag, L. S., Pickett, K. E., Kasza, K. E., & Loeber, R. (2006). Is prenatal smoking associated with a developmental pattern of conduct problems in young boys? *Journal of the American Academy of Child and Adolescent Psychiatry, 45,* 461–467.

Walderhaug, E., Krystal, J. H., & Neumeister, A. (2011). In D. M. Benedek & G. H. Wynn (Eds.), *Clinical manual for management of PTSD* (pp. 45–68). Arlington, VA: American Psychiatric Publishing.

Waldinger, M. D. (2015). Psychiatric disorders and sexual dysfunction. *Handbook of Clinical Neurology, 130,* 469–489.

Walker, E. F., Cornblatt, B. A., Addington, J., Cadenhead, K. S., Cannon, T. D., McGlashan, T. H., Perkins, D. O., Seidman, L. J., Tsuang, M. T., Woods, S. W., & Heinssen, R. (2009). The relation of antipsychotic and antidepressant medication with baseline symptoms and symptom progression: A naturalistic study of the North American Prodrome Longitudinal Sample. *Schizophrenia Research, 115,* 50–57.

Walker, E. F., Kestler, L., Bollini, A., & Hochman, K. M. (2004). Schizophrenia: Etiology and course. *Annual Review of Psychology, 55,* 401–430.

Walkup, J. T., Albano, A. M., Piacentini, J., Birmaher, B., Compton, S. N., Sherrill, J. T., et al. (2008). Cognitive behavioral therapy, sertraline, or a combination in childhood anxiety. *New England Journal of Medicine, 359*(26), 2753–2766.

Walkup, J. T., Ferraõ, Y., Leckman, J. F., Stein, D. J., & Singer, H. (2010). Tic disorders: Some key issues for *DSM-V. Depression and Anxiety, 27,* 600–610.

Wallace, E. R., IV, & Gach, J. (Eds.). (2008). *History of psychiatry and medical psychology: With an epilogue on psychiatry and the mind-body relation.* New York: Springer Science.

Wampold, B. E. (2015). How important are the common factors in psychotherapy? An update. *World Psychiatry, 14*(3), 270–277.

Wang, P. S., Aguilar-Gaxiola, S., Alonso, J., Angermeyer, M. C., Borges, G., & Bromet E. J. (2007). Use of mental health services for anxiety, mood, and substance disorders in 17 countries in the WHO World Mental Health surveys. *Lancet, 370,* 841–850.

Wang, S., & Blazer, D. G. (2015). Depression and cognition in the elderly. *Annual Review of Clinical Psychology, 11,* 331–360.

Wanic, R., & Kulik, J. (2011). Toward an understanding of gender differences in the impact of marital conflict on health. *Sex Roles, 65*(5–6), 297–312.

Warren, J. I., Burnette, M., South, S. C., Chauhan, P., Bale, R., & Friend, R. (2002). Personality disorders and violence among female prison inmates. *Journal of the American Academy of Psychiatry and the Law, 30*(4), 502–509.

Warren, J. I., Murrie, D. C., Chauhan, P., Dietz, P. E., & Morris, J. (2004). Opinion formation in evaluating sanity at the time of the offense: An examination of 5175 pre-trial evaluations. *Behavioral Sciences and the Law, 22,* 171–186.

Wassertheil-Smoller, S., Arredondo, E. M., Cai, J., Castaneda, S. F., Choca, J. P., Gallo, L. C., et al. (2014). Depression, anxiety, antidepressant use, and cardiovascular disease among Hispanic men and women of different national backgrounds: Results from the Hispanic Community Health Study/Study of Latinos. *Annals of Epidemiology, 24*(11), 822–830.

Watson, D. (2009). Differentiating the mood and anxiety disorders: A quadripartite model. *Annual Review of Clinical Psychology, 5,* 221–247.

Watson, D., Clark, L. A., & Chmielewski, M. (2008). Structures of personality and their relevance to psychopathology: II. Further articulation of a comprehensive unified trait structure. *Journal of Personality, 76,* 1545–1585.

Watson, J. B. (1930). *Behaviorism.* Chicago: University of Chicago Press.

Watson, J. B., & Raynor, R. (1920). Conditioned emotional reactions. *Journal of Experimental Psychology, 3,* 1–14.

Watson, M., Haviland, J. S., Greer, S., Davidson, J., & Bliss, J. M. (1999). Influence of psychological response on survival in breast cancer: A population-based cohort study. *Lancet, 354,* 1331–1336.

Waugh, M. H., Hopwood, C. J., Krueger, R. F., Morey, L. C., Pincus, A. L., & Wright, A. G. (2017). Psychological assessment with the DSM-5 Alternative Model for Personality Disorders: Tradition and innovation. *Professional Psychology: Research and Practice, 48*(2), 79–89.

Webb, R. L., & Murphy, M. P. (2012). ß-Secretases, Alzheimer's disease, and Down syndrome. *Current Gerontology and Geriatrics Research, 2012,* 362839.

Webster-Stratton, C., & Reid, M. J. (2017). The Incredible Years Parents, Teachers, and Children Training Series: A multifaceted treatment approach for young children with conduct problems. In J. R. Weisz & A. E. Kazdin (Eds.), *Evidence-based psychotherapies for children and adolescents* (3rd ed., pp. 122–141). New York: Guilford.

Wechsler, H., Lee, J. E., Kuo, M., Seibring, M., Nelson, T. F., & Lee, H. (2002). Trends in alcohol use, related problems and experience of prevention efforts among U.S. college students 1993 to 2001: Results from the 2001 Harvard School of Public Health College Alcohol Study. *Journal of American College Health, 50,* 203–217.

Weems, C. F., Pina, A. A., Costa, N. M., Watts, S. E., Taylor, L. K., & Cannon, M. F. (2007). Predisaster trait anxiety and negative affect predict posttraumatic stress in youths after Hurricane Katrina. *Journal of Counseling and Clinical Psychology, 75,* 154–159.

Weinberg, A., & Klonsky, E. D. (2012). The effects of self-injury on acute negative arousal: A laboratory simulation. *Motivation and Emotion, 36,* 242–254.

Weiner, B. A., & Wettstein, R. M. (1993). *Legal issues in mental health care.* New York: Plenum Press.

Weiner, L., & Avery-Clark, C. (2017). *Sensate focus in sex therapy: The illustrated manual.* Taylor & Francis.

Weissman, M., & Cuijpers, P. (2017). Psychotherapy over the last four decades. *Harvard Review of Psychiatry, 25*(4), 155–158.

Weissman, M. M., Markowitz, J. C., & Klerman, G. J. (2017). *The guide to interpersonal psychotherapy: Updated and expanded edition.* New York: Oxford University Press.

Weissman, M. M., & Verdeli, H. (2013). Interpersonal psychotherapy: Evaluation, support, triage. *Clinical Psychology & Psychotherapy, 19,* 106–112.

Werner, K. B., Few, L. R., & Bucholz, K. K. (2015). Epidemiology, comorbidity, and behavioral genetics of antisocial personality disorder and psychopathy. *Psychiatric Annals, 45*(4), 195–199.

Wersebe, H., Sijbrandij, M., & Cuijpers, P. (2013). Psychological group-treatments of social anxiety disorder: A meta-analysis. *PLoS ONE, 8,* e79034.

Westefeld, J. S., Gann, L. C., Lustgarten, S. D., & Yeates, K. J. (2016). Relationships between firearm availability and suicide: The role of psychology. *Professional Psychology: Research and Practice, 47*(4), 271–277.

Westen, D. (1998). The scientific legacy of Sigmund Freud: Toward a psychodynamically informed psychological science. *Psychological Bulletin, 124,* 333–371.

Westermeyer, J., Bouafuely, M., Neider, J., & Callies, A. (1989). Somatization among refugees: An epidemiologic study. *Psychosomatics, 30,* 34–43.

Westrin, A., & Lam, R. W. (2007). Seasonal affective disorder: A clinical update. *Annals of Clinical Psychiatry, 19,* 239–246.

Wetherell, J. L., Lenze, E. J., & Stanley, M. A. (2005). Evidence-based treatment of geriatric anxiety disorders. *Psychiatric Clinics of North America, 28,* 871–896.

Wetzel, E., Brown, A., Hill, P. L., Chung, J. M., Robins, R. W., & Roberts, B. W. (2017). The narcissism epidemic is dead; long live the narcissism epidemic. *Psychological Science, 28*(12), 1833–1847.

Wexler, L., Chandler, M., Gone, J. P., Cwik, M., Kirmayer, L. J., LaFromboise, T., et al. (2015). Advancing suicide prevention research with rural American Indian and Alaska Native populations. *American Journal of Public Health, 105*(5), 891–899.

Whalley, B., Thompson, D. R., & Taylor, R. S. (2014). Psychological interventions for coronary heart disease: Cochrane systematic review and meta-analysis. *International Journal of Behavioral Medicine, 21*(1), 109–121.

Wheeler, J., Newring, K. A. B., and Draper, C. (2008). Transvestic fetishism: Psychopathology and theory. In D. R. Laws & W. T. O'Donohue (Eds.), *Sexual deviance: Theory, assessment, and treatment* (pp. 272–284). New York: Guilford Press.

White, H. R., Xie, M., & Thompson, W. (2001). Psychopathology as a predictor of adolescent drug use trajectories. *Psychology of Addictive Behaviors, 15,* 210–218.

WHO World Mental Health Survey Consortium. (2004). Prevalence, severity, and unmet need for treatment of mental disorders in the World Health Organization World Mental Health Surveys. *JAMA, 291,* 2581–2590.

Whooley, M. A., de Jonge, P., Vittinghoff, E., Otte, C., Moos, R., Carney, R. M., Ali, S., Dowray, S., Na, B., Feldman, M. D., Schiller, N., & Browner, W. S. (2008). Depressive symptoms, health behaviors, and risk of cardiovascular events in patients with coronary heart disease. *JAMA, 300,* 2379–2388.

Whooley, M. A., & Wong, J. M. (2013). Depression and cardiovascular disorders. *Annual Review of Clinical Psychology, 9,* 327–354.

Widiger, T. A. (2002). Values, politics, and science in the construction of the *DSM*s. In J. Z. Sadler (Ed.), *Descriptions and prescriptions: Values, mental disorders, and the* DSMs (pp. 25–41). Baltimore: Johns Hopkins University Press.

Widiger, T. A., & Costa, P. T. C., Jr. (2013). *Personality disorders and the five-factor model of personality* (3rd ed.) Washington, DC: American Psychological Association.

Widiger, T. A., & Mullins-Sweatt, S. N. (2009). Five-factor model of personality disorder: A proposal for *DSM-V. Annual Review of Clinical Psychology, 5,* 197–220.

Widom, C. S., DuMont, K., & Czaja, S. J. (2007). A prospective investigation of major depressive disorder and comorbidity in abused and neglected children grown up. *Archives of General Psychiatry, 64,* 49–56.

Wiewel, E. W., Torian, L. V., Merchant, P., Braunstein, S. L., & Shepard, C. W. (2016). HIV diagnoses and care among transgender persons and comparison with men who have sex with men: New York City, 2006–2011. *American Journal of Public Health, 106*(3), 497–502.

Wilens, T. E., Biederman, J., & Spencer, T. J. (2002). Attention deficit/hyperactivity disorder across the lifespan. *Annual Review of Medicine, 53,* 113–131.

Wilfley, D. E., Pike, K. M., & Striegel-Moore, R. H. (1997). Toward an integrated model of risk for binge-eating disorder. *Journal of Gender, Culture, & Health, 2,* 1–32.

Williams, C., Firn, M., Wharne, S., & Macpherson, R. (eds.) (2011). *Assertive outreach in mental healthcare: Current perspectives.* Oxford: Wiley-Blackwell.

Williams, D. H., IV, & Johnson, B. A. (2016). Clinical evaluation and treatment of disorders of ejaculation. In L. Lipshultz, A. Pastuszak, A. Goldstein, A. Giraldi, & M. Perelman (Eds.). *Management of sexual dysfunction in men and women* (pp. 139–157). New York: Springer.

Williams, D. L. (2010). *Developmental language disorders: Learning, language, and the brain.* San Diego, CA: Plural.

Williams, J. M. G., Barnhofer, T., Crane, C., Hermans, D., Raes, F., Watkins, E., & Dalgleish, T. (2007). Autobiographical memory specificity and emotional disorder. *Psychological Bulletin, 133,* 122–148.

Williams, L. M. (1995). Recovered memories of abuse in women with documented child sexual victimization histories. *Journal of Traumatic Stress, 8,* 649–673.

Williams, R. B. (2008). Psychosocial and biobehavioral factors and their interplay in coronary heart disease. *Annual Review of Clinical Psychology, 4,* 349–365.

Williams, R. B., Barefoot, J. C., Haney, T. L., & Harrell, F. E. (1988). Type A behavior and angiographically documented coronary atherosclerosis in a sample of 2,289 patients. *Psychosomatic Medicine, 50,* 139–152.

Williamson, G. L. (1993). Postpartum depression syndrome as a defense to criminal behavior. *Journal of Family Violence, 8,* 151–165.

Wilps, R. F., Jr. (1990). Male bulimia nervosa: An autobiographical case study. In A. E. Andersen (Ed.), *Males with eating disorders* (pp. 9–29). New York: Brunner/Mazel.

Wilson, A. D., Roos, C. R., Robinson, C. S., Stein, E. R., Manuel, J. A., Enkema, M. C., et al. (2017). Mindfulness-based interventions for addictive behaviors: Implementation issues on the road ahead. *Psychology of Addictive Behaviors, 31*(8), 888–896.

Wilson, G. R., Loeb, K. L., Walsh, B. T., Labouvie, R., Petkova, E., Xinhua, L., & Waternaux, C. (1999). Psychological versus pharmacological treatments of bulimia nervosa: Predictors and processes of change. *Journal of Consulting & Clinical Psychology, 67,* 451–459.

Wilson, G. T., Fairburn, C. C., Agras, W. S., Walsh, B. T., & Kraemer, H. (2002). Cognitive-behavioral therapy for bulimia nervosa: Time course and mechanisms of change. *Journal of Consulting & Clinical Psychology, 70,* 267–274.

Wilson, K. A., & Hayward, C. (2005). A prospective evaluation of agoraphobia and depression symptoms following panic attacks in a community sample of adolescents. *Journal of Anxiety Disorders, 19,* 87–103.

Wincze, J. P., Bach, A. K., & Barlow, D. H. (2008). Sexual dysfunction. In D. H. Barlow (Ed.), *Clinical handbook of psychological disorders* (4th ed., pp. 615–661). New York: Guilford.

Wincze, J. P., & Weinberg, R. B. (2015). *Sexual dysfunction: A guide for assessment and treatment* (3rd ed.). New York: Guilford.

Winger, G., Hofmann, F. G., & Woods, J. H. (1992). *Handbook on drug and alcohol abuse.* New York: Oxford University Press.

Winger, G., Hofmann, F. G., & Woods, J. H. (2004). *Handbook on drug and alcohol abuse: The biomedical aspects* (4th ed.). New York: Oxford University Press.

Winkelmann, J., Schormair, B., Lichtner, P., et al. (2007). Genome-wide association study of restless legs syndrome identifies common variants in three genomic regions. *Nature Genetics, 39,* 1000–1006.

Wintemute, G. J., Parham, C. A., Beaumont, J. J., Wright, M., & Drake, C. (1999). Mortality among recent purchasers of handguns. *New England Journal of Medicine, 341,* 1583–1589.

Wintersteen, M. B., Mensinger, J. L., & Diamond, G. S. (2005). Do gender and racial differences between patient and therapist affect therapeutic alliance and treatment retention in adolescents? *Professional Psychology: Research and Practice, 36,* 400–408.

Witkiewitz, K., Van der Maas, H. L. J., Hufford, M. R., & Marlatt, G. A. (2007). Nonnormality and divergence in posttreatment alcohol use: Reexamining the project MATCH data "another way." *Journal of Abnormal Psychology, 116,* 378–394.

Wittchen, H.-U., Gloster, A. T., Beesdo-Baum, K., Fava, G., & Craske, M. G. (2010). Agoraphobia: A review of the diagnostic classificatory position and criteria. *Depression and Anxiety, 27,* 113–133.

Witthöft, M., Kerstner, T., Ofer, J., Mier, D., Rist, F., Diener, C., & Bailer, J. (2016). Cognitive biases in pathological health anxiety: The contribution of attention, memory, and evaluation processes. *Clinical Psychological Science, 4*(3), 464–479.

Wolfe, B. E., Baker, C. W., Smith, A. T., & Kelly-Weeder, S. (2009). Validity and utility of the current definition of binge eating. *International Journal of Eating Disorders, 42,* 674–686.

Wolfson, A. R. (2010). Adolescents and emerging adults' sleep patterns: New developments. *Journal of Adolescent Health, 46,* 97–99.

Wollert, R., & Cramer, E. (2011). Sampling extreme groups invalidates research on the paraphilias: Implications for *DSM-5* and sex offender risk assessments. *Behavioral Sciences & the Law, 29,* 554–565.

Wonderlich, S. A., Gordon, K. H., Mitchell, J. E., Crosby, R. D., & Engel, S. G. (2009). The validity and clinical utility of binge eating disorder. *International Journal of Eating Disorders, 42,* 687–705.

Wong, C., Odom, S. L., Hume, K. A., Cox, A. W., Fettig, A., Kucharczyk, S., et al. (2015). Evidence-based practices for children, youth, and young adults with autism spectrum disorder: A comprehensive review. *Journal of Autism and Developmental Disorders, 45*(7), 1951–1966.

Wong, J. M., Na, B., Regan, M. C., & Whooley, M. A. (2013). Hostility, health behaviors, and risk of recurrent events in patients with stable coronary heart disease: Findings from the Heart and Soul Study. *Journal of the American Heart Association, 2*(5), e000052.

Wong, Q. J., & Rapee, R. M. (2016). The aetiology and maintenance of social anxiety disorder: A synthesis of complementary theoretical models and formulation of a new integrated model. *Journal of Affective Disorders, 203,* 84–100.

Wong Sarver, N., & Gros, D. F. (2014). A modern behavioral treatment to address fetishism and associated functional impairment. *Clinical Case Studies, 13*(4), 336–351.

Woods, D. W., & Houghton, D. C. (2014). Diagnosis, evaluation, and management of trichotillomania. *Psychiatric Clinics of North America, 37*(3), 301–317.

Woody, M. L., McGeary, J. E., & Gibb, B. E. (2014). Brooding rumination and heart rate variability in women at high and low risk for depression: Group differences and moderation by COMT genotype. *Journal of Abnormal Psychology, 123,* 61–67.

World Health Organization (WHO). (2014). *Global status report on alcohol and health.* Geneva, Switzerland: Author.

World Health Organization (WHO). (2017). Suicide prevention. http://www.who.int/mental_health/suicide-prevention/en/ (accessed May 14, 2018).

World Health Organization (WHO). (2018a). Cardiovascular diseases (CVDs). http://www.who.int/en/news-room/fact-sheets/detail/cardiovascular-diseases-(cvds). Retrieved July 5, 2018.

World Health Organization (WHO). (2018b). HIV/AIDS. http://www.who.int/en/news-room/fact-sheets/detail/hiv-aids. Retrieved July 5, 2018.

World Health Organization (WHO). (2018c). Obesity. Retrieved June 21, 2018, from http://www.who.int/topics/obesity.

World Health Organization (WHO). (2018d). WHO releases new international classification of diseases (ICD 11). http://www.who.int/news-room/detail/18-06-2018-who-releases-new-international-classification-of-diseases-(icd-11). Retrieved July 4, 2018.

Worthman, C. M., & Panter-Brick, C. (2008). Homeless street children in Nepal: Use of allostatic load to assess the burden of childhood adversity. *Development and Psychopathology, 20,* 233–255.

Wright, A. G. C., Calabrese, W. R., Rudick, M. M., Yam, W. H., Zelazny, K., Williams, T. F., et al. (2015). Stability of the DSM-5 Section III pathological personality traits and their longitudinal associations with psychosocial functioning in personality disordered individuals. *Journal of Abnormal Psychology, 124,* 199–207.

Wright, A. G. C., Thomas, K. M., Hopwood, C. J., Markon, K. E., Pincus, A. L., & Krueger, R. F. (2012). The hierarchical structure of DSM-5 pathological personality traits. *Journal of Abnormal Psychology, 121,* 951–957.

Wurtzel, E. (1995). *Prozac nation.* New York: Berkley.

X

Xu, M.-Q., Sun, W.-S., Liu, B.-X., Feng, G.-Y., Yu, L., Yang, L., He, G., Sham, P., Susser, E., St. Clair, D., & He, L. (2009). Prenatal malnutrition and adult schizophrenia: Further evidence from the 1959–1961 Chinese famine. *Schizophrenia Bulletin, 35,* 568–576.

Xu, Y., Schneier, F., Heimberg, R. G., Princisvalle, K., Liebowitz, M. R., Wang, S., & Blanco, C. (2012). Gender differences in social anxiety disorder: Results from the national epidemiologic sample on alcohol and related conditions. *Journal of Anxiety Disorders, 26*(1), 12–19.

Y

Yang, J., Dai, X., Yao, S., Cai, T., Gao, B., McCrae, R. R., & Costa, P. T. (2002). Personality disorders and the five-factor model of personality in Chinese psychiatric patients. In P. T. Costa & T. A. Widiger (Eds.), *Personality disorders and the five-factor model of personality* (2nd ed., pp. 215–221). Washington, DC: American Psychological Association.

Yanovski, S. Z., & Yanovski, J. A. (2014). Long-term drug treatment for obesity: A systematic and clinical review. *JAMA, 311*(1), 74–86.

Yapko, M. D. (1997). *Breaking the patterns of depression.* New York: Golden Books.

Yarbrough, E. (2018). *Transgender mental health.* Washington, DC: American Psychiatric Association.

Yeh, M., & Weisz, J. R. (2001). Why are we here at the clinic? Parent-child (dis)agreement on referral problems at outpatient treatment entry. *Journal of Consulting & Clinical Psychology, 69,* 1019–1025.

Yehuda, R., Blair, W., Labinsky, E., & Bierer, L. M. (2007). Effects of parental PTSD on the cortisol response to dexamethasone administration in their adult offspring. *American Journal of Psychiatry, 164,* 163–166.

Yehuda, R., Pratchett, L., & Pelcovitz, M. (2012). Biological contributions to PTSD: Differentiating normative from pathological response. In J. G. Beck & D. M. Sloan (Eds.), *The Oxford handbook of traumatic stress disorders* (pp. 159–174). New York: Oxford University Press.

Yim, I. S., Tanner Stapleton, L. R., Guardino, C. M., Hahn-Holbrook, J., & Dunkel Schetter, C. (2015). Biological and psychosocial predictors of postpartum depression: Systematic review and call for integration. *Annual Review of Clinical Psychology, 11,* 99–137.

Yip, S. W. & Potenza, M. N. (2014). *Current Treatment Options in Psychiatry, 1,* 189–203.

Yoshikawa, H., Aber, J. L., & Beardslee, W. R. (2012). The effects of poverty on the mental, emotional, and behavioral health of children and youth: Implications for prevention. *American Psychologist, 67*(4), 272–284.

Young, E., & Korzun, A. (1999). Psychoneuroendocrinology of depression: Hypothalamic-pituitary-gonadal axis. *Psychiatric Clinics of North America, 21,* 309–323.

Young-Wolff, K. C., Kendler, K. S., Ericson, M. L., & Prescott, C. A. (2011). Accounting for the association between childhood maltreatment and alcohol-use disorders in males: A twin study. *Psychological Medicine, 41,* 59–70.

Yusuf, S., Hawken, S., Ounpuu, S., Dans, T., Avezum, A., Lanas, F., Budaj, A., Pais, P., Varigos, J., & Lisheng, L. (2004). Effect of potentially modifiable risk factors associated with myocardial infarction in 52 countries (the INTERHEART study): Case-control study. *Lancet, 364,* 937–952.

Z

Zadra, A., Desautels, A., Petit, D., & Montplaisir, J. (2013). Somnambulism: Clinical aspects and pathophysiological hypotheses. *Lancet Neurology, 12*(3), 285–294.

Zalta, A. K., Gillihan, S. J., Fisher, A. J., Mintz, J., McLean, C. P., Yehuda, R., & Foa, E. B. (2014). Change in negative cognitions associated with PTSD predicts symptom reduction in prolonged exposure. *Journal of Consulting and Clinical Psychology, 82,* 171–175.

Zanarini, M. C., Frankenburg, F. R., Reich, D. B., & Fitzmaurice, G. (2012). Attainment and stability of sustained symptomatic remission and recovery among patients with borderline personality disorder and axis II comparison subjects: A 16-year prospective follow-up study. *American Journal of Psychiatry, 169,* 476–483.

Zanarini, M. C., Schulz, S. C., Detke, H., Zhao, F., Lin, D., Pritchard, M., Deberdt, W., Fitzmaurice, G., & Corya, S. (2012). Open-label treatment with olanzapine for patients with borderline personality disorder. *Journal of Clinical Psychopharmacology, 32,* 398–402.

Zanarini, M. C., Skodol, A.-E., Bender, D., Dolan, R., Sanislow, C., Schaefer, E., Morey, L., Grilo, C. M., Shea, M. T., McGlashan, T. H., & Gunderson, G. (2000). The Collaborative Longitudinal Personality Disorders Study: Reliability of Axis I and II diagnoses. *Journal of Personality Disorder, 14,* 291–299.

Zayas, L. H., Lester, R. J., Cabassa, L. J., & Fortuna, L. R. (2005). Why do so many Latina teens attempt suicide? A conceptual model for research. *American Journal of Orthopsychiatry, 75,* 275–287.

Zdanys, K. F., & Steffens, D. C. (2015). Sleep disturbances in the elderly. *Psychiatric Clinics, 38*(4), 723–741.

Zelt, D. (1981). First person account: The Messiah quest. *Schizophrenia Bulletin, 7,* 527–531.

Zhang, B., & Wing, Y.-K. (2006). Sex differences in insomnia: A meta-analysis. *Sleep, 29,* 85–93.

Zhang, X., Beaulieu, J. M., Sotnikova, T. D., Gainetdinov, R. R., & Caron, M. G. (2004). Tryptophan hydroxylase-2 controls brain serotonin. *Science, 305,* 217.

Zhu, B., Chen, C., Loftus, E. F., He, Q., Chen, C., Lei, X., Lin, C., & Dong, Q. (2012). Brief exposure to misinformation can lead to long-term false memories. *Applied Cognitive Psychology, 26,* 301–307.

Ziegelstein, R. C., Fauerbach, J. A., Stevens, S. S., Romanelli, J., Richter, D. P., & Bush, D. E. (2000). Patients with depression are less likely to follow recommendations to reduce cardiac risk during recovery from a myocardial infarction. *Archives of Internal Medicine, 160,* 1818–1823.

Zigler, E., Gilliam, W. S., & Jones, S. M. (2006). *A vision for universal preschool education.* New York: Cambridge University Press.

Zigler, E., & Hodapp, R. M. (1991). Behavioral functioning in individuals with mental retardation. *Annual Review of Psychology, 42,* 29–50.

Zigler, E., & Styfco, S. J. (2004). Applying the findings of developmental psychology to improve early childhood intervention. In M. A. Feldman (Ed.), *Early intervention: The essential readings* (pp. 54–72). Malden, UK: Blackwell.

Zigler, E., & Styfco, S. J. (2008). America's Head Start program: An effort for social justice. In C. Wainryb, J. Smetana, & E. Turiel (Eds.), *Social development, social inequalities, and social justice* (pp. 53–80). New York: Taylor & Francis Group/ Lawrence Erlbaum.

Zilboorg, G., & Henry, G. W. (1941). *A history of medical psychology.* New York: W. W. Norton.

Zimmerman, M., Rothschild, L., & Chelminski, I. (2005). The prevalence of *DSM-IV* personality disorders in psychiatric outpatients. *American Journal of Psychiatry, 162,* 1911–1918.

Zintzaras, E., Kitsios, G. D., Papathanasiou, A. A., Konitsiotis, S., Miligkos, M., Rodopoulou, P., & Hadjigeorgiou, G. M. (2010).

Randomized trials of dopamine agonists in restless legs syndrome: A systematic review, quality assessment, and meta-analysis. *Clinical Therapeutics, 32,* 221–237.

Zinzow, H. M., Resnick, H. S., McCauley, J. L., Amstadter, A. B., Ruggiero, K. J., & Kilpatrick, D. G. (2012). Prevalence and risk of psychiatric disorders as a function of variant rape histories: Results from a national survey of women. *Social Psychiatry and Psychiatric Epidemiology, 47,* 893–902.

Zucker, K. J. (2018). The myth of persistence: Response to "A critical commentary on follow-up studies and 'desistance' theories about transgender and gender non-conforming children" by Temple Newhook et al. (2018). *International Journal of Transgenderism, 19,* 231–235.

Zucker, K. J., & Cohen-Kettenis, P. T. (2008). Gender identity disorder in children and adolescents. In D. L. Rowland & L. Incrocci (Eds.), *Handbook of sexual and gender identity disorders* (pp. 376–422). Hoboken, NJ: Wiley.

Zucker, K. J., & Duschinsky, R. (2016). Dilemmas encountered by the Sexual and Gender Identity Disorders Work Group for DSM-5: An interview with Kenneth J. Zucker. *Psychology & Sexuality, 7*(1), 23–33.

Zucker, K. J., Lawrence, A. A., & Kreukels, B. P. (2016). Gender dysphoria in adults. *Annual Review of Clinical Psychology, 12,* 217–247.

Zucker, K. J., & Wood, H. (2011). Assessment of gender variance in children. *Child and Adolescent Psychiatric Clinics of North America, 20,* 665–680.

Zucker, R. A., Chermack, S. T., & Curran, G. M. (1999). Alcoholism: A lifespan perspective on etiology and course. In M. Lewis & A. J. Sameroff (Eds.), *Handbook of developmental psychopathology* (2nd ed.). New York: Plenum Press.

Zucker, R. A., Heitzeg, M. M., & Nigg, J. T. (2011). Parsing the undercontrol–disinhibition pathway to substance use disorders: A multilevel developmental problem. *Child Development Perspectives, 5*(4), 248–255.

Zucker, R. A., Kincaid, S. B., Fitzgerald, H. E., & Bingham, C. R. (1995). Alcohol schema acquisition in preschoolers: Differences between children of alcoholics and children of nonalcoholics. *Alcoholism: Clinical & Experimental Research, 19,* 1011–1017.

Zuvekas, S. H., & Vitiello, B. (2012). Stimulant medication use in children: A 12-year perspective. *American Journal of Psychiatry, 169,* 160–166.

Zvolensky, M. J., & Smits, J. A. J. (Eds.). (2008). *Anxiety in health behaviors and physical illness.* New York: Springer Science & Business Media.

Zwerdling, D. (2009, November 11). Walter Reed officials asked: Was Hasan psychotic? http://www.npr.org/templates/story/story.php?storyId=120313570.

NAME INDEX

B

C

D

E

F

H

I

J

K

M

P

Q

R

S

T

U

V

W

X

Y

Z

SUBJECT INDEX

D

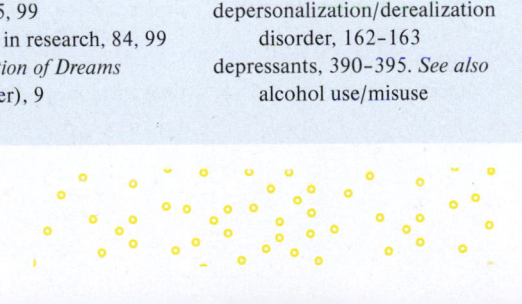

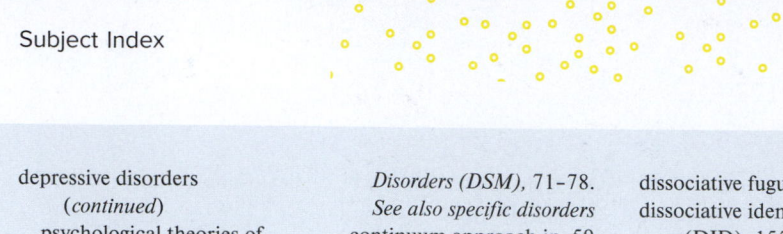

E

F

G

H

N

Q

R

S

T

U

V

W

X

Y

Z